Using 1-2-3® for DOS Release 3.1+

Special Edition

Que Development Group

Using 1-2-3® for DOS Release 3.1, Special Edition
Copyright© 1992 by Que® Corporation.

All rights reserved. Printed in the United States of America. No part of this book may be used or reproduced in any form or by any means, or stored in a database or retrieval system, without prior written permission of the publisher except in the case of brief quotations embodied in critical articles and reviews. Making copies of any part of this book for any purpose other than your own personal use is a violation of United States copyright laws. For information, address Que Corporation, 11711 N. College Ave., Carmel, IN 46032.

Library of Congress Catalog No.: 91-66198

ISBN: 0-88022-843-1

This book is sold *as is*, without warranty of any kind, either express or implied, respecting the contents of this book, including but not limited to implied warranties for the book's quality, performance, merchantability, or fitness for any particular purpose. Neither Que Corporation nor its dealers or distributors shall be liable to the purchaser or any other person or entity with respect to any liability, loss, or damage caused or alleged to have been caused directly or indirectly by this book.

93 92 91   5 4 3 2 1

Interpretation of the printing code: the rightmost double-digit number is the year of the book's printing; the rightmost single-digit number, the number of the book's printing. For example, a printing code of 91-1 shows that the first printing of the book occurred in 1991.

Art by Hartman Publishing.

Screens reproductions in this book were created with Inset from Inset Systems, Brookfield, CT.

Using 1-2-3 for DOS Release 3.1+, Special Edition covers Lotus 1-2-3 Release 3.1+, and the earlier Releases 3 and 3.1.

Publisher: Lloyd J. Short

Associate Publisher: Karen A. Bluestein

Product Development Manager: Mary Bednarek

Managing Editor: Paul Boger

Book Design: Scott Cook

Production Team: Scott Boucher, Martin Coleman, Brook Farling, Sandy Grieshop, Dennis C. Hager, Betty Kish, Phil Kitchel, Bob LaRoche, Laurie Lee, Anne Owen, Juli Pavey, Howard Peirce, Cindy L. Phipps, Tad Ringo, Bruce Steed, Mary Beth Wakefield, Sue VandeWalle, Johnna VanHoose

Product Director
Joyce J. Nielsen

Production Editor
Robin Drake

Technical Editors
David Maguiness
Joyce J. Nielsen
Robin Drake

*Composed in Garamond and Macmillan
by Que Corporation*

About the Authors

Rebecca Bridges Altman has a degree in economics from Stanford and owns a microcomputer training and consulting business. Her specialty is developing computer training materials. She was the technical editor for Que's *Absolute Reference: The Journal for 1-2-3 and Symphony Users*, and the revision author for Que's *1-2-3 Release 2.2 Quick Reference*; *1-2-3 QueCards*, Second Edition; and *Using Symphony*, Second Edition.

Rosemary Colonna is a software engineer who has developed course materials and trained instructors on networking and operating systems (such as DOS, UNIX, and ULTRIX). She has worked as a software quality assurance engineer for several computer companies, and is the author of user and system administrator manuals for a variety of computer products. She also is the author of *1-2-3 Release 2.3 Quick Reference*, and a coauthor of *Using Symphony*, Special Edition, and *Using UNIX*.

Joseph Desposito is a microcomputer consultant and free-lance writer specializing in microcomputer topics. Currently, he is a contributing editor for *Computer Craft* magazine. Desposito has held the position of editor-in-chief of *PC Clones* magazine and has worked as senior project leader at *PC Magazine's* PC Labs. He also has served as technical editor for several magazines, including *Creative Computing*, *Computers and Electronics*, and *Popular Electronics*. Desposito is a coauthor of *Using 1-2-3 for DOS Release 2.3*, Special Edition, and a revision author for *1-2-3 Quick Reference for Release 3.1*; *Using 1-2-3 Release 3.1*; *1-2-3 Macro Library*, Third Edition; and *Using 1-2-3 Release 2.2*.

David Paul Ewing is the president and publisher of New Riders Publishing Company. Prior to his position with New Riders, he was the publishing director of the Best Sellers editorial group at Que Corporation. He is the author of Que's *1-2-3 Macro Library* and *Using 1-2-3 Workbook and Instructor's Guide*; coauthor of Que's *Using 1-2-3 for DOS Release 2.3*, Special Edition; *Using Symphony*, Special Edition; *Using Q&A*; *Using Javelin*; and *1-2-3 Macro Workbook*; and contributing author for *Using 1-2-3*, Special Edition; *1-2-3 QuickStart*; and *Upgrading to 1-2-3 Release 3*.

Bill Fletcher is a Quality Assurance and Documentation manager at Lotus Development Corporation. He is a coauthor of Que's *Using 1-2-3 for DOS Release 2.3*, Special Edition, as well as a number of books on using microcomputer software in business applications, and is a revision author for *Using 1-2-3 Release 3.1*.

David Alan Knispel is a Senior Programmer/Systems Analyst for Macmillan Computer Publishing. He graduated from Anderson University with a bachelor of arts in Computer Science. He has been the technical editor for a number of Que books, including *Using 1-2-3 Release 3*; *1-2-3 Graphics Techniques*; and *Using Your Hard Disk*.

David Maguiness, a financial analyst with Blue Cross and Blue Shield of Indiana, was editor-in-chief of *Absolute Reference: The Journal for 1-2-3 and Symphony Users*. He also was a product development specialist with expertise in spreadsheet, database, and integrated software. He is the revision author for *1-2-3 for Business*, Second Edition, and a coauthor of *Using 1-2-3*, Special Edition; *1-2-3 Quick Reference*; *Upgrading to 1-2-3 Release 3*; and *Using Symphony*, Special Edition.

Timothy S. Stanley has worked for Que since 1985 as a technical editor. In addition to technical editing a number of Que's books, he has contributed to *Using 1-2-3 Release 3*; *Upgrading to 1-2-3 Release 3*; *1-2-3 Macro Library*; *Using WordPerfect 5.1*, Special Edition; and *Using Symphony*, Special Edition. Stanley also is the author of *Windows 3 Quick Reference*.

Brian Underdahl, an independent consultant in Reno, Nevada, studied electrical engineering at the University of Minnesota. He later worked at Graybar Electric for 18 years where, most recently, he was responsible for all PC-related projects. He is the author of *Que's Upgrading to MS-DOS 5*; a coauthor of *Using Symphony*, Special Edition; and a contributing author for *1-2-3 Beyond the Basics*; and has contributed to Que's *Absolute Reference: The Journal for 1-2-3 and Symphony Users*.

Trademark Acknowledgments

Que Corporation has made every effort to supply trademark information about company names, products, and services mentioned in this book. Trademarks indicated below were derived from various sources. Que Corporation cannot attest to the accuracy of this information.

1-2-3, DIF, Symphony, and VisiCalc are registered trademarks and Lotus Manuscript is a trademark of Lotus Development Corporation.

Apple and LaserWriter are registered trademarks of Apple Computer, Inc.

Bitstream is a registered trademark of Bitstream Inc.

dBASE, dBASE II, dBASE III Plus, and dBASE IV are registered trademarks of Ashton-Tate Corporation.

Epson is a registered trademark of Seiko Epson Corporation.

HP, LaserJet, and ThinkJet are registered trademarks and DeskJet is a trademark of Hewlett-Packard Company.

IBM, OS/2, and IBM Quietwriter are registered trademarks and ProPrinter is a trademark of International Business Machines Corporation.

Microline is a registered trademark of Oki America, Inc.

Microsoft Windows, Microsoft Windows Write, and MS-DOS are registered trademarks of Microsoft Corporation.

NEC is a registered trademark of NEC Information Systems, Inc.

OKIDATA is a registered trademark of Oki America, Inc.

PageMaker is a registered trademark of Aldus Corporation.

Paradox is a registered trademark of Borland International, Inc.

PostScript is a registered trademark of Adobe Systems Incorporated.

R:BASE is a registered trademark of Microrim, Inc.

Rolodex is a registered trademark of Rolodex Corporation.

Ventura Publisher is a registered trademark of Ventura Software, Inc.

Xerox is a registered trademark of Xerox Corporation.

Acknowledgments

Using 1-2-3 for DOS Release 3.1+, Special Edition, is the result of the efforts of many dedicated people. Que Corporation thanks the following people for their contributions to the revision of this book: Brian Underdahl, Joyce Nielsen, Robin Drake, David Maguiness, and the Que production staff. Special thanks to Doug Mills for his financial expertise.

Also, many thanks to the editorial team from the previous edition of this book: David Ewing, Alice Martina Smith, Mike La Bonne, Rob Lawson, Lisa Hunt Tally, Dave Knispel, Rob Perry, Tim Stanley, Debbie Walkowski, and Jerry Ellis.

Contents at a Glance

Introduction 1

Part I — Building the 1-2-3 Worksheet

Chapter 1	An Overview of 1-2-3 Release 3.1+ 9
Chapter 2	Getting Started 33
Chapter 3	Learning Worksheet Basics 61
Chapter 4	Using Fundamental 1-2-3 Commands 93
Chapter 5	Formatting Cell Contents 161
Chapter 6	Using @Functions in the Worksheet 203
Chapter 7	Managing Files 381

Part II — Creating 1-2-3 Reports and Graphs

Chapter 8	Printing Reports 317
Chapter 9	Using Wysiwyg To Enhance and Print Reports ... 365
Chapter 10	Creating and Printing Graphs 407
Chapter 11	Enhancing and Printing Graphs in Wysiwyg 469

Part III — Customizing 1-2-3

Chapter 12	Managing Data 495
Chapter 13	Using Macros 573
Chapter 14	Introducing the Advanced Macro Commands 599

Part IV — 1-2-3 Release 3.1+ Command Reference

Part V — Appendixes

Appendix A	Installing 1-2-3 Release 3.1+ 869
Appendix B	Using the Auditor Add-In 881
Appendix C	Using the Solver and Backsolver Add-Ins 891
Appendix D	Using the Viewer Add-In 917
Appendix E	Compose Sequences for the Lotus Multibyte Character Set 927

Index 935

Table of Contents

Introduction 1

I Building the 1-2-3 Worksheet

1 An Overview of 1-2-3 Release 3.1+ 9

Comparing Releases 3.1 and 3.1+ to Earlier Versions 10
Seeing 1-2-3 as an "Electronic" Accountant's Pad 11
Creating Formulas 15
Playing "What-If" 16
Examining Functions 16
    Mathematical Functions 17
    Statistical Functions 17
    Financial Functions 17
    Logical Functions 17
    Special Functions 17
    Date and Time Functions 18
    String Functions 18
Using the Command Menus 18
    Using the 1-2-3 Main Menu 19
    Using the Wysiwyg Menu 22
Understanding 1-2-3 File Management 23
Taking Advantage of File and Worksheet Protection 24
Enhancing Worksheets with 1-2-3 Graphics 24
Getting Acquainted with 1-2-3 Database Management 25
    Using the /Data Table Command 26
    Applying Multiple Regression and Simultaneous Equations 26
    Using the /Data External Command 27
Printing Reports and Graphs 27
Using Macros and the Advanced Macro Commands 28
Understanding 1-2-3 Hardware Requirements and Options 29
    Which Video Displays Does Release 3.1+ Support? 31
    Which Printers Does Release 3.1+ Support? 31
Summary 32

2 Getting Started 33

Starting 1-2-3 from the Operating System 34
    Starting 1-2-3 34
    Starting Wysiwyg 35
    Exiting 1-2-3 36
Using the 1-2-3 Access System 37
    Starting and Exiting 1-2-3 from the 1-2-3 Access System 39
    Using the Install Program 39
    Using the Translate Program 40
Learning the 1-2-3 Keyboard 41
    The Alphanumeric Keys 43
    The Numeric Keypad and the Cursor-Movement Keys 44
    The Function Keys 44
    The Special Keys 44
Using the Mouse with 1-2-3 47
    Understanding Mouse Terminology 47
    Using the Mouse To Select Menu Commands 48
Learning the 1-2-3 Screen Display 49
    The Control Panel 49
    The Mode Indicators 51
    The Status Indicators 52
    The File and Clock Indicator 53
    The Error Messages Area 54
Using the 1-2-3 Help Features 54
    Finding On-Screen Help 55
    Taking the 1-2-3 Tutorial 56
Using 1-2-3 Release 3.1+ with Windows 57
    Starting 1-2-3 Release 3.1+ from Windows 58
    Using 1-2-3 Release 3.1+ in Windows 58
    Transferring 1-2-3 Release 3.1+ Data by Using Windows 59
Summary 60

3 Learning Worksheet Basics 61

Understanding Worksheets and Files 62
    Introducing Multiple Worksheets 63
    Linking Files 64
    Using the Workspace 64
    Understanding the Multiple-Worksheet Display 65
Moving around the Worksheet 66
    Keyboard Control of the Cell Pointer 66
    Mouse Control of the Cell Pointer 67
    Using the Basic Movement Keys 68

Table of Contents

Entering Data into the Worksheet 73
    Entering Labels 73
    Entering Numbers 76
    Entering Formulas 77
    Changing Cell Formats 82
    Adding Notes to a Cell 83
Editing Data in the Worksheet 83
    Keyboard Editing 83
    Wysiwyg Editing 84
Using the Undo Feature 84
Using Multiple Worksheets 86
    Moving around Multiple Worksheets 87
    Entering Formulas with Multiple-Worksheet Files 90
    Entering Formulas That Link Files 90
    Choosing between Multiple-Worksheet Files and Linked Files 91
Summary 92

4   Using Fundamental 1-2-3 Commands 93

Selecting Commands from Command Menus 94
Saving Your Files 98
Using Ranges 99
    Typing the Addresses of the Range 100
    Specifying a Range in POINT Mode 100
    Specifying a Range with Range Names 106
    Using Ranges in Files with Multiple Worksheets 110
Setting Column Widths 111
Setting Row Heights 114
Erasing and Deleting Rows, Columns, and Worksheets 115
    Erasing Ranges 115
    Deleting Rows and Columns 116
    Using GROUP Mode To Change All the Worksheets in a File 117
    Deleting Worksheets and Files 117
    Clearing the Entire Workspace 119
Inserting Rows, Columns, and Worksheets 120
Using Window Options 121
    Changing the Display Format 121
    Splitting the Screen 122
    Zooming and Moving between Windows 124
    Displaying a Graph in a Worksheet 125
Freezing Titles On-Screen 126
Using Wysiwyg Display Options 128
    Changing the Display Mode 128
    Adjusting the Number of Rows and Columns 129

Changing the Display Colors 129
　　　Changing the Appearance of the Worksheet 129
　　Protecting and Hiding Worksheet Data 130
　　　Protecting Cells from Change 131
　　　Using /Range Input 132
　　　Hiding Data 133
　　　Sealing a File To Prevent Tampering 136
　　　Saving a File with a Password To Prevent Access 136
　　Controlling Recalculation 137
　　　Understanding Recalculation Methods 137
　　　Using Iteration To Solve Circular References 138
　　Moving the Contents of Cells 140
　　　Moving the Contents of a Single Cell 140
　　　Moving the Contents of a Range 141
　　Copying the Contents of Cells 144
　　　Copying the Contents of a Cell 145
　　　Copying a Formula with Relative Addressing 145
　　　Copying a Formula with Absolute Addressing 146
　　　Copying One Cell's Contents Several Times 147
　　　Copying One Cell's Contents to a Range of Cells 147
　　　Copying the Contents of a Range 149
　　　Copying with Mixed Addressing 151
　　　Using Range Names with /Copy 152
　　　Using /Range Value To Convert Formulas to Values 152
　　　Using /Range Transpose 154
　　Finding and Replacing Data 155
　　Accessing the Operating System 158
　　Summary 159

5　Formatting Cell Contents 161

　　Setting Worksheet Global Defaults 161
　　Setting Range and Worksheet Global Formats 163
　　　The Available Formats 164
　　　The Contents versus the Format of a Cell 165
　　　Using the Format Commands of the Main Menu 166
　　　　General Format 170
　　　　Fixed Format 171
　　　　Comma Format 171
　　　　Currency Format 172
　　　　Percent Format 173
　　　　Scientific Format 173
　　　　The +/- Format 174
　　　　Date and Time Formats 175

Table of Contents

    Text Format 180
    Hidden Format 180
    Label Format 181
    Automatic Format 181
    Parentheses Format 183
    Color Format 184
    International Formats 184
Changing Label Prefixes 185
Justifying Text 186
Suppressing the Display of Zeros 188
Using the :Format Commands of the Wysiwyg Menu 189
    Font Formats 190
    Underline Formats 192
    Changing Range Colors 192
    Line Formats 193
    Shade Formats 194
    Manipulating Formats 194
    Manipulating Text 197
Summary 202

6   Using @Functions in the Worksheet 203

Learning How To Enter a 1-2-3 @Function 204
Using Mathematical @Functions 206
    General Mathematical @Functions 206
Using Date and Time @Functions 210
    @D360—Dealing with 360-Day Years 212
    @DATE—Converting Date Values to Serial Numbers 212
    @DATEVALUE—Changing Date Strings to Serial Numbers 214
    @DAY, @MONTH, and @YEAR—Converting Serial Numbers
      to Dates 215
    @NOW and @TODAY—Finding the Current Date and Time 215
    @TIME—Converting Time Values to Serial Numbers 216
    @TIMEVALUE—Converting Time Strings to Serial Values 218
    @SECOND, @MINUTE, and @HOUR—Converting Serial
      Numbers to Time Values 218
Using Financial and Accounting @Functions 218
    @IRR—Calculating Internal Rate of Return 220
    @PV—Calculating Present Value of an Annuity 225
    @FV—Calculating Future Value 226
    @TERM—Calculating the Term of an Investment 227
    @CTERM—Calculating the Term of a Compounding Investment 228
    @SLN—Calculating Straight-Line Depreciation 229
    @DDB—Calculating Double Declining-Balance Depreciation 230

@SYD—Calculating Sum-of-the-Years'-Digits Depreciation 231
@VDB—Calculating Variable Declining-Balance Depreciation 232
Using Statistical @Functions 233
@AVG—Computing the Arithmetic Mean 234
@COUNT—Counting Cell Entries 235
@MAX and @MIN—Finding Maximum and Minimum Values 236
@STD and @STDS—Calculating the Standard Deviation 237
@SUM—Totaling Values 238
@SUMPRODUCT—Multiplying Lists of Values 239
@VAR and @VARS—Calculating the Variance 240
Using Database @Functions 241
@DSTDS and @DVARS—Calculating Deviation and Variance 243
@DGET—Extracting a Value or Label 244
@DQUERY—Working with External Tables 244
Using Logical @Functions 245
@IF—Creating Conditional Tests 246
@ISERR and @ISNA—Trapping Errors in Conditional Tests 248
@TRUE and @FALSE—Checking for Errors 249
@ISRANGE—Checking for a Range Name 249
@ISSTRING and @ISNUMBER—Checking the Cell's Aspect 250
Using String @Functions 251
@FIND—Locating One String within Another 253
@MID—Extracting One String from Another 254
@LEFT and @RIGHT—Extracting Strings from Left and Right 255
@REPLACE—Replacing a String within a String 256
@LENGTH—Computing the Length of a String 257
@EXACT—Comparing Strings 257
@LOWER, @UPPER, and @PROPER—Converting the Case
  of Strings 257
@REPEAT—Repeating Strings within a Cell 259
@TRIM—Removing Blank Spaces from a String 259
@N and @S—Testing for Strings and Values 259
@STRING—Converting Values to Strings 260
@VALUE—Converting Strings to Values 260
@CLEAN—Removing Nonprintable Characters from Strings 261
Using @Functions with Character Sets 261
Using Logarithmic @Functions 263
@LOG—Computing Logarithms 263
@EXP—Finding Powers of *e* 264
@LN—Computing Natural Logarithms 264
Using Trigonometric @Functions 264
@PI—Computing Pi 264
@COS, @SIN, and @TAN—Computing Trigonometric Functions 265

Table of Contents

@ACOS, @ASIN, @ATAN, and @ATAN2—Computing
  Inverse Trigonometric Functions 265
Using Special @Functions 267
  @@—Referencing Cells Indirectly 268
  @CELL and @CELLPOINTER—Checking
    Cell Attributes 269
  @COORD—Creating a Cell Address 271
  @CHOOSE—Selecting an Item from a List 272
  @COLS, @ROWS, and @SHEETS—Finding the Dimensions
    of Ranges 272
  @ERR and @NA—Trapping Errors 273
  @HLOOKUP and @VLOOKUP—Looking Up Entries in a Table 274
  @INDEX—Retrieving Data from Specified Locations 275
  @INFO—Getting System Information about the Current Session 277
Summary 279

7 Managing Files 281

Managing Active Files in Memory 282
Naming Files 283
Changing Directories 284
Saving Files 285
Retrieving Files from Disk 287
  Using Wild Cards for File Retrieval 287
  Retrieving Files from Subdirectories 288
  Retrieving a File Automatically 289
  Opening a New File in Memory 289
Multiple-File Applications 290
Extracting and Combining Data 291
  Extracting Information 291
  Combining Information from Other Files 295
  Using /File Combine Copy 297
  Using /File Combine Add and /File Combine Subtract 299
Protecting Files 301
  Using Passwords for File Protection 301
  Using /File Admin Seal for File Protection 302
  Using File Reservation for Protecting Files 303
  Using /Worksheet Global Prot for File Protection 303
Erasing Files 303
Creating Lists and Tables of Files 304
Transferring Files 305
  Transferring Files with /File Import 305
  Transferring Files with the Translate Utility 307

Using Earlier Versions of 1-2-3 and Symphony Files in Release 3 308
    Using External Databases 309
Using 1-2-3 in a Multiuser or Networking Environment 309
    File Sharing Guidelines 310
    Descriptions of /File Admin Commands 310
Summary 313

II Creating 1-2-3 Reports and Graphs

8 Printing Reports 317

Getting Started from the Main Print Menu 319
Understanding the Print Default Settings 321
    Current Printer Status 321
    Default Hardware-Specific Options 322
    Default Page-Layout Options 323
    Other Default Options: Wait, Setup, and Name 324
Printing Your Reports 325
    Printing a Short Report 326
    Printing a Multiple-Page Report 329
    Printing Multiple Ranges 333
    Hiding Segments within the Designated Print Range 336
Designing Your Reports 341
    Creating Headers and Footers 341
    Printing a Listing of Cell Contents 344
    Printing Borders 346
    Setting Page Layout: Margins and Page Length 347
Enhancing Your Reports 348
    Improving the Layout 350
    Selecting Fonts 354
    Using Setup Strings 355
    Selecting Color 358
Controlling Your Printer 358
    Choosing the Printer 358
    Controlling the Movement of the Paper 359
    Setting Your Printing Priorities 360
    Holding a Print Job (Hold) 360
    Pausing the Printer (Suspend and Wait) 361
    Stopping the Printer (Cancel and Quit) 361
    Printing a Graph with Text (Image) 362
    Naming and Saving the Current Print Settings 362
    Clearing the Print Options 363

Table of Contents

    Preparing Output for Use in Other Programs 363
    Summary 364

9 Using Wysiwyg To Enhance and Print Reports 365

    Loading Wysiwyg 366
    Understanding How 1-2-3 and Wysiwyg Work Together 367
        Understanding the Wysiwyg Menu 367
        Saving Your Wysiwyg Formatting 369
        Understanding the Wysiwyg Screen 369
        Specifying Cell Ranges in Wysiwyg 370
    Formatting with Wysiwyg 371
        Understanding Fonts 371
        Changing Formatting Attributes 375
        Drawing Lines and Boxes 377
        Adding Shades 378
        Using Formatting Sequences 378
        Adjusting Column Widths and Row Heights 380
    Managing Your Formats 381
        Copying and Moving Formats 381
        Using Named Styles 382
        Importing Formats 383
        Exporting Formats 384
    Printing with Wysiwyg 384
        Configuring Your Printer 385
        Specifying a Print Range 386
        Previewing on Your Screen 388
        Inserting Page Breaks 388
        Setting Up the Page 389
        Specifying Print Settings 394
        Printing to a File 395
    Setting Display Characteristics 395
        Mode 396
        Zoom 396
        Colors 396
        Options 397
        Font Directory 399
        Rows 399
        Default 399
    Using Wysiwyg Text Commands 400
        Typing or Correcting Text 400
        Formatting Characters 402
        Aligning Labels 403

Using 1-2-3 for DOS Release 3.1+, Special Edition

      Reformatting Paragraphs 404
      Setting and Clearing Text Attributes 406
  Summary 406

10 Creating and Printing Graphs 407

  Working with Wysiwyg 408
  Determining Hardware and Software Needs 408
  Understanding Graphs 408
  Creating Simple Graphs 409
      Selecting a Graph Type 412
      Specifying Data Ranges 412
      Constructing the Default Line Graph 418
  Enhancing the Appearance of a Basic Graph 419
      Adding Descriptive Labels and Numbers 420
      Altering the Default Graph Display 425
      Modifying the Graph Axes 427
      Adding a Second Y Scale 433
      Using Other Features Menu Options 435
      Using Advanced Graph Options 437
  Viewing Graphs 443
      Viewing Graphs from the Worksheet 443
      Viewing Graphs in a Screen Window 443
      Viewing Graphs in Wysiwyg 443
      Viewing a Graph in Color 444
  Saving Graphs and Graph Settings 445
      Saving Graphs on Disk 445
      Saving Graph Settings 445
  Resetting the Current Graph 446
  Developing Alternative Graph Types 447
      Selecting an Appropriate Graph Type 447
      Building All Graph Types 448
  Printing Graphs 460
      Installing a Printer to Print Graphs 460
      Changing the Appearance of Printed Graphs 461
      Printing a Graph with Default Settings 463
      Printing a Graph with Customized Print Settings 464
      Saving Graph Print Settings 465
      Including Graphs in Reports 466
  Summary 467

11 Enhancing and Printing Graphs in Wysiwyg 469

Adding a Graph 469
Repositioning a Graph 471
   Moving a Graph 471
   Resizing a Graph 472
   Removing a Graph 472
Specifying Graph Settings 472
Using the Graphics Editor 473
   Adding Objects 474
   Selecting Objects 478
   Editing Objects 479
   Changing the Display of the Graphic Editing Window 484
   Rearranging Objects 487
   Transforming Objects 489
Summary 492

III Customizing 1-2-3

12 Managing Data 495

Defining a Database 496
Designing a 1-2-3 Database 497
Creating a Database 498
   Entering Field Names 499
   Entering Data 500
   Modifying a Database 501
Sorting Database Records 502
   Using the One-Key Sort 503
   Using the Two-Key Sort 504
   Using the Extra-Key Sort 505
   Determining the Sort Order 505
   Restoring the Presort Order 507
Searching for Records 507
   Using Minimum Search Requirements 507
   Listing All Specified Records 511
   Handling More Complicated Criteria Ranges 514
   Performing Other Types of Searches 522
Joining Multiple Databases 524
Creating Data Tables 527
   General Terms and Concepts 528

The Four Types of Data Tables	528
Creating a Type 1 Data Table	528
Analyzing a 1-2-3 Database with /Data Table 1	530
Creating a Type 2 Data Table	531
Analyzing a 1-2-3 Database with /Data Table 2	532
Creating a Type 3 Data Table	533
Analyzing a Three-Dimensional Database	535
Creating a Labeled Data Table	537
Analyzing a 1-2-3 Database with /Data Table Labeled	546
Filling Ranges	548
Filling Ranges with Numbers	548
Using Formulas and Functions to Fill Ranges	549
Filling Ranges with Dates or Times	549
Creating Frequency Distributions	550
Using the /Data Regression Command	551
Using the /Data Matrix Command	555
Loading Data from Other Programs	556
Using the /Data Parse Command	557
Using Caution with /Data Parse	560
Working with External Databases	561
Understanding External Database Terminology	562
Using an Existing External Table	562
Listing External Tables	563
Creating a New External Table	565
Deleting an External Table	568
Using Other /Data External Commands	568
Disconnecting 1-2-3 and the External Table	570
Summary	571

13 Using Macros 573

Introducing Macros	574
Developing Your Own Macros	574
Writing Some Sample Macros	575
Writing a Macro That Enters Text	575
Writing a Simple Command Macro	577
Using Macro Key Names	578
Guidelines for Developing Macros	580

Table of Contents

    Formatting Macros 580
    Naming and Running Macros 581
  Planning the Layout of a Macro 585
  Documenting Macros 587
    Using Descriptive Names 587
    Using the /Range Name Note Feature 587
    Including Comments in the Worksheet 588
    Keeping External Design Notes 588
  Protecting Macros 588
  Building a Simple Macro Library 589
    A Macro To Define Printer Setup Strings 589
    A Macro To Print a Report 590
    A Macro To Set Worksheet Recalculation 591
    A Macro To Add a New Worksheet 591
  Recording and Testing Macros 591
    Creating Macros with Record 592
    Using Playback To Repeat Keystrokes 595
    Using Record To Test Macros 595
    Watching for Common Errors in Macros 597
  Moving Up to the Advanced Macro Commands 598
  Summary 598

14 Introducing the Advanced Macro Commands 599

  Why Use the Advanced Macro Commands? 599
  What Are the Advanced Macro Commands? 600
  Understanding the Elements of Advanced Macro Command Programs 602
  Understanding Advanced Macro Command Syntax 603
  Creating, Using, and Debugging Advanced Macro Command Programs .. 603
  Understanding the Advanced Macro Command Categories 605
    Using Commands that Accept Input 605
    Using Commands That Control Programs 612
    Using Commands That Make Decisions 625
    Using Commands That Manipulate Data 627
    Using Commands That Enhance Programs 632
    Using Commands That Manipulate Files 639
  Summary 646

xxiii

IV 1-2-3 Release 3.1+ Command Reference

V Appendixes

A Installing 1-2-3 Release 3.1+ 869

Checking DOS Configuration 869
Starting the Install Program 870
    Registering Your Original Disks 870
    Choosing Files To Copy 870
    Creating a Directory for the 1-2-3 Files 871
    Copying Files 871
    Configuring 1-2-3 for Your Computer 871
Installing the Release 3.1+ Add-Ins 875
    Understanding the System Requirements 875
    Checking Available Memory 875
    Installing the Add-Ins 876
Changing 1-2-3's Equipment Configuration 877
    Changing the Selected Display or Printer 877
    Changing the Selected Country 879
Changing Wysiwyg Options 880

B Using the Auditor Add-In 881

Attaching and Detaching Auditor 881
Invoking and Using Auditor 882
Understanding the Auditor Menu 883
    Setting the Audit Range 883
    Changing the Audit Mode 884
    Finding Cells Used by One Formula (Precedents) 884
    Finding Formulas That Refer to One Cell (Dependents) 885
    Finding Formulas 885
    Examining Recalculation Order 886
    Examining Circular References 887
    Resetting Auditor Options 888

C Using the Solver and Backsolver Add-Ins 891

Attaching and Detaching
    Solver and Backsolver 891
Invoking Solver 892

Table of Contents

Using Solver 893
   Understanding Solver Terminology 893
   Optimizing Production for Maximum Profit 894
      Creating a Sample Worksheet for Solver 894
      Evaluating Solver's Answers 898
Supplying Guesses 899
Understanding Best and Optimal Answers 900
   Displaying Attempted Answers 900
   Selecting an Answer 900
Using the Solver Reports 901
   The Answer Report 901
   The How Solved Report 902
   The What-If Report 904
   The Differences Report 905
   The Inconsistent Constraints Report 905
   The Unused Constraints Report 908
   The Cells Used Report 909
Using Functions with Solver 909
Using Solver with Macros 910
Using Backsolver 912

D   Using the Viewer Add-In 917

Attaching and Detaching Viewer 917
Invoking and Using Viewer 918
Understanding the Viewer Menu and Screen 918
Navigating Viewer 920
Retrieving a File 920
   Viewing a File Before Retrieving 921
   Returning to the List Window 921
Changing the Display Sort Order 922
Opening Files with Viewer 922
Linking Files with Viewer 922
Browsing Files with Viewer 924

E   Compose Sequences for the Lotus Multibyte Character Set 927

Group 0 928
Group 1 932

Index 935

xxv

Introduction

Since 1983, Que has helped millions of spreadsheet users learn the commands, features, and functions of Lotus 1-2-3. *Using 1-2-3*—through six editions—has become the standard guide to 1-2-3 for both new and experienced 1-2-3 users worldwide. This book provides complete coverage of 1-2-3 Release 3.1+ to help new spreadsheet users, and users who have upgraded to Release 3.1+, take advantage of the capabilities in this version of 1-2-3.

Que's unprecedented experience with 1-2-3—and 1-2-3 users—helped produce this high-quality, highly informative book. But a book such as *Using 1-2-3 for DOS Release 3.1+* does not develop overnight. This book represents long hours of work from a team of expert authors and dedicated editors who developed the first, second, and this special edition covering Release 3.1+.

Que began developing the first edition of *Using 1-2-3 Release 3* immediately after Lotus designers announced that they were planning a new version of 1-2-3. Even before the software was developed, Que's product development editors began searching for the best team of 1-2-3 experts available. This team of authors had to be able to cover the complex, powerful new program comprehensively, accurately, and clearly.

In March 1989, Que's team of authors traveled to the Lotus Development Corporation in Boston for a preview of Release 3. The team met with the Release 3 developers and discussed the new product in depth. On seeing Release 3 demonstrated, the authors prepared to begin detailed use of the product, ready to discover the wealth of capabilities provided by the program's new features.

The authors outlined the strategies needed to produce the best book possible on Release 3. Team members reviewed comments from users, critiqued competing products, and analyzed the traits that made previous editions of *Using 1-2-3* the most popular 1-2-3 books on the market. When Lotus announced 1-2-3 Release 3.1+ in the spring of 1991, Que authors began updating the second edition of *Using 1-2-3 Release 3.1* to cover and illustrate the powerful Release 3.1+ enhancement add-ins. The authors tested and developed applications using the add-ins, and supplemented the previous edition of this book with new add-in material. The result is a comprehensive tutorial and reference, written in the easy-to-follow style expected from Que books.

Because of these efforts, *Using 1-2-3 for DOS Release 3.1+* is the best available reference to 1-2-3 Releases 3, 3.1, and 3.1+. Whether you are using 1-2-3 for inventory control, statistical analysis, or portfolio management, this book is designed for you. Like all previous editions of this title, *Using 1-2-3 for DOS Release 3.1+* leads you step-by-step from spreadsheet basics to the advanced features of Releases 3, 3.1, and 3.1+. Whether you are a new user or an experienced user upgrading to Release 3.1+, this book will occupy a prominent place next to your computer, as a tried and valued reference to your most-used spreadsheet program.

Who Should Read This Book?

Using 1-2-3 for DOS Release 3.1+ is written and organized to meet the needs of a wide range of readers, from those for whom 1-2-3 Release 3.1+ is their first spreadsheet product, to those who are experienced 1-2-3 Release 2.01, 2.2, 3, and 3.1 users who have upgraded to Release 3.1+.

If Release 3.1+ is your first 1-2-3 package, then this book will help you learn the basics so that you can quickly begin using 1-2-3 for your needs. The first five chapters in particular teach you basic concepts for understanding 1-2-3—commands, the differences and organization of the two command menus in Release 3.1+ (the 1-2-3 command menu and the Wysiwyg command menu), special uses of the keyboard and mouse, features of the 1-2-3 screen, and methods for creating and modifying 1-2-3 worksheets.

If you are an experienced 1-2-3 Release 3 user and have upgraded to Release 3.1+, you learn the new desktop publishing features in Release 3.1+ and how to apply them as you develop worksheet applications, create graphs, and print reports and graphs. If you are upgrading from Release 3 or 3.1 to 3.1+, you also learn about the Release 3.1+ enhancement add-ins. In addition, you learn how to use the mouse to highlight ranges, move from one part of the worksheet to another, select commands, and access the 1-2-3 Help screens. You also learn how to change the way your 1-2-3 worksheet appears on-screen by adding grid lines, changing colors of screen elements, and changing the size and style of characters on the worksheet. *Using 1-2-3 for DOS Release 3.1+* quickly and easily teaches you how to use Wysiwyg features to produce professional-quality graphs and reports.

Introduction 3

Whether you are new to 1-2-3 or have upgraded to Release 3.1+, *Using 1-2-3 for DOS Release 3.1+* provides the tips and techniques you need to get the most from 1-2-3. As you continue to use 1-2-3 Release 3.1+, you will find that the 1-2-3 Command Reference, with its easy-to-use format, is a frequently used guide for providing you with the steps, reminders, tips, and cautions for using Release 3.1+ commands.

The Organization of This Book

If you browse quickly through this book, you can get a better sense of its organization and layout. The book is organized to follow the natural flow of learning and using 1-2-3.

Part I—Building the 1-2-3 Worksheet

Chapter 1, "An Overview of 1-2-3 Release 3.1+," covers the uses, features, and commands in Release 3.1+ that are the same as those in Releases 3 and 3.1, as well as uses, features, and commands specific to Release 3.1+. This chapter explains the "What-you-see-is-what-you-get" desktop publishing capabilities for displaying and printing high-quality worksheets and graphs, as well as the enhancement add-ins. Also, this chapter introduces the general concepts for understanding 1-2-3 as a spreadsheet program, and introduces the program's major uses—creating worksheets, databases, graphics, and macros.

Chapter 2, "Getting Started," helps you begin using 1-2-3 Release 3.1+ for the first time, and includes starting and exiting from the program, learning special uses of the keyboard and mouse with 1-2-3, understanding features of the 1-2-3 screen display, getting on-screen help, and using the 1-2-3 tutorial.

Chapter 3, "Learning Worksheet Basics," introduces the concepts of worksheets and files, and teaches you how to move the cell pointer around the worksheet, enter and edit data, and use Undo. You also learn how to build multiple worksheets and multiple-worksheet files with Release 3.1+, and how to create formulas that link cells among different files.

Chapter 4, "Using Fundamental 1-2-3 Commands," teaches you how to use the 1-2-3 Release 3 command menus and the most fundamental commands for building worksheets. For example, in this chapter you learn how to change the width of a column, clear data from the worksheet, and control the way data appears on-screen. You also learn how to save your worksheet files and leave 1-2-3 temporarily to return to the operating system.

Chapter 5, "Formatting Cell Contents," shows you how to change the way data appears on-screen, including the way values, formulas, and text are displayed. You also learn how to suppress the display of zeros.

Chapter 6, "Using @Functions in the Worksheet," covers the following @functions available in Release 3: mathematical, trigonometric, statistical, financial, accounting, logical, special, date, time, logarithmic, database, and string.

Chapter 7, "Managing Files," covers commands for saving, erasing, and listing files, as well as commands for combining data from several files, extracting data from one file to another, and opening more than one file in memory at a time. Besides introducing you to these commands, Chapter 7 teaches you how to transfer files between different programs and how to use 1-2-3 in a multiuser environment.

Part II—Creating 1-2-3 Reports and Graphs

Chapter 8, "Printing Reports," shows you how to print a report immediately, create a file for delayed printing, or create a file to be read by another program. You learn how to print a basic report by using only a few commands. Also, you learn how to enhance a report by using other commands that change page layout, type size, character and line spacing, and enable you to add such elements as headers and footers.

Chapter 9, "Using Wysiwyg To Enhance and Print Reports," focuses on the Wysiwyg formatting and printing features of Release 3.1 and 3.1+. The chapter introduces you to the Wysiwyg commands, covering in particular how the 1-2-3 commands and Wysiwyg work together. You learn how to design a worksheet with different sizes and types of characters, and highlight worksheet data with special elements such as underlining, shading, boxes, and grids. Finally, Chapter 9 teaches you how to use the word processing capabilities available through the :Text command.

Chapter 10, "Creating and Printing Graphs," teaches you how to create graphs from worksheet data manually and automatically. This chapter also covers the options available to change the type of graph, label and title a graph, enhance a graph with a background grid, change the scaling of a graph, and view a graph in full- or partial-screen mode. Release 3 enables you print to graphs directly from the /Print menu, and the process is less complicated than printing graphs in previous releases. This chapter covers the commands in the /Print menu and steps for printing graphs in Release 3.

Chapter 11, "Enhancing and Printing Graphs in Wysiwyg," shows you how to modify and embellish graphs through the :Graph command on the Wysiwyg menu. You learn how to change the position of a graph on the page; adjust graph settings; add, modify, and rearrange text and geometric shapes; and change the size and rotation of objects displayed on graphs.

Part III—Customizing 1-2-3

Chapter 12, "Managing Data," introduces you to the advantages and limitations of 1-2-3's database and shows you how to create, modify, and maintain data records, including sorting, locating, and extracting data. Chapter 12 also covers the special commands and features of 1-2-3 data management, such as database statistical functions, parsing data to use in the worksheet, regression analysis, and accessing and manipulating data in a table in an external database.

Chapter 13, "Using Macros," is an introduction to the powerful macro capability of Release 3. This chapter teaches you how to create, name, and run macros and build a macro library. Also, the chapter covers macro features special to Release 3, such as creating a macro by automatically recording keystrokes, naming macros with descriptive names, and invoking macros from a menu.

Chapter 14, "Introducing the Advanced Macro Commands," explains the powerful advanced macro commands in Release 3 and includes a complete reference of advanced macro commands with many examples of their use.

Part IV—1-2-3 Release 3.1+ Command Reference

"1-2-3 Command Reference" is a quick, easy-to-use, and comprehensive guide to the procedures for using almost every command on the command menus. This section also gives many reminders, important cues, and cautions that greatly simplify and expedite your day-to-day use of 1-2-3.

Appendixes

Appendix A shows you how to install 1-2-3 Release 3.1+ for your hardware and operating system. Instructions for installing the enhancement add-ins are also provided.

Appendix B contains information on using the Auditor add-in with Release 3.1+ to check and verify worksheet formulas.

Appendix C provides examples on using the Solver and Backsolver add-ins of Release 3.1+ to evaluate solutions to "what-if" scenarios.

Appendix D shows you how to use the Release 3.1+ Viewer add-in to quickly link, retrieve, and browse your 1-2-3 worksheets.

Appendix E presents a table of the Lotus Multibyte Character Set—characters not on your keyboard that can appear on your monitor and print with your printer. Your specific equipment determines which characters in this list you can display and print.

A pull-out command chart that lists the menu hierarchy of all 1-2-3 Release 3.1+ commands (including Wysiwyg and the enhancement add-ins) is included in the back of this book.

Other Titles To Enhance Your Personal Computing

Although *Using 1-2-3 for DOS Release 3.1+* is a comprehensive guide to Release 3, no single book can fill all your 1-2-3 and personal computing needs. Que Corporation publishes a full line of microcomputer books that complement this best-seller.

Several Que books can help you learn and master your operating systems. *Using MS-DOS 5* is an excellent guide to the MS-DOS operating system. Its counterpart—written for all DOS users—is *Que's MS-DOS 5 User's Guide*, Special Edition. Both books provide the same type of strong tutorial and complete Command Reference found in *Using 1-2-3 for DOS Release 3.1+*. If you prefer to "get up and run" with DOS fundamentals in a quick and easy manner, try Que's *MS-DOS 5 QuickStart*. This graphics-based tutorial helps you teach yourself the fundamentals of DOS.

If you are using 1-2-3 on a personal computer equipped with a hard disk drive, you may already know that the key to efficient computer use is effective hard disk management. Que's *Using Your Hard Disk* shows you how to get the most from your hard disk by streamlining your use of directories, creating batch files, and more. This well-written text is an invaluable addition to your library of personal computer books.

1-2-3 Release 3.1+ requires the use of powerful equipment to operate quickly and efficiently. If you find your current computer hardware not quite up to the task, examine Que's *Upgrading and Repairing PCs*. This informative text shows you how to get the most from your current hardware, and how to upgrade your system to handle the new breed of high-powered software—such as 1-2-3 Release 3.1+. Mark Brownstein of *InfoWorld* called *Upgrading and Repairing PCs* "one of the best books about the workings of personal computers I've ever seen; it will be a useful, easy-to-read, and interesting addition to most anyone's library."

Learning More about 1-2-3

If *Using 1-2-3 for DOS Release 3.1+* whets your appetite for more information about 1-2-3, you're in good company. Over one million *Using 1-2-3* readers have purchased one or more additional Que books about 1-2-3.

1-2-3 Release 3.1+ Quick Reference is an affordable, compact reference to the most commonly used Release 3.1+ commands and functions. It's a great book to keep near your computer when you need to find quickly the function of a command and the steps for using it.

1-2-3 Beyond the Basics covers all DOS releases of 1-2-3 through Release 3.1 and presents hundreds of tips and techniques to help you get the most from the program. This book covers Release 2.3 and 3.1's spreadsheet publishing capability, new graphics features, database and macro techniques, and information on using 1-2-3 with other software programs.

Besides these books, Que publishes books for new Release 3.1+ users, such as *1-2-3 for DOS Release 3.1+ QuickStart*. Keep in mind that Que also publishes a complete line of books for 1-2-3 Release 2 users, covering Releases 2.01, 2.2, and 2.3.

All these books can be found in better bookstores worldwide. In the United States, you can call Que at 1-800-428-5331 to order books or obtain further information.

Part I

Building the 1-2-3 Worksheet

An Overview of 1-2-3 Release 3.1+

Getting Started

Learning Worksheet Basics

Using Fundamental 1-2-3 Commands

Formatting Cell Contents

Using @Functions in the Worksheet

Managing Files

An Overview of 1-2-3 Release 3.1+

For more than eight years, 1-2-3 has been the dominant spreadsheet software product used in businesses worldwide. Today, 1-2-3 is used by over 10 million people and continues to be the standard.

When first introduced in 1983, 1-2-3 revolutionized microcomputing by replacing the dominant spreadsheet product at the time, VisiCalc, and soon became the program identified with the IBM PC as the established tool for financial analysis. With the introduction of Release 3.1+ in 1991, 1-2-3 remains the leader in microcomputer spreadsheet software by maintaining the overall functionality, command structure, and screen and keyboard features of its earlier versions.

Note: In this book, the term *Release 3* is used to refer to features available in 1-2-3 Releases 3, 3.1, and 3.1+. Features available only in Releases 3.1 and 3.1+ are clearly indicated in the text.

Release 3 uses extended memory beyond 1 megabyte. This feature enables you to create and open multiple worksheets as well as to do file linking. At the same time, however, with Releases 3.1 and 3.1+, Lotus Development Corporation has responded to the growing needs of users and the capabilities available in state-of-the-art microcomputers.

Why is 1-2-3 so popular? 1-2-3 provides three fundamental applications integrated in one program. Without having to learn three separate kinds of software, you can perform financial analysis with the 1-2-3 worksheet, create database applications, and generate graphics. Commands enabling users to develop all three types of applications are combined in one main menu. These commands are easily accessed, and when you select them, prompts guide you through each step needed to perform a task.

Reminder:
1-2-3 is three applications in one: spreadsheet, database, and graphics.

Besides enabling you to work in the traditional keyboard mode, Releases 3.1 and 3.1+ let you work with a mouse in an interactive graphical work environment. By moving the mouse and pressing its control buttons, you can perform actions normally done with a series of keystrokes. Release 3.1+ adds four enhancement add-ins to the core Release 3.1 program.

If you are upgrading from an earlier release of 1-2-3, this chapter gives you a general introduction to the differences between earlier releases and Releases 3.1 and 3.1+ and identifies many of the features and commands unique to these versions. Specifically in this chapter, you learn about the following topics:

- The features special to Release 3.1 and 3.1+ (developed for those readers who are planning to upgrade or have just upgraded from Release 2.01, 2.2, 2.3, or 3 to Release 3.1 or 3.1+)
- The general capabilities of 1-2-3 (presented especially for those readers who are new to 1-2-3 as well as Release 3.1 or 3.1+)
- The commands available for using 1-2-3 worksheets
- 1-2-3 file management and worksheet and file protection
- 1-2-3 graphics, including an introduction to those enhancements in Release 3.1 and 3.1+ graphics not available in earlier releases
- Database management with 1-2-3
- Printing reports and graphs
- Using the Wysiwyg commands of Releases 3.1 and 3.1+
- Macros and the advanced macro commands
- The system requirements for 1-2-3 Releases 3.1 and 3.1+

Comparing Releases 3.1 and 3.1+ to Earlier Versions

If you have used a previous version of 1-2-3, you will find the program unchanged in its primary functions. You can still use 1-2-3 for simple-to-complex financial applications; for organizing, sorting, extracting, and finding information; and for creating graphs that are useful for analyzing data or for using in presentations.

1-2-3 Release 3.1+ is a minor upgrade to Release 3.1. Release 3.1+ specifically adds four enhancement add-ins to the previous version. These add-ins—Auditor, Solver, Backsolver, and Viewer—are discussed in the Appendixes.

Reminder:
1-2-3 Releases 3.1 and 3.1+ offer Wysiwyg and mouse capabilities.

The major enhancement to 1-2-3 Releases 3.1 and 3.1+ over all earlier releases is the interactive Wysiwyg work environment with mouse support. Mouse control makes 1-2-3 easier than ever to use. With a click of the mouse, you can adjust column widths or row heights, select ranges, and make menu selections from pull-down menus. *Mouse-driven icons*—position the mouse pointer on the icon and click the mouse control button to activate—can be used to scroll through worksheets or to access help. What appears on-screen is exactly the way printed documents appear thanks to Wysiwyg. This "visual fix" gives you better control of fonts, colors, lines, borders, and graphs.

Major enhancements included in Release 3 and retained in Releases 3.1 and 3.1+ include the following:

- ◆ The capacity to have up to 256 worksheets in one file and multiple files in memory at a time
- ◆ The capacity to cancel printing from the /Print menu, create graphs automatically, and enter dates in many different formats
- ◆ The option to access external databases
- ◆ The improved quality of printed reports and on-screen and printed graphs

Releases 1A through 2.3 of 1-2-3 did not have multiple worksheet and multiple file capabilities. These earlier releases of 1-2-3 limited you to one worksheet per file; only one file could be opened at a time. Release 3 breaks this barrier, taking advantage of advances in hardware technology and operating system enhancements by providing up to 256 worksheets in a single file and multiple files in memory at one time.

What are the advantages to multiple worksheet and file capability? First of all, it's ideal for consolidations—of regional sales, of department budgets, of product forecasts, and so on. You can easily create formulas that reference cells in other worksheets and other files and are immediately updated when changes are made.

Besides consolidation applications, Release 3's multiple worksheet and file capability has many other uses. Rather than scatter separate applications and macros over one large worksheet, you can reserve a separate worksheet for each application—a workheet on one, a database on another, and a macro library on a third. Using separate worksheets helps you avoid accidentally deleting or overwriting data when you delete a column or row or move and copy data from one part of the worksheet to another. Another valuable use for multiple worksheets is for "what-if" applications. If you want to play out different business scenarios by changing a few assumptions within an original worksheet, you can copy a single worksheet to many other worksheets, change assumptions on each, and create graphs to show the results of each change.

Cue:
Use separate worksheets in the same file for applications and macros.

Seeing 1-2-3 as an "Electronic" Accountant's Pad

1-2-3 Release 3, as well as earlier versions, is like an electronic accountant's pad, or electronic spreadsheet. When you start Release 3, your computer screen displays a column and row area into which you can enter text, numbers, or formulas as an accountant would on one sheet of a columnar pad (and with the help of a calculator). The multiple worksheet and file capability of Release 3 extends this analogy further. Although Releases 1, 1A, 2.01, 2.2, and 2.3 each can be thought of as a single, large spreadsheet, Release 3 provides you with multiple accounting sheets containing data that is instantly accessible (see fig. 1.1).

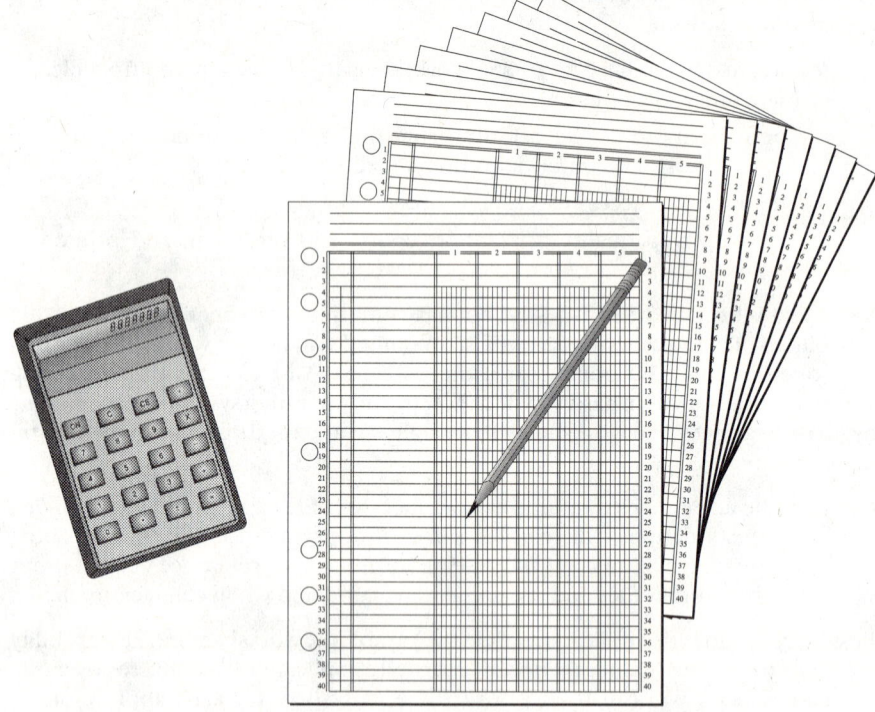

Fig. 1.1.

The multiple worksheet capability offered in 1-2-3 Release 3.

Release 3 frees you from the limitations and inconveniences of the single worksheet available with Releases 1A through 2.3 of 1-2-3. Release 2.3, for example, offers a single 256-column-by-8192-row grid on which to work. Of course, only a small part of this worksheet is visible at any one time. Organizing applications on such a large grid can be very cumbersome. When you create multiple worksheets in Release 3, one behind another, you can easily page through, using special combinations of the keys on your keyboard, and view three consecutive worksheets on-screen at one time. Depending on the amount of memory in your machine, you can add up to 255 worksheets behind (or in front of) the original worksheet that appears on-screen when you first start 1-2-3.

With Release 3, as with earlier versions of 1-2-3, the worksheet is the basis for the whole product. Whether you are working with a database application or creating graphs, the task is done within the structure of the worksheet. Commands are initiated from the menu commands that appear at the top of your screen (see fig. 1.2 for an example of a main 1-2-3 menu or fig. 1.3 for an example of a Wysiwyg menu). Graphs are created from data entered in the worksheet, database operations are performed on data organized into the worksheet's column and row format, and macro programs are stored in cells of the worksheet.

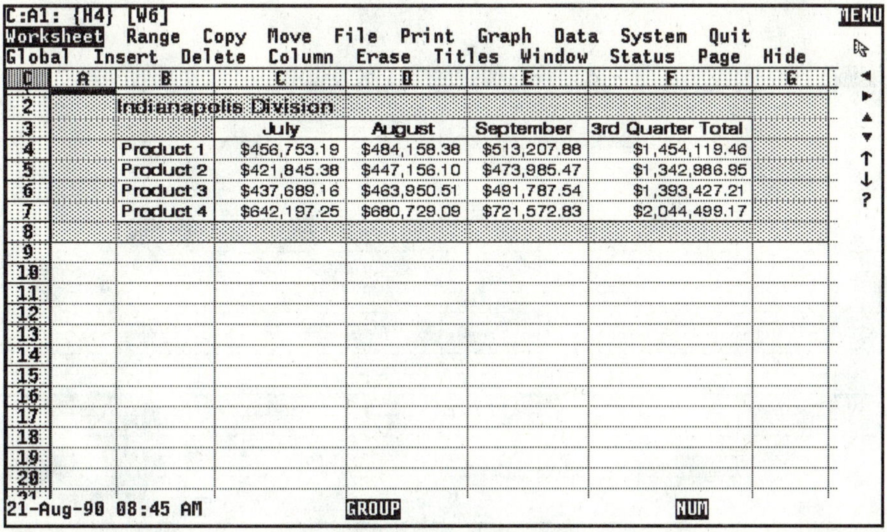

Fig. 1.2.
The main 1-2-3 command menu at the top of the screen.

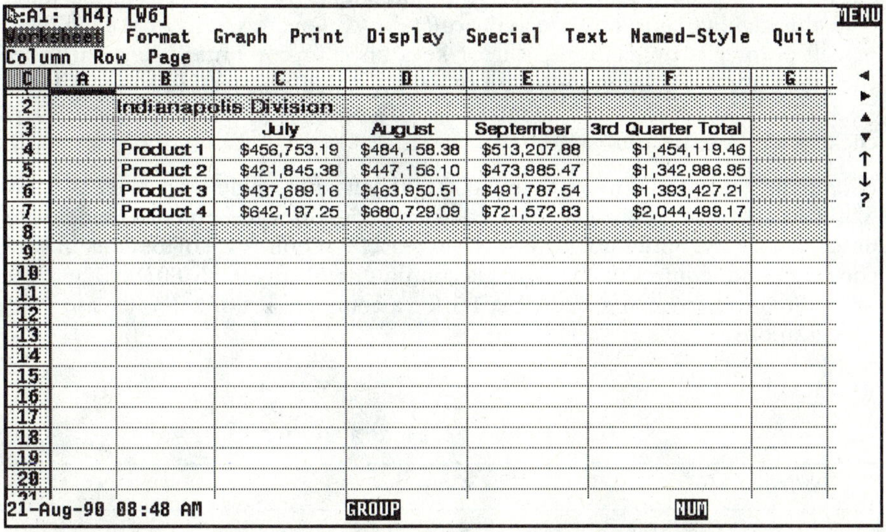

Fig. 1.3.
The Wysiwyg command menu at the top of the screen.

All data—text, numbers, or formulas—is stored in individual cells in the worksheet. 1-2-3 sets aside a rectangular area, its location indicated by the intersection of a particular column and row on the worksheet. If you type a number in the cell two rows down from the top border and three columns to the right of the left border, you are entering the number in cell C3 (see fig. 1.4). Columns in the worksheet are marked alphabetically from A to Z, then AA to AZ, then BA to BZ, and so on up to IA to IV; rows are marked by numbers from 1 to 8192. If you decide to open two or more worksheets, a cell is further identified by a letter prefix indicating which worksheet the cell is on. The letter A represents the first worksheet in the stack; B, the second; C, the third; and so on.

14 Part I ♦ Building the 1-2-3 Worksheet

Fig. 1.4.
1-2-3 worksheet cell.

A worksheet cell

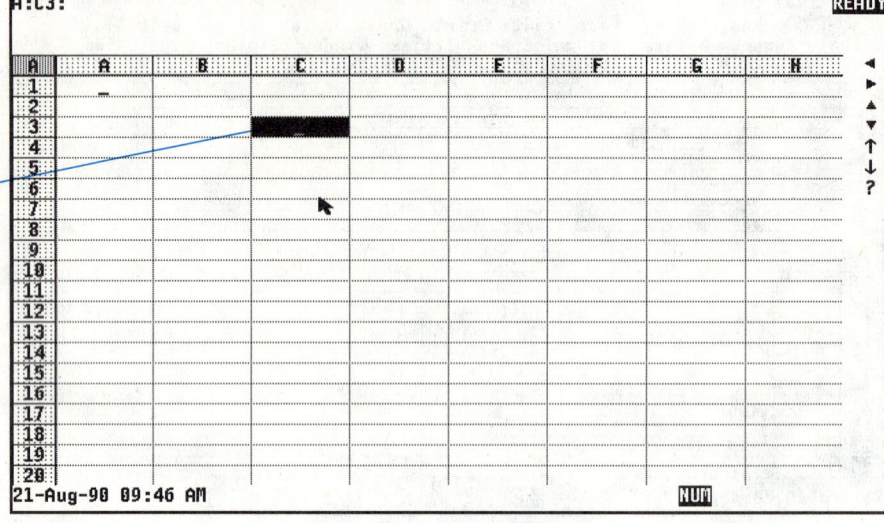

Reminder:
Use the cursor keys or the mouse to move the cell pointer around the worksheet.

As you are working in the worksheet, 1-2-3 highlights the cell where you can enter data; this highlight is referred to as the *cell pointer*. One way to move the highlight or cell pointer is by using the cursor keys on your computer's keyboard (see Chapter 3 for more information on moving the cell pointer). Releases 3.1 and 3.1+ offer you another way to move the cell pointer: by moving a mouse and clicking a mouse button.

Potentially, you can fill more than 2,000,000 cells in a single worksheet and 256 worksheets in a file. Few users will need or have computer equipment to handle this much data. At the minimum, though, Release 3.1+ requires 1M of memory in your computer and requires that you have a computer with an 80286, 80386SX, 80386, or 80486 microprocessor. See table 1.1 for a complete list of 1-2-3 Release 3.1+ specifications.

Table 1.1
1-2-3 Release 3.1+ at a Glance

Published by:

    Lotus Development Corporation
    55 Cambridge Parkway
    Cambridge, Massachusetts 02142

System Requirements:

    IBM PC AT or compatible 80286/80386SX/80386/80486 machine, or
      PS/2 Model 50, 60, 70, or 80
    Hard disk drive with at least one floppy disk drive

Chapter 1 ♦ An Overview of 1-2-3 Release 3.1+

System Requirements:

    Display: VGA, EGA, or high-resolution CGA or Hercules Graphics Adapter

    Disk capacity: 5M (6M with the Release 3.1+ enhancement add-ins)

    Memory size: 1M (1.5M recommended for Wysiwyg)

    Maximum usable memory: 640K conventional memory
                                 16M of extended memory
                                 8M of expanded memory (LIM Specification version 3.2)
                                 32M of expanded memory (LIM Specification version 4.0)

    Operating System: DOS V3.0 or later

    Optional hardware: color/graphics adapter, printer, plotter, expanded memory, 80287, 80387SX, 80387 math coprocessor

Price: $595

Creating Formulas

Because the primary use of 1-2-3 is for financial applications, 1-2-3's capacity to develop formulas is one of its most sophisticated and yet easy-to-use features. Creating a formula may be as simple as adding the values in two cells on the same worksheet:

    +A1+B1

Entered in another cell, such as C1, this formula indicates that the value stored in cell A1 will be added to the value stored in B1. The formula does not depend on the specific values contained in A1 and B1 but adds whatever values are entered. If A1 originally contains the value 4, and B1 the value 3, the formula computes to 7. If you change the value in A1 to 5, the formula automatically recalculates to 8.

You can create formulas that have *operators*: addition (+), subtraction (−), multiplication (*), and division (/). The capability of Release 3 formulas, however, is best shown by linking data across worksheets and across files. By referencing cells in other worksheets and other files, formulas can calculate results from numerous, separate worksheet applications.

Reminder:
With Release 3, you can use formulas to link worksheets across files.

When you create a formula linking data across worksheets, you first indicate what worksheet the data is located in (indicated by letter A through IV); then you follow this letter with a colon (:) and enter the cell address. The following example shows a formula that links data across three worksheets:

+A:B3+B:C6+D:B4

If the formula links data across files, the file name is entered in the formula. The following formula is an example of this technique:

+A:C6+<<SALES1.WK3>>A:C5..A:C5

See Chapter 3 for more information on creating formulas that link data across files.

Playing "What-If"

Because 1-2-3 does not simply calculate values but remembers the relationships between cells, you can change a value in a cell and see what happens when your formulas automatically recalculate. This "what-if" capability makes 1-2-3 an incredibly powerful tool for many types of analysis. You can, for example, analyze the effect of an expected increase in the cost of goods and determine what kind of price increase for your product is needed to maintain current profit margins.

With Release 3's multiple worksheet capability, you can play "what-if" by creating a series of worksheets and accompanying graphs showing the effects of certain changes from one worksheet to another. One worksheet, for example, might show the effect of an increase in the cost of goods without an accompanying increase in product price. Another worksheet might show the expected effect of special advertising or product promotion. You can easily create such a series of "what if" worksheets by simply copying the data on one worksheet to others and then changing each worksheet as needed to test various assumptions.

Examining Functions

Reminder:
1-2-3 Release 3.1+ has 103 predefined functions.

Building applications in 1-2-3 would be quite difficult if you couldn't calculate complex mathematical, statistical, logical, financial, and other types of formulas. Release 3.1+ provides 103 useful functions that let you create complex formulas for a wide range of applications, including business, scientific, and engineering applications. Instead of entering complicated formulas containing numerous operators and parentheses, you can use functions as a shortcut. All functions in 1-2-3 begin with the @ sign followed by the name of the function—for example, @SUM, @RAND, and @ROUND. Many functions require that you enter an *argument*—that is, the specifications the function needs to calculate the formula—after the function name.

Release 3 includes seven categories of functions: mathematical and trigonometric, statistical, financial and accounting, logical, special, date and time, and string.

Mathematical Functions

Mathematical functions, which include logarithmic and trigonometric functions, provide convenient tools that let you easily perform a variety of standard arithmetical operations such as adding and rounding values or calculating square roots. For engineering and scientific applications, 1-2-3 includes all standard trigonometric functions, such as those to calculate sine (@SIN), cosine (@COS), and tangent (@TAN).

Reminder: *Mathematical functions include logarithmic and trigonometric functions.*

Statistical Functions

Release 3 includes a set of 10 statistical and 11 database statistical functions that allow you to perform all the standard statistical calculations on your worksheet data or in a 1-2-3 database. These functions allow you to find minimum and maximum values (@MIN and @MAX), calculate averages (@AVG), and compute standard deviations and variances (@STD and @VAR). Database statistical functions are specialized versions of the statistical functions that apply only to 1-2-3 databases.

Financial Functions

One of the most used categories of functions is financial functions. These functions allow you to perform a series of discounted cash flow, depreciation, and compound-interest calculations that ease considerably the burden and tedium of investment analysis and accounting or budgeting for depreciable assets. Specifically, Release 3 includes two functions that calculate returns on investments (@IRR and @RATE), one function that calculates loan investments (@PMT), two functions for calculating present values (@NPV and @PV), one function that calculates future values (@FV), two functions that perform compound-growth calculations (@TERM and @CTERM), and four functions that calculate asset depreciation (@SLN, @DDB, @SYD, and @VDB).

Logical Functions

Logical functions let you add standard Boolean logic to your worksheet and use the logic either alone or as part of other worksheet formulas. Essentially, each of the logical functions allows you to test whether a condition—either one you've defined or one 1-2-3 has predefined—is true or false. The @IF function, for example, tests a condition and returns one result if the condition is true and another if the condition is false.

Special Functions

Special functions are tools for dealing with the worksheet itself. For example, one special function returns information about specific cells. Other functions count the number of rows, columns, or worksheets in a range. For example, @CELL and

@CELLPOINTER can return up to nine different characteristics of a cell, including the type of address and prefix, the format, and the width of a cell. @COORD specifies a cell address as absolute, relative, or mixed. @INFO lets you retrieve system-related information. The special functions are often used in macro programs.

Date and Time Functions

Cue:
Use the date and time functions to perform date and time arithmetic.

Date and time functions allow you to convert dates, such as September 7, 1991, and times, such as 11:00 A.M., to serial numbers and then use these serial numbers to perform date and time arithmetic. These functions are a valuable aid when dates and times affect worksheet calculations and logic. Date and time functions also are useful for documenting your worksheets and printed reports. For example, at the beginning of your worksheet, you can enter date and time functions that display the current date and time. When you print a report, if you include in your print range the cells containing these functions, the report shows the exact date and time you prepared the report for printing.

String Functions

String functions help you manipulate text. You can use string functions to repeat text characters, to convert letters in a string to uppercase or lowercase, and to change strings to numbers and numbers to strings. You also can use string functions to locate or extract characters and replace characters.

Using the Command Menus

The worksheet is the basis for all applications you create, modify, and print from in 1-2-3. Into your worksheet cells, you enter data in the form of text, numbers, and formulas. You perform operations on this data with two command menus in Release 3.1 and Release 3.1+: the main 1-2-3 command menu and the Wysiwyg command menu. The 1-2-3 menu lets you format, copy, move, print, create a graph, and perform database operations on this data. The Wysiwyg menu lets you enhance the look of text and numbers you enter, as well as enhance the look of graphs you create. Figure 1.5, for example, shows a worksheet with numbers formatted as currency. The worksheet has been dressed up with lines, shadows, and fonts selected from the Wysiwyg menu.

Reminder:
1-2-3 Release 3 has over 800 commands, some of which you use every time you create or modify a worksheet.

The commands in the main and Wysiwyg menus lead to many sublevels of commands, in total over 800 commands. Some commands you use frequently whenever you create or modify a worksheet application. Other commands, such as specialized database commands, you may rarely or never use. The following sections briefly introduce the commands you probably use most frequently—those commands related to creating and modifying worksheet applications.

Chapter 1 ◆ An Overview of 1-2-3 Release 3.1+   19

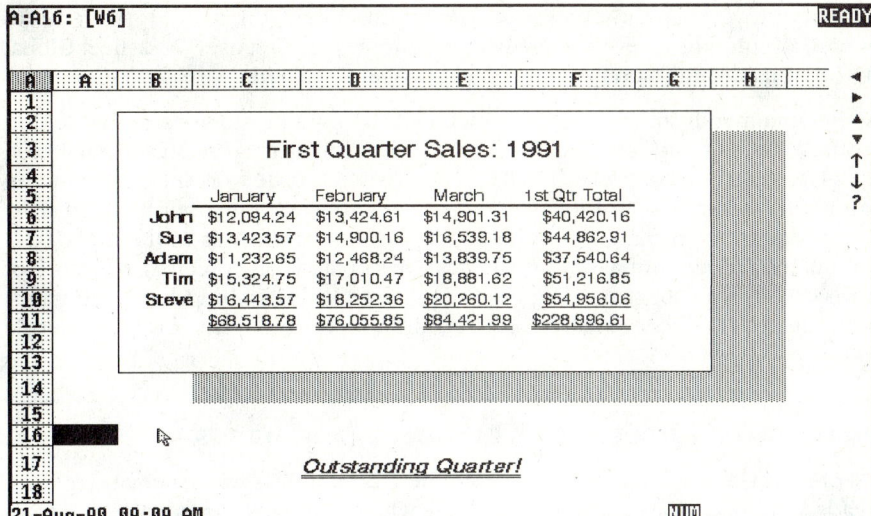

Fig. 1.5.
Numbers in a worksheet formatted with the Wysiwyg menu.

The 1-2-3 Menu and the Wysiwyg Menu

The 1-2-3 main menu is always available whenever you start 1-2-3. You access the 1-2-3 menu by pressing the / key. If you want to use the Wysiwyg menu and the mouse, however, you must first load the Wysiwyg feature into memory. If you want, you can install the Wysiwyg feature so that it loads automatically whenever you start 1-2-3 (install the Wysiwyg menu and mouse control using the Add-In feature). Once the Wysiwyg menu is loaded, you access it by pressing the : key.

Using the 1-2-3 Main Menu

In addition to the activities accessed by the main command menu, 1-2-3 provides menu commands that allow you to save and retrieve your worksheet as a file on disk, manage and change these files, and read files in formats different from a 1-2-3 worksheet file format. Still another command on the main 1-2-3 menu lets you temporarily leave a worksheet, return to the operating system, and then return to your original worksheet location.

Understanding the 1-2-3 worksheet structure and the effect of certain commands on the worksheet is the first step in using 1-2-3 successfully for your applications. When you begin to investigate the 1-2-3 command menu, you find that some commands affect a whole, single worksheet. And if you have multiple worksheets and want these commands to affect not just one but all, you need to use a special command, /Worksheet Global Group Enable from the main menu, before using the other commands. If you want, for example, to widen all columns on one worksheet, you use the /Worksheet Global Col-Width command. If you want to widen all columns on every worksheet in your file, you first use /Worksheet Global Group Enable and then use /Worksheet Global Col-Width.

Other commands in the 1-2-3 main menu affect only a portion or block of cells in your worksheet, referred to as a *range*. This range may be as small as a single cell or as large as thousands of cells, all contained on the same worksheet or spanning multiple worksheets. Multiple cell ranges are always a contiguous block of cells, either square or rectangular in shape. One of the commands in the main 1-2-3 menu, the /**R**ange command, affects only a designated cell or rectangular block of cells in your worksheet. As a beginning 1-2-3 user, keep in mind whether you want a command to affect a single worksheet, all worksheets at once, or just a specific range.

Using /Worksheet and :Worksheet Commands

Reminder:
The main menu /Worksheet commands enable you to change the way data and graphs appear on-screen; the Wysiwyg menu :Worksheet commands enable you to adjust the width of columns and the height of rows.

/Worksheet, the first command on both the 1-2-3 and Wysiwyg command menus, leads to those options that affect either the whole worksheet or columns and rows on the worksheet. With /Worksheet commands from the main menu, you can change the way numbers and formulas appear on a single worksheet or multiple worksheets—in percentage format, in currency format, in comma format, and so on. Other commands that affect the overall worksheet include those for inserting and deleting columns, rows, or individual worksheets in a file containing multiple worksheets. The /Worksheet menu provides a command that lets you clear the current file from your screen and computer memory, and replaces the screen with a new, clean worksheet. You also can hide a worksheet or worksheets to keep data confidential or from printing on a report.

Some main menu /Worksheet commands let you change the way data and graphs appear on-screen. You may, for example, freeze certain columns or rows so that they remain on-screen even though you move the cell pointer to other areas of the worksheet. You also can split your screen and display two areas of the worksheet—or different worksheets or files—at one time or split the screen so that worksheet data is displayed on the left side and a graph on the right. Finally, /Worksheet also gives you a status report displaying such information as how much memory is available for you to use and what settings are in effect for the worksheet.

The :**W**orksheet commands from the Wysiwyg menu let you adjust the width of columns and the height of rows. The Wysiwyg features of Releases 3.1 and 3.1+ let you enhance text and numbers by changing the typeface and type size. Although 1-2-3 automatically adjusts the height of a row to accommodate an enlarged typeface, the :**W**orksheet **R**ow command gives you manual control over this feature. The Wysiwyg :**W**orksheet menu also lets you insert page breaks into rows or columns of a worksheet.

Using /Range Commands

Apart from the commands for copying and moving data from one area of the worksheet to another or from one worksheet to another, one other command, /Range, on the main 1-2-3 command menu affects single cells or a square/rectangular block of cells. Some /Range commands control the way data in one cell or block of cells appears on-screen and on paper. You may, for example, change the way numbers and formulas are displayed; indicate whether you want text to be aligned to the left, right, or center of the cell; and justify the right margin of a block of text that spans many rows of the worksheet. You also can change data from displaying in column format to row format and vice versa. /Range lets you protect certain areas of your worksheet so that you or other users do not accidentally change, erase, or overwrite data. If you want to erase data in one cell or block of cells, use /Range Erase.

One of the most useful /Range commands lets you attach a name to a single cell or block of cells. You can create a formula, for example, that will total a column of numbers by simply entering the function @SUM followed in parentheses by the column's *range name*—@SUM(QTR1). Range names also are useful for printing. Rather than having to define the exact cell boundaries for an area you want to print, you can give that area a name and enter the name when you are asked to indicate the part of the worksheet you want to print. Other uses for range names include naming parts of a single worksheet or naming parts of many worksheets, and permitting easy movement of the cell pointer from one area to another. These are only a few of the many uses of range names. As you become accustomed to using range names, you find many occasions when they simplify your work and save time as you create and use worksheet applications.

Reminder:
Range names make the /Range commands easier to use.

Using /Copy and /Move Commands

As indicated in the previous sections, /Worksheet and /Range are two of the most frequently used 1-2-3 commands. Two other commands, however, also are used commonly for creating and modifying worksheet applications. As their names indicate, /Copy and /Move allow you to copy and move data from one cell or block of cells to another on the same worksheet or from one cell or block of cells to another worksheet.

The /Copy command saves you hours of time by letting you duplicate text, numbers, divider and formatting lines, and formulas. Copying formulas is one of the most important functions of this command. You can create a few key formulas and then copy these formulas to other parts of the worksheet where they can calculate values different from those that the original formula calculates.

When you use /Move, you can move not only the contents of one cell to another but also the contents of a large block of cells to another area of the worksheet or another worksheet. You move a large block simply by issuing the /Move command, highlighting the cells you want to move, and indicating the top left cell where you want the data to be relocated.

Using the Wysiwyg Menu

In addition to the 1-2-3 menu, Releases 3.1 and 3.1+ have the Wysiwyg menu, which is like the menu used with the add-in utility program Impress, and similar to the Allways menu of Release 2.2. (1-2-3 Release 2.3 also offers the Wysiwyg menu.) The Wysiwyg menu with mouse support does not load automatically. You must first install a mouse driver for your mouse, start 1-2-3, and then load the Wysiwyg menu. You can press Alt-F10, select Load from the menu that appears, and then choose Wysiwyg from the list of files that appears.

Reminder:
Pressing the right mouse button toggles between the 1-2-3 menu and the Wysiwyg menu.

Once you load Wysiwyg, you bring up the Wysiwyg menu by typing : or, if you have a mouse, by simply moving the arrow to the control panel. Pressing the right mouse button toggles between the main menu and the Wysiwyg menu.

As you have seen in previous sections, some Wysiwyg commands are the same as 1-2-3 commands. Other Wysiwyg commands are described in the following sections.

Using :Format Commands

The Wysiwyg :Format command leads to options that improve the appearance of text and numbers when printed. :Format options let you specify the font for a range and add or remove bold, italics, and underline attributes. The :Format command also lets you add or remove horizontal and vertical lines, outlines, and drop shadows from ranges, as well as add or remove single, double, or thick underlines from a range. Other options let you specify colors for background, text, and negative values in a range. The :Format Shade command lets you add or remove light, dark, or solid shading from a range.

Using :Display Commands

The Wysiwyg :Display command leads to options that change the way 1-2-3 displays worksheets on the screen. Using :Display, you can specify colors for all parts of the worksheet, namely the worksheet background, data, cell pointer, grid, frame, lines, drop shadows, negative values, and data in unprotected ranges. The :Display Mode command lets you switch the screen display between graphics display mode and text display mode, or between color and black and white. :Display Mode also lets you display page breaks and grid lines in a worksheet and lets you display up to 60 rows at one time on the screen.

Using :Text Commands

The Wysiwyg :Text command gives you more control over labels than with any previous version of 1-2-3. For example, the :Text Edit command lets you edit labels directly in the worksheet rather than in the control panel. The :Text Reformat command formats a column of long labels so that they fit within a text range and look like a paragraph. :Text Align, a command similar to 1-2-3's /Range Label command, aligns text at the right, left, or center of a text range.

Using the :Special and :Named-Style Commands

The Wysiwyg :Special command lets you copy or move formats from one part of a worksheet to another, or lets you copy a format from one file to another. These commands are useful when you want to have identical formats in several areas of a worksheet or when you want to format worksheets that have identical structures, such as monthly expense statements.

The Wysiwyg :Named-Style command lets you assign a name to a collection of Wysiwyg formats taken from a single cell. Then you can apply the style to one or more ranges in the current file. Up to eight named styles can exist in each file.

Understanding 1-2-3 File Management

The type of file you create most often when using Release 3 is a *worksheet file*. A worksheet file saves all the data, formulas, and text you enter into a worksheet and also saves such things as the format of cells, the alignment of text, names of ranges, and settings for ranges that are protected. Saved as Release 3 files, these files are stored with a WK3 extension. Worksheet files also may have a BAK extension, indicating that a backup file is saved on disk. A WK1 extension indicates that the file is a Release 2.01, 2.2, or 2.3 worksheet.

Reminder: *You use a worksheet file to store all the data, formulas, and text you enter into a worksheet.*

Four other types of Release 3.1+ files may be created: text files, denoted by a PRN extension; encoded print-image files denoted by an ENC extension; graph-image files denoted by a PIC extension; and files in graphic metafile graph-image format denoted by a CGM extension. With Releases 3.1 and 3.1+, Wysiwyg files are denoted by an FM3 extension.

One of the commands on the 1-2-3 menu lets you perform most of the file operations you need when creating and using worksheet applications. The /File command provides a wide range of file management, modification, and protection capabilities. Some of these commands are similar to your operating system commands, such as those that enable you to erase or list files. Other commands relate to specific 1-2-3 tasks and applications. You can, for example, combine data from several files, extract data from one file to another file, and open more than one file in memory at a time. "Reserving" a file is also possible so that only one user is permitted to write information to and update the file. The /File command is particularly important for those who are using 1-2-3 Release 3 on a network.

In addition to the 1-2-3 menu's options for managing, modifying, and protecting files, the Translate utility lets you "translate" several file formats that differ from the 1-2-3 worksheet file format. You can, for example, convert files from the following programs and read them into 1-2-3 Release 3.1+: dBASE II, III, and III Plus; Multiplan in the SYLK format; and other files in DIF format. You also can convert Release 3.1+ files to formats that can be read by 1-2-3 Releases 1A, 2, 2.01, 2.2, 2.3, 3, and 3.1; dBASE II, III, and III Plus; Symphony; and other programs that use the DIF format. You do not need to use the Translate utility to read worksheet files created by 1-2-3 Releases 1A, 2, 2.01, 2.2, 2.3, 3, and 3.1 and Symphony 1, 1.01, 1.1, 1.2, and 2.

Taking Advantage of File and Worksheet Protection

Cue:
You can protect all or part of a worksheet with 1-2-3's protection capabilities.

In addition to letting you assign "reservation" status to a file, Release 3 allows you to assign a password to a file so that file retrieval is restricted to those people who know that password. You may, however, want to give other users access to a file but restrict their ability to make changes or delete data, intentionally or unintentionally, in the application. For that reason, the /**W**orksheet **G**lobal **P**rot and /**R**ange **P**rot commands allow you to "lock out" changes to your worksheet. See Chapter 4 for more information on /**W**orksheet **G**lobal **P**rot and /**R**ange **P**rot.

The /**F**ile **A**dmin **S**eal command (discussed in Chapter 7) provides a different kind of protection to data in a worksheet. Using this command allows you to guard range names, worksheet global settings, and column settings from being changed.

Enhancing Worksheets with 1-2-3 Graphics

When 1-2-3 was first introduced, business users quickly recognized the advantages of being able to analyze worksheet data as instant graphs produced by the same worksheet program. Release 3 lets you create seven types of graphs: line, bar (both vertical and horizontal), XY, stacked-bar, pie, high-low-close-open, and mixed (a bar graph overlaid with a line graph). Depending on how data is organized in your worksheet, 1-2-3 can create a graph automatically. If you position the cell pointer within the matrix of data in consecutive columns and rows, 1-2-3 creates a graph automatically when you press the Graph (F10) key. You also can create a graph by using the /Graph Group command and highlighting a range of data.

Reminder:
Save a graph so that you can use it again.

Beyond creating a simple graph, 1-2-3 /Graph commands let you enhance and customize graphs for your needs. You can, for example, add titles and notes, label data points, change the format of values displayed on a graph, create a grid, and change the scaling along the x-axis or y-axis. By naming the settings you have entered to create a graph and saving the name, you can display the graph again whenever you access the file in the future. You also can use graph names to print graphs from the 1-2-3 /**P**rint menu.

Some earlier 1-2-3 releases provided the necessary tools for analyzing data in graph form but were primitive in their capacity to produce high-quality graphs on-screen and in printed form. Exceptions are Release 2.2 combined with the Allways add-in, Release 2.3 with the Wysiwyg add-in, and Release 3. Releases 3.1 and 3.1+, like their most recent predecessors, support the most advanced monitor adapters as well as high-quality printers. Depending on your monitor, graphs can be viewed either in full-screen view or in combination with the 1-2-3 worksheet. The quality of Release 3.1 and 3.1+ graphs can be enhanced by options on both the main and Wysiwyg menus.

The main menu lets you change type font and size, color, and hatch patterns. The Wysiwyg menu lets you enhance a graph with text, lines, arrows, polygons, rectangles, ellipses, or symbols. It also allows you to choose colors from a pallet of 224 choices. Release 3 prints graphs through the /**P**rint menu, the same menu you use to print worksheet data. If you are printing a graph in Release 3.1 or 3.1+ which has been enhanced with Wysiwyg, print through the :**P**rint menu. Unlike Releases 1A through 2.2, Release 3 does not require that you use a separate PrintGraph program.

Getting Acquainted with 1-2-3 Database Management

The column-row structure used to store data in the 1-2-3 worksheet is similar to the structure of a relational database. 1-2-3 provides true database management commands and functions, allowing you to sort, query, extract, and perform statistical analysis on data, and even access and manipulate data from an external database. One important advantage of 1-2-3's database manager over independent database programs is that its commands are similar to the other commands used in the 1-2-3 program. The user therefore learns how to use the 1-2-3 database manager along with the rest of the 1-2-3 program.

After a database has been built in 1-2-3 (an activity that is no different from building any other worksheet application), you can perform a variety of functions on the database. Some of these tasks are accomplished with standard 1-2-3 commands. For example, /**W**orksheet **I**nsert **R**ow adds records to a database. /**W**orksheet **I**nsert **C**olumn adds fields to a database. Editing the contents of a database cell is as easy as editing any other cell; you simply move the cursor to that location, press Edit (F2), and start typing.

Reminder: You build databases in 1-2-3 the same way you build any other worksheet application.

Data also can be sorted. You can perform sorts using alphabetic or numeric keys in ascending or descending order. In addition, various kinds of mathematical analyses can be performed on a field of data over a specified range of records. For example, you can count the number of items in a database that match a set of criteria; compute a mean, variance, or standard deviation; and find the maximum or minimum value in the range. The capacity to perform statistical analysis on a database is an advanced feature for database management systems on any microcomputer.

A 1-2-3 database can be queried in several ways. You may use /**D**ata **Q**uery **U**nique or /**D**ata **Q**uery **F**ind. After specifying the criteria on which you are basing your search, you ask the program either to point to each selected record in turn or to extract the selected records to a separate area of the worksheet. You also can ask the program to delete records that fit your specified criteria. The *criteria* refer to fields in the database and set the conditions that data must meet in order to be selected.

Several commands help the user make inquiries and remove duplicated data. All these commands, which are subcommands of /**D**ata **Q**uery, require that you specify one or more criteria for searching the database.

1-2-3 allows a great deal of latitude in defining criteria. As many as 256 cells across, each containing multiple criteria, may be included in the criteria range. Criteria can include complex formulas as well as simple numbers and text entries. Two or more criteria in the same row are considered to be joined with *AND*. Criteria in different rows are assumed to be combined with *OR*. Criteria may also include wild-card characters, which stand for other characters.

1-2-3 also has a special set of statistical functions that operate only on information stored in the database. Like the query commands, the statistical functions use criteria to determine the records on which they operate.

The statistical database functions are these: @DCOUNT, @DGET, @DSUM, @DAVG, @DSTD, @DSTDS, @DMAX, @DMIN, @DQUERY, @DVAR, and @DVARS. These functions perform essentially the same tasks as their spreadsheet counterparts. For example, @DMIN finds the minimum number in a given range. @DCOUNT counts all the nonzero entries in a range. @DSTD computes the standard deviation of the items in the range. @DQUERY selects a record from an external database.

The combination of these functions and 1-2-3's database commands makes this program a capable data manager. Although 1-2-3's data management capabilities are not equivalent to such dedicated database programs as dBASE III Plus, dBASE IV, or R:BASE, 1-2-3 really shines when used as an analytical tool in conjunction with a database. Because of Release 3's capability to access external disk-based databases, you can import records from another database, such as dBASE III, into a 1-2-3 worksheet. (1-2-3's data management capabilities are covered in detail in Chapter 12.)

Using the /Data Table Command

Reminder:
Data tables enable you to look at the outcome of a set of conditions.

One of the most useful, but most misunderstood, commands in 1-2-3's menu of /Data commands is /Data Table. A *data table* merely offers you a way to look at all the outcomes of a set of conditions without having to enter each set into the equation manually. The command allows you to build a table that defines the formula you want to evaluate and contains all the values you want to test. A data table is similar to the X-Y decision grids you probably built as a math student in high school.

You can structure a variety of "what-if" problems by using the /Data Table command. When combined with 1-2-3's database and statistical functions, /Data Table can solve complex problems. (Chapter 12 explains in detail the /Data Table command and gives examples that help you master this powerful tool.)

Applying Multiple Regression and Simultaneous Equations

1-2-3's multiple regression command significantly expands the program's capacity for statistical analysis. If you use regression analysis, the regression command could save you the cost of a stand-alone statistical package. For business applications, the /**Data R**egression command probably meets all your regression-analysis needs.

The /**Data M**atrix command lets you solve systems of simultaneous equations. This capability, although likely to be of greater interest to scientific and engineering users, is available to all.

Using the /Data External Command

One of the most significant single commands in Release 3 is the /**D**ata **E**xternal command. This command makes accessing data from many types of external databases a simple process. When you use the options available after selecting /**D**ata **E**xternal, you can access tables located in an *external database*—a file created and maintained by a database program such as dBASE III. Using the /**D**ata **E**xternal command to access data from an external table is possible only if a special driver file exists, making the transferral of data between the database and 1-2-3 possible. Release 3.1+ provides drivers for dBASE III and Paradox.

If the right driver file exists and a connection, or *link*, is established between 1-2-3 and an external database, you can perform several tasks. First, you can find and manipulate data in the external database and then work with that data in your worksheet. Second, you can use formulas and database functions to perform calculations based on data in the external database. And third, you can create a new external database that contains data from your worksheet or from an existing external database. (See Chapter 12 for more information on the /**D**ata **E**xternal command.)

Cue:
The /**D**ata **E**xternal command enables you to access tables located in an external database maintained by another application.

Printing Reports and Graphs

By using 1-2-3's **P**rint command from either the 1-2-3 menu or the Wysiwyg menu, you can access several levels of print options that let you print worksheet data and graphs for either draft review or more formal presentations. The /**P**rint command lets you send data and graphs directly from 1-2-3 to the printer or save worksheet data in a text file so that the data can be incorporated in another program, such as a word processing program. You save data and graphs to a file format that retains your selected report enhancements (such as boldface type, underlining, and italic) so that you can print later with an operating system command.

With the Wysiwyg menu's **:P**rint command, you can combine text and graphics anywhere on a page for sophisticated, publishing-quality output; you can preview all pages, including text and graphics, before printing; you can print in portrait or landscape mode on laser printers; and you can automatically compress a worksheet print range to fit a single page.

Cue:
Use **:P**rint to combine text and graphics on a report.

Release 3 provides a great deal of flexibility in printing reports. Unlike Releases 1A through 2.3, Release 3 does not limit you to entering one type of print range—

a contiguous block of cells on one worksheet. With Release 3, you can enter a single worksheet range to print, but you can also enter the following:

- ◆ A range that spans multiple worksheets or 1-2-3 main menu files
- ◆ A series of noncontiguous ranges from the same worksheet or from different worksheets or files

The /Print menus in 1-2-3 give you considerable control over the design of printed output—from simple one-page reports to longer reports that incorporate data from many worksheets and include graphs. One command available from both the 1-2-3 and Wysiwyg /Print and :Print menus provides options for developing page-layout features—setting margins, indicating text for headers and footers, telling 1-2-3 to print certain column or row data on every page, and setting the length of the page. A second /Print command available on the 1-2-3 menu lets you enhance your report by changing type size, character and line spacing, or printing in color. A third set of options, also available on the 1-2-3 menu, is used specifically for printing graphs; these options enable you to rotate the position of the graph on the page, change the graph size, and print in draft or final quality.

Keep in mind, however, that when you are working in the interactive graphics environment of Release 3.1 or 3.1+, it's possible to make font and color changes right on the screen and also combine numbers, text, and graphs on one or more worksheets. If you use these features, you probably do not need to use the second and third sets of commands just described.

Reminder:
With 1-2-3 Release 3, you can specify settings used to print a report, save those settings, and reuse them whenever you want.

Besides the commands that affect how your report and graph look when printed, other commands give you greater control over the printing process and operation of your printer. If you want to reuse settings you have entered to print a report, you can name these settings, save them with the file, and recall them at a later time. You also can easily clear settings—all or only certain settings—and reenter new ones in their place. Release 3 lets you temporarily stop the process of entering print settings, return to the worksheet to make a change, and then turn back to enter settings again, all without losing the initial settings.

For greater printer control, Release 3 lets you stop your printer to change the paper, ribbon, or toner cartridge and then resume printing at the point where it stopped. Also, unlike Releases 1A through 2.3, Release 3 lets you cancel printing from the main /Print menu. One of the major benefits of printing with Release 3 rather than with Releases 1A through 2.2 is that as you start printing, you may return to work within the worksheet while the printing job runs in the background.

Using Macros and the Advanced Macro Commands

Cue:
Use macros to simplify and speed up your work in 1-2-3.

One of 1-2-3's most useful features is its macro capability, which allows you to automate and customize 1-2-3 for your special applications. 1-2-3's macro and advanced macro command capability allows you to create, inside the 1-2-3 worksheet, user-defined programs to be used for a variety of purposes. At the simplest level, these programs save time. Just like the memory function keys of some telephones, which "remember" a set of buttons for a frequently used phone number, the macro commands reduce, from many to two, the number of keystrokes for a 1-2-3 operation. At a more complex level, 1-2-3's advanced macro commands give the user full-featured programming capability.

By using Release 3's Record mode, you can easily create a macro that records a series of keystrokes automatically. These keystrokes may then be copied to the worksheet as macros. In addition to naming a macro with the backslash (\) and a single letter, Release 3 lets you name a macro with a name consisting of up to 15 characters.

Whether you use 1-2-3's programming capability as a typing alternative or as a programming language, you will find that it simplifies and automates many of your 1-2-3 applications. When you create typing-alternative macros, you group together and name a series of normal 1-2-3 commands, text, or numbers. After you name a macro or advanced macro command program, you can activate its series of commands and input data by pressing two keys—the Alt key and a letter key— or by accessing a menu to select the macro name.

The implications for such typing-alternative macros are limited only by 1-2-3's capabilities. For example, typing the names of months as column headings is a task frequently performed in budget building. A 1-2-3 macro can easily reduce these multiple keystrokes down to a couple of keys. Macro programs also can make decisions. These decisions can be based either on values found in the worksheet or on input from the user at the time the sequence is executed. By combining the typing-alternative features of 1-2-3's macro capability with the advanced macro commands, you can create interactive programs that pause and wait for user input.

Cue:
Use macros to reduce the number of keystrokes you use to perform an operation.

When you begin to use 1-2-3's advanced macro commands, you discover the power available for your special needs. The application developer finds that the advanced macro commands are much like a programming language (such as BASIC). The programming process, however, is simplified significantly by all the powerful features of 1-2-3's spreadsheet, database, and graphics commands. Whether you want to use 1-2-3 to create typing-alternative macros or to program, Chapters 13 and 14 give you the information you need to get started.

Understanding 1-2-3 Hardware Requirements and Options

Because Release 3 contains many features not included in previous versions, Release 3 places more demands on computer hardware than any version of 1-2-3 previously written. Consider the following five factors in determining whether your system can run Release 3:

1. The type of architecture used by the computer
2. The type of microprocessor used by the computer
3. The amount of random-access memory (RAM) in your computer
4. The amount of available storage on the computer's hard disk
5. The type of operating system under which you plan to run Release 3

The following paragraphs explain the specific requirements for each of these five items needed to run Release 3.1+.

Because of the system architecture required by Release 3, many users will find their current systems unable to run the program. Also, much more memory is required than is required for Releases 1A through 2.3.

> **Reminder:**
> *You need at least an AT-class computer to run 1-2-3 Release 3.*

The specific hardware requirements for running Release 3.1+ are the following. At minimum, you need an AT type of system (a computer with an 80286 microprocessor).

The minimum requirements for running Release 3 under DOS are the following:

- System with AT type of architecture
- DOS V3.0 or higher
- 1M of memory or more (1.5M recommended for Wysiwyg)
- 5M of free disk space plus 1M for the enhancement add-ins of Release 3.1+

Release 3 does not run on a PC or XT type of system. The following types of systems can run Release 3:

Industry Standard Architecture (ISA) AT type of bus
- 80286 CPU
- 80386SX CPU
- 80386 CPU
- 80486 CPU

PS/2 Micro Channel Architecture (MCA) bus
- 80286 CPU (16-bit MCA)
- 80386SX CPU (32-bit MCA)
- 80386 CPU (16-bit MCA)
- 80486 CPU (32-bit MCA)

Extended Industry Standard Architecture (EISA) AT type of bus
- 80386 CPU
- 80486 CPU

> **Reminder:**
> *More powerful processors increase processing speed.*

Release 3 runs exactly the same on systems with 80286, 80386SX, 80386, or 80486 processors. The program makes no real distinction about which processor your system has, and no additional features are enabled for those who use more powerful chips. The only advantages for systems with more powerful processors include increased processing speed and greater efficiency in switching modes with the DOS-extender program.

Chapter 1 ♦ An Overview of 1-2-3 Release 3.1+

A few PC or XT systems actually have an 80286 or 80386 processor for increased performance. These systems usually have one or more 8-bit slots of the same system bus design featured on the original IBM PC. These PC and XT systems cannot run 1-2-3 Release 3 under DOS because they cannot run in the protected mode of 80286 or higher, a requirement of running Release 3 with the DOS-extender program.

Which Video Displays Does Release 3.1+ Support?

Release 3 supports all the existing display systems available on the market today. These systems include the following:

- Monochrome Display Adapter (MDA)
- Color Graphics Adapter (CGA)
- Multicolor Graphics Array (MCGA)
- Enhanced Graphics Adapter (EGA)
- Video Graphics Array (VGA)

In addition, Release 3 supports the following graphics products:

- Hercules Graphics Card
- Hercules InColor Card

Although Release 3 runs on a Monochrome Display Adapter (MDA), you cannot display graphics with such a system. The Release 3.1 and 3.1+ Wysiwyg enhancement works only on VGA, EGA, high-resolution CGA, or the Hercules Graphics Adapter. Which color display, though, is best for Release 3? Because a Video Graphics Array (VGA) system provides the best graphics resolution of the color adapters in the preceding list, it is the best choice for Release 3. Also, because VGA may display 25, 34, or 60 lines on-screen at one time, you can take advantage of Release 3's capability to toggle between different display modes. If you install 1-2-3 for two different modes, you can use a command to switch between, for example, the 25-line mode when you need large characters and overall clarity, and 60-line mode when you want to see a much larger area of your worksheet on-screen.

Reminder:
You cannot display graphics on an MDA system.

Which Printers Does Release 3.1+ Support?

In some of its early releases, 1-2-3 did not provide much support for laser printers. With Release 3, however, you can use a laser printer for professional-looking documents.

The following are some of the printers you can install with Release 3:

- Apple LaserWriter
- Epson FX Series, MX-80
- Epson LQ, LQ 800/1000, LQ 1500, LQ 2500
- HP ColorPro 7440A Plotter
- HP DeskJet
- HP ThinkJet
- HP LaserJet
- HP LaserJet+, 500+
- HP LaserJet II
- HP LaserJet IIP (Releases 3.1 and 3.1+ only)
- HP LaserJet III (Releases 3.1 and 3.1+ only)
- HP PaintJet
- HP PaintJet XL (Releases 3.1 and 3.1+ only)
- IBM Graphics Printer
- IBM ProPrinter
- IBM ProPrinter II/XL
- IBM ProPrinter X24/XL24
- IBM Quietwriter I, II, or III
- NEC Pinwriter P5
- Okidata Microline 84, 92, 93, 290I
- Toshiba 351 Series
- Xerox 4045 (Releases 3.1 and 3.1+ only)

Release 3 also supports other printers that are compatible with those in the preceding list. Simply select the compatible printer during installation.

Summary

1-2-3 Release 3 is the impressive successor in the line of 1-2-3 releases that revolutionized computing during the 1980s. With its tremendous power and capability, 1-2-3 Release 3 will foster another generation of computer users—businesses where the capacity of Release 3 will replace outdated software and machines, providing what many businesses until now depended on from larger computers. Release 3's capacity to create and manipulate data across many worksheets, link data among files, and produce high-quality graphics and printing will make 1-2-3 the new standard of the 1990s.

This chapter has described in general terms the capabilities that make 1-2-3 Releases 3, 3.1, and 3.1+ impressive programs. Turn now to the remaining chapters of the book and learn how to use Release 3, 3.1, and 3.1+ features quickly, easily, and productively.

Getting Started

2

This chapter helps you get started using 1-2-3 for the first time. If you are new to computers and are using DOS for the first time, several books published by Que Corporation can give you a basic introduction to your operating system. If you are using 1-2-3 with DOS, the *MS-DOS 5 QuickStart* provides a visually oriented approach to learning MS-DOS. Other Que titles that can serve as a reference when learning DOS include *Using MS-DOS 5* and *Que's MS-DOS 5 User's Guide*, Special Edition.

If you are familiar with 1-2-3 but new to Release 3.1+, you may find introductory material too basic. If you want to begin using the 1-2-3 worksheet immediately, first read through the tables in this chapter, and then skip to Chapter 3. The tables include important reference information about Release 3.1+.

This chapter covers the following topics:

- Starting 1-2-3 and Wysiwyg
- Exiting 1-2-3 and Wysiwyg
- Using the 1-2-3 Access System
- How 1-2-3 uses the computer keyboard and mouse
- How 1-2-3 uses the screen display
- Finding on-screen help
- Using the 1-2-3 Tutorial

The last section in this chapter presents information on the 1-2-3 Tutorial. Many first-time users find the Tutorial a helpful introduction to 1-2-3. If you are new to 1-2-3, you can use the Tutorial as you read through this book for the first time. If you have worked with 1-2-3, but are new to Release 3.1+, read through the appropriate parts of the Tutorial.

Part I ♦ Building the 1-2-3 Worksheet

Before you begin, be sure that 1-2-3 is installed on your computer system. Follow the instructions in Appendix A to complete the installation for your system.

Starting 1-2-3 from the Operating System

Two different methods of starting 1-2-3 are available. You can start from within the 1-2-3 Access System or directly from DOS. Most users start directly from the operating system because this method is easier, faster, and uses less memory. Starting from the operating system is covered in the following sections. Starting from the 1-2-3 Access System is covered later in the chapter.

Starting 1-2-3

If you have installed 1-2-3 according to the directions in Appendix A, the 1-2-3 program is now in a subdirectory named \123R3.

To start 1-2-3 directly from the operating system, use the following steps:

1. Change to the drive on which you installed 1-2-3. In most systems, this is drive C, but you may have installed 1-2-3 on drive D, E, or another drive. If 1-2-3 is installed on drive C and drive C is not the current drive, type **C:** and press Enter.
2. Type **CD \123R3** and press Enter to change to the \123R3 directory.
3. Type **123** and press Enter to start 1-2-3.

To simplify this process, you can create a start-up batch file or add 1-2-3 to a start-up menu. You can use a text editor or word processor to create an unformatted or nondocument text file if you are creating a batch file. The specific instructions depend on the program and operating system you use.

Cue:
Use a batch file to start 1-2-3.

The following steps show one way to create a start-up batch file by using the DOS COPY command. In most systems, batch files are kept in a directory called \BATCH, \BIN, or \UTILITY. In some systems, the batch files are in the \DOS or the root directory. In any case, the directory that contains the batch file should be a part of your PATH statement in your AUTOEXEC.BAT file. The following example uses the \BATCH directory:

1. Change to the directory in which you keep your batch files. Type **CD \BATCH**, for example, and press Enter.
2. Type **COPY CON 123R3.BAT** and press Enter.
3. Type **C:** (or the name of the drive on which you have installed 1-2-3), and then press Enter.
4. Type **CD \123R3** and press Enter.
5. Type **123** and press Enter.
6. Type **CD** and press Enter.
7. Press Ctrl-Z (press and hold the Ctrl key and press the Z key).

After creating this batch file, you need only type **123R3** and press Enter to start 1-2-3.

After you start 1-2-3, the registration screen appears for a few seconds while the program loads. Then a blank worksheet appears, and you are ready to start using 1-2-3.

Starting Wysiwyg

To take advantage of the new Wysiwyg features of 1-2-3 Release 3.1 and 3.1+, you have to load the Wysiwyg add-in into memory. This multistep procedure must be performed each time you start 1-2-3—unless you set 1-2-3 to load and invoke Wysiwyg automatically. If you want to learn how to set up your system to invoke Wysiwyg automatically, skip the discussion in the next three paragraphs.

To load Wysiwyg manually, press Alt-F10 (press and hold the Alt key and press F10). A menu, called the *Add-in menu*, appears in the control panel above the worksheet. You choose Load, the first choice on the menu, either by typing **L** (for Load) or by pressing Enter (because Load is already highlighted). After you choose Load, a list of add-in files appears. The file you should select is `WYSIWYG.PLC`. If the file is highlighted, just press Enter to select it. If not, use the right-arrow key to move the highlight to the file, and then press Enter.

When you select the file, a submenu appears. This menu lets you attach the Wysiwyg add-in to one of three function keys. Attaching an add-in to a function key means you can *invoke* the add-in (bring up the add-in menu) by pressing the Alt key and a function key.

This procedure is not recommended for Wysiwyg, however, because there are easier ways to invoke the add-in. It's best to simply select No-Key by pressing **N** (for **No**-Key) or pressing Enter. If for some reason you do want to attach Wysiwyg to a function key, select **1**, **2**, or **3** (for function keys Alt-F7, Alt-F8, or Alt-F9), either by typing the number or by highlighting it first and then pressing Enter. Once you make your selection, the Wysiwyg copyright screen appears, and then the Wysiwyg worksheet appears. You must select **Q**uit to leave the Add-in menu.

Loading Wysiwyg manually this way can take time because you have to do it whenever you start 1-2-3. You can save time by configuring your system to load Wysiwyg automatically. The procedure to set up your system to invoke Wysiwyg automatically requires the following steps:

1. Load Wysiwyg by pressing Alt-F10.
2. Choose **S**ettings **S**ystem **S**et either by typing **sss** or by highlighting each choice and pressing Enter.
3. Select `WYSIWYG.PLC` from the list of files that appears.
4. Select **Y**es (to automatically start the application when it is read into memory).

Reminder:
You must load the Wysiwyg feature after you start 1-2-3; alternatively, set up 1-2-3 to load Wysiwyg automatically.

5. Decide whether or not you want to attach Wysiwyg to a function key. It's best to select **No-Key**.

6. Choose **Update Quit**. This step completes the procedure.

The next time you start 1-2-3, and each time thereafter, the 1-2-3 worksheet loads, and then Wysiwyg loads automatically.

Reminder:
You must load the mouse driver separately from the Wysiwyg feature.

If you want to use a mouse with the Wysiwyg feature, you have to load a mouse driver before starting 1-2-3. If you are using a batch file to start 1-2-3, like the one described in the previous section, you can add commands to it that load the mouse driver. You also can load the mouse driver by adding it to your AUTOEXEC.BAT file, the file that automatically executes commands when you power up your PC.

1-2-3 Release 3.1+ does not provide the mouse driver; the company that manufactures the mouse does. Directions for adding a mouse driver are in the documentation you received with your mouse.

If you load a mouse driver before starting 1-2-3, a pointer arrow appears in the upper left portion of the screen when Wysiwyg is loaded into memory. The mouse controls the movement of the pointer—if you move the mouse, the pointer moves. You can use the mouse to select commands by pointing to the command and clicking the left mouse button. For example, to leave the Add-in menu, you move the pointer to **Quit** and click the left mouse button.

Exiting 1-2-3

To exit 1-2-3, you must use the 1-2-3 main menu. Press the slash (/) key, and the 1-2-3 menu containing 10 options appears across the top of the worksheet (see fig. 2.1). Selecting the **/Quit** option allows you to exit the worksheet and return to the operating system.

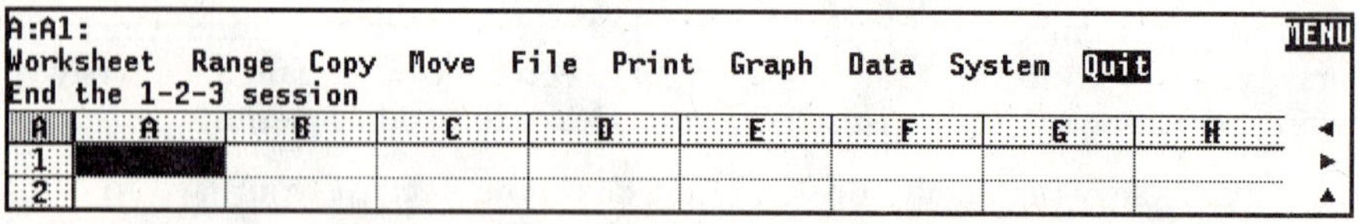

Fig. 2.1.
The 1-2-3 main command menu.

Caution:
Save your work before you quit the worksheet.

To select **/Quit**, use the right and left arrows to move the menu pointer or highlight to **Quit** and press Enter. You must verify your choice before you exit 1-2-3. Unless you have saved them, all worksheet files and temporary settings are lost when you quit 1-2-3. No is the default answer; to verify that you want to exit, move the highlight to **Yes** and press Enter (see fig. 2.2). If you made changes to any worksheets and did not save them, 1-2-3 prompts you a second time to verify this choice before you exit (see fig. 2.3).

If you want to save your files first, leave the highlight at **No** and press Enter to cancel the **/Quit** command. The commands to save files are introduced in Chapter 4 and covered in detail in Chapter 7. If you do not want to save your files and want to quit, highlight **Yes** and press Enter.

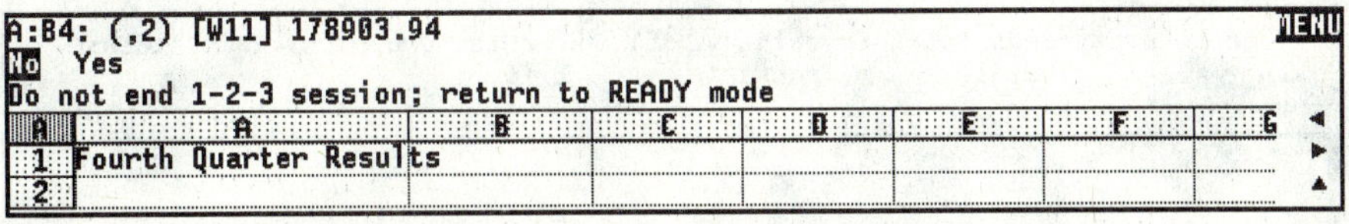

```
A:B4: (,2) [W11] 178903.94                                          MENU
No  Yes
Do not end 1-2-3 session; return to READY mode
         A           B          C          D          E          F          G
1   Fourth Quarter Results
2
```

Fig. 2.2.
The confirmation prompt to quit 1-2-3.

```
A:B4: (,2) [W11] 178903.94                                          MENU
No  Yes
WORKSHEET CHANGES NOT SAVED!   End 1-2-3 anyway?
         A           B          C          D          E          F          G
1   Fourth Quarter Results
2
```

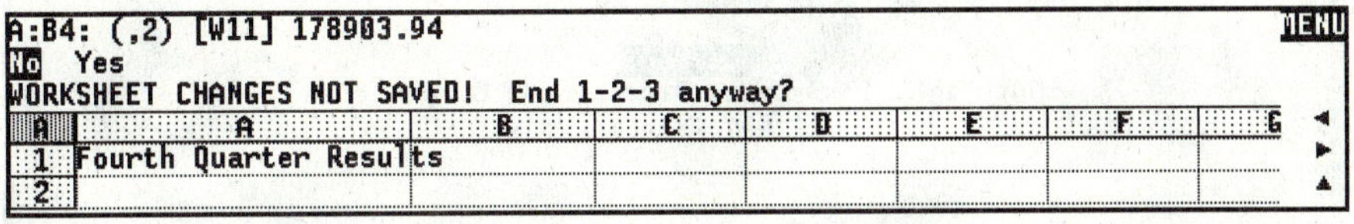

Fig. 2.3.
The second confirmation prompt to quit 1-2-3.

Mouse users can exit 1-2-3 another way, provided Wysiwyg is loaded into memory. First move the mouse pointer to the control panel above the worksheet frame. The mere act of moving the pointer arrow to this section of the display brings up either the Wysiwyg or the 1-2-3 menu. Clicking the right mouse button toggles between the two menus.

When you see the 1-2-3 menu, simply point to **Quit**, click the left mouse button, and then click **Yes**. Like before, if you made changes to any worksheets and did not save them, 1-2-3 prompts you a second time to verify this choice before you exit. Click **Yes** again to end your 1-2-3 session.

Using the 1-2-3 Access System

The 1-2-3 Access System is a way to use menus to access not only the 1-2-3 worksheet but also the Install and Translate programs (see fig. 2.4).

Use the Install program to change any installation settings, such as the type of printer and display, and different Wysiwyg options. (See Appendix A for a complete discussion of the Install program.) You use the Translate program to transfer files between 1-2-3 and other programs, such as dBASE II, III, and III Plus; Lotus Manuscript; programs that can read and write to the DIF format; and previous versions of 1-2-3 and Symphony. (See Chapter 7 for more information on the Translate program.)

Cue:
Appendix A contains complete installation instructions.

If you have installed 1-2-3 according to the directions in Appendix A, the 1-2-3 Access System is now in a subdirectory named \123R3. Use the following steps to start the 1-2-3 Access System:

1. Change to the drive on which you installed 1-2-3. In most systems, this is drive C, but you may have installed 1-2-3 on drive D, E, or another drive. If 1-2-3 is installed on drive C and drive C is not the current drive, type **C:** and press Enter.

2. Type **CD \123R3** and press Enter to change to the \123R3 directory.

3. Type **LOTUS** and press Enter to start 1-2-3.

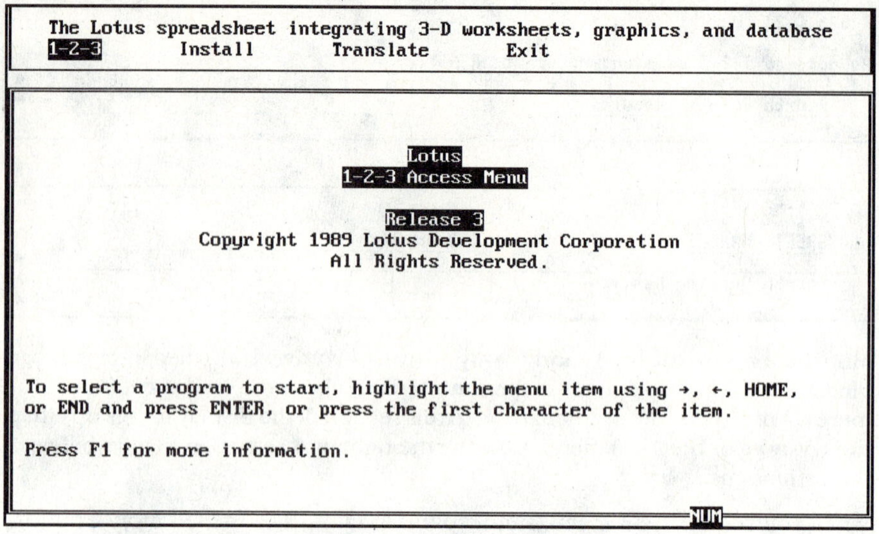

Fig. 2.4.
The 1-2-3 Access System menu.

```
The Lotus spreadsheet integrating 3-D worksheets, graphics, and database
 1-2-3      Install       Translate       Exit


                          Lotus
                    1-2-3 Access Menu

                         Release 3
              Copyright 1989 Lotus Development Corporation
                      All Rights Reserved.




        To select a program to start, highlight the menu item using →, ←, HOME,
        or END and press ENTER, or press the first character of the item.

        Press F1 for more information.


                                                                    NUM
```

Cue:
Use a batch file to start 1-2-3 from the Access System.

To simplify this process, you can create a start-up batch file or add 1-2-3 to a start-up menu. You can use a text editor or word processor to create an unformatted or text file if you are creating a batch file. The specific instructions depend on the program and operating system you use.

The following steps show one way to create a start-up batch file by using the DOS COPY command. In most systems, batch files are kept in a directory called \BATCH, \BIN, or \UTILITY. In some systems, the batch files are in the \DOS or the root directory. In any case, the directory that contains the batch file should be a part of your PATH statement in your AUTOEXEC.BAT file. The following example uses the \BATCH directory.

1. Change to the directory in which you keep your batch files. Type, for example, **CD \BATCH** and press Enter.
2. Type **COPY CON LOTUS.BAT** and press Enter to name the batch file LOTUS.BAT. If you want to name the batch file ACCESS.BAT, type **COPY CON ACCESS.BAT** and press Enter.
3. Type **C:** (or the name of the drive on which you installed 1-2-3) and press Enter.
4. Type **CD \123R3** and press Enter.
5. Type **LOTUS** and press Enter.
6. Type **CD** and press Enter.
7. Press Ctrl-Z (press and hold the Ctrl key and press the Z key).

If you have a mouse, keep in mind that you should add commands to load the mouse driver to this batch file. This step is not necessary if you load the mouse driver with the AUTOEXEC.BAT file.

After creating this batch file, type **LOTUS** and press Enter from the DOS prompt to start the 1-2-3 Access System. If you changed the batch-file name to ACCESS.BAT in Step 2, type **ACCESS** and press Enter to start the 1-2-3 Access System.

The 1-2-3 Access System menu appears (see fig. 2.4). The command menu includes the following four options:

> 1-2-3   Install   Translate   Exit

To select any of these options, highlight the menu entry and press Enter, or type the first letter of the menu entry.

Starting and Exiting 1-2-3 from the 1-2-3 Access System

The first option in the 1-2-3 Access System menu, **1-2-3**, starts 1-2-3. When the access menu appears, the highlight is on this option. To select the option, press Enter. If you have moved the highlight to another option, use the right-arrow or left-arrow key to return to the first option, and then press Enter. After you start 1-2-3, the registration screen appears for a few seconds while the program loads. A blank worksheet appears, and you are ready to start using 1-2-3.

To exit the 1-2-3 program, press the slash (/) key to access the 1-2-3 main menu. Use the right or left arrow to move the highlight to the **Quit** option, and then press Enter. You must verify this choice before you exit 1-2-3; when you quit 1-2-3, all worksheet files and temporary settings are lost unless you have saved them. To verify that you want to exit, move the highlight to **Yes** and press Enter.

If you made changes to any worksheets and did not save them, 1-2-3 prompts you a second time to verify this choice before you exit. To verify that you want to exit, move the highlight to **Yes** again and press Enter. Using the mouse, move the arrow pointer to the control panel and click the right button, if necessary, to display the 1-2-3 menu. Then make selections as just described, pointing to and clicking the left button for each choice you want to make.

Reminder: *When you quit the program, 1-2-3 prompts you to make sure that you want to abandon any changes you made.*

If you start 1-2-3 from the Access System, you return to the 1-2-3 Access System menu (see fig. 2.4) when you choose **Quit**. To exit the 1-2-3 Access System and return to the operating system, choose **Exit**.

Using the Install Program

Choose Install from the 1-2-3 Access Menu to access the Install program, which you can use to change the options you set during the initial installation. Complete installation instructions are found in Appendix A. You can run Install to prepare 1-2-3 for a different display or printer, or to select various Wysiwyg options.

Part I ◆ Building the 1-2-3 Worksheet

You can access up to two displays and up to 16 printers and plotters from within 1-2-3. You also can select Wysiwyg fonts and change mouse settings. But you must first use Install to tell 1-2-3 that these devices and fonts are available.

Cue:
When you add a new display or printer, 1-2-3 may prompt you to insert driver or font disks.

When you choose the **Install** option, you may be asked to place one or more of the driver or font disks into drive A to continue. Follow the prompts and insert any disks requested; then press Enter to continue the Install process.

You can go directly from the operating system to Install without using the 1-2-3 Access System. To start Install directly from the operating system, follow these steps:

1. Change to the drive on which you installed 1-2-3. In most systems, this is drive C, but you may have installed 1-2-3 on drive D, E, or another drive. If 1-2-3 is installed on drive C and drive C is not the current drive, type **C:** and press Enter.
2. Type **CD \123R3** and press Enter.
3. Type **INSTALL** and press Enter.

To exit Install, select `End Install Program` from the 1-2-3 menu. From the Exit screen, choose **No** to return to the 1-2-3 menu, or **Yes** to exit Install. If you start Install from the Access System menu, you return to the Access System menu when you exit Install. If, however, you start Install directly from the operating system, you return to the operating system.

Using the Translate Program

Cue:
Use Translate to exchange data among many different programs.

Choose **Translate** from the 1-2-3 Access System menu to reach the Translate program. The Translate utility provides a method to convert files so that they can be read by a different program. To execute Translate, you must copy the Translate file onto your hard disk by using the Install program. (See Appendix A for details.)

You can convert files *to* 1-2-3 Release 3.1+ format from the following programs:

- ◆ dBASE II, III, and III Plus
- ◆ Multiplan using the SYLK format
- ◆ Products that use the DIF format

You do not have to convert files from previous releases of 1-2-3 or Symphony. Release 3 can retrieve these files directly. See Chapter 7 for information about translating and accessing files from previous versions of 1-2-3 and Symphony.

You can convert files *from* 1-2-3 Release 3.1+ format to the following programs:

- ◆ 1-2-3 Release 1A, 2, 2.01, 2.2, 2.3, 3, and 3.1
- ◆ Symphony Release 1, 1.01, 1.1, 1.2, 2, and 2.2
- ◆ dBASE II, III, and III Plus
- ◆ Products that use the DIF format

When you convert 1-2-3 Release 3 files to previous releases of 1-2-3 or Symphony, you lose some information if you use any features of Release 3.1 and 3.1+ that do not appear in previous products, such as Wysiwyg (does not appear in any previous products), multiple-worksheet files (do not appear in Release 1A through 2.3), and functions such as @SUMPRODUCT (do not appear in Release 1A through 2.3).

If, however, you do not use advanced features of Release 3.1+, you do not need to translate the files. Just save the files with a WK1 extension (see Chapter 7 for details). These files can be read directly into previous releases of 1-2-3 and Symphony.

You can go directly from the operating system to the Translate program without using the 1-2-3 Access System. To start Translate directly from the operating system, follow these steps:

1. Change to the drive on which you installed 1-2-3. In most systems, this is drive C, but you may have installed 1-2-3 on drive D, E, or another drive. If 1-2-3 is installed on drive C and drive C is not the current drive, type **C:** and press Enter.
2. Type **CD \123R3** and press Enter.
3. Type **TRANS** and press Enter.

To exit Translate from the opening screen, press Esc. At the `Do you want to end Translate?` prompt, select either **No**, in case you decide to stay in Translate, or **Yes**. 1-2-3 returns you to either the Access System or the operating system.

Caution:
When you translate data from one program to another, you can lose some information.

Cue:
*Type **TRANS** to start the Translate program directly from the operating system.*

Learning the 1-2-3 Keyboard

The most common configurations for keyboards on IBM and IBM-compatible personal computers are shown in figures 2.5, 2.6, and 2.7. The enhanced keyboard, shown in figure 2.7, is now the standard keyboard on all new IBM personal computers and most compatibles. Some compatibles, especially laptops, have different keyboards.

The keyboards are divided into four or five sections: the *alphanumeric keys* in the center, the *numeric keypad* on the right, and the *function keys* on the left or across the top. The *special keys* are found in various locations. The *cursor-movement* keys are found in a separate section on the enhanced keyboard only.

Most keys in the alphanumeric section match the keys on a typewriter, and most maintain their normal functions in 1-2-3. Several keys, however, take on new and unique functions or are not found on typewriter keyboards.

You use the keys on the numeric keypad (on the right side of the keyboard) to enter numbers or to move the cell pointer around the screen.

The function keys provide special actions. For example, they can be used to access 1-2-3's editing functions, to display graphs, and to call up help messages. These keys are located across the top of the enhanced keyboard and on the left side of the other two keyboards.

Reminder:
Some keys take on special meaning in 1-2-3.

42   Part I ♦ Building the 1-2-3 Worksheet

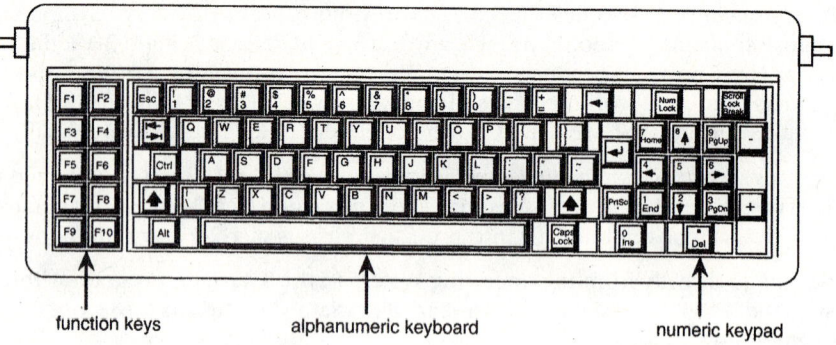

Fig. 2.5.
The original IBM PC keyboard.

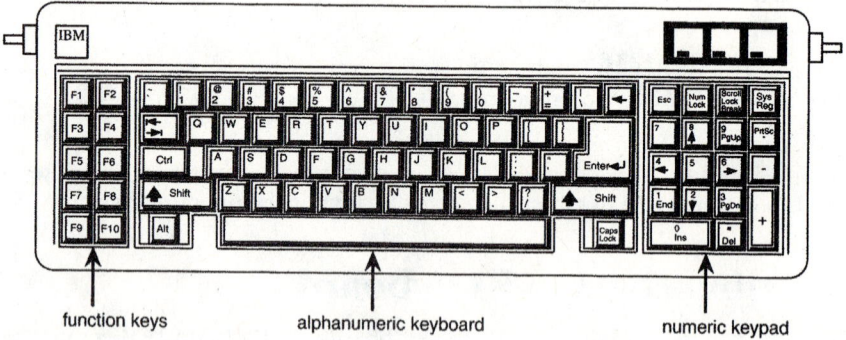

Fig. 2.6.
The original IBM AT keyboard.

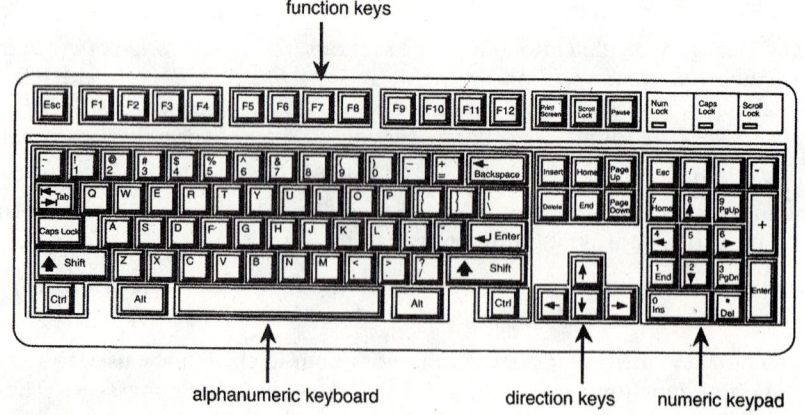

Fig. 2.7.
The enhanced keyboard.

The special keys are Del (Delete), Ins (Insert), Esc (Escape), Num Lock (Number Lock), Scroll Lock, Break, and Pause. These keys, which provide certain special actions, are located in different places on different keyboards.

Only the enhanced keyboard has a separate section for cursor-movement keys—the up-, down-, left-, and right-arrow keys. Use the enhanced keyboard's numeric keypad—actually, a cursor/numeric keypad—to enter numbers and use the keyboard's cursor-movement keys to move easily around the worksheet.

Reminder: *Use the enhanced keyboard's numeric keypad to enter numbers; use the separate arrow keys to move around the worksheet.*

The Alphanumeric Keys

Although most of the alphanumeric keys shown in figures 2.5, 2.6, and 2.7 have the same functions as on a typewriter, several keys have special functions in 1-2-3. These keys and their functions are listed in table 2.1. The meaning of these keys becomes more clear as they are used and explained in later chapters.

Table 2.1
Alphanumeric Key Operation

Key	Function
→| (Tab)	Moves cell pointer one screen to the right.
|← (Shift-Tab)	Moves cell pointer one screen to the left.
Caps Lock	Shifts the letter keys to uppercase.
	Note: Unlike the shift-lock key on a typewriter, Caps Lock has no effect on numbers and symbols.
↑ (Shift)	Used with another key, shifts the character produced. Used with a letter, produces an uppercase letter. Used with a number or symbol, produces the shifted character on that key. Used with the numeric keypad, produces a number. Used with Caps Lock and a letter, produces a lowercase letter. Used with Num Lock and the numeric keypad, produces a cursor-movement key.
Ctrl	A special type of shift key. Used with several keys to change their functions.
Alt	A special type of shift key. Used with the function keys, provides different functions. Used with letter keys, invokes macros.
Backspace	During cell definition or editing, erases the preceding character. Cancels a range during some prompts that display the old range. Displays the previous help screen when using Help.
/ (slash)	Starts a command from READY mode. Used as the division sign when entering data or editing a formula in a cell

continued

Table 2.1—(continued)

Key	Function
< (less-than sign)	Used as an alternative to the slash (/) to start a command from READY mode. Also used in logical formulas.
. (period)	When used in a range address, separates the address of the cell at the beginning of the range from the address of the cell at the end of the range.
: (colon)	Starts a Wysiwyg command from READY mode.

The Numeric Keypad and the Cursor-Movement Keys

The keys in the numeric keypad on the right side of IBM PC-style and AT-style keyboards are used mainly for cursor movement (see figs. 2.5 and 2.6). When Num Lock is off, these keys are used as movement keys. When Num Lock is on, these keys serve as number keys. You can reverse the setting of Num Lock by holding the Shift key before you press one of the numeric keys. The enhanced keyboard has separate keys for cursor movement (see fig. 2.7). The functions of the cursor-movement keys are explained in Chapter 3; the other special keys on the numeric keypad are discussed later in this chapter.

Cue:
Macros can solve numeric-keypad problems on PC-style and AT-style keyboards.

If you do not have an enhanced keyboard, you can use a macro to move the cell pointer every time you press Enter. You can then keep Num Lock on and use the numeric keypad to enter numbers. You can use different macros to move the cell pointer in different directions.

The Function Keys

The 10 function keys, F1 through F10, are used for special actions in 1-2-3. These keys are located across the top of the enhanced keyboard and on the left side of the other two keyboards. The enhanced keyboard has 12 function keys, but 1-2-3 uses only the first 10. These keys can be used alone or with the Alt key. Table 2.2 lists the function keys and an explanation of each key's action.

The Special Keys

Reminder:
Use Esc to cancel a menu or an action; use Break to cancel a menu or a macro.

The special keys provide some important 1-2-3 functions. For example, certain special keys cancel an action. Both Esc and Break cancel a menu. Also, Esc cancels an entry, and Break cancels a macro. The Del key deletes a character when you are editing a cell.

**Table 2.2
Function Key Operation**

Key	Function
F1 (Help)	Accesses the on-line help facility.
F2 (Edit)	Puts 1-2-3 into EDIT mode to change the current cell.
F3 (Name)	Displays a list of names any time a command or formula can accept a range name or a file name. After @ is used in a formula, displays a list of functions. After a left brace({) is typed in a label, displays a list of macro key names and advanced macro commands. Whenever a list of names is on the third line of the control panel, this key produces a full-screen display of all available names.
F4 (Abs)	Changes a cell or range address from relative to absolute to mixed and back to relative.
F5 (GoTo)	Moves the cell pointer to a cell address or range name.
F6 (Window)	Moves the cell pointer to another window or worksheet when the screen is split.
F7 (Query)	In READY mode, repeats the last /Data Query command. During a /Data Query Find, switches between FIND and READY mode.
F8 (Table)	Repeats the last /Data Table command.
F9 (Calc)	In READY mode, recalculates all worksheets in memory. If entering or editing a formula, converts the formula to its current value.
F10 (Graph)	Displays the current graph if one exits. If no current graph exists, displays the data around the cell pointer.
Alt-F1 (Compose)	Creates international characters that cannot be typed directly using the keyboard.
Alt-F2 (Record)	Allows you to save up to the last 512 keystrokes in a cell or to repeat a series of commands.
Alt-F3 (Run)	Runs a macro.
Alt-F4 (Undo)	Reverses the last action.
Alt-F5	Not defined in Release 3.
Alt-F6 (Zoom)	Enlarges a split window to full size.
Alt-F7 (App1)	Starts an add-in program assigned to this key.
Alt-F8 (App2)	Starts an add-in program assigned to this key.
Alt-F9 (App3)	Starts an add-in program assigned to this key.
Alt-F10 (Add-in)	Accesses the Add-in menu.

Some special keys change the actions of other keys. When you edit data in a cell, you can use the Ins key to change the mode from insert to overtype. Num Lock changes the meaning of the keys on the numeric keypad from movement keys to number keys. Scroll Lock changes how the arrow keys move the display. The functions and locations of the special keys on the different keyboards are listed in table 2.3.

Table 2.3
Special Key Operation

Cue:
Note the differences between the enhanced, PC-style, and AT-style keyboards.

Key	Function
Break	Cancels a macro or cancels menu choices and returns to READY mode. *Note:* On the PC and AT keyboards, Break is Ctrl-Scroll Lock. On the enhanced keyboard, Break is Ctrl-Pause.
Del	When editing a cell, deletes one character at the cursor. In the Install program, reverses the selection of the highlighted display or printer choice.
Esc	When accessing the command menus, cancels the current menu and backs up to the previous menu. If at the 1-2-3 menu, returns to READY mode. When entering or editing data in a cell, clears the edit line. Cancels a range during some prompts that display the old range. Returns from the on-line help facility. *Note:* On the original PC keyboard, Esc is to the left of the 1 key in the alphanumeric section. On the AT-style keyboard, Esc is at the upper left of the numeric keypad. On the enhanced keyboard, Esc is to the left of the F1 key.
Ins	When editing a cell, changes mode to overtype. Any keystrokes replace whatever is at the cursor position in the cell. If you toggle Ins to return to insert mode, any keystrokes are inserted at the cursor position.
Num Lock	Shifts the actions of the numeric keypad from cursor-movement keys to numbers. On the PC and AT keyboards, Ctrl-Num Lock serves as the Pause key. *Note:* On both the original PC and the enhanced keyboard, Num Lock is at the upper left of the numeric keypad. On the AT-style keyboard, Num Lock is next to Esc on the numeric keypad.
Pause	Pauses a macro, a recalculation, and some commands until you press any key. *Note:* On the PC and AT keyboards, Pause is Ctrl-Num Lock. On the enhanced keyboard, Pause is a separate key to the right of Scroll Lock.
Scroll Lock	Scrolls the entire window when you use the arrow keys.

Note: On the PC and AT keyboards, Ctrl-Scroll Lock serves as the Break key. On the PC and AT keyboards, Scroll Lock is to the right of the Num Lock on the numeric keypad. On the enhanced keyboard, Scroll Lock is to the right of the function keys.

Using the Mouse with 1-2-3

When you load Wysiwyg into memory (Release 3.1 or 3.1+ only), your mouse (if one is installed) can replace some of the activities normally done from the keyboard. The mouse pointer, a small arrow, points to the center of the screen when Wysiwyg is loaded. Pressing either the right or left mouse button enables you to select commands, switch between the 1-2-3 and Wysiwyg menus, move the cell pointer, and select ranges. Before using the mouse, you should be familiar with some terms, as well as be acquainted with using the mouse.

Cue:
Use the mouse to perform an action instead of pressing several keyboard keys.

Understanding Mouse Terminology

One of the terms that you have become acquainted with is the *mouse pointer*, the arrow that moves on the screen as you move the mouse. Additional terms to become familiar with are *point*, *click*, *click-and-drag*, and *icon*.

To *point* means to move the mouse until the tip of the arrow is pointing on something. For example, if you are instructed to point to cell B5, then you must move the mouse until the tip of the arrow is *over* cell B5.

When you *click* the mouse, you press and immediately release one of the two buttons on the mouse. (If your mouse has three buttons, only the two outside buttons are active. The center button is not used.) Normally, you only click a mouse button after you have pointed with the mouse. The left button on the mouse acts as the Enter key. The right button has two functions. Normally, the right button acts as the Esc key; if you are typing text into a cell, for example, pressing the right button erases the text from the edit line and returns 1-2-3 to READY mode. The second function of the right mouse button is to switch between the 1-2-3 menu and the Wysiwyg menu.

When installing 1-2-3, you can reverse the operations of the mouse buttons. That is, you can make the right button the Enter button and the left button the Esc/Switch button. This is helpful if you are left-handed because the reversal of the buttons allows the primary button to be pressed with the index finger and the secondary button to be pressed with the middle finger.

Cue:
If you are left-handed, reverse the operations of the two mouse buttons when installing 1-2-3.

Click-and-drag is a combination of pointing, clicking, and moving the mouse. When you are using this method, you normally are highlighting a range. To click-and-drag, move the mouse pointer to the desired beginning location. Press and hold the left mouse button; do not release the button at this time. Move the mouse to the desired ending location and release the mouse button. To select a range from B5 through D10, point to cell B5, press and hold the left mouse button, and point to cell D10; then release the left mouse button.

An *icon* is a character that represents an action. Notice the right side of the screen shown in figure 2.8. There are four triangles, two arrows, and one question mark. These are icons. When you point and click on one of the icons, you invoke an action. Clicking any of the triangles has the same action as pressing one of the arrow keys; the cell pointer moves one cell in the direction indicated by the triangle. Clicking the arrows is the same as pressing the Ctrl-PgUp or Ctrl-PgDn keys; the up arrow is the Ctrl-PgUp key and the down arrow is the Ctrl-PgDn key. Finally, clicking the question mark selects Help, just as if you pressed the F1 function key.

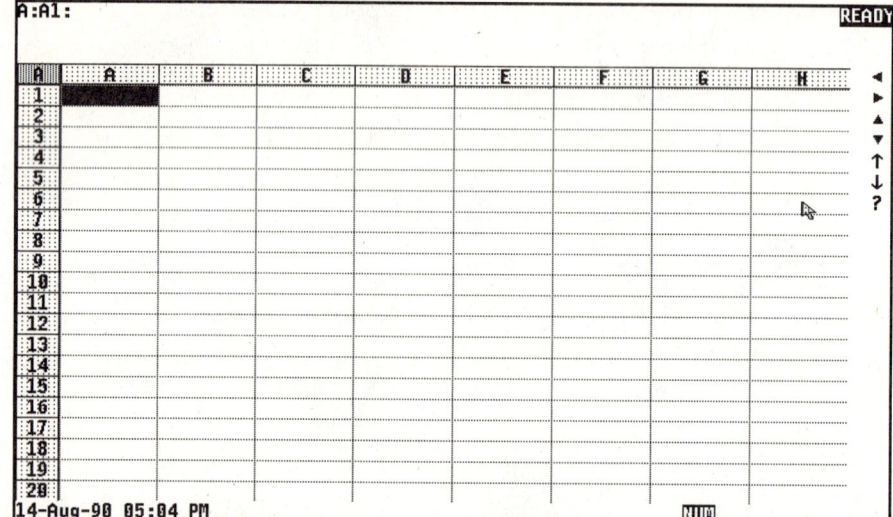

Fig. 2.8.

The seven mouse icons on the right side of the Release 3.1 and 3.1+ screen.

Using the Mouse To Select Menu Commands

Reminder:

Press the right mouse button to switch between the 1-2-3 and Wysiwyg menus.

When you move the mouse pointer into the control panel area, a menu automatically appears on the screen as if you pressed the slash or colon key. The menu that appears (1-2-3 or Wysiwyg) depends on the last menu that was active. Pressing the right mouse button switches between the 1-2-3 and Wysiwyg menus.

Using the mouse to select an option from a menu is easy. First, activate a menu by moving the mouse pointer to the control panel. Once a menu is active, point to a menu option, and click the left mouse button. All options from menus are selected in the same way. If the command requires you to type additional information, you may do so, pressing either Enter or the left mouse button in the control panel to accept the entry.

Using the mouse can greatly increase your speed and productivity. If, however, you have used 1-2-3 in the past, you may be more comfortable using the keyboard. Experiment with using the mouse, the keyboard, or a combination of both to find which combination is best for you.

Chapter 2 ♦ Getting Started   49

Learning the 1-2-3 Screen Display

The main 1-2-3 display is divided into three parts: the *control panel* at the top of the screen, the *worksheet area* itself, and the *status line* at the bottom of the screen (see fig. 2.9). The reverse-video *worksheet frame* marks the worksheet area. This border contains the letters and numbers that mark columns and rows.

The *cell pointer* marks the location of the current cell in the worksheet area; that is, the intersection of a column and a row. When you enter data into the worksheet, the data goes into the location marked by the cell pointer.

A *file* is made up of 1 to 256 separate worksheets. More than one file can be in memory at one time. You can change the display to show multiple worksheets in two or three windows. These subjects are covered in later chapters. For now, this chapter looks at the display with one file and one worksheet in memory and one window.

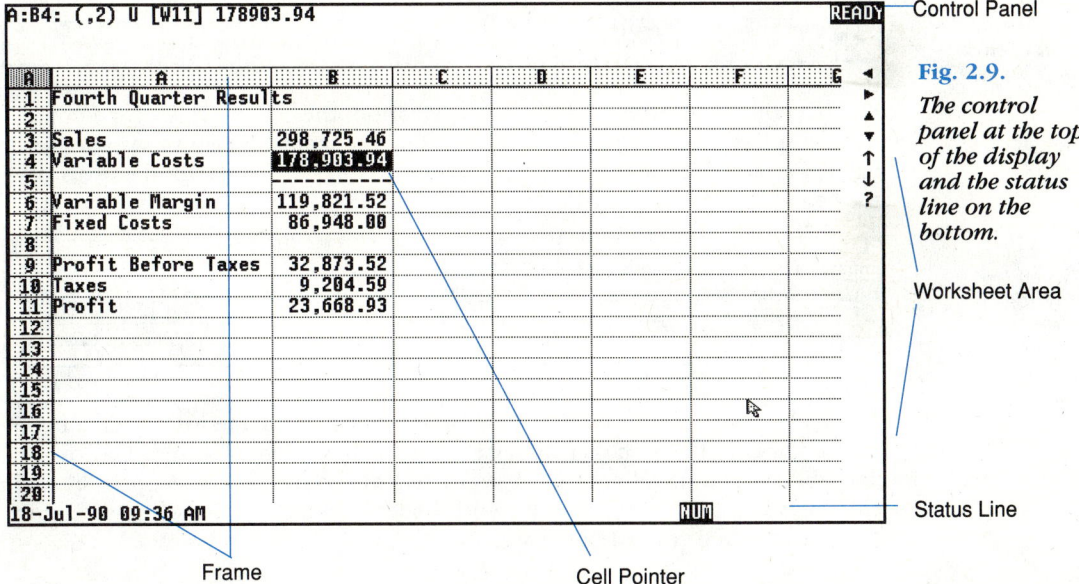

Fig. 2.9.

The control panel at the top of the display and the status line on the bottom.

The Control Panel

The three-line control panel is the area above the reverse-video border. The first line contains information about the current cell. This information can include the address of the cell, the cell's contents, and the protection status (U if unprotected or PR if protected). The format and column width are included if different from the default; these attributes are explained in later chapters. When Wysiwyg is active, information applicable to Wysiwyg, such as row height, graph, and text format, is also in the control panel.

Cue:
The third line of the control panel displays an explanation of the highlighted command or a preview of the next menu.

The cell's address is the worksheet, the column, and the row in the form A:B4 for worksheet A, column B, row 4. If the file contains only one worksheet, the worksheet is always A.

When you use the command menus, the second line of the control panel displays the menu choices, and the third line contains explanations of the current menu item or the next hierarchical menu (see fig. 2.10). As you move the pointer from one item to the next in a command menu, the explanation on the third line of the control panel changes.

To better understand this change in information that occurs on the third line, compare the third line of the control panel in figure 2.10 (with the Worksheet command highlighted) to the third line of the control panel in figure 2.1 (with the Quit command highlighted).

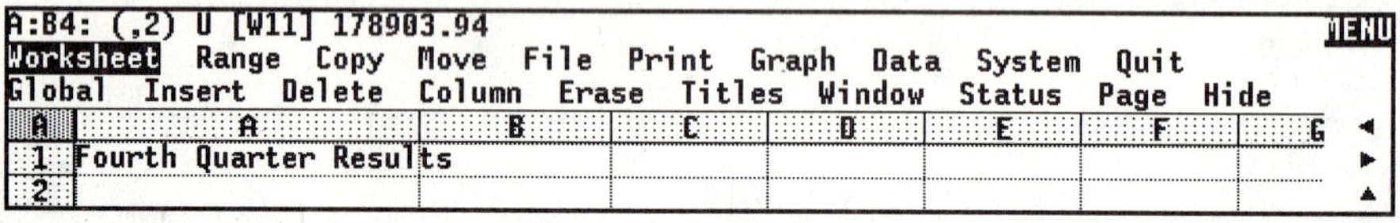

Fig. 2.10.
The 1-2-3 menu with the Worksheet menu option highlighted.

```
A:B4: (,2) U [W11] 178903.94                                    MENU
Worksheet  Range  Copy  Move  File  Print  Graph  Data  System  Quit
Global  Insert  Delete  Column  Erase  Titles  Window  Status  Page  Hide
```

When a command prompts you for information, the second line of the control panel displays the prompt (see fig. 2.11). When a command prompts you for a file name, a range name, a graph name, or a print settings name, the third line displays the beginning of this list of names.

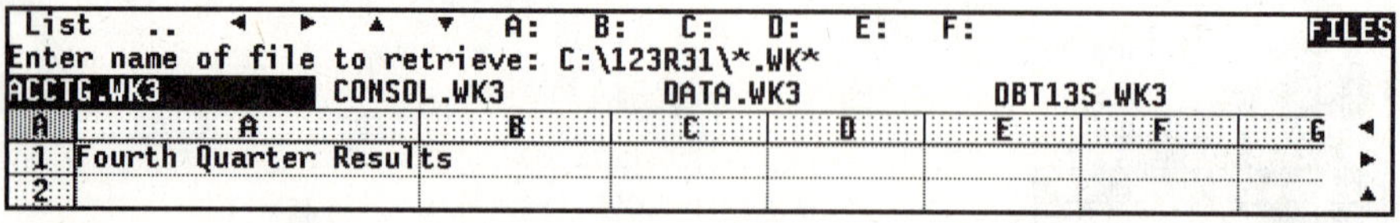

Fig. 2.11.
The display showing command prompts on the second line.

```
List     ..  ◄  ►  ▲  ▼    A:    B:    C:    D:    E:    F:       FILES
Enter name of file to retrieve: C:\123R31\*.WK*
ACCTG.WK3          CONSOL.WK3          DATA.WK3          DBT13S.WK3
```

When you enter or edit data in a cell, the second line contains the data being entered or edited. When you enter or edit data that is too long to display on one line, the control panel area enlarges to accommodate the largest possible cell entry, which is 512 characters. The worksheet area is pushed down to make room for the expanded control panel area (see fig. 2.12).

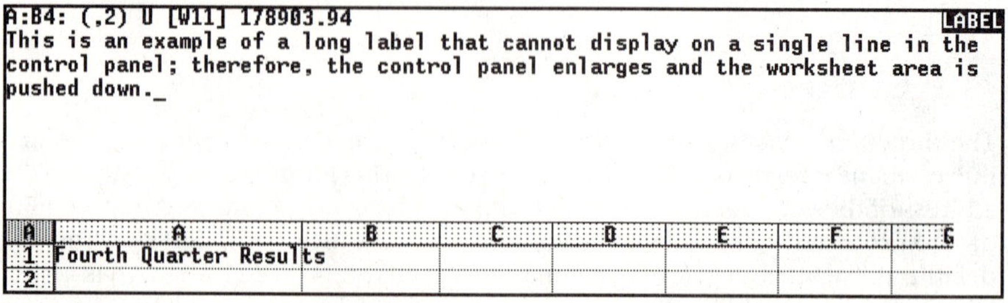

Fig. 2.12.
The control panel enlarged to accommodate the display of a long label.

```
A:B4: (,2) U [W11] 178903.94                                    LABEL
This is an example of a long label that cannot display on a single line in the
control panel; therefore, the control panel enlarges and the worksheet area is
pushed down._
```

The Mode Indicators

The *mode indicator* is located in the upper right corner of the control panel. This indicator tells you what mode 1-2-3 is in and what you can do next. When 1-2-3 is waiting for your next action, the mode indicator is READY (see figs. 2.9 and 2.13). Table 2.4 lists the mode indicators and their meanings.

Table 2.4
Mode Indicators

Indicator	Description
EDIT	You are editing a cell entry.
ERROR	1-2-3 encountered an error, or you used Break to cancel a macro. Press Enter or Esc to clear the error message (located in the lower left corner of the screen) and return to READY mode.
FILES	1-2-3 prompted you to select a file name from a list of files. Either type a file name or point to an existing file and press Enter.
FIND	1-2-3 is in the middle of a /Data Query Find operation.
HELP	You are in the Help facility. Press Esc to return to the worksheet.
LABEL	You are entering a label into a cell.
MENU	You are selecting command options from one of the command menus.
NAMES	1-2-3 prompted you to select a range name, graph name, print setting, database driver, external database, or an external table name, and then displayed a list of names. Either type an appropriate name and press Enter or point to an existing name with the mouse and click.
POINT	Either 1-2-3 prompted you to select a range or you used the cursor-movement keys to specify a range while entering a formula. You type either the cell coordinates or the name of the range, or you highlight the range using the cursor-movement keys or the mouse; then press Enter.
READY	1-2-3 is waiting for your next entry or command.
STAT	1-2-3 is displaying a status screen.
VALUE	You are entering a number or a formula into a cell.
WAIT	1-2-3 is in the middle of some activity. Do not proceed until the activity finishes and the WAIT indicator disappears.

The Status Indicators

Reminder:
Status indicators tell you about the state of the system.

1-2-3 displays the *status indicators* in the middle and right side of the status line at the bottom of the display. These indicators give you information about the state of the system. Each indicator displays in reverse video in the same area (see fig. 2.13). These indicators and their meanings are listed in table 2.5.

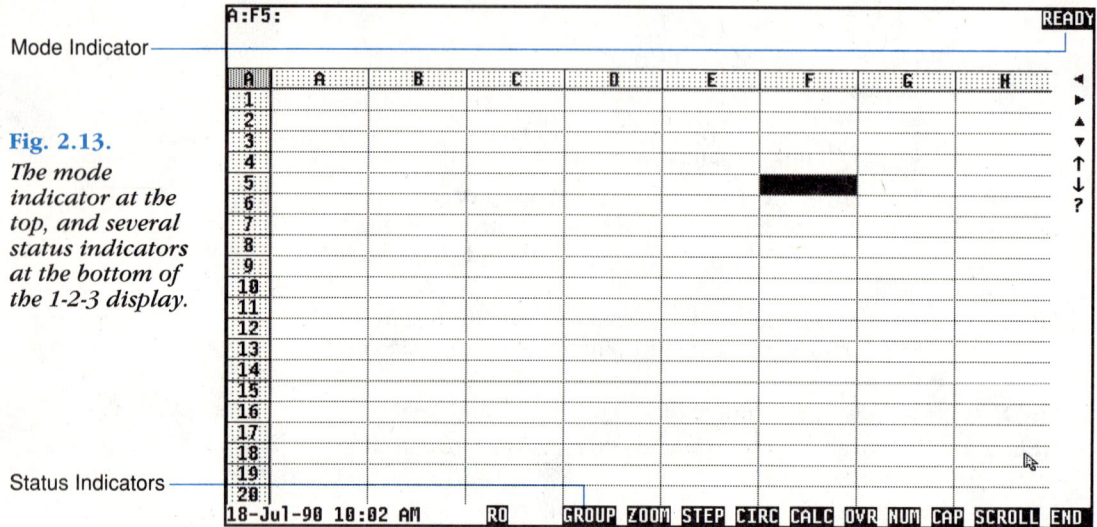

Mode Indicator

Fig. 2.13.
The mode indicator at the top, and several status indicators at the bottom of the 1-2-3 display.

Status Indicators

Table 2.5
Status Indicators

Indicator	Description
CALC	If the CALC indicator is in white and is not flashing, the file is set to manual recalculation, and there has been a change since the last calculation. Warns you that parts of the file may not be current. Press Calc (F9) to force a recalculation and clear the indicator.
	If the CALC indicator is in red on color monitors, or is flashing on monochrome monitors, the file is set to automatic recalculation and is in the middle of a background recalculation. You can continue to work, but the values of some formulas may change during the recalculation.
CAP	You pressed Caps Lock. All letters are entered as uppercase. Press Caps Lock again to turn off the indicator.
CIRC	There is a circular reference in the worksheet. Use the /Worksheet Status command to find one of the cell addresses in the circular reference.
CMD	You are running a macro.

Chapter 2 ♦ Getting Started   **53**

Indicator	Description
END	You pressed the End key.
FILE	You pressed Ctrl-End, the File key. When combined with an arrow key, the File key moves across multiple files in memory.
GROUP	You selected /Worksheet Global Group Enable to modify multiple worksheets in a file together.
MEM	You have less than 4,096 characters of memory left.
NUM	You pressed Num Lock. The keys on the numeric keypad now act as numbers, not cursor-movement keys. To use them as cursor-movement keys, press Num Lock again or press the Shift key.
OVR	You pressed Ins while editing a cell to change to overtype mode. Any keystrokes replace whatever is at that cursor position in the cell. Press Ins again to return to insert mode. Keystrokes are then inserted at the cursor position.
PRT	Indicates a background print is in progress.
RO	The current file is read-only. The file can only be saved with a different name. Applies to files used on a network or multiuser system. Sometimes occurs if you run out of memory while reading a file.
SCROLL	You pressed Scroll Lock. Whenever you use an arrow key, the entire window moves in the direction of the arrow. To use the arrow keys to move the cursor from cell to cell, press Scroll Lock again.
SST	You are executing a macro in single-step mode.
STEP	You turned on single-step mode for macros, but you are not currently running a macro. When you start a macro, this indicator changes to SST.
ZOOM	You used /Worksheet Window to split the screen into multiple windows and then pressed Alt-F6 to enlarge the current window to fill the entire screen. To return the display to multiple windows, press Alt-F6 again.

The File and Clock Indicator

The lower left corner of the screen shows the file name of the current file. If you have just built the worksheet and you have never saved it, this area displays the date and time (see fig. 2.13).

Part I ♦ Building the 1-2-3 Worksheet

The Error Messages Area

Cue:
If the mode indicator changes to ERROR, look at the lower left corner of the screen for an error message.

When 1-2-3 encounters an error, the mode indicator changes to ERROR and an error message replaces the file or clock message in the lower left corner of the screen (see fig. 2.14). Errors can be caused by many different situations. For example, you may have specified an invalid cell address or range name in response to a prompt or tried to retrieve a file that does not exist. Press Esc or Enter to clear the error and return to READY mode.

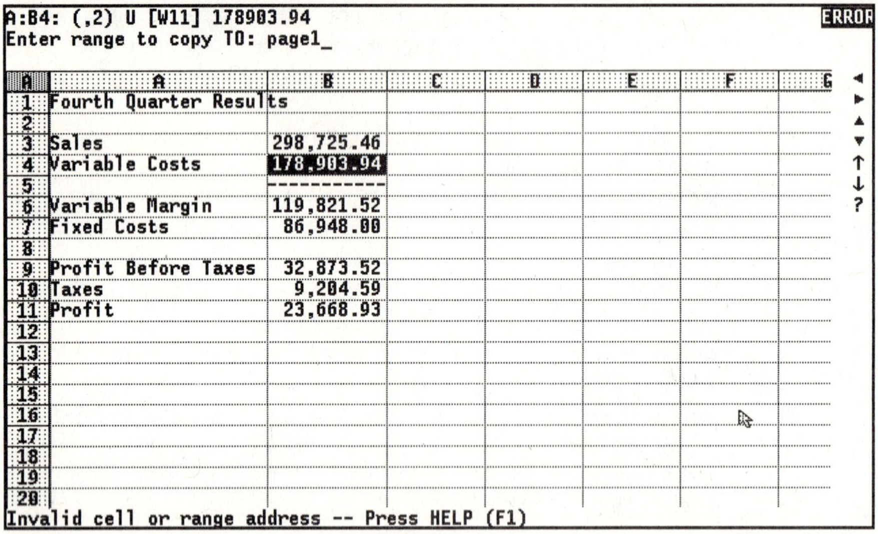

Fig. 2.14.
An error message displayed at the lower left corner of the screen.

Now that you have learned about several important features of the screen, it may be good to see them all together. Figure 2.15 represents a sample screen with all its parts labeled.

Using the 1-2-3 Help Features

Cue:
Use the Help facility and the Tutorial to get assistance with 1-2-3.

1-2-3 includes features that provide help to users: the keyboard help facility and the 1-2-3 Tutorial.

1-2-3 provides on-line help at the touch of a key. You can be in the middle of any operation and press the Help (F1) key at any time to get one or more screens of explanations and advice on what to do next.

Lotus also includes in its documentation a printed Tutorial to help you learn 1-2-3. This self-paced instructional manual leads you through a series of actual 1-2-3 worksheets that use important features of the program.

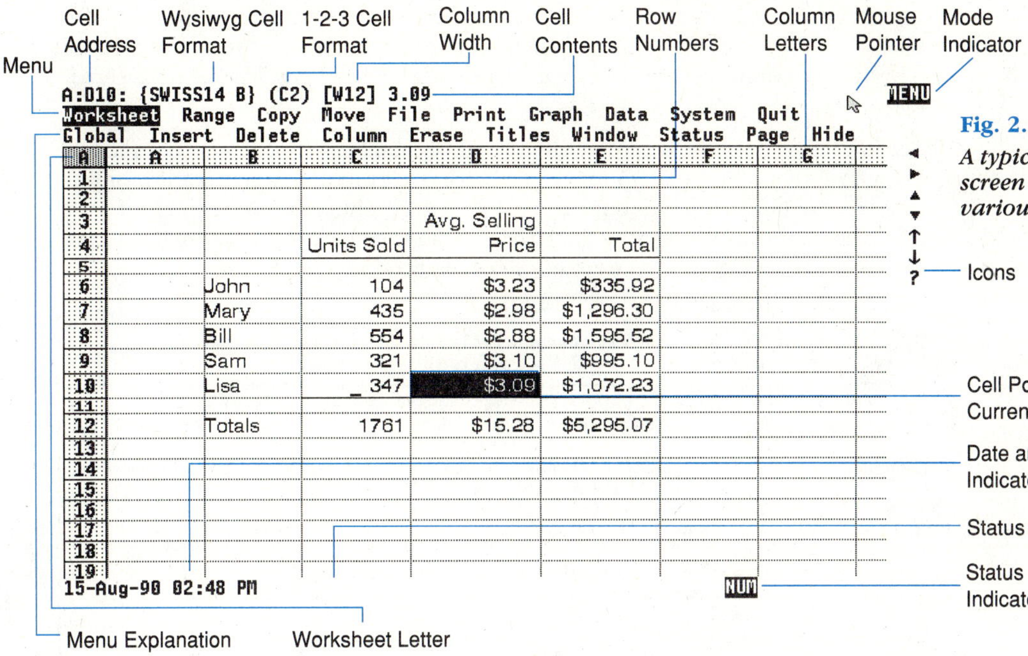

Chapter 2 ◆ Getting Started   **55**

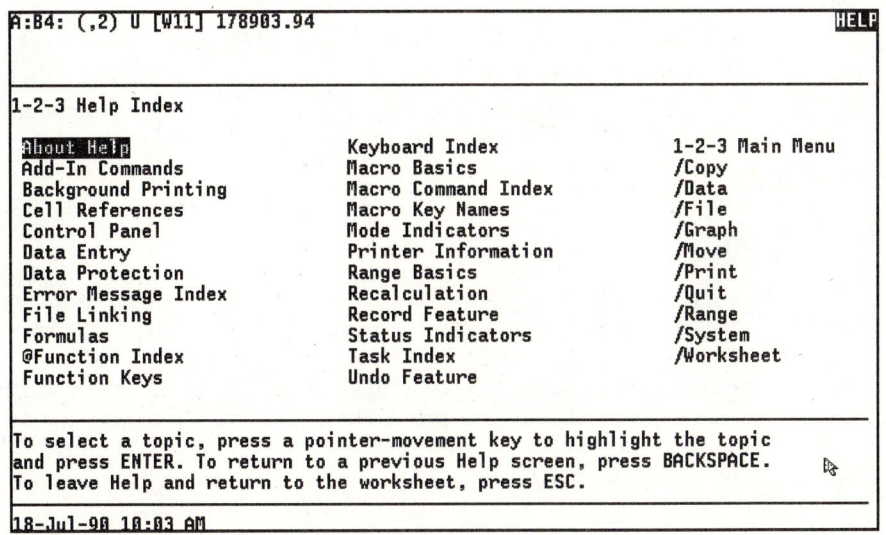

Fig. 2.15.

A typical 1-2-3 screen and its various parts.

Finding On-Screen Help

Press Help (F1) at any time to get to the on-line help facility. If you press Help while in READY mode, the Help Index appears (see fig. 2.16). Choose any of the topics in the Help Index to get to the other help screens.

Fig. 2.16.

The 1-2-3 Help Index screen.

Reminder:
The Help (F1) key is context-sensitive.

You can press the Help (F1) key at any time, even while executing a command or editing a cell. The Help key is context-sensitive. For example, if you are executing a particular command when you press Help (F1), 1-2-3 gives you a help screen about that command (see fig. 2.17).

Certain parts of the help screen identify additional help topics. These topics are displayed in boldface on a monochrome monitor or in green on a color monitor. To get more information about a topic, move the highlight to that topic and press Enter. An option to return to the Help Index as well as one or more additional topics are always located at the bottom of the screen.

Fig. 2.17.
A context-sensitive help screen that explains the /Worksheet commands.

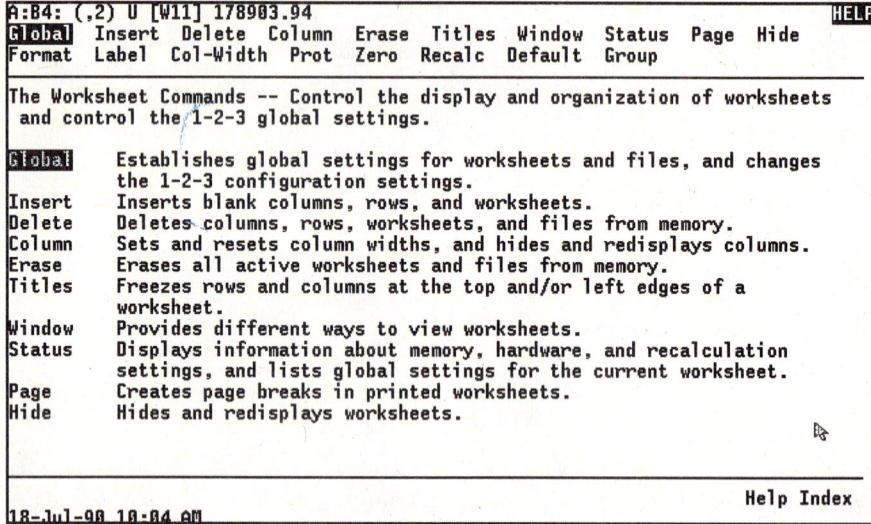

Press the Backspace key to view a previous help screen. Press the Esc key to return to the 1-2-3 worksheet when you finish consulting the help facility.

Cue:
Make sure that the Wysiwyg menu is displayed if you want help on a Wysiwyg feature.

If you are working from the Wysiwyg command menu, pressing F1 brings up the Wysiwyg help screen shown in figure 2.18. This help facility is completely separate from the 1-2-3 help screens. Therefore, if you want help on a Wysiwyg feature, you should display the Wysiwyg menu first.

Taking the 1-2-3 Tutorial

Lotus offers a self-paced series of lessons in a Tutorial manual, a book that comes with the 1-2-3 documentation. The lessons are arranged in order of increasing difficulty and build on each other. The Tutorial does not cover all of 1-2-3's functions and commands but covers enough to give you a basic understanding of the program. Also, the tutorial does not provide any assistance for users who want to use Wysiwyg or the mouse. Before you use the Tutorial, you must successfully install 1-2-3 on your hard disk.

Chapter 2 ◆ Getting Started

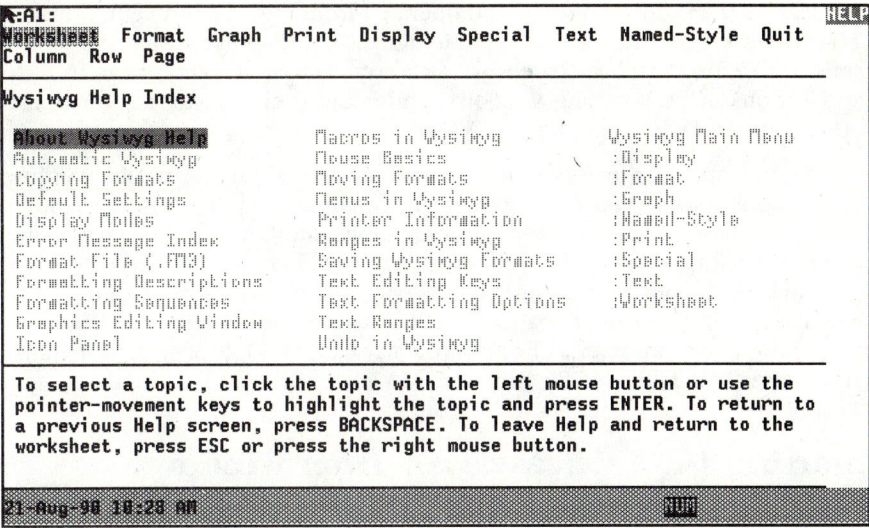

Fig. 2.18.
The Wysiwyg Help Index screen.

The Tutorial is divided into 5 chapters with 17 lessons. Chapter 1 covers the basics of starting 1-2-3: entering and editing data; using command menus, formulas, functions, and ranges; formatting; and printing. Chapter 2 is about graphs. Chapter 3 is about using multiple worksheets and files. Chapter 4 covers databases, and Chapter 5 is about macros.

If you are new to 1-2-3, the best approach is to do one or two lessons at a time until you complete Chapter 1. After each lesson, work with 1-2-3 for a while before you tackle the more advanced topics. Only after you feel comfortable with all the material in Chapter 1 of the Tutorial should you try the other chapters. You can learn about the more specialized topics, such as the database or macros, without going through all the preceding lessons.

If you are familiar with 1-2-3 Release 3, you should skip the Tutorial and instead go straight to the Wysiwyg Publishing and Presentation documentation and try out the new Wysiwyg features. If you are familiar with earlier releases of 1-2-3 but not with Release 3, you should read through the entire Tutorial and try out the new features. Then you should read the Wysiwyg Publishing and Presentation documentation and try out the new Wysiwyg features.

For further details on 1-2-3 functions and commands, you can refer to the Command Reference section or other appropriate sections of this book or to the 1-2-3 documentation.

Cue:
If you are new to 1-2-3, complete Lesson 1 of the Tutorial to get a basic understanding of the program.

Using 1-2-3 Release 3.1+ with Windows

Windows is a very popular operating environment for DOS. Windows enables you to easily start programs, manage directories and files, and run multiple programs at the same time in multiple windows on your screen. Release 3.1, unlike earlier

Cue:
You can use 1-2-3 Release 3.1+ with the Windows 3 operating environment.

releases of 1-2-3, can be started and operated from this environment. Although 1-2-3 Release 3.1 cannot take full advantage of Windows like a program written specifically for Windows (such as Microsoft Excel), it can return to 1-2-3 applications without exiting Windows, and it can even transfer information to other programs while operating in Windows.

Windows 3 operates in three modes. *Real mode* is used to run old Windows applications. *Standard Mode* operates on a computer equipped with an 80286 microprocessor, such as an IBM AT or compatible. Another mode, which works on computers with an 80386 microprocessor, is called *386-Enhanced Mode*. Although 1-2-3 Release 3.1 operates in either mode, you will find that 1-2-3's speed is better in Standard Mode. In 386-Enhanced Mode, however, transferring information to other programs is more versatile. Also, you may have multiple programs operating at the same time while in 386-Enhanced Mode.

Starting 1-2-3 Release 3.1+ from Windows

1-2-3 Release 3.1+ includes a special file, called a *Program Information File* (PIF), which contains information that Windows must have for 1-2-3 to operate from Windows. This information includes the amount of memory that 1-2-3 requires, whether 1-2-3 will run in a window, and whether 1-2-3 requires the entire screen.

You can create an icon in Windows' Program Manager to start 1-2-3. You can do it manually or let Windows create the icon using the Windows Setup utility found in the Main program group of the Program Manager. Activating this icon starts 1-2-3 from Windows 3.

Using 1-2-3 Release 3.1+ in Windows

If you are using 1-2-3 in Window's Standard Mode or Wysiwyg in 386-Enhanced Mode, then you must run 1-2-3 in *full-screen* mode. That is, 1-2-3 takes the entire screen. You may use the Alt-Esc key to switch from 1-2-3 back to Windows. When you switch back to Windows, 1-2-3 stops whatever it was doing. When you switch back to 1-2-3, however, 1-2-3 picks up where it left off.

Cue:
Use 1-2-3 Release 3.1+ with Windows 3 to facilitate the transfer of information between programs.

Using 1-2-3 in Windows' 386-Enhanced Mode has certain restrictions. If you are using Wysiwyg, you must operate with 1-2-3 in full-screen mode. However, if you install 1-2-3 for a CGA screen, you may run 1-2-3 in a window (as shown in fig. 2.19).

1-2-3 operates in Windows just as it does if you do not use Windows. One benefit of using Windows is that you can transfer information from 1-2-3 into a Windows document.

Chapter 2 ◆ Getting Started   59

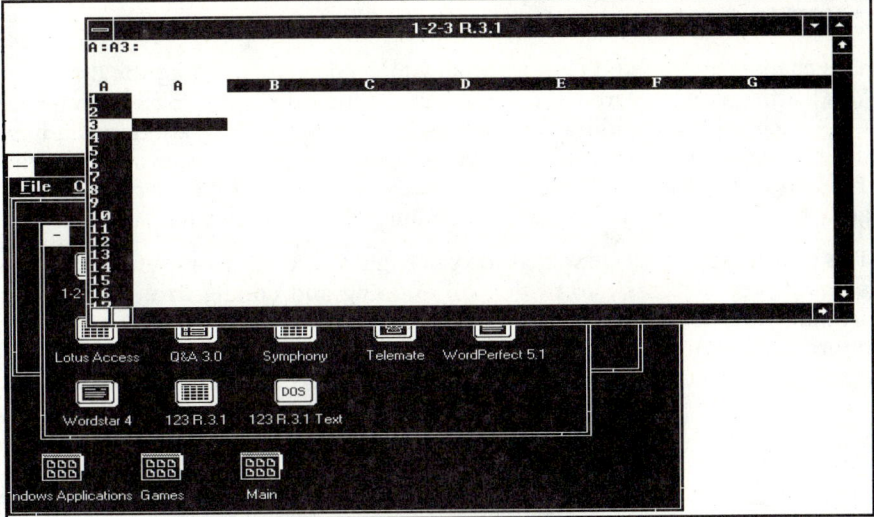

Fig 2.19.
Running 1-2-3 in a window of Windows 3.

Transferring 1-2-3 Release 3.1+ Data by Using Windows

While using 1-2-3 with Windows, you can copy information from your 1-2-3 screen and place it in other Windows applications, for example a word processor like Windows Write. If you are using 1-2-3 in a window, you can select information to copy to another program as shown in figure 2.20. However, if you are using 1-2-3 in the full-screen mode, you must transfer the entire screen.

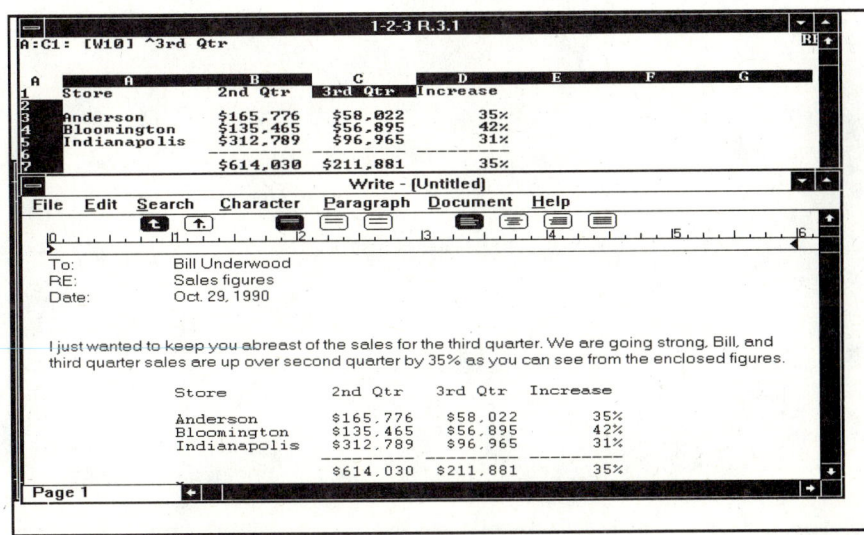

Figure 2.20.
Information included in a word processor that was copied from 1-2-3.

Summary

This chapter presented the information you need to use 1-2-3 for the first time. You learned how to start and exit 1-2-3 from either the operating system or the 1-2-3 Access System and how to start and exit Wysiwyg. You also learned how to implement the Install and Translate programs. The features provided in the 1-2-3 display and how 1-2-3 uses the keyboard and mouse also were presented. In addition, you learned how to use the on-line help facility and the Tutorial.

This chapter sets the stage so that you can begin to use 1-2-3 for useful work. The next chapter presents information on entering and editing data and moving around worksheets and files. Chapter 3 also presents multiple worksheets and information about using Wysiwyg.

Learning Worksheet Basics

3

This chapter presents the skills needed to use 1-2-3, the powerful electronic spreadsheet. If this is your first experience with spreadsheet software, you learn how to use a spreadsheet for data analysis. If you are familiar with electronic spreadsheets but are new to 1-2-3 or to Release 3.1+, you can find information in this chapter to help you understand the conventions and features of the program.

1-2-3 refers to its spreadsheet as a *worksheet*. This chapter helps you access the power of 1-2-3 by familiarizing you with moving around the worksheet. Most of the actions you perform on a worksheet change it in some way. Several of these actions, such as entering and editing data, are covered in this chapter. This chapter also covers the Undo feature, which enables you to reverse any changes made in error.

You use 1-2-3 to do *data analysis*—to manipulate and analyze data, numbers, and formulas. Because the worksheet is also used to report the results of your analysis, you need a method to organize the material. This chapter shows you how to use titles, headings, names, comments, descriptions, and a variety of other entries, called *labels*, that make your final worksheet clear and easy to follow. This chapter also shows you how to use the mouse and some commands from the Wysiwyg menu of 1-2-3 Releases 3.1 and 3.1+.

The 1-2-3 worksheet, a two-dimensional grid of columns and rows, can be expanded to a three-dimensional array with multiple-worksheet files. In this chapter and later chapters, you learn how to build multiple-worksheet files. The multiple-worksheet file approach is useful for consolidating information. For example, you can link files by writing formulas in one file that refer to cells in another file. If you need to work with large amounts of data or data from different sources, you can work with a number of files in the computer's memory at the same time.

This chapter begins by introducing the basic skills of using a single worksheet. These skills are then expanded to cover using multiple-worksheet files, linked files, and multiple files in memory.

This chapter enables you to do the following:

- Work with worksheets and files
- Move the cell pointer around the worksheet with mouse or keyboard
- Enter data
- Edit data
- Use the Undo feature
- Use multiple worksheets
- Use the linking features
- Use the Wysiwyg features

Understanding Worksheets and Files

Reminder:
A file can be made up of one or more worksheets.

When you first start 1-2-3, you start with a blank worksheet file and build a worksheet in the computer's memory. To keep your worksheet, you save it in a file on disk with a file name. (Chapter 7 covers files in detail.) In 1-2-3, a file can be one worksheet (the simplest type of file), or a file can be made up of multiple worksheets. A multiple-worksheet file can contain up to 256 worksheets. Each worksheet in the file has a worksheet letter. The first worksheet is called A; the second, B; the 27th, AA; and so on to IV, the 256th worksheet in the file.

Whenever you enter data into the worksheet, the entry goes into the cell at the location of the cell pointer. This highlighted cell is called the *current cell*. To move around the worksheet, you move the cell pointer. By moving the cell pointer, you control where you put data in the worksheet. In figure 3.1, for example, any data you type goes into cell C7 until you move the cell pointer.

The name of the current file may be displayed in the lower left corner of the screen once you save the worksheet. In figure 3.1, the current file is PROFIT.WK3. The current worksheet itself is displayed on-screen. If you use the window options to display more than one worksheet, the *current worksheet* is the one that displays the cell pointer.

Note: You can change 1-2-3 so that the date and time, rather than the file name, display in the lower left corner of the screen.

Reminder:
Formulas make 1-2-3 an electronic worksheet.

Formulas are operations or calculations that you want 1-2-3 to perform on the data. Formulas make 1-2-3 an electronic worksheet, not just a computerized method of displaying data. You enter the numbers and the formulas, and 1-2-3 performs the calculations. If you change a number, 1-2-3 changes the results of all the formulas that use that number. If you change the number in cells C4 or C5 in figure 3.1, the results of all the cells containing formulas that depend on these cells change automatically.

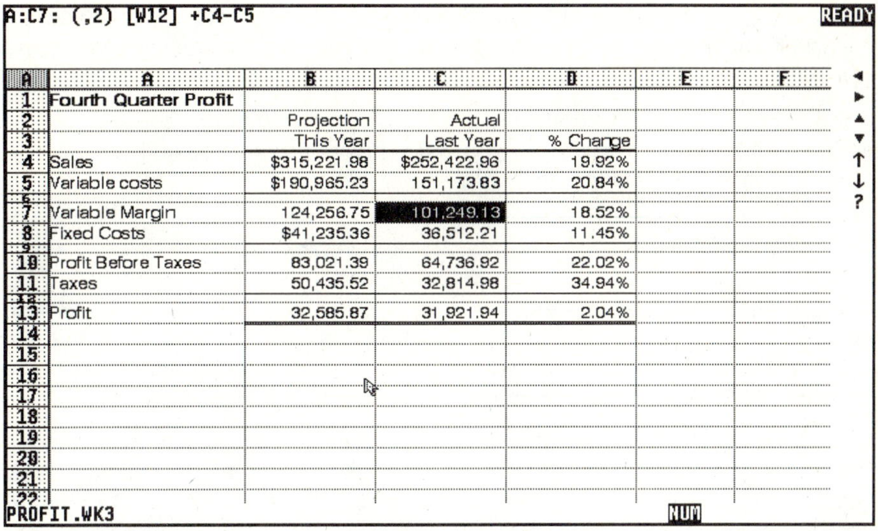

Chapter 3 ♦ Learning Worksheet Basics **63**

```
A:C7: (,2) [W12] +C4-C5                                    READY
```

	A	B	C	D	E	F
1	Fourth Quarter Profit					
2		Projection	Actual			
3		This Year	Last Year	% Change		
4	Sales	$315,221.98	$252,422.96	19.92%		
5	Variable costs	$190,965.23	151,173.83	20.84%		
6						
7	Variable Margin	124,256.75	101,249.13	18.52%		
8	Fixed Costs	$41,235.36	36,512.21	11.45%		
9						
10	Profit Before Taxes	83,021.39	64,736.92	22.02%		
11	Taxes	50,435.52	32,814.98	34.94%		
12						
13	Profit	32,585.87	31,921.94	2.04%		

PROFIT.WK3   NUM

Fig. 3.1.
A sample worksheet.

Introducing Multiple Worksheets

You use multiple-worksheet files in two basic situations:

First, multiple-worksheet files are ideal for consolidations. If you need a worksheet for many departments, you can build a separate, identical worksheet for each department. Each worksheet is smaller and easier to understand and use than a single large worksheet that contains all the data for each department. One of the worksheets can be a consolidation that combines the data from the individual departments.

Cue:
Use multiple worksheets for consolidations.

For example, you can put a formula in a cell in one worksheet that refers to cells in other worksheets. An example of this technique is found in the section "Using Multiple Worksheets," later in this chapter. Use multiple-worksheet files for any consolidations that contain separate parts, such as products, countries, or projects.

Second, you can use multiple-worksheet files to put separate sections of an application into separate worksheets. You can put input areas, reports, formulas, notes, assumptions and constants, and macros in separate worksheets. Each worksheet, which is therefore smaller and more manageable, can be customized for its particular purpose. This technique includes using global formats and setting column widths as described in Chapters 4 and 5.

Reminder:
Using multiple worksheets means you can make changes to one worksheet without affecting the others.

Using multiple worksheets in effect creates a set of separate worksheets for a large file. One important advantage this technique provides is that you can make changes to one worksheet without risking accidental changes to the other worksheets. When the entire file is composed of one worksheet, you can insert or delete a row or column in one area and accidentally destroy part of another area that shares the same row or column. With multiple-worksheet files, you can design each worksheet so that you can insert and delete rows and columns anywhere and not affect any other part of the file.

Another common error is to accidentally write over formulas that are part of input areas. With multiple worksheets, you can separate input areas and formulas so that this error is less likely.

Linking Files

Reminder:
File linking is working with multiple worksheets in separate files.

Using multiple-worksheet files in the same file is just one way to work with multiple worksheets. You also can work with worksheets in separate files. You can put a formula in a cell in one worksheet that refers to cells in worksheets in another file. This procedure is called *file linking* or *creating file links*.

With this capability, you can consolidate data in separate files easily. Suppose that you have data from separate departments or divisions to consolidate. Each department's data is in a separate file. Your consolidation file can use formulas to combine the data from each separate file. The process also works in reverse. You can have a central database file as well as separate files to distribute to each department. The individual department files can contain formulas that refer to data in the central database file.

Using linked files instead of one large file has several advantages:

- ◆ You can use file linking to build large worksheet systems that are too large to fit into memory all at once.
- ◆ You can link files that come from different sources.
- ◆ You can more easily build formulas in one file that refer to cells in another file if both files are in memory at one time.
- ◆ You can develop a separate macro library file. (See Chapter 13 for more information on creating macros and macro libraries.)

Using the Workspace

The *workspace* is made up of the worksheets and files that you have in memory at any one time. With 256 columns and 8192 rows in a single worksheet, the potential size of your workspace is formidable. You can visualize the size of this single worksheet as an enormous piece of paper almost 20 feet wide and over 110 feet long. At its maximum, the worksheet can be over 500 feet wide. 1-2-3's large work area—over 500 million cells—gives you flexibility when you design your worksheets. You do not have to crowd everything together to save space. You can lay out different parts of the worksheet in different places to make the data easier to use and understand.

If you try to build a single worksheet that uses all possible rows and columns, you produce a worksheet that is complex, difficult to use, and possibly too large for your computer's memory. A more typical large worksheet might contain

Chapter 3 ◆ Learning Worksheet Basics

information about thousands of employees or inventory items. This type of worksheet uses a few columns and many rows. Another typical worksheet might contain a series of related reports that uses many columns but just a few rows.

You start out building small, simple worksheets. As you increase your skills using 1-2-3, you feel comfortable building larger, more complex worksheets. The generous workspace lets you build your worksheets without worrying about running out of room.

When you start to build more complex models, use multiple-worksheet files. The two-dimensional environment of a single worksheet's horizontal rows and vertical columns is enhanced by using multiple-worksheet files. This technique adds a third dimension to your work.

You can have a total of up to 256 worksheets in memory at one time. You can have a single file with 256 worksheets, or many files, each containing one or more worksheets. In most cases, you are limited by the amount of memory in your computer.

Reminder:
1-2-3's workspace is large enough so that you don't have to crowd information together.

Understanding the Multiple-Worksheet Display

You can change the screen to view one worksheet or multiple worksheets in different ways. These window options are covered in detail in Chapter 4. The default screen display is a single window that shows part of one worksheet. For example, the worksheet in figure 3.1 could be a single-worksheet file or part of a multiple-worksheet file.

In figure 3.2, the screen is in *perspective view*. Perspective view lets you see parts of up to three worksheets at one time. In this file, worksheet B is used for assumptions and notes; worksheet C contains macros to automate certain worksheet tasks—typical uses for multiple-worksheet files.

Cue:
You can view multiple worksheets at one time with window options.

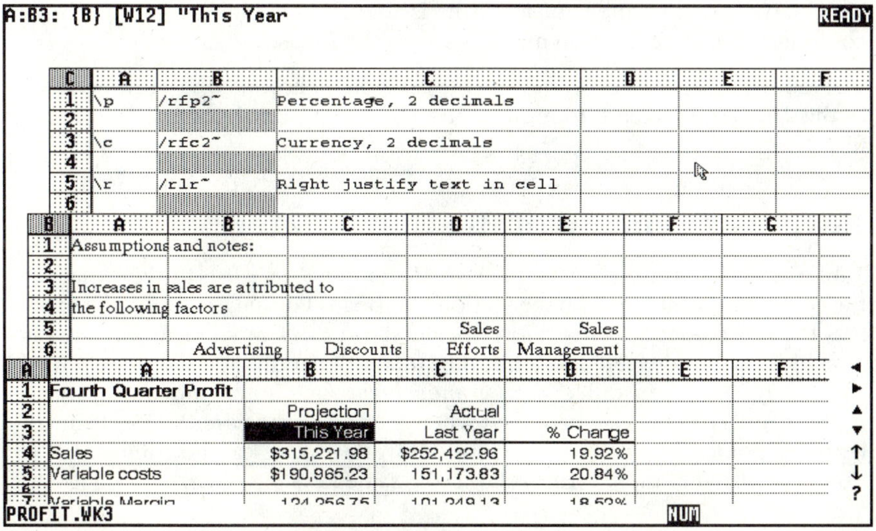

Fig. 3.2.

A file with three worksheets in perspective view.

The name of the current file is displayed in the lower left corner of the screen once you save the file. In figure 3.2, the current file is PROFIT.WK3. If you use the window options to display more than one worksheet, the current worksheet is the one that displays the cell pointer. In figure 3.2, the current worksheet is A, and the current cell is A:B3.

> **Reminder:**
> *The current worksheet is the one that displays the cell pointer.*

To determine the current worksheet in figure 3.2, you can make a couple of observations: the cell pointer is in worksheet A, and the cell address in the control panel begins with A:. If a file has more than three worksheets, you cannot see all the worksheets at the same time.

Most features of 1-2-3 apply to either a single worksheet or to multiple worksheets in a file. In this and later chapters, you learn to use 1-2-3 with one worksheet first and then extend your knowledge to work with multiple-worksheet files, linked files, and multiple files in memory.

Moving around the Worksheet

> **Reminder:**
> *The cell pointer is on the worksheet; the cursor is in the control panel.*

Moving around the worksheet means moving the *cell pointer*—the bright rectangle that highlights and identifies an entire cell. In figure 3.2, the cell pointer is in cell A:B3. Characters within the cell pointer appear in reverse video on the highlighted background. Any data typed into the worksheet goes into the cell at the location of the cell pointer. The *cursor* is the blinking line in the control panel when you enter or edit data in a cell. The cursor shows you the position of the next character typed. Within a menu, the *menu pointer* is the highlight used to select a command.

Because you can enter data only at the location of the cell pointer, you must know how to move the cell pointer to the location you want before you enter data. Also, because you can display only a small part of the worksheet at any one time, it is helpful to know how to move the cell pointer to see different parts of the worksheet at different times. The cell pointer is controlled either with keyboard keys or—as long as the mouse driver is loaded, a mouse is attached to the computer, and Wysiwyg is in memory—with the mouse.

The following sections cover moving the cell pointer around *one* worksheet. Later in this chapter, you learn to move around multiple-worksheet files and multiple files.

Keyboard Control of the Cell Pointer

> **Reminder:**
> *The same keys are used to move the cell pointer and the cursor, depending on the current mode.*

Table 3.1 (in the section "Using the Basic Movement Keys") lists the keys that move the cell pointer. Table 3.2 (in the section "Keyboard Editing," later in this chapter) lists the movement keys that move the cursor in EDIT mode. Many of the same keys move either the cell pointer or the cursor, depending on the current mode. These keys are often called *pointer-movement keys* when they move the cell pointer, and *cursor-movement keys* when they move the cursor. This distinction between pointer-movement and cursor-movement keys can be confusing if you do not realize that these terms refer to the same keys.

Chapter 3 ♦ Learning Worksheet Basics

This section discusses the movement of the cell pointer. Cursor movement is covered later in this chapter during the discussion of editing data in the worksheet. Menu-pointer movement for commands is discussed in Chapter 4.

When 1-2-3 is in READY or POINT mode, the movement keys move the cell pointer. In LABEL or VALUE mode, the movement keys end the entry, return to READY mode, and move the cell pointer. In EDIT mode, some movement keys move the cursor in the control panel; other movement keys end the edit, return to READY mode, and move the cell pointer. In MENU mode, the movement keys move the menu pointer to menu choices.

The current cell address is displayed in the upper left corner of the display in the following format: A:B3. This format represents the worksheet letter, the column letter, and the row number. When you work with one worksheet, the worksheet letter is always A. The worksheet letter is also found in the upper left corner of the reverse-video border. In figure 3.2, the worksheet at the bottom of the screen is A, the one in the middle is B, and the one on the top is C.

If Wysiwyg is not loaded into memory, another way to find the current location of the cell pointer is by observing the reverse-video border. The column border and row border contrast with the rest of the border. Exactly how it contrasts depends on the type of monitor you use.

Reminder:
The control panel shows the worksheet, column, and row of the current cell.

Mouse Control of the Cell Pointer

You can use the mouse to move the cell pointer in READY or POINT mode. When in LABEL, VALUE, or EDIT mode, the left mouse button ends the entry and returns to READY mode. You also can use the mouse to move the menu pointer to menu choices when in MENU mode.

There are several ways to move the cell pointer with the mouse. The simplest way is to point to a cell and click the left mouse button. Another way is to use the icons on the right side of the worksheet. This set of icons, called the *icon panel*, contains four solid triangles, each pointing in a different direction (see fig. 3.1).

Cue:
Use the icon panel at the side of the screen with the mouse to move the cell pointer.

Pointing to one of the triangles and clicking the left mouse button moves the cursor one cell in the direction of the triangle. If you hold the left mouse button down, the cell pointer keeps moving in the direction of the triangle. If you want to move the cell pointer to a cell not shown on the display, point to the appropriate triangle and hold the left mouse button until the worksheet starts to scroll. When you reach the row or column you want, release the mouse button.

A different way to move the cell pointer to a cell not shown on the display is by holding the left mouse button and moving the mouse in the direction of the cell to which you want to move. When the mouse pointer moves past the edge of the worksheet, the screen begins scrolling. When you release the mouse button, the scrolling stops. For example, suppose the cell pointer is in cell A:A5. To move to a cell not currently shown on the screen, such as A:AA5, hold the left mouse button and move the mouse to the right beyond the rightmost column displayed,

Reminder:
Hold the mouse button and move the pointer to scroll the screen.

column H. When you move the mouse beyond the H column, the entire worksheet scrolls to the left and the column letters change. When you get to column AA, release the mouse button.

To return to the original cell, hold the left mouse button and move the mouse to the left. When you move beyond the leftmost column, the entire worksheet scrolls to the right and the column letters change again.

If you want to move to a cell below those shown on the display, hold the left mouse button and move the mouse down below the last row shown on the display. The entire worksheet scrolls up and the row numbers on the worksheet frame increase.

To move to a cell above those shown on the display, hold the left mouse button and move the mouse above the top row shown on the display into the area of the top frame of the worksheet. The entire worksheet scrolls down and the row numbers on the frame decrease. If you ever use the mouse to try to move past the edge of the worksheet, 1-2-3 beeps a warning.

Using the Basic Movement Keys

Reminder:
Use the arrow keys on the keyboard to move the cell pointer.

The four directional-arrow keys that move the cell pointer are located on the numeric keypad and on the separate pad of the enhanced keyboard. The cell pointer moves in the direction of the arrow on the key. If you press and hold the arrow key, the cell pointer continues to move in that direction. When the cell pointer reaches the edge of the screen, the worksheet continues to scroll in the direction of the arrow. If you try to move past the edge of the worksheet, 1-2-3 beeps a warning.

You can use several other keys to page through the worksheet by moving the cell pointer one screen at a time. Press the PgUp and PgDn keys to move up or down one screen. Press Ctrl-→ or Tab to move one screen to the right; press Ctrl-← or Shift-Tab (hold the Shift key and press Tab) to move one screen to the left. The size of one screen depends on the type of display driver in your system and whether one or more windows are present on-screen. (Windows are discussed in Chapter 4.)

Table 3.1 summarizes the action of the movement keys. Press the Home key to move the cell pointer directly to the home position—usually cell A1. In Chapter 4, you learn how to lock titles on-screen. Locked titles can change the home position. The other keys listed in table 3.1 are covered in the following sections.

Reminder:
Use Scroll Lock to activate or deactivate the scroll function.

Scrolling the Worksheet

The Scroll Lock key toggles the scroll function on and off. When you press the Scroll Lock key, you activate the scroll function, and the SCROLL status indicator appears at the bottom right of the screen.

Table 3.1
Movement-Key Operation with One Worksheet

Key	Description
→	Moves the cell pointer one cell to the right.
←	Moves the cell pointer one cell to the left.
↑	Moves the cell pointer one cell up.
↓	Moves the cell pointer one cell down.
Ctrl-→ or Tab	Moves the cell pointer right one screen.
Ctrl-← or Shift-Tab	Moves the cell pointer left one screen.
PgUp	Moves the cell pointer up one screen.
PgDn	Moves the cell pointer down one screen.
Home	Moves the cell pointer to the home position (usually cell A1).
End Home	Moves the cell pointer to the lower right corner of the active area.
End →, End ↓, End ←, End ↑	Moves the cell pointer in the direction of the arrow to the next cell that contains data (the intersection between a blank cell and a cell that contains data).
F5 (GoTo)	Prompts for a cell address or range name, and then moves the cell pointer directly to that cell.
F6 (Window)	If the window has been split, moves the cell pointer to the next window.
Scroll Lock	Toggles the scroll function on and off; when on, moves the entire window when you press one of the four arrow keys.

When you use the mouse to move the cell pointer, you see no obvious change in operation until you try to move to a cell not on the display. For example, to view columns to the right of the current screen, press the left mouse button and move the mouse pointer past the right frame of the worksheet. To view columns to the left of the current screen, press the left mouse button and move the mouse pointer past the left edge of the worksheet. Scrolling up and down is done in a similar manner.

When you press an arrow key with Scroll Lock on, the cell pointer stays in the current cell, and the entire window moves opposite the direction of the arrow key. When the cell pointer reaches the end of the display, if you continue to press the same arrow key, the cell pointer moves to the next cell as the entire window scrolls. If the SCROLL status indicator is on, press the Scroll Lock key again to turn it off.

Use the scroll function with the arrow keys if you want to see part of the worksheet that is off the screen without moving the cell pointer from the current cell. For example, in figure 3.2, the cell pointer is in B3. Suppose that you want to see the data in column G before you change the contents of B3. If you turn on the scroll function and press the right-arrow key once, the entire window moves to the left. You can see column G, and the cell pointer stays in B3 (see fig. 3.3). To get the same result without using Scroll Lock, you move the mouse until column G appears, and then you click cell B3, or you press the right arrow five times to display column G, and then press the left arrow five times to return to B3.

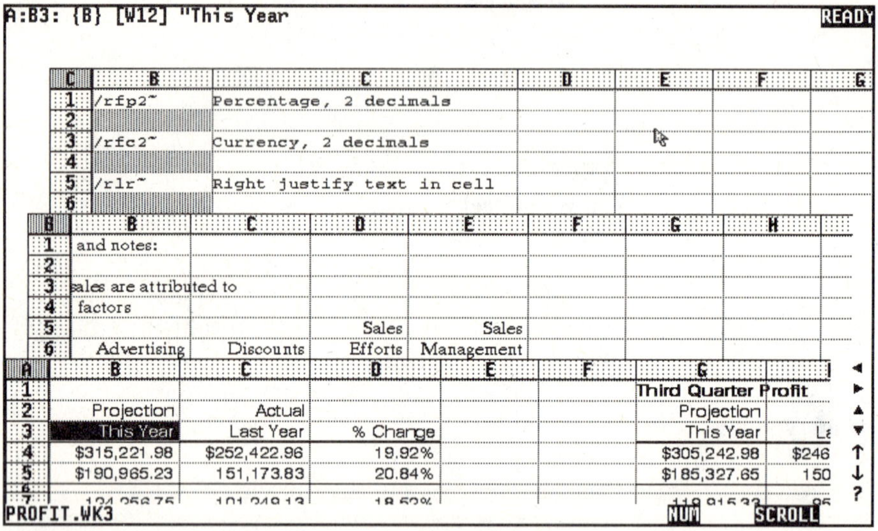

Fig. 3.3.
The Scroll Lock key used to move an entire window.

Reminder:
Check the SCROLL indicator if the cell pointer does not move the way you expect.

Scroll Lock has no effect on the other movement keys. If the cell pointer does not move the way you expect, check to see whether Scroll Lock has been accidentally turned on. Check for the SCROLL indicator in the lower right corner of the screen, as shown in figure 3.3. Press Scroll Lock again to turn it off.

Using the End Key

Reminder:
Use End and an arrow key or icon to move to the next intersection of a blank cell and a cell that contains data.

The End key is used in a special way in 1-2-3. When you press and release the End key, the END status indicator appears on the last line of the display. If you then click one of the triangle icons with the mouse or press one of the arrow keys, the cell pointer moves in the direction of the triangle or arrow key to the next intersection of a blank cell and a cell that contains data. The cell pointer always stops on a cell that contains data if possible. If there are no cells that contain data in the direction of the triangle or arrow key, the cell pointer stops at the edge of the worksheet.

For example, figure 3.4 shows the cell pointer in cell B3. The END status indicator at the bottom right corner of the screen shows that the End key has been pressed. If you now click the triangle that points to the right or press the right-arrow key,

Chapter 3 ◆ Learning Worksheet Basics 71

the cell pointer moves right to the first cell that contains data. In this case, the cell pointer moves to D3, as shown in figure 3.5. If you press the End key, and then click the triangle that points right or press the right-arrow key again, the cell pointer moves to the last cell that contains data before a blank cell. In this case, the cell pointer moves to G3, as shown in figure 3.6.

If no other data is in the worksheet and you press the End key and then click the right triangle or press the right-arrow key again, the cell pointer moves to the end of the worksheet to cell IV3. If you press End and then click the down triangle or press the down-arrow key from G3, the cell pointer moves to G14.

Cue:
Use the End key to move directly to the end of a list of data.

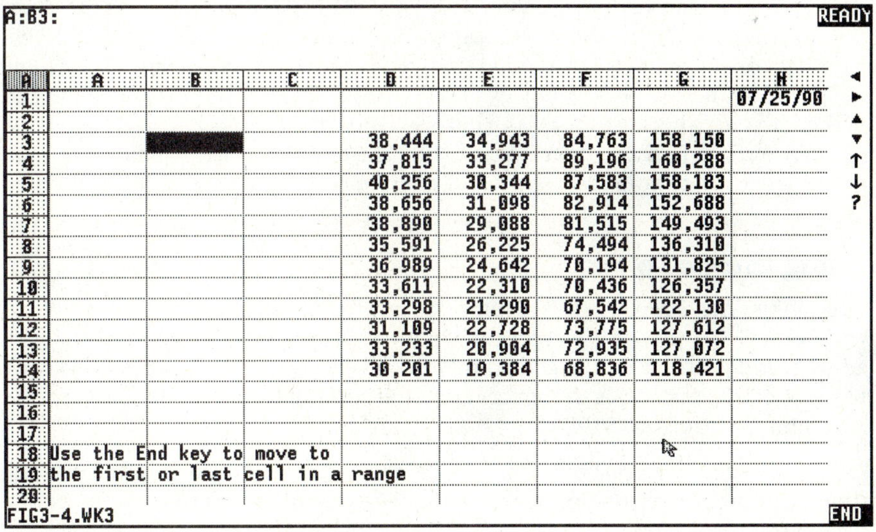

Fig. 3.4.
The END key status indicator.

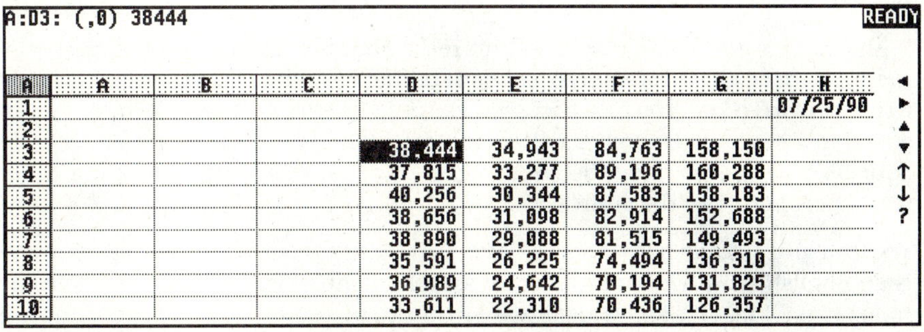

Fig. 3.5.
The cell pointer moved to the first cell that contains data after pressing End →.

The End key works the same way with the left and up triangles and left-arrow and up-arrow keys. In figure 3.6, pressing End ← or pressing End and clicking the left triangle takes you to D3. From D3, End ← takes you to D1 (the edge of the worksheet). After you press the End key, the END indicator stays on only until you click a triangle icon or press an arrow key or the End key again. If you press End in error, just press End again and the END status indicator goes off.

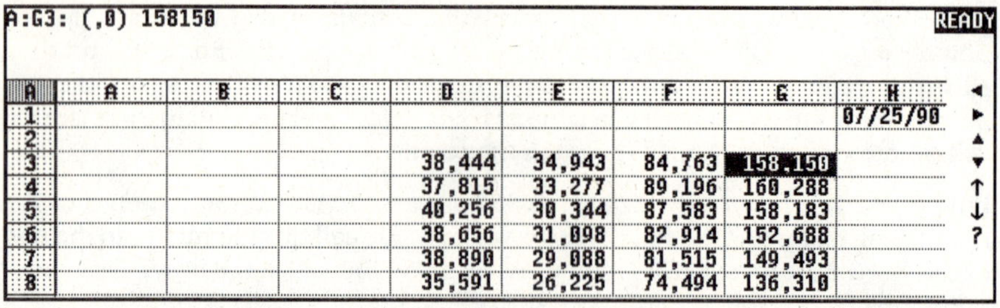

Fig. 3.6.
The cell pointer moved to the last cell that contains data after pressing End → again.

```
A:G3: (,0) 158150                                    READY
          A      B      C      D       E       F       G       H
    1                                                         07/25/90
    2
    3                          38,444  34,943  84,763  158,150
    4                          37,815  33,277  89,196  160,288
    5                          40,256  30,344  87,583  158,183
    6                          38,656  31,098  82,914  152,688
    7                          38,890  29,088  81,515  149,493
    8                          35,591  26,225  74,494  136,310
```

If you press the End key and then the Home key, the cell pointer moves to the lower right corner of the active area. The *active area* includes all rows and all columns that have data or cell formats (covered in Chapter 5). If you press End and then Home in figure 3.4, the cell pointer moves to H19. 1-2-3 considers this blank cell the end of the active area because there is an entry in column H (in H1) and an entry in row 19 (in A19). Use End and then Home to find the end of the active area if you want to add a section to your worksheet and not interfere with any existing data.

Using the GoTo Key

Reminder:
Use GoTo (F5) to jump to any cell in the worksheet.

You can use the GoTo (F5) key to jump directly to any cell in the worksheet. When you press GoTo (F5), 1-2-3 prompts you for an address. When you type the cell address and press Enter, the cell pointer moves directly to that address. With one worksheet, the address is in the format of the column letter from A to IV and the row number from 1 to 8192.

If you have a large worksheet, you may have to hold the mouse button for a long time or press one of the pointer-movement keys many times to move from one part of the worksheet to another. With the GoTo key, you can move across large parts of the worksheet at once.

With a large worksheet, it is difficult to remember the addresses for each part of the worksheet. GoTo's requirement of a specific cell address can make it difficult to use the GoTo key. You can, however, use range names with the GoTo key so that you don't have to remember cell addresses. You also can list commonly used addresses on a separate worksheet; then press Ctrl-PgUp to access the other worksheet and view the addresses.

Cue:
You can use range names with the GoTo (F5) key.

You can give a range name to a cell or a rectangular group of cells. A *range name* is an English synonym for a cell address; for example, you can give cell B56 the range name PROFIT. Range names are easier to remember than cell addresses. If you include range names in your worksheet, you can press GoTo, and then type the range name instead of the cell address. If the range name refers to more than one cell, the cell pointer moves to the upper left corner of the range. More information about ranges and range names is found in Chapter 4.

Entering Data into the Worksheet

To enter data into a cell, move the cell pointer to that cell, type the entry, and then press Enter or click the left mouse button. As you type, the entry appears on the second line of the control panel. When you press Enter or click the mouse button, the entry appears in the current cell and on the first line of the control panel. If you enter data into a cell that already contains information, the new data replaces the earlier entry.

If you plan to enter data into more than one cell, you do not have to press Enter or click the mouse button and then move the cell pointer to the next cell. You can type the entry into the cell and move the cell pointer with one operation; either click a triangle icon with the mouse or press one of the pointer-movement keys (such as the arrow keys, Tab, PgUp, or PgDn) after typing the entry.

The two types of cell entries are labels and values. A *label* is a text entry. A *value* is either a number or a formula. 1-2-3 determines the type of cell entry from the first character that you enter. 1-2-3 treats your entry as a value (a number or a formula) if you begin with one of the following numeric characters:

0 1 2 3 4 5 6 7 8 9 + − . (@ # $

If you begin by entering any other character, 1-2-3 treats the entry as a label. As soon as you type the first character, the mode indicator changes from READY to either VALUE or LABEL.

Cue:
Use the movement keys to complete an entry and move to the next cell.

Entering Labels

Labels make the numbers and formulas in your worksheets understandable. The labels in figures 3.1 and 3.2 tell you what the data means. In figures 3.4 through 3.6, the numbers and formulas have no labels, and you have no idea what this data represents.

Because a label is a text entry, it can contain any string of characters and can be up to 512 characters long. Labels can include titles, headings, explanations, and notes, all of which can help make your worksheet more readable.

When you enter a label, 1-2-3 adds a label prefix to the beginning of the cell entry. The label prefix is not visible on the worksheet, but is visible in the control panel (see fig. 3.7). 1-2-3 uses the label prefix to identify the entry as a label and determine how it is displayed and printed.

You can assign one of the following five label prefixes:

Reminder:
Labels make the numbers and formulas in the worksheet more understandable.

Prefix	Meaning
'	Left-aligned (default)
"	Right-aligned
^	Centered
\	Repeating
|	Left-aligned and nonprinting

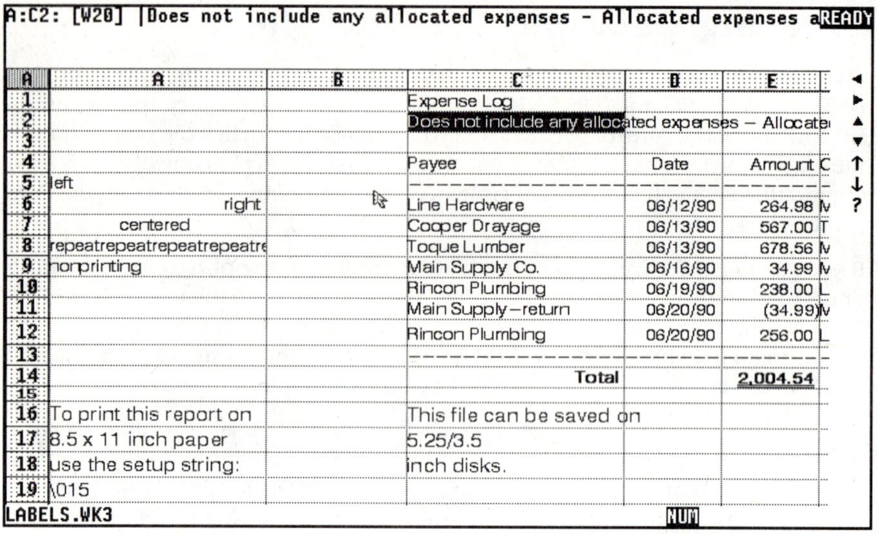

Fig. 3.7.
Examples of different label prefixes.

```
A:C2: [W20] |Does not include any allocated expenses - Allocated expenses a   READY

         A                  B              C              D           E
 1                                     Expense Log
 2                                     Does not include any allocated expenses — Allocate
 3
 4                                     Payee          Date         Amount  C
 5    left                             ------------   ----------   ----------
 6                       right         Line Hardware  06/12/90       264.98 N
 7              centered               Cooper Drayage 06/13/90       567.00 T
 8    repeatrepeatrepeatrepeatre       Toque Lumber   06/13/90       678.56 N
 9    nonprinting                      Main Supply Co. 06/16/90       34.99 N
10                                     Rincon Plumbing 06/19/90      238.00 L
11                                     Main Supply—return 06/20/90   (34.99) N
12                                     Rincon Plumbing 06/20/90      256.00 L
13                                     ------------                ----------
14                                              Total              2,004.54
15
16    To print this report on          This file can be saved on
17    8.5 x 11 inch paper              5.25/3.5
18    use the setup string:            inch disks.
19    \015
LABELS.WK3                                                         NUM
```

Cue:
Use right-aligned labels for column headings over columns of numbers or numeric formulas.

When you enter a label, 1-2-3 by default adds the apostrophe (') for a left-aligned label. To use a different label prefix, type the prefix as the first character of the label.

In figure 3.7, column A shows examples of the different label prefixes so that you can compare how they display. Columns C through E show how to use these label prefixes in a typical worksheet. A column of descriptions such as in C6..C12 usually looks best if left-aligned—the normal way to line up text. Column headings should align with the data below, such as the heading in C4, which is left-aligned to match the *Payee* descriptions. When the entries fill the cell width, as do the dates in column D, the column heading can be aligned either left, right, or center. In this example, the *Date* heading is centered. A centered label is best when the column heading is shorter than the data below it. Because numbers and numeric formulas are always right-aligned, the *Amount* column heading in E4 is also right-aligned.

Reminder:
A repeating label automatically changes length to match the column width.

The dashed lines in rows 5 and 13 are repeating labels. The repeating labels fill the entire width of the cell. If you change the column width, the label changes length to fill the new column width. Keep in mind, however, that Wysiwyg lets you create solid lines in your worksheet. In most cases, a solid line is preferable to a dashed line. Solid lines are covered in detail later in this chapter.

The note in cell C2 of figure 3.7 has a nonprinting label prefix (|). The prefix displays left-aligned but does not print if the print range starts in the same row as the label. In this example, if the print range starts in C1, the note in C2 does not print. If the print range starts in A1, the note does print. Printing and nonprinting labels are covered in more detail in Chapter 8.

Chapter 3 ◆ Learning Worksheet Basics

To use a label-prefix character as the first character of a label, first type a label prefix and then type the label-prefix character you want to use as the first character of the label (see cell A19 in fig. 3.7). If you type \015 into A19, the cell displays 015015015015015015 as a repeating label. You must first type a label prefix, in this case an apostrophe, and then \015.

Reminder:
You must type a label prefix to make another label prefix the first character of the label.

You must type a label prefix if the first character of the label is a numeric character. If not, as soon as you type the numeric character, 1-2-3 switches to VALUE mode and expects a valid number or formula. If the label is a valid formula, 1-2-3 evaluates it. If it is invalid, 1-2-3 refuses to accept the entry and places you in EDIT mode. (EDIT mode is explained later in this chapter.)

In cell C17 of figure 3.7, you must type a label prefix to precede the label 5.25/3.5. If you do not, 1-2-3 treats the entry as a formula and displays the result of 5.25 divided by 3.5, which is 1.5.

Reminder:
You must type a label prefix before an entry that looks like a valid formula.

In A17 in figure 3.7, you must type a label prefix to precede the label 8.5 x 11 inch paper, or 1-2-3 treats it as an invalid formula. You often encounter this problem when you enter an address such as **11711 N. College Ave**.

If a label is longer than the cell width, the label displays across the cells to the right as long as these cells are blank (see cells C2..E2 in fig. 3.7). The cell display can even continue into the next window to the right as long as all these cells are blank. The label in C2 in figure 3.7 is too long to be displayed in the window. You can see the continuation of the label in the next window to the right (see fig. 3.8).

Reminder:
A long label appears across blank cells to its right.

1-2-3 includes several commands that can change many label prefixes at one time. This subject is covered in Chapter 5.

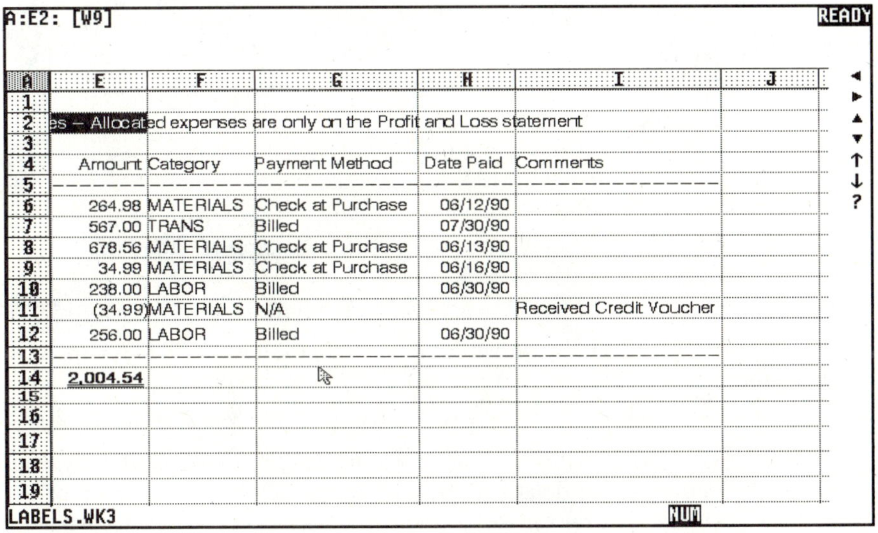

Fig. 3.8.
A long label continuing into the next window.

Entering Numbers

To enter a valid number, you can type any of the 10 digits (0 through 9) and certain other characters according to the following rules:

1. The number can start with a plus sign (+); the sign is not stored when you press Enter.

    +123 is stored as 123

2. The number can begin with a minus sign (–); the number is stored as a negative number.

    –123 is stored as –123

3. The number can be placed within parentheses ( ); the number is stored as a negative number. The parentheses are dropped, and the number is preceded by a minus sign.

    (123) is stored as –123

4. The number can begin with a dollar sign ($); the sign is not stored when you press Enter.

    $123 is stored as 123

5. You can include one decimal point.

6. Three digits must follow each comma included; commas are not stored when you press Enter.

    123,345,789 is stored as 123345789

7. The number can end with a percent sign (%); the number is divided by 100, and the percent sign is dropped.

    123% is stored as 1.23

8. You can type a number in scientific notation. A number is stored in scientific notation only if it requires more than 20 digits.

    123E3 is stored as 123000
    1.23E30 is stored as 1.23E+30
    123E–4 is stored as 0.0123
    1.23E–30 is stored as 1.23E–30

9. If you enter a number with more than 18 digits, it is rounded off to 18 digits.

    123456789987654321 98 is stored as 123456789987654322 00

10. If you enter a number with more than 20 digits, it is stored in scientific notation.

    123456789987654321987 is stored as 1.23456789987654322E+20.

Reminder: *Commas, dollar signs, and parentheses are not stored with the number.*

If the number is too long to display normally in the cell, 1-2-3 tries to display what it can. If the cell uses the default General format and the integer part of the number can fit in the cell width, 1-2-3 rounds off any part of the decimal part of the number that does not fit. In figure 3.9, the numbers in columns C, D, and E are the same; only the column widths are different. In E5, 25.54321 displays rounded off to 26. In C6, 1675.123456789 displays rounded off to 1675.123. Cell formats are described in detail in Chapter 5.

If the cell uses the default **General** format and the integer part of the number does not fit in the cell, 1-2-3 displays the number using scientific notation. Example cells in figure 3.9 are C4, C7, and C9. If the cell uses a format other than **General** or the cell width is too narrow to display in scientific notation and the number cannot fit into the cell width, 1-2-3 displays asterisks (see fig. 3.9).

Caution:
If the column width is too narrow to display a number, 1-2-3 displays asterisks.

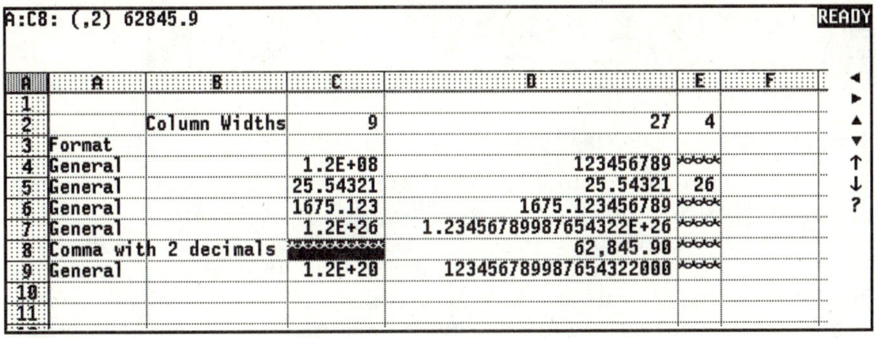

Fig. 3.9.
Asterisks displayed in place of a number too long for the cell width.

Entering Formulas

The real power of 1-2-3 comes from its capability to perform calculations on formulas you enter. In fact, formulas make 1-2-3 an electronic worksheet—not just a computerized way to assemble data for reports. You enter the numbers and formulas into the worksheet; 1-2-3 calculates the results of all the formulas. As you add or change data, you never have to recalculate the effects of the changes; 1-2-3 does it automatically for you. In figure 3.2, if you change the Sales or Variable Costs, 1-2-3 automatically recalculates the Variable Margin. In figure 3.7, the total expense in E14 is recalculated each time you add or change an expense amount.

You can enter formulas that operate on numbers, labels, and other cells in the worksheet. Like labels, a formula can be up to 512 characters long.

There are three different types of formulas: numeric, string, and logical. *Numeric formulas* work with numbers, other numeric formulas, and numeric functions. *String formulas* work with labels, other string formulas, and string functions. *Logical formulas* are true/false tests that can test either numeric or string values. Functions are covered in Chapter 6. This chapter covers each type of formula.

Formulas can operate on numbers in the cell, such as 8+26. This formula uses 1-2-3 just as a calculator. A more useful formula uses cell references in the calculation. The formula in cell F1 in figure 3.10 is +B1+C1+D1+E1. The control panel shows the formula. The worksheet shows the result of the calculation; in this case, 183. The power and usefulness of this formula is that the result in F1 changes automatically any time you change any of the numbers in the other cells. This automatic recalculation capability is a powerful feature of the 1-2-3 electronic worksheet.

Reminder:
Formulas make 1-2-3 an electronic worksheet by preventing you from having to perform calculations manually.

Reminder:
The formula appears in the control panel; the result of the calculation appears in the worksheet.

Notice that the formula begins with a plus sign (+B1). If a formula begins with the characters **B1**, 1-2-3 assumes that you are entering a label, and no calculation is performed.

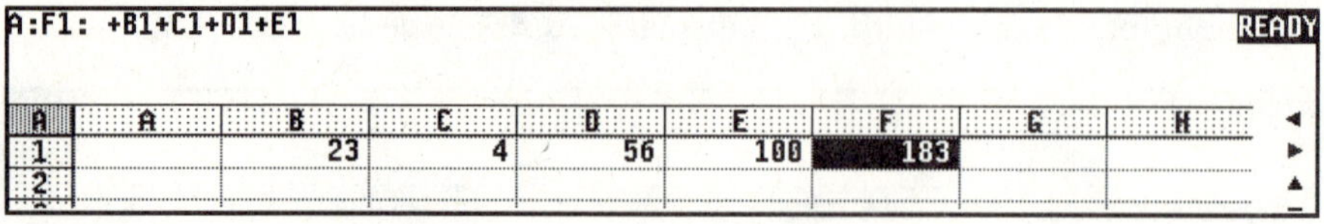

Fig. 3.10.
The result of the calculation displayed in the worksheet.

```
A:F1: +B1+C1+D1+E1                                          READY

       A        B        C        D        E        F        G        H
   1            23       4        56       100      183
   2
```

Using Operators in Numeric Formulas

Reminder:
Use operators to specify which calculations a formula is to perform.

A formula is an instruction to 1-2-3 to perform a calculation. You use *operators* to specify the calculations to perform. The numeric operators are addition, subtraction, multiplication, division, and exponentiation (raising a number to a power). The formula in figure 3.10 uses the plus sign—the addition operator. The simplest numeric formula uses just the plus sign to repeat the value in another cell. In figure 3.9, D4 and E4 both contain the formula +C4. The other cells in columns D and E are also formulas that refer to the corresponding cells in column C. In each case, the value of the cell in column C is repeated in columns D and E.

When 1-2-3 evaluates a formula, it calculates terms within the formula in a specified sequence. Following are the arithmetic operators listed in order of precedence:

Operator	Meaning
^	Exponentiation
+, −	Positive, Negative
*, /	Multiplication, Division
+, −	Addition, Subtraction

Cue:
Use parentheses in a formula to change the order of precedence of the calculations.

If a formula uses all these operators, 1-2-3 calculates exponentiation operations first, and then works down the list. If two operators are equal in precedence, 1-2-3 calculates from left to right. This order of precedence has a definite effect on the result of many formulas. To override the order, use parentheses. Operations inside a set of parentheses are always evaluated first.

The following examples show how 1-2-3 uses parentheses and the order of precedence to evaluate complex formulas. In these examples, numbers are used instead of cell references to make it easier to follow the calculations.

Formula	Evaluation	Result
5+3*2	5+(3*2)	11
(5+3)*2	(5+3)*2	16
−3^2*2	−(3^2)*2	−18
−3^(2*2)	−(3^(2*2))	−81
5+4*8/4−3	5+(4*(8/4))−3	10

Formula	Evaluation	Result
5+4*8/(4–3)	5+((4*8)/(4–3))	37
(5+4)*8/(4–3)	(5+4)*8/(4–3)	72
(5+4)*8/4–3	(5+4)*(8/4)–3	15
5+3*4^2/6–2*3^4	5+(3(*(4^2)/6)–(2*(3^4))	–149

Using Operators in String Formulas

String formulas have different rules than numeric formulas. A *string* is either a label or string formula. There are only two string formula operators. You can repeat another string, or you can join (*concatenate*) two or more strings.

The simplest string formula uses only the plus sign to repeat the string in another cell. In figure 3.11, the formula in A6 is +A3. The formula to repeat a numeric cell and to repeat a string cell is the same. In figure 3.9, the formula in cell D4 is a numeric formula because it refers to a cell with a number. In figure 3.11, the formula in cell A6 is a string formula because it refers to a cell with a string.

Reminder:
There are only two types of string formulas; formulas that repeat strings and formulas that join strings.

Fig. 3.11.
String formulas used to repeat or concatenate strings.

The string concatenation operator is the ampersand (&). The formula in A7 in figure 3.11 is +A3&B3. The first operator in a string formula must be a plus sign; any other operators in the formula must be ampersands. If you do not use the ampersand, but use any of the numeric operators, 1-2-3 treats the formula as a numeric formula. A cell that contains a label has a numeric value of zero. If you enter the formula +A3+B3 in the worksheet in figure 3.11, the formula is treated as a numeric formula and evaluates to zero.

Reminder:
A string is treated as a value of zero in numeric formulas.

If you use an ampersand in a formula, 1-2-3 treats it as a string formula. If you also use any numeric operators (after the plus sign at the beginning), 1-2-3 considers it an invalid formula. The formulas +A3&B3+C3 and +A3+B3&C3 are invalid. When you enter an invalid formula, 1-2-3 puts you in EDIT mode. EDIT mode is covered later in this chapter.

Cue:
You can insert a string directly into a string formula if you enclose it in quotation marks.

In figure 3.11, the names run together in A7, so you want to put a space between the first and last names. You can insert a string directly into a string formula by enclosing the string in quotation marks (" "). The formula in B8 is +A3&" "&B3. The formula in B10 is +D3&", "&E3.

You can write more complex string formulas with string functions, which are covered in Chapter 6.

Using Operators in Logical Formulas

Logical formulas are true/false tests. They compare two values and evaluate to 1 if the test is true and 0 if the test is false. Used mainly in database criteria ranges, logical formulas are covered in more detail in Chapters 6 and 12.

The logical operators include the following:

Operator	Meaning
=	Equals
>	Greater than
<	Less than
>=	Greater than or equal to
<=	Less than or equal to
<>	Not equal
#NOT#	Reverses the results of a test (changes the result from true to false or from false to true)
#OR#	Logical OR to join two tests; the result is true if *either* test is true.
#AND#	Logical AND to join two tests; the result is true if *both* tests are true.

Figure 3.12 shows examples of logical formulas.

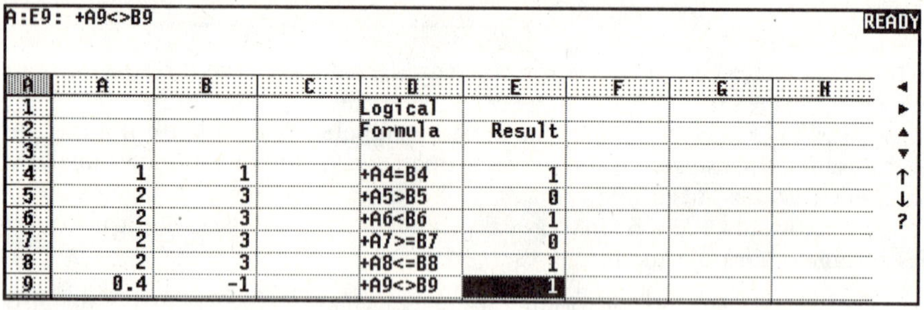

Fig. 3.12.
Logical formulas evaluate to 1 if true or 0 if false.

```
A:E9: +A9<>B9                                                READY

          A       B       C       D         E      F    G    H
  1                               Logical
  2                               Formula   Result
  3
  4       1       1               +A4=B4    1
  5       2       3               +A5>B5    0
  6       2       3               +A6<B6    1
  7       2       3               +A7>=B7   0
  8       2       3               +A8<=B8   1
  9       0.4    -1               +A9<>B9   1
```

Pointing to Cell References

Cue:
Point to the cell you want a formula to use.

Formulas consist mainly of operators and cell references. The formula in figure 3.10 has four cell references. You can type each address, but there is a better way. Whenever 1-2-3 expects a cell address, you can use the mouse or the movement keys to point to the cell. If you use the mouse, you must also use the triangle icons in the icon panel to move the cell pointer. As soon as you move the cell pointer, 1-2-3 changes to POINT mode, and the address of the cell pointer appears in the formula in the control panel.

Move the cell pointer until it is on the correct cell address for the formula you are creating. If this location marks the end of the formula, press Enter. If there are more terms in the formula, type the next operator and continue the process until you are finished; then press Enter. You can type some addresses and point to others. You have no way to tell if the cell references in the formula in figure 3.10 were entered by typing or pointing.

Typing an incorrect address in a formula is easy. Pointing to cells is not only faster but more accurate than typing. The only time it is easier to type an address than point to the cell is when the cell reference is very far from the current cell and you happen to remember the cell address. For example, if you enter a formula in Z238 and you want to refer to cell I23, it may be faster to just type **I23** than point to it. Experienced 1-2-3 users rarely type addresses.

Reminder: *Pointing to, rather than typing, cell addresses is faster and more accurate.*

Correcting Errors in Formulas

If, in error, you enter a formula that 1-2-3 cannot evaluate, the program beeps, changes to EDIT mode, and moves the cursor to the place in the formula where it encountered an error. You cannot enter an invalid formula into a worksheet. For more information about changing a cell in EDIT mode, see "Editing Data in the Worksheet" later in this chapter.

Common errors that make a formula invalid are missing or extra parentheses and mixing numeric and string operators. Other sources of errors are misspelled function names and incorrect arguments in functions (covered in Chapter 6). Some common simple errors are as follows:

Formula	Reason Why It's Incorrect
+A1+A2&A3	Mixing numeric and string operators
+A1/(A2–A3	Missing right parentheses
@SIM(A1..A3)	Misspelled @SUM function

You may not know what is wrong or how to fix the formula. You may also want to use the Help facility to check the format of a function. Before you can do anything else, you must clear the error. If you press Esc or click the right mouse button, you erase the entire entry. If you press Esc or click the mouse again, you are back to READY mode, but you have lost the entire formula.

If you know what is wrong with the formula, follow the procedures in "Editing Data in the Worksheet" later in this chapter. If you do not know how to correct the formula, convert it to a label. Because all labels are valid entries, this technique clears the error and lets you continue working. Follow these steps to convert a formula to a label, clear EDIT mode, and return to READY mode:

Cue: *To fix a formula that is in error, temporarily convert it to a label and move it to another cell.*

1. Press Home to move to the beginning of the formula.
2. Type an apostrophe as the label prefix (1-2-3 accepts anything preceded by an apostrophe as a label).
3. Press Enter.

You can now use the Help facility or look at another part of the worksheet that has a similar formula. When you find the error, correct the formula and remove the apostrophe.

Addressing Cells

Reminder:
When you copy a formula to another location and the cell references change, this is called relative addressing.

A cell address in a formula, such as the one in figure 3.10, is known as a *cell reference*. The formula in F1 has four cell references. Normally, when you copy a formula from one cell to another cell, the cell references adjust automatically. If you use the /Copy command to copy the formula in F1 of figure 3.10 to F2, the cell references change to +B2+C2+D2+E2. This automatic change of cell references is called *relative addressing*.

You can use cell references in formulas that are absolute instead of relative. An *absolute address* in a formula does not change when you copy the formula to another cell. You specify an absolute address when you type a formula by preceding the column and row address with a dollar sign ($). For example, +$A$1 is an absolute address. If this address were in cell C10 and you copied it to cell E19, the cell reference would still be +$A$1. To specify an absolute cell address in POINT mode, press the ABS (F4) key. You also can make a reference to a cell in a specific worksheet absolute. For example, +$A:$A$1 always refers to cell A1 in worksheet A, no matter what cell or worksheet the address is copied to.

In addition to relative and absolute cell addresses, there are also *mixed addresses*. In a mixed address, part of the address is relative and part is absolute. For example, +A$1 is a mixed address; the column letter can change, but the row number cannot.

Whether a cell reference is relative, absolute, or mixed has no effect on how the formula is calculated. This type of addressing matters only when you copy the formula to another cell. Copying and cell addressing are covered in detail in Chapter 4.

Changing Cell Formats

Several commands change the way numbers and formulas display in the worksheet. These commands, /Worksheet Global Format and /Range Format, are covered in detail in Chapter 5.

For example, you can force a fixed number of decimal digits so that the numbers in a column line up; add commas and currency symbols; show numbers as percents; and even hide the contents of the cell. The value in cell D8 in figure 3.9 is formatted to include a comma between thousands and hundreds and to show 2 decimal places. The Wysiwyg menu also enables you to change cell formats. The :Format command changes the appearance of numbers and labels in the worksheet. This command is covered in detail in Chapter 5.

In addition, 1-2-3 includes special formats and functions to handle dates and times. These topics are explained in Chapters 5 and 6.

For example, you can change the font, style (bold, italic, underline), and color of a number or label, and change the color of negative numbers. Additionally, you can change the color of cells, reverse data and cell colors, and add lines, boxes, shadows, and shading to cells.

Adding Notes to a Cell

You can add a note to a cell that contains a value. This technique is useful to explain a number or a formula. Immediately after the number or formula, type a semicolon (;) and then type the note. Do not type a space between the semicolon and the first character of the note. A note displays in the control panel but not in the worksheet.

Cue:
Add a note to a cell by preceding the note with a semicolon.

Editing Data in the Worksheet

After you make an entry in a cell, you may want to change it. You may have misspelled a word in a label or created an incorrect formula. You can change an existing entry by either using the keyboard and mouse with the 1-2-3 menu or using the keyboard and mouse with the Wysiwyg menu.

Keyboard Editing

You can replace the contents of a cell by typing a new entry. The new entry completely replaces the old entry. You also can change (edit) the contents of the cell. To edit a cell's contents, move the cell pointer to the cell and press the Edit (F2) key to go into EDIT mode. You also can press Edit (F2) while you are typing an entry. If you make an error entering a formula, 1-2-3 forces you into EDIT mode.

Reminder:
Edit the contents of a cell by highlighting the cell, pressing Edit (F2), and making the changes.

If the cell entry can fit on one line, the entry displays on the second line in the control panel. If the entry is too large to display on one line, the entire worksheet area drops down to enlarge the entry area to display a full 512-character entry.

Table 3.2 describes the action of keys in EDIT mode. While in EDIT mode, a cursor is in the entry area in the control panel. You use the keys in table 3.2 to move the cursor. As you edit the cell, the contents of the cell as displayed in the first line of the control panel and in the worksheet do not change. The cell's contents change only when you click the left mouse button or press Enter to complete the edit. Keep in mind that the mouse cannot move the cursor while in EDIT mode.

Reminder:
The mouse does not move the cursor while you are in EDIT mode.

If you click the right mouse button or press Esc while in EDIT mode, you clear the edit area. If you then click the mouse or press Esc or Enter with a blank edit area, you do not erase the cell; you cancel the edit, and the cell reverts to the way it was before you pressed Edit (F2).

Cue:
Press Esc twice to cancel editing and restore the cell to its original contents.

Table 3.2
Key Actions in EDIT Mode

Key	Action
←	Moves the cursor one character to the left.
→	Moves the cursor one character to the right.
↑	If the entry fits on one line, completes the edit and moves the cell pointer up one row. If the entry is on more than one line, moves the cursor up one line.
↓	If the entry fits on one line, completes the edit and moves the cell pointer down one row. If the entry is on more than one line, moves the cursor down one line.
Ctrl-← or Shift-Tab	Moves the cursor left five characters.
Ctrl-→ or Tab	Moves the cursor right five characters.
Home	Moves the cursor to the beginning of the entry.
End	Moves the cursor to the end of the entry.
Backspace	Deletes the character to the left of the cursor.
Del	Deletes the character at the cursor.
Ins	Toggles between insert and overtype mode.
Esc	Clears the edit line.
Esc Esc	Cancels the edit and makes no change to the cell.
F2 (Edit)	Switches to VALUE or LABEL mode.
Enter	Completes the edit.

Wysiwyg Editing

The :Text command on the Wysiwyg menu provides you with additional editing features. With this command, you can edit labels right in the worksheet instead of in the control panel. When you choose :Text Edit and specify a cell or range of cells, a vertical-line cursor appears in front of the first character in the label. Move the cursor by clicking the triangle icons with the mouse or using the cursor-arrow keys. Delete characters with the Del and Backspace keys; insert characters by typing. End the edit either by clicking the right mouse button or by pressing Esc.

The :Text command also lets you reformat columns of long labels to look like a paragraph. When you choose :Text Reformat from the Wysiwyg menu and specify a range of labels, Wysiwyg reformats the labels to look like a paragraph.

Reminder:
Use the :Text Reformat command to reformat columns of long labels to look like a paragraph.

Using the Undo Feature

When you type an entry or edit a cell, you change the worksheet. If you change the worksheet in error, you can press the Undo (Alt-F4) key to reverse the last change. For example, if you type over an existing entry, you can undo the new entry and

Chapter 3 ◆ Learning Worksheet Basics

restore the old one. When you select commands from either the 1-2-3 menu or the Wysiwyg menu, you often change the worksheet. In most cases, you can press Undo to reverse the changes you have made with the command menus.

Initially, the Undo feature is disabled, so you must use commands to enable Undo. To turn on the Undo feature, choose /**W**orksheet **G**lobal **D**efault **O**ther **U**ndo **E**nable. To make this change permanent, choose /**W**orksheet **G**lobal **D**efault **U**pdate. When Undo is enabled, 1-2-3 must remember the last action that changed the worksheet. This action requires memory. How much memory Undo requires changes with different actions. You should enable Undo on your system and disable it again with /**W**orksheet **G**lobal **D**efault **O**ther **U**ndo **D**isable only if you get low on memory.

Caution:
To use Undo, you first must enable it.

When you press Undo (Alt-F4), you get a menu with two choices: **No** and **Yes**. You must press **Y** to actually undo the last change. In this book, when you are asked to undo or press the Undo key, remember that you must also press **Y**.

Reminder:
*Press **Y** after you press Undo (Alt-F4) to actually undo the last change.*

Remember that you can undo only the last change; if you make an error, undo it immediately or the old data may be lost.

If you Undo a change but then decide to restore it, you cannot undo the Undo. If you press Undo at the wrong time and undo an entry, you cannot recover it.

Caution:
You can Undo only the last change.

Undo is very useful and powerful. It is also tricky and can surprise you, so use Undo carefully. 1-2-3 remembers the last change to the worksheet and reverses this change when you press Undo. You must understand what 1-2-3 considers a change. A *change* occurs between the time 1-2-3 is in READY mode and the next time it is in READY mode. Suppose, for example, that you press Edit (F2) to go into EDIT mode to change a cell. You can make any number of changes to the cell, and then press Enter to save the changes and return to READY mode. If you then press Undo, 1-2-3 returns the worksheet to the way it was at the last READY mode. In this case, it returns the cell to the way it was before you edited it.

You can change many cells at one time or even erase everything in memory with one command. These commands are covered in Chapter 4. If you press Undo after a command, you undo all the effects of the command.

With some commands, such as /**P**rint (Chapter 8); /**G**raph (Chapter 10); and /**D**ata (Chapter 12), you can execute many commands before you return to READY mode. If you press Undo then, you reverse all the commands executed since the last time 1-2-3 was in READY mode.

For example, suppose that you type an entry into cell K33, press Enter, and then press Home. The cell pointer moves to A1. If you press Undo now, you not only undo the Home key, you undo the entry in cell K33 as well.

Caution:
What 1-2-3 considers the last change may not be the last action you performed, so you may be surprised by the effects of Undo.

A change can refer to either a change to one or more cells or a change to command settings. For example, to print a report, you must specify a print range. Specifying a command setting does not change any data in the worksheet; it only changes the previous setting. If you press Undo the next time you are in READY mode, you undo the print range you specified.

Some commands do not change any cells or settings. Examples of such commands are /File Save, /File Xtract, /File Erase, and /Print Printer Page. If you make an entry in a cell, save the file, and then press Undo, you undo the last change, which is the cell entry.

Reminder:
You may not have enough memory to store the status of the worksheet before making a change.

The more extensive a change, the more memory 1-2-3 needs to remember the status of the worksheet before the change. If you do not have enough memory to save the status before the change, 1-2-3 pauses and presents you with the following menu:

    Proceed Disable Quit

Choose **P**roceed to disable Undo temporarily and complete the command. Undo is reenabled as soon as the command completes. Choose **D**isable to disable Undo and complete the command. Undo remains disabled until you quit and restart 1-2-3 or enable Undo again with /Worksheet Global Default Other Undo Enable.

Choose **Q**uit to cancel the command in progress. You do not quit 1-2-3; you return to READY mode. The command may have been partially completed before 1-2-3 ran out of memory. For example, if you copy a range multiple times (explained in Chapter 4), run out of memory, and choose **Q**uit from the preceding menu, the range may have been copied to part of the range you specified as the TO range. Check your work carefully to determine the effects of the last command.

In most cases, choose **P**roceed. Be sure, however, that you want to perform the command because you cannot undo it. If you executed the command in error, choose **Q**uit now, and then immediately undo whatever the command changed. If you see this menu often and it is slowing you down, choose **D**isable. Although you won't be stopped by this menu again, you won't be able to use Undo.

Using Multiple Worksheets

Multiple-worksheet files make it much easier to organize large, complex files. If you are new to 1-2-3, get comfortable with the basics by starting with one worksheet. When you are ready to design worksheets that are more complex than simple reports, you can use multiple-worksheet files, file linking, and multiple files in memory at the same time.

The following sections cover moving around multiple worksheets as well as entering data and formulas with multiple worksheets and files. Chapter 4 discusses the commands needed to create and use multiple-worksheet files. Chapter 7 introduces the commands to read files into memory and save them.

Some commands related to multiple worksheets include the following:

Command	Action
/Worksheet Insert Sheet	Adds one or more new worksheets to the current file
/Worksheet Delete Sheet	Deletes one or more existing worksheets from the current file
/File Open	Reads a file from disk and adds it to memory; does not replace existing files in memory
/File New	Opens a new, blank file and adds it to memory; does not replace existing files in memory
/Worksheet Delete File	Removes an active file from memory when more than one file is in memory at the same time
/Worksheet Window Perspective	Displays three worksheets at once in a perspective view
/Worksheet Global Group Enable	Changes the scope of many /Worksheet commands such as Insert, Global Format, and Global Col-Width so that they affect all worksheets in the file, not just the current worksheet

Moving around Multiple Worksheets

Moving around multiple worksheets or files with the mouse is as easy as moving around a single worksheet—you simply point to a cell in a worksheet or file and click the left mouse button to move to that worksheet or file. Alternatively, you can point to the up-arrow icon at the right side of the worksheet and click the left mouse button to move to the next worksheet or file, or click the down-arrow icon to move to the previous worksheet or file.

All the movement keys in table 3.1 work the same way with multiple-worksheet files and multiple files in memory; however, these keys keep the cell pointer in the current worksheet. Table 3.3 shows the additional keys needed with multiple-worksheet files and multiple files in memory. The most important key combinations in table 3.3 are Ctrl-PgUp (to move to the next worksheet) and Ctrl-PgDn (to move to the previous worksheet). Do not be concerned with the other movement keys at this time. You can learn them when you build large worksheet files.

Table 3.3
Movement-Key Operation with Multiple Worksheets

Key	Description
Ctrl-PgUp	Moves the cell pointer to the next worksheet.
Ctrl-PgDn	Moves the cell pointer to the previous worksheet.
Ctrl-Home	Moves the cell pointer to the home position in the first worksheet in the file (usually A:A1).
End Ctrl-Home	Moves the cell pointer to the end of the active area in the last worksheet in the file.
End Ctrl-PgUp or End Ctrl-PgDn	Moves the cell pointer through the worksheets to the next cell that contains data (the intersection between a blank cell and a cell that contains data).
Ctrl-End Ctrl-PgUp	Moves the cell pointer to the next file.
Ctrl-End Ctrl-PgDn	Moves the cell pointer to the previous file.
Ctrl-End Home	Moves the cell pointer to the first file in memory.
Ctrl-End End	Moves the cell pointer to the last file in memory.
F5 (GoTo)	Prompts for a cell address or range name and then moves the cell pointer directly to that cell (which can be in another worksheet or file).
F6 (Window)	If the screen has been split, moves the cell pointer to the next window (which can contain another worksheet or file).

Cue:
Use multiple-worksheet files for consolidations.

Figure 3.13 displays a multiple-worksheet file. Worksheet A is the consolidation worksheet. Worksheet B contains the detail data for Region 1, and worksheet C contains the detail data for Region 2. So that you can see the entire set of worksheets in perspective view, this file contains only three worksheets; each contains very little data. Point to cell B:B3 and click the left mouse button or press Ctrl-PgUp to move the cell pointer from A:B3 to B:B3.

Cue:
Use file links for consolidations.

Figure 3.14 shows a different way to get the same consolidation as the one in figure 3.13 with multiple files. Each worksheet in figure 3.14 is a separate file. The consolidated file is named CONSOL2. The other two files are named REGION1 and REGION2. Because the cell pointer is in CONSOL2, you see `CONSOL2` as the file name at the lower left corner of the screen. Click the mouse on cell A:B3 or press Ctrl-PgUp to move the cell pointer to A:B3 in the file REGION1.

Cue:
Use GoTo to move between worksheets.

The GoTo (F5) key works the same within a worksheet or with multiple worksheets. If you press GoTo and then type a cell address that includes only the column and row, the cell pointer moves to that address in the current worksheet. Include a worksheet letter in the cell address to move the cell pointer to another worksheet in the file. To move the cell pointer to B:A1 in the file in figure 3.13, press GoTo (F5), type **B:A1**, and press Enter.

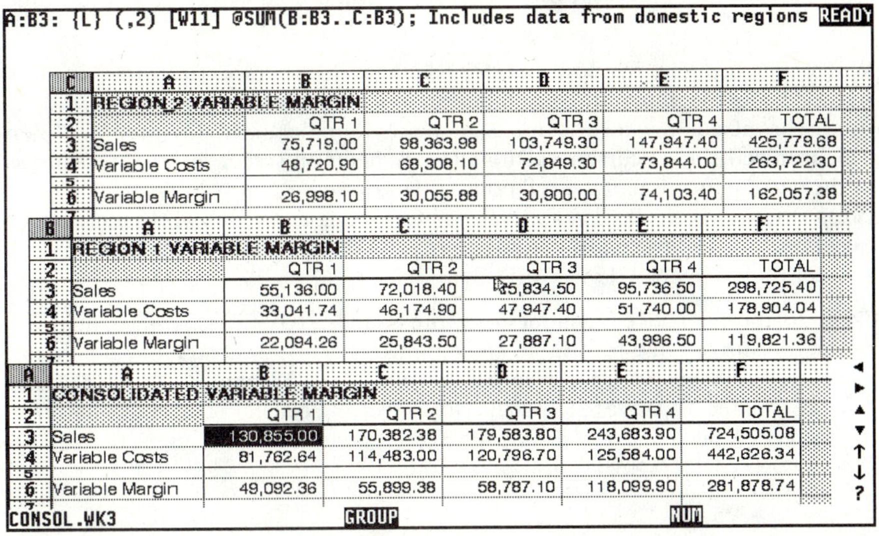

```
A:B3: {L} (,2) [W11] @SUM(B:B3..C:B3); Includes data from domestic regions      READY
```

	A	B	C	D	E	F
1	REGION 2 VARIABLE MARGIN					
2		QTR 1	QTR 2	QTR 3	QTR 4	TOTAL
3	Sales	75,719.00	98,363.98	103,749.30	147,947.40	425,779.68
4	Variable Costs	48,720.90	68,308.10	72,849.30	73,844.00	263,722.30
5						
6	Variable Margin	26,998.10	30,055.88	30,900.00	74,103.40	162,057.38

	A	B	C	D	E	F
1	REGION 1 VARIABLE MARGIN					
2		QTR 1	QTR 2	QTR 3	QTR 4	TOTAL
3	Sales	55,136.00	72,018.40	75,834.50	95,736.50	298,725.40
4	Variable Costs	33,041.74	46,174.90	47,947.40	51,740.00	178,904.04
5						
6	Variable Margin	22,094.26	25,843.50	27,887.10	43,996.50	119,821.36

	A	B	C	D	E	F
1	CONSOLIDATED VARIABLE MARGIN					
2		QTR 1	QTR 2	QTR 3	QTR 4	TOTAL
3	Sales	130,855.00	170,382.38	179,583.80	243,683.90	724,505.08
4	Variable Costs	81,762.64	114,483.00	120,796.70	125,584.00	442,626.34
5						
6	Variable Margin	49,092.36	55,899.38	58,787.10	118,099.90	281,878.74

CONSOL.WK3   GROUP   NUM

Fig. 3.13.
A file with three worksheets used to consolidate regional data.

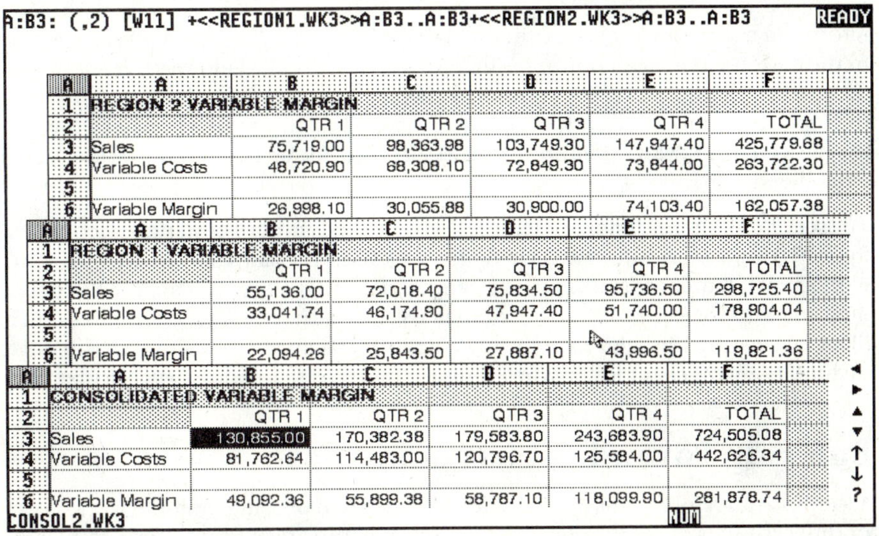

```
A:B3: (,2) [W11] +<<REGION1.WK3>>A:B3..A:B3+<<REGION2.WK3>>A:B3..A:B3      READY
```

	A	B	C	D	E	F
1	REGION 2 VARIABLE MARGIN					
2		QTR 1	QTR 2	QTR 3	QTR 4	TOTAL
3	Sales	75,719.00	98,363.98	103,749.30	147,947.40	425,779.68
4	Variable Costs	48,720.90	68,308.10	72,849.30	73,844.00	263,722.30
5						
6	Variable Margin	26,998.10	30,055.88	30,900.00	74,103.40	162,057.38

	A	B	C	D	E	F
1	REGION 1 VARIABLE MARGIN					
2		QTR 1	QTR 2	QTR 3	QTR 4	TOTAL
3	Sales	55,136.00	72,018.40	75,834.50	95,736.50	298,725.40
4	Variable Costs	33,041.74	46,174.90	47,947.40	51,740.00	178,904.04
5						
6	Variable Margin	22,094.26	25,843.50	27,887.10	43,996.50	119,821.36

	A	B	C	D	E	F
1	CONSOLIDATED VARIABLE MARGIN					
2		QTR 1	QTR 2	QTR 3	QTR 4	TOTAL
3	Sales	130,855.00	170,382.38	179,583.80	243,683.90	724,505.08
4	Variable Costs	81,762.64	114,483.00	120,796.70	125,584.00	442,626.34
5						
6	Variable Margin	49,092.36	55,899.38	58,787.10	118,099.90	281,878.74

CONSOL2.WK3   NUM

Fig. 3.14.
Three separate files in memory at the same time.

To move the cell pointer to the current cell in worksheet B, press GoTo (F5), type **B:**, and then press Enter. 1-2-3 remembers a current cell for every worksheet in memory. In some cases, 1-2-3 returns to the cell pointer's last location in a worksheet. For example, if you are in cell A:B3 in figure 3.13 and press GoTo (F5) to go to B:C15, the cell pointer jumps to C15 in worksheet B, but it remembers the last location in worksheet A. If you then press GoTo to go to worksheet A, the cell pointer returns to cell B3 in worksheet A.

Note: When you use GoTo to move among worksheets, remember that each worksheet's current cell varies depending on whether you are viewing a full-screen worksheet or using the window options to view multiple worksheets at the same time.

When you use the window options, such as the perspective view used in figure 3.13, the current cells in each worksheet can be synchronized or unsynchronized. Synchronizing is explained in detail in Chapter 4. When synchronized, the current cell for all worksheets on-screen is the same address as the current location of the cell pointer. For example, if you are in cell A:B3 and press GoTo to go to B:C15, the cell pointer jumps to C15 in worksheet B. C15 becomes the current cell. If you then press GoTo to go to worksheet A, the cell pointer moves to cell C15 in worksheet A.

To go to another active file in memory, press GoTo (F5) and then type the name of the file surrounded by double angle brackets (<< >>). To move directly to REGION2 in figure 3.13, for example, press GoTo (F5), type **<<REGION2>>**, and press Enter. To move to a specific worksheet and cell in REGION2, include the worksheet and cell address. To move to cell A:F6 in REGION2, press GoTo (F5), type **<<REGION2>>A:F6**, and press Enter.

> **Reminder:**
> Synchronized worksheet cells change the operation of the GoTo key.

Entering Formulas with Multiple-Worksheet Files

A formula can refer to cells in other worksheets by including the worksheet letter in the address. If the cell pointer is in A:A1, to refer to cell C4 in worksheet B, type **+B:C4**. To point to a cell in another worksheet, press **+**, use the mouse to click the up-arrow and down-arrow icons to move to the other worksheet, or use the movement keys Ctrl-PgUp and Ctrl-PgDn to move to the cell in the other worksheet.

> **Reminder:**
> You can create formulas that refer to cells in multiple worksheets by the pointing method.

To see how three-dimensional files are used for consolidations, consider figure 3.13. The formula in A:B3 in figure 3.13 sums the sales data in the other two worksheets. Similar formulas in the range A:B3..A:E4 sum the data for the other quarters and for costs. Writing formulas using multiple-worksheet files is much like writing formulas with a single worksheet. The only difference is that you must include the worksheet letter when you use an address in another worksheet.

Entering Formulas That Link Files

A formula can refer to cells in other files. This method of using multiple worksheets in different files is called *file linking*. Figure 3.14 shows three separate files in memory. The formula in A:B3 in CONSOL2 refers to cell A:B3 in REGION1 and cell A:B3 in REGION2. This powerful feature lets you consolidate data from separate files automatically.

You can use file linking on a network or other multiuser environment. If you believe that one or more of these linked files were updated since you last read the file that contained the links, use /File Admin Link-Refresh to update these formulas.

When you write a formula that refers to a cell in another file in memory, you can point to the cell just as if it were a worksheet in the same file. 1-2-3 includes the path and file name as part of the cell reference (see fig. 3.14). If the file is not in memory, you must type the entire cell reference including the file name and extension inside double angle brackets, as in the following example:

+<<REGION1.WK3>>A:B3

If the file is in another directory, you must include the entire path, as in the following example:

+<<E:\DATA\123\REGION1.WK3>>A:B3

As you can see, a formula that links files is very long. If possible, when you build a formula that refers to a cell or a range in another file, try to have that file in memory so that you can point to the cells instead of typing the complete address. Once the formulas are built, the linked files do not all have to be in memory at the same time. Because formulas are longer and more complex with multiple worksheets and files, try to use POINT mode whenever you enter a formula.

Whenever you read from the disk a file containing formulas that refer to cells in another file, 1-2-3 can read the referenced cells from each linked file and recalculate each linked formula. The linked files are not read into memory. This fact allows you to build worksheet systems that are linked but are too large to fit into memory all at the same time. This feature allows you to build large consolidation models that update automatically without running out of memory.

You can read the CONSOL2 file in figure 3.14 without reading the REGION1 and REGION2 files (see fig. 3.15). All the formulas in the file—except for formulas that link to other files—are updated when you read the file. To update the file links, use /File Admin Link-Refresh. You can update REGION1 and save it, and then update REGION2 and save it. Then retrieve CONSOL2 and select /File Admin Link-Refresh to get the correct consolidated data.

Note: Examine the formulas in the control panels of figures 3.13 and 3.14. Figure 3.13 uses a function to sum the values across the worksheets in the same file. Figure 3.14, however, uses a formula to achieve the same results. You must use formulas when linking worksheets in different files; functions do not work.

Choosing between Multiple-Worksheet Files and Linked Files

Figure 3.13 shows a consolidation using a multiple-worksheet file. Figure 3.14 shows the same consolidation using linked files. The method you choose depends on the specific circumstances. If each regional worksheet is updated by a different person, separate files are necessary. If each regional file is so large that you don't have enough memory to put them all into one file, separate files are required.

Reminder:
If the other file is in memory, 1-2-3 includes the file name in the address when you point to it.

Cue:
For speed and accuracy, use POINT mode to enter cell references in formulas.

Cue:
Use separate files to hold worksheets if the worksheets are updated by different people or if the worksheets are too large to fit together into memory.

Fig. 3.15.
A formula that refers to cells in files which are on disk and not in memory.

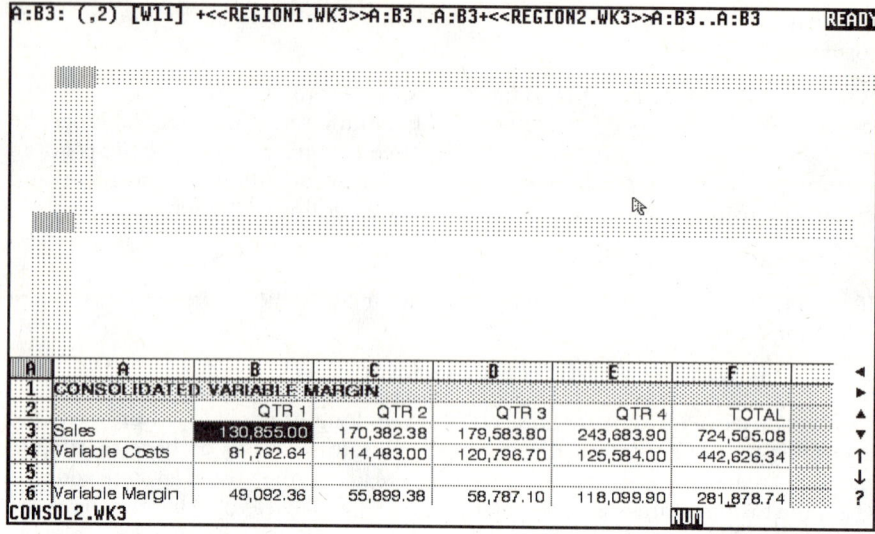

If you have many regions but each regional worksheet is small, use a single, multiple-worksheet file. It is easy to sum a range of any size in a multiple-worksheet file (see fig. 3.13). Ranges, however, cannot include multiple files, so you must write long formulas with individual cell addresses as shown in figure 3.14. A formula can be no more than 512 characters long. Normally, you exceed this amount with a formula that includes 16 or more regions, depending on the names of the path to the subdirectories you use to store your worksheet files. Another consideration is recalculation time. A multiple-worksheet file takes longer to recalculate than separate linked files.

If memory and recalculation time are not at issue and you do not have to distribute parts of the file to others, multiple-worksheet files are easier to build and update in most cases.

Summary

In this chapter, you learned how to organize your work into single worksheets, multiple-worksheet files, and linked files. The process of moving around worksheets and files and entering and editing data was explained. You learned how to build different types of formulas, including formulas that refer to other worksheets and files. Pointing to cells in formulas and using the various operators was also covered. The important Undo feature, which you can use to undo a change made in error, was introduced.

This chapter gives you the basic skills to use 1-2-3. In the next chapter, you learn the basic commands that provide the tools to build and use worksheets effectively.

Using Fundamental 1-2-3 Commands

4

Much of the power of 1-2-3 comes from your use of its commands. You use commands to tell 1-2-3 to perform a specific task or sequence of tasks. Commands can change the operation of the 1-2-3 program itself, or they can operate on a file, a worksheet, or a range. You use commands to change how data displays in the cell, to arrange the display of worksheets in windows on-screen, to print reports, to graph data, to save and retrieve files, to copy and move cells, and to perform many other tasks.

1-2-3 includes over 800 commands. Certain commands are used every time you use the program; others are used rarely, if ever. Some commands perform general tasks that apply to all worksheets; other specialized commands apply only to special circumstances. This chapter covers using command menus and the most fundamental 1-2-3 commands. Later chapters cover more specific commands.

You also learn the limitations on these commands. You cannot do certain actions, such as formatting a diskette, within 1-2-3. In this chapter, you learn how to access the operating system without quitting 1-2-3 so that you can perform operations such as formatting a diskette.

In addition to the detailed explanation of the most important commands in this chapter, this book includes a separate Command Reference section that lists and describes all the commands in alphabetical order.

This chapter shows you how to do the following:

- ◆ Use command menus
- ◆ Save files
- ◆ Use ranges and range names
- ◆ Set column widths
- ◆ Clear data from rows, columns, and worksheets

- Insert rows, columns, and worksheets
- Use window options
- Use display options
- Freeze titles on-screen
- Protect and hide data
- Control recalculation
- Move and copy data
- Reference cells with relative and absolute addressing
- Find and replace particular data
- Access the operating system without quitting 1-2-3

Selecting Commands from Command Menus

Reminder:
You can access the 1-2-3 and Wysiwyg menus from READY mode only.

You execute 1-2-3 commands through a series of menus. To access the 1-2-3 menu, which displays in the second line of the control panel, press the slash (/) key from READY mode. To access the Wysiwyg menu, press the colon (:) key from READY mode. In either case, the mode indicator changes to MENU (see figs. 4.1 and 4.2). To access these menus with the mouse, just move the mouse pointer into the control panel, and one of the menus appears. To toggle between the 1-2-3 and Wysiwyg menus, press the right mouse button. These menus give you access to over 800 commands.

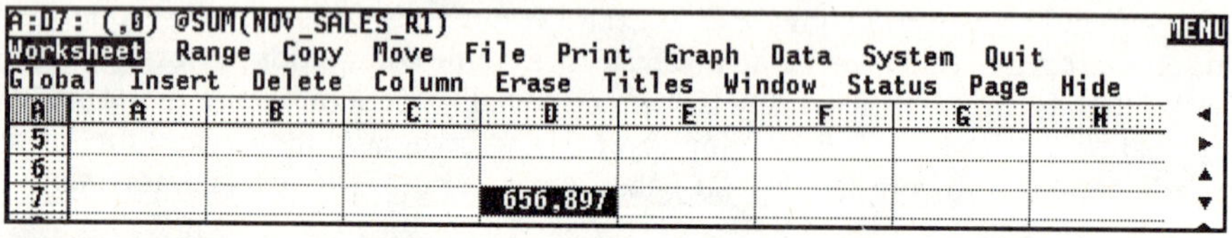

Fig. 4.1.
The 1-2-3 command menu.

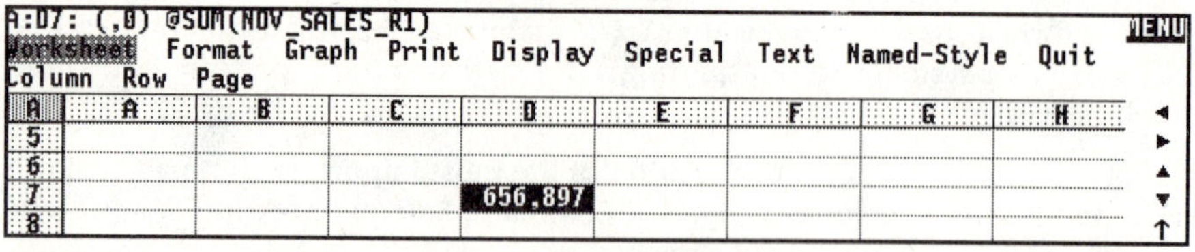

Fig. 4.2.
The Wysiwyg command menu.

When you first press the slash or the colon key or move the mouse into the control panel area, the Worksheet command is highlighted. Keep in mind that both the 1-2-3 and Wysiwyg menus have a Worksheet command, and each command leads to submenus. You can determine which menu you are in by looking at the rest of the commands in the menu or by observing the color of the command highlight. Below the menu options, on the third line, is either an explanation of the highlighted menu option or a list of the options in the next menu. In figure 4.1, the third line lists the /Worksheet menu options of the 1-2-3 menu.

Chapter 4 ♦ Using Fundamental 1-2-3 Commands   95

To select a menu option, use the cursor keys to move the highlight to a choice and press Enter, or point to the choice with the mouse and press the left mouse button. Table 4.1 shows the keys that move the *menu pointer*, also called the *highlight*. As you highlight each menu item, the next set of commands displays on the screen's third line. Figure 4.3 shows the menu after you select /Worksheet from the 1-2-3 menu. Notice that the third line in figure 4.1 has moved up to become the menu line in figure 4.3. Continue to make menu selections until you get to the command you want. Some commands prompt you to specify ranges, file names, values, or other information.

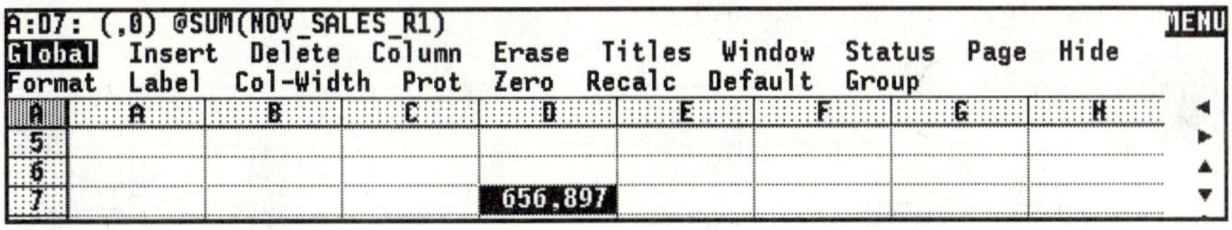

Fig. 4.3.
The /Worksheet menu.

Table 4.1
Menu Pointer Movement Keys

Key	Function
→	Moves the pointer one command to the right. If at the last command, wraps to the first command.
←	Moves the pointer one command to the left. If at the first command, wraps to the last command.
Home	Moves the pointer to the first command.
End	Moves the pointer to the last command.
Enter	Selects the command highlighted by the menu pointer.
Esc	Cancels the current menu and returns to the previous menu. If at the 1-2-3 menu, cancels the menu and returns to READY mode.
Ctrl-Break	Cancels the menu and returns to READY mode.

Once you become familiar with the command menus, you can use a different method to select commands. Just type the first letter of each command. You may find this technique faster than highlighting the command and pressing Enter. Every option on a menu begins with a different character, so 1-2-3 always knows which menu option you want. Most users type the first letter of the commands they know well and point to commands they don't often use.

Cue:
Type the first character of a command name to select the command from a menu.

One of the first commands you use is /**R**ange **E**rase. To erase a cell or a range of cells from the keyboard, first press / from READY mode. Select **R**ange, and then select **E**rase. The prompt `Enter range to erase:` appears (see fig. 4.4). If you want to erase just the current cell, press Enter (see fig. 4.5). If you want to erase a range, specify the range to erase and press Enter. You learn how to specify ranges in the section "Using Ranges" later in this chapter.

Part I ♦ Building the 1-2-3 Worksheet

To perform the same operation by using the mouse, move the mouse pointer to the control panel to display the 1-2-3 menu (press the right mouse button, if necessary, to toggle the menu). Point to **R**ange and press the left mouse button. The same prompt appears as before (see fig. 4.4). To erase the current cell, point to the cell and press the left mouse button twice (see fig. 4.5). If you want to erase a range, specify the range to erase and press the left mouse button. You learn how to specify ranges with the mouse in the section "Using Ranges" later in this chapter.

Fig. 4.4.
The /Range Erase prompt.

A:D15: [W11] 'Dept 13						POINT
Enter range to erase: A:D15..A:D15						

	A	B	C	D	E	F	G
1	Sales Forecast				This	Next	Following
2					Year	Year	Year
3				Dept 1	23456	34198	37650
4				Dept 2	17693	28762	31495
5				Dept 3	33418	31690	34893
6				Dept 4	16933	19761	23061
7				Dept 5	28610	33388	38964
8				Dept 6	18793	21931	25593
9				Dept 7	23691	27647	32264
10				Dept 8	31520	36784	42927
11				Dept 9	17621	20564	23998
12				Dept 10	16918	19743	23040
13				Dept 11	35971	41978	48988
14				Dept 12	26918	31413	36659
15				Dept 13			

Fig. 4.5.
The current cell erased by using /Range Erase.

A:D15: [W11]						READY

	A	B	C	D	E	F	G
1	Sales Forecast				This	Next	Following
2					Year	Year	Year
3				Dept 1	23456	34198	37650
4				Dept 2	17693	28762	31495
5				Dept 3	33418	31690	34893
6				Dept 4	16933	19761	23061
7				Dept 5	28610	33388	38964
8				Dept 6	18793	21931	25593
9				Dept 7	23691	27647	32264
10				Dept 8	31520	36784	42927
11				Dept 9	17621	20564	23998
12				Dept 10	16918	19743	23040
13				Dept 11	35971	41978	48988
14				Dept 12	26918	31413	36659
15							

You can point to each menu option (using either the mouse or the cursor keys) or type the first letter of the option. In this book, the entire command name is shown; the first letter is in boldface. You type only the first letter. For example, to erase a range, press **/re** (**/R**ange **E**rase).

As you make menu selections, you can make an occasional error. To correct an error, press Esc or press the right mouse button to return to the previous menu. If you press Esc at the top level of the 1-2-3 or Wysiwyg menus, you clear the menu and return to READY mode. If you press Ctrl-Break from any menu, you return

Chapter 4 ◆ Using Fundamental 1-2-3 Commands 97

directly to READY mode. To clear a top-level menu with the mouse, move the mouse pointer to the worksheet area and press the right mouse button.

You can explore the command menus without actually executing the commands. Using the cursor keys to highlight each menu option in the 1-2-3 menu (see fig. 4.1), read the third line in the control panel to find out more about the option or to see the next menu. Then select each menu option to get to the next menu (see fig. 4.3). Continue to select the menu options you want to explore until there are no more menus. Use the Command Chart at the back of this book to help guide you through the menus. Figure 4.6 shows the /Worksheet Window Display menu. You can select one of two display options from this menu.

Cue:
Use the arrow keys and the Esc key to explore the command menus.

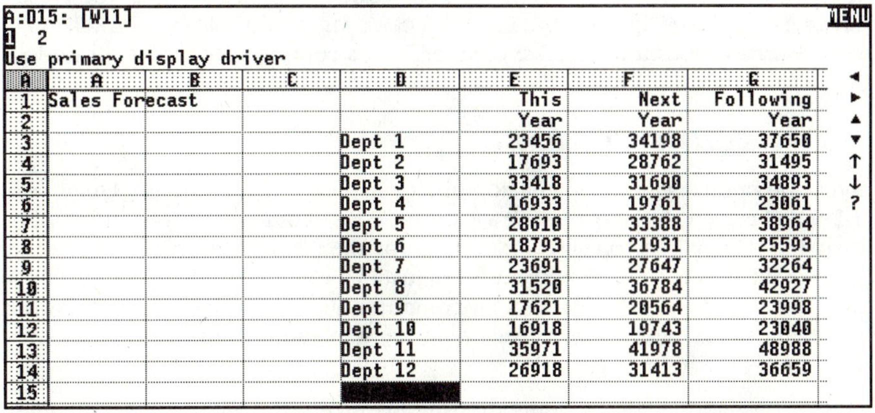

Fig. 4.6.

The /Worksheet Window Display menu.

Use the Esc key or press the right mouse button to back out of a menu to the next higher menu without actually executing the command. Figure 4.7 shows the result after you press Esc at the /Worksheet Window Display menu in figure 4.6. You can now explore another /Worksheet Window option.

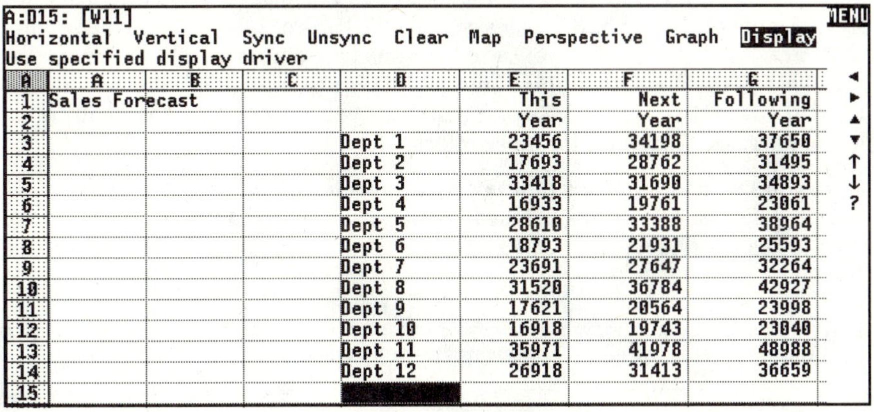

Fig. 4.7.

The /Worksheet Window menu after you press Esc from the /Worksheet Window Display menu.

Reminder:
A /Worksheet command may refer to a worksheet, to a file, or to 1-2-3 as a whole.

The 1-2-3 and Wysiwyg menu choices (see figs. 4.1 and 4.2) help guide you to the correct command. For example, all the graph commands are accessed through **/Graph** or **:Graph**, and all the data-management commands are accessed through **/Data**. There is one important exception: The **/Worksheet** and **:Worksheet** commands can refer to a single worksheet, to a file, or to 1-2-3 as a whole. For example, use **/Worksheet Global Default** to change overall 1-2-3 defaults, such as the choice of printer. Versions 1A through 2.3 of 1-2-3 enable you to work with only one worksheet and one file at a time. The **/Worksheet** and **:Worksheet** commands in Release 3.1+ affect a larger area than any other command, such as **/Range**.

If you execute a command in error, you can Undo it. For example, if you erase a range in error (see figs. 4.4 and 4.5), you can press Undo (Alt-F4) and select **Yes** to recover the erased range. See Chapter 3 for a complete discussion of Undo.

Saving Your Files

A file you build exists only in the computer's memory. When you use **/Quit** to exit 1-2-3 and return to the operating system, you lose your work if you did not first save it to disk. When you save a file, you copy the file in memory to the disk and give it a file name. The file then exists not just in memory but as a duplicate file on disk after you quit 1-2-3 or turn off the computer. When you make changes to a file, the changes are made only in the computer's memory until you save the new version of the file to disk.

More information about file operations is included in Chapter 7. In that chapter, you learn how to read in, use, and save multiple files in memory at the same time. For now, you can learn to save your work by using the **/File Save** command. This chapter covers saving only one file in memory.

First, choose **/File Save** from the 1-2-3 menu. If you have only one file in memory, 1-2-3 prompts for the name of the file to save and displays a default path and file name for the file. If you have never saved the file before, 1-2-3 displays the prompt `Enter name of file to save:` and assigns a default file name such as FILE0001.WK3. Do not use this name, but type a meaningful file name, such as DEPT1BUD (a budget file for Department 1). If you have more than one file open in memory, see Chapter 7 for more information.

Once you save a file, the next time you save it the default file name is the name you supplied the last time you saved the file, such as DEPT1BUD (see fig. 4.8). To save the file again and keep the same name, just press Enter or press the left mouse button.

Fig. 4.8.
The default file name is the name used the last time the file was saved.

```
A:A1: 'Department 1 Budget                                          EDIT
Enter name of file to save: C:\123R31\FILES\DEPT1BUD.WK3
       A         B         C         D         E         F         G         H
   1 Department 1 Budget
   2
```

Chapter 4 ◆ Using Fundamental 1-2-3 Commands   99

To save the file with a different name, type the file name. The file name you type replaces the existing name. If the file already exists on the disk, 1-2-3 displays the following three-option menu:

    Cancel Replace Backup

Choose **Replace** to write over the previous file. Once you choose **Replace**, however, you lose the previous file. If you make an error in a file, and then save it with the same name and choose **Replace**, you cannot read in the previous file.

Choose **Cancel** to void the /**File Save**. If you type a file name in error that matches another file name, **Cancel** the command so that you do not lose the other file.

If you choose **Backup**, 1-2-3 renames the existing file on disk with a BAK extension, and then saves the new file. By using this choice, you have both the new file and the previous file on disk.

Caution:
If you choose Replace, the previous file with that name is lost.

Cue:
Choose Backup to keep a backup copy of your file and save a new version.

Using Ranges

A *range*, a rectangular group of cells, is defined by the cell addresses of two opposite corners and is separated by two periods. As shown in figure 4.9, a range can be a single cell (E1..E1), part of a row (A1..C1), part of a column (G1..G5, D13..D20, and F14..F15), or a rectangle that spans multiple rows and columns (B4..E9 and A13..B15). A range also can span multiple worksheets. A range can be an entire worksheet or file, but it cannot span multiple files.

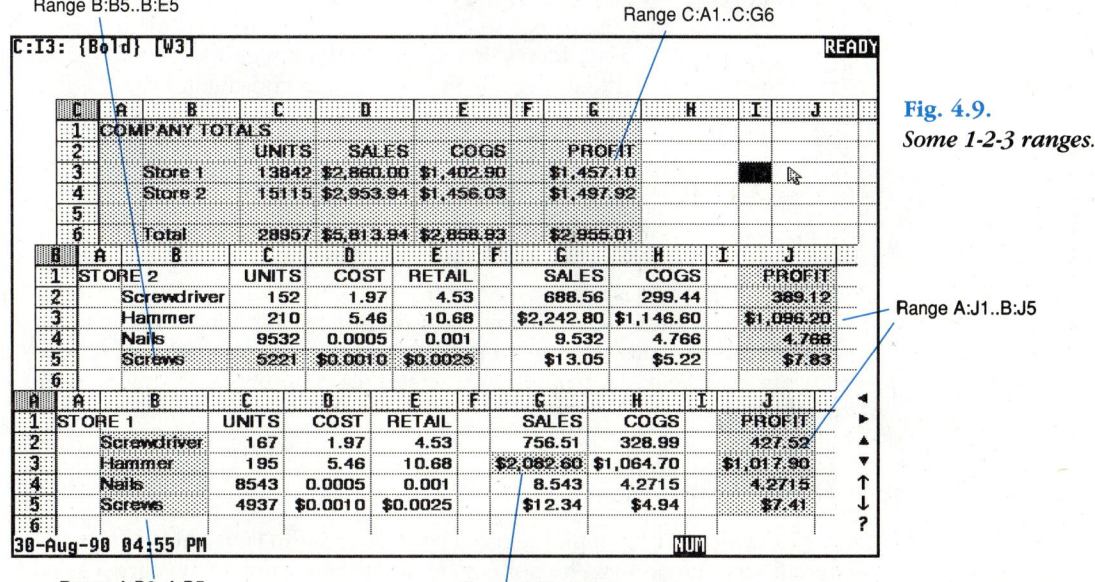

Fig. 4.9.
Some 1-2-3 ranges.

Many commands act on one or more ranges. For example, the /Range Erase command in figure 4.4 prompts you for the range to erase. In this example, the range is a single cell. You can respond to a prompt for a range in several different ways. At different times, each one of these methods may be the most convenient. To specify a range, you can use any of the following methods:

- Type the addresses of the corners of the range
- Highlight the cells in the range in POINT mode by using the arrow keys or the mouse
- Type the range name or press Name (F3) and point to the range name if one has been assigned

Each method is covered in the following sections.

Typing the Addresses of the Range

Reminder:
Typing the addresses of the range is the method most prone to error.

The first method, typing the addresses of the range, is used the least because it is the most prone to error. This method requires you to type the addresses of any two opposite corners of the range.

You can specify a range by typing the address of the upper left corner, one or two periods, and the address of the lower right corner. 1-2-3 always stores a range with two periods to separate the addresses, but you need to type only one period. 1-2-3 always stores a range using the upper left and lower right addresses. You may, if you wish, type the upper right and lower left addresses or reverse their order and type the lower address first and then the upper address. 1-2-3 always stores the range using the upper left and lower right coordinates.

For example, to specify the range A1..G6 in worksheet C of figure 4.9, type A1..G6 or A1.G6 or G6..A1 or G6.A1. You also can use the other two opposite corners: A6..G1 or G1..A6. In all cases, 1-2-3 stores the range as A1..G6.

You may type cell addresses to specify a range in several situations: when the range does not have a range name; when the range you want to specify is far from the current cell, and it is not convenient to use POINT mode; or when you happen to know the cell addresses of the range. Experienced 1-2-3 users rarely type cell addresses. Instead, they use one of the following alternative methods: specifying a range in POINT mode, typing range names, or pointing to a range name that already exists.

Specifying a Range in POINT Mode

The second method, highlighting the cells in the range in POINT mode, is the most common technique. It can be done with either the mouse or the cursor keys.

You can point to and highlight a range that has been written into commands and functions just as you can point to a single cell in a formula. Any special considerations for highlighting ranges in functions are covered in Chapter 6.

Chapter 4 ◆ Using Fundamental 1-2-3 Commands　　**101**

Highlighting a Range

Figure 4.10 is a sample sales forecast. Suppose that because of a reorganization you have to erase all the forecasts and enter new data. Figure 4.10 shows the Enter range to erase: prompt that appears when you execute /**R**ange **E**rase. The default range in the control panel is the address of the cell pointer, in this example A:E3..A:E3. The single cell is shown as a one-cell range. When the prompt shows a single cell as a one-cell range, the cell is said to be *anchored*. Most /**R**ange commands use an anchored, one-cell range as the default range. When the cell is anchored, as you *drag* the mouse (move the mouse while holding the left mouse button) or move the cell pointer, you highlight a range.

```
A:E3: [W11] 23456                                              POINT
Enter range to erase: A:E3..A:E3

        A         B         C         D         E         F         G
   1 Sales Forecast                                This      Next    Following
   2                                               Year      Year      Year
   3                                     Dept 1   23456     34198     37650
   4                                     Dept 2   17693     28762     31495
   5                                     Dept 3   33418     31690     34893
   6                                     Dept 4   16933     19761     23061
   7                                     Dept 5   28610     33388     38964
   8                                     Dept 6   18793     21931     25593
   9                                     Dept 7   23691     27647     32264
  10                                     Dept 8   31520     36784     42927
  11                                     Dept 9   17621     20564     23998
  12                                     Dept 10  16918     19743     23040
  13                                     Dept 11  35971     41978     48988
  14                                     Dept 12  26918     31413     36659
  15
  16
  17
  18
  19
  20
02-Aug-90 08:11 AM                                              NUM
```

Fig. 4.10.

A one-cell range at the location of the cell pointer.

Figure 4.11 shows the screen after you drag the mouse to A:G14 and release the left mouse button or press End down-arrow and then End right-arrow. You also can press End Home, which is quicker and uses fewer keystrokes. As you move the cell pointer, the highlight expands from the anchored cell. The highlighted range becomes A:E3..A:G14, which is the range that appears in the control panel. When you press the left mouse button or press Enter, 1-2-3 executes the command by using the highlighted range (see fig. 4.12).

Cue:
Check the control panel to see whether the cell is anchored.

Typically, pointing and highlighting is faster and easier than typing the range addresses. Also, because you can see the range as you specify it (see fig. 4.11), you make fewer errors pointing than typing.

Use the End key when you highlight ranges from the keyboard. The End key moves to the end of a range of occupied cells. To highlight the range from A:E3..A:G14 in figure 4.11, you can press End down-arrow and End right-arrow, as in the previous example. Without the End key, you have to press the right-arrow twice and the down-arrow 11 times.

Cue:
Use the End key with the arrow keys to highlight ranges quickly.

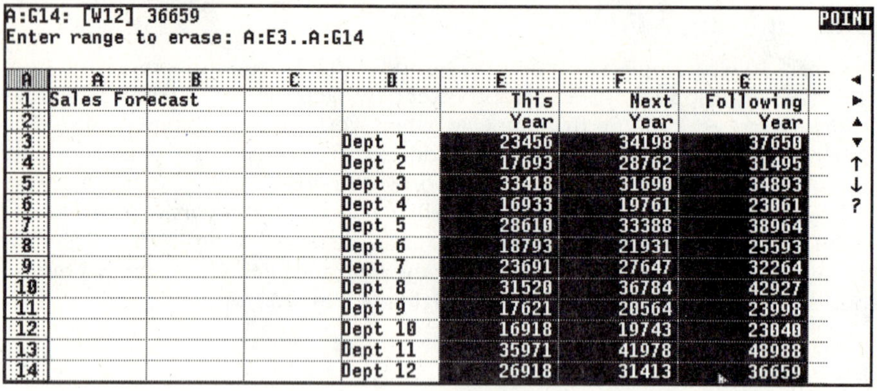

Fig. 4.11.
A range highlighted as the cell pointer is moved.

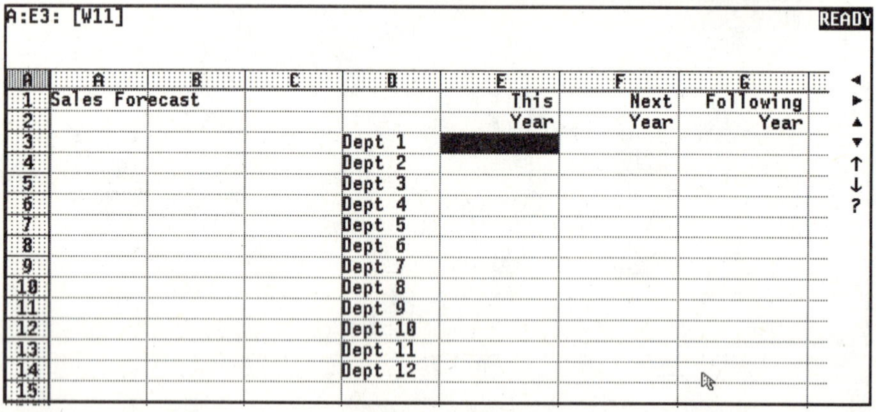

```
A:G14: [W12] 36659                                          POINT
Enter range to erase: A:E3..A:G14
```

	A	B	C	D	E	F	G
1	Sales Forecast				This	Next	Following
2					Year	Year	Year
3				Dept 1	23456	34198	37650
4				Dept 2	17693	28762	31495
5				Dept 3	33418	31690	34893
6				Dept 4	16933	19761	23061
7				Dept 5	28610	33388	38964
8				Dept 6	18793	21931	25593
9				Dept 7	23691	27647	32264
10				Dept 8	31520	36784	42927
11				Dept 9	17621	20564	23998
12				Dept 10	16918	19743	23040
13				Dept 11	35971	41978	48988
14				Dept 12	26918	31413	36659

Fig. 4.12.
The highlighted range erased.

```
A:E3: [W11]                                                 READY
```

	A	B	C	D	E	F	G
1	Sales Forecast				This	Next	Following
2					Year	Year	Year
3				Dept 1			
4				Dept 2			
5				Dept 3			
6				Dept 4			
7				Dept 5			
8				Dept 6			
9				Dept 7			
10				Dept 8			
11				Dept 9			
12				Dept 10			
13				Dept 11			
14				Dept 12			
15							

With some commands, such as /**R**ange Erase in this example, the anchored cell starts at the position of the cell pointer. You should move the cell pointer to the upper left corner of the range before you start the command. In figure 4.10, the cell pointer started at A:E3, the upper right corner of the range to erase.

Figure 4.13 shows what happens if the cell pointer is in the wrong cell when you start a /**R**ange Erase. The cell pointer was in F4; after you drag the mouse to A:G14 or press End-down arrow and End-right arrow, the range A:F4..A:G14 is highlighted.

Whenever you highlight a range, the other cell in the range, the one opposite the anchored cell, is called the *free cell*. You can identify the position of the free cell by observing the cell address shown in the upper left corner of the display. In figure 4.13, the free cell is G14. The highlight expands or contracts from the free cell when you use the mouse or one of the movement keys. If the wrong cell is anchored, as in figure 4.13, you can move the anchor cell and the free cell by pressing the period key (.). Every time you press the period key while in POINT mode, the free cell moves to another corner of the highlighted range.

Chapter 4 ◆ Using Fundamental 1-2-3 Commands   **103**

```
A:G14: [W12] 36659                                          POINT
Enter range to erase: A:F4..A:G14
```

	A	B	C	D	E	F	G
1	Sales Forecast				This	Next	Following
2					Year	Year	Year
3				Dept 1	23456	34198	37650
4				Dept 2	17693	28762	31495
5				Dept 3	33418	31690	34893
6				Dept 4	16933	19761	23061
7				Dept 5	28610	33388	38964
8				Dept 6	18793	21931	25593
9				Dept 7	23691	27647	32264
10				Dept 8	31520	36784	42927
11				Dept 9	17621	20564	23998
12				Dept 10	16918	19743	23040
13				Dept 11	35971	41978	48988
14				Dept 12	26918	31413	36659
15							

Fig. 4.13.
The wrong range highlighted.

To highlight the correct range in figure 4.13, first press the period key twice. You can tell that the free cell moves from G14 to F4 (see fig. 4.14) by observing the cell address shown in the upper left corner of the display. (When specifying a range, the first cell is always the anchored cell. The second cell is the free cell. In the range A:F4..A:G14, F4 is the anchored cell and G14 is the free cell.) Now press the right-arrow and left-arrow keys to highlight the correct range (see fig. 4.15).

```
A:F4: [W11] 28762                                           POINT
Enter range to erase: A:G14..A:F4
```

	A	B	C	D	E	F	G
1	Sales Forecast				This	Next	Following
2					Year	Year	Year
3				Dept 1	23456	34198	37650
4				Dept 2	17693	28762	31495
5				Dept 3	33418	31690	34893
6				Dept 4	16933	19761	23061
7				Dept 5	28610	33388	38964
8				Dept 6	18793	21931	25593
9				Dept 7	23691	27647	32264
10				Dept 8	31520	36784	42927
11				Dept 9	17621	20564	23998
12				Dept 10	16918	19743	23040
13				Dept 11	35971	41978	48988
14				Dept 12	26918	31413	36659
15							

Fig. 4.14.
The free cell moved to F4.

Press the right mouse button, Esc, or Backspace to clear an incorrectly highlighted range. The highlight collapses to the anchor cell only, and the anchor is removed. Thus, if you press the right mouse button, Esc, or Backspace in figure 4.13, the highlight becomes just F4 and the cell becomes unanchored (see fig. 4.16). Observe that the cell address in the control panel in figure 4.16 is the single address A:F4, not the one-cell range A:F4..A:F4.

Cue:
Press Esc or Backspace to clear a highlighted range.

Now move the cell pointer to E3 and press the left mouse button or the period key to anchor the cell again. The control panel shows the one-cell range A:E3..A:E3. This anchored cell represents the same situation as shown in figure 4.10. Now highlight the range A:E3..A:G14 and complete the command.

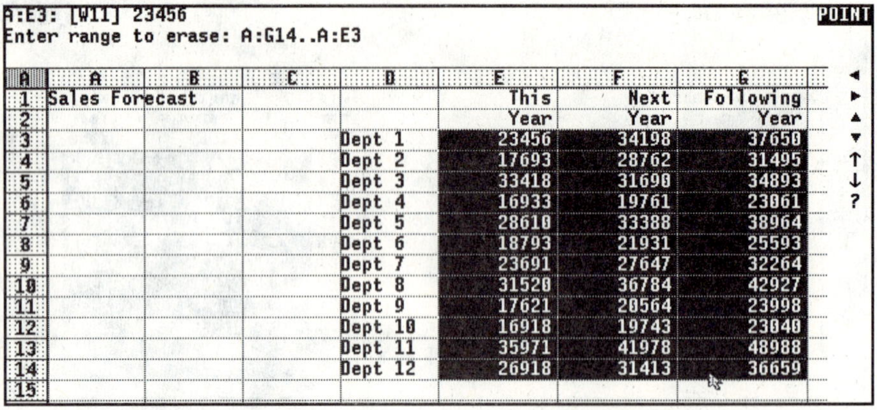

Fig. 4.15.
The correct range highlighted after the free cell is moved to E3.

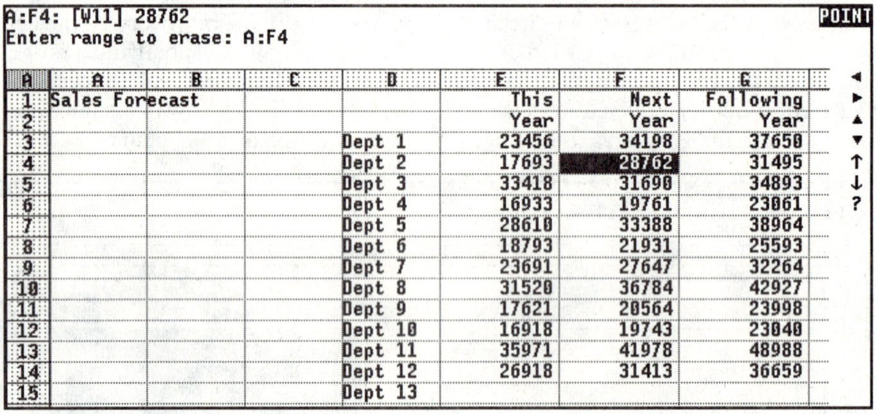

```
A:E3: [W11] 23456                                              POINT
Enter range to erase: A:G14..A:E3
```

	A	B	C	D	E	F	G
1	Sales Forecast				This	Next	Following
2					Year	Year	Year
3				Dept 1	23456	34198	37650
4				Dept 2	17693	28762	31495
5				Dept 3	33418	31690	34893
6				Dept 4	16933	19761	23061
7				Dept 5	28610	33388	38964
8				Dept 6	18793	21931	25593
9				Dept 7	23691	27647	32264
10				Dept 8	31520	36784	42927
11				Dept 9	17621	20564	23998
12				Dept 10	16918	19743	23040
13				Dept 11	35971	41978	48988
14				Dept 12	26918	31413	36659
15							

Fig. 4.16.
The highlighted range and the anchor cleared.

```
A:F4: [W11] 28762                                              POINT
Enter range to erase: A:F4
```

	A	B	C	D	E	F	G
1	Sales Forecast				This	Next	Following
2					Year	Year	Year
3				Dept 1	23456	34198	37650
4				Dept 2	17693	28762	31495
5				Dept 3	33418	31690	34893
6				Dept 4	16933	19761	23061
7				Dept 5	28610	33388	38964
8				Dept 6	18793	21931	25593
9				Dept 7	23691	27647	32264
10				Dept 8	31520	36784	42927
11				Dept 9	17621	20564	23998
12				Dept 10	16918	19743	23040
13				Dept 11	35971	41978	48988
14				Dept 12	26918	31413	36659
15				Dept 13			

While in the /**R**ange **E**rase state, 1-2-3 expects the range to start at the current location of the cell pointer and gives this cell an anchored cell status. This procedure is followed when using certain other commands, including all the /Range commands (except /Range Search), /Copy and /Move from the 1-2-3 menu, and :**F**ormat, :**S**pecial, :**T**ext, and :**N**amed-Style from the Wysiwyg menu.

However, when using other commands (including /**D**ata, /**G**raph, /**P**rint, and /**R**ange Search from the 1-2-3 menu, and :**G**raph and :**P**rint from the Wysiwyg menu), at the Enter range: prompt, 1-2-3 does not expect the range to start at the current location of the cell pointer. The control panel shows the current cell address, A:M1, as a single address (see fig. 4.17). And because 1-2-3 expects the range to start at a different location, the cell pointer is not anchored. When you use the movement keys, the address in the control panel changes to the single address of the current location of the cell pointer. To anchor the first corner of the range, press the period key. Figure 4.18 shows the screen after you move the cell pointer to A:M3 and press the period key. The address in the control panel changes to a one-cell range. If you want a larger range than A:M3, move the cell pointer to highlight the range and press Enter. Unlike the cursor keys, the mouse always causes cells to become anchored whether they are anchored or not. As soon as you press the left mouse button to drag the mouse, the unanchored cell becomes anchored.

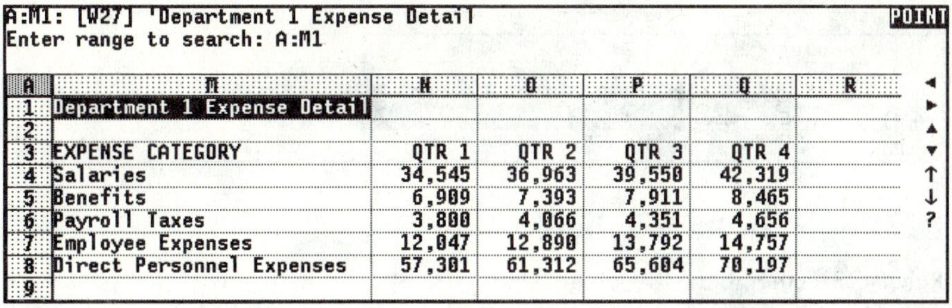

```
A:M1: [W27] 'Department 1 Expense Detail                           POINT
Enter range to search: A:M1
```

A	M	N	O	P	Q	R
1	Department 1 Expense Detail					
2						
3	EXPENSE CATEGORY	QTR 1	QTR 2	QTR 3	QTR 4	
4	Salaries	34,545	36,963	39,550	42,319	
5	Benefits	6,909	7,393	7,911	8,465	
6	Payroll Taxes	3,800	4,066	4,351	4,656	
7	Employee Expenses	12,047	12,890	13,792	14,757	
8	Direct Personnel Expenses	57,301	61,312	65,604	70,197	
9						

Fig. 4.17.
An unanchored current cell.

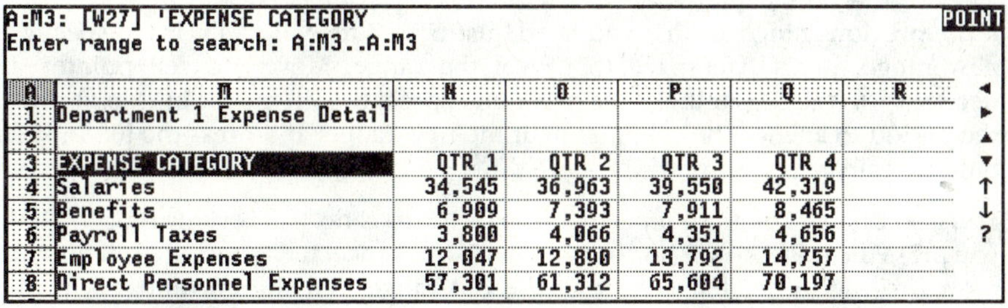

```
A:M3: [W27] 'EXPENSE CATEGORY                                      POINT
Enter range to search: A:M3..A:M3
```

A	M	N	O	P	Q	R
1	Department 1 Expense Detail					
2						
3	**EXPENSE CATEGORY**	QTR 1	QTR 2	QTR 3	QTR 4	
4	Salaries	34,545	36,963	39,550	42,319	
5	Benefits	6,909	7,393	7,911	8,465	
6	Payroll Taxes	3,800	4,066	4,351	4,656	
7	Employee Expenses	12,047	12,890	13,792	14,757	
8	Direct Personnel Expenses	57,301	61,312	65,604	70,197	

Fig. 4.18.
An anchored cell after the period key is pressed.

Preselecting a Range

Before issuing a command, you can select the range to be affected by the command. This technique is called *preselecting a range*. Why preselect a range instead of selecting the range after you issue the command? When you preselect a range, you can issue several Wysiwyg formatting commands that affect the range. The range that you preselect remains selected. For example, if you want to change the font of some numbers and then outline the cells that contain the numbers, preselect the range and perform both commands. You can preselect a range only when Wysiwyg is active.

You can preselect a range in one of two ways. If you are using the keyboard, move the cell pointer to the beginning of the range. Next, press F4. The mode indicator changes from READY to POINT, and an anchored range address appears in the control panel. Using the arrow keys, select the range. Figure 4.19 shows the screen when preselecting the range A:C3..A:F4. After selecting the desired range, press Enter to accept the range setting.

If you are using a mouse, press and hold the Ctrl key. Move the mouse to the corner cell of the range and press and hold the left mouse button. 1-2-3 enters POINT mode. Drag the mouse to highlight the range, and then release both the Ctrl key and the left mouse button. You do not have to press Enter to complete the selection. Releasing the mouse button completes the selection. After you press

Part I ♦ Building the 1-2-3 Worksheet

and hold the left mouse button, you can release the Ctrl key. 1-2-3 remains in POINT mode until you release the left mouse button.

Fig. 4.19.

Preselecting the range A:C3..A:F4.

| A:F4: (C0) 61478 | | | | | POINT |
| A:C3..A:F4 | | | | | |

	A	B	C	D	E	F	G	H
1	All Departments							
2			Qtr 1	Qtr 2	Qtr 3	Qtr 4		
3		Sales	$96,487	$98,523	$92,874	$99,861		
4		Expenses	$68,512	$63,521	$66,885	$61,478		
5		Profit	$27,975	$35,002	$25,989	$38,383		

Dealing with Remembered Ranges

Cue:
1-2-3 remembers the previous range with some commands.

Release 3 remembers the range when you specify it. When you repeat such commands as /Data, /Graph, /Print, and /Range Search from the 1-2-3 menu and :Graph and :Print from the Wysiwyg menu, 1-2-3 highlights the previous range.

If the previous range is what you need, just press Enter. If you want to specify a new range, press Backspace to cancel the range. Move the cell pointer, if necessary, to the beginning of the new range, press the left mouse button or press the period to anchor the cell, highlight the new range, and press the left mouse button again or press Enter.

You also can use the right mouse button or Esc to cancel a previous range. When you press the right mouse button or press Esc to cancel the range, the cell pointer moves to the upper left corner of the old range, not the current cell in the worksheet. For example, suppose the cell pointer is in M1, and you want to print this part of the worksheet. The range previously printed was A:A2..A:G18. When you choose /Print Printer Range, 1-2-3 remembers the old range. If you press Backspace now, 1-2-3 cancels the old range and returns the cell pointer to M1. If you press the right mouse button or Esc now, 1-2-3 cancels the old range but moves the cell pointer to A2, the upper left corner of the old range.

Specifying a Range with Range Names

Cue:
You can use a range name any time 1-2-3 expects a range or cell address.

The third method for specifying a range at the prompt involves giving the range a name. Range names, which should be descriptive, can include up to 15 characters and can be used as part of formulas and commands. Whenever 1-2-3 expects a cell or range address, you can specify a range name. There are two ways to specify a range name. You can type the range name, or you can press Name (F3) and point to the range name.

Using range names has a number of advantages. Range names are easier to remember than addresses. It is sometimes faster to use a range name rather than point to a range in another part of the worksheet. Range names also make formulas easier to understand. For example, if you see the range name NOV_SALES_R1 in a formula, you may remember that the entry represents "November Sales for Region 1." Utilizing range names as mnemonic devices in formulas and commands can serve better than a numerical address, such as C:D7..C:D10 (see fig. 4.20).

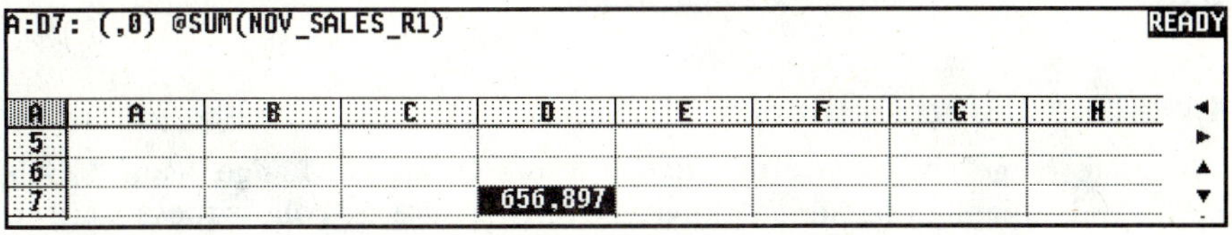

Fig. 4.20.
A formula that uses a range name.

If you have more than one file in memory, 1-2-3 displays a list of range names in the current file, as well as a list of the other files in memory. To select a range name in another file, first select the file name to see the display of range names in that file. Then select the range name in that file.

When you press Name (F3), the third line of the control panel lists the first four range names in alphabetical order. Use the mouse or movement keys to point to the correct range name, and then either press the left mouse button or press Enter. If you have many range names, press Name (F3) again; 1-2-3 displays a full screen of range names (see fig. 4.21).

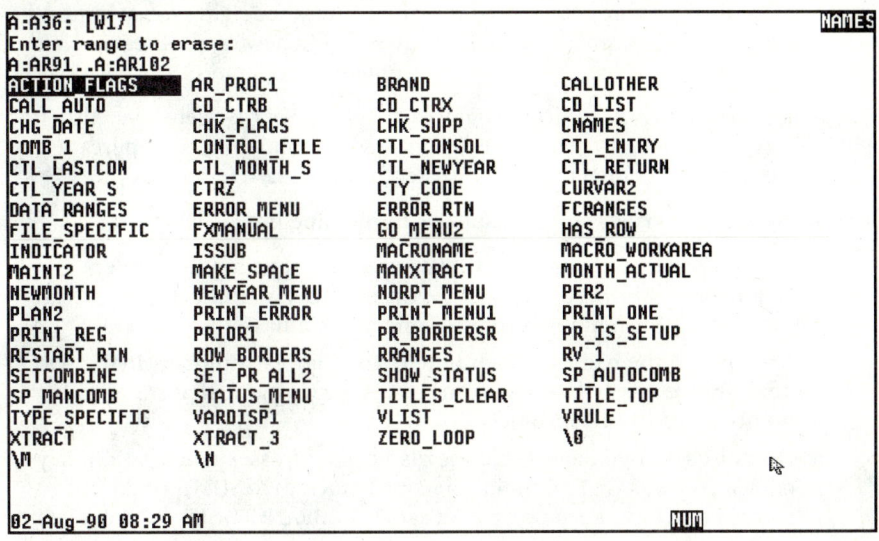

Fig. 4.21.
A full-screen display of range names.

If the command calls for a single cell address, such as with **/Data Sort Primary-Key** or GoTo (F5), 1-2-3 can specify a range whether you type an English name or a cell address. If the prompt calls for a single cell address, such as when using GoTo (F5), and you type a range name that applies to a multiple-cell range, 1-2-3 uses the upper left corner of the range. If you type a nonexistent range name, 1-2-3 displays an error message. Press the left or right mouse button, Esc, or Enter to clear the error and try again.

Cue:
You can use the Name (F3) key in commands, functions, and multiple worksheets in conjunction with the GoTo (F5) key.

Because a single cell is considered a valid range, you can name a single cell as a range. Whenever 1-2-3 expects a cell address, you can type the address, point to the cell, or type the single-cell range name.

Creating Range Names

To create range names, use the /**R**ange **N**ame **C**reate or /**R**ange **N**ame **L**abels commands to assign names to individual cells or ranges. Follow these steps to create range names with the /**R**ange **N**ame **C**reate command:

1. Move to the upper left corner of the range you want to name.
2. Choose /**R**ange **N**ame **C**reate.
3. Type the name, and then press the left mouse button or press Enter at the `Enter name:` prompt. 1-2-3 displays the `Enter range:` prompt.
4. If you type a new range name, 1-2-3 shows the current cell as an anchored range. Highlight the range or type the address or addresses of the cell or range; then press the left mouse button or press Enter.

    If you type an existing range name, 1-2-3 highlights the existing range. Use the arrow keys to extend the range, press the right mouse button, or press Esc to cancel the range; then specify a new range. Press the left mouse button or press Enter to complete the operation.

Cue:
You can specify range names by using any combination of uppercase and lowercase letters, although all characters are stored as uppercase.

Range names can include up to 15 characters and are not case-sensitive. Although you can type or refer to the name using any combination of uppercase and lowercase letters, all range names are stored as uppercase letters.

Following are a few rules and precautions for naming ranges:

- ◆ Do not use spaces or special characters (except for the underscore character (_) in range names. If you use special characters, you can confuse 1-2-3 when you use the name in formulas.
- ◆ Do not start the name with a number. You may use numbers in the rest of the range name, but you cannot use a range name that starts with a number as part of a formula.
- ◆ Do not use range names that are also cell addresses (such as P2), key names (such as GoTo), function names (such as @SUM), or advanced macro command keyword names (such as BRANCH). If you use a cell address as a range name, when you type the range name, 1-2-3 uses the cell address instead.

Certain other errors can occur when you use range names in formulas. These errors are covered in Chapter 6.

You also can create range names with the /**R**ange **N**ame **L**abels command. Use this command to assign range names to many individual cells at one time. You can use /**R**ange **N**ame **L**abels to assign range names to single-cell ranges only. When using /rnl, use labels already typed into the worksheet as range names for adjacent cells. In figure 4.22, for example, you can use the labels in cells B5..B8 to name the cells

Chapter 4 ◆ Using Fundamental 1-2-3 Commands   **109**

with sales data in C5..C8. Because you want to name the cells to the right of the labels, use /**Range Name Labels Right**. Specify a range of B5..B8 and press the left mouse button or press Enter. Now C5 has the range name DEPT_1, C6 has the name DEPT_2, and so on.

```
A:B2: 'Fourth Quarter Sales                                    READY

         A           B          C          D        E        F       G
  1
  2                      Fourth Quarter Sales
  3
  4
  5                   Dept_1      7,565
  6                   Dept_2     49,484
  7                   Dept_3     53,783
  8                   Dept_4     32,783
  9                                ---------
 10  Total for Region:      65   143,615
```

Fig. 4.22.
Labels that can be used for range names.

The other options with /**Range Name Labels** are **Left**, **Down**, and **Up**. These commands only assign range names to labels in the range you specify. If you specify a range of B2..B10 in figure 4.22, the blank cells in B3, B4, B9, and the number in B10 are ignored. The first 15 characters in the label in B2 become the range name for C2: Fourth Quarter. You do no harm if you include cells that are blank, or include numbers or formulas in a /**Range Name Labels** range; but do not include other labels, or you end up with unwanted range names.

Adding Notes about Ranges

Once you create a range name, you can append a note to a range name with /**Range Name Note Create**. First, select the range name you want to annotate, and then type a note of up to 512 characters. Use this feature to explain the meaning of the range or how it is used. You also can use this command to change an existing note. You can list these notes with /**Range Name Note Table**.

Listing All Range Names and Notes

1-2-3 includes two commands that can create a table of named ranges in your worksheet. /**Range Name Table** creates a list of range names and addresses. /**Range Name Note Table** creates a list of range names, addresses, and notes. Using these commands is the only way to see your range-name notes (see fig 4.23). This table is part of the documentation for the worksheet file and can be put in a worksheet separate from the actual data.

To delete an unwanted range name, use /**Range Name Delete**. Use caution when using the /**Range Name Reset** command, however. The command immediately deletes all the range names in the file.

Caution:
The /Range Name Reset command deletes all range names.

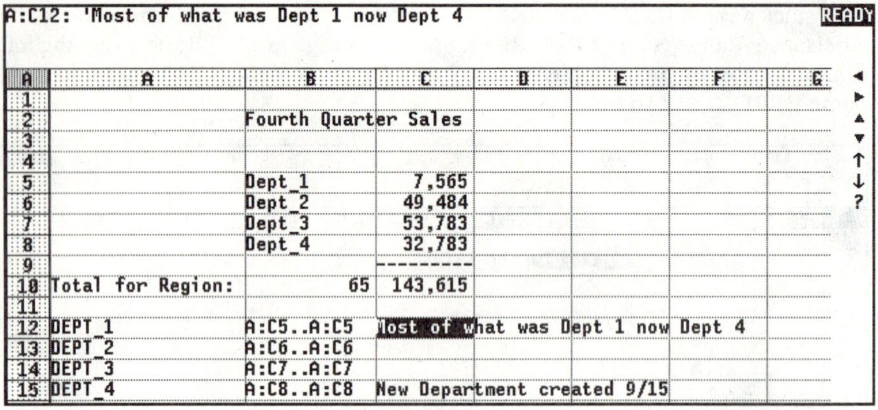

Fig. 4.23.
A table of range names, addresses, and notes created with /Range Name Note Table.

```
A:C12: 'Most of what was Dept 1 now Dept 4                    READY
         A              B            C          D        E        F        G
 1
 2                  Fourth Quarter Sales
 3
 4
 5                  Dept_1          7,565
 6                  Dept_2         49,484
 7                  Dept_3         53,783
 8                  Dept_4         32,783
 9                                 --------
10   Total for Region:        65   143,615
11
12   DEPT_1         A:C5..A:C5   Most of what was Dept 1 now Dept 4
13   DEPT_2         A:C6..A:C6
14   DEPT_3         A:C7..A:C7
15   DEPT_4         A:C8..A:C8   New Department created 9/15
```

Using Ranges in Files with Multiple Worksheets

If your file has more than one worksheet, you can specify three-dimensional ranges. A range cannot span more than one file, but you can specify a range in one file that refers to a two-dimensional or three-dimensional range in another file. A three-dimensional range must have the shape of a three-dimensional rectangle.

For example, you can specify a /Data Query Input range in FILE A that refers to a range in FILE B. When you execute /Data Query Extract in FILE A, the input range used is in FILE B. /Data Query thus allows you to use data from a number of files. More information on this process is found in Chapter 12.

By using the /Print menu, you can print a range in FILE A that refers to a range in FILE B. This two-dimensional range enables you to print a report that combines data from multiple files. This process is covered in Chapter 8.

Figures 4.24, 4.25, and 4.26 display examples of three-dimensional ranges. To create the range B:B2..D:B2 in figure 4.24, start with the cell pointer in B:B2. Use the mouse to click the up-arrow in the icon panel twice to move up to worksheet D. Click the mouse pointer anywhere in the worksheet to complete the operation. From the keyboard, press the period key to anchor the range. Then press Ctrl-PgUp twice to move up to worksheet D. Press Enter to complete the operation.

To create the range B:B2..C:B4 in figure 4.25, again start with the cell pointer in B:B2. Drag the mouse to B:B4 to highlight B:B2..B:B4. Then release the mouse button and click the up-arrow in the icon panel. To complete the operation, click the mouse pointer anywhere in the worksheet. From the keyboard, press the period key to anchor the range. Press the down-arrow key twice to highlight B:B2..B:B4, and then press Ctrl-PgUp to move up to worksheet C. Press Enter to complete the operation.

Chapter 4 ◆ Using Fundamental 1-2-3 Commands

To create the range B:B2..D:D5 in figure 4.26, once again start with the cell pointer in B:B2. Drag the mouse to B:D5 to highlight B:B2..B:D5. Then release the mouse button and click the up-arrow in the icon panel twice. To complete the operation, click the mouse pointer anywhere in the worksheet. From the keyboard, press the period key to anchor the range. Press the down-arrow key three times and the right-arrow key twice to highlight B:B2..B:D5, and then press Ctrl-PgUp twice to move up to worksheet D. Press Enter to complete the operation.

Three-dimensional ranges can be useful with consolidation worksheets. *Consolidations* are worksheets that combine data from many different worksheets that each contain data from one department, region, product, and so on.

It is much easier to highlight a range than to type the corner addresses. If you type the address, make sure that you use the correct worksheet letters. The corners are the upper left of the first worksheet and the lower right of the last worksheet.

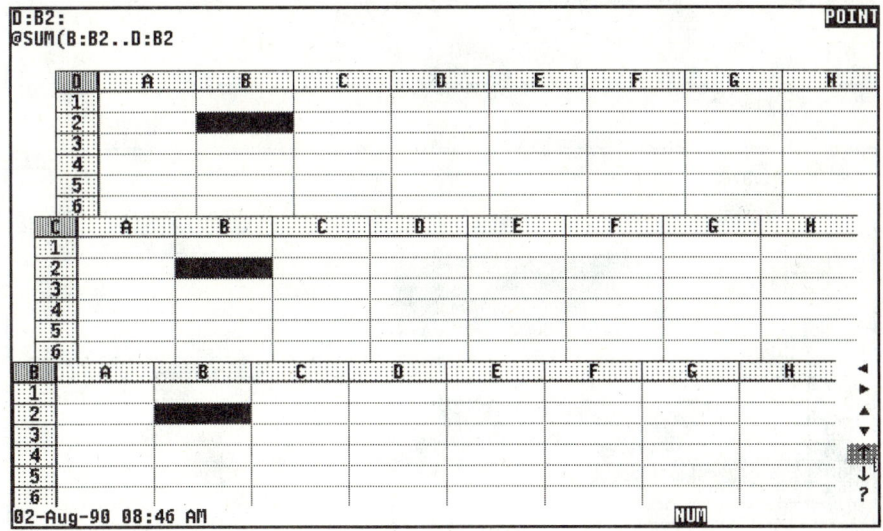

Fig. 4.24.
Three-dimensional range that includes a single cell across three worksheets.

Setting Column Widths

When you start a new worksheet, all columns are 9 characters wide. You can change this default column width and the width of each individual column to best accommodate your data. If columns are too narrow, numbers display as asterisks, and labels are truncated if the adjacent cell is full. If columns are too wide, you cannot see as much on-screen or print as much on one page. Figure 4.27 shows a worksheet with a default column width of 5 characters and an individual column width of 15 for column A. The number in cell J8 is too wide for the column and displays as a row of asterisks. The label in A5 is too long for the column width and is truncated by the number in B5. Any column width other than the default is displayed in the control panel.

Fig. 4.25.

A three-dimensional range that includes three cells in a column across two worksheets.

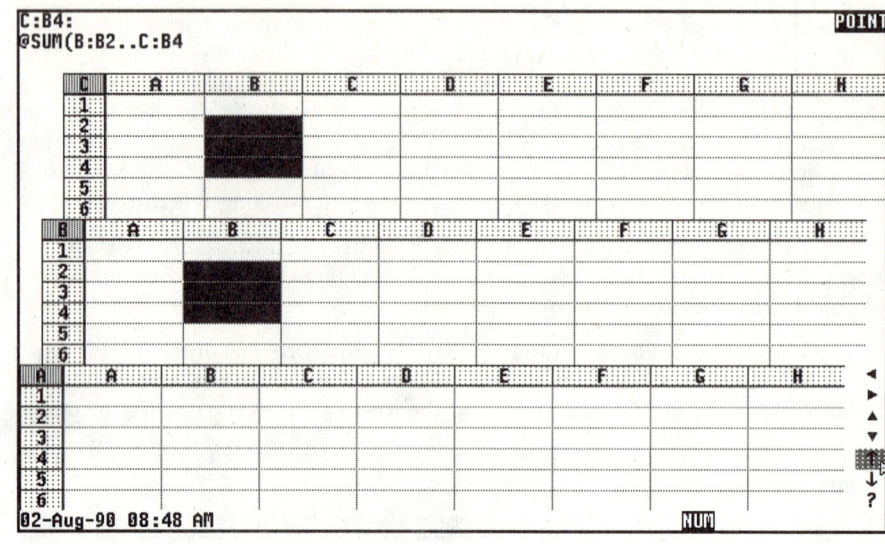

Fig. 4.26.

A three-dimensional range that includes a rectangular range across three worksheets.

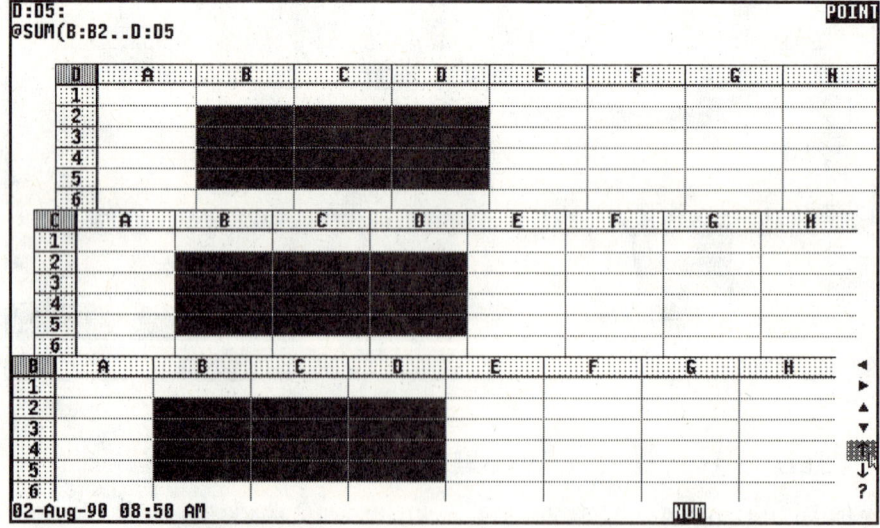

Whether a number can fit into a cell depends on both the column width and the format. In general, a number's width must be one character less than the column width. Some negative numbers display with parentheses, which take two extra characters. If a number displays as a row of asterisks, change either the column width, the format, or both.

Use /Worksheet Global Col-Width to change the default column width for the entire worksheet. At the prompt, type a number between 1 and 240 and press the left mouse button or press Enter.

Chapter 4 ◆ Using Fundamental 1-2-3 Commands 113

```
A:J8: (F1) @SUM(I8..B8)                                           READY

       A         B    C    D    E    F    G    H    I    J    K    L
  1  Work Schedule
  2  ----------------------------------Week--------------------------
  3              1.0  2.0  3.0  4.0  5.0  6.0  7.0  8.0 TOTAL
  4              ---  ---  ---  ---  ---  ---  ---  ---  ---
  5  Write proposal 22.0                                      22.0
  6  Present plan        4.5                                   4.5
  7  Get approval        2.5                                   2.5
  8  Research           16.0 28.0 30.5 35.5 24.0 10.5        *****
  9  Compile notes                          12.0 16.0         28.0
 10  Write final                                  8.0 32.0 40.0
 11  Present                                          8.0  8.0
 12
```

Fig. 4.27.

A worksheet with a global column width of 5 and individual column widths.

When using the mouse to set the width of one column, move the mouse pointer to the top border of the worksheet and point to the vertical line that marks the end of a particular column. When you hold the left mouse button, the pointer changes to a double-headed arrow pointing to the right and left as shown in figure 4.28. To increase the width of the column, move the mouse to the right while continuing to hold the left mouse button. To decrease the width of the column, move the mouse to the left while continuing to hold the left mouse button.

```
A:B1: [W11]                                                       READY

       A         B         *  C         D         E         F         G         H
  1
  2
```

Fig. 4.28.

Changing the width of a column with the mouse.

You can set the width of a column through menu choices, too. When using the Wysiwyg menu to set the width of one column, move the cell pointer to the appropriate column and choose :Worksheet Column Set-Width. Press the left mouse button twice to select the column, or press Enter. At the prompt, type a number between 1 and 240 and press the left mouse button or press Enter. To do the same thing using the 1-2-3 menu, move the cell pointer to the column you want to change and use /Worksheet Column Set-Width. At the prompt, type a number between 1 and 240 and press Enter.

To change column widths for more than one column at a time with the Wysiwyg menu, choose :Worksheet Column Set-Width, and then select a range of columns by dragging the mouse, using the cursor keys, or typing in the range address or range name; then type the column width and press the left mouse button or press Enter. This procedure operates on a contiguous set of columns only.

To set a range of column widths from the 1-2-3 menu, use /Worksheet Column Column-Range Set-Width. At the first prompt, highlight the range of columns to set; then type the column width and press the left mouse button or press Enter. This method works on a contiguous set of columns only.

An individual column width overrides the global column width. If you change the global column width shown in figure 4.27, the width of column A does not change.

Cue:
Use the arrow keys to set column widths instead of typing the width value.

If you are not sure of the exact column width you want, use the left-arrow and right-arrow keys instead of typing a number. Each time you press the left-arrow key, the column width decreases by one. Each time you press the right-arrow key, the column width increases by one. When the display looks the way you want, press Enter. This technique works for individual columns, column-ranges, and global column widths.

Use :**W**orksheet **C**olumn **R**eset-Width, /**W**orksheet **C**olumn **R**eset-Width, or /**W**orksheet **C**olumn **C**olumn-**R**ange **R**eset-Width to remove individual or multiple column widths and reset the width(s) to the global default.

If the window of a single worksheet is split when you change column widths, the column width applies only to the current window. When you clear a split window, the column widths in the upper or left window are saved. Any column widths in the lower or right window are lost. Column widths and global column widths apply to just the current worksheet unless you turn on GROUP mode with /**W**orksheet **G**lobal **G**roup. In GROUP mode, all worksheets in the file change column widths at the same time.

Use GROUP mode when all the worksheets in a file have the same format; for example, when each worksheet contains the same data for a different department or division. In GROUP mode, any formatting change (such as setting column widths) that you make to one worksheet in the file affects all the worksheets in the file.

Setting Row Heights

The Wysiwyg features of Release 3.1 make it possible to view a variety of type fonts on-screen (see fig. 4.29). However, many fonts are too large to fit in a normal size cell. 1-2-3 automatically adjusts the height of a row to compensate for the size of the font. 1-2-3 also lets you adjust the row height manually. To adjust the height of a single row with the mouse, move the mouse pointer over to the left border of the worksheet and point to the horizontal line that marks the bottom of a particular row. When you press and hold the left mouse button, a double-headed arrow appears pointing up and down (see fig. 4.30). To increase the row height, drag the mouse down; to decrease the row height, drag the mouse up.

Adjust the height of a range of rows by selecting :**W**orksheet **R**ow **S**et-Height. At the first prompt, highlight the range of rows to set; then type a number between 1 and 240 and press the left mouse button or press Enter. You can adjust the height of a single row with this method by selecting a single row as the range.

Once you set the height of a row or rows by using :**W**orksheet **R**ow **S**et-Height, the height does not automatically adjust when you change the font size for that row. To make the row sizes automatically adjust again, select the command :**W**orksheet **R**ow **A**uto, and select the rows you want to reset.

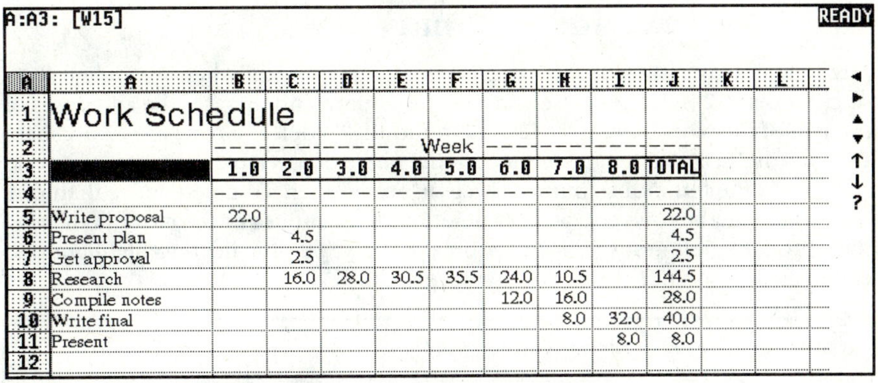

Chapter 4 ◆ Using Fundamental 1-2-3 Commands   **115**

Fig. 4.29.
Wysiwyg enables you to view a variety of type fonts on the screen.

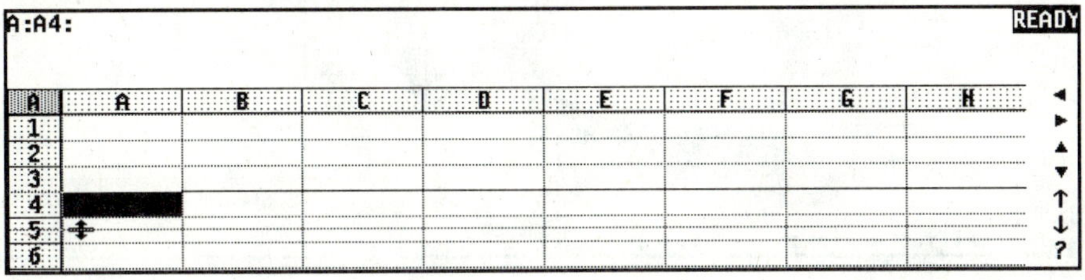

Fig. 4.30.
Changing the height of a row with the mouse.

Erasing and Deleting Rows, Columns, and Worksheets

You can clear parts or all of your work in several ways. Any data that you clear is removed from the workspace in memory, but does not affect the files on disk until you use the /File commands explained in Chapter 7. There are two ways to clear part of your work in memory. If you erase the work, you remove all the contents of the cells. If you delete the work, you remove not only the contents but also the cells from the workspace.

Erasing Ranges

Use the /Range Erase command to erase sections of a file in memory. You can erase a single cell, a range within one worksheet, or a range that spans multiple worksheets in one file. You cannot, however, erase cells in more than one file with one /Range Erase command.

When you erase a range, only the contents are lost. Characteristics such as format, protection status, and column width remain.

After you choose /Range Erase, 1-2-3 prompts you for the range you want eliminated. Highlight a range or type a range name and press the left mouse button or press Enter. You also can press Name (F3) for a list of range names. To erase only the current cell, press the left mouse button twice or press Enter.

Part I ◆ Building the 1-2-3 Worksheet

Deleting Rows and Columns

After you erase a range, the blank cells remain. In contrast, when you delete rows or columns, 1-2-3 deletes the entire row or column and updates the addresses of the rest of the worksheet to reflect the removal. To delete a row, use /Worksheet Delete Row. You are then prompted for the range of rows to delete. To delete one row, press the left mouse button twice or press Enter. To delete more than one row, highlight the rows you want to delete with the mouse or the movement keys; then press the left mouse button or press Enter. You only need to highlight one cell in each row—not the entire row (see fig. 4.31).

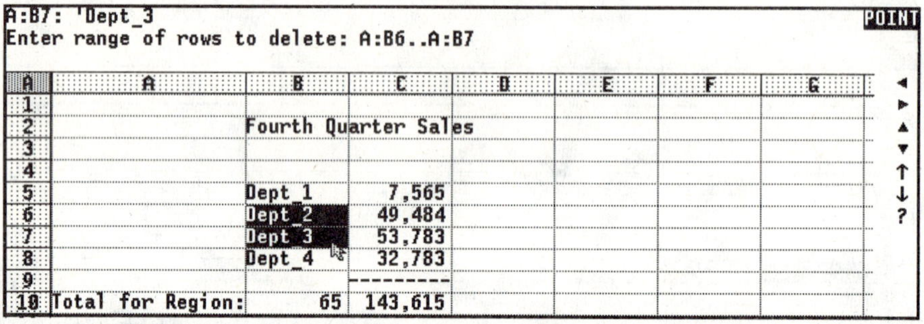

Fig. 4.31.

One cell in each row highlighted for deletion.

When you press the left mouse button or press Enter, the rows that contain highlighted cells are deleted (see fig. 4.31). The rest of the worksheet then moves up (see fig. 4.32). 1-2-3 automatically adjusts all addresses, range names, and formulas. Follow the same procedure to delete columns, selecting /Worksheet Delete Columns.

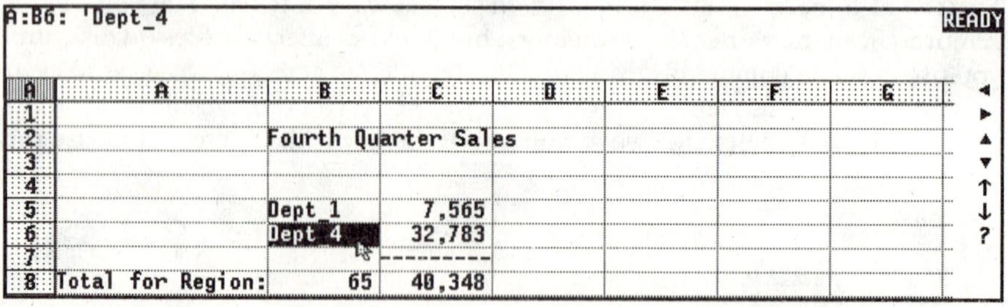

Fig. 4.32.

The worksheet after rows are deleted.

Caution:

When you delete rows, columns, or worksheets, ERR can occur anywhere in the file if the file contains formulas that refer to deleted cells.

If you delete rows or columns that are part of a range name or a range in a formula, 1-2-3 automatically adjusts the range. If the deleted rows or columns contain cells referenced by formulas in the remaining part of the worksheet, the references change to ERR and the formulas become invalid (see fig. 4.33). This action can be a serious consequence of deleting rows and columns. These formulas do not have to be visible on-screen; they can be anywhere in the file, or even in other worksheets or files.

Chapter 4 ◆ Using Fundamental 1-2-3 Commands   **117**

```
A:D15: (,0) +ERR                                          READY

        A         B         C         D         E         F         G
   1
   2              Fourth Quarter Sales
   3
   4
   5              Dept 1    7,565
   6              Dept 4   32,783
   7              ----------
   8   Total for Region:   65   40,348
   9
  10
  11
  12              Yearly Sales
  13                        QTR 1-3    QTR 4   Yearly TOTAL
  14              Dept 1    17,891     7,565    25,456
  15              Dept 2   117,030      ERR      ERR
  16              Dept 3   127,197      ERR      ERR
  17              Dept 4    77,532    32,783   110,315
  18
  19
  20
02-Aug-90 09:20 AM                                        NUM
```

Fig. 4.33.
ERR replacing cell addresses in formulas referring to deleted cells.

Using GROUP Mode To Change All the Worksheets in a File

Normally, deleting rows or columns affects only the current worksheet. However, if you have multiple worksheets in the file and GROUP mode is turned on, when you delete (or add) rows or columns to one worksheet, you delete (or add) the same rows or columns in all worksheets in the file.

Choose /Worksheet Global Group Enable to turn on GROUP mode. The GROUP status indicator appears on the status line (see fig. 4.34). If you now delete the columns highlighted in figure 4.34, you delete the same columns in all worksheets in the file (see fig. 4.35).

GROUP mode applies to all commands that affect the status of a worksheet, such as /Worksheet Global Col-Width (discussed in this chapter) and /Worksheet Global Format, covered in Chapter 5.

Deleting Worksheets and Files

If the file has multiple worksheets, you can delete an entire worksheet the same way you delete a row or a column. Use /Worksheet **Delete Sheet** to delete one or more worksheets from a file. You cannot delete all the worksheets from a file; at least one worksheet must remain after the deletion. If you try to delete all worksheets in a file, you receive an error message, and no worksheets are deleted.

If you have multiple files in memory, you can remove a file from the workspace with /Worksheet Delete File. When you issue this command, a set of menu items appears on the first line of the control panel as shown in figure 4.36. Selecting List

Part I ♦ Building the 1-2-3 Worksheet

with the mouse gives a full screen list of files and subdirectories in the current directory in the current drive. Selecting the directory icon (..) with the mouse shows the files and subdirectories in the next higher subdirectory on the current drive. This information appears on the third line of the control panel. The triangles move the menu pointer in the direction shown when you click them with the mouse, and the drive letter(s) replace(s) the current drive letter and path. These menu items also appear for any other command that automatically lists files, such as /File **R**etrieve. For commands such as /File **S**ave that do not automatically list files, the menu items appear when you press the right mouse button or press Esc.

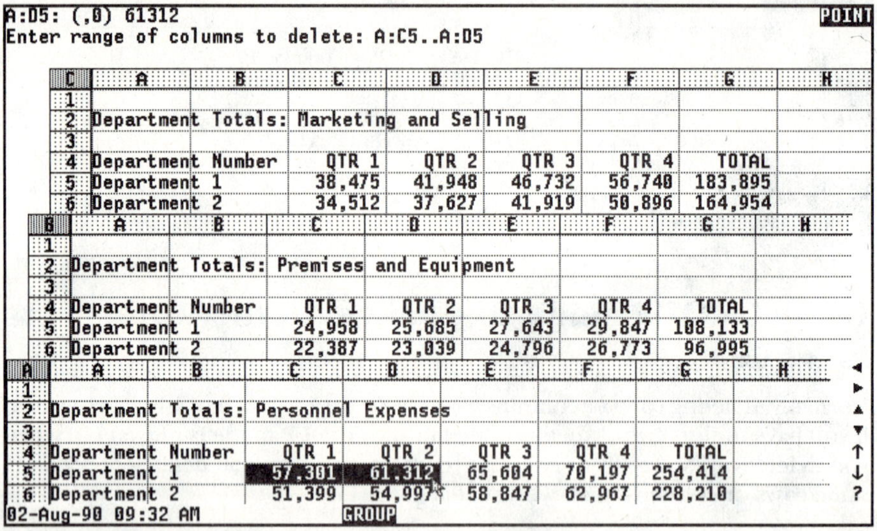

Fig. 4.34.
A multiple-worksheet file in GROUP mode before columns are deleted.

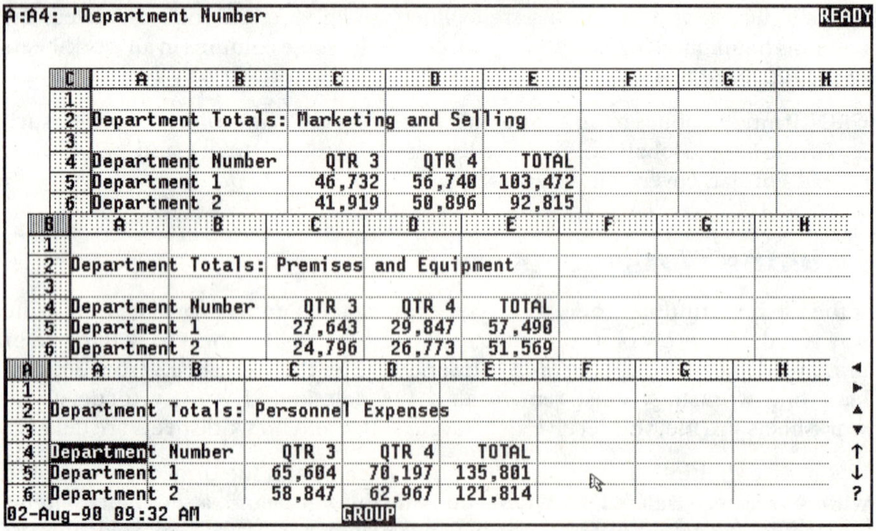

Fig. 4.35.
The multiple-worksheet file in GROUP mode after columns are deleted.

Chapter 4 ◆ Using Fundamental 1-2-3 Commands   **119**

To continue with the /**W**orksheet **D**elete **F**ile operation, point to the file from the list of active files in memory and press the left mouse button or press Enter. Although up to three single worksheet files can be visible at one time (see fig. 4.36), more files can be active in memory. At the `Enter name of file in memory to delete:` prompt, the first four files in memory are listed on the third line. Click List or press Names (F3) to see all the file names in memory. If you have not saved the file, all changes made to the file are lost when you delete it. (See Chapter 7 for more information on files.) After you delete a file from memory, more memory is available; you can add data to the existing files in memory or open another file.

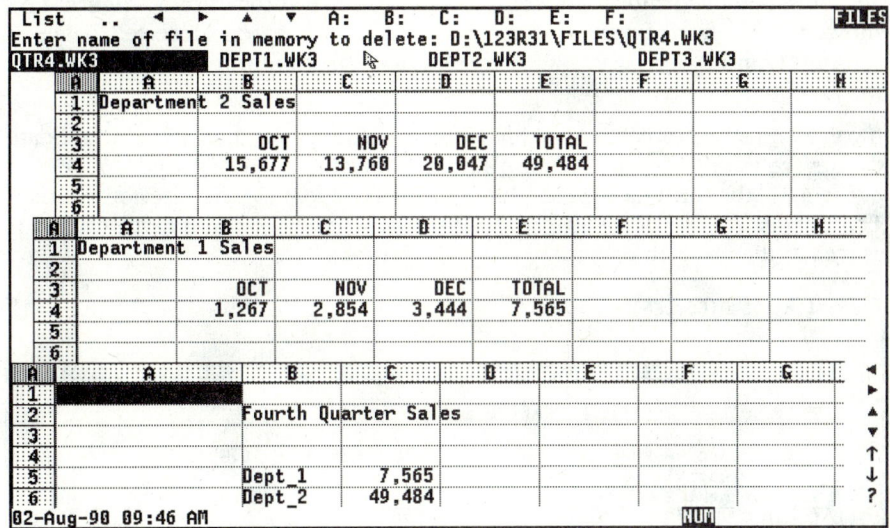

Fig. 4.36.
The list of file names presented at the prompt.

Clearing the Entire Workspace

You can clear all files from memory with /**W**orksheet **E**rase **Y**es. The command deletes *all* worksheets and files from memory, not just a single worksheet. This command's name, which some find confusing, is a holdover from earlier versions of 1-2-3, which allowed only one file and one worksheet in memory at one time. /**W**orksheet **E**rase **Y**es also restores all the global default settings. The effect is the same as if you quit 1-2-3 and restarted it from the operating system.

When you finish working on a system with multiple files in memory, you can use /**W**orksheet **E**rase **Y**es to clear all of them from memory. You then can retrieve another file or read in another worksheet system. Remember to use /**F**ile **S**ave before you use /**W**orksheet **E**rase **Y**es. 1-2-3 provides no method of reclaiming worksheets after /**W**orksheet **E**rase **Y**es is executed.

Caution:
/Worksheet Erase Yes deletes all files in memory, not just the current worksheet.

120 Part I ◆ Building the 1-2-3 Worksheet

Inserting Rows, Columns, and Worksheets

You can delete rows, columns, and worksheets; you also can insert them anywhere in the file. Insert rows with /**W**orksheet **I**nsert **R**ow and columns with /**W**orksheet **I**nsert **C**olumn. You can insert one or more rows or columns at one time. At the `Enter insert range:` prompt, highlight the number of rows or columns you want to insert and press the left mouse button or press Enter.

Reminder:
When you insert columns or rows, all addresses in formulas and range names adjust automatically.

When you insert rows, all rows below the cell pointer are pushed down. When you insert columns, all columns to the right of the cell pointer are pushed to the right. All addresses in formulas and range names adjust automatically. Figure 4.37 shows the file from figure 4.35 after one column has been inserted between columns C and D. Because GROUP mode is still on, a column is inserted in every worksheet in the file.

If you insert a row or column within a range, the range expands to accommodate the new rows or columns. In figure 4.35, the formula in E5 is @SUM(C5..D5). In figure 4.37, the formula is pushed to F5 to make room for the inserted column. The formula now reads @SUM(C5..E5) and includes the columns in the old range as well as the inserted column.

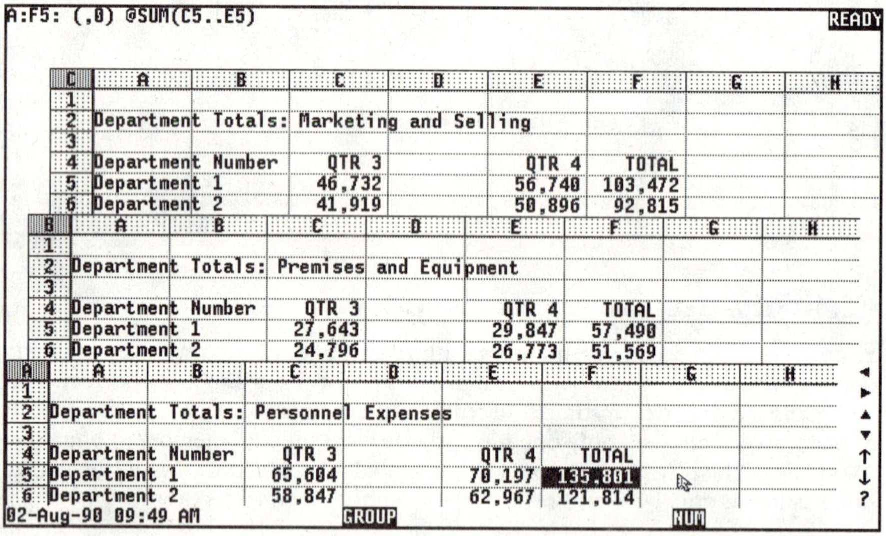

Fig. 4.37.
Addresses automatically adjusted after column insertion.

Use /**W**orksheet **I**nsert **S**heet to insert one or more new worksheets into the file. 1-2-3 then prompts you to insert the new worksheets either **B**efore or **A**fter the current worksheet. In most cases, select **A**fter to insert the new worksheet(s) behind the current worksheet. Figure 4.38 shows the file from figure 4.37 after a new worksheet was inserted between worksheets A and B.

If you introduce worksheets into the middle of a multiple-worksheet file, all the worksheets behind the new ones receive new worksheet letters. As in figure 4.38, if you insert a new worksheet after worksheet A, and worksheet B already exists, the new worksheet becomes B, and old worksheet B becomes C. All addresses and formulas adjust automatically. If you insert a worksheet within a range that spans worksheets, the range expands automatically to accommodate the new worksheet.

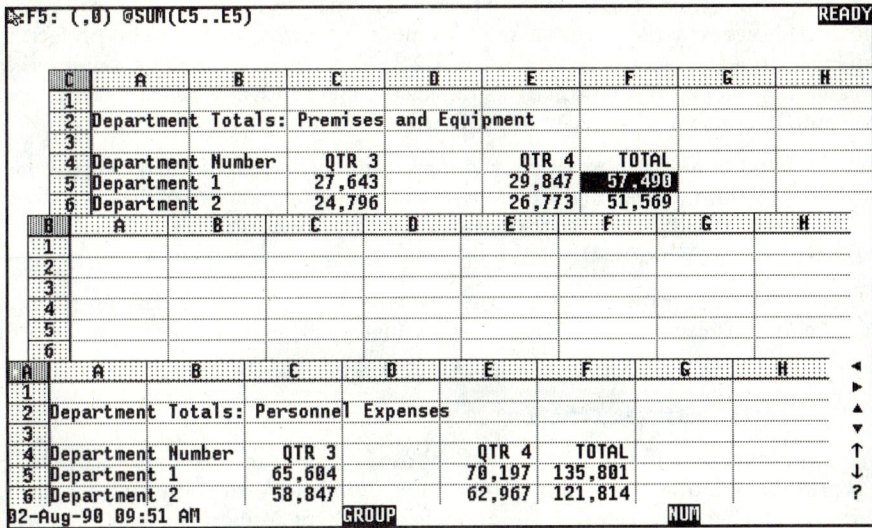

Fig. 4.38.
Addresses of worksheets behind the inserted worksheet adjusted automatically.

Using Window Options

You can change the way you view the worksheets in memory in a number of different ways. You can change the display format to view more rows and columns at one time. You can split the screen into two windows either vertically or horizontally, and you can view parts of three worksheets at once in perspective, three-dimensional view. These options give you the ability to see different parts of your work at the same time.

Changing the Display Format

When you work with large databases, reports, or tables of data, you cannot see all the data at one time. If your display hardware supports it, you can change the display to view more columns and rows of data at the same time. The more data you can see at one time, the easier it is to compare different months or different departments.

Many displays give you a choice of formats besides the standard 80-character by 25-line (80x25) display. You choose these display formats when you install 1-2-3 (see Appendix A). For example, if your system has a Hercules Graphics Adapter, you can choose an 80x25 or 90x43 display. With EGA, you can choose an 80x25 or 80x43 display. With VGA, you can choose an 80x25, 80x34, or 80x60 display.

Cue:
Use /Worksheet Window Display Secondary to view more data at one time if your hardware permits it.

If you have a monochrome display adapter (no graphics), a Color Graphics Adapter, or EGA with only 64K of video memory, you can display data in the 80x25 format only.

If your display hardware gives you a choice of formats, you can choose two of them at installation. This setup allows you to switch formats from within 1-2-3. Your first format choice is marked with a 1 and becomes the *primary* display. This preferred display appears when you first load 1-2-3. The second format becomes the *secondary* display. If you want to display a worksheet with more columns than the default, use the /Worksheet Window Display 2 command.

You may want to do most of your work in standard 80x25 format because it's the sharpest and easiest on the eyes. When you want to see more of the worksheet at one time, switch to the higher-density secondary display format. To switch back, use /Worksheet Window Display 1.

Another way to vary the display is to use the :Display Rows and the :Display Zoom commands. These commands are discussed later in this chapter.

Splitting the Screen

You can split the screen either horizontally or vertically into two windows by using /Worksheet Window Horizontal or /Worksheet Window Vertical. These commands are useful when you are using large, single worksheet applications, enabling you to see different parts of the worksheet at the same time.

Split the screen vertically when you want to see the totals column to the right of the data, as in figure 4.39. Split the screen horizontally when you want to see the totals row at the bottom of the data. With a split screen, you can change data in one window and at the same time see how the totals change in the other window. This capability is well-suited for "what-if" analysis.

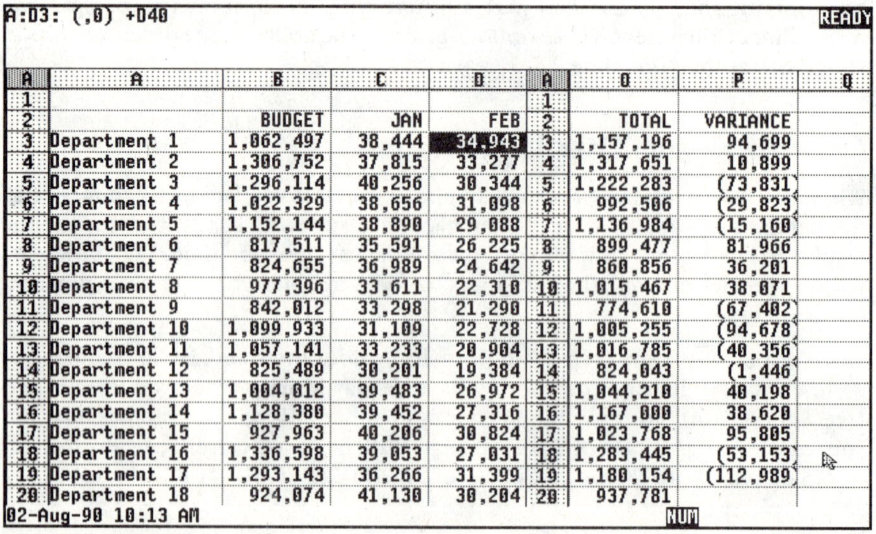

Fig. 4.39.
The screen split vertically.

```
A:D3: (,0) +D40                                                    READY

╔═══╤═══════════════╤══════════╤═════════╤════════╦═══╤══════════╤══════════╤═══╗
║ A │       A       │    B     │    C    │    D   ║ A │    O     │    P     │ Q ║
╠═══╪═══════════════╪══════════╪═════════╪════════╬═══╪══════════╪══════════╪═══╣
║ 1 │               │          │         │        ║ 1 │          │          │   ║
║ 2 │               │  BUDGET  │   JAN   │   FEB  ║ 2 │  TOTAL   │ VARIANCE │   ║
║ 3 │ Department  1 │1,062,497 │  38,444 │ 34,943 ║ 3 │1,157,196 │   94,699 │   ║
║ 4 │ Department  2 │1,306,752 │  37,815 │ 33,277 ║ 4 │1,317,651 │   10,899 │   ║
║ 5 │ Department  3 │1,296,114 │  40,256 │ 30,344 ║ 5 │1,222,283 │  (73,831)│   ║
║ 6 │ Department  4 │1,022,329 │  38,656 │ 31,098 ║ 6 │  992,506 │  (29,823)│   ║
║ 7 │ Department  5 │1,152,144 │  38,890 │ 29,088 ║ 7 │1,136,984 │  (15,160)│   ║
║ 8 │ Department  6 │  817,511 │  35,591 │ 26,225 ║ 8 │  899,477 │   81,966 │   ║
║ 9 │ Department  7 │  824,655 │  36,989 │ 24,642 ║ 9 │  860,856 │   36,201 │   ║
║10 │ Department  8 │  977,396 │  33,611 │ 22,310 ║10 │1,015,467 │   38,071 │   ║
║11 │ Department  9 │  842,012 │  33,298 │ 21,290 ║11 │  774,610 │  (67,402)│   ║
║12 │ Department 10 │1,099,933 │  31,109 │ 22,728 ║12 │1,005,255 │  (94,678)│   ║
║13 │ Department 11 │1,057,141 │  33,233 │ 20,904 ║13 │1,016,785 │  (40,356)│   ║
║14 │ Department 12 │  825,489 │  30,201 │ 19,384 ║14 │  824,043 │   (1,446)│   ║
║15 │ Department 13 │1,004,012 │  39,483 │ 26,972 ║15 │1,044,210 │   40,198 │   ║
║16 │ Department 14 │1,128,380 │  39,452 │ 27,316 ║16 │1,167,000 │   38,620 │   ║
║17 │ Department 15 │  927,963 │  40,206 │ 30,824 ║17 │1,023,768 │   95,805 │   ║
║18 │ Department 16 │1,336,598 │  39,053 │ 27,031 ║18 │1,283,445 │  (53,153)│   ║
║19 │ Department 17 │1,293,143 │  36,266 │ 31,399 ║19 │1,180,154 │ (112,989)│   ║
║20 │ Department 18 │  924,074 │  41,130 │ 30,204 ║20 │  937,781 │          │   ║
╚═══╧═══════════════╧══════════╧═════════╧════════╩═══╧══════════╧══════════╧═══╝
02-Aug-90 10:13 AM                                                    NUM
```

A split screen also is helpful when you write macros. You can write the macro in one window and see the data that the macro operates on in the other window. Macros are covered in Chapter 13.

The window splits at the position of the cell pointer, so be sure that you first move the cell pointer to the desired position before splitting the screen.

Reminder:
Move the cell pointer to the position where you want the screen to split.

When you split the screen vertically, the left window includes the columns to the immediate left of the cell pointer but does not include the cell pointer's column. In figure 4.39, the cell pointer was in column E when the window was split. Columns A-D (the columns to the left of the cell pointer) became the left window. The right window was then scrolled to display the TOTAL and VARIANCE columns O and P. These two columns are always visible as you scroll the left window.

When you split the screen horizontally, the top window includes the rows above the cell pointer. To display rows 10-20 in the upper window, scroll the display so that row 10 is at the top of the display, and then move the cell pointer to row 21 and select /Worksheet Window Horizontal. Because a split screen has two frames, you cannot display quite as much data at one time as you can with a full screen.

As you move down the worksheet in figure 4.39, both windows scroll together. If you move the cell pointer below row 20, both windows scroll up so that you can see row 21. In this particular example, *synchronized scrolling* of data is what you want. No matter where the cell pointer is in the left window, you can see the total for that department in the right window.

At other times, you may want to see two unrelated views of the same worksheet. For example, when one window contains data and the other window contains macros, you want the two windows to scroll separately. Use /Worksheet Window Unsync to stop the synchronized scrolling and /Worksheet Window Sync to restore it.

Reminder:
When you want two windows to scroll separately, use /Worksheet Window Unsync.

In figure 4.39, the two windows display different parts of the same worksheet. If you have multiple worksheets or files in memory, you can use the split screen to display different worksheets. When you use Ctrl-PgUp, Ctrl-PgDn, or the other movement keys to move between worksheets and files, you affect only the current window. The file in figure 4.39 has multiple worksheets. With the cell pointer in the left window, if you press Ctrl-PgUp, the left window displays cumulative information from another file in memory rather than the detailed information shown in figure 4.39; the right window is unchanged (see fig. 4.40).

You can use the mouse to move between worksheets and files when the window is split horizontally, but not vertically. When the window is split horizontally, the icon panel displays as usual, and you click the down- or up-arrow icons to move between worksheets and files. When the window is split vertically, the icon panel disappears, and you must use the keyboard to move between worksheets and files.

To clear a split screen, use /Worksheet Window Clear. No matter what window you are in, the cell pointer moves to the left or upper window when you clear a split screen.

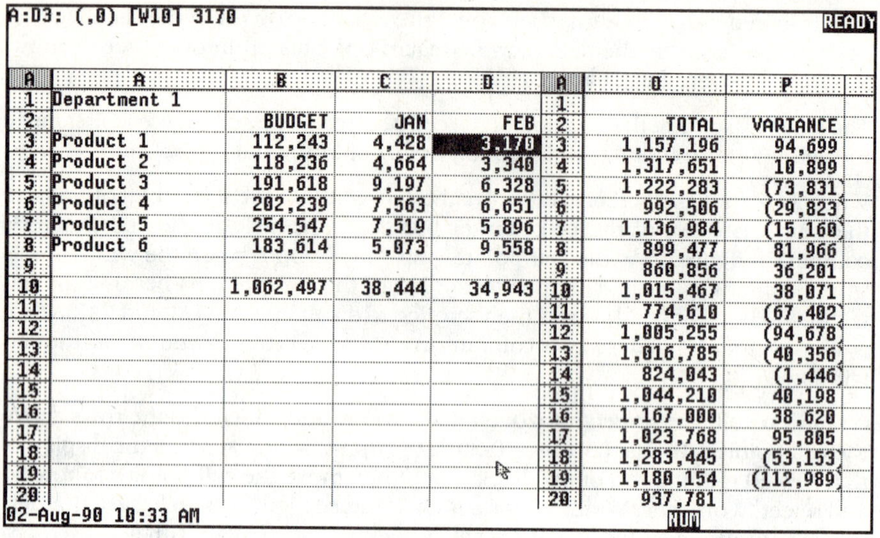

Fig. 4.40.

Two different worksheets displayed in a split window.

```
A:D3: (,0) [W10] 3170                                              READY
┌───┬──────────────┬──────────┬────────┬────────┬───┬──────────┬──────────┐
│ A │      A       │    B     │   C    │   D    │ A │    O     │    P     │
├───┼──────────────┼──────────┼────────┼────────┼───┼──────────┼──────────┤
│ 1 │Department 1  │          │        │        │ 1 │          │          │
│ 2 │              │  BUDGET  │  JAN   │  FEB   │ 2 │  TOTAL   │ VARIANCE │
│ 3 │Product 1     │ 112,243  │ 4,428  │ 3,170  │ 3 │1,157,196 │  94,699  │
│ 4 │Product 2     │ 118,236  │ 4,664  │ 3,340  │ 4 │1,317,651 │  10,899  │
│ 5 │Product 3     │ 191,618  │ 9,197  │ 6,328  │ 5 │1,222,283 │ (73,831) │
│ 6 │Product 4     │ 202,239  │ 7,563  │ 6,651  │ 6 │  992,506 │ (29,823) │
│ 7 │Product 5     │ 254,547  │ 7,519  │ 5,896  │ 7 │1,136,984 │ (15,160) │
│ 8 │Product 6     │ 183,614  │ 5,073  │ 9,558  │ 8 │  899,477 │  81,966  │
│ 9 │              │          │        │        │ 9 │  860,856 │  36,201  │
│10 │              │1,062,497 │38,444  │34,943  │10 │1,015,467 │  38,071  │
│11 │              │          │        │        │11 │  774,610 │ (67,402) │
│12 │              │          │        │        │12 │1,005,255 │ (94,678) │
│13 │              │          │        │        │13 │1,016,785 │ (40,356) │
│14 │              │          │        │        │14 │  824,043 │  (1,446) │
│15 │              │          │        │        │15 │1,044,210 │  40,198  │
│16 │              │          │        │        │16 │1,167,000 │  38,620  │
│17 │              │          │        │        │17 │1,023,768 │  95,805  │
│18 │              │          │        │        │18 │1,283,445 │ (53,153) │
│19 │              │          │        │        │19 │1,180,154 │(112,989) │
│20 │              │          │        │        │20 │  937,781 │          │
└───┴──────────────┴──────────┴────────┴────────┴───┴──────────┴──────────┘
02-Aug-90 10:33 AM                                                    NUM
```

Cue:

In perspective view, each window displays a separate worksheet.

You also can split the screen by using /**W**orksheet **W**indow **P**erspective. Figure 4.38 displays three worksheets as if they were stacked up on your desk. This command always presents three worksheets. If there are fewer than three worksheets in memory, you see blank worksheets. In perspective view, each window displays a separate worksheet.

You can have either a split screen or a perspective view, but not both at the same time. To go from one option to the other, first use /**W**orksheet **W**indow **C**lear, and then choose the other window option.

Zooming and Moving between Windows

To move between windows, use the mouse or the Window (F6) key. While in a split screen, you move back and forth between the two windows. In perspective view, you move up from the first worksheet to the second, the third, and then back down to the first worksheet. Window (F6) moves only between windows on-screen. If you have worksheets that are not visible in a window, press the down- and up-arrow icons in the icon panel or use Ctrl-PgUp and Ctrl-PgDn (or other worksheet-movement keys) to get to these other worksheets. Ctrl-PgUp and Ctrl-PgDn also move through the visible worksheets in perspective view.

Cue:

Use Zoom (Alt-F6) to enlarge a window to full-screen size.

You can make the current window expand to full-screen size by using the Alt-F6 (Zoom) key. The ZOOM status indicator appears in the status line at the bottom of the display. To return to the separate windows, press Alt-F6 again. Do not confuse the Zoom (Alt-F6) key with the **:D**isplay **Z**oom command.

When you use a split screen or perspective view, the view in each window is smaller than a full screen. Perspective view is useful when you move among different worksheets in memory (see fig. 4.38), but you can see only six rows in each worksheet at one time. When you want to work with one of the worksheets

Chapter 4 ◆ Using Fundamental 1-2-3 Commands **125**

for a while, use Zoom (Alt-F6) to display the worksheet in a full-screen view so that you can see a full 20 rows. In figure 4.40, you can see only two months in the left window. If you want to work on the data in the left window, you can use Zoom (Alt-F6) to see five months at once (see fig. 4.41).

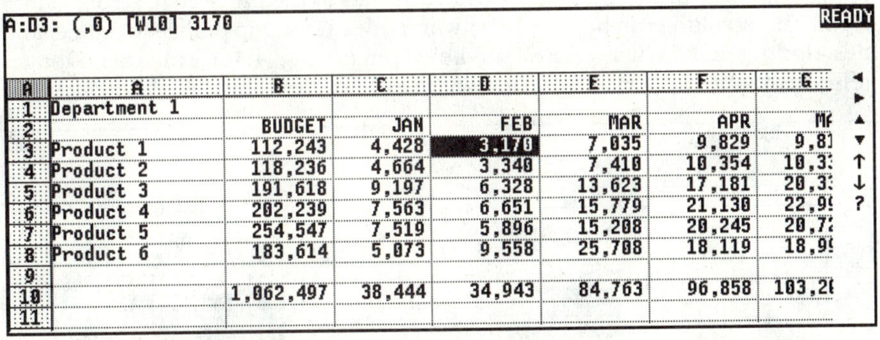

Fig. 4.41.

A window expanded to full-screen size after Zoom (Alt-F6) is pressed.

When you are in ZOOM mode, you can click the down- and up-arrow icons or use the F6 key to move between windows as if they were all on-screen at the same time. These techniques provide ways to move quickly between full-screen windows.

Displaying a Graph in a Worksheet

The /Worksheet Window Graph command applies only when you are using graphs. Use /Worksheet Window Graph to split the screen into a data window and a graph window. The graph changes automatically as you change the data in the worksheet. Figure 4.42 shows a display with a graph window. You cannot use /Worksheet Window Graph with a Color Graphics Adapter (CGA) because of the CGA's low resolution. Graphing is covered in detail in Chapter 10.

Cue:
The /Worksheet Window Graph command visibly changes the graph as you change the data.

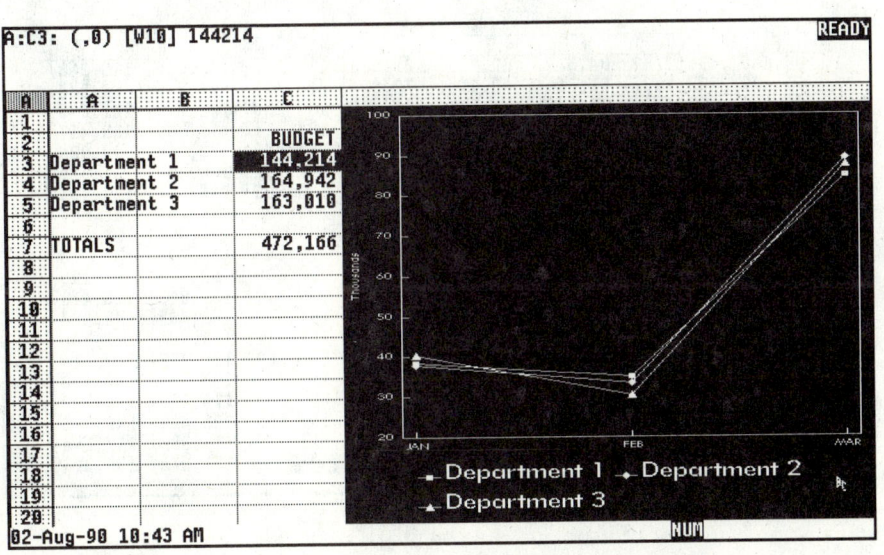

Fig. 4.42.

The screen split into a data window and a graph window.

Freezing Titles On-Screen

Most worksheets are much larger than can be displayed on-screen at any one time (see fig. 4.43). As you move the cell pointer, you scroll the display. New data appears at one edge of the display while the data at the other edge scrolls out of sight. This scrolling can be a problem when titles at the top of the worksheet and descriptions at the left also scroll off the screen (see fig. 4.44). You can no longer tell what month and what department the cell pointer is in.

Fig. 4.43.
Part of the data visible on the worksheet.

	A	B	C	D	E	F	G
1							
2		BUDGET	JAN	FEB	MAR	APR	MAY
3		-------	------	------	------	------	------
4	Department 1	1,062,497	38,444	34,943	84,763	96,858	103,208
5	Department 2	1,306,752	37,815	33,277	89,196	102,014	114,444
6	Department 3	1,296,114	40,256	30,344	87,583	99,494	100,902
7	Department 4	1,022,329	38,656	31,098	82,914	81,070	82,164
8	Department 5	1,152,144	38,890	29,088	81,515	84,552	94,339
9	Department 6	817,511	35,591	26,225	74,494	71,451	77,039
10	Department 7	824,655	36,989	24,642	70,194	69,684	70,397
11	Department 8	977,396	33,611	22,310	70,436	80,645	85,278
12	Department 9	842,012	33,298	21,290	67,542	65,139	63,960
13	Department 10	1,099,933	31,109	22,728	73,775	80,675	87,451
14	Department 11	1,057,141	33,233	20,904	72,935	76,787	76,582
15	Department 12	825,489	30,201	19,384	68,836	66,229	64,752
16	Department 13	1,004,012	39,483	26,972	88,458	86,954	85,819
17	Department 14	1,128,380	39,452	27,316	77,631	84,475	84,958
18	Department 15	927,963	40,206	30,824	83,885	85,593	83,618
19	Department 16	1,336,598	39,053	27,031	79,099	88,476	96,329
20	Department 17	1,293,143	36,266	31,399	83,595	96,031	102,120

Fig. 4.44.
Titles scrolled off the screen.

	F	G	H	I	J	K	L	M
11	80,645	85,278	94,573	89,930	101,855	112,147	107,505	110,268
12	65,139	63,960	61,859	63,816	72,814	76,413	74,336	84,535
13	80,675	87,451	95,946	91,237	97,179	106,256	101,739	101,695
14	76,787	76,582	77,168	87,049	91,263	102,511	117,095	133,417
15	66,229	64,752	68,199	69,717	77,374	81,448	90,362	96,034
16	86,954	85,819	88,136	88,982	100,413	102,132	106,083	117,625
17	84,475	84,958	97,580	105,054	113,707	123,865	135,457	133,949
18	85,593	83,618	87,550	90,958	95,834	102,781	107,194	102,687
19	88,476	96,329	102,805	112,787	126,434	142,381	148,858	159,124
20	96,031	102,120	100,656	100,477	104,720	118,063	133,833	137,228
21	76,666	78,599	80,706	85,320	87,898	87,780	93,524	97,195
22	86,527	87,790	94,518	97,008	109,718	120,212	129,861	128,478
23	85,202	93,413	105,694	105,462	117,647	131,858	143,433	142,984
24	84,600	81,160	90,441	95,263	102,109	109,412	115,484	123,748
25	87,025	88,474	98,334	106,361	102,079	100,780	114,475	113,714
26	89,205	96,984	98,131	110,968	105,654	113,232	129,970	137,182
27	81,786	82,917	86,394	95,328	98,459	111,142	116,253	130,518
28	95,053	92,801	100,399	110,693	108,741	116,136	123,405	140,470
29	90,392	91,276	87,232	99,806	111,139	115,585	110,389	117,164
30	88,648	85,422	96,165	100,969	106,450	111,513	127,378	136,305

Chapter 4 ◆ Using Fundamental 1-2-3 Commands   **127**

Use the /**W**orksheet **T**itles command to prevent titles from scrolling off the screen.

To lock titles, follow these steps:

1. Position the display so that the titles to lock are at the top and left of the display (see fig. 4.43).
2. Move the cell pointer to the first row below the titles and the first column to the right of the titles. In figure 4.43, the titles are in rows 2-3 and column A; the cell pointer is in B4.
3. Choose /**W**orksheet **T**itles **B**oth to lock both horizontal and vertical titles.

Once these titles are locked, the data below row 3 and to the right of column A can scroll off the screen, but the locked titles in rows 2-3 and column A remain on-screen (see fig. 4.45).

Cue:
Use the /Worksheet Titles command to prevent titles from scrolling off the screen.

```
A:K30: (,0) [W9] 111513                                          READY

     A              G        H        I        J        K        L
  2                MAY      JUN      JUL      AUG      SEP      OCT
  3               ------   ------   ------   ------   ------   ------
 13 Department 10  87,451   95,946   91,237   97,179  106,256  101,739
 14 Department 11  76,582   77,168   87,049   91,263  102,511  117,095
 15 Department 12  64,752   68,199   69,717   77,374   81,448   90,362
 16 Department 13  85,819   88,136   88,982  100,413  102,132  106,883
 17 Department 14  84,958   97,580  105,054  113,707  123,865  135,457
 18 Department 15  83,618   87,550   90,958   95,834  102,781  107,194
 19 Department 16  96,329  102,805  112,787  126,434  142,381  148,858
 20 Department 17 102,120  100,656  100,477  104,720  118,063  133,833
 21 Department 18  78,599   88,706   85,320   87,898   87,780   93,524
 22 Department 19  87,790   94,518   97,008  109,718  120,212  129,861
 23 Department 20  93,413  105,694  105,462  117,647  131,858  143,433
 24 Department 21  81,160   90,441   95,263  102,109  109,412  115,484
 25 Department 22  88,474   93,834  106,361  102,079  100,780  114,475
 26 Department 23  96,984   98,131  110,968  105,654  113,232  129,970
 27 Department 24  82,917   86,394   95,328   98,459  111,142  116,253
 28 Department 25  92,801  100,399  110,693  108,741  116,136  123,405
 29 Department 26  91,276   87,232   99,806  111,139  115,585  110,389
 30 Department 27  85,422   96,165  100,969  106,450  111,513  127,378
02-Aug-90 10:55 AM
```

Fig. 4.45.
Locked titles on-screen.

With locked titles, pressing Home moves the cell pointer to the position following the titles rather than to A1. In this case, the Home position is B4 (see fig. 4.43). You cannot use the mouse or the movement keys to move into the titles area, but you can use the GoTo (F5) key. When you use GoTo to move to a cell in the titles area, the title rows and columns display twice (see fig. 4.46). This double set of titles can be confusing. You can move into the titles area in POINT mode and see the same double display as in figure 4.46.

Use /**W**orksheet **T**itles **C**lear to cancel the locked titles so that you can move freely in the titles area. You also can lock just the rows at the top of the screen with /**W**orksheet **T**itles **H**orizontal or just the columns at the left with /**W**orksheet **T**itles **V**ertical. To change the locked titles, use /**W**orksheet **T**itles **C**lear first, and then specify the new locked titles.

Reminder:
To move freely in the titles area, use /Worksheet Titles Clear.

With a split screen, locking titles affects only the current window. With a multiple-worksheet file, locking titles affects only the current worksheet unless you are in GROUP mode.

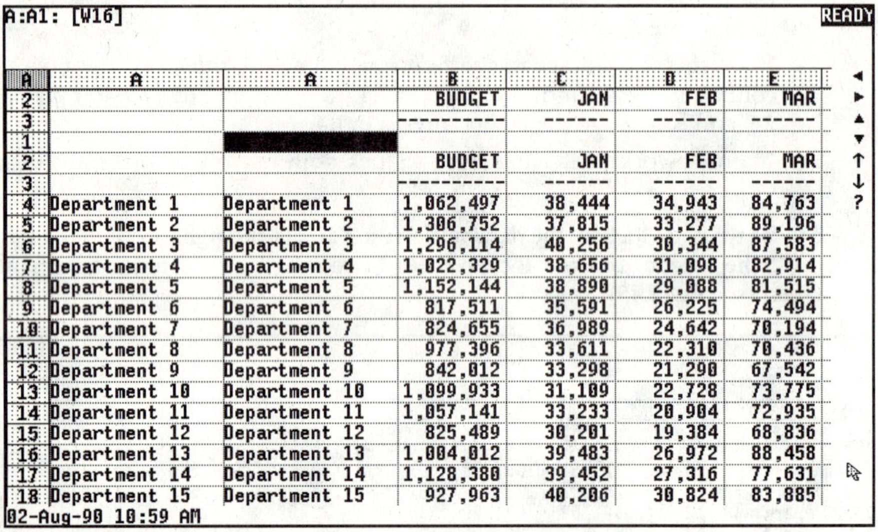

Fig. 4.46.
Double display with the cell pointer in the titles area.

A:A1: [W16]					READY
		BUDGET	JAN	FEB	MAR
		BUDGET	JAN	FEB	MAR
Department 1	Department 1	1,062,497	38,444	34,943	84,763
Department 2	Department 2	1,306,752	37,815	33,277	89,196
Department 3	Department 3	1,296,114	40,256	30,344	87,583
Department 4	Department 4	1,022,329	38,656	31,098	82,914
Department 5	Department 5	1,152,144	38,890	29,088	81,515
Department 6	Department 6	817,511	35,591	26,225	74,494
Department 7	Department 7	824,655	36,989	24,642	70,194
Department 8	Department 8	977,396	33,611	22,310	70,436
Department 9	Department 9	842,012	33,298	21,290	67,542
Department 10	Department 10	1,099,933	31,109	22,728	73,775
Department 11	Department 11	1,057,141	33,233	20,904	72,935
Department 12	Department 12	825,489	30,201	19,384	68,836
Department 13	Department 13	1,004,012	39,483	26,972	88,458
Department 14	Department 14	1,128,380	39,452	27,316	77,631
Department 15	Department 15	927,963	40,206	30,824	83,885

02-Aug-90 10:59 AM

Using Wysiwyg Display Options

You can change the way worksheets look on your display by changing worksheet colors, enlarging or reducing the size of cells so that a greater or lesser number of them appear on the display, adding grid lines and page breaks to worksheets, and changing the way the cell pointer looks. You can even make 1-2-3 look just like it does when Wysiwyg is not loaded into memory.

Changing the Display Mode

Two basic display modes are available in 1-2-3 Release 3.1: graphics mode and text mode. Graphics mode is the default when Wysiwyg is loaded into memory. In this mode, you can type numbers and labels in a variety of type styles and sizes. When Wysiwyg is not loaded into memory, the mode is text mode. In this mode, every character you type appears in the same style and size on the display. You can switch to text mode with the **:Display Mode Text** command, and then switch back to graphics mode with the **:Display Mode Graphics** command.

The **:Display Mode** command also enables you to display your worksheets either in color or black and white. The default display mode is color. You can switch to black and white with the **:Display Mode B&W** command. To switch back to color again you use the **:Display Mode Color** command.

Adjusting the Number of Rows and Columns

The Wysiwyg menu gives you two ways to adjust the number of rows that appear on the display. You can show as many as 75 rows or as few as five by selecting **:Display Zoom Manual** and typing in a number from 25 to 400. The numbers represent the percent of reduction or enlargement of the cell size. You can also choose standard reductions or enlargements of 63% (**Tiny**), 87% (**Small**), 125% (**Large**), and 150% (**Huge**). You return to normal size by selecting **:Display Zoom Normal**. The second way to adjust the number of displayed rows is to choose **:Display Rows**. When the prompt `Enter number of rows (16..60):` appears, you type in the number of rows you want and press the left mouse button or press Enter.

There is a difference between using **:Display Zoom** or **:Display Rows** and using **/Worksheet Window Display**. The **/Worksheet Window Display** command selects a different mode that is built into your display hardware. The Wysiwyg commands change the way in which Wysiwyg displays the worksheet on the screen, no matter which **/Worksheet Window Display** mode is active.

Reminder:
Wysiwyg commands change how the worksheet is displayed on-screen.

Changing the Display Colors

1-2-3 gives you complete control over the colors of the display. When you select **:Display Colors**, a menu appears with 11 choices. These options enable you to change the colors of the worksheet background, text, unprotected text, cell pointer, frame, grid, lines, negative values, and shadows. For each of these options you can select one of eight colors: black, white, red, green, dark blue, cyan, yellow, or magenta. For example, to change the color of the cell pointer to red, you choose **:Display Colors Cell-Pointer Red**. If you don't like the shades of the default colors, you can change them with **:Display Colors Replace**. This command brings up a menu of eight colors. When you select a color, the prompt `Enter color value (0..63):` appears. You can modify the color that appears on the display (but not on the printer) by typing a number between 0 and 63 and pressing the left mouse button or pressing Enter.

Changing the Appearance of the Worksheet

By using **:Display Options**, you can change the entire appearance of the worksheet. You can modify the worksheet frame in a variety of ways or make it disappear altogether. You can change the look of the cell pointer, and add a grid to the worksheet.

To modify the worksheet frame, select **:Display Options Frame**. At this point you have five choices. Select **1-2-3** for the standard frame design. Select **Enhanced** to have lines drawn around each row number and column letter (as shown in the figures in this chapter). Select **Relief** to have a gray sculpted worksheet frame. Select **None** to make the worksheet frame disappear. One other choice, **Special**, lets you set the worksheet frame to correspond to type measurements in 10-point characters, inches, centimeters, or points and picas. Use this option when you

Tip:
To exert greater control over the type fonts of a printed report, use :Display Options Frame Special.

need to exert greater control over the type fonts of a printed report. When you select one of the **S**pecial options, the worksheet column letters and row numbers are replaced by rulers. Figure 4.47 shows the result of choosing **:**Display Options Frame Special Inches.

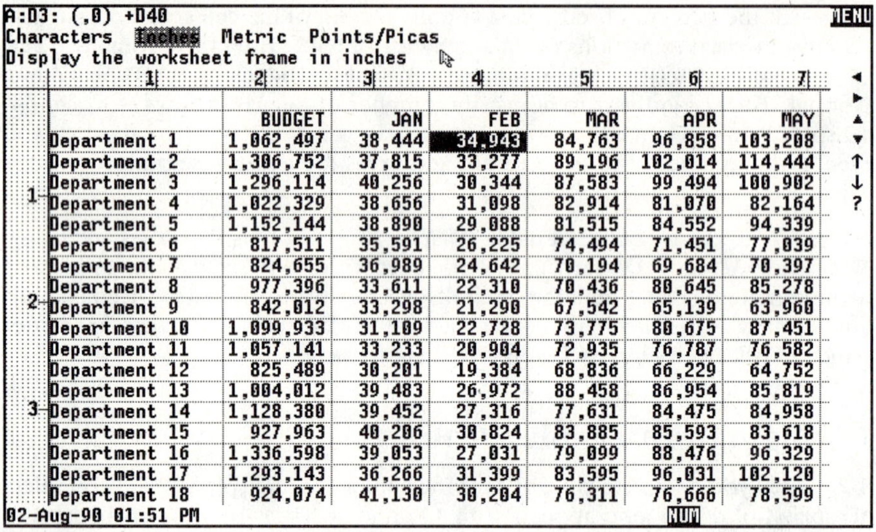

Fig. 4.47.

The worksheet borders replaced with inch rulers.

```
A:D3: (,0) +D40                                                      MENU
Characters  Inches  Metric  Points/Picas
Display the worksheet frame in inches
          1|         2|         3|         4|         5|         6|         7|
                 BUDGET       JAN       FEB       MAR       APR       MAY
   Department  1  1,062,497    38,444    34,943    84,763    96,858   103,208
   Department  2  1,306,752    37,815    33,277    89,196   102,014   114,444
   Department  3  1,296,114    40,256    30,344    87,583    99,494   100,902
1- Department  4  1,022,329    38,656    31,098    82,914    81,070    82,164
   Department  5  1,152,144    38,890    29,088    81,515    84,552    94,339
   Department  6    817,511    35,591    26,225    74,494    71,451    77,039
   Department  7    824,655    36,989    24,642    70,194    69,684    70,397
   Department  8    977,396    33,611    22,310    70,436    80,645    85,278
2- Department  9    842,012    33,298    21,290    67,542    65,139    63,960
   Department 10  1,099,933    31,109    22,728    73,775    80,675    87,451
   Department 11  1,057,141    33,233    20,904    72,935    76,787    76,582
   Department 12    825,489    30,201    19,384    68,836    66,229    64,752
   Department 13  1,004,012    39,483    26,972    88,458    86,954    85,819
3- Department 14  1,128,380    39,452    27,316    77,631    84,475    84,958
   Department 15    927,963    40,206    30,824    83,885    85,593    83,618
   Department 16  1,336,598    39,053    27,031    79,099    88,476    96,329
   Department 17  1,293,143    36,266    31,399    83,595    96,031   102,120
   Department 18    924,074    41,130    30,204    76,311    76,666    78,599
02-Aug-90 01:51 PM                                                    NUM
```

Other options let you change how the cell pointer looks and how the body of the worksheet looks. Usually the cell pointer is a solid color, but you can change it so that it outlines a cell. Use the command **:**Display Options Cell-Pointer Outline to make this change. Usually the body of the worksheet is blank, but you can add a grid to it to better define the boundaries of each cell. To do this choose **:**Display Options Grid Yes.

If you make changes and then decide you don't want them, you can restore the original settings by selecting **:**Display Default Restore. Any changes you make with the **:**Display menu can be made permanent by choosing **:**Display Default Update. Once you select Update, however, these settings become the default settings. You cannot restore them to the previous settings.

Protecting and Hiding Worksheet Data

A typical 1-2-3 file contains numbers, labels, formulas, macros, and at least one worksheet. When you first build a file, you can lay out the worksheets for an entire year. The budget model in figure 4.43 contains all the labels and formulas for a yearly budget. Once you build this file, you do not want the labels and formulas to change. However, the detailed budget figures may change many times as different versions are submitted for approval or submitted to different departments for revision.

Once the budget is approved, you add actual expense data each month. Each time someone changes the detailed data, you run the risk of accidentally changing a formula or a label. If a formula is changed, all the totals can be wrong.

If different people add data to the file, someone may want to change a formula that seems incorrect. For example, a model may use factors for inflation, growth, or foreign exchange rates. These factors may be decided by the Finance Department and should apply equally to all departments. Some department heads, however, may want to use their own factors. This situation can invalidate the overall budget that is submitted for approval.

1-2-3 includes a variety of features that protect data from accidental or deliberate change. For example, parts of a file might contain confidential data such as salaries or cost factors. 1-2-3 includes a method of protection that enables someone to use the file but not to see certain areas of the file. Unfortunately, hiding formulas and other data may not prevent people from finding this hidden information if they know enough about 1-2-3.

A more effective form of protection is to password-protect a file that contains confidential data when you save it. This security measure completely prevents access to the file by anyone who does not know the password.

Reminder:
If a formula is changed, all the totals can be wrong.

Reminder:
To prevent access to files by unauthorized persons, password-protect the files.

Protecting Cells from Change

Every worksheet has areas containing formulas and labels that do not change over time. Other areas of the worksheet contain data that can change. You can protect the cells that should not change and still allow changes to other cells by using two related commands: **/R**ange **U**nprot marks the cells that allow changes; **/W**orksheet **G**lobal **P**rot **E**nable turns on protection for all other cells.

You must tell 1-2-3 to use the cell-protection feature. When you start a new worksheet, protection is disabled, and all cells in the worksheet are accessible. To enable the protection feature, use **/W**orksheet **G**lobal **P**rot **E**nable. Initially, all cells in the worksheet are protected, and the symbol PR appears in the control panel for every protected cell. If you enable protection and try to change a protected cell, 1-2-3 displays an error message and does not make the change.

To unprotect the cells you want to change when worksheet protection is enabled, select **/R**ange **U**nprot. At the Enter range to unprotect: prompt, highlight the range of cells. The letter U appears in the control panel for every unprotected cell. Cells that contain data and are unprotected display in green on color monitors and in boldface on monochrome monitors. Once you unprotect a range of cells, you can protect them again with **/R**ange **P**rot.

You can protect or unprotect ranges with global protection either enabled or disabled. Typically, when you build a new worksheet, you leave global protection disabled. When you finish the worksheet, and you think that all the formulas and labels are correct, you can unprotect the data input areas and enable global protection.

Tip:
To protect all worksheets in a multiple-worksheet file, enable the GROUP mode.

/**W**orksheet **G**lobal **P**rot affects only the current worksheet in a multiple-worksheet file. You can have some worksheets in a file with global protection enabled and other worksheets with global protection disabled. If you are in GROUP mode, you change the global protection status of all worksheets at the same time. When you enable GROUP mode, all worksheets change to the global protection status of the current worksheet.

As you build a worksheet, you want protection disabled so that you can change all cells. When the worksheet is complete and you enable protection, you might build another worksheet in the same file, perhaps for macros, a consolidation, or a summary report. You want to leave protection disabled in this new worksheet until you are finished building it. Or you may have some worksheets in a file that are used as input areas. You want these worksheets unprotected to let users add data and to insert rows and columns. The other worksheets in the file with formulas, reports, and macros would have protection enabled.

Caution:
Protection does not stop anyone from deliberately tampering with a file unless the file is sealed.

If you need to change a protected cell for any reason, you can unprotect the cell, change it, and then protect it again. You also can disable global protection, change the cell or cells, and then enable it again. Because of this flexible feature of /**W**orksheet **G**lobal **P**rot, 1-2-3's protection features protect only against accidental change, not from deliberate alteration of the worksheet by an unauthorized person. To prevent unauthorized tampering, you must seal the file as explained in the section on sealing files found later in this chapter and in Chapter 7.

Using /Range Input

When you use /**W**orksheet **G**lobal **P**rot **E**nable, you restrict changes to cells that are range-unprotected. You can go one step further and restrict the cell pointer to unprotected cells in a specified range by using the /**R**ange **I**nput command.

You use /**R**ange **I**nput with data entry areas or forms, such as the one in figure 4.48. The range J28..J34 is unprotected; the other cells are protected. Typically, you use /ri when you build worksheets for others to use for data entry. In this case, you want whoever does the data entry to see the entire range I22..J34, but to be able to move the cell pointer only in the range J28..J34.

When you choose /**R**ange **I**nput, the `Enter data-input range:` prompt appears; you specify the input range, and then press the left mouse button or press Enter. In figure 4.48, the data-input range is I22..J34. 1-2-3 positions the display at the beginning of the data-input range and moves the cell pointer to the first unprotected cell in the range, in this case J28.

While /**R**ange **I**nput is active, you can move the cell pointer only to unprotected cells in the input range. If you press Home, the cell pointer moves to J28; use the mouse or press End to go to J33. If you are in J33 and click a cell below it, or click the down-triangle icon, or click the down-arrow key, you "wrap" to J28. If you are in J29 and click the right-triangle, or press the right-arrow key, the cell pointer moves to J30 because there are no unprotected cells to the right of J29.

```
A:J28: U [W22] 'Chris                                              READY
     I               J            K         L         M         N
 22 Customer Name and Address Data
 23
 24 Please complete all entries
 25
 26 Press Enter when complete
 27
 28 First Name    Chris
 29 Last Name     Palin
 30 Street        96 Hobart Drive
 31 City          San Francisco
 32 ST            CA
 33 Zip           94131-0112
 34
 35
```

Fig. 4.48.
An input form used with /Range Input.

While /Range Input is active, you can type entries and edit any unprotected cells, but you cannot execute commands. If you press the slash key, you enter the slash character into a cell. To deactivate /Range Input, press Enter or Esc in READY mode. The cell pointer then returns to its former position.

Reminder:
You cannot execute commands while /Range Input is active.

You can use /Range Input for convenience as well as security. /Range Input can be used if you work with novice users who know little about 1-2-3. Because these users can only move the cell pointer to unprotected cells while /Range Input is in effect, they cannot accidentally change protected cells. /Range Input is almost always executed by a macro as part of a data entry system. (Macros are covered in Chapters 13 and 14.) The advanced macro command FORM is another way to create and use data entry forms.

Hiding Data

Sometimes you want to do more than just stop someone from changing data or formulas; you want to prevent others from even seeing the information. To do this, you can hide cells, columns, and worksheets.

You can hide data so that the data is not easily visible, but you cannot hide confidential data to prevent someone from seeing it if that person knows how to use 1-2-3.

Caution:
You cannot hide data from someone who knows how to use 1-2-3.

To hide a cell or range of cells, use /Range Format Hidden. Hidden cells display as blank cells in the worksheet. If you move the cell pointer to a hidden cell, and the cell is protected with global protection enabled, the cell contents do not display in the control panel. To display the cell contents again in the worksheet, use any other range format as described in Chapter 5. Or use /Range Format Reset to reset the cell to the global format.

You cannot use the hidden format to hide data completely unless all the cells in the file are protected. If you can change the format or the protection status, you can see the contents of the cell. If the file is sealed, you cannot change the format or the protection status, but you can still determine the value in the hidden cell. Just enter a formula in an unprotected cell that refers to the hidden cell. If you want to determine the formula in the hidden cell, you can use the CONTENTS macro command. These techniques are discussed in Chapter 5. The CONTENTS macro command is covered in Chapter 14.

To completely hide columns, use /**W**orksheet **C**olumn **H**ide and highlight the columns you want to hide. You need to highlight only one cell in each column. A hidden column does not display in the window but retains its column letter. Figure 4.49 shows a worksheet with some columns about to be hidden. Figure 4.50 shows the worksheet after the columns are hidden. Note that in the column borders, column letters C..E are skipped. The columns are still there, but they do not display, and you cannot move the cell pointer to them.

Fig. 4.49. */Worksheet Column Hide used to hide columns.*

```
A:E3: (,0) [W8] 84763                                         POINT
Specify columns to hide: A:C3..A:E3
```

A	A	B	C	D	E	F	G
1							
2		BUDGET	JAN	FEB	MAR	TOTAL	VARIANCE
3	Department 1	144,214	38,444	34,943	84,763	158,150	13,936
4	Department 2	164,942	37,815	33,277	89,196	160,288	(4,654)
5	Department 3	163,010	40,256	30,344	87,583	158,183	(4,827)
6	Department 4	156,855	38,656	31,098	82,914	152,668	(4,187)
7	Department 5	154,556	38,890	29,088	81,515	149,493	(5,063)
8	Department 6	128,374	35,591	26,225	74,494	136,310	7,936
9	Department 7	114,947	36,989	24,642	70,194	131,825	16,878
10	Department 8	133,835	33,611	22,310	70,436	126,357	(7,478)
11	Department 9	119,778	33,298	21,290	67,542	122,130	2,352
12	Department 10	116,507	31,109	22,728	73,775	127,612	11,105
13	Department 11	116,584	33,233	20,904	72,935	127,072	10,488
14	Department 12	116,221	30,201	19,384	68,836	118,421	2,200
15							

Fig. 4.50. *The worksheet with hidden columns.*

```
A:F3: (,0) [W9] @SUM(C3..E3)                                  READY
```

A	A	B	F	G	H	I	J
1							
2		BUDGET	TOTAL	VARIANCE			
3	Department 1	144,214	158,150	13,936			
4	Department 2	164,942	160,288	(4,654)			
5	Department 3	163,010	158,183	(4,827)			
6	Department 4	156,855	152,668	(4,187)			
7	Department 5	154,556	149,493	(5,063)			
8	Department 6	128,374	136,310	7,936			
9	Department 7	114,947	131,825	16,878			
10	Department 8	133,835	126,357	(7,478)			
11	Department 9	119,778	122,130	2,352			
12	Department 10	116,507	127,612	11,105			
13	Department 11	116,584	127,072	10,488			
14	Department 12	116,221	118,421	2,200			

When you print a range with hidden columns, the hidden columns do not print. Although you can change the appearance of the display and reports with hidden columns, this technique is not an effective way to hide sensitive information. Whenever you are in POINT mode, 1-2-3 displays the hidden columns so that you can include cells in the hidden columns in the ranges. This is true even if the file is sealed as described in the following section.

Chapter 4 ◆ Using Fundamental 1-2-3 Commands

To hide a worksheet in a multiple-worksheet file, use /Worksheet Hide Enable and highlight the worksheets you want to hide. The worksheets and all the data still exist, but you cannot move the cell pointer to a hidden worksheet. Figure 4.51 shows a file similar to the one in figure 4.49, but the monthly detail has been moved to worksheet B, and the two remaining columns moved to the left to fill in the gap. Figure 4.52 shows the file after worksheet B is hidden.

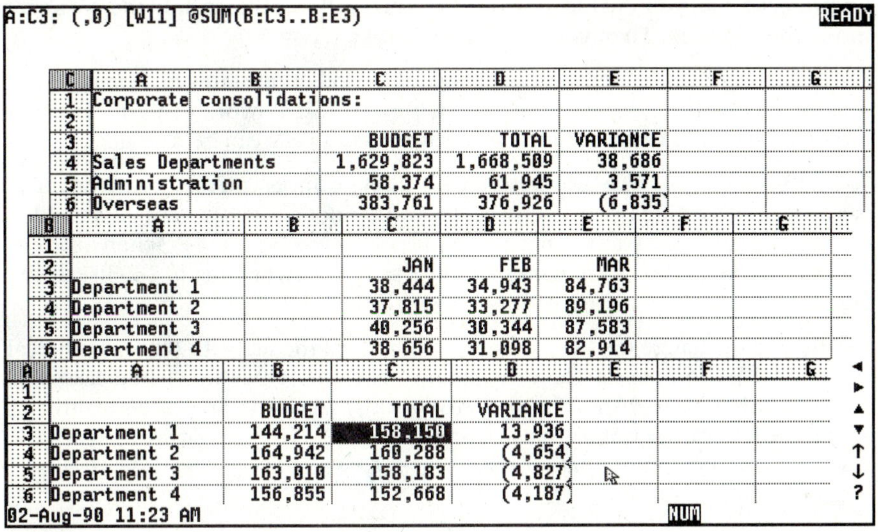

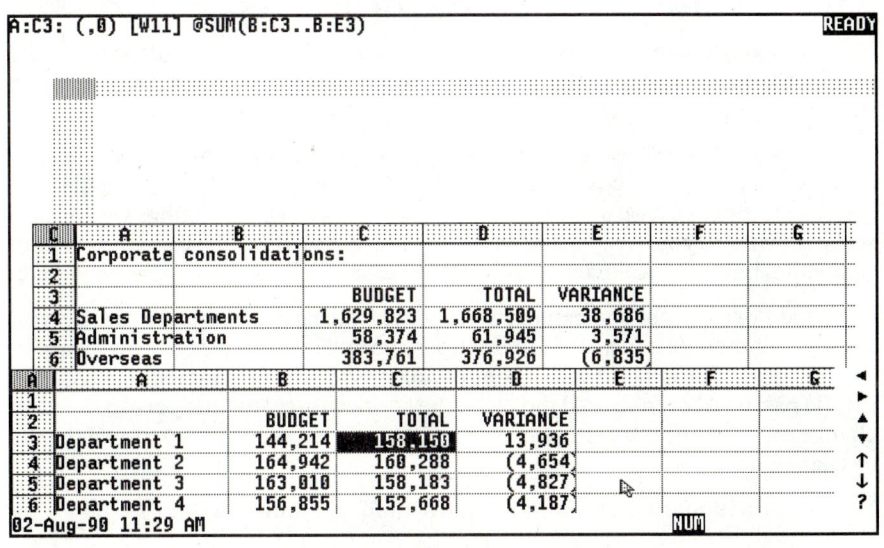

Fig. 4.51.
A multiple-worksheet file with details in worksheet B.

Fig. 4.52.
The worksheet file with worksheet B hidden.

Like hidden columns, you can't use hidden worksheets to hide sensitive data. Whenever you are in POINT mode, 1-2-3 displays the hidden worksheets. This is true even if the file is sealed as described in the next section.

Part I ♦ Building the 1-2-3 Worksheet

Sealing a File To Prevent Tampering

Cue:
Seal a file to protect it from being tampered with by others.

/File Admin Seal File provides the maximum protection for a file that is used by others. Even someone who is very knowledgeable about 1-2-3 cannot tamper with a sealed file. You can be sure that the protected formulas and labels, the formats, and the worksheet and range settings remain unchanged.

To protect a file, you enable global protection and unprotect only the cells that should be changed. Then you seal the file with a password.

Once you seal the file, no one can change the protection status or format of any cells or change the global protection without the password. This means that protected cells are really secure. Only unprotected cells can be changed.

To seal a file, choose /File Admin Seal File. 1-2-3 prompts you for a password. The password can include up to 15 characters and cannot contain spaces. As an added security measure, the password does not display as you type it. 1-2-3 then prompts you for the password again. If you type the same password again, 1-2-3 seals the file.

Caution:
If you lose the password, you cannot unseal the file and change it.

If you need to change the file, you must first unseal the file with /File Admin Seal Disable. 1-2-3 prompts you for the password. You must type the original password or you cannot unseal the file and change it. Passwords are case-sensitive. A lowercase letter does not match an uppercase letter. You should write down the password and keep it in a safe place.

Saving a File with a Password To Prevent Access

Reminder:
Save the file with a password to completely prevent access to its data.

To completely prevent access to a file, save the file with a password. Without the password, no one can read the file or get any information from the file. If you lose the password, you cannot access any information in the file.

Sealing and saving files are two separate file-protection schemes. These two actions and the two passwords are completely independent. If you seal a file, you can read the file, but you cannot change any protected cells or settings without the seal password. If you save the file with a password, you need the password to read in the file, but once you have read the file into memory, you can change the file.

For added protection, you can combine these two methods; that is, you can seal the file and then save it with a different password. For example, you may want to use this type of protection with a confidential personnel file. Someone must have the file password even to read the file. If the file also is sealed, that person then can change only the unprotected cells. You are the only person who can unseal the file to change it.

More information on password-protection of files is found in Chapter 7.

Controlling Recalculation

The commands discussed so far have shown you how to view, clear, and protect data in worksheets and files. This section covers how you can control the way 1-2-3 updates the file as you change it.

Whenever a value in a file changes, 1-2-3 recalculates all other cells that depend on the changed value. This is the essence of an electronic worksheet. 1-2-3 provides a number of recalculation options for different circumstances.

Understanding Recalculation Methods

Normally 1-2-3 recalculates the file whenever any cell changes. This feature is called *automatic recalculation*. Most of the earlier versions of 1-2-3 took a long time to recalculate large worksheets. With Release 3, however, recalculation is optimal and in the background.

Optimal recalculation means that the only cells recalculated are those cells containing formulas that refer to the changed cell. If you change a cell in a large file, and that cell is used in only one formula, only that one formula is recalculated. Recalculation is therefore very fast.

Background means that you can continue to work while 1-2-3 recalculates the file. You may have many numbers to add or change, and they each can affect hundreds of calculations in the file. As you enter each number, 1-2-3 starts a recalculation, but you are not locked out of continuing to enter numbers to the worksheet. As long as you change cells faster than 1-2-3 can recalculate the file, the CALC indicator stays on in the status line at the bottom of the display. As soon as 1-2-3 completes the recalculation, the CALC indicator disappears.

> **Reminder:**
> *You can continue to work while 1-2-3 recalculates the file by using background recalculation.*

Because of these recalculation routines, recalculation is best left in the default automatic mode most of the time. However, you can tell 1-2-3 not to recalculate the worksheet when there is a change to make by using /**W**orksheet **G**lobal **R**ecalc **M**anual. To force a recalculation, press the Calc (F9) key. Pressing F9 produces a foreground calculation. Until the recalculation is complete, the mode indicator is set to WAIT, and you cannot use 1-2-3.

Automatic recalculation can slow down macro execution because the recalculation is not done in the background. If you use macros, you may prefer to have the macro set the recalculation to manual while the macro executes, and then reset recalculation to automatic before the macro ends. There are special considerations for macros when recalculation is manual. These are covered in Chapter 14.

During recalculation, 1-2-3 determines which formulas depend on which cells and sets up a recalculation order to ensure the correct answer. This process is called the *natural order of recalculation*. Spreadsheet programs before 1-2-3 did not use this approach and sometimes required many successive recalculations before they arrived at the right answer in all cells.

> **Reminder:**
> *The* natural order of recalculation *sets up a recalculation order to ensure the correct answer.*

Part I ◆ Building the 1-2-3 Worksheet

These early spreadsheet programs could only recalculate either columnwise or rowwise. Columnwise recalculation starts in cell A1 and calculates the cells down column A, then down column B, and so on. Rowwise recalculation starts in cell A1 and calculates the cells across row 1, then across row 2, and so on. **C**olumnwise and **R**owwise are options in the /**W**orksheet **G**lobal **R**ecalc menu, but as a rule you should ignore them and leave recalculation on **N**atural.

Using Iteration To Solve Circular References

When a *circular reference* occurs, the natural order of recalculation does not ensure the correct answer for all cells. A circular reference is a formula that depends, either directly or indirectly, on its own value. Usually a circular reference is an error, and you should eliminate it immediately. Whenever 1-2-3 performs a recalculation and finds a circular reference, the CIRC indicator appears in the status line at the bottom of the display. Figure 4.53 shows a typical erroneous circular reference in which the @SUM function includes itself. In this example, the sum of cells B2, B3, and B4 (3300) is added to itself, making 6600.

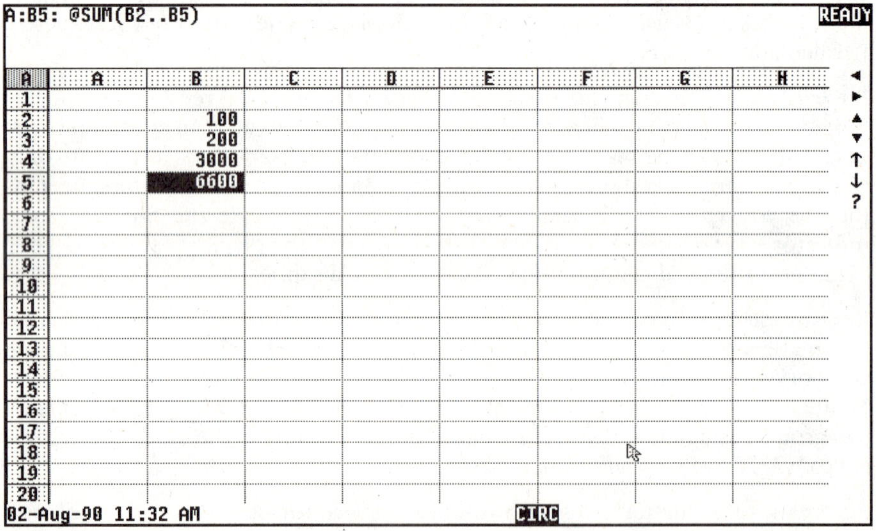

Fig. 4.53.
A circular reference that produces the CIRC indicator.

Cue:
Use /**W**orksheet **S**tatus to find the location of a circular reference.

If you are not sure of the reason when the CIRC indicator appears, use /**W**orksheet **S**tatus for a basic status display (see fig. 4.54). This display points out the cell that caused the circular reference. In this case, you can fix the error. In other cases, the source of the problem may not be so obvious and you may have to check every cell referred to in the formula cell.

In some special cases, a circular reference is deliberate. Figure 4.55 shows a worksheet with a deliberate circular reference. In this example, a company sets aside 10 percent of its net profit for employee bonuses. The bonuses themselves, however, represent an expense that reduces net profit. The formula in C5 shows that the amount of bonuses is net profit in D5 times .1, or 10%. But net profit is profit before bonuses minus bonuses (B5 – C5). The value of Employee Bonuses depends on the value of Net Profit, and the value of Net Profit depends on the value of Employee Bonuses. In figure 4.55, C5 depends on D5 and D5 depends on C5. This is a classic circular reference.

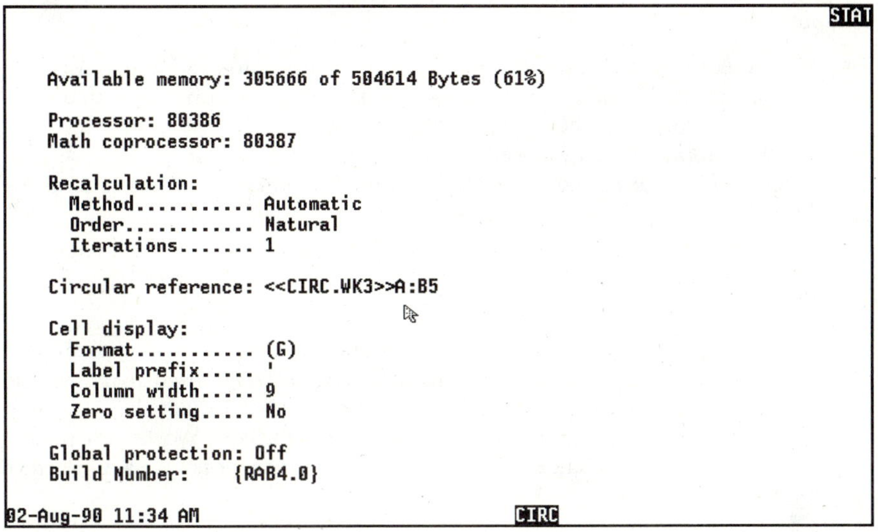

```
                                                                    STAT

     Available memory: 305666 of 504614 Bytes (61%)

     Processor: 80386
     Math coprocessor: 80387

     Recalculation:
       Method........... Automatic
       Order............ Natural
       Iterations....... 1

     Circular reference: <<CIRC.WK3>>A:B5

     Cell display:
       Format........... (G)
       Label prefix..... '
       Column width..... 9
       Zero setting..... No

     Global protection: Off
     Build Number:    {RAB4.0}

02-Aug-90 11:34 AM                          CIRC
```

Fig. 4.54.
The circular reference displayed by the /Worksheet Status screen.

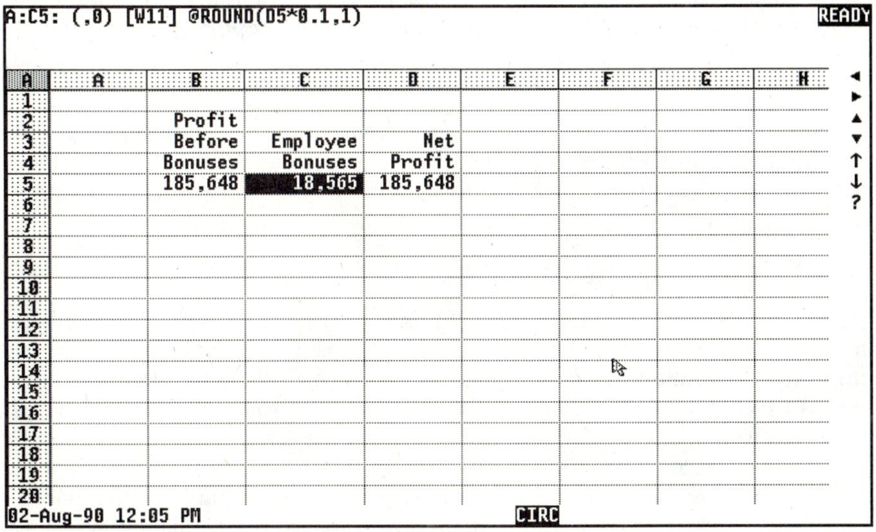

```
A:C5: (,0) [W11] @ROUND(D5*0.1,1)                     READY

     A      B         C         D      E    F    G    H
  1
  2         Profit
  3         Before  Employee   Net
  4         Bonuses Bonuses    Profit
  5         185,648  18,565    185,648
  6
  7
  ...
 20
02-Aug-90 12:05 PM                          CIRC
```

Fig. 4.55.
A worksheet with a deliberate circular reference.

Each time you recalculate the worksheet, the answers change by a smaller amount with a legitimate circular reference. Eventually, the changes become insignificant. This is called *convergence*. Note that the erroneous circular reference in figure 4.53 never converges, and the @SUM result gets bigger every time you recalculate.

The worksheet in figure 4.55 needs five recalculations before the changes become less than one dollar. Once you establish this number, you can tell 1-2-3 to recalculate the worksheet five times every time it recalculates with /Worksheet Global Recalc Iteration. Press 5; then press the left mouse button or press Enter. In most cases, you can handle a converging circular reference with a macro (see Chapter 14).

Reminder:
Use /Worksheet Status to locate circular references.

Use /Worksheet Status (see fig. 4.54) to see a mixture of information that includes the memory available; the processor in your computer; the current recalculation method; default formats, label prefix, and column width for the current worksheet; and whether global protection is enabled in the current worksheet. The main use of this status display is to check on the amount of memory available and to locate circular references.

Moving the Contents of Cells

When you build worksheets, you often enter data and formulas in one part of the worksheet and later want to move them somewhere else. Use the /Move command to move the contents of a cell or range from one part of a worksheet file to another. You can move the cell or range to another part of the same worksheet or to a different worksheet in the same file. Unfortunately, you cannot move a range from one file to another file.

Use /Move to move other data out of the way so that you can add to a list, a report, or a database. You also use /Move to rearrange a report so that it prints out in the exact format you want. When you first start to lay out a report, you often are not sure how you want it to look. After some trial-and-error and moving the data around, you get the report format you want.

When you move a range, you also move the format and protection status. You do not, however, move the column width. The original cells still exist after you move their contents, but they are blank, and any protection or formatting is removed.

Moving the Contents of a Single Cell

Figure 4.56 shows three numbers in column B and their sum in B5. These cells are formatted to display with commas and two decimal places. The numbers are unprotected. To move the sum in B5 to D6, move the cell pointer to B5 and start the /Move command. The Enter range to move FROM: prompt asks you what cells you want to move. To move just one cell, press the left mouse button twice or press Enter. The next prompt, Enter range to move TO:, asks where you want the cells to go. Move the cell pointer to D6 and press the left mouse button twice or press Enter. The result is shown in figure 4.57. The exact formula that was in B5 is now in D6.

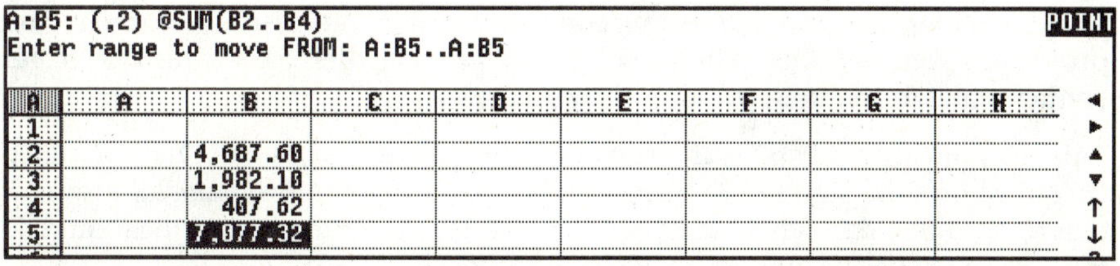

Chapter 4 ◆ Using Fundamental 1-2-3 Commands

Fig. 4.56.
A formula before being moved.

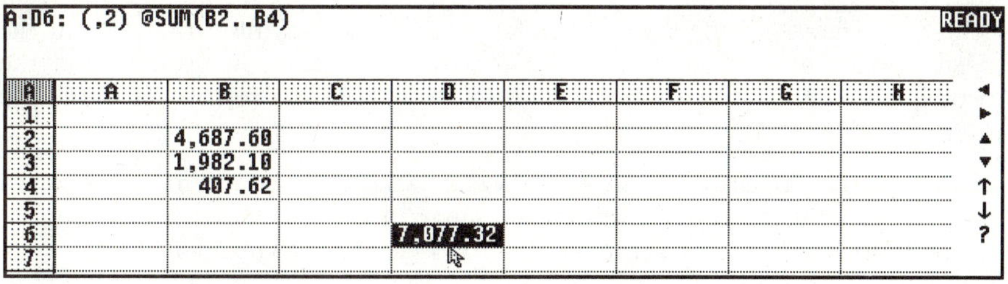

Fig. 4.57.
The formula after being moved.

Moving the Contents of a Range

To move a range, move the cell pointer to the upper left corner of the range and start the /Move command. At the Enter range to move FROM: prompt, highlight the range of cells to move, as in figure 4.58. This prompt starts with the address of the cell pointer as an anchored range. When you move the cell pointer, you highlight the range starting at the original location of the cell pointer to the corner where you move. Press the left mouse button or press Enter to lock in the FROM range. At the Enter range to move TO: prompt, move the cell pointer to the upper left corner of the new location and press the left mouse button twice or press Enter. This prompt's address is not anchored. In figure 4.59, the range was moved to C1. Like all commands that prompt for ranges, you can type addresses, point and highlight, or use range names.

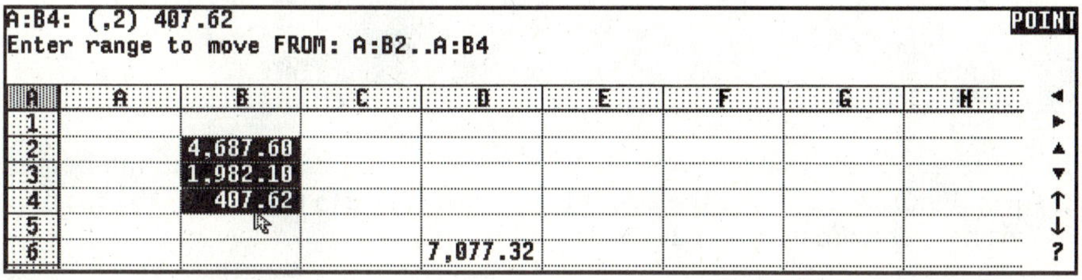

Fig. 4.58.
A range of numbers before being moved.

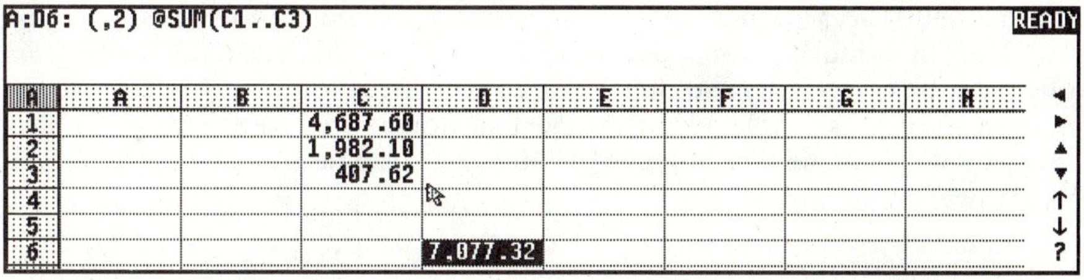

Fig. 4.59.
The formula adjusted after the numbers are moved.

142   Part I ♦ Building the 1-2-3 Worksheet

In figure 4.59, not only were the contents moved, but also the formats and protection. The original cells in column B are still there, but they no longer contain data, formatting, or unprotected status.

This self-adjusting capability is a very important feature of /Move. The formula in D6 still shows the sum of the three numbers. When you move data, all formulas that refer to that data adjust their cell references to refer to the new location. The formula in D6 has changed from @SUM(B2..B4) to @SUM(C1..C3).

Caution:

When you move cells, ERR can occur anywhere in the file if there are formulas that refer to the range you moved to.

When you move a range, you completely eliminate anything that was in the destination range before the move. You lose the data, the format, and the protection status. If any formulas refer to those cells, the references change to ERR.

You can move ranges of any size; you also can move them between worksheets. If you build a large model by starting with one worksheet, you can move parts of it into different worksheets as the model grows (see figs. 4.60 and 4.61).

Fig. 4.60.

The worksheet before data is moved to another worksheet.

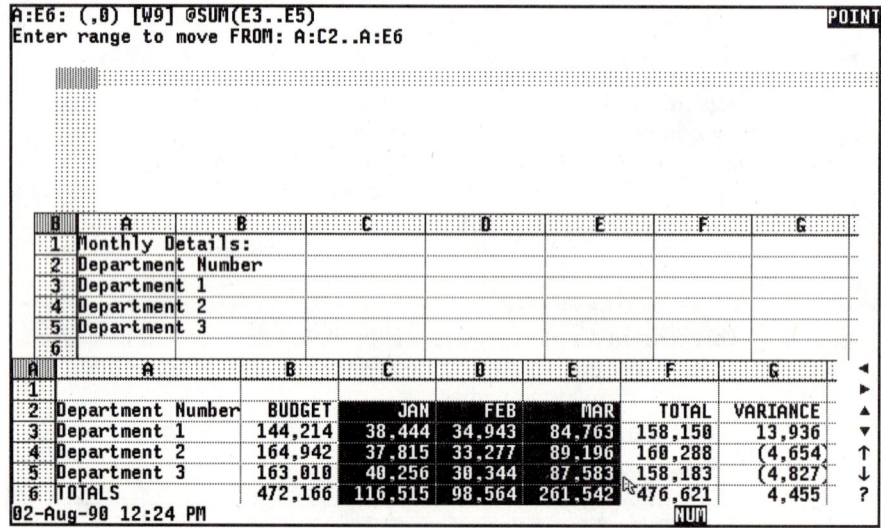

In figure 4.62, you want to replace the numbers in C1..C3 with the numbers in H1..H3. Figure 4.63 shows the result if you move H1..H3 to C1..C3. The formula in D6 changes from @SUM(C1..C3) to @SUM(ERR).

This change is permanent unless you immediately press Alt-F4 (Undo) to undo the move. Otherwise, you must manually reenter the formula in D6. You can have hundreds of formulas throughout the file that refer to the cells C1..C3, and every one must be corrected. (You don't have to type every formula; you can use the /Copy command as explained in the next sections.) Because of this potentially undesirable result, be very careful with /Move; you can destroy a worksheet if you use /Move incorrectly.

The correct way to replace the data in C1..C3 with the data in H1..H3 (see fig. 4.62) is to copy H1..H3 to C1..C3, and then use /Range Erase on H1..H3.

Chapter 4 ♦ Using Fundamental 1-2-3 Commands   **143**

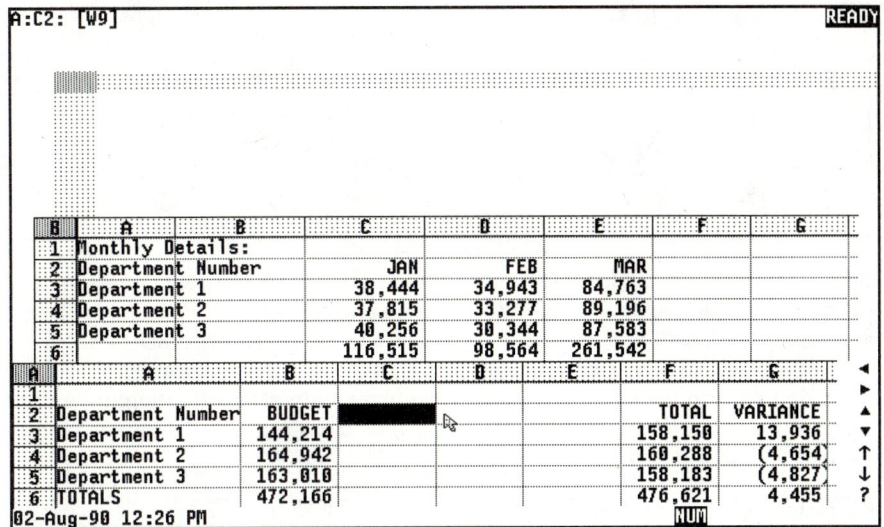

Fig. 4.61.
The worksheet after data is moved to another worksheet.

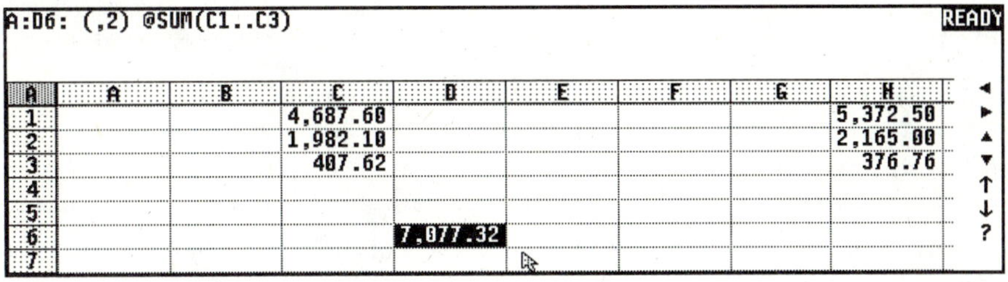

Fig. 4.62.
The worksheet before data is moved into cells already used in a formula.

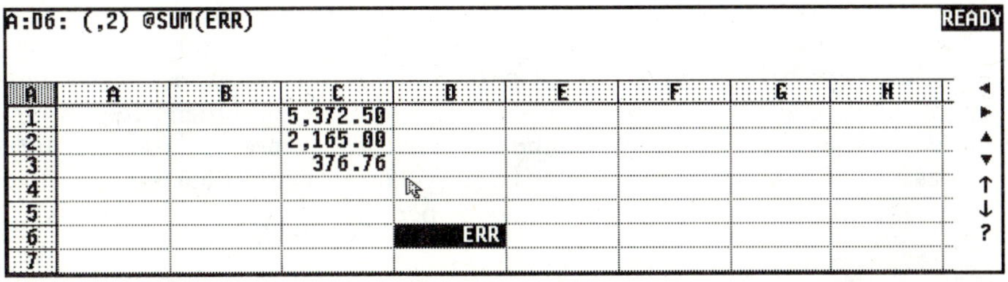

Fig. 4.63.
A formula changed to ERR when data is moved into cells already used in formulas.

The FROM range and the TO range can overlap, and the /Move command still works correctly. If you move just one corner of a range used in a formula, the range expands or contracts. Figure 4.64 shows what happens after you move E2..G6 to F2. The overlapping range caused no problems. A common use of /Move is to make room for a new row or column in a range of data.

Before the move shown in figure 4.64, the formula in F3 (now G3) was @SUM(C3..E3). Because of the range move, the formula expanded to keep all the necessary cells in the formula. The formula expanded to @SUM(C3..F3).

Fig. 4.64.

The range expanded and formulas adjusted automatically as one corner of the range is moved out.

```
G3: (,0) [W9] @SUM(C3..F3)                                          READY

      A         B          C          D          E          F          G          H          I
  1
  2           BUDGET      JAN        FEB                            MAR      TOTAL    VARIANCE
  3           144,214   38,444     34,943                         84,763   158,150     13,936
  4           164,942   37,815     33,277                         89,196   160,288     (4,654)
  5           163,010   40,256     30,344                         87,583   158,183     (4,827)
  6           472,166  116,515     98,564                        261,542   476,621      4,455
  7
```

If you move the range F2..H6 in figure 4.64 back to E2, the formulas revert to their original form (see fig. 4.65). ERR does not display even though part of the range was eliminated. ERR only occurs if you move a range on top of one of the corner cells in a range. In figure 4.63, a range was moved on top of the corner cells in the range in the formula in row D6, so the formulas changed to ERR. In figure 4.65, a range moved on top of the middle portion of the range; the formulas do not change to ERR but just contract the range.

Fig. 4.65.

The range contracted and the formulas adjusted automatically as one corner of the range is moved in.

```
F3: (,0) [W9] @SUM(C3..E3)                                          READY

      A         B          C          D          E          F          G          H          I
  1
  2           BUDGET      JAN        FEB        MAR      TOTAL    VARIANCE
  3           144,214   38,444     34,943     84,763   158,150     13,936
  4           164,942   37,815     33,277     89,196   160,288     (4,654)
  5           163,010   40,256     30,344     87,583   158,183     (4,827)
  6           472,166  116,515     98,564    261,542   476,621      4,455
  7
```

The cell pointer does not need to be at the top of the range when you start the /Move command. Sometimes it's easier to start at the destination range. At the Enter range to move FROM: prompt, press the right mouse button or press Esc to unanchor the range. Move the cell pointer to the range that you want to move; drag the mouse to highlight the range, or press the period key to anchor the range and use the cursor keys to highlight the range to move; and then press the left mouse button or press Enter. At the Enter range to move TO: prompt, 1-2-3 moves back to the original location of the cell pointer. Press the left mouse button twice or press Enter to complete the move operation.

Copying the Contents of Cells

You use /Move to rearrange data in a file. You use /Copy to make duplicate copies of a range in a file or to copy from one file to another file. In a typical file, most formulas are duplicated many times. For example, in figure 4.65, the formula in F3 is duplicated in F4..F6. The same is true for the formulas in column G. This list could include hundreds of rows. It is long and tedious to type each formula separately. Fortunately, if you need the same number, label, or formula in a number of places in a file, you can enter them once and copy them.

Chapter 4 ◆ Using Fundamental 1-2-3 Commands

You use /Copy more than any other 1-2-3 command. Copying can be very simple or quite complicated. This section begins with simple examples and progresses to more complex examples.

You can copy a single cell or a range to another part of the worksheet, to another worksheet in the file, or to another worksheet in another file. When you copy, you can make a single copy or many copies at the same time. When you copy a range, you also copy the format and protection status. You do not, however, copy the column width. The original cells are unchanged after you copy them. When you copy, the duplicate cells overwrite anything that was in the destination range before the copy. You lose the destination range's data as well as its format and protection status.

Reminder:
When you copy, you lose the destination range's data and its format and protection status.

Copying the Contents of a Cell

The simplest example is to copy a label from one cell to another. Figure 4.66 shows the beginnings of a budget application. A repeating label in B6 separates the department detail from the totals in row 7. To copy this label from B6 to C6, move the cell pointer to B6 and select /Copy. At the prompt Enter range to copy FROM:, press the left mouse button twice or press Enter to specify the one-cell range at B6. At Enter range to copy TO:, move to C6 and press the left mouse button twice or press Enter. The result is displayed in figure 4.67. Unlike the /Move command, /Copy produces the label in both places.

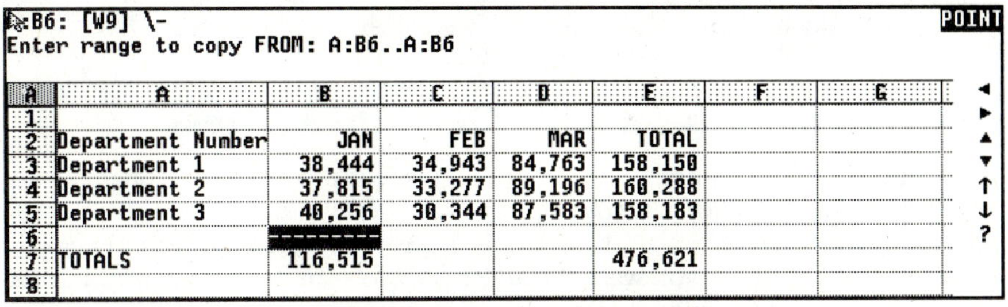

Fig. 4.66.
A worksheet before a label is copied.

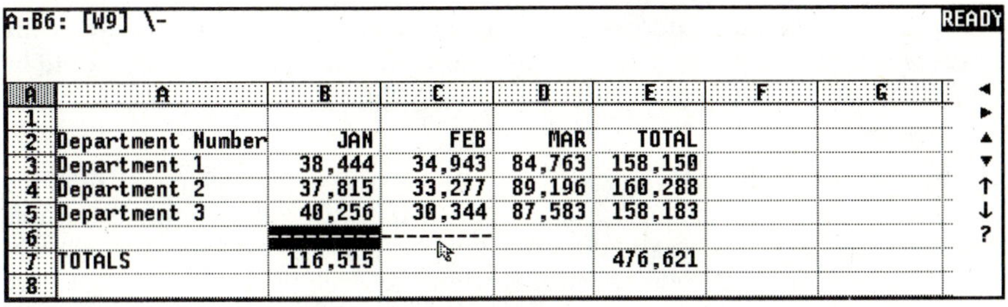

Fig. 4.67.
The worksheet after a label is copied.

Copying a Formula with Relative Addressing

The real power of /Copy shows up when you copy a formula. The formula in B7 is @SUM(B3..B5). When you copy B7 to C7, the formula in C7 is @SUM(C3..C5) (see fig. 4.68). This *relative addressing* concept is very important in 1-2-3. When you copy a formula, 1-2-3 adjusts the new formula so that its cell references are in the same relative location as they were in the original formula.

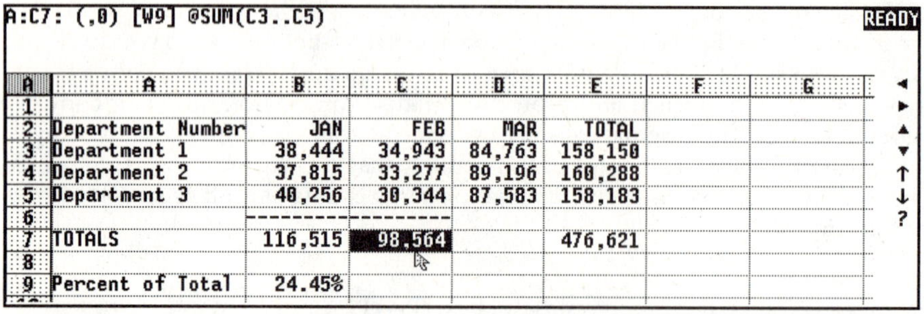

Fig. 4.68.
The addresses adjusted automatically when a formula is copied.

```
A:C7: (,0) [W9] @SUM(C3..C5)                                    READY

      A              B         C         D         E        F       G
 1
 2  Department Number  JAN       FEB       MAR      TOTAL
 3  Department 1     38,444    34,943    84,763   158,150
 4  Department 2     37,815    33,277    89,196   160,288
 5  Department 3     40,256    30,344    87,583   158,183
 6                  ────────  ────────  ────────  ────────
 7  TOTALS          116,515    98,564             476,621
 8
 9  Percent of Total 24.45%
```

The best way to understand relative addressing is to understand how 1-2-3 actually stores addresses in formulas. The formula in B7 is @SUM(B3..B5). In other words, this formula means "sum the contents of all the cells in the range from B3 to B5." But that is not the way 1-2-3 really stores this formula. To 1-2-3, the formula is "sum the contents of all the cells in the range from the cell 4 rows above this cell to the cell 2 rows above this cell." When you copy this formula to C7, 1-2-3 uses the same relative formula but displays it as C3..C5.

In most cases, when you copy a formula, you want the addresses to adjust automatically. Sometimes you do not want some addresses to adjust, or you want part of an address to adjust. These situations are examined separately.

Copying a Formula with Absolute Addressing

The formula in B9 in figure 4.68 is +B7/E7. This figure represents January's sales as a percentage of the total. If you copy this formula to C9, you get +C7/F7. Sales for February, C7, is correct. F7, however, is incorrect; F7 is a blank cell. When you copy the formula in B9, you want the address E7 to copy as an absolute address; you do not want it to change after you copy it to C9.

Cue:
Specify absolute addresses when you write the formula, not when you copy it.

To specify an absolute address, type a dollar sign ($) before each part of the address you want to remain "absolutely" the same. The formula in B9 should be +B7/$E$7. When you copy this formula to C9, the formula becomes +C7/$E$7 (see fig. 4.69).

Instead of typing the dollar signs, you can press Abs (F4) after you type the address; the address changes to absolute. In this case, the complete formula becomes +C7/$A:$E$7. If an address is in the same worksheet as the cell that contains the formula, and the worksheet reference is relative, 1-2-3 does not store the worksheet letter in the address, such as the C7 part of the formula in C9. If the worksheet reference is absolute, the worksheet letter is stored in the formula, such as the $A:$E$7 part of the formula in C9.

Chapter 4 ◆ Using Fundamental 1-2-3 Commands   **147**

Notice that when the formula appears in the control panel of figure 4.69, the worksheet reference does not appear as it did when you first entered it. If, however, that formula is copied to another worksheet, the formula is displayed in the control panel with the worksheet reference. For example, if the formula in C9 of worksheet A (see fig. 4.69) is copied to B:C9, the formula displays as +C7/$A:$E$7 in the control panel.

```
A:C9: (P2) [W9] +C7/$E$7                                        READY

       A               A         B         C         D         E         F         G
   1
   2   Department Number       JAN       FEB       MAR     TOTAL
   3   Department 1         38,444    34,943    84,763   158,150
   4   Department 2         37,815    33,277    89,196   160,288
   5   Department 3         40,256    30,344    87,583   158,183
   6                        ----------------------------
   7   TOTALS              116,515    98,564              476,621
   8
   9   Percent of Total     24.45%    20.68%
```

Fig. 4.69.
An absolute address that remains unchanged when copied.

You can enter dollar signs while pointing to addresses in a formula. As you point to a cell to include it in a formula, press Abs (F4) to make the address absolute. If you forget to make an address absolute, just press F2 (Edit) to go into EDIT mode, move the cursor in the control panel to the address you want to make absolute, and then press F4.

If you want to change an absolute reference (with dollar signs) back to a relative reference, press F2 (Edit), move the cursor to the reference, and then press F4 (Abs) a number of times until there are no dollar signs. Press the right mouse button or press Esc to reenter the formula.

Another kind of addressing is called *mixed addressing*. Mixed addressing can be very complex and is covered later in this chapter.

Copying One Cell's Contents Several Times

In figure 4.68, one cell was copied one time. The idea, however, is to copy the formula in B7 to C7 and D7. You can replicate a cell's contents in one copy operation. The FROM range is still B7, but at the `Enter range to copy TO:` prompt, move the cell pointer to C7, drag the mouse to highlight D7, and press the left mouse button; or press the period to anchor the cell, highlight D7 using the right-arrow key, and then press Enter. The formula in B7 is copied to both cells (see fig. 4.70).

Copying One Cell's Contents to a Range of Cells

You can copy a single cell to a range on the same worksheet or a range that spans multiple worksheets. Figure 4.71 shows a simple price-forecasting model. The current prices are in column B. The formula in C3 increases the price by the percentage established in B1. To copy this formula through the table in worksheet A, copy from C3 to C3..G10. The result is displayed in figure 4.72.

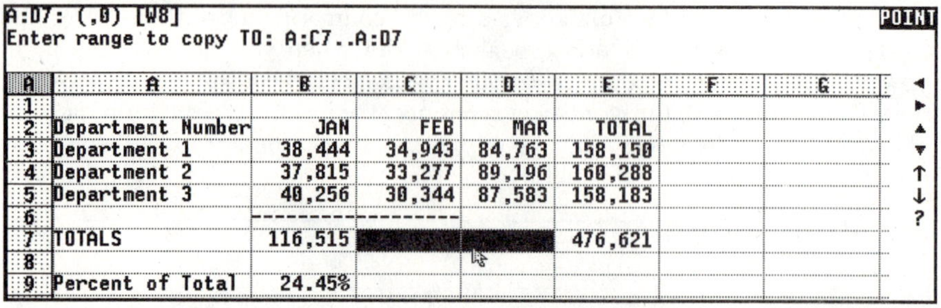

Fig. 4.70.

A cell copied to two cells in one copy operation.

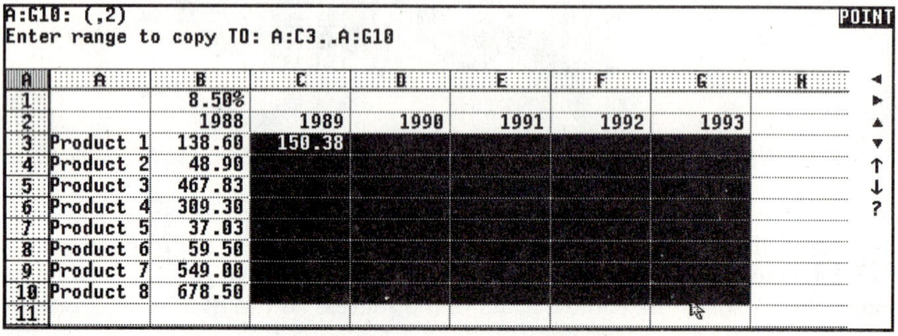

```
A:D7: (,0) [W8]                                                    POINT
Enter range to copy TO: A:C7..A:D7
     A              A            B         C         D         E         F         G
  1
  2  Department Number          JAN       FEB       MAR      TOTAL
  3  Department 1            38,444    34,943    84,763    158,150
  4  Department 2            37,815    33,277    89,196    160,288
  5  Department 3            40,256    30,344    87,583    158,183
  6                         ----------
  7  TOTALS                  116,515                        476,621
  8
  9  Percent of Total         24.45%
```

Fig. 4.71.

A cell copied to a number of rows and columns in one copy.

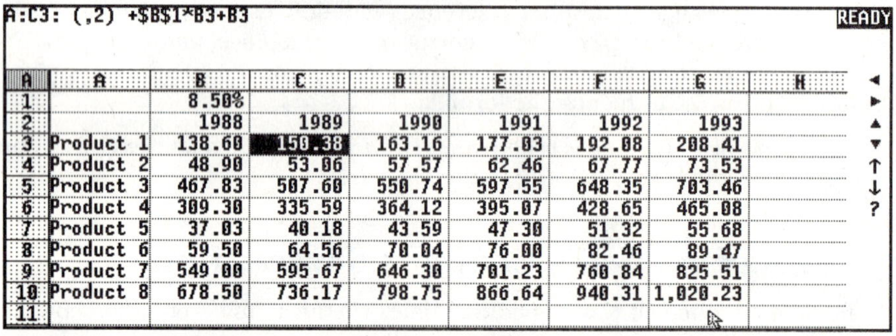

```
A:G10: (,2)                                                        POINT
Enter range to copy TO: A:C3..A:G10
     A              A            B         C         D         E         F         G         H
  1                            8.50%
  2                            1988      1989      1990      1991      1992      1993
  3  Product 1                138.60    150.38
  4  Product 2                 48.90
  5  Product 3                467.83
  6  Product 4                309.30
  7  Product 5                 37.03
  8  Product 6                 59.50
  9  Product 7                549.00
 10  Product 8                678.50
 11
```

Fig. 4.72.

The worksheet after the copy.

```
A:C3: (,2) +$B$1*B3+B3                                             READY
     A              A            B         C         D         E         F         G         H
  1                            8.50%
  2                            1988      1989      1990      1991      1992      1993
  3  Product 1                138.60    150.38    163.16    177.03    192.08    208.41
  4  Product 2                 48.90     53.06     57.57     62.46     67.77     73.53
  5  Product 3                467.83    507.60    550.74    597.55    648.35    703.46
  6  Product 4                309.30    335.59    364.12    395.07    428.65    465.08
  7  Product 5                 37.03     40.18     43.59     47.30     51.32     55.68
  8  Product 6                 59.50     64.56     70.04     76.00     82.46     89.47
  9  Product 7                549.00    595.67    646.30    701.23    760.84    825.51
 10  Product 8                678.50    736.17    798.75    866.64    940.31  1,020.23
 11
```

When you copy a single cell, there is no harm if you include the FROM cell in the TO range, as in figure 4.71. As a general rule, the first cell in the FROM range can be the same cell as the first cell in the TO range. In most other cases, an overlapping FROM and TO range can destroy the data before it is copied.

You can copy a single cell to multiple worksheets. If the same pricing model for different departments is found in different worksheets, for example, you can fill in multiple worksheets with one three-dimensional copy. Figure 4.73 is the result of copying from A:C3 to A:C3..C:G10. To highlight the TO range across multiple worksheets, highlight the TO range on the first sheet being copied to—in this example, A:C3..AG10. Click the up-arrow icon or press Ctrl-PgUp to copy this same range through to the next worksheet. In this example, click the up-arrow icon twice or press Ctrl-PgUp twice to extend the range to A:C3..C:G6.

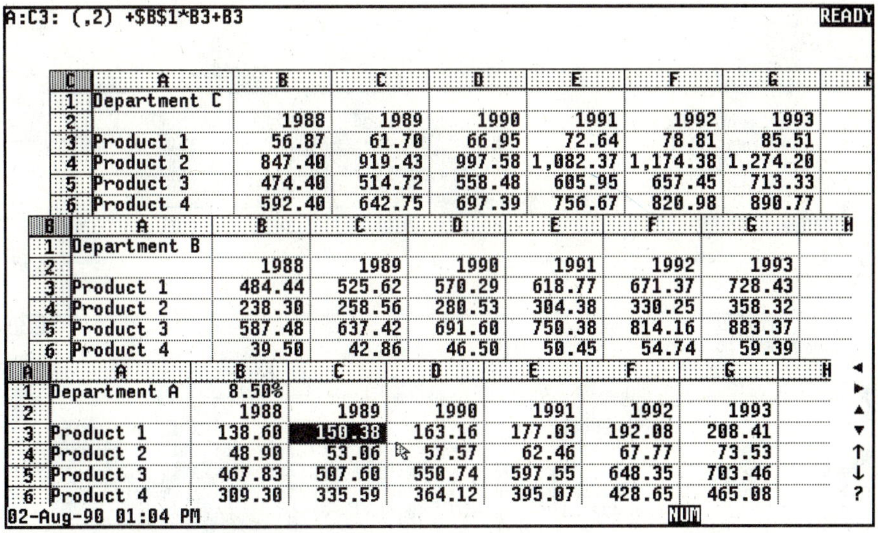

Chapter 4 ◆ Using Fundamental 1-2-3 Commands   **149**

Fig. 4.73.
A cell copied to multiple rows, multiple columns, and multiple worksheets in one /Copy operation.

Copying the Contents of a Range

In previous examples, one cell at a time was copied. You can copy a row or a column of cells to a number of locations.

In figure 4.74, suppose that you want to copy the label in C6 and the formula in C7 across the other columns. Copy from C6..C7 to D6..F6. Figure 4.74 shows the screen after the TO range is highlighted. In this example, a range down one column is copied a number of times across a row. Note that the TO range is only across row 6, highlighting only the top cell where each copy goes. 1-2-3 remembers the size of each copy and the contents of the cells in the FROM range and fills in the lower cells of the target range accordingly. The result is displayed in figure 4.75.

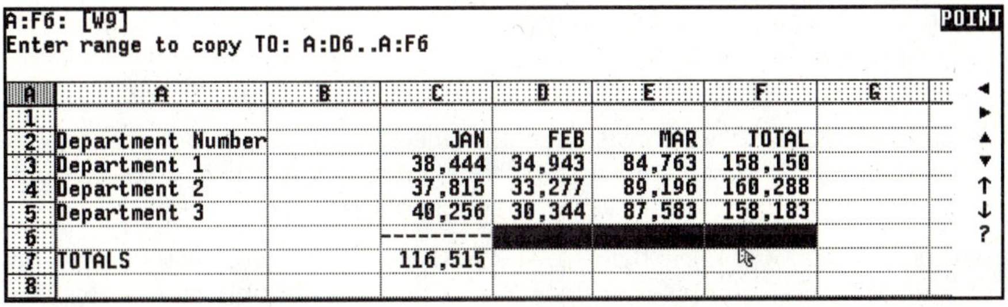

Fig. 4.74.
Copying a single-column range across a row.

You also can copy a range across one row down a number of columns. In figure 4.76, you want to copy the TOTAL in F3 and the VARIANCE in G3 down the column. Copy from F3..G3 to F4..F6. Figure 4.76 displays the screen after the TO range is highlighted. The result is displayed in figure 4.77.

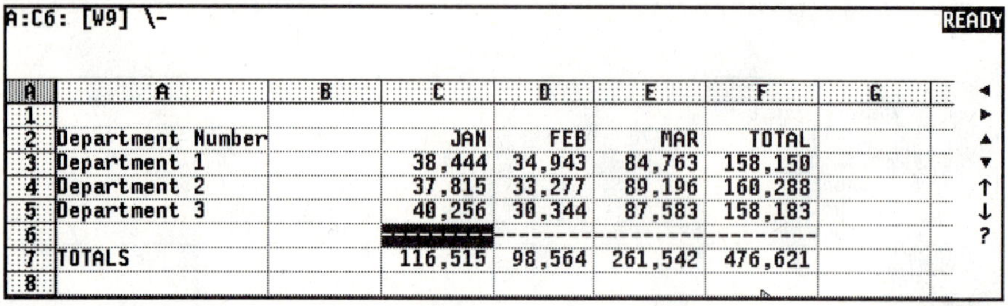

Fig. 4.75.

The worksheet after two cells down a column are copied across three columns.

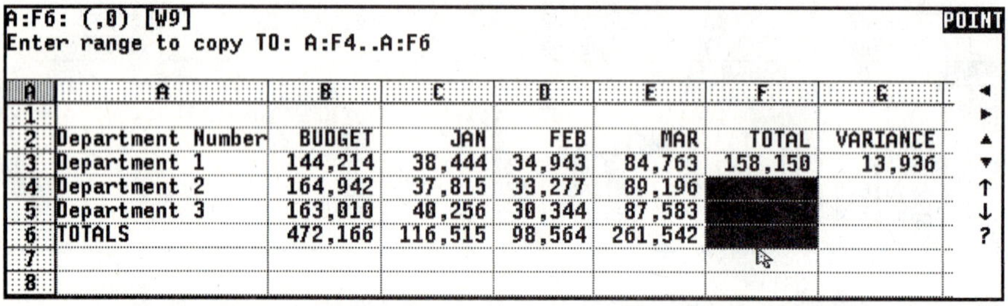

```
A:C6: [W9] \-                                                    READY
       A              B        C       D       E       F       G
  1
  2  Department Number        JAN     FEB     MAR    TOTAL
  3  Department 1          38,444  34,943  84,763  158,150
  4  Department 2          37,815  33,277  89,196  160,288
  5  Department 3          40,256  30,344  87,583  158,183
  6  ----------------------------------------------------
  7  TOTALS               116,515  98,564 261,542  476,621
  8
```

Fig. 4.76.

Copying a single-row range down a column.

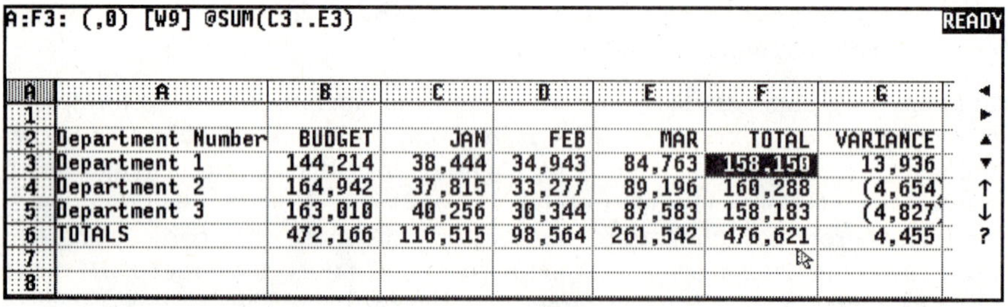

```
A:F6: (,0) [W9]                                                  POINT
Enter range to copy TO: A:F4..A:F6
       A              B        C       D       E       F       G
  1
  2  Department Number  BUDGET   JAN     FEB     MAR    TOTAL  VARIANCE
  3  Department 1      144,214 38,444  34,943  84,763 158,150   13,936
  4  Department 2      164,942 37,815  33,277  89,196
  5  Department 3      163,010 40,256  30,344  87,583
  6  TOTALS            472,166 116,515 98,564 261,542
  7
  8
```

Fig. 4.77.

The worksheet after two cells across a row are copied down two columns.

```
A:F3: (,0) [W9] @SUM(C3..E3)                                     READY
       A              B        C       D       E       F       G
  1
  2  Department Number  BUDGET   JAN     FEB     MAR    TOTAL  VARIANCE
  3  Department 1      144,214 38,444  34,943  84,763 158,150   13,936
  4  Department 2      164,942 37,815  33,277  89,196 160,288   (4,654)
  5  Department 3      163,010 40,256  30,344  87,583 158,183   (4,827)
  6  TOTALS            472,166 116,515 98,564 261,542 476,621    4,455
  7
  8
```

Copying a range a number of times is very useful. When you build worksheets, you use this technique often. The technique, however, does have limitations. The following is the general rule: if the FROM range is only one cell wide in a dimension, you can copy it a number of times in that dimension.

A single cell is one cell wide in all directions; it is part of one row, one column, and one worksheet. You can copy a single cell across a row, down a column, and through multiple worksheets, as shown in figures 4.70 through 4.73.

Because the FROM range in figure 4.74 (C6..C7) occupies two rows, you can copy this range across columns (see fig. 4.74) or through multiple worksheets. You cannot copy this range down rows. Whether you specify a TO range in figure 4.74 of D6..F7 or D6..F100, you get the same result as in figure 4.75. The rows are ignored in the TO range because they are fixed in the FROM range.

A two-dimensional range can be copied only once to each worksheet in the file. If you copy more than once, any data from the previous copy operation is overwritten. For example, the range C3..G10 in figure 4.72 can be copied

Cue:

If the FROM range is only one cell wide in a dimension, you can copy it a number of times in that dimension.

anywhere on this worksheet one time. If you highlight more than a single cell as the TO range, 1-2-3 uses the upper left corner and ignores the rest. You also can copy this range through multiple worksheets. If the price forecasts in worksheets B and C in figure 4.73 are blank, you can copy from A:C3..A:G10 to B:C3..C:C3 to complete the other two worksheets.

A three-dimensional range, such as A:C3..C:G10, can be copied only once. The three-dimensional range of the copy is successful only if there are enough worksheets in the file.

In figure 4.73, you can copy the range A:C3..C:G10 to any position in worksheet A, such as A:I3. This process duplicates the data in all three worksheets. If you try to copy the range A:C3..C:G10 to any position in worksheet B or C, such as B:I3, 1-2-3 displays the error message `Cannot Move or Copy data beyond worksheet boundaries`. The TO range is three worksheets deep. You are trying to copy data from worksheets A-C into worksheets B-D. Because no worksheet D exists, the copy fails.

Copying with Mixed Addressing

Figure 4.78 shows a price-forecast worksheet similar to the one in figure 4.71, but this time there is a different price increase percentage for each year. Now the formula in C3 is more complex. When you copy this formula down column C, you do not want the reference to C1 to change, but when you copy the formula across row 3, you want the reference to change for each column. A *mixed reference* is relative for the column and absolute for the row or vice versa. The formula in C3 is `+B3*(1+$A:B$1)`. When you copy this formula down one row to C4, the formula becomes `+B4*(1+$A:B$1)`. The relative address B3 became B4, but the mixed address `$A:B$1` is unchanged. When you copy the formula to D3, the formula becomes `+C3*(1+$A:C$1)`. The relative address B3 becomes C3, and the mixed address becomes `$A:C$1`. You can copy from C3 to C3..G10 and create the correct formula throughout the worksheet.

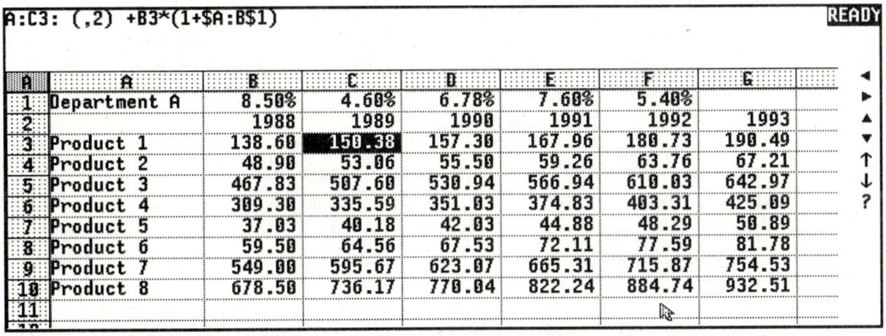
A:C3: (,2) +B3*(1+$A:B$1)   READY

A	A	B	C	D	E	F	G
1	Department A	8.50%	4.60%	6.78%	7.60%	5.40%	
2		1988	1989	1990	1991	1992	1993
3	Product 1	138.60	150.38	157.30	167.96	180.73	190.49
4	Product 2	48.90	53.06	55.50	59.26	63.76	67.21
5	Product 3	467.83	507.60	530.94	566.94	610.03	642.97
6	Product 4	309.30	335.59	351.03	374.83	403.31	425.09
7	Product 5	37.03	40.18	42.03	44.88	48.29	50.89
8	Product 6	59.50	64.56	67.53	72.11	77.59	81.78
9	Product 7	549.00	595.67	623.07	665.31	715.87	754.53
10	Product 8	678.50	736.17	770.04	822.24	884.74	932.51
11							

Fig. 4.78. *A mixed address in a formula adjusted when copied in one direction and remaining the same when copied in another direction.*

To make an address mixed without typing the dollar signs, use the Abs (F4) key. The first time you press F4, the address becomes absolute. As you continue to press F4, the address cycles through all the possible mixed addresses and returns to relative. The complete list of relative, absolute, and mixed addresses is found in table 4.2. To obtain the address in figure 4.78, press F4 twice.

Table 4.2
Using Abs (F4) To Change Address Type

Number of Times To Press Abs (F4)	Result	Explanation
1	$A:$B$1	Completely absolute
2	$A:B$1	Absolute worksheet and row
3	$A:$B1	Absolute worksheet and column
4	$A:B1	Absolute worksheet
5	A:$B$1	Absolute column and row
6	A:B$1	Absolute row
7	A:$B1	Absolute column
8	A:B1	Returned to relative

Caution:

Decide whether you want the worksheet part of the address to be absolute when using absolute and mixed addresses.

When you work with multiple worksheets, you must be very careful with absolute and mixed addresses. When you first press F4 (Abs), the worksheet is absolute. In many cases you do not want this. Consider the worksheet in figure 4.78. The term $A:B$1 in cell C3 forces the B$1 reference to always look at sheet A. If you plan to expand this model to multiple worksheets, as in figure 4.73, you want each worksheet to reference the growth range for that sheet. You want the worksheet letter to change relative to its new worksheet; you therefore want a term of A:B$1 and not the original $A:B$1. In this case, the correct formula in C3 would be +B3*(1+A:B$1). To get the last address in the formula correct, you press the F4 key six times.

Using Range Names with /Copy

With all commands that prompt for a range, you can use range names for the FROM range, the TO range, or both. Just type the range name or press the Name (F3) key and point to the range name. Unfortunately, 1-2-3 makes it impossible to use range names with mixed addresses.

To specify an absolute address, you must type the dollar sign before the range name. To use the range name SALES in a formula as an absolute address, you type **$SALES**. You cannot use Abs (F4) with range names. You cannot specify a range name and make it a mixed address. You must use the actual cell addresses.

Using /Range Value To Convert Formulas to Values

/Range Value is a special type of copy command. When you use **/Range Value** on a cell that contains a label or a number, this command works exactly like **/Copy**. When you use **/Range Value** on a cell that contains a formula, the current value, not the formula, is copied. You use /Range Value to freeze the value of formulas so that they won't change. Figure 4.79 shows a model that forecasts profits for future years. You update the forecasts each quarter, but you want to keep track of the forecasts from the previous quarter for comparison. You can achieve this type of comparison by converting the formula results in row 16 into values in row 18. In this way, next quarter's changes won't affect row 18.

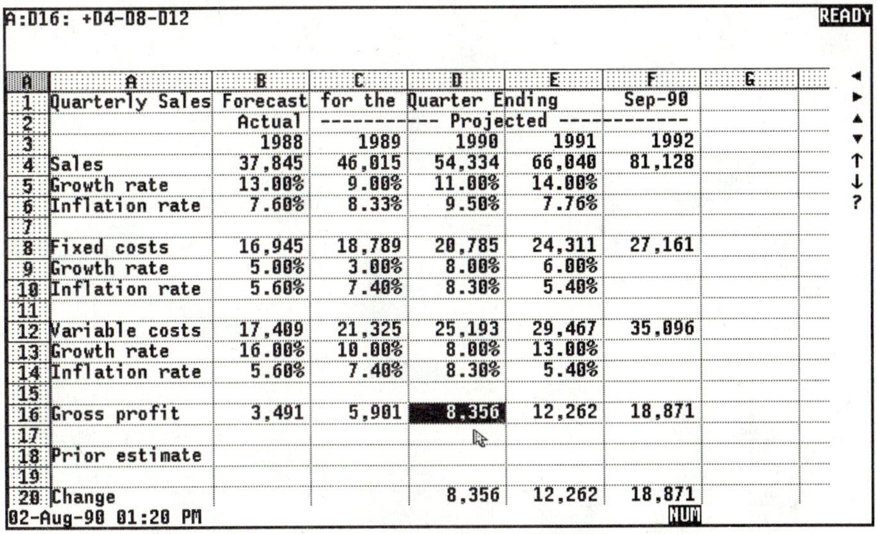

Fig. 4.79.

A worksheet before a /Range Value operation.

The profit figures in figure 4.79 are formulas. To obtain the prior estimate in row 18, use /Range Value from B16..F16 to B18. The prior estimate is a copy of the gross profit converted to numbers.

The result is shown in figure 4.80. The numbers in row 18 are the current values of the formulas in row 16.

In figure 4.81, the various rates were updated, and 1-2-3 calculated new gross profits. Because the prior estimates in row 18 did not change, you can compare the newest estimate with the prior one and calculate the difference in row 20.

Formulas take more memory than numbers; they also take time to recalculate. You can convert (to numbers) formulas that never change. For example, the years for projections in row 3 in figure 4.81 are formulas that add 1 to the previous year. The formula in C3 is +B3+1. To convert these formulas to numbers, use /Range Value from C3..F3 to C3. The trick here is to use /Range Value to convert the formulas to themselves.

Cue:
Use /Range Value to convert formulas to numbers.

There is a danger when using /Range Value if you have recalculation set to manual. If you use /Range Value on a formula that is not current, you freeze the old value. This problem is even worse if you convert formulas to numbers and the formulas are not current. You lose the formulas, and the resulting numbers are wrong. In figure 4.82, the CALC indicator shows that the worksheet is not current. If you use

/Range Value on the formula in B5, you freeze an incorrect value. If your worksheet is set to manual recalculation and the CALC indicator is on, press Calc (F9) before you use /Range Value.

Fig. 4.80.
The worksheet after the /Range Value operation that locked in the prior estimate figures.

```
A:D18: 8356                                                    READY
     A              B        C         D         E        F       G
 1 Quarterly Sales Forecast for the Quarter Ending  Sep-90
 2                 Actual   ---------- Projected ------------
 3                 1988     1989      1990      1991      1992
 4 Sales           37,845   46,015    54,334    66,040    81,128
 5 Growth rate     13.00%   9.00%     11.00%    14.00%
 6 Inflation rate  7.60%    8.33%     9.50%     7.76%
 7
 8 Fixed costs     16,945   18,789    20,785    24,311    27,161
 9 Growth rate     5.00%    3.00%     8.00%     6.00%
10 Inflation rate  5.60%    7.40%     8.30%     5.40%
11
12 Variable costs  17,409   21,325    25,193    29,467    35,096
13 Growth rate     16.00%   10.00%    8.00%     13.00%
14 Inflation rate  5.60%    7.40%     8.30%     5.40%
15
16 Gross profit    3,491    5,901     8,356     12,262    18,871
17
18 Prior estimate  3,491    5,901     8,356     12,262    18,871
19
20 Change                             0         0         0
02-Aug-90 01:21 PM                                              NUM
```

Fig. 4.81.
The worksheet with new profit figures after the rates are updated.

```
A:D18: 8356                                                    READY
     A              B        C         D         E        F       G
 1 Quarterly Sales Forecast for the Quarter Ending  Sep-90
 2                 Actual   ---------- Projected ------------
 3                 1988     1989      1990      1991      1992
 4 Sales           37,845   46,015    54,534    64,492    77,836
 5 Growth rate     13.00%   8.30%     8.00%     12.00%
 6 Inflation rate  7.60%    9.43%     9.50%     7.76%
 7
 8 Fixed costs     16,945   18,789    21,087    25,701    28,985
 9 Growth rate     5.00%    4.50%     12.54%    7.00%
10 Inflation rate  5.60%    7.40%     8.30%     5.40%
11
12 Variable costs  17,409   21,325    24,873    29,550    34,572
13 Growth rate     16.00%   8.60%     9.70%     11.00%
14 Inflation rate  5.60%    7.40%     8.30%     5.40%
15
16 Gross profit    3,491    5,901     8,574     9,241     14,279
17
18 Prior estimate  3,491    5,901     8,356     12,262    18,871
19
20 Change                             218       (3,021)   (4,592)
02-Aug-90 01:27 PM                                              NUM
```

Using /Range Transpose

/Range Transpose is another special type of copy command. /Range Transpose converts rows to columns, columns to rows, and changes formulas to values at the same time. In figure 4.83, the range F12..N19 is the result of the command /Range

Chapter 4 ♦ Using Fundamental 1-2-3 Commands **155**

Transpose from A2..H10 to F12. The rows and columns are transposed, and the formulas in row 10 become numbers in column N.

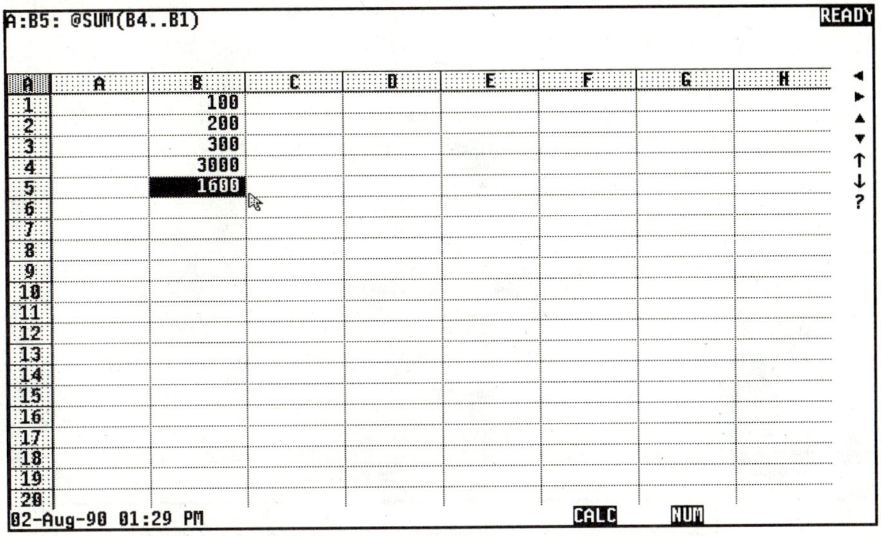

```
A:B5: @SUM(B4..B1)                                          READY
     A      B      C      D      E      F      G      H
 1          100
 2          200
 3          300
 4         3000
 5         1600
 6
 7
 ...
02-Aug-90 01:29 PM                              CALC    NUM
```

Fig. 4.82.
An incorrect value locked in when /Range Value is selected while the CALC indicator is on.

As with /Range Value, you can freeze incorrect values if recalculation is set to manual. Make sure that the CALC indicator is off before you transpose a range.

Caution:
Press Calc (F9) before you transpose a range.

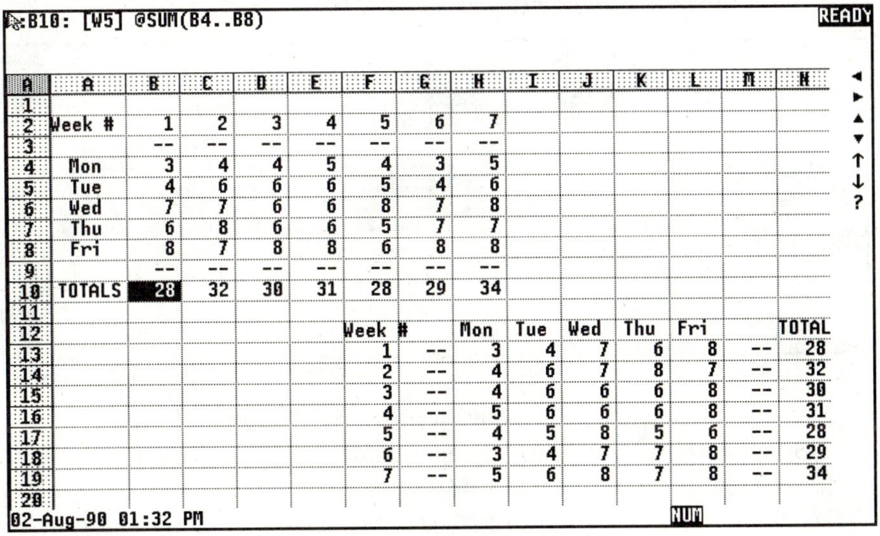

```
B10: [W5] @SUM(B4..B8)                                      READY
       A    B   C   D   E   F   G   H   I   J   K   L   M   N
 1
 2  Week #  1   2   3   4   5   6   7
 3         --  --  --  --  --  --  --
 4  Mon     3   4   4   5   4   3   5
 5  Tue     4   6   6   6   5   4   6
 6  Wed     7   7   6   6   8   7   8
 7  Thu     6   8   6   6   5   7   7
 8  Fri     8   7   8   8   6   8   8
 9         --  --  --  --  --  --  --
10  TOTALS 28  32  30  31  28  29  34
11
12                          Week # Mon Tue Wed Thu Fri  TOTAL
13                             1   --   3   4   7   6   8  --   28
14                             2   --   4   6   7   8   7  --   32
15                             3   --   4   6   6   6   8  --   30
16                             4   --   5   6   6   6   8  --   31
17                             5   --   4   5   8   5   6  --   28
18                             6   --   3   4   7   7   8  --   29
19                             7   --   5   6   8   7   8  --   34
20
02-Aug-90 01:32 PM                                      NUM
```

Fig. 4.83.
A table after /Range Transpose was used to transpose the rows and columns.

Finding and Replacing Data

/Range Search searches a range of cells to find a string of characters in labels and formulas. This feature works much like the search-and-replace feature in many

Caution:
Always save the file before you use /Range Search.

word processing packages. An incorrect search and replace operation can destroy a file, so always save the file first.

Suppose that you have a list of department names as labels (see fig. 4.84), and you want to shorten the labels from "Department" to "Dept". To search and replace a label, choose /Range Search, and then follow these steps:

1. At the prompt, highlight the range to search, A3..A10 (see fig. 4.84), and then press the left mouse button or press Enter.

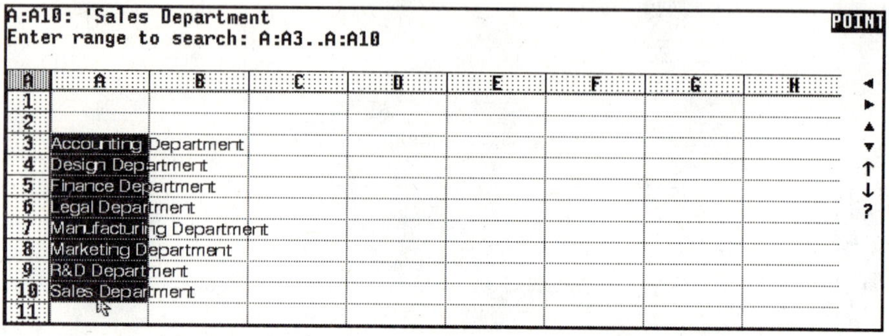

Fig. 4.84.

A column of labels before a /Range Search operation to replace Department *with* Dept.

2. Type the search string (**department**), and then press the left mouse button or press Enter.

3. At the menu (see fig. 4.85), choose to search Formulas, Labels, or Both. Choose Labels to replace cells with labels.

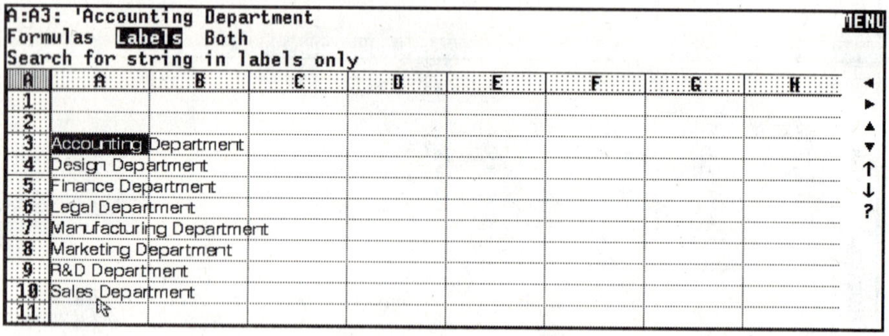

Fig. 4.85.

The /Range Search menu with Labels selected.

4. At the Find or Replace menu (see fig. 4.86), choose **Replace**.

5. At the prompt, type the replacement string (**Dept**), and then press the left mouse button or press Enter.

6. The cell pointer moves to the first cell with a matching string (A3) and gives you the following menu (see fig. 4.87):

   Replace All Next Quit

Choose Replace to replace Department with Dept in this one cell and move to the next matching cell. Choose All to replace Department with

Dept in all cells in the range. Choose **Quit** to stop the search and replace operation and return to READY mode. Choose **Next** to skip the current cell without changing it and move to the next matching cell. A good idea is to choose **Replace** for the first cell and make sure that the change is correct. If it is correct, choose **All** to replace the rest. If you made an error on the first **Replace**, choose **Quit** and redo the command.

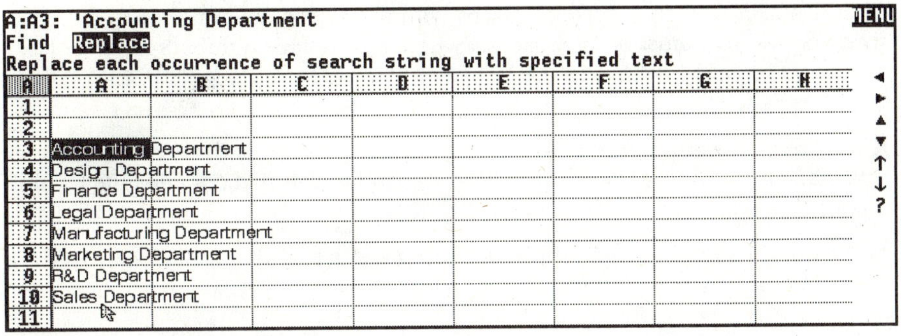

Fig. 4.86.
The /Range Search menu with Replace highlighted.

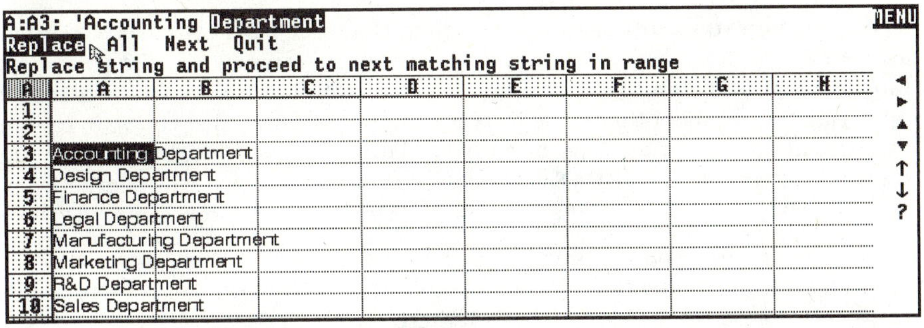

Fig. 4.87.
The /Range Search menu after Replace is selected.

The result is shown in figure 4.88. Case is not used with a search string (department matches Department, for example), but case is important in the replacement string.

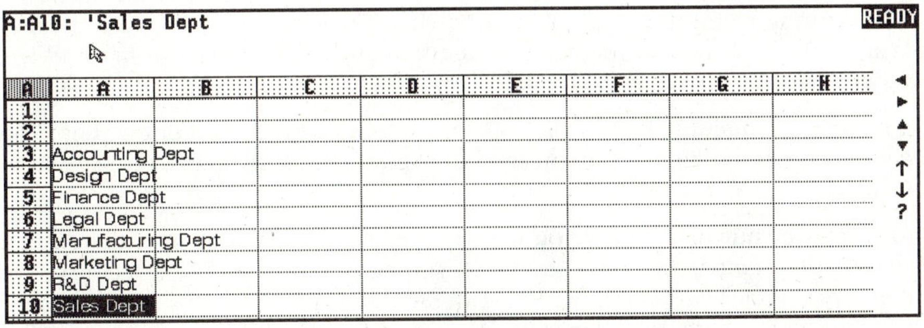

Fig. 4.88.
The labels after the /Range Search Replace command is used.

If you choose **F**ind instead of **R**eplace in the menu in figure 4.86, the cell pointer moves to the first cell in the range with a matching string and gives you a menu with the options **N**ext or **Q**uit. Choose **N**ext to find the next occurrence or **Q**uit to return to READY mode. If there are no more matching strings, 1-2-3 stops with an error message.

You also can use /**R**ange Search to modify formulas. If you have many formulas that round to 2 decimal places, such as @ROUND(A1*B1,2), you can change the formulas to round to 4 decimal places with a search string of ,2) and a replace string of ,4). You must be very careful when you replace numbers in formulas. If you try to replace 2 with 4 in the last example, the formula @ROUND(A2*B2,2) becomes @ROUND(A4*B4,4).

If your replacement makes a formula invalid, 1-2-3 cancels the replacement and returns to READY mode with the cell pointer at the cell that contains the formula it could not replace.

At the end of a **R**eplace operation, the cell pointer is at the last cell replaced.

Accessing the Operating System

In this chapter, you learned how to use many different 1-2-3 commands to build and modify your worksheet files. At times, however, you may need to perform a function that you cannot do in 1-2-3, but one which requires you to use the operating system or another program. For example, suppose that you want to save a file on a diskette, but you have no formatted diskettes available. In this case, you want to use the DOS FORMAT command. Or, while you are working in 1-2-3, someone may ask you to print a letter you created in word processing.

In these situations, you can save your files and exit 1-2-3. Then, when you are finished with the other task, you can restart 1-2-3 and read in the files again. However, you do not have to exit 1-2-3; there is a faster way.

Use /**S**ystem to temporarily suspend 1-2-3 and access the operating system (DOS). Once in the operating system, you can copy files, format diskettes, execute other system functions, or even execute another program, if you have enough memory available. To return to 1-2-3, type **exit** and then press Enter. You return to 1-2-3 with the same status that you had when you left. The same worksheets and files are in memory, and the cell pointer is in the same place. Window settings and any other defaults are exactly as you left them.

If not enough memory is available, 1-2-3 cannot invoke the operating system. You can recover some memory if you save your files and close them as described in Chapter 7.

Caution:
Save your work before you use /System. You may not be able to return to 1-2-3.

Always save your files before you use /**S**ystem. If you execute any program that remains in memory (memory-resident), you cannot reenter 1-2-3. Examples of memory-resident programs include SideKick and SideKick Plus from Borland International, Lotus Magellan, the DOS MODE and PRINT commands, print spoolers, and many other programs. If you do not save your files and you cannot reenter 1-2-3, your work cannot be accessed or saved.

Summary

In this chapter, you learned to use the fundamental 1-2-3 commands that work with most worksheets and files. You learned how to use command menus, how to specify and name ranges, and how to save files. The process of controlling how data is displayed on-screen was discussed, and you learned how to change column widths, split the screen into windows, and freeze titles. Erasing ranges and inserting and deleting rows, columns, and worksheets were presented as ways to change the layout of your worksheets and files. You learned how to customize the worksheet as to color, size of cells, and in many other ways.

You learned how to protect and hide data and files. Just as important, you learned the limitations of these techniques and how they can be overridden.

You learned how to use /Move and /Copy, two basic commands that are used when you rearrange data and build worksheets and files. You also learned how to use 1-2-3's search-and-replace feature to find data or to change it.

Finally, you learned how to suspend 1-2-3 so that you can perform actions that you cannot do in 1-2-3, and then return to the program just as you left it.

Learning all the commands in 1-2-3 is a formidable task. Fortunately, many commands perform very specialized tasks; you can learn them as you need to perform these tasks. The following chapters cover these more specialized commands.

Formatting Cell Contents

5

Using 1-2-3 to manipulate data is only the first step in using an electronic spreadsheet. Making the results clear and easy to understand can be as important as calculating the correct answer. In this chapter, you learn to use the tools that control how data within cells appears on-screen. Changing how data displays is called *formatting*. 1-2-3 offers three types of formatting commands: the Wysiwyg :Format commands affect the display of individual cells; the /Range commands also affect individual cells; and the /Worksheet Global commands affect the display of an entire worksheet or file. You use these commands to customize the display of data.

When you format data, you change only the way the data displays. You do not change the value of the data itself. Formatting options are also available when you print reports. Those printing capabilities are covered in Chapter 8.

This chapter shows you how to do the following:

- ◆ Set worksheet global default settings
- ◆ Set range and worksheet global formats
- ◆ Use the format commands to change how cells display
- ◆ Change label alignment in the cell
- ◆ Justify long labels across columns
- ◆ Suppress the display of zeros within cells

Setting Worksheet Global Defaults

1-2-3 includes a number of overall settings that define how 1-2-3 operates or how the screen looks. These settings can be changed. Some settings must be selected with the Install program (see Appendix A). For example, you use Install to specify the type of display and the printers that are connected to your computer. Other settings can be changed as you work in 1-2-3. The main command to change these settings when you are in 1-2-3 is /Worksheet Global Default. The menu that appears contains the following options:

> **Printer   Dir   Status   Update   Other   Graph   Temp   Ext   Autoexec   Quit**

Choose **Printer** to change the printer defaults, as described in Chapter 8. Choose **Dir** and **Ext** to change the defaults for directories and files (see Chapter 7). Choose **Graph** to change the graphing defaults (see Chapter 10). Choose **Autoexec** to control macros that execute when you retrieve a file (see Chapter 13). Choose **Other** from the menu for the following additional choices:

> **International   Help   Clock   Undo   Beep**

Choose **Clock** to change the default file and clock indicator at the lower left corner of the screen. Choose **Undo** to activate the Undo feature (Chapter 3). **Help** is an obsolete command that was left on the menu by Lotus for compatibility reasons.

Another selection from the **Other** menu is **Beep**. Normally, 1-2-3 Release 3 beeps when you make an error. You can turn off the beep with /Worksheet Global Default Other Beep No and turn the beep back on with /Worksheet Global Default Other Beep Yes. You may want to turn off the beep when you work in an area where the beep may disturb others, such as in a library. You may also turn off the beep when you demonstrate a 1-2-3 system to others so that it's not so obvious if you press a key in error.

Choose **International** for the International menu. You use this menu for additional formatting options. The choices on this menu include the following:

> **Punctuation   Currency   Date   Time   Negative   Release-2   File-Translation   Quit**

Cue:
Use /Worksheet Global Default Status to see all the global defaults at one time.

To see the current status of all these settings, use /Worksheet Global Default Status (see fig. 5.1). Any setting changes you make are effective only until you exit 1-2-3. The next time you start 1-2-3, these settings revert to their original values. To permanently update the changed settings, choose /Worksheet Global Default Update. This command updates a configuration file that 1-2-3 uses to determine the default for these settings.

Caution:
Update the global defaults, or all changes are lost when you quit 1-2-3.

Use /Worksheet Status (see fig. 5.2) to see a mixture of information that includes the memory available; the processor in your computer; the current recalculation method; default formats, label prefix, and column width for the current worksheet; and whether the current worksheet is using global protection. The main use of this status display is to check the amount of memory available and to find circular references. (See Chapter 4 for more information on circular references.)

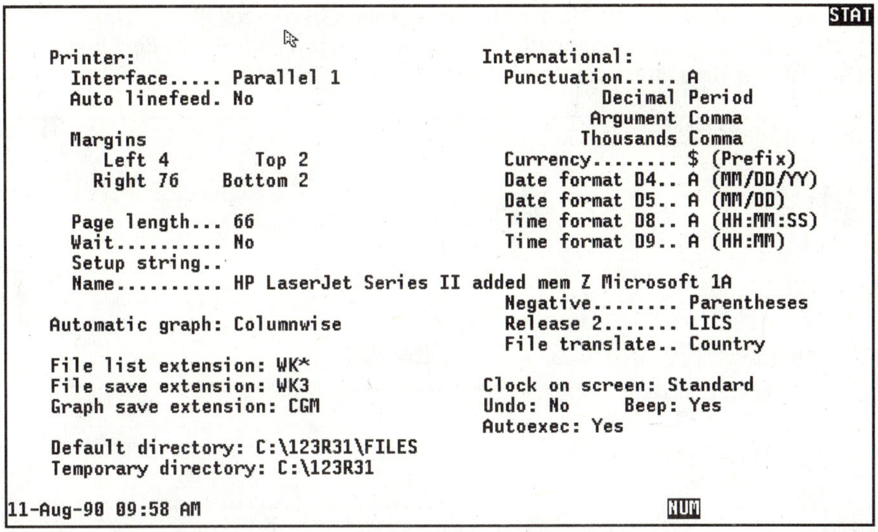

Chapter 5 ◆ Formatting Cell Contents **163**

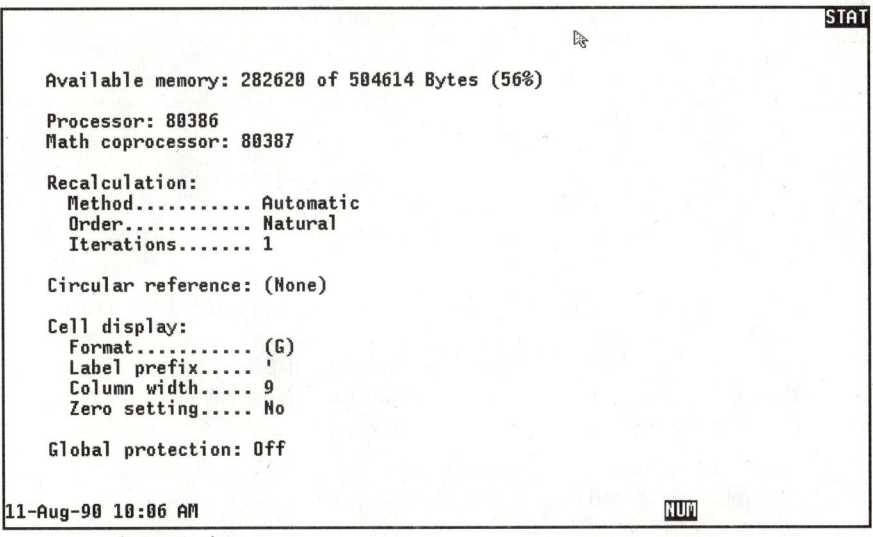

Fig. 5.1.
The /Worksheet Global Default Status screen.

Fig. 5.2.
The /Worksheet Status screen.

Setting Range and Worksheet Global Formats

Data in a cell has two characteristics: contents and formatting. These two characteristics are not the same, but they are related. The contents of the current cell are shown in the control panel; the formatted display of the contents shows in the worksheet (see fig. 5.3). A cell may contain a formula, such as +B8 in cell

C8, but the current value of the formula displays in the cell. The formula in C8 displays as 1,234.30. Other factors, such as the column width, can affect how a cell displays, but the cell format is the most important factor.

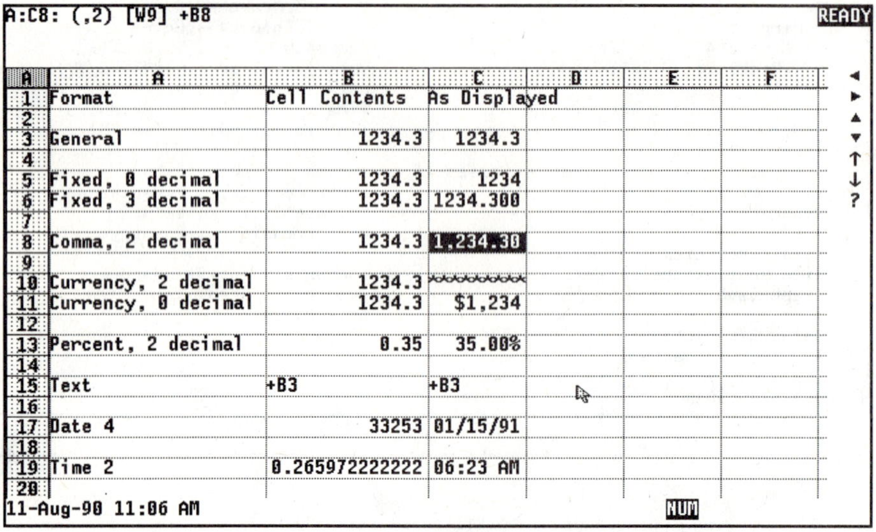

Fig. 5.3.

A worksheet showing various formats.

```
A:C8: (,2) [W9] +B8                                              READY
      A              B              C         D         E        F
 1 Format          Cell Contents  As Displayed
 2
 3 General                 1234.3     1234.3
 4
 5 Fixed, 0 decimal        1234.3       1234
 6 Fixed, 3 decimal        1234.3   1234.300
 7
 8 Comma, 2 decimal        1234.3   1,234.30
 9
10 Currency, 2 decimal     1234.3  *********
11 Currency, 0 decimal     1234.3     $1,234
12
13 Percent, 2 decimal        0.35     35.00%
14
15 Text            +B3            +B3
16
17 Date 4                   33253   01/15/91
18
19 Time 2         0.265972222222   06:23 AM
20
11-Aug-90 11:06 AM                                               NUM
```

The Available Formats

You can display data in a cell in a number of different formats. Table 5.1 lists the formats available from the 1-2-3 menu. Other formats are available from the Wysiwyg menu.

Most of the formats available from the 1-2-3 menu apply only to numeric data (numeric formulas and numbers). If you format a label as **Fixed** or **Currency**, for example, the format has no effect on how the label displays. A few formats, such as **Hidden**, can apply to labels and string formulas. Figure 5.3 shows examples of some of the possible formats.

The formats available from the Wysiwyg menu apply equally to numeric data and labels. For example, if you format a cell or range of cells with a particular font, the contents appear in that font, whether numbers or labels.

No matter what the format, numeric data is right-aligned. The rightmost digit always appears in the second position from the right. The extreme right position is reserved for a percent sign or right parenthesis. The result of a string (text) formula is always left-aligned, even if the formula refers to a label with another alignment.

The width of a cell is controlled by the column width setting, as described in Chapter 4. If the column is not wide enough to display a numeric entry, asterisks fill the cell (see C10 in fig. 5.3). To display the data, you must change either the format or the column width.

**Table 5.1
Display Formats**

Format	Example	Application
General	1234.5	Numeric data
Fixed	1234.50	Numeric data
, (Comma)	1,234.50	Numeric data
Currency	$1,234.50	Numeric data
Percent	35.4%	Numeric data
Sci (scientific)	1.2345E+03	Numeric data
+/–	+++++	Numeric data
Date	10/10/91	Special date serial numbers
Time	06:23 AM	Special time fractions
Text	+C6	All formulas
Hidden	No display	All data
Label	57 Main St.	Blank cells before labels are entered
Automatic	1,234.50	Blank cells before data is entered
Parentheses	(1,234.50)	Numeric data
Color	–1,234.50	Negative numeric data displays in color

If you use the 1-2-3 text display, the extreme right position of a cell is reserved for a percent sign or right parenthesis. Therefore, a number must fit into the cell using one character less than the column width. If the column width is 9, the formatted number must fit into 8 positions not counting a percent sign or right parenthesis. Negative numbers appear with either a minus sign or parentheses, which means that a negative number requires an extra character to display. With a column width of 9, a negative number must fit into 7 positions. The 1-2-3 graphics display reserves a position for a right parenthesis but not a percent sign. However, the number of characters that appear in a column with a width of 9 depends on the font that is used. For example, a 12-point Roman font displays eight characters, and a 24-point Swiss font displays just four.

Cue:
If numeric data appears as asterisks, either change the format or change the column width.

The Contents versus the Format of a Cell

Remember that *formatting* changes how the data appears, not the data itself. For example, the number 1234 can appear as `1,234`, `$1,234.00`, `123400%` and many other combinations. With the new Wysiwyg feature, the data can be any font and any color. No matter how the number displays, it remains the same number.

Some formats display a number as if it were rounded. If you format 1234.5 in **Fixed** format with zero decimal places, the number displays as `1235`, but the actual value of 1234.5 is used in formulas. In figure 5.4, the sales total in C8 looks like an addition error. Actually, the formula in C6 is +B6*1.1, projecting 10 percent higher sales next year. The value of the formula in C6 is 95.7. The display,

Caution:
The number that displays in a cell may not be the exact value of the cell because of rounding.

however, shows 96 formatted **Fixed** with zero decimal places. The value of the formula in C7 is 83.6, but the display shows 84. The value of the sum in C8 is 179.3, but the display shows 179. The value appears as 96+84=179. This result is an apparent error produced by rounding the display.

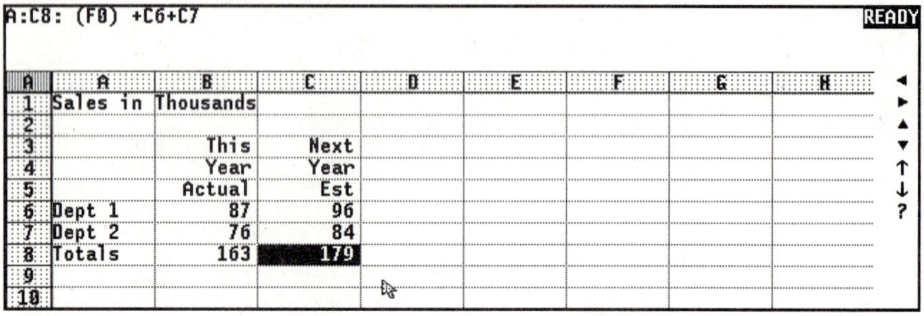

Fig. 5.4.
An apparent error caused by rounding.

```
A:C8: (F0) +C6+C7                                              READY
     A            B        C        D       E       F       G       H
 1  Sales in Thousands
 2
 3                      This     Next
 4                      Year     Year
 5                      Actual   Est
 6  Dept 1              87       96
 7  Dept 2              76       84
 8  Totals              163      179
 9
10
```

Cue:

Use formats to change how a number appears; use @ROUND to round the decimal precision of the value in the cell.

To avoid rounding errors, you need to round the actual value of the formulas in figure 5.4, not just the displayed value. To round the value of a formula, use the @ROUND function, as explained in Chapter 6.

Using the Format Commands of the Main Menu

You change the format of a cell or range of cells with the **/Range Format** command on the 1-2-3 menu (see fig. 5.5). You then select one of the formats from the menu or choose **Other** for additional choices (see fig. 5.6). For comma format, you press the comma key (,).

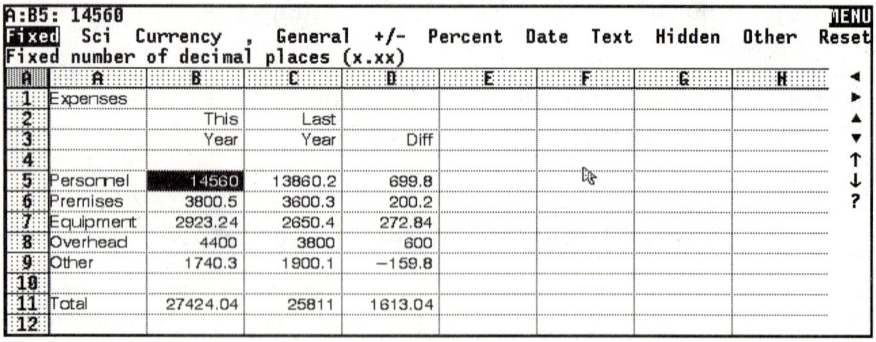

Fig. 5.5.
The /Range Format menu.

```
A:B5: 14560                                                    MENU
Fixed  Sci  Currency  ,  General  +/-  Percent  Date  Text  Hidden  Other  Reset
Fixed number of decimal places (x.xx)
     A            B        C        D       E       F       G       H
 1  Expenses
 2
 3                      This     Last
 4                      Year     Year     Diff
 5  Personnel           14560    13860.2  699.8
 6  Premises            3800.5   3600.3   200.2
 7  Equipment           2923.24  2650.4   272.84
 8  Overhead            4400     3800     600
 9  Other               1740.3   1900.1   -159.8
10
11  Total               27424.04 25811    1613.04
12
```

If you choose **Fixed**, **Sci** (scientific), **,** (comma), **Currency**, or **Percent**, you are prompted for the number of decimal places (see fig 5.7). Whenever this prompt appears, 1-2-3 shows a default of 2 decimal places. Press Enter to accept the default, or type another number from 0 to 15 and press Enter or press the left mouse button. The **Date** and **Time** formats have additional menus that are covered later in this chapter. The **Time** format is an option on the **Date** menu.

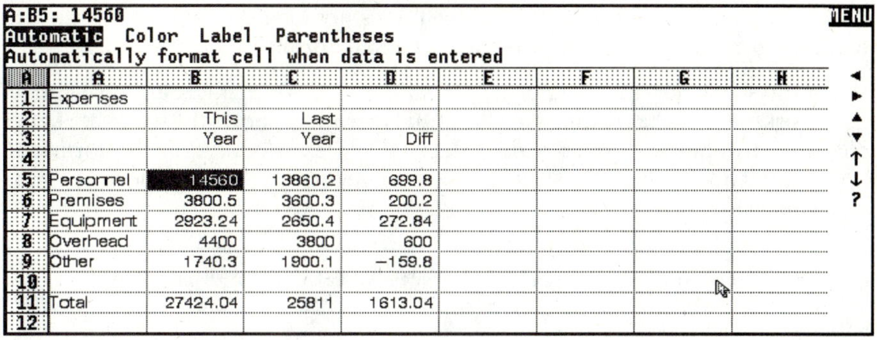

Chapter 5 ◆ Formatting Cell Contents

Fig. 5.6.
The /Range Format Other menu.

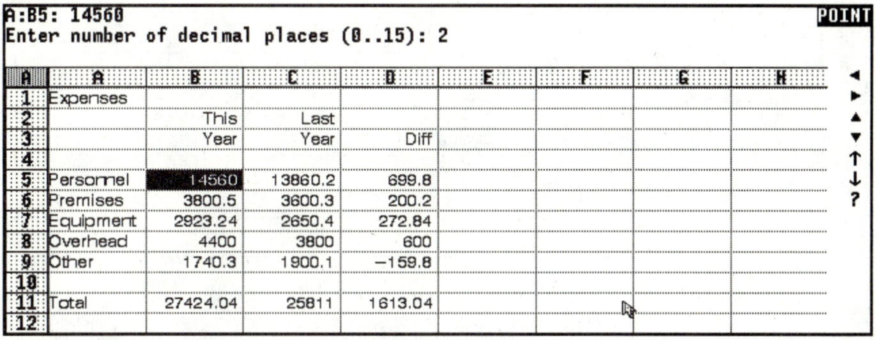

Fig. 5.7.
The prompt to enter the number of decimal places.

After you select a format and any options, the program prompts you for the range to format. Highlight the range and press Enter or press the left mouse button. Figure 5.8 shows the result after you use **/R**ange Format Fixed with 2 decimal places on the range B5..B11. An abbreviation of the format appears in the control panel when the current cell has a range format. In figure 5.8, (F2) in the control panel indicates that B5 has been range-formatted as **F**ixed with 2 decimal places. If the cell has no range format, no format indicator appears in the control panel.

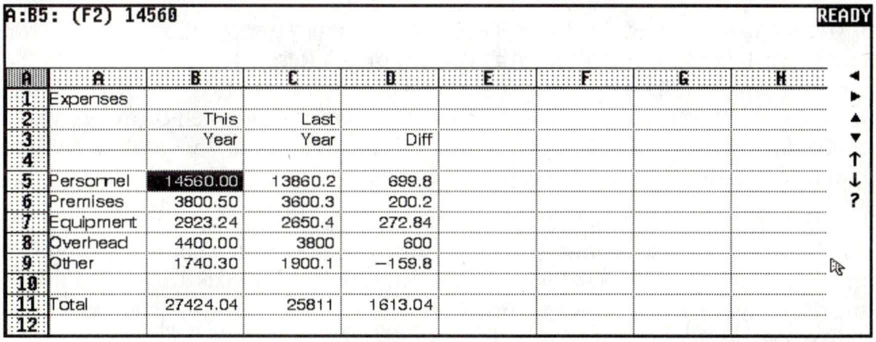

Fig. 5.8.
A range formatted as Fixed with 2 decimal places.

When you start a new worksheet, no cells have a range format. For example, in figure 5.7, no cells have a range format. In figure 5.8, only the cells in the range

Reminder:
When you start a new file, the global format is General.

Cue:
A range format overrides the global format.

B5..B11 have a range format. When a cell does not have a range format, the cell takes the format specified by /**W**orksheet **G**lobal **F**ormat.

When you start a new file, the global format is General. To change the global format, use /**W**orksheet **G**lobal **F**ormat (see fig. 5.9). Figure 5.10 shows the worksheet after changing to comma format with 2 decimal places. Notice that the format in B5..B11 did not change. These cells have a range format; the global format affects only the cells with no range format.

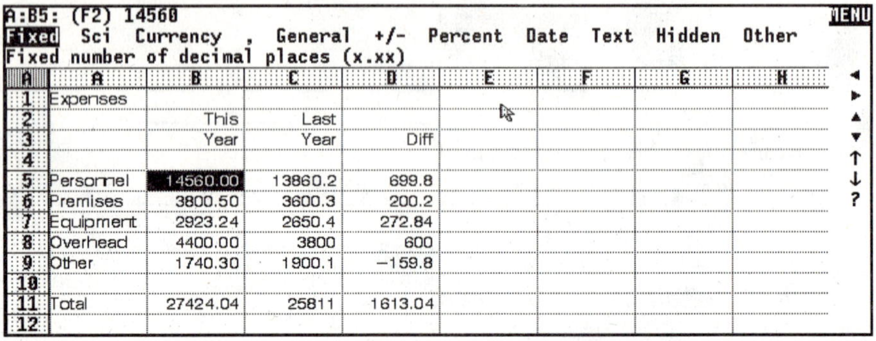

Fig. 5.9.
The /Worksheet Global Format menu.

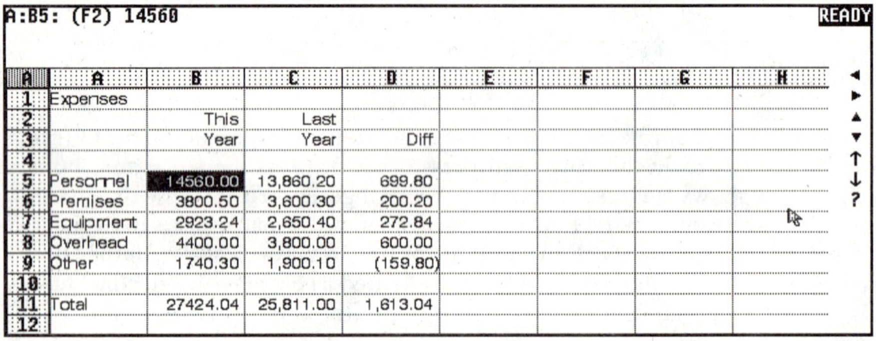

Fig. 5.10.
The worksheet with a global format of comma (,) with 2 decimal places.

If you want a cell or range that has a range format to have the global format, you can remove range formatting with /**R**ange **F**ormat **R**eset. Figure 5.11 shows the worksheet after a /**R**ange **F**ormat **R**eset operation in the range B5..B11. This range now displays with the global comma format. If you want a cell or range with a range format to have a different range format, execute the /**R**ange **F**ormat command again and choose a different format.

For the global format, select the format that you expect to use most in the worksheet. Then use /**R**ange **F**ormat to format ranges you want to display with other formats. Most worksheets look best if a variety of formats are used to match the data. Figure 5.11A shows a worksheet with a global comma format, as well as **C**urrency and **P**ercent range formats.

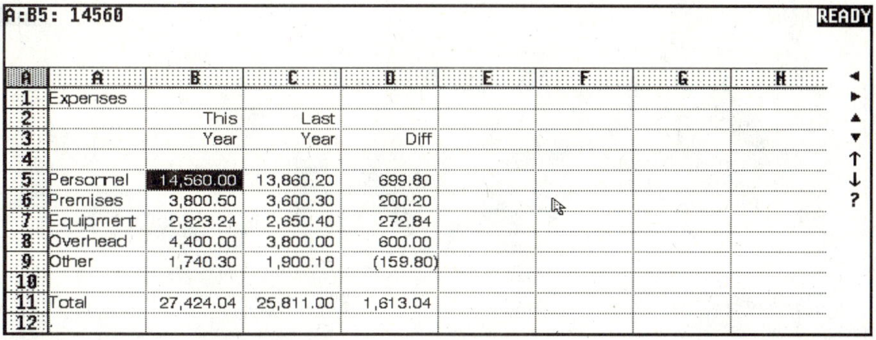

Chapter 5 ◆ Formatting Cell Contents   **169**

```
A:B5: 14560                                                    READY
```

	A	B	C	D	E	F	G	H
1	Expenses							
2		This	Last					
3		Year	Year	Diff				
4								
5	Personnel	14,560.00	13,860.20	699.80				
6	Premises	3,800.50	3,600.30	200.20				
7	Equipment	2,923.24	2,650.40	272.84				
8	Overhead	4,400.00	3,800.00	600.00				
9	Other	1,740.30	1,900.10	(159.80)				
10								
11	Total	27,424.04	25,811.00	1,613.04				
12								

Fig. 5.11.
The range B5..B11 takes on the default comma format with 2 decimals after using /Range Format Reset.

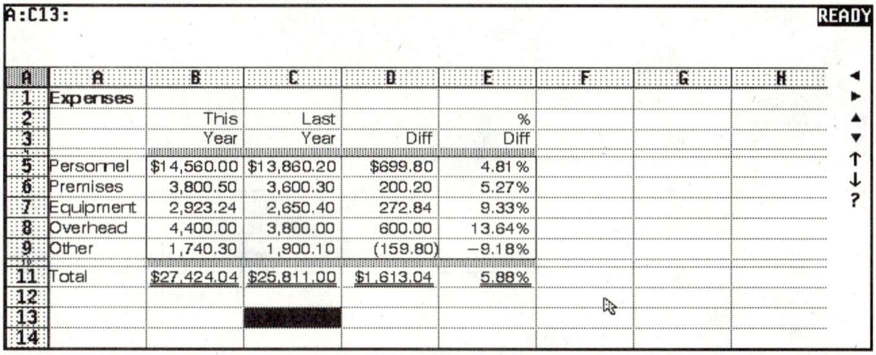

```
A:C13:                                                         READY
```

	A	B	C	D	E	F	G	H
1	Expenses							
2		This	Last		%			
3		Year	Year	Diff	Diff			
5	Personnel	$14,560.00	$13,860.20	$699.80	4.81%			
6	Premises	3,800.50	3,600.30	200.20	5.27%			
7	Equipment	2,923.24	2,650.40	272.84	9.33%			
8	Overhead	4,400.00	3,800.00	600.00	13.64%			
9	Other	1,740.30	1,900.10	(159.80)	−9.18%			
11	Total	$27,424.04	$25,811.00	$1,613.04	5.88%			
12								
13								
14								

Fig. 5.11A.
A worksheet with a global comma format, as well as Currency and Percent formats.

/Worksheet Global Format applies to the current worksheet. If you change /Worksheet Global Format in a file with multiple worksheets, you change only the current worksheet. If you want all the worksheets in the file to have the same global format, turn on GROUP mode with /Worksheet Global Group. If every worksheet in the file has the same layout, such as the file in figure 5.12, you use GROUP mode so that changes to one worksheet affect all worksheets. Notice that in figure 5.12, the **Global** format is changed to comma with 2 decimals. If each worksheet in the file has a different layout, such as situations in which separate worksheets are used for input areas, notes and assumptions, reports, and macros, you want GROUP mode off so that you can format each worksheet separately.

GROUP mode also affects the /Range Format and :Format commands. With GROUP mode enabled, if you format a range in one worksheet, the same range is formatted in all worksheets in the file. Figure 5.13 shows the effects of /Range Format Percent with 4 decimal places on the range A:E5..A:E11. Even though the range includes only worksheet A, the same range in the other worksheets also changes formats.

The following sections describe each 1-2-3 menu format in detail. Each format can be used with /Worksheet Global Format or /Range Format.

Reminder:
In GROUP mode, /Range Format applies to all worksheets in the file.

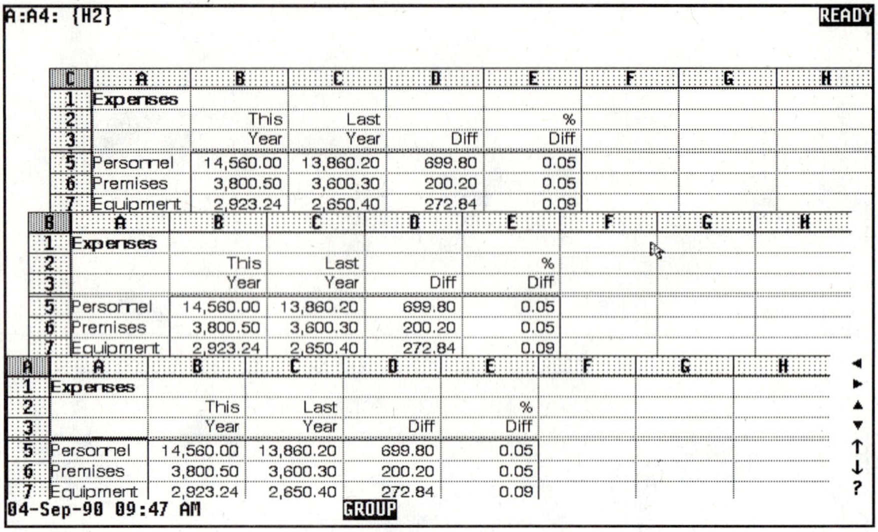

Fig. 5.12.
All worksheets with the same global format in GROUP mode.

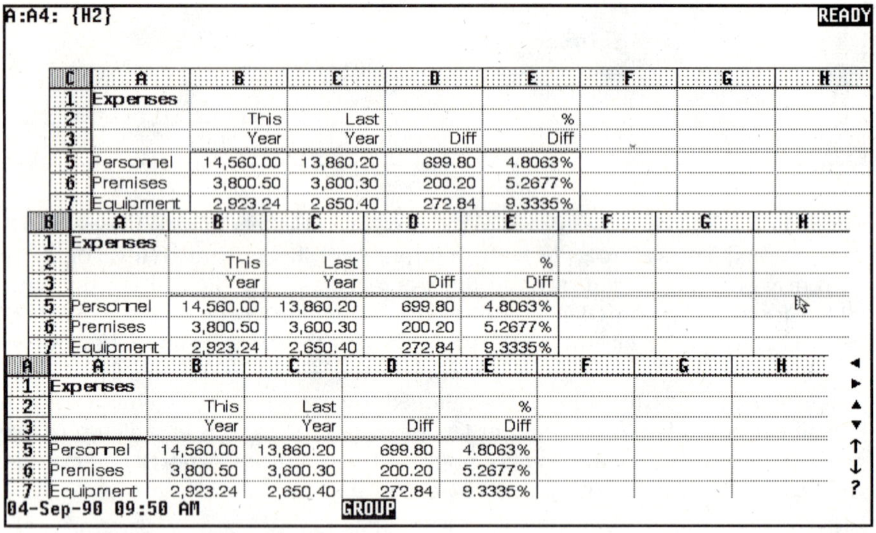

Fig. 5.13.
The same range in all worksheets range-formatted at the same time.

General Format

General format, the default for all new worksheets, displays only the number in cells containing values. If the number is negative, it is preceded by a minus sign. If the number contains decimal digits, it can contain a decimal point. If the number contains too many digits to the right of the decimal point to fit in the column width, the decimal portion is rounded. If the number is too large or small to display normally, it displays in Sci (scientific) format. 123400000 displays as `1.2E+08`, and 0.0000000012 displays as `1.2E-09`. Negative numbers in Sci (scientific) format display with a leading minus sign.

Following are several examples of General format in cells that have a column width of 9 and a :Format Font format of 12-point Times Roman:

Typed Entry	Cell Format	Display Result
123.46	(G)	123.46
–123.36	(G)	-123.36
1.2345678912	(G)	1.234568
150000000	(G)	1.5E+08
–.00000002638	(G)	-2.64E-08

(G) appears in the control panel of cells that have been formatted with /Range Format General.

Fixed Format

Use the Fixed format when you want a column of numbers to line up on the decimal point. 1-2-3 displays the fixed number of decimal places, from 0 to 15, that you specify. If the number has more decimal digits than the format you specify, the number is rounded on the display, but not in the value used for calculation.

Following are several examples of Fixed format in cells that have a column width of 9 and a :Format Font format of 12-point Times Roman:

Typed Entry	Cell Format	Display Result
123.46	(F0)	123
123.46	(F1)	123.5
–123.46	(F2)	-123.46
123.46	(F4)	123.4600
–123.46	(F4)	-123.4600
12345678	(F2)	***********

In all cases, the full number in the cell is used in calculations. Negative numbers display with a leading minus sign.

(F*n*) appears in the control panel of cells that have been formatted with /Range Format Fixed. *n* represents the number of decimal places.

Reminder:
When a cell is filled with asterisks, the contents of the cell are wider than the cell can display. Increase the column width by using /Worksheet Column Set-Width.

Comma Format

Like the Fixed format, the comma (,) format displays data with a fixed number of decimal places (from 0 to 15). In addition, comma format separates thousands, millions, etc., with commas. Positive numbers less than 1,000 display the same way in Fixed format and comma format. The comma format is used most often for financial data.

If the number has more decimal digits than the format you specify, the number is rounded on the display. The full value in the cell is used in calculations.

Use the comma format instead of Fixed format for large numbers. It is easier to read `12,300,000.00` than `12300000.00`. With comma format, negative numbers display in parentheses. –1234 displays as `(1,234)` with 0 decimal places.

You can change the setting so that negative numbers display with a leading minus sign by using **/Worksheet Global Default Other International Negative Sign**. –1234 then appears as `-1,234`. To return to parentheses for negative numbers, use **/Worksheet Global Default Other International Negative Parentheses**. This default applies to 1-2-3 as a whole, not to any one worksheet or file.

`(,n)` appears in the control panel of cells that have been formatted with **/Range Format , (comma)**. *n* represents the number of decimal places.

Following are several examples of comma (,) format in cells that have a column width of 9 and a **:Format Font** format of 12-point Times Roman:

Typed Entry	Cell Format	Display Result
123.46	(,0)	123
1234.6	(,2)	1,234.60
–1234.6	(,0)	(1,235)
		–1,235 (with a default negative sign)
–1234567	(,2)	************

Currency Format

Currency format works much like comma format but includes a leading dollar sign. Because of the dollar sign, you need an extra position in the column width to display a number in Currency format. Negative numbers are handled the same as with comma format.

The dollar sign, the default currency symbol, can be changed if you are using a different currency. Use **/Worksheet Global Default Other International Currency** to specify a different currency symbol and whether the symbol is a prefix or a suffix. This default applies to 1-2-3 as a whole, not to any one worksheet or file.

Caution:
If you change the currency symbol, the change affects all open files on your computer.

For example, suppose that you create a file using **Currency** format for U.S. dollars and save the file. You later create a file that uses the British pound (£). You can change the currency symbol to the British pound by issuing the **/Worksheet Global Default Other International Currency** command. When the prompt `Currency Symbol: $` appears, you delete the dollar sign and substitute the British pound sign by pressing Alt-F1 (Compose) and then typing **L=**. Then you press Enter or press the left mouse button and select **Prefix**. When you later retrieve another file, any cells formatted with **Currency** display the pound as the currency symbol.

(C*n*) appears in the control panel of cells formatted with /**R**ange **F**ormat **C**urrency. *n* represents the number of decimal places.

Following are several examples of **C**urrency format in cells that have a column width of 9 and a **:F**ormat **F**ont format of 12-point Times Roman:

Typed Entry	Cell Format	Display Result
123	(C2)	$123.00
		£123.00 (using the pound symbol as the default)
–123.124	(C2)	($123.12)
		–$123.12 (with a default negative sign)
1234.12	(C0)	$1,234
–123456.12	(C2)	************

Percent Format

Use the **P**ercent format to display percentages. You specify the number of decimal places from 0 to 15. The number displayed is the value of the cell multiplied by 100, followed by a percent sign. If the number has more decimal digits than the format you specify, the number is rounded on the display.

Note that the number of decimal places you specify is the number as a percent, not as a whole number. The number displays as multiplied by 100, but the value of the cell is unchanged. To display 50% in a cell, you type **.5** and format for **P**ercent. If you type **50** and format for **P**ercent with zero decimal places, 5000% displays.

Reminder: *Enter percentages as decimal fractions, not as whole numbers.*

(P*n*) appears in the control panel of cells formatted with /**R**ange **F**ormat **P**ercent. *n* represents the number of decimal places.

Following are several examples of **P**ercent format in cells that have a column width of 9 and a **:F**ormat **F**ont format of 12-point Times Roman:

Typed Entry	Cell Format	Display Result
.3	(P2)	30.00%
–.3528	(P2)	–35.28%
30	(P0)	3000%
30	(P4)	************

Scientific Format

Use **Sci** (scientific) format to display very large or very small numbers. Very large and very small numbers usually have a few significant digits and many zeroes as placeholders to tell you how large or how small the number is.

A number in scientific notation has two parts: a *mantissa* and an *exponent*. The mantissa is a number from 1 to 10 that contains the significant digits. The exponent tells you how many places to move the decimal point to get the actual value of the number. You specify the number of decimal places in the mantissa from 0 to 15. If the number has more significant digits than the format you specify, the number is rounded on the display.

1230000000000 displays as `1.23E+12` in scientific format with 2 decimal places. `E+12` signifies that you must move the decimal point 12 places to the right to get the actual number. 0.000000000237 displays as `2.4E-10` in scientific format with 1 decimal place. `E-10` means that you must move the decimal point 10 places to the left to get the actual number.

A number too large to display in a cell in **General** format displays in **Sci** (scientific) format.

(S*n*) appears in the control panel of cells formatted with **/Range Format Sci**. *n* represents the number of decimal places.

Following are several examples of Sci format in cells that have a column width of 9 and a **:Format Font** format of 12-point Times Roman:

Typed Entry	*Cell Format*	*Display Result*
1632116750000	(S2)	1.63E+12
1632116750000	(S0)	2E+12
–1632116750000	(S1)	-1.6E+12
–1632116750000	(S4)	************
–.00000000012	(S0)	-1E-10

The +/– Format

The **+/–** format creates a horizontal bar chart based on the number in the cell. A positive number appears as a row of plus signs; a negative number appears as a row of minus signs; and a zero (or any other number less than 1, but greater than –1) appears as a period. The number of pluses or minuses can be no wider than the cell.

This format was originally devised to create imitation bar charts in spreadsheets that had no graphing capability. The format has little use today.

(+) appears in the control panel of cells formatted with **/Range Format +/–**.

If you display cells with this format, and you are using **:Format Font** to change the appearance of cells, use a nonproportional font (such as Courier) for cells formatted with **/Range Format +/–**. Using a proportional font causes the minus signs to look like a solid bar on screen. Using the nonproportional font gives each minus sign its own position, distinguishing one minus sign from another.

Following are several examples of +/– format in cells that have a column width of 9 and a **:Format Font** format of 12-point Courier:

Typed Entry	Cell Format	Display Result
6	(+)	++++++
4.9	(+)	++++
–3	(+)	---
0	(+)	.
17.2	(+)	**********
.95	(+)	.

Date and Time Formats

All the formats mentioned so far deal with regular numeric values. Use **Date** and **Time** formats when you deal with date and time calculations or time functions. These functions are covered in Chapter 6.

Choose /**R**ange **F**ormat **D**ate or /**W**orksheet **G**lobal **F**ormat **D**ate for the five **D**ate format options, or to choose a **T**ime format. The menu for /**R**ange **F**ormat **D**ate or /**W**orksheet **G**lobal **F**ormat **D**ate is as follows:

1 (DD-MMM-YY) **2** (DD-MMM) **3** (MMM-YY) **4** (Long Intn'l) **5** (Short Intn'l) **T**ime

Choose /**R**ange **F**ormat **D**ate **T**ime or /**W**orksheet **G**lobal **F**ormat **D**ate **T**ime for the four **T**ime format options, which are as follows:

1 (HH:MM:SS AM/PM) **2** (HH:MM AM/PM) **3** (Long Intn'l) **4** (Short Intn'l)

Date Formats

When you use date functions, 1-2-3 stores the date as a serial number representing the number of days since January 1, 1900. The serial date number for January 1, 1900 is 1. The serial date number for January 15, 1991 is 33253. The latest date that 1-2-3 can handle is December 31, 2099, with a serial number of 73050. If the number is less than 1 or greater than 73050, a **D**ate format displays as asterisks; however, in Wysiwyg, the cell displays as blank. **D**ate formats ignore any fraction. 33253.99 with format D4 (long international) displays as 01/15/91. The fraction represents the time, a fractional portion of a 24-hour clock.

Don't be concerned about which serial date number refers to which date. Let 1-2-3 format the serial date number to appear as a textual date.

Actually, all the date serial numbers starting with March 1, 1900, are off by one day. The calendar inside 1-2-3 treats 1900 as a leap year; it is not. A date serial number of 60 displays as 02/29/00—a date that does not exist. Unless you compare dates before February 28, 1900, to dates after February 28, 1900, this error has no effect on your worksheets. However, dates can be off by one day if you export data to a database.

When you choose /**R**ange **F**ormat **D**ate, the **D**ate menu appears. Five **D**ate formats can format serial numbers to look like dates. Table 5.2 lists these formats. Long international and short international each have four different formats. The defaults

Caution:
Lotus 1-2-3 is one day off in serial-number calculations starting with March 1, 1900. This only has an effect, however, when comparing dates to those before March 1, 1900.

are those that are most common in the United States. If you prefer one of the other international **Date** formats, use **/W**orksheet **G**lobal **D**efault **O**ther **I**nternational **D**ate and choose from formats **A** through **D**.

**Table 5.2
Date Formats**

Menu Choice	Format	Description	Example
1	(D1)	Day-Month-Year DD-MMM-YY	15-Jan-91
2	(D2)	Day-Month DD-MMM	15-Jan
3	(D3)	Month-Year MMM-YY	Jan-91
4	(D4)	Long International*	
A		MM/DD/YY	01/15/91
B		DD/MM/YY	15/01/91
C		DD.MM.YY	15.01.91
D		YY-MM-DD	91-01-15
5	(D5)	Short International*	
A		MM/DD	01/15
B		DD/MM	15/01
C		DD.MM	15.01
D		MM-DD	01-15

*Use the **/W**orksheet **G**lobal **D**efault **O**ther **I**nternational **D**ate command to select one of the international formats (**A**, **B**, **C**, or **D**).

Cue:
Type an entry that looks like a date. 1-2-3 automatically converts it to a date serial number.

You can enter date serial numbers without using date functions. You simply type what looks like a date, and 1-2-3 converts it to a serial date number. This method is often the fastest way to enter dates. You can enter a date in either **Date 4** format, such as **1/15/91**, or **Date 1** format, such as **15-Jan-91**, and 1-2-3 converts the entry to the date serial number 33253. If you enter a date in **Date 2** format, such as **15-Jan**, 1-2-3 assumes that you want the current year. If the internal clock in the computer says it is 1991, **15-Jan** converts to 33253, the date serial number for January 15, 1991. If you type **15-Jan** during 1990, you get 32888, the date sequence number for January 15, 1990. If you meant the entry **1/15/91** to be the formula 1 divided by 15 divided by 91, however, you must enter the formula with a preceding value prefix: **+1/15/91**.

Cue:
*Format blank cells with **D**ate format before you enter dates.*

1-2-3 does not format the cell. For a number to display as a date, either the global format or the range format must be a **Date** format. You can use **/R**ange **F**ormat on the cell either before or after you enter the date in the cell. If you know that you will enter dates in certain cells, format the blank cells with a **Date** format. You won't see the date serial numbers in the cells, just the formatted dates.

Chapter 5 ♦ Formatting Cell Contents

You cannot enter dates as date serial numbers by using the other date formats. If you enter a date in **Date 3** format, such as **Jan-91**, 1-2-3 treats the entry as a label. If you enter a date in **Date 5** format, such as **1/15**, 1-2-3 treats it as a formula and converts it to a number, in this case `0.066667`. This operation can be confusing.

For example, suppose that a cell is formatted as **Date 4**. You type **1/15/91** and press Enter or press the left mouse button. 1-2-3 converts the entry to the serial date number `33253`.

`(Dn)` appears in the control panel of cells formatted with **/R**ange Format Date. *n* represents the Date format selection (**1–5**) in the Format Date menu.

Following are several examples of **Date** format in cells that have a column width of 9 and a **:**Format Font format of 12-point Times Roman:

Typed Entry	*Cell Format*	*Display Result*	*Cell Contents*
10/12/91	(D1)	************	33523
10/12/91	(D2)	12-Oct	33523
10/12/91	(D3)	Oct-91	33523
10/12/91	(D4)	10/12/91	33523
10/12/91	(D5)	10/12	33523
15	(D4)	01/15/00	15
33253	(D4)	01/15/91	33253
33253.4538	(D4)	01/15/91	33253.4538
–33253	any date	************	–33253
12-Oct-91	(D4)	10/12/91	33523
12-oct (during 1991)	(D4)	10/12/91	33523
Oct-91	any date	Oct-91	'Oct-91
10/12	any date	************	0.833333333333333333

Following are several examples of **Date 1** format in cells that have a column width of 10 and a **:**Format Font format of 12-point Times Roman (Date 1 format cannot display in a cell with a default column width of 9 and this font):

Typed Entry	*Cell Format*	*Display Result*	*Cell Contents*
10/12/91	(D1)	12-Oct-91	33523
12-Oct-91	(D1)	12-Oct-91	33523
12-oct (during 1991)	(D1)	12-Oct-91	33523

Time Formats

1-2-3 maintains times in a special format called *time fractions*. You can then format these time fractions so that they look like a time of the day.

Caution:
If you enter a date in **Date 5** *format, 1-2-3 treats it as a formula and converts it to a number.*

Cue:
Date 1 format cannot display in a cell with the default column width of 9.

When you enter a time function, 1-2-3 stores the time as a decimal fraction from 0 to 1 that represents the fraction of the 24-hour clock. The time fraction for 3 a.m. is 0.125; the time fraction for noon is 0.5; and the time fraction for 6 p.m. is 0.75. You can ignore the actual fractions and let 1-2-3 display the fraction as a time.

When you choose /**Range Format Date Time**, the **Time** menu appears. 1-2-3 includes four **Time** formats that display fractions as times. Table 5.3 lists these formats. Long international and short international each have four different formats. The defaults are those most common in the United States. If you prefer one of the other international time formats, use /**Worksheet Global Default Other International Time** and choose from the formats **A–D**, which represent the four choices.

Cue:
Type an entry that looks like a time, and 1-2-3 automatically converts it to a time fraction.

You can enter a time fraction without using time functions. To do so you type what looks like a time, and 1-2-3 converts it to a time fraction. You can enter a time in any **Time** format. You can use regular time (AM/PM) or 24-hour military time. Seconds are optional.

If you enter **6:23, 6:23:00, 6:23AM**, or **6:23:00 am**, 1-2-3 converts the entry to the time fraction `0.265972`. (Actually, 1-2-3 stores fractions with up to 19 significant digits but 6–8 are shown in these examples.) If you enter **6:23:57** or **6:23:57 AM**, 1-2-3 converts the entry to the time fraction 0.266632. If you enter **6:23 pm** or **18:23**, 1-2-3 converts the entry to the time fraction 0.765972.

You do not have to type **AM** for times before noon. For times after noon, type **PM** or type the hour from 12 to 23. The AM or PM can be in uppercase or lowercase and can follow a space after the time.

Table 5.3
Time Formats

Menu Choice	Format	Description	Example
1	(D6)	Hour:Minute:Second HH:MM:SS AM/PM	06:23:57 PM
2	(D7)	Hour:Minute HH:MM AM/PM	06:23 PM
3	(D8)	Long International*	
A		HH:MM:SS	18:23:57
B		HH.MM.SS	18.23.57
C		HH,MM,SS	18,23,57
D		HHhMMmSSs	18h23m57s
4	(D9)	Short International*	
A		HH:MM	18:23
B		HH.MM	18.23
C		HH,MM	18,23
D		HHhMMm	18h23m

* Use the /**Worksheet Global Default Other International Time** command to select one of the international formats (**A**, **B**, **C**, or **D**).

Chapter 5 ◆ Formatting Cell Contents

1-2-3 does not format the cell. For a number to display as a time, either the global format or the range format must be a **Time** format. You can use **/Range Format** on the cell either before or after you enter the time in the cell. However, if you enter the time into a cell with **General** format, the time fraction can be confusing. If you know that you will enter times in certain cells, format the blank cells with a **Time** format. You won't see the time fractions in the cells, just the formatted times.

Cue:
*Format blank cells with a **Time** format before you enter times.*

If the number is greater than 1, **Time** formats ignore the integer portion; 33253.75 with format D7 (**Time 2** or Lotus standard short form) displays as `06:00 PM`. Negative numbers represent the fraction of a day before midnight; –0.75 (or –33253.75) is the same as 0.25 and displays as `06:00 AM`. The time –0.125 is the same as 0.875 and displays as `9:00 PM`.

(D*n*) appears in the control panel of cells range-formatted with **/Range Format Date Time**. *n* represents the **Time** format selection (6–9).

1-2-3 identifies **Time** formats in a confusing way. If you choose **Date Time 1**, 1-2-3 displays (D6) in the control panel, not (T1). **Date Time 2** displays (D7), **Date Time 3** displays (D8), and **Date Time 4** displays (D9).

Following are several examples of **Time** format in cells that have a column width of 9 and a **:Format Font** format of 12-point Times Roman:

Typed Entry	Cell Format	Display Result	Cell Contents
6:23 AM	(D6)	************	0.265972
6:23 AM	(D7)	06:23 AM	0.265972
6:23	(D8)	06:23:00	0.265972
6:23	(D9)	06:23	0.265972
6:23:57	(D7)	06:23 AM	0.266632
6:23:57	(D8)	06:23:57	0.266632
6:23 pm	(D7)	06:23 PM	0.765972
6:23:57 pm	(D8)	18:23:57	0.766632
18:23	(D7)	06:23 PM	0.765972
2	(D7)	12:00 AM	2
–.25	(D7)	06:00 PM	–.25

Following are several examples of **Time 1** (D6) format in cells that have a column width of 12 and a **:Format Font** format of 12-point Times Roman (**Time 1** format cannot display in a cell with the default column width of 9 and this font):

Cue:
Time 1 format cannot display in a cell with the default column width of 9; a column width of 12 is required.

Typed Entry	Cell Format	Display Result	Cell Contents
6:23	(D6)	06:23:00 AM	0.265972
6:23:57	(D6)	06:23:57 AM	0.266632
18:23:57	(D6)	06:23:57 PM	0.766632

Text Format

Use the **Text** format to display in a cell both numeric and string formulas instead of their current values. Numbers formatted for **Text** display in the **General** format. If the formula being displayed in **Text** Format is too long to display in the column width, it is truncated, or shortened; it does not display across blank cells to the right like a long label. If you attach a note to the number or formula in a cell, the note displays if the column is wide enough.

The entries in figure 5.14 are formatted as **Text**. The labels are unaffected. The numbers in B3..B4 display in **General** format. The number in B5 has a note attached and displays with the note left-aligned. The formula and note in B7 display instead of the current value of the formula.

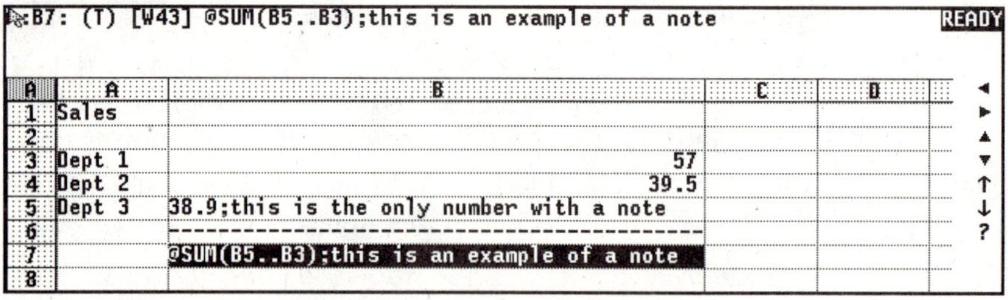

Fig. 5.14.
Samples of Text format.

```
B7: (T) [W43] @SUM(B5..B3);this is an example of a note           READY

         A                      B                    C         D
  1  Sales
  2
  3  Dept 1                                 57
  4  Dept 2                               39.5
  5  Dept 3    38.9;this is the only number with a note
  6  -----------------------------------------------
  7            @SUM(B5..B3);this is an example of a note
  8
```

One use of the **Text** format is for criteria ranges with **/D**ata **Q**uery commands, which are covered in Chapter 12. You can also use **Text** format when you enter or debug complex formulas, or to see formulas with **/D**ata **T**able. You can temporarily change the format of a formula to text so that you can see the formula in one cell as you build a similar formula in another cell. You may need to widen the column temporarily as you do this.

(T) appears in the control panel of cells formatted with **/R**ange **F**ormat **T**ext.

Hidden Format

A cell formatted as **Hidden** displays as blank no matter what the cell contains. Use this format for intermediate calculations that you don't want to display, or to hide sensitive formulas. The contents of a hidden cell do not display in the control panel when you move the cell pointer to that cell if the cell is protected and global protection is enabled. In other cases, you can see the contents of the cell in the control panel. **Hidden** format is also discussed in Chapter 4.

You cannot use **Hidden** format to completely hide data unless the file contains no unprotected cells. If you can change the format or the protection status, you can see the contents of the cell. If the file is not sealed (see Chapter 4), you can use **/R**ange **F**ormat to change the format, and the contents of the cell then become visible.

If the file is sealed, you cannot change the format or the protection status, but you can use a formula in any unprotected cell to determine the value in the hidden cell.

Chapter 5 ◆ Formatting Cell Contents   **181**

The worksheet in figure 5.15 has global protection enabled; the file is sealed with **/File Admin Seal File**. **/Range Prot** and **/Range Format Hidden** have been used on cell A1. The range C1..C5 is unprotected. The formula in C1 is +A1. This simple formula shows you the value of the hidden cell.

```
A:C1: U +A1                                                    READY
     A        B        C        D        E        F        G        H
1                    409.7721
2
3                    {contents C5,A1,25,117}
4
5                    @SUM(M1..M15)*1.47469
6
7
```

Fig. 5.13.
The appearance of the worksheet changed by use of Hidden format. Sensitive data or formulas remain open.

To determine the formula in A1, you need a macro. The CONTENTS macro in C3 puts the contents of A1 into C5 in **Text** format. See Chapter 13 for more about the CONTENTS command.

(H) appears in the control panel of cells formatted with **/Range Format Hidden**.

Label Format

Use **/Range Format Other Label** to assign the **Label** format. Use this format on blank cells to make it easier to enter labels. With this format, all entries are considered labels, and 1-2-3 precedes the entry with the default label prefix. This step makes it easier to enter labels that look like numbers, or formulas that begin with a numeric character.

As an example, suppose that you typed **57 Main Street** and pressed Enter. 1-2-3 considers the entry an invalid numeric entry and puts you in EDIT mode. You must manually type the label prefix.

In the next example, suppose that you typed **10/15** and pressed Enter. 1-2-3 considers **10/15** a formula, converts it to a number, and displays 0.666667. To make this entry a label, you must reenter the label with a label prefix. In both cases, if you format the range as **Label** before you type the entry, 1-2-3 precedes the entry with a label prefix, and the entry becomes a text label. If you change existing numeric entries to **Label** format, they do not become labels; the number displays in **General** format. The **Label** format has no effect on existing labels.

Cue:
Use the Label format before you type a series of numbers or addresses you want as labels.

(L) appears in the control panel of cells formatted **/Range Format Other Label**.

Automatic Format

Use **/Range Format Other Automatic** to assign the **Automatic** format. When you enter data into a cell with an **Automatic** format, 1-2-3 analyzes the format of the data and selects a format. Table 5.4 lists examples of **Automatic** formatting.

In table 5.4, the first column lists the data that you type into a cell formatted Automatic. When you complete the entry, 1-2-3 analyzes the data and stores it in the cell with the format shown in the second column. This format is what you would see in the control panel. The third and fourth columns show how 1-2-3 stores the data (to 10 places) and how the data displays in the worksheet. (This table assumes a column width of 10.)

Once you enter a number into a cell and 1-2-3 applies an Automatic format, this format stays with the cell. Use /Range Format to change the format after having used Automatic. Automatic format only works for the first item entered after formatting. The format does not change when a number with a different format is entered.

Table 5.4
Automatic Formatting Examples

Data Entered	Data Format	Stored Data	Data Displayed
57 Main	(L)	'57 Main	57 Main
@SUM(xxxx	(L)	'@SUM(xxxx	@SUM(xxxx
258	(F0)	258	258
258.46	(F2)	258.46	258.46
258.00	(F2)	258	258.00
1,258	(,0)	1258	1,258
1,258.69	(,2)	1258.69	1,258.69
0,087.00	(,2)	87	87.00
$258.00	(C2)	258	$258.00
25%	(P0)	0.25	25%
2.50%	(P2)	0.025	2.50%
1.2E4	(S1)	12000	1.2E+04
2.587E–16	(S3)	2.587E–16	2.587E–16
25.87E–17	(S2)	2.587E–16	2.59E–16
15-jan-91	(D1)	33253	15-Jan-91
15-jan	(D2)	33253*	15-Jan
jan-91	(L)	'jan-91	jan-91
1/15/91	(D4)	33253	01/15/91
10/15	(A)	0.6666666667	0.6666667
6:23:57 am	(D6)	0.2666319444	06:23:57 AM
6:23:57	(D8)	0.2666319444	06:23:57
6:23:57 pm	(D6)	0.7666319444	06:23:57 PM
6:23 am	(D7)	0.2659722222	06:23 AM
6:23	(D9)	0.2659722222	06:23
6:23 PM	(D7)	0.7659722222	06:23 PM
18:23:57	(D8)	0.7666319444	018:23:57
18:23	(D9)	0.7659722222	18:23

*If the current year is 1991

Chapter 5 ◆ Formatting Cell Contents

1-2-3 normally treats an invalid entry as just that—an invalid entry. Consider these entries: **57 Main Street; @SUM(ABCD**. When you type one of these entries and press Enter, 1-2-3 changes to Edit mode, and enables you to correct the entry. With Automatic formatting, however, 1-2-3 precedes the entry with a label prefix and considers it a label.

If you type a number containing decimal places, 1-2-3 formats it with the same amount of decimal places. If you use no other formatting characters, 1-2-3 uses the Fixed format. If you type **123.4**, 1-2-3 makes the format Fixed with **1** decimal place (F1). If you type **123.40**, 1-2-3 drops the last zero in the control panel but makes the format Fixed with **2** decimal places (F2).

If you precede the number with a dollar sign (or other one-character currency symbol specified with /Worksheet Global Default Other International Currency), 1-2-3 formats the cell as Currency. If you type a number with commas, 1-2-3 drops the commas but formats the cell with comma format. If you follow the number with a percent sign (%), 1-2-3 drops the percent sign, divides the number by 100, and formats the cell with Percent format. (Ordinarily, if you enter a number with a percent sign, 1-2-3 divides the number by 100 and enters the result in the cell.)

If the number looks like one of the long Date or Time formats, 1-2-3 uses that Date format. 1-2-3 does not recognize the short Date formats D3: MMM-YY or D5: MM/DD (see table 5.2).

If you enter a formula into a cell, the format stays Automatic. If you enter a number into the cell later, 1-2-3 applies a format. If the cell contains a numeric formula and you convert it to a number with Edit (F2), 1-2-3 applies a format at that time.

Cue:
Use the Automatic format before you make cell entries.

(A) appears in the control panel of cells formatted with /Range Format Other Automatic. When you first make an entry into the cell, the format changes to match the entry's format.

Parentheses Format

Use the **Parentheses** format to enclose numbers in parentheses. In certain situations, you want a number to appear in parentheses, but you do not want to enter it as a negative number. In these cases, use /Range Format Other Parentheses Yes. You can combine this format with the other formats. Use /Range Format Other Parentheses No to remove the parentheses.

/Worksheet Global Format Other Parentheses Yes results in parentheses around all numbers in the default format only. The command does not affect numbers with range formats or labels. Use /Worksheet Global Format Other Parentheses No to remove the parentheses from all numeric cells with the default format.

Part I ◆ Building the 1-2-3 Worksheet

This format can be confusing, so use it with care. For example, 456 displays as (456). If you apply this format to a negative number, the number still shows as negative. In General format, –1234 displays as(–1234). In comma format with 2 decimal places, –1234 displays as ((1,234.00)). The double set of parentheses is confusing.

(()) appears in the control panel of cells formatted with /Range Format Other Parentheses, in addition to any other format indicators.

Color Format

Cue:
Display negative numbers in color if you want them to stand out.

Use /Range Format Other Color Negative to display negative numbers in color on a color monitor, or in boldface with a monochrome monitor. This method is a handy way to make negative numbers stand out. The minus sign or parentheses displays also. As with all formatting options, you can use this option on the entire worksheet or on a range only.

Use /Range Format Other Color Reset to turn off the color display of negative numbers.

(–) appears in the control panel of cells formatted with /Range Format Other Color Negative, in addition to any other format indicators.

International Formats

You can change some Date and Time formats and the characters 1-2-3 uses for currency, the decimal point, and the thousands separator. Because different countries have different formatting standards, these are called *international formatting options*. If you work with U.S. dollars in the United States, you can stay with the defaults and ignore these options. Use the /Worksheet Global Default Other International command to access the menu to change the defaults as shown:

Punctuation Currency Date Time Negative Release-2 File-Translation Quit

Then use /Worksheet Global Default Update to make the change permanent.

Choose Date and Time to change the international Date and Time formats. The format options are listed in tables 5.2 and 5.3. Choose Currency to change the currency symbol from the dollar sign ($) to another symbol and specify whether it is a prefix or suffix. You can use multiple characters and special Lotus Multibyte Character Set (LMBCS) characters. (For more on LMBCS characters, see Chapter 6 and Appendix E.)

Choose Punctuation to change the characters used for the decimal point, the argument separator, and the thousands separator. Eight different combinations are available. Choose Negative to specify the way to show negative numbers in comma and Currency formats. The default is Parentheses, but you can change it to a minus sign.

Changing Label Prefixes

Most formats on the 1-2-3 menu apply to numeric data. Almost all numeric data formats have one thing in common; the numbers display right-aligned in the cell. With labels, however, you can align the text in different ways. Label alignment is based on the label prefix. The label prefixes include the following:

Prefix	Alignment
'	left-aligned
"	right-aligned
^	center-aligned
\	repeating
|	nonprinting

Labels and label prefixes are covered in Chapter 3. If you want a repeating or nonprinting label, you must type the label prefix. If you type a label with another prefix and you want to change it to repeating or nonprinting, you must edit the cell, delete the old prefix, and type the new one.

You can, however, change the label alignment of a cell or range to left, right, or center with the /**R**ange **L**abel command or **:T**ext **A**lign command (covered later in this chapter). You can also change the default label prefix that 1-2-3 inserts when you enter a label and do not type a prefix.

When you enter a label without a label prefix, 1-2-3 automatically enters the default label prefix. With a new worksheet file, the default is left-aligned ('). You can change this default by using /**W**orksheet **G**lobal **L**abel. Changing the default has no effect on existing labels. This method is different from the way 1-2-3 handles formats. When you change the global format, you change all cells that have not been range-formatted.

To change the label prefix of existing labels, use /**R**ange **L**abel. Choose **L**eft, **R**ight, or **C**enter, and then specify the range. These steps are usually faster than typing individual label prefixes as you enter labels.

Figure 5.16 shows left-aligned column headings that do not line up with the data. Figure 5.17 shows the headings after /**R**ange **L**abel **R**ight is selected. Right-alignment starts one position from the extreme right edge of the column. Right-aligned labels match the alignment of numeric data.

When you work with a multiple-worksheet file, GROUP mode affects the /**R**ange **L**abel and **:T**ext **A**lign commands. With GROUP mode enabled, if you use /**R**ange **L**abel or **:T**ext **A**lign to change the label prefix in a range in one worksheet, the label prefix changes in the same range in all worksheets in the file.

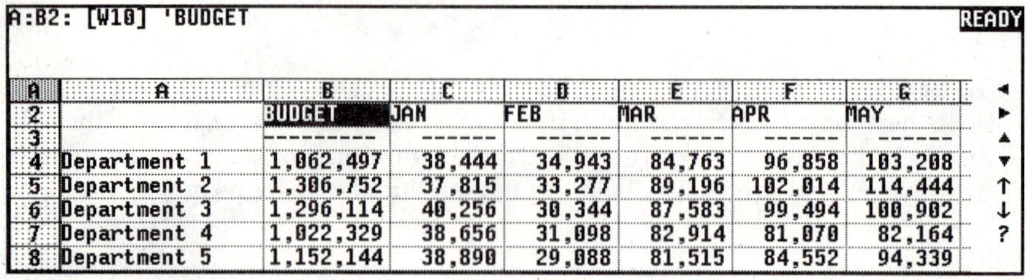

Fig. 5.16.

Left-aligned column headings that do not line up with numeric data.

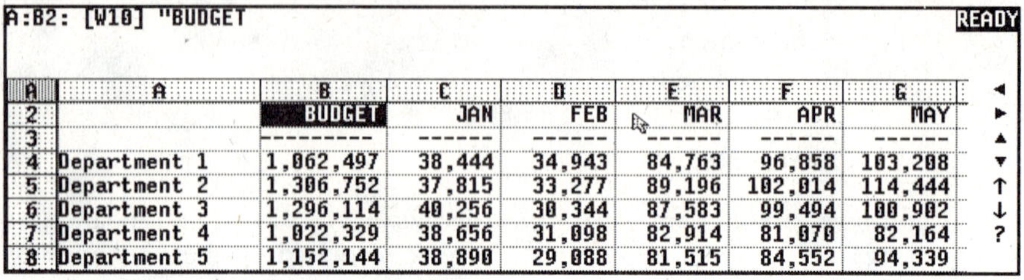

```
A:B2: [W10] 'BUDGET                                              READY
     A             B         C         D         E         F         G
2              BUDGET     JAN       FEB       MAR       APR       MAY
3              ------    ------    ------    ------    ------    ------
4  Department 1  1,062,497  38,444    34,943    84,763    96,858   103,208
5  Department 2  1,306,752  37,815    33,277    89,196   102,014   114,444
6  Department 3  1,296,114  40,256    30,344    87,583    99,494   100,902
7  Department 4  1,022,329  38,656    31,098    82,914    81,070    82,164
8  Department 5  1,152,144  38,890    29,088    81,515    84,552    94,339
```

Fig. 5.17.

Headings aligned after /Range Label Right is executed.

```
A:B2: [W10] "BUDGET                                              READY
     A             B         C         D         E         F         G
2              BUDGET       JAN       FEB       MAR       APR       MAY
3              ------    ------    ------    ------    ------    ------
4  Department 1  1,062,497  38,444    34,943    84,763    96,858   103,208
5  Department 2  1,306,752  37,815    33,277    89,196   102,014   114,444
6  Department 3  1,296,114  40,256    30,344    87,583    99,494   100,902
7  Department 4  1,022,329  38,656    31,098    82,914    81,070    82,164
8  Department 5  1,152,144  38,890    29,088    81,515    84,552    94,339
```

Justifying Text

At times, you want to include in a worksheet several lines, or even a paragraph, that explain a table, graph, or report. 1-2-3 includes word wrap features like word processing software if you use the **:Text Edit** command from the Wysiwyg menu (covered later in this chapter). Otherwise, everything you type goes into one cell until you press Enter or the left mouse button. You can type one line of text into each cell, but entering and editing paragraphs in this way is slow and imprecise. You may get something like the ragged text in figure 5.18; some of it is off the screen.

One way to justify labels is to use the **/Range Justify** command from the 1-2-3 menu; another way is to use the **:Text Reformat** command from the Wysiwyg menu (covered later in this chapter).

You can type text into one cell or multiple cells down a column as in figure 5.19 and use **/Range Justify** to arrange it. At the `Enter justify range:` prompt, highlight the rows that contain the labels and include any additional rows for the labels to expand into. Highlight across the columns to show how wide each label can be. When you press Enter or the left mouse button, 1-2-3 rearranges the text to fit the area you highlighted (see fig. 5.19). Labels are wrapped only at spaces. Where 1-2-3 breaks a label, it eliminates the space. Where 1-2-3 combines all or parts of two labels into one label, it adds a space.

If you add more text, use **/Range Justify** again to rejustify the text. If you specify a one-row range, 1-2-3 justifies the entire "paragraph." Figure 5.20 shows the data in figure 5.19 after you use **/Range Justify** on the range A1..F1. This practice, however, is very dangerous. 1-2-3 justifies the labels and uses as many rows as it needs, but it moves any data in Column A down to make room. If fewer rows are needed, it moves any data in Column A up. In figure 5.20, the department numbers no longer line up with each department's data.

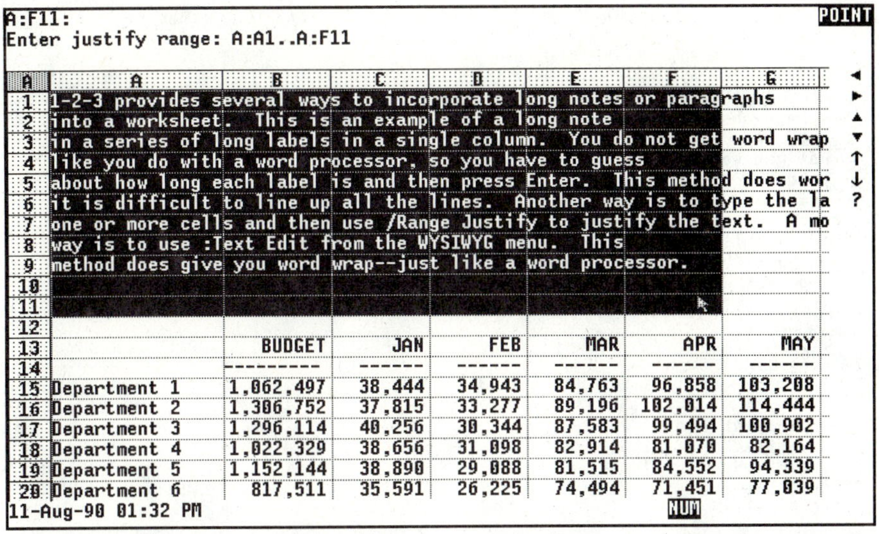

Chapter 5 ◆ Formatting Cell Contents

Fig. 5.18.
A column of long labels for a note is difficult to line up correctly.

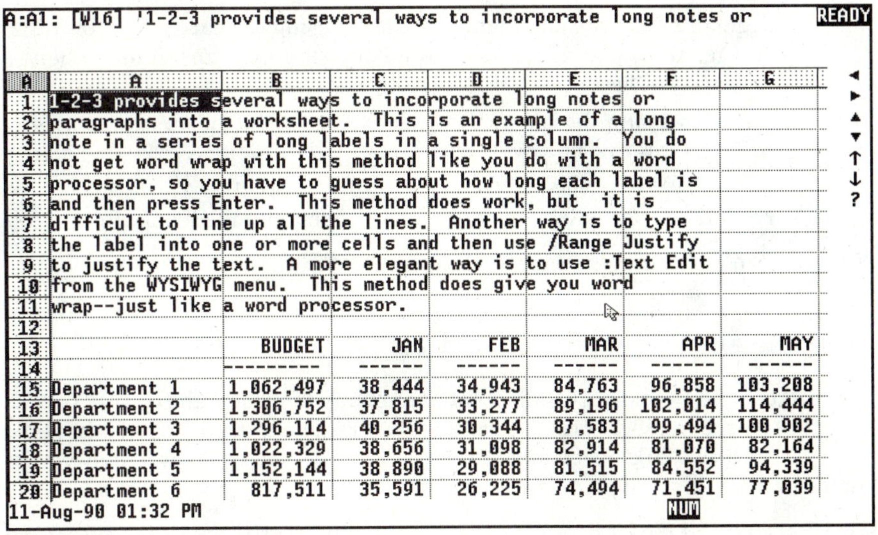

Fig. 5.19.
A series of long labels after a /Range Justify operation.

You cannot justify more than one column of labels at one time. When 1-2-3 reaches a blank or numeric cell in the first column, it stops. The labels must all be in the first column of the highlighted range. In figure 5.20, all the labels are in column A. Any labels in column B would be ignored.

Caution:
Don't use /Range Justify with a one-row range if data is present below the labels.

Follow these steps to justify labels with /**R**ange **J**ustify:

1. Move the cell pointer to the first cell in the range of text by using either the cursor keys or mouse.

2. Choose /**R**ange **J**ustify.

Fig. 5.20.

A one-row /Range Justify operation that pushes down the data below it (in column A).

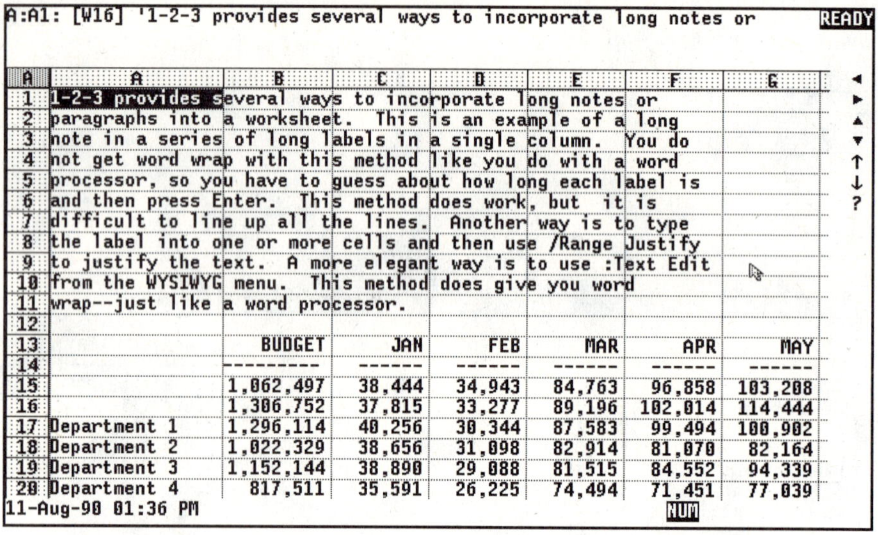

```
A:A1: [W16] '1-2-3 provides several ways to incorporate long notes or         READY

        A              B          C          D          E          F          G
 1  1-2-3 provides several ways to incorporate long notes or
 2  paragraphs into a worksheet.  This is an example of a long
 3  note in a series of long labels in a single column.  You do
 4  not get word wrap with this method like you do with a word
 5  processor, so you have to guess about how long each label is
 6  and then press Enter.  This method does work, but it is
 7  difficult to line up all the lines.  Another way is to type
 8  the label into one or more cells and then use /Range Justify
 9  to justify the text.  A more elegant way is to use :Text Edit
10  from the WYSIWYG menu.  This method does give you word
11  wrap--just like a word processor.
12
13                   BUDGET       JAN        FEB        MAR        APR        MAY
14                   ------      ------     ------     ------     ------     ------
15                  1,062,497   38,444     34,943     84,763     96,858    103,208
16                  1,306,752   37,815     33,277     89,196    102,014    114,444
17  Department 1    1,296,114   40,256     30,344     87,583     99,494    100,902
18  Department 2    1,022,329   38,656     31,098     82,914     81,070     82,164
19  Department 3    1,152,144   38,890     29,088     81,515     84,552     94,339
20  Department 4      817,511   35,591     26,225     74,494     71,451     77,039
11-Aug-90 01:36 PM                                                            NUM
```

3. Highlight the rows that contain labels by using the cursor keys or the mouse; allow enough extra rows for the labels to expand into when they are justified.

4. Again, by using the cursor keys or mouse, highlight the number of columns to show how wide each label can be. In figure 5.20, the text displays from Columns A–F.

5. Press Enter or the left mouse button to complete the justification.

You also can perform steps 3 and 4 in reverse order.

Suppressing the Display of Zeros

You can use the /Worksheet Global Zero command to change the display of cells that contain the number zero or formulas that evaluate to zero. To hide the zeros completely, use /Worksheet Global Zero Yes. The zero cells display as if they were blank.

This feature can be useful with worksheets in which zeros represent missing or meaningless information. Making these cells appear blank can improve the appearance of the worksheet. However, it can also cause confusion if you or other users are not sure if the cell is blank because you forgot to enter the data.

You can also display a label of your choice instead of the zero or blank. Use /Worksheet Global Zero Label and type the label you want to display instead of the zero. Common labels are none, zero, and N A (not available). Figure 5.21 is a worksheet with the /Worksheet Global Zero Label set to display none.

Use /Worksheet Global Zero No to cancel the option and display zeros as zeros.

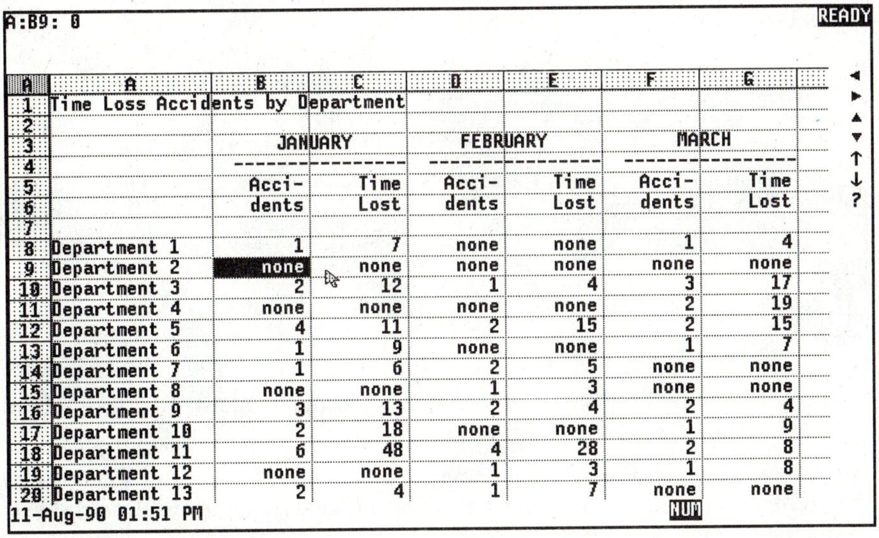

A:B9: 0 READY

	A	B	C	D	E	F	G
1	Time Loss Accidents by Department						
2							
3		JANUARY		FEBRUARY		MARCH	
4		-------	-------	-------	-------	-------	-------
5		Acci-	Time	Acci-	Time	Acci-	Time
6		dents	Lost	dents	Lost	dents	Lost
7							
8	Department 1	1	7	none	none	1	4
9	Department 2	none	none	none	none	none	none
10	Department 3	2	12	1	4	3	17
11	Department 4	none	none	none	none	2	19
12	Department 5	4	11	2	15	2	15
13	Department 6	1	9	none	none	1	7
14	Department 7	1	6	2	5	none	none
15	Department 8	none	none	1	3	none	none
16	Department 9	3	13	2	4	2	4
17	Department 10	2	18	none	none	1	9
18	Department 11	6	48	4	28	2	8
19	Department 12	none	none	1	3	1	8
20	Department 13	2	4	1	7	none	none

11-Aug-90 01:51 PM NUM

Fig. 5.21.
A worksheet with zero values set to display as none.

When you work with a multiple-worksheet file, GROUP mode affects the /**W**orksheet **G**lobal **Z**ero command. With GROUP mode disabled, the command affects only the current worksheet. With GROUP mode enabled, the command affects all worksheets in the file.

Using the :Format Commands of the Wysiwyg Menu

You change the format of a cell or range of cells with the **:F**ormat command of the Wysiwyg menu. The commands on the **:F**ormat menu are as follows:

Font **B**old **I**talics **U**nderline **C**olor **L**ines **S**hade **R**eset **Q**uit

Cue:
The :Format commands affect the way data is presented on the display and on printed reports.

You then pick one of the formats from the menu. These format commands affect the way data is presented on the display and on printed reports. If you choose **B**old or **I**talics, you get two choices: **S**et and **C**lear. You choose **S**et to add bold or italics to a range. When prompted for a range to format, highlight the range and press Enter or the left mouse button. You choose **C**lear to remove the format from a range. When prompted for a range to clear, highlight the range and press Enter or the left mouse button. The **F**ont, **U**nderline, **C**olor, **L**ines and **S**hade formats have additional menus that are covered later in this chapter. The **R**eset command removes all formatting from a range and restores the default font.

The name or an abbreviation of the format appears in the control panel when the current cell has a format. One cell can contain several formats. In figure 5.22, {Bold Italic U1} displayed in the control panel indicates that cell A1 has been formatted as **B**old, **I**talics and **U**nderline **S**ingle. If the cell has no format, no format indicator appears in the control panel.

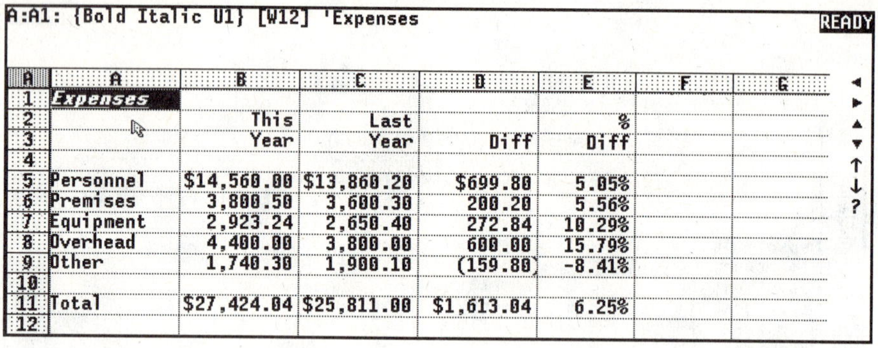

Part I ◆ Building the 1-2-3 Worksheet

Fig. 5.22.
Cell A1's multiple formats are shown in the control panel.

```
A:A1: {Bold Italic U1} [W12] 'Expenses                              READY
         A        B         C         D         E        F       G
 1  Expenses
 2                This     Last                 %
 3                Year     Year       Diff      Diff
 4
 5  Personnel  $14,560.00 $13,860.20  $699.80   5.05%
 6  Premises    3,800.50   3,600.30   200.20    5.56%
 7  Equipment   2,923.24   2,650.40   272.84   10.29%
 8  Overhead    4,400.00   3,800.00   600.00   15.79%
 9  Other       1,740.30   1,900.10  (159.80)  -8.41%
10
11  Total     $27,424.04 $25,811.00 $1,613.04   6.25%
12
```

When you start a new file, none of the cells has a format. When a cell does not have a format, it displays in the default font.

GROUP mode affects the **:Format** command. With GROUP mode enabled, when you format a range in one worksheet, the same range is formatted in all worksheets in the file.

The following sections describe each format in detail.

Font Formats

Use the **Font** formats to change the typeface and size of text and numbers that appear on the display. When you choose Font, the names of eight fonts appear on the screen similar to that shown in figure 5.23. Each font is given a number. You choose a font by selecting its corresponding number from the Font menu. After you select a number, you are prompted to highlight a range, as shown in figure 5.24. The result of formatting range A:A2..A:E11 with the Bitstream Dutch 12-Point font is shown in figure 5.25.

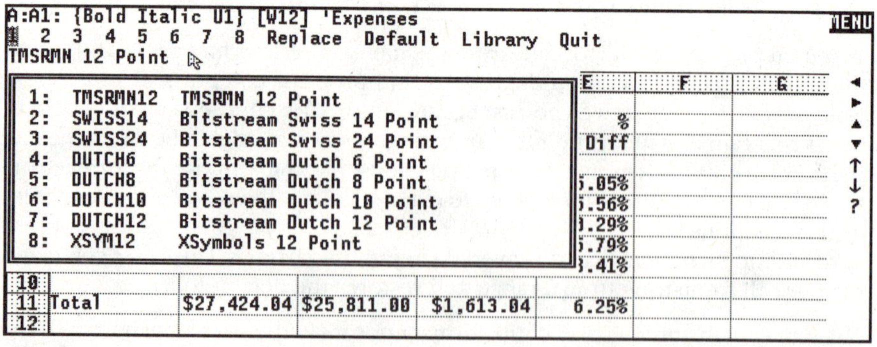

Fig. 5.23.
Font names displayed with the :Format Font command.

```
A:A1: {Bold Italic U1} [W12] 'Expenses                              MENU
  1  2  3  4  5  6  7  8  Replace  Default  Library  Quit
TMSRMN 12 Point
                                                  E       F       G
  1:  TMSRMN12   TMSRMN 12 Point
  2:  SWISS14    Bitstream Swiss 14 Point                %
  3:  SWISS24    Bitstream Swiss 24 Point               Diff
  4:  DUTCH6     Bitstream Dutch 6 Point
  5:  DUTCH8     Bitstream Dutch 8 Point              5.05%
  6:  DUTCH10    Bitstream Dutch 10 Point             5.56%
  7:  DUTCH12    Bitstream Dutch 12 Point            10.29%
  8:  XSYM12     XSymbols 12 Point                   15.79%
                                                     -8.41%
10
11  Total     $27,424.04 $25,811.00 $1,613.04   6.25%
12
```

Reminder:
You are not limited to choosing one of the eight fonts shown in the Font menu.

You are not limited to choosing one of the eight fonts shown in the Font menu. You can replace any font in the menu with a different font by selecting **Replace** from the Font menu. When you select **Replace**, the font numbers appear in the menu, as shown in figure 5.26. When you select one of the numbers, a menu

Chapter 5 ◆ Formatting Cell Contents 191

appears with four typefaces and **Other**, as shown in figure 5.26. If you choose a typeface, you are prompted for a point size from 3 to 72. If you select **Other**, a full page list of typefaces appears, as shown in figure 5.27. After you select a typeface you are prompted for a point size from 3 to 72. You enter the point size and then press Enter or the left mouse button to complete the replacement. The next time you select a font, the list will include the new font at the number where the old font had been.

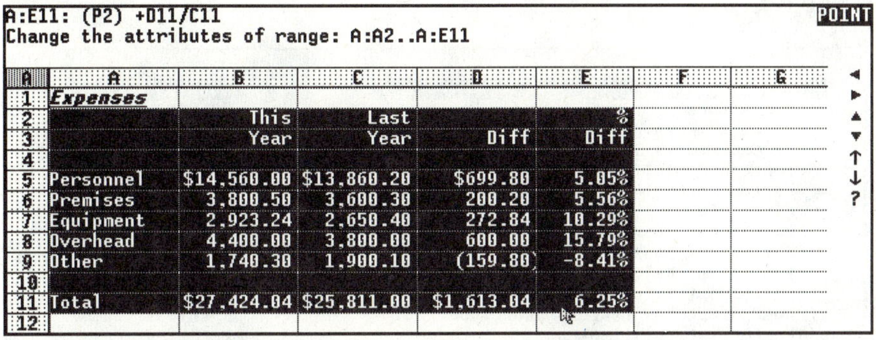

Fig. 5.24.
The prompt to specify a range with :Format Font.

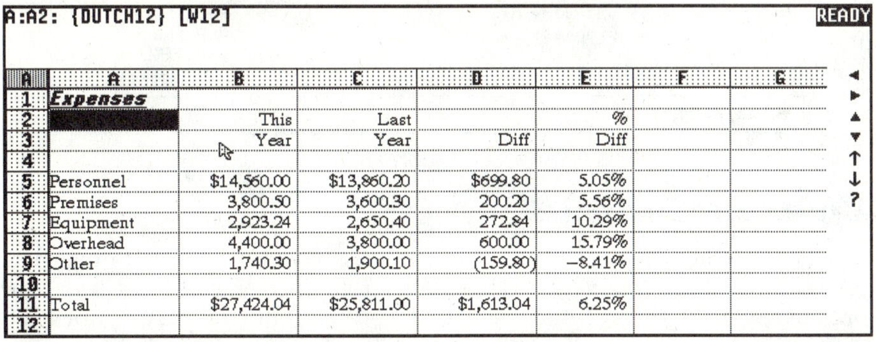

Fig. 5.25.
Formatting a range with the Bitstream Dutch 12-Point font.

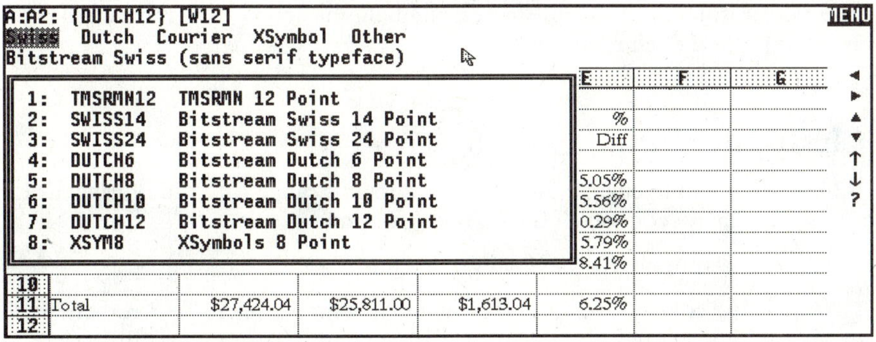

Fig. 5.26.
The :Format Font Replace menu after selecting a number.

To switch back to the old font set, select **Default Restore** from the Font menu. To make this new font set the default set, select **Default Update**. To save this set for future use without having to make it the default set, select **Library Save**. When the prompt `Enter the name of the fontset library:` appears, enter a name and press Enter or the left mouse button. To retrieve this font set at a later date, select **Library Retrieve** and enter the name at the prompt or select it from the list that appears. To delete this font set from the disk, select **Library Erase** and enter the name at the prompt or select it from the list that appears. Font set files have an AF3 extension.

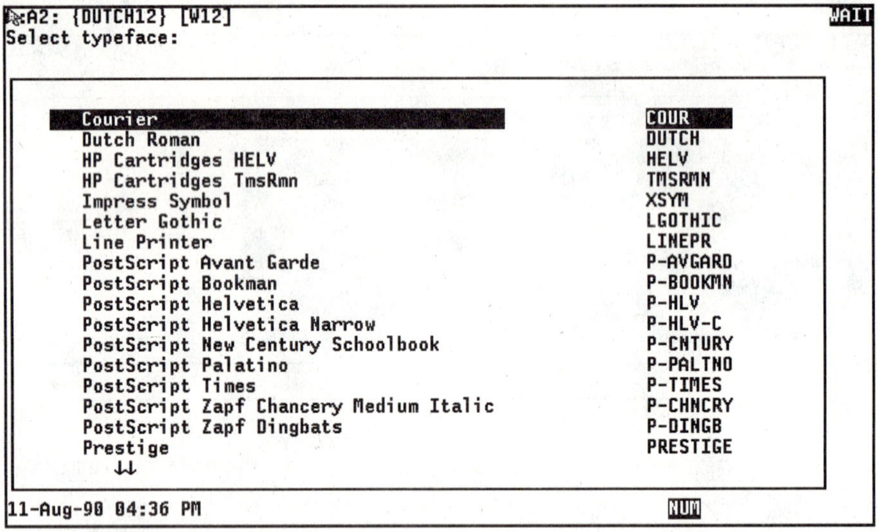

Fig. 5.27.
A full-page list of typefaces appears when you select Other.

Underline Formats

Use the Underline formats to add a single, double or wide underline to a range of text and numbers. When you choose **Underline**, a menu appears with four options: **Single**, **Double**, **Wide**, and **Clear**. You select one of these options and then highlight a cell or range of cells to underline. To delete the underline format, select **Clear** from the Underline menu, highlight the appropriate range, and press Enter or press the left mouse button.

Changing Range Colors

Reminder:
The only color options that exist for negative numbers are the default color and red.

1-2-3 enables you to change the default colors in a range with the **:Format Color** menu. This menu consists of the following options:

   Test Background Negative Reverse Quit

To change the colors of labels and numbers in a range, select **Text**. A menu with six colors plus Normal (the default color) appears. These menu options are as follows:

   Normal Red Green Dark-Blue Cyan Yellow Magenta

When you select a color, the prompt `Change the attributes of range:` **appears**. You highlight the range and press Enter or the left mouse button.

Chapter 5 ◆ Formatting Cell Contents   **193**

You change the background color of a range in a similar way. You change the color of negative numbers in a range to red by selecting **N**egative and then choosing **R**ed. The only color options that exist for negative numbers are the default color and red. After selecting **R**ed, you highlight the range and press Enter or the left mouse button.

To reverse the colors of data and background in a range, choose **R**everse from the Color menu, highlight the range, and press Enter or the left mouse button. For any color menu options to take effect, you must be in Graphics and Color modes (selected from the **:D**isplay Mode menu, as explained in Chapter 4).

Line Formats

Use line formats to replace the hyphenated lines that appear in many worksheets created with older versions of 1-2-3, and to generally enhance the overall appearance of worksheets and printed reports. When you select Lines from the **:**Format menu, the following menu appears:

Outline Left Right Top Bottom All Double Wide Clear Shadow

The first six options of the menu let you draw single lines around an entire range, along the right side of the range, along the left side of the range, along the top of the range, along the bottom of the range, or around each cell of the range. For example, if you want to draw a single line around each cell of a range, select **A**ll, highlight the range, and press Enter or the left mouse button. Figure 5.28 shows a **L**ine format of this type (the worksheet grid has been removed for clarity).

Cue:
Use line formats to replace the hyphenated lines appearing in worksheets created with older versions of 1-2-3.

	A	B	C	D	E	F
1						
2		Expenses				
3						
4			This Year	Last Year	Difference	% Difference
5						
6		Personnel	$14,560.00	$13,860.20	$699.80	5.05%
7		Premises	3,800.50	3,600.30	200.20	5.56%
8		Equipment	2,923.24	2,650.40	272.84	10.29%
9		Overhead	4,400.00	3,800.00	600.00	15.79%
10		Other	1,740.30	1,900.10	(159.80)	−8.41%
11						
12		Total	$27,424.04	$25,811.00	$1,613.04	6.25%

Fig. 5.28.
The :Format Lines All command outlines each cell in the range with a single line.

The next two menu options let you perform the same operations with double and wide lines as you do with single lines. Select **D**ouble or **W**ide and choose one of the line-formatting options. For example, to double underline the range that includes the totals shown in figure 5.28, select **D**ouble **B**ottom, highlight the range (B12..F12), and press Enter or the left mouse button. This move produces the double underline shown in figure 5.29.

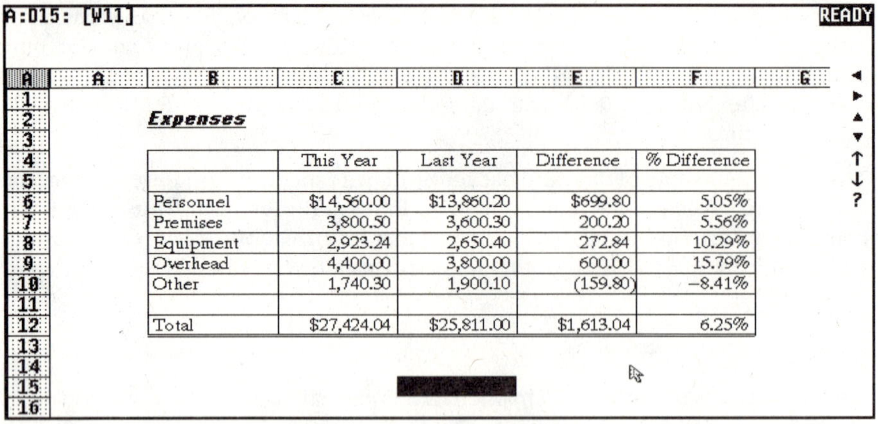

Fig. 5.29.
A worksheet with a double underline under the totals.

```
A:D15: [W11]                                                    READY

        A         B           C           D           E          F        G
 1
 2    Expenses
 3
 4                         This Year   Last Year   Difference  % Difference
 5
 6    Personnel           $14,560.00  $13,860.20     $699.80        5.05%
 7    Premises              3,800.50    3,600.30      200.20        5.56%
 8    Equipment             2,923.24    2,650.40      272.84       10.29%
 9    Overhead              4,400.00    3,800.00      600.00       15.79%
10    Other                 1,740.30    1,900.10     (159.80)      -8.41%
11
12    Total               $27,424.04  $25,811.00   $1,613.04        6.25%
13
14
15
16
```

To add a drop shadow to a range, select **:Format Lines Shadow Set**, highlight the range, and press Enter or the left mouse button. To clear a drop shadow, use **:Format Lines Shadow Clear**.

Reminder:
To clear any kind of single-, double-, or wide-line format, select Clear from the Lines menu.

To clear any kind of single-, double- or wide-line format, select **Clear** from the **Lines** menu. Then select from among **O**utline, **L**eft, **R**ight, **T**op, **B**ottom and **A**ll. Finally, highlight the range and press Enter or press the left mouse button.

Shade Formats

Caution:
Solid shading obscures data unless you select a color for the data.

Use **S**hade formats to emphasize certain data in the worksheet, such as totals or the highest and lowest amounts in a table. When you select **S**hade from the **:F**ormat menu, the following four options appear:

   Light **D**ark **S**olid **C**lear

Light adds light shading to a range; **D**ark adds dark shading to a range. Light shading is shown in figure 5.30. When you shade a range, you may also want to format labels and numbers in the range in boldface to create more contrast. Whereas light and dark shading highlight data in a range, solid shading actually obscures data unless you select a color for the data with **:Format Color Text**. When you select a color, the data appears in the selected color on top of the solid shading. To clear shading from a range, use **:Format Shade Clear**.

Manipulating Formats

Use **:S**pecial from the Wysiwyg menu when you want to transfer the format from one range to another part of the worksheet or to another worksheet or file. Use **:S**pecial **C**opy to copy the formats—not the data—to a different part of the same worksheet or to another worksheet in the same file, as shown in figure 5.31. Use **:S**pecial **M**ove to move the formats—not the data—to a different part of the same worksheet or to another worksheet in the same file.

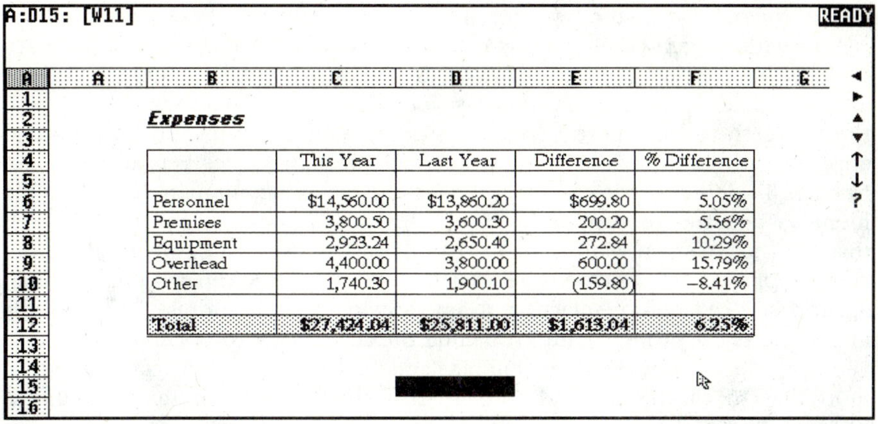

Chapter 5 ◆ Formatting Cell Contents   **195**

Fig. 5.30.
A worksheet with a light shading added to the totals, and the text and numbers in boldface to improve contrast.

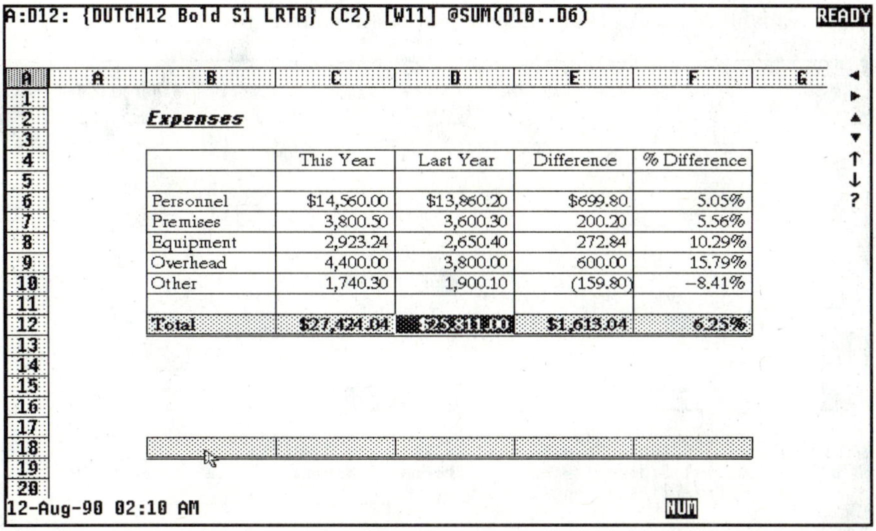

Fig. 5.31.
Copying formats—not data—to a range with :Special Copy.

Formats can be moved from one file to another with **:S**pecial Import and **:S**pecial Export. Use the former when you want to import formats from a Wysiwyg (FM3), Impress (FMT), or Allways (ALL) format file on disk into a worksheet. Use the latter when you want to export formats from the current worksheet to a Wysiwyg format file on disk. When you import a format file, you are presented with the following menu:

   All Named-Styles Fonts Graphs

This menu gives you the option of importing all formats, just fonts, or just graphs. You may also import a file's named Styles, which are explained in the following paragraph.

Reminder:
Using :Named-Style makes it easy to format ranges with certain combinations of formats.

One of the options on the Wysiwyg menu, **:Named-Style**, makes it easy to format ranges with certain combinations of formats. For example, suppose that each time you have a row of totals, you format the row with boldface, double underline, and light shading. To get these formats, you begin by selecting **:Named-Style**, and the menu shown in figure 5.32 appears. You then select **Define** and a menu appears with eight styles. If you haven't defined any styles yet, all styles are Normal. To define a style named Totals, select one of the numbered styles on the menu. When the prompt `Cell defining the style:` appears, point to the cell that has the style you want to name. In this case, you point to any totals cell in row 12, or type a cell name, such as A:D12. (If you place the cell pointer in an appropriate cell before selecting **:Named-Style**, the cell address automatically appears after the prompt.) After you enter the cell address, press Enter. The `Style name:` prompt appears. Here you enter a name such as Totals—the name cannot be more than six characters—and press Enter or the left mouse button. At the next prompt, `Style description:`, you describe the style, such as `Bold Double Underline Light Shading`, and press Enter or the left mouse button. This style is now available from the **:Named-Style** menu shown in figure 5.33.

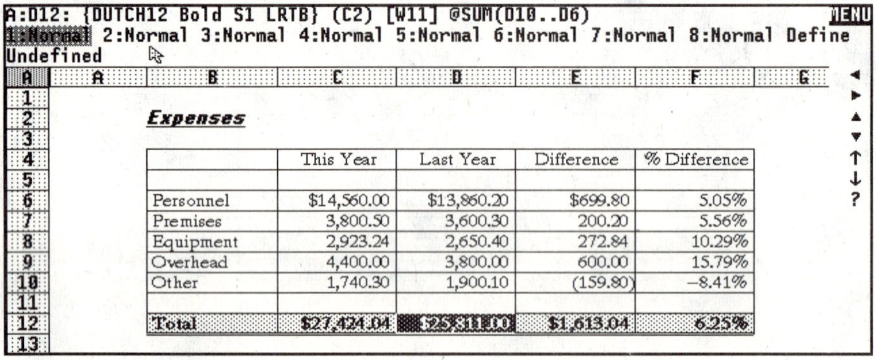

Fig. 5.32.
The :Named-Style menu.

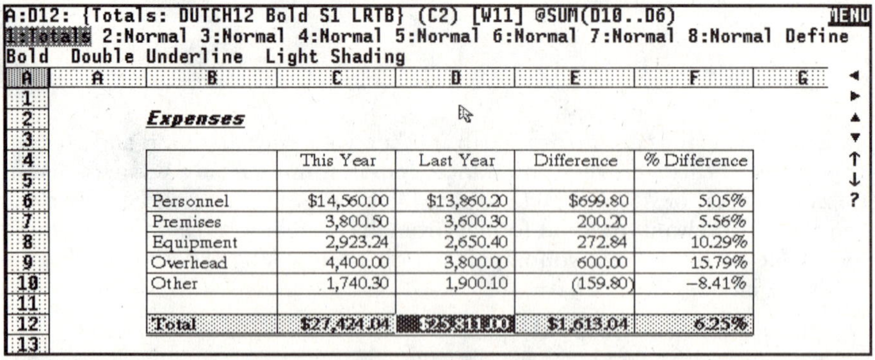

Fig. 5.33.
A named style called Totals added to the :Named-Style menu in the first position.

Use a named style whenever you want to format a cell or range of cells in that style. For example, to format a range with the named style Totals, select **:Named-Style** **1**:Totals, highlight the range, and press Enter or the left mouse button.

The control panel shows the format in braces (see fig. 5.34).

Chapter 5 ◆ Formatting Cell Contents **197**

```
A:D12: {Totals: DUTCH12 Bold S1 LRTB} (C2) [W11] @SUM(D10..D6)          READY
```

	A	B	C	D	E	F	G
1							
2		*Expenses*					
3							
4			This Year	Last Year	Difference	% Difference	
5							
6		Personnel	$14,560.00	$13,860.20	$699.80	5.05%	
7		Premises	3,800.50	3,600.30	200.20	5.56%	
8		Equipment	2,923.24	2,650.40	272.84	10.29%	
9		Overhead	4,400.00	3,800.00	600.00	15.79%	
10		Other	1,740.30	1,900.10	(159.80)	−8.41%	
11							
12		Total	$27,424.04	$25,811.00	$1,613.04	6.25%	
13							

Fig. 5.34.
The named style of a cell (displayed in the control panel).

Manipulating Text

Use **:Text** from the Wysiwyg menu when you want to edit lines or paragraphs right on the worksheet. This feature supports word wrap, just like a word processor. When you select **:Text**, the menu shown in figure 5.35 appears. Select **Edit** any time you want to enter text right on the worksheet. After you select **Edit**, the prompt `Select text range:` appears. You highlight the range and press Enter or the left mouse button. This action makes the mouse pointer disappear. The pointer is replaced by the vertical line text cursor shown in figure 5.36.

Cue:
The Wysiwyg **:Text** menu supports word wrap, just like a word processor.

```
A:A1: [W16]                                                              MENU
      Align  Reformat  Set  Clear
Edit text directly in the worksheet
```

	A	B	C	D	E	F	G
1							
2							
3							
4							
5							
6							
7							
8							
9							
10							
11							
12							
13			BUDGET	JAN	FEB	MAR	APR	MAY
14			------	---	---	---	---	---
15	Department 1	1,062,497	38,444	34,943	84,763	96,858	103,208
16	Department 2	1,306,752	37,815	33,277	89,196	102,014	114,444
17	Department 3	1,296,114	40,256	30,344	87,583	99,494	100,902
18	Department 4	1,022,329	38,656	31,098	82,914	81,070	82,164
19	Department 5	1,152,144	38,890	29,088	81,515	84,552	94,339
20	Department 6	817,511	35,591	26,225	74,494	71,451	77,039

```
13-Aug-90 09:44 AM                                              NUM
```

Fig. 5.35.
The :Text menu.

The mouse cannot control this cursor directly; however, you can move the cursor with the mouse by clicking on the triangle icons in the icon panel. You can also move the text cursor with the arrow keys and other editing keys as explained in table 5.5. You may find the keyboard of more use than the mouse when editing text.

You end a text-editing session by pressing Esc or pressing the right mouse button. To return to text editing with the mouse, just double-click the mouse on any text range; to do it with the menu, select :Text Edit, highlight the range, and press Enter or the left mouse button. The text cursor appears in the upper left corner of the range. A text range displays the label {Text} after the cell address in the control panel.

Table 5.5
Text Cursor-Movement Keys

Key	Operation
← or →	Moves cursor one character to the left or right in the text range
↑ or ↓	Moves cursor one line up or down in the text range
Backspace	Deletes the character to the left of the cursor
Ctrl-←	Moves the cursor left to the beginning of the preceding word
Ctrl-→	Moves the cursor right to the end of the following word
Home	Moves the cursor to the left of the first character in a line
Home Home	Moves the cursor to the left of the first character in a paragraph
End	Moves the cursor to the right of the last character in a line
End End	Moves the cursor to the right of the last character in a paragraph
PgUp	Moves the cursor up one screen
PgDown	Moves the cursor down one screen

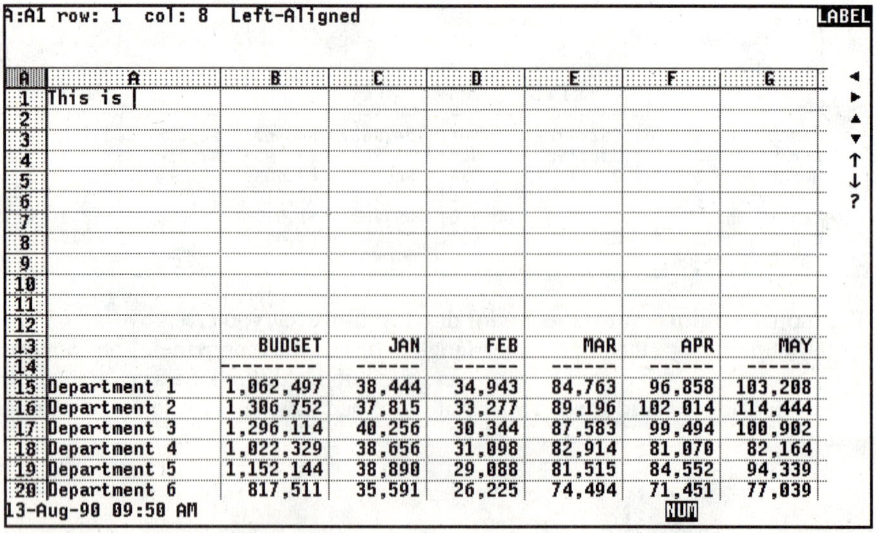

Fig. 5.36.

The text cursor is a vertical line.

Chapter 5 ◆ Formatting Cell Contents   **199**

If you enter text in a worksheet the "old-fashioned" way, with line-by-line labels, you can reformat the text to look like a paragraph by using the **:Text R**eformat command. This command is similar to the /**R**ange **J**ustify command of the 1-2-3 menu. The main difference is that **:T**ext **R**eformat formats a range as {Text}.

You align text in a cell or range of cells with the **:Text A**lign command. This command works just like the /**R**ange **L**abel command for a label in a single cell. However, you can also align text in a range with this command. When you select **:T**ext **A**lign, a menu with four options appears, as shown in figure 5.37. Select **L**eft to left-justify text in a range, select **R**ight to right-justify text in a range, select **C**enter to center text in a range, and select **E**ven to right-justify and left-justify text in a range. For example, the text in figure 5.38 was aligned with **:T**ext **A**lign **E**ven. Note that the right edge of the text is not ragged as it was when /**R**ange **J**ustify was used in figure 5.19.

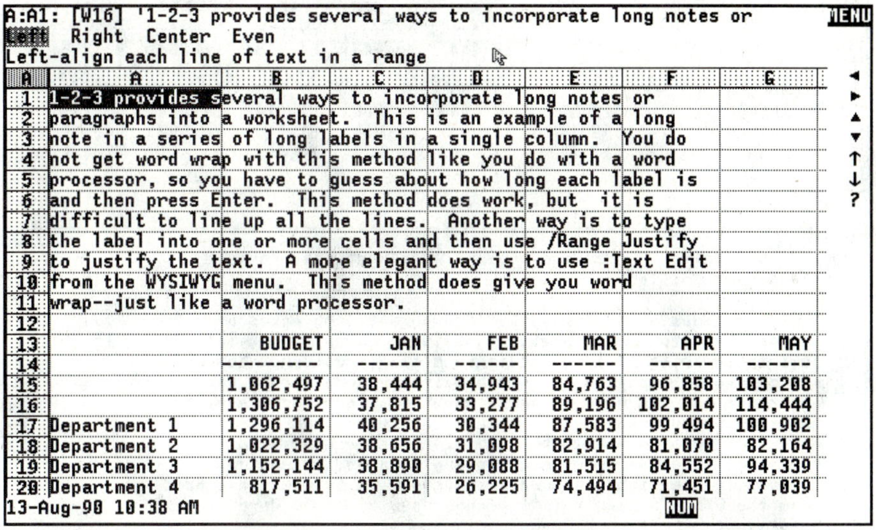

Fig. 5.37.
The **:T***ext* **A***lign menu.*

The alignment of the paragraph is remembered. If you **R**eformat the range, and had aligned the paragraph as **E**ven, then the **E**ven alignment is retained.

Wysiwyg formatting options available for cells and ranges are available also for text ranges. To format a word or group of words in a text range, move the text cursor to the left of the word, and press F3. The menu shown in figure 5.39 appears. The symbols + and – in the menu let you format words or numbers as superscripts and subscripts, respectively. The option **O**utline formats text as shown in figure 5.40. Notice that all text is formatted from the beginning of the text cursor to the end of the line. If you want to format a single word such as "several" in the paragraph in figure 5.40, you must move the cursor to the right of the word and return the format of the remaining words to normal by pressing F3 and selecting **N**ormal from the menu (see fig. 5.41). With this method, you can alter the format of any word that appears in a text range. Other choices, such as **F**ont and **C**olor, bring up additional menus. When you choose **F**ont, a menu appears with numbers 1

Cue:
Add a subscript to your text by pressing F3– (minus) while working in a text range.

Part I ◆ Building the 1-2-3 Worksheet

through 8, which represent eight font styles. When you choose Colors, a menu appears with six colors and Normal options.

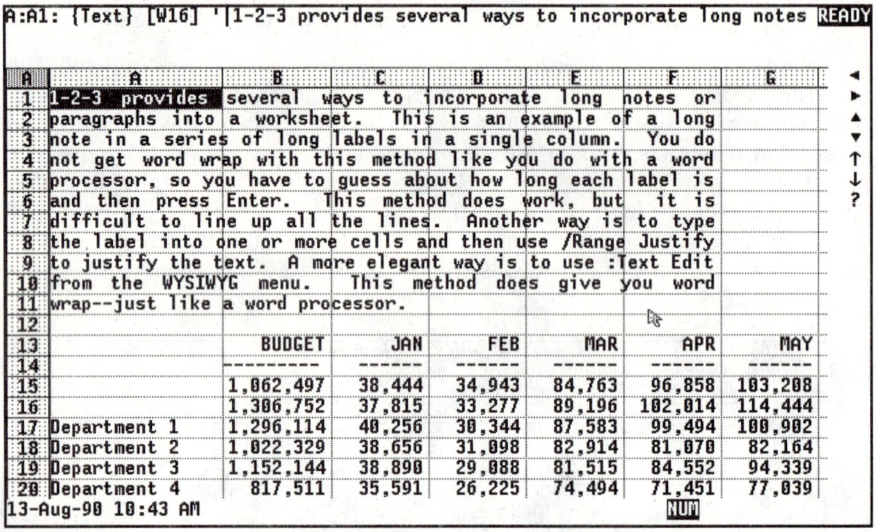

Fig. 5.38.

A paragraph with right and left justification done with the :Text Align Even command.

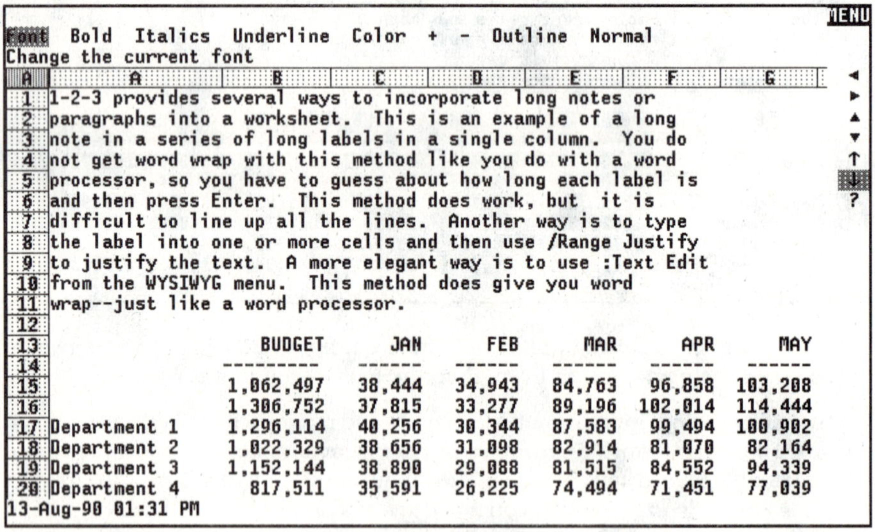

Fig. 5.39.

Pressing F3 while editing a text range to bring up the formatting menu.

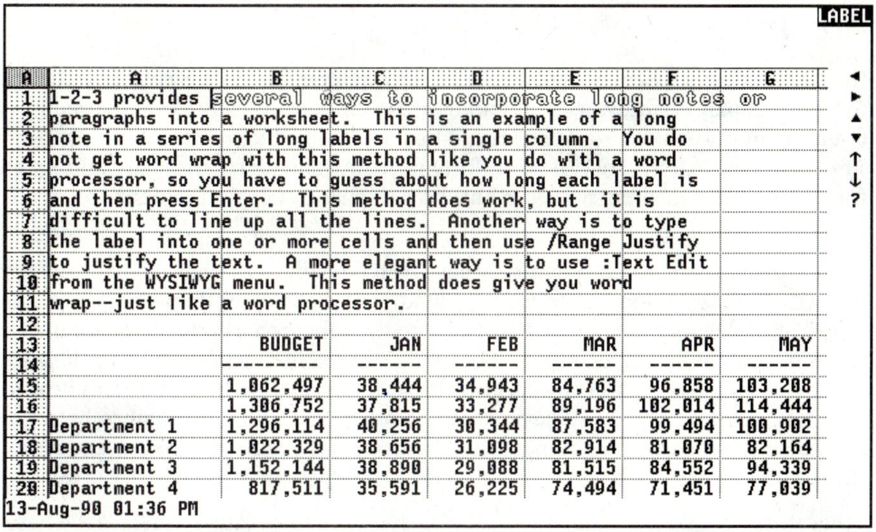

Fig. 5.40.

Adding an Outline format to several words in a line of text.

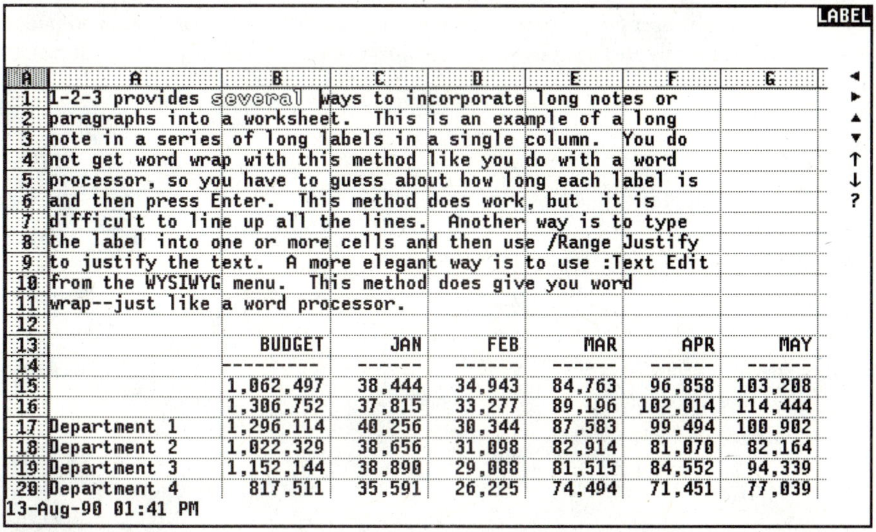

Fig. 5.41.

Adding an Outline format to a single word in a line of text.

Use the **:Text Set** command to format a range as text without entering the **:Text Edit** mode. Use **:Text Clear** to remove the text attribute from a range. **:Text Clear** also clears **Right**, **Center** and **Even** alignment from a text range, though not from an individual cell.

Summary

In this chapter, you learned how to: display numeric data in a variety of different formats, display formulas as text, and hide the contents of cells. You learned how to enter and format dates and times and how to change the International **Date** and **Time** formats. You learned how to format blank cells with **Automatic** and **Label** formats to make data entry easier, and how to change label alignment and justify blocks of text.

Additionally, you learned how to display any type of data in a variety of formats by using the Wysiwyg menu of Releases 3.1 and 3.1+. You learned how to change the typeface, style, and size of data, and how to add lines, shadows and shading to a worksheet to enhance its appearance. You learned how to move, copy, import, and export formats. You learned how to name format combinations and how to edit text directly in the worksheet. And you learned the differences between similar commands such as **/R**ange Label from the 1-2-3 menu and **:T**ext Align from the Wysiwyg menu.

You can now build and format worksheets and reports because you have the basic skills to use 1-2-3 constructively. The next chapter extends your skills to performing data analysis. Chapter 6 covers the extensive library of @functions that you use to manipulate data beyond simple formulas, and opens up the vast analytical power of 1-2-3.

Using @Functions in the Worksheet

6

In addition to the worksheet formulas you can create, you can take advantage of a variety of ready-made formulas provided by 1-2-3. These built-in formulas—called *@functions*—enable you to take advantage of 1-2-3's analytical capability. You can use @functions by themselves, in your own formulas, or in macros and advanced macro command programs to calculate results and solve problems.

1-2-3 provides you with @functions in the following categories:

- Mathematical
- Date and time
- Financial and accounting
- Statistical
- Database
- Logical
- String
- Logarithmic
- Trigonometric
- Special

The mathematical, logarithmic, and trigonometric @functions are useful in engineering and scientific applications. However, these @functions are also convenient tools you can use to perform a variety of standard arithmetic operations, such as rounding values or calculating square roots.

The date and time @functions enable you to convert dates, such as November 26, 1959, and times, such as 6:00 p.m., to serial numbers. You can then use the serial numbers to perform date and time arithmetic. These @functions are a valuable tool when dates and times affect calculations and logic in your worksheets.

The financial and accounting @functions enable you to perform a variety of business-related calculations. These calculations include discounting cash flows, calculating depreciation, and analyzing the return on investments. This set of @functions helps you perform investment analysis and accounting, or budgeting for depreciable assets.

A set of statistical and database statistical @functions rounds out the data analysis capabilities of 1-2-3. These @functions enable you to perform all the standard statistical calculations on data in your worksheet or in a 1-2-3 database. You can find minimum and maximum values, calculate averages, and compute standard deviations and variances. (In some cases, the database statistical @functions are considered a separate @function type; in practice, however, they are used as specialized versions of the statistical @functions, applied to 1-2-3 databases.)

Database @functions enable you to perform in one simple statement calculations that would otherwise require several statements. Among other uses, these @functions enable you to find the number of items in a list, sum the items, and find the minimum, maximum, standard deviation, variance, and arithmetic mean of the items.

With the logical @functions, you can add standard Boolean logic to your worksheet and use the logic either alone or as part of other worksheet formulas. Essentially, each of the logical @functions enables you to test whether a condition—one that you have defined or one of 1-2-3's predefined conditions—is true or false. These logical tests are important for using @functions that make decisions; the function or its result acts differently, depending on a condition elsewhere in your worksheet.

Tip:
A handy trick for creating worksheet and row boundaries and visual borders is to use @string functions to repeat text characters.

Another set of 1-2-3 @functions is the string @functions, which manipulate text. You can use string @functions to repeat text characters (a handy trick for creating worksheet and row boundaries and visual borders), to convert letters in a string to uppercase or lowercase, to change strings into numbers, and to change numbers into strings. String @functions also can be important when you convert data for use by other programs, such as word processing mailing lists.

1-2-3 also provides a set of special @functions. You use these special tools to deal with the worksheet itself. For example, one special @function returns information about specific cells. Other special @functions count the number of rows, columns, or worksheets in a range.

This chapter describes the basic steps for using 1-2-3 @functions, and then provides discussions and examples of specific @functions.

Learning How To Enter a 1-2-3 @Function

To enter a 1-2-3 @function into a worksheet, follow this four-step process:

1. Type the @ sign to tell 1-2-3 that you want to enter an @function.
2. Type the @function name.

Chapter 6 ♦ Using @Functions in the Worksheet   205

   3. Type within parentheses any information or arguments that the @function needs.
   4. Press Enter.

An example of an @function is @AVG. If you type the @function **@AVG(*1,2,3*)**, 1-2-3 returns the calculated result 2, which is the average of the three numbers 1, 2, and 3.

All @functions begin with—and are identified by—the @ character. In effect, by typing @ you tell 1-2-3 that you are entering a function.

The next step is to enter the name of the @function. 1-2-3 helps you remember the name of the @function by using short, three-to-five-character abbreviations for @functions. These abbreviations assist you in identifying and remembering those @functions you use most often. For example, the @function to calculate the average, a statistical function, is @AVG; the @function to calculate the internal rate of return, a financial @function, is @IRR; and the function to round numbers, a mathematical function, is @ROUND.

A feature that can help you select the function you need is to type the @ symbol, and then press F3 (NAMES). 1-2-3 shows a full-screen display of all @functions. To select a function from the list, highlight it with your cell pointer and press Enter.

After typing @ and the function name, enter any of the arguments or inputs the function needs to perform its calculations. You place an @function's arguments inside parentheses that immediately follow the @function's name. If the @function has multiple arguments, you separate them with commas. You can also use a semicolon or period to separate @function arguments.

Entering @functions is straightforward. Suppose, for example, that you want to calculate the average monthly revenue from four products. To calculate the result, type the following:

   @AVG(1000,5000,6000,8000)

1-2-3 returns 5000, which is the average of the numbers entered as arguments. Notice that the @function begins with the @ character, followed by the function name AVG, and that the @function's arguments are included inside parentheses and separated by commas.

In the preceding example, the arguments use actual numeric values. You also can use cell addresses and range names as arguments. For example, if you store the monthly revenue values of these products or the formulas that produce these revenue values in worksheet cells B1, B2, B3, and B4, you can type the following function:

   @AVG(B1,B2,B3,B4)

Or, if you name each of the four cells that contain the revenue values or formulas with each product's name or product number, you can type the following function:

   @AVG(PART12,PART14,PART21,PART22)

Reminder:
All @functions begin with—and are identified by—the @ sign.

Cue:
1-2-3 uses short, three-to-five-character abbreviations for @functions. These abbreviations help you identify and remember the @functions you use most frequently.

Cue:
After you type @, press F3 to present a full-screen display of all 1-2-3 @functions.

Reminder:
Some @functions do not require arguments.

Some @functions do not require arguments or inputs, so you don't use parentheses. For example, the mathematical function @PI returns „ ; and the mathematical function @RAND produces a random number.

Using Mathematical @Functions

1-2-3 provides 17 mathematical @functions that enable you to perform most of the common—and some of the more specialized—mathematical operations. The operations you can perform include general, logarithmic, and trigonometric calculations.

General Mathematical @Functions

1-2-3 offers nine general mathematical @functions. Table 6.1 summarizes these @functions.

Table 6.1
General Mathematical @Functions

@Function	Description
@ABS(*number* or *cell_reference*)	Computes the absolute value of the argument
@EXP(*number* or *cell_reference*)	Computes the number *e* raised to the power of the argument
@INT(*number* or *cell_reference*)	Computes the integer portions of a specified number
@LN(*number* or *cell_reference*)	Calculates the natural logarithm of a specified number
@LOG(*number* or *cell_reference*)	Calculates the common, or base 10, logarithm of a specified number
@MOD(*number,divisor*)	Computes the remainder, or modulus, of a division operation
@ROUND(*number* or *cell reference,precision*)	Rounds a number to a specified precision
@RAND	Generates a random number
@SQRT(*number* or *cell_reference*)	Computes the square root of a number

Reminder:
@ABS calculates the absolute value of a number.

@ABS—Computing Absolute Value

The @ABS function calculates the absolute value of a number. Use the following format for this function:

@ABS(*number* or *cell_reference*)

The @ABS function has one argument, which can be either a numeric value or a cell reference to a numeric value. The result of @ABS is the positive value of its argument. @ABS converts a negative value into its corresponding positive value. @ABS has no effect on positive values.

Figure 6.1 shows how the @ABS function can be used to convert the negative result of a calculation to a positive value. Cell B8 contains the formula `@ABS(B15)`; this formula returns to cell B8 the absolute value of the value contained in cell B15. Although B15 contains negative 33, the formula in B8 returns positive 33. The other cells in row 8 contain similar formulas.

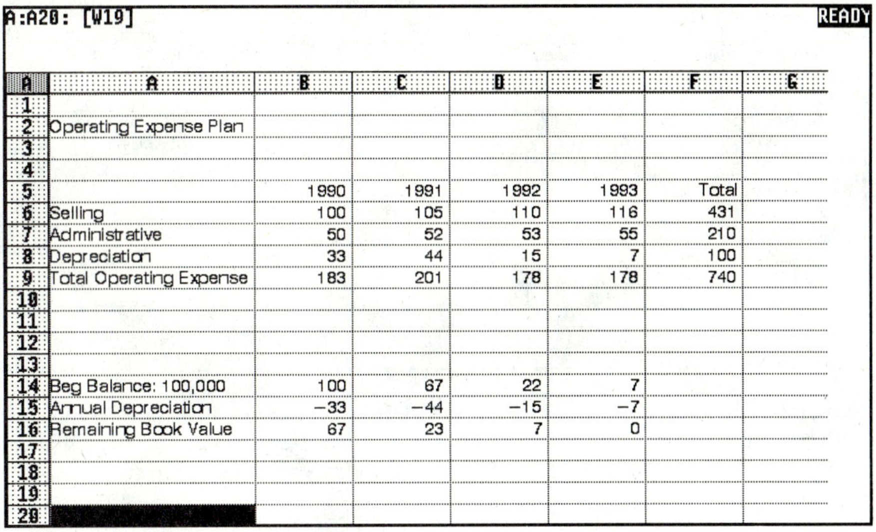
A:A20: [W19] READY

A	A	B	C	D	E	F	G
1							
2	Operating Expense Plan						
3							
4							
5		1990	1991	1992	1993	Total	
6	Selling	100	105	110	116	431	
7	Administrative	50	52	53	55	210	
8	Depreciation	33	44	15	7	100	
9	Total Operating Expense	183	201	178	178	740	
10							
11							
12							
13							
14	Beg Balance: 100,000	100	67	22	7		
15	Annual Depreciation	−33	−44	−15	−7		
16	Remaining Book Value	67	23	7	0		
17							
18							
19							
20							

Fig. 6.1. *Using the @ABS function to convert a negative number to a positive number.*

You can also use @ABS in data entry macros to ensure that an entered value results in a positive number, no matter what value was typed. @ABS is also essential in trigonometric calculations.

@INT—Computing the Integer

The @INT function converts a decimal number into an integer, or whole number. @INT creates an integer by truncating, or removing, the decimal portion of a number. @INT uses the following format:

@INT(*number* or *cell_reference*)

@INT has one argument, which can be either a numeric value or a cell reference to a numeric value. The result of applying @INT to the values 3.1, 4.5, and 5.9 yields integer values of 3, 4, and 5.

@INT is useful for computations in which the decimal portion of a number is irrelevant or insignificant. Suppose, for example, that you have $1,000 to invest in XYZ company and that shares of XYZ sell for $17 each. You divide 1,000 by 17 to compute the total number of shares that can be purchased. Because you cannot purchase a fractional share, you can use @INT to truncate the decimal portion (see figure 6.2).

Fig. 6.2.
The @INT function used to calculate the number of shares that can be purchased.

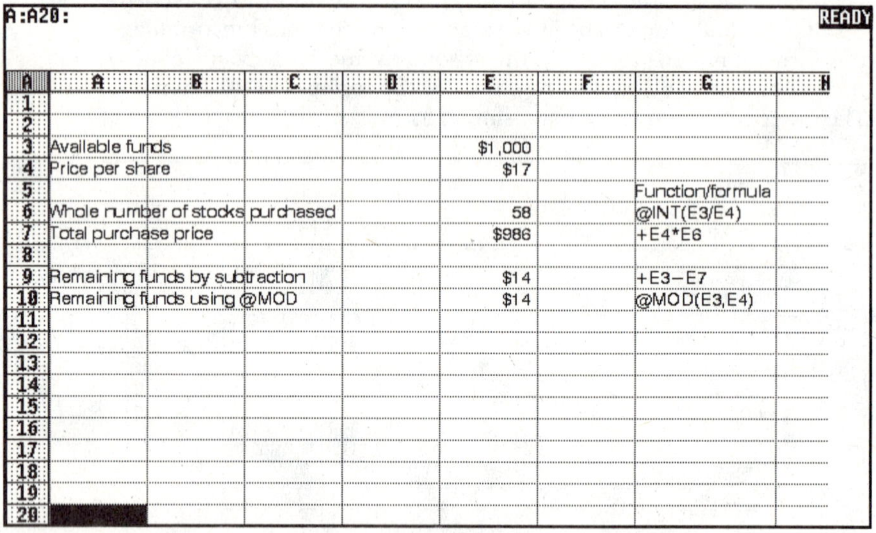

	A	B	C	D	E	F	G	H
1								
2								
3	Available funds				$1,000			
4	Price per share				$17			
5							Function/formula	
6	Whole number of stocks purchased				58		@INT(E3/E4)	
7	Total purchase price				$986		+E4*E6	
8								
9	Remaining funds by subtraction				$14		+E3−E7	
10	Remaining funds using @MOD				$14		@MOD(E3,E4)	

Remember the difference between the @ROUND and @INT @functions: @ROUND with a positive precision argument rounds decimal numbers to the next highest integer; @INT removes the decimal portion and leaves the integer only.

@MOD—Finding the Modulus or Remainder

Cue:
@MOD computes the remainder of a division operation.

The @MOD function computes the remainder, or modulus, that results when one number is divided by another. @MOD uses two arguments that can be either numeric values or cell references. The @MOD function uses the following syntax:

@MOD(*number,divisor*)

The *number* being divided determines the sign of the remainder, or modulus. The *divisor* cannot be zero, or @MOD returns ERR.

You can use the @INT function to calculate the number of shares of XYZ as shown in figure 6.2. Use @MOD, also shown in figure 6.2, to determine the remainder or the amount left over after the purchase.

@ROUND—Rounding Numbers

The @ROUND function rounds values to a precision you specify. The function uses two arguments: the value you want to round, and the precision you want to use in the rounding. @ROUND uses the following format:

@ROUND(*number* or *cell_reference,precision*)

The *precision* argument determines the number of decimal places and can be a numeric value between −100 and +100. You use positive precision values to specify places to the right of the decimal place, and negative values to specify places to the left of the decimal place. A precision value of 0 rounds decimal values to the nearest integer. Figure 6.3 shows how @ROUND is used to round results before totaling them.

A:A20: [W8] READY

A	A	B	C	D	E	F	G
1							
2							
3		Value	Precision	Result		Function	
4		123.456	2	123.46		@ROUND(B4,C4)	
5		123.456	1	123.5		@ROUND(B5,C5)	
6		123.456	0	123		@ROUND(B6,C6)	
7		123.456	−1	120		@ROUND(B7,C7)	
8		123.456	−2	100		@ROUND(B8,C8)	
9		123.456	−3	0		@ROUND(B9,C9)	
10							
11		Use @ROUND to round values before totalling:					
12							
13				Tax			
14		Price	Percent	Amount			
15		$45.67	6.5%	$2.97		@ROUND(B15*C15,2)	
16		$43.89	6.5%	$2.85		@ROUND(B16*C16,2)	
17		$12.02	6.5%	$0.78		@ROUND(B17*C17,2)	
18			Total Tax	$6.60			
19							
20							

Fig. 6.3.
The @ROUND function used to round values.

Note: The @ROUND function and the /**R**ange **F**ormat command perform differently. @ROUND actually changes the contents of a cell; /**R**ange **F**ormat alters only how the cell's contents are displayed.

Caution:
The formatted number you see on-screen or in print may not be the number used in calculations.

In 1-2-3, the formatted number you see on-screen or on a printed report may not be the number used in calculations. This difference can cause errors in the magnitude of thousands of dollars in worksheets that calculate mortgage tables. To prevent errors, use @ROUND to round formula results or the numbers used in your formulas so that the calculated numbers are the same as those displayed by 1-2-3.

As you work with rounding, keep in mind that @ROUND rounds a number according to the following standard rule: If the number is less than 0.5, it is rounded down to 0; if the number is 0.5 or more, it is rounded up to 1.

Cue:
Round up to the nearest integer by adding 0.5 to the number you need to round.

Finally, the @ROUND function is most useful for rounding a value being used in other formulas or @functions, such as @AVG or @SUM. If you need to round up to the nearest integer, add 0.5 to the number you need to round.

@RAND—Producing Random Numbers

You use the @RAND function to generate random numbers. The function requires no arguments, and uses the following syntax:

@RAND

Reminder:
Use @RAND to model problems that involve random occurrences.

@RAND returns a randomly generated number between 0 and 1, to a 17-decimal-place precision. If you want a random number greater than 1, multiply the @RAND function by the maximum random number you want. If you want a random number in a range of numbers, use a formula similar to the following:

+10+@RAND*20

In this example, the random numbers generated will be between 10 and 30. Enclose random number calculations in an @INT function if you need random integers.

Note that new random numbers are generated each time you recalculate. To see the results from new random numbers, press Calc (F9).

@SQRT—Calculating the Square Root

The @SQRT function calculates the square root of a positive number. The function uses one argument, the number whose square root you want to find. @SQRT uses the following format:

@SQRT(*number* or *cell_reference*)

The value must be either a nonnegative numeric value or a cell reference to such a value. If @SQRT is a negative value, then the function returns ERR. Figure 6.4 shows some examples of @SQRT. The second example shows how the @ABS function can change a negative number into a positive one before @SQRT finds the square root.

Using Date and Time @Functions

1-2-3's date and time @functions enable you to convert dates, such as November 26, 1959, and times, such as 6:00 p.m., to serial numbers. You can then use the serial numbers in date arithmetic and time arithmetic, which are valuable tools when dates and times affect worksheet calculations and logic.

As you review the examples showing the mechanics of 1-2-3's date and time @functions, you should develop a better appreciation of their potential contributions to your applications. The date and time @functions available in 1-2-3 are summarized in table 6.2.

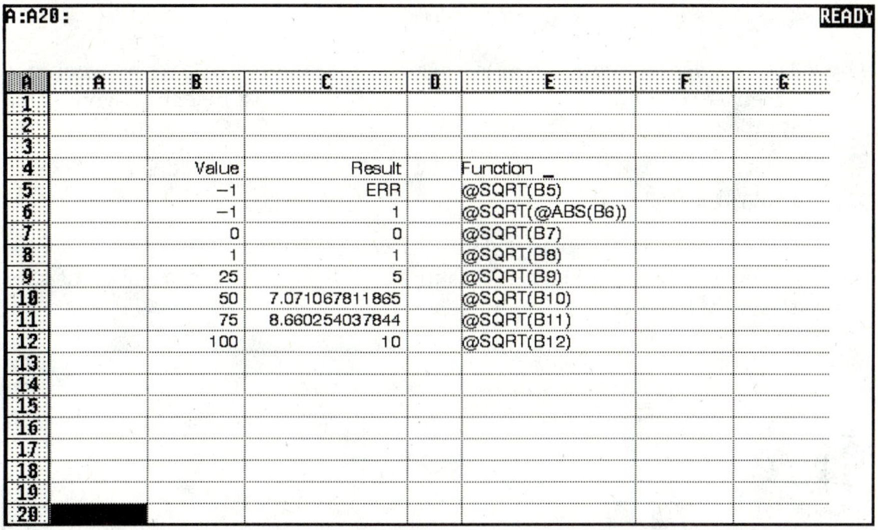

Chapter 6 ◆ Using @Functions in the Worksheet **211**

```
A:A20:                                                              READY

       A         B         C         D         E         F         G
  1
  2
  3
  4            Value     Result              Function
  5              -1       ERR                @SQRT(B5)
  6              -1         1                @SQRT(@ABS(B6))
  7               0         0                @SQRT(B7)
  8               1         1                @SQRT(B8)
  9              25         5                @SQRT(B9)
 10              50    7.071067811865        @SQRT(B10)
 11              75    8.660254037844        @SQRT(B11)
 12             100        10                @SQRT(B12)
 13
 14
 15
 16
 17
 18
 19
 20
```

Fig. 6.4.
The @SQRT function used to find the square root of numbers.

Table 6.2
Date and Time @Functions

@Function	Description
@D360(*date1,date2*)	Calculates the number of days between two dates, based on a 360-day year
@DATE(*y,m,d*)	Calculates the serial number that represents the described date
@DATEVALUE (*date_string*)	Converts a date expressed as a quoted string into a serial number
@DAY(*date*)	Extracts the day number from a serial number
@HOUR(*time*)	Extracts the hour number from a serial number
@MINUTE(*time*)	Extracts the minute number from a serial number
@MONTH(*date*)	Extracts the month number from a serial number
@NOW	Calculates the serial date and time from the current system date and time
@SECOND(*time*)	Extracts the seconds from a serial number
@TIME(*h,m,s*)	Calculates the serial number representing the described time
@TIMEVALUE (*time_string*)	Converts a time expressed as a string into a serial number
@TODAY	Calculates the serial number for the current system date
@YEAR(*date*)	Extracts the year number from a serial number

@D360—Dealing with 360-Day Years

Cue:
@D360 enables you to calculate the number of days between two dates, based on a 360-day year.

The @D360 function enables you to calculate the number of days between two dates, based on a 360-day year. Both date arguments must be expressed as valid serial numbers; otherwise, the function returns ERR. @D360 uses the following format:

@D360(*date1,date2*)

The @D360 function proves helpful in cases where interest calculations are made by using a 360-day year. Figure 6.5 shows, for example, the number of days between sets of dates based on a 360-day year.

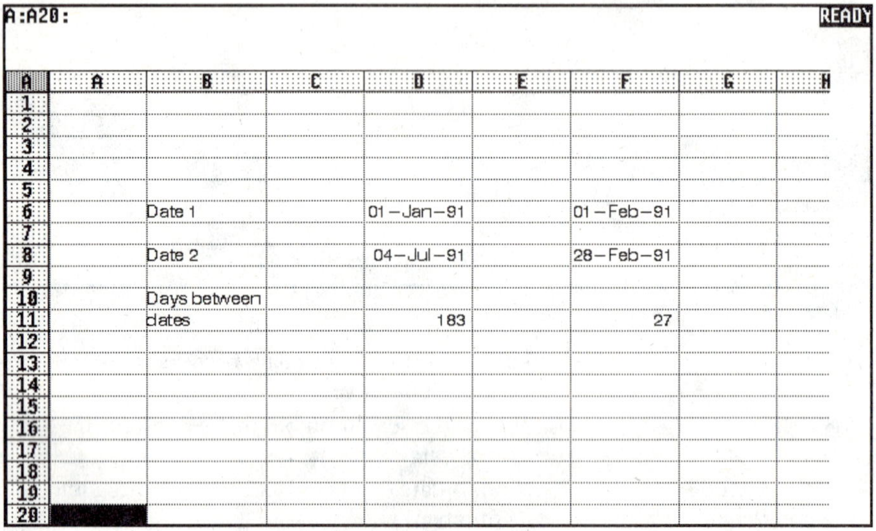

Fig. 6.5.
The @D360 function used to calculate the difference between two dates, based on a 360-day year.

	A	B	C	D	E	F	G	H
6		Date 1		01–Jan–91		01–Feb–91		
8		Date 2		04–Jul–91		28–Feb–91		
10		Days between						
11		dates		183		27		

@DATE—Converting Date Values to Serial Numbers

The first step in using dates in arithmetic operations is to convert the dates to serial numbers, which you can then use in addition, subtraction, multiplication, and division operations. Probably the most frequently used date @function is @DATE. This function converts any date into a number that you can use in arithmetic operations, and—just as important—that 1-2-3 can display as a date. @DATE uses the following format:

@DATE(*year,month,day*)

You use numbers to identify a year, month, or day. For example, you enter the date November 26, 1959, which also can be expressed as 11-26-59, into the @DATE function in the following way:

@DATE(59,11,26)

Chapter 6 ♦ Using @Functions in the Worksheet   **213**

The numbers you enter to represent the year, month, and day need to comprise a valid date, or 1-2-3 returns ERR. For example, 1-2-3 is programmed so that you can specify the day argument in February as 29 only during leap years, and you never can specify the day as 30 or 31 for February. When you specify the month as 1, which represents January, 30 and 31 are valid day arguments because January has 31 days.

As you begin using the @DATE function, keep in mind several guidelines. First, 1-2-3's internal calendar begins with the serial number 1, which is the first date that 1-2-3 recognizes, and that serial number represents January 1, 1900. A single day is represented by an increment of 1; thus, 1-2-3 represents January 2, 1900, as 2.

Second, even though 1900 wasn't a leap year, 1-2-3 assigns the serial number 60 to the date February 29, 1900. Although this assignment generally should not be a problem, you may have difficulty if you transfer data between 1-2-3 and other programs. In that case, you may need to adjust your applications for this error yourself.

Figure 6.6 shows an example of the @DATE function being used to calculate the number of days a bill is overdue.

	A	B	C	D	E	F	G	H	I
1									
2									
3									
4									
5									
6					14-Jun-90				
7								Days	
8		Year	Month	Day	Date	Firm	Amount	overdue	
9		90	2	12	12-Feb-90	Mountain Sports	455.98	122	
10		90	2	24	24-Feb-90	Chez Diner	23.45	110	
11		90	3	2	02-Mar-90	ElectroTek	657	104	

Fig. 6.6.
The @DATE function used to calculate the number of days a bill is overdue.

Dates created or entered with the @DATE function appear on an unformatted worksheet as a number—the number of days since the beginning of the century. To make that serial number display as a text date, format the cell with the /**R**ange **F**ormat **D**ate command. When you format the dates, 1-2-3 works with the dates as serial numbers, but displays them in reports and on-screen in the date format you've selected. (The /**R**ange Format commands and the various Date and Time formats available are discussed in detail in Chapter 5, "Formatting Cell Contents.")

Part I ◆ Building the 1-2-3 Worksheet

Finally, you can type dates directly into a cell if you use one of the formats that 1-2-3 recognizes—for example, Jan-12-90. First, you must preformat the cell by choosing /Range Format Other Automatic, and then enter the date into the cell.

@DATEVALUE—Changing Date Strings to Serial Numbers

@DATEVALUE computes the serial number for a text string typed into a referenced cell. The text string must use one of the formats recognized by 1-2-3. @DATEVALUE requires the following format:

@DATEVALUE(*date_string*)

Reminder:
You need to enclose the date string in quotation marks.

The date string must look like one of the date formats you can select when you choose /Range Format. If 1-2-3 cannot recognize the format, the function results in ERR.

Note: If you have reset the default date format for 1-2-3 so that you can use international date formats, you need to type one of the date formats for the country you selected.

Figure 6.7 shows @DATEVALUE converting the date strings in column B into serial numbers in column C. Use /Range Format Date to format a cell containing @DATEVALUE so that the cell displays the serial date number as a text date.

Fig. 6.7.
The @DATEVALUE function used to convert date strings into serial date numbers.

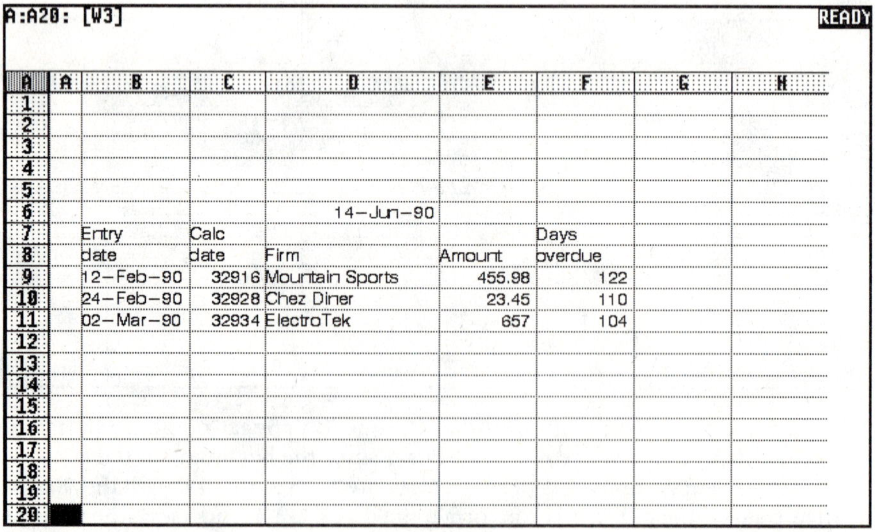

```
A:A20: [W3]                                                    READY

   A      B         C        D              E        F        G       H
 1
 2
 3
 4
 5
 6                           14-Jun-90
 7       Entry     Calc                              Days
 8       date      date      Firm           Amount   overdue
 9       12-Feb-90 32916     Mountain Sports 455.98  122
10       24-Feb-90 32928     Chez Diner      23.45   110
11       02-Mar-90 32934     ElectroTek      657     104
12
13
14
15
16
17
18
19
20
```

Chapter 6 ◆ Using @Functions in the Worksheet

@DAY, @MONTH, and @YEAR—Converting Serial Numbers to Dates

The @DAY, @MONTH, and @YEAR @functions convert serial numbers into a numeric day, month, or year, respectively. These @functions use the following respective formats:

@DAY(*date*)

@MONTH(*date*)

@YEAR(*date*)

The @DAY function accepts a valid serial number as its single argument and returns the day of the month—which is a number from 1 to 31. The @MONTH function accepts a valid date serial number as its single argument and returns the month of the year—which is a number from 1 to 12. The @YEAR function accepts a valid serial date number as its single argument and returns the number of the year—which is a number from 0 (1900) to 199 (2099).

Figure 6.8 illustrates the mechanics of these three date @functions, which enable you to extract just the component of a date—year, month, or day—that you want to manipulate.

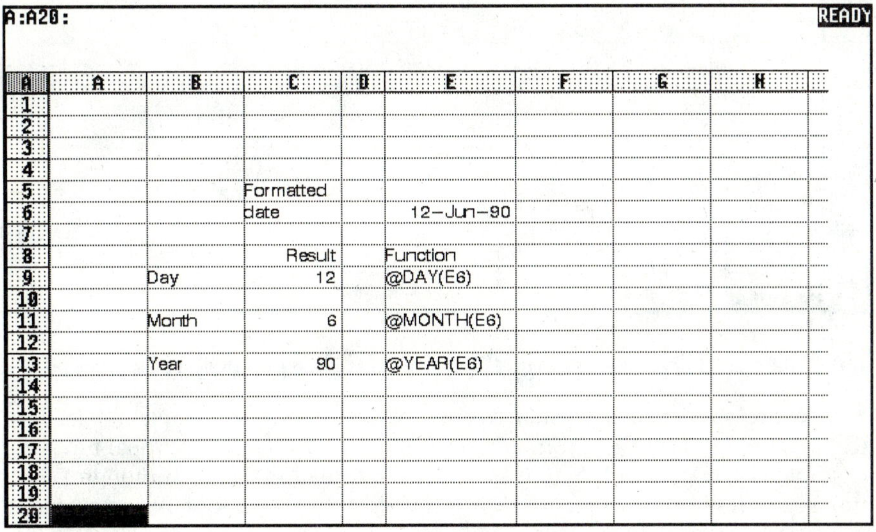

Fig. 6.8.

The @YEAR, @MONTH, and @DAY @functions used to extract parts of date serial numbers.

	A	B	C	D	E	F
5			Formatted			
6			date		12-Jun-90	
7						
8			Result		Function	
9		Day	12		@DAY(E6)	
10						
11		Month	6		@MONTH(E6)	
12						
13		Year	90		@YEAR(E6)	

@NOW and @TODAY—Finding the Current Date and Time

1-2-3 provides two @functions, @NOW and @TODAY, that extract information from the system date and time. The @NOW function retrieves as a serial number both the current system date and the current system time. The decimal places to the left of the decimal point specify the date; the decimal places to the right of the decimal point specify the time. The @TODAY function is similar to @NOW except that @TODAY retrieves only the system date and not the system time. These two @functions provide a convenient tool for recording the dates and times when worksheets are modified or printed. Neither function requires any arguments.

Use the @INT function to calculate the date or time portion of the @NOW function. Use the /**R**ange Value command to freeze either @NOW or @TODAY into an unchanging value. The easiest way to accomplish this task is to create a macro that enters @NOW into a cell, formats the cell, and freezes it with the /**R**ange Value command.

Figure 6.9 illustrates the results of using both @functions. Column C shows the serial numbers, which represent the system date and time. Columns D and E show the results of the two @functions formatted as dates and times, respectively.

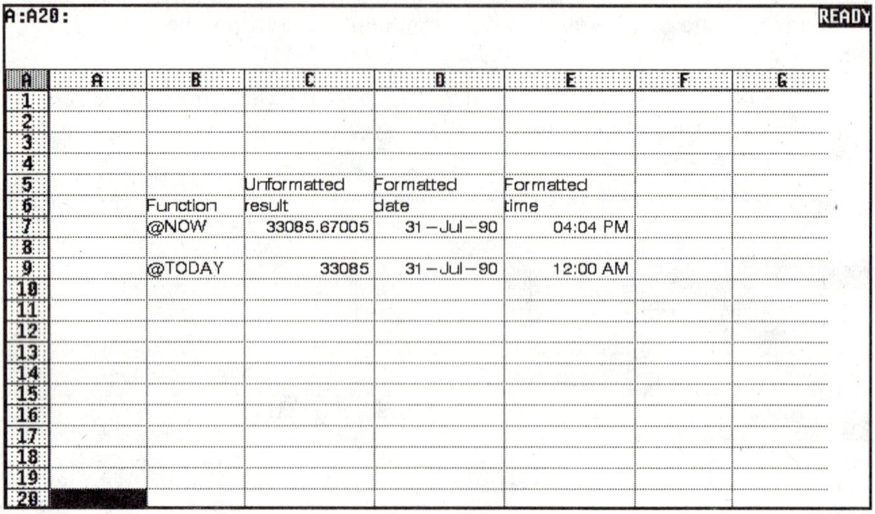

Fig. 6.9.
The @NOW and @TODAY @functions used to insert the date and time on a worksheet.

	A	B	C	D	E
5			Unformatted	Formatted	Formatted
6		Function	result	date	time
7		@NOW	33085.67005	31–Jul–90	04:04 PM
8					
9		@TODAY	33085	31–Jul–90	12:00 AM

@TIME—Converting Time Values to Serial Numbers

Reminder:
1-2-3 expresses time in fractions of serial numbers between 0 and 1.

1-2-3 expresses time as a decimal fraction of a full day. For example, 0.5 is equal to 12 hours (or 12:00 p.m.). In addition, 1-2-3 works on international time. For example, 10:00 p.m. in U.S. time is 22:00 in international time. Although 1-2-3's timekeeping system may seem a little awkward at first, you soon become used to it. Following are some guidelines to help you understand the system:

Time Increment	Numeric Equivalent
1 hour	0.0416666667
1 minute	0.0006944444
1 second	0.0000115741

The @TIME function produces a serial number for a specified time of day. @TIME uses the following format:

Chapter 6 ◆ Using @Functions in the Worksheet   217

@TIME(*hour,minute,second*)

You can use @TIME to produce a range of times just as you use @DATE to generate a range of dates. One way to produce a range of times is to use the /Data Fill command. For example, to produce a range of times from 8:00 a.m. to 5:00 p.m. in 15-minute increments, follow these steps:

1. Choose /Data Fill.
2. Specify the range where you want the times to appear.
3. Type **@TIME(8,0,0)** as the Start value.
4. Type **@TIME(0,15,0)** as the Step value.
5. Type **@TIME(17,0,0)** as the Stop value.
6. Press Enter.
7. Choose /Range Format Date Time, and select the time format you want.
8. Widen the column to at least 12 with the /Worksheet Column Set-Width command.

In figure 6.10, B7..B14 was selected as the range where the times appear in time format 7—HH:MM AM/PM.

	A	B	C	D	E	F	G
1							
2							
3							
4							
5			Instrument		Reading variance		
6		Time	reading		at 15 min. intervals		
7		08:00 AM	354				
8		08:15 AM	358		4		
9		08:30 AM	363		5		
10		08:45 AM	360		−3		
11		09:00 AM	359		−1		
12		09:15 AM	365		6		
13		09:30 AM	370		5		
14		09:45 AM	368		−2		
15				Average var.	2		

Fig. 6.10.
An example of the @TIME function.

Be aware that the numeric arguments have certain restrictions. First, *hour_number* must be between 0 and 23. Second, both *minute_number* and *second_number* must be between 0 and 59. Finally, although 1-2-3 accepts numeric arguments that contain integers and decimals, only the integer portion is used.

After 1-2-3 has interpreted a time as a fraction of a serial number, you can use /Range Format Date Time, and choose a format to display the time in a more recognizable way (for example, 10:42 PM). 1-2-3's time formats are discussed in the following section on @TIMEVALUE.

@TIMEVALUE—Converting Time Strings to Serial Values

Like @DATEVALUE and @DATE, the @TIMEVALUE @function is a variation of @TIME. Like @TIME, @TIMEVALUE produces a serial number from the hour, minute, and second information you supply to the function. Unlike @TIME, however, @TIMEVALUE uses string arguments rather than numeric arguments. You can type a time as text, and the @TIMEVALUE function converts the entry into a serial date number. @TIMEVALUE requires the following format:

@TIMEVALUE(*time_string*)

Reminder:
If the string you supply doesn't conform to an acceptable format, 1-2-3 returns ERR.

The time string must appear in one of four time formats:

HH:MM:SS	AM/PM
HH:MM	AM/PM
HH:MM:SS	(24 hour)
HH:MM	(24 hour)

If the string conforms to one of the time formats, 1-2-3 displays the appropriate serial number fraction. If you then format the cell, 1-2-3 displays the appropriate time of day.

@SECOND, @MINUTE, and @HOUR—Converting Serial Numbers to Time Values

With the @SECOND, @MINUTE, and @HOUR @functions, you can extract different units of time from the decimal portion of a serial date number. These @functions use the following formats, respectively:

@SECOND(*time*)

@MINUTE(*time*)

@HOUR(*time*)

Figure 6.11 shows that these three @functions are, in a sense, the inverse of the @TIME function, just as the @DAY, @MONTH, and @YEAR @functions are the inverse of the @DATE function.

Using Financial and Accounting @Functions

1-2-3 provides 12 financial and accounting @functions that perform a variety of calculations for discounting cash flows, loan amortization, and asset depreciation. The 1-2-3 financial @functions include two that calculate return on investment (@IRR and @RATE), one that calculates loan payments (@PMT), two that calculate present value (@NPV and @PV), one that calculates future value (@FV), two that perform compound growth calculations (@TERM and @CTERM), and four that calculate asset depreciation (@SLN, @DDB, @SYD, and @VDB). Table 6.3 summarizes the financial and accounting @functions available in 1-2-3.

	A	B	C	D	E	F
1						
2						
3						
4						
5			Start time	09:30 AM		
6						
7		Result		Function/formula		
8		9		@HOUR(D5)		
9						
10		30		@MINUTE(D5)		
11						
12		0		@SECOND(D5)		
13						
14		The time in two hours is				
15		11:30:00 AM		@TIME(D5+2,B10,B12)		

Fig. 6.11.
The @SECOND, @MINUTE, and @HOUR @functions compared to the @TIME function.

Table 6.3
Financial and Accounting @Functions

Investment @Function	Description
@IRR(*guess,cashflows*)	Calculates the internal rate of return on an investment
@RATE(*future_value, present_value,term*)	Calculates the periodic return required to increase the present-value investment to the size of the future value in the length of time indicated (*term*)
@PMT(*principal, interest,term*)	Calculates the loan payment amount
@NPV(*interest, cashflows*)	Calculates the present value (today's value) of a stream of cash flows of uneven amounts, but at evenly spaced time periods, when the payments are discounted by the periodic interest rate
@PV(*payment, interest,term*)	Calculates the present value (today's value) of a stream of periodic cash flows of even payments discounted at a periodic interest rate
@FV(*payment,interest, term*)	Calculates the future value (value at the end of payments) of a stream of periodic cash flows compounded at the periodic interest rate

continued

Table 6.3—(continued)

Depreciation @Function	Description
@TERM(*payment, interest,future_value*)	Calculates the number of times an equal payment must be made in order to accumulate the future value when payments are compounded at the periodic interest rate
@CTERM(*interest, future_value, present_value*)	Calculates the number of periods required for the present-value amount to grow to a future-value amount given a periodic interest rate
@SLN(*cost,salvage,life*)	Calculates straight-line depreciation
@DDB(*cost,salvage,life, period*)	Calculates 200 percent declining-balance depreciation
@SYD(*cost,salvage,life, period*)	Calculates sum-of-the-years'-digits depreciation
@VDB(*cost,salvage,life, start,end,[depreciation], [switch]*)	Calculates the depreciation, using the variable-rate declining-balance method

@IRR—Calculating Internal Rate of Return

The @IRR function calculates the internal rate of return on an investment. @IRR uses the following format:

@IRR(*guess,cashflows*)

Cue:
The guess *argument should be a decimal between 0 and 1.*

The *guess* argument typically should be a guess at the interest rate and entered as a decimal between 0 and 1. The first cash flow must be a negative amount, the amount initially invested at time 0 or at the start of the investment.

You should start the calculation with a guessed interest rate that is as close as possible. From this guess, 1-2-3 attempts to converge to a correct interest rate, with .0000001 precision within 20 iterations. If the program cannot do so, the @IRR function returns ERR. If ERR occurs, try again with another guess.

The initial cash flow at time 0 is negative because it flows out from your initial investment. Cash flows in the range after that may be negative (payments by you) or positive (payments to you). Cash flows occur at the end of equally spaced periods with the initial payment by you being at time 0. 1-2-3 ignores empty cells in the range of cash flows and treats cells containing labels as zero.

Figure 6.12 shows the @IRR function calculating the internal rate of return on an investment with uneven cash flows. Notice that during some time periods the investor had to inject additional cash into the investment. Notice also that multiplying the monthly amount by 12 converts the monthly internal rate of return to an annual rate.

```
A:A20: [W8]                                                    READY

        A      B         C      D        E   F      G        H
  1
  2
  3
  4    Period Description       Amount                 Formula
  5       0   Initial Invest.   -540000      Guess   0.010
  6      Feb  End of Feb        0            IRR     0.301   @IRR(G5,D5..D13)*12
  7      Mar  End of Mar        0
  8      Apr  End of Apr        -12000
  9      May  End of May        25000
 10      Jun  End of Jun        -20000
 11      Jul  End of Jul        15000
 12      Aug  End of Aug        0
 13      Sep  EOM Sold          650000
 14
 15
 16
 17
 18
 19
 20
```

Fig. 6.12.
The internal rate of return calculated with the @IRR function.

Although the internal-rate-of-return method is widely used as a measure of profitability, you should be aware that the IRR method has several drawbacks when used to analyze investments. Note that the problem is with the internal-rate-of-return method itself, not with the @IRR function.

One problem is evident when you use the internal-rate-of-return measure on an investment that has multiple internal rates of return. In theory, for example, the formula for calculating the internal rate of return for an investment with cash flows over 10 years is a 10th-root polynomial equation with up to 10 correct solutions. In practice, an investment has as many correct internal rates of return as there are sign changes in the cash flows.

Cue:
An investment may have multiple internal rates of return.

A sign change occurs when the cash flow changes from positive to negative, or vice versa, between periods. Accordingly, even if you get the @IRR function to return an internal rate of return with your first guess, try other guesses to see whether another correct internal-rate-of-return answer is evident; you probably should not use the measure when it delivers multiple solutions.

A serious problem with the @IRR method is that it tends to overestimate a positive rate of return from the investment and neglects to account for additional outside investments that must be injected into the investment over its life span. The overestimate on return occurs because the @IRR method assumes that positive cash flows are reinvested at the same rate of return earned by the total investment. Actually, it is rare that a small return can be reinvested at the same high rate as that of a large investment. This situation is especially true in the analysis of large fixed assets and land investments.

An alternative and more accurate method of evaluating investments is to calculate your investment's net present value. You use 1-2-3's @NPV function to perform net present-value analysis, which is discussed later in this chapter.

@RATE—Calculating Compound Growth Rate

The @RATE function calculates the compound growth rate for an initial investment that grows to a specified future value over a specified number of periods. The rate is the periodic interest rate and not necessarily an annual rate. @RATE uses the following format:

  @RATE(*future_value,present_value,term*)

For the @RATE calculation, the formula is rearranged to compute the interest rate in terms of the initial investment, the future value, and the number of periods.

The actual formula for calculating the interest rate is the following:

  Interest rate = (future value/present value)$^{1/term}$ − 1

Cue:
Use @RATE to determine the yield of a zero-coupon bond.

You can use @RATE to determine, for example, the yield of a zero-coupon bond sold at a discount of its face value. Suppose that for $350 you can purchase a zero-coupon bond with a $1,000 face value, maturing in 10 years. What is the implied annual interest rate? The answer, shown in figure 6.13, is 11.07 percent.

The @RATE function is useful also in forecasting applications to calculate the compound growth rate between current and projected future revenues, earnings, and so on.

@PMT—Calculating Loan Payment Amounts

You use the @PMT function to calculate the periodic payments necessary to pay the entire principal on an amortizing loan. To use @PMT you need to know the loan amount (*principal*), periodic interest rate, and term, as follows:

  @PMT(*principal,interest,term*)

@PMT assumes that payments are to be made at the end of each period—an ordinary annuity. The @function uses the following formula to make the payment calculation:

  Payment = principal * periodic interest / 1 − (periodic interest + 1)$^{-term}$

A:A20: READY

A	A	B	C	D	E	F	G	H
1								
2								
3							Formula	
4		Future value			$1,000.00			
5		Present value			$350.00			
6		Term – years			10			
7								
8		Interest rate			11.07%		@RATE(E4,E5,E6)	
9								
10								
11								
12								
13								
14								
15								
16								
17								
18								
19								
20								

Fig. 6.13. *The @RATE function used to calculate the zero-coupon yield.*

Figure 6.14 shows the @PMT function being used to calculate the monthly car payment on a $12,000 car loan. The loan is repaid over 48 months, and the loan rate is 1 percent—12 percent divided by 12 periods per year.

A:A20: READY

A	A	B	C	D	E	F	G
1							
2							
3							
4		Loan principal			12000		Function/formula
5		Interest – monthly			0.01		
6		Term in months			48		
7							
8		Ordinary annuity			$316.01		@PMT(E4,E5,E6)
9							
10		Annuity due			$312.88		@PMT(E4,E5,E6)/(1+E5)
11							
12							
13							
14							
15							
16							
17							
18							
19							
20							

Fig. 6.14. *The @PMT function used to calculate loan payments.*

You can modify the calculated result of the @PMT function if payments are to be made at the beginning of the period—an annuity due. The modified format for the function is as follows:

@PMT(*principal,interest,term*)/(1+*interest*)

Whether you are calculating ordinary annuities or annuities due, you need to keep two important guidelines in mind. First, calibrate the interest rate as the rate-per-payment period. Second, express the loan term in payment periods. Accordingly, if you make monthly payments, you should enter the interest rate as the monthly interest rate and enter the term as the number of months you will be making payments. Alternatively, if you make annual payments, you should enter the interest rate as the annual interest rate, and the term as the number of years you will be making payments.

@NPV—Calculating Net Present Value

Cue:
The @NPV function closely resembles the @PV function.

The @NPV function closely resembles the @PV function except that @NPV can calculate the present value of a varying, or changing, stream of cash flows. @NPV uses this format:

@NPV(*interest,cashflows*)

Figure 6.15 shows how you can use @NPV to calculate the present value of a stream of varying cash flows.

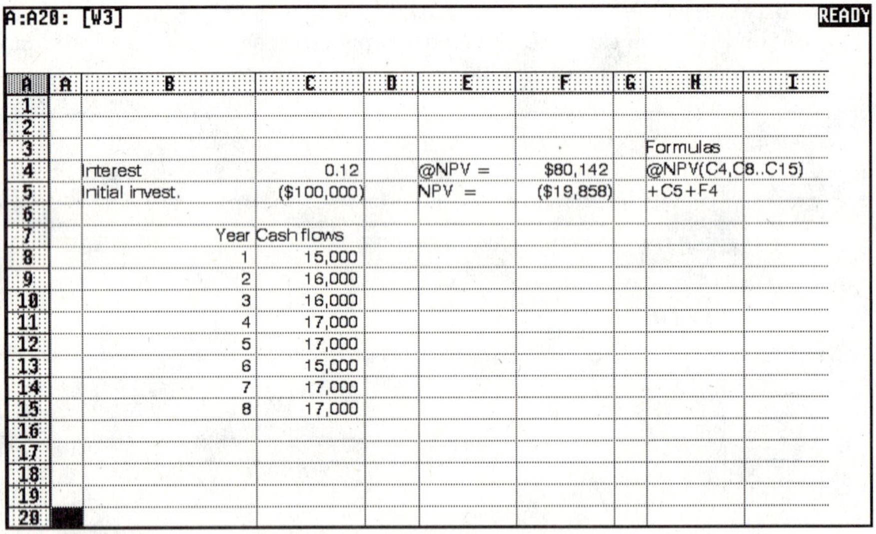

Fig. 6.15.
The @NPV function used to calculate the present value of varying cash flows.

	A	B	C	D	E	F	G	H	I
1									
2									
3								Formulas	
4		Interest	0.12		@NPV =	$80,142		@NPV(C4,C8..C15)	
5		Initial invest.	($100,000)		NPV =	($19,858)		+C5+F4	
6									
7			Year	Cash flows					
8			1	15,000					
9			2	16,000					
10			3	16,000					
11			4	17,000					
12			5	17,000					
13			6	15,000					
14			7	17,000					
15			8	17,000					

The @NPV function assumes that the first cash flow occurs at the end of the first period; the function, therefore, is actually a flexible present-value function. Any time you use the @PV function, you can also use the @NPV function to obtain the same result.

Accountants and financial analysts use the term *net present value* to refer to a measure of an investment's profitability, using the following formula:

$$NPV = \sum_{n=1}^{x} \frac{C_n}{(1+i)^n}$$

where

C_n = Cash flow at *n*th period x = Number of cash flows
i = Interest rate n = The current iteration (1 through *n*)

To calculate the actual profitability measure, or net present value, you need to subtract the initial investment from the result of the @NPV function. When you construct a formula that uses the @NPV function in this way, you are essentially testing whether the investment meets, exceeds, or falls short of the interest rate specified in the @NPV function. Such a formula would be as follows:

+INITL_AMOUNT+@NPV(*interest,cashflows*)

The value in the cell named INITL_AMOUNT is negative because the amount is money you invested, or paid out.

If the calculated result of the preceding formula is a positive amount, the investment produces a return that exceeds the interest rate specified in the @NPV function. If the calculated result equals zero, the investment produces a return that equals the interest rate specified in the @NPV function. Finally, if the calculated result is a negative amount, the investment produces a return that falls short of the interest rate specified in the @NPV function.

Cue:
To calculate the actual profitability measure, or net present value, subtract the initial investment from the result of the @NPV function.

@PV—Calculating Present Value of an Annuity

The @PV function closely resembles the @NPV function in that @PV calculates the present value of a stream of cash flows. The only difference is that @PV calculates the present value of a stream of equal cash flows occurring at the end of the period. This stream of equal cash flows is called an *ordinary annuity*, or *payments in arrears*. The @PV function uses the following format:

@PV(*payment,interest,term*)

The @PV function uses the following formula:

$$PV = payment * \frac{1-(1+interest)^{-term}}{interest}$$

Figure 6.16 shows the result of using @PV to calculate the present value of 24 payments of $1,000 each.

Fig. 6.16.
The @PV function used to calculate the present value of 24 payments of $1,000 each.

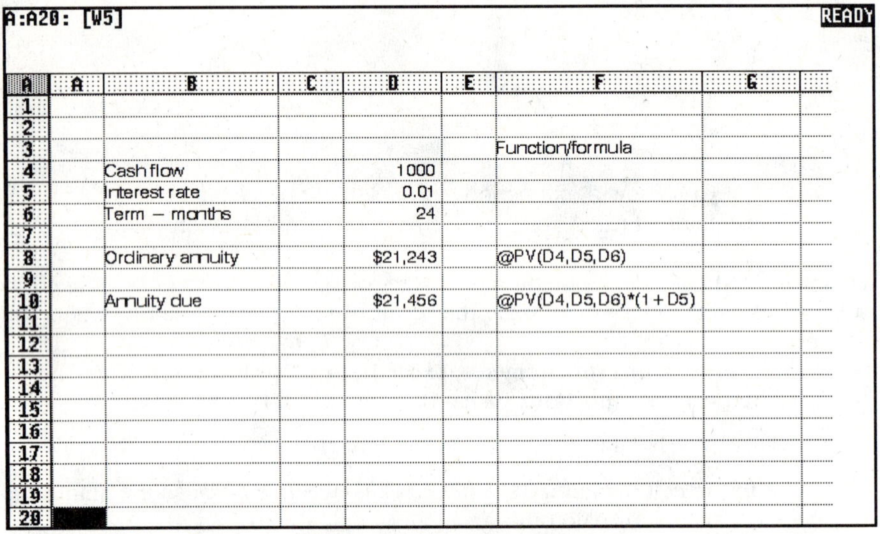

```
A:A20: [W5]                                                    READY
```

	A	B	C	D	E	F	G
1							
2							
3						Function/formula	
4		Cash flow		1000			
5		Interest rate		0.01			
6		Term — months		24			
7							
8		Ordinary annuity		$21,243		@PV(D4,D5,D6)	
9							
10		Annuity due		$21,456		@PV(D4,D5,D6)*(1+D5)	

Keep in mind that the @PV function assumes that the equal-amount cash flows, or payments, occur at the *end* of the period. If the cash flows occur at the *beginning* of the period—called an annuity due or payments in advance—you use the following formula:

@PV(*payment,interest,term*)*(1+*interest*)

@FV—Calculating Future Value

The @FV function calculates what a current amount will grow to, based on an interest rate and number of years you specify. The function is helpful for estimating future balances that current savings and investments will grow to. The @FV function requires this format:

@FV(*payment,interest,term*)

The function uses the following formula:

$$FV = payment * \frac{(1+interest)^{term} - 1}{interest}$$

Suppose that you want to use the @FV function to calculate the estimated size of your vacation savings 24 months from now. Figure 6.17 shows such a calculation, assuming monthly contributions of $1,000 and an annual interest rate of 12 percent.

Chapter 6 ◆ Using @Functions in the Worksheet **227**

```
A:A20:                                                          READY

     A         B              C     D      E        F          G
 1
 2
 3                                                Function/formula
 4         Cash flow                $1,000
 5         Interest rate/period       0.01
 6         Term in months              24
 7
 8         Ordinary annuity        $26,973     @FV(D4,D5,D6)
 9
10         Annuity due             $27,243     @FV(D4,D5,D6)*(1+D5)
11
12
13
14
15
16
17
18
19
20
```

Fig. 6.17.
The @FV function used to calculate vacation savings.

To calculate the future value of an annuity due, you use a formula similar to the one that calculates present value of an annuity due. Use the following formula:

> Future Value of
> an Annuity Due = @FV(*payment,interest,term*)*(1+*interest*)

In addition to calculating the future value of a stream of periodic cash-flow payments (using the @FV function), you may want to calculate the future value of amounts you've already set aside. The following formula calculates the future value of a present value:

> Future value = present value * (1 + interest)^{term}

@TERM—Calculating the Term of an Investment

The @TERM function calculates the number of periods required to accumulate a specified future value by making equal payments into an interest-bearing account at the end of each period. This number of periods is the term for an ordinary annuity. The @TERM function uses the following formula:

> @TERM(*payment,interest,future_value*)

@TERM is similar to @FV, with one exception. Instead of finding the future value of a stream of payments over a specified period, @TERM finds the number of periods required to reach the given future value. The following equation calculates the number of periods:

$$\text{Term} = \frac{@LN(1+(interest*future\ value)/payment)}{@LN(1+interest)}$$

Reminder:
@TERM finds the number of periods required to reach the given future value.

Suppose that you want to determine the number of months required to accumulate $5,000 by making a monthly payment of $50 into an account that pays 8 percent annual interest compounded monthly (0.67 percent per month). Figure 6.18 shows how @TERM can help you get the answer, which is almost 77 months.

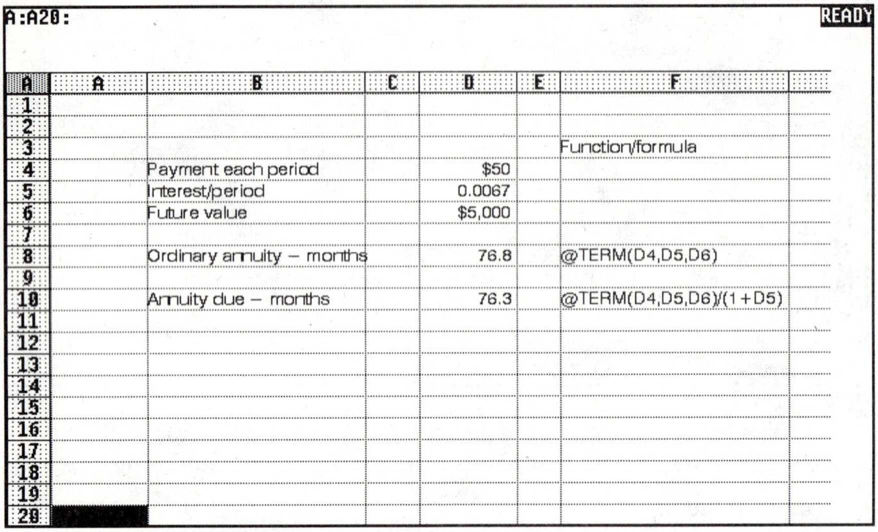

Fig. 6.18.
The @TERM function used to calculate the number of months required to reach a specified future value.

```
A:A20:                                                              READY
     A         B                   C       D      E         F
 1
 2
 3                                                     Function/formula
 4          Payment each period           $50
 5          Interest/period               0.0067
 6          Future value                  $5,000
 7
 8          Ordinary annuity — months     76.8      @TERM(D4,D5,D6)
 9
10          Annuity due — months          76.3      @TERM(D4,D5,D6)/(1+D5)
11
12
13
14
15
16
17
18
19
20
```

To calculate the term for an annuity due, in which payments are made at the beginning of the period, use the following equation:

Term for an
annuity due = @TERM(*payment,interest,future_value*/(1+*interest*))

@CTERM—Calculating the Term of a Compounding Investment

The @CTERM function calculates the number of periods required for an initial investment, earning a specified interest rate, to grow to a specified future value. While the @TERM function calculates the number of periods needed for a series of payments to grow to a future value, the @CTERM function calculates the number of periods needed for the present value of a single initial amount to grow to a future value. The @CTERM function uses the following format:

@CTERM(*interest,future_value,present_value*)

The @CTERM function uses the following formula:

$$\text{Term} = \frac{@LN(\text{future value}/\text{present value})}{@LN(1+\text{interest})}$$

@CTERM is useful in determining the term an investment needs to achieve a specified future value. For example, suppose that you want to determine how many years it will take for $2,000 invested in an IRA at 10 percent interest to grow to $10,000. Figure 6.19 shows how to use the @CTERM function to determine the answer, which is just over 16 years and 10 months.

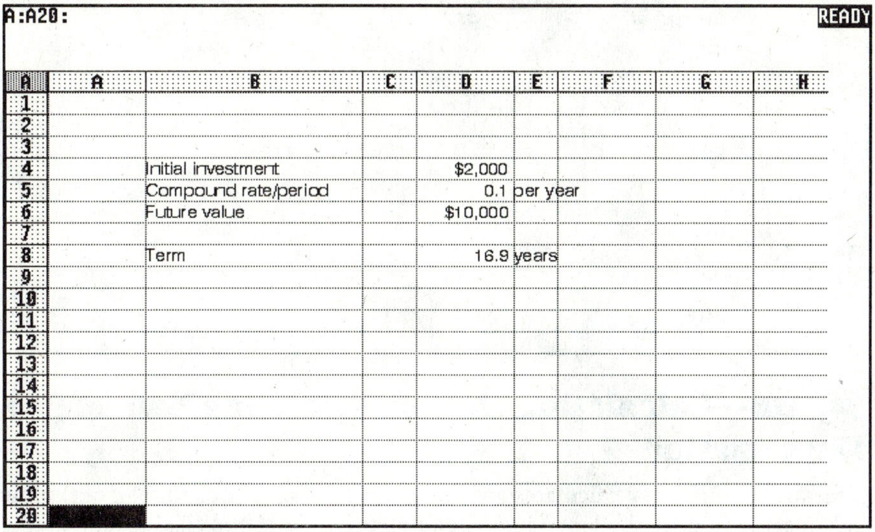

	A	B	C	D	E	F	G	H
1								
2								
3								
4		Initial investment		$2,000				
5		Compound rate/period		0.1	per year			
6		Future value		$10,000				
7								
8		Term		16.9	years			

Fig. 6.19.
The @CTERM function used to calculate the number of years for $2,000 to grow to $10,000 at 10 percent interest.

@SLN—Calculating Straight-Line Depreciation

The @SLN function calculates straight-line depreciation, given the asset's cost, salvage value, and depreciable life. The @SLN function uses the following format:

@SLN(*cost,salvage,life*)

The following formula calculates @SLN:

SLN = (cost−salvage)/life

@SLN conveniently calculates straight-line depreciation for an asset. Suppose, for example, that you have purchased a machine for $5,000 that has a useful life of three years and a salvage value estimated to be 10 percent of the purchase price ($500) at the end of the machine's useful life. Figure 6.20 shows how to use @SLN to determine the straight-line depreciation for the machine, which is $1,500 per year.

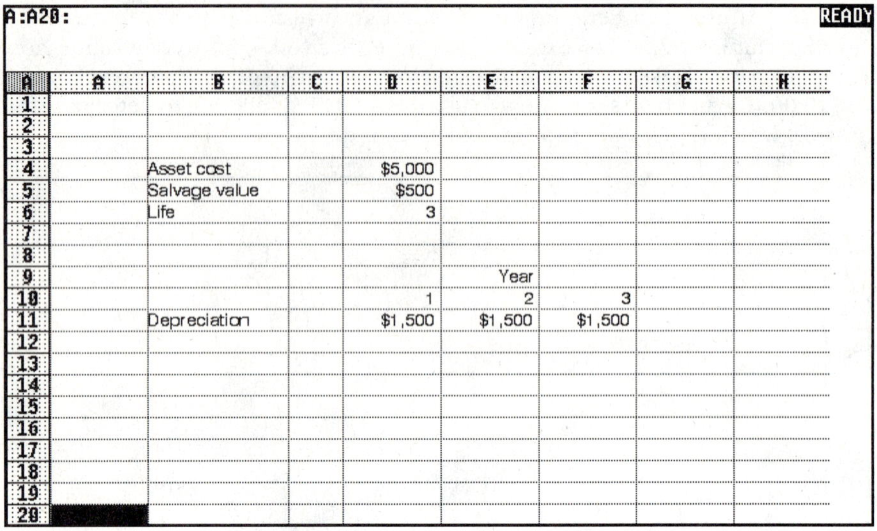

Fig. 6.20.
The @SLN function used to calculate straight-line depreciation.

```
A:A20:                                                        READY

     A         B            C        D         E        F        G        H
 1
 2
 3
 4             Asset cost            $5,000
 5             Salvage value         $500
 6             Life                  3
 7
 8
 9                                             Year
10                                    1         2        3
11             Depreciation         $1,500    $1,500   $1,500
12
13
14
15
16
17
18
19
20
```

@DDB—Calculating Double Declining-Balance Depreciation

The @DDB function calculates depreciation by using the double declining-balance method, with depreciation ending when the book value equals the salvage value. The double declining-balance method accelerates depreciation so that greater depreciation expense occurs in the earlier periods rather than in the later ones. Book value in any period is the purchase price less the total depreciation in all prior periods. @DDB uses the following format:

@DDB(*cost,salvage,life,period*)

Generally, the double declining-balance depreciation in any period is the following:

book value*2/*n*

In this formula, the book value is the book value in the period, and *n* is the depreciable life of the asset. 1-2-3 adjusts the result of this formula in later periods, however, to ensure that total depreciation does not exceed the purchase price less the salvage value.

Reminder:
When you use the double declining-balance depreciation method for an asset with a small salvage value, the asset will not be fully depreciated in the final year.

Figure 6.21 shows how the @DDB function can calculate depreciation on an asset purchased for $5,000, with a depreciable life of three years and an estimated salvage value of $500.

Keep in mind that when you use the double declining-balance depreciation method for an asset with a small salvage value, the asset will not be fully depreciated in the final year. If this is the case with one of your assets, you need to use the @VDB function, discussed later in this section.

Chapter 6 ◆ Using @Functions in the Worksheet **231**

```
A:D11: (C0) @VDB($D$4,$D$5,$D$6,D13,D14,1.5)                    READY
```

	A	B	C	D	E	F	G	H
1								
2								
3								
4		Asset cost		$5,000				
5		Salvage value		$500				
6		Life		3				
7								
8								
9						Year		
10				1	2	3	4	Total
11		Depreciation		$1,250	$1,875	$938	$438	4500
12								
13		Start period		0	0.5	1.5	2.5	
14		End period		0.5	1.5	2.5	3	

```
FIG_0623.WK3                                                    NUM
```

Fig. 6.21.
The @DDB function used to calculate double declining-balance depreciation.

@SYD—Calculating Sum-of-the-Years'-Digits Depreciation

The @SYD function calculates depreciation by the sum-of-the-years'-digits method. Similar to double-declining balance, this method accelerates depreciation so that earlier periods of the item's life reflect greater depreciation than do later periods. @SYD uses the following format:

@SYD(*cost,salvage,life,period*)

The cost is the purchase cost of the asset, and the salvage is the estimated value of the asset at the end of the depreciable life. The life is the depreciable life of the asset, and the period is the period for which depreciation is to be computed.

@SYD calculates depreciation with the following formula:

$$SYD = \frac{(cost\_salvage)*(life\_period+1)}{life*(life+1)/2}$$

The expression (life_period+1) in the numerator shows the life of the depreciation in the first period, decreased by 1 in each subsequent period. This expression reflects the declining pattern of depreciation over time. The expression in the denominator, life*(life+1)/2, is equal to the sum of the digits, as in the following:

1 + 2 +...+ life

The name *sum-of-the-years'-digits* originated from this expression.

Figure 6.22 shows how the @SYD function can calculate depreciation for an asset costing $5,000 with a depreciable life of three years and an estimated salvage value of $500.

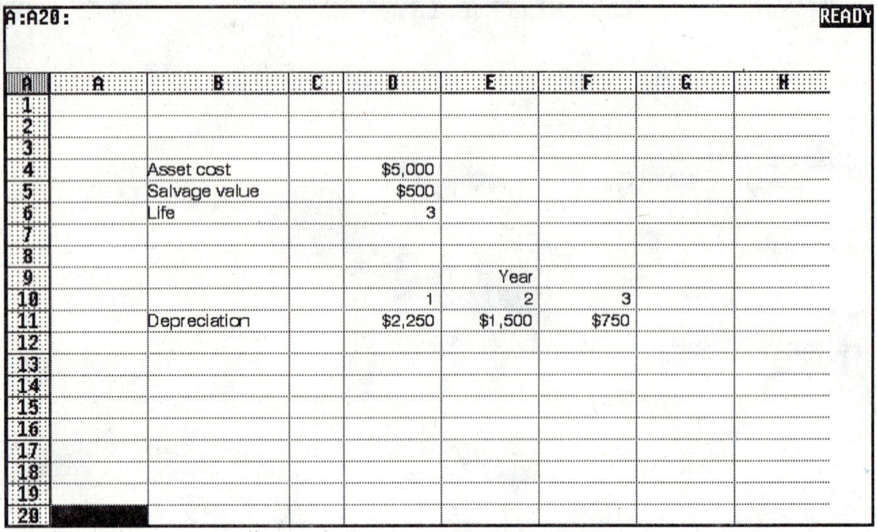

Fig. 6.22.
The @SYD function used to calculate sum-of-the-year's-digits depreciation.

```
A:A20:                                                              READY
       A          B          C          D          E          F          G          H
  1
  2
  3
  4            Asset cost            $5,000
  5            Salvage value           $500
  6            Life                       3
  7
  8
  9                                             Year
 10                                     1         2         3
 11            Depreciation        $2,250    $1,500      $750
 12
 13
 14
 15
 16
 17
 18
 19
 20
```

@VDB—Calculating Variable Declining-Balance Depreciation

The @VDB function calculates depreciation by using a variable-rate declining-balance method. The variable-rate depreciation method gives you accelerated depreciation during the early part of the term. If you do not specify a depreciation rate, 1-2-3 uses 200 percent to produce double declining-balance depreciation. Normally, @VDB automatically switches from accelerated depreciation to straight-line depreciation when it is most advantageous. However, you can set a switch in the @VDB argument if you do not want automatic switchover to straight-line depreciation. The start-period and end-period correspond to the beginning and end of the asset's life, respectively, relative to the fiscal period. For example, to find the first year's depreciation of an asset purchased at the beginning of the third quarter of the fiscal year, the start-period would be zero and the end-period would be .50 (half of the year).

The @VDB function uses the following format:

@VDB(*cost,salvage,life,start,end,[depreciation],[switch]*)

Figure 6.23 shows how the @VDB function can calculate depreciation on an asset purchased for $5,000, with a depreciable life of three years, an estimated salvage value of $500, and placed into service at the beginning of the third quarter of the first fiscal year. The optional percent argument is set at 150 percent.

An easy way to enter the start and end period for each fiscal year is to create a table, as shown in figure 6.23. After entering the initial start and end periods for the first year, you can use a formula to calculate the subsequent years' start and end periods. Or you can use 1-2-3's /Data Fill command to enter the values for you. Either way, this method eliminates the need for you to type in the start and end period's decimal fractions required to calculate the depreciation for that year.

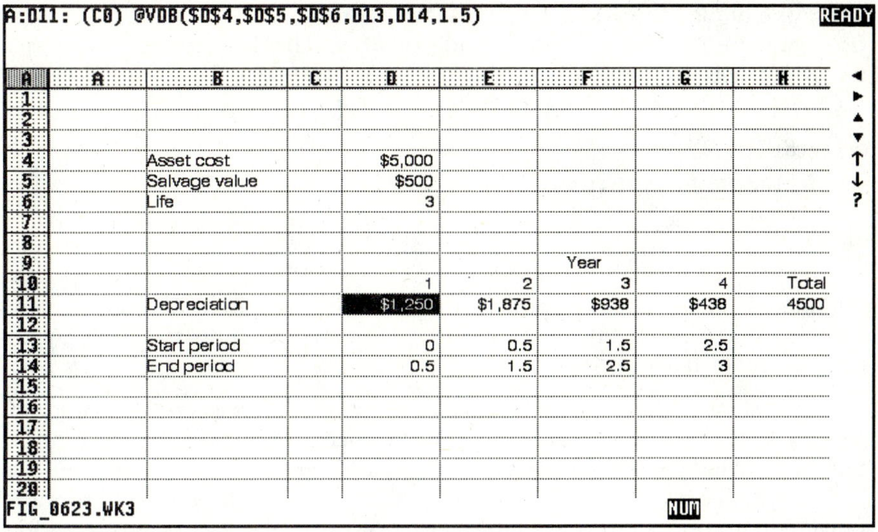

Fig. 6.23.
The @VDB function used to calculate 150 percent declining-balance depreciation.

Using Statistical @Functions

1-2-3 provides 10 statistical @functions. Table 6.4 lists the @functions, their arguments, and the statistical operations they perform.

Table 6.4
Statistical @Functions

@Function	Description
@AVG(*list*)	Calculates the arithmetic mean of a list of values
@COUNT(*list*)	Counts the number of cells that contain entries
@MAX(*list*)	Returns the maximum value in a list of values
@MIN(*list*)	Returns the minimum value in a list of values
@STD(*list*)	Calculates the population standard deviation of a list of values
@STDS(*list*)	Calculates the sample population standard deviation of a list of values
@SUM(*list*)	Sums a list of values
@SUMPRODUCT(*range1,range2*)	Multiplies *range1* by *range2* and sums the values
@VAR(*list*)	Calculates the population variance of a list of values
@VARS(*list*)	Calculates the sample population variance of a list of values

Reminder:
Every statistical @function except @SUMPRODUCT uses the list *argument.*

Every one of the statistical @functions except one—@SUMPRODUCT—uses the *list* argument. This argument can be individually specified values or cell addresses, a range of cells, or multiple ranges of cells. For example, 1-2-3 considers each of the following formats (or any combination) valid:

@SUM(1,2,3,4)

@SUM(B1,B2,B3,B4)

@SUM(B1..B4)

@SUM(B1..B2,B3..B4)

Although the preceding examples use the @SUM function (which totals the values included as arguments), the principles that these examples illustrate apply equally to each of the statistical @functions.

Note that some of the statistical @functions perform differently when you specify cells individually instead of as ranges. The @functions that perform differently in this case include @AVG, @MAX, @MIN, @STD, @STDS, @VAR, and @VARS. When you specify a range of cells, 1-2-3 ignores empty cells within the specified range. When you specify cells individually, however, 1-2-3 takes empty cells into consideration for the particular @functions mentioned.

Suppose, for example, that you are looking for the minimum value in a range that includes an empty cell and cells containing the entries 1, 2, and 3; in this case, 1-2-3 returns the value 1 as the minimum value. Suppose, however, that you instead specify individually a cell that is empty, along with cells containing the entries 1, 2, and 3; in this case, 1-2-3 returns the value 0 as the minimum.

The reason that 1-2-3 makes this distinction is that empty cells actually contain zeros, although they are invisible. Accordingly, 1-2-3 assumes that if you go to the extra effort of actually specifying an individual cell—even if it is empty—you must want it included in the calculation.

Reminder:
1-2-3 treats cells containing labels as zeros.

When you specify cells, keep in mind also that 1-2-3 treats cells containing labels as zeros. This is the case when the cell is included as part of a range or when you specify the cell individually.

@AVG—Computing the Arithmetic Mean

To calculate the average of a set of values, you add all the values and then divide the sum by the number of values. Essentially, the @AVG function produces the same result as if you divided @SUM(*list*) by @COUNT(*list*), two @functions described later in this section. You may find the @AVG function a helpful tool for calculating the arithmetic mean—a commonly used measure of a set of values' averages. Use the following format for @AVG:

@AVG(*list*)

As noted earlier, the *list* argument can be values, cell addresses, cell names, cell ranges, range names, or a combination of these.

Figure 6.24 shows an example of the @AVG function calculating the mean price per share of an imaginary company. In the figure, the function's argument is D5..D16. As long as cells D6..D7 and D13..D14 are empty and are included in the list argument only as part of a range, the values of these cells—actually zero—are ignored in the average calculation.

```
A:H5: (C2) @AVG(D5..D16)                                    READY

       A        B         C          D        E      F           G         H
  1
  2
  3
  4            Date      Day      Stock Price
  5         01-Jun-90    Fri       $125.83         Average Price        $124.17
  6         02-Jun-90    Sat                       Maximum Price        $125.98
  7         03-Jun-90    Sun                       Minimum Price        $121.21
  8         04-Jun-90    Mon       $121.87
  9         05-Jun-90    Tue       $121.21         Days Counted              8
 10         06-Jun-90    Wed       $125.40
 11         07-Jun-90    Thu       $125.98         Std. Dev. - Pop.    1.699275
 12         08-Jun-90    Fri       $124.13         Std. Dev. - Sample  1.816602
 13         09-Jun-90    Sat
 14         10-Jun-90    Sun
 15         11-Jun-90    Mon       $123.65
 16         12-Jun-90    Tue       $125.28
 17
 18
 19
 20
```

Fig. 6.24.

The @AVG function used to calculate the average price per share.

@COUNT—Counting Cell Entries

The @COUNT function totals the number of cells that contain entries of any kind, including labels, label-prefix characters, or the values ERR and NA. Use the following format for @COUNT:

@COUNT(*list*)

The *list* argument can be values, cell addresses, cell names, cell ranges, range names, or a combination of these.

For example, you can use @COUNT to show the number of share prices included in the @AVG calculation made in figure 6.24. Figure 6.25 shows this calculation being made in cell G9.

You should use ranges as the argument in the @COUNT function. If you specify a cell individually, 1-2-3 counts that cell as if it has an entry even if the cell is empty. If you absolutely must specify a cell individually, but want it counted only if it actually contains an entry, you need to use the @@ function. That function is described in the section covering 1-2-3's special @functions later in this chapter.

Fig. 6.25.
The @COUNT function used to count the number of prices per share in average calculations.

```
A:H9: @COUNT(D5..D16)                                          READY
```

	A	B	C	D	E	F	G	H
1								
2								
3								
4		Date	Day	Stock Price				
5		01–Jun–90	Fri	$125.83		Average Price		$124.17
6		02–Jun–90	Sat			Maximum Price		$125.98
7		03–Jun–90	Sun			Minimum Price		$121.21
8		04–Jun–90	Mon	$121.87				
9		05–Jun–90	Tue	$121.21		Days Counted		8
10		06–Jun–90	Wed	$125.40				
11		07–Jun–90	Thu	$125.98		Std. Dev. – Pop.		1.699275
12		08–Jun–90	Fri	$124.13		Std. Dev. – Sample		1.816602
13		09–Jun–90	Sat					
14		10–Jun–90	Sun					
15		11–Jun–90	Mon	$123.65				
16		12–Jun–90	Tue	$125.28				
17								
18								
19								
20								

@MAX and @MIN—Finding Maximum and Minimum Values

Reminder:
@MAX finds the largest value included in the list *argument.*

The @MAX function finds the largest value included in the *list* argument; the @MIN function finds the smallest value included in the *list* argument. The @functions use the following formats:

  @MAX(*list*)

  @MIN(*list*)

Figure 6.26 shows information concerning prices per share of an imaginary company shown earlier. The @MAX and @MIN functions can help you find the highest and the lowest prices, respectively. Note that the argument of @MAX in the control panel is D5..D16. The argument of @MIN, which isn't shown in the figure, is identical to the @MAX argument. Although the example shows only eight values, the true power of these @functions is most evident when your list consists of several dozen or several hundred items.

If you are familiar with statistics, you'll recognize that these two @functions also provide the two pieces of data you need to calculate a popular statistical measure—a range. A *range*, which is one measure of variability in a list of values, is the difference between the highest value and the lowest value in a list of values. (A range as a statistical measurement is not the same thing as a worksheet range, which is a rectangular block of cells.)

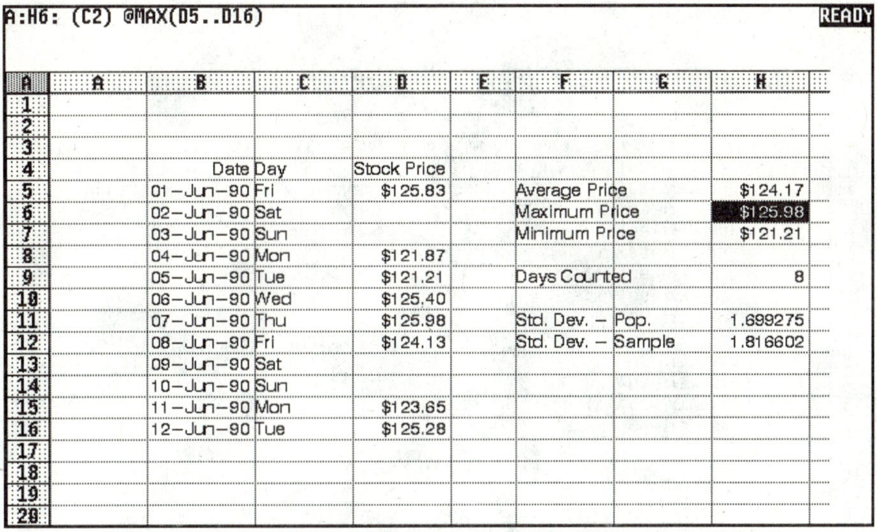

Fig. 6.26.
The @MAX function used to show the highest price per share.

@STD and @STDS—Calculating the Standard Deviation

The @STD function uses the *n*, or population, method of calculating standard deviation; the @STDS function uses the *n–1*, or sample population, method of calculating the standard deviation. Use the following formats for these @functions:

@STD(*list*)

@STDS(*list*)

Essentially, the standard deviation is a measure of how individual values vary from the mean or average of the other values in the list. Figure 6.27 shows the @STD function as used to calculate the standard deviation of stock price values.

The precise definitions of the two standard deviation formulas are best shown by the formulas 1-2-3 uses to calculate them. These formulas are as follows:

$$STD = \sqrt{\frac{\sum_{n=1}^{N}(X_n - avg)^2}{N}} \qquad STDS = \sqrt{\frac{\sum_{n=1}^{N}(X_n - avg)^2}{N-1}}$$

where

N = Number of items in list
X_n = The *n*th item in list
avg = Arithmetic mean of list

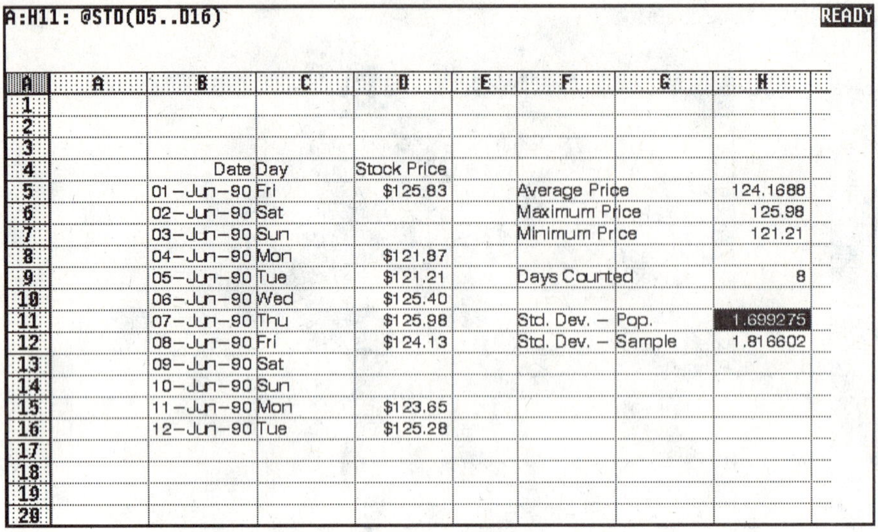

Fig. 6.27.
The @STD function used to calculate standard deviation.

```
A:H11: @STD(D5..D16)                                          READY
```

	A	B	C	D	E	F	G	H
1								
2								
3								
4		Date	Day	Stock Price				
5		01-Jun-90	Fri	$125.83		Average Price		124.1688
6		02-Jun-90	Sat			Maximum Price		125.98
7		03-Jun-90	Sun			Minimum Price		121.21
8		04-Jun-90	Mon	$121.87				
9		05-Jun-90	Tue	$121.21		Days Counted		8
10		06-Jun-90	Wed	$125.40				
11		07-Jun-90	Thu	$125.98		Std. Dev. – Pop.		1.699275
12		08-Jun-90	Fri	$124.13		Std. Dev. – Sample		1.816602
13		09-Jun-90	Sat					
14		10-Jun-90	Sun					
15		11-Jun-90	Mon	$123.65				
16		12-Jun-90	Tue	$125.28				
17								
18								
19								
20								

Essentially, the standard deviation is a measure of dispersion about or around an average. A smaller standard deviation indicates less dispersion, or variation, while a larger standard deviation indicates greater dispersion, or variation. Perhaps not surprisingly, a standard deviation of 0 indicates that there is no dispersion—meaning that every value in the list of values is the same.

To choose the correct @function, you need to know whether you are dealing with the entire population or with a sample. If you are measuring, or including, every value in a calculation, you are working with a *population*. However, if you are measuring, or including, only a subset or portion of the values in a calculation, you are working with a *sample*. The @STDS function uses the *n*–1, or sample population, method to calculate standard deviation for sample populations. This method adjusts the standard deviation so that it is slightly higher to compensate for possible errors because the entire population was not used.

@SUM—Totaling Values

The @SUM function provides a convenient way to add a list of values. Of all the statistical @functions that 1-2-3 provides, @SUM is the one you probably use most often. @SUM uses the following format:

@SUM(*list*)

Figure 6.28 shows subtotals in column E. You may calculate a total of these subtotals with the following formula:

+E5+E6+E7+E8+E9+E10+E11

This method, however, is inefficient and prone to error. A better way to total the column is to use the @SUM function over the range of the subtotals.

Chapter 6 ♦ Using @Functions in the Worksheet   **239**

```
A:A20:                                                    READY
     A       B         C       D       E       F      G      H
 1
 2
 3         Price      Tax             Subtotal Function
 4         -----     -----            --------
 5         $45.67    6.5%             $2.97
 6         $34.00    6.5%             $2.21
 7         $43.20    6.5%             $2.81
 8         $22.15    6.5%             $1.44
 9         $16.78    6.5%             $1.09
10         $43.89    6.5%             $2.85
11         $12.02    6.5%             $0.78
12                                    ------
13                 Total Tax          $14.15 @SUM(E4..E12)
14
15
16
17
18
19
20
```

Fig. 6.28.
The @SUM function used to calculate the subtotals in column E.

When you sum a range of cells with @SUM, you can insert more cells or delete cells from the middle of the range, and 1-2-3 will continue to calculate accurate results. You can insert a row accidentally at one end of an @SUM range, however, so that new data entered at that spot appears to be included in the @SUM formula range but is not. To prevent such an occurrence, you can include a *placeholder* (a blank or text-filled cell) at the top or bottom of the range of cells being summed. (If filled with text, the cell will not affect the total because the cell equals zero). If you use this technique regularly, rows or columns inserted above or below the first and last number still will be inside the placeholders that mark the end points of the range being summed.

@SUMPRODUCT—Multiplying Lists of Values

The @SUMPRODUCT function gets its name because it sums the products of the two ranges specified as its arguments. The format for @SUMPRODUCT is the following:

   @SUMPRODUCT(*range1,range2*)

You can use @SUMPRODUCT to calculate, for example, the total dollars of inventory (see figure 6.29). In effect, the @SUMPRODUCT function performs the calculations @SUM(C8*D8,C9*D9,...) and then totals the results, called *products*.

Because @SUMPRODUCT multiplies two ranges and totals the result, you can use this @function to calculate weighted averages.

Reminder:
@SUMPRODUCT multiplies the two ranges specified as its arguments.

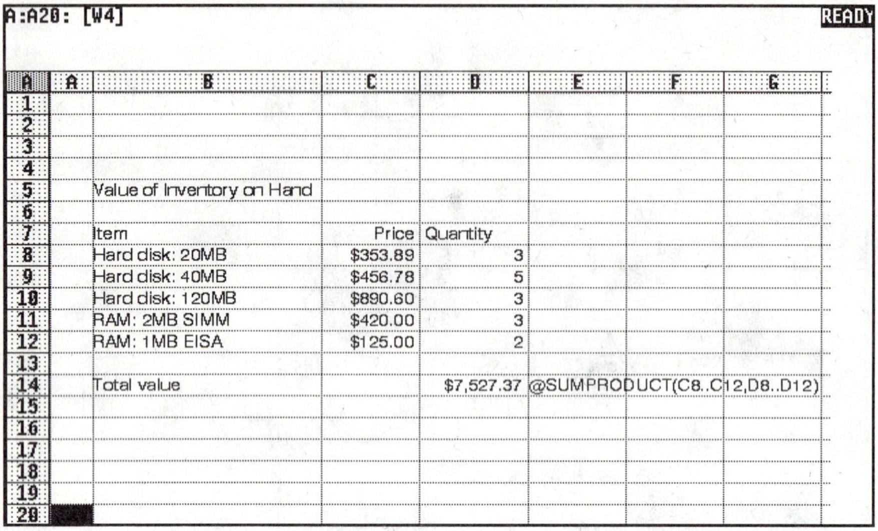

Fig. 6.29.
@SUMPRODUCT used to calculate the total dollars of inventory.

```
A:A20: [W4]                                                    READY

      A    B                        C         D       E       F       G
 1
 2
 3
 4
 5         Value of Inventory on Hand
 6
 7         Item                      Price     Quantity
 8         Hard disk: 20MB           $353.89          3
 9         Hard disk: 40MB           $456.78          5
10         Hard disk: 120MB          $890.60          3
11         RAM: 2MB SIMM             $420.00          3
12         RAM: 1MB EISA             $125.00          2
13
14         Total value                         $7,527.37 @SUMPRODUCT(C8..C12,D8..D12)
15
16
17
18
19
20
```

@VAR and @VARS—Calculating the Variance

The variance, like the standard deviation, is a measure of dispersion about, or around, an average. The @VAR function calculates the variance by using the population, or *n*, method. The @VARS function calculates the variance by using the sample population, or *n*–1, method. These @functions use the following formats:

@VAR(*list*)

@VARS(*list*)

Note that calculating a statistical variance is an intermediate step in calculating the standard deviations described in the discussion of the @STD and @STDS @functions. By comparing the following two formulas, you can see that the standard deviation is simply the square root of the variance:

$$\text{VAR} = \frac{\sum_{n=1}^{N}(X_n - \text{avg})^2}{N} \qquad \text{VARS} = \frac{\sum_{n=1}^{N}(X_n - \text{avg})^2}{N-1}$$

where
    N = Number of items in list
    X_n = The *n*th item in list
    avg = Arithmetic mean of list

For explanations of the terms *population* and *sample*, refer to the earlier discussion of the @STD and @STDS @functions.

Using Database @Functions

1-2-3's database @functions are similar to the worksheet @functions, but have been modified to manipulate database fields. Like the standard @functions, the database @functions perform in one simple statement calculations that may otherwise require several statements. This efficiency and ease of application make these @functions excellent tools. The database @functions are described in table 6.5.

Cue:
Use the database @functions to summarize your database selectively.

Table 6.5
Database @Functions

Function	Description
@DCOUNT	Gives the number of items in a list that match the selected criteria
@DSUM	Sums the values of items in a list that match the selected criteria
@DMIN	Gives the minimum value of items in a list that match the selected criteria
@DMAX	Gives the maximum value of items in a list that match the selected criteria
@DSTD	Gives the standard deviation of items in a list that match the selected criteria
@DVAR	Gives the variance of items in a list that match the selected criteria
@DAVG	Gives the arithmetic mean of items in a list that match the selected criteria
@DGET	Extracts a value or label from a field in a database that matches the selected criteria
@DQUERY	Sends a command to an external database management program
@DSTDS	Calculates the sample standard deviation of values in a field of a database that match the selected criteria
@DVARS	Calculates the sample variance of values in a field of a database that match the selected criteria

The general format of these @functions is as follows:

@DSUM(*input_range,offset,criteria_range*)

The one exception to this format is @DQUERY, which is discussed later in this section.

The *input_range* and *criteria_range* are the same as those used by the /Data Query command. The *input_range* specifies the database or part of a database to be scanned, and the *criteria_range* specifies which records are to be selected. The offset indicates which field to select from the database records; the *offset* value must be either zero or a positive integer. A value of zero indicates the first column in the database, a one indicates the second column, and so on.

Cue:
Remember that all the database @functions consider that the first column in a database is offset zero.

Suppose that you want to compute the mean, variance, and standard deviation of the average interest rates offered by money market funds for a given week.

Figure 6.30 shows the money market database and the results of the various database @functions. Notice that the @functions to find the count, sum, maximum, and minimum rates of return are also included. Also, the database formulas from column E are repeated in column F with /Range Format Text applied.

Figure 6.30 shows that the week's mean return for 17 different money market funds works out to an annual percentage rate of 7.7 (cell E5), with a variance of .057 (cell E6). One standard deviation below a mean of 7.7 is 7.46. One standard deviation above a mean of 7.7 is 7.94.

Fig. 6.30.
Database @functions used with the money market database.

```
A:E3: (F8) [W9] @DCOUNT(A3..B20,1,D13..D14)                    READY

     A                              B    C    D                   E           F               G
 1  Money Market Database (7 days average yield)
 2                                            Database Statistics
 3  Name                         Week 1      Count                17  @DCOUNT(DB,1,CRIT)
 4  Alliance Group                 7.7       Sum               131.7  @DSUM(DB,1,CRIT)
 5  Bull & Bear Reserves           7.7       Mean           7.747059  @DAVG(DB,1,CRIT)
 6  Carl's Cash Securities         7.4       Variance          0.057  @DVAR(DB,1,CRIT)
 7  Colonial Money Market          7.9       Std Dev           0.238  @DSTD(DB,1,CRIT)
 8  Ed's Money Market Account      7.8       Maximum             8.2  @DMAX(DB,1,CRIT)
 9  Fred's Group Cash Reserves     8.0       Minimum             7.3  @DMIN(DB,1,CRIT)
10  Kemper Money Funds             7.7
11  Len Smith Money Market         8.1
12  Market Management              7.8       Criterion Range
13  Paine Webber Cash              7.9       Week 1
14  Prudential Bache               7.4       +WEEK 1>7
15  Saint Brian Money Market, Inc. 7.6
16  Shearson T-Fund                8.2
17  Shorty's Income Fund           7.9
18  Standaway Reserves             7.6
19  Summit Cash Reserves           7.3
20  Value Line Cash Fund           7.7
19-Jul-90 02:38 PM                                                           NUM
```

The result of the @DMIN function (cell E9) shows that Summit Cash Reserves returns the lowest rate at 7.3 percent (row 19). This value is almost two standard deviations below the mean. That figure—two standard deviations below the mean—is computed as follows:

$$7.7 - (2 \times .238) = 7.22$$

Because approximately 95 percent of the population falls within plus or minus two standard deviations of the mean, Summit Cash Reserves is close to being in the lowest 2.5 percent of the population of money market funds for that week; 5 percent is divided by 2 because the population is assumed to be normal.

Conversely, the Shearson T-Fund returns 8.2 percent, the highest rate. The @DMAX function has determined the highest rate (cell B16) to be just over two standard deviations above the mean, the highest 2.5 percent of the population.

By setting up the proper criteria, you can analyze any portion of the database you want. How do the statistics change if funds returning less than 7.5 percent are excluded from the statistics? Figure 6.31 gives the answer.

```
A:D14: (T) [W12] +WEEK 1>7.5                                       READY

     A                              B    C    D                 E    F         G
  1  Money Market Database (7 days average yield)
  2                                           Database Statistics
  3  Name                          Week 1     Count                 14 @DCOUNT(DB,1,CRIT)
  4  Alliance Group                 7.7       Sum                109.6 @DSUM(DB,1,CRIT)
  5  Bull & Bear Reserves           7.7       Mean            7.828571 @DAVG(DB,1,CRIT)
  6  Carl's Cash Securities         7.4       Variance           0.031 @DVAR(DB,1,CRIT)
  7  Colonial Money Market          7.9       Std Dev            0.175 @DSTD(DB,1,CRIT)
  8  Ed's Money Market Account      7.8       Maximum              8.2 @DMAX(DB,1,CRIT)
  9  Fred's Group Cash Reserves     8.0       Minimum              7.6 @DMIN(DB,1,CRIT)
 10  Kemper Money Funds             7.7
 11  Len Smith Money Market         8.1
 12  Market Management              7.8       Criterion Range
 13  Paine Webber Cash              7.9       Week 1
 14  Prudential Bache               7.4       +WEEK 1>7.5
 15  Saint Brian Money Market, Inc. 7.6
 16  Shearson T-Fund                8.2
 17  Shorty's Income Fund           7.9
 18  Standaway Reserves             7.6
 19  Summit Cash Reserves           7.3
 20  Value Line Cash Fund           7.7
19-Jul-90 02:39 PM                                                 NUM
```

Fig. 6.31.
Money market fund analysis with funds earning less than 7.5 percent excluded.

Obviously, the database @functions can tell you a great deal about the database as a whole and about how to interpret the values contained in it. If you add a few more weeks' data to the database, as shown in figure 6.32, the database @functions also can be used to analyze all or part of the larger database.

You can use all the methods you have seen so far to interpret the statistics in figure 6.32. Note, however, that you must adjust the input (or database) range address and the offset used in the database formulas to access the data from the third week. The input range is now A3..D20 and the offset must be adjusted to 3. Although the figure shows "Week 3" in cell E13 for clarity, you may recall that any database field name can be used when the criteria range uses a formula instead of a value.

@DSTDS and @DVARS—Calculating Deviation and Variance

The two database @functions @DSTDS and @DVARS calculate the sample standard deviation and variance, respectively. Compare these @functions with @DSTD and @DVAR, which calculate the population standard deviation and variance, respectively. When you are evaluating a small number of observations, the sample standard deviation and variance values give more accurate results than the population values.

Fig. 6.32.
Additional money market fund data.

```
A:F9: [W9] @DMIN(DB,3,CRIT)                                          READY

     A                              B        C       D     E                F        G
 1  Money Market Database (7 days average yield)
 2                                                        Database Statistics
 3  Name                         Week 1  Week 2  Week 3  Count              17
 4  Alliance Group                 7.7     7.8     7.9  Sum              133.5
 5  Bull & Bear Reserves           7.7     7.8     7.8  Mean          7.852941
 6  Carl's Cash Securities         7.4     7.5     7.5  Variance         0.058
 7  Colonial Money Market          7.9     7.9     7.9  Std Dev          0.240
 8  Ed's Money Market Account      7.8     7.9     7.9  Maximum            8.3
 9  Fred's Group Cash Reserves     8.0     8.1     8.1  Minimum            7.4
10  Kemper Money Funds             7.7     7.8     7.8
11  Len Smith Money Market         8.1     8.2     8.2
12  Market Management              7.8     7.9     7.9  Criterion Range
13  Paine Webber Cash              7.9     8.0     8.0  Week 3
14  Prudential Bache               7.4     7.5     7.5  +WEEK 3>7
15  Saint Brian Money Market, Inc. 7.6     7.7     7.7
16  Shearson T-Fund                8.2     8.3     8.3
17  Shorty's Income Fund           7.9     8.0     8.1
18  Standaway Reserves             7.6     7.7     7.8
19  Summit Cash Reserves           7.3     7.4     7.4
20  Value Line Cash Fund           7.7     7.7     7.7
19-Jul-90 02:40 PM                                                      NUM
```

@DGET—Extracting a Value or Label

The database @function @DGET extracts a value or label from a field in the database. The format for @DGET is the following:

   @DGET(*input_range*,*offset*,*criteria_range*)

The *input_range*, *offset*, and *criteria_range* arguments are used in exactly the same manner as in the other database @functions. @DGET returns the value or label in the specified field of the record that matches the specified criteria.

To see how @DGET works, suppose that you want to find the name of the firm offering the highest third-week return—8.3 percent (shown in cell F8). In cell E14, enter the criterion **+WEEK 3=8.3**. In cell E10 enter "**Name**" and in cell F10, type the following formula:

   @DGET(A3..D20,"NAME",E13..E14)

The @DGET function returns `Shearson T-Fund`, which is the only firm on the list that offers an 8.3 percent return (see figure 6.33). If no elements in the database match the criteria, @DGET returns ERR. More important, @DGET returns ERR if more than one element in the database matches the criteria. Therefore, if you use @DGET and it returns ERR, you must determine what has caused the error. Notice also that the rest of the database @functions now show exactly the expected results when only one record matches the criteria.

@DQUERY—Working with External Tables

A function for use with external tables is @DQUERY, which is similar to the /Data External Other Command command. With @DQUERY, you may use in the criteria range for record selection an @function that belongs to the external database management program. @DQUERY uses the following format:

@DQUERY (*external_function,arguments,arg2*...)

```
A:E14: (T) [W12] +WEEK 3=8.3                                      READY
         A                        B      C      D      E              F         G
 1  Money Market Database (7 days average yield)
 2                                                    Database Statistics
 3  Name                       Week 1 Week 2 Week 3  Count              1
 4  Alliance Group               7.7    7.8    7.9   Sum                8.3
 5  Bull & Bear Reserves         7.7    7.8    7.8   Mean               8.3
 6  Carl's Cash Securities       7.4    7.5    7.5   Variance           0.000
 7  Colonial Money Market        7.9    7.9    7.9   Std Dev            0.000
 8  Ed's Money Market Account    7.8    7.9    7.9   Maximum            8.3
 9  Fred's Group Cash Reserves   8.0    8.1    8.1   Minimum            8.3
10  Kemper Money Funds           7.7    7.8    7.8   Name        Shearson T-Fund
11  Len Smith Money Market       8.1    8.2    8.2
12  Market Management            7.8    7.9    7.9   Criterion Range
13  Paine Webber Cash            7.9    8.0    8.0   Week 3
14  Prudential Bache             7.4    7.5    7.5   +WEEK 3=8.3
15  Saint Brian Money Market, Inc. 7.6  7.7    7.7
16  Shearson T-Fund              8.2    8.3    8.3
17  Shorty's Income Fund         7.9    8.0    8.1
18  Standaway Reserves           7.6    7.7    7.8
19  Summit Cash Reserves         7.3    7.4    7.4
20  Value Line Cash Fund         7.7    7.7    7.7
19-Jul-90 02:42 PM                                                            NUM
```

Fig. 6.33.
The results of the @DGET function.

The *external_function* is the name of the function in the external database management program, and the *arguments* are the values that the external function uses. You can include any additional arguments (*arg2*...) required by the external function; the arguments are separated by a comma.

To understand how @DQUERY works, suppose that your database management program contains a function to match data phonetically. The function is called LIKE, and it has one argument, the data you are matching. For example, LIKE("SMITH") matches the names Smith, Smyth, and Smythe.

In the criteria range, you type **@DQUERY("LIKE","SMITH")**. The @DQUERY function causes the matches to be phonetic because of the use of the LIKE function from the external database management program.

When you enter the @DQUERY function in the cell, the result that you see in the cell is the external function name. In other words, when you type the function **@DQUERY("LIKE","SMITH")**, LIKE is displayed in the cell.

Using Logical @Functions

The logical @functions enable you to use Boolean logic within your worksheets. Most of the logical @functions test whether a condition is true or false.

Cue:
Logical @functions add Boolean logic to your worksheet.

For most logical @functions, both the test and the answer the function returns based on the test are built into the function. The @ISSTRING function is a good example because it tests whether the argument is a string, and returns a 1 if the test is true or a 0 if the test is false. For one of the logical @functions, @IF, you describe the test and what the function result should be, based on the test. @IF tests a condition and returns one value or label if the test is true, or another value or label if the test is false.

The eight logical @functions that 1-2-3 provides are summarized in table 6.6. In the text that follows, the logical @functions are described in order of complexity.

Table 6.6
Logical @Functions

@Function	Description
@FALSE	Equals 0, the logical value for false
@IF(*test,true,false*)	Tests the condition and returns one result if the condition is true and another result if the condition is false
@ISERR(*cell_reference*)	Tests whether the argument results in ERR
@ISNA(*cell_reference*)	Tests whether the argument results in NA
@ISNUMBER(*cell_reference*)	Tests whether the argument is a number
@ISRANGE(*cell_reference*)	Tests whether the argument is a defined range
@ISSTRING(*cell_reference*)	Tests whether the argument is a string
@TRUE	Equals 1, the logical value for true

@IF—Creating Conditional Tests

The @IF function represents a powerful tool—one you can use both to manipulate text within your worksheets and to affect calculations. For example, you can use the @IF statement to test the condition "Is the inventory on hand below 1,000 units?" and then return one value or string if the answer to the question is true, or another value or string if the answer is false. The @IF function uses the following format:

@IF(*test,true,false*)

Figure 6.34 shows several examples of the @IF function in action. To show clearly the @functions, their arguments, and their results, the first column displays the value, the second column shows the calculated results of the function, and the third column shows the formula.

The first two @IF @functions check whether the content of cell B5 or B6 is between 4 and 10. The second two @IF @functions check whether a cell contains the text string "Wrench." The third example checks whether the dates in B11 and B12 are after December 1, 1990. (Substitute B12 for B11 in the formula in cell D12.)

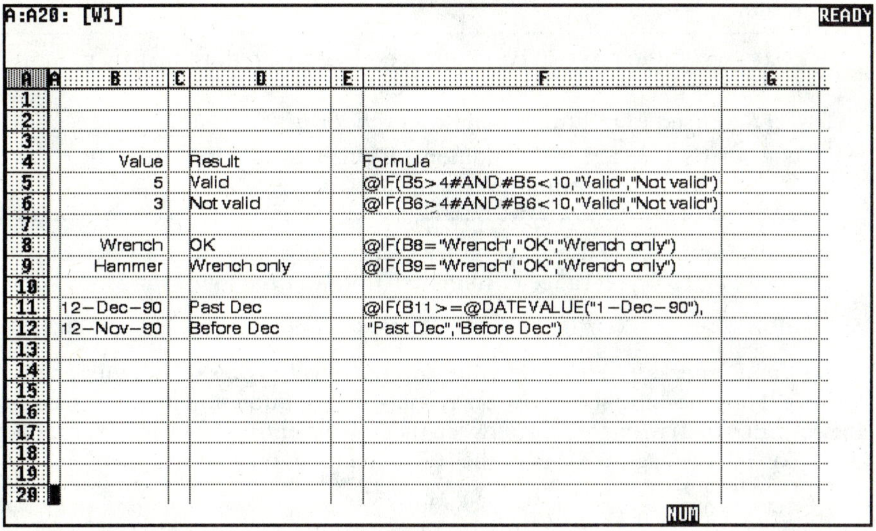

```
A:A20: [W1]                                                    READY
   A    B        C           D          E              F                              G
 1
 2
 3
 4      Value    Result                 Formula
 5        5      Valid                  @IF(B5>4#AND#B5<10,"Valid","Not valid")
 6        3      Not valid              @IF(B6>4#AND#B6<10,"Valid","Not valid")
 7
 8      Wrench   OK                     @IF(B8="Wrench","OK","Wrench only")
 9      Hammer   Wrench only            @IF(B9="Wrench","OK","Wrench only")
10
11    12-Dec-90  Past Dec               @IF(B11>=@DATEVALUE("1-Dec-90"),
12    12-Nov-90  Before Dec             "Past Dec","Before Dec")
13
14
15
16
17
18
19
20                                                                                   NUM
```

Fig. 6.34.
Examples of the @IF function using strings and values.

The @IF function can use six operators when testing conditions. These operators are summarized in table 6.7.

Table 6.7
Logical Test Operators

Operator	Description
<	Less than
<=	Less than or equal to
=	Equal to
>=	Greater than or equal to
>	Greater than
<>	Not equal to

As figure 6.34 shows, the @IF function is a powerful tool for worksheets, enabling you to add decision-making logic to your worksheets. The logical test can be based on strings or numeric comparison, and the function can return either string or numeric values. You can further expand the power of @IF @functions by using compound tests.

In addition, you can do complex conditional tests by using @IF @functions with logical operators that enable you to test multiple conditions in one @IF function. These complex operators are summarized in table 6.8.

Table 6.8
Complex Operators

Operator	Description
#AND#	Used to test two conditions, both of which must be true in order for the entire test to be true
#NOT#	Used to test that a condition is *not* true
#OR#	Used to test two conditions; if either condition is true, the entire test condition is true

One simple but valuable use for complex @IF @functions is to test whether data entries are in the correct range of numbers. Consider the following formula:

@IF(B12>=5#AND#B12<=20,"","Enter a number between 5 and 20.")

This formula checks whether the value entered in cell B12 is within the range of 5 to 20. If it is, nothing shows up as a result—that is, quotation marks appear (in the control panel) with nothing between them. If the entry is not within the range, the following message appears in the cell containing the @IF function:

```
Enter a number between 5 and 20.
```

You also can specify within an @IF function the true or false result of another @IF function. Putting @IF @functions inside other @IF @functions is a common and important logical tool. This technique, called *nesting IF statements*, enables you to construct sophisticated logical tests and operations in your 1-2-3 worksheets.

@ISERR and @ISNA—Trapping Errors in Conditional Tests

The @ISERR function tests whether the argument equals ERR. If the test is true, the function returns the value 1; if the test is false, the function returns the value 0. @ISERR uses the following format:

@ISERR(*cell_reference*)

Reminder:
To trap errors produced in one location that can cause more drastic results in other locations, use @ISERR.

This function is helpful because you can use it to trap errors produced in one location that can cause more drastic results in other locations. Figure 6.35 shows how to use @ISERR to trap a possible division-by-zero error or a serious data entry error that would cause an error to appear on-screen or in the printout. When you use this function, the letters NA appear on-screen in place of ERR.

The @ISNA function works similarly to @ISERR. @ISNA tests whether the argument you include is equal to NA. If the test is true, the function returns the value 1; if the test is false, the function returns the value 0. The @ISNA function uses the following format:

@ISNA(*cell_reference*)

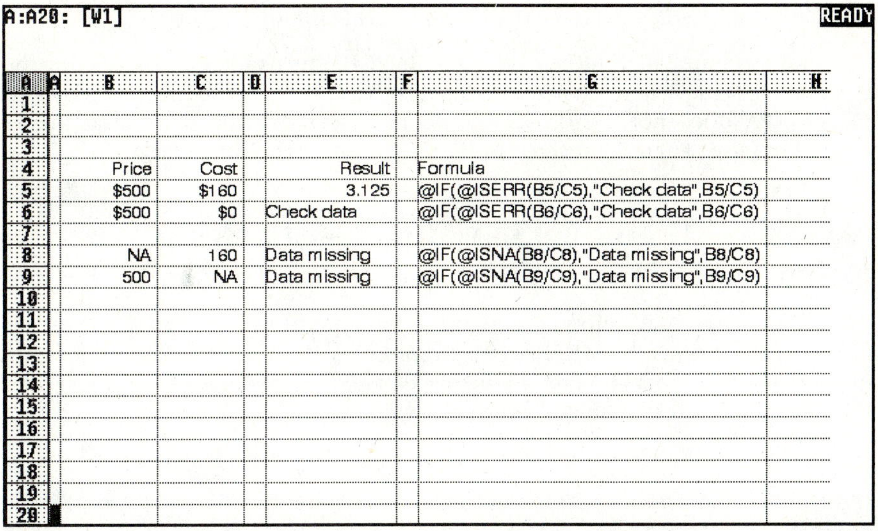

Chapter 6 ◆ Using @Functions in the Worksheet

```
A:A20: [W1]                                                              READY
    A     B       C      D       E        F              G                  H
 1
 2
 3
 4        Price   Cost          Result   Formula
 5        $500    $160          3.125    @IF(@ISERR(B5/C5),"Check data",B5/C5)
 6        $500    $0            Check data @IF(@ISERR(B6/C6),"Check data",B6/C6)
 7
 8        NA      160           Data missing  @IF(@ISNA(B8/C8),"Data missing",B8/C8)
 9        500     NA            Data missing  @IF(@ISNA(B9/C9),"Data missing",B9/C9)
10
...
20
```

Fig. 6.35.
The @ISERR and @ISNA @functions used to test for errors.

You can use the @ISNA function to trap NA values in worksheets in which you have been using the @NA function. The @NA function, which represents "Not Available," is discussed in the section "Using Special @Functions" later in this chapter.

@TRUE and @FALSE—Checking for Errors

You use the @TRUE and @FALSE @functions to check for errors. Neither function requires arguments, but both are useful for providing documentation for formulas and advanced macro commands. The @TRUE function returns the value 1, the Boolean logical value for true. The @FALSE function returns the value 0, the Boolean logical value for false.

@ISRANGE—Checking for a Range Name

@ISRANGE checks whether the argument is a range name. If it is, the function returns the value 1; otherwise, the function returns the value 0. @ISRANGE uses the following format:

@ISRANGE(*cell_reference*)

The argument can be either a cell reference to a string or the string itself. The string does not need to be a text label; the string can be either a cell reference containing a text label or a formula that returns a text label.

One of the best uses of @ISRANGE is within macro programs that test for the existence of range names. The following function from a print macro, for example, tests for the existence of the range name PRINTAREA:

{IF @ISRANGE(PRINTAREA)=1}{BRANCH SUBPRINT}

If the range name PRINTAREA exists, @ISRANGE returns the value 1, making the IF statement true. Then the macro branches to a subroutine to print the range. If PRINTAREA does not exist, @ISRANGE returns the value 0, making the IF statement false. Then the macro continues without branching and printing.

@ISSTRING and @ISNUMBER—Checking the Cell's Aspect

Two @functions that help you determine the type of value stored in a cell are @ISSTRING and @ISNUMBER. They are often used with @IF to check for data entry errors—numbers entered in the place of text, or text entered in the place of numbers. For @ISNUMBER, use the following format:

@ISNUMBER(*cell_reference*)

If the argument is a number, the numeric value of the function is 1 (true). If the argument is a string, including the null string (" "), the numeric value of the function is 0 (false).

Suppose, for example, that you want to test whether the value entered in cell B3 is a number. If the value is a number, you want to show the label number in the current cell; otherwise, you want to show the label string. You can use the following statement:

@IF(@ISNUMBER(B3),"number","string")

With this statement, you can be fairly certain that the appropriate label will appear in the current cell. The @ISNUMBER function, however, gives the numeric value 1 to empty cells as well as to numbers. Obviously, the function itself is incomplete because it will assign the label number to the current cell if cell B3 is empty. For complete reliability, the function must be modified to handle empty cells.

You can distinguish between a number and an empty cell by using this formula (cell AA3 must contain the label B3..B3):

@IF(@ISNUMBER(B3),@IF(@COUNT(@@(AA3)),"number","blank"),"string")

This function first tests whether the cell contains a number, NA, ERR, or is blank. If the test detects a number, NA, ERR, or finds that the cell is blank, the function then uses the @COUNT function to test whether the range B3..B3 contains an entry. (Recall that @COUNT assigns the value 0 to blank cells and assigns the value 1 to cells with an entry when the argument used is a range rather than a cell reference. See this chapter's discussion of the @COUNT function for a detailed explanation.) If the cell contains an entry, the label number is displayed. Otherwise, the label blank is displayed. If the cell does not contain a number or a blank, the cell must contain a string, and the string label is displayed.

Alternatively, you may want to use the @ISSTRING function. @ISSTRING works in nearly the same way as @ISNUMBER. The @ISSTRING function, however, determines whether a cell entry is a string value. The format of @ISSTRING is the following:

@ISSTRING(*cell_reference*)

If the argument for @ISSTRING is a string, the value of the function is 1 (true). If the argument is a number or a blank, however, the value of the function is 0 (false).

Returning to the earlier example about discriminating between a number and an empty cell, you can also complete the function with the help of @ISSTRING. Use the following formula (again, note that cell AA3 must contain the label B3..B3):

@IF(@ISSTRING(B3),"string",@IF(@COUNT(@@(AA3))>0,"number","blank"))

The first step that this function performs is to test whether string data is present in cell B3. If string data is present, the function results in the label string. Otherwise, the @COUNT function is used to determine whether the range B3..B3 contains a number or is empty. If the data is a number, the label number is the result. Otherwise, the label blank is the result.

@ISNUMBER tests for a number (or NA or ERR), although the function's principal weakness is that it cannot distinguish between numbers and blank cells. In many applications, however, @ISNUMBER provides sufficient testing of values, especially when you are certain that a cell is not blank. @ISSTRING provides the capability to test for a string. When used with the @COUNT function, @ISSTRING can distinguish blank cells from strings. The @COUNT function combined with both @ISNUMBER and @ISSTRING can help you distinguish between blank cells, strings, and numbers.

Additionally, you can use the @CELL and @CELLPOINTER @functions within formulas or macros to test whether a cell contains a number, a text string, or a blank.

Using String @Functions

1-2-3 offers a variety of @functions that provide you significant power to manipulate text strings.

Strings are labels or portions of labels. More specifically, strings are data consisting of characters (alphabetic, numeric, blank, and special) enclosed in quotation marks, such as "total". The @functions specifically designated as string @functions are one category of 1-2-3 @functions that take advantage of the power and flexibility of strings. Logical, error-trapping, and special @functions use strings as well as values. The string @functions, however, are specifically designed to manipulate strings. Table 6.9 summarizes the string @functions available in 1-2-3.

**Table 6.9
String @Functions**

@Function	Description
@FIND(*search_string, string,start_number*)	Locates the start position of one string within another string
@MID(*string,start_number,number*)	Extracts a string of a specified number of characters from the middle of another string, beginning at the starting position
@LEFT(*string,number*)	Extracts the leftmost specified number of characters from the string
@RIGHT(*string,number*)	Extracts the rightmost specified number of characters from the string
@REPLACE(*original_string,start_number,length,replacement_string*)	Replaces a number of characters in the original string with new string characters, starting at the character identified by the start position
@LENGTH(*string*)	Returns the number of characters in the string
@EXACT(*string1,string2*)	Returns 1 (true) if *string1* and *string2* are exact matches; otherwise, returns 0 (false)
@LOWER(*string*)	Converts all characters in the string to lowercase
@UPPER(*string*)	Converts all characters in the string to uppercase
@PROPER(*string*)	Converts the first character in each word in the string to uppercase, and converts the remaining characters to lowercase
@REPEAT(*string,number*)	Copies the string the specified number of times in a cell
@TRIM(*string*)	Removes blank spaces from the string
@STRING(*numeric_value,decimal_places*)	Converts a value to a string showing the specified number of decimal places
@VALUE(*string*)	Converts a string to a value
@CLEAN(*string*)	Removes nonprintable characters from the string
@CHAR(*number*)	Converts a code number into an ASCII/LMBCS character
@CODE(*string*)	Converts the first character in the string into an ASCII/LMBCS code
@N(*range*)	Returns as a value the contents of the cell in the upper left corner of a range
@S(*range*)	Returns as a label the contents of the cell in the upper left corner of a range

Chapter 6 ◆ Using @Functions in the Worksheet

You can link strings to other strings by using the concatenation operator (&). The discussion of the individual string @functions in this section shows several examples of the use of the concatenation operator. Keep in mind that you cannot link strings to cells that contain numeric values or that are empty. If you try, 1-2-3 returns ERR. Use @STRING if you want to concatenate a number with text.

Avoid mixing data types in string @functions. For instance, some @functions produce strings, but other @functions produce numeric results. If an @function's result is not of the data type you need, use the @STRING and @VALUE @functions to convert a numeric value to a string value, or a string value to a numeric value.

The numbering scheme for positioning characters in a string begins with zero and continues to the number corresponding to the last character in the label. The prefix before a label is not counted for numeric positioning. Negative position numbers are not allowed.

Reminder:
You can link strings to other strings by using the concatenation operator (&).

@FIND—Locating One String within Another

The @FIND function locates the starting position of one string within another string. For instance, you can use @FIND to determine at what position the blank space occurs within the string `Jim Johnson`. The position number of the blank space can then be used with the @LEFT and @RIGHT @functions to separate `Jim` and `Johnson` into two separate cells for use in a mailing list database. (Although this example shows a search for the single blank-space character, @FIND will also find the location of multiple character strings, such as `Calif`, within longer strings.)

Reminder:
@FIND performs only exact searches; uppercase and lowercase are significant.

The @FIND function uses the following format:

@FIND(*search_string,string,start_number*)

The *search_string* argument is the string you want to locate. In this example, the search string is " ". The string being searched is "Jim Johnson". And *start_number* is the position number in the string where you want to start the search. If you want to start at the first character and search through the contents of cell A6 for a blank space, use the following statement:

@FIND(" ",A6,1)

In this example, with "Jim Johnson" as the string, the @FIND function returns the value 4. In figure 6.36, @FIND locates the last name Lange, starting at the ninth character in cell C13.

You can search for a second occurrence of the search string by adding 1 to the result of the first @FIND function. This move starts the next @FIND at the character location after the blank space that was already found. Following is a formula that searches for the character position of the second blank space:

@FIND(" ",A6,@FIND(" ",A6,1)+1)

When @FIND cannot find a match, the result is ERR.

Fig. 6.36.
The @FIND function used to find the text string specified in D6.

```
A:A20: [W16]                                                      READY
        A            B         C              D                E
 1
 2
 3
 4
 5
 6                            Search string   Lange
 7
 8
 9  Function      Result    Name            Street           Address
10  @FIND($D$6,C10,0)  ERR  Karen Kuehnle   2628 Juniper Dr. Toledo, OH 43614
11  @FIND($D$6,C11,0)  ERR  Susan Nanzini   256 35th Ave.    Nonsence, UT 43076
12  @FIND($D$6,C12,0)  ERR  Joe Calabash    212 Alta Vista Dr. Floral Gables, FL 23009
13  @FIND($D$6,C13,0)    9  Ralph J. Lange  98 Singletree Rd. Dry Well, TX 57063
14
15
16
17
18
19
20
```

@MID—Extracting One String from Another

Whereas @FIND helps you locate one string within another, the @MID function enables you to extract one string from within another. @MID uses the following format:

@MID(*string,start_number,number*)

The *start_number* argument is a number representing the character position in the string where you want to begin extracting characters. The *number* argument, which indicates the length of the string, is the number of characters to extract. For example, to extract the first name from a label containing the full name `Page Davidson`, use the following statement:

@MID("Page Davidson",0,4)

This function extracts the string starting in position 0 (the first character) and continuing for a length of 4 characters—the string `Page`.

Cue:
Use @MID with @FIND to extract first and last names from a list of full names.

Now suppose that you want to extract the first and last names from a column of full names and you want to put those two extracted names in separate columns. To accomplish both tasks, use the @MID and @FIND @functions. Because you know that a blank space separates the first and last names, you can use @FIND to locate the position of the blank space in each full name. Using this character position, you can then set up the @functions to extract the first and last names.

If cell C9 contains the full name `Karen Kuehnle`, as shown in figure 6.37, place the following function in cell A9:

@MID(C9,0,@FIND(" ",C9,0))

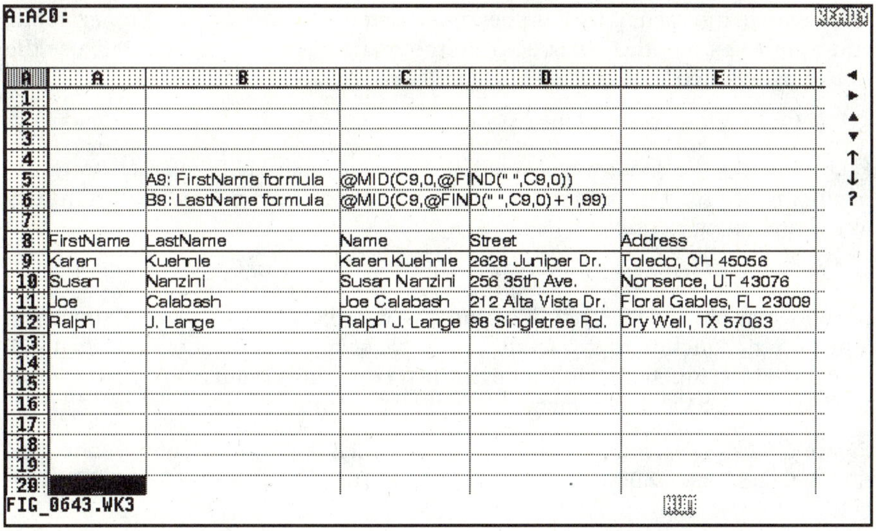

Chapter 6 ♦ Using @Functions in the Worksheet

Fig. 6.37.
The @MID and @FIND @functions used to locate and extract first and last names.

The value of this function will appear as Karen because @FIND(" ",C9,0) will return a value of 6 for the *number* argument.

Next place the following function statement in cell B9:

@MID(C9,@FIND(" ",C9,0)+1,99)

Here the @FIND function indicates that the start position is one character beyond the blank space. In addition, the length of the string to be extracted is 99 characters. Although a length of 99 is greater than you need, no ERR results for this excess. The string that 1-2-3 extracts is Kuehnle.

If you use this type of formula to convert a long string in a database into shorter strings, you may want to convert the string formulas (first and last names) into values before using the database. To make these conversions, use the /Range Value command to copy the string formulas onto themselves. This technique replaces the formulas with the formula results.

@LEFT and @RIGHT—Extracting Strings from Left and Right

The @LEFT and @RIGHT @functions are variations of @MID and are used to extract one string of characters from another, beginning at the leftmost and rightmost positions in the string. These @functions require the following formats:

@LEFT(*string,number*)

@RIGHT(*string,number*)

Cue:
Use @RIGHT to extract the ZIP code from an address.

The *number* argument is the number of characters to be extracted. If, for example, you want to extract the ZIP code from the string Cincinnati, Ohio 45243, use the following @function statement:

@RIGHT("Cincinnati, Ohio 45243",5)

@LEFT works the same way as @RIGHT except that @LEFT extracts from the beginning of a string. For instance, use the following statement to extract the city in the preceding example:

@LEFT("Cincinnati, Ohio 45243",10)

In most cases, use @FIND(",","Cincinnati, Ohio 45243",0) instead of 10 for the length in the function to extract the city from the address. To replace the @LEFT or @RIGHT @functions with their results, copy the formulas onto themselves with the /Range Value command.

Figure 6.38 shows a mailing list database in which the original entries contained the city, state, and ZIP code in a single cell. The @FIND, @MID, @LEFT, and @RIGHT @functions were used to separate the long strings into separate cells.

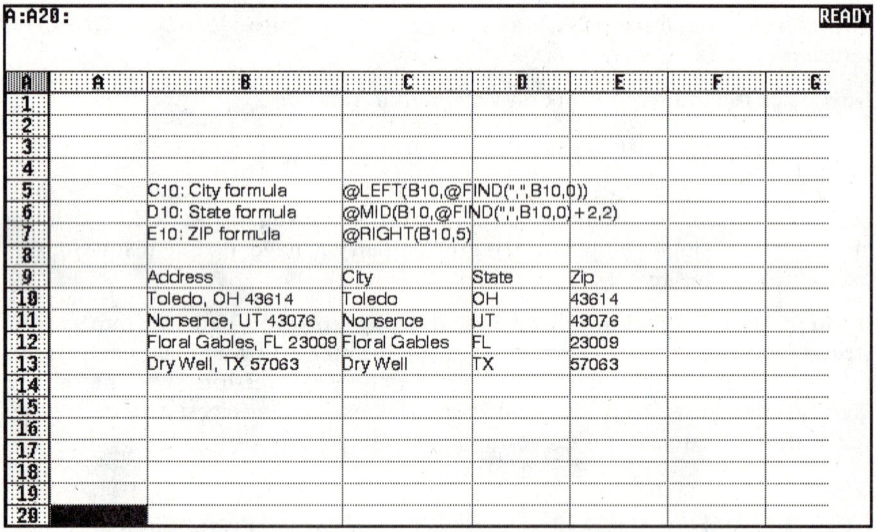

Fig. 6.38.
The @FIND, @MID, @LEFT, and @RIGHT @functions used to separate long strings.

```
A:A20:                                                              READY

      A         B                    C                    D        E        F        G
  1
  2
  3
  4
  5             C10: City formula    @LEFT(B10,@FIND(",",B10,0))
  6             D10: State formula   @MID(B10,@FIND(",",B10,0)+2,2)
  7             E10: ZIP formula     @RIGHT(B10,5)
  8
  9             Address              City                 State    Zip
 10             Toledo, OH 43614     Toledo               OH       43614
 11             Nonsence, UT 43076   Nonsence             UT       43076
 12             Floral Gables, FL 23009  Floral Gables    FL       23009
 13             Dry Well, TX 57063   Dry Well             TX       57063
 14
 15
 16
 17
 18
 19
 20
```

@REPLACE—Replacing a String within a String

The @REPLACE function replaces one group of characters in a string with another group of characters. @REPLACE is a valuable tool for correcting a frequently-incorrect text entry without retyping it. Use this format for @REPLACE:

@REPLACE(*original_string,start_number,length,replacement_string*)

The *start_number* argument indicates the position where 1-2-3 will begin removing characters in the original string. The *length* argument shows how many

Chapter 6 ◆ Using @Functions in the Worksheet   257

characters to remove, and *replacement_string* contains the new characters to replace the removed ones. @REPLACE numbers the character positions in a string starting with zero and continuing to the end of the string (up to 239).

@LENGTH—Computing the Length of a String

The @LENGTH function calculates the length of a string. @LENGTH uses the following format:

@LENGTH(*string*)

@LENGTH is frequently used to calculate the length of a string being extracted from another string. This function can also be used to check for data entry errors. The function returns ERR as the length of numeric values or formulas, empty cells, and null strings.

@EXACT—Comparing Strings

The @EXACT function compares two strings, returning the value 1 (true) for strings that are exactly the same, or returning the value 0 (false) for strings that are different. @EXACT uses the following format:

@EXACT(*string1,string2*)

The @EXACT function's method of comparison is similar to the = operator in formulas except that the = operator checks for a match regardless of uppercase and lowercase, and @EXACT checks for an exact match that distinguishes between uppercase and lowercase. If, for example, cell B7 holds the string Wrench and cell D7 holds the string wrench, the logical value of B7=D7 is 1 because the two strings are an approximate match. But the value of @EXACT(B7,D7) is 0 because the two @functions are not an exact match; their cases are different.

The *string1* and *string2* arguments can be text, the result of text formulas, or references to cells containing text or text formulas. The examples in figure 6.39 demonstrate the use of @EXACT. Notice in the fourth and fifth examples that @EXACT cannot compare nonstring arguments. In fact, if either argument is a nonstring value of any type (including numbers), 1-2-3 returns ERR. (Note that you can use the @S function, explained later in this chapter, to ensure that the arguments used within @EXACT have string values.)

Cue:
Use @S to ensure that the argument of @EXACT is a string.

@LOWER, @UPPER, and @PROPER—Converting the Case of Strings

1-2-3 offers three different @functions for converting the case of a string value:

@LOWER(*string*)   Converts all letters in a string to lowercase.

@UPPER(*string*)   Converts all letters in a string to uppercase.

Part I ♦ Building the 1-2-3 Worksheet

@PROPER(*string*) Capitalizes the first letter in each word of a label. (Words are defined as groups of characters separated by blank spaces.) @PROPER goes on to convert the remaining letters in each word to lowercase.

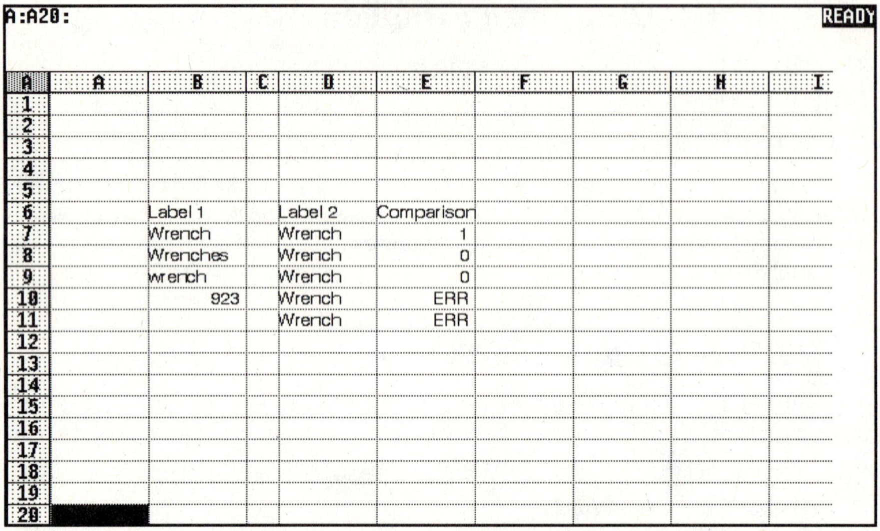

Fig. 6.39.
Strings compared with the @EXACT function.

```
A:A20:                                                    READY
     A         B          C         D         E      F      G      H      I
 1
 2
 3
 4
 5
 6            Label 1              Label 2   Comparison
 7            Wrench               Wrench              1
 8            Wrenches             Wrench              0
 9            wrench               Wrench              0
10                  923            Wrench            ERR
11                                 Wrench            ERR
12
...
20
```

Figure 6.40 gives an example of the use of each case @function.

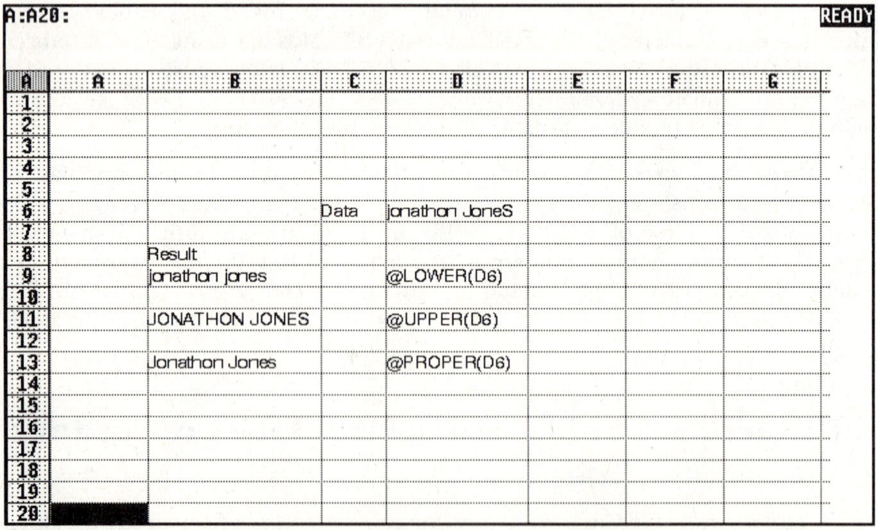

Fig. 6.40.
@Functions used to convert the case of alphanumeric strings.

```
A:A20:                                                    READY
     A              B                C         D          E     F     G
 1
 2
 3
 4
 5
 6                              Data    jonathon JoneS
 7
 8            Result
 9            jonathon jones            @LOWER(D6)
10
11            JONATHON JONES            @UPPER(D6)
12
13            Jonathon Jones            @PROPER(D6)
...
20
```

These three @functions work with string values or references to strings. If a cell contains a number or a null string (" "), 1-2-3 returns ERR for each of these @functions. (Note that you can use the @S function, explained later in this chapter, to ensure that the arguments of these @functions have string values.)

You can use @LOWER, @UPPER, or @PROPER to modify the contents of a database so that all entries in a field appear with the same capitalization. This technique produces reports that appear consistent. Capitalization will also affect sorting order. Uppercase and lowercase letters do not sort together. To ensure that data with different capitalization sorts together, create a column, using one of the @functions that references the data, and then sort on this new column.

@REPEAT—Repeating Strings within a Cell

The @REPEAT function repeats strings a specified number of times, much as the backslash (\) repeats strings to fill a cell. But @REPEAT has some distinct advantages over the backslash. With @REPEAT, you can repeat the string the precise number of times you want. If the result is wider than the cell width, the result is displayed in empty adjacent cells to the right. @REPEAT uses the following format:

@REPEAT(*string,number*)

The *number* argument indicates the number of times you want to repeat a string in a cell. For example, if you want to repeat the string "-**-" three times, you can enter @REPEAT("-**-",3). The resulting string will be "-**--**--**-". This string follows 1-2-3's rule for long labels. That is, the string is displayed beyond the right boundary of the column, provided that no entry is in the cell to the right. When you use the backslash to repeat a string, however, 1-2-3 fills the column to the exact column width.

Reminder:
@REPEAT copies strings beyond the current column width.

@TRIM—Removing Blank Spaces from a String

The @TRIM function eliminates unwanted blank spaces from the beginning, end, or middle of a string. If multiple adjacent spaces are within a string, they are reduced to a single space. Use the following format for @TRIM:

@TRIM(*string*)

@TRIM is useful for trimming spaces from data as it is entered into a macro, or for trimming unwanted spaces from data in a database. Such spaces in a database can cause the sort order to be different from what you expect.

@N and @S—Testing for Strings and Values

The @N and @S @functions convert cell contents into either numeric values or string values. These @functions are important when you are using other @functions that operate on numeric values only, or @functions that operate on string values only. When you are in doubt as to whether a cell contains a numeric or text value, use @N or @S to force the contents into becoming a number or text.

@N converts the contents of a cell to a number. If the cell is blank or contains a label, @N returns the value 0. @N will always have a numeric value.

@S converts the contents of a cell to text. If the cell contains a string or a formula that evaluates to a string, @S returns this string. If the cell contains a number or is empty, @S returns the null string (" "). @S always will have a string value. This function can be especially useful when you want to concatenate numeric values and text values. For example, you may want to put a calculated amount due within a text sentence.

The @N and @S @functions have the following respective formats:

@N(*range*)

@S(*range*)

The argument must be a range or a single-cell reference. If you use a single-cell reference, 1-2-3 adjusts the argument to range format and returns the numeric or string value of the single cell. If the argument is a multicell range, @N or @S returns the numeric or string value of the upper left corner of the range.

@STRING—Converting Values to Strings

The @STRING function enables you to convert a number to its text-string equivalent so that you can work with the number as text. For example, @STRING can override 1-2-3's automatic right-justification of numbers and display a number justified to the left. You can also use @STRING to convert a number to text and then concatenate the result into a text sentence.

Use the following format for @STRING:

@STRING(*numeric_value,decimal_places*)

1-2-3 uses the Fixed format for the @STRING function. The *decimal_places* argument represents the number of decimal places to be included in the string. 1-2-3 rounds the resulting textual number to match the number of decimal places you specify. Note also that @STRING ignores all numeric formats you placed on the cell and operates on just the numeric contents of the cell. Figure 6.41 shows examples of values being used as strings.

@VALUE—Converting Strings to Values

The @VALUE function converts a number that is a string into a numeric value that can be used in calculations. The string must be text or a label that is made up only of numbers. The *string* argument within @VALUE must contain only numbers; it cannot contain alphabetical characters. One valuable feature of @VALUE is that it converts text fractions into decimal numbers. The function is useful, therefore, in converting stock data from database or wire services into numbers that you can analyze and graph. @VALUE requires the following format:

@VALUE(*string*)

Chapter 6 ◆ Using @Functions in the Worksheet   **261**

```
A:A20:                                                    READY

       A         B         C        D                E
   1
   2
   3
   4
   5             Cell
   6             contents   Result   Function/formula
   7             Values
   8                        45   45.00     @STRING(B8,2)
   9                        53.25  You owe $53.25  +"You owe $"&@STRING(B9,2)
  10                        6    There are 6 left  +"There are "&@STRING(B10,0)&" left"
  11             Labels
  12             22 1/2          22.5    @VALUE(B12)
  13             22 3/8          22.375  @VALUE(B13)
  14             22.5%           0.225   @VALUE(B14)
  15
```

Fig. 6.41.
The @STRING and @VALUE @functions used to convert strings and values.

A few rules are important when you use @VALUE. Although 1-2-3 usually does not object to extra spaces left in a string, the program has trouble with some extra characters, such as trailing percent signs. Currency signs (such as $) that precede the string are acceptable, however. Try experimenting with different extra characters to see how @VALUE reacts. Another point to remember is that when a numeric value is supplied as an argument for @VALUE, it simply returns the original number value.

@CLEAN—Removing Nonprintable Characters from Strings

Sometimes when you import strings with /File Import, particularly with a modem, the strings will contain nonprintable characters. The @CLEAN function removes the nonprintable characters from the strings (see fig. 6.42). @CLEAN uses the following format:

   @CLEAN(*string*)

The argument used with @CLEAN must be either a string value or a cell reference to a cell containing a string value. 1-2-3 will not accept a cell entry containing @CLEAN with a range argument specified.

Cue:
@CLEAN removes nonprintable characters from data imported into your worksheet from other sources.

Using @Functions with Character Sets

1-2-3 offers a few special @functions for working with the Lotus Multibyte Character Set (LMBCS). This character set replaces the Lotus International Character Set (LICS) used in previous releases of 1-2-3. The complete set of LMBCS characters, listed in Appendix E of this book, includes everything from the copyright sign (©) to the lowercase *e* with the grave accent (è).

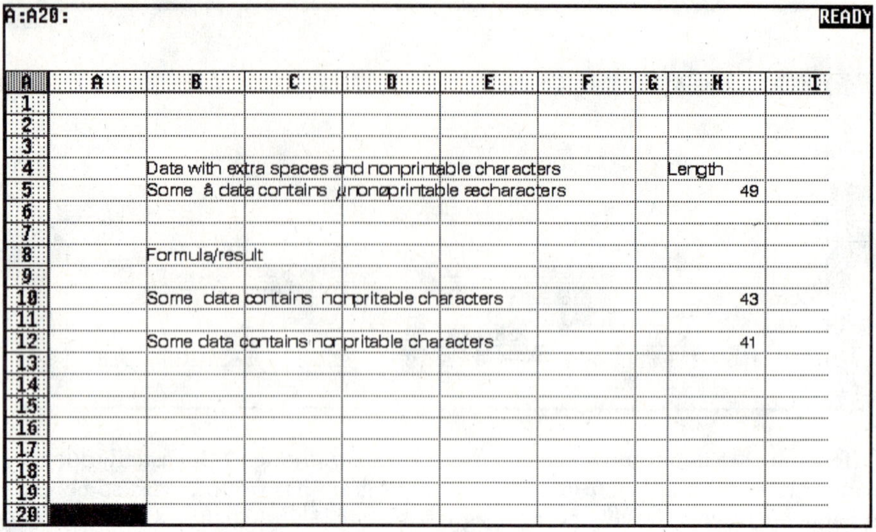

Part I ◆ Building the 1-2-3 Worksheet

Fig. 6.42.
The @CLEAN function used to remove nonprintable characters.

```
A:A20:                                                    READY
         A         B         C         D         E    F    G    H         I
  1
  2
  3
  4           Data with extra spaces and nonprintable characters     Length
  5           Some  a data contains  nonprintable  characters           49
  6
  7
  8           Formula/result
  9
 10           Some data contains nonpritable characters                 43
 11
 12           Some data contains nonpritable characters                 41
 13
 14
 15
 16
 17
 18
 19
 20
```

@CHAR—Displaying LMBCS Characters

The @CHAR function produces on-screen the LMBCS equivalent of a number which specifies that character. @CHAR uses the following format:

@CHAR(*number*)

Figure 6.43 shows several examples of the use of @CHAR.

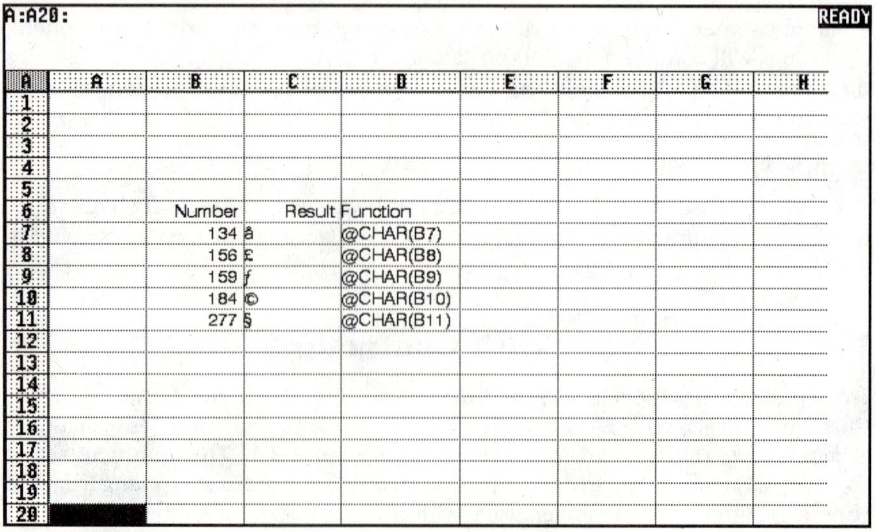

Fig. 6.43.
Examples of the @CHAR function.

```
A:A20:                                                    READY
         A         B         C         D         E    F    G    H
  1
  2
  3
  4
  5
  6          Number      Result  Function
  7            134  â            @CHAR(B7)
  8            156  £            @CHAR(B8)
  9            159  f            @CHAR(B9)
 10            184  ©            @CHAR(B10)
 11            277  §            @CHAR(B11)
 12
 13
 14
 15
 16
 17
 18
 19
 20
```

@CODE—Computing the LMBCS Code

The @CODE function performs the opposite action of @CHAR. Whereas @CHAR takes a number and returns the LMBCS, @CODE examines the LMBCS character and returns a number. @CODE uses the following format:

@CODE(*string*)

Suppose that you want to find the LMBCS code for the letter *a*. You enter @CODE("A") in a cell, and 1-2-3 returns the number 65. If you enter @CODE("Aardvark"), 1-2-3 still returns 65, the code of the first character in the string.

Using Logarithmic @Functions

1-2-3 has three logarithmic @functions—@LOG, @EXP, and @LN. Each of these @functions has one argument, which can be a numeric value or a cell reference to a numeric value. Figure 6.44 shows examples of @LOG, @EXP, and @LN.

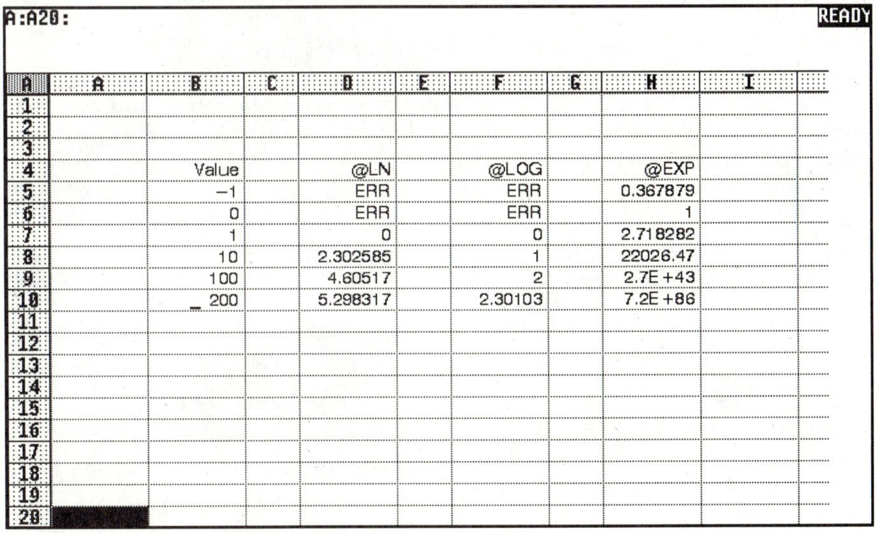

```
A:A20:                                                          READY

      A       B         C        D         E        F        G        H         I
  1
  2
  3
  4            Value              @LN               @LOG              @EXP
  5             -1                ERR               ERR               0.367879
  6              0                ERR               ERR               1
  7              1                  0                  0              2.718282
  8             10                2.302585            1               22026.47
  9            100                4.60517             2               2.7E+43
 10            200                5.298317            2.30103         7.2E+86
 11
 12
 ...
 20
```

Fig. 6.44.
Examples of the logarithmic @functions @LN, @LOG, and @EXP.

@LOG—Computing Logarithms

The @LOG function computes the base 10 logarithm. @LOG uses the following format:

@LOG(*value* or *cell_reference*)

You cannot use a negative value with this function. If you use a negative value with @LOG, ERR is returned.

@EXP—Finding Powers of *e*

The @EXP function calculates *e* raised to the power of the argument. The format of @EXP is the following:

@EXP(*value* or *cell_reference*)

Do not use an argument larger than 709. With @EXP, you can quickly create very large numbers. If the @function's resulting value is too large to be displayed, asterisks are displayed.

@LN—Computing Natural Logarithms

The @LN function computes the natural, or base *e*, logarithm. @LN uses the following format:

@LN(*value* or *cell_reference*)

If you use a negative argument with @LN, ERR is returned.

Using Trigonometric @Functions

1-2-3 provides eight trigonometric @functions for engineering and scientific applications. Table 6.10 lists the @functions, their arguments, and the operations they perform.

Table 6.10
Trigonometric @Functions

@Function	Description
@PI	Calculates the value of π
@SIN(*angle*)	Calculates the sine, given an angle in radians
@COS(*angle*)	Calculates the cosine, given an angle in radians
@TAN(*angle*)	Calculates the tangent, given an angle in radians
@ASIN(*angle*)	Calculates the arcsine, given an angle in radians
@ACOS(*angle*)	Calculates the arccosine, given an angle in radians
@ATAN(*angle*)	Calculates the arctangent, given an angle in radians
@ATAN2(*number1, number2*)	Calculates the four-quadrant arctangent

@PI—Computing Pi

The @PI function results in the value of π. The function uses no arguments. Its syntax is simply @PI.

Chapter 6 ♦ Using @Functions in the Worksheet

@PI returns the value 3.14159265358979324. Use @PI to calculate the area of circles and the volume of spheres. In addition, @PI is needed to convert angle measurements in degrees to angle measurements in radians.

Reminder:
@PI returns the value 3.14159265358979324.

@COS, @SIN, and @TAN—Computing Trigonometric Functions

The @COS, @SIN, and @TAN @functions calculate the cosine, sine, and tangent, respectively, for an angle. Each function uses one argument—an angle measured in radians. Use these formats for the @functions:

@COS(*angle*)

@SIN(*angle*)

@TAN(*angle*)

Be sure to convert angle measurements into radians before you use these @functions. Because 2*π radians are in 360 degrees, you can calculate radian angles by multiplying the number of degrees by @PI and dividing by 180, as shown in figure 6.45.

Cue:
Convert angle measurements into radians before you use the trigonometric @functions.

```
A:A20: [W6]                                                        READY
     A        B          C        D         E        F        G        H        I        J
 1
 2  @PI=    3.141593
 3
 4          Degrees              Radians            @COS              @SIN              @TAN
 5              0                   0                 1                 0                 0
 6             45                0.785398          0.707107          0.707107             1
 7             90                1.570796             0                 1               ERR
 8            135                2.356194         -0.70711           0.707107            -1
 9            180                3.141593            -1                 0                 0
10            225                3.926991         -0.70711          -0.70711             1
11            270                4.712389         1.1E-19              -1            -9.2E+18
12            315                5.497787         0.707107          -0.70711            -1
13            360                6.283185             1                 0                 0
```

Fig. 6.45.
Examples of the @COS, @SIN, @PI, and @TAN @functions.

@ACOS, @ASIN, @ATAN, and @ATAN2— Computing Inverse Trigonometric Functions

The @ACOS, @ASIN, @ATAN, and @ATAN2 @functions calculate the arccosine, the arcsine, the arctangent, and the four-quadrant arctangent, respectively. @ACOS computes the inverse of cosine; @ASIN computes the inverse of sine—a radian angle between –π/2 and π/2 (–90 and +90 degrees). @ATAN computes the inverse of tangent—a radian angle between $-\pi/2$ and $\pi/2$ (-90 and $+90$ degrees). @ATAN2 calculates the four-quadrant arctangent, using the ratio of its two arguments.

@ACOS and @ASIN each use one argument:

@ACOS(*angle*)

@ASIN(*angle*)

Reminder:
Because all cosine and sine values lie between -1 and 1, @ACOS and @ASIN work only with values between -1 and 1.

Because all cosine and sine values lie between -1 and 1, @ACOS and @ASIN work only with values between -1 and 1. Either function returns ERR if you use an argument outside this range. @ASIN returns angles between $-\pi/2$ and $+\pi/2$, whereas @ACOS returns angles between 0 and $\pi/2$. Figure 6.46 shows examples of the @ACOS, @ASIN, and @ATAN @functions.

Fig. 6.46.
Examples of the @ACOS, @ASIN, and @ATAN @functions.

```
A:A20: [W6]                                                          READY

      A        B         C         D         E         F         G         H         I        J
 1
 2
 3
 4            Value               @ACOS               @ASIN               @ATAN
 5              1                   0               1.570796            0.785398
 6           0.70711            0.785394            0.785403            0.615482
 7              0               1.570796               0                   0
 8          -0.70711            2.356199            -0.7854             -0.61548
 9             -1               3.141593            -1.5708             -0.7854
10
11
12
13
14
15
16
17
18
19
20
```

Like @ACOS and @ASIN, the @ATAN function uses one argument. @ATAN can use any number and returns a value between $-\pi/2$ and $+\pi/2$. The format of @ATAN is the following:

@ATAN(*angle*)

@ATAN2 computes the angle whose tangent is specified by the ratio *number2/number1*—the two arguments. At least one of the arguments must be a number other than zero. @ATAN2 returns radian angles between $-\pi$ and $+\pi$. Use this format for @ATAN2:

@ATAN2(*number1,number2*)

Using Special @Functions

The special @functions are listed together in a special category because they provide information about cell or range contents or about worksheet location. @CELL, @CELLPOINTER, and @COORD are three of 1-2-3's most powerful special @functions and have many different capabilities. @CELL and @CELLPOINTER can return up to 58 different characteristics of a cell. These characteristics are known as *attributes*. @COORD specifies a cell address as absolute, relative, or mixed. @NA and @ERR enable you to trap errors that may otherwise appear in your worksheet. With @ROWS, @COLS, and @SHEETS, you can determine the size of a range. The @@ function enables you to reference indirectly one cell with another cell within the worksheet. With @CHOOSE, @HLOOKUP, @VLOOKUP, and @INDEX, you can use specified keys in the @functions' arguments to look up values in tables or lists. @INFO enables you to retrieve system-related information.

Reminder: @INFO enables you to retrieve system-related information.

Table 6.11 lists 1-2-3's special @functions.

Table 6.11
Special @Functions

@Function	Description
@@(*cell_reference*)	Returns the contents of the cell referenced by the cell address in the argument
@CELL(*attribute,range*)	Returns the designated attribute for the cell in the upper left corner of the referenced range
@CELLPOINTER(*attribute*)	Returns the designated attribute for the current cell
@CHOOSE(*offset,list*)	Locates in a list the entry that is offset a specified amount from the beginning of the list
@COLS(*range*)	Computes the number of columns in a range
@COORD(*worksheet, column,row,absolute*)	Constructs a cell address from values corresponding to rows and columns
@ERR	Displays ERR in the cell
@HLOOKUP(*key,range, row_offset*)	Locates the specified key in a lookup table and returns a value from that row of the range
@INDEX(*range,column, row,[worksheet]*)	Returns the contents of a cell specified by the intersection of a row and column within a range on a designated worksheet
@INFO(*attribute*)	Retrieves system information
@NA	Displays NA in the cell
@ROWS(*range*)	Computes the number of rows in a range
@SHEETS(*range*)	Computes the number of worksheets in a range
@VLOOKUP(*key,range, column_offset*)	Locates the specified key in a lookup table and returns a value from that column of the range

@@—Referencing Cells Indirectly

Cue:
@@ provides a way of indirectly referencing one cell through another cell.

The @@ function provides a way of indirectly referencing one cell through the contents of another cell. @@ uses the following format:

@@(*cell_reference*)

Simple examples show how the @@ function works. If cell A1 contains the label 'A2, and cell A2 contains the number 5, then the function @@(A1) returns the value 5. If the label in cell A1 is changed to 'B10, and cell B10 contains the label "hi there", the function @@(A1) returns the string value "hi there".

The argument of the @@ function must be a cell reference of a cell containing an address. This address is an indirect address. Similarly, the cell referenced by the argument of the @@ function must contain a string value that evaluates to a cell reference. This cell can contain a label, a string formula, or a reference to another cell, as long as the resulting string value is a cell reference.

The @@ function is useful primarily in cases where several formulas have the same argument, and the argument must be changed from time to time during the course of the application. 1-2-3 enables you to specify the argument of each formula through a common indirect address, as shown in figure 6.47.

```
A:A20: [W1]                                                        READY
     A    B       C    D          E    F         G    H                    I
  1
  2
  3       Interest      Reference
  4       rates         cell            Result        Formula
  5       0.09          B6              $96.50        @PMT(10000,@@(D5)/12,20*12)
  6       0.10                          $193.00       @PMT(20000,@@(D5)/12,20*12)
  7       0.11                          $289.51       @PMT(30000,@@(D5)/12,20*12)
  8       0.12                          $386.01       @PMT(40000,@@(D5)/12,20*12)
  9       0.13                          $482.51       @PMT(50000,@@(D5)/12,20*12)
 10       0.14                          $579.01       @PMT(60000,@@(D5)/12,20*12)
 11
 12
 13
 14
 15
 16
 17
 18
 19
 20
```

Fig. 6.47.
The @@ function used to reference indirectly one cell through another cell.

In figure 6.47, column F contains a variety of financial @functions, all of which use the @@ function to reference 1 of 6 interest rates in column B indirectly through cell D5. When you are ready to change the cell being referenced, you have to change only the label in cell D5 instead of editing all six formulas in column F.

@CELL and @CELLPOINTER—Checking Cell Attributes

The @CELL and @CELLPOINTER @functions provide an efficient way to determine the nature of a cell because these @functions return up to 58 different cell characteristics, such as a cell's number or value, color, and width. @CELL and @CELLPOINTER are used primarily in macros and advanced macro command programs (see Chapters 13 and 14). Use the following formats for @CELL and @CELLPOINTER:

@CELL(*attribute,range*)

@CELLPOINTER(*attribute*)

Because you want to examine a cell's attributes, both @functions have *attribute* as a string argument. @CELL, however, also requires the specification of a range; @CELLPOINTER works with the current cell.

The following examples illustrate how the @CELL function can be used to examine some cell attributes:

- @CELL("address",SALES)

    If the range named SALES is C187..E187, 1-2-3 returns the absolute address $C$187. This statement is convenient for listing the upper left corner of a range's address in the worksheet.

- @CELL("prefix",C195..C195)

    If cell C195 contains the label 'Chicago', 1-2-3 returns ' (indicating left alignment). If cell C195 is blank, however, 1-2-3 returns nothing; in other words, the current cell appears blank.

- @CELL("format",A10)

    1-2-3 returns the format of cell A10 as a text string, using the same notation as that used on the worksheet. For example, a Currency format with 2 decimal places appears as C2.

- @CELL("width",B12..B12)

    1-2-3 returns the width of column B.

The attribute argument is text and must be enclosed in quotation marks. You can use one of two forms. An attribute preceded by an *s* is the attribute of global settings. An attribute without an *s* is the attribute of the specified cell. If a range of cells is specified, the returned value refers to the top left cell in the range.

Table 6.12 lists the full set of attributes that can be examined with @CELL and @CELLPOINTER.

Cue:
@CELL and @CELLPOINTER provide an efficient way to determine the nature of a cell.

Reminder:
An attribute argument is text and must be enclosed in quotation marks.

Table 6.12
Attributes Used with @CELL and @CELLPOINTER

Attribute	What the @Function Returns
"address"	The abbreviated absolute cell address
"col"	Column letter, from 1 to 256
"color"	1 - Cell is formatted for color
	2 - Cell is not formatted for color
"contents"	Cell contents
"filename"	Name of file that contains the cell
"format"	**Fixed decimal**, F0 to F15
	Scientific, S0 to S15
	Currency, C0 to C15
	Comma, ,0 to ,15
	G for **General**, label, or blank
	+ for **+/−**
	Percent, P0 to P15
	Date/Time, D1 to D9
	Automatic, A
	Text, T
	Label, L
	Hidden, H
	Color, −
	Parentheses, ( )
"prefix"	Same as label prefixes; blank if no label
"protect"	1 if protected; 0 if not
"row"	Row number, 1 to 8192
"sheet"	Worksheet letter, 1 to 256
"type"	b is blank, v is value, and l is label
"width"	Column width

Figure 6.48 illustrates the use of the @CELLPOINTER function.

The @CELLPOINTER function works well within @IF @functions to test whether data entered into a cell is numeric or text. @CELL and @CELLPOINTER are frequently used within macros to examine the current contents or format of cells. {IF} macros can then use the results to change the worksheet accordingly.

The difference between @CELL and @CELLPOINTER is important. The @CELL function examines the string attribute of a cell you designate in a range format, such as A1..A1. If you use a single range format, such as A1, 1-2-3 changes to the range format (A1..A1) and returns the attribute of the single-cell range. If you define a range larger than a single cell, 1-2-3 evaluates the cell in the upper left corner of the range.

Chapter 6 ◆ Using @Functions in the Worksheet   **271**

```
A:A20:                                                    READY
     A      B        C       D              E      F      G
 1
 2
 3
 4
 5                            123
 6
 7           Result     Formula
 8           $D$5       @CELLPOINTER("address")
 9           5          @CELLPOINTER("row")
10           4          @CELLPOINTER("col")
11           123        @CELLPOINTER("contents")
12           v          @CELLPOINTER("type")
13                      @CELLPOINTER("prefix")
14           1          @CELLPOINTER("protect")
15           9          @CELLPOINTER("width")
16           G          @CELLPOINTER("format")
17
18
19
20
```

Fig. 6.48.
@CELLPOINTER function used to determine cell attributes.

The @CELLPOINTER function operates on the *current* cell—the cell where the cell pointer was positioned when the worksheet was last recalculated. The result remains the same until you enter a value or press Calc (F9) if your worksheet is in automatic recalculation mode, or until you press Calc (F9) in manual calculation mode.

For example, to determine the address of the current cell, you can enter @CELLPOINTER("address") in cell B22. If recalculation is set to automatic, the value displayed in that cell is displayed as the absolute address $B$22. This same address remains displayed until you recalculate the worksheet by making an entry elsewhere in the worksheet or by pressing Calc (F9). The address that appears in cell B22 changes to reflect the position of the cell pointer when the worksheet was recalculated. If recalculation is set to manual, you can change the address only by pressing Calc (F9).

Reminder:
If recalculation is set to manual, you can change the address only by pressing Calc (F9).

@COORD—Creating a Cell Address

You use @COORD to create an absolute, relative, or mixed cell address. @COORD uses the following format:

@COORD(*worksheet,column,row,absolute*)

The *worksheet* argument corresponds to the worksheet containing the referenced cell. The *column* and *row* arguments refer, respectively, to the column and row containing the cell address. And the *absolute* argument refers to the exact type of reference—absolute, relative, or mixed—that you want the function to return. All the arguments (*worksheet, column, row, absolute*) of the @COORD function require that you enter numbers as follows:

worksheet	Enter 1–256 (worksheet A=1, B=2, C=3,...IV=256)
column	Enter 1–256 (column A=1, B=2, C=3,...IV=256)
row	Enter the row number of the cell (1–8192)
absolute	Enter the number for the type of reference (see table 6.13)

When you use @COORD, the function returns the actual address, not a value.

**Table 6.13
Values of Absolute**

Value	Worksheet	Column	Row	Example
1	Absolute	Absolute	Absolute	$A:$A$1
2	Absolute	Relative	Absolute	$A:A$1
3	Absolute	Absolute	Relative	$A:$A1
4	Absolute	Relative	Relative	$A:A1
5	Relative	Absolute	Absolute	A:$A$1
6	Relative	Relative	Absolute	A:A$1
7	Relative	Absolute	Relative	A:$A1
8	Relative	Relative	Relative	A:A1

@CHOOSE—Selecting an Item from a List

Reminder:
@CHOOSE selects an item from a list.

The @CHOOSE function selects an item from a list according to the item's position in the list. The format of the function is the following:

@CHOOSE(*offset,list*)

The function selects the item in the specified position, or offset, in the list. Keep in mind that positions in the list are numbered starting with 0. For example, the first position is 0, the second is 1, the third is 2, and so on.

Figure 6.49 shows examples of the @CHOOSE function. Use the @INT function combined with formulas if you need to choose from a list but are given indexes that span a range.

@COLS, @ROWS, and @SHEETS—Finding the Dimensions of Ranges

The @COLS, @ROWS, and @SHEETS @functions describe the dimensions of ranges. Use the following formats for these @functions:

@COLS(*range*)
@ROWS(*range*)
@SHEETS(*range*)

Chapter 6 ◆ Using @Functions in the Worksheet   **273**

```
A:A20: [W19]                                                    READY
     A              B         C    D             E         F         G
 1
 2
 3
 4
 5  Type a number                       Formula
 6  to enter text              1 West   @CHOOSE(B6,"East","West","North",
 7                                      "South")
 8  Choose a commission
 9  by dollar amount      $1,532  0.07  @CHOOSE(@INT(B9/1000),0.05,0.07,0.085,0.11)
10                                      0.11)
11  Calculate a day
12  from a date        24-Dec-91 Tues   @CHOOSE(@MOD(B12,7),"Sat","Sun","Mon","Tues
13                                      "Tues","Wed","Thu","Fri")
14
15
16
17
18
19
20
```

Fig. 6.49.
The @CHOOSE function used to select an item from a list.

Suppose that you want to determine the number of columns in a range called PRICE_TABLES, which has the cell coordinates A:D4..C:G50, and display that value in the current cell. To calculate the number of columns, you use @COLS(PRICE_TABLES). Similarly, you can enter @ROWS(PRICE_TABLES) to display the number of rows in the range, and @SHEETS(PRICE_TABLES) to display the number of worksheets in the range.

@COLS, @ROWS, and @SHEETS are useful within macros to determine the size of a range. Once the size of a range is determined, you can use {FOR} loops to step the macro through all the cells within the range.

If you specify a single cell (such as C3) as the argument for the @COLS, @ROWS, or @SHEETS function, 1-2-3 changes the argument to range format (C3..C3) and returns the value 1 for the function.

@ERR and @NA—Trapping Errors

When you create templates for other users, you may want to use @NA or @ERR to screen out unacceptable values for cell entries. Suppose, for example, that you are developing a checkbook-balancing macro in which checks with values less than or equal to zero are unacceptable. One way to indicate the unacceptability of these checks is to use @ERR to signal that fact. You can use the following version of the @IF function:

   @IF(B9<=0,@ERR,B9)

In plain English, this statement says, "If the amount in cell B9 is less than or equal to zero, then display ERR on the screen; otherwise, use the amount." Notice that the @ERR function controls the display in almost the same way that @NA does in

Tip:
To screen out unacceptable values for cell entries when you create templates, use @NA or @ERR.

a previous example. A better technique, however, is to display a message to the user that indicates the specific error. Note the following example:

@IF(B9<=0,"Enter positive amounts",B9)

1-2-3 also uses ERR as a signal for unacceptable numbers—for example, a division by zero or mistakenly deleted cells. ERR often shows up temporarily when you are reorganizing the cells in a worksheet. If ERR persists, you may have to do some careful analysis to determine the reason.

1-2-3 displays ERR (as it does for NA) in any cells that depend on a cell with an ERR value. Sometimes the ERR cascades through other dependent cells. Use Undo (Alt-F4) to return the worksheet to the way it was before the change. See Chapter 3, "Learning Worksheet Basics," for more information about Undo.

@HLOOKUP and @VLOOKUP—Looking Up Entries in a Table

The @HLOOKUP and @VLOOKUP @functions retrieve a string or value from a table, based on a specified key used to find the information. The operation and format of the two @functions are essentially the same except that @HLOOKUP looks through horizontal tables (hence, the H in the function's name) and @VLOOKUP looks through vertical tables (the source of the V in its name). These @functions use the following formats, respectively:

@HLOOKUP(*key,range,row_offset*)

@VLOOKUP(*key,range,column_offset*)

Cue:

When you use numeric keys, make sure that the key values ascend in order.

When you use numeric keys, make sure that the key values ascend in order; otherwise, 1-2-3 returns ERR. (In contrast, if the keys are strings, the keys can be listed in any order.) And with numeric keys, both @HLOOKUP and @VLOOKUP are actually searching for the largest value that is less than or equal to the key. Therefore, if either of these @functions can't find a value that is equal, the function selects the largest value that is less than the numeric key.

The *range* argument is the area that makes up the entire lookup table. *Offset* specifies which row or column contains the data you are looking up. The *offset* argument is always a number, in ascending order, ranging from 0 to the highest number of columns or rows in the lookup table. Number 0 marks the column or row containing key data. The next column or row is 1, the next is 2, and so on. When you specify an offset number, it cannot be negative or exceed the correct number of columns or rows.

The best way to grasp the mechanics of @HLOOKUP or @VLOOKUP is to review examples. Figure 6.50 shows a table for @HLOOKUP. You can easily see how this @function (or @VLOOKUP) is useful for finding any type of value you would have to look up manually in a table, such as a tax amount, shipping zones, or interest charges.

```
A:A20:                                                    READY

     A         B           C         D         E         F         G         H
 1
 2
 3
 4                                          Formulas
 5            Amount of sale          $22,456
 6            Product class                 2
 7            Commission rate            0.06 @HLOOKUP(D6,B12..E17,2)
 8            Commission            $1,347 +D5*D7
 9
10                        Table of Commissions
11                        Product Class
12            Sales $             1         2         3
13             $5,000          0.04      0.06      0.04
14            $10,000          0.05      0.06      0.05
15            $50,000          0.06      0.07      0.06
16           $100,000          0.08      0.07      0.07
17           $500,000          1.00      0.07      0.08
18
19
20
```

Fig. 6.50.

The @HLOOKUP @function used to retrieve strings and values from tables.

Watch for three common errors when you use @HLOOKUP and @VLOOKUP. First, when you use a string as the *key* argument, the LOOKUP function returns an error if the function can't find the string in the lookup table. If either function with a string key returns ERR, make sure that you haven't misspelled the string either in the function or in the lookup table.

A second error is to fail to include the columns or rows that contain key strings or values in the range of the lookup table; the result is an ERR condition. The examples in figure 6.50 use cell addresses to specify the table so that you can easily understand the examples. You may want to name your lookup tables with the /Range Name Create command; however, naming them can make spotting missing rows or columns more difficult.

A third error, which is simple to avoid or correct, is to place the key strings or values in the wrong column. Remember that the key strings or values belong in the first column or row and that column and row numbering starts at 0. Accordingly, the first offset is 0 containing the key, the second is 1, the third is 2, and so on.

@INDEX—Retrieving Data from Specified Locations

@INDEX, a data-management @function, is similar to the table-lookup @functions described earlier. But @INDEX has some unique features. @INDEX uses the following format:

@INDEX(*range,colum,row,*[*worksheet*])

Like @HLOOKUP and @VLOOKUP, @INDEX finds a value within a table. But unlike the lookup @functions, @INDEX does not compare a key value against values in the first row or column of the table. Instead, @INDEX requires you to indicate the column offset and row offset of the range from which you want to retrieve data. For example, the following function, shown in figure 6.51, returns the value .8934:

@INDEX(C10..G14,D6,D5)

Here D6 is the column offset, and D5 is the row offset.

Notice that the number 0 corresponds to the first column, 1 corresponds to the second column, and so on. The same numbering scheme applies to rows. Using 3 for the *column* argument and 2 for the *row* argument indicates that you want an item from the fourth column, third row.

Fig. 6.51.

An example of the @INDEX function.

	A	B	C	D	E	F	G	H
1								
2								
3								
4					Formula			
5		Row		3				
6		Column		2				
7		Lookup value		0.8934	@INDEX(C10..G14,D6,D5)			
8								
9		Row/Col	0	1	2	3	4	
10		0	0.9607	0.8420	0.6832	0.5807	0.3613	
11		1	0.0750	0.8046	0.0900	0.1908	0.0183	
12		2	0.7510	0.2387	0.5111	0.5044	0.6056	
13		3	0.8077	0.7784	0.8934	0.5328	0.0618	
14		4	0.4608	0.5651	0.3505	0.3820	0.0362	

Reminder:

With @INDEX, you cannot use column, row, or worksheet numbers that fall outside the relevant range.

With the @INDEX function, you cannot use column, row, or worksheet numbers that are outside the range. Using negative numbers or numbers too large for the range causes 1-2-3 to return ERR.

@INDEX is useful when you know the exact position of a data item in a range of cells and you want to locate the item quickly. For example, @INDEX works well for rate quotation systems. Figure 6.52 shows an example of a system for quoting magazine advertising rates.

In the example, the following function returns a value of 1,000:

@INDEX(C10..G13,C4,C3)

This value corresponds to the amount in the third column and the fourth row of the index range. If 5 is entered for the frequency (in this case, the number of times an advertisement is run), the ERR message appears instead of a valid dollar amount.

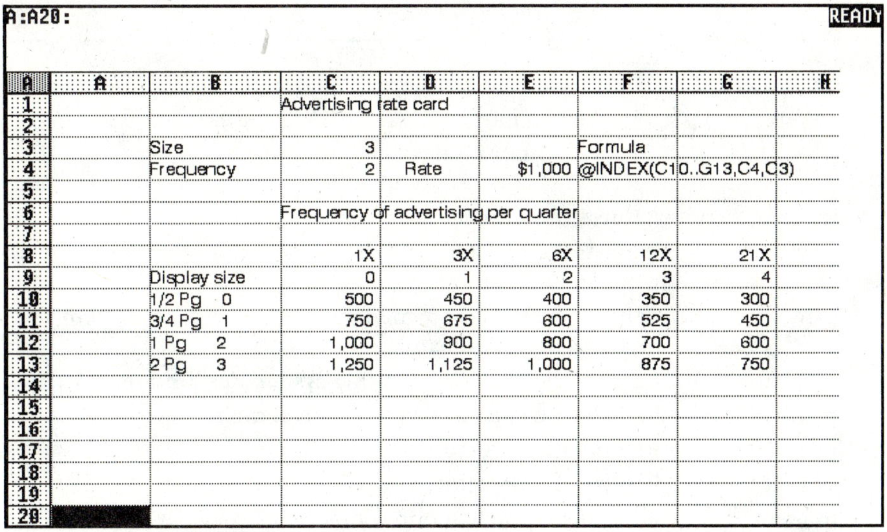

Chapter 6 ◆ Using @Functions in the Worksheet 277

```
A:A20:                                                          READY

       A       B          C        D        E        F        G       H
  1                    Advertising rate card
  2
  3          Size          3                        Formula
  4          Frequency     2        Rate     $1,000 @INDEX(C10..G13,C4,C3)
  5
  6                    Frequency of advertising per quarter
  7
  8                        1X       3X       6X      12X      21X
  9          Display size   0        1        2       3        4
 10          1/2 Pg   0    500      450      400     350      300
 11          3/4 Pg   1    750      675      600     525      450
 12          1 Pg     2   1,000     900      800     700      600
 13          2 Pg     3   1,250    1,125    1,000    875      750
 14
 ...
 20
```

Fig. 6.52.
The @INDEX function used for advertising rate quotations.

The *worksheet* number enables you to work in three-dimensional ranges. Offset numbering starts at zero: the first worksheet in a range is specified as 0, the second worksheet is specified as 1, and so on. The *worksheet* argument is optional.

@INFO—Getting System Information about the Current Session

The @INFO function enables you to tap system information about your current 1-2-3 session. Table 6.14 summarizes the attributes you can check by using @INFO.

Table 6.14
@INFO Session Attributes

Attribute	Description
"directory"	Returns the current directory path
"memavail"	Returns the memory available
"mode"	Returns a numeric code indicating one of these modes:
	0 = WAIT mode
	1 = READY mode
	2 = LABEL mode
	3 = MENU mode
	4 = VALUE mode
	5 = POINT mode
	6 = EDIT mode

continued

Part I ♦ Building the 1-2-3 Worksheet

Table 6.14—(continued)

Attribute	Description
	`10` = HELP mode
	`99` = All other modes (such as those set by the {INDICATE} command)
"numfile"	Returns the number of currently open files
"origin"	Returns the cell address of the first cell in the window with the cell pointer
"osreturncode"	Returns the value returned by the most recent /System or {SYSTEM} command
"osversion"	Returns the current operating system description
"recalc"	Returns the current recalculation setting
"release"	Returns the 1-2-3 release number
"system"	Returns the name of the operating system
"totmem"	Returns the total amount of memory (amount used plus amount available)

Figure 6.53 shows some of the system information returned.

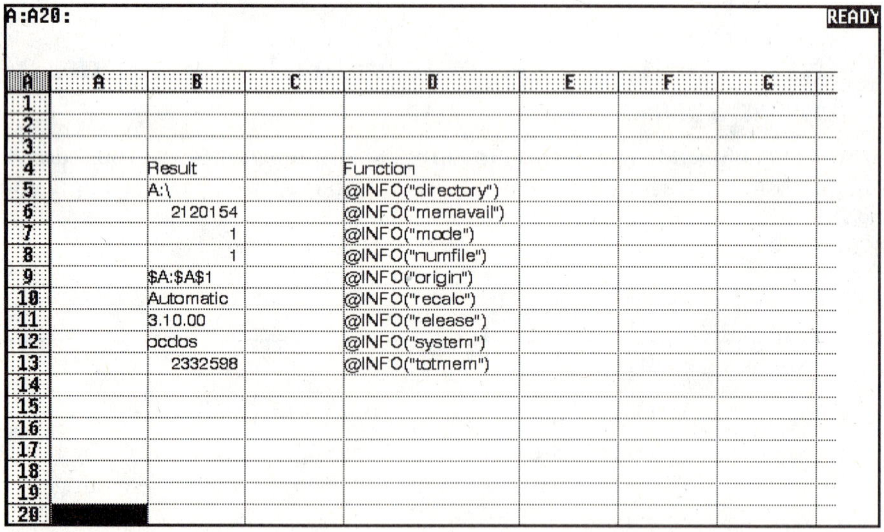

Fig. 6.53.

The @INFO function returning information about system attributes.

	A	B	C	D
4		Result		Function
5		A:\		@INFO("directory")
6		2120154		@INFO("memavail")
7		1		@INFO("mode")
8		1		@INFO("numfile")
9		$A:$A$1		@INFO("origin")
10		Automatic		@INFO("recalc")
11		3.10.00		@INFO("release")
12		pcdos		@INFO("system")
13		2332598		@INFO("totmem")

The values returned by @INFO are useful in macros for monitoring such items as application memory size, the current mode, or the current directory. Given this information, you can advise users to take the appropriate action in their 1-2-3 session.

Summary

This chapter described the @functions that 1-2-3 provides to make formula and worksheet construction easier and, usually, more error-free. After you become proficient in the use of the @functions, you can regularly incorporate them into your worksheet models, and use this chapter as a reference for the formats and the types of arguments the @functions require.

In the next chapter, you learn how to save, retrieve, and manage files with 1-2-3.

Managing Files

7

The commands available when you select /File from 1-2-3's main menu provide a wide range of file management, modification, and protection functions. Some commands, such as /File Erase and /File List, are similar to operating system commands. Other commands are related to specific 1-2-3 tasks and applications. Through the File menu, you can, for example, combine data from several files, extract data from one file and put it in another file, and open more than one file in memory at a time. You can also give a file "reservation" status so that only one user is permitted to write information to and update the file. This chapter covers the /File commands and good 1-2-3 file management.

This chapter shows you how to do the following:

- Manage the active files in memory
- Name files
- Change directories
- Save files to disk
- Retrieve files from disk
- Extract and combine data
- Protect files
- Erase files from disk
- List different types of files
- Transfer files between different programs
- Use 1-2-3 in a multiuser environment

To work with 1-2-3's commands for managing worksheet files, you access the /File option on the command menu. From that menu option, you can read files, combine information into the current file, and create new files. A brief description of these commands follows. The rest of the chapter covers the /File commands in more detail.

To read a file from disk and make the file active, you can use one of two commands. Use /File Retrieve to replace the current file with a new one. Use /File Open to add another active file to memory. Any files active, or in memory, before the execution of the /File Open command are still active afterward.

If you want to combine information into the current file, use /File Combine or /File Import. With the former, you can read all or part of a 1-2-3 worksheet file and combine the data into the current file. With the latter, you can read a text file and combine the data into the current file.

To create a new file, use /File Save or /File Xtract. /File Save saves one or all active files on the disk. /File Xtract saves part of a file as a new file.

When you first start 1-2-3, you have a blank worksheet. If you want to build a new worksheet, just use the blank one. If you want to start with an existing file, use /File Retrieve. To build a new worksheet file when you have one or more existing files in memory, use /File New.

At any one time, you usually work with data files in one directory on your disk. To change the default data directory, use /File Dir (Directory). To see a list of all or some of the files in the current directory, use /File List. To save a list of files as a table in a worksheet, use /File Admin Table.

If you want to erase unneeded files on your disk to make room for other files, use /File Erase.

If you work with shared files in a network or other multiuser environment, you can use /File Admin Reservation to control write-access to files. If you have files with formulas that refer to cells in shared files, use /File Admin Link-Refresh to update these formulas manually.

Cue:
To seal a file so that no one can change the protection settings without giving a password, use /File Admin Seal.

To seal a file so that no one can change the protection settings without giving a password, use /File Admin Seal.

Managing Active Files in Memory

In 1-2-3 Release 3, the word *file* refers to two types of files—disk files and RAM files or worksheets. A disk-based file stores computer information magnetically for the long term. When you build or change worksheets in memory, the information is lost unless you save it to a disk-based file.

Alternatively, a file can consist of one or more worksheets that form an integral group in the computer's memory, even if the worksheets have not yet been saved to a disk-based file. When you first build a new worksheet, you are starting this second type of file. You can enter data into the worksheet, and you can insert additional worksheets into the same file. When you save a file to disk, you save all the file's worksheets together. When you read a file from disk, you read into memory all the file's worksheets.

Chapter 7 ◆ Managing Files   **283**

Reading a file from disk produces in the computer's memory an exact copy of the disk file. The file still exists unchanged on disk.

When you save a file, you store on the disk an exact copy of the file that is in the computer's memory. The file still exists unchanged in memory. To manage files on disk, you must understand how to manage files in memory.

The computer's memory is your work area. Files in memory are called *active files*. When you use the **/Q**uit command or the **/W**orksheet **E**rase command, you lose all active files from memory. When you use **/F**ile **R**etrieve, you replace the current file in memory with another file from the disk. The current file is the file containing the cell pointer. Use **/W**orksheet **D**elete **F**ile to remove an active file from memory (see "Deleting Worksheets and Files" in Chapter 4). If you save a file before removing it from memory, you can read the file again from disk. If you make changes to a file and do not save it to disk, the changes are lost if you delete the file or replace it in memory.

Caution:
When you use the /Quit command or the /Worksheet Erase command, you lose all active files from memory.

Naming Files

The exact rules for file names depend on the operating system you use. In this book, the assumption is that you use a version of MS-DOS or PC DOS. File names consist of a 1- to 8-character name plus an optional file extension of 1 to 3 characters. The extension usually identifies the type of file. An example of a file name is BUDGET.WK3. Usually, you choose the file name, and 1-2-3 supplies the extension.

A file name in DOS can contain letters, numbers, and the following characters:

~ ! @ $ % ^ & ( ) - _ { } # '

Spaces are not allowed. All letters convert automatically to uppercase. A file name should include only letters, numbers, the hyphen (-), and the underline character (_). Other characters may work now but may not work in later versions of DOS or other operating systems. For example, the characters # and ' work with current versions of DOS but not with OS/2. Whether you plan to switch to OS/2 or not, a future release of DOS may well make these two characters invalid in file names.

Reminder:
A file name should include only letters, numbers, the hyphen, and the underline character.

The standard extension for 1-2-3 Release 3 worksheet files is WK3. When you type a file name, simply type the 1- to 8-character part of the name. 1-2-3 adds the extension for you. 1-2-3 Release 3.1+ uses the following extensions:

Extension	Description
WK3	For Releases 3, 3.1, and 3.1+ worksheet files
BAK	For backup worksheet files
WK1	For Releases 2, 2.01, 2.2, and 2.3 worksheet files
PRN	For print-image text files with no special characters
ENC	For encoded print-image files with graphics and/or formatting characters specific to one printer
PIC	For files in Lotus graph-image format
CGM	For files in graphic metafile graph-image format

You can override these standard extensions and type your own. In addition, 1-2-3 can read worksheets that have the following extensions:

Extension	Description
WKS	For Release 1A worksheet files
WRK	For Symphony Releases 1 and 1.01 worksheet files
WR1	For Symphony Releases 1.1, 1.2, 2, and 2.2 worksheet files

When you execute most file commands, 1-2-3 assumes that you want to see the existing files that have WK* extensions and so lists these files in the control panel. The asterisk (*) means "any character"; W K * therefore designates such extensions as WK3, WK1, and WKS. If you create a file whose extension does not start with W K, 1-2-3 does not list that file name as a default.

Reminder:
Keeping the macro file hidden would prevent you from accidentally retrieving the file outside of the macro.

To read a file that has a nonstandard extension, you must type the complete file name and extension. You may want to save a file with a nonstandard extension so that the file does not show up when 1-2-3 lists the worksheet files. For example, you may want to use a nonstandard extension with a file that is part of a macro-controlled system, in which macros retrieve or open the file. Keeping the macro file hidden would prevent you from accidentally retrieving the file outside of the macro. The nonstandard extension "hides" the file from any list of worksheet files. When you want to retrieve the file outside of the macro environment, perhaps to change it, simply type the entire file name and extension.

To change the file list's default extension from WK* to something else, use /**W**orksheet **G**lobal **D**efault **E**xt **L**ist and specify the new default extension. To list only Release 3 worksheets, type **WK3**. To list 1-2-3 and Symphony worksheet files, type **W***.

You do not have to accept the default WK3 extension when you save a file. You can type any extension you want. If you use the WK1 extension, 1-2-3 saves the file in Release 2 format, and the file can be read with either Release 2 or Release 3. This arrangement works only if the file contains just one worksheet and uses only functions or macros available in Release 2.

If you must pass files between Release 2 and Release 3, and you don't use any features, functions, or macros that are not in Release 2, you can change the default extension to WK1. Use /**W**orksheet **G**lobal **D**efault **E**xt **S**ave and specify the new default extension—in this case, WK1. To change these defaults permanently, use /**W**orksheet **G**lobal **D**efault **U**pdate.

Changing Directories

A hard disk is logically separated into several directories (also called *subdirectories*). The set of directories leading from the root to the directory containing a file you want is called the *path*, or *directory path*. When you perform file operations in 1-2-3, you usually deal with one directory at a time.

To select the default directory when you start 1-2-3, use /Worksheet Global Default Dir. Type the path to the directory that contains the files you use most often (see fig. 7.1, which shows the sample path name D:\123R31); press Enter. To save the name of the path permanently, use /Worksheet Global Default Update.

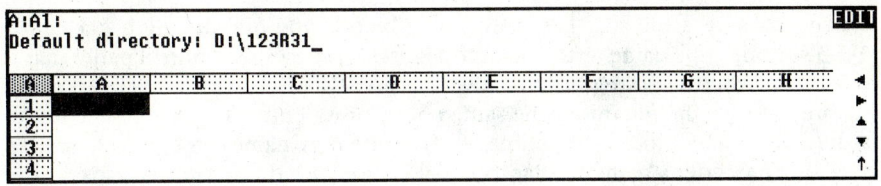

Fig. 7.1.
The sample default directory D:\123R31.

To change the current directory, use /File Dir. 1-2-3 displays the current directory path (see fig. 7.2). You can ignore the current path and type a new one. As soon as you type a character, the old path clears. To erase part of the path, use the End, left-arrow, right-arrow, Del, and Backspace keys. Type the directory path that you want to use; press Enter. When you perform any other file commands, such as /File Retrieve, 1-2-3 assumes that you want to use the current directory and displays the current path.

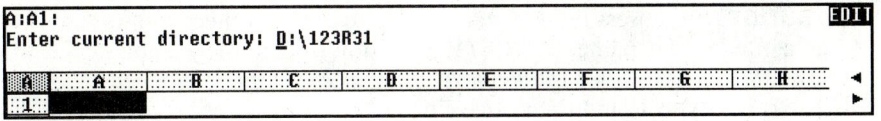

Fig. 7.2.
The current directory, following a prompt for a directory path.

Saving Files

The /File Save command enables you to store on disk a copy of one or all active files in memory, including all the formats, names, and settings.

When you save a file for the first time, the file has no name. 1-2-3 supplies the default file name FILE0001.WK3 (see fig. 7.3). If this file name already exists in the current directory, 1-2-3 uses FILE0002.WK3, and so on. Do not accept this default file name; instead, type a more meaningful name. As soon as you begin to type a new name, 1-2-3 clears the default name but leaves the path. Figure 7.4 shows the control panel after you type the letter **b** as the first character of the file name BUDGET. You do not need to use Backspace to erase the default name. After you type the file name, press Enter.

```
A:G13:                                                           EDIT
Enter name of file to save: D:\123R31\FILE0001.WK3
         A            B         C         D        E        F        G
  1:  Department 1   QTR 1     QTR 2     QTR 3    QTR 4   TOTALS
  2:                 -----     -----     -----    -----   ------
  3:  Product 1      4,428     3,170     7,035    9,829   24,462
  4:  Product 2      4,664     3,340     7,410   10,354   25,768
```

Fig. 7.3.
The default file name FILE0001.WK3, supplied by 1-2-3.

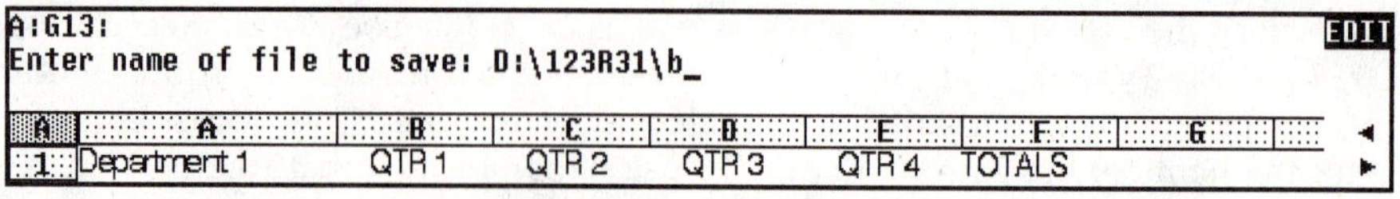

Fig. 7.4.

Clearing the default file name after the first letter of the new file name is typed.

```
A:G13:                                                      EDIT
Enter name of file to save: D:\123R31\b_

        A           B        C        D        E        F        G
  1: Department 1   QTR 1    QTR 2    QTR 3    QTR 4    TOTALS
```

When you save a file that has been saved before, the file already has a name. 1-2-3 supplies this name as the default. Figure 7.5 shows the control panel that is on-screen when you are about to save the file BUDGET, which has been saved before. To save the file under the same name, press Enter. To save the file under a different name, ignore the old name, type the new name, and press Enter. To save the file under a name similar to the old name, use the arrow, Backspace, and Del keys to erase part of the old name; then type any additional characters.

Fig. 7.5.

The default file name BUDGET.WK3, supplied by 1-2-3 for a file previously saved under that name.

```
A:G13:                                                      EDIT
Enter name of file to save: D:\123R31\budget.wk3_

        A           B        C        D        E        F        G
  1: Department 1   QTR 1    QTR 2    QTR 3    QTR 4    TOTALS
```

For example, suppose that you build a worksheet and are about to save it for the first time. You don't want the default file name FILE0001.WK3, so you ignore it, type **BUDGET**, and press Enter. Later you add to the worksheet and want to save it again, under the name BUDGET1. You don't want the default file name BUDGET.WK3, so you use the left-arrow key to move the cursor after the *T* in BUDGET, you type **1**, and then press Enter. Renaming different versions of the same worksheet is a good way to keep several backup copies accessible while you build a new worksheet. If you make a catastrophic error and don't discover it until after you have saved the file, you have earlier versions to go back to.

If another file exists in the same directory under the same file name you have chosen, 1-2-3 gives you three options: **C**ancel, **R**eplace, and **B**ackup (see fig. 7.6). If you do not want to write over the old file on disk, choose **C**ancel to cancel the command and start over. You then can save your file under a different name.

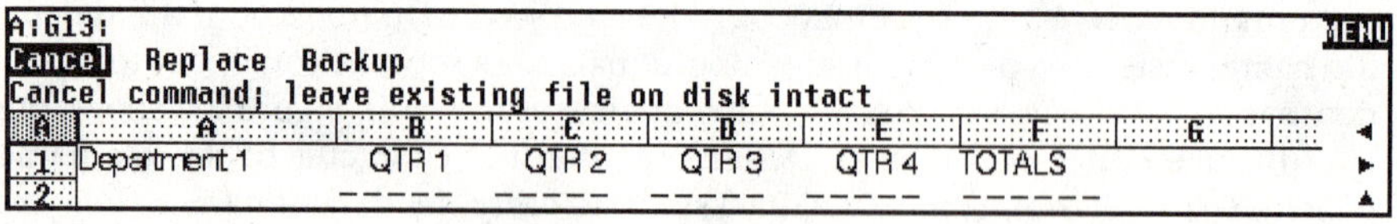

Fig. 7.6.

The menu that appears when you try to save a file under an existing name.

```
A:G13:                                                      MENU
Cancel  Replace  Backup
Cancel command; leave existing file on disk intact

        A           B        C        D        E        F        G
  1: Department 1   QTR 1    QTR 2    QTR 3    QTR 4    TOTALS
  2:                -----    -----    -----    -----    ------
```

If you want to write over the old file, choose **R**eplace. The old file with the same name is lost permanently. When you choose **R**eplace, 1-2-3 first deletes the old file from the disk. If you get a `Disk full` message while saving a file, you must save the file on another disk or erase some existing files to make room to save the file. If you do not successfully save the file, both the new version in memory and the old version on disk are lost.

If you want to save your file under the same name but not lose the old file on disk, choose **B**ackup. Backup renames the old file with a BAK extension, then saves the new file under the same file name, with a WK3 extension. You thus have both files on disk.

The **B**ackup option saves only one file as a backup. If you save the file again and choose **B**ackup, 1-2-3 deletes the current backup file, renames the WK3 file with a BAK extension, and saves the new file under a WK3 extension. If you want to keep the old file with a BAK extension, you must copy the file to a different disk or directory, or you must rename the file.

Retrieving Files from Disk

Two commands enable you to read a file from disk into memory. /**F**ile **R**etrieve replaces the current file with the new file. If you just started 1-2-3, or if nothing but a blank worksheet is in memory, use this command. If you have a current file in memory and you changed the file since the last time you saved it, those changes are lost if you use /**F**ile **R**etrieve with another file. 1-2-3 gives no warning if you are about to replace a file you have changed.

Caution:
/*F*ile *R*etrieve replaces the current file; if you made changes to this file since the last /*F*ile *S*ave operation, the changes are lost.

/**F**ile **O**pen reads a file from disk into the computer's memory. Unlike /**F**ile **R**etrieve, this command does not replace the current file in memory. With /**F**ile **O**pen, you can continue to read files into memory until you run out of memory.

When more than one file is in memory, or is active, you can easily move the cell pointer among the files to update one file and then another. As explained in Chapter 3, when both files are in memory, you can more easily create formulas that link files. Also, you can use commands that span multiple files. For example, you can copy data from one file to another, print reports with data from multiple files, graph data in multiple files in the same graph, and use /**D**ata **Q**uery **E**xtract to move data from one file to another.

After you select /**F**ile **O**pen, choose either **B**efore or **A**fter to tell 1-2-3 to put the file either before or after the current file. In perspective view, *before* means toward the bottom of the screen, and *after* means toward the top. In figure 7.7, FILE2 is after FILE1 and before FILE3.

With either /**F**ile **R**etrieve or /**F**ile **O**pen, at the prompt requesting you to enter the file name, 1-2-3 lists the files on disk. You can either type the file name or point to the file from the list in the control panel. If several files are in the directory, press **N**ame (F3) for a full-screen display of file names (see fig. 7.8). Files are listed in alphabetical order as you read from left to right. Point to the file you want to retrieve; then press Enter.

Cue:
Press Name (F3) for a full-screen list of file names.

Using Wild Cards for File Retrieval

Whenever 1-2-3 prompts you for a file name, you can include the asterisk (*) and the question mark (?) as *wild cards* in the file name. Wild cards are characters that enable you to make one file name match several files. Although wild cards can be used with many of the /**F**ile commands, you probably use these special characters most often with /**F**ile **R**etrieve.

Fig. 7.7. *Three files in perspective view.*

```
List   ..   ◄   ►   ▲   ▼   A:   B:   C:   D:   E:                      FILES
Enter name of file to retrieve: D:\123R31\DATA\*.WK*
          2SHEET.WK3    07-Jul-90      06:07 PM          1824
2SHEET.WK3        ACCTG.WK3          BUDGET.WK3          CONSOL.WK3
DATA.WK3          DBT13S.WK3         DBT14S.WK3          EXTEXAM.WK3
EXTRACT.WK3       FIG723.WK3         FIG724.WK3          FIG732.WK3
FIG734.WK3        FILE0001.WK3       FILE1.WK3           FILE2.WK3
```

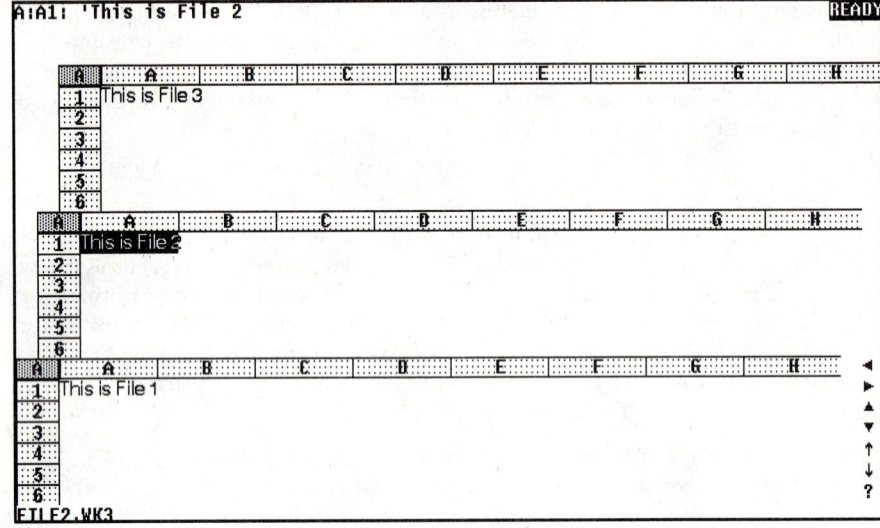

Fig. 7.8. *A full-screen list of file names, produced by pressing Name (F3).*

The ? matches any one character in the name (or no character if the ? is the last character in the file name's main part or extension). The * matches any number of characters (or no character).

Reminder: *When you use wild cards in response to a file name prompt, 1-2-3 lists only the files whose names match the wild-card pattern.*

When you use wild cards in response to a file name prompt, 1-2-3 lists only the files whose names match the wild-card pattern; 1-2-3 does not actually execute the command (unless you use /File List). For example, if you use wild cards after you select /**F**ile **R**etrieve, /**F**ile **O**pen, /**F**ile **C**ombine, or /**F**ile **I**mport, 1-2-3 does not try to read a file but lists only the files that match the wild-card pattern.

Suppose that you type **DEPT?BUD** at the prompt shown in figure 7.8. 1-2-3 lists all file names that start with DEPT, followed by any character, followed by BUD—such as DEPT1BUD, DEPT2BUD, and DEPTXBUD. If you type **BUDGET***, 1-2-3 lists all file names that start with BUDGET—such as BUDGET, BUDGET1, BUDGETX, and BUDGET99.

Retrieving Files from Subdirectories

Whenever 1-2-3 prompts you for a file name and gives you a default, the program also lists the complete path, such as D:\123R31\DATA\BUDGET.WK3.

To change the current directory, use /File Dir. To retrieve or save a file in another directory without changing the current directory, press Esc twice to clear the old path; then type a new path. You also can edit the existing path in the prompt.

When 1-2-3 lists the files in the current directory, the program lists any subdirectories below the current directory, placing a backslash (\) before each directory's name. To read a file in one of the subdirectories, point to the subdirectory name and press Enter. 1-2-3 then lists the files and any subdirectories in that subdirectory. To list the files in the parent directory (the directory above the one displayed), press Backspace; 1-2-3 lists the files and subdirectories in the parent directory. You can move up and down the directory structure this way until you find the file you want.

Reminder:
Press Backspace to list a parent directory; select a subdirectory to list the files in that subdirectory.

For those who want to learn more about directories, Que Corporation has many books available. Users new to DOS should try *MS-DOS 5 QuickStart*. Intermediate users who want to learn more about DOS file and directory management should consult *Using MS-DOS 5*; *Que's MS-DOS 5 User's Guide*, Special Edition; or *Using Your Hard Disk*.

Retrieving a File Automatically

Usually, when you first start 1-2-3, you have a blank worksheet. If you are in the default directory and save a file under the name AUTO123, however, 1-2-3 retrieves that file automatically when 1-2-3 starts. This capability is useful if you work with macro-driven worksheet files. You can use the AUTO123 file to provide the first menu of a macro-driven system or a menu of other files to retrieve.

Opening a New File in Memory

You can start a new file without clearing any existing files from memory. /File New creates a new, blank file in the computer's memory. The newly created file has the default font set, named styles, :Print Configuration settings, :Print Layout settings, and :Print Settings settings for the current Wysiwyg session. Using the /File New command does not affect the :Display settings for the current Wysiwyg session. Any files that were active before you issued this command remain active after you insert the new file. As with /File Open, described earlier, use /File New when you want to work with more than one active file in memory.

Cue:
Use /File New to start a new worksheet and leave the active files in memory.

After you select /File New, choose either Before or After to insert the blank worksheet file either before or after the current file. When you start a new file, 1-2-3 prompts you for a file name, offers a default such as FILE0001.WK3 (see the earlier section "Saving Files"), and then writes a blank file to disk.

Figure 7.9 shows the workspace in figure 7.7 after the cell pointer has been moved to FILE3 and the /File New After command has been issued to create a new file named FILE4. (Because FILE4 is a new file, it is blank.) The perspective mode allows you to view three files at the same time. Notice that FILE1 dropped off, so that FILE2, FILE3, and FILE4 are displayed.

Part I ◆ Building the 1-2-3 Worksheet

Fig. 7.9.
A new file opened after the existing files in memory.

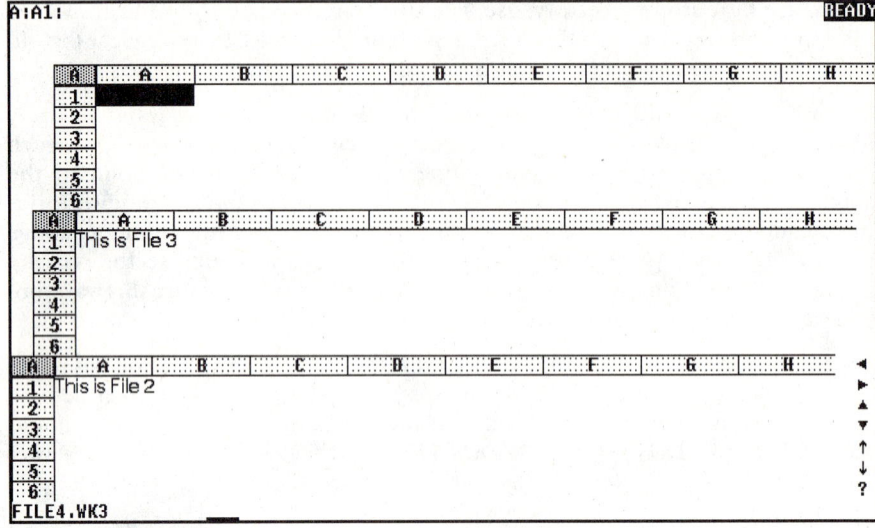

If you want to build a new worksheet file and remove all other files and worksheets, you can clear the workspace with /Worksheet Erase. This command clears all files in memory, not just the current worksheet or file. 1-2-3 asks you to confirm **No** or **Yes** before it clears the workspace. If you changed any active files since you last saved them, 1-2-3 warns you with another **No** or **Yes** menu. To save the changes, choose **No** and save the file; then execute /Worksheet Erase again.

Reminder:
*You can read a WK3 file into memory with Release 3.1+ by using either /**F**ile **O**pen or /**F**ile **R**etrieve.*

You can read a WK3 file into memory with Release 3.1+ by using either /**F**ile **O**pen or /**F**ile **R**etrieve. 1-2-3 reads the formatting information into memory from the Wysiwyg format file (with the extension FM3) with the same name, provided that one exists. This differs with a WK1 file. When reading a WK1 file into memory, 1-2-3 reads the formatting information into memory from either an Impress format file (FMT) or Allways format file (with the extension ALL), if one exists.

The rules determining which format file 1-2-3 retrieves with the WK1 files depend on which files have been formatted with Impress and which have been formatted with Allways. The rules apply in the following order:

◆ 1-2-3 retrieves the FMT file if an Impress format file with the same name as the WK1 file exists. If there is an Allways format file (ALL) with the same name, the ALL file is ignored and the Impress format file has priority.

◆ 1-2-3 retrieves the ALL file with the same name as the WK1 file if there is no Impress format file.

Multiple-File Applications

1-2-3 enables you to work with multiple files in memory. This capability makes it possible for you to refer to data that is stored in another file, to copy data from one file to another, to create formulas that refer to information in different files, and to change data in one file as a result of changes in another file.

The /**File O**pen command is the tool that makes these tasks possible. When you have multiple files in memory, you can save one file and have no effect on the other files in memory or on disk. You also can save each file that you have modified or all the files at once. Refer to Chapter 3 for a detailed explanation of using multiple files.

Extracting and Combining Data

You can take the data from part of a file and use that data to create another, smaller file. For example, you may have a large budget file that contains information from many departments. For each department, you can create an input file that contains only the data for that department.

You then may want to reverse the procedure; you may have many departmental input files and want to combine them into one file for company-wide analysis and reporting.

1-2-3 provides the /**File X**tract command so that you can save a part of the current file as a new file. When using Release 3, it is wise to note that if you extract a range of data from an active file and save it in a worksheet file on disk with /**File X**tract, a format file for the new worksheet is not created. 1-2-3 also offers the /**File C**ombine command so that you can combine data from another file into the current file.

Extracting Information

The /**File X**tract command enables you to save a range in the current file as a separate file. You can use this command to save part of a file before you change it, to break a large file into smaller files so that it can be read in another computer that has less memory, to create a partial file for someone to work on, or to pass information to another file.

The extracted range can be a single cell or a two-dimensional or three-dimensional range. The extracted file contains the contents of the cells in the range, including the cells' formats and protection status; all range names in the file; and all file settings, such as column widths, window options, print ranges, and graph options.

To extract part of a worksheet, choose /**File X**tract and select either **F**ormulas or **V**alues. When you select **F**ormulas, any cells in the extract range in the current file that contain formulas are copied into the extracted file as formulas. When you select **V**alues, any cells in the extract range in the current file that contain formulas are converted into their current values, and these values are copied into the extracted file. 1-2-3 then acts as if you were saving a file for the first time. 1-2-3 prompts for a file name, offering the default FILE0001.WK3. Type a file name and press Enter. Then specify the range to extract and press Enter. For the range, you can type addresses, highlight the range, type a range name, or press Name (F3) and point to

Caution:
*If you use /**F**ile **X**tract to extract a range of data from an active file and save it in a worksheet file, no format file for the new worksheet is created.*

a range name. If there is another file with the same name, you get the **Cancel Replace Backup** menu (as shown in fig. 7.6).

The extracted range can start anywhere in the current file (see fig. 7.10). The upper left corner of the extracted range becomes cell A:A1 in the new file (see fig. 7.11). All range names adjust to their new positions.

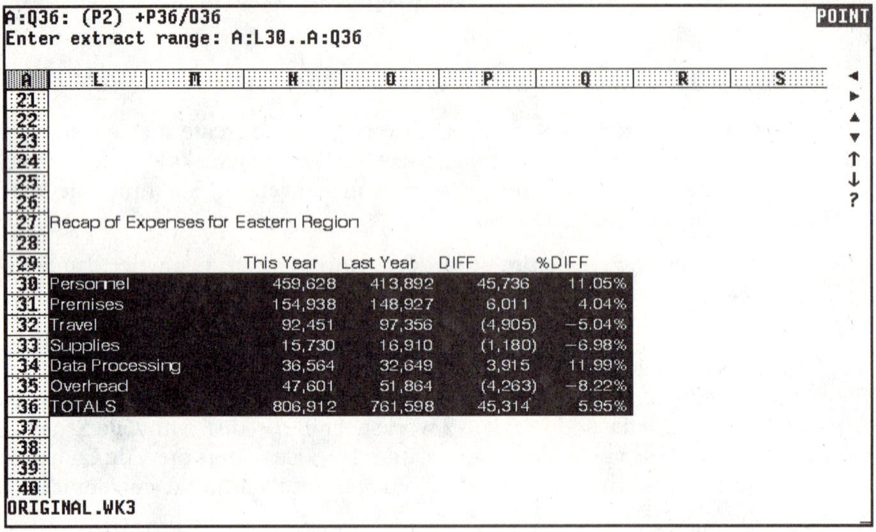

Fig. 7.10.
A highlighted range to be extracted.

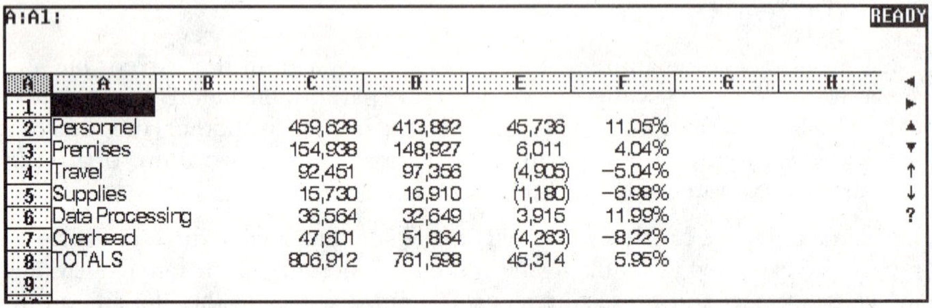

Fig. 7.11.
The extracted range, which starts in cell A:A1 of the new file.

Compare the range name table in the file SALES (see fig. 7.12) with the range name table in the file XVALUES (see fig. 7.13). The XVALUES file was created with /**F**ile **X**tract **V**alues from the range F1..F9 in the SALES file, and a range name table was added to the extracted file.

In the original file (shown in fig. 7.12), GRAND_TOT refers to F9. In the new file (shown in fig. 7.13), GRAND_TOT refers to A9. All other range names are adjusted as well. Be aware that range names to the left or above the upper left of the extract range "wrap" to the end of the worksheet, as shown in the range name table in figure 7.13. Most of these range names refer to blank cells and really have no meaning in this worksheet. The only meaningful range names are those completely within the extract range—in this case, TOTALS and GRAND_TOT.

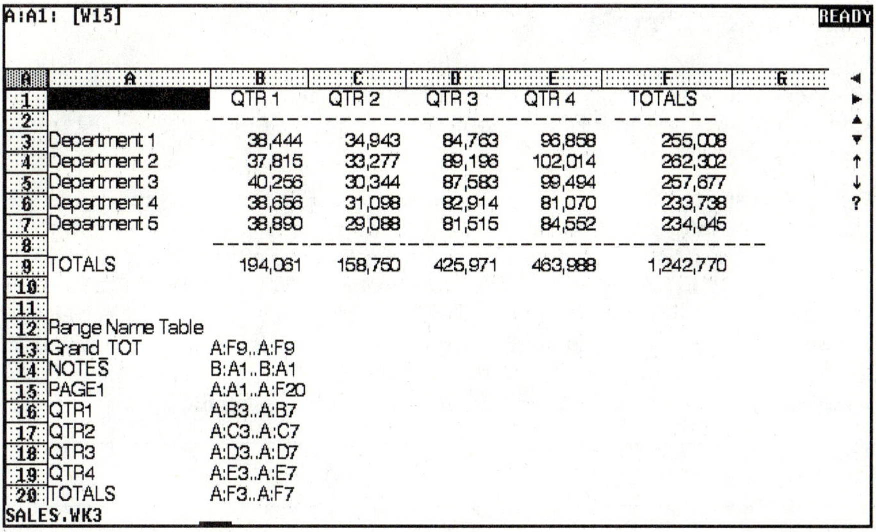

Chapter 7 ◆ Managing Files 293

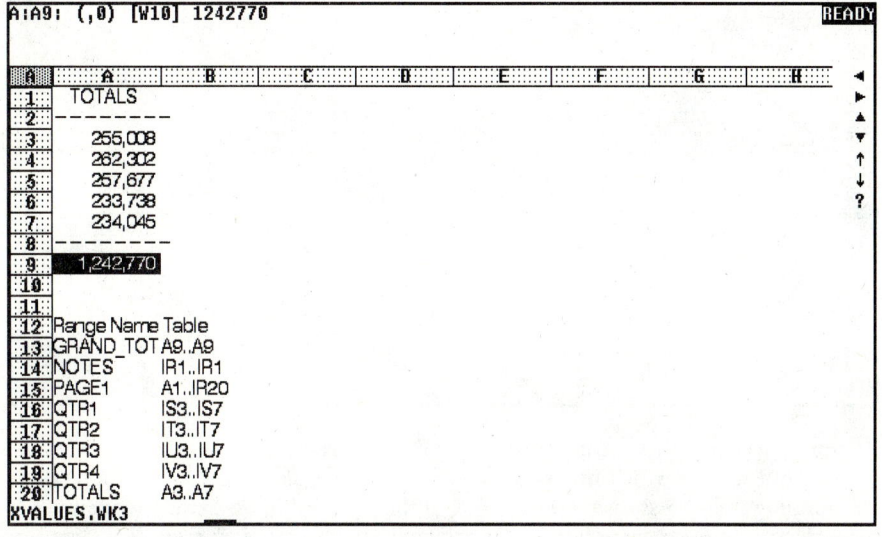

Fig. 7.12.
The SALES file.

Fig. 7.13.
The extracted file XVALUES, created by /File Xtract Values, with a range name table added.

The extracted file also has all the other settings of the original file, including print, graph, and data ranges. These settings adjust, as do the range names. For example, the print range in SALES (see fig. 7.12) is A1..F20. In XVALUES (see fig. 7.13), the print range is A1..IR20. The /Graph **X** range is A3..A7 in SALES and IR3..IR7 in XVALUES. As with range names, do not use /**P**rint, /**G**raph, or /**D**ata settings in an extract file unless the entire settings range is within the range extracted. In this example, the /**P**rint and /**G**raph settings are meaningless.

Extracting Formulas

Caution:
Extract formulas only if those formulas refer solely to cells in the extract range.

You should extract formulas only when the formulas in the extract range refer solely to other cells in the extract range. The formulas in figure 7.12 were converted to values in figure 7.13. This fact is important because the formulas in F3..F7 sum a range that was not extracted.

Figure 7.14 shows the XFORMULA file created with /File **X**tract **F**ormulas from the range F1..F9 in the SALES file in figure 7.12. This range is the same one extracted with /File **X**tract **V**alues in figure 7.13. In the SALES file, the formula in F3 is @SUM(E3..B3). In figure 7.14, this formula becomes @SUM(IS3..IV3). The formula was summing cells from four cells to the left through one cell to the left. This relative addressing is carried through to the extracted file just as it would if you copied or moved the cells in a worksheet. Notice that the extracted file retains the column width and cell formats as well as the values from the original file.

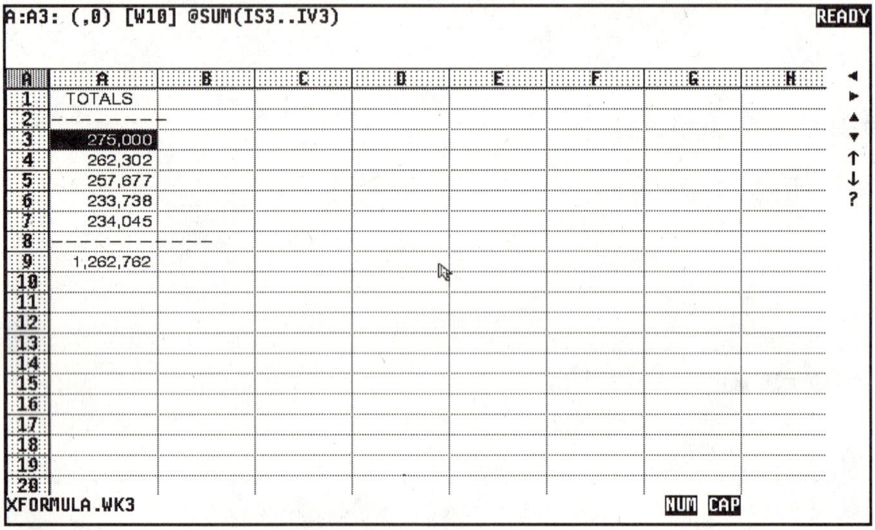

Fig. 7.14.
Meaningless results produced by /File Xtract Formulas.

```
A:A3: (,0) [W10] @SUM(IS3..IV3)                                    READY
       A         B        C        D        E        F        G        H
 1  TOTALS
 2  --------
 3   275,000
 4   262,302
 5   257,677
 6   233,738
 7   234,045
 8  --------
 9  1,262,762
10
...
XFORMULA.WK3                                                    NUM CAP
```

At times, you need to extract formulas. Suppose, for example, that you want to extract one of the worksheets from the SALES file discussed in the preceding section. Figure 7.15 shows worksheet C of the SALES file. To extract worksheet C and place it in a separate file for Department 1 personnel to complete, use the command /File **X**tract **F**ormulas and specify the range C:A1..C:F10. You might name this extract file XSALES1 to remind yourself that it is an extract file from SALES for Department 1 (see fig. 7.16). Because all formulas refer to cells in the extracted range, the formulas are still valid. The worksheet data in figure 7.16 is identical to the data in worksheet C in figure 7.15.

Cue:
Even absolute values adjust with /File Xtract.

When you extract formulas, the formulas adjust even if they are absolute. The resulting formulas are still absolute, but they have new addresses. If the formula in F3 in figure 7.12 were @SUM($E$3..$B$3), the formula in A3 in figure 7.14 would be @SUM($IS$3..$IV$3).

Chapter 7 ◆ Managing Files   **295**

```
C:A1: 'Department 1                                              READY
```

	A	B	C	D	E	F	G	H
1	Department	QTR 1	QTR 2	QTR 3	QTR 4	TOTALS		
2		-----	-----	-----	-----	------		
3	Product 1	4,428	3,170	7,035	9,829	24,462		
4	Product 2	4,664	3,340	7,410	10,354	25,768		
5	Product 3	9,197	6,328	13,623	17,181	46,329		
6	Product 4	7,563	6,651	15,779	21,130	51,123		
7	Product 5	7,519	5,896	15,208	20,245	48,868		
8	Product 6	5,073	9,558	25,708	18,119	58,458		
9		-----	-----	-----	-----	------		
10		38,444	34,943	84,763	96,858	255,008		

Fig. 7.15.
Worksheet C of the original SALES file.

```
A:A1: [W15] 'Department 1                                        READY
```

	A	B	C	D	E	F	G
1	Department 1	QTR 1	QTR 2	QTR 3	QTR 4	TOTALS	
2		-----	-----	-----	-----	------	
3	Product 1	4,428	3,170	7,035	9,829	24,462	
4	Product 2	4,664	3,340	7,410	10,354	25,768	
5	Product 3	9,197	6,328	13,623	17,181	46,329	
6	Product 4	7,563	6,651	15,779	21,130	51,123	
7	Product 5	7,519	5,896	15,208	20,245	48,868	
8	Product 6	5,073	9,558	25,708	18,119	58,458	
9		-----	-----	-----	-----	------	
10		38,444	34,943	84,763	96,858	255,008	
11							
12							
13							
14							
15							
16							
17							
18							
19							
20							

XSALES1.WK3

Fig. 7.16.
The XSALES1 file, extracted from SALES using /File Xtract Formulas.

Extracting Values

When you extract values, you get the current value of any formulas in the extract range. If recalculation is set to manual and the CALC indicator is on, press Calc (F9) to calculate the worksheet before you extract a range; otherwise, you may inadvertently extract old values.

Caution:
If the CALC indicator is on, press Calc (F9) to calculate the worksheet before you use /File Xtract Values.

Combining Information from Other Files

You can combine information from one or more files into the current file. Depending on your needs, you can do this either with formulas or with the /File Combine command. The /File Combine command does not include information from the corresponding format file. A formula can include references to cells in other files, as in figure 7.17. The formula in B3 of the file LINKED, at the bottom of the screen, refers to the total sales for Department 1 in B10 of the file LINKED1, in the middle of the screen. Linked worksheets and formulas are described in Chapter 3.

Cue:
/File Combine does not read the formatting information into memory from any corresponding format file.

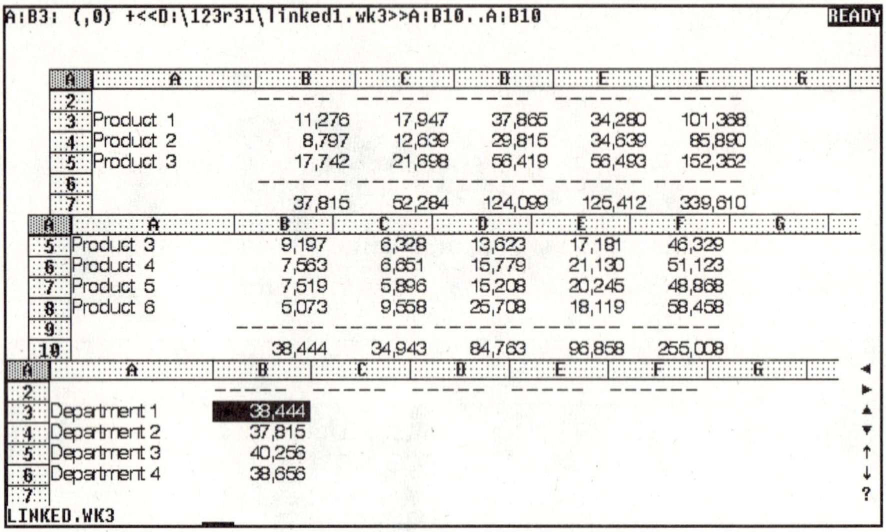

Fig. 7.17.
A worksheet with references to cells in other files.

In certain situations, you do not want to use linked files for consolidations. If you use formulas that link many external files, then each time you read in the consolidation file, 1-2-3 must read parts of each linked file to update the linked formulas. This process may take too long.

You may not want to update the consolidation automatically every time you read in the file. You may want to update the consolidation only once a month, for instance, when all the new detail data is available. The rest of the time, you may use the consolidation file for "what if" analysis, using the previous month's data.

When you want manual control over when and how you update a file with data from other files, use /File Combine. This command combines the cell contents of all or part of another file into the current file, starting at the location of the cell pointer.

Reminder:
When you want manual control over when and how you update a file with data from other files, use /File Combine.

/File Combine offers three options: Copy, Add, and Subtract. Copy enables you to replace data in the current file with data from an external file. With Add, you sum the values of the cells in the external file with the values of the cells in the current file. Subtract enables you to subtract the data in the external file from the data in the current file.

Caution:
You can make an error if you use range addresses because you can't see the external file that the data is coming from.

You can use any of the /File Combine options with either an entire file or a range. The menu choices are Entire-File or Named/Specified-Range. The range can be a single cell, a two-dimensional range, or a three-dimensional range. You can specify range addresses, but you should use range names if possible. You can easily make an error if you specify range addresses because when you execute the command, you can't see the external file that the data is coming from.

When you use the /File Combine options, blank cells in the external file are ignored. Cells with data in the external file update the corresponding cells in the current file.

Using /File Combine Copy

In the section "Extracting and Combining Data," /File Xtract was used with a consolidated file to create separate files for the individual departments. In this section, the process is reversed. /File Combine Copy is used to update the consolidated file from the individual departmental files. These examples are typical of how you use /File Xtract and /File Combine. You start with the consolidated file, and each month (or other time period) you extract the departmental files for input, then combine them for consolidated analysis and reporting.

You would use /File Combine Copy, for example, if you needed to update the SALES file with new data contained in another file—the file XSALES2, for instance (see fig. 7.18). Making sure that you are in the receiving worksheet, move the cell pointer to the upper left corner of the range to receive the combined data—in this case, B25 (see fig. 7.19)—and execute /File Combine Copy. After selecting /File Combine Copy, you have the choice of combining the whole file or only a range. If you want to include, for example, only the values in the range B3..E5 in XSALES2, choose Named/Specified-Range; then specify the range B3..E5 and press Enter. Finally, specify the external file—in this case, XSALES2—where the range B3..E5 comes from. Figure 7.20 shows how the data in figure 7.19 has been replaced by the data in figure 7.18.

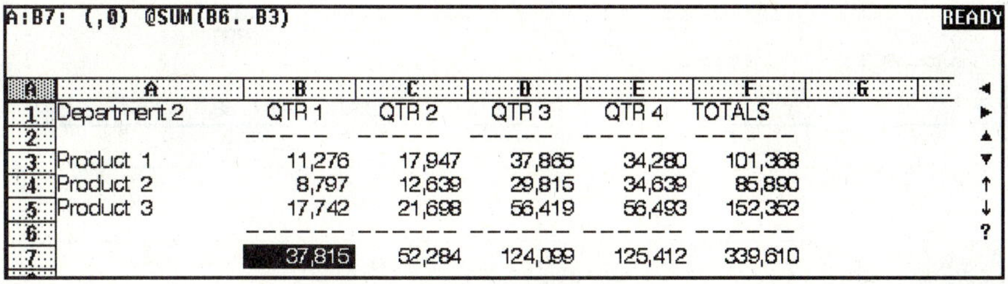

Fig. 7.18.
The XSALES2 file, to be combined into SALES.

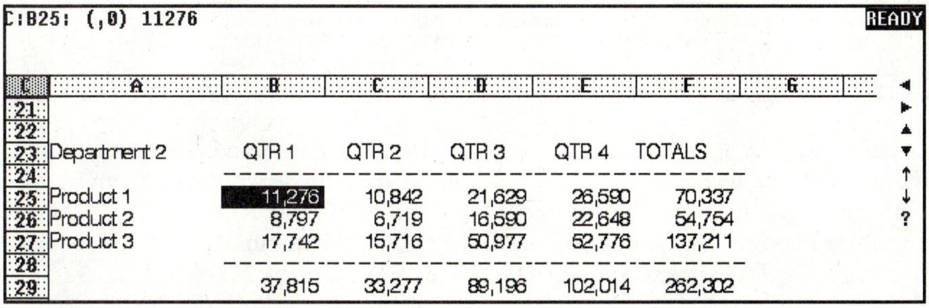

Fig. 7.19.
The SALES file before the incorporation of new data.

In this case, the old data and the new data had a known format, with no blank cells. Each cell in the external file replaced the data in the current file. If there are blank cells in the external file, however, they are ignored, and the corresponding cell in the current file is left unchanged; the corresponding cell is not blanked out.

Fig. 7.20.
The SALES file after the incorporation of new data.

```
C:B25: (,0) 11276                                                    READY

          A              B          C          D          E          F        G
 21
 22
 23  Department 2      QTR 1      QTR 2      QTR 3      QTR 4     TOTALS
 24       ---------  ---------  ---------  ---------  ---------
 25  Product 1         11,276     17,947     37,865     34,280    101,368
 26  Product 2          8,797     12,639     29,815     34,639     85,890
 27  Product 3         17,742     21,698     56,419     56,493    152,352
 28       ---------  ---------  ---------  ---------  ---------
 29                    37,815     52,284    124,099    125,412    339,610
```

Figure 7.21 is a variation of the input file shown in figure 7.18. In figure 7.21, Product 3 is canceled and the sales data erased. If you repeat the /File Combine Copy command to update the file in figure 7.20 with the data shown in figure 7.21, you get figure 7.22. Note that the old sales figures for Product 3 are not erased and that the totals for the department are wrong. To avoid this error, erase the range in the current file before you incorporate the new data. In this case, erase C:B25..C:E27.

Fig. 7.21.
An input worksheet with blank cells, to be incorporated into the SALES file shown in figure 7.20.

```
A:A1: [W15] 'Department 2                                            READY

          A              B          C          D          E          F        G
  1  Department 2      QTR 1      QTR 2      QTR 3      QTR 4     TOTALS
  2       ---------  ---------  ---------  ---------  ---------
  3  Product 1         11,276     17,947     37,865     34,280    101,368
  4  Product 2          8,797     12,639     29,815     34,639     85,890
  5  Product 3       cancelled                                          0
  6       ---------  ---------  ---------  ---------  ---------
  7                    20,073     30,586     67,680     68,919    187,258
```

Fig. 7.22.
Incorrect results in the SALES file, produced because the blank cells did not update the file.

```
C:B25: (,0) 11276                                                    READY

          A              B          C          D          E          F        G
 23  Department 2      QTR 1      QTR 2      QTR 3      QTR 4     TOTALS
 24       ---------  ---------  ---------  ---------  ---------
 25  Product 1         11,276     17,947     37,865     34,280    101,368
 26  Product 2          8,797     12,639     29,815     34,639     85,890
 27  Product 3       cancelled    21,698     56,419     56,493    134,610
 28       ---------  ---------  ---------  ---------  ---------
 29                    20,073     52,284    124,099    125,412    321,868
```

In these examples, only numbers, not formulas, were combined. You can combine formulas if you also combine the data referenced in those formulas. From figures 7.18 and 7.21 you could have incorporated B3..F7 and included the TOTALS formulas in row 7 and column F. Because you also combined the data for these formulas, the formulas would have been correct in figures 7.20 and 7.22.

Cue:
Even absolute values adjust with /File Combine Copy.

Be careful when you use /File Combine Copy with formulas. Formulas—even absolute ones—adjust automatically to their new location after the execution of /File Combine Copy. In figures 7.18 and 7.21, for example, the formula for the total for QTR 1 in cell A:B7 is @SUM(B6..B2). If you combine this formula into SALES in figures 7.19 and 7.22, the formula adjusts to @SUM(B28..B24) in cell C:B29. If the formula in cell A:B7 were @SUM($B$6..$B$2), the formula would adjust, after the execution of /File Combine, to @SUM($B$28..$B$24) in cell C:B29.

If you simply combine the formulas without the data, the formulas are meaningless, and you get incorrect results. Figure 7.23 shows the master consolidation in worksheet A for the SALES file. Because the detail exists in another worksheet, you could decide to combine only the totals from B7..E7 in figure 7.21 directly into B4..E4. The formula in B7 in figure 7.21 is @SUM(B6..B2). In figure 7.23, the formula adjusts to @SUM(B3..B8191), which is clearly wrong. This formula makes the figures for Department 2 wrong and causes a circular reference. To get what you want in this case, use /File Combine Add, as described in the text that follows.

A:A4: [W15] 'Department 2 READY

	A	B	C	D	E	F	G
1		QTR 1	QTR 2	QTR 3	QTR 4	TOTALS	
2		-------	-------	-------	-------	-------	
3	Department 1	38,444	34,943	84,763	96,858	255,008	
4	Department 2	670,318	303,230	797,649	849,360	2,620,557	
5	Department 3	40,256	30,344	87,583	99,494	257,677	
6	Department 4	38,656	31,098	82,914	81,070	233,738	
7	Department 5	38,890	29,088	81,515	84,552	234,045	
8		-------	-------	-------	-------	-------	
9		826,564	428,703	1,134,424	1,211,334	3,601,025	
10							
11							
12							
13							
14							
15							
16							
17							
18							
19							
20							

SALES.WK3 CIRC

Fig. 7.23.
An erroneous formula in the SALES file, caused by the omission of data when /File Combine Copy was used with formulas.

Using /File Combine Add and /File Combine Subtract

/File Combine Add works somewhat like **/File Combine Copy** but differs in some important ways. **/File Combine Subtract** is identical to **/File Combine Add** except that you subtract instead of add. With that exception, everything that follows about **/File Combine Add** applies to **/File Combine Subtract** as well.

Instead of replacing the contents of cells in the current file, **/File Combine Add** adds the values of the cells in the external file to the values of cells in the current file that contain numbers or are blank. In other words, this command adds a number or a formula result to a number or a blank cell. If the cell in the current file contains a formula, the formula is unchanged by **/File Combine Add**.

To update the totals correctly for Department 2 in figure 7.23, move the cell pointer to B4 and use **/Range Erase** to erase B4..E4. Then use **/File Combine Add Named/Specified-Range** to add B7..E7 from file XSALES2 in figure 7.21. The result is shown in figure 7.24.

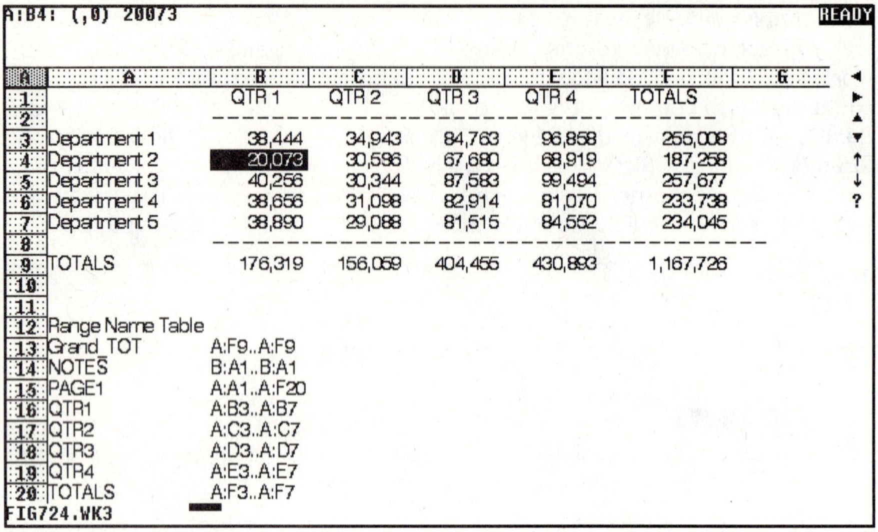

Fig. 7.24.
The SALES file after being updated with /File Combine.

```
A:B4: (,0) 20073                                                    READY

        A           B        C        D        E        F           G
                   QTR 1    QTR 2    QTR 3    QTR 4    TOTALS
 1
 2     ─────────────────────────────────────────────────────
 3     Department 1   38,444   34,943   84,763   96,858   255,008
 4     Department 2   20,073   30,596   67,680   68,919   187,258
 5     Department 3   40,256   30,344   87,583   99,494   257,677
 6     Department 4   38,656   31,098   82,914   81,070   233,738
 7     Department 5   38,890   29,088   81,515   84,552   234,045
 8     ─────────────────────────────────────────────────────
 9     TOTALS        176,319  156,059  404,455  430,893  1,167,726
10
11
12     Range Name Table
13     Grand_TOT     A:F9..A:F9
14     NOTES         B:A1..B:A1
15     PAGE1         A:A1..A:F20
16     QTR1          A:B3..A:B7
17     QTR2          A:C3..A:C7
18     QTR3          A:D3..A:D7
19     QTR4          A:E3..A:E7
20     TOTALS        A:F3..A:F7
FIG724.WK3
```

/File Combine Add adds to the current file the current value of any formulas in the external file. Because you erased the range B4..E4 in SALES, these blank cells are treated as zeros.

If you had specified a /File Combine Add range of B7..F7 instead of B7..E7, you would have gotten the same result. The total in F7 in figure 7.21 would not be added to the contents of F4 in figure 7.23 because F4 contains the formula @SUM(E4..B4). This formula remains @SUM(E4..B4) after the /File Combine Add because this command has no effect on formulas in the current file.

Caution:
Make sure that the CALC indicator is off before you save a file that might be used for a /File Combine Add or Subtract operation.

Be aware that with /File Combine Add you can add incorrect formula results. Because /File Combine Add converts formulas in the external file to their current values before the command adds them, these values must be current in order to get the correct result. If XSALES2 in figure 7.21 were set to manual calculation and the CALC indicator had been on the last time the file was saved, incorrect data could have been added during the execution of the /File Combine command. You can do nothing about this problem when you issue the /File Combine Add command. You must press Calc (F9) to calculate the external file before it is saved.

Reminder:
You can use /File Combine Add to sum the values from two or more files into one consolidation.

The other way to use /File Combine Add is to sum the values from two or more files into one consolidation. If all you wanted was the single row of totals in B9..F9 in figure 7.24, you could add the totals from all the input worksheets directly. First use /Range Erase to erase A3..F7 because you won't be keeping department totals in this example. Make sure that F9 contains @SUM(B9..E9). Then move the cell pointer to B9 and use /Range Erase on B9..E9. Finally, use /File Combine Add to add the totals from each input file (XSALES1, XSALES2, and so on). This process accumulates the totals from each department.

If you have a separate file for credits or returns, you can use /File Combine Subtract to subtract these returns. If the returns are entered as negative numbers, however, you should use **/File Combine Add** to add the negative numbers and thereby correctly decrease the sales totals.

Protecting Files

File protection is offered in a variety of ways with 1-2-3 Release 3. You learn how to simply password-protect a file or how to ensure protection for a file accessed in a multiuser or networking environment. The following sections describe the file protection methods available.

Using Passwords for File Protection

You can protect worksheet files by using passwords. Once a file is password-protected, no one can read the file without first issuing the password. This restriction applies to **/File** Retrieve, **/File** Open, **/File** Combine, and the Translate Utility (from the Lotus 1-2-3 Access Menu).

You password-protect a file when you specify the file name during a **/File Save** or **/File X**tract operation. Type the file name, press the space bar once, type **p** (see fig. 7.25), and then press Enter. 1-2-3 prompts you to type a password of 1–15 characters. The password cannot contain spaces. As you type, asterisks (*) appear on the screen in place of the actual characters you type to provide additional security.

Fig. 7.25.
The file name followed by the letter p, which tells 1-2-3 to password-protect the file.

After you type the password, press Enter; you are prompted to type the password again. Type it again (see fig. 7.26, which shows asterisks where the words have been typed); then press Enter. If both passwords are identical, the file is saved in a special format, and neither you nor anyone else has access to the file without first giving the password. If the two passwords do not match, 1-2-3 gives you an error message, and you must type the passwords again.

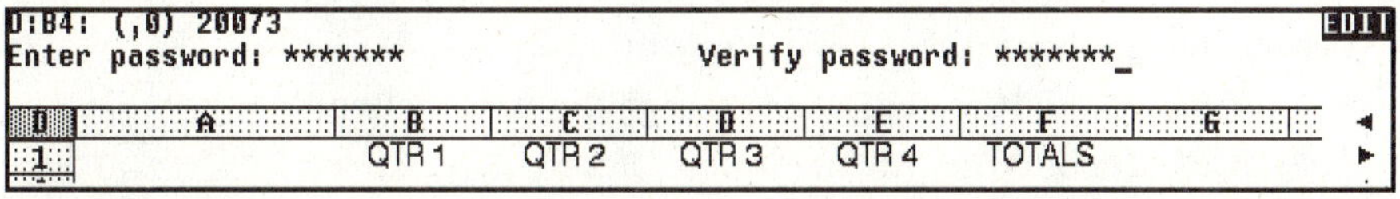

Fig. 7.26.
The control panel after you have typed the password twice.

Passwords are case-sensitive: if a password includes a lowercase letter, that letter does not match the corresponding uppercase letter. When you first assign a password, check the Caps Lock indicator so that you know how you are entering letters.

Caution:
If you forget the password, you cannot access a password-protected file.

When you use /File Retrieve, Open, or Combine with a password-protected file, 1-2-3 prompts you for the password. Only if you type the password correctly can you access the file.

When you save a file that has already been saved with a password, 1-2-3 displays the message [PASSWORD PROTECTED] after the file name (see fig. 7.27). To save the file with the same password, just press Enter. To delete the password, press Backspace once to clear the [PASSWORD PROTECTED] message; then press Enter. To change the password, press Backspace once to clear the [PASSWORD PROTECTED] message; then press the space bar once, type **p**, and press Enter. Finally, assign a new password.

Fig. 7.27.
A password-protected file that is about to be saved again.

If you have several files in memory and you execute /File Save, 1-2-3 displays [ALL MODIFIED FILES] instead of a file name. To save a file and add, delete, or change the password, press Esc or Edit (F2) to change the prompt to the current file name. Then you can proceed as explained earlier.

Using /File Admin Seal for File Protection

The /File Admin Seal method of file protection is used in the multiuser or networking environment. (See the descriptions of the /File Admin commands later in this chapter for more detailed information.) Because the multiuser and networking environments provide more than one user simultaneous access to a file, using /File Admin Seal protects or seals the current file or just the current file's reservation setting by requiring the use of a password.

When /File Admin Seal is used, the following commands are sealed and cannot be used to change the file:

- /File Admin Reservation Setting
- /Graph Name [Create, Delete, Reset]
- /Print [Printer, File, Encoded] Options Name [Create, Delete, Reset]
- /Range [Format, Label, Prot, Unprot]
- /Range Name [Create, Delete, Labels, Reset, Undefine]
- /Range Name Note [Create, Delete, Reset]
- /Worksheet Column Hide
- /Worksheet Global [Col-Width, Format, Group, Label, Prot, Zero]

Reminder:
When you use /File Admin Seal, you cannot change the settings that were sealed in the file.

You are able to read a sealed file into memory, but you cannot change the settings that were sealed in the file.

Using File Reservation for Protecting Files

Once again, this method of file protection is intended for multiuser or networking environments. To make certain that network users who share your data files cannot write over your work, 1-2-3 provides controls called *reservations*. A reservation provides the user with a guarantee that other network users cannot make changes to a file and save this file using the same file name.

To obtain a file reservation, you need to access the /**F**ile **A**dmin **R**eservation command. Once you activate this command, you can make all the changes you desire even though other users may be using the same file at the same time.

Using /Worksheet Global Prot for File Protection

This method of protection is used to protect the worksheet data. A file protected with /**W**orksheet **G**lobal **P**rot can be read into memory, but no changes are allowed to data in protected cells. You can check if the cell pointer is on a protected cell by looking at the control panel where 1-2-3 displays PR to indicate global protection is on.

Erasing Files

Every time you save a file under a different file name, you use up some space on your disk. Eventually you run out of disk space if you do not occasionally erase unneeded files from the disk. Even if you still have disk space left, you have a harder time finding the files you want to read if the disk contains many obsolete files. Before you erase some old files, you may want to save them to a diskette in case you ever need them again.

When you use /**W**orksheet **D**elete **F**ile, you clear the file from memory, but you do not erase the file from disk. You can still retrieve or open the file. To erase an unneeded file from disk, use /**F**ile **E**rase. This command removes the file from disk and frees up the disk space for other files. If you have not saved other files to the disk, a deleted file may be recovered by using a special utility program. Once the disk has been written to, however, the deleted file's space on the disk may have been replaced with new data. You also can use DOS's ERASE or DEL command to erase files on disk. Within 1-2-3, you can erase only one file at a time.

Caution:
Once you erase a file from disk, you cannot recover it without using a special utility program.

When you choose /**F**ile **E**rase, you get the menu shown in figure 7.28. Use this menu to select the type of file you want to erase. If you choose **W**orksheet, 1-2-3 lists all files in the current directory that have WK* extensions (unless you change the default with /**W**orksheet **G**lobal **D**efault **E**xt **L**ist). If you choose **P**rint, 1-2-3 lists all files contained in the current directory that have PRN extensions. Choosing **G**raph produces a list of all files contained in the current directory that have CGM extensions (unless you change the default by using /**W**orksheet **G**lobal **D**efault **G**raph **PIC**). Choosing **O**ther produces a list of all files in the current directory. *Other*, in this case, really means *all*.

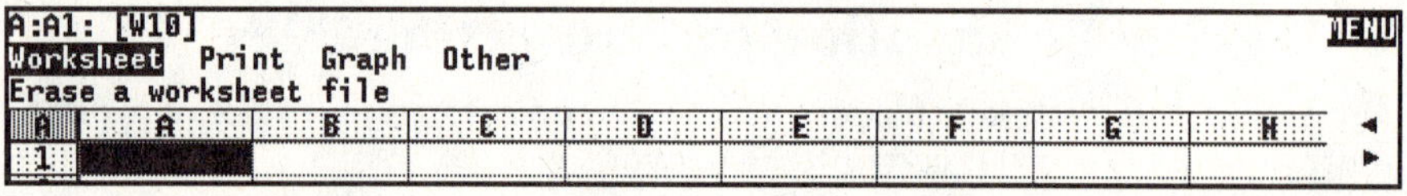

Fig. 7.28.
The /File Erase menu.

```
A:A1: [W10]                                                          MENU
Worksheet  Print  Graph  Other
Erase a worksheet file
```

To list some other set of files, choose any of the options in figure 7.28; then press Edit (F2) and change the file specification. To list all worksheet files that start with BUDGET, type **BUDGET*.WK***; to list all backup files, type ***.BAK**. When the file you want to erase is listed, highlight the file name and press Enter. Choose **Yes** to confirm that you want to erase the file. 1-2-3 erases the file.

When you select a file to erase, 1-2-3 also erases the corresponding Wysiwyg format file (with the extension FM3), Impress format file (with the extension FMT) or Allways format file (with the extension ALL), if one exists.

Creating Lists and Tables of Files

1-2-3 provides commands to help you keep track of the files you have on disk. You can either list the files or save a table of files in your worksheet. If you work with many files, you may forget the names of certain files or the times they were last updated. In addition, you can list the files that are active in memory. This capability is handy if you work with many files in memory at the same time.

To see a list of files, use **/File List**. The menu shown in figure 7.29 appears. The **Worksheet**, **Print**, **Graph**, and **Other** options provide the same lists that they provide with the /File Erase menu described earlier. Choose **Active** to list all files currently in memory. Figure 7.30 shows a sample active list, which indicates whether an active file has been modified since the last time it was saved. M O D means *modified*; U N M O D means *unmodified*. Choose Linked from the /File List menu to list all files referenced in formulas in the current file.

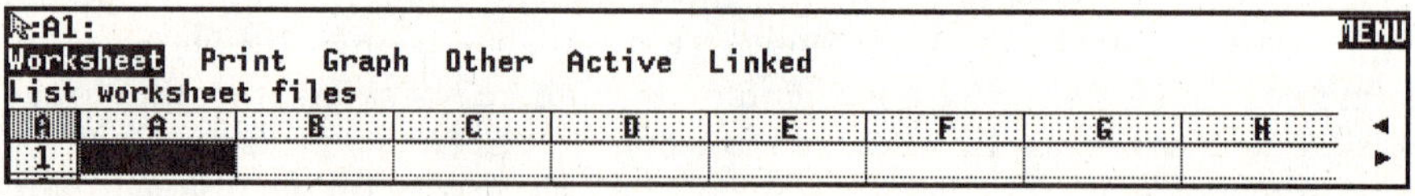

Fig. 7.29.
The /File List or /File Admin Table menu.

```
A1:                                                                  MENU
Worksheet  Print  Graph  Other  Active  Linked
List worksheet files
```

Fig. 7.30.
An active files list.

```
List    ..  ◄  ►  ▲  ▼   A:   B:   C:   D:   E:              FILES
Enter names of files to list:
EXTEXAM.WK3   08-Jul-90    06:02 PM      1605          3    UNMOD
(no name)               ACCTG.WK3          2SHEET.WK3      BUDGET.WK3
EXTEXAM.WK3
```

To save a file list as a table in your worksheet, use **/File Admin Table**. You get the same menu as in figure 7.29. If you choose **Active**, you create a table starting at the position of the cell pointer, like the table in figure 7.31. You may have to change the column widths to see all the information.

```
A:A1: 'BUDGET.WK3                                              READY
      A          B          C           D       E    F    G
  1  BUDGET.W   07-Jul-91  03:46:30 PM  1846    1    0    1
  2  EXTEXAM.W  08-Jul-91  06:02:40 PM  1605    3    0    1
  3  EXTRACT.W  08-Jul-91  11:13:36 PM  1546    1    0    1
  4  (no name)  01-Jan-00  12:00:00 AM     0    1    1    1
  5
```

Fig. 7.31.
A table of active files.

The first column lists the file name. The second column lists the date of the last save. The third column lists the time of the last save. You have to format the second and third columns in **Date** and **Time** format; 1-2-3 does not format them for you. The fourth column lists the size, in bytes, of the file. You get these first four columns by choosing any of the **Table** options. When you choose Linked, the file name includes the complete path.

With **Active**, you get three additional columns. The fifth column lists the number of worksheets in the file. The sixth column shows 0 if you have not modified the file since the last save, and 1 if you have modified it. The seventh column shows 1, which indicates that you have the reservations and can save the file. A 0 appears in this column only when the file is shared on a network or marked read-only and you do not have the file reservation.

Transferring Files

1-2-3 provides several ways to pass data between itself and other programs. The simplest file format is straight text, called also an *ASCII file*. Most programs, including spreadsheets, word processing packages, and database management systems, can create text files. To create a text file in 1-2-3, use /Print File, which Chapter 8 covers in detail. To read a text file into a worksheet, use /File Import.

Transferring Files with /File Import

/**File Import** is a special type of /File Combine. You combine the information into the current worksheet, starting at the position of the cell pointer. Any existing data in these cells is overwritten. When you execute the /File Import command, 1-2-3 lists the files contained in the current directory ending with PRN extensions. To list files that have another extension—TXT, for example—type the appropriate characters (such as *.**TXT**) and press Enter.

Caution:
When you use /**File Import**, existing data in the worksheet is overwritten.

Importing Unstructured Text Files

The typical text file contains lines of data, each line ending with a carriage return. Except for the carriage returns, these text files have no structure. You combine them by using /**File Import Text**. Figure 7.32 shows the result of importing a typical text file into a worksheet. This data may have come from a mainframe or minicomputer personnel program. Each line in the text file becomes a long label in a cell. All the

Part I ♦ Building the 1-2-3 Worksheet

data is in column A. If you import a list of names or simply want to see this data, you are finished. In most cases, however, you want to work with this data in separate cells; you want numbers as numbers and dates as dates, not labels. To make this data usable, use the /Data Parse command. See Chapter 12, "Managing Data," for a complete discussion of the /Data Parse command.

Fig. 7.32.
An unstructured text file imported with /File Import Text as long labels.

```
A:A4:   'Cheryl Morgan        4      10/27/88    Temp                    READY

         A              B       C       D          E        F        G        H
  1
  2
  3
  4    Cheryl Morgan    4     10/27/88  Temp              12.15
  5    V.R. Colonna     1     05/01/83  C-01              3,178.00   1/30/89
  6    Amanda Morgan    2     03/18/78  Executive         6,700.00   12/31/89
  7    Vinnie Charles   6     10/10/82  B-04              3,378.00   10/31/89
  8    Rick Morgan      1     01/15/54  A-07              4,213.00   01/31/90
  9    Nick Charles     1     03/14/78  A-01              4,528.00   03/31/90
 10    Charles Colonna  5     06/29/59  B-03              3,750.00   06/30/90
 11    Sarah Jones      1     01/18/58  B-03              3,680.00   01/31/90
 12    Angie Morgan     1     01/25/86  Executive         5,850.00   12/31/89
```

Importing Delimited Files

Some ASCII files are in a special format that enables them to be imported into separate cells without being parsed. This special format is called the *delimited* format. There is a delimiter between each field, and labels are enclosed in quotation marks. A delimiter can be a space, comma, colon, or semicolon. If the labels are not enclosed in quotation marks, they are ignored, and only the numbers are imported.

To import a delimited file, use /File Import Numbers. In spite of the name, this command really means "file import delimited." Figure 7.33 is an example of a delimited file. Figure 7.34 shows the results after the execution of /File Import Numbers.

Fig. 7.33.
A delimited ASCII file.

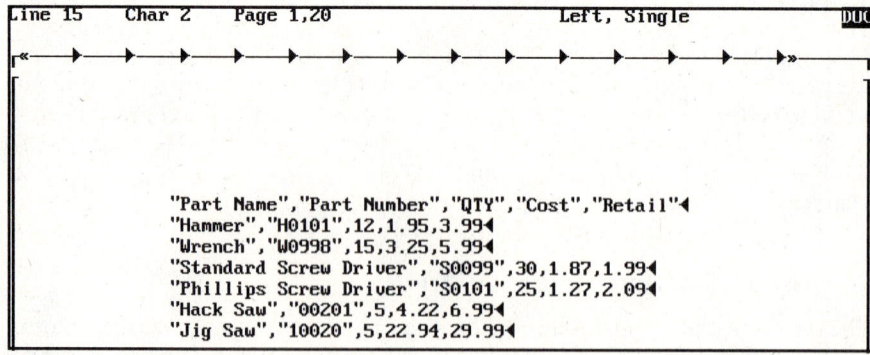

Chapter 7 ♦ Managing Files **307**

```
A:C2: [W5] 12                                                    READY
```

	A	B	C	D	E
1	Part Name	Part Number	Qty	Cost	Retail
2	Hammer	H0101	12	1.95	3.99
3	Wrench	W0998	15	3.25	5.99
4	Standard Screw Driver	S0099	30	1.87	1.99
5	Phillips Screw Driver	S0101	25	1.27	2.09
6	Hack Saw	00201	5	4.22	6.99
7	Jig Saw	10020	5	22.94	29.99
8					

Fig. 7.34.
The delimited ASCII file after the execution of /File Import Numbers.

Transferring Files with the Translate Utility

The Translate Utility is not part of the 1-2-3 worksheet program but is a separate program. Type **trans** from the operating system prompt to execute Translate, or choose **Translate** from the Lotus 1-2-3 Access Menu.

Use Translate to convert files so that they can be read by a different program. You can convert files to 1-2-3 Release 3 format from the following formats:

- ♦ dBASE II, III, and III Plus
- ♦ DisplayWrite and Manuscript, using the RFT/DCA format
- ♦ Multiplan with SYLK format
- ♦ Products that use the DIF format

You can convert files from 1-2-3 Release 3 to the following formats:

- ♦ 1-2-3 Releases 1A, 2, 2.01, 2.2, and 2.3
- ♦ Symphony Releases 1, 1.01, 1.1, 1.2, 2, and 2.2
- ♦ dBASE II, III, and III Plus
- ♦ Multiplan with SYLK format
- ♦ Products that use the DIF format

When you convert 1-2-3 Release 3 files to earlier formats of 1-2-3 or Symphony, you lose some information if you have used any of the features unique to Release 3.

To use Translate, first move the menu pointer to choose the format or program that you want to translate from; then choose the format or program that you want to translate to (see fig. 7.35). Finally, choose the file that you want to translate. Type the file name of the output file to be created by Translate and press Enter.

When you translate from Release 3, you can translate one worksheet in the file or all worksheets into separate files. When you translate to dBASE format, you can translate the entire file or a named range. Usually, the file contains data in addition to the Input range, so make sure that you use **/R**ange **N**ame to name the database **I**nput range. When you translate a file into dBASE format, the range or entire file must consist only of a database **I**nput range.

Fig. 7.35.
The menu of choices to translate to and from.

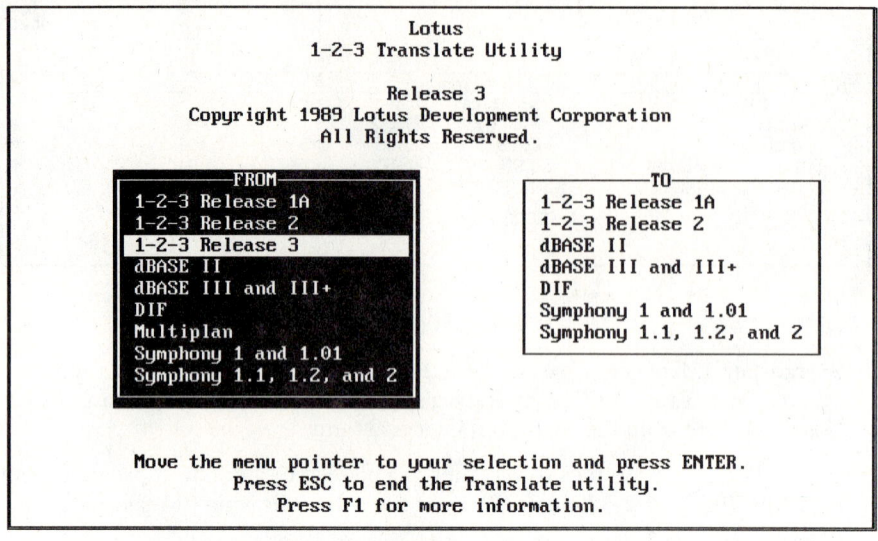

Using Earlier Versions of 1-2-3 and Symphony Files in Release 3

1-2-3 Release 3 can read files created by all prior releases of 1-2-3 and Symphony. Just use /**F**ile **R**etrieve or /**F**ile **O**pen and specify the complete file name and extension; you do not need to use Translate. The Translate menu (shown in fig. 7.35) seems to give you the option of translating files to 1-2-3 Release 3 format from the formats for prior releases of 1-2-3 and Symphony. If you choose one of these formats, however, you simply get a message telling you that you do not need to translate the file.

1-2-3 Release 3 can write files in 1-2-3 Release 2 format if you haven't used any features unique to Release 3. Just use /**F**ile **S**ave and specify a file name with a WK1 extension. Symphony Releases 1.1, 1.2, 2, and 2.2 also can read these files.

Reminder:
You cannot save a file in Release 2 format if the file contains multiple worksheets or is sealed.

You cannot save a file in Release 2 format if the file contains multiple worksheets or is sealed. Functions that are new with Release 3 or that contain new arguments are treated like Release 2 add-in functions. New functions or those containing new arguments evaluate to NA in the worksheet. Formats and settings new with Release 3, as well as notes, are lost. Labels larger than 240 characters are truncated. Formulas larger than 240 characters remain in the cell, but the cell cannot be edited in Release 2 or Symphony.

To create a file in Release 3 that can be read by 1-2-3 Release 1A or Symphony Releases 1 or 1.01, you must use Translate.

Using External Databases

You can read and create dBASE III files directly from within the 1-2-3 worksheet. Lotus provides a special "driver" program that enables you to access and create dBASE III files by using /Data External commands. Using /Data External with drivers is covered in Chapter 12. Other vendors of database management programs supply their own drivers that enable 1-2-3 to access and create files for their programs. If you use a database management program and want to share files with 1-2-3, contact the vendor and find out whether it has such a driver available.

Using 1-2-3 in a Multiuser or Networking Environment

When you use 1-2-3 in a network or other multiuser environment, you must be aware that two or more people can try to access or update the same file simultaneously. The network administrator sets up shared disks so that some files can be shared and some cannot. You do not have to worry about those files on a network server that you alone can read.

Reminder:
When you use 1-2-3 on a network, some disks can share data and some cannot.

Different programs handle the problems of multiple access in different ways. With a database management system such as dBASE III Plus, the program itself controls access so that many users can access the database at the same time. With most programs, such as word processing packages, the network administrator makes sure that these files are identified as *nonsharable*. This means that only one person can access any one file at one time. If you are working with a word processing file, no one else can read the file until you close it. Then it is available to the next person who wants it.

As discussed earlier in this chapter, 1-2-3 uses reservations to handle file sharing. In order for the 1-2-3 file reservation system to work properly, your work group must use only 1-2-3 Release 2.2, 2.3, 3, 3.1, or 3.1+; 1-2-3 Networker; or any other product that supports file sharing. If you attempt to share data files without these types of software, you may experience data loss.

Caution:
If you attempt to share data files without using file-sharing software, you may suffer data loss.

You should not use a program other than 1-2-3 Release 3, 3.1, or 3.1+ to modify a file for which you have a reservation. This prevents loss of data or, as is possible in some environments, equipment failure.

When attempting to read a shared file that was created in 1-2-3 Release 1A or 2 format without the WK* extension (for example, Symphony WR1 files), 1-2-3 Release 3 reads the file into memory and renames it in memory with the WK3 extension. If no WK3 file with the same name exists, 1-2-3 gets a reservation for the new file; however, if a file exists with the same name, 1-2-3 gives the file in memory read-only status and displays the RO indicator with an error message. In order to save the file, you have to rename it first.

1-2-3 displays the WAIT indicator if you try to read a file from disk while another user is doing so or if you try to read a file while another user is saving it on disk.

The WAIT indicator remains on screen until the first user completes the process of reading or saving the file. The WAIT indicator should never display very long. You can use Ctrl-Break to interrupt the wait cycle and return to the position you were in before you tried to read or save the file. An error message appears if 1-2-3 cannot read or save the file within one wait cycle.

File Sharing Guidelines

If you create or save a shared file and then release the reservation or perhaps decide to end 1-2-3, another user may get the file's reservation and save changes. Such a file change and save by another user would alter the file before you read it into memory again. To determine when the changes were last saved to a file, you can use the /File List command (explained earlier in this chapter).

Caution:
If you make changes to a file without a reservation, and later save those changes to the same file name, you may inadvertently write over another user's work.

If you make changes to a file without a reservation and decide to save the changes in a file with a different name, do not copy your file over the original file after the reservation for the original file is available. In doing so, you may inadvertently write over another user's work.

If you need to access a file for read-only purposes and it has an Automatic reservation setting in memory, remember to release the reservation so another user can get it.

Descriptions of /File Admin Commands

The /File Admin commands control reservations for sharing worksheet files, creating tables of information about files, sealing some settings in worksheet files and recalculating all formulas in active files. In this section, you look at the individual commands responsible for performing these tasks.

/File Admin Reservation

To avoid concurrent updates of the same shared file, 1-2-3 provides a reservation option. At any one time, only one user can have a file's reservation. The reservation status therefore is either available or unavailable. Before reading a file into memory, 1-2-3 checks the reservation status and acts accordingly.

Reminder:
Only the user who has the file reservation can save changes to a file with the same file name.

If the reservation is available, and the reservation setting is Automatic, 1-2-3 reads the file into memory with its reservation.

If the reservation is not available, and the reservation setting is Automatic, 1-2-3 displays a prompt asking if you want to read the file into memory without a reservation (see fig. 7.36). If you choose Yes, you can access the file in read-only status. In other words, you can look at the file, but any changes you make are not saved in the file with the original file name.

The RO status indicator at the bottom of the screen warns you that you cannot save the file under its current name (see fig. 7.37). If you want to save the file, you must give it a different name.

Chapter 7 ◆ Managing Files   **311**

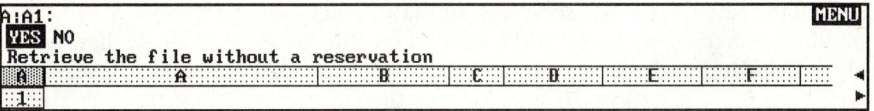

Fig. 7.36.
A file already in use, prompting whether you want to read it without a reservation.

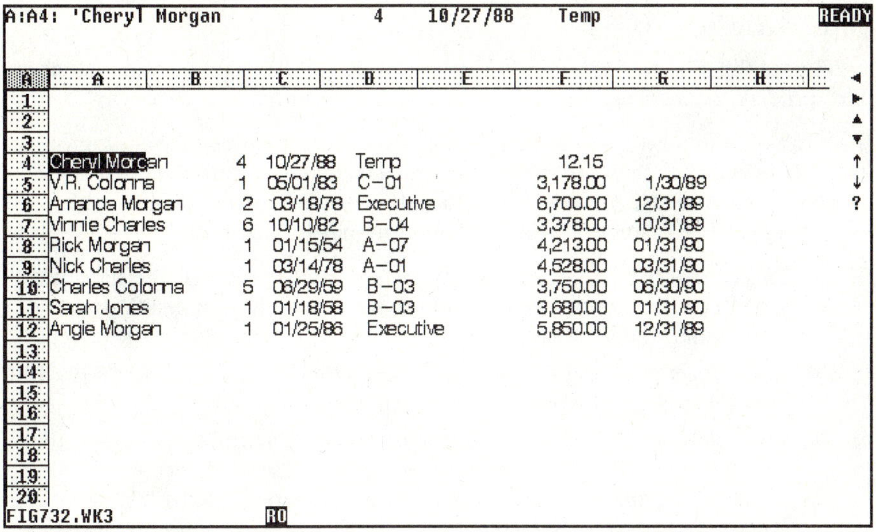

Fig. 7.37.
The RO status indicator, warning you that you cannot save the file under its current name.

Network users can assign a file read-only status, or a network file may be in a read-only network directory. If either of these situations is present, you cannot get a reservation for a file of this type even if no other user has the reservation. In network situations such as this, the network commands take precedence over the 1-2-3 reservation status.

If you have the reservation for a file, you keep the reservation until you remove the file (under the same name) from your worksheet. You can remove the file with /**Quit**, /**Worksheet Erase**, /**Worksheet Delete File**, or /**File Retrieve**. You also can release the reservation with /**File Save** if you save the file under a different name. You can release the reservation manually with /**File Admin Reservation Release**. You still have the file in memory, but you cannot save the file.

This reservation system also works manually. If many people can read a file but only one can update it, you can assign the reservation manually. Use /**File Admin Reservation Setting Manual** so that the first person to read a file does not get the reservation. Everyone who reads the file has read-only access until one person gets the reservation with /**File Admin Reservation Get**. In general, using manual reservation settings is a bad idea because you cannot ensure that only authorized people get the reservation. The network administrator may be able to set up restricted access for those people who can read but should not write to a file.

Cue:
To make the reservation setting permanent, save the file.

Automatic sets the file's reservation so that the first person to read the file into memory gets the reservation while **Manual** sets the file reservation so that no one automatically gets the reservation and the user must use /**File Admin R**eservation **G**et. To make the setting permanent, save the file.

/File Admin Table

1-2-3 uses the /**File Admin T**able command to create a table of information about files on disk, active files, or files linked to the current file.

Caution:
Make certain that the designated location in the worksheet is blank, because 1-2-3 writes over the existing data to create the table.

The **T**able command lists varied information about the files, depending on the type of file you specify. Make certain that the designated location in the worksheet is blank, because 1-2-3 writes over the existing data to create the table. The following is a breakdown of what information may be obtained:

- The names of all relevant files in the specified directory, the date and time each file was last saved, and the size of the file on disk in bytes is listed when the **W**orksheet, **P**rint, **G**raph, or **O**ther option is selected.
- The information listed above plus the path and the file name of each linked file is listed when **L**inked is selected.
- When you select **A**ctive, in addition to the information listed above, the fifth column of the table displays the number of worksheets in each file; the sixth column displays 1 if you have modified the active file and 0 if you have not modified the file; the seventh column displays 1 if you have the file's reservation and 0 if you do not.

/File Admin Seal

1-2-3 uses the /**File Admin S**eal command to seal the current file or the reservation setting of a file so that no one can change it. If this command is used to seal the current file, you can prevent changes to some graph, print, range, and worksheet settings in addition to the reservation setting of a file. (See "Protecting Files," earlier in this chapter for a listing of these changes.)

Reminder:
Once a file is sealed with a password, the only way to unseal it is to use the /File Admin Seal Disable command.

Once a file is sealed with a password, the only way to unseal it is to use the /**File Admin S**eal **D**isable command.

/File Admin Link-Refresh

When you have a file that contains references to other files, 1-2-3 updates these formulas when you read the file and use /**File Admin L**ink-**R**efresh to update these formulas.

Although executing the /**File Admin L**ink-**R**efresh command requires simply selecting the command and pressing Enter, you may need to insert a note in your files reminding you to update files when necessary. See Chapter 3 for more information on linking files and using /**File Admin L**ink-**R**efresh.

Summary

In this chapter, you learned how to manage files on disk and how to save and read whole files and extract and combine partial files. You learned how to combine text files and translate files to other formats. You learned the different methods of protecting files as a single user and in a multiuser or networking environment. You also learned how to use lists and tables of files to help you keep track of your files on disk and in memory. Finally, you learned the special considerations for using 1-2-3 on a network.

Part II

Creating 1-2-3 Reports and Graphs

Printing Reports

Using Wysiwyg To Enhance and Print Reports

Creating and Printing Graphs

Enhancing and Printing Graphs in Wysiwyg

Printing Reports

8

1-2-3 is a powerful tool for developing and manipulating tabular information. You can enter and edit your worksheet and database files on-screen, as well as store the data on disk. But to make good use of your data, you often need it in printed form—for example, as an income forecast, a budget analysis, or a detailed reorder list to central stores.

Release 3.1 offers two options to meet your printing needs. You can use the /**P**rint **P**rinter command sequence to print directly from 1-2-3 to the printer. Or you can print with Wysiwyg's :**P**rint command. If you are not using Wysiwyg, you must use /**P**rint to print your reports. If Wysiwyg is attached, you have the option of using either command. Both of these commands enable you to print worksheets and graphs, and will neatly format multipage reports. So how do you know when to use /**P**rint and when it is more beneficial to use :**P**rint?

First of all, you must use Wysiwyg's :**P**rint command whenever you enhance your spreadsheet with any of Wysiwyg's formatting options. For example, if you use :**F**ormat **B**old to boldface a row of column headings, you must print the report with :**P**rint. (1-2-3's /**P**rint command will ignore Wysiwyg enhancements.) Also, if you have inserted a graph into a worksheet range by using the :**G**raph **A**dd command, you must print the inserted graph with :**P**rint.

If your spreadsheet has not been formatted with Wysiwyg options, you may print the report with either the 1-2-3 or Wysiwyg **P**rint command; it doesn't matter which you use. Thus, feel free to use either /**P**rint or :**P**rint for your first drafts that you haven't yet formatted with Wysiwyg, and for your simple internal reports that don't need fancy formatting.

This chapter is devoted to 1-2-3's /**P**rint command. Printing with Wysiwyg's :**P**rint command is discussed in Chapter 9.

317

Part II ♦ Creating 1-2-3 Reports and Graphs

Note that the /Print menu is one of the most complex menus in 1-2-3. The menu is complex because 1-2-3 gives you considerable control over the design of printed output—from simple one-page reports to longer reports that incorporate data from many worksheets and include sophisticated graphs. Several levels of menus offer commands that you can use to design reports, enhance reports, and control the printer.

Figure 8.1 shows the /Print menu, with its various menu levels presented as horizontal bars. Notice that the middle portion of the menu contains primarily the commands you use to design your reports, such as commands for setting headers and footers, margins, and page length. The lower left portion of the menu offers commands for enhancing your reports, such as commands for improving the layout, choosing fonts, and selecting color. In the lower right portion of the menu are commands for printing graphs.

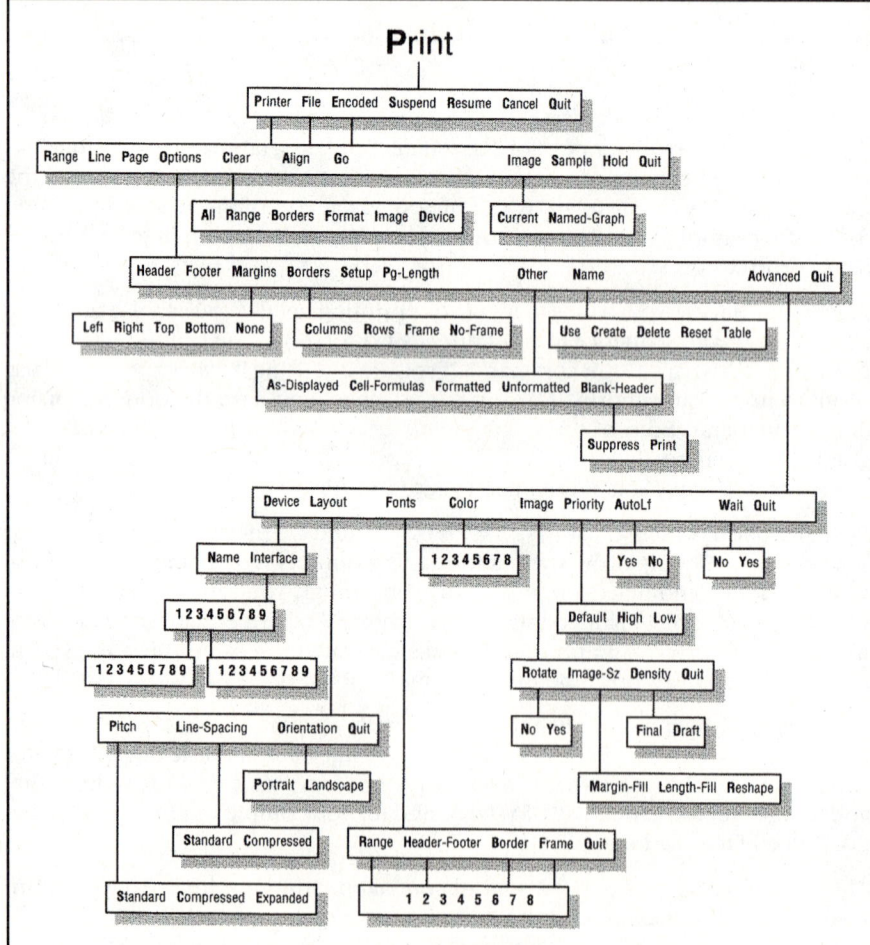

Fig. 8.1.
An illustration of the /Print menu.

Although earlier versions of 1-2-3 required the use of a separate program to print graphs, you now can print graphs from the /**P**rint menu. Graph printing is covered separately in Chapters 10 and 11.

This chapter shows you how to do the following:

- Print a report immediately, create a file for delayed printing, or create a file for word processing
- Print a report by using 1-2-3's default settings
- Print a multiple-page report
- Print multiple ranges
- Exclude segments within a designated print range
- Change the default settings for page layout and printer control
- Print worksheet formulas
- Enhance the readability and effect of a report by using different type styles, sizes, fonts, and colors
- Control paper movement

As indicated in previous chapters, 1-2-3's three-dimensional capability enables you to have as many as 256 worksheets in memory at one time. A printed report can contain data from a single worksheet or from two or more worksheets. Because most print commands work the same whether you are printing from a single worksheet or from multiple worksheets, you work primarily with one worksheet in this chapter. Techniques for printing from multiple worksheets are covered in the section "Printing Multiple Ranges."

Reminder:
With 1-2-3's three-dimensional capability, you can have as many as 256 worksheets in memory at one time.

1-2-3 uses the term *print job* to refer to data ranges and graphs which are sent to the printer or a disk file. A job begins when you select **G**o from the /**P**rint **P**rinter, /**P**rint **F**ile, or /**P**rint **E**ncoded menu. A job ends when you exit from the /**P**rint menu by selecting **Q**uit, pressing Esc, selecting /**P**rint **C**ancel, or pressing Ctrl-Break.

Getting Started from the Main Print Menu

You must start any /**P**rint command sequence from the 1-2-3 command menu. After choosing /**P**rint, you must select one of the first three options: **P**rinter, **F**ile, or **E**ncoded. You use the next three options—**S**uspend, **R**esume, and **C**ancel—only when a print job is in progress. These options are covered later in the chapter. The seventh option, **Q**uit, returns you to READY mode.

To send your report directly to the current printer, choose **P**rinter. (See "Choosing the Printer" later in this chapter for details on how to specify a printer.)

To create a text file on disk, select **F**ile. A text file can contain data but no graphs or special printer codes. Later, you can print the text file from the operating system prompt, or you can incorporate the text file into a word processing file.

Reminder:
An encoded file is not suitable for transferring data to another program.

To create a disk file that includes instructions on printing, choose **Encoded**. An encoded file can contain data, graphs, and printer codes for 1-2-3 print options, such as fonts, colors, and line spacing. An encoded file can be printed from the operating system prompt, but such a file is not suitable for transferring data to another program.

If you choose **File** or **Encoded**, you must respond to the prompt for a file name by typing a name that contains up to eight characters. You need not add a file extension because 1-2-3 automatically assigns the PRN (print file) or ENC (encoded file) extension. You can specify a different extension if you want.

You use an encoded file for printing at another time or from another computer while preserving all the special print options available in 1-2-3. When you create an encoded file, be sure that the selected printer is the same as the one you use eventually to print the file. An encoded file contains printer codes that control special printer features, such as fonts and line spacing. Because these codes are printer-specific, an encoded file created for one printer may not print correctly on another printer. The printer control codes embedded in the encoded file ensure that the final output looks the same as output printed directly from 1-2-3.

To print an encoded file, you use the operating system COPY command with the /B option. Consider the following example:

    COPY C:\123R3\SALES.ENC/B LPT1:

This command prints the file SALES.ENC, located in directory C:\123R3, on the printer connected to the port LPT1 (usually the default printer port). Other printer ports are LPT2, COM1, and COM2.

After you select **Printer**, **File**, or **Encoded**, the second line of the control panel displays a menu with 11 options. Throughout the chapter, this menu is referred to as the /Print [**P,F,E**] menu. The notation /Print [**P,F,E**] indicates that options on this menu are available when you select /Print Printer, /Print File, or /Print Encoded. Occasionally, an abbreviated notation is used in a command sequence, such as /Print [**P,E**] Options Advanced Fonts. This sequence indicates that the option being discussed—in this case, Fonts—does not affect your text file.

The /Print [**P,F,E**] menu offers the following choices:

Menu Item	Description
Range	Indicates the section(s) of the worksheet to be printed
Line	Advances the paper in the printer by one line
Page	Advances the paper in the printer to the top of the next page
Options	Changes default print settings and offers a number of print enhancements
Clear	Erases some or all of the previously entered print settings
Align	Signals that the paper in the printer is set to the beginning of a page
Go	Starts printing
Image	Selects a graph to print

Menu Item	Description
Sample	Prints a sample worksheet
Hold	Returns to READY mode without closing the current print job
Quit	Exits from the **P**rint menu and closes the current print job

In 1-2-3, the most frequently used (or least dangerous) commands are usually on the left side of a menu. In any print command sequence, you start with /**P**rint; branch to **P**rinter, **F**ile, or **E**ncoded; and then proceed to the next menu. Regardless of which branch you select, you must specify a **R**ange to print, choose **A**lign, select **G**o to begin printing, and then select **Q**uit or press Esc twice to return to the worksheet. All other selections are optional.

Selecting **A**lign ensures that printing begins at the top of all succeeding pages after the first page. Make sure in particular that you reposition your printer paper and use the **A**lign command whenever you have aborted a print job.

You use **P**age to move the paper to the top of the next page. **P**age also can be used to eject a blank page, making it easier for you to get the last page of your report.

Before you learn which print commands to use for performing specific tasks or operations, you need a general understanding of 1-2-3's default print settings. These settings are discussed in the next section.

Reminder:
*Select **A**lign to ensure that printing begins on the top of all succeeding pages after the first page.*

Understanding the Print Default Settings

To minimize the keystrokes necessary for a basic print operation, 1-2-3 includes default settings based on certain assumptions about how typical users want to print their reports. The default print operation produces 72 characters per line and 56 lines per page on 8 1/2-by-11-inch continuous-feed paper, and uses the first parallel printer installed. You should check the current settings for your 1-2-3 program, however, because another user may have changed them.

Current Printer Status

Check the global default settings before you print. To check these settings, you invoke the /**W**orksheet **G**lobal **D**efault command. In this menu, three of the options (**P**rinter, **S**tatus, and **U**pdate) pertain directly to print settings. You use **P**rinter to change a setting for the current work session, and **U**pdate to use that setting every time you reload 1-2-3. To view the current settings, you choose **S**tatus; the current printer settings appear in a status report similar to that shown in figure 8.2.

Cue:
*Use /**W**orksheet **G**lobal **D**efault **S**tatus to check the current default print settings.*

The settings relevant to printing are in the upper left corner of the status screen. The first two settings contain hardware-specific information. The `Margins` and `Page length` sections show page layout information. `Wait...No` is the setting for continuous-feed paper, and no setup string is in effect. Finally, `Name` indicates which printer is current.

Fig. 8.2.

A sample default status report.

```
                                                                    STAT
Printer:                          International:
   Interface..... Parallel 1         Punctuation..... A
   Auto linefeed. No                       Decimal Period
                                          Argument Comma
   Margins                                Thousands Comma
      Left  4      Top    2         Currency........ $ (Prefix)
      Right 76     Bottom 2         Date format D4.. A (MM/DD/YY)
                                    Date format D5.. A (MM/DD)
   Page length... 66                Time format D8.. A (HH:MM:SS)
   Wait.......... No                Time format D9.. A (HH:MM)
   Setup string..
   Name.......... Toshiba P351 Series P351
                                       Negative........ Parentheses
Automatic graph: Columnwise            Release 2....... LICS
                                       File translate.. Country
File list extension: WK*
File save extension: WK3            Clock on screen: None
Graph save extension: PIC           Undo: No    Beep: Yes
                                    Autoexec: Yes
Default directory: C:\123R3
Temporary directory: C:\
```

Default Hardware-Specific Options

If you want to change any of the print settings shown in the default status report, you invoke the /Worksheet Global Default Printer command. The first two options, Interface and AutoLf, are the same as the first two settings in the default status report.

The **Interface** option specifies one of the following connections between your computer and your printer:

1 Parallel 1 (the default)
2 Serial 1
3 Parallel 2
4 Serial 2
5 Output Device LPT1
6 Output Device LPT2
7 Output Device LPT3
8 Output Device COM1
9 Output Device COM2

Choices **5** through **9** are applicable only if your computer is part of a local area network (LAN). If you select either of the serial port options (**2** or **4**), another menu appears. From that menu, you must specify one of the following baud rates (data transmission speeds):

1 110 baud
2 150 baud
3 300 baud

4   600 baud
5   1200 baud
6   2400 baud
7   4800 baud
8   9600 baud
9   19200 baud

For example, a 1200 baud rate equals approximately 120 characters per second.

The baud rate that you select must match the printer's baud rate setting. In addition, the printer must be configured for 8 data bits, 1 stop bit (2 stop bits at 110 baud), and no parity. Check your printer manual for information about the interface and baud rate settings, as well as other print settings.

The AutoLf setting specifies the printer's end-of-line procedure. **Yes** indicates that the paper is automatically advanced one line when the printer receives a carriage return; **No** means that a line is *not* automatically advanced when the printer receives a carriage return. With most printers, you should leave AutoLf in its default setting of **No**. To determine whether the setting is correct, you can print a range of two or more rows. If the output is double-spaced or if the paper does not advance between lines, just change AutoLf to the opposite setting.

Default Page-Layout Options

For page layout, you must consider the length and width of the paper in the printer, the number of lines that print on one page (lines per inch), and the number of characters per line. The default page length is 66 lines, for 11-inch-long paper and a printer output of 6 lines per inch. The page length for laser printers should be 60 lines. The default line length is 80 characters (1/4 inch at either edge of the paper is not available for printing) for 8 1/2-inch-wide paper and a printer output of 10 characters per inch. However, because of 1-2-3's default margin settings (2-line margins at the top and bottom, and 4-character margins at the right and left), the full page width and length are not used. To maximize the amount of information per printed page, set the top, bottom, and left margins to 0; set the right margin to the maximum (1000).

The following options on the /Worksheet Global Default Printer menu determine default page-layout characteristics:

Menu Item	Message
Left	`Default left margin (0..1000):4`
Right	`Default right margin (0..1000):76`
Top	`Default top margin (0..240):2`
Bottom	`Default bottom margin (0..240):2`
Pg-Length	`Default lines per page (1..1000):66`

324 Part II ♦ Creating 1-2-3 Reports and Graphs

In each message, the numbers enclosed in parentheses indicate the minimum and maximum values you can select. The number after the colon is the current setting.

Reminder:
The right margin is measured in characters from the left edge of the paper.

Both the left and right margins refer to the number of characters from the left edge of the paper. To calculate the width of your report, subtract the left margin setting (4) from the right margin setting (76). Your report is printed with 72 characters per line.

To calculate how many lines of your worksheet print on each page, you need to subtract not only the lines for the top and bottom margins, but also the lines that 1-2-3 automatically reserves for a header and footer (see fig. 8.3). If, for example, you are using all default settings, the actual number of worksheet lines (or rows) that print is 56. You get this number of lines because 1-2-3 assigns 2 lines each for the top and bottom margins, and reserves 3 lines each for the header and footer. These 6 lines are reserved even if you do not supply a header or footer—unless you select /**P**rint [**P,F,E**] **O**ptions **O**ther **B**lank-Header **S**uppress. Because the default page length is 66, you subtract 4 lines for the top and bottom margins and 6 lines reserved for the header and footer to get 56 lines printed. (For more information about including headers and footers in your printed reports, refer to the section "Creating Headers and Footers.")

Other Default Options: Wait, Setup, and Name

The final three options for default printer settings control the way paper is fed to the printer (**W**ait), printer codes (**S**etup), and the specific printer you use (**N**ame).

Reminder:
*To hand-feed single sheets of paper, set the **W**ait option to **Y**es, and the printer pauses after each page.*

If you are using continuous-feed paper or a sheet-feeder bin, do not change the **W**ait option's default setting of **N**o. If you are hand-feeding single sheets of paper, select **Y**es to change the default setting; printing pauses at the end of each page so that you can insert a new sheet of paper. After you insert the page, select /**P**rint **R**esume to continue printing.

The default setting for **S**etup is no setup string. No special printer-control features, such as italic or double-striking, are in effect. (For more information about setup strings, see the section "Using Setup Strings.")

The menu that appears after you select **N**ame depends on decisions you made during installation. Suppose, for example, that you have a portable computer and you installed your 1-2-3 program to print on two different printers: an Epson printer at home and a Hewlett-Packard LaserJet printer at work. And suppose that because each printer uses a parallel port, you set Interface to **1** (parallel 1). In that case, selecting **N**ame produces a menu that offers option **1** (the Epson printer) and option **2** (the LaserJet printer). If you are at home, choose **1**; if you are at work, choose **2**.

Remember that if you use the /**W**orksheet **G**lobal **D**efault **P**rinter command to change print settings, the new settings remain in effect for the current work session. For the settings to remain the defaults whenever you start 1-2-3, you must use the /**W**orksheet **G**lobal **D**efault **U**pdate command after you have made the changes you want.

Chapter 8 ◆ Printing Reports **325**

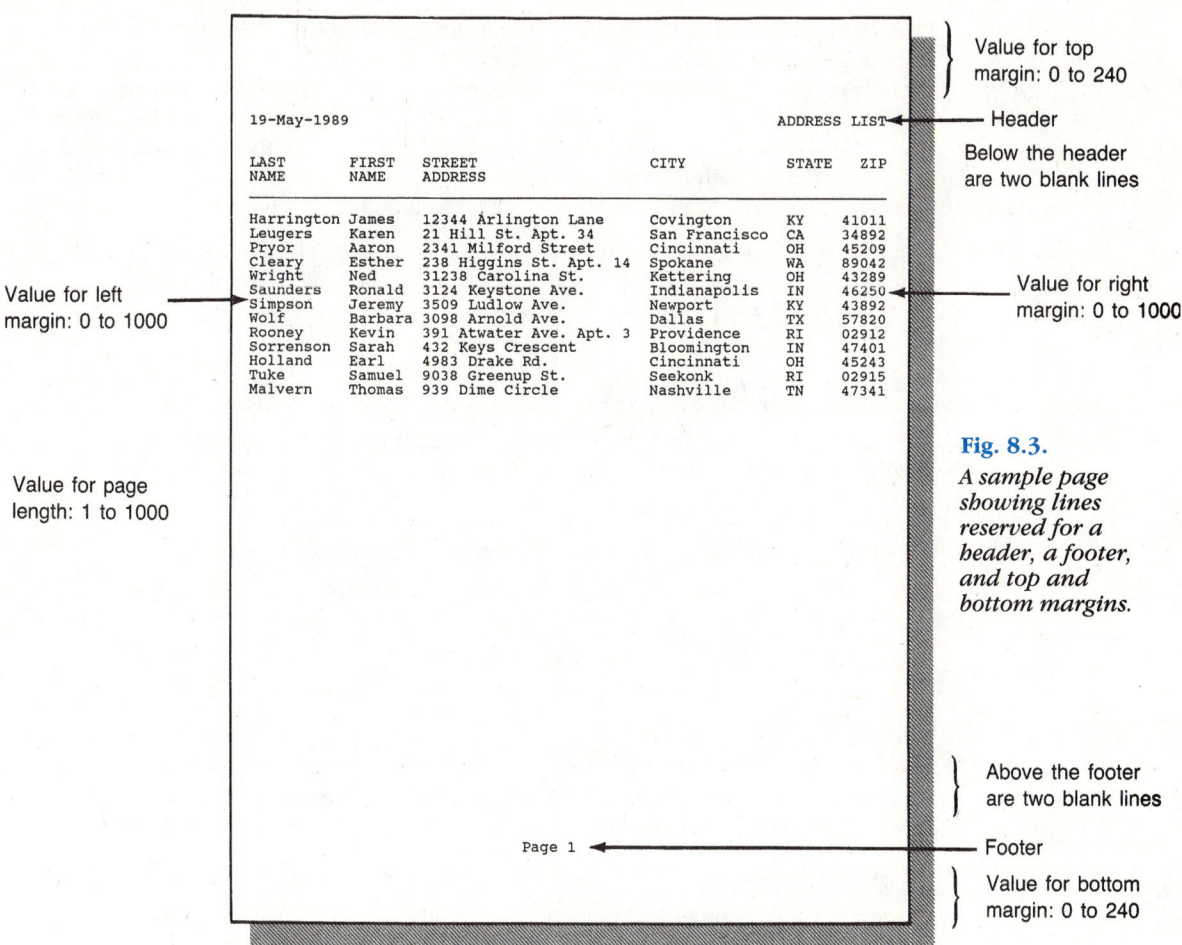

Fig. 8.3.
A sample page showing lines reserved for a header, a footer, and top and bottom margins.

Printing Your Reports

The 1-2-3 /Print menu is designed to accommodate your worksheet printing needs, from simple single-page printouts to more complex multiple-page reports. If your report does not require special print settings, such as those for paper size, header, footer, or a different style of type, you can print a report very quickly. All you need to do is specify a print range. If, on the other hand, your report has special requirements, you need to explore the /Print [**P,F,E**] Options menu.

This section shows you how to print reports quickly and efficiently by using a minimum of commands on the /Print [**P,F,E**] menu. First, you learn how to print a short report and then a multiple-page report. In the next section, you learn how to include headers and footers in your reports, print worksheet formulas rather than their results, and print borders on each page. Later in the chapter, you become familiar with the commands that enhance your reports, enabling you to control such features as type style, line spacing, and color.

Figure 8.4 shows a large model, occupying the range A:A1..A:W130. This model, which is referenced throughout the chapter, is used only as an example of a complex worksheet from which you may want to generate reports.

Printing a Short Report

For most print jobs, when the defaults and the printer are already set up, printing a single-page report involves only a few steps. These steps include the following:

1. Choosing /Print **P**rinter.
2. Using **R**ange to select the worksheet area you want printed.
3. Selecting **A**lign to signal 1-2-3 that the printer is positioned at the start of a page.
4. Choosing **G**o to begin printing.
5. Choosing **P**age to eject the paper.

If you are certain that all default settings are correct, you can easily print a report by completing the following operations. First, check that your printer is on-line and that your paper is positioned at the top of a page. Next, choose /**P**rint **P**rinter. The following menu appears:

Range **L**ine **P**age **O**ptions **C**lear **A**lign **G**o **I**mage **S**ample **H**old **Q**uit

Indicate the part of the worksheet you want to print by selecting **R**ange and specifying the rectangular range. You can either type the cell addresses of the range corners or highlight the area with the keyboard or the mouse.

You can use PgUp, PgDn, and End to designate ranges when you print. If you want to designate a range that includes the entire active area of the worksheet, first press Home, type a period (.) to anchor the corner of the print range, and then press End, followed by Home again. You must press Enter to finish the selection.

For many reports, a single, two-dimensional range—one rectangular region in a single worksheet—is all you need. You also can specify multiple ranges for a single print job. (You learn how to do that later in the chapter.)

After specifying the exact range you want printed, select **A**lign and then **G**o. Figure 8.5 shows the Cash Flow Projector worksheet with the range A1..G17 highlighted for printing, and figure 8.6 shows the resulting report. After you select **G**o, choose **P**age to eject the page, and then select **Q**uit to return to READY mode.

Chapter 8 ◆ Printing Reports **327**

Fig. 8.4.
The Cash Flow Projector worksheet.

	Oct	Nov	Dec	Jan	Feb	Mar	Apr	May	Jun	Jul	Aug	Sep	Oct	Nov	Dec	Total
CASH FLOW PROJECTOR Copyright (C) 1989 Que Corporation																
BALANCES IN WORKING CAPITAL ACCOUNTS																
Assets																
Cash			$17,355	$31,643	$34,333	$36,657	$35,614	$29,146	$20,000	$20,000	$20,000	$176,623	$186,131	$337,995	$582,796	$570,036
Accounts Receivable			493,151	510,780	533,597	551,287	577,314	614,997	641,802	750,544	879,211	989,501	1,097,616	1,170,646	1,218,036	358,228
Inventory			163,833	169,209	176,671	189,246	206,788	228,828	269,990	296,527	324,230	345,629	352,687	358,926	358,926	1,716,633
Liabilities																1,254,073
Accounts Payable			125,000	130,754	139,851	150,186	163,731	180,350	203,669	225,085	243,320	258,740	261,621	272,747	275,041	1,490,000
Line of Credit			0	0	0	0	0	0	1,834	8,327	2,035				0	
Net Working Capital			$549,339	$580,878	$604,750	$627,003	$655,984	$692,620	$726,289	$833,659	$978,146	$1,153,013	$1,368,812	$1,594,820	$1,884,718	
SALES	Oct	Nov	Dec	Jan	Feb	Mar	Apr	May	Jun	Jul	Aug	Sep	Oct	Nov	Dec	Total
Profit Center 1	$27,832	$23,864	$26,125	$31,336	$37,954	$43,879	$51,471	$55,953	$53,145	$54,140	$53,614	$52,015	$48,902	$44,091	$42,536	
Profit Center 2	13,489	21,444	20,140	22,572	24,888	25,167	32,588	40,140	37,970	34,587	33,483	28,939	24,153	27,060	26,701	
Profit Center 3	126,811	124,382	123,618	131,685	129,044	131,723	139,221	141,879	149,803	147,108	147,032	153,440	149,990	145,198	150,510	
Profit Center 4	94,285	92,447	89,010	95,473	98,008	96,986	95,318	103,538	108,146	108,642	106,065	110,401	112,018	111,956	107,522	
Profit Center 5										115,000	175,000	225,000	300,000	325,000	359,000	
Total Sales	$262,417	$262,137	$258,893	$281,066	$289,894	$297,755	$318,598	$342,510	$349,064	$459,477	$515,174	$569,795	$635,063	$653,305	$677,269	$5,380,970
Percent of	Cash	10%	10%	10%	10%	10%	10%	10%	10%	10%	10%	10%	10%	10%	10%	
Collections	30 Days	20%	20%	20%	20%	20%	20%	20%	20%	20%	20%	20%	20%	20%	20%	
	60 Days	50%	50%	50%	50%	50%	50%	50%	50%	50%	50%	50%	50%	50%	50%	
	90 Days	20%	20%	20%	20%	20%	20%	20%	20%	20%	20%	20%	20%	20%	20%	
Cash Collections				$263,437	$267,077	$280,066	$292,571	$304,827	$322,258	$350,735	$386,447	$459,566	$526,948	$582,275	$629,878	$4,664,085
PURCHASES	Oct	Nov	Dec	Jan	Feb	Mar	Apr	May	Jun	Jul	Aug	Sep	Oct	Nov	Dec	Total
Cost of Goods Sold																
Profit Center 1	33%	33%	33%	33%	33%	33%	33%	33%	33%	33%	33%	33%	33%	33%	33%	
	$9,185	$7,875	$8,621	$10,341	$12,525	$14,480	$16,985	$18,794	$17,538	$17,866	$17,693	$17,165	$16,138	$14,550	$14,037	$189,112
Profit Center 2	29%	29%	29%	29%	29%	29%	29%	29%	29%	29%	29%	29%	29%	29%	29%	
	$3,912	$6,219	$5,841	$6,546	$7,218	$7,298	$9,451	$11,641	$11,011	$10,030	$9,704	$8,392	$7,004	$7,847	$7,743	$103,886
Profit Center 3	50%	50%	50%	50%	50%	50%	50%	50%	50%	50%	50%	50%	50%	50%	50%	
	$63,406	$62,191	$61,809	$65,843	$64,522	$65,862	$69,611	$70,940	$74,902	$73,554	$73,516	$76,720	$74,995	$72,599	$75,255	$858,317
Profit Center 4	67%	67%	67%	67%	67%	67%	67%	67%	67%	67%	67%	67%	67%	67%	67%	
	$63,171	$61,939	$59,637	$63,967	$65,665	$64,981	$63,863	$69,370	$72,458	$72,790	$71,064	$73,969	$75,052	$75,011	$72,040	$840,229
Profit Center 5	30%	30%	30%	30%	30%	30%	30%	30%	30%	30%	30%	30%	30%	30%	30%	
	$0	$0	$0	$0	$0	$0	$0	$0	$0	$34,500	$52,500	$67,500	$90,000	$97,500	$105,000	$447,000
Total Cost of Goods Sold	$139,673	$138,224	$135,908	$146,696	$149,930	$152,621	$159,910	$170,745	$175,908	$208,741	$224,476	$243,746	$263,189	$267,507	$274,075	$2,437,543
Inventory	0 Days in Advance	5%	5%	5%	5%	5%	5%	5%	5%	5%	5%	5%	5%	5%	5%	5%
Purchasing	30 Days in Advance	50%	50%	50%	50%	50%	50%	50%	50%	50%	50%	50%	50%	50%	50%	
Schedule	60 Days in Advance	30%	30%	30%	30%	30%	30%	30%	30%	30%	30%	30%	30%	30%	30%	
	90 Days in Advance	15%	15%	15%	15%	15%	15%	15%	15%	15%	15%	15%	15%	15%	15%	
Inventory Purchases	$138,873	$141,363	$148,015	$152,072	$157,391	$165,196	$177,452	$192,785	$217,071	$235,277	$252,180	$265,145	$270,247	$273,747	$274,075	$2,832,637
Payment	Cash	30%	30%	30%	30%	30%	30%	30%	30%	30%	30%	30%	30%	30%	30%	30%
Schedule	30 Days	40%	40%	40%	40%	40%	40%	40%	40%	40%	40%	40%	40%	40%	40%	40%
	60 Days	30%	30%	30%	30%	30%	30%	30%	30%	30%	30%	30%	30%	30%	30%	30%
Payment for Purchases			$142,612	$147,237	$152,451	$158,137	$166,531	$178,375	$195,471	$215,247	$234,886	$250,999	$262,786	$269,766	$272,795	$2,504,680

Fig. 8.4.
(Continued)

	Oct	Nov	Dec		Jan	Feb	Mar	Apr	May	Jun	Jul	Aug	Sep	Oct	Nov	Dec	Total
OPERATING EXPENSES																	
Profit Center 1	$20,458	$20,760	$20,963		$21,529	$22,329	$22,802	$23,108	$24,099	$24,422	$24,431	$25,060	$25,646	$26,515	$26,639	$26,881	$293,461
Profit Center 2	14,377	15,002	15,587		15,846	16,790	17,355	17,739	18,195	18,610	19,412	19,546	20,348	20,860	21,729	21,785	228,315
Profit Center 3	25,921	26,393	27,339		27,554	28,286	28,464	29,275	29,292	29,578	30,246	30,358	31,041	31,680	32,048	32,525	360,347
Profit Center 4	13,922	14,885	15,801		16,130	16,800	17,651	18,039	18,789	19,704	20,400	20,939	21,589	21,833	22,024	22,154	236,052
Profit Center 5						10,000	14,000	18,000	20,000	22,000	22,470	22,837	22,995	23,384	24,023	24,806	224,495
Corporate Overhead	14,944	15,262	15,801		16,332	16,474	16,933	17,616	18,575	18,640	19,278	19,544	20,225	21,142	21,565	22,378	228,702
Total Expenses	$89,622	$92,302	$95,491		$97,491	$110,679	$117,205	$123,777	$128,950	$132,954	$136,237	$138,284	$141,844	$145,394	$148,028	$150,529	$1,571,372
Payment Schedule Cash	70%	70%	70%		70%	70%	70%	70%	70%	70%	70%	70%	70%	70%	70%	70%	
30 Days	20%	20%	20%		20%	20%	20%	20%	20%	20%	20%	20%	20%	20%	20%	20%	
60 Days	10%	10%	10%		10%	10%	10%	10%	10%	10%	10%	10%	10%	10%	10%	10%	
Total Payment for Expenses			$94,266		$96,572	$106,523	$113,928	$121,153	$126,741	$131,236	$134,852	$137,342	$140,571	$143,973	$146,883	$149,515	$1,549,288

	Jan	Feb	Mar	Apr	May	Jun	Jul	Aug	Sep	Oct	Nov	Dec	Total
CASH FLOW SUMMARY													
Collection of Receivables	$263,437	$267,077	$280,066	$292,571	$304,827	$322,258	$350,735	$386,447	$459,566	$526,948	$580,275	$629,878	$4,664,085
Other Cash Receipts	0	0	0	0	0	0	0	0	0	0	0	50,000	50,000
Cash Disbursements													
Payment for Purchases on Credit	141,237	152,451	158,137	166,531	178,375	195,471	215,247	234,886	250,999	262,786	269,766	272,795	2,504,680
Operating Expenses	96,572	106,523	113,928	121,153	126,741	131,236	134,852	137,342	140,571	143,973	146,883	149,515	1,549,288
Long-Term Debt Service													
Interest Payment on Line of Credit													137
Interest Rate	13.50%	13.50%	13.50%	13.50%	13.50%	13.50%	13.50%	13.50%	13.50%	13.50%	13.50%	13.50%	
Payment	5,340	5,413	5,677	5,930	6,179	6,532	7,109	7,833	9,315	10,681	11,762	12,767	94,538
Income Tax Payments						21		94	23				
Other													
Total Cash Disbursements	243,149	264,387	277,742	293,614	311,295	333,238	357,228	380,154	400,908	417,440	428,411	435,077	4,148,643
Net Cash Generated This Period	$14,288	$2,690	$2,324	($1,043)	($6,468)	($10,980)	($6,493)	$6,293	$58,658	$109,508	$151,864	$244,801	$565,441

	Dec	Jan	Feb	Mar	Apr	May	Jun	Jul	Aug	Sep	Oct	Nov	Dec
ANALYSIS OF CASH REQUIREMENTS													
Beginning Cash Balance		$17,355	$31,643	$34,333	$36,657	$35,614	$29,146	$18,166	$(6,293)	$20,000	$76,623	$186,131	$337,995
Net Cash Generated This Period		14,288	2,690	2,324	(1,043)	(6,468)	(10,980)	(6,493)	6,293	58,658	109,508	151,864	244,801
Cash Balance before Borrowings		31,643	34,333	36,657	35,614	29,146	18,166	13,507	26,293	78,658	186,131	337,995	582,796
Minimum Acceptable Cash Balance		20,000	20,000	20,000	20,000	20,000	20,000	20,000	20,000	20,000	20,000	20,000	20,000
Amount above/(below) Minimum Acceptable Balance		11,643	14,333	16,657	15,614	9,146	(1,834)	(6,493)	6,293	58,658	166,131	317,995	562,796
Current Short-Term Borrowings	0	0	0	0	0	0	1,834	6,493	(6,293)	(2,035)	0	0	0
Total Short-Term Borrowings		0	0	0	0	0	1,834	8,327	2,035				
Ending Cash Balance		$31,643	$34,333	$36,657	$35,614	$29,146	$20,000	$20,000	$20,000	$76,623	$186,131	$337,995	$582,796

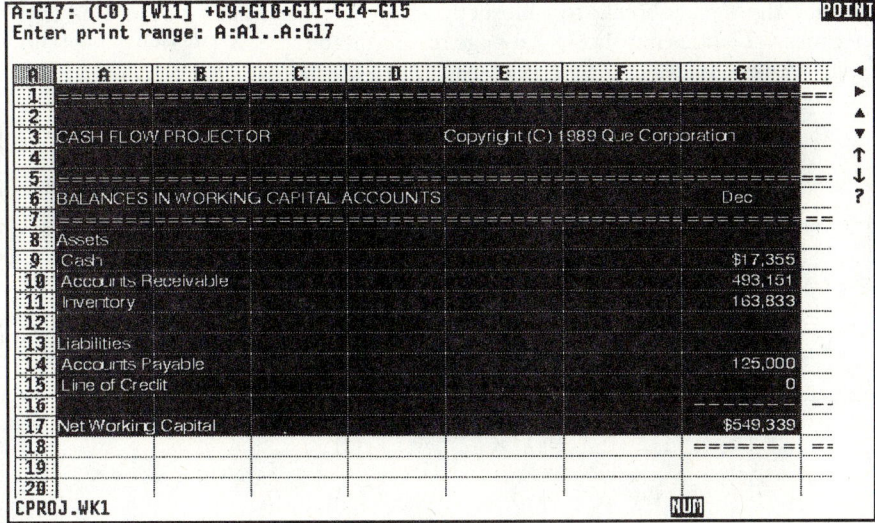

Fig. 8.5.
The Cash Flow Projector worksheet with the range highlighted.

```
===========================================================================

CASH FLOW PROJECTOR                     Copyright (C) 1989 Que Corporation

===========================================================================
BALANCES IN WORKING CAPITAL ACCOUNTS                                  Dec
============================================================== =========
Assets
 Cash                                                            $17,355
 Accounts Receivable                                             493,151
 Inventory                                                       163,833

Liabilities
 Accounts Payable                                                125,000
 Line of Credit                                                        0
                                                                --------
Net Working Capital                                             $549,339
```

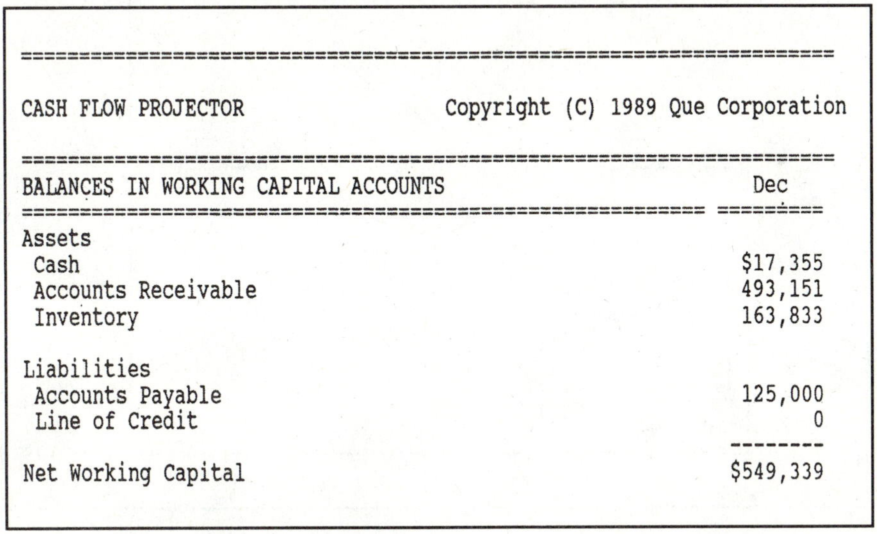

Fig. 8.6.
The printed report.

Printing a Multiple-Page Report

If your print range contains more rows or columns than can fit on a single page, 1-2-3 automatically prints the report on multiple pages. You follow the same steps for printing a short report as described in the preceding section. Figure 8.7 shows how 1-2-3 breaks into pages a print range from A1 through X150.

When printing a multiple-page report, you must pay attention to where 1-2-3 splits the worksheet between pages, both vertically and horizontally. 1-2-3 sometimes splits pages at inappropriate locations, resulting in a report that is hard to read.

Getting these page breaks to fall exactly where you want them can be a bit tricky because 1-2-3 does not show your page breaks on the screen. (Wysiwyg does show page breaks—see Chapter 9 for details.)

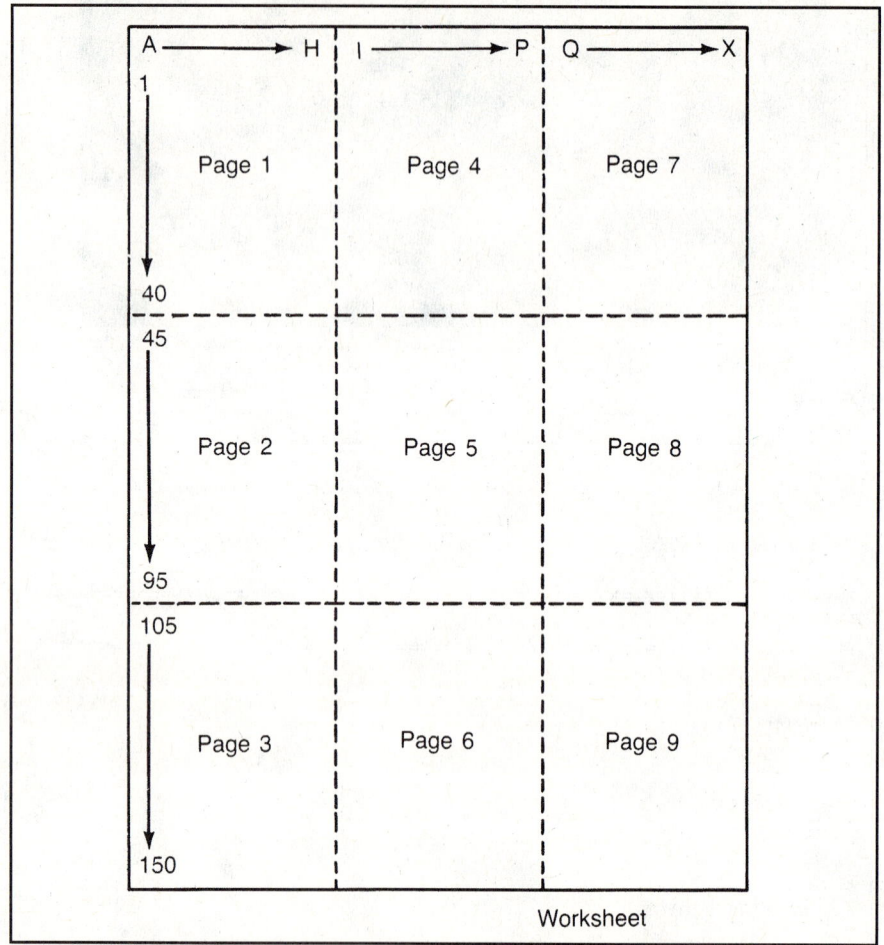

Fig. 8.7.
A large print range automatically printed on multiple pages.

Vertical Page Breaks

Vertical page breaks are always placed between worksheet columns. A single column is never split between two pages. The number of columns that print across a page is determined by the widths of the worksheet columns, the width of the page, and the print pitch. As discussed earlier in this chapter, the page width is defined in terms of standard characters and is equal to the right-margin number minus the left-margin number. During printing, a column that extends past the right margin is made the first column on the next page.

1-2-3's default settings print eight columns per page (see fig. 8.8). This number is calculated by dividing the default page width (72) by the default column width (9). Any additional columns, if included in the print range, appear on subsequent pages.

```
     Jan       Feb       Mar       Apr       May       Jun       Jul       Aug
  ========  ========  ========  ========  ========  ========  ========  ========

  $31,643   $34,333   $36,657   $35,614   $29,146   $20,000   $20,000   $20,000
   510,780   533,597   551,287   577,314   614,997   641,802   750,544   879,271
   169,209   176,671   189,246   206,788   228,828   269,990   296,527   324,230

   130,754   139,851   150,186   163,731   180,350   203,669   225,085   243,320
         0         0         0         0         0     1,834     8,327     2,035
   -------   -------   -------   -------   -------   -------   -------   -------
  $580,878  $604,750  $627,003  $655,984  $692,620  $726,289  $833,659  $978,146
```

Fig. 8.8.
Eight worksheet columns printed on a single page.

If the width of a column in the range is increased to 10, the situation changes. Because the total width of the eight columns is now 73, they will not fit on a 72-character-wide page. The eighth column is printed on a subsequent page (see fig. 8.9).

To determine where a vertical page break occurs, follow these steps:

1. Determine the page width by selecting /**W**orksheet **G**lobal **D**efault **P**rinter and checking the **L**eft and **R**ight margin settings. Subtract the left margin from the right margin.

2. Return to your worksheet and, starting in the first column in the print range, move the cell pointer across the worksheet, adding up column widths as you go.

A vertical page break goes before the column that causes the column-width total to exceed the page width.

To move a vertical page break to the right (that is, to print more columns on a given page), do one or more of the following:

1. Either decrease the setting of the left margin or increase the setting of the right margin. (Use the **O**ptions **M**argin command on the /**P**rint menu.)

2. Decrease the width of one or more columns in the print range.

Finally, to move a vertical page break to the left (that is, to print fewer columns on a given page), complete one or more of the following:

1. Either increase the setting of the left margin or decrease the setting of the right margin.

2. Increase the width of one or more columns in the print range.
3. Insert one or more blank columns in the print range.

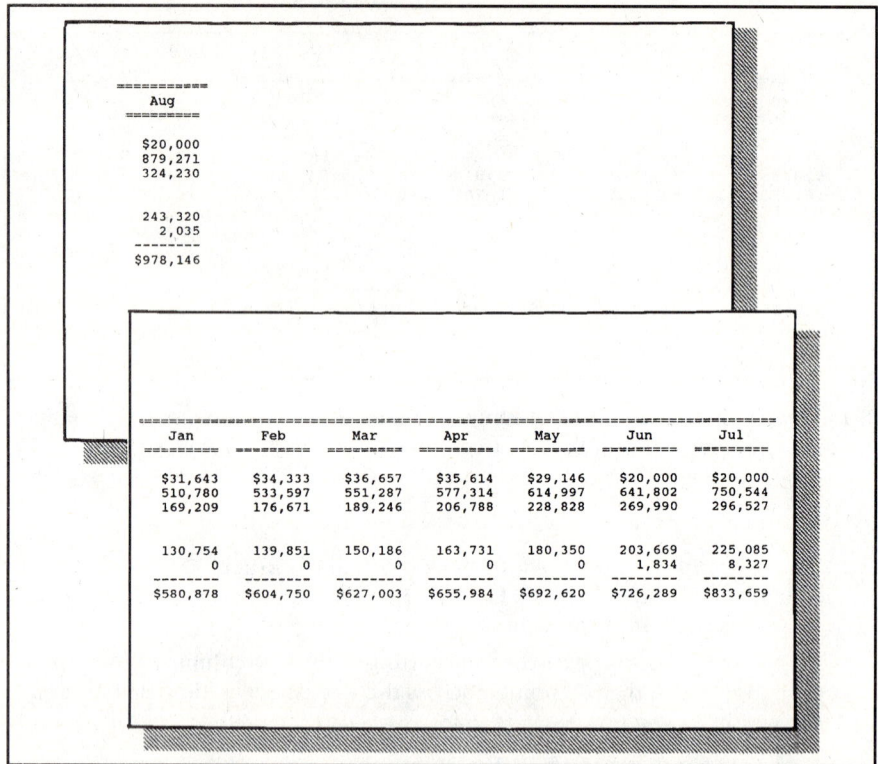

Fig. 8.9.
Seven worksheet columns printed on the first page; the eighth column printed on a second page.

With these techniques, you can position vertical page breaks to improve the appearance of your reports. The Wysiwyg menu offers an option for vertical page breaks. See Chapter 9 for information on using the :Worksheet Page Column command.

Remember that 1-2-3 treats numbers and labels differently when placing vertical page breaks. Numbers print completely on a single page because they can span only one cell. A label, however, can span two or more cells if it is wider than the column and if the cell(s) to the right of the label are blank. If a label spans a vertical page break, part of the label prints on one page, and part on another. If you "paste" several vertical pages to create a wide report, you may be able to position the pages so that these split labels come together again.

Horizontal Page Breaks

Horizontal page breaks are inserted between worksheet rows; the row just before a horizontal page break is printed at the bottom of one page, and the row just below the break is printed at the top of the next page. When printing, 1-2-3 automatically inserts a horizontal page break after every *n*th row, where *n* is the setting for lines per page, as discussed earlier in this chapter.

Reminder:
1-2-3 automatically inserts horizontal page breaks.

Look again at figure 8.4, which shows the entire Cash Flow Projector worksheet, and at figure 8.10, which shows the report that results from printing range A1..G72 of that worksheet with 1-2-3's default print settings. Note that the Purchases section (which begins in row 42) is split across two pages. 1-2-3 automatically inserted a horizontal page break after row 56.

The report may be easier to read if the entire Purchases section were printed on one page. To improve the readability of the report, you can insert a page break into the worksheet by using a command sequence or by typing a page-break symbol (|::).

To insert a page break by using 1-2-3's commands, you move the cell pointer to the first column in the print range, and then to the row at which you want the page break to occur. Select the /**W**orksheet **P**age command, which automatically inserts a new blank row containing a page-break symbol (|::).

Suppose, for example, that you want to insert a page break just above the first separating line in the Purchases section of the Cash Flow Projector worksheet. To do this, you position the cell pointer on A42 and then execute the command. Figure 8.11 shows the inserted row with the page-break symbol. To remove the inserted row and the page-break symbol after you finish printing, use the /**W**orksheet **D**elete **R**ow command.

As an alternative, you can insert a blank row into your worksheet where you want a page break, and then type a page-break symbol (|::) into the leftmost column of the print range in that row. The contents of cells in any row marked by the page-break symbol will not print.

The modified report is shown in figure 8.12. By having the entire Purchases section on one page, readability is greatly improved.

Be careful when you alter a worksheet. You may alter formula results by inserting rows, or you may accidentally delete the wrong row after you finish printing. You can possibly avoid these problems by typing the page-break symbol into the leftmost column in the print range of a row that is already blank in your worksheet. Check first to be sure that the row is blank; use End and the arrow keys to scan the row. Using the page-break symbol in a row that is not entirely blank keeps that row from printing.

Caution:
Inserting a blank row for a page-break symbol may alter formulas or cause other problems.

Printing Multiple Ranges

For many reports, a single two-dimensional print range, like those used in the preceding examples, is all you need. You can, however, create a print job that includes more than one two-dimensional range in one or more worksheets, one or more three-dimensional ranges, or a combination of these.

Fig. 8.10.

The Purchases section split between two pages.

```
Total Cost of Goods Sold            $139,673    $138,224    $135,908
                                    ========    ========    ========
Inventory          0 Days in Advance     5%          5%          5%
Purchasing        30 Days in Advance    50%         50%         50%
Schedule          60 Days in Advance    30%         30%         30%
                  90 Days in Advance    15%         15%         15%

Inventory Purchases                 $138,873    $141,363    $148,015

Payment         Cash                    30%         30%         30%
Schedule        30 Days                 40%         40%         40%
                60 Days                 30%         30%         30%
                                                            --------
Payment for Purchases                                        $142,612
                                                            ========
```

```
================================================================
CASH FLOW PROJECTOR              Copyright (C) 1989 Que Corporation
================================================================
BALANCES IN WORKING CAPITAL ACCOUNTS                          Dec
================================================================
Assets
  Cash                                                    $17,355
  Accounts Receivable                                     493,151
  Inventory                                               163,833

Liabilities
  Accounts Payable                                        125,000
  Line of Credit                                                0
                                                         --------
Net Working Capital                                      $549,339
                                                         ========


================================================================
SALES                             Oct        Nov         Dec
================================================================
Profit Center 1                $27,832    $23,864     $26,125
Profit Center 2                 13,489     21,444      20,140
Profit Center 3                126,811    124,382     123,618
Profit Center 4                 94,285     92,447      89,010
Profit Center 5
                              --------   --------    --------
Total Sales                   $262,417   $262,137    $258,893
                              ========   ========    ========

              Cash                 10%        10%         10%
Percent of    30 Days              20%        20%         20%
Collections   60 Days              50%        50%         50%
              90 Days              20%        20%         20%

Cash Collections


================================================================
PURCHASES                         Oct        Nov         Dec
================================================================
Cost of Goods Sold
  Profit Center 1                  33%        33%         33%
                                $9,185     $7,875      $8,621
  Profit Center 2                  29%        29%         29%
                                $3,912     $6,219      $5,841
  Profit Center 3                  50%        50%         50%
                               $63,406    $62,191     $61,809
  Profit Center 4                  67%        67%         67%
                               $63,171    $61,939     $59,637
  Profit Center 5                  30%        30%         30%
                                    $0         $0          $0
                              --------   --------    --------
```

Chapter 8 ◆ Printing Reports **335**

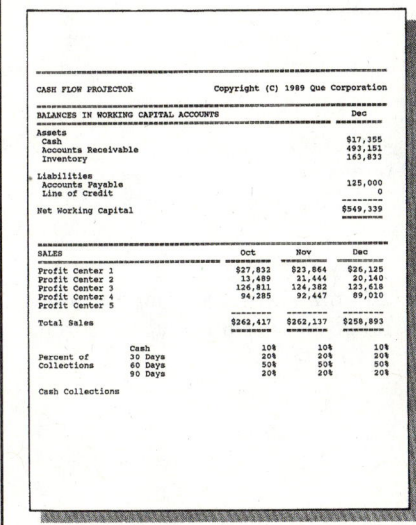

Fig. 8.11.
The result of inserting a page-break symbol in the worksheet.

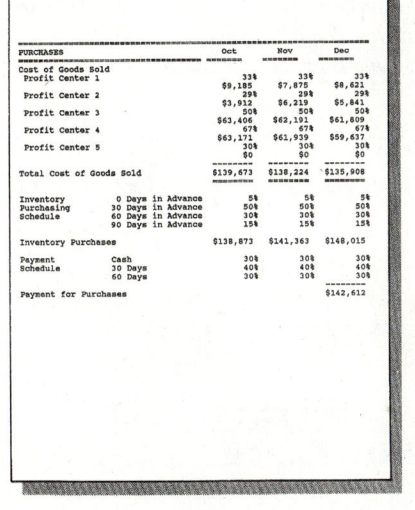

Fig. 8.12.
The entire Purchases section printed on a single page, after a page-break was inserted.

You specify a three-dimensional print range just as you specify a two-dimensional range—by entering cell addresses or an assigned range name, or by pointing. When pointing, remember that Ctrl-PgUp and Ctrl-PgDn are used to move up and down through active worksheets. With the mouse, you can click on the up- and down-arrows in the icon panel to move to the next or previous worksheet. Figure 8.13 shows a worksheet with a three-dimensional print range selected, and figure 8.14 shows the resulting printout.

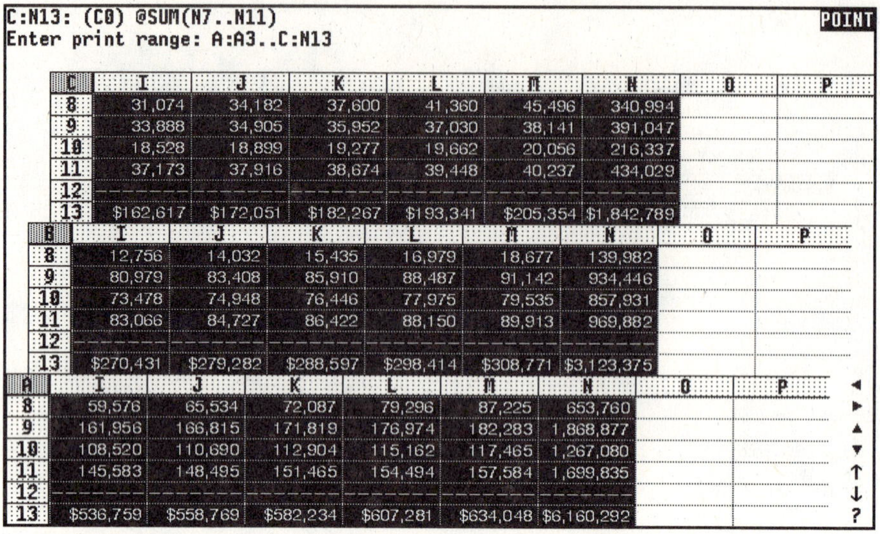

Fig. 8.13.
A worksheet with a three-dimensional print range selected.

```
C:N13: (C0) @SUM(N7..N11)                                    POINT
Enter print range: A:A3..C:N13
```

	I	J	K	L	M	N	O	P
8	31,074	34,182	37,600	41,360	45,496	340,994		
9	33,888	34,905	35,952	37,030	38,141	391,047		
10	18,528	18,899	19,277	19,662	20,056	216,337		
11	37,173	37,916	38,674	39,448	40,237	434,029		
12								
13	$162,617	$172,051	$182,267	$193,341	$205,354	$1,842,789		

	I	J	K	L	M	N	O	P
8	12,756	14,032	15,435	16,979	18,677	139,982		
9	80,979	83,408	85,910	88,487	91,142	934,446		
10	73,478	74,948	76,446	77,975	79,535	857,931		
11	83,066	84,727	86,422	88,150	89,913	969,882		
12								
13	$270,431	$279,282	$288,597	$298,414	$308,771	$3,123,375		

	I	J	K	L	M	N	O	P
8	59,576	65,534	72,087	79,296	87,225	653,760		
9	161,956	166,815	171,819	176,974	182,283	1,868,877		
10	108,520	110,690	112,904	115,162	117,465	1,267,080		
11	145,583	148,495	151,465	154,494	157,584	1,699,835		
12								
13	$536,759	$558,769	$582,234	$607,281	$634,048	$6,160,292		

Cue:
To include more than one range in a print job, separate the entered ranges with a range separator symbol (; or ,).

To specify multiple print ranges, enter each range as you would enter a single print range, and enter an argument separator after each range. You can use the semicolon (;) or the comma (,). Figure 8.15 shows how to specify multiple print ranges; the first range has been entered, and the second is highlighted. Figure 8.16 shows the resulting printout.

You can specify any combination of two- and three-dimensional ranges. The following examples are valid multiple print ranges:

A:A1..A:H10;B:C5..B:E12;C:C1..C:D5

A:A1..C:D10;A:F10..D:H20;C:C1..C:H10

In a print job, each range prints below the last, in the order specified when you entered the ranges. If you prefer to have each range on a separate page, insert page breaks at the bottom of each range.

Hiding Segments within the Designated Print Range

Though you can print only rectangular blocks from the worksheet, you can suppress the display of cell contents within the range. You can eliminate one or more rows, exclude one or more columns, or remove from view a segment that occupies only part of a row or column. If you use the default settings, each of the illustrations discussed here is printed on one page.

Chapter 8 ◆ Printing Reports 337

NATIONAL MICRO

	Jan	Feb	Mar	Apr	May	Jun	Jul	Aug	Sep	Oct	Nov	Dec	Total
SALES REPORT													
Northeast	$31,366	$34,503	$37,953	$41,748	$45,923	$50,515	$55,567	$61,123	$67,236	$73,959	$81,355	$89,491	$670,739
Southeast	30,572	33,629	36,992	40,691	44,760	49,237	54,160	59,576	65,534	72,087	79,296	87,225	653,760
Central	131,685	135,636	139,705	143,896	148,213	152,659	157,239	161,956	166,815	171,819	176,974	182,283	1,868,877
Northwest	94,473	96,362	98,290	100,256	102,261	104,306	106,392	108,520	110,690	112,904	115,162	117,465	1,267,080
Southwest	126,739	129,274	131,859	134,496	137,186	139,930	142,729	145,583	148,495	151,465	154,494	157,584	1,699,835
Total Sales	$414,835	$429,404	$444,799	$461,087	$478,343	$496,647	$516,086	$536,759	$558,769	$582,234	$607,281	$634,048	$6,160,292

	Jan	Feb	Mar	Apr	May	Jun	Jul	Aug	Sep	Oct	Nov	Dec	Total
COST OF GOODS													
Northeast	$10,341	$11,375	$12,513	$13,764	$15,140	$16,654	$18,320	$20,152	$22,167	$24,384	$26,822	$29,504	$221,135
Southeast	6,546	7,201	7,921	8,713	9,584	10,542	11,597	12,756	14,032	15,435	16,979	18,677	139,982
Central	65,843	67,818	69,853	71,948	74,107	76,330	78,620	80,979	83,408	85,910	88,487	91,142	934,446
Northwest	63,967	65,246	66,551	67,882	69,240	70,625	72,037	73,478	74,948	76,446	77,975	79,535	857,931
Southwest	72,314	73,760	75,235	76,740	78,275	79,840	81,437	83,066	84,727	86,422	88,150	89,913	969,882
Total Cost of Goods Sold	$219,011	$225,401	$232,073	$239,048	$246,346	$253,992	$262,011	$270,431	$279,282	$288,597	$298,414	$308,771	$3,123,375

	Jan	Feb	Mar	Apr	May	Jun	Jul	Aug	Sep	Oct	Nov	Dec	Total
OPERATING EXPENSES													
Northeast	$21,529	$23,682	$26,050	$28,655	$31,521	$34,673	$38,140	$41,954	$46,149	$50,764	$55,841	$61,425	$460,382
Southeast	15,946	17,541	19,295	21,224	23,347	25,681	28,249	31,074	34,182	37,600	41,360	45,496	340,994
Central	27,554	28,381	29,232	30,109	31,012	31,943	32,901	33,888	34,905	35,952	37,030	38,141	391,047
Northwest	16,130	16,453	16,782	17,117	17,460	17,809	18,165	18,528	18,899	19,277	19,662	20,056	216,337
Southwest	32,361	33,008	33,668	34,342	35,029	35,729	36,444	37,173	37,916	38,674	39,448	40,237	434,029
Total Operating Expenses	$113,520	$119,064	$125,027	$131,447	$138,368	$145,834	$153,899	$162,617	$172,051	$182,267	$193,341	$205,354	$1,842,789

Fig. 8.14.
A printout of the selected three-dimensional range in landscape mode.

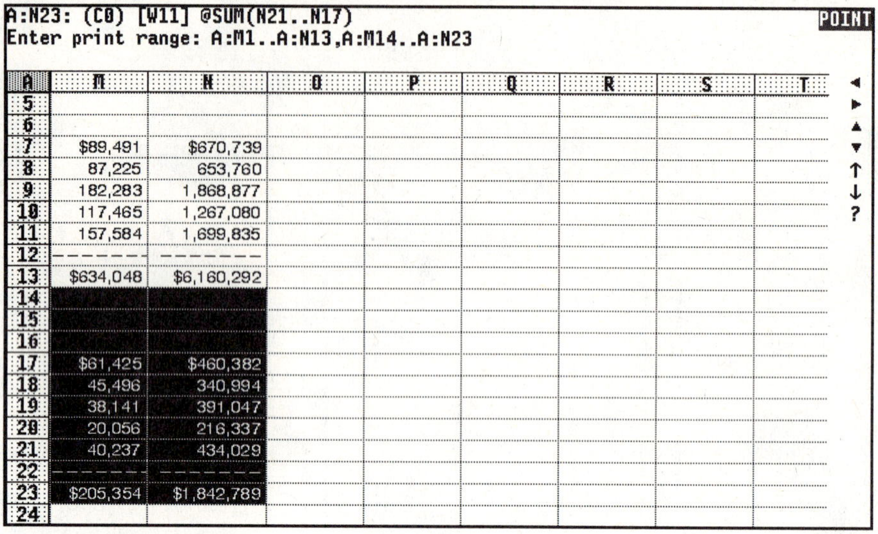

338   Part II ♦ Creating 1-2-3 Reports and Graphs

Fig. 8.15.

A worksheet with multiple print ranges specified.

```
A:N23: (C0) [W11] @SUM(N21..N17)                                    POINT
Enter print range: A:M1..A:N13,A:M14..A:N23
```

	M	N	O	P	Q	R	S	T
5								
6								
7	$89,491	$670,739						
8	87,225	653,760						
9	182,283	1,868,877						
10	117,465	1,267,080						
11	157,584	1,699,835						
12	--------	----------						
13	$634,048	$6,160,292						
14								
15								
16								
17	$61,425	$460,382						
18	45,496	340,994						
19	38,141	391,047						
20	20,056	216,337						
21	40,237	434,029						
22	--------	----------						
23	$205,354	$1,842,789						
24								

Fig. 8.16.

A printout of the specified multiple print ranges.

```
NATIONAL MICRO


                        ================  ================
                            Jan        Feb        Dec       Total
                        ================  ================
SALES REPORT
    Northeast          $31,366    $34,503    $89,491    $670,739
    Southeast           30,572     33,629     87,225     653,760
    Central            131,685    135,636    182,283   1,868,877
    Northwest           94,473     96,362    117,465   1,267,080
    Southwest          126,739    129,274    157,584   1,699,835
                       --------   --------   --------  ---------
Total Sales           $414,835   $429,404   $634,048  $6,160,292


                        ================  ================
                            Jan        Feb        Dec       Total
                        ================  ================
OPERATING EXPENSES
    Northeast          $21,529    $23,682    $61,424    $460,382
    Southeast           15,946     17,541     45,496     340,994
    Central             27,554     28,381     38,141     391,047
    Northwest           16,130     16,453     20,056     216,337
    Southwest           32,361     33,008     40,237     434,029
                       --------   --------   --------  ---------
Total Operating Expenses $113,520 $119,064   $205,354  $1,842,789
```

Excluding Rows

To prevent a row from printing, you type two vertical bars (||) in the row's leftmost cell within the print range. Only one vertical bar appears on-screen, and neither bar appears on the printout. A row marked in this way will not print, but the suppressed data remains in the worksheet and is used in any applicable calculations.

Suppose, for example, that you want to print the Cash Flow Summary line descriptions from the Cash Flow Projector worksheet. When you specify a range to print, you indicate A:A94..A:D111. The resulting printout is shown in figure 8.17.

```
=================== ================
CASH FLOW SUMMARY
===================================
Collection of Receivables
Other Cash Receipts

Cash Disbursements
 Payment for Purchases on Credit
 Operating Expenses
 Long-Term Debt Service
 Interest Payment on Line of Credit
  Interest Rate
  Payment
 Income Tax Payments
 Other

Total Cash Disbursements
```

Fig. 8.17.
A printout of Cash Flow Summary line descriptions.

Now suppose that you do not want the printout to show the cash-disbursements details (rows 100 through 108). Don't use a worksheet command to delete the rows! Instead, keep the rows from printing by typing two vertical bars in the leftmost cell of each row. The simplest method is to insert a new column (column A) at the left edge of the print range and to narrow that column to a width of 1. Then type || (hold down the Shift key and press the backslash key twice) in cell A:A100 and copy that entry to cells A:A101..A:A108.

The new column must be included in the print range, or the double vertical bar (||) will have no effect. After you insert the new column A, the print range should be adjusted to A:A94..A:E111. Figure 8.18 shows the resulting printout.

```
======================================
CASH FLOW SUMMARY
======================================
Collection of Receivables
Other Cash Receipts

Total Cash Disbursements
```

Fig. 8.18.
The printout with itemized cash-disbursements rows omitted.

To restore the worksheet after you have finished printing, you simply delete the column containing the double vertical bars.

Excluding Columns

As you learned in Chapter 4, you can use 1-2-3's /**W**orksheet **C**olumn **H**ide command to indicate columns that you do not want displayed on-screen. If these marked columns are included in a print range, they will not appear on the printout.

Suppose, for example, that you are working with the Cash Flow Projector worksheet and that you want to print the Sales information for January through March only. That information is contained in range A:A21..A:J40. Select the /**W**orksheet **C**olumn **H**ide command and specify columns A:E1..A:G1 to suppress the data for October through December. The resulting printout is shown in figure 8.19.

Fig. 8.19.
The printout after hiding columns E, F, and G.

```
==============================================================================
SALES                                          Jan         Feb         Mar
====================================== =========   =========   =========
Profit Center 1                           $31,336     $37,954     $43,879
Profit Center 2                            22,572      24,888      25,167
Profit Center 3                           131,685     129,044     131,723
Profit Center 4                            95,473      98,008      96,986
Profit Center 5
                                         --------    --------    --------
Total Sales                              $281,066    $289,894    $297,755
                                         ========    ========    ========

                  Cash                        10%         10%         10%
Percent of        30 Days                     20%         20%         20%
Collections       60 Days                     50%         50%         50%
                  90 Days                     20%         20%         20%
                                         --------    --------    --------
Cash Collections                         $263,437    $267,077    $280,066
                                         ========    ========    ========
```

To restore the columns, select /**W**orksheet **C**olumn **D**isplay. When the hidden columns (marked with an asterisk) reappear on-screen, you can specify which column or columns to display by highlighting them and pressing Enter.

Excluding Ranges

If you want to hide only part of a row or column, or an area that spans one or more rows and columns, you use the /**R**ange **F**ormat **H**idden command to mark the ranges.

Perhaps your worksheet includes documentation that you want to save on disk but omit from a printed report. For example, you may want to omit the copyright message in the third row of the Cash Flow Projector worksheet. To omit that message, you select /**R**ange **F**ormat **H**idden and specify cell E3. (Although the message spans several cells, it is entered in E3.) Then print the range A:A1..A:G7 (see fig. 8.20).

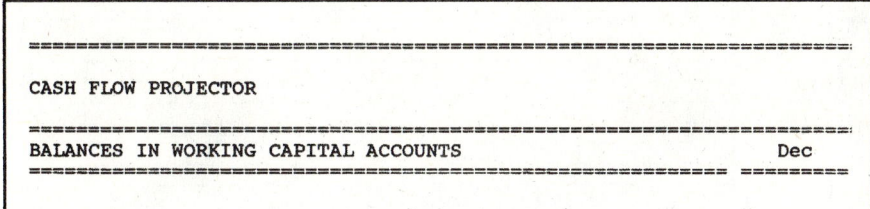

Fig. 8.20.
The printout after hiding cell E3.

After you finish printing, you select /**R**ange **F**ormat **R**eset and specify the cell E3 to restore the copyright message.

If you find yourself repeating certain print operations (such as hiding the same columns or suppressing and then restoring the same documentation messages), remember that you can save time and minimize frustration by developing and using print macros. For more information on using macros, refer to Chapter 13.

Designing Your Reports

As indicated earlier in the chapter, you can use the /**W**orksheet **G**lobal **D**efault **P**rinter command to change the default print settings. Another method is available for changing the print settings. You can use the /**P**rint [**P,F,E**] **O**ptions menu shown in figure 8.21. The **M**argins, **S**etup, and **P**g-Length options override the settings in /**W**orksheet **G**lobal **D**efault **P**rinter. The **H**eader, **F**ooter, and **B**orders settings are unique to this menu; they are provided to help you improve the readability of your reports. Two selections, **O**ther and **N**ame, lead to other menus containing a number of options that enable you to design your reports, and to name and save the current settings. All of these menu items are discussed in this section.

One menu item—**A**dvanced—leads to additional menus with options for enhancing your worksheet for printing, and controlling the printer. These **A**dvanced options are discussed later in the chapter.

Whatever print settings you select are saved with the worksheet file when you execute /**F**ile **S**ave. When you retrieve the file, the settings are still in effect. You also can save sets of printer options with the **N**ame command, which is discussed in the section "Naming and Saving the Current Print Settings."

Creating Headers and Footers

On each printed page, 1-2-3 reserves three lines for a header and an additional three lines for a footer. You can either retain the six lines (regardless of whether you use them) or eliminate all six lines by selecting **O**ther **B**lank-Header **S**uppress from the /**P**rint [**P,F,E**] **O**ptions menu. This option is discussed later in the chapter.

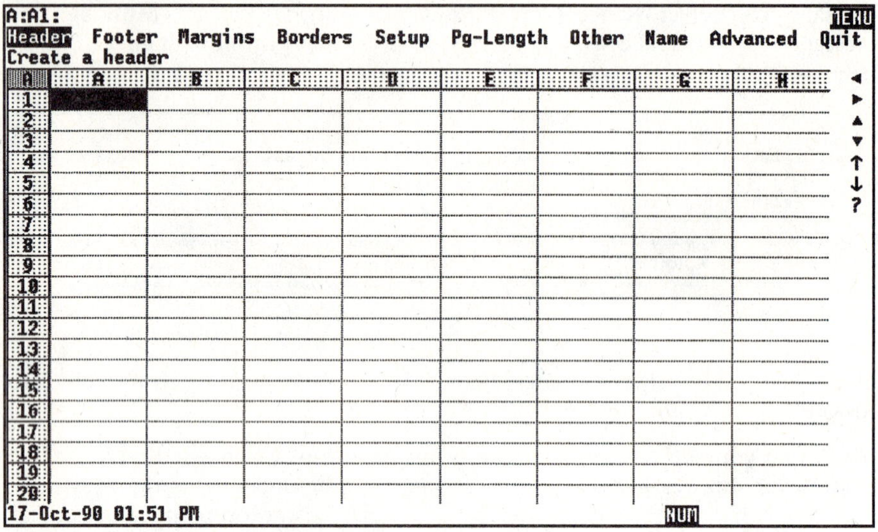

Fig. 8.21.
*The /Print
[P, F, E]
Options menu.*

```
A:A1:                                                                    MENU
Header  Footer  Margins  Borders  Setup  Pg-Length  Other  Name  Advanced  Quit
Create a header
```

Reminder:
To print the footer on the last page of a report, issue the /Print [P, F, E] Page command.

The header text, which is printed on the first line after the current top-margin lines, is followed by two blank header lines (for spacing). The footer text line is printed above the current bottom-margin lines and below two blank footer lines (for spacing).

Both the **Header** and **Footer** options enable you to specify up to 512 characters of text in one line. Portions of the header or footer can be positioned at the left, right, or center of the page. The overall header or footer length, however, cannot exceed the page width.

1-2-3 provides special characters you can include in a header or footer. These characters print the page number, the current date, or the contents of a worksheet cell. Also available are special characters to control the positioning of text within a header or footer. These special characters include the following:

Character	Function

Reminder:
To include the date and page number in headers and footers, use the @ and # symbols, respectively.

#	Automatically prints page numbers, starting with 1
@	Automatically includes the current system date (in the form 25-Jun-91)
|	Automatically separates text. If this character is not present, the entire header or footer is left-justified. Text to the right of the first | is centered. Text to the right of a second | is right-justified. (You insert a | by pressing the Shift key and typing a backslash.)

Character	Function
\	When followed by a cell address or range name, fills the header or footer with the contents of the indicated cell. After supplying the backslash, you can use POINT mode to indicate the desired cell. To point to the cell with the mouse, you must move the cell pointer by clicking the appropriate symbols in the icon panel. When you include a backslash, the contents of the indicated cell are the only text in the header or footer and are left-aligned.

To see how these special characters affect a printed report, create a header that includes three of the preceding characters. To add the header, select /Print [**P,F,E**], select **R**ange and specify A:A1..A:G17, and then select **O**ptions **H**eader. At the prompt Enter Header:, type the following:

@|**NATIONAL MICRO**|@

Then select **Q**uit from the **O**ptions menu, choose **A**lign, select **G**o, and select **P**age to eject the paper, if necessary. If you compare the printed report shown in figure 8.22 with that shown in figure 8.6, you can see how the header improves the report's appearance and legibility.

```
08-May-89                    NATIONAL MICRO                          1

=================================================================
CASH FLOW PROJECTOR              Copyright (C) 1989 Que Corporation

=================================================================
BALANCES IN WORKING CAPITAL ACCOUNTS                        Dec
==============================================           =========
Assets
  Cash                                                    $17,355
  Accounts Receivable                                     493,151
  Inventory                                               163,833

Liabilities
  Accounts Payable                                        125,000
  Line of Credit                                                0
                                                         --------
Net Working Capital                                      $549,339
```

Fig. 8.22.
A printed header.

Whenever the print range is too large to fit on a single page, the header is reproduced on each succeeding page, and the page number is increased by one. If you have used the special character for including page numbers (#) and you want to print your report a second time before you leave the /Print menu, you can reset the page number to 1 and set the top of the form by selecting **A**lign before you select **G**o.

Part II ♦ Creating 1-2-3 Reports and Graphs

If you have specified a header line, but the centered or right-justified text doesn't print, make sure that the right-margin setting is appropriate for the current pitch and paper width. To remove the header, choose /Print [**P,F,E**] Options Header, press Esc to remove the header text, and then press Enter.

Formatted or Unformatted Output

> **Cue:**
> When using /**P**rint **F**ile to prepare data for other programs, select **U**nformatted to suppress headers, margins, and other formatting.

Selecting **U**nformatted from the /Print [**P,F,E**] Options Other menu suppresses the printing of headers, footers, and page breaks. Unformatted output is often appropriate when you are using /Print File to create a data file to be imported by another program, such as a word processing package. (Exporting data is covered later in the chapter.) You select **F**ormatted to turn the headers, footers, and page breaks back on.

Blank-Header

The **B**lank-Header option from the /Print [**P,F,E**] Options Other menu enables you to specify whether 1-2-3 leaves three blank lines at both the top and bottom of each printed page when no header or footer has been specified. If you select **B**lank-Header **S**uppress, the three blank lines are omitted at both the top and bottom of the page, but only if neither a header nor a footer has been provided. You cannot suppress blank lines at only the top or bottom of the page—it's both or neither. The **S**uppress option enables you to print six more lines of data per page. Selecting **B**lank-Header **P**rint reinstates the six blank lines.

Printing a Listing of Cell Contents

Developing and debugging a complex worksheet can take days of hard work. You should safeguard your work, of course, by making backup disk copies of important files. For both backup and reference purposes, you also can make regular printouts of your worksheet's cell contents, including formulas and formatting information.

> **Cue:**
> Select **C**ell-Formulas to print a listing of the worksheet formulas; **A**s-Displayed, the default, prints the range as it is displayed on-screen.

To print cell contents instead of cell values, you select **C**ell-Formulas from the /Print [**P,F,E**] Options Other menu. Choosing Cell-Formulas produces a printout that consists of one line for each cell in the print range. The line shows the cell's width and format (if different from the default), protection status, and contents. By subsequently selecting **A**s-Displayed, you restore the default setting that prints the range as it appears on-screen.

Figure 8.23 shows a Cell-Formulas printout of the range A:A1..A:G18 from the Cash Flow Projector worksheet. Notice that within the specified print range, all the cells in the first row are listed before the cells in the next row.

Information within parentheses indicates a range format established independently of the global format in effect. For example, the (C0) in cell G17 indicates that the cell was formatted (with a /**R**ange Format command) as

Currency, with zero decimal places. Information within square brackets indicates a column width set independently of the global column width in effect. For example, the [W11] in cell G17 indicates that column G was set specifically to be 11 characters wide.

```
A:A1:  [W9]  \=
A:B1:  [W9]  \=
A:C1:  [W9]  \=
A:D1:  [W9]  \=
A:E1:  [W12] \=
A:F1:  [W11] \=
A:G1:  [W11] \=
A:A3:  [W9]  'CASH FLOW PROJECTOR
A:E3:  [W12] 'Copyright (C) 1990 Que Corporation
A:A5:  [W9]  \=
A:B5:  [W9]  \=
A:C5:  [W9]  \=
A:D5:  [W9]  \=
A:E5:  [W12] \=
A:F5:  [W11] \=
A:G5:  [W11] \=
A:A6:  [W9]  'BALANCES IN WORKING CAPITAL ACCOUNTS
A:G6:  [W11] ^Dec
A:A7:  [W9]  \=
A:B7:  [W9]  \=
A:C7:  [W9]  \=
A:D7:  [W9]  \=
A:E7:  [W12] \=
A:F7:  [W11] \=
A:G7:  [W11] '  =========
A:A8:  [W9]  'Assets
A:A9:  [W9]  ' Cash
A:G9:  (C0) [W11] 17355
A:A10: [W9]  ' Accounts Receivable
A:G10: (,0) [W11] 493151
A:A11: [W9]  ' Inventory
A:G11: (,0) [W11] 163833
A:A13: [W9]  'Liabilities
A:A14: [W9]  ' Accounts Payable
A:G14: (,0) [W11] 125000
A:A15: [W9]  ' Line of Credit
A:G15: (,0) [W11] 0
A:G16: [W11] '  --------
A:A17: [W9]  'Net Working Capital
A:G17: (C0) [W11] +G9+G10+G11-G14-G15
A:G18: [W11] '  ========
```

Fig. 8.23.
A listing produced with the Cell-Formulas option.

Cell contents are printed after the information for range format and column width. For example, the formula in G17 results in the $549,339 for Net Working Capital.

Printing Borders

A printed report containing numbers without descriptive headings can be difficult, if not impossible, to interpret. You can make your report easier to understand by using a special 1-2-3 feature that enables you to print specified columns and/or rows repeatedly on a multiple-page report. In addition, you can include the worksheet frame (the row numbers located on the left of the screen, and the column letters located at the top).

Column and Row Borders

If you use the default print settings to print the Cash Flow Projector worksheet, the report contains all the necessary information. But without descriptions of what each line of numbers represents, some pages may be hard to interpret.

To improve the printed report, you can add column and row labels—called *borders*—in 1-2-3. With /Print [**P,F,E**] **O**ptions **B**orders **C**olumns, you can specify one or more columns of labels that print at the left edge of every page, serving to identify the rows on the page. Likewise, **B**orders **R**ows designates one or more rows of labels that print at the top of every page, identifying the columns on the page. Setting borders in a printout is analogous to freezing titles in the worksheet: **B**orders **C**olumns produces a border like a frozen vertical title display, and **B**orders **R**ows produces a border like a frozen horizontal title display.

To understand the process of creating borders, you can modify only a small portion of the Cash Flow Projector worksheet—the Balances in Working Capital Accounts section, contained in the range A:A1..A:S18. You can omit the blank columns (E and F) as well as the initial December column (G), and use the **B**orders **C**olumns command to repeat the account names in columns A through D.

Select /**P**rint **P**rinter **R**ange and specify **A:H1..A:S18**, and then select **O**ptions **B**orders **C**olumns. When the message `Enter Border Columns:` appears in the control panel, specify A1..D1. The account names are repeated to coincide with the dollar amounts for January through December. Figure 8.24 shows page 2 of the report.

Remember that the print range and the border range must not overlap, or you get the borders printed twice on some pages. If you want to print information with a horizontal border on every page, select **B**orders **R**ows. For example, you can use that option to print only the Liabilities information in rows 13 through 15 (refer to fig. 8.4). To cancel borders, you select /**P**rint **P**rinter **C**lear **B**orders.

Frame Borders

Cue:
Select /Print [P, F, E] Options Borders Frame to include the worksheet frame on each page of your printout.

To include the worksheet frame (vertical row numbers and horizontal column letters) on each page of your printed report, you select /**P**rint [**P,F,E**] **O**ptions **B**orders **F**rame. Each page includes the worksheet frame (see fig. 8.25). To turn off the frame, you select **O**ptions **B**orders **N**o-**F**rame. The **F**rame option is particularly useful during worksheet development when you want your printouts to show the location of data and formulas within a large worksheet. To make the frame stand-out from the worksheet, you can specify a different font. See "Selecting Fonts" for details.

```
===============================================================
    CASH FLOW PROJECTOR
===============================================================
    BALANCES IN WORKING CAPITAL ACCOUNTS    Apr         May         Jun
    ===================================  =========   =========   =========
    Assets
      Cash                                 $35,614     $29,146     $20,000
      Accounts Receivable                  577,314     614,997     641,802
      Inventory                            206,788     228,828     269,990

    Liabilities
      Accounts Payable                     163,731     180,350     203,669
      Line of Credit                             0           0       1,834
                                          --------    --------    --------
    Net Working Capital                   $655,984    $692,620    $726,289
                                          ========    ========    ========
```

Fig. 8.24.
Page 2 of a report printed with column borders.

```
    A      H          I          J          K          L          M
    6     Jan        Feb        Mar        Apr        May        Jun
    7   ========   ========   ========   ========   ========   ========
    8
    9    $31,643    $34,333    $36,657    $35,614    $29,146    $20,000
   10    510,780    533,597    551,287    577,314    614,997    641,802
   11    169,209    176,671    189,246    206,788    228,828    269,990
   12
   13
   14    130,754    139,851    150,186    163,731    180,350    203,669
   15          0          0          0          0          0      1,834
   16   --------   --------   --------   --------   --------   --------
   17   $580,878   $604,750   $627,003   $655,984   $692,620   $726,289
   18   ========   ========   ========   ========   ========   ========
```

Fig. 8.25.
The worksheet frame printed on a report.

Setting Page Layout: Margins and Page Length

To change the page layout of the current worksheet, you use the /**Print** [**P,F,E**] **Options** menu. If you want to change the margins, select **Margins** and then choose **Left**, **Right**, **Top**, **Bottom**, or **None** from the menu. The following list indicates the message for each menu item:

Menu Item	Message
Left	`Set left margin (0..1000):XX`
Right	`Set right margin (0..1000):XX`
Top	`Set top margin (0..240):XX`
Bottom	`Set bottom margin (0..240):XX`
None	`Clear all margin settings`

The numbers in parentheses are the minimum and maximum for each margin setting. The X X at the end of each line denotes the current setting, which you can change. Selecting **None** sets the left, top, and bottom margins to 0 and the right margin to 1000. Before you make any changes, review the section "Understanding the Print Default Settings" at the beginning of the chapter.

Be sure that you set left and right margins that are consistent with the width of your paper and the established pitch (characters per inch). The right margin must be greater than the left margin. Make sure also that the settings for the top and bottom margins are consistent with the paper's length and the established number of lines per inch.

The specified page length must not be less than the top margin *plus* the header lines *plus* one line of data *plus* the footer lines *plus* the bottom margin—unless you use /Print [P,F,E] Options Other Unformatted to suppress all formatting. To maximize the output on every printed page of a large worksheet, you can combine the Unformatted option with commands that condense printing and increase the number of lines per inch.

Enhancing Your Reports

Now that you have examined the /Print menu options for designing your reports, you should become familiar with the menu options for enhancing your printed reports. The /Print [P,E] Options Advanced menu offers a number of enhancements. These same enhancements are also available in Wysiwyg. Wysiwyg has the advantage of allowing you to see your enhancements on the screen, plus it offers additional options. Refer to Chapter 9 for information on formatting your worksheets with Wysiwyg.

Reminder:
Select /Print Printer Sample Go to create a sample printout that demonstrates the capabilities of your printer.

Some printers do not support all the advanced options. You can use /Print [P,F,E] Sample to print a sample printout that shows which of the advanced options your printer supports. Selecting /Print [P,F,E] Sample Go prints a sample to the currently selected device or file (encoded or text). This sample includes the following information:

1. A list of your current print settings (see fig. 8.26)
2. A small predefined worksheet printed with the current print options, except **Borders** (see fig. 8.26)
3. Printer capabilities, including fonts 1 through 8, colors 1 through 8, and the various options for pitch and line spacing (see fig. 8.26)
4. A sample graph using the current graph options (see fig. 8.27), plus samples of font options and text sizes for graphs (see fig. 8.28)

The sample shown in figures 8.26, 8.27, and 8.28 was printed with a Hewlett-Packard LaserJet Series II printer. For more information on designing and printing graphs, refer to Chapter 10.

PRINTER SETTINGS

Header =
Footer =
Margins:
  Left = 4, Right = 76 , Top = 2 , Bottom = 2
Borders:
  Columns = , Rows = , No-Frame
Setup =
Pg-Length = 66
Other:
  Cell-Formulas , Formatted , Print Blank-Header
Device:
  Name = Apple LaserWriter Plus Times/Helvetica
  Interface = Parallel 2
Layout:
  Standard Pitch , Standard Line-Spacing , Portrait
Fonts:
  Range = 0 , Header/Footer = 0 , Border = 0 , Frame = 0
Image:
  No Rotate , Margin-Fill , Final Density

Color = 0, Default Priority , No AutoLf, No Wait

SAMPLE WORKSHEET

Left-aligned label	54	69	$84.00
Right-aligned label	599	614	$629.00
Centered label	-1144	-1159	($1,174.00)

PRINTER CAPABILITIES

FONT 1 and COLOR 1 were used to print this text.
FONT 2 and COLOR 2 were used to print this text.
FONT 3 and COLOR 3 were used to print this text.
FONT 4 and COLOR 4 were used to print this text.
FONT 5 and COLOR 5 were used to print this text.
FONT 6 and COLOR 6 were used to print this text.
FONT 7 and COLOR 7 were used to print this text.
FONT 8 and COLOR 8 were used to print this text.

This text is in STANDARD PITCH.
This text is in COMPRESSED PITCH.
This text is in EXPANDED PITCH.

STANDARD LINE SPACING was used for these three lines of text.
STANDARD LINE SPACING was used for these three lines of text.
STANDARD LINE SPACING was used for these three lines of text.
COMPRESSED LINE SPACING was used for these three lines of text.
COMPRESSED LINE SPACING was used for these three lines of text.
COMPRESSED LINE SPACING was used for these three lines of text.

SAMPLE GRAPH AND GRAPH TEXT OPTIONS

Fig. 8.26.
The first page of the sample printout, showing print settings, a predefined worksheet, and printer font and color capabilities.

350 Part II ◆ Creating 1-2-3 Reports and Graphs

Fig. 8.27.
The second page of the sample printout, showing a predefined graph.

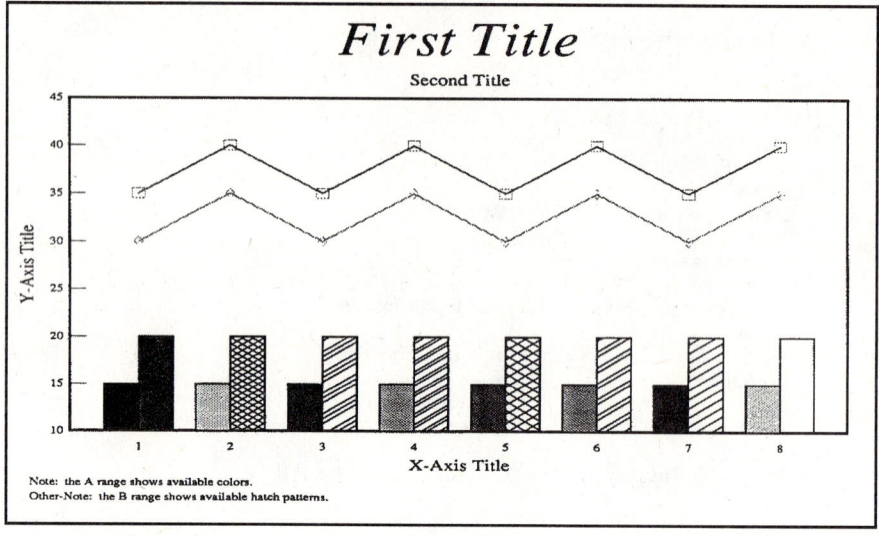

Fig. 8.28.
The third page of the sample printout, showing text sizes and styles available in graphs.

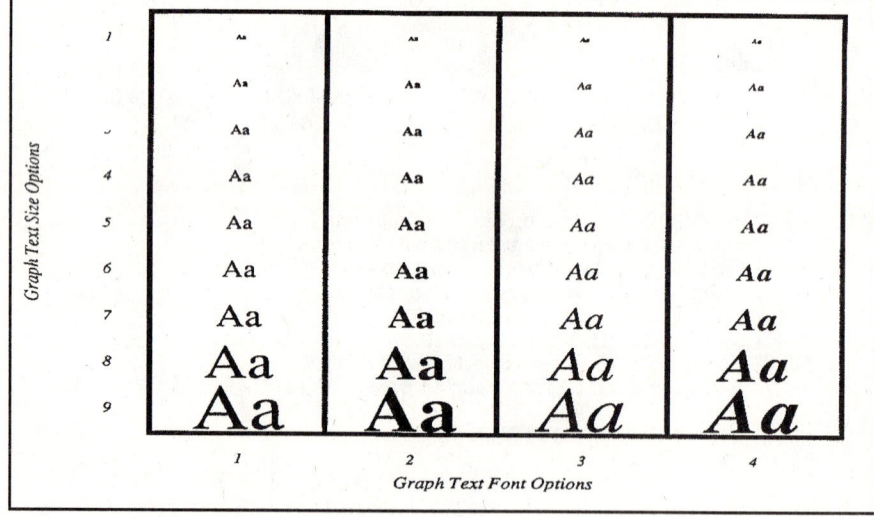

Improving the Layout

With the /**Print** [**P,E**] **Options Advanced Layout** menu, you can specify the pitch (character spacing), line spacing, and orientation of your printed pages. These options enable you to customize the layout of your report.

Changing the Pitch

The *pitch* affects character size and thus the number of characters printed on each line. The choices available with the **Pitch** option are **Standard**, **Compressed**, and **Expanded**. Again, the actual effect of each of these options depends on your printer. Typical pitch settings are 5 characters per inch (cpi) for **Expanded**, 10 cpi for **Standard**, and 17 cpi for **Compressed**. You do not see the pitch change on the screen. Wysiwyg, on the other hand, does show you type sizes on the screen.

Reminder: *When you change the pitch, 1-2-3 does not show the change on-screen.*

Changing Line Spacing

The **Line-Spacing** options are **Standard** (the default) and **Compressed**. Like pitch, the line spacing that results with each of these options depends on your printer. For many printers, **Standard** spacing is 6 lines per inch, and **Compressed** spacing is 8 lines per inch. Changing line spacing also affects the number of lines printed on each page.

Note that when you use the **Options Advanced Layout** menu to change either line spacing or pitch, 1-2-3 automatically makes an adjustment for the different number of characters per line or lines per page. You do not need to adjust manually the settings for margins or page length.

Suppose that you want to produce a printed report of the Cash Flow Projector worksheet shown in figure 8.4. Because the worksheet is large, printing all of it requires many pages. You can put more data on each printed page by using the **Pitch** and **Line-Spacing** menu options.

First, select **/Print Printer Range** and then designate the entire worksheet as the print range. Next, select **Options Advanced Layout Pitch Compressed** and then choose **Line-Spacing Compressed**. Finally, select **Quit Quit Quit Align** and then **Go**.

Printing with compressed pitch and line spacing enables you to get much more information on each page of your printed report. Figure 8.29 shows the first page of the Cash Flow Projector worksheet printed with standard pitch and line spacing. Compare this figure with figure 8.30, which shows the first page printed with compressed pitch and line spacing. Of course, the readability of the results depends on your specific printer.

Choosing Orientation

With the **Orientation** option, you can specify whether the output is printed in **Landscape** or **Portrait** mode. In **Portrait** mode (the default), the lines of text are printed on the paper in the usual manner, with the page situated vertically. In **Landscape** mode, the page is situated horizontally, and the lines of text are printed sideways on the page. Landscape printing is useful for fitting wide worksheets onto single pages.

Part II ◆ Creating 1-2-3 Reports and Graphs

Fig. 8.29.

The worksheet page printed with standard line spacing and pitch.

```
==================================================================
CASH FLOW PROJECTOR                    Copyright (C) 1989 Que Corporation
==================================================================
BALANCES IN WORKING CAPITAL ACCOUNTS                       Dec
==================================================================
Assets
  Cash                                                  $17,355
  Accounts Receivable                                   493,151
  Inventory                                             163,833

Liabilities
  Accounts Payable                                      125,000
  Line of Credit                                              0
                                                       --------
Net Working Capital                                   $549,339
                                                       ========


==================================================================
SALES                             Oct        Nov        Dec
==================================================================
Profit Center 1                $27,832    $23,864    $26,125
Profit Center 2                 13,489     21,444     20,140
Profit Center 3                126,811    124,382    123,618
Profit Center 4                 94,285     92,447     89,010
Profit Center 5
                              --------   --------   --------
Total Sales                   $262,417   $262,137   $258,893
                              ========   ========   ========

                  Cash            10%        10%        10%
Percent of        30 Days         20%        20%        20%
Collections       60 Days         50%        50%        50%
                  90 Days         20%        20%        20%

Cash Collections


==================================================================
PURCHASES                         Oct        Nov        Dec
==================================================================
Cost of Goods Sold
  Profit Center 1                 33%        33%        33%
                               $9,185     $7,875     $8,621
  Profit Center 2                 29%        29%        29%
                               $3,912     $6,219     $5,841
  Profit Center 3                 50%        50%        50%
                              $63,406    $62,191    $61,809
  Profit Center 4                 67%        67%        67%
                              $63,171    $61,939    $59,637
  Profit Center 5                 30%        30%        30%
                                  $0         $0         $0
```

Reminder:

When you select Landscape mode, you must adjust margins and page length manually.

Not all printers support Landscape mode, although all laser printers do. If your printer cannot print in Landscape, selecting this mode will have no effect on the output. When you select Landscape mode, 1-2-3 does not automatically adjust margins and page length; you must change these settings manually to reflect the new orientation.

Fig. 8.30.
The worksheet page printed with compressed line spacing and pitch.

Selecting Fonts

With the **/Print [P,E] Options Advanced Fonts** option, you can specify the fonts, or type styles, that will be used to print different sections of each page. 1-2-3 offers eight different fonts, numbered as shown here:

Font 1	Normal serif
Font 2	Bold serif
Font 3	Italic serif
Font 4	Bold italic serif
Font 5	Normal sans serif
Font 6	Bold sans serif
Font 7	Italic sans serif
Font 8	Bold italic sans serif

You can see what these fonts look like by referring to figure 8.26. How many of these fonts will be available to you depends on your printer. Some printers have all eight fonts, and other printers have only one or two. To see what fonts your printer supports, select **/Print Printer Sample G**o to produce the sample printout, as described earlier in this chapter.

You can specify different fonts for different areas of the report. After selecting **Options Advanced Fonts**, select one of the following: **Range**, **Header/Footer**, **Border**, or **Frame**. 1-2-3 next displays the numbers 1–8, corresponding to the preceding fonts. Choose the desired font. Selecting **Quit** returns you to the Options Advanced menu.

Figure 8.31 shows a report printed with one font for the main print range and a different font for the borders.

Fig. 8.31.
A report printed with two different fonts.

```
==================================================================
SALES                              OCT        Nov        Dec
==============================  =========  =========  =========
Profit Center 1                   $27,832    $23,864    $26,125
Profit Center 2                    13,489     21,444     20,140
Profit Center 3                   126,811    124,382    123,618
Profit Center 4                    94,285     92,447     89,010
Profit Center 5
                                ---------  ---------  ---------
Total Sales                      $262,417   $262,137   $258,893
                                =========  =========  =========

                     Cash            10%        10%        10%
Percent of           30 Days         20%        20%        20%
collections          60 Days         50%        50%        50%
                     90 Days         20%        20%        20%
```

If no fonts are specified, or if your printer does not support the specified font, 1-2-3 uses font 1 for all sections of the report.

Using Setup Strings

A *setup string* is a code that you send to the printer to change a printing characteristic, such as compressing the print, underlining, or boldfacing. In 1-2-3, you type a setup string consisting of one or more backslashes (\), followed by a three-digit decimal number corresponding to the desired code. Some codes have multiple strings (for example, \027\069). Because different printers use different codes, you need to refer to your printer manual (look under the topics of *escape codes* or *printer control codes*). A setup string has a maximum length of 512 characters.

Setup strings are not necessary in Wysiwyg because you can specify print characteristics by choosing menu options for any range of cells. For example, you can choose :Format Bold or :Format Underline and then highlight a range.

You can use one of the following methods to send a setup string from 1-2-3 to your printer:

1. Use the /Print [P,E] Options Setup command to provide a setup string. The setup string is sent to the printer at the start of every print job. The setup string also is saved with the worksheet and used the next time you retrieve the worksheet file.

2. Use the /Worksheet Global Default Printer Setup command to provide a default setup string, and then select Update from the /Worksheet Global Default menu. The setup string is in effect whenever you use 1-2-3. The Options Setup string can be combined with or override the default setup string, depending on the setup strings used.

3. Embed one or more setup strings in the worksheet itself. To use this method, you type two vertical bars (||) and the setup string in the first cell of a blank row in the print range. Because an embedded setup string is sent to the printer only when printing reaches the row that contains the setup string, a setup string can be used to affect only portions of a report. The setup string affects the entire width of all worksheet rows below the row in which the setup string is located. A second setup string can change or cancel the effect of the first.

You should not use setup strings to change print attributes, such as line spacing and type size, that can be controlled from the /Print [P,E] Options Advanced Layout menu. When you use the Layout menu, 1-2-3 automatically adjusts margins and lines per page to accommodate the new line spacing and type size. If you use setup strings to change either of these settings, you have to make the adjustments for margins and page length. You should use setup strings to make print enhancements not available on 1-2-3 menus, or to change the print style in only part of a report.

Reminder:
Use setup strings to make print enhancements not available on 1-2-3 menus.

Part II ◆ Creating 1-2-3 Reports and Graphs

To see how setup strings work, print portions of the Sales information from the range A:A21..A:G31 of the Cash Flow Projector worksheet. For these examples, assume that a Hewlett-Packard LaserJet II printer is being used.

Use the first method to send a setup string that prints a report in emphasized mode. Select /Print [P,E] Range and specify the range A:A21..A:G31, choose Options Setup, and then type the following setup string:

\027(s3B

Note that a setup string can consist of a combination of codes. The special capabilities of your printer and the codes used to control them are detailed in your printer instruction manual. For example, the code \027, which corresponds to Esc, is used as the first element in many setup strings.

Next, select Quit to return to the /Print [P,F,E,] menu, select Align, and choose Go. The printed report is shown in figure 8.32. Compare this report to the one shown in figure 8.33. Figure 8.33 was printed without the setup string embedded in the worksheet, and thus displays the printer's default 10 cpi draft-quality output.

Fig. 8.32.
The report printed in emphasized mode.

```
========================================================
SALES                            Oct       Nov       Dec
========================================    ========  ========  ========
Profit Center 1              $27,832   $23,864   $26,125
Profit Center 2               13,489    21,444    20,140
Profit Center 3              126,811   124,382   123,618
Profit Center 4               94,285    92,447    89,010
Profit Center 5
                             --------  --------  --------
Total Sales                 $262,417  $262,137  $258,893
                             ========  ========  ========
```

Fig. 8.33.
The report printed in default draft mode.

```
========================================================
SALES                            Oct       Nov       Dec
========================================    ========  ========  ========
Profit Center 1              $27,832   $23,864   $26,125
Profit Center 2               13,489    21,444    20,140
Profit Center 3              126,811   124,382   123,618
Profit Center 4               94,285    92,447    89,010
Profit Center 5
                             --------  --------  --------
Total Sales                 $262,417  $262,137  $258,893
                             ========  ========  ========
```

To remove a setup string, select **Setup** from the **/Print [P,E] Options** menu, press **Esc**, and then press Enter. However, removing a printer code from the **Setup** option does not cancel the code in the printer. Even though you have removed the setup string, your printer remembers the last code it was sent until it is turned off or until another code is sent. To cancel the previous setup string sent to the printer, you can either turn the printer off or enter a reset code in the **Setup** option. The reset code for a LaserJet printer is \027E.

A printer code entered in the **Setup** option affects all output from the current print operation. In the example, the contents in the entire print range were printed in emphasized mode. If headers, footers, or borders had been included, they would have been printed in emphasized mode also.

If you want only selected rows within a print range to reflect a special printing characteristic, you can use the third method—embedding a setup string in the worksheet. In this demonstration, you include setup strings in the Cash Flow Projector worksheet so that the range printed in figure 8.33 prints with the row for Profit Center 3 underlined.

Cue:
For special print enhancements that affect only part of a report, use embedded setup strings.

First, insert two blank rows—one above and one below row 26. These new rows are rows 26 and 28. In cell A:A26, type the following control codes to turn underlining on:

   ||\027&d#D

In cell A:A28, type these codes to turn underlining off:

   ||\027&d@

Figure 8.34 shows the worksheet with the control codes (setup strings) included. If you print range A:A21..A:G33, the printout appears as shown in figure 8.35.

```
A:A8:  ||\027&d@                                                    READY

       A              B         C         D         E         F         G         H
 1  =========================================================================
 2  SALES                                          Oct       Nov       Dec
 3  =========================================================================
 4  Profit Center 1                              $27,832   $23,864   $26,125
 5  Profit Center 2                               13,489    21,444    20,140
 6  |\027&d#D
 7  Profit Center 3                              126,811   124,382   123,618
 8  \027&d@
 9  Profit Center 4                               94,285    92,447    89,010
10  Profit Center 5
11                                               -------   -------   -------
12  Total Sales                                 $262,417  $262,137  $258,893
13                                              =======   =======   =======
```

Fig. 8.34.
A worksheet with embedded printer control codes.

Fig. 8.35.
A printout of the worksheet range, with the data row for Profit Center 3 underlined.

```
==================================================================
SALES                              Oct        Nov        Dec
==================================================================
Profit Center 1                 $27,832    $23,864    $26,125
Profit Center 2                  13,489     21,444     20,140
Profit Center 3                 126,811    124,382    123,618
Profit Center 4                  94,285     92,447     89,010
Profit Center 5
                                --------   --------   --------
Total Sales                    $262,417   $262,137   $258,893
                                ========   ========   ========
```

When you have finished printing, just delete the rows containing the setup strings. Remember that these codes are for a Hewlett-Packard LaserJet printer; they do not work properly on other printers.

When using embedded printer setup strings, keep the following points in mind:

1. The setup string must be inserted in a blank row, in the leftmost column in the print range.
2. Any other cell contents in the row containing the setup string are ignored and do not print. The row is not counted as part of the page length.
3. A second setup string is needed if you want to return printing to normal.

Selecting Color

With the **Color** option, you can select whatever color you want to use for your printed report. Headers, footers, and the print range are printed in the selected color. You can choose from as many as eight colors, depending on your printer. If negative numbers are displayed on-screen in red (in other words, if you have selected /**W**orksheet **G**lobal **F**ormat **O**ther **C**olor **N**egative), those numbers are printed in red also, if possible.

Controlling Your Printer

Some of the print commands deal directly with controlling the printer hardware. You need to understand these commands so that you can create your printed reports efficiently.

Choosing the Printer

Reminder:
Use /**P**rint [**P,E**] **O**ptions **A**dvanced **D**evice to specify which installed printer to use.

/**P**rint **P**rinter **O**ptions **A**dvanced **D**evice enables you to choose the **N**ame and the **I**nterface of the printer to be used. You select **D**evice **N**ame to choose from the list of printers selected during the Install procedure. Next, you select **D**evice **I**nterface to indicate the port to which the printer is attached. If the port is a serial port, you also must specify the baud rate.

Controlling the Movement of the Paper

If you print a range containing fewer lines than the default page length, the paper does not advance automatically to the top of the next page. Likewise, if you print a range containing more lines than the default page length, 1-2-3 automatically inserts page breaks between pages, but the paper does not advance to the top of the next page after the last page has printed. In both cases, the next print job begins wherever the preceding operation ended.

If you want to advance to a new page after printing less than a full page, select **/Print Printer Page**. Whenever you issue this command, the printer advances to the start of the next page. (You learned earlier in the chapter how to embed a page-break symbol in the print range in order to instruct 1-2-3 to advance automatically.)

To print an existing footer on the last page of a report, use the **Page** command at the end of the printing session. If you select the **Quit** command from the **/Print** menu without issuing the **Page** command, this final footer does not print. If this happens, reissue the **/Print Printer** command and select **Page**, and the footer prints when the page ejects.

If you want to advance the paper one line at a time (for example, to separate several ranges that fit on one printed page), you issue the **/Print Printer Line** command.

When you are using a dot-matrix printer and continuous-feed paper, 1-2-3 must know the position of the perforations between pages if the printed output is to be positioned properly on the paper. The top of a page is initially marked by the print head's position when you turn on the printer and load 1-2-3. At the start of each work session, be sure that the paper is positioned so that the print head is at the top of the page, and then turn on the printer.

> **Reminder:**
> *When you begin each work session, be sure the paper is set so that the print head is at the top of the page.*

During the work session, do not advance the paper manually—use the **Page** or **Line** commands. Because 1-2-3 coordinates a line counter with the current page-length setting, any lines you advance manually are not counted, and page breaks may crop up in strange places. Whenever you or someone else manually advances the paper, 1-2-3 and the printer get "out of sync." When that happens, page breaks may appear midpage, resulting in blank areas in your reports. To prevent this problem, you should select **Align** before selecting **Go** whenever you begin a print job at the top of a page.

As printing progresses, both the printer and 1-2-3 maintain internal line counters that indicate the print head's current position on the page. If these two pointers get "out of sync," you are likely to get output that is printed on top of the perforations as lines in the middle of pages are skipped. If this problem occurs, take the following steps:

1. Turn off the printer.
2. Advance the paper manually until the print head is at the top of a page, and then turn the printer back on.
3. Select **Align** from the **/Print Printer** menu.

Note that the **Align** command resets 1-2-3's page number counter. If you are including page numbers in your report, you may want to skip the third step.

Setting Your Printing Priorities

As indicated at the beginning of the chapter, a print job begins when you select **G**o from the **/P**rint [**P,F,E**] menu. The print job ends when you exit from the **/P**rint menu by selecting **Q**uit, pressing Esc, or pressing Ctrl-Break. When a print job ends, the printing does not stop—you simply have finished defining the job. You can end one print job and then specify additional jobs as the first one is still printing. 1-2-3 automatically puts multiple jobs in a queue and prints them in order.

You can use **/P**rint **P**rinter **O**ptions **A**dvanced **P**riority to set the priority for the current print job within the print queue. If no other jobs are in the queue, this priority setting has no effect (the job is printed immediately). The following **P**riority menu items are available:

Menu Item	Description
Default	Puts the current job ahead of low-priority jobs and behind all other jobs
Low	Puts the current job behind all other jobs
High	Puts the current job behind high-priority jobs and ahead of all other jobs

The **P**riority setting takes effect when you exit from the **/P**rint menu. A job that is actually printing will not be interrupted by a job with a higher priority.

1-2-3 can send data to the printer as you continue to work in the worksheet. This capability is known as *background printing*. As a worksheet is printing, the message PRT appears at the bottom of the screen. If a printer error—for example, running out of paper—occurs during background printing, 1-2-3 displays an error message on-screen. Because this background error does not cause 1-2-3 to go into ERROR mode, you can continue working in the worksheet if you want. You can either correct the printer problem and continue printing with **/P**rint **R**esume, or cancel all print jobs with **/P**rint **C**ancel.

Holding a Print Job (Hold)

The **/P**rint **P**rinter **H**old option enables you to return to 1-2-3 READY mode while keeping the current print job open. In READY mode, you can perform a number of tasks, including the following:

1. Importing new data into the worksheet.
2. Changing column widths, cell formats, or other aspects of worksheet display.
3. Modifying **/W**orksheet **G**lobal settings.

Reminder:
If you return to READY mode by any means besides HOLD, you have to start again to define the print job.

After finishing your tasks in READY mode, you can return to the **/P**rint [**P,F,E**] menu and continue creating the same print job. If you return to READY mode by any means other than **H**old, the current print job closes, and you have to start again to define the print job.

Chapter 8 ◆ Printing Reports **361**

Note that **H**old does not affect the printer itself. If a print job is in progress—actually printing—the **H**old option does not stop the printer. To pause or stop the printer, use /**P**rint **S**uspend or /**P**rint **C**ancel.

Pausing the Printer (Suspend and Wait)

You can temporarily pause the printer by invoking the /**P**rint **S**uspend command. Printing pauses as soon as the printer's internal buffer empties. Do not turn the printer off, or you will lose part of your report! You may lose only a few lines or several pages, depending on the printer. Use /**P**rint **S**uspend to perform such tasks as refilling the paper bin or changing the ribbon.

/**P**rint **R**esume restarts printing that was paused in one of the following ways:

1. You invoked a /**P**rint **S**uspend command.
2. You selected /**P**rint **P**rinter **O**ptions **A**dvanced **W**ait **Y**es or /**W**orksheet **G**lobal **D**efault **P**rinter **W**ait **Y**es, and the printer is at the end of a page, waiting for another sheet of paper.
3. A printer error has occurred. After correcting the error, you invoke /**P**rint **R**esume to clear the error message and resume printing.

Select **W**ait **Y**es if you are hand-feeding paper to the printer; 1-2-3 stops sending data to the printer at the end of each page. The printer pauses, enabling you to insert a new sheet of paper. **R**esume then continues printing with the next page. This option is different from **S**uspend, which temporarily pauses printing under user control, and from **C**ancel, which permanently ends all print jobs.

Stopping the Printer (Cancel and Quit)

After starting one or more print jobs, you may realize that you have made an error in the worksheet data or print settings and that you need to correct the error before the report is printed. Selecting /**P**rint **C**ancel stops the current print job and removes any other print jobs from the queue. Once you have canceled the current print jobs, you cannot restart them. This command cancels reports printed in 1-2-3 (/**P**rint **P**rinter) and Wysiwyg (**:P**rint).

When you select /**P**rint **C**ancel, printing may not stop immediately if the printer has an internal print buffer or if a software print spooler has been installed. Turning the printer off for a few seconds clears the printer buffer. If printing resumes when you turn the printer back on, a print spooler probably is installed. Refer to the documentation for your print spooler for instructions on how to clear it.

The /**P**rint **C**ancel command resets 1-2-3's page and line counters to 1. If the printer stops in the middle of a page, you need to take one of the following steps to realign the paper:

1. Turn the printer off, advance the paper manually to the top of the page, turn the printer back on, and select /**P**rint **P**rinter **A**lign.

Cue:
*Use /**P**rint **S**uspend to halt printing temporarily. Use /**P**rint **C**ancel to end all print jobs permanently.*

2. With the printer on, use **/P**rint **P**rinter **L**ine to advance the paper, one line at a time, to the top of the next page; and then select **A**lign.

You cannot cancel an individual print job; you must cancel all print jobs or none.

Printing a Graph with Text (Image)

Thus far, this chapter has dealt with printing text alone (without a graph). You also can include 1-2-3 graphs in your reports, placing a graph on a separate page or on a page containing text. (Graph printing is covered in detail in Chapters 10 and 11.) You can use three methods to print a graph as part of a report:

1. Use the Wysiwyg **:G**raph **A**dd command to indicate the worksheet range in which you want the graph to print. See Chapter 11 for details.
2. In 1-2-3, print the text portion of the report without form-feeding the page. Then select **I**mage from the **/P**rint [P,E] menu, specify the graph to print, and select **G**o again. The selected graph prints immediately after the text.
3. After specifying the worksheet range to print, but before pressing Enter, type a range separator (; or ,) and an asterisk followed by the name of the graph to print. For example, look at the following print range:

    B1..H20;*PROFITS;K10..N15

    This range prints the text in B1..H20, followed by the graph named PROFITS and the text in K10..N15.

Before printing a graph, you may need to modify its size, rotation, or density. To make these changes, use the **/P**rint [P,E] **O**ptions **A**dvanced **I**mage menu, which is discussed in Chapter 10.

Naming and Saving the Current Print Settings

1-2-3 enables you to save all current print settings under a unique name, recall the settings with that name, and reuse the settings without having to specify them individually. To use this feature, you select **/P**rint [P,F,E] **O**ptions **N**ame. The following choices are presented:

Menu Item	Description
Create	Assigns a name to the current print settings. You select this command and then enter a name in response to the prompt. The name can contain up to 15 characters and can include any combination of letters, numbers, and symbols—except for two "less than" symbols (<<). If you type a print-settings name already in use, the original settings associated with that name are replaced by the current settings.

Chapter 8 ◆ Printing Reports **363**

Menu Item	Description
Delete	Deletes a print-settings name. You select this command and then select the print-settings name to delete.
Reset	Deletes all print-settings names from the current file.
Table	Creates a list of all print-settings names in the current file. You select this command and then position the cell pointer at the worksheet location where you want the table to appear. The table occupies one column and as many rows as there are print-settings names.
Use	Makes current the print settings associated with a particular print-settings name.

Clearing the Print Options

With **/P**rint **P**rinter **C**lear, you can eliminate all or some of the **/P**rint options you chose earlier. When you select **C**lear, the following menu appears:

    All   **R**ange   **B**orders   **F**ormat   **I**mage   **D**evice

You can choose **A**ll to clear every **/P**rint option, including the print range, or you can be more specific by using one of the following choices:

Menu Item	Description
Range	Clears existing print range specifications
Borders	Cancels **C**olumns and **R**ows specified as borders
Format	Eliminates **M**argins, **P**g-Length, and **S**etup string settings
Image	Clears graphs selected for printing
Device	Returns device name and interface to defaults

Preparing Output for Use in Other Programs

Many word processing programs and other software packages accept ASCII text files—the kind created by 1-2-3's **/P**rint **F**ile option. You can maximize your chances of successfully exporting 1-2-3 files to other programs if you use several **/P**rint command sequences to eliminate unwanted formatting from the output.

You begin by selecting **/P**rint **F**ile to direct output to an ASCII PRN file. After specifying a file name and the **R**ange to print, you choose **O**ptions **O**ther **U**nformatted. Selecting Unformatted removes all headers, footers, and page breaks from the output.

You then set the left margin to 0 and the right margin to 255. Do not worry about worksheet lines shorter than 255 characters. The line ends after the last printed character, not at 255.

Next, you select **Q**uit to leave the **O**ptions menu, create the PRN file on disk by selecting **G**o, and select **Q**uit to exit the /**P**rint File menu. You should then follow the instructions provided with your word processing program or other software package in order to import the specially prepared 1-2-3 disk file.

Refer also to your word processing manual for more information about ASCII or text file retrieval. Before retrieving the PRN file, be sure that your word processing margins are set as wide as or wider than your print range. After retrieving the PRN file, use a search-and-replace command to remove unwanted hard carriage returns at the ends of lines.

To restore the default print settings for headers, footers, and page breaks, you issue the /**P**rint **P**rinter **O**ptions **O**ther **F**ormatted command. Ordinarily, you select Formatted for printing to the printer or an encoded (ENC) file, and Unformatted for printing to a PRN file.

Summary

This chapter showed you how to create printed reports from your 1-2-3 worksheets. You learned first how to print reports with the default settings, and then how to change those defaults through either the /**W**orksheet menu or the /**P**rint menu. To make your reports more readable, you learned how to break the worksheet into pages; provide headers, footers, and borders; and change the margins and page length. You also discovered how to take full advantage of your printer's font, color, and line-spacing capabilities by using 1-2-3's advanced print options as well as setup strings.

Using a variety of options to print reports from large worksheets takes practice and careful study of your printer manual. Use this chapter as a reference as you continue to experiment.

Using Wysiwyg To Enhance and Print Reports

9

The Wysiwyg add-in offers Release 3.1 and 3.1+ users a graphical interface. In Wysiwyg (a name based on the acronym WYSIWYG, meaning "what you see is what you get"), the screen reflects all special formatting (lines, shading, and fonts, for example), and the worksheet prints almost exactly as it appears on-screen. With Wysiwyg, you also can use a mouse to move the cell pointer, size rows and columns, access the menu, and select ranges.

Although not a full-featured desktop publishing program, Wysiwyg may be all you need for many desktop publishing tasks involving 1-2-3 reports and graphs. Using the add-in, you can produce printed 1-2-3 reports that incorporate a variety of type fonts, lines, shadings, and other formatting features (boldface, underline, and so on). Compare a report printed from the 1-2-3 /Print command (see fig. 9.1) with the same report formatted and printed with Wysiwyg (see fig. 9.2). As you can see, the difference in presentation quality is dramatic. (All printed figures in this chapter were produced on a Hewlett-Packard LaserJet II laser printer.)

In addition to providing enhanced text formatting, Wysiwyg enables you to embed 1-2-3 graphs into your printouts and use a graphics editor to embellish your graphs. The graphing aspects of Wysiwyg are covered in Chapter 11. This chapter focuses on Wysiwyg's formatting and printing features. Specifically, you learn the following in this chapter:

- ◆ How to load Wysiwyg
- ◆ How 1-2-3 and Wysiwyg work together
- ◆ How to format worksheets with fonts and other print attributes
- ◆ How to manage formats

Part II ♦ Creating 1-2-3 Reports and Graphs

- ♦ How to print in Wysiwyg, including how to fine-tune the page layout and add titles and borders
- ♦ How to change the appearance of the screen
- ♦ How to use Wysiwyg's text commands

```
LaserPro Corporation
Balance Sheet
October 1, 1990


ASSETS
                                This Year    Last Year     Change
Current Assets
Cash                              247,886      126,473        96%
Accounts receivable               863,652      524,570        65%
Inventory                          79,071       53,790        47%
Prepaid expenses                    9,257       11,718       -21%
Investments                       108,577       31,934       240%
     Total Current Assets       1,308,443      748,485        75%

Fixed Assets
Machinery and equipment           209,906      158,730        32%
Vehicles                          429,505      243,793        76%
Office furniture                   50,240       36,406        38%
(Accumulated depreciation)       (101,098)     (64,394)       57%
     Total Fixed Assets           588,553      374,535        57%
                               $1,896,996   $1,123,020        69%


LIABILITIES AND SHAREHOLDERS' EQUITY

                                This Year    Last Year     Change
Current Liabilities
Accounts payable trade            426,041      332,845        28%
Notes payable                      45,327       23,486        93%
Accrued liabilities                34,614       26,026        33%
Income taxes payable               88,645       51,840        71%
     Total Current Liabilities    594,627      434,197        37%

Noncurrent Liabilities
Long-term debt                    488,822      349,253        40%
Deferred federal tax              147,844       92,101        61%
     Total Noncurrent Liabilities 636,666      441,354        44%

Shareholders' equity
Common stock                        1,000        1,000         0%
Opening retained earnings         246,469       82,531       199%
Profit (loss) for the period      418,234      163,938       155%
     Total Shareholders' Equity   665,703      247,469       169%
                               $1,896,996   $1,123,020        69%
```

Fig. 9.1.

A report printed with the 1-2-3 /Print command.

Loading Wysiwyg

Before you can use Wysiwyg, it must be loaded into memory. To load Wysiwyg, press Alt-F10 to display the Add-In menu; then select **L**oad. Choose `WYSIWYG.PLC` from the list that appears on-screen. You are then asked to select a function key for invoking the Wysiwyg menu. Choose **N**o-Key, because the easiest way to invoke the menu is with the mouse or the colon (:) key. (See the section "Understanding the Wysiwyg Menu" for further information.) Finally, choose **Q**uit to exit the Add-In menu.

Because you will probably want to use Wysiwyg every time you use 1-2-3, you should change the default settings so that the add-in is loaded automatically after 1-2-3 is loaded. To do so, press Alt-F10 to display the Add-In menu. Choose **S**ettings **S**ystem **S**et and select `WYSIWYG.PLC`. In response to the question `Automatically start this application when it is read into memory?`, **type N** for **N**o. (If you type **Y** for **Y**es, the Wysiwyg menu appears in the control panel every time you load 1-2-3.) Choose **N**o-Key and then **U**pdate to save the settings.

Fig. 9.2.
The report formatted and printed with Wysiwyg.

Understanding How 1-2-3 and Wysiwyg Work Together

1-2-3 Releases 3.1 and 3.1+ and Wysiwyg are very closely integrated—much more closely than Allways is integrated into Release 2.2. You do not need to switch between the graphical and the standard interface, because there is now only one interface: graphical. When Wysiwyg is loaded, your screen looks similar to figure 9.3. You are in READY mode, so you can move the cell pointer, make cell entries, or bring up the menu by pressing the slash key. But with the Wysiwyg add-in attached, there's a lot more you can do, as you soon find out.

Understanding the Wysiwyg Menu

When you are in Wysiwyg, two menus are available. As always, pressing the slash key displays the standard 1-2-3 menu. To display the Wysiwyg menu, press the colon (:). The Esc key backs you out of whatever menu is currently displayed.

Another way to display the menus is with the mouse. A menu automatically appears when you place the mouse pointer in the control panel. The particular menu displayed depends on which menu you were in last.

Fig. 9.3.
The worksheet screen when Wysiwyg is loaded.

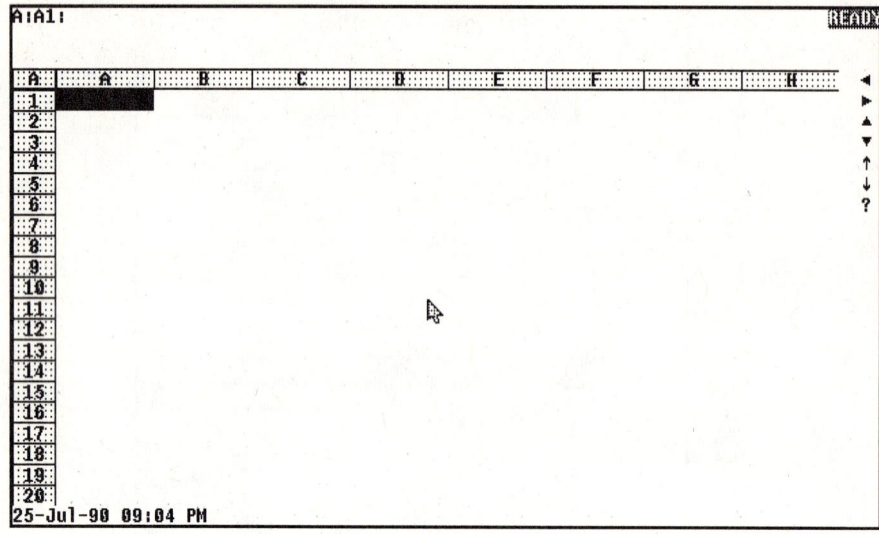

The Wysiwyg menu offers the following choices:

    Worksheet Format Graph Print Display Special Text Named-Style Quit

Although some of the option names are similar to the ones on your standard 1-2-3 menu, the submenus and their functions are quite different. The following is a summary of each main menu option.

Option	Description
Worksheet	Sets column widths, row heights, and page breaks
Format	Adds boldface, lines, shading, fonts, and so on
Graph	Inserts a graph into a worksheet range; enhances the graph
Print	Prints the formatted worksheet or graph; specifies page layout
Display	Alters the screen characteristics (for example, colors)
Special	Copies, moves, imports, and exports formats
Text	Edits, aligns, and reformats a range of text
Named-Style	Assigns names to commonly used format combinations
Quit	Returns to READY mode

Cue:
Use **:P**rint if you have used **:F**ormat commands to enhance the worksheet; use **/P**rint if you haven't used Wysiwyg formatting commands.

Note that both the 1-2-3 and Wysiwyg menus offer a **P**rint option. How do you know when you should use **/P**rint (1-2-3) or **:P**rint (Wysiwyg)? Use **:P**rint if you have used any of Wysiwyg's **:F**ormat commands to enhance the worksheet or if you have inserted a graph into a worksheet range. Use **/P**rint if you haven't used Wysiwyg formatting commands on the worksheet or graph you want to print.

Wysiwyg menus work the same way as 1-2-3 menus: select a command by typing the first letter of the command or by highlighting the command name and pressing Enter. Each of the Wysiwyg options is explained in detail in this chapter.

Saving Your Wysiwyg Formatting

Wysiwyg stores enhanced formatting information in its own file, separate from the worksheet file. The Wysiwyg file has the same first name as your 1-2-3 file but bears the extension FM3. For example, if Wysiwyg is loaded and you save a worksheet file called BUDGET.WK3, Wysiwyg saves an associated BUDGET.FM3 file. This file contains all the formatting enhancements selected with Wysiwyg.

Wysiwyg saves enhanced formatting information only when you use the 1-2-3 /**File Save** command to save the current 1-2-3 worksheet. If you press Alt-F10 and choose **Detach**, Wysiwyg is erased immediately from memory, and therefore no enhanced formatting can be saved. If Wysiwyg is detached before you save the worksheet, your FM3 file is not updated, and you may lose an extensive amount of formatting work.

Do not modify the structure of a Wysiwyg-formatted worksheet when the add-in is not attached. If you delete, insert, or move anything, the formatting will not match up with the proper cells the next time you attach Wysiwyg.

Reminder: *Wysiwyg stores its formatting information in a separate file that has the extension FM3.*

Reminder: *If Wysiwyg is detached before you save the worksheet, the FM3 file is not updated and you may lose extensive formatting work.*

Understanding the Wysiwyg Screen

The 1-2-3 and Wysiwyg screens are similar in structure. Figure 9.4 points out the different areas of the Wysiwyg screen. You see the worksheet frame (column letters and row numbers), the clock at the bottom left corner of the screen, and the READY mode indicator in the upper right corner. As with the 1-2-3 screen, the top three lines make up the Wysiwyg screen's control panel. The only difference here is that Wysiwyg format abbreviations are indicated between the current cell address and the cell contents. For example, {Bold} indicates boldface.

The right side of the Wysiwyg screen displays an *icon panel* for use with the mouse. Table 9.1 describes the function of each of these symbols. To select an icon, place the mouse pointer on the icon and press the left mouse button. Press and hold down the button to scroll continuously.

Table 9.1
The Wysiwyg Screen's Icon Panel

Symbol	Function
◄ (solid left triangle)	Moves the cell pointer one cell to the left
► (solid right triangle)	Moves the cell pointer one cell to the right
▲ (solid up triangle)	Moves the cell pointer up one cell
▼ (solid down triangle)	Moves the cell pointer down one cell

continued

Table 9.1—(continued)

Symbol	Function
↑ (up arrow)	Moves the cell pointer to next worksheet
↓ (down arrow)	Moves the cell pointer to previous worksheet
? (question mark)	Help

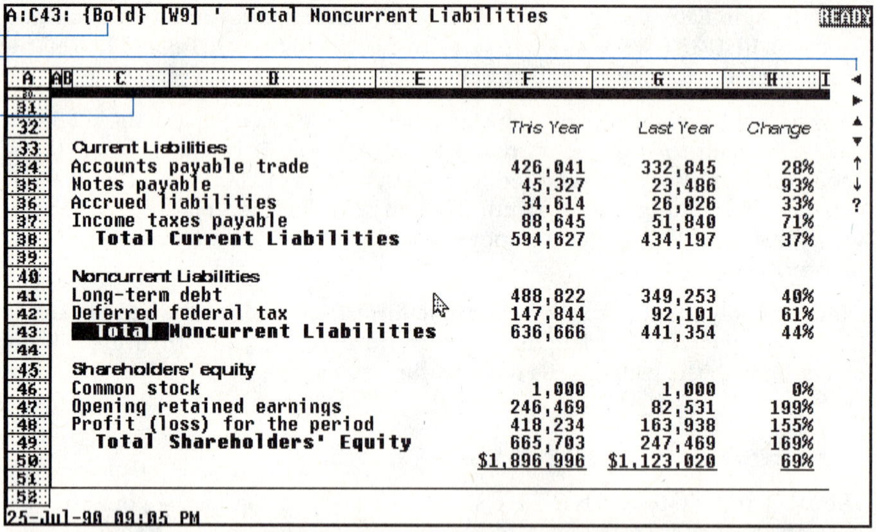

Fig. 9.4.
The parts of the Wysiwyg screen.

(Screenshot labeled with: Attribute, Icon panel, Frame)

Specifying Cell Ranges in Wysiwyg

Many Wysiwyg commands require you to specify a range. You can specify a range by using any of the following techniques:

- Typing the cell references or range name
- Pressing Name (F3) and choosing the name from a list
- Using the arrow keys to point to the range
- Using the mouse to point to the range

To highlight a range with the mouse, click the mouse on the upper left corner of the range, hold the mouse button down, drag the mouse to the lower right corner of the range, and release the mouse button.

Cue:
To specify multiple ranges, type a comma or semicolon between each range.

Wysiwyg lets you indicate more than one range when you are specifying a range to format. To specify multiple ranges, insert a comma or semicolon between each range and press Enter when you have finished defining ranges. For example, to select the ranges A:A1..A:A5 and A:C1..A:C5, type **A:A1..A:A5,A:C1..A:C5** or **A:A1..A:A5;A:C1..A:C5**. You can select each range by using any of the techniques described earlier, except the mouse. Although you can use it to select the first range, the mouse does not work reliably for selecting later ranges.

Wysiwyg also lets you specify a single range *before* you invoke a command. The preselected range applies to all commands until you change the range specification. Prespecifying a range saves time when you want a series of commands (for example, those for shading, lines, and boldface) to apply to the same range.

To select a range when you are in READY mode, place the cell pointer in the upper left corner of the range, press F4 to anchor, and then move to the lower right corner of the range. If you are using the mouse, hold down the Ctrl key as you highlight the range with the press-and-drag technique. Once the range is selected, you can invoke the Wysiwyg menu and issue as many commands as you like. Wysiwyg automatically uses the highlighted range and does not prompt you for one.

Cue:
You can prespecify a Wysiwyg range that applies automatically to a series of commands.

Formatting with Wysiwyg

The heart of Wysiwyg's power is its capability to add professional formatting touches. The 1-2-3 formats—numeric display and label alignment—carry through automatically to Wysiwyg. Wysiwyg's formats determine printed typeface, character size, boldfacing, and other stylistic features such as lines and shading.

Wysiwyg's additional formats provide many ways to enhance the appearance of printed text. To assign a Wysiwyg format to a cell or range, use the Wysiwyg **:Format** command. To determine the format of a cell, move the cell pointer to the cell. The format displays at the top of the screen, next to the current-cell address. If you use Wysiwyg in graphics mode (the default), you can actually see the formatting on the screen. See "Setting Display Characteristics" later in this chapter for information on changing the display mode.

Understanding Fonts

Most of Wysiwyg's formatting effects result from the use of different fonts. In Wysiwyg, a *font* is a particular typeface—for example, Times Roman—in a particular point size. A *point*, a printer's unit of measure, is 1/72 inch (an inch contains 72 points). The larger the point size, the larger the type. The fonts you have to choose from depend on your printer. Wysiwyg can use any font your printer is capable of printing.

Wysiwyg comes with four soft fonts from Bitstream: Swiss, Dutch, Courier, and XSymbol. A *soft font* is a file on disk that specifies to a printer how to make a font. Soft fonts are sent to the printer's memory before the document is printed, so that the printer can use the information to print the document. If you have a dot-matrix printer, Wysiwyg uses your printer's graphics mode to produce these fonts. If you have a laser printer, these four fonts are downloaded automatically to your printer when you use them. Your printer, however, may not have enough memory for many different fonts or larger point sizes.

If your printer provides additional fonts, these also are available to Wysiwyg. The Hewlett-Packard LaserJet II comes with two built-in fonts (Courier and Line Printer), for example, and you can buy dozens of cartridges to access additional fonts.

Reminder:
For worksheet text, Wysiwyg can use any additional laser printer fonts you have.

Each worksheet can use up to eight different fonts. These eight fonts are stored in a *font set*. The font list displayed in figure 9.5 is the default font set, composed primarily of Swiss and Dutch fonts. Figure 9.6 shows examples of the default fonts.

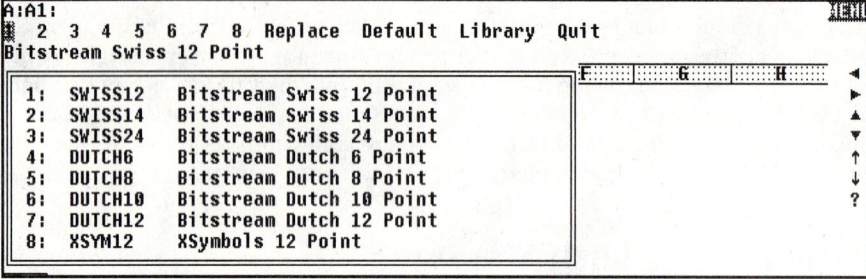

Fig. 9.5.
The default font set offered in Wysiwyg.

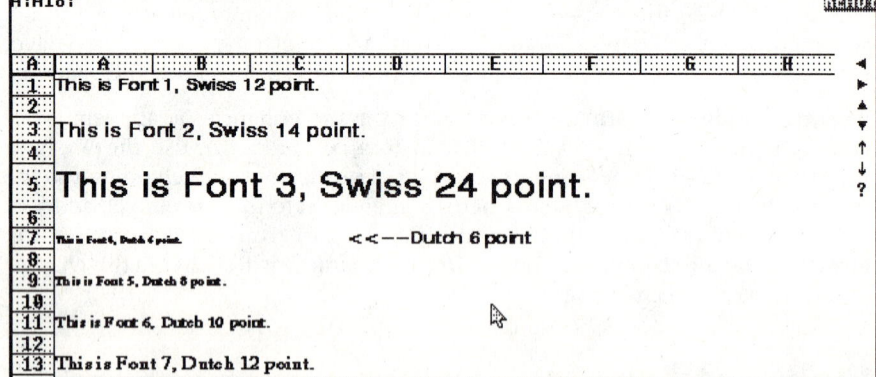

Fig. 9.6.
Examples of the default fonts.

Using Fonts

With Wysiwyg, you can format each cell or range of cells with a different font. You can use up to eight fonts for a single worksheet, but by default, all cells are assigned to font 1.

You assign a font to a cell or range by using the Wysiwyg :Format Font command. A description of each font (typeface and point size) appears in a box below the menu. Highlight the desired font number on the menu and press Enter, or click the number. (Alternatively, you can type the number.) Wysiwyg then prompts you for a range. When you supply the range and press Enter, the selected font is applied to the specified range. If necessary, Wysiwyg adjusts the height of the row to conform to the tallest point size used.

If you change the font size of a paragraph of text, you may find that the text occupies more or fewer columns than it originally did. To respace the text, use the **:Text Reformat** command. This command is similar to 1-2-3's **/Range Justify** command, which word-wraps text within the range you define. (See "Reformatting Paragraphs" later in the chapter.)

Replacing Fonts

If a font you want to use is not in the default font set, shown in figure 9.5, you can substitute that font for any of the default fonts. Because you are limited to eight fonts per worksheet, you must replace one of the existing fonts in the list; you cannot add fonts to the list.

Reminder: You cannot have more than eight fonts in the font list, although you can replace fonts in the list.

To replace one of the fonts in the current set with a font not currently shown, select **:Format Font Replace**. Choose the number associated with the font you want to replace (choose a font you don't need in the current worksheet). The following menu appears:

    Swiss **D**utch **C**ourier **X**Symbol **O**ther

The soft fonts included with Wysiwyg represent four of the most common types of fonts: proportional sans serif (**Swiss**), proportional serif (**Dutch**), fixed-pitch (**Courier**), and special-effects characters (**XSymbol**). Table 9.2 defines some of these terms.

Table 9.2
Terms Used To Describe Fonts

Term	Definition
Proportional	Characterizing a font in which the actual width of each character determines how much space the character occupies when printed
Fixed-space	Characterizing a font in which each printed character occupies the same amount of space regardless of character width
Serif	Having short cross-lines (serifs), or decorative "tails," at the ends of many characters' main strokes
Sans serif	Without the short cross-lines

The **X**Symbol font contains special characters such as arrows and circled numbers. Figure 9.7 shows different letters and numbers formatted with the **X**Symbol font. For example, if you enter a lowercase *a* into a cell and format it to **X**Symbol font, a right-pointing arrow is displayed. These special characters are sometimes referred to as *dingbats*.

*Reminder: The **X**Symbol font contains special characters such as arrows and circled numbers.*

The **O**ther option on the **:Format Font Replace** menu lets you select from a list of other typefaces. For example, if you have an HP LaserJet II, you can choose the printer's built-in Line Printer font or a font cartridge. Note that your printer may not be able to use all typefaces on the list. If you select a font your printer can't use, Wysiwyg substitutes a similar typeface.

Once you have chosen the typeface, indicate a type size. Although the screen prompts you to enter a size between 3 and 72 points, not all point sizes are available. For example, the Line Printer font comes in only one size: 8 point. If you choose a size that is not available in a certain typeface, Wysiwyg substitutes a similar typeface in the size you specified (for example, Courier 10 point in place of a nonexistent Line Printer 10 point). If you generated the Basic font set, the following high-resolution type sizes are available for each typeface: 4, 6, 8, 9, 10, 12, 14, 16, 18, 20, and 24. The Medium font set contains 36 point in addition to all the sizes in the Basic set. The Extended set has 19 high-resolution sizes ranging from 4 to 72 points. To generate a more complete font set, you can run the Install program again.

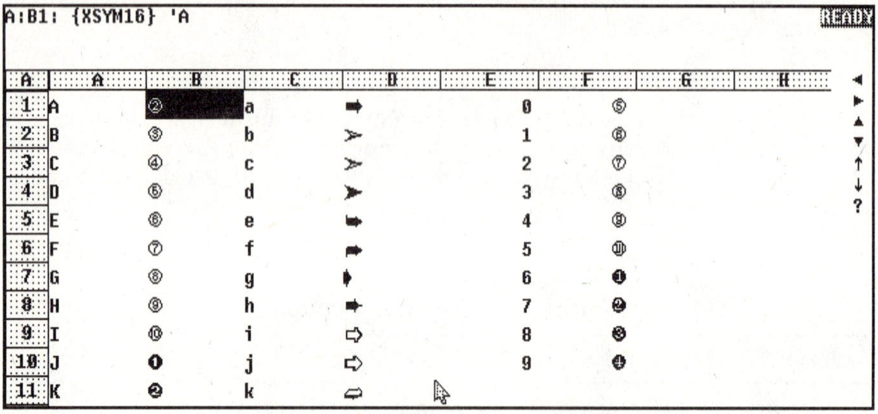

Fig. 9.7.
Examples of the XSymbol font characters (dingbats).

Once you enter the font size, the new font is listed in the font set and can be used immediately or at a later time. To use the newly added font, select the number from the :Format Font menu, highlight the range to which you want to apply the font, and press Enter.

When you replace fonts, any worksheet cells formatted with that particular font number automatically change. Suppose that you use :Format Font Replace to replace Swiss 12 with Courier 10. All worksheet cells previously formatted as Swiss 12 are automatically reformatted as Courier 10.

Reminder:
Font 1 is assigned automatically to all cells.

As mentioned earlier, font 1 is assigned automatically to all cells. Thus, when you replace font 1 with a different font, all cells—except for the ones assigned to other font numbers—automatically change to the new font 1. You do *not* need to choose :Format Font 1 and highlight a range.

Creating Font Libraries

Cue:
Save in a font library those font sets you are likely to use with other worksheets.

When you use :Format Font Replace to customize the font list for the current worksheet, you may want to save the font set for use with another worksheet file. The font set can be named and saved in a font library to be used over again in any other worksheet. Create font libraries for combinations of fonts you are likely to use in other worksheets. Creating a font library saves you from using the :Format Font Replace command in each worksheet.

Chapter 9 ◆ Using Wysiwyg To Enhance and Print Reports   375

To save the current font set in a library, select **:Format Font Library Save**. Wysiwyg prompts you to enter a file name. Type a file name of up to eight characters and press Enter. The file is saved with the extension AF3.

When you want to use a font library, select **:Format Font Library Retrieve**. Wysiwyg displays a list of library files with the AF3 extension. Highlight the name of the library you want to use; then press Enter. The eight fonts saved in this library are displayed in the font box, and you can use any of these fonts on the current worksheet.

If you know you want to use the fonts stored in another file, but you haven't saved them to a library, you can still use those fonts in the current file. Use the **:Special Import Fonts** command as described in the "Importing Formats" section.

If you frequently retrieve the same font library, make it the default font set. To do so, retrieve the font library that is to become the default and select **:Format Font Default Update**.

Cue:
Make your most frequently used font library the default.

Some laser printers have a restricted amount of memory. In general, the larger the point size of a font, the more memory the font takes in the printer's memory. When you download soft fonts to a laser printer, the printer stores the fonts in its memory for use during the printing process. If you get an `Out of memory` message when you print, your printer does not have enough memory to support the font set downloaded to it. Try replacing the large fonts with smaller fonts or using an internal or cartridge font.

Reminder:
Your laser printer may not have enough memory to download soft fonts of large point sizes.

Changing Formatting Attributes

Font formats are only one type of formatting you can apply to a cell or a range. You also can apply boldface, italics, and underline attributes. In addition, you can change the color of a range of cells; if you have a color printer, you can then print in different colors. Figure 9.8 shows examples of these formatting attributes. The headings (for example, Operating Expenses) appear in boldface, the other labels (for example, Payroll) are italicized, and the last number before the total is underlined.

You can use bold or italic formatting to enhance column headings, totals, or other ranges you want to emphasize. To boldface a range, select **:Format Bold Set** and indicate the range to which you want to apply the attribute. Use **:Format Italics Set** to italicize a range. Boldfaced text appears heavier on the screen; italicized text slants to the right. The first line of the control panel indicates the attribute with `{Bold}` or `{Italics}`.

Use the Wysiwyg underline formatting option instead of the 1-2-3 repeating label to create underlines. In 1-2-3, you have to enter \– to create a single underline and \= to produce a double underline. This method has several disadvantages. First, you must enter these labels into blank cells, consuming valuable worksheet space. Second, the underlines are not solid and don't look very professional.

Cue:
Use Wysiwyg to create professional-looking underlines in your worksheet.

Wysiwyg solves these problems by offering true underlining—the same as is available in word processing. You do not use blank rows for the underlines;

underlines are solid and appear directly underneath existing cell entries, not in separate cells.

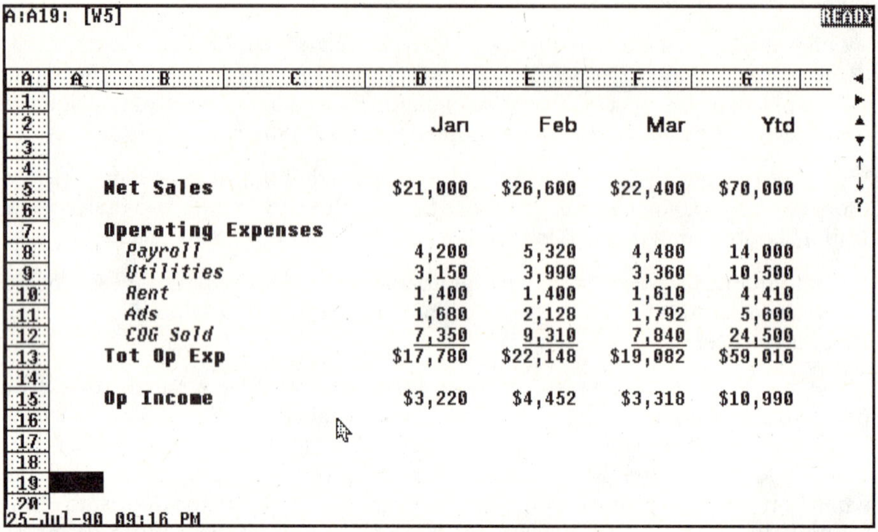

Fig. 9.8.
A worksheet formatted with boldface, italics, and single underlines.

```
A:A19: [W5]                                                          READY
     A       B                  C          D          E          F
 1
 2                             Jan        Feb        Mar        Ytd
 3
 4
 5          Net Sales        $21,000    $26,600    $22,400    $70,000
 6
 7          Operating Expenses
 8            Payroll         4,200      5,320      4,480     14,000
 9            Utilities       3,150      3,990      3,360     10,500
10            Rent            1,400      1,400      1,610      4,410
11            Ads             1,680      2,128      1,792      5,600
12            COG Sold        7,350      9,310      7,840     24,500
13          Tot Op Exp      $17,780    $22,148    $19,082    $59,010
14
15          Op Income        $3,220     $4,452     $3,318    $10,990
16
17
18
19
20
25-Jul-90 09:16 PM
```

The Underline option on the **:Format** menu offers three types of underlining: **Single**, **Double**, and **Wide**. The **Single** underline option can be used at the bottom of a column of numbers, above a total. This option underlines only the characters in the cell, not the full width of the cell. If the single underline is not long enough, use the **:Format Lines Bottom** command (see "Drawing Lines and Boxes" later in this chapter for details). You will probably use the **Single** option only when the last number in the column is the longest number. The **Double** option is ideal for double-underlining grand totals. To get a thicker line, use the **Wide** underline option. You can cancel boldface and underlining by using the **:Format Bold Clear** and **:Format Underline Clear** commands.

Reminder:
You can print up to seven different colors if your printer has the capability.

If you have a color printer, such as the HP PaintJet, you may want to enhance your printouts by using different colors. You can print up to seven different colors if your printer has the capability. To change the color of a range, select **:Format Color**. The following menu appears:

Text Background Negative Reverse Quit

The **Text** option defines the color of the characters in the range, whereas **Background** refers to the color behind the characters. You can select from the following colors:

Normal (the default color)

Red

Green

Dark-Blue

Cyan

Yellow

Magenta

Use the **Reverse** option to switch the text and background colors for a range. The **Negative** option lets you display negative values in red.

Drawing Lines and Boxes

You can make your worksheet look more professional by adding horizontal or vertical lines and creating boxes. Figure 9.9 shows how lines can enhance a worksheet.

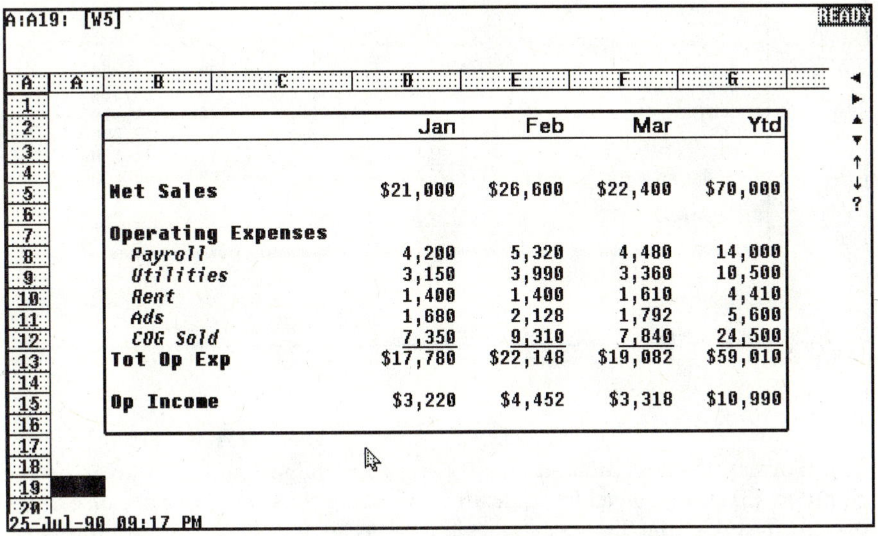

Fig. 9.9.

Lines created with the :Format Lines command.

The **:Format Lines** command enables you to place lines around any part of a cell or range, using the options **Outline**, **Left**, **Right**, **Top**, **Bottom**, and **All**. With the **Outline** option, you can draw lines around the entire range, forming a single box. The worksheet in figure 9.9 has an outline border around it. The **Left**, **Right**, **Top**, and **Bottom** options enable you to draw a line along the appropriate side of each selected cell in the range. Using the **All** option, you can draw lines around each cell in the range, boxing each cell. Choosing this option is the equivalent of choosing **Left**, **Right**, **Top**, and **Bottom** for each cell in the range.

If you choose one of these options on the Lines menu, a single, thin line is drawn in the specified range. However, Wysiwyg offers two other line styles: **Double** and **Wide**. To draw a double line, choose **:Format Lines Double** and then select the line location (Outline, Left, Right, Top, Bottom, or All). The **:Format Lines Wide** command creates a thicker line. If you need even thicker lines, you can use the **:Format Shade Solid** formatting option. (See the next section for details.)

Reminder:

Use :Format Lines Outline to draw a box around a range of cells.

Cue:
To create a drop shadow, use :Format Lines Outline and :Format Lines Shadow.

The final option on the Lines menu, Shadow, enables you to create a special three-dimensional effect called a *drop shadow*, shown in figure 9.10. There are two steps to creating a drop shadow. First, draw a box around the range, using the :Format Lines Outline command. Second, use :Format Lines Shadow on the same range. Use :Format Lines Clear to cancel your line drawing from a range.

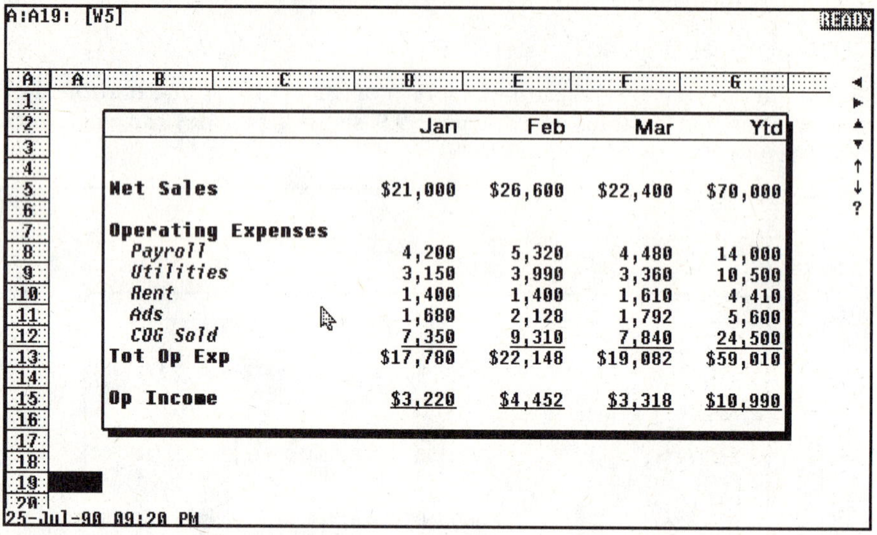

Fig. 9.10.
A box with a drop shadow.

```
A:A19: [W5]                                                    READY
     A        B          C         D        E        F        G
 1
 2                                         Jan      Feb      Mar      Ytd
 3
 4
 5            Net Sales                  $21,000  $26,600  $22,400  $70,000
 6
 7            Operating Expenses
 8               Payroll                   4,200    5,320    4,480   14,000
 9               Utilities                 3,150    3,990    3,360   10,500
10               Rent                      1,400    1,400    1,610    4,410
11               Ads                       1,680    2,128    1,792    5,600
12               COG Sold                  7,350    9,310    7,840   24,500
13            Tot Op Exp                 $17,780  $22,148  $19,082  $59,010
14
15            Op Income                   $3,220   $4,452   $3,318  $10,990
16
17
18
19
20
25-Jul-90 09:20 PM
```

Adding Shades

The :Format Shade command enables you to highlight important areas on the printed worksheet. The column headings in figure 9.11 stand out because of the background shading. Shades can be Light (as in fig. 9.11), Dark, or Solid (black). The Dark shade is not as dark as it appears on-screen—you should have no problem reading text in a dark-shaded area on a printed report. Using the Solid shade on blank cells, you can create thick horizontal and vertical lines. The thick line under the column headings in figure 9.11, for example, is the result of using the Solid shade on a narrow row. (A later section explains how to adjust row heights.) You cannot see the cell contents if you assign Solid to cells containing data. To create a border around a shaded area, use :Format Lines Outline. To remove shading, choose :Format Shade Clear.

Using Formatting Sequences

Reminder:
Formatting sequences enable you to boldface or italicize a single word in a cell.

The options on the :Format menu let you format cells and ranges. To format individual characters within a cell, you can use *formatting sequences*. With formatting sequences, you can bold or italicize a single word in a cell, for example. Formatting sequences are codes you enter as you are typing or editing text in the control panel. The codes appear in the control panel, but when you press Enter, they are replaced with the actual formatting.

Chapter 9 ◆ Using Wysiwyg To Enhance and Print Reports   379

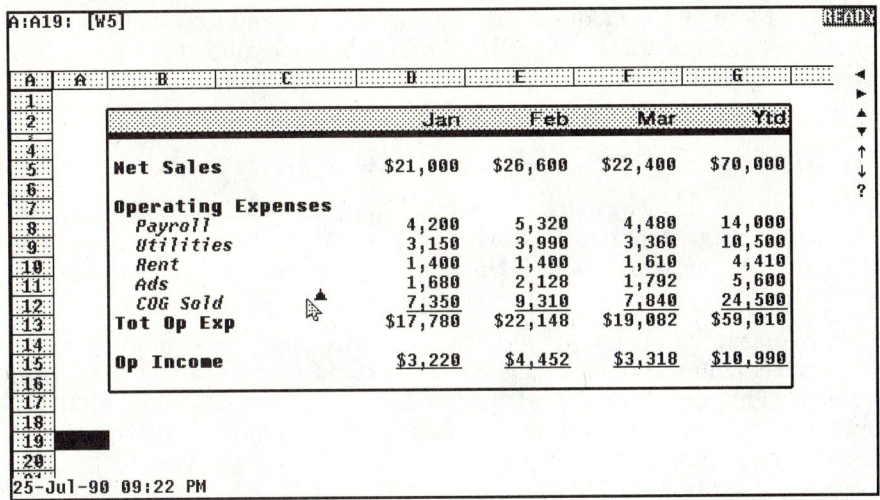

Fig. 9.11.

Headings emphasized with light and solid shades.

The code to insert when you begin entering a formatting sequence is Ctrl-A (for *attribute*). The symbol appears. You then type the one-character or two-character code for the attribute. Table 9.3 lists these codes. Be sure to type the exact uppercase or lowercase characters listed in the table. To end the formatting sequence, press Ctrl-N.

Table 9.3
Attribute Codes

Code	Description	Code	Description	Code	Description
b	Bold	1c	Default color	1F	Font 1
i	Italics	2c	Red	2F	Font 2
u	Superscript	3c	Green	3F	Font 3
d	Subscript	4c	Dark-Blue	4F	Font 4
o	Outline	5c	Cyan	5F	Font 5
x	Flip x-axis	6c	Yellow	6F	Font 6
y	Flip y-axis	7c	Magenta	7F	Font 7
8c	Reverse colors			8F	Font 8
1_	Single underline				
2_	Double underline				
3_	Wide underline				
4_	Box around characters				

To specify multiple attributes, press Ctrl-A and the first attribute code, followed by Ctrl-A and the second code, and so on. For example, to boldface and italicize a word, press Ctrl-A and type **b**, and press Ctrl-A and type **i**. At the end of the word, press Ctrl-N to cancel all formatting sequences. If you want to cancel just one of the attributes, press Ctrl-E followed by the attribute code you want to discontinue (for example, **i** for italic).

Adjusting Column Widths and Row Heights

When you start changing fonts, you may discover a need to adjust column widths. If you use a larger font size, the labels may truncate, and the values may display asterisks. The menus in both 1-2-3 and Wysiwyg offer options for adjusting column widths; you can use either menu.

The **:W**orksheet **C**olumn **S**et-Width command is the exact equivalent of the **/W**orksheet **C**olumn **C**olumn-Range **S**et-Width command. Before you indicate the column width, you are prompted to select the range of columns whose width you want to change. As in 1-2-3, you can adjust the column width in Wysiwyg by using the left and right arrows to change the width one character at a time.

Wysiwyg does not offer a way to change column widths globally; to do that you must use 1-2-3's **/W**orksheet **G**lobal **C**ol-Width command. Wysiwyg does, however, provide an option for returning a range of columns to the global column width: the **:W**orksheet **C**olumn **R**eset-Width command.

Wysiwyg offers yet another way to adjust column widths: with the mouse. Place the mouse pointer on the vertical line to the right of the column letter and then press and hold down the left mouse button. As shown in figure 9.12, the mouse pointer turns into a cross with left- and right-pointing arrows, and vertical dotted lines define the column width. Keeping the mouse button pressed down, move the mouse pointer to the left or right until the column is the proper width. Then release the mouse button.

Fig. 9.12.
Adjusting a column width with the mouse.

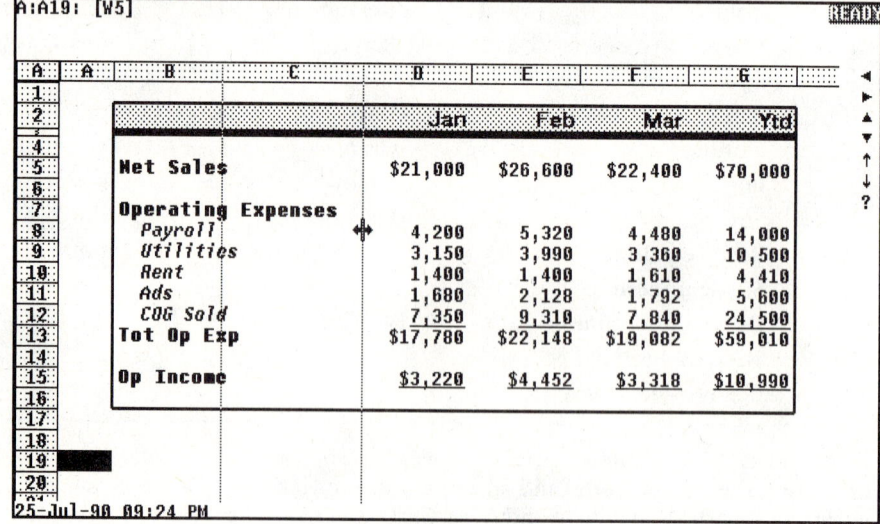

Chapter 9 ◆ Using Wysiwyg To Enhance and Print Reports

You can adjust only one column at a time with the mouse. Also, the mouse technique works only if the worksheet frame is displayed with the Enhanced or Relief option. (The worksheet frame display is changed with the :Display Options Frame command.)

By default, the height of the rows in Wysiwyg automatically adjusts to accommodate the largest font in the row. The row height is approximately 20 percent greater than the font size. For example, if the font size is 10 points, the row height is 12 points. The :Worksheet Row Set-Height command enables you to set the height of a single row or a range of rows. This command essentially "freezes" the row to the height you specify. The row height remains frozen until you change it again or until you return the row-height setting to automatic with :Worksheet Row Auto.

Reminder:
Wysiwyg row height automatically adjusts to accommodate the largest font in the row.

To enter a row height, either type the new point size when prompted or press the up- and down-arrows to adjust the height of the row one point size at a time. (When specifying the number of points for the row height, remember that one inch equals 72 points.) The current row height is displayed when you select :Worksheet Row Set-Height.

Reminder:
One inch equals 72 points.

Another way to adjust row heights is with the mouse. Place the mouse pointer on the horizontal line underneath the row number and then press and hold down the left mouse button. The mouse pointer turns into a cross with up- and down-pointing arrows, and horizontal dotted lines define the row height. Keeping the mouse button pressed down, move the mouse pointer up or down until the row is the proper height. Then release the mouse button.

Managing Your Formats

Because formatting is really the heart of Wysiwyg, the program offers several commands for dealing with the formats assigned to your cells. You can copy and move formats—not the cell contents, but the formats associated with the cell. You can assign a name to the set of formatting instructions in a cell and then apply this format to any range. And you can save *all* the formats associated with the file and apply them to another file.

Copying and Moving Formats

If one cell or range should be formatted the same way as another cell or range, you can use the :Special Copy command to copy the formatting instructions. For example, if you have formatted a range to 14-point Swiss, in boldface with shading and an outline, you save a lot of time by copying the format to another range rather than using four separate :Format commands. The command copies formats only, not cell contents. 1-2-3's /Copy command copies cell contents *and* formats (assuming that Wysiwyg is attached). The formatting that can be copied with :Special Copy includes the font, boldface, italics, underline, shading, color, and lines. You should find that Wysiwyg's :Special Copy command saves you time in formatting.

Cue:
Use :Special Copy to format ranges quickly in your worksheet.

When you invoke Wysiwyg's :Special Copy command, you are asked to enter the range to copy attributes from (the cell or cells containing the formatting) and the range to copy the attributes to (the target cell or cells). You can copy formats between any active worksheet or file. To copy a format from one file to another, use the /File Open command to retrieve each file before invoking :Special Copy. Use cursor-movement keys or mouse icons to indicate ranges in other files.

The :Special Move command also copies formats from the source range to the target range, but at the same time resets all source-range formats to the defaults. The source range is set to font 1, and all special formatting (boldface, italics, underline, shading, lines, and colors) is cleared. Like :Special Copy, this command does not affect the cell contents of either the source or the target range.

Because the command resets your source-range formats, use it with care. In some cases, using :Special Copy and resetting source-range formats as necessary with :Format may be safer.

Like :Special Move, 1-2-3's /Move command reverts the source range to the default format settings. However, /Move moves the cell contents in addition to the format.

Using Named Styles

Reminder:
Create named styles for the formats you use frequently.

Another way to apply a format from one cell to another is by creating and using named styles. You may want to create named styles for the formats you use frequently. Suppose, for example, that your worksheet contains 10 subheadings, and you want all of them to be in 14-point Swiss bold with a heavy shade. To ease the formatting process and to ensure consistency, you can name this particular formatting style SUB and then apply this style to all the subheadings.

Another advantage to using named styles is that you can make format changes rapidly. If you decide that you want your subheadings to have a light instead of a heavy shade, you need only change the format of one cell.

Here's how the task is done. To define a style, format a cell so that it has the attributes you want and then choose :Named-Style Define. As the menu indicates, up to eight different styles can be defined per file. At first, all eight styles have the name `Normal`. As you define styles, the names you specify (instead of `Normal`) appear next to the number. Choose any number.

The definition process entails specifying the cell that contains the formats, assigning a six-character name, and giving a brief description of the style. Once the style is defined, the style name appears in the :Named-Style menu.

To apply a format style to a cell or range, choose :Named-Style and then select the desired style from the menu of eight style names. Indicate the range by typing the cell coordinates or a range name, or by using the arrow keys or mouse in POINT mode. When a cell has been formatted with a named style, the style name appears inside the format braces. For example, if you created the style SUB, discussed earlier, the formatting instructions would be `{SUB: SWISS14 Bold S2}`. *SWISS14 Bold S2* is the format code associated with the style (14-point Swiss bold with a dark shade).

One reason to use named styles is that they make global formatting changes easy. Changing the format of an existing style requires two simple steps. First, go to any cell formatted with the style you want to change and modify the format. At this point, the cell is no longer associated with the named style. But that's no problem—you just need to redefine the style. Thus the second step is to use the **:Named-Style Define** command and assign the same style number and name to the cell. Change the description if necessary. Now all cells with that style name automatically reflect the format change.

As mentioned in the preceding paragraph, when you change the format of a cell that was formatted with a named style, the cell is no longer associated with the style name.

Importing Formats

Wysiwyg offers the **:Special Import** command to apply the formats contained in another format file on disk to the current worksheet. You can import the following types of formatting: the font set, graphs, named styles, or all formatting.

:Special Import is similar to 1-2-3's **/File Combine Copy**, but the Wysiwyg command imports only formatting and printing instructions, not the data. If a series of files have identical structures (for instance, a series of budget worksheets), you can eliminate the need to format each worksheet: just import all the formatting. Or if you want to use a set of fonts or named styles contained in another file, you can restrict your copying to just these settings.

To import formats from another file, select **:Special Import** and choose one of the following:

Option	Description
All	Copies individual cell formats, the font set, named styles, graphs, print range, orientation, bin, settings, and layout
Named-Styles	Replaces the styles in the current file with the styles in the specified format file
Fonts	Replaces the font set in the current file with the font set in the specified format file (similar to **:Format Font Library Retrieve**)
Graphs	Places graphs in the same location and with the same enhancements as in the specified format file

You are prompted to enter the name of the format file from which you want to import. You are allowed to import from Wysiwyg, Impress, or Allways format files. Wysiwyg automatically displays a list of files that have the FM* extension (either Wysiwyg FM3 files or Impress FMT files). You can import from an Allways file by including the ALL extension when you type the file name.

The **:Special Import All** command completely strips all formatting from the current worksheet and replaces the formats with imported ones. The imported

Reminder:
Using named styles makes global formatting changes easier.

Caution:
When you use :Special Import All, your current worksheet must be organized identically to the worksheet from which you are importing formats.

formats appear in the same locations in the current worksheet as they appear in the imported worksheet. If the two worksheets are not organized identically, formats may appear in unexpected cells. You may be able to fix minor problems by using :Special Move to move imported cell formats that do not match up exactly with the current file.

If you don't like the results of importing the formats from another file, you can undo the formats by pressing Alt-F4 and selecting Yes (if Undo is enabled).

Exporting Formats

When you use the /File Save command with Wysiwyg attached, two files are stored: the 1-2-3 worksheet file (WK3 extension) and the Wysiwyg format file (FM3 extension). If you want to save the format file only, use the :Special Export option. This command creates a file on disk that contains the current file's formatting, graphing, and printing instructions. The exported file can be a Wysiwyg FM3 file, an Impress FMT file, or an Allways ALL file. The file contains individual cell formats; the current font set; named styles; graph placement and enhancements (but not the actual graphs); and the print range, settings, orientation, and layout.

Reminder:
If the file contains formatting commands unavailable in Allways, these formats will not be saved in the ALL file.

One possible use of the :Special Export command is to create a format file that can be used in Impress or Allways. Be aware that if the file contains formatting commands unavailable in Allways, these particular formats will not be saved in the ALL file. For example, Allways does not have double or wide lines, so these formats are not stored in the ALL file.

Printing with Wysiwyg

The following sections examine each of the options available with the Wysiwyg :Print command. The :Print menu displays a full-screen settings sheet as shown in figure 9.13. With a quick glance, you can immediately see your current print settings. This feature is not offered on the 1-2-3 /Print menu. Notice that each corner of the settings sheet contains a different category of print information. The upper left corner displays the page layout, the margins are in the upper right corner, the print settings are in the lower right corner, and the configuration is in the lower left side of the screen. Because your worksheet is hidden when the settings sheet is displayed, the Info command on the :Print menu lets you temporarily hide the settings sheet. Choose Info again to redisplay the settings sheet. You also can use the F6 key to toggle the settings sheet on and off.

In the following sections, you learn how to configure your printer, specify a print range, preview the report on the screen, lay out a page, set page breaks, specify print settings, and print to an encoded file.

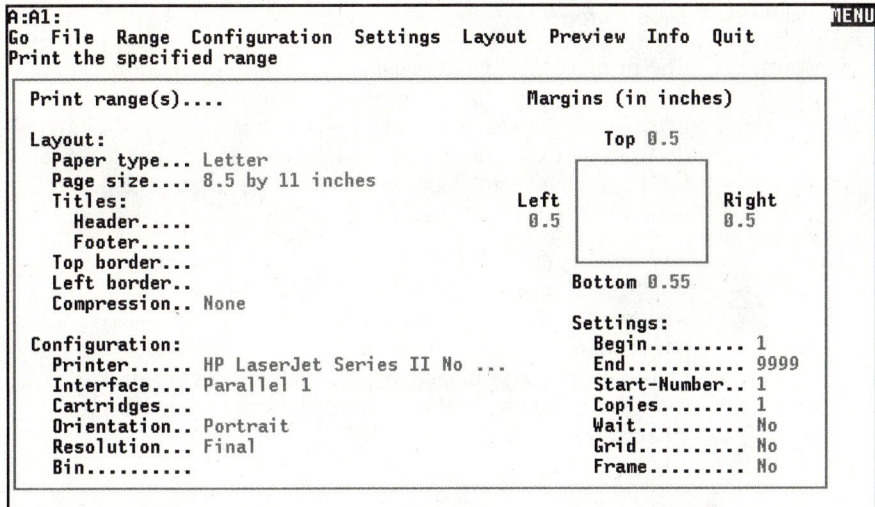

Fig. 9.13.
Wysiwyg's print settings sheet.

Configuring Your Printer

Before you print, select **:P**rint **C**onfiguration and check the settings sheet to make sure that Wysiwyg is set up to work with your printer. Figure 9.13 displays the configuration for an HP LaserJet Series II printer.

Not all the options on the **:P**rint **C**onfiguration menu apply to all printers. For example, an Epson RX-80 does not have cartridges or bins, nor can it print with the landscape orientation.

Following is a description of the **:P**rint **C**onfiguration options:

Option	Description
Printer	The printer to be used. When multiple printers have been selected in the Install program, you can use the **P**rinter option to specify which printer you want to use.
Interface	The printer port to which your printer is attached (Parallel 1, Serial 1, Parallel 2, Serial 2, or one of the following output devices: LPT1, LPT2, LPT3, COM1, or COM2).
1st-Cart	Your primary printer cartridge. Some printers have separate cartridges or cards you can buy to get additional fonts for your printer. The HP LaserJet, for example, offers a "B" cartridge that includes 14-point Helvetica and 8-point and 10-point Times Roman.
2nd-Cart	Your secondary cartridge.
Orientation	The orientation of the page to be printed: **P**ortrait (vertical) or **L**andscape (horizontal). This setting is saved in the current worksheet's format file.

Option	Description
Resolution	The print quality: **Final** or **Draft**. The **Draft** resolution prints faster but with poorer quality. Not all printers have two print qualities. The HP LaserJet, for example, does not have draft mode except when printing graphs. If you select **Draft** for a worksheet range and either nothing or garbage prints, your printer does not have draft mode.
Bin	The feeding method, if your printer offers more than one way to feed paper. Your printer may provide multiple paper trays and a way to feed paper manually. If you want to feed paper manually, select **Manual**. (If you feed paper manually, you also may want to choose **:Print Settings Wait** to pause between pages.) This setting is saved in the current worksheet's format file.

Specifying a Print Range

Reminder:
Print ranges entered in 1-2-3 are not transferred to Wysiwyg.

Wysiwyg's **:Print Range Set** command is the equivalent of 1-2-3's **/Print Printer Range** command. If you enter a print range in 1-2-3, however, it is not transferred to Wysiwyg. You must set the print range in Wysiwyg before you print.

To specify a Wysiwyg print range, select **:Print Range Set** and indicate the range just as you do in 1-2-3: highlight the range with the cursor-movement keys or the mouse, type the range, or use a 1-2-3 range name. If you want to use a range name, type the range name or press F3 to choose from a list of names when prompted for the print range. The print range can include ranges in other worksheets in the same file but not ranges in other open files. Use worksheet-movement keys (for example, Ctrl-PgUp to go to the next worksheet) to display other worksheets when you are selecting a range. Mouse users can press the up-arrow and down-arrow icons to view other worksheets.

Reminder:
To print multiple ranges, separate each range with a comma or semicolon.

To print multiple ranges, separate each range with a comma or semicolon. For example, to print the two noncontiguous ranges A:A1..A:D15 and A:S20..A:Y50, specify the print range **A:A1..A:D15;A:S20..A:Y50** or **A:A1..A:D15,A:S20..A:Y50**. If you want blank space between each print range, be sure to include blank rows at the top or bottom of the ranges. To print each range on a separate page, include a page break at the bottom of each range (except for the last one). Refer to "Inserting Page Breaks" later in this chapter for more details on using page breaks.

After you define the print range, dashed borders appear around the area. To see these lines, either select **Quit** from the **:Print** menu or choose **Info** to display the worksheet. If the print area is large, dashed lines appear around each page. To change where the pages break, you can insert your own breaks. If you have defined multiple print ranges, each range is enclosed in the dashed borders (see fig. 9.14). Notice that the outer edges of the print ranges have larger dashes than the inner edges. The smaller dashes indicate that the print range continues and is not the beginning or end of a page.

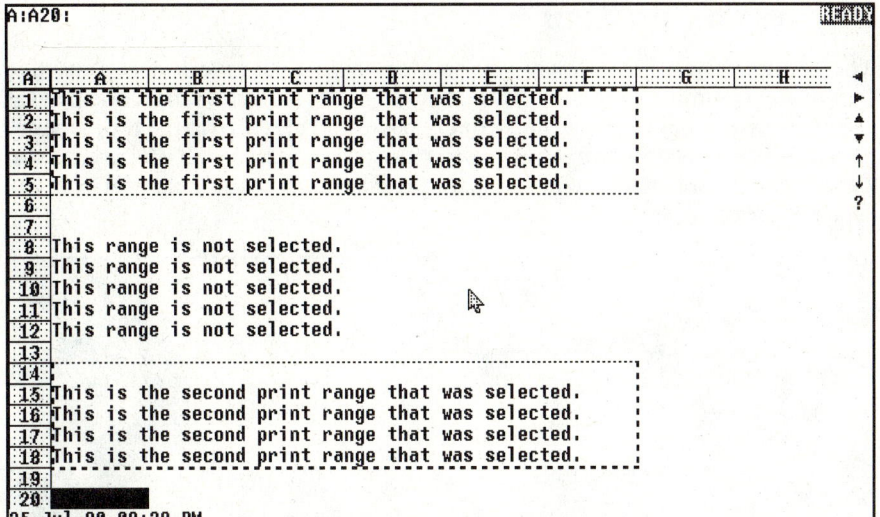

Fig. 9.14.
Multiple print ranges selected.

If you want to print a Wysiwyg graph, you must first define its range with **:G**raph **A**dd, as explained in Chapter 11. Be sure to include the entire graph range in the print range.

You also can select the range to print before choosing **:P**rint **R**ange. To preselect the range, place the cell pointer in the top left cell in the range, press F4, and extend the highlight to the lower right corner of the desired range. Using the mouse, hold down the Ctrl key while you click-and-drag. Then, when you use **:P**rint **R**ange **S**et, Wysiwyg automatically highlights the selected range; press Enter to accept it.

To print the range, assuming that the print configuration is defined properly, select **G**o from the **:P**rint menu. If the selected range exceeds both the width and length of the page, Wysiwyg (like 1-2-3) prints the left part of the range from top to bottom and then prints the right parts of the range from top to bottom until the entire range is printed. The dashed lines on the screen let you know where the page breaks occur.

Laser printers have varying amounts of memory. Your laser printer may not have enough memory to accept downloaded fonts with large point sizes, or several different fonts on a page. If you get an `Out of memory` message when you print, specify smaller font sizes, make fewer font selections, or use an internal or cartridge font.

Like 1-2-3, Wysiwyg prints in the background, allowing you to continue working while the document is printing. The indicator PRT appears at the bottom of the screen to let you know that printing is in progress. You can continue working on the same file, open or retrieve other files, or print additional ranges. To stop a report from printing, use 1-2-3's /**P**rint **C**ancel command. This command cancels all print jobs.

Reminder:
Your laser printer may not have enough memory to print graphics at a high resolution or accept downloaded fonts with large point sizes.

Previewing on Your Screen

Cue:
Preview your report on-screen before printing.

The **:Print Preview** option gives you an idea of what your worksheet looks like before you commit it to paper. This option displays your print range, one page at a time; press any key to display subsequent pages and to return to the **:Print** menu. Although you probably won't be able to read every character on the screen, you can see your overall page layout and page breaks. Figure 9.15 displays an example of a previewed page.

Fig. 9.15.
A previewed page.

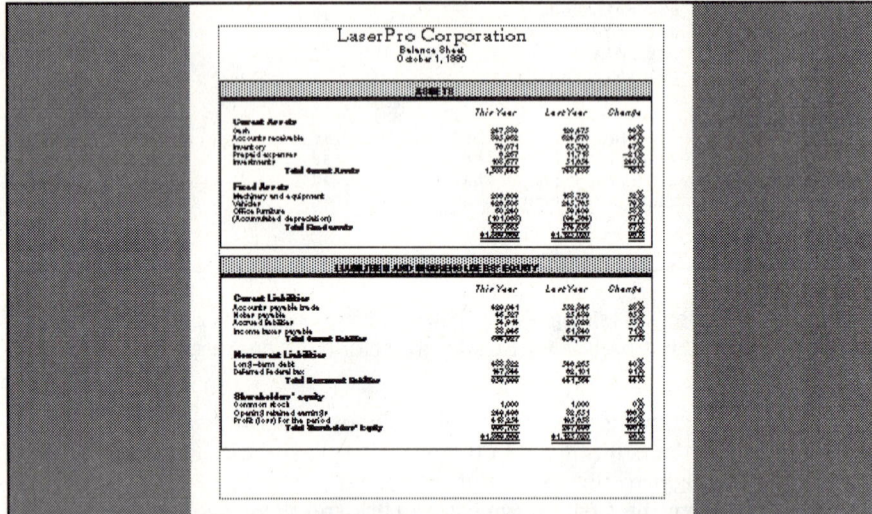

Inserting Page Breaks

After you choose a print range, you see dashed lines around each page. If you don't like where the page breaks are, use **:Worksheet Page** to set new page breaks before you print. You can specify the row or column on which you want Wysiwyg to start a new page.

To set a horizontal page break, select **:Worksheet Page Row**. Position the pointer on the first row of the new page and press Enter. As shown in figure 9.16, a dashed line appears above the specified row to indicate the new page break.

1-2-3 also offers an option for inserting horizontal page breaks: **/Worksheet Page**. Feel free to use either 1-2-3's or Wysiwyg's page-break option; both types of breaks are honored when you print in Wysiwyg.

To tell Wysiwyg at which column to start a new page, choose **:Worksheet Page Column**. Position the cell pointer on the first column of the new page and press Enter. A dashed line appears to the left of the specified column to indicate the new page break.

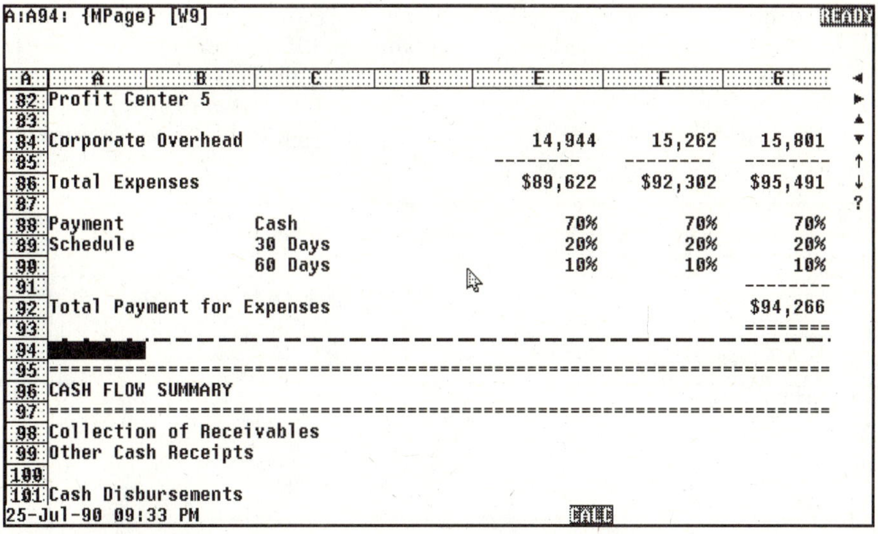

Fig. 9.16.
A worksheet with a page break added at row 94.

To remove a page break you inserted in Wysiwyg, place the cell pointer on the first row or column of the page and select **:W**orksheet **P**age **D**elete. The dashed page-break line immediately disappears.

Setting Up the Page

Use the **:P**rint **L**ayout command to fine-tune the page layout. Figure 9.17 shows the **:P**rint **L**ayout menu and the print settings sheet. All the **L**ayout settings are located in the top half of the screen. Notice that many of the options are similar to those offered in 1-2-3's /**P**rint **P**rinter **O**ptions menu. However, the headers, footers, margins, and borders you enter in 1-2-3 do not transfer into Wysiwyg. If you defined headers and footers in 1-2-3, you must use the Wysiwyg **:P**rint **L**ayout command to set them up again. The following sections explain how to use the various options on the **L**ayout menu.

Reminder:
Any headers, footers, margins, and borders specified in 1-2-3 must be respecified in Wysiwyg.

Defining the Page Layout

The default page size is standard letter size (8 1/2 inches by 11 inches). Using **:P**rint **L**ayout **P**age-**S**ize, you can choose from several different sizes. If your paper size does not fall in any of the predefined dimensions, you can choose **C**ustom. The **C**ustom option lets you define the page width and page length as any size you need. You can enter the size in either inches or millimeters. The current unit of measurement appears in the top right corner of the **L**ayout screen. To change to a different unit of measurement, follow the number by **mm** (millimeters) or **in** (inches).

Wysiwyg's **M**argins option is similar to 1-2-3's, with several important differences. In 1-2-3, the right and left margins are entered in terms of characters, and the top and bottom margins are entered in terms of lines. In Wysiwyg, all margins are entered in inches, millimeters, or centimeters. (If you enter a number in centimeters [for example, 1cm], Wysiwyg automatically converts the number to millimeters [10mm].) In 1-2-3, the right margin is the number of characters from the left edge of the page. In Wysiwyg, the right margin is the space between the printed worksheet and the right edge of the page.

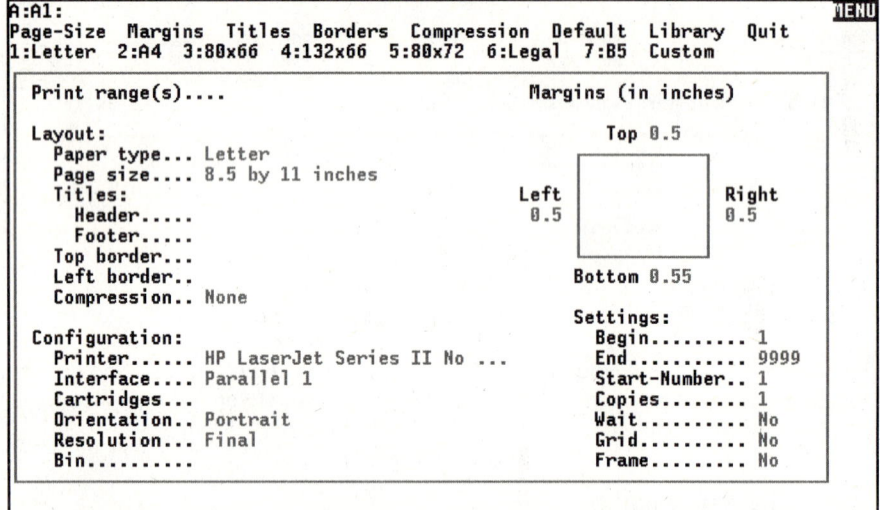

Fig. 9.17.

The :Print Layout menu and settings sheet.

Remember, page orientation (landscape and portrait) is on the **:Print** Configuration menu. (You might expect page orientation to be on the Layout menu, but it is not.)

Printing Titles and Borders

Wysiwyg's **:Print** Layout Titles command is the equivalent of 1-2-3's **/Print** Printer Options Header and Footer commands. A header is a one-line title at the top of every page; a footer is a line that prints at the bottom of each page. You do not see these titles on-screen with Wysiwyg unless you preview the range with **:Print** Preview.

As with 1-2-3, in Wysiwyg you can include special characters in a header or footer. Including the @ symbol prints the current day's date in that position; including the # symbol prints the page number. Including vertical bar characters (|) separates the text into left-justified, centered, and right-justified sections.

If you type a header as @|**Projection**|**Page #**, the printed header appears as in figure 9.18.

In your Wysiwyg headers and footers, you can enter formatting sequences to assign an attribute to all or part of the text. See "Using Formatting Sequences" earlier in the chapter for details.

```
          07/25/90                    Projection                    Page 1


          ==========================================================
          CASH FLOW PROJECTOR          Copyright (C) 1990 Que Corporation
          ==========================================================
          BALANCES IN WORKING CAPITAL ACCOUNTS               Dec
          ==========================================================
          Assets
           Cash                                          $17,355
           Accounts Receivable                           493,151
           Inventory                                     163,833

          Liabilities
           Accounts Payable                              125,000
           Line of Credit                                      0
                                                        --------
          Net Working Capital                           $549,339
                                                        ========



          ==========================================================
          SALES                           Oct      Nov      Dec
          ==========================================================
          Profit Center 1              $27,832  $23,864  $26,125
          Profit Center 2               13,489   21,444   20,140
          Profit Center 3              126,811  124,382  123,618
          Profit Center 4               94,285   92,447   89,010
          Profit Center 5
                                       -------  -------  -------
          Total Sales                 $262,417 $262,137 $258,893
                                       =======  =======  =======

                           Cash           10%      10%      10%
          Percent of       30 Days        20%      20%      20%
          Collections      60 Days        50%      50%      50%
                           90 Days        20%      20%      20%

          Cash Collections
```

Fig. 9.18.
A printed worksheet with a header.

Wysiwyg reserves three lines on the printout for each header and footer. Remember to figure in these extra lines when you calculate how many lines of text fit on a printed page. Unlike 1-2-3, Wysiwyg does not reserve lines for titles if you don't have any titles. To cancel headers or footers, use the **:Print Layout Titles Clear** command.

The **Layout** menu's **Borders** option is the same as 1-2-3's **/Print Printer Options Borders** command. This command specifies a worksheet range (rows or columns) to be printed on every page of a multipage printout. Suppose that the balance sheet shown in figure 9.2 included columns for five years instead of two. You would need several pages to print the report, with the leftmost column as the first column on each page so that you know what each row of data signifies. Using the **Borders** option, you can specify the columns to print at the left side of each page when the worksheet is wide. You can also specify the rows to print at the top of each page if the worksheet is long.

To repeat a column or row of text on other pages of the report, follow these steps:

1. Use the Wysiwyg **:Print Range Set** command to specify a range that includes the entire report except for the border columns and rows.

Reminder:
When you calculate how many lines of text fit on a printed page, remember to figure in three lines for each header and footer.

2. Select :**P**rint **L**ayout **B**orders **L**eft and highlight any cell in the border column and/or select **B**orders **T**op and highlight any cell in the border row. If the border has multiple rows or columns, press the period (.) key to anchor the highlight and extend the highlight over the additional rows or columns (or highlight them with the mouse). Press Enter.

3. Print the report, using :**P**rint **G**o.

The border columns and rows should print on each page. Make sure that the border range is not included in the print range, or the border range is printed twice. To cancel borders, use the :**P**rint **L**ayout **B**orders **C**lear command.

Compressing the Print

Cue:
Use the :Print Layout Compression option to fit a large worksheet on one page.

The **C**ompression option on the **L**ayout menu offers an ideal way to fit a large worksheet on one page. Rather than guess at the font size needed to print a report on a single page, you can use the :**P**rint **L**ayout **C**ompression **A**utomatic command. Wysiwyg will then determine how much the font size needs to be reduced. Wysiwyg calculated that the worksheet in figure 9.19 needed to be reduced 38 percent. A worksheet cannot be reduced to less than 15 percent of its original size. (And 15 percent is so tiny that it's barely legible.) If your print range is too large for the maximum-allowed reduction, the worksheet will print on multiple pages.

Compressed type does not look any different on the screen, although the dashed lines around the print range accurately reflect the page breaks. Any manual page breaks that you have entered with :**W**orksheet **P**age or /**W**orksheet **P**age are still in effect. If you don't want these page breaks in the compressed printout, delete them before printing. To get an idea of what the page looks like with the compressed print, use the :**P**rint **P**review command.

The **C**ompression command also offers a **M**anual option, by which you can enter your own reduction or enlargement percentage. To reduce the type, enter a number greater than or equal to 15 but less than 100. To spread the type across and down the page, enter a number greater than 100.

To remove the automatic or manual compression factors you have entered, use the :**P**rint **L**ayout **C**ompression **N**one command.

Saving Layout Settings

Cue:
Use :Print Layout Default to change the layout settings permanently.

The :**P**rint **L**ayout **D**efault and **L**ayout **L**ibrary commands enable you to modify all the layout settings at once. To return all the layout settings to the default values, choose :**P**rint **L**ayout **D**efault **R**estore. To change the default settings permanently to those currently displayed, use :**P**rint **L**ayout **D**efault **U**pdate. Use the latter command if you find yourself constantly changing the layout settings to the same values. That way any new worksheets you create in the future will automatically have the layout values you normally use.

Chapter 9 ◆ Using Wysiwyg To Enhance and Print Reports

Use **:Print Layout Library** to save a disk file of your layout settings. If you need certain combinations of layout settings for different types of worksheets, you can save each group of settings and then retrieve them to use later with any worksheet.

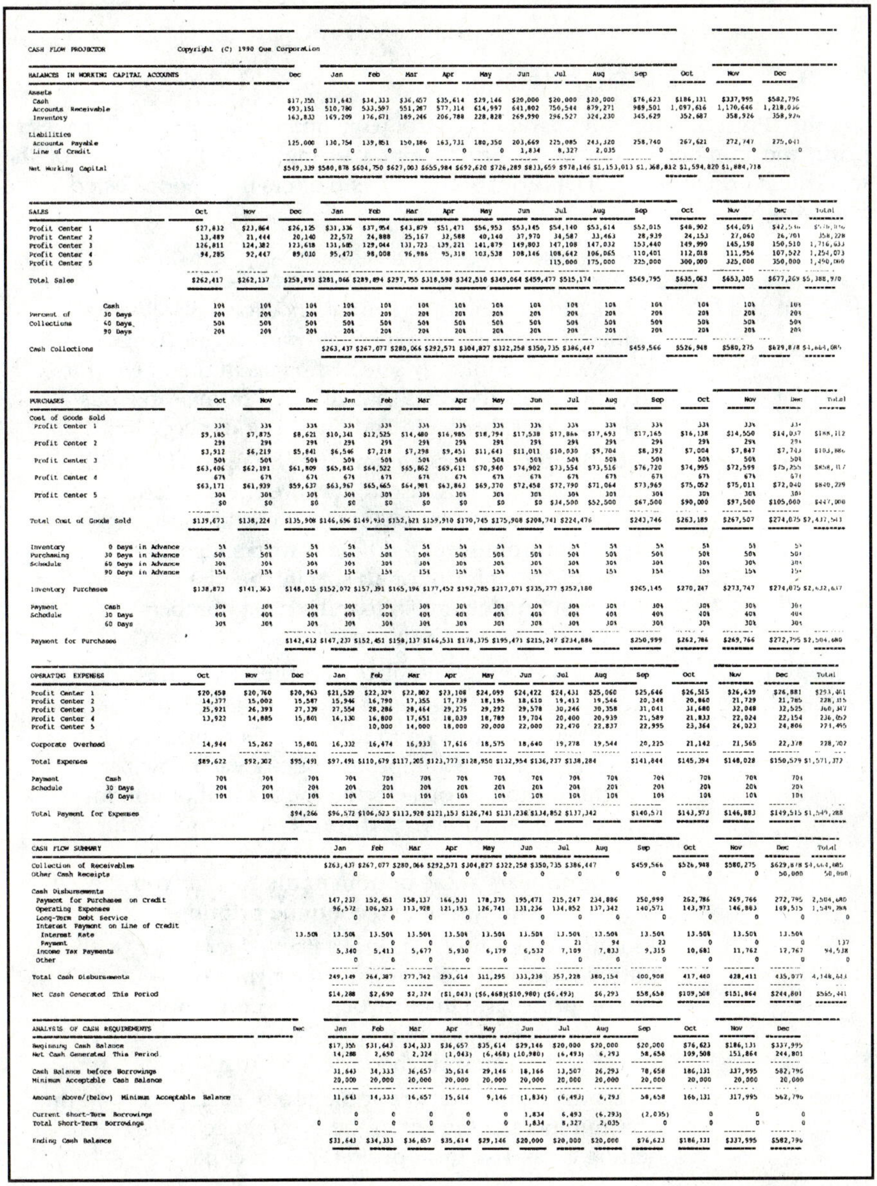

Fig. 9.19.
Automatic compression.

To save the current page-layout settings in a library, use **:Print Layout Library Save** and specify a file name. The file is given the extension AL3. When you want to use the settings with another worksheet, use **:Print Layout Library Retrieve**. If you no longer need a library file, delete it by using **:Print Layout Library Erase**.

Specifying Print Settings

Use the **:Print Settings** command to control page numbering, ranges of pages to print, the number of copies to print, print pausing, and the printing of the worksheet grid or frame. The **:Print Settings** menu offers the options listed in the following chart.

Option	Description
Begin and End	Prints the specified page numbers. Normally, Wysiwyg prints the entire range specified with **:Print Range Set**. If you want to print only selected pages in the range (for instance, only the ones that changed from a previous printing), set the **Begin** and **End** options accordingly.
Start-Number	Specifies the first page number to be printed in a title. The page number is inserted where the # symbol appears in the header or footer. If you are printing your document from several different worksheets, for example, use this option to specify the first page number of each subdocument so that the page numbers are continuous. The default setting is 1.
Copies	Prints the specified number of copies.
Wait	Pauses the printer between pages. The default setting is **No**. If you want to feed individual sheets into the printer, select **Yes** to pause the printer before each new page. Use this option if you selected the **Manual** option for **:Print Configuration Bin**. If you set **Wait** to **Yes**, the message `Insert next sheet of paper and select Resume` appears at the bottom of the screen. You should then use **/Print Resume** to continue printing.
Grid	Produces a printout that looks like ledger paper, with dotted lines enclosing every cell on your printout. This option prints grid lines through the entire printout. If you want to enclose only part of your printout in a grid, use **:Format Lines All** and specify a range.
Frame	Prints the column letters at the top of each page, and the row numbers to the left of the print range if the **Frame** setting is on. Use this option for draft copies.
Reset	Restores the Wysiwyg default print settings for the document.
Quit	Leaves the **:Print Settings** menu.

Cue:
*To create a printout that looks like ledger paper, use the **G**rid print setting.*

Printing to a File

Create an encoded file if you want to print the worksheet on a remote printer and if the computer connected to this printer doesn't have 1-2-3 and Wysiwyg. The print file you create contains all the necessary data and formatting instructions so that it can be printed from DOS. Before you print to a file, make sure that the following conditions are met:

- The final destination printer is selected under :Print Configuration Printer.
- The fonts you have chosen for your worksheet are available on the final destination printer.
- The print range is selected.

To create the encoded file, choose :Print File. You are prompted for a file name; Wysiwyg supplies the default extension ENC (for encoded) if you don't specify an extension.

When you're ready to print the file, issue the following DOS command:

COPY *filename*/B *device*

The argument *filename* is the full name of your file (for example, ASSET.ENC), and *device* is the name of the DOS port or logical device to which your printer is connected. Parallel port 1, for instance, has the device name LPT1:. Be sure to include the /B switch, or DOS may interpret certain binary codes in the file as end-of-file markers and terminate the printout prematurely. The DOS command to print ASSET.ENC to a printer connected to the first parallel port is as follows:

COPY ASSET.ENC/B LPT1:

Reminder:
Be sure to include the /B switch, or DOS may interpret certain binary codes as end-of-file markers and prematurely end the printout.

Setting Display Characteristics

With Wysiwyg, you can change many of the characteristics of the screen. Among other things, you can set the screen colors, display the worksheet in graphics mode ("what you see is what you get") or in text mode (like the default display in 1-2-3), display grid lines between worksheet columns and rows, change the brightness of the screen, and specify a cell pointer style.

In addition, you can change the size of the characters on the screen. You can reduce the characters so that you can see more of the worksheet at once or magnify them to see small fonts more clearly. The :Display commands do not affect the report printout; they simply change how the worksheet looks on-screen. When you select :Display, this menu of options appears:

Mode Zoom Colors Options Font-Directory Rows Default Quit

The following sections describe each of these options.

Mode

Reminder:
You must have a graphics monitor to use graphics mode.

Choose between the **Graphics** and **Text** options and between **B&W** (black and white, or monochrome) and **Color**. In graphics mode, formatting shows on-screen close to how it prints. You must have a graphics monitor to use graphics mode. You cannot see formatting on-screen in text mode, although the control panel displays the formatting instructions for the current cell.

Even if you have a color monitor, you may want to use **B&W** mode occasionally to see how the worksheet will look printed on a black-and-white printer.

Zoom

Choose from **Tiny**, **Small**, **Normal**, **Large**, and **Huge** character display. Figure 9.20 shows **Tiny** magnification; figure 9.21 shows **Large**. The zoom feature does not work in text mode.

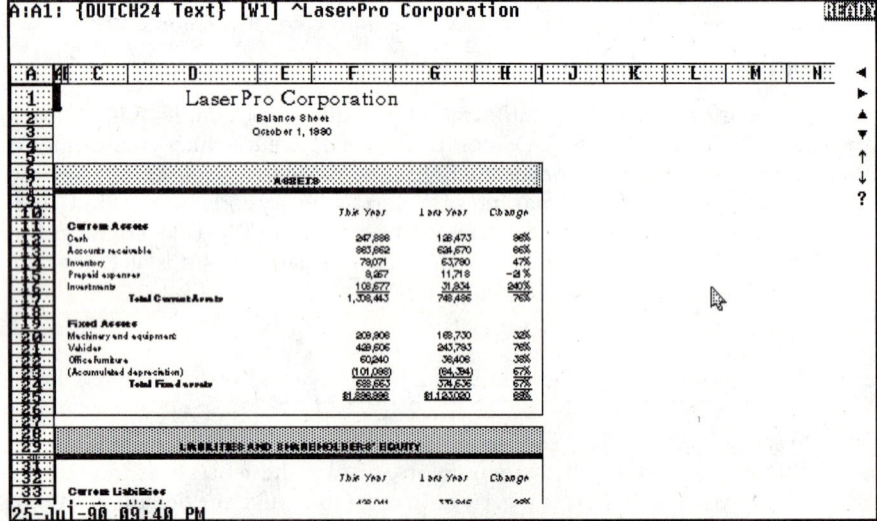

Fig. 9.20.
A worksheet zoomed to the Tiny magnification size.

Colors

This option enables you to select the colors for different parts of the screen: background, text (the characters), unprotected cells, cell pointer, grid lines, worksheet frame, negative numbers, lines, and drop shadows. Wysiwyg can use the following eight colors: black, white, red, green, dark blue, cyan, yellow, and magenta. On a monochrome monitor, you can switch the background from white to black if you prefer a dark background on your screen.

Reminder:
The screen colors you select do not affect the printed report.

For the most part, the screen colors you select do not affect the printed report. If you have a color printer, though, the negative values, lines, and drop shadows will print in the color you specified.

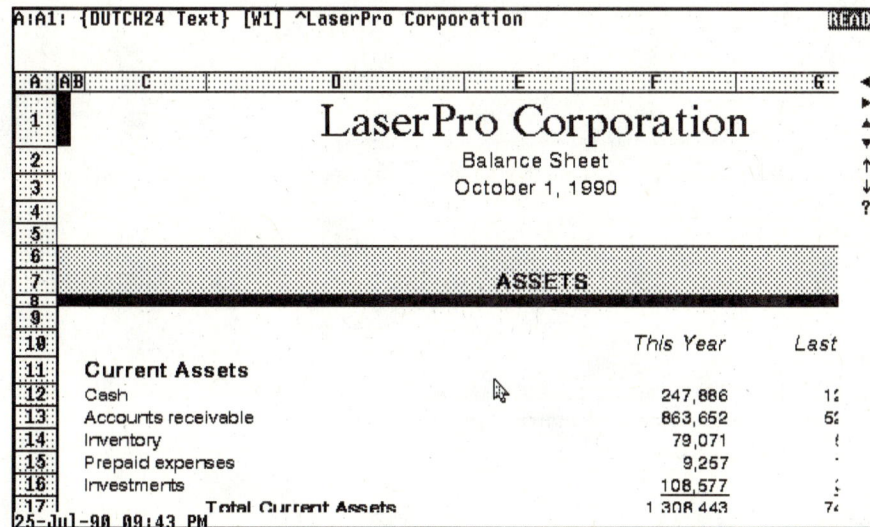

Fig. 9.21.
A worksheet zoomed to the Large magnification size.

The **R**eplace option on the **:D**isplay **C**olors menu enables you to define the palette setting for each color. To change the shade of a color, choose **:D**isplay **C**olors **R**eplace, select the color, and enter a number between 0 and 63. To make the color-change permanent, use the **:D**isplay **D**efault **U**pdate command.

Options

You can set options for the following screen aspects: **F**rame, **G**rid, **P**age-Breaks, **C**ell-Pointer, and **I**ntensity. Each of these options is described in the following section.

Frame

The **F**rame option controls how the worksheet column letters and row numbers are displayed. The default frame display is **E**nhanced—rectangles enclose each column letter and row number. The **R**elief option displays a bright, sculpted worksheet frame. The **1**-2-3 frame is similar to the one you see in 1-2-3 without Wysiwyg attached.

The **S**pecial option displays measurements in the worksheet frame instead of the standard column letters and row numbers. You can display **C**haracters, **I**nches, **M**etric (centimeters), or **P**oints/Picas. The Inches frame is shown in figure 9.22. Because the use of 1-2-3 depends so heavily on cell coordinates, you probably wouldn't want to work with a **S**pecial frame setting all the time. These settings are ones you would temporarily turn on to check the worksheet dimensions; then you would immediately revert to your normal frame display.

398 Part II ◆ Creating 1-2-3 Reports and Graphs

Fig. 9.22.
Inches displayed in the worksheet frame.

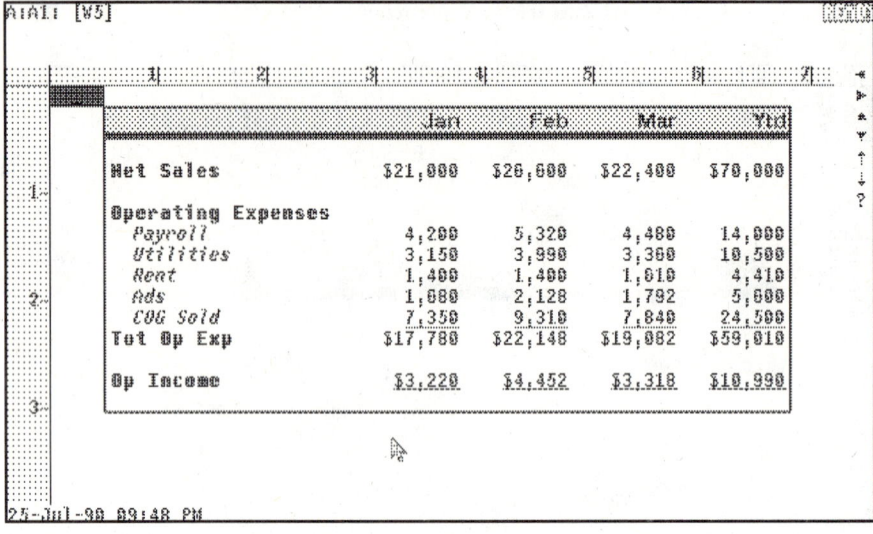

The last **Frame** option, **None**, turns off the display of the frame. You might want to use this option in macros when it's not important to have column letters and row numbers on the screen—for example, when an information screen is displayed.

Grid

Cue:
When grid lines are displayed, it's easier to determine cell coordinates on the screen.

The **Grid** option on the **:Display Options** menu enables you to display dotted lines between columns and rows, as shown in figure 9.23. With grid lines displayed, your electronic worksheet more closely resembles accountant's ledger paper. It's also easier to determine the cell coordinates of the cells displayed on the screen.

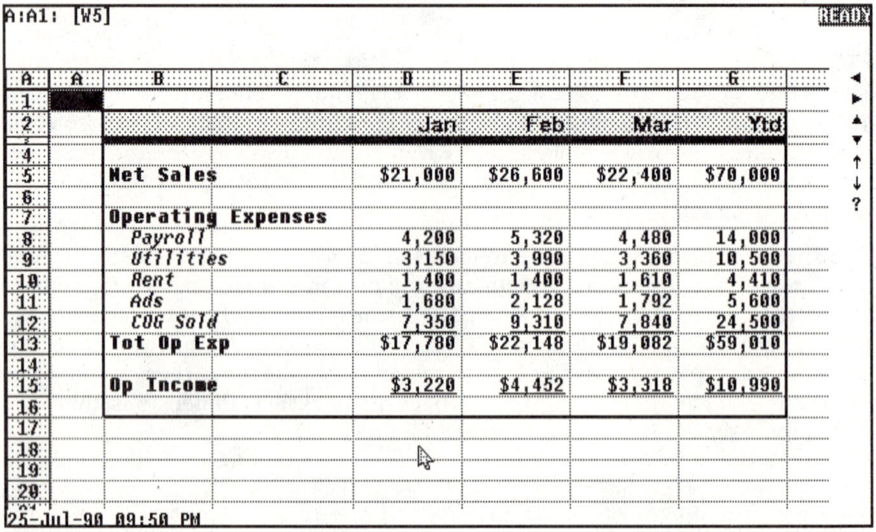

Fig. 9.23.
Grid lines.

Chapter 9 ◆ Using Wysiwyg To Enhance and Print Reports   **399**

Turning on the grid with **:D**isplay **O**ptions **G**rid **Y**es does not mean that the grid appears on your printed report. If you want the grid to print, use the **:P**rint **S**ettings **G**rid command.

Page Breaks

With the **P**age-**B**reaks option, you control whether the dashed print borders are displayed on the screen. These borders normally display when you define your print range with **:P**rint **R**ange **S**et and when you insert page breaks with **:W**orksheet **P**age. To turn off their display, choose **N**o for the **P**age-**B**reaks option.

Regardless of whether the page breaks are displayed, they will be used when you print the report.

Cell Pointer

The **C**ell-**P**ointer option controls the style of your cell pointer: **S**olid or **O**utline. The cell pointer can be displayed as a solid rectangular bar (the default) or as an outline around the cell. This option also controls how ranges are highlighted. With the **O**utline style, the highlighted range is not actually highlighted: it is enclosed in an outline border. The cell pointer is more difficult to see in **O**utline style, especially when the grid is turned on.

Cue:
Make the cell pointer solid if you turn on the grid.

Intensity

Two **I**ntensity settings are offered: **N**ormal (the default) and **H**igh. If you prefer a brighter screen, change the screen intensity to **H**igh.

Font Directory

Use the **F**ont-**D**irectory option to indicate the directory in which your screen and print fonts are located. When the Install program creates the Bitstream soft fonts, the files are stored in the WYSIWYG directory. If you move these fonts to another directory, or if you want to use fonts located in another directory, enter the path with the **F**ont-**D**irectory option.

Rows

The **R**ows option enables you to specify how many worksheet rows are displayed on the screen. Enter a value between 16 and 60. This option applies only when the screen is in graphics mode (**:D**isplay **M**ode **G**raphics).

Default

The settings you change on the **:D**isplay menu are temporary. They are valid for the current 1-2-3 session only and are lost when you quit the program. To save the

> **Reminder:**
> To save the :Display settings permanently, choose :Display Default Update.

:Display settings permanently, choose :Display Default Update. Your current settings will then be active every time you use 1-2-3 and Wysiwyg.

To cancel your current display settings and return them to their default values, choose :Display Default Restore.

Using Wysiwyg Text Commands

By using Wysiwyg's :Text commands, you can manipulate the labels in your worksheet in several different ways. With the :Text Align command, you can align a label over a defined worksheet range. This option is great for centering a title over a worksheet table. With the :Text Edit command, you can type text directly into the worksheet, and the words will wrap just like in a word processing package. You can even change the format of individual characters. For example, you can underline or italicize a single word. The :Text Reformat command adjusts a column of long labels so that they fit into a designated range. You use this command after you have edited or changed the font of a range, and some or all of the lines in the text block are no longer the correct width.

All the :Text commands require that you define a text range. Once you have manipulated a text range, the code {Text} appears in the control panel.

Typing or Correcting Text

> **Cue:**
> Use :Text Edit to type word-wrapped paragraphs.

Many people love 1-2-3 so much that they even use it to type short letters and memos. However, typing and editing in a spreadsheet program are much more cumbersome than typing and editing in a word processing program—that is, until Wysiwyg came along. Now you can type directly into the worksheet, and Wysiwyg automatically word-wraps when you get to the end of the line. You have a cursor that you can position on any character in the text range, and you can then edit the characters—insert, delete, overtype, or format them.

In addition to typing letters and memos, you can use :Text Edit to type a paragraph or two of descriptive information about the purpose of a worksheet.

You can use the :Text Edit command to modify existing worksheet labels or to type new text. When you select :Text Edit, you are prompted for a text range. Be sure to include the complete width and length of the range you want to edit. If you are going to insert text, you need to include blank rows or columns or both in your text range. Otherwise, you will encounter the error message Text input range full. If this happens, press Esc twice: once to clear the error, and the second time to return to READY mode. Then redefine your text range.

> **Reminder:**
> When you are in :Text Edit mode, the screen shows a small vertical-line cursor.

As shown in figure 9.24, several important changes occur when you are in the text editor. First, the cell pointer and mouse pointer disappear, and you have a small vertical-line cursor. The arrow keys move the cursor within the defined text range. Second, the mode indicator displays LABEL. Third, once you start typing or moving the cursor, the control panel displays the following information: the cell the current line of text was typed into, the cursor's row and column number position, and the line's alignment (Left-Aligned, Centered, and so on). The row number corresponds to the row in the defined text range, not the actual worksheet row. For example, if worksheet row 13 is the first row in the current text range, the row number is 1. The column number refers to the number of characters over from the beginning of the line.

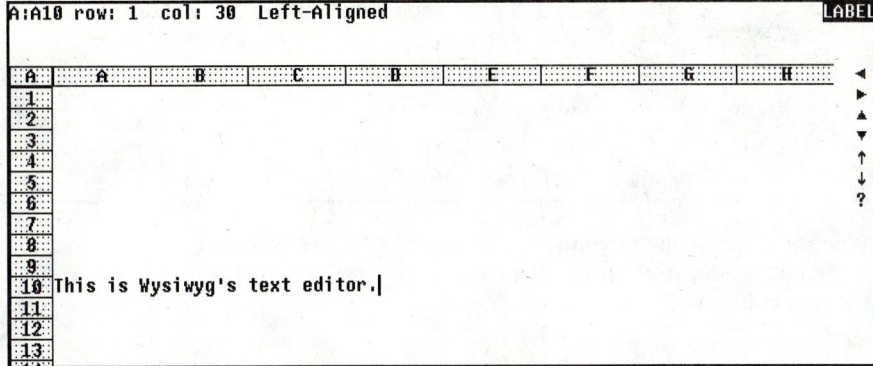

Fig. 9.24.
Wysiwyg's text editor.

As you type text, the words automatically wrap to the next line as necessary. When you want to start a new paragraph, take one of three actions, depending on how you want the text to look:

- ◆ Press Enter twice, leaving a blank line between paragraphs.
- ◆ Press Enter once and press the space bar one or more times at the beginning of the paragraph.
- ◆ Press Ctrl-Enter to insert a paragraph symbol.

The preceding paragraph rules come into play when you reformat the text. (See "Reformatting Paragraphs" for additional information.)

Table 9.4 lists the cursor-movement and editing keys you can use with :Text Edit. Many of these keys are similar to the ones you can use in 1-2-3's EDIT mode.

**Table 9.4
Cursor-Movement and Editing Keys Available in :Text Edit**

Key	Description
Ctrl-←	Beginning of the previous word
Ctrl-→	End of the next word
PgDn	Next screen
PgUp	Previous screen
Home	Beginning of line
Home Home	Beginning of paragraph
End	End of line
End End	End of paragraph

continued

Table 9.4—(continued)

Key	Description
Backspace	Deletes character to the left of cursor
Del	Deletes character to the right of cursor
Ins	Toggles between insert mode (the default) and overtype mode
Enter	Begins a new line
Ctrl-Enter	Begins a new paragraph
F3	Displays a format menu
Esc	Returns to READY mode

When you are finished typing and editing the text, press Esc to exit the text editor. In READY mode, you can see that each line of text is actually entered into cells in the first column of the text range.

Formatting Characters

Earlier in the chapter you learned how to use formatting sequences to assign attributes to individual characters in a cell. You press Ctrl-A and a code and then press Ctrl-N to cancel the attribute. The text editor offers an easier way to format characters: the F3 key. You don't need to remember codes because pressing F3 displays a menu.

Cue:

In the text editor, use F3 to format individual characters.

To add formatting attributes, you must first give the :Text Edit command and define the text range. Be sure to include the entire width of the long labels, not just the column they are typed into. Place the cursor just to the left of the first character you want to format and press F3. A menu of attributes appears in the control panel.

The first several attributes (Font, Bold, Italics, Underline, and Color) should already be familiar to you. The last four attributes are unique to the F3 key. The + option superscripts the text; the – option subscripts the text; Outline traces the outside of the letter forms, leaving the inside hollow; and the Normal option removes formatting. Examples of the Superscript, Subscript, and Outline attributes are shown in figure 9.25.

Fig. 9.25.

Some of the format attributes that can be added to individual characters in the text editor.

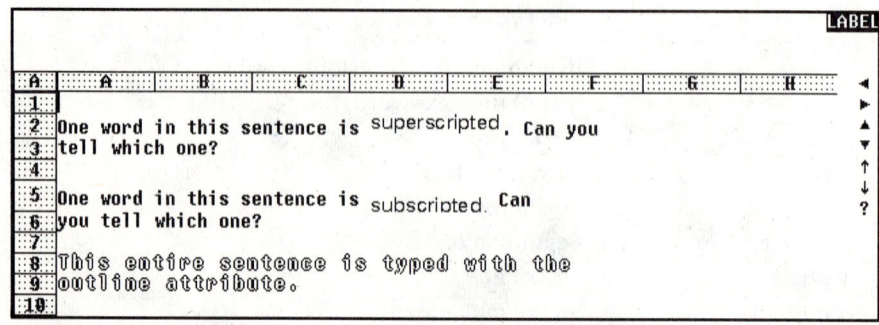

Chapter 9 ◆ Using Wysiwyg To Enhance and Print Reports   **403**

If superscripted or subscripted text is cut off at the top or bottom, you can increase the row height. You must first escape text-editing mode (press Esc) and issue the **:Worksheet Row Set-Height** command.

After you select the attribute you want, everything from the right of the cursor through the end of the line appears with this attribute. Your next step is to indicate where you want the attribute to stop (for example, at the end of a word). Place the cursor to the right of the last character you want to format and press F3. Choose **Normal** or select a different font.

Because some of the attributes change the size of characters, you may notice that your paragraphs are no longer neatly aligned after you format. When this misalignment happens, use the **:Text Reformat** command to adjust the paragraphs. (See "Reformatting Paragraphs" for additional information on reformatting.)

Character formatting is not limited to existing text; you also can apply attributes as you type new text in text-edit mode. Simply press F3 and select the format before you begin typing. Type the text, and when you want to discontinue this attribute, press F3 and choose **Normal**.

Aligning Labels

Wysiwyg's **:Text Align** command is a souped-up version of 1-2-3's **/Range Label [Left, Right, Center]** command. 1-2-3's command aligns a label within the current column width. A label that exceeds the column width aligns on the left. Wysiwyg's command aligns a label within a specified range. Thus you can center a label across a range of cells so that the label is centered over the worksheet. Figure 9.26 shows titles that were entered into A1..A3 and centered over the range A1..H3.

Cue:
Use :Text Align to center a title over a worksheet.

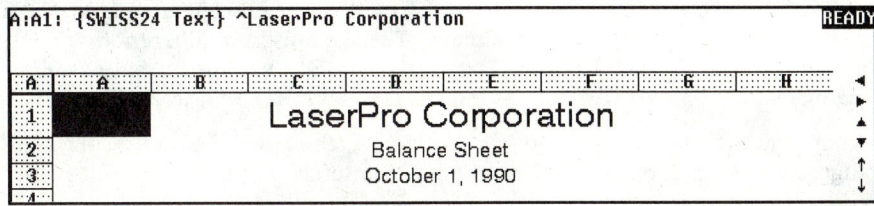

Fig. 9.26.
Lines centered with :Text Align.

Once you choose **:Text Align**, Wysiwyg offers four choices: **Left, Right, Center,** and **Even. Left** is the default alignment. **Right** aligns the label on the right edge of the rightmost cell in the text range, **Center** aligns the text in the middle of the range, and **Even** stretches the text between the left and the right edge of the text range (spaces are inserted between words to create the smooth margins). Figure 9.27 shows examples of each type of alignment.

Once you make your alignment selection, you are prompted for a text range. Highlight the rows for which you want to change the alignment. If you want the text aligned in the current range, you need only highlight the first column of the range. For example, the text range for the even-aligned paragraph in figure 9.27 is A:A14..A:A18. To align the text in a wider range, highlight the entire width of the text range.

Fig. 9.27.

The four types of alignment: Left, Right, Center, and Even.

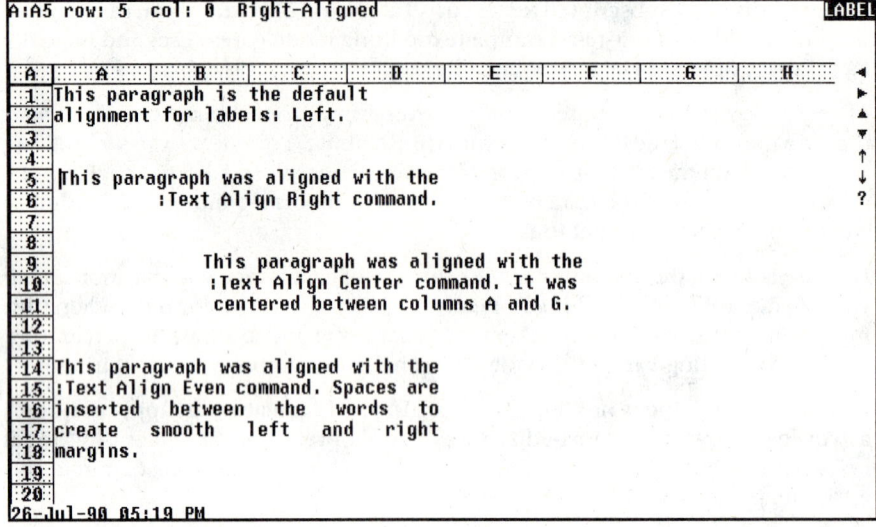

Wysiwyg uses the following symbols to identify each type of alignment:

Symbol	Description
'	Left
"	Right
^	Center
|	Even

You may notice that these symbols correspond to the label-alignment symbols inserted with the **/R**ange **L**abel command. The symbols have different functions, however, when the cell has the {Text} attribute. You can insert these symbols manually in 1-2-3's EDIT mode, as long as the cell has the {Text} attribute.

When you are editing in Wysiwyg's text editor, the control panel displays the alignment of the current line (**L**eft-Aligned, **C**entered, and so on).

Reformatting Paragraphs

Reminder:

*Use **:T**ext **R**eformat to realign paragraphs after editing and formatting text.*

One of the advantages of using the text editor is that you can easily correct typing mistakes, reword a passage, or insert additional text. Once you start editing and formatting, however, you will notice that your paragraphs are no longer properly aligned. For instance, some lines may be too short. The first paragraph in figure 9.28 shows a paragraph from which words have been deleted. The second paragraph illustrates how the text readjusts after the **:T**ext **R**eformat command is issued.

:Text **R**eformat is actually quite similar to 1-2-3's **/R**ange **J**ustify command, and in many cases the two can be used interchangeably. The main difference between them is that **/R**ange **J**ustify ignores Wysiwyg alignment commands and

Chapter 9 ◆ Using Wysiwyg To Enhance and Print Reports

consequently left-aligns all the labels when it reformats. :Text Reformat, on the other hand, retains the alignment commands as it reformats.

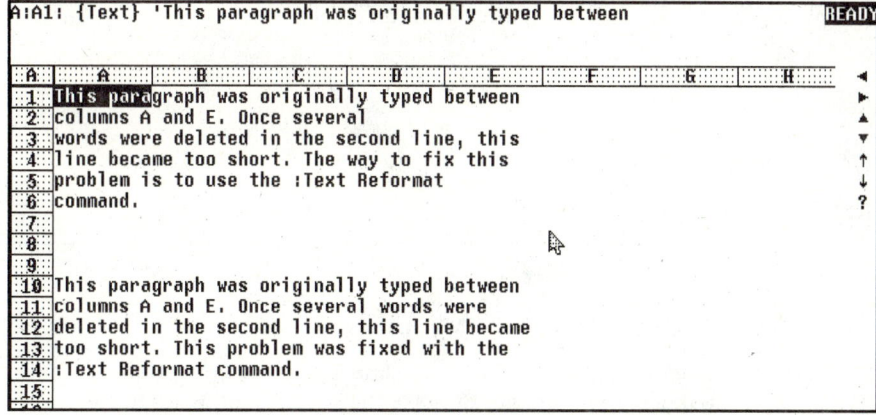

Fig. 9.28.
Using the :Text Reformat command.

To invoke the :Text Reformat command, you must be in READY mode. (If you are in the text editor, press Esc.) The range you last indicated in the :Text Edit command is automatically highlighted for you. If this range is acceptable, press Enter, and the text will readjust. To indicate a different range, press Esc or Backspace and then highlight the width and length of the range you want.

:Text Reformat rearranges the text within each paragraph and, when necessary, brings text up from subsequent lines to fit into the reformat range you specified. This command does not combine text from separate paragraphs, assuming that you followed the paragraph rules defined in the "Typing or Correcting Text" section.

Another reason to use the :Text Reformat command is to align the text into a different number of columns. Suppose, for example, that the range currently spans four columns, and you want it to go across six. To make longer lines of text, simply include these extra columns in your reformat range.

Making lines of text shorter is another story, however. If your reformat range contains fewer columns than your text range, nothing happens when you reformat—the command is ignored. The reason Wysiwyg snubs your request is that all columns in your text range contain the {Text} attribute. For example, in figure 9.29, all cells in the range A:A1..A:G3 have the {Text} attribute. You must remove this attribute from the extra columns before you can reformat. Thus, if you want the range in figure 9.29 to be reformatted to columns A through E, you must clear the {Text} attribute from columns F and G. Use :Text Clear to eliminate the attribute. If you find the multiple steps too awkward, you can use the /Range Justify command (it doesn't require the extra step).

Another consideration when reformatting to fewer columns is that your text range will become longer than it currently is. Therefore, you will need to include additional blank rows at the bottom of the range. If you don't, you get the message Text input range full. When this happens, press Esc to clear the error message, reissue the :Text Reformat command, but include a longer range.

Cue:
:Text Reformat also can be used to align text into a different number of columns.

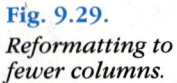
Fig. 9.29.
Reformatting to fewer columns.

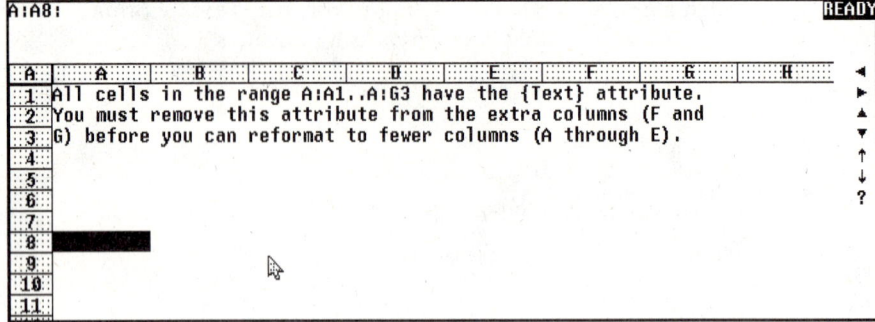

Setting and Clearing Text Attributes

The **:Text** menu offers two more options: **Set** and **Clear**. The **Set** option assigns the {Text} attribute to a cell or a range. Because the **:Text Align**, **Edit**, and **Reformat** commands automatically assign the {Text} attribute, you probably won't need to use this option very often. You will use **:Text Set** if you accidentally clear the {Text} attribute from a cell (for example, with the **:Text Clear** or **:Format Reset** commands).

Another reason you may want to define a text range with **:Text Set** is so that you can use the mouse to invoke the text editor. If you have a mouse, you don't need to use the **:Text Edit** command. Once a text range has been defined (with **:Text Set** or any of the other **Text** commands), you can place the mouse pointer anywhere in the text and press the left mouse button twice. Your cursor then moves to the beginning of the text range. The right mouse button cancels **:Text Edit** mode and returns you to READY mode.

As mentioned previously, use the **:Text Clear** command to eliminate the {Text} attribute from cells you don't want included in the reformat range.

Summary

In this chapter, you learned how to use Wysiwyg to enhance your 1-2-3 worksheets. Wysiwyg's extensive formatting capability is this add-in's feature attraction. You can emphasize important areas of the worksheet by changing fonts, or by adding lines, colors, boldface, italics, and shading. By using Wysiwyg's formatting options, you can create attractive, professional-looking reports.

Although formatting is key in Wysiwyg, it is not the only thing you can do with the add-in. The text editor is another powerful feature. This simple word processing system lets you type, edit, format, and align text.

Graph enhancement is yet another capability of Wysiwyg. This subject is covered in Chapter 11.

Creating and Printing Graphs

10

Keeping detailed worksheets that show real or projected data is worthless if the data cannot be readily understood. That's where 1-2-3 business graphics can help out. It's often easier to spot a trend or analyze data by using a graph than by working with a sea of numbers.

To help decision-makers who are pressed for time or unable to draw conclusions from countless rows of numeric data, 1-2-3 offers graphics capabilities. The program offers seven types of basic business graphs as well as sophisticated options for enhancing the graphs' appearance. The real strength of 1-2-3's graphics, however, lies in its integration with the worksheet.

This chapter shows you how to do the following:

- ◆ Create graphs from worksheet data
- ◆ Use 1-2-3's automatic graphing capability
- ◆ Add descriptive labels and numbers to a graph
- ◆ Save graphs and graph settings for later use
- ◆ Select an appropriate graph type
- ◆ Print graphs that you create in 1-2-3
- ◆ Include one or more graphs in a printed report

Also in this chapter, you learn how to apply most of 1-2-3's graph options to a line graph. Then you learn how to construct all the other types of 1-2-3 graphs.

Working with Wysiwyg

Graphing commands are also available in Wysiwyg. However, the options on the :Graph menu are primarily for enhancing the graphs you created with 1-2-3's /Graph menu. Wysiwyg contains a built-in graph editor that you can use to annotate your graphs. Here are a few things you can do with your graphs in Wysiwyg:

- Insert a graph in any worksheet range
- Type text anywhere on the graph
- Draw arrows, lines, circles and other shapes
- Print graphs and worksheet data on the same page

Although the Wysiwyg commands are not covered in this chapter, pertinent :Graph commands are referred to when appropriate. Chapter 11 contains a thorough explanation of the :Graph commands.

Determining Hardware and Software Needs

Reminder:
To view a graph on-screen, you need graphics-capable video hardware.

Before creating your first graph, you must determine whether your hardware supports viewing and printing graphs, and whether your 1-2-3 software is correctly installed. You also should be familiar with the various graph types so that you know which type of graph is best suited for presenting specific numeric data.

To view a graph on-screen, you need graphics-capable video display hardware. Almost all systems have such hardware. Without it, you can construct, save, and print 1-2-3 graphs, but you cannot view graphs on-screen.

To print a graph, you need a graphics printer or plotter supported by 1-2-3. Graph printing is described at the end of this chapter.

Understanding Graphs

To understand 1-2-3's graphics, you need to be familiar with a few terms concerning plotting a graph. The two basic terms—x-axis and y-axis—are illustrated in figure 10.1.

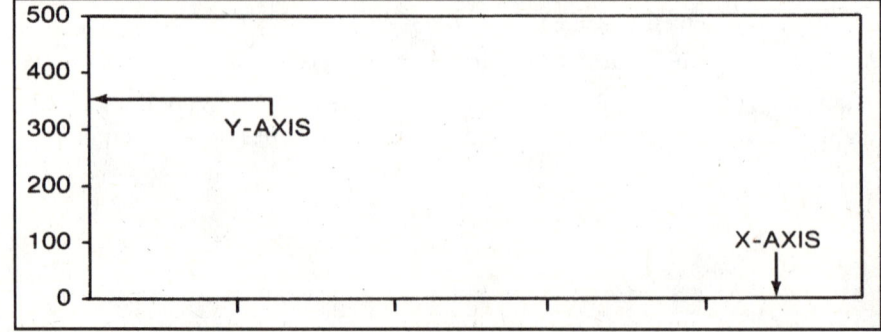

Fig. 10.1.
A graph's x- and y-axes.

All graphs (except pie graphs) have two axes: the *y-axis* (the vertical left edge) and the *x-axis* (the horizontal bottom edge). 1-2-3 automatically provides tick marks for both axes. The program also scales the numbers on the y-axis, based on the minimum and maximum figures included in the plotted data range(s).

Every point plotted on a graph has a unique *x,y* location. The *x* represents the horizontal position, corresponding to the category associated with the data point (for example, Gross Sales, Expenses, or January). The *y* represents the vertical position, corresponding to the second value associated with the data point (for example, Dollars or Percent Profit). In figure 10.2, for example, the *x* variable is Month and the *y* variable is a dollar value.

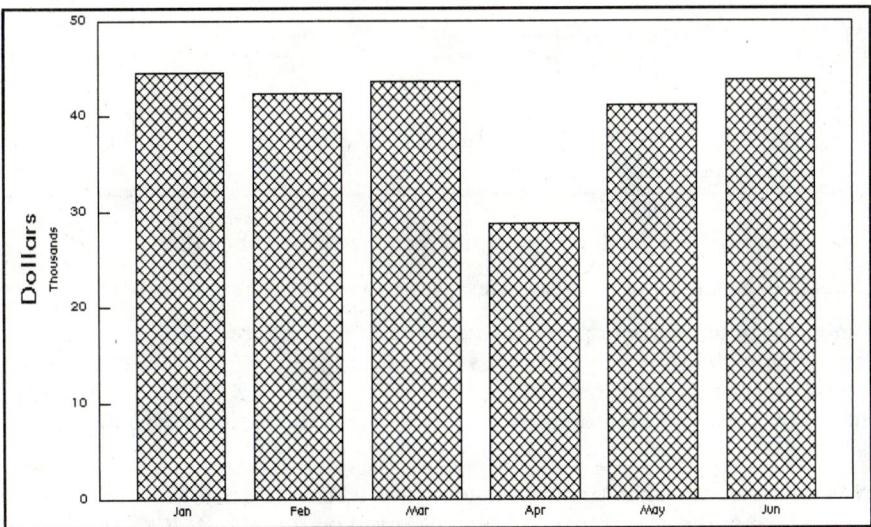

Fig. 10.2.
A basic bar graph in which the x variable is Month and the y variable is a dollar value.

The intersection of the y-axis and the x-axis is called the *origin*. Notice that the origin of the axes in figure 10.2 is zero for both *x* and *y* (0,0). Although graphs can be plotted with a nonzero origin, you should use a zero origin in your graphs to minimize misinterpretation of graph results and to make graphs easier to compare. Later in this chapter, you learn how you can manually change the upper or lower limits of the scale initially set by 1-2-3.

Creating Simple Graphs

To create a graph, you first must load 1-2-3 and retrieve the file that contains the data you want to graph. Many of the examples in this chapter are based on the Sales Data worksheet shown in figure 10.3.

To graph information from the Sales Data worksheet, you need to know which numeric data you can plot and which data (numeric or label) you may be able to use to enhance the graph. In figure 10.3, time period labels are listed across row 6. Category identifiers are located in column A. The numeric entries in rows 9 and 10, as well as the formula results in rows 11 and 12, are suitable for graphing as data points.

Fig. 10.3.
A sample sales data worksheet.

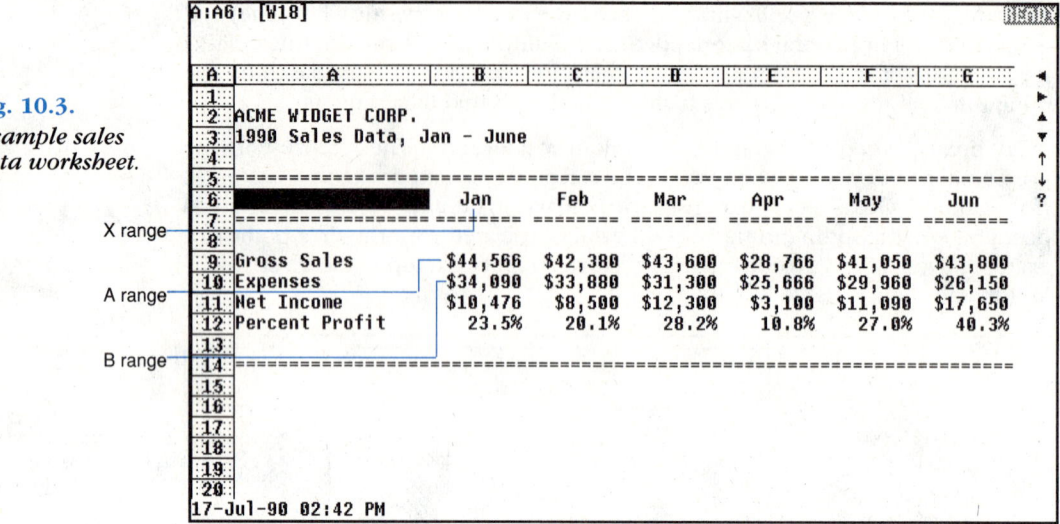

Select /Graph from the 1-2-3 command menu to display the following menu:

Type **X A B C D E F** Reset View Save Options Name Group Quit

Only two options from the main **Graph** menu are required. You must indicate which **Type** of graph you want, unless you are using **Line**, which is the default. And you must define at least one data series from the choices **X**, **A**, **B**, **C**, **D**, **E**, and **F**. After you have specified these two options, you can select **View** to display the graph.

X is the range for labels along the x-axis (the horizontal axis). Units of time (for example, months or years) are usually displayed on this axis. **A**, **B**, **C**, **D**, **E**, and **F** are data ranges that are plotted along the y-axis (the vertical axis). You can plot as many as six sets of data. The result is a basic graph that depicts relationships between numbers or trends across time.

Look at the sample worksheet in figure 10.3. To create a basic graph, suitable for a quick on-screen look at the data, issue the following command sequences. After each range specification, press Enter.

/Graph Type Bar

A A:B9..A:G9 (Gross Sales, data range A)

B A:B10..A:G10 (Expenses, data range B)

View

The resulting graph is shown in figure 10.4. In this graph, the six sets of bars represent monthly data. The bars are graphed in order from left to right, starting with the January data. Within each set of bars, the left-hand bar represents the Gross Sales figure and the right-hand bar, the corresponding Expenses figure. This minimal graph shows a fairly steady sales rate over the six-month period, with the exception of the fourth month, which had significantly lower sales. Expenses remained relatively constant.

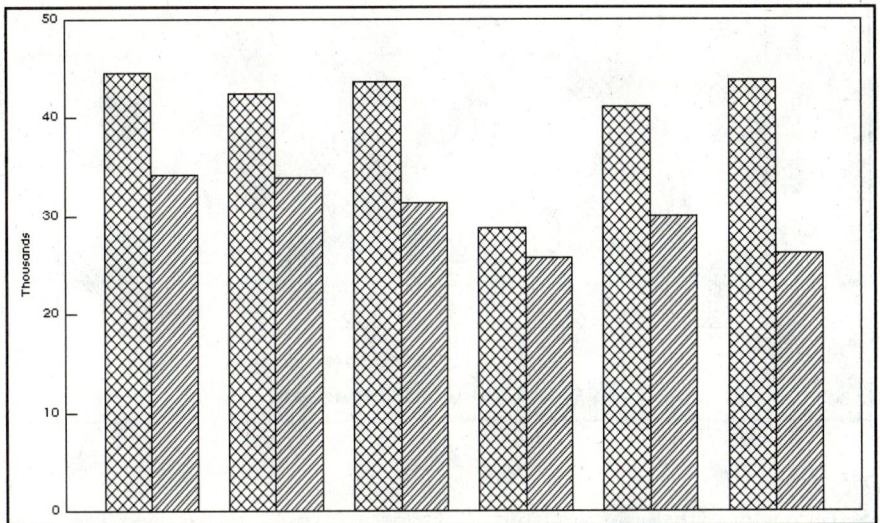

Fig. 10.4.
A basic bar graph.

The graph in figure 10.4 is not, however, something you want to show to your boss. 1-2-3 has numerous options that enable you to improve the appearance of your graphs and produce labeled final-quality output suitable for business presentations. To convert the graph in figure 10.4 to presentation-quality, select the following commands from the /Graph menu. (These options are explained in detail later in the chapter.) Press Enter after each range or text specification.

Reminder:
To return to the worksheet when a graph is displayed, press any key.

    X A:B6..A:G6 (Monthly headings below x-axis)

    Options Titles First **ACME WIDGET CORP.**

        Titles Second **1990 Sales Data, Jan – June**

        Titles X-Axis **East Coast Operations**

        Titles Y-Axis **Dollars**

        Legend A **Gross Sales**

        Legend B **Expenses**

        Grid Horizontal

        Scale Y-Scale Format Currency **0**

        Quit Quit View

The resulting graph is shown in figure 10.5. As you can see, even those who are unfamiliar with the data can understand the contents of an enhanced graph.

Fig. 10.5.
The enhanced, presentation-quality graph.

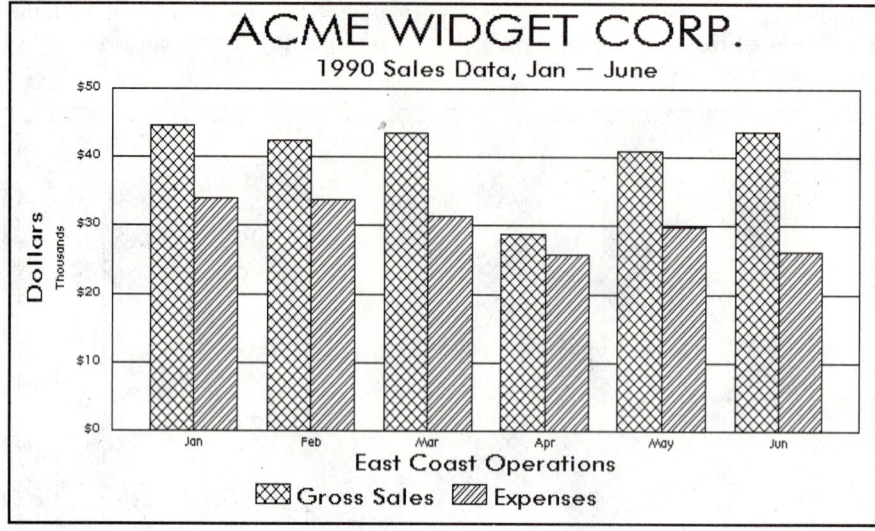

Selecting a Graph Type

Selecting one of the seven available graph types is easy. When you select **Type** from the /Graph menu, the following menu appears:

   Line Bar XY Stack-Bar Pie HLCO Mixed Features

By selecting one of the first seven options, you set that graph type, and automatically restore the /Graph menu to the control panel. By selecting **Features**, you go to a submenu that enables you to set certain graph options, which are discussed later in this chapter.

Of the seven 1-2-3 graph types, all but the pie graph display both x- and y-axes. The line, bar, stacked-bar, HLCO (high-low-close-open), and mixed graphs display numbers (centered on the tick marks) along the y-axis. The x-axis of these graph types can display user-defined labels centered on the tick marks. The XY graph displays numbers on both axes. Some graph types can have a second y-axis, at the right edge of the graph.

Specifying Data Ranges

You cannot type data directly on a 1-2-3 graph, except with Wysiwyg. The data to be graphed must be present in the current worksheet, either as values or as the result of formula calculations. Do not confuse the process of specifying data points, which are always numeric, with that of typing descriptions, such as titles. (Typing descriptions is illustrated later in this chapter.)

You must specify which data in the currently displayed worksheet should be graphed. A graph data range consists of one or more rectangular ranges of numbers. If the range contains labels or blank cells, these cells are given a value of zero. If the data is in adjacent rows or columns, you can use 1-2-3's automatic

> **Reminder:** *Specify worksheet data to be graphed by entering or highlighting data ranges.*

graph feature (discussed later in this section) to assign the data ranges. Otherwise, you must assign the data ranges manually.

Specifying Data Ranges Manually

To specify a graph data range manually, you first select **A**, **B**, **C**, **D**, **E**, or **F** from the /Graph menu, and then specify the range just as you do any other 1-2-3 range—by entering cell addresses or a range name, or by using the mouse or arrow keys in POINT mode.

The **X** data range option is used for numeric data only with the **XY** graph type. For the other graph types (except pie), this option is used to specify x-axis labels.

Before you start building a graph, read the following general statements about the choice(s) required for each graph type:

Graph type	Option(s)
Line	Enter as many as six sets of data in ranges **A**, **B**, **C**, **D**, **E**, and **F**. 1-2-3 creates one graph line for each range; each point on a line represents one value in the range. The data points in each data range are marked by a unique symbol and/or color when graphed (see table 10.1).
Bar	Enter as many as six data ranges: **A**, **B**, **C**, **D**, **E**, and **F**. 1-2-3 creates one set of bars for each range; each bar in a set represents one value in the range. The bars for multiple data ranges appear within each x-axis group on the graph in alphabetical (A–F) order from left to right. On a monochrome monitor, the bars for each data range are displayed with a unique shading. On a color monitor, they are displayed with a unique color (limited by the maximum number of colors possible on your hardware). Shading and screen colors are summarized in table 10.1.
XY	Choose **X** from the main /Graph menu and select the data range that contains the independent variable (the x-axis variable). Enter as many as six dependent variable ranges: **A**, **B**, **C**, **D**, **E**, and **F**. 1-2-3 creates one set of points for each dependent variable range. The data points for each data range are marked by a unique symbol when graphed. The symbols are the same as the Line symbols shown in table 10.1.
Stack-Bar	Follow the bar graph instructions. In a stacked-bar graph, multiple data ranges are stacked on top of each other, with the **A** range on the bottom.
Pie	Enter only one data series by selecting **A** from the main /Graph menu. For each value in the **A** range, 1-2-3 creates a pie "slice." The **X** range describes each pie slice. (To shade and "explode" pieces of the pie, also select a **B** range, as explained later in this chapter.)

Graph type	Option(s)
HLCO	The **A**, **B**, **C**, and **D** ranges specify respectively the high, low, closing, and opening values. The **E** range is used for the bars in the lower portion of the graph, and the **F** range is used for the single graph line (see the section on HLCO graphs later in this chapter).
Mixed	Mixed graphs contain a bar graph overlaid with line graphs. The **A**, **B**, and **C** ranges are used for the bar portion of the graph, and the **D**, **E**, and **F** ranges for the line portion.

As you build your own graphs, refer to the preceding comments about graph types and to the information in table 10.1.

Table 10.1
Graph Symbols and Shading

Data Range	Line Graph Symbols	Bar Graph B&W Shading	On-Screen Color
A	■	▨	Red
B	◆	▨	Green
C	▲	▨	Blue
D	⊟	⊠	Yellow
E	◇	▨	Magenta
F	△	▨	Light Blue

This table shows each data range with the corresponding default assignments for line symbols, bar shading, and color.

Specifying Data Ranges Automatically

In some circumstances, 1-2-3 can automatically perform some or all the work of specifying data ranges for a graph. An automatic graph creates an entire graph with a single keystroke. A graph group enables you to specify multiple graph data ranges in one step. These 1-2-3 features can be great time savers.

Automatic Graphs

1-2-3's automatic graph feature enables you to create certain types of graphs with a single keystroke. For an automatic graph, the position of the cell pointer—not the settings of the /Graph **X** and /Graph **A** through **F** options—determines which data is included in the graph. Creating an automatic graph requires that the following two conditions be met:

- The /Graph **X** and **A** through **F** settings are cleared (with the /**G**raph **R**eset **R**ange command).
- The cell pointer is in a section of the worksheet that can be interpreted as an automatic graph (explained later in this section).

If these conditions are satisfied, displaying an automatic graph requires only that you position the cell pointer anywhere within the worksheet data range and press Graph (F10) or select /**G**raph **V**iew.

The following criteria for an automatic graph range are strict, but can be met by many common arrangements of data in a worksheet:

- An automatic graph range must contain data that can be divided, by either rows or columns, into the X and A through F ranges for the graph.
- An automatic graph range must be separated by at least two blank rows and columns from other data in the worksheet.
- The data in an automatic graph range must be arranged by columns or rows with the X data range first, the A data range second, and so on. The first row or column in the range can contain labels.

1-2-3 divides an automatic graph range into rows or columns, depending on the setting of /**W**orksheet **G**lobal **D**efault **G**raph, which can be set to **C**olumnwise or **R**owwise. Use **R**owwise when each data range is located in a row; use **C**olumnwise when each data range is in a column. The type of graph created depends on the setting of /**G**raph **T**ype; if no setting has been made, the default graph type, **L**ine, is created. Data assignments are made as follows:

- The first column or row that contains numbers is used as the **A** data range. XY graphs use this column or row for the **X** data range. Adjacent columns or rows are used for additional data ranges, in order. Labels in these ranges are treated as zeros.
- For all graph types except XY, a column or row of labels preceding the first numerical data range is used as the **X** data range. This range must contain only labels. If such a column or row doesn't exist, no **X** range assignment is made.

An automatic graph makes use of all current /**G**raph menu selections, such as **T**ype, **F**eatures, and **O**ptions. The only part of an automatic graph that is "automatic" is the assignment of data ranges. Once an automatic graph exists, it can be treated as any other graph—named, saved, printed, and so on.

Consider the worksheet shown in figure 10.6. The data in the range A:A2..A:D6 is a valid automatic graph range. If /**W**orksheet **G**lobal **D**efault **G**raph **C**olumnwise is in effect (the default), and you have selected /**G**raph **T**ype **B**ar, then positioning the cell pointer anywhere in that range and pressing Graph (F10) displays the graph in figure 10.7. Note that the other data ranges in figure 10.6 are not valid automatic graph ranges, because they are not separated by at least two rows or columns from other worksheet data.

Fig. 10.6.
Valid and invalid automatic graph ranges.

Valid automatic graph range

Invalid automatic graph ranges

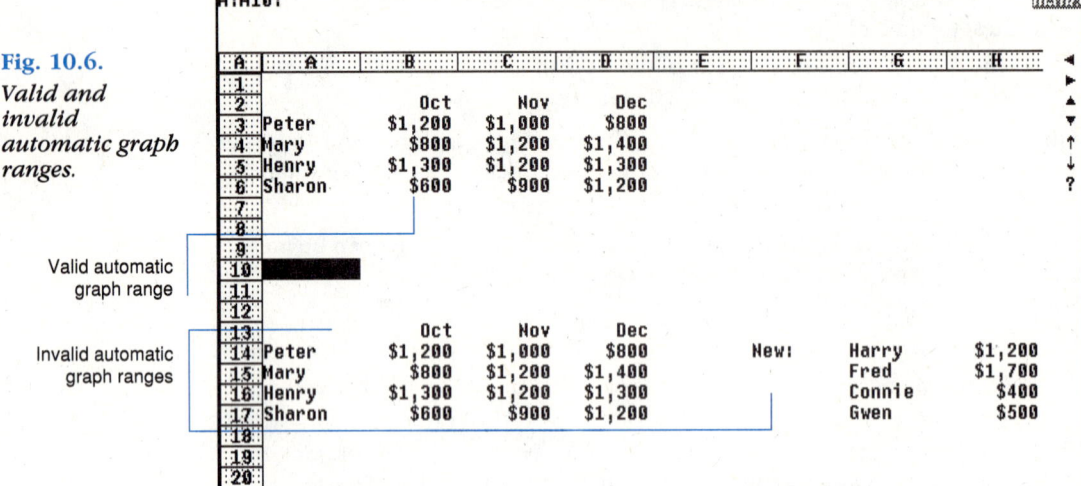

Fig. 10.7.
An automatic bar graph created from the data in figure 10.6.

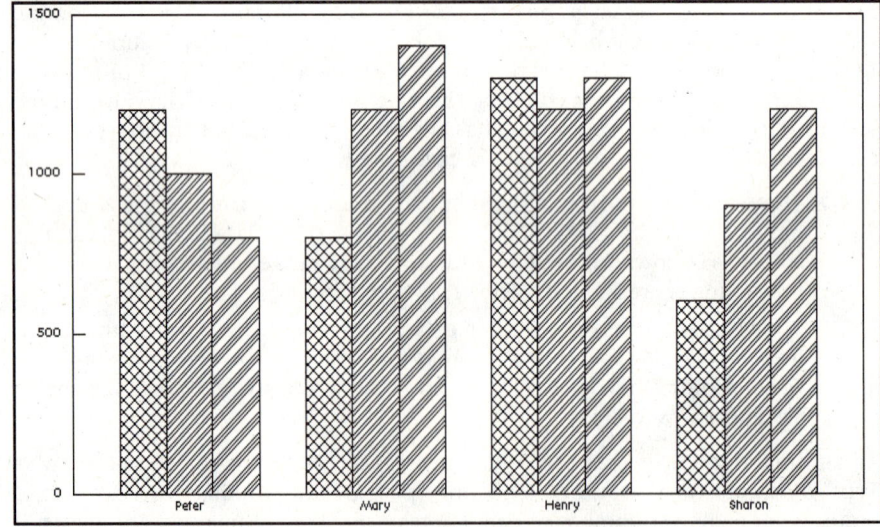

/Graph Group

Reminder:
Use /Graph Group to save keystrokes when the X and A-F data ranges are in adjacent rows or in columns.

When your data ranges for 1-2-3 graphs are in adjacent worksheet rows or columns, you can use /Graph Group to save a significant number of keystrokes. The **Group** option enables you to specify all graph data ranges, **X** and **A** through **F**, in one operation. The procedure is as follows:

1. Select /Graph Group.
2. Indicate the rectangular range to be divided into data ranges. You can enter cell addresses or range names, or use the mouse or arrow keys

Chapter 10 ◆ Creating and Printing Graphs   **417**

in POINT mode. This range should not include the data range descriptions (that is, the legends).

3. Select **C**olumnwise or **R**owwise to indicate whether the data ranges are located in columns or rows.

Consider the small worksheet shown in figure 10.8. To graph this data as rows in a bar graph, you first set **T**ype to **B**ar. In this figure, /**G**raph **G**roup has been selected, and POINT mode is being used to indicate the range A:B2..A:D5. When prompted, choose **R**owwise followed by **V**iew, and the graph in figure 10.9 appears.

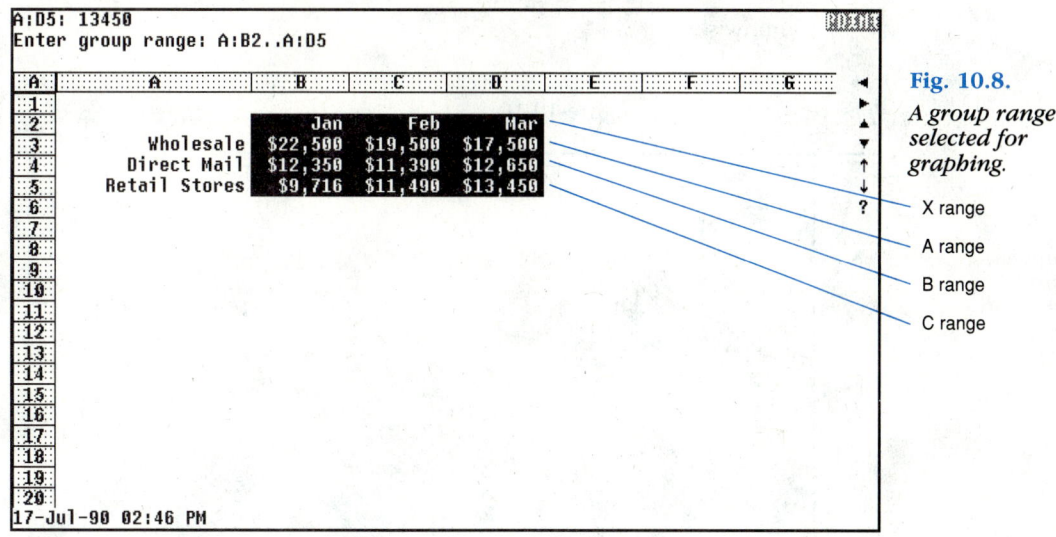

Fig. 10.8.

A group range selected for graphing.

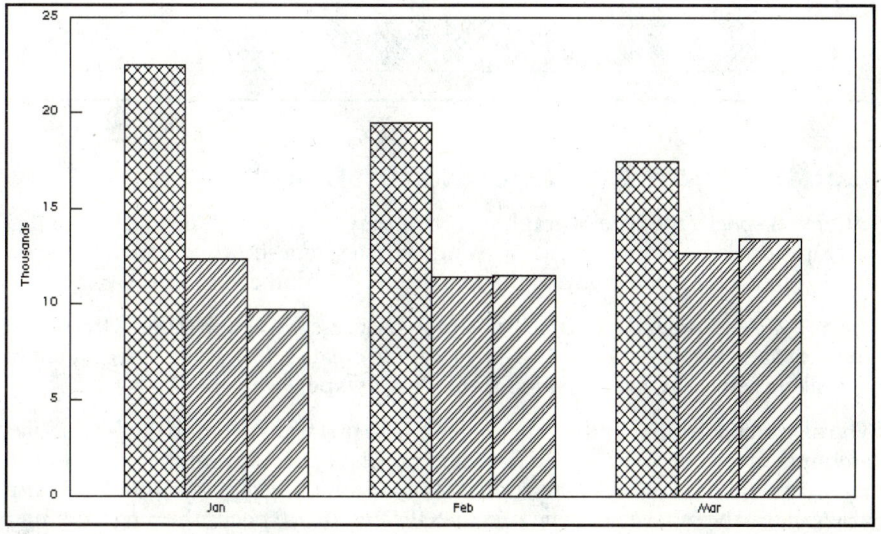

Fig. 10.9.

A Rowwise graph created from the data in figure 10.8.

The following /Graph data range assignments have been made automatically:

X A:B2..A:D2
A A:B3..A:D3
B A:B4..A:D4
C A:B5..A:D5

You can graph the same data as columns with the following command sequence:

/Graph Group A:A3..A:D5
Columnwise
View

The result is shown in figure 10.10.

Fig. 10.10.
Group data graphed columnwise.

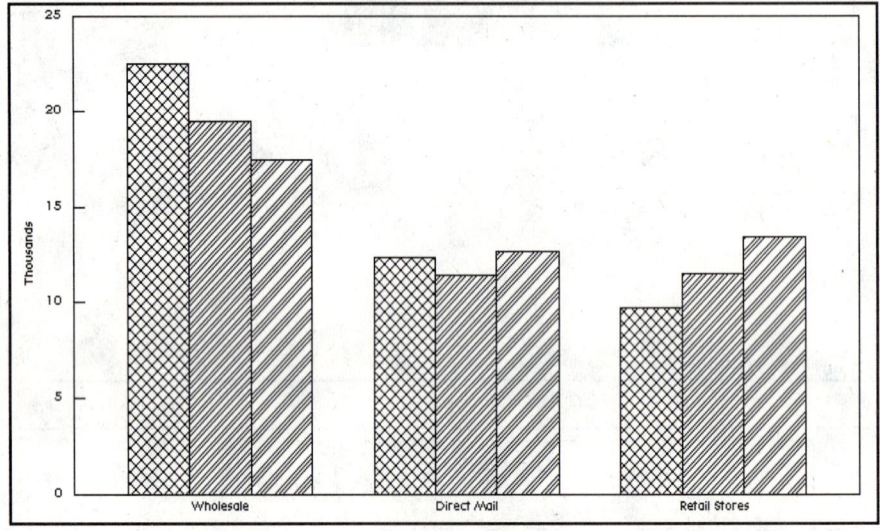

Constructing the Default Line Graph

After you specify the type of graph you want for your data and the location of that data, producing a graph is easy. By using the sales data shown in figure 10.3, you easily can create a line graph of the January through June amounts.

From 1-2-3's command menu, select **/Graph** to access the Graph menu. Ordinarily, the next step is to select **Type**. But if you want to create a line graph, you don't have to make a selection, because **Line** is the default type.

The next step is to specify the data range(s). You first want to graph the Gross Sales amounts in row 9. To enter the first data range, choose **A** from the main /Graph menu and then respond to the control-panel prompt by typing **A:B9..A:G9**. You also can use the mouse or arrow keys in POINT mode to specify the range, or enter the range name if one has been assigned.

By specifying the type of graph and the location of data to plot, you have completed the minimum requirements for creating a graph manually. If you choose View, you see a graph similar to the one shown in figure 10.11.

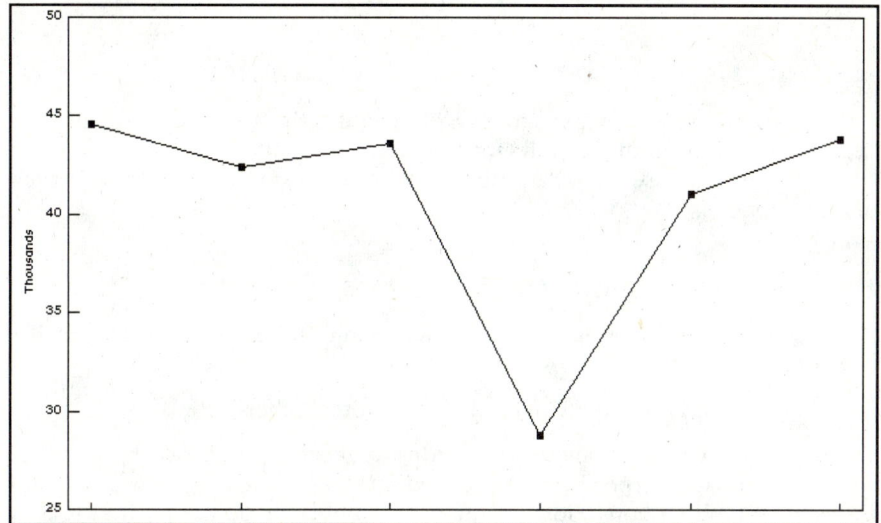

Fig. 10.11.
A basic line graph.

Although *you* know what this graph represents, it won't mean much to anyone else. The six data points corresponding to the January-through-June figures have been plotted, but the points have not been labeled to indicate what they represent. Nor have the graph axes been labeled (except for the Thousands indicator on the y-axis). Notice also that the y-axis origin on this initial graph is not zero, which makes the April decrease seem larger than it really is. Clearly, there's room for improvement here. The text that follows shows you how to enhance this basic graph.

Enhancing the Appearance of a Basic Graph

Many of 1-2-3's graph features apply equally to all seven graph types. The next section of this chapter takes you from start to finish, step-by-step, in the creation of a line graph from data in the worksheet in figure 10.3. Later, the chapter covers some graph features that are specific to the other graph types.

Most of the 1-2-3 features for enhancing a graph's appearance are accessed through **Options** on the /Graph menu. When you make this selection, the following menu appears:

    Legend Format Titles Grid Scale Color B&W Data-Labels Advanced Quit

As you work with this menu to add enhancements to your graphs, you should check the results frequently. To see the most recent version of your graph, press F10; you do not need to return to the main /Graph menu to select View. Press any

Reminder:
To see the most recent version of your graph, press F10.

key to exit the graph display and restore the /Graph menu to the screen. Or, depending on your video hardware, you can use the /**W**orksheet **W**indow **G**raph command to display the graph in a screen window (see this chapter's section called "Viewing Graphs in a Screen Window").

Adding Descriptive Labels and Numbers

To add descriptive information to a graph, you use the **T**itles, **D**ata-Labels, and **L**egend options from the /**G**raph **O**ptions menu. In addition, for all graph types except XY, you can use the **X** data range option. The text that follows covers each of these options.

Using the Titles Option

If you select /**G**raph **O**ptions **T**itles, the following options are displayed in the control panel:

First   Second   X-Axis   **Y**-Axis   **2Y**-Axis   **N**ote   **O**ther-Note

The **F**irst and **S**econd options are for entering titles centered above the graph. The first title is in larger type above the second title. After selecting **F**irst or **S**econd from the /**G**raph **O**ptions **T**itles menu, you can either type the desired title in response to the prompt, or enter a backslash followed by the address of the worksheet cell containing the label or number to be used as the title.

The **X**-Axis, **Y**-Axis, and **2Y**-Axis options are for labeling the graph axes. **X**-Axis centers a horizontal label below the x-axis. **Y**-Axis places a vertical label just to the left of the left y-axis. **2Y**-Axis places a vertical label just to the right of the right y-axis. You can type the labels directly, or enter a cell address or range name preceded by a backslash.

The **N**ote and **O**ther-Note options are for entering "footnotes" that appear in the lower left corner of the graph. Again, the notes can be typed directly or entered as a cell address.

Figure 10.12 shows the positions of the various titles as they appear on a graph.

Suppose that you want to enhance the basic line graph of the sales data amounts shown in figure 10.3. You can enter four titles by using cell references for two of the titles and typing new descriptions for the others.

Reminder:
You can enter four titles by using cell references for two of the titles, and typing new descriptions for the others.

First, select /**G**raph **O**ptions **T**itles **F**irst. Next, when 1-2-3 prompts you for a title, type **\A2** to reference the cell that contains ACME WIDGET CORP., the first title, and then press Enter. The **O**ptions menu (*not* the **T**itles menu) reappears. Next, select **T**itles **S**econd and type **\A3** to make the label in cell A3 the second title centered above the graph.

Then, to label the x-axis, select **T**itles **X**-Axis and type **MONTH**. To enter the fourth title, select **T**itles **Y**-Axis and type **Dollars**. Now, to check the graph, press F10. Your graph should look like the enhanced graph shown in figure 10.13.

Chapter 10 ◆ Creating and Printing Graphs — 421

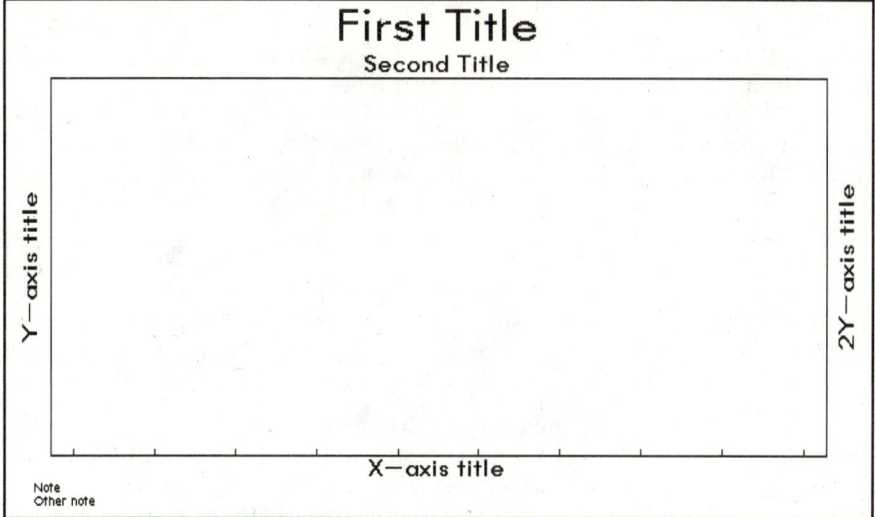

Fig. 10.12.
Graph positions of the seven types of titles.

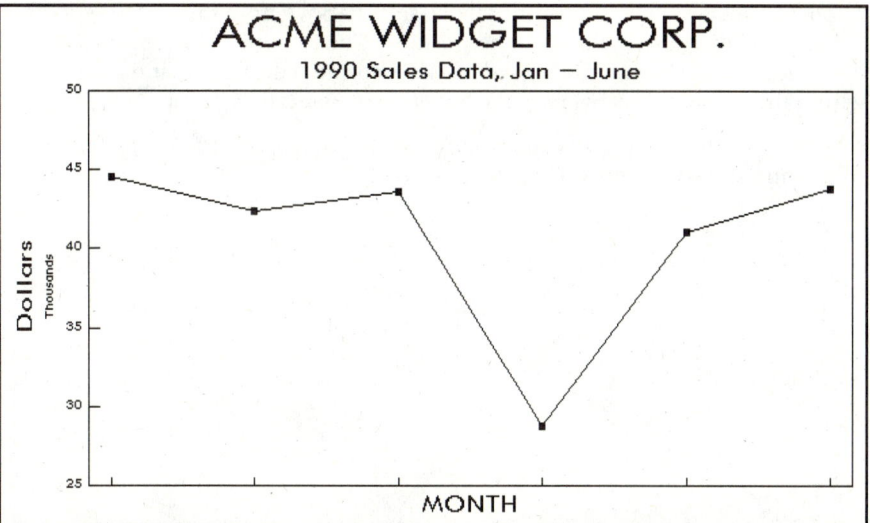

Fig. 10.13.
The line graph enhanced with titles.

To edit a title, use the command sequence you used for creating the title. The existing text, cell reference, or range name appears in the control panel, ready for editing. To eliminate a title, press Esc, and then press Enter.

Entering Data Labels within a Graph

Sometimes you may want to have labels on the graph itself to explain each of the data points. You can add these labels by selecting **Data-Labels** from the **/G**raph **O**ptions menu and selecting from the following menu that appears:

Cue:
Use /**G**raph **O**ptions **D**ata-Labels to place descriptive labels within a graph.

A B C D E F Group Quit

From this menu, select the data range to which you are assigning data labels. Select **Group** if the data labels for multiple ranges are in adjacent columns. You cannot type the data labels directly, except with Wysiwyg; instead, you must specify a worksheet range that contains the labels. You can specify the range by typing cell addresses, by pointing, or by entering a range name. After you specify the data label range, the following menu appears:

Center Left Above Right Below

The selection you make from this menu determines where each data label is displayed in relation to the corresponding data point. The labels (or numbers) in the data-label range are assigned to data points in the order that the labels appear in the worksheet.

Continue to enhance your sample line graph by entering as data labels the Jan–Jun headings from row 4 of the worksheet. First, select /**G**raph **O**ptions **D**ata-Labels, and then select **A** to assign labels to the **A** range (the only range on the graph). To enter the six abbreviated monthly headings from row 6 of the worksheet, select **A**, type **A:B6..A:G6** in response to the prompt for a label range, and press Enter. Then, to specify a position for the labels, select **A**bove from the next menu. Each set of data labels can have only one position. For example, you cannot position one cell within a data-label range *above* its associated data point and another cell within that same data-label range *below* its associated data point.

Now, press F10 to display the graph on-screen. Your graph should appear similar to the one shown in figure 10.14.

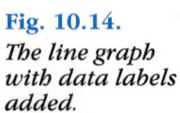

Fig. 10.14.
The line graph with data labels added.

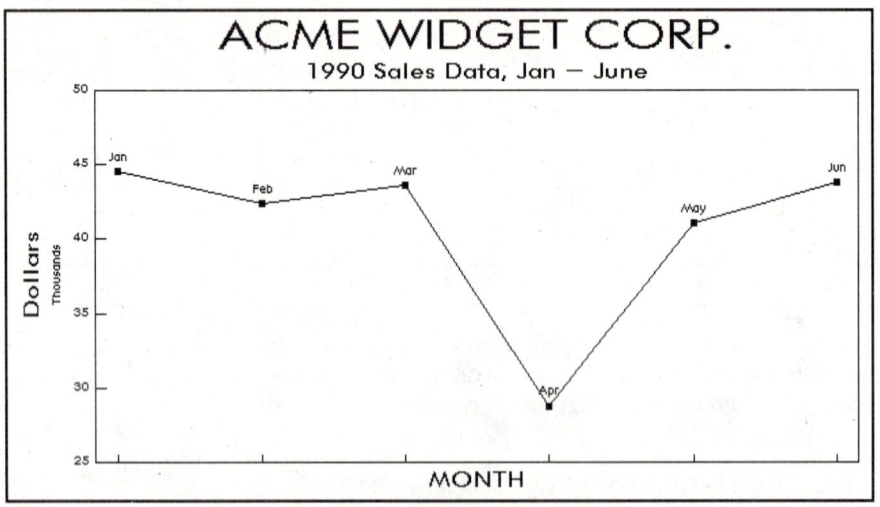

If you graph more than one data series, attach the data labels to the data range that includes the largest numeric values. Then select **A**bove to position the data labels above the data points. These steps place the data labels as high as possible in the graph, where they won't obscure the data points.

Another possibility is to use the data label text itself as the plotted points by following these steps:

1. Select /**G**raph **O**ptions **F**ormat **A** **N**either, which results in neither lines nor symbols being plotted for the specified data range.
2. Select **C**enter for the data label position, which centers the labels over the positions where the data points would have appeared.

By using this technique with a "dummy" data range, you can place labels anywhere on the graph. Wysiwyg offers a more direct way to place text on your graphs; see Chapter 11 for details.

To edit either the range or position of the data labels, use the same command sequence you used to create the data labels. Enter a different data-label range or specify a different position.

To remove data labels from a data range, follow the same steps used when first creating the data labels, but this time specify a single empty cell as the data-label range. You cannot eliminate the existing range by pressing Esc, as you did to eliminate an unwanted title. Alternatively, you can remove data labels by resetting the data range. Be careful, because this method removes not only the data labels but also the data range and any other associated options.

Caution: *You cannot use the **D**ata-Labels option with a pie graph.*

Entering Labels below the X-Axis

Instead of placing descriptive information within a graph, you may prefer to enter label information along the x-axis. With all graph types except pie and XY, the /**G**raph menu's **X** option can be used to position labels below the x-axis.

If you want to enter the Jan–Jun labels below the x-axis, select /**G**raph **X** and enter the range that contains the data labels: **A:B6..A:G6.** Then select **V**iew. Your graph should appear as in figure 10.15. Compare this graph to that in figure 10.14.

The cells you specify for the **X** range or for a data-label range can contain either labels or values. If values, they are displayed on the graph in the same format as they are displayed on the worksheet.

Keep the **X** labels for now. If you later need to eliminate the x-axis labels, select /**G**raph **R**eset **X**.

Using the Legend Option

A *data legend* is a key or label on the graph that explains the meaning of a symbol, line color, or hatch pattern. Data legends are particularly useful on graphs that include multiple data ranges.

Fig. 10.15.
The graph with an X range specified.

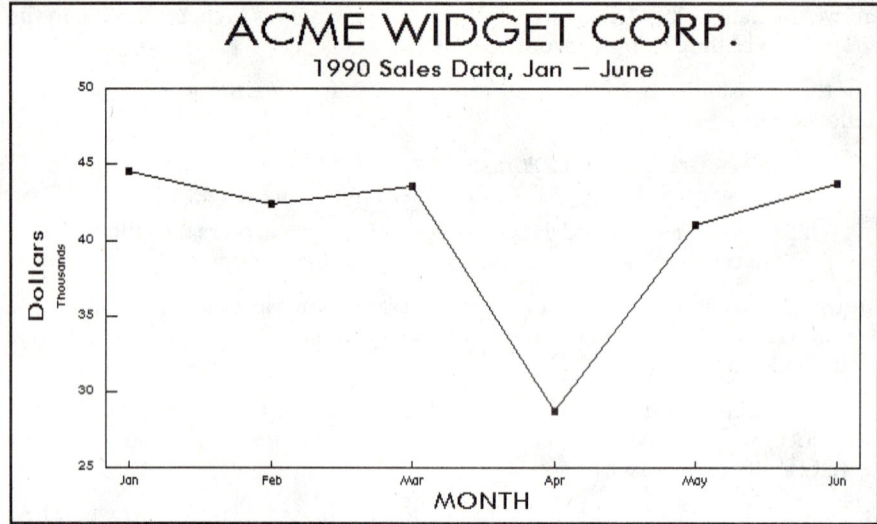

When a graph contains more than one data range, you need to distinguish between the different ranges. If you are using a color monitor and select **Color** from the /Graph Options menu, 1-2-3 differentiates data ranges with color. If the **B&W** (black and white) option is in effect, data ranges are marked with different symbols in line graphs and with different hatching patterns in other types. (Refer to table 10.1 for a summary of the assignments specific to each data range.)

To add legends to a graph, select **Options Legend** from the /Graph menu. The following menu appears:

   A B C D E F Range

Select the data range to which you are assigning a legend. Then, in response to the prompt, type the text for the legend or enter a backslash followed by the address of the worksheet cell containing the legend text. Select **Range** to specify a worksheet range containing legend text for all the data ranges.

To illustrate the use of legends, you can add a second data range to the Sales Data line graph, and then add legends to identify the two data ranges. Suppose, for example, that you want the graph to reflect two items: Gross Sales and Expenses.

To add the second data range, select **/Graph**, choose **B**, and then enter the range for the Expenses data: **A:B10..A:G10**. Next, select Options Legend, and choose **A** to specify the legend for the first data range. Enter **Gross Sales** or, alternatively, **\A9**. The program returns to the Options menu. To specify the legend for the second data range, again select Legend, choose **B**, and enter either **Expenses** or **\A10**. Finally, press F10 to display the graph. The modified graph should appear similar to the one shown in figure 10.16.

To edit a legend, use the same command sequence you used to create the legend. The existing text, cell reference, or range name appears in the control panel, ready for you to edit. To eliminate a legend, press Esc, and then press Enter.

Cue:
To edit a data legend or a graph label, follow the same steps used to create the legend or label.

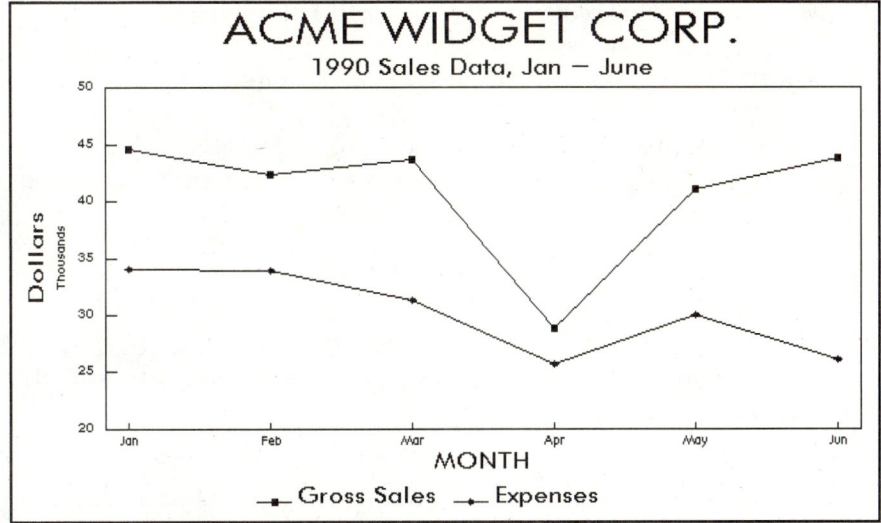

Fig. 10.16.
A graph with two data ranges and their legends.

Legends are appropriate only for graphs with two or more data series. You cannot use the Legend option for pie graphs, which have only one data series.

Altering the Default Graph Display

The graph enhancements discussed so far all involved making additions to a basic, simple graph. Other enhancements are possible by modifying the default settings 1-2-3 uses to create a simple graph. In this section, you learn to enhance the basic line graph by changing some of 1-2-3's defaults. This chapter's "Building All Graph Types" section discusses some default settings that apply to other graph types.

Selecting the Format for Data in Graphs

The /Graph Options Format selection enables you to specify the format of the lines in graphs that include lines: line, XY, mixed, and HLCO graphs. (The option affects only the line portions of mixed and HLCO graphs.) When you select Format from the Options menu, the following menu appears:

   Graph A B C D E F Quit

Select the data range whose format you want to specify, or select Graph to set the format for all data ranges. Next, the following menu appears:

   Lines Symbols Both Neither Area

The selections have the following effects:

   Lines   The data points are connected by lines, but no symbols are displayed.

Symbols   A symbol is displayed at each data point, but the symbols are not connected by lines.

Both   Both symbols and connecting lines are displayed. This is the default.

Neither   Neither symbols nor lines are displayed. (This option is used with centered data labels, as described in a preceding section).

Area   The space between the indicated line and the line below it (or the x-axis) is filled with a color or hatch pattern. If **Area** format is specified for more than one data range, the lines are stacked. Negative values in the line are treated as zeros.

Experiment with these settings to see the effect. For example, selecting /Graph Options Format Graph Area results in the sample graph as shown in figure 10.17.

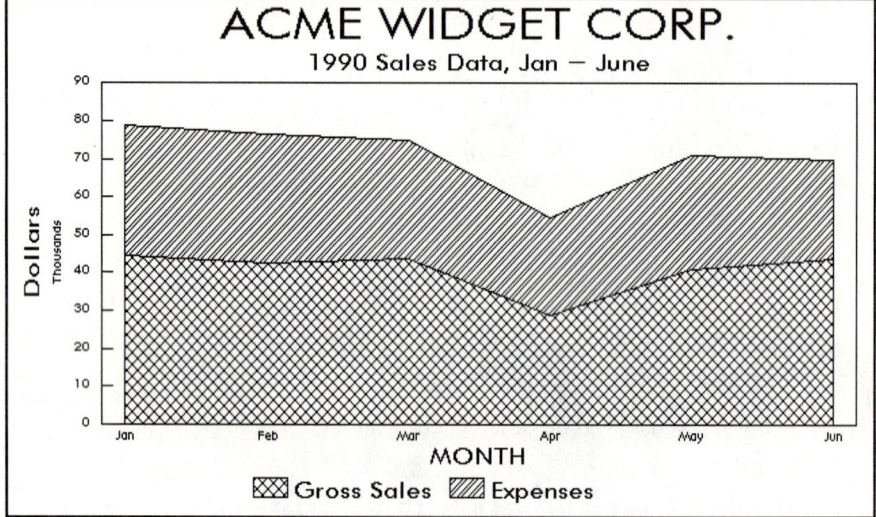

Fig. 10.17.
An area graph.

Setting a Background Grid

Grid lines can help make your data-point values easier to read. 1-2-3 enables you to specify horizontal and/or vertical grid lines. Horizontal grid lines are shown in figure 10.18.

Selecting /Graph Options Grid produces the following menu:

   Horizontal   Vertical   Both   Clear   Y-Axis

The selections on this menu have the following effects:

Reminder:
Use /Graph Options Grid to display a vertical grid, horizontal grid, or both on your graph.

Horizontal   Draws across the graph a series of horizontal lines, spaced according to the tick marks on the y-axis

Vertical   Draws across the graph a series of vertical lines, spaced according to the tick marks on the x-axis

Both   Draws both horizontal and vertical lines

Y-Axis Determines whether Horizontal grid lines are drawn according to tick marks on the left y-axis, the right y-axis, or both

Clear   Clears all grid lines from the graph

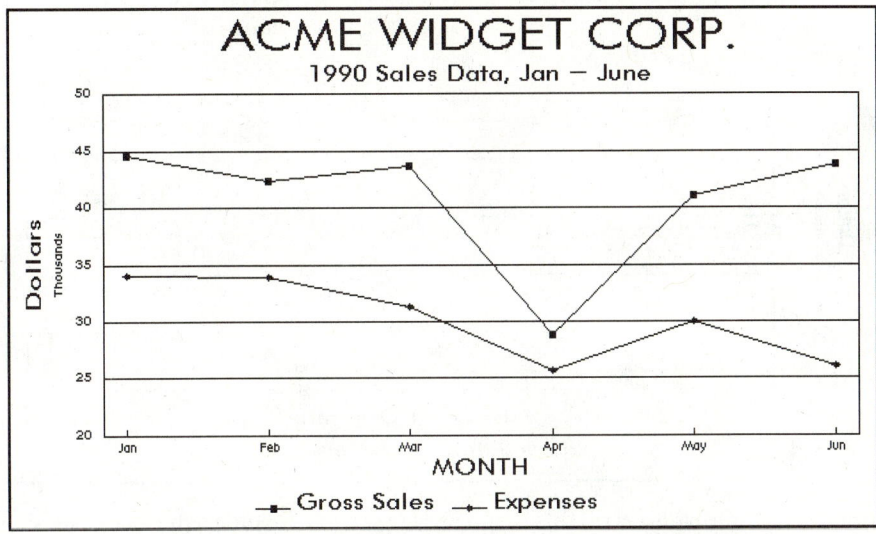

Fig. 10.18.
A graph with horizontal grid lines.

To add horizontal lines to the sample graph, select /Graph Options Grid Horizontal and press F10. The graph should look like the one shown in figure 10.18 (assuming that you first selected Options Format Graph Both to turn off the area graph option).

Experiment with different grids, repeating the command sequence and specifying other options. Whenever you want to eliminate a grid display, select /Graph Options Grid Clear.

Reminder:
You cannot add a grid to a pie graph.

Modifying the Graph Axes

The Scale option takes you to a series of menus that enable you to control various aspects of how the graph's axes are displayed. When you select /Graph Options Scale, the following menu appears:

    Y-Scale X-Scale Skip 2Y-Scale

If you choose Skip, you can specify that you want the graph to display only every *n*th data point in the X range. The *n* variable can range from 0 to 8192, although you almost always use low values such as 2 or 5.

If you select /Graph Options Scale Skip and enter a value of 2, the resulting graph looks similar to the one shown in figure 10.19. Notice that only Jan, Mar, and May are displayed on the x-axis scale; Feb, Apr, and Jun have been skipped. In this case

Reminder:
Scale options do not apply to pie graphs.

Cue:
Use /Graph Options Scale Skip when you have too many x-axis values to display together.

using **Skip** does not improve the graph's appearance. If the month names were spelled out in full, however, they would look too crowded if all were displayed. Using **Skip** then would make the x-axis more legible.

Fig. 10.19.
The graph with Skip set to 2.

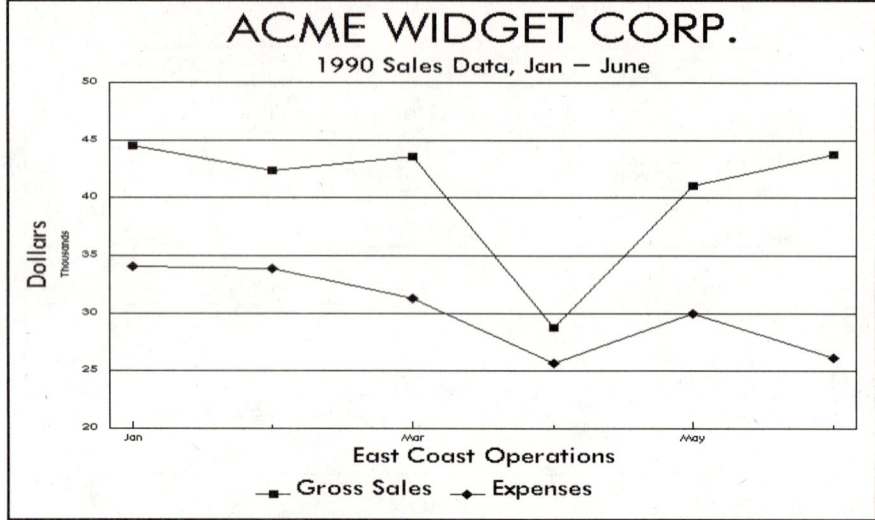

The other three options on this menu are for selecting which axis to change: the y-axis, the x-axis, or the second (right) y-axis. Whichever axis you select, the series of menus and options that appears after you select an axis is the following:

Automatic Manual Lower Upper Format Indicator Type Exponent Width Quit

Remember that any changes made from this menu apply only to the specific graph axis selected in the previous step.

Minimum and Maximum Axis Values

Reminder:
1-2-3 automatically includes a y-axis scale.

When you create a graph with 1-2-3, the program automatically sets the scale, or minimum-maximum range, of the y-axis based on the smallest and largest numbers in the data range(s) plotted. This default applies as well to the second y-axis when it is used. For XY graphs, 1-2-3 also automatically establishes the x-axis scale based on values in the **X** data range.

To set your own scale, you first select **Manual** and then choose **Lower** and enter the minimum axis value. Finally, you select **Upper** and enter the maximum axis value. Selecting **Automatic** returns 1-2-3 to the default automatic scaling.

Caution:
If you set the axis range too small to include all the data points, some data points are not plotted. 1-2-3 does not warn you when this happens.

Although you can change the minimum and maximum axis values, you cannot determine the size of the tick mark increment; 1-2-3 automatically sets this increment. Also, be aware that it is possible to set an axis range that is too small to include all the data points. If this happens, some data points are not plotted. 1-2-3 does not warn you when this happens.

Suppose that you want to change the y-axis origin on the sample graph. First, select /Graph Options Grid Clear to get rid of the grid lines. Next, select Scale Y-Scale Manual. Select Lower and enter 0, and then select Upper and enter 50000. Finally, press F10 to display the graph shown in figure 10.20.

Notice how the perspective of the graph has changed. Earlier, with automatic scaling, the y-axis range was from 20000 to 50000. The April dip in sales appeared more severe than it actually was. By setting the scale manually so that the y-axis origin is at 0, the visual impression of the graph more accurately reflects the actual figures.

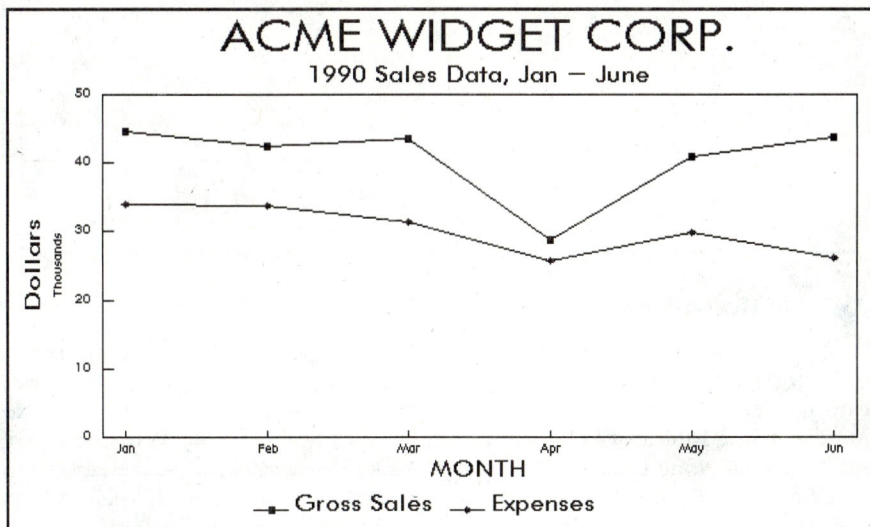

Fig. 10.20.
The graph with the y-axis scale set from 0-50000.

Axis Number Format

1-2-3's default is to display the axis scale values in General format, the same format that is the default for the screen display of worksheet values. You can display axis scale values in any of 1-2-3's numeric formats. Select Format from the /Graph Options Scale [Y-Scale, X-Scale, 2Y-Scale] menu, and the following choices appear:

    Fixed Sci Currency , General +/– Percent Date Text Hidden

Making a format choice here is exactly like selecting a format for a worksheet range with /Range Format. This process includes specifying the number of decimal places and the particular Date or Time format desired (refer to Chapter 5 for details). Note that /Graph Options Scale [Y,X,2] Format is a different command from /Graph Options Format, which controls the way lines are displayed.

For the sample graph, a currency format is appropriate for the y-axis. Select /Graph Options Scale Y-Scale Format Currency and enter 0 for the number of decimal places. Pressing Graph (F10) displays the graph as shown in figure 10.21.

Fig. 10.21.
The graph with the y-axis scale values in Currency format.

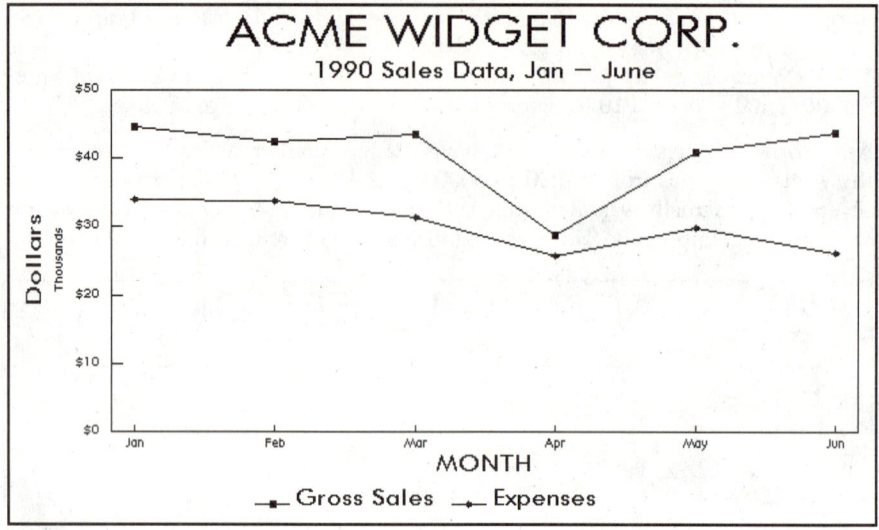

Axis Scale Indicator

When axis scale values are some multiple of 10, 1-2-3 automatically displays a scale indicator, such as *Thousands* or *Millions*, between the axis and the axis title. You can suppress display of the scale indicator or enter your own scale indicator text. After selecting **Indicator** from the /Graph Options Scale [**Y**,**X**,**2**] menu, you have three choices. **None** suppresses display of the scale indicator. **Manual** enables you to define the indicator; you can type the scale indicator text or specify a cell address preceded by a backslash. **Yes** turns the automatic indicator display back on.

To change the y-axis indicator in the sample graph, select /Graph Options Scale **Y**-Scale Indicator Manual, and then enter **X 1000**. You also can specify a cell address or a range name for the indicator text, preceded by \. If you display the graph by pressing F10, the graph appears as shown in figure 10.22.

Axis Type

The **Type** command on the /Graph Options Scale [**Y**,**X**,**2**] menu enables you to specify whether the graph axis will have a linear scale (the default) or a logarithmic scale. On a linear scale, equal distances on the axis correspond to linear increments in value—10, 20, 30, and so on. On a logarithmic scale, equal distances on the axis correspond to logarithmic (base 10) increments in value—10, 100, 1000, and so on. Although you generally use linear scales, logarithmic scales are appropriate for graphing data sets that span a wide range of values when small fluctuations at the lower end of the data range must be visible.

Consider the data shown in figure 10.23. If you graph this data as a line graph with a linear Y-scale, you get the graph shown in figure 10.24. The small values A through H are essentially hidden in this graph. Changing the y-axis to a logarithmic scale yields the graph shown in figure 10.25. This graph shows the entire range while preserving the minor fluctuations of points A through H.

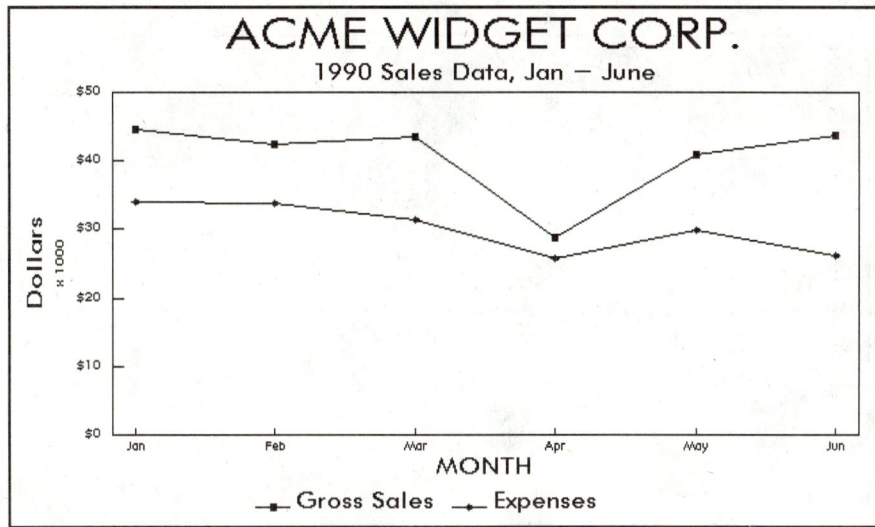

Fig. 10.22.
The graph with a manual y-scale indicator.

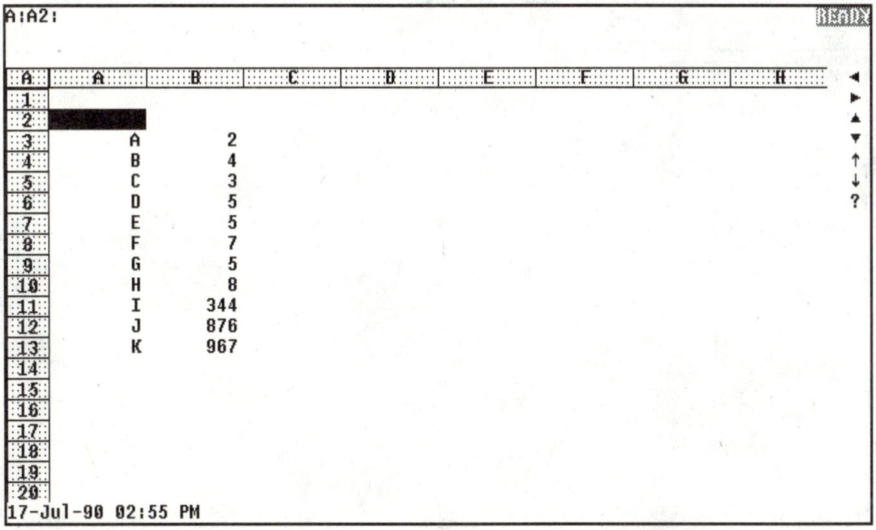

Fig. 10.23.
Sample worksheet data for linear and logarithmic plotting.

Scale Number Exponent

The *scale number exponent* is the power of 10 by which scale numbers must be multiplied to reflect the actual values in the graph. In the sample sales data graph, 1-2-3 automatically has selected an exponent of 3. The scale values—for example, 30, 40, and 50—must be multiplied by 1000 (10 to the third power) when you read the graph values. If you don't like 1-2-3's automatic selection (which is usually the most appropriate), you can manually select a scale exponent, a value between –95 and 95.

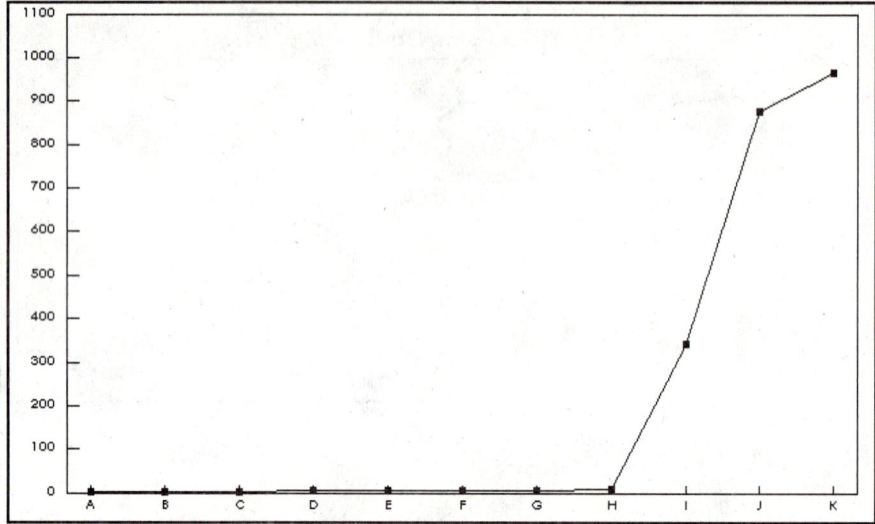

Fig. 10.24.

The data from figure 10.23 plotted on a linear y-axis.

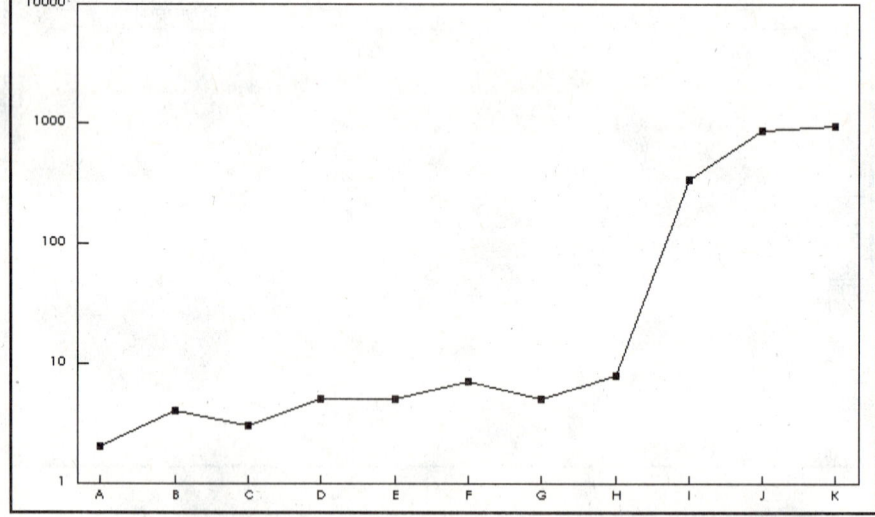

Fig. 10.25.

The data from figure 10.23 plotted on a logarithmic y-axis.

To change the exponent on the Sales Data graph, select /Graph Options Scale Y-Scale Exponent Manual and enter an exponent of 0. You also need to select Options Scale Y-Scale Indicator Yes to remove the manual scale indicator **X 1000** entered earlier. The graph now should appear as shown in figure 10.26.

Chapter 10 ◆ Creating and Printing Graphs   **433**

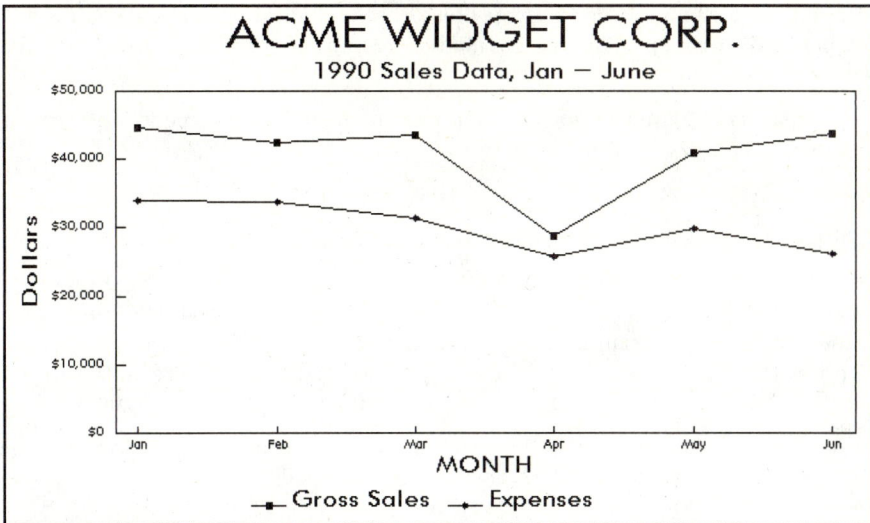

Fig. 10.26.
The y-scale exponent set manually to 0.

Scale Number Width

When you select **Width** from the /**Graph Options Scale [Y,X,2]** menu, you have two choices for specifying the maximum width of the scale numbers displayed. Choose **Automatic** (the default) to have 1-2-3 set the maximum width for scale numbers. Choose **Manual** to specify a maximum width between 0 and 50 (excluding 0). If a scale number is longer than the maximum width minus 1, 1-2-3 displays asterisks instead of the number.

Adding a Second Y Scale

1-2-3 enables you to create graphs that have two separate y-axes with different scales. The second y-axis, called the 2Y-axis, is displayed on the right side of the graph. By using dual y-axes, you can include on the same graph data sets that encompass widely different ranges of values.

Cue:
Use dual y-axes to plot data ranges that differ widely.

When you assign data ranges to graph ranges **A** through **F** in the /**Graph** menu, the ranges automatically are assigned to the first y-axis. To create a 2Y-axis, select /**Graph Type Features**. You are presented with the following menu:

   Vertical Horizontal Stacked 100% 2Y-Ranges Y-Ranges Quit

The fifth and sixth options are relevant to double y-axis graphs. (The other menu options are covered in the next section.) Select **2Y-Ranges** to display the following menu:

   Graph **A B C D E F** Quit

Selecting **Graph** assigns all data ranges (which you initially selected from the /**Graph** menu) to the 2Y-axis. Selecting **A** through **F** assigns the indicated data range to the 2Y-axis. Note that you don't enter actual ranges here—you do that from the /Graph menu. The choices made here only move existing ranges from the first to the second y-axis.

If you select **Y-Ranges** from the **Features** menu, the same menu appears, as follows:

> Graph **A B C D E F** Quit

The selections here are used to move data ranges back from the 2Y-axis to the y-axis.

To illustrate the advantages of having dual y-axes, you can modify the sample graph to display Gross Profit and Percent Profit. Select **/Graph B**, press Esc to cancel the current **B** range, and enter **A:B12..A:G12** as the **B** range. Next, select **Options Legend B** and change the **B** legend to read **Percent Profit**. When you display the graph by pressing F10, the graph appears as shown in figure 10.27.

Where are the data points for Percent Profit? These data points are in the range .10–.30, and the y-axis is scaled from 0 through 50000. The Percent Profit data points are therefore plotted almost right on top of the x-axis.

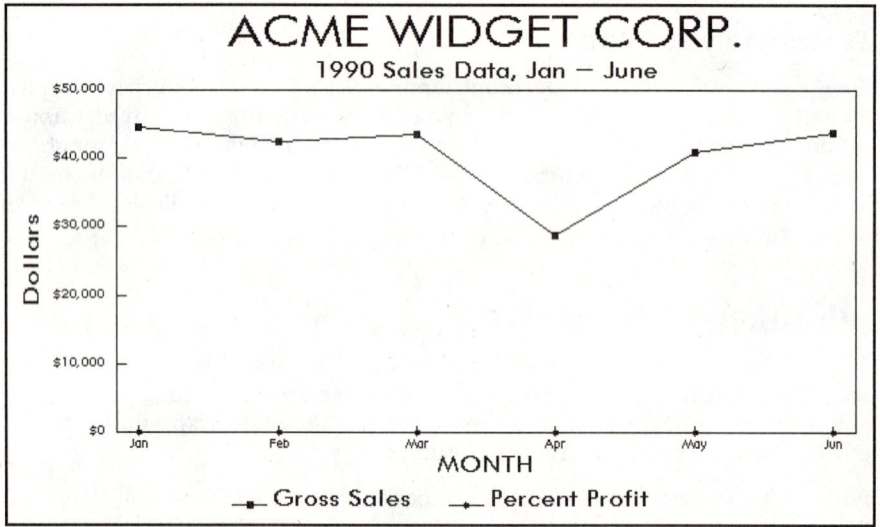

Fig. 10.27.
Gross Sales and Percent Profit graphed on a single y-axis.

To rectify this problem, return to the /Graph menu by pressing Esc, and then select **Type Features 2Y-Ranges B** to assign the **B** data range (Percent Profits) to the 2Y-axis. Next, select **Quit Quit Options Scale 2Y-Scale Format Percent** and enter **0** for the number of decimal places. Choose **Manual Lower 0** and **Upper 50%**. Then select **Quit Titles 2Y-Axis** and enter **% Profit**. Finally, press F10, and the graph shown in figure 10.28 appears. With dual axes, both the Gross Sales and the Percent Profit data ranges can be displayed clearly.

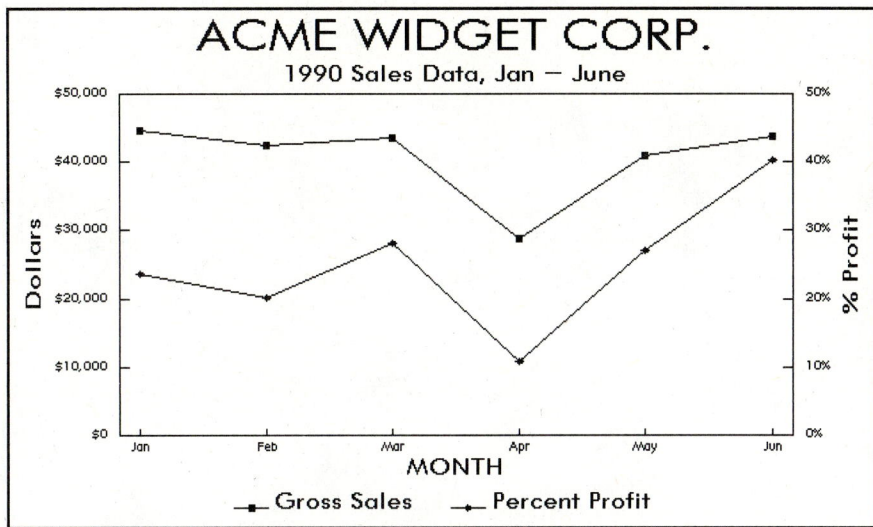

Fig. 10.28.

Gross Sales and Percent Profit graphed on dual y-axes.

Using Other Features Menu Options

The **Features** menu contains other options besides those dealing with 2Y-axes:

Vertical	Displays the graph upright, which is the default
Horizontal	Reverses the x- and y-axes. (An example is shown in this chapter's section on bar graphs.)
Stacked	This option can be used with line, bar, mixed, and XY graphs that have two or more data ranges. All the values in the data range are "stacked" on top of each other rather than being plotted relative to the x-axis.
100%	This option applies to bar, line, mixed, stacked-bar, and XY graphs that include at least two data ranges. Values in each data range are plotted as a percentage of the total value.

Figure 10.29 shows an example of a graph created without the Stacked option. The graph shows Expenses plotted as range **A** and Net Income plotted as range **B**, with **Stacked** (the default) turned off. After displaying this graph, return to the /Graph menu, select **Type Features Stacked Yes Quit**, and redisplay the graph. The graph then should appear as shown in figure 10.30. Note that the **B** range, Net Income, is stacked on, or added to, the **A** range. Because Net Profits plus Expenses equals Gross Sales, this graph actually is displaying three sets of information, even though Gross Sales is not an explicitly selected data range. Continue to enhance the graph by selecting **O**ptions **F**ormat **G**raph **A**rea. The result is shown in figure 10.31.

To illustrate the type of graph produced with the **100%** option on the **Features** menu, consider the budget worksheet shown in figure 10.32.

Fig. 10.29.
Expenses and Net Income plotted on a nonstacked line graph.

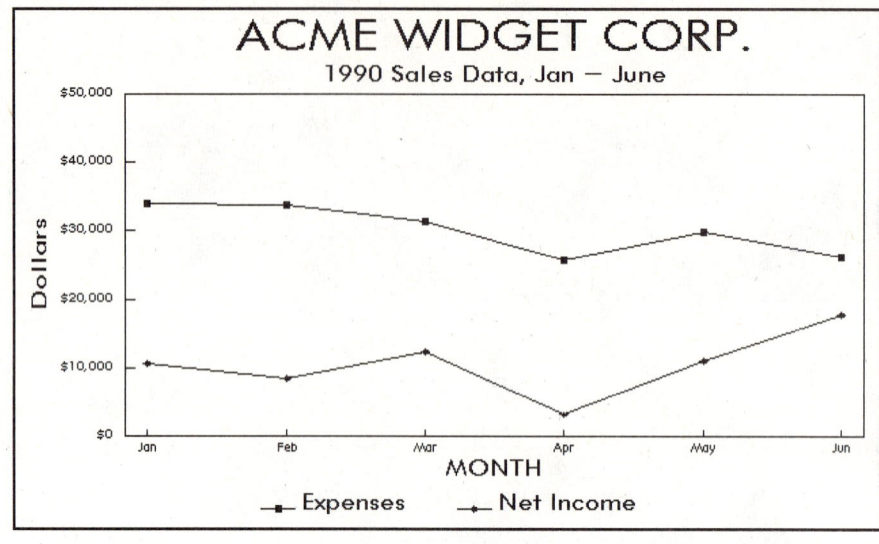

Fig. 10.30.
Expenses and Net Income plotted as a stacked line graph.

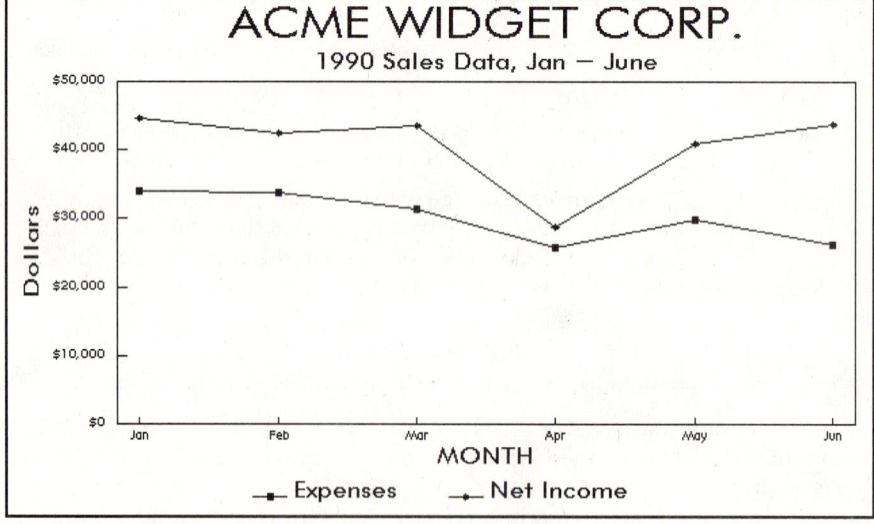

You can create a stacked-bar graph from the budget worksheet data by using the following command sequence:

/Graph Type Stack-Bar

Group A:C18..A:E22 Rowwise

Options Legend Range A:B19..A:B22

Reminder:
Use the Type Feature 100% option to plot each data range as a percentage of the total.

The resulting graph, shown in figure 10.33, shows for each month the total dollar amount spent in each of the four categories. Now, return to the /Graph menu, select Type Features 100% Yes, and redisplay the graph. The result, shown in figure

10.34, is a graph that shows the *percentage* of each month's total expenses that went to each category. For certain types of data, such as sources of income or expense categories, the 100% graph can be quite useful.

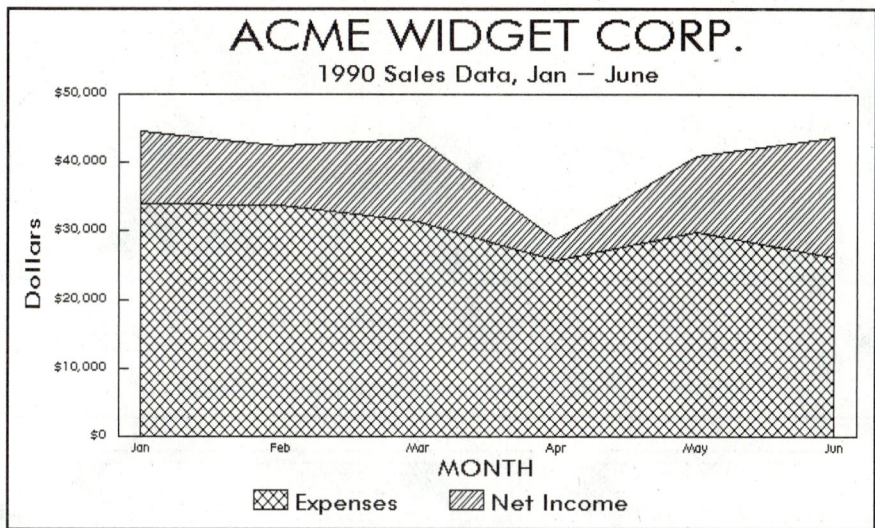

Fig. 10.31.

An area format specified to further enhance the graph.

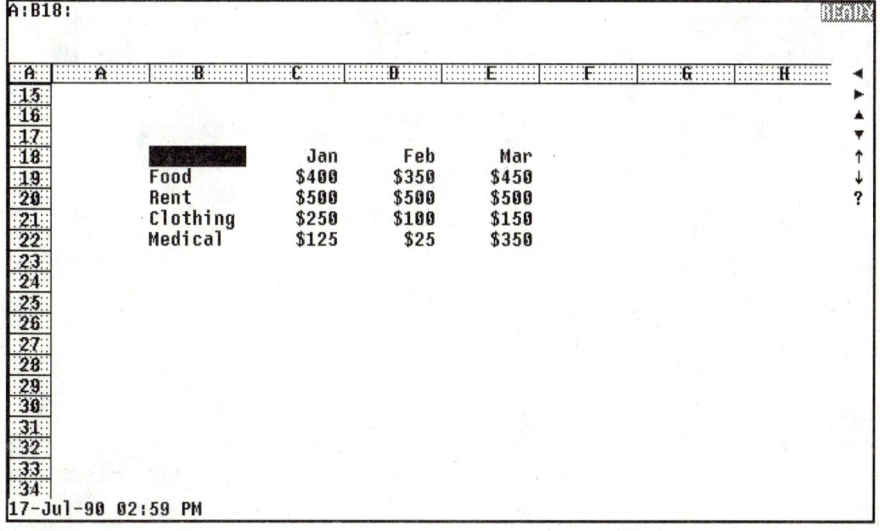

Fig. 10.32.

A three-month household expenses worksheet.

Using Advanced Graph Options

Selecting **A**dvanced from the /**G**raph **O**ptions menu takes you to the following menu:

Colors   Text   Hatches   Quit

Fig. 10.33.
The budget worksheet shown as a stacked-bar graph.

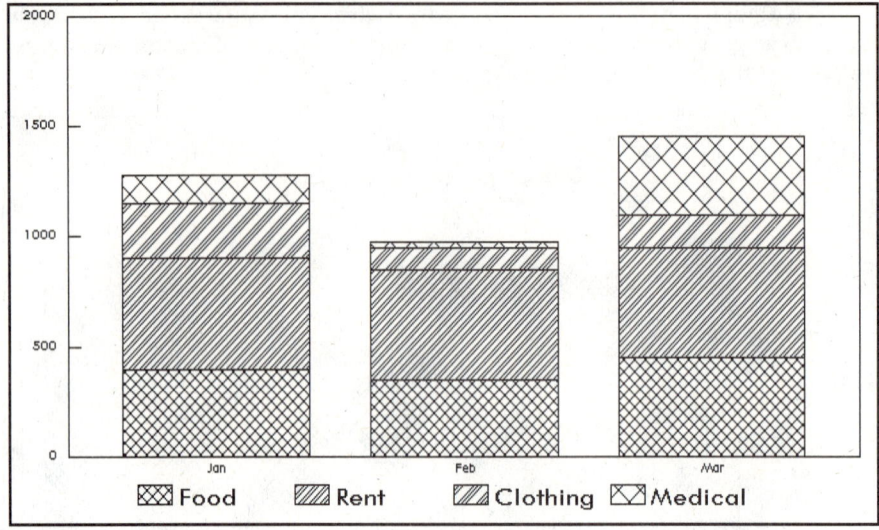

Fig. 10.34.
The budget worksheet shown as a 100% stacked-bar graph.

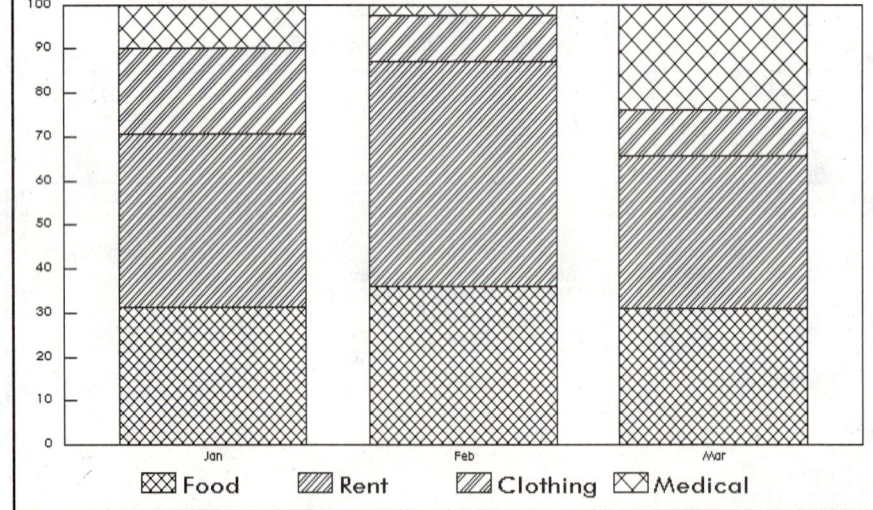

You need not use any of the Advanced options when creating a graph. The Advanced options do not add any new data or information to a graph; rather, they modify certain aspects of the way existing information on the graph is displayed and printed.

Colors

Selecting Advanced Colors specifies colors for the **A** through **F** data ranges and also enables you to hide one or more of the **A** through **F** ranges. The colors specified here are used in the graph display and also during printing (if you have a color printer). After you select **Colors**, the following menu appears:

A B C D E F Quit

Select the range whose color you want to specify. After you specify the range, the following menu appears:

1 2 3 4 5 6 7 8 Hide **R**ange

The effects of these choices are as follows:

1-8   The color that corresponds to the selected number is used for all values in the specified data range. The particular colors that correspond to the numbers 1 through 8 depend on your graphics hardware and your printer.

Hide   The selected data range is not displayed.

Range   This option enables you to specify a worksheet color range that contains the color numbers to be assigned to individual values in the selected data range. The color range must be the same size as the data range, and can contain values from 1 through 14. The color values are assigned, in order, to the values in the data range.

Although the **A**dvanced **C**olors menu provides only 8 colors, by using a color range you can specify 14 different colors. Actual display or printing of these 14 colors depends on your hardware.

By using a conditional @ function in the color range, you can display data points in a color that depends on their value. For example, to display values above 10000 in color 4 and values less than or equal to 10000 in color 7, follow these steps (assuming that the **A** data range is A:C4..A:C13):

1. Select a worksheet location for the color range—for example, A:D4..A:D13.

2. In cell A:D4, enter the formula **@IF(C4>10000,4,7)**, and then copy it to A:D4..A:D13.

3. Assign the color range by selecting /**G**raph **O**ptions **A**dvanced **C**olors **A R**ange and entering **A:D4..A:D13**.

By entering formulas in your color range, you can emphasize certain aspects of your data with colors.

Note: The default colors for data ranges **A** through **F** are colors 2 through 7, respectively. When you use a color range, the first color in the range is used for the legend key (if any) for that data range. A negative value in the colors range hides the corresponding value in the data range.

The /**G**raph **O**ptions **A**dvanced **C**olors **A R**ange setting is used for pie graphs only under certain conditions. If the graph display is set to **C**olor and colors have not been specified with a **B** data range (as discussed later in this chapter's section on

Reminder:
By using a conditional @ function in the color range, you can display data points in a color that depends on their value.

pie graphs), then the /Graph Options Advanced Colors A Range setting controls the colors used to display a pie graph. Otherwise, the setting is ignored.

Wysiwyg also offers ways to change the colors in your graph. To change the color of the area where the titles print (the *background*), use the :Graph Edit Color Background command. To change the color of each graph range, use :Graph Edit Color Map. See Chapter 11 for further information.

Hatches

The Hatches menu choice specifies the hatch patterns used for the bars in bar, stacked-bar, mixed, and HLCO graphs; the areas between lines in area graphs; and the slices in pie graphs. You use this option much like the way you set Advanced Colors. Select Advanced Hatches, and then select the desired data range A through F. Next, select 1 through 8 or Range.

1-8	Assigns the corresponding hatch pattern to the selected data range. Displayed hatch patterns 1 through 8 are the same for all monitors, but printed hatch patterns may differ depending on your printer.
Range	Lets you specify a worksheet *hatch range* that contains the hatch numbers to be assigned to individual values in the selected data range. The hatch range must be the same size as the data range, and can contain values from 1–14. The hatch values are assigned, in order, to the values in the data range.

Using a hatch range enables you to specify 14 different hatch patterns, although the Advanced Hatch menu provides only 8 patterns. The 6 additional selections are gray scales. Negative numbers in the hatch range hide the corresponding data value. The first hatch pattern in the hatch range is used for the legend key of the corresponding data range.

By using a conditional formula in the hatch range, you can display individual data values in different hatch patterns, depending on their value. This step is done in the same way as the color range, explained earlier in this chapter.

Cue:
You can display and print colored hatches by using both Advanced Colors and Advanced Hatches.

The /Graph Options Advanced Hatches A Range setting controls pie graph hatch patterns only when graph display is set to Color or when graph display is set to B&W and hatch patterns are not specified with a B range (as discussed later, in this chapter's section on pie graphs).

Text

The Advanced Text selection enables you to specify attributes for the text displayed and printed on graphs. When you select Advanced Text, the following menu appears:

   First   Second   Third   Quit

Use this menu to specify the exact text whose attributes you want to change:

First The first line of the graph title

Second The second line of the graph title, the axis titles, and legend text

Third The scale indicators, axis labels, data labels, and footnotes

After you select the text group to be changed, the following menu appears:

Color Font Size Quit

The **Color** option selects the color to be used for the specified text group. The settings made here are displayed only when the graph display is set to **Color**, and are printed on a color printer. After selecting **Color**, select color **1** through **8**, or **Hide**. As before, the colors that correspond to the color numbers 1-8 depend on your graphics hardware and your printer. **Hide** suppresses display of the selected text whether display is set to **Color** or **B&W**.

The **Font** option enables you to select the font, or typestyle, used for the specified text group. You can select font **1** through **8**, or **Default** to use the default font for that text group. The defaults are font 1 for the first text group and font 3 for the second and third text groups. To see examples of your printer's eight fonts, use the **/Print Printer Sample Go** command (see Chapter 8).

Cue:
You can specify different fonts for different parts of the graph.

The **Size** menu choice is used to specify the size of text to be used in the graph. Select a size (**1** through **9**), or **Default** to use the default size for that text group. The defaults are size 7 for the first text group, size 4 for the second text group, and size 2 for the third text group. Larger numbers correspond to larger type size.

Note: While you can specify nine text sizes, 1-2-3 uses only three of them for screen display. Settings **1-3** display in the smallest text size, settings **4-6** in the medium size, and settings **7-9** in the largest size. The sizes available for printed graphs depend on your printer and on the font selected with **Advanced Text Font**. You can use the print sample to get an indication of your printer's text size capabilities.

If the text size you specify won't fit on the graph (both displayed and printed), 1-2-3 automatically reduces the text size (if a smaller size is available). If the text still won't fit, it is truncated.

The Wysiwyg commands offer a way to proportionally magnify or reduce all the text in the chart. For example, you can increase the text size by 120 percent. Use the **:Graph Edit Options Font-Magnification** command. See Chapter 11 for further information.

Figure 10.35 displays a graph using 1-2-3's defaults for all features that can be changed on the **/Graph Options Advanced** menu. Compare that figure with figure 10.36, which displays some changes in hatching and text size. These figures should give you some idea of the flexibility that 1-2-3's **Advanced** graph options provide.

Fig. 10.35.
A bar graph displayed with default settings.

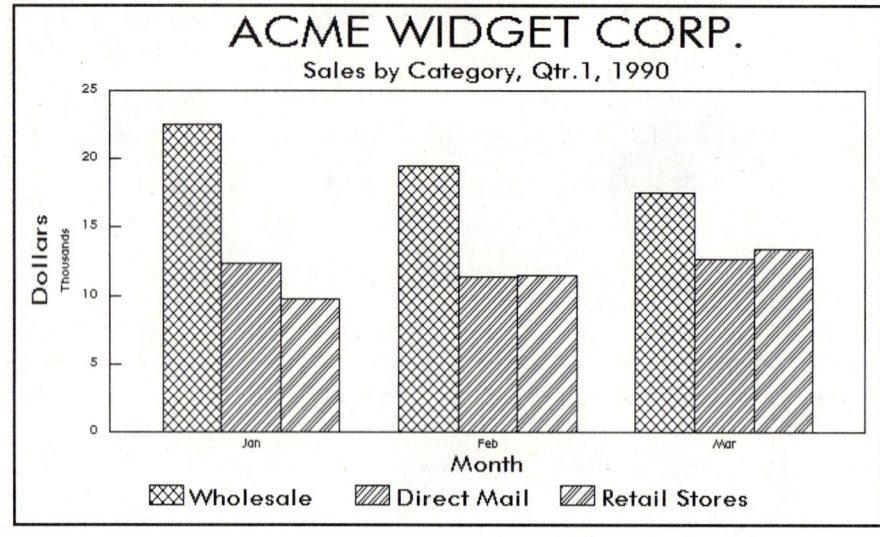

Fig. 10.36.
The same graph with modifications to text size and hatch styles.

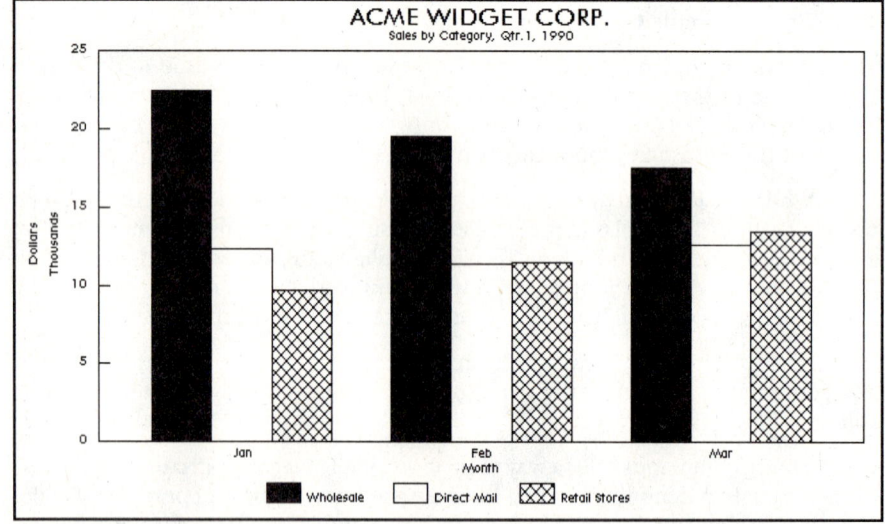

The **Advanced** options give you a great amount of control over the final appearance of printed graphs. The options provide just a bit less control over displayed graphs. Of course, a lot depends on your specific hardware setup. If you have a VGA graphics display and a laser printer, you have a lot more flexibility than if you have a CGA display and a dot-matrix printer. The best approach is to use this chapter as a guide as you experiment with your setup.

Viewing Graphs

Several options are available in 1-2-3 for viewing a graph on-screen. You can view a graph from within the worksheet, by using the entire screen to display the graph. Depending on your video hardware, you may be able to display a graph in a screen "window," leaving the worksheet visible in the remainder of the screen. You also can decide whether to view the graph in color or in black and white.

Viewing Graphs from the Worksheet

While working in a worksheet, you can view a graph in two ways. You either can press **Graph** (F10) or issue the **/Graph View** command. If a graph is currently defined, 1-2-3 clears the screen and displays the graph. If no graph is defined, 1-2-3 attempts to create an automatic graph (discussed earlier in this chapter) based on the position of the cell pointer. If the cell pointer is in a valid automatic graph range, the automatic graph appears. If not, 1-2-3 beeps and displays a blank screen. Pressing Esc returns you to your worksheet.

After you have defined a graph, you can use Graph (F10) and Esc to alternate quickly between the worksheet and the graph. This technique can be used for "what-if" scenarios; as you modify worksheet data, you can quickly see the effects of the changes graphically.

Cue:
Use Graph (F10) to toggle between graph display and worksheet display.

Viewing Graphs in a Screen Window

One useful feature of 1-2-3 is the ability to view a graph in a screen window. Selecting **/Worksheet Window Graph** splits the screen vertically at the column to the right of the cell pointer. The current graph, if any, is displayed in the right window, and the worksheet remains displayed in the left window. Any changes made in the worksheet data or in the graph settings are reflected immediately in the graph display. Figure 10.37 shows a 1-2-3 screen with a graph displayed in a window.

Displaying a graph in a window can be extremely useful during graph development. You can see instantly on-screen the effects of changes in data ranges, options, or graph types. Note that **/Worksheet Window Graph** does not work with all video hardware. With certain video adapters, you can display graphs full-screen, but not in a window.

Viewing Graphs in Wysiwyg

Wysiwyg offers yet another way to view your graphs. After defining the graph with 1-2-3's **/Graph** commands, you can insert it into a worksheet range with Wysiwyg's **:Graph Add** command. As with 1-2-3's graph window, you can simultaneously see your worksheet data and its chart. See Chapter 11 for details.

Fig. 10.37.
The /Worksheet Window Graph command used to display the current graph in a screen window.

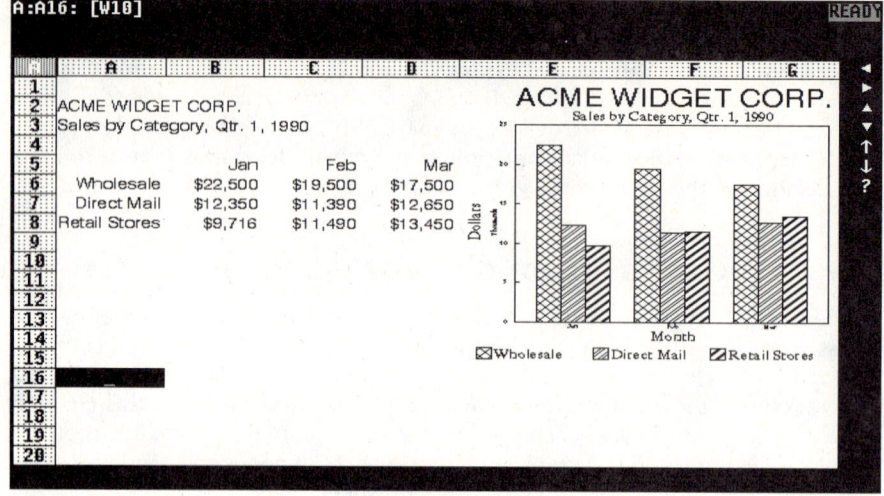

Viewing a Graph in Color

The /Graph Options Color and B&W (black and white) options determine whether graphs are displayed in monochrome or color. For color display, of course, you need a color monitor. You can select B&W with either a color or monochrome monitor.

When a graph is displayed in color, each data range is displayed in a different color. When displayed in monochrome, data ranges are differentiated by symbols, shapes, or shading patterns. Some of 1-2-3's shading patterns are shown in the graph in figure 10.38. You see more patterns in this chapter's section on bar graphs.

Fig. 10.38.
1-2-3's hatch patterns.

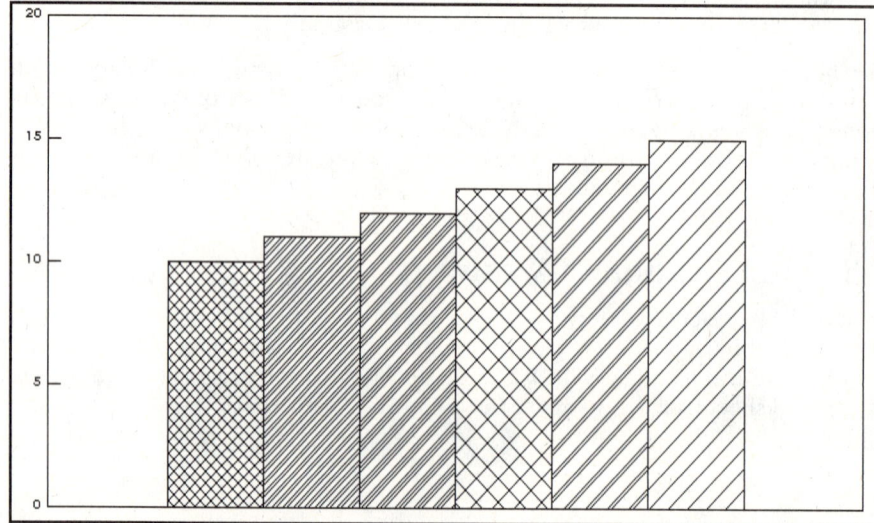

Saving Graphs and Graph Settings

You have learned how to create a basic graph and how to use options to enhance the display of that graph. This section shows you how to use the **S**ave option to save the graph for use by other programs. With the **N**ame option, you can save the settings for one or more graphs for later recall within the worksheet.

Cue:
*Use /**G**raph **N**ame to save a graph for later recall in the worksheet.*

Saving Graphs on Disk

Unlike earlier versions of 1-2-3, Release 3 does not require that a graph be saved to disk before printing. You can, however, save a graph in a disk file for later modification by other programs.

1-2-3 can save graphs in either of two file formats: *Picture* or *Metafile.* **P**icture is the standard graph file format used in all versions of 1-2-3 and Symphony. **M**etafile is a file format recognized by many other programs. For example, desktop publishing programs (such as PageMaker and Ventura Publisher) are able to import **M**etafile format files. Which format you use depends on the **/W**orksheet **G**lobal **D**efault **G**raph setting. To determine the current setting, select **/W**orksheet **G**lobal **D**efault **S**tatus and look for the entry under Graph save extension:. If PIC is listed, then graphs are saved in **P**icture file format. If C G M is displayed, **M**etafile format is used. To change the setting, select **/W**orksheet **G**lobal **D**efault **G**raph, and then select **M**etafile or **P**IC.

To save a graph, select **/G**raph **S**ave. You are then prompted for the file name. You can use the arrow keys to highlight an existing name, or type a name that is as many as eight characters long. 1-2-3 automatically supplies the PIC or CGM extension, depending on the format selected. If a file by the same name exists in the current directory, you see a **C**ancel/**R**eplace menu similar to that which appears when you try to save a worksheet file under an existing name. To overwrite the contents of the existing file, select **R**eplace. To abort storage of the current graph, select **C**ancel.

If you have set up subdirectories for disk storage, you can store the graph in a subdirectory other than the current one without first having to issue a **/F**ile **D**irectory command to change directories. To store the graph, select **/G**raph **S**ave. Press Esc twice to remove all existing current directory information. Then type the name of the subdirectory in which you want to store this particular graph, followed by the file name.

Saving Graph Settings

Although using 1-2-3 to construct a graph from existing data in a worksheet is easy, having to rebuild the graph whenever you want to print or display it on-screen would be tedious. Graphs saved to disk cannot be recalled into 1-2-3. You can, however, save the settings for one or more graphs and recall them later. These settings are not saved in a separate file, but are kept as part of the worksheet itself.

Reminder:
Graphs saved to disk cannot be recalled into 1-2-3.

Part II ◆ Creating 1-2-3 Reports and Graphs

To save the current graph settings, you issue the /Graph Name command to access the following menu:

Use   Create   Delete   Reset   Table

These commands perform the following actions:

Use   Displays a list of named graphs, and makes current the one you select.

Create Saves the current graph setting under a user-specified name.

Delete Deletes a single named graph.

Reset   Deletes all named graphs (Be careful!).

Table   Creates a listing of all named graphs in the current worksheet. Move the cursor to the cell where you want the listing to appear and press Enter. The listing occupies three columns and as many rows as there are named graphs. For each named graph, the listing gives the name, the type of graph (line, bar, and so on), and the first graph title. This list overwrites any existing worksheet data.

Reminder:
Use Create before you reset or change settings for the next graph.

When designing multiple graphs, be sure to use the Create option before you reset or change any settings for the next graph. If you forget, you may end up changing the previous graph's settings. Also, be sure to save the worksheet even if the actual data has not changed.

Resetting the Current Graph

You may have noticed that, throughout this chapter, instructions for editing or removing options have been given at the end of each new topic. These instructions are important because 1-2-3 continues to use an enhancement in the next version of the same graph, or in a new graph, unless you take specific actions to remove that enhancement. For example, you can build a series of six different bar graphs by specifying the graph type (with the Type option) for only the first one. Recall, for example, that after you specified the titles in the sample Sales Data graph, you did not have to specify them again for the subsequent versions of the graph.

Reminder:
To speed up the process when making substantial changes in a graph, use /Graph Reset.

If you want to make changes to only a few items in a graph's design, you can do so from the Options menu. However, if the next graph you construct is substantially different from the current one, you may want to use the /Graph Reset command. Selecting /Graph Reset produces the following menu:

Graph   X   A   B   C   D   E   F   Ranges   Options   Quit

You use these menu options in the following ways:

Graph   Cancels all current graph settings. This command resets the type, data ranges, options—everything!

X   Cancels labels displayed below the x-axis, pie-slice labels, and x-axis information for an XY graph. Clears any associated legends.

Chapter 10 ◆ Creating and Printing Graphs   447

A-F Cancels the specified data range and any associated legends.

Ranges Cancels all data ranges, including **Group** ranges, without affecting **Options**.

Options Cancels all /Graph **Options** settings, returning them to the defaults where appropriate.

Developing Alternative Graph Types

You can use 1-2-3 to build seven types of graphs: line, bar, XY, stacked-bar, mixed, HLCO, and pie. In some cases, more than one graph type can accomplish the desired presentation. Choosing the best graph for a given application can sometimes be strictly a matter of personal preference. For example, line, bar, or pie format is appropriate if you plan to graph only a single data range. At other times, however, only one graph type will do the job. For instance, HLCO graphs are specialized for presenting certain types of stock market information. Before you work through the remainder of this chapter, take a moment to learn or review the primary uses of each graph type. Then go on to learn how to construct each type of graph.

Selecting an Appropriate Graph Type

A brief summary of each graph type and its purpose follows. This list in not exhaustive, of course. Your creativity and ingenuity are the only real limiting factors when applying 1-2-3's graph types to your data.

Type	*Purpose*
Line	To show the trend of numeric data across time.
Bar	To compare related data at one point in time, or to show the trend of numeric data across time.
XY	To show the relationship between one numeric independent variable and one or more numeric dependent variables.
Stack-Bar	To show two or more data ranges in terms of the proportion of the total contributed by each data point.
Pie	To graph a single data series, showing what percentage of the total each data point contributes. Do not use this type of graph if your data contains negative numbers.
HLCO	To show fluctuations in a stock's high-low-close-open prices over time. Other types of data with high/low values (such as test scores and temperatures) can be plotted as HLCO also.
Mixed	A combination of line and bar graphs, to display in a single graph data best shown in bar format and data best shown in line format.

Reminder:
1-2-3 offers seven different graphs that can be used for any number of simple to complex applications.

Building All Graph Types

Throughout this chapter, examples of line graphs have been used to illustrate most of 1-2-3's graph enhancements. Most of the options described can be used for all the other graph types as well. This section focuses briefly on each of the graph types, giving an example and discussing any enhancements that apply particularly to that type. In this section, the example graphs are based on the worksheet shown in figure 10.39.

Fig. 10.39.
A sales-by-category worksheet.

```
A:A1: [W18]                                                      READY

         A              B          C        D        E        F       G
 1
 2  ACME WIDGET CORP.
 3  Sales by Category, Qtr. 1, 1990
 4
 5  ===========================================================
 6                              Jan      Feb      Mar     Total
 7  ======================     ======  ======   ======   ======
 8
 9          Wholesale          $22,500  $19,500  $17,500  $59,500
10          Direct Mail        $12,350  $11,390  $12,650  $36,390
11          Retail Stores      $9,716   $11,490  $13,450  $34,656
12
13  ===========================================================
14          Total Sales        $44,566  $42,380  $43,600  $130,546
15
16
17
18
19
20
17-Jul-90 03:04 PM
```

Line Graphs

Suppose that you want to create a line graph that shows the steady increase in retail store sales during the 1st quarter. To create this graph, first select /Graph Reset Graph to reset any existing graph settings. Because Line is the default graph type, you do not need to specify a type. Use the following command sequence to select the data ranges (press Enter after specifying the ranges and titles):

   /Graph A A:C11..A:E11

Next, select the X data range:

   X A:C6..A:E6

Finally, enter the graph titles:

   Options Titles First \A:A2

   Titles Second \A:A11

When you press F10, the graph shown in figure 10.40 appears.

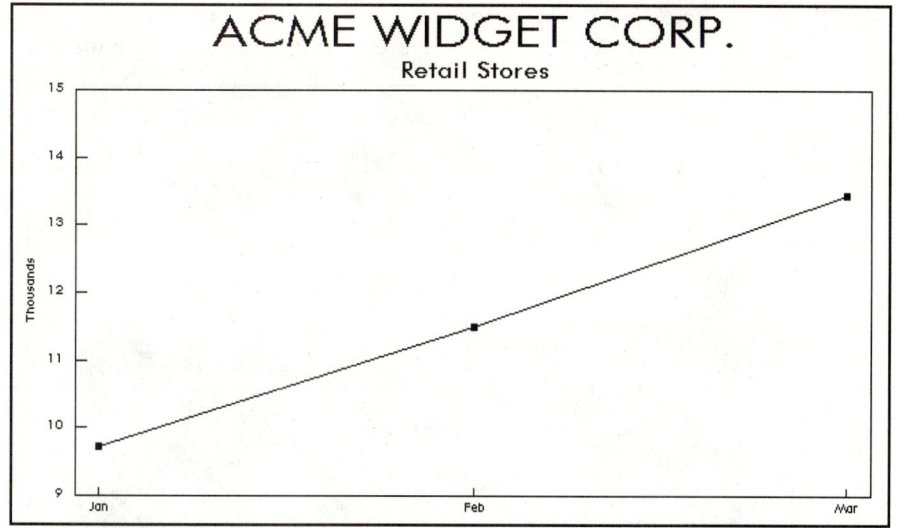

Fig. 10.40.
A line graph depicting first quarter retail sales.

Bar Graphs

Suppose that you want to create a bar graph that shows each month's sales by category. A bar graph is appropriate for this data because the differences in sales figures can be clearly shown by the different bar heights.

First, select /**G**raph **R**eset **G**raph to reset any existing graph settings. Next, use the following command sequence to select the graph type and the data ranges (press Enter after specifying ranges and titles):

/**G**raph **T**ype **B**ar

A A:C9..A:E9

B A:C10..A:E10

C A:C11..A:E11

Next, select an **X** data range and specify a range for data legends:

X A:C6..A:E6

Options **L**egend **R**ange A:A9..A:A11

Finally, specify graph titles and a y-axis title:

Titles **F**irst \A:A2

Titles **S**econd \A:A3

Titles **Y**-Axis **D**ollars

The resulting graph, shown in figure 10.41, shows that Wholesale sales have been decreasing, Direct Mail sales have been holding about steady, and Retail Store sales have been increasing. In this graph, each of the three bars clustered around a tick mark on the x-axis represents sales from a certain category for that month. In each set of bars, the leftmost bar represents data range **A**; the next, data range **B**; and the next, data range **C**. Monthly headings are centered under the x-axis tick marks.

Fig. 10.41.
Data from figure 10.39 graphed as a bar graph.

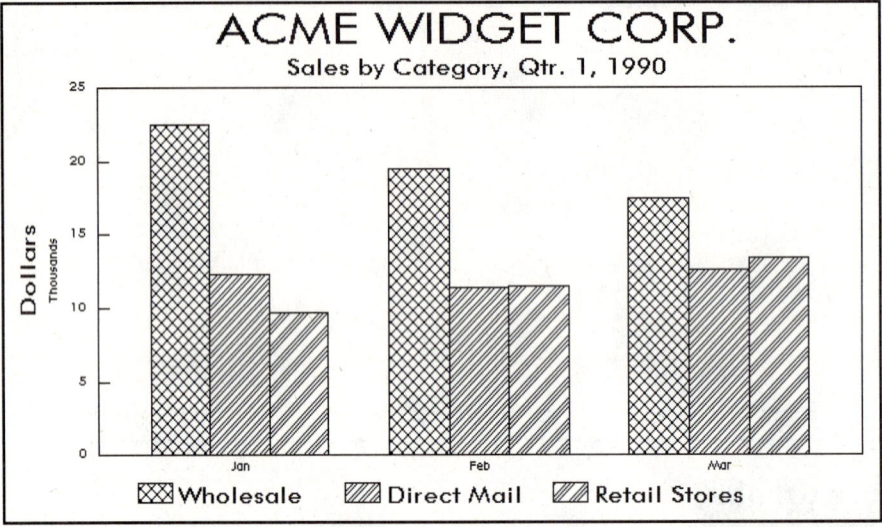

Because you need this graph for later examples, assign it a name by selecting /Graph Name Create and entering **Q1SALES**. Now you can modify the graph in the next examples, and then recall it in its original form when needed.

Reminder:
A bar graph can be displayed either vertically or horizontally.

Suppose that you want to display this graph horizontally. To do so, select **Type Features Horizontal**. The graph now is displayed as shown in figure 10.42. Horizontal display can be used with other graph types (except pie), but seems particularly appropriate for bar graphs. Selecting between **Vertical** and **Horizontal** is usually a matter of personal preference.

Stacked-Bar Graphs

You may want to experiment with different graph types when you plot multiple time-series data. If the data ranges combine in amounts to produce a meaningful figure (for example, the total monthly sales for the Acme Widget Corp.), try using Stack-Bar as a graph type. These bars are plotted in the order **A B C D E F**, with the **A** range closest to the x-axis. After having entered the command sequences to create figure 10.42, for example, you can create the stacked-bar graph shown in figure 10.43 by selecting **Type Features Vertical** to return to vertical graph display. Then select **Type Stack-Bar** from the /Graph menu, and select **View** to display the graph on-screen.

All the options you set to produce the bar graph in figure 10.42 are carried over to the new stacked-bar graph. 1-2-3 also adjusts automatically the upper and lower limits of the y-axis. In a stacked-bar graph, the lower limit must always be zero.

Chapter 10 ◆ Creating and Printing Graphs   **451**

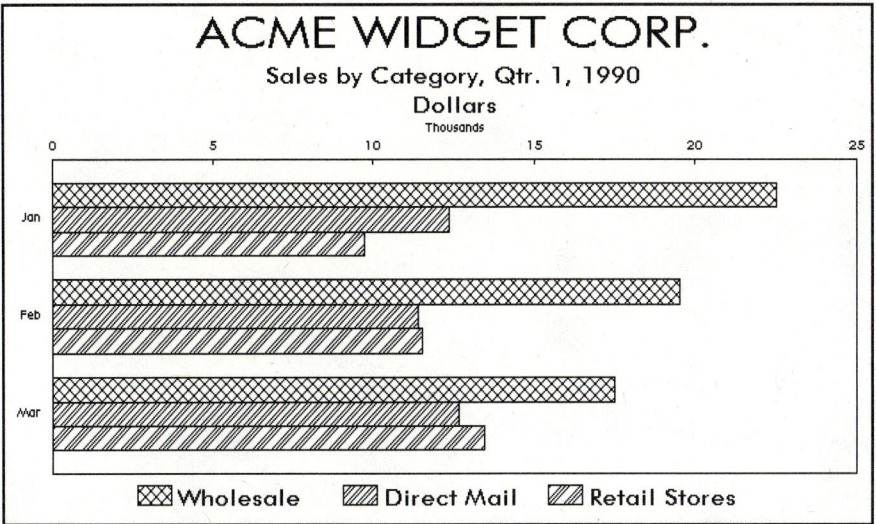

Fig. 10.42.
The graph from figure 10.41 graphed horizontally.

Distinguishing between certain patterns of crosshatches can be difficult if those patterns appear next to each other. For example, look at the patterns that represent Retail Stores and Direct Mail—the uppermost two bar sections for each month in figure 10.43. To solve this problem, assign a different hatch pattern to range C. Assuming that the current graph is shown in figure 10.43, use the following command sequences to produce the graph shown in figure 10.44:

/Graph Options Advanced Hatches **C 5**

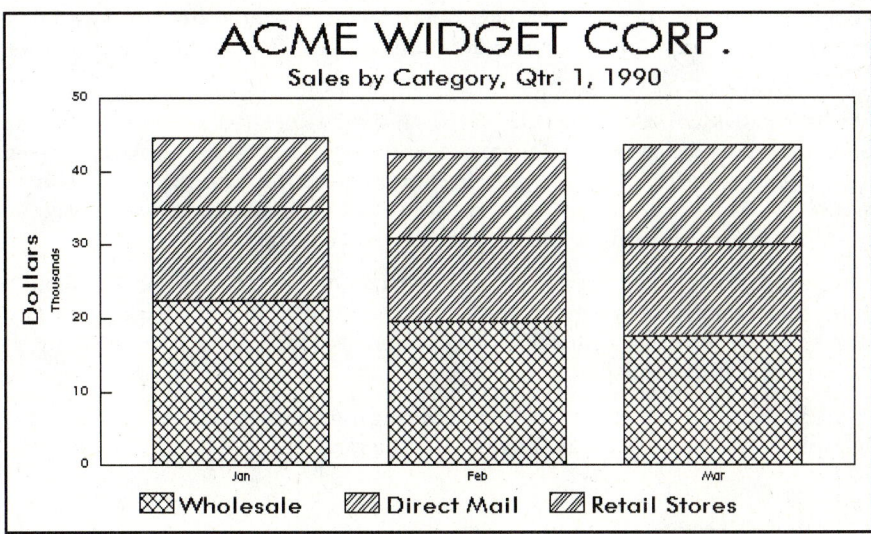

Fig. 10.43.
The graph from figure 10.42 displayed as a stacked-bar graph.

Fig. 10.44.
The hatch style for range C changed for increased legibility.

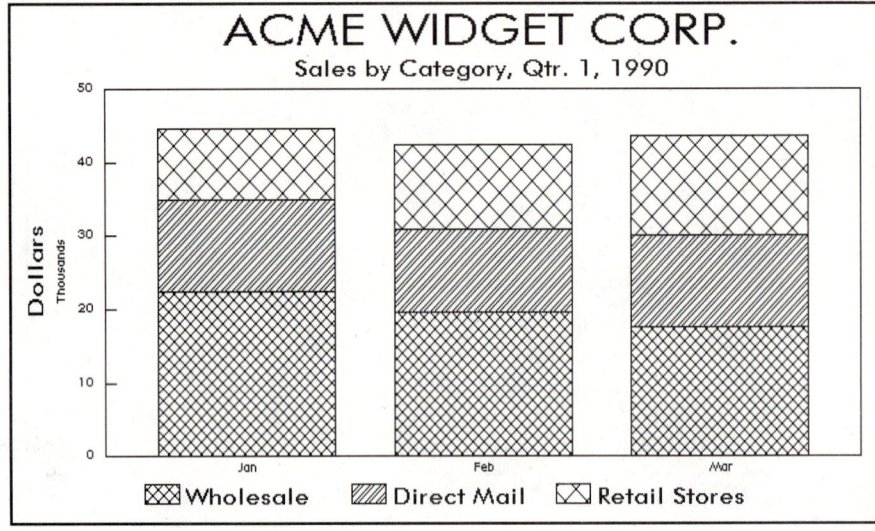

Cue:
To view a stacked-bar graph in color, assign different colors to consecutive bars.

If you compare figures 10.43 and 10.44, you can see that changing the patterns of crosshatches makes the information easier to read. If you intend to view the stacked-bar graph in color, be sure to assign different colors to consecutive bars; otherwise, you won't be able to differentiate between two distinct data items.

Mixed Graphs

A mixed graph is nothing more than a combination of the line and bar types. Data ranges **A**, **B**, and **C** are plotted as bars, and ranges **D**, **E**, and **F** are plotted as lines. Otherwise, all graph options and restrictions apply.

Suppose that you want to modify the graph in figure 10.41 to be a mixed graph that displays individual sales categories as bars and total sales as a line. First, recall the settings (remember, you saved them as a named graph) by selecting /**G**raph **N**ame **U**se, highlighting Q1SALES, and pressing Enter. The graph is displayed as shown in figure 10.41. Return to the /**G**raph menu, select **T**ype **M**ixed, and redisplay the graph. You may be surprised to see that it hasn't changed.

The graph didn't change because only the "bar" ranges, **A–C**, have been assigned. If no "line" ranges are assigned, a mixed graph displays just as a bar graph does. The converse is true as well: if line ranges but no bar ranges are assigned, a mixed graph displays as a line graph does.

You can complete the mixed graph by entering the following commands from the /**G**raph menu (press Enter after specifying the ranges):

D A:C14..A:E14

Options **L**egend **D** \A:A14

Quit **V**iew

The result is the graph shown in figure 10.45. The message of this graph is that although individual sales categories are changing, Total Sales remains relatively constant.

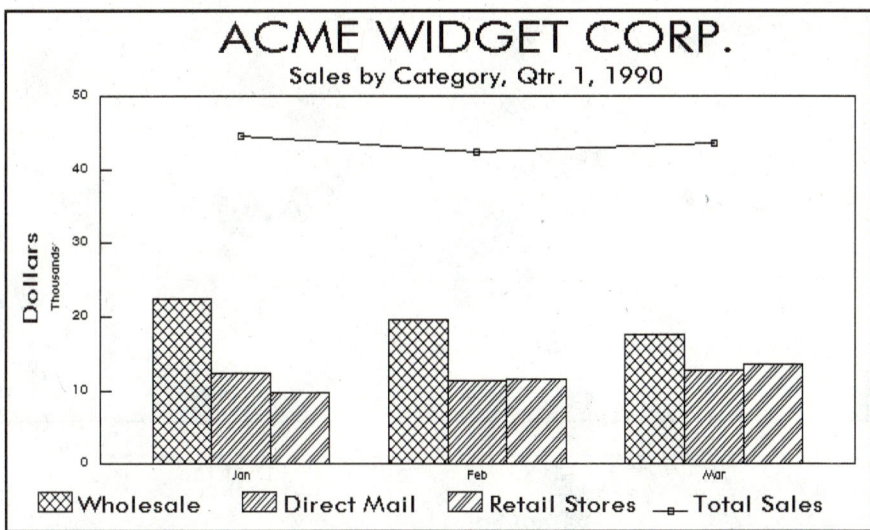

Fig. 10.45.
A mixed graph.

Pie Graphs

You use a pie graph only for plotting a single data range that contains positive numbers. Many of the /Graph menu's options, including all those dealing with graph axes, do not apply to pie graphs.

Suppose that you want to construct a pie graph from the data shown in figure 10.39, and that you want to graph the percentage of Total Sales for the quarter from each category. You start by selecting /Graph Reset Graph. Next, you select Type Pie and specify A:F9..A:F11 as data range A. When you display the graph, it appears as shown in figure 10.46.

1-2-3 automatically calculates and displays parenthetically the percentage of the whole represented by each pie slice. These percentage values can be suppressed by using a C range, as described in the text that follows.

You can enhance this basic pie graph by adding titles and an X range of explanatory labels. For example, you can use the labels in column A as the X range by entering the following command sequence (press Enter after specifying ranges and titles):

/Graph X A:A9..A:A11

Options Titles First \A:A2

Titles Second Total Sales by Category

Quit View

The resulting graph is shown in figure 10.47.

Fig. 10.46.
A default pie graph.

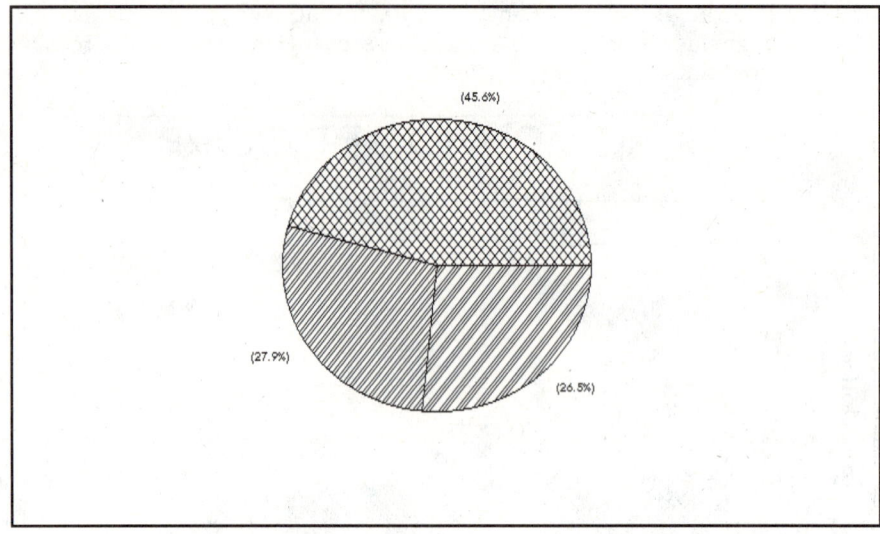

Fig. 10.47.
A pie graph enhanced with titles and labels.

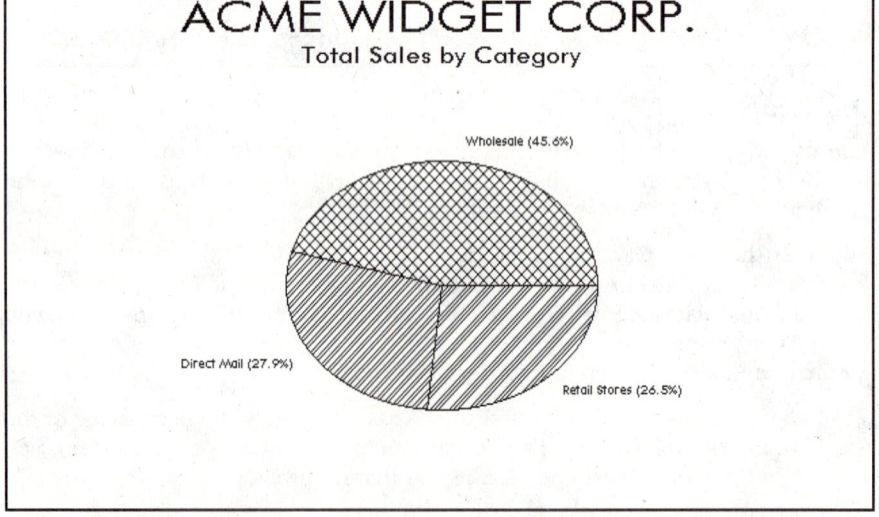

1-2-3 provides eight different shading patterns for monochrome display, eight different colors for EGA color display, and four colors for CGA color display.

Figure 10.48 shows the pie graph shading patterns associated with each code number.

1-2-3 automatically displays the pie slices in different colors or hatch patterns, depending on whether **Options B&W** or **Options Color** is in effect. You can modify the assignment of colors or hatching, and optionally "explode" individual pie slices for emphasis. You do this by using the **B** data range to enter codes for the pattern or colors for each pie slice. The **B** range can be any range of your

Cue:

*Use the **B** data range to specify colors or hatch patterns for the wedges of a pie graph.*

worksheet that is the same size as the **A** data range being plotted as a pie graph. The codes for color *or* hatch pattern, depending on whether the graph is displayed in black and white or color, are as follows:

0	An unshaded pie slice without an outer border
1-7	A specified hatch pattern or color
8	An unshaded pie slice with an outer border
Negative value	A hidden slice

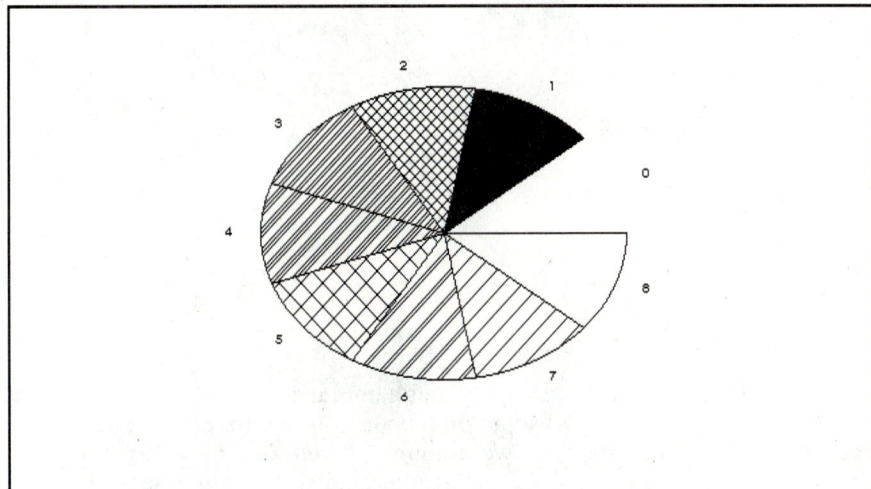

Fig. 10.48.
The pie graph hatch patterns associated with each code number.

Adding 100 to the preceding codes results in an exploded pie slice.

Suppose that you want to add shading or exploding codes to the Sales-by-category worksheet graph. Although you can put the **B** range anywhere in the worksheet, put it adjacent to the **A** range for this example. In cells A:G9..A:G11, enter the values **4**, **5**, and **106**, in that order. Then, from the /Graph menu, specify those three cells as the **B** range. Selecting **View** displays the graph shown in figure 10.49.

To assign both colors and hatch patterns to a pie graph, use /**G**raph **O**ptions **A**dvanced **H**atches **A R**ange (as described in this chapter's "Using Advanced Graph Options" section). To hide a pie slice, include a negative number in the corresponding cell of the **B** range.

To suppress the display of percentage values on the pie graph, assign a **C** range in the same manner as the **B** range. A value of 0 in a cell in the **C** range suppresses the percentage display for the corresponding pie slice. A blank cell retains the percentage display. Note: You can have a **C** range with no **B** range.

Fig. 10.49.
A pie graph with an exploded slice.

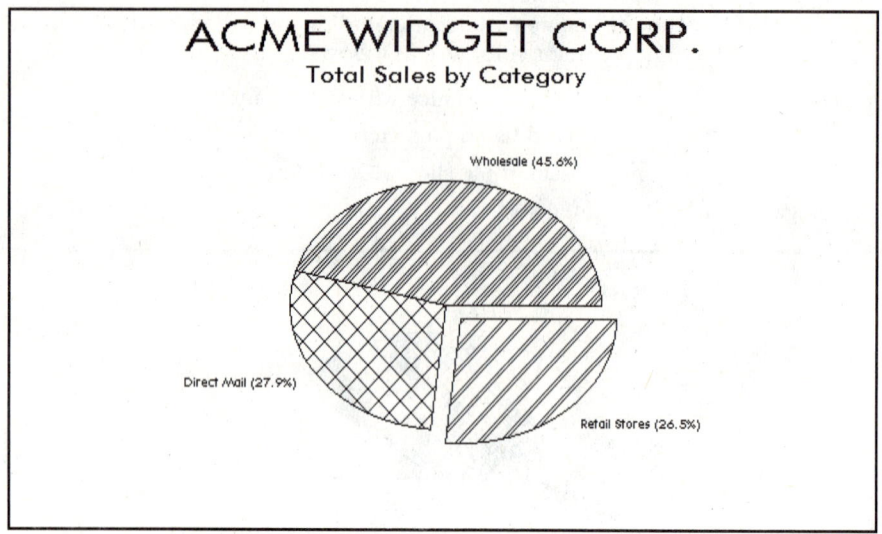

XY Graphs

The XY graph, often called a *scatter plot*, is a unique variation of a line graph. In an XY graph, a data point's position on the x-axis is determined by a numerical value rather than by a category. Two or more different data items from the same data range can have the same X value. Rather than showing time-series data, XY graphs illustrate the relationships between different attributes of data items—age and income, for example, or educational achievements and salary. You must think of one data item (X) as the *independent variable* and consider the other item (Y) to be dependent on the first—that is, the *dependent variable*. Use the /Graph menu's **X** data range to specify the range containing the independent variable, and one or more of the **A B C D E F** options to enter the dependent variable(s).

Suppose that you want to create a graph that shows the relationship between the amount spent on advertising each month and the sales generated. For the example, you can use the data in figure 10.50, which shows the advertising budget and sales by month for an entire year. Note that a line graph would be an appropriate type for plotting Sales as a function of Month. For Sales vs. Advertising Budget, however, you must use an XY graph.

Chapter 10 ◆ Creating and Printing Graphs

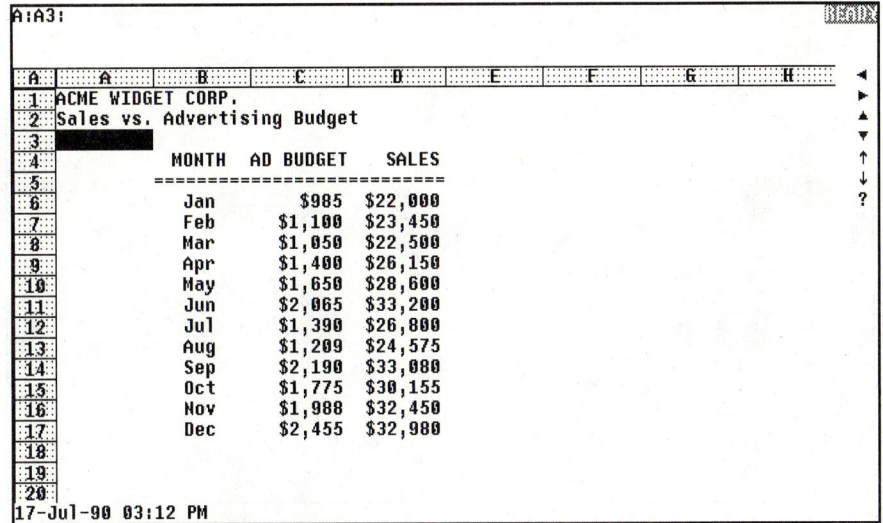

Fig. 10.50.

Data to be plotted on an XY graph.

To create the XY graph, enter the following commands (press Enter after specifying ranges):

/Graph Type XY

X A:C6..A:C17

A A:D6..A:D17

The resulting graph is shown in figure 10.51.

Notice that the data points are connected by lines, making the graph difficult to interpret. This problem results because 1-2-3 orders the data points from right to left based on the values in the **X** range (smallest to largest), while the points are connected in the order they appear in your worksheet. Therefore, for XY graphs, you usually set Format to Symbols. Setting Format to Symbols plots each data point as a symbol without lines connecting the symbols. Use the following /Graph commands to make that change and to add some other enhancements (press Enter after specifying the titles):

/Graph Options Format Graph Symbols Quit

Titles First \A:A1

Titles Second \A:A2

Titles X-Axis \A:C4

Titles Y-Axis \A:D4

The resulting graph is shown in figure 10.52.

Cue:

To create a scatter plot, use an XY graph with Format set to Symbols.

Fig. 10.51.
The basic XY graph.

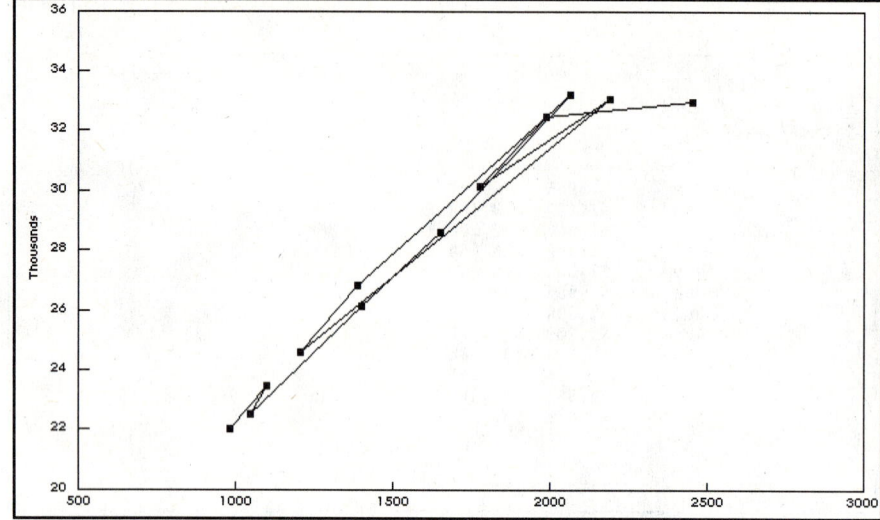

Fig. 10.52.
The enhanced XY graph.

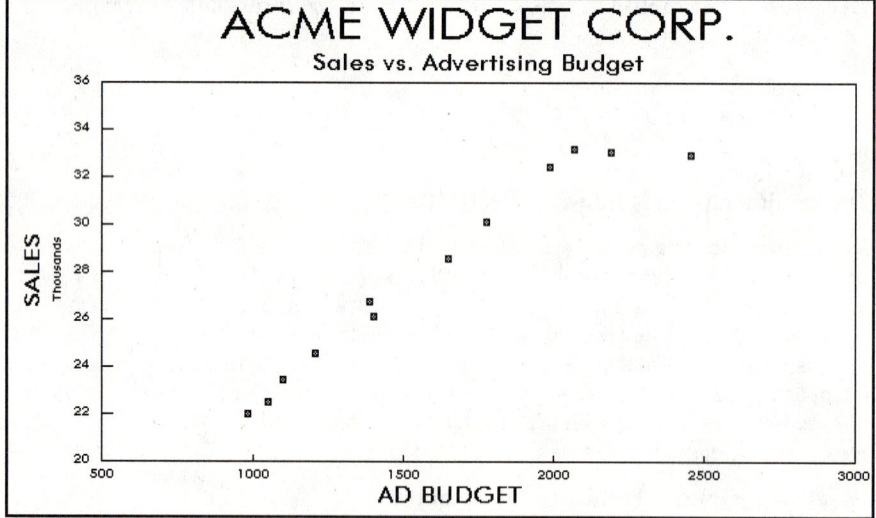

This graph clearly shows a trend between advertising expenditures and sales. As the advertising budget goes up, so do sales. Note, however, that the plot "flattens out" at the top, suggesting that once advertising expenditures increase beyond $2000 per month, they are not having any additional effect on sales.

HLCO Graphs

HLCO stands for high-low-close-open. This graph is a special type used in graphing data about the price of stock over time. The meanings of the values are as follows:

High	The stock's highest price in the given time period
Low	The stock's lowest price in the given time period
Close	The stock's price at the end, or close, of the time period
Open	The stock's price at the start, or open, of the time period

Reminder: *Use an HLCO graph to plot stock market information.*

While HLCO graphs are specialized for stock market information, they also can be used to track other kinds of fluctuating data over time, such as daily temperature or currency exchange rates.

Each set of data—four figures representing high, low, close, and open values—is represented on the graph as one vertical line. The vertical extent of the line (that is, the length) is from the low value to the high value. The close value is represented by a tick mark extending right from the line, and the open value by a tick mark extending left. The total number of lines on the graph depends on the number of time periods included.

An HLCO graph also can include a set of bars and a line across the graph. The bars and line can be used for any quantity you want. In the financial world, the bars often are used to illustrate daily trading volume for the stock.

Data ranges for an HLCO graph are assigned as follows:

Range	Values or elements
A	The high values
B	The low values
C	The closing values
D	The opening values
E	The bars
F	The line

If you specify only some of these ranges, only the corresponding part of the graph is plotted. The minimum requirements are that the **A** and **B** ranges must be specified, *or* the **E** range, *or* the **F** range. The graph in figure 10.53, for example, shows an HLCO plot of common stock data for a fictional company. Graph enhancements, such as an **X** range, titles, and axis labels, are added, as with the other graph types.

Part II ♦ Creating 1-2-3 Reports and Graphs

Fig. 10.53.
An HLCO graph of stock market information.

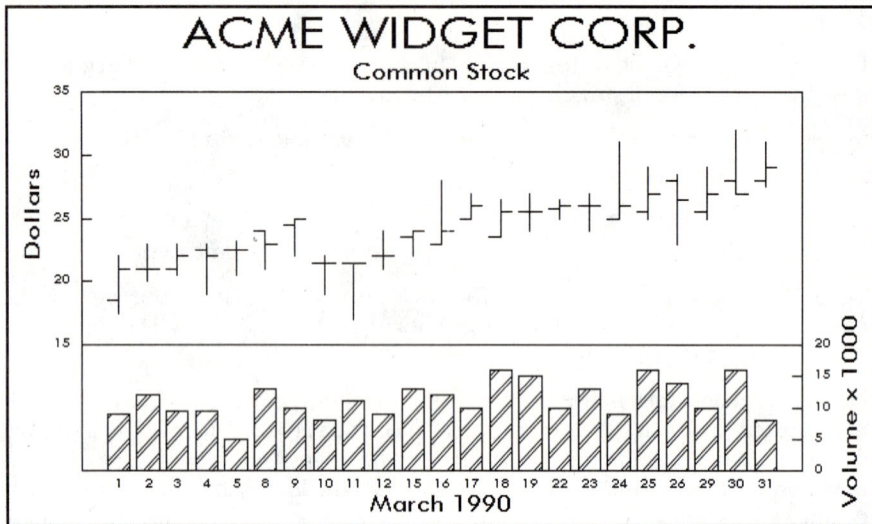

Stock market figures are often downloaded from on-line information services as text labels in the form '45 3/8. To change these labels to values that can be used in an HLCO graph, use the @VALUE function, as described in Chapter 6.

Printing Graphs

The first part of this chapter showed you how to create 1-2-3 graphs that are displayed on-screen. Screen graphs are fine as far as they go, but you often need to create printed copies that can be distributed to colleagues, used in business presentations, or filed for future reference.

If you have used earlier versions of 1-2-3, you may notice a major change in the way graphs are printed in Release 3. Rather than using a separate PrintGraph program, you now can print graphs from within the main 1-2-3 program itself. Furthermore, 1-2-3's background printing capability enables you to continue working in your worksheet while a graph is printing.

The text in this section shows you how to print graphs you created in 1-2-3. You also learn how to modify the quality, size, and orientation of printed graphs. In addition, you learn how to include one or more graphs in a printed report.

Another way to print graphs is through the Wysiwyg **:Graph Add** and **:Print** commands. Chapters 9 and 11 include complete information on this process.

Installing a Printer to Print Graphs

To print a graph, you must have installed a graphics-capable printer during the 1-2-3 Install procedure, and have it connected to your computer and on-line. If you installed only one printer, you are ready to go.

If you installed more than one graphics-capable printer, you can select the one to be used for graph printing. Issue the /**Print Printer Options Advanced Device Name** command and choose a printer (**1**, **2**, etc.). To see which printer is associated with which number, highlight the numbers and read the descriptions. You can determine the currently selected printer with /**Worksheet Global Default Status**, which presents a screen display of various default settings, including the selected printer. (See Chapter 8 for more information on the printing commands.)

Reminder:
If you installed more than one graphics-capable printer, select the one to be used for graph printing.

You print graphs from the /**Print** menu. A graph, or a report containing a graph, can be sent directly to the printer or to an encoded disk file for later printing. To print immediately, select /**Print Printer**. To send output to an encoded file, select /**Print Encoded**, and then enter the desired file name. Chapter 8 includes detailed information on creating and using encoded files.

Reminder:
To print immediately, select /Print Printer; to send output to an encoded file, select /Print Encoded.

After choosing between /**Print Printer** and /**Print Encoded**, select **Image**. Next, select either **Current** or **Named-Graph**. The **Current** option prints the current graph—that is, the graph that is displayed on-screen by selecting /**Graph View** or pressing Graph (F10). The **Named-Graph** option prints a graph you have saved with /**Graph Name Create**. Highlight the desired name from the list presented and press Enter. You can select any named graph from any active file.

After specifying the image to print, you are returned to the /**Print** [**P,E**] menu. Make sure that the printer is on-line. Position the paper, then select **Align** from the menu. Select **Go** to start printing. You then can select **Quit** to return to your worksheet. You can continue working on the worksheet, even specifying additional graphs and reports to print. If you do so, the additions are placed in 1-2-3's print queue and printed in order according to their priority.

The procedure for printing a graph is identical in many respects to printing a text-only report. The same principles of background printing, print jobs, headers and footers, margins, and print priority that were covered in Chapter 8 apply to graph printing as well. Before continuing with this chapter, you should therefore be familiar with the material in Chapter 8.

Note: Background printing works only when you have selected /**Print Printer**. If you have selected /**Print Encoded** *filename*, you have to wait until the printing process is completed before being able to perform other worksheet tasks.

Reminder:
Background printing works only when you have selected /Print Printer.

Changing the Appearance of Printed Graphs

Most aspects of a graph's appearance are decided when you design the graph for screen display. For example, colors, fonts, text size, and hatch patterns are specified as you create the graph on the screen. You cannot modify these features during printing. Note, however, that the final appearance of the printed graph may differ somewhat from its appearance on-screen, particularly with regard to fonts and, if using a color printer, colors. The printed appearance of fonts and colors depends to a large extent on the specifics of your printer. To get an idea of your printer's capabilities, select /**Print Printer Sample Go** to print a sample worksheet and sample graph, containing graph, color, and font examples. Keep this sample worksheet available for reference when you create your next graph.

> **Reminder:**
> *You specify some aspects of a graph's appearance at print time.*

Some aspects of a graph's appearance are specified at print time. Selecting **Options Advanced Image** from the **/Print [P,E]** menu displays the following menu options:

Rotate Image-Sz Density Quit

Rotate

> **Reminder:**
> *The Rotate option has no effect if your printer cannot rotate graphs.*

The **Rotate** option determines whether your graph is printed upright on the page or sideways. **Rotate No**, the default setting, prints graphs upright on the page. Select **Rotate Yes** to print graphs rotated 90 degrees counterclockwise. If your printer cannot rotate graphs, selecting **Yes** has no effect.

When you rotate a graph, its size depends on your **Image-Sz** settings. When you use the default **Margin-Fill** size, the graph's 4:3 (width:length) ratio does not change when the graph is rotated, but the right-left margin space is considered the length rather than the width. When using the **Length-Fill** size setting, the length you specified is considered the width when the graph is rotated.

Rotate affects only graphs and does not affect the orientation used to print a data range. To rotate both data ranges and graphs, select **/Print [P,E] Options Advanced Layout Orientation Landscape**. This command sequence has an effect only if supported by your printer.

Image-Sz

> **Cue:**
> *Use the Image-Sz option to specify the size and shape of printed graphs.*

The **Image-Sz** option is used to specify the size and shape of printed graphs. The default graph shape is a rectangle with a 4:3 (width:length) ratio; the default size is a graph that fills the width of the page between the margins. By using the default page margin settings, you get a graph that is approximately 6 1/2 inches wide and 5 inches high.

The **Image-Sz** options are as follows:

Length-Fill	You enter a graph length in standard lines (6 per inch). 1-2-3 creates the largest possible graph using that length, while maintaining the default 4:3 (width:length) ratio.
Margin-Fill	1-2-3 creates a graph of the default shape that fills the page between the left and right margins. This is the default **Image-Sz** setting.
Reshape	You enter a graph length in standard lines (6 per inch) and a graph width in standard characters (10 per inch). 1-2-3 creates a graph of the specified size and shape. If the specified width or length exceeds the page size, 1-2-3 resizes the graph to fit on the page.

Chapter 10 ♦ Creating and Printing Graphs   463

If you have previously printed a data range or another graph on part of a page, select /**P**rint **P**rinter **P**age to have the next graph print on a new page. If you do not advance the paper to the next page, and the graph does not fit on the remaining portion of the page, 1-2-3 automatically advances to the next page before starting the new graph.

To print the largest possible graph on its own page, select **R**eshape, and then enter a length and width that exceed the dimensions of the page. 1-2-3 resizes the graph to the largest size that fits on a page.

When **L**ength-**F**ill or **R**eshape has been selected and a graph length is entered that is longer than a page, 1-2-3 prints the largest possible graph, centering it both vertically and horizontally on the page. With **M**argin-**F**ill, the graph is centered horizontally but not vertically.

Density

The **D**ensity option offers you two choices: **D**raft or **F**inal. **D**raft produces a lower-density printout with an image that is not as dark as **F**inal. On some printers, graphs in **D**raft density are printed significantly faster than those in **F**inal density. **D**raft density also puts less wear on printer ribbons and toner cartridges. While you are experimenting to see how your graphs look on paper, use **D**raft density; then switch to **F**inal for the final printed copy.

Note: 1-2-3 supports only one density on some printers. In this case, the **D**ensity selection has no effect.

Cue:
Use **D**raft density while you are experimenting on paper; switch to **F**inal for the final printed graph.

Printing a Graph with Default Settings

Assuming that your printer is properly installed and connected, printing the current graph with the default settings is simple. Select /**P**rint **P**rinter **I**mage **C**urrent **G**o **Q**uit, and your graph is printed.

Note: With laser printers, you may have to select **P**age before the graph can print. Using a sample graph from earlier in this chapter, you get output as shown in figure 10.54.

Fig. 10.54.
A graph printed with the default /Print [P,E] Options Advanced Image settings.

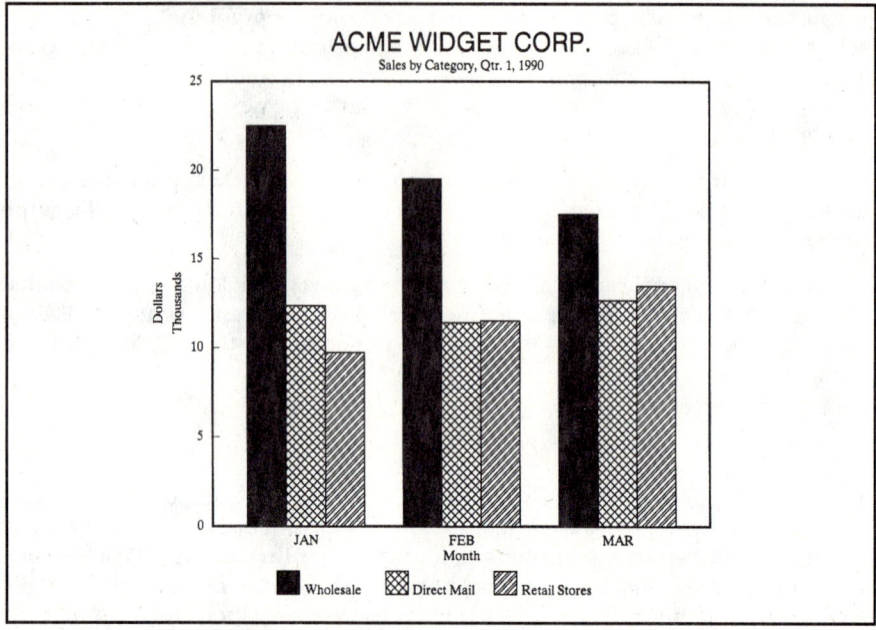

To print a graph that is not current, but is a named graph, the procedure is only slightly different. Select **/P**rint **P**rinter **I**mage **N**amed-Graph, highlight the name of the desired graph, and press Enter. Next, select **G**o **Q**uit, and the graph is printed.

Printing a Graph with Customized Print Settings

To see the effect of changing the graph size, select **/P**rint **P**rinter **O**ptions **A**dvanced **I**mage **I**mage-Sz **R**eshape, and in response to the prompts, enter **30** for width and **44** for length. Select **Q**uit three times to return to the **/P**rint **[P,E]** menu, and then select **G**o **Q**uit. You do not need to specify **I**mage again, because this image is already selected as the one to be printed. The printed graph now looks like the one in figure 10.55.

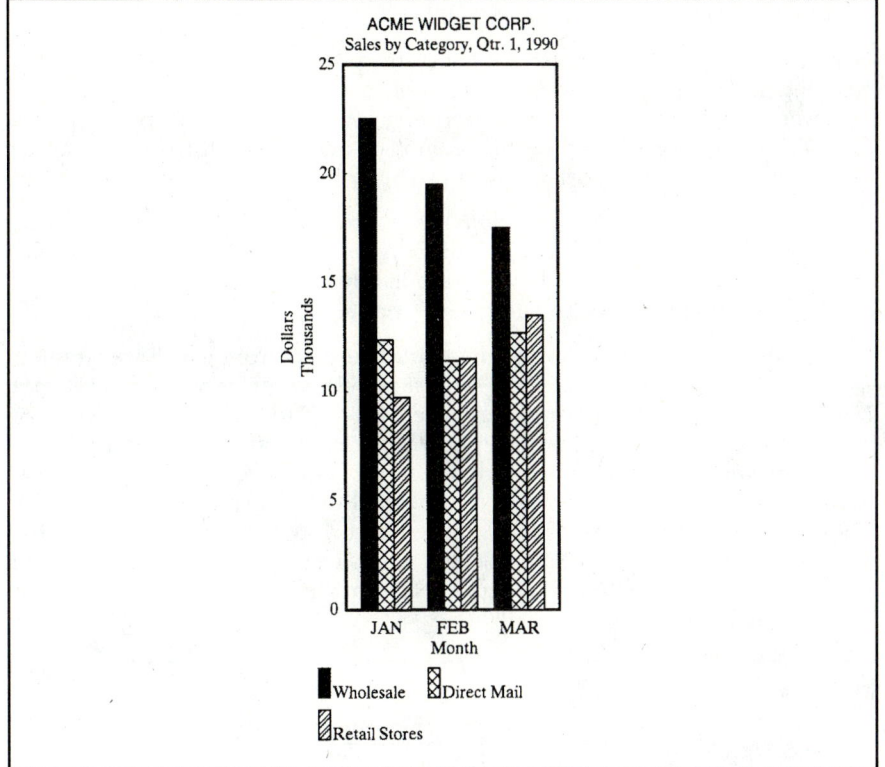

Fig. 10.55.
The graph from figure 10.54 printed with a width of 30 and a length of 44.

Saving Graph Print Settings

Keep in mind that graph size settings are not saved with the graph. You can, however, save them as a named print setting, as explained in Chapter 8. To save the print settings that produced figure 10.55, for example, you select **Options Name Create** from the **/Print [P,E]** menu. You are prompted for a name to assign to the current print settings. Because these settings produce a tall, narrow graph, type **narrow** followed by Enter. The print settings are saved under that name when you save the worksheet with **/File Save**.

Cue:
Save graph size settings as a named print setting.

The next time you want to print a graph with these settings, you can recall them by selecting **Options Name Use** from the **/Print [P,E]** menu, highlighting NARROW, and pressing Enter.

Including Graphs in Reports

Cue:
You can use two methods for printing worksheet data and graphs on a single page.

Printing your graphs on separate pages from the worksheet data and then collating them to produce a report is a simple matter. A more effective approach, however, is to have a graph and its supporting data on one page. If your graph size supports this arrangement, you can accomplish this easily with 1-2-3. You can use two techniques to print worksheet data and graphs on a single page.

In the first technique, you specify *both* the graph and the text as part of the same print job. As mentioned in Chapter 8 on printing reports, this step is performed by including the name of the graph, preceded by an asterisk, as part of the print range. This method works with all types of printers.

Figure 10.56, for example, shows the worksheet data from which the graph in figure 10.54 was generated. In this worksheet, the command sequence /**G**raph **N**ame **C**reate was used to assign the name DEFAULT to this graph. Figure 10.56 shows the screen after selecting /**P**rint **P**rinter **R**ange and entering a two-part range specification. The range consists of the worksheet data range A1..F17 followed by a semicolon and the graph name DEFAULT preceded by an asterisk. This range specification tells 1-2-3 to print the worksheet range A1..F17 and then print the graph DEFAULT. Note that the worksheet range specified includes a couple of blank lines at the end to separate it from the graph. The resulting output is shown in figure 10.57.

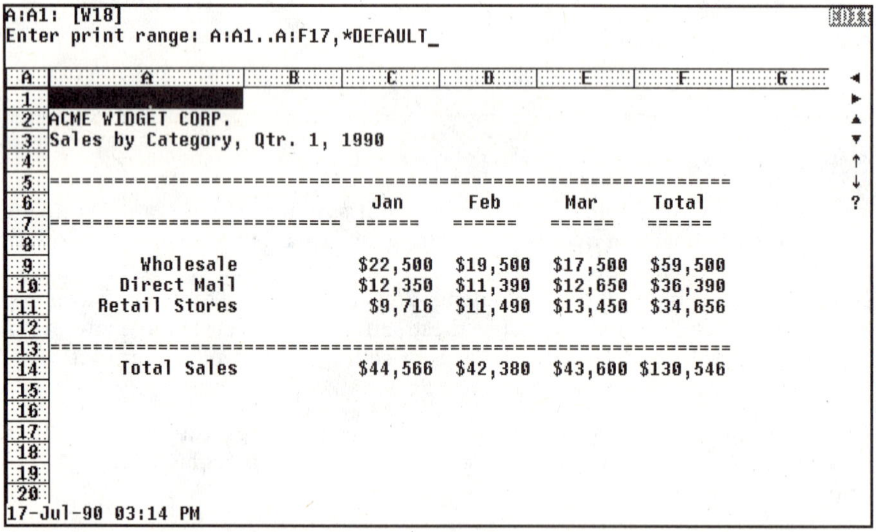

Fig. 10.56.
A print range specified that includes worksheet data.

```
A:A1: [W18]
Enter print range: A:A1..A:F17,*DEFAULT_

         A              B        C       D       E        F         G
 1
 2  ACME WIDGET CORP.
 3  Sales by Category, Qtr. 1, 1990
 4
 5  ==================================================================
 6                            Jan     Feb     Mar     Total
 7  ==================================================================
 8
 9          Wholesale      $22,500 $19,500 $17,500  $59,500
10          Direct Mail    $12,350 $11,390 $12,650  $36,390
11          Retail Stores   $9,716 $11,490 $13,450  $34,656
12
13  ==================================================================
14          Total Sales    $44,566 $42,380 $43,600 $130,546
15
16
17
18
19
20
17-Jul-90 03:14 PM
```

A second technique you can use to print worksheet data and graphs on the same page is offered in Wysiwyg. You first use the **:G**raph **A**dd command to insert the graph into a worksheet range. You then use the **:P**rint **R**ange **S**et command and highlight the worksheet data and the graph. See Chapter 11 for details.

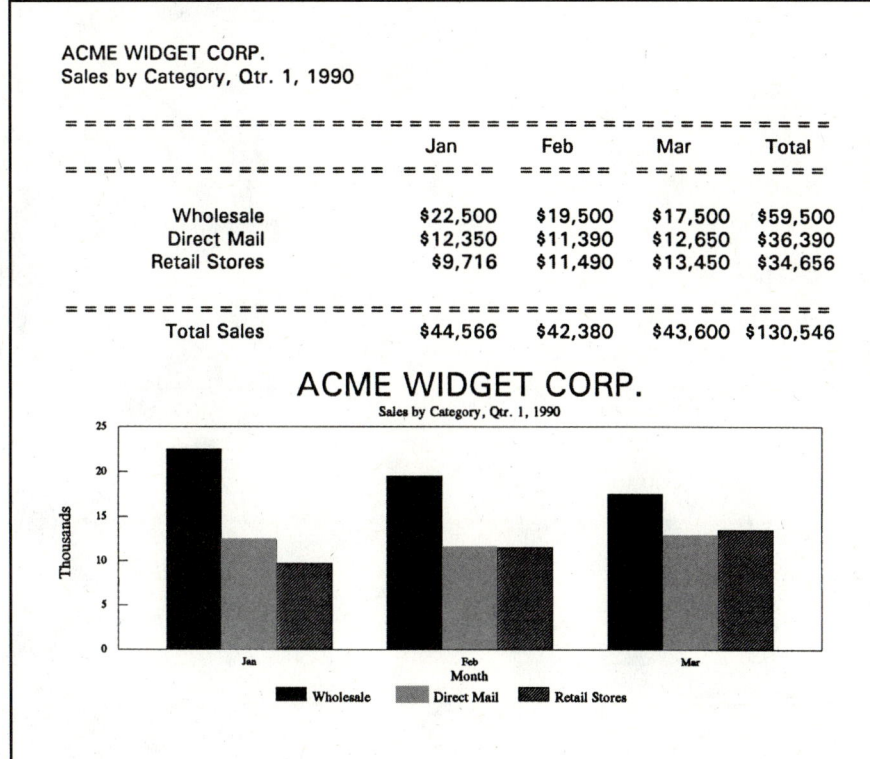

Fig. 10.57.
A worksheet range and a graph printed on the same page.

Summary

You have learned a great deal about 1-2-3 graphs from this chapter: how to create and enhance all seven graph types, and how to store graphs for recall in the worksheet as well as for use by other programs. You also have had an introduction to 1-2-3's many advanced graph features, which can be used, along with your imagination, to produce attractive and informative graph displays.

In addition, you learned how to print graphs, how to modify their orientation, size, and shape, and how to incorporate graphs and worksheet data on the same page. By experimenting with the techniques presented in this chapter and in Chapter 8 on printing reports, you soon will be able to create printed reports that effectively present your data in tabular and graphical form.

Enhancing and Printing Graphs in Wysiwyg

11

In the previous chapter, you learned how to create and print business graphs with 1-2-3's /Graph and /Print commands. As you see in this chapter, Wysiwyg offers its own set of graphing commands in Releases 3.1 and 3.1+. However, the Wysiwyg :Graph commands are not for creating graphs; they are primarily for embellishing graphs you have created in 1-2-3 and other graphics programs. (You can even create your own drawings with the Wysiwyg :Graph commands.) A graphics editor lets you add geometric shapes, rotate and flip objects, and perform other advanced operations.

The following topics are covered in this chapter:

- Including your 1-2-3 graphs in a Wysiwyg-formatted report
- Changing a graph's position on the page
- Adjusting graph settings
- Adding, modifying, and rearranging text and geometric shapes
- Transforming the size and rotation of objects

Adding a Graph

Before you can include a 1-2-3 graph in a Wysiwyg-formatted report, you must add the graph to the worksheet with the :Graph Add command. By using this command, you define the worksheet range in which you want the graph to appear—you actually see the graph in the worksheet. After you select :Graph Add, you see the following choices:

Option	Description
Current	Inserts the current 1-2-3 graph (the one you see when you press F10).
Named	Inserts a 1-2-3 graph that you have named with the /Graph Name Create command.
PIC	Inserts a 1-2-3 graph that has been created with the /Graph Save command (any version of 1-2-3). The file has the extension PIC.
Metafile	Inserts a graphic that was saved in metafile format. This file could have been created in 1-2-3 Release 3, 3.1, or 3.1+, or an external graphics package. The file has the extension CGM.
Blank	Inserts an empty placeholder. Use this option if you haven't created the graph yet, but want to reserve space for it. Also use this option if you want to create your own graphic drawing.

Cue:
Insert a Blank placeholder when you want to create your own graphic drawing.

Choose the **Current** option only if the worksheet contains a single graph. If your worksheet has multiple graphs, the graph in your worksheet is replaced with the new current graph every time you issue the /Graph Name Use command. Therefore, when your worksheet currently contains or may contain more than one graph, you should name the graph before adding it.

Cue:
Use :Graph View to see a PIC or Metafile graph before you add it.

Depending on which of the :Graph Add options you select, you are prompted for information. If you select **Named**, for example, you must type the name of the graph. If you select **P**IC or **Metafile**, a list of PIC or CGM files in the current directory appears; select one of the names or choose a different directory. If you can't remember which PIC or Metafile graph you want, cancel the :Graph Add command (press Esc until you are back in READY mode) and choose :Graph View to display the graphs on the screen so that you can choose the correct one.

Next, specify the range over which you want to paste the graph. The size and shape of the range you specify determines the size and shape of the graph when it is printed. The graph is automatically scaled (down or up) to fit in the specified range.

To print the graph in the middle of a worksheet report, insert blank rows or columns where you want the graph to appear before you add the graph. If you don't, the graph overlays worksheet data. Be sure that you insert enough rows and columns to make the graph the size you want.

Suppose that you want to paste the current 1-2-3 bar graph in the middle of a worksheet and then print the worksheet and graph. Figure 11.1 shows the worksheet with the graph added. Notice that the graph actually appears in the worksheet. This graph was added to the worksheet by choosing :Graph Add Current and selecting the range A:B18..A:G31.

Reminder:
You don't have to remove one graph before adding another graph in the same location.

If you discover you added the wrong graph, or you later create a graph you want in the same perfectly sized graph range, you can replace the existing graph with another. You do not have to remove one graph before adding another in the same location. Just select :Graph Settings Graph. First indicate the graph you want to replace by moving the cell pointer to one cell in the graph range. If your cell pointer is not near the graph, you can press Name (F3) and select the graph name from a list. Now answer some questions about the replacement graph. You must indicate the type of graph (**C**urrent, **N**amed, **P**IC, **M**etafile, or **B**lank), and specify the name if prompted.

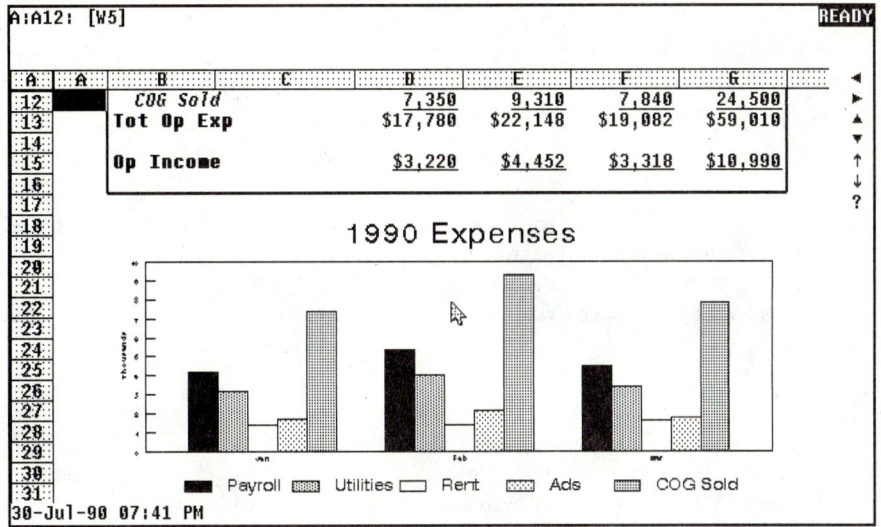

Fig. 11.1.
A graph inserted in a worksheet range.

Any enhancements (such as annotations) you added to the initial graph also appear in the new graph. If you don't want these enhancements in the new graph, don't use the **:G**raph **S**ettings **G**raph command. Instead, use **:G**raph **R**emove to delete the initial graph, and then insert the new graph with **:G**raph **A**dd.

Repositioning a Graph

After adding a graph, you may realize that the range isn't appropriate for your graph, or you may want to position the graph in a different area of the worksheet. The **:G**raph menu offers several commands for changing your graph's position. You can move, remove, or resize the graph.

If your worksheet is large or has many graphs, you can use the **:G**raph **G**oto command to move the cell pointer to a specific graph before repositioning the graph. After choosing **:G**raph **G**oto, select the name of the graph from the list, or press Name (F3) to see a full-screen list.

Reminder:
Use **:G**raph **G**oto to move to a specific named graph in the worksheet.

Moving a Graph

To move a graph from one worksheet location to another, use the **:G**raph **M**ove command. This command retains the graph's original size and shape (that is, the number of rows and columns), only changing the graph's position in the worksheet. When prompted for the graph to move, you can place the cell pointer anywhere in the graph, or press Name (F3) to select the name of the graph from a list. After you press Enter, you are prompted for the target location. Place the cell

Reminder:
:Graph **M**ove moves a graph from an existing location in the worksheet to a new location, without changing the size and shape of the graph.

pointer in the upper left corner of the target range and press Enter. (You don't have to highlight the entire range.) The graph moves to its new location, retaining its original size and shape. If the new location has different row heights or column widths, the moved graph has a slightly different size and shape.

Resizing a Graph

Reminder:
Use :Graph Settings Range to resize a graph.

Once you add a graph, you may realize that the range you specified is either too large or too small for the graph. The :**G**raph Settings **R**ange command enables you to resize an existing graph.

Once you select the graph to resize, the current graph range is highlighted on-screen. Type the new range, or move the cell pointer to highlight a larger or smaller area. If you want to specify a new range entirely different from the existing one, press Esc or Backspace to cancel the old range before specifying the new one.

Removing a Graph

To erase a graph from the worksheet report, use :**G**raph **R**emove. 1-2-3 prompts you for the graph to remove. Either move the cell pointer to the graph range, or press Name (F3) and highlight the name of the graph you want to remove. Press Enter, and the graph disappears. :**G**raph **R**emove does not delete the graph name or the graph's settings.

Specifying Graph Settings

In the previous sections, you looked at two of the options on the :**G**raph Settings menu (**G**raph and **R**ange). These two settings enable you to replace and resize a graph. The :**G**raph Settings menu offers several more options which are discussed in this section. Each of these options can be applied to individual graphs. To turn on any of these options for all graphs in the worksheet, specify a range that includes all the graphs you have added.

Cue:
Turn the Display setting off to speed up screen redrawing.

The :**G**raph Settings **D**isplay command controls whether you see the graphs you add in the worksheet. By default, all graphs are displayed. Depending on your computer's speed, however, redrawing the screen can be slow when a graph is on-screen. If you set the **D**isplay option to **N**o, Wysiwyg displays a shaded rectangle in the graph range (see fig. 11.2). The rectangle is replaced with the actual graph when you print. Of course, you want to see the graph as you are editing and enhancing it, but once this is done, you may want to turn off its display so that you don't have to wait for the screen to redraw the graph.

The :**G**raph Settings **S**ync command controls whether the graph is synchronized with your worksheet data. By default, every time you change a number in the worksheet, 1-2-3 redraws the graph to reflect the new values. This synchronization allows you to play what-if games with your worksheet: type different values, and the picture instantly changes.

Chapter 11 ◆ Enhancing and Printing Graphs in Wysiwyg   **473**

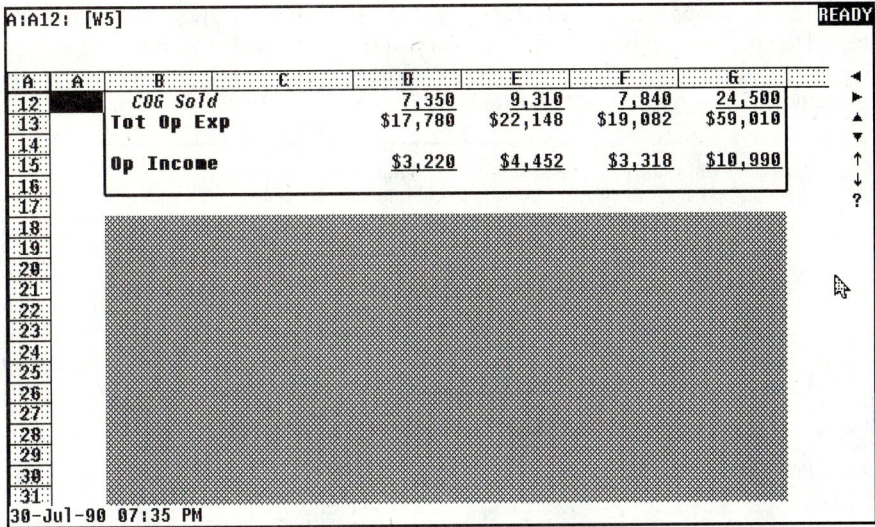

Fig. 11.2.
A graph range with the graph display turned off.

Because redrawing the screen takes time, you may want to unsynchronize the graph and data. Choose :Graph Settings Sync No and point to a cell in the graph. Now, whenever your data changes, the graph remains static. To update the graph, choose :Graph Compute or turn on the synchronization with :Graph Settings Sync Yes. The :Graph Compute command redraws all graphs in the file; :Graph Settings Sync Yes turns on synchronization for only the specified graphs.

The :Graph Settings Opaque command controls whether the graph hides any data typed in cells within the graph range. By default, the graph is opaque and underlying data is hidden. To view the contents of the cells through the graph, choose :Graph Settings Opaque No. Turning off the Opaque setting is useful if you have entered text in a cell in the graph range that you want to appear as a note or label on the graph.

Cue:
To view the contents of the cells underneath the graph, turn off the Opaque graph setting.

Using the Graphics Editor

Included in Wysiwyg is a graphics editor that enables you to add and manipulate graphic objects. With this text editor, you can add text, arrows, boxes, and other geometric shapes. Once you add these special objects, you can modify them, rearrange them, duplicate them, and transform them.

You have two ways to place a graph in the graphics editing window. You can choose :Graph Edit and then choose which graph you want to edit by placing the cell pointer anywhere in that graph's range. Alternatively, you can place the mouse pointer on the graph and double-click the mouse.

Cue:
To place a graph in the graphics editing window, double-click the mouse on the graph.

Figure 11.3 shows the graphics editing window with a graph in place. When you are in the graphics editing window, you are almost in a different world. You see only the graph—not the worksheet. This arrangement lets you concentrate on the task at hand: enhancing the graph. Furthermore, the editing menu always remains at the top of the screen and is active at all times; you cannot press Esc or the right mouse button to clear the menu. The only way to exit the graphics editor is to choose the Quit menu option or press Ctrl-Break.

Fig 11.3.
The graphics editing window.

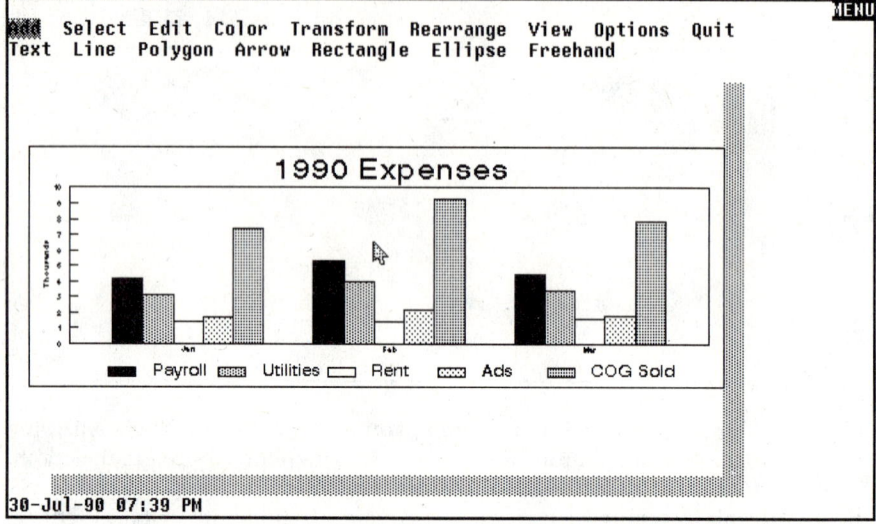

Caution:
The Undo command does not work in the graphics editing window.

The Undo command does not work on options in the :Graph Edit menu. You can, however, undo all the additions and modifications made in the current graph-editing session. Select **Q**uit from the :Graph Edit menu, press Undo (Alt-F4), and choose **Y**es.

Adding Objects

Wysiwyg lets you add the following types of objects to your graph: text, lines, polygons, arrows, rectangles, and ellipses. You also can draw freehand. The objects Wysiwyg provides are designed to help you annotate your graphs. For example, you can add a brief explanation of why a data point is unusually high or low. Figure 11.4 shows how text, an arrow, and an ellipse are used to point out a value on the graph.

To create an object for your graph, choose **A**dd from the :Graph Edit menu and then select the type of object you want to add. The following sections describe how to add each type of object.

Adding Text

The **A**dd **T**ext command lets you insert titles or comments anywhere on the graph. You do not type text directly on the graph. Instead, you add the text in two steps:

select **Add Text** from the **:Graph Edit** menu and type the text at the `Text:` prompt at the top of the screen; then position the complete phrase where you like. The text phrase can be up to 512 characters long. To insert the contents of a cell as text on a graph, type a backslash followed by the cell's address or range name. Once you type the text and press Enter, indicate where you want to place the text. If you can't see the phrase, press the down arrow or move the mouse until it appears. Continue using the mouse or the arrow keys to position the text in its final destination. The arrow keys move in such small increments that you will probably prefer to use the mouse if you have one.

Cue:
Use the mouse to quickly position the text you add to a graph.

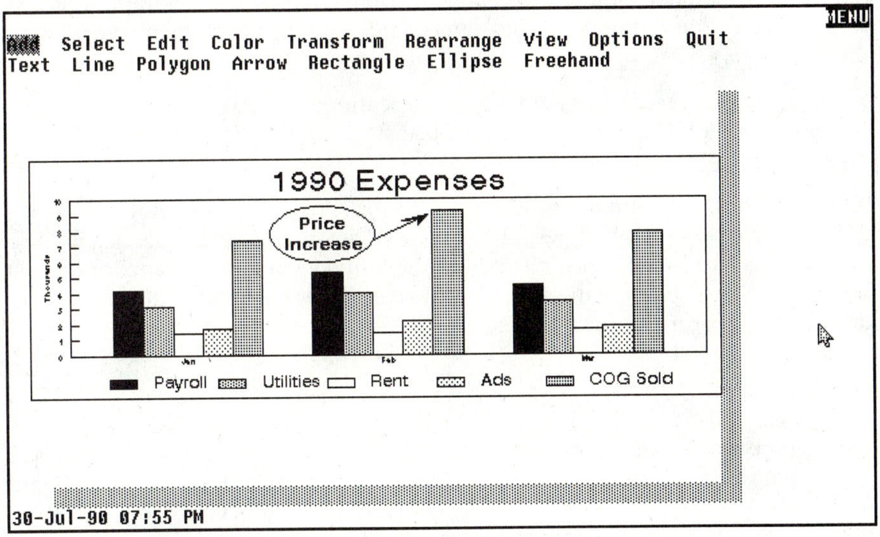

Fig. 11.4.
A graph annotated with the graphics editor.

To confirm the target location for the text, either press the left mouse button or press Enter. Small solid squares, called *selection indicators*, surround the text. These boxes mean that the object is selected and that you can perform another operation on it (such as move it, change its font, and the like). To change the font, use the **Edit Font** command. To change the content of the text, use the **Edit Text** command. These editing options are discussed in "Editing Objects," later in this chapter.

The text you add can include formatting sequences (for example, boldface, italic, outline, and fonts). Chapter 9 describes how to format text.

Reminder:
The text you add can include formatting sequences, such as boldface and italics.

Adding Lines and Arrows

The processes you follow to draw lines and arrows are identical. The only difference is the end result: the arrow has an arrowhead at one end of the line. Follow these basic steps to draw a line or arrow after you have selected **Line** or **Arrow** from the **:Graph Edit Add** menu:

1. When 1-2-3 prompts you to `Move to the first point,` use the mouse or the arrow keys to move the pointer on the graph to one end of the line you want to draw.

2. Press the left mouse button or the space bar to anchor this point.

3. When 1-2-3 prompts you to Stretch the line to the next point, use the mouse or the arrow keys to move the pointer to the other end of the line.

4. Press the left mouse button twice or press Enter to complete the line.

Cue:
To switch the direction of the arrow, use the Edit Arrowheads option.

The line or arrow is drawn on the screen, and the selection indicator appears in the center of the line. If you are adding an arrow, the arrowhead appears at the second point you indicated. To switch the direction of the arrow, use the :Graph Edit Edit Arrowheads option. To change the line width, use the :Graph Edit Edit Width option. See "Editing Objects" later in this chapter for more information on these options.

You can connect several lines together by repeating steps 2 and 3 of the preceding procedure for each line-ending. When you finish drawing a line, click twice or press Enter.

Cue:
To create perfectly straight lines, hold the Shift key before you anchor the last point.

When drawing horizontal, vertical, or diagonal lines, you may notice that it's difficult to draw straight lines; the lines end up being somewhat jagged. To prevent this jagged look, press and hold the Shift key before you anchor the last point. The line segment automatically snaps to 45-degree angles, allowing you to draw perfectly straight lines.

Adding Polygons

A *polygon* is a multisided object—the object can have as many connecting lines as you want. You don't need to concern yourself with connecting the last side with the first because Wysiwyg automatically connects this segment for you. The steps for creating a polygon are similar to the ones you use for creating lines and arrows:

1. Choose :Graph Edit Add Polygon.

2. When 1-2-3 prompts you to Move to the first point, use the mouse or the arrow keys to move the pointer to the first point of the polygon.

3. Press the left mouse button or the space bar to anchor this point.

4. When 1-2-3 prompts you to Stretch the line to the next point, use the mouse or the arrow keys to move the pointer to the opposite end of the first line.

5. Press the left mouse button or the space bar to anchor this point.

6. Repeat steps 3 and 4 for each side of the polygon.

7. Press the left mouse button twice or press Enter to complete the polygon.

Adding Rectangles and Ellipses

Use rectangles and ellipses to enclose text and other objects on your graph. For example, figure 11.5 shows text with a rectangle drawn around it.

Chapter 11 ◆ Enhancing and Printing Graphs in Wysiwyg

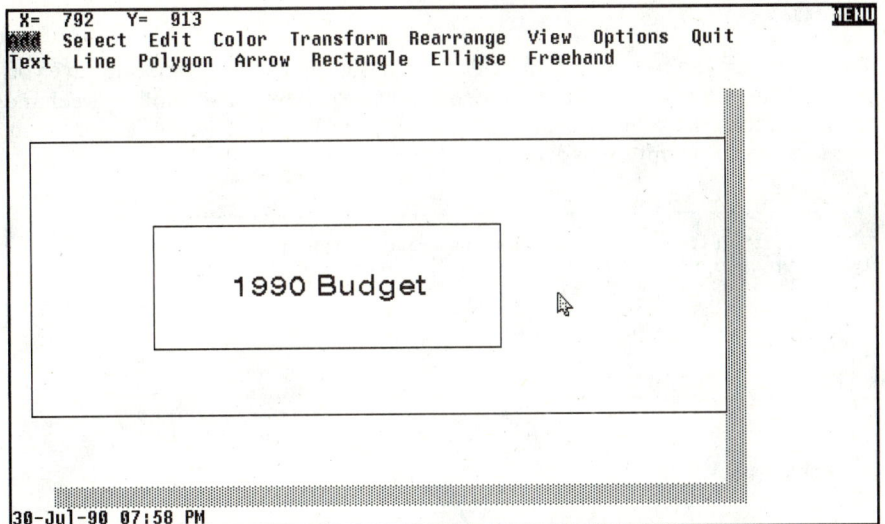

Fig. 11.5.
Text enclosed with a rectangle.

If you are drawing rectangles and ellipses with a mouse, use the click-and-drag method to define the shape. Press and hold the left mouse button in the upper left corner of the object. Then drag the mouse to create the object in the desired size. Whether you are creating a rectangle or an ellipse, a rectangle appears on the screen—that is, until you release the mouse button. As soon as you let go of the button, the shape you chose is drawn.

To draw rectangles and ellipses with the keyboard, follow these steps:

1. Choose **:G**raph **E**dit **A**dd **R**ectangle or **E**llipse.
2. Place the cursor on the upper left corner of the range where you want the rectangle or ellipse to be located.
3. Press the space bar to anchor the corner.
4. Use the arrow keys to stretch the box to its desired size. (A box appears regardless of whether you are drawing a rectangle or ellipse; the box is called the *bounding box*.)
5. Press Enter.

In the middle of each side of the rectangle or ellipse are selection indicators. To change the type of line (solid, dashed, or dotted) used in the rectangle or ellipse, use the **:G**raph **E**dit **E**dit **L**ine-Style command. This option is discussed in "Editing Objects" later in this chapter.

To create a circle when you have chosen Ellipse, or a square when you have chosen **R**ectangle, press and hold the Shift key before you set the object size. Although the object may not appear perfectly circular or square on the screen, it prints accurately.

Reminder:
Use the click-and-drag method to define the shape and size of rectangles and ellipses.

Cue:
To create a perfect circle or square, hold the Shift key before you set the ellipse or rectangle size.

Adding Objects Freehand

When you use the **:G**raph **E**dit **A**dd **F**reehand option, it's as if someone gave you a pencil and let you draw on the screen. Unless you have artistic ability, freehand drawing looks more like freehand scribbling (see fig. 11.6); therefore, you may want to leave this option to the professionals.

Caution:
Unless you have artistic ability, freehand drawing looks more like freehand scribbling.

Fig. 11.6.
Freehand drawing (scribbling).

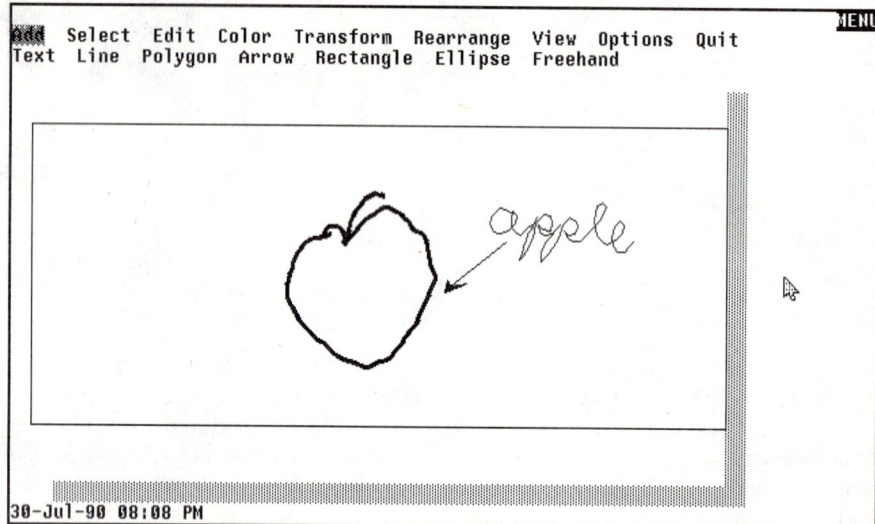

You must have a mouse to draw freehand. Simply place the pointer where you want to begin drawing, press and hold the left mouse button, and move the mouse to draw. Release the mouse button when you are finished drawing a segment of the graphic. Each segment of the freehand drawing displays a selection indicator. To change the type of line (solid, dashed, or dotted), use the **:G**raph **E**dit **E**dit **L**ine-**S**tyle command. This option is discussed in "Editing Objects," later in this chapter.

Selecting Objects

You can do many things to objects once you add them to a graph. For example, you can change the line-style and font, and you can move, delete, or copy the objects. Regardless of which operation you perform on the object, you must select the object or objects you want to change. If you just added the object, it is selected automatically. When an object is selected, selection indicators (small solid boxes) appear on the object.

Mouse users have several different selection techniques available to them (see "Selecting with the Mouse"). Keyboard users use the **S**elect menu to select objects (see "Selecting with the Menu").

Reminder:
Select the object before issuing a command.

Normally, you select the object or objects you want to change before issuing a command. If no object is selected, you are prompted to point to the object.

Selecting with the Mouse

Mouse users can select a single object by clicking on it. (You can select an object only when the **:G**raph **E**dit menu is displayed.) Check the selection indicators to make sure that they are around the object you want to change. If two objects are close together, you may have to click several times until the correct object is selected.

Sometimes, you may want to select more than one object. For example, you may want to change the font of all the text you have added. To select multiple objects, press and hold the Shift key as you click the mouse on each object. If you accidentally select the wrong object, keep the Shift key down and click the object again.

Cue:
To select multiple objects, hold the Shift key as you click the mouse on each object.

Selecting with the Menu

To select a single object with the keyboard, you use the **S**elect option, and choose **O**ne. Wysiwyg displays the prompt `Point to desired object.` Use the arrow keys to move the pointer to the object, and press Enter. The selection indicators appear on the object.

Another way to select an object is with the **S**elect **C**ycle command. This option cycles through all the objects one at a time, letting you select one or more objects. Each time you press an arrow key, a different object displays small boxes that look similar to selection indicators, except that the boxes are hollow. When an object you want to select (or deselect) displays the hollow selection boxes, press the space bar. Continue pressing the arrow keys and space bar until you have selected (or deselected) all the objects you want. When you are finished, press Enter. Mouse users may want to use the **S**elect **C**ycle option if they are having trouble selecting an object that is close to another object.

Cue:
*Use **S**elect **C**ycle to display each object in turn; press space bar to select an object.*

The **S**elect menu offers several other ways to select objects. The **A**ll option selects all objects you have added except for the graph itself. The **N**one option deselects everything—the objects and the graph. **G**raph selects only the underlying graph. The **M**ore/**L**ess option lets you select an additional object or deselect one of the currently selected objects. If you point to an object that is not selected, 1-2-3 selects it; if the object is selected already, the selection is removed.

Editing Objects

As mentioned throughout the "Adding Objects" section earlier in this chapter, the graphics editor provides ways to fine-tune the objects you add. Following is a list of the options you can change on your objects:

- ◆ Text content, alignment, and font
- ◆ Position of the arrowhead on an arrow
- ◆ Line-style and width
- ◆ Sharpness of angles

Part II ♦ Creating 1-2-3 Reports and Graphs

The following sections examine each of the options on the :Graph Edit Edit menu. Remember to select the object or objects you want to edit before you issue the command.

Editing Text

Cue:
To correct a typing mistake, use Edit Text.

The **Text** option on the :**G**raph **E**dit **E**dit menu lets you edit text you have added with the :**G**raph **A**dd **T**ext command. You cannot edit text that was added with the /**G**raph commands (for example, titles and legends) or that was part of the PIC or Metafile graph you added. When you choose Edit Text, a copy of the text appears at the top of the screen. To correct or insert text, use the editing keys you normally use in EDIT mode. (See Chapter 3 for a list of editing keys.) Press Enter when you are finished, and the text is corrected.

Centering Text

The **C**entering option aligns text with respect to the text's original location. If you choose **L**eft, the left edge of the text is aligned with the text's original center point. If you choose **C**enter, the center of the text is aligned with the text's original left edge. If you choose **R**ight, the text goes back to its original position.

Because of the way text is aligned, the Centering option is not very useful. You may find it easier to position text with the :**G**raph **E**dit **R**earrange **M**ove command.

Changing Fonts

To change the font (typeface and size) of the text you added with the :**G**raph **E**dit **A**dd **T**ext command, use the :**G**raph **E**dit **E**dit **F**ont option. You cannot change the font of text that was part of the graph before you added it to your worksheet. To adjust the typeface and size of your titles, labels, and legends, use the /**G**raph **O**ptions **A**dvanced **T**ext command. (See Chapter 10 for more detailed information.)

Reminder:
Use the :Format Font Replace command to use a different font in the graphics editing window.

When you choose Edit Font, a list displays the eight fonts currently available in the worksheet. Choose the desired font number to change all the selected text. If the font you want to use is not listed, exit the graphics editor by choosing **Q**uit. Then use the :**F**ormat **F**ont **R**eplace command to replace one of the existing eight fonts with the font you want to use.

Changing Line-Style

Using the Line-Style option, you can display different types of lines in your objects. Figure 11.7 shows examples of each of the six line styles. **S**olid is the default. You can change the line styles of lines, arrows, rectangles, polygons, ellipses, and freehand drawings.

Chapter 11 ♦ Enhancing and Printing Graphs in Wysiwyg   481

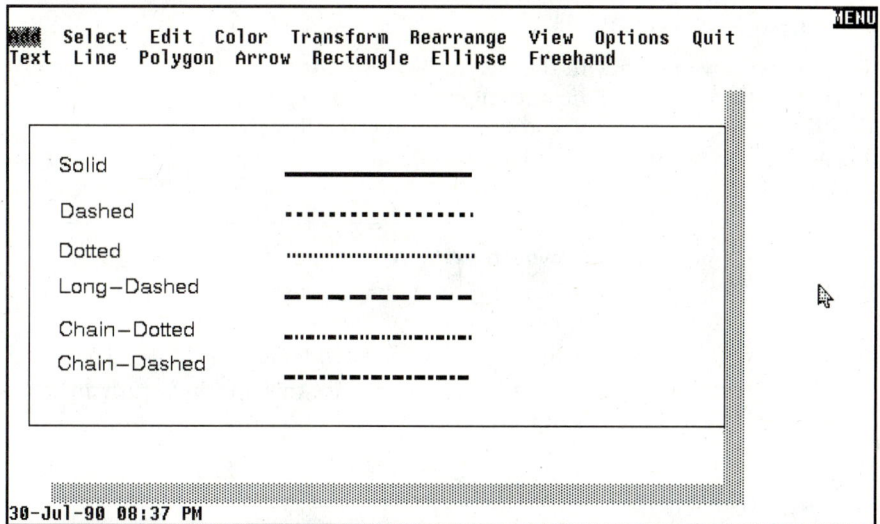

Fig. 11.7.

Examples of the six line styles.

Changing Line Width

By default, line widths are quite thin. Use the **:G**raph **E**dit **E**dit **W**idth option to change the width of the lines in arrows, rectangles, polygons, ellipses, lines, and freehand drawings. Of course, only the lines in the selected object or objects are affected. Figure 11.8 shows examples of the five line widths.

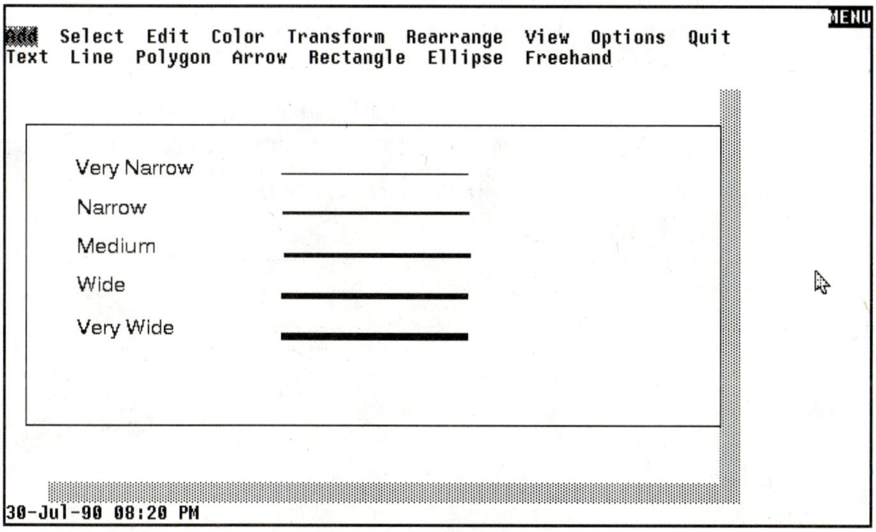

Fig. 11.8.

Examples of the five line widths.

Changing Arrowheads

When you draw arrows with the :Graph Edit Add Arrow option, the arrowhead automatically points from the line ending (the second point you indicated). Using the :Graph Edit Edit Arrowhead option, you can adjust arrowhead positioning. The following four options are available:

Option	Description
Switch	Moves the arrowhead to the opposite end of the line
One	Adds an arrowhead to a line (you can use this option to turn a line into an arrow)
Two	Adds an arrowhead to each end of the line
None	Removes all arrowheads (you can use this option to turn an arrow into a line)

Smoothing Angles

> **Cue:**
> *By using the Smoothing option, you can create smooth curves out of sharp angles.*

By using the Smoothing option, you can create smooth curves out of sharp angles. You can smooth rectangles, polygons, freehand drawings, and line segments that are connected together. The Smoothing menu displays the following options:

Option	Description
None	Returns a smoothed object to its original angles
Tight	Slightly smooths or rounds the object's angles
Medium	Provides the maximum smoothing available; smooths the angles to a greater degree than the Tight option

Figure 11.9 shows a rectangle with None, Tight, and Medium smoothing.

Fig. 11.9.
The three types of smoothing.

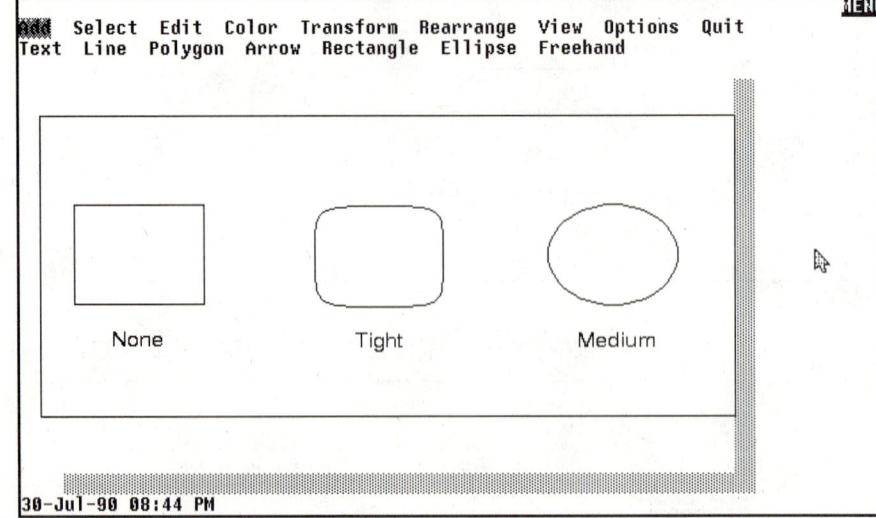

Adding Patterns and Colors

The **Color** option on the **:Graph Edit** menu enables you to assign colors or patterns to the following areas of your graph:

Area	Description
Lines	Lines, arrows, and object outlines
Inside	The space inside the rectangle, ellipse, or polygon
Text	Text added with **:Graph Edit Add Text** (not legends or titles entered with /Graph commands)
Background	In the defined graph range, the area behind the graph (where the titles, legends, and scale indicators appear)

Note: The options listed do not apply to the underlying 1-2-3 graph.

To change the colors or patterns of any elements in the 1-2-3 graph, you can use either color mapping (discussed later in this section) or the /Graph Options Advanced command. Refer to Chapter 10 for more information about the /Graph commands.

To change a color, first select the object or objects you want to modify and then choose **Colors** from the **:Graph Edit** menu. Then select one of the four areas in which you want to change the color (**Lines**, **Inside**, **Text**, or **Background**). If you select the **Lines** or **Text** option, choose from a menu of the following colors:

Black	White
Red	Green
Dark-Blue	Cyan
Yellow	Magenta
Hidden	

If you select the **Inside** or **Background** option, a color palette appears on the screen. If you have a monochrome monitor, the palette displays different patterns. Either type the number that appears next to the desired color/pattern, or use the arrow keys to move the box to the color/pattern and press Enter. If you have a mouse, you can point to the color/pattern and press the left mouse button.

The **:Graph Edit Color Map** option enables you to change the fill colors and patterns of the underlying graph. For example, suppose that you don't like the shade of green of the bars in a bar graph. You can use color mapping to adjust the shade, or you can use a different pattern. You cannot use this option to change the color of lines or text.

Cue:
Use the Color Map option to change the fill colors and patterns of the underlying graphic.

You can change the graph with up to 16 different colors; the Map menu indicates the 16 choices with the numbers 1 through 9 and the letters A through G. The numbers 1 through 7 correspond to 1-2-3 graph objects: **1** is the graph text, **2** is the **A** range, **3** is the **B** range, **4** is the **C** range, and so on. The remaining nine color choices refer to colors that may appear in other types of underlying graphics (for example, in a Metafile graphic).

After you choose the color number or letter, the color palette appears. The current color/pattern is boxed. Select the color/pattern you want to replace it with by typing the number that appears next to the desired color/pattern, or by using the arrow keys to move the box to the color/pattern and pressing Enter. Mouse users can point to the color/pattern and press the left mouse button.

Suppose that you want to change the color of the **A** range. From the **Color Map** menu, select **2**; the color palette displays a box around one of the colored squares. To choose a different color or pattern, use the arrow keys to move the box to another colored square and press Enter. The original **A** range color changes to the color or pattern you just selected.

The procedure for changing the colors in a Metafile-format graphic is actually a trial-and-error process. You must check the color palette for each of the numbers (1 through 7) and letters (A through G) until you find the color you want to change. For example, suppose that a Metafile-format graphic contains a shade of yellow that you detest; you want to replace it with a shade of teal. From the **Color Map** menu, choose **1** and look at the boxed shade in the color palette. If the color is yellow, you are in luck—you found the correct color number and can now highlight the teal shade you want to replace it with. If color **1** is not yellow, press Esc and continue choosing options on the **Color Map** menu until you see the yellow color boxed on the color palette.

Cue:
*To see how colors translate into grey shades, use the **:D**isplay **M**ode **B&W** command.*

If you have a color monitor but plan to print the graph on a black-and-white printer, you may want to view the graph in black and white before you print. Viewing the graph in black and white enables you to see how the colors translate into gray shades. Use the **:D**isplay **M**ode **B&W** command to change to a black and white display.

Changing the Display of the Graphic Editing Window

The graphic editor's **O**ptions and **V**iew menus provide ways to change the graphic editing window's display. The **O**ptions menu offers the following options: **G**rid, **C**ursor, and **F**ont-Magnification. The **V**iew menu enables you to size and reposition the contents of the editing window. The **V**iew menu offers the following options: **F**ull, **I**n, **P**an, **+**, **–**, **U**p, **D**own, **L**eft, and **R**ight.

Using the :Graph Edit Options Menu

Cue:
*Use the **G**rid option or press F4 to turn on and off the display of grid lines in the worksheet.*

The **G**rid option on the **:G**raph Edit **O**ptions menu enables you to display dotted lines to define the cells in the underlying worksheet. Grid lines can help you line up the objects you create with worksheet cells. The cell coordinates are not displayed—just the cell outlines. Alternatively, you can press F4 to toggle the display of grid lines in the graphics editor.

The **C**ursor option lets you define the size of the cursor: **B**ig or **S**mall. By default, the graph editor's cursor is a small cross. A big cursor is also a cross, but its lines extend completely across the editing window. Figure 11.10 shows a rectangle being drawn with a big cursor. A large cursor makes it easy to line up one edge of an object with another.

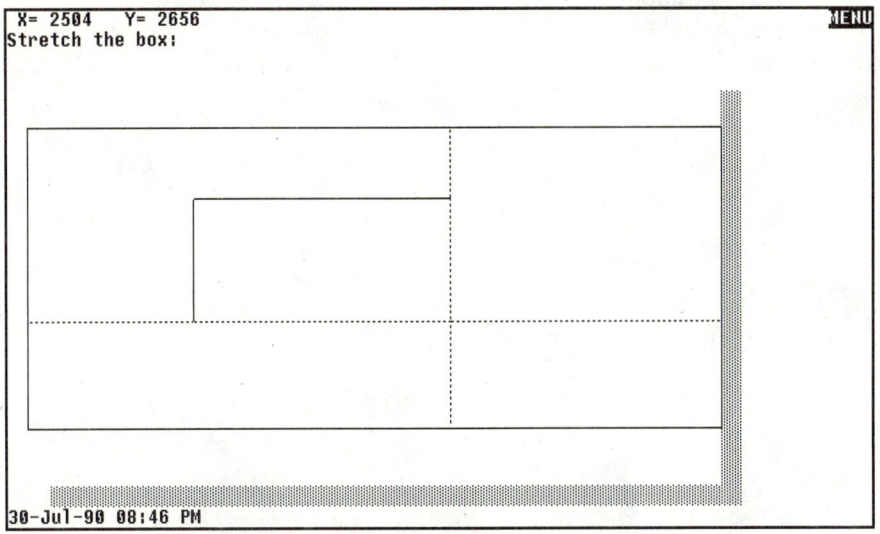

Fig. 11.10.
A rectangle being drawn with a big cursor.

Using the Font-Magnification option, you can scale the size of all text up or down. This option applies to text inserted with **:Graph Edit Add Text** as well as the text in the underlying graph (that is, titles and legends). Font-Magnification saves you from having to change the font size of each piece of text in your graph. For example, if all your titles and legends are too large, you can use Font-Magnification to reduce them all at once, instead of using the /Graph Options Advanced Text command to change each individually.

Cue:
To scale the size of all text (up or down), use the Font-Magnification option.

The font-magnification value is a percentage between 0 and 1000. The default value is 100. To scale down the sizes, enter a value under 100. For example, to reduce the text to 80% of its current size, type **80**. To magnify the text, enter a value over 100. For example, to double the size of the text, enter **200**. To display the text at its original point size—instead of at the size Wysiwyg scaled it when you added the graph—enter **0** for the font-magnification value.

Using the :Graph Edit View Menu

The **:Graph Edit View** menu lets you size and reposition the contents of the graphics editing window. You can use the options on the menu to concentrate on an area you are modifying. None of the View menu options changes the actual size of the graphic.

The **Full** option restores the graphic to its normal full size after you have resized or repositioned it with the other View options.

The **In** option lets you zoom in on a selected area of the graphic. Figure 11.11 shows a zoomed-in graphics window. When you select this option, the prompt `Move to the first corner` appears. Indicate the area you want to zoom in on by drawing a box around the range. Mouse users should use the click-and-drag technique to stretch the box around the area. Keyboard users should use the arrow keys to position the pointer on the first corner, press Enter, use the arrow keys to stretch the box so that the area is surrounded, and then press Enter again.

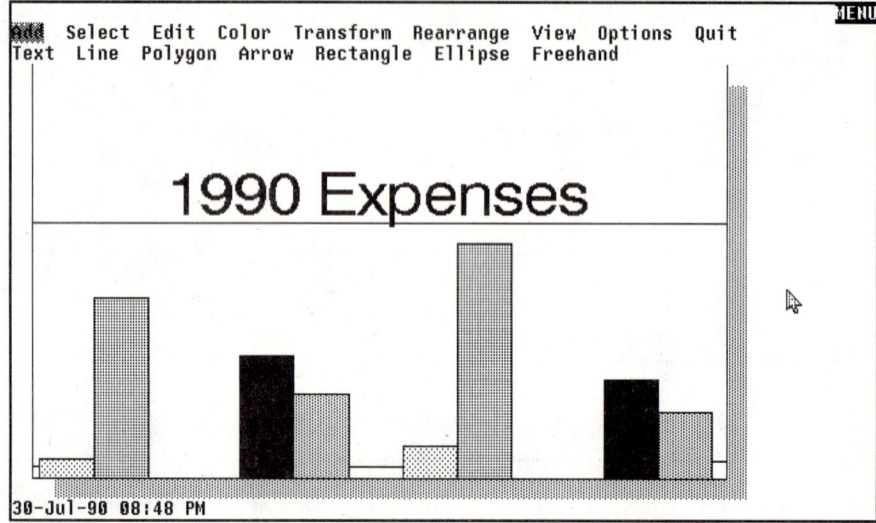

Fig. 11.11.
A zoomed-in graph.

Mouse users have a second zooming method available. From the :Graph Edit menu, press and hold Ctrl while clicking-and-dragging a box around the area. To unzoom, press and hold Ctrl and click anywhere in the graph.

Cue:
Press + to zoom in further or – to unzoom.

After you zoom in on an area, you may want to zoom in even further, or move the graph slightly in one direction. The remaining View options allow you to make these adjustments. Use the + option to zoom in further, or the – option to unzoom. Each time you choose +, you zoom in further. From the normal full size, you can zoom five times. (Actually, you don't even need to access the View menu to use the + and – options; you can press + and – from the :Graph Edit menu.)

The **Up**, **Down**, **Left**, and **Right** options on the View menu let you see parts of a zoomed graph not currently in the window. Each of these options moves the display one-half screen in the specified direction. To move the display up or down when you are at the :Graph Edit menu, press the up- or down-arrow key.

Cue:
Use View Pan to zoom, unzoom, and move the display around.

The View Pan option is a way to zoom, unzoom, and move the display around all at once. View Pan is essentially the +, –, Up, Down, Left, and Right options rolled into one. When you choose View Pan, the following message explains what to do: `Use cursor keys to move view, +/- to zoom, Enter to leave.` Thus, you can press + to zoom, – to unzoom, and the arrow keys to display a different part of the graph in the window. Once you are satisfied with the window contents, press Enter. Choose View Full to restore the screen to its original size and arrangement.

Rearranging Objects

The **R**earrange option on the **:G**raph **E**dit menu enables you to delete, copy, and move the objects you added to your graph with **:G**raph **E**dit **A**dd. Before you choose one of the **R**earrange options, select the object or objects you want to rearrange. See "Selecting Objects," earlier in this chapter, for details on selecting objects with the mouse or the **:G**raph **E**dit **S**elect menu.

Deleting and Restoring Objects

The **R**earrange **D**elete option removes the selected object or objects from the graph. Although Wysiwyg does not ask you to confirm your intention to delete, you can use the **R**earrange **R**estore command to retrieve the last deleted object or group of objects. Suppose that you select three objects at once and then choose **R**earrange **D**elete. All three objects are deleted. If you choose **R**earrange **R**estore, all three objects are retrieved into their original locations. But if you select and delete a line, and then select and delete a rectangle, you cannot restore the deleted line; you can retrieve only the deleted rectangle.

As an alternative to using the **R**earrange **D**elete command, you can simply select the object or objects you want to delete and press Del. Press Ins to restore the most recently deleted object or group of objects. Make sure that no object is selected when you press Ins to restore a deleted object; when an object is selected and you press Ins, that object is copied.

Reminder:
You can restore the last deleted object.

Moving Objects

To reposition an object, use the **R**earrange **M**ove option. If you haven't already done so, you are asked to select the objects you want to move. Either use the arrow keys to move the pointer to the object and press Enter, or click the mouse on the object. (You must click directly on the outline of rectangles, ellipses, or polygons. If you click inside the object, you cancel the command.) After you make your selection, a copy of the object appears inside a dotted rectangle (the *bounding box*). A hand also appears inside the bounding box, indicating that you are moving the object. Use the mouse or the arrow keys to move the bounding box to the target location and press the left mouse button or press Enter. Figure 11.12 shows a rectangle being moved.

If you have a mouse, you do not have to use the **R**earrange **M**ove option; from the **:G**raph **E**dit menu, you can simply use the click-and-drag technique to reposition an object.

Reminder:
Move the copy of the object in the dotted box to the new location and press Enter or click the mouse.

Copying Objects

Once you create an object, you may want to clone it. Using the **R**earrange **C**opy command ensures that two or more objects are the same size, with the same options. For example, if you create a shaded rectangle with wide lines, the copy of the rectangle is also shaded and has wide lines. When you copy an object, the following :Graph Edit options are copied along with the object:

- Edit options (Font, Line-Style, Width, Arrowheads, Smoothing)
- Color settings
- Transform options: Size, Rotate, Quarter-Turn, X-Flip, Y-Flip, Horizontal, Vertical (see "Transforming Objects" later in this chapter for more information)

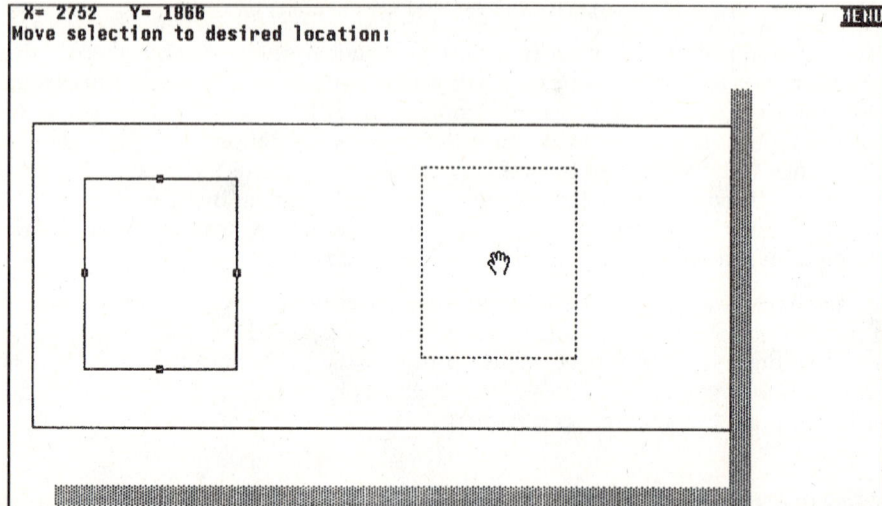

Fig. 11.12.
A rectangle being moved.

If an object is selected when you choose the **Rearrange Copy** command, a duplicate is placed slightly to the right of and below the original object. If no object was selected when you choose **Rearrange Copy**, you are prompted to select the objects to copy. The **Copy** command does not prompt you for a target location; you must use the **Rearrange Move** command to put the object into place. Thus copying is a two-step process.

Cue:
To copy an object, select it and press Ins.

Instead of using the **Rearrange Copy** command, you can simply select the object and press the Ins key. Like the **Rearrange Copy** command, Ins places the duplicated object next to the original; you must use the **Rearrange Move** command to put the object into position. If you don't have an object selected when you press Ins, the last deleted object is restored.

Moving an Object to the Back or Front

When a colored or shaded object is positioned on top of an existing object, it can obscure the objects underneath it. Suppose that you add some text, draw an ellipse around it, and then add a pattern to the ellipse. After adding the pattern, you can no longer see the text because the ellipse is on top of the text (see the left ellipse in fig. 11.13). To see the text, you need to bring the text in front of the ellipse, or place the ellipse in back of the text. You can select the ellipse and choose **Rearrange Back**, or select the text and choose **Rearrange Front**. The ellipse on the right side of figure 11.13 shows how the text reappears after the ellipse is moved to the back.

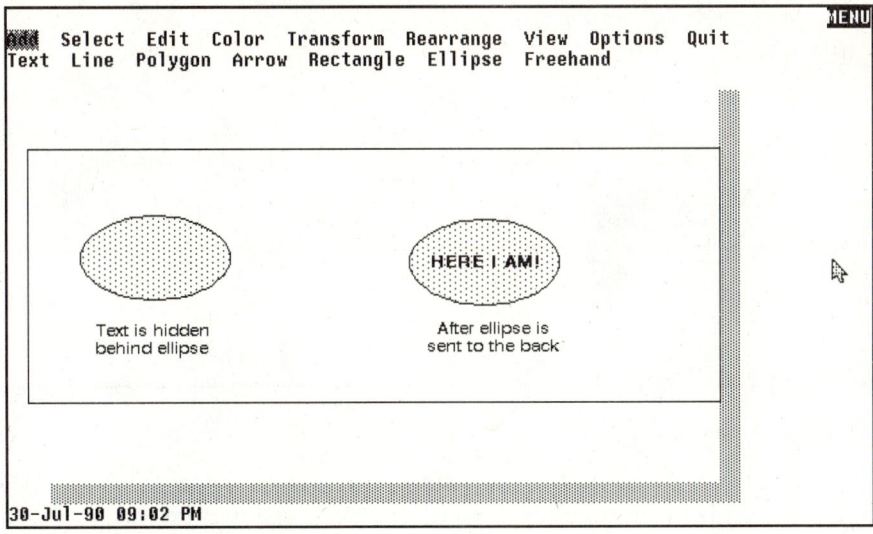

Fig. 11.13.
Using the Rearrange Back command.

When objects seem to have disappeared mysteriously, it's quite possible that they are hidden by an overlaying object. Use the **Rearrange Front** and **Back** options to find such missing objects.

Locking an Object

Once you have an object the perfect size, in the perfect location, with the perfect options, you may want to use the **Rearrange Lock** option to prevent it from being changed. When you lock an object, you cannot delete it, move it, transform it, color it, or edit it. You can copy it, however, but the duplicate is not locked. If you later need to make a change to the locked object, use the **Rearrange Unlock** option.

Cue:
To prevent an object from being changed accidentally, use the Rearrange Lock command.

Transforming Objects

With the options on the **:G**raph Edit Transform menu, you can change basic geometric shapes. The shape in figure 11.14 (originally a basic rectangle) was altered with several of the **T**ransform options. If you aren't happy with the transformed object, you can use Transform Clear to clear all transformations made to the selected objects.

Fig. 11.14.
A transformed rectangle.

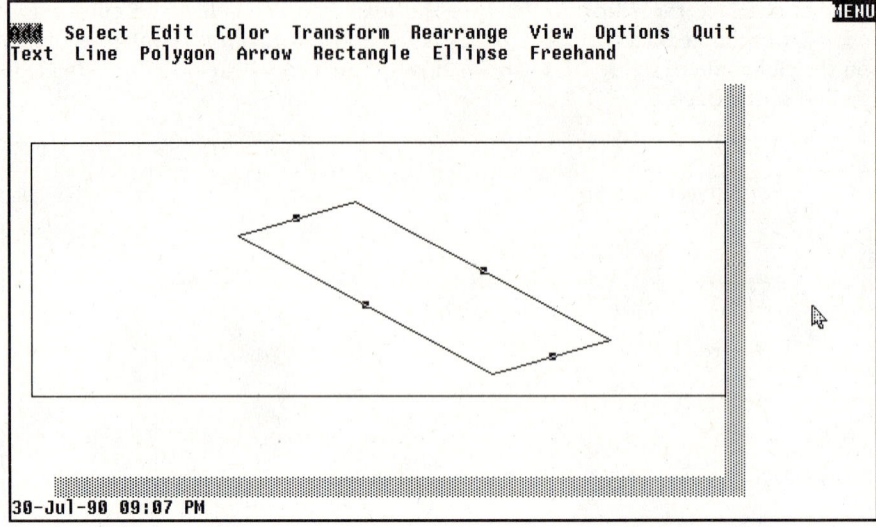

Sizing an Object

Reminder:
Use **T***ransform* **S***ize to change the height and width of any added objects.*

You can change the size (height and width) of any added objects except text with the **:Graph Edit Transform Size** command. (To change the text size, specify a different font with the **:Graph Edit Edit Font** command.) When you choose the **Transform Size** command, the selected object is surrounded by a bounding box. The upper left corner of the box is anchored, and the cursor is in the lower right corner. Control the size of the object by pressing the arrow keys or by moving the mouse until the bounding box is the desired size. Then press Enter or the left mouse button to change the object's size.

Another way to adjust an object's size is with the **Transform Horizontal** or **Transform Vertical** options. These options also change the angles of the objects. See "Adjusting the Slant," later in this chapter, for further information.

Rotating an Object

Cue:
To rotate an object, use **T***ransform* **Q***uarter-Turn or* **R***otate.*

The **Transform** menu offers two ways to rotate an object. The **Quarter-Turn** option rotates the selected object or objects in 90-degree increments. The turns are made in a counterclockwise direction. Figure 11.15 shows two objects (the ellipse and the text inside it) before and after a **Quarter-Turn**.

If you want to rotate an object in increments other than 90 degrees, use the **Transform Rotate** option; you can rotate the selected object or objects to any angle. An axis extends from the center of the object to outside the bounding box. Think of this axis as a handle that pulls the object in the direction you press the arrow keys or move the mouse. As you rotate, the original object remains intact, and a copy of the object rotates. As soon as you press Enter or the left mouse button, the rotated copy is replaced with the original.

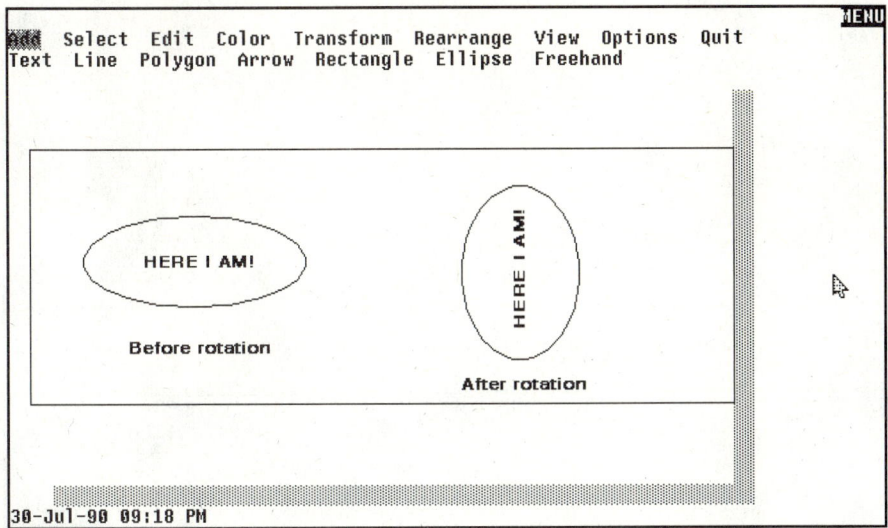

Fig. 11.15. *Objects before and after a Quarter-Turn rotation.*

Some printers can print text rotated only in 90-degree increments. The HP LaserJet Series II and PostScript printers can print text at any angle.

Flipping an Object

Imagine that the selected object is a pancake, and that the **X**-Flip and **Y**-Flip options are spatulas. **X**-Flip flips the object over, positioning the original upper left corner in the upper right corner. **Y**-Flip turns the object upside down, positioning the upper left corner in the lower left corner. If you choose the wrong flip direction, you can reverse the action by choosing the same direction again. For example, if you choose **X**-Flip and don't like the results, flip the object back to its original position by choosing **X**-Flip again.

You do not notice any effect when you flip lines, rectangles, or ellipses that are in a 90-degree angle position.

Adjusting the Slant

The **Transform Horizontal** and **Transform Vertical** options let you change the slant (angles) and size of the selected object or objects. You can even flip the object in the same step. Consider figure 11.16. The rectangle is being transformed horizontally. The upper line is anchored. As you press the arrow keys or move the mouse, you see the bounding box stretch freely in the direction you move the cursor. To flip the object, position the bounding box above the selected object. When the bounding box is the desired size and shape, press Enter or the left mouse button. The object is moved into the position of the bounding box.

When you transform an object vertically, the left side of the object is anchored. To flip the object, position the bounding box to the left of the selected object.

Cue:
Use **T**ransform **H**orizontal *or* **T**ransform **V**ertical *to change the angles and size of an object.*

Part II ◆ Creating 1-2-3 Reports and Graphs

Fig. 11.16.
A rectangle being transformed horizontally.

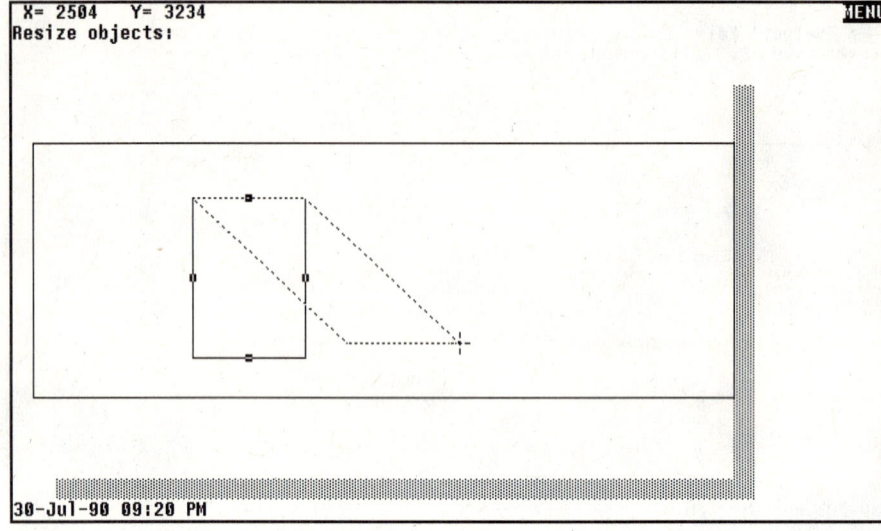

Summary

This chapter showed you how to use Wysiwyg's graphing commands and options. At the simplest level, you can insert a graph so that you can include it with a Wysiwyg-formatted report. You can then take the 1-2-3 graph and make annotations to point out key data values. At another level, you can use the graphics editor to create your own graphic drawings that include text and geometric objects.

Part III

Customizing 1-2-3

Managing Data

Using Macros

Introducing the Advanced Macro Commands

Managing Data

12

In addition to the electronic spreadsheet and business graphics, 1-2-3 has a third capability: data management. These three elements, along with Release 3.1+'s virtual memory capability, give 1-2-3 users a powerful software package.

Virtual memory is a technique that enables 1-2-3 to use files that are too large to fit in main memory. Virtual memory automatically uses a temporary file on the hard disk as an extension to main memory.

Release 3 provides many new levels of features, including some of the relational enhancements and larger databases of products like dBASE. Because the entire database normally resides in the worksheet within main memory (RAM), 1-2-3's database feature is fast, easy to access, and easy to use.

The 1-2-3 database has easy access because Lotus Development Corporation made the entire database visible within the worksheet. You can view the contents of the whole database by using worksheet windows and cursor-movement keys to scroll through the database.

The program is easy to use because it integrates data management with worksheet and graphics functions. The commands to add, modify, and delete items in a database are the same commands that you have already used to manipulate cells or groups of cells within a worksheet. Creating graphs from ranges in a database is as easy as creating graphs in a worksheet.

This chapter shows you how to do the following:

- ◆ Understand the advantages and limitations of 1-2-3's database
- ◆ Create, modify, and maintain data records
- ◆ Sort, locate, extract, and edit data entries
- ◆ Create three-dimensional and labeled data tables

- Use database functions
- Load data from ASCII files and other programs
- Access and manipulate data in a table within an external database

Defining a Database

A *database* is a collection of related information. It is data organized so that you can list, sort, or search its contents. A database can contain any kind of information, from addresses to tax-deductible expenditures. For example, a telephone book is one kind of database; personal address books, personal checkbooks, and Rolodex files also are common databases.

In 1-2-3, the word *database* means a range of cells that spans at least one column and more than one row. Because a database is actually a list, its manner of organization sets it apart from ordinary cells. Just as a list must be organized to be useful, a database must be organized to permit access to the information it contains.

Generally, you have three kinds of database organization. The simplest database organization in 1-2-3 is a single database contained in a single worksheet. This organization is used in most of the examples in this chapter, as well as in most real-world applications. You also have multiple databases, with each one occupying a different portion of one worksheet. Finally, with 1-2-3's three-dimensional capabilities, you have multiple databases on two or more worksheet "levels." Note, however, that a single database table cannot span different worksheet levels; the database must be located entirely within one worksheet level. As you see later in this chapter, you can "relate" databases that are on different worksheet levels, and thus produce a more efficient overall database structure.

Remember that in 1-2-3 a database is similar to any other group of cells. This knowledge may help you as you learn about the different /Data commands covered in this chapter. In many instances, you can use these database commands in what you may consider "nondatabase" applications.

Databases are made up of fields and records. A *field*, or single data item, is the smallest unit in a database. For example, if you were to develop an information base of companies you do business with, you could include the following six pieces, or fields, of information on each company:

Name
Address
City
State
ZIP
Phone

Reminder:
In 1-2-3, a field is a single cell, and a record is a row of cells within a database.

A *record* is a collection of associated fields. That is, the accumulation of all data on one company makes one record. For example, the six fields in the preceding paragraph represent one record on one company. In 1-2-3, a field is a single cell, and a record is a row of cells within a database.

A database must be set up so that you can access the information it contains. Retrieval of information usually involves key fields. A database *key field* is any field on which you base a list, sort, or search operation. For example, you can use ZIP as a key field to sort the data in the company database and to assign contact representatives to specific geographic areas.

Do not confuse *database table* with *data table,* which only refers to the data table created with the /**D**ata **T**able command. *Database table* is often used with relational databases because a single database may contain several tables of related information. Because most 1-2-3 databases contain only one table, however, the term *database* is often used in place of database table. Later in this chapter, you examine two database tables used to create a relational structure.

Designing a 1-2-3 Database

A 1-2-3 database resides within the worksheet's row-and-column format. Figure 12.1 shows the general organization of a 1-2-3 database. Labels, or *field names,* that describe the data items appear as column headings. Information about each specific data item (field) is entered in a cell in the appropriate column. In figure 12.1, cell A4 represents data (A1 Computing) for the first field (COMPANY) in the database's first record.

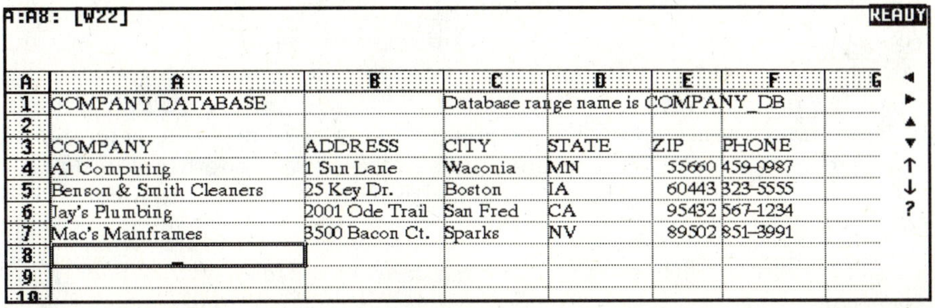
A:A8: [W22] READY

A	A	B	C	D	E	F	G
1	COMPANY DATABASE		Database range name is COMPANY_DB				
2							
3	COMPANY	ADDRESS	CITY	STATE	ZIP	PHONE	
4	A1 Computing	1 Sun Lane	Waconia	MN	55660	459-0987	
5	Benson & Smith Cleaners	25 Key Dr.	Boston	IA	60443	323-5555	
6	Jay's Plumbing	2001 Ode Trail	San Fred	CA	95432	567-1234	
7	Mac's Mainframes	3500 Bacon Ct.	Sparks	NV	89502	851-3991	
8							
9							
10							

Fig. 12.1.
Organization of a 1-2-3 database.

Theoretically, the maximum number of records you can have in a 1-2-3 database corresponds to the maximum number of rows in the worksheet (8,192 rows minus 1 row for the field names). Realistically, however, the number of records in a specific database is limited by the amount of available memory: internal memory (RAM), plus disk storage for virtual memory, and the room needed within the database to hold data extracted by the /**D**ata **Q**uery commands.

When you estimate the maximum database size you can use on your computer equipment, be sure to include enough blank rows to accommodate the maximum output you expect from extract operations. You may also be able to split a large 1-2-3 database into separate database tables on different worksheet levels if all the data does not have to be sorted or searched as a unit. For example, you may be able to separate a telephone list database by name (A through M in one file; N through Z in another) or area code.

You access the menu of **/Data** commands from the 1-2-3 command menu. Because all the options (**W**orksheet, **R**ange, **C**opy, **M**ove, **F**ile, **P**rint, and **G**raph) that precede **D**ata on the main menu work as well on databases as they do on worksheets, the power of 1-2-3 is at your fingertips.

Reminder:
You can translate files between 1-2-3 and dBASE for your database applications.

You can also use 1-2-3's file-translation capabilities (refer to Chapter 7), or 1-2-3's **/D**ata **E**xternal command, covered later in this chapter, to access database files created with dBASE and the @BASE add-in for earlier versions of 1-2-3 and Symphony. This feature enables you to take advantage of 1-2-3's data and graph commands.

When you select **/D**ata from the 1-2-3 command menu, the following options appear in the control panel's second line:

    Fill **T**able **S**ort **Q**uery **D**istribution **M**atrix **R**egression **P**arse **E**xternal

The **S**ort and **Q**uery (search) options are true data management operations. Most of the other options (**F**ill, **T**able, **D**istribution, **M**atrix, **R**egression, and **P**arse) are considered, more appropriately, data-creation and data-manipulation operations. Finally, the **E**xternal option is used to access database files created with other database programs. All nine options are discussed in this chapter.

Creating a Database

Caution:
Locate your database where it won't be affected by inserted columns, deleted rows, or changed column widths.

You can create a database as a new worksheet file or as part of an existing worksheet. If you decide to build a database as part of an existing worksheet, choose a worksheet area that you do not need for anything else. This area should be large enough to accommodate the number of records you plan to enter during the current session and in the future. A better idea is to add another worksheet to the current file so that the database and any existing worksheets do not interfere with each other.

To add another worksheet for the new database, first use the **/W**orksheet **I**nsert **S**heet command. You can add the worksheet before or after the current worksheet, and you can accept **1** as the number of worksheets to add. Next, use the **/W**orksheet **G**lobal **G**roup **D**isable command to make sure that the two worksheets do not interfere with each other. This step prevents column width settings as well as row or column insertions (or deletions) in one worksheet from applying to the other worksheet. Finally, use Ctrl-PgUp or Ctrl-PgDn to move between the two worksheets. If you want both worksheets on-screen together, use **/W**orksheet **W**indow **P**erspective to arrange the display.

After you have decided which area of the worksheet to use, you create a database by specifying field names across a row and entering data in cells as you would for any other 1-2-3 application (see fig. 12.2). The mechanics of entering database contents are simple; the most critical step in creating a useful database is choosing your fields properly.

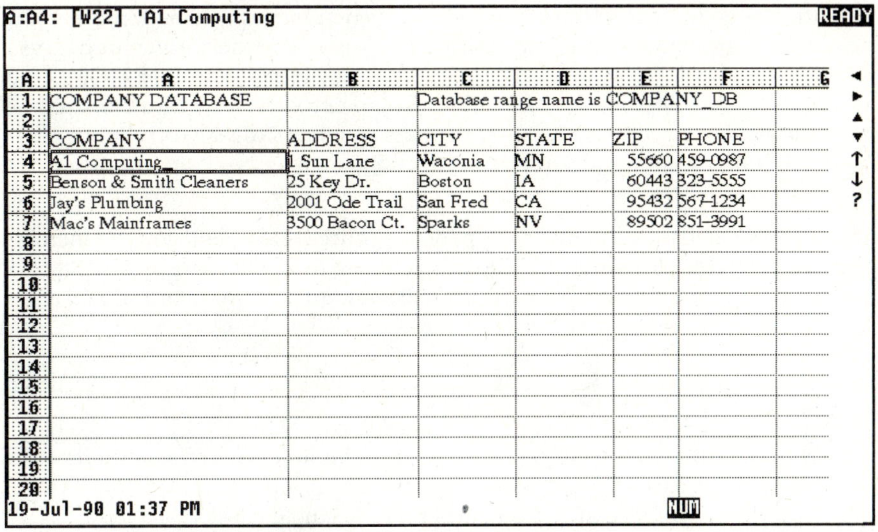

```
A:A4: [W22] 'A1 Computing                                                    READY

          A                    B              C          D       E      F          G
   1  COMPANY DATABASE                   Database range name is COMPANY_DB
   2
   3  COMPANY               ADDRESS       CITY       STATE    ZIP    PHONE
   4  A1 Computing          1 Sun Lane    Waconia    MN       55660  459-0987
   5  Benson & Smith Cleaners 25 Key Dr.  Boston     IA       60443  323-5555
   6  Jay's Plumbing        2001 Ode Trail San Fred  CA       95432  567-1234
   7  Mac's Mainframes      3500 Bacon Ct. Sparks    NV       89502  851-3991
   8
   ...
  20
19-Jul-90 01:37 PM                                                         NUM
```

Fig. 12.2.

The first field of the first database record.

Entering Field Names

1-2-3's data-retrieval techniques rely on locating data by field names. You may want to write down the output you expect from the database before you begin typing the data items. You also need to consider any source documents already in use that can provide input to the file. For example, you can use the following information from the sample company database:

Name
Address
City
State
ZIP
Phone

When you are ready to set up these items in your database, you must specify for each item of information a field name, the column width, and the type of entry.

You can make a common error in setting up your database if you choose a field name (and enter data) without thinking about the output you want from that key field. For example, suppose that you established ORDERDATE as a field name to describe the last date an order was made. Then you entered record dates as labels, in the general form MMM-DD-YYYY (such as JAN-01-1991). Although you may search for an ORDERDATE that matched a specific date, you may not be able to perform a math-based search for all ORDERDATEs within a specified period of time or before a certain date. To get maximum flexibility from 1-2-3's data commands, you should use one of 1-2-3's date formats or date functions to enter dates in your databases (see Chapter 6 for more information on functions).

Cue:
Although you may enter dates by using @DATE, Release 3 recognizes the simpler MM/DD/YY form as a date entry.

You then need to choose the level of detail needed for each item of information, select the appropriate column width, and determine whether you enter data as a number or a label. For example, if you want to be able to sort by area code all records containing telephone numbers, you should enter telephone numbers as two separate fields: area code (XXX) and the base number (XXX-XXXX). Because you probably won't want to perform math functions on telephone numbers, you can enter them as labels.

If you enter database content from a standard source document, you can increase the speed of data entry by setting up the field names in the same order as that of the corresponding data items on the form. Be sure to plan your database carefully before you establish field names and enter data.

Entering Data

Reminder:
The format of your data (date, labels, or numbers) affects how the data is sorted and searched.

After you have planned your database, you can build it. To understand how the process works, create a Company database as a new database on a blank worksheet (in READY mode). Enter the field names across a single row (A3..F3 in fig. 12.1).

The field names must be labels, even if they are the numeric labels '1, '2, and so on. Although you can use more than one row for the labels, 1-2-3 uses only the values that appear in the bottom row as the field names. For example, if you typed **STREET** in cell B2, the second field name in the Company database is still only ADDRESS, not STREET ADDRESS.

Reminder:
Keep all field names unique; repetition of field names confuses 1-2-3.

Keep in mind that all field names must be unique; any repetition of names confuses 1-2-3 when you search or sort the database.

To control the manner in which cells are displayed on-screen, you use 1-2-3's /Range Format and /Worksheet Column Set-Width options. In figure 12.1, notice that the column widths on the worksheet vary from seven to 22 characters.

Cue:
Insert blank columns between fields to prevent crowding of data.

Note also that whenever a right-justified column of numeric data is adjacent to a left-justified column of label information (such as ZIP and PHONE), the data looks crowded. You can insert blank columns to change the spacing between fields; if you plan to search values in the database, however, do not leave any blank rows.

After you have altered the column widths, entered titles and field names, and added spacing columns, you can add records to the database. To enter the first record, move the cursor to the row directly below the field-name row, and then enter the data across the row. To enter the first record, for example, type the following entries in these cells:

- A4: **A1 Computing**
- B4: **'1 Sun Lane**
- C4: **Waconia**
- D4: **MN**
- E4: **55660**
- F4: **'459-0987**

Chapter 12 ◆ Managing Data **501**

Notice that the contents of the ADDRESS and PHONE fields are entered as labels by typing a ' label character; contents of the ZIP field are entered as numbers in this example.

This sample company database is used periodically throughout this chapter to illustrate the results of using various /Data commands. In this book, the fields are limited to a single screen display. In "real life" applications, however, you would track many more data items. You can maintain 256 fields (the number of columns available) in a 1-2-3 database.

Modifying a Database

After you have collected the data for your database and decided which field types, widths, and formats to use, creating a database is easy. Thanks to 1-2-3, maintaining the accuracy of the database content is easy also.

To add and delete records in a database, use the same commands for inserting and deleting rows that you use for any other application in 1-2-3. Because records correspond to rows, you insert a record with the /Worksheet Insert Row command. You then fill in the various fields in the row with the appropriate data. Figure 12.3 shows a record being inserted in the middle of a database. Instead of inserting a record in the middle of a database, however, you may add new records at the end, and then use 1-2-3's sorting capabilities, illustrated in the next section, to rearrange the physical order of database records.

Cue:
If your database is contained in a multi-level worksheet file, use /Worksheet Global Group Disable to ensure that rows or columns inserted or deleted in one worksheet aren't also inserted or deleted in other worksheet(s).

Fig. 12.3.
Inserting a record in the database.

A	A	B	C	D	E	F	G
1	COMPANY DATABASE		Database range name is COMPANY_DB				
2							
3	COMPANY	ADDRESS	CITY	STATE	ZIP	PHONE	
4	A1 Computing	1 Sun Lane	Waconia	MN	55660	459-0987	
5	Benson & Smith Cleaners	25 Key Dr.	Boston	IA	60443	323-5555	
6							
7	Jay's Plumbing	2001 Ode Trail	San Fred	CA	95432	567-1234	
8	Mac's Mainframes	3500 Bacon Ct.	Sparks	NV	89502	851-3991	
9							
10							

To delete records, move your cell pointer to the row you want to delete and select the /Worksheet Delete Row command. Be extremely careful when you specify the records to be deleted if you are not using Undo (Alt-F4). If you want to remove only inactive records, consider first using the /Data Query Extract command to store the extracted inactive records in a separate file before you delete the records. (This chapter shows you how.)

You modify fields in a database the same way you modify the contents of cells in any other application. As you learned in Chapter 3, you change the cell contents either by retyping the cell entry or by using Edit (F2) and editing the entry.

To add a new field to a database, you place the cell pointer anywhere in the column that is to the right of the newly inserted column. You issue the /Worksheet

Cue:
Use /Data Query Extract to archive inactive records before deleting them from the main database.

Reminder:
Add new fields to your database with /Worksheet Insert Column; delete fields with /Worksheet Delete Column.

Insert Column command and then fill the field with values for each record. For example, to insert an AREA field between the ZIP and PHONE fields, place the cell pointer on any cell in the PHONE column, issue the /Worksheet Insert Column command, and then type the new field name (**AREA**) in cell E3 (see figure 12.4).

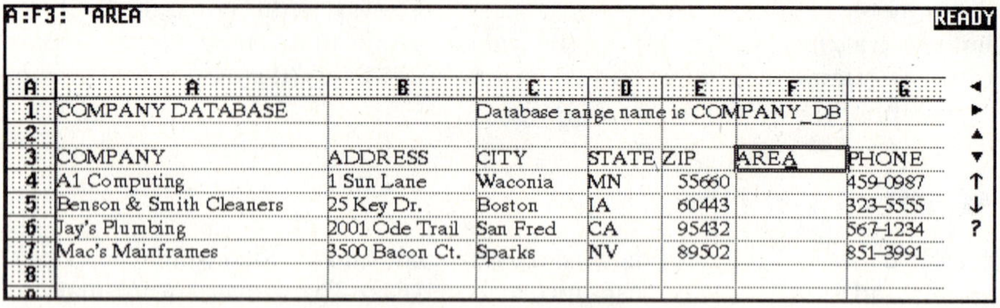

Fig. 12.4.
Inserting a column for a new field.

```
A:F3: 'AREA                                                          READY

       A                    B              C          D      E       F          G
  1  COMPANY DATABASE                   Database range name is COMPANY_DB
  2
  3  COMPANY              ADDRESS        CITY       STATE  ZIP     AREA       PHONE
  4  A1 Computing         1 Sun Lane     Waconia    MN     55660              459-0987
  5  Benson & Smith Cleaners 25 Key Dr.  Boston     IA     60443              323-5555
  6  Jay's Plumbing       2001 Ode Trail San Fred   CA     95432              567-1234
  7  Mac's Mainframes     3500 Bacon Ct. Sparks     NV     89502              851-3991
  8
```

To delete a field, place the cell pointer anywhere in the column you want to remove, and then select the /Worksheet Delete Column command.

All other commands, such as those for moving cells, formatting cells, and displaying the contents of worksheets, work the same way in both database and worksheet applications.

Sorting Database Records

1-2-3's data management capability enables you to change the order of records by sorting them according to the contents of the fields. You can use the /Data Sort command only with a worksheet database, not with an external database. Selecting /Data Sort produces the following menu:

> Data-Range Primary-Key Secondary-Key Extra-Key Reset Go Quit

To sort the database, you start by designating a **Data-Range**. This range must include all the records to be sorted and also be wide enough to include all the fields in each record. If you do not include all fields when sorting, you destroy the integrity of your database because parts of one record end up with parts of other records. In figure 12.4, the Company database covers the range from A4..G7. Notice, however, that the **Data-Range** must not include the field name row. (If you are unfamiliar with how to designate ranges or how to name them, refer to Chapter 4.)

Caution:
*Make sure that the **D**ata-Range does not include the field name row. Otherwise the field name row is one of the records to be sorted and your database may be damaged.*

The **Data-Range** does not necessarily have to include the entire database. If part of the database already has the organization you want, or if you do not want to sort all the records, you can sort only a portion of the database.

After choosing the **Data-Range**, you must specify the keys for the sort. The field with the highest precedence is the **Primary-Key**, and the field with the next highest precedence is the **Secondary-Key**. You must set a **Primary-Key**, but the **Secondary-Key** is optional.

After you have specified the range to sort, specified the sort key(s) on which to base the reordering of the records, and indicated whether the sort order—based on the sort key—is ascending or descending, you select **Go** to execute the command. For safety, use **/File Save** before performing the sort, so you can retrieve the original database if something goes wrong with your sort operation.

Cue:
Use /File Save before sorting your database, in case you later need to restore the original order.

Using the One-Key Sort

One of the simplest examples of a database sorted according to a primary key (often called a single-key database) is the white pages of the phone book. All the records in the white pages are sorted in ascending alphabetical order, with the last name used as the primary key.

You can use 1-2-3's sorting capability to reorder records alphabetically on the STATE field. If you have not already specified the **Data-Range** (to sort by ZIP as in figure 12.5, for example), select **/Data Sort Data-Range**. At the prompt for a range to sort, highlight A4..G7. After you specify the range, the **/Data Sort** menu returns to the screen. This is one of 1-2-3's menus that remain displayed and active until you select **Quit**. This is helpful because you do not have to specify **/Data Sort** at the beginning of each command.

```
A:A3: [W22] 'COMPANY                                              READY

     A                   B            C         D      E      F         G
 1  COMPANY DATABASE                  Database range name is COMPANY_DB
 2
 3  COMPANY             ADDRESS       CITY      STATE  ZIP    AREA      PHONE
 4  A1 Computing        1 Sun Lane    Waconia   MN     55660            459-0987
 5  Benson & Smith Cleaners 25 Key Dr. Boston   IA     60443            323-5555
 6  Mac's Mainframes    3500 Bacon Ct. Sparks   NV     89502            851-3991
 7  Jay's Plumbing      2001 Ode Trail San Fred CA     95432            567-1234
 8
```

Fig. 12.5.
The database sorted by ZIP code.

After choosing the **Data-Range**, select **Primary-Key** and then type or point to any cell (including blank or field-name cells) in the column containing the primary-key field. For example, type **D3** (for STATE) as the **Primary-Key**. 1-2-3 then asks you to enter a sort order (A or D). *A* stands for ascending, and *D* for descending. For this example, choose **A** for ascending order and press Enter. Finally, select **Go** from the menu to execute the sort. Figure 12.6 shows the database sorted in ascending order by state.

```
A:A3: [W22] 'COMPANY                                              READY

     A                   B            C         D      E      F         G
 1  COMPANY DATABASE                  Database range name is COMPANY_DB
 2
 3  COMPANY             ADDRESS       CITY      STATE  ZIP    AREA      PHONE
 4  Jay's Plumbing      2001 Ode Trail San Fred CA     95432            567-1234
 5  Benson & Smith Cleaners 25 Key Dr. Boston   IA     60443            323-5555
 6  A1 Computing        1 Sun Lane    Waconia   MN     55660            459-0987
 7  Mac's Mainframes    3500 Bacon Ct. Sparks   NV     89502            851-3991
 8
```

Fig. 12.6.
The database sorted by STATE.

Part III ◆ Customizing 1-2-3

You can add a record to a sorted database without having to insert a row manually to place the new record in the proper position. Simply add the new record to the bottom of the current database, expand the **Data-Range**, and then sort the database again using the desired sort key.

Using the Two-Key Sort

A double-key sort uses both a primary and a secondary sort key. In the telephone book's yellow pages, records are sorted first according to business type (the primary key) and then by business name (the secondary key). To see how a double-key sort works (first sorting by one key and then by another key within the first sort order), you can add a new record to the end of the Company database and then reorder it first by STATE and then by CITY within STATE.

Place the cursor in cell A8 and add the following entries to the indicated cells:

  A8: **Ralph's Bar**
  B8: **'10 Lilac**
  C8: **Carmel**
  D8: **CA**
  E8: **95309**
  G8: **'369-2468**

Your database should now look like figure 12.7.

Fig. 12.7.

The database after adding Ralph's Bar.

```
A:G8: '369-2468                                                       READY

      A                  B              C         D    E      F       G
 1 COMPANY DATABASE                     Database range name is COMPANY_DB
 2
 3 COMPANY              ADDRESS         CITY      STATE ZIP    AREA    PHONE
 4 Jay's Plumbing       2001 Ode Trail  San Fred  CA    95432         567-1234
 5 Benson & Smith Cleaners 25 Key Dr.   Boston    IA    60443         323-5555
 6 A1 Computing         1 Sun Lane      Waconia   MN    55660         459-0987
 7 Mac's Mainframes     3500 Bacon Ct.  Sparks    NV    89502         851-3991
 8 Ralph's Bar          10 Lilac        Carmel    CA    95309         369-2468
 9
```

After adding Ralph's record, select **/Data Sort Data-Range**. Notice that A4..G7 is still highlighted. To include the new record, use the down-arrow key to extend the highlighted area down so that A4..G8 is highlighted. The STATE field is still selected as the **Primary-Key**, so you don't have to respecify it. Select **Secondary-Key**, enter C3, and choose **A** for ascending for the sort order by CITY. Figure 12.8 shows the results of issuing the **G**o command after you have specified the two-key sort.

As you can see, records are now grouped first by state in alphabetical order (California, Iowa, Minnesota, and Nevada), and then by city within state (Carmel, California, before San Fred, California). When you determine whether to use a primary or secondary sort key, be sure to request a reasonable sort. For example, you probably don't want to sort first by CITY and then by STATE within CITY.

Chapter 12 ♦ Managing Data **505**

A:G8: '851-3991							READY
A	**A**	**B**	**C**	**D**	**E**	**F**	**G**
1	COMPANY DATABASE		Database range name is COMPANY_DB				
2							
3	COMPANY	ADDRESS	CITY	STATE	ZIP	AREA	PHONE
4	Ralph's Bar	10 Lilac	Carmel	CA	95309		369-2468
5	Jay's Plumbing	2001 Ode Trail	San Fred	CA	95432		567-1234
6	Benson & Smith Cleaners	25 Key Dr.	Boston	IA	60443		323-5555
7	A1 Computing	1 Sun Lane	Waconia	MN	55660		459-0987
8	Mac's Mainframes	3500 Bacon Ct.	Sparks	NV	89502		851-3991
9							
10							

Fig. 12.8.

The company database sorted by CITY within STATE.

Using the Extra-Key Sort

The **Extra-Key** option enables you to specify as many as 253 sort keys to be used in addition to the primary and secondary sort keys. These extra keys are used to determine the sort order when two or more records contain identical values in both the primary- and secondary-key fields. The extra keys are numbered from 1 through 253 and are applied in order: **Extra-Key 1** is used to break ties in the secondary-key field, **Extra-Key 2** is used to break ties in extra-key field 1, and so on.

You assign an extra key essentially the same way that you assign primary and secondary keys. Select **Extra-Key** from the **/Data Sort** menu and then enter the number (**1-253**) of the extra key you are assigning. Next, enter the field (column) to be used for the extra key, followed by the sort order (**A** for ascending or **D** for descending).

To understand how an extra-key sort works, look at the database shown in figure 12.8. Suppose that as your database grew, several of the records were "tied" in their CITY and STATE fields. You can sort this database on the CITY and STATE fields, specifying COMPANY as an extra key to break the ties.

To remove an extra sort key, you assign its number to the data field being used by a "higher" sort key. For example, to cancel **Extra-Key 2**, you select **/Data Sort Extra-Key**, type **2**, and specify the column being used by **Extra-Key 1**. To cancel **Extra-Key 1**, you assign it to the data field being used by the **Secondary-Key**.

Determining the Sort Order

Certain aspects of the sort order are determined by the collating sequence setting that you established when 1-2-3 was installed on your system. The three options for this setting are Numbers First, Numbers Last, and ASCII. When you select ascending sort order, the effects of each setting are shown in table 12.1 (selecting descending order reverses the orders shown).

For Numbers First and Numbers Last, capitalization is ignored. For ASCII, uppercase letters precede lowercase letters (*Jay's* comes before *benson*, for example).

When you specify numbers as labels, a problem can occur because 1-2-3 sorts from left to right, one character at a time. For example, if you were to sort the company database in ascending order according to ADDRESS (column B), the results of the sort would resemble those shown in figure 12.9.

Table 12.1
Collating Sequences for Ascending Order

Collating Sequence	Sort Order
Numbers First	Blank cells
	Labels beginning with numbers in numeric order
	Labels beginning with letters in alphabetical order
	Labels beginning with other characters in ASCII value order
	Values
Numbers Last	Blank cells
	Labels beginning with letters in alphabetical order
	Labels beginning with numbers in numeric order
	Labels beginning with other characters in ASCII value order
	Values
ASCII	Blank cells
	All labels in ASCII value order
	Values

Fig. 12.9.
An erroneous ascending sort.

```
A:G8:  '851-3991                                                    READY

     A                  B              C         D    E      F       G
 1 COMPANY DATABASE                Database range name is COMPANY_DB
 2
 3 COMPANY            ADDRESS       CITY      STATE ZIP   AREA  PHONE
 4 A1 Computing       1 Sun Lane    Waconia   MN    55660       459-0987
 5 Ralph's Bar        10 Lilac      Carmel    CA    95309       369-2468
 6 Jay's Plumbing     2001 Ode Trail San Fred CA    95432       567-1234
 7 Benson & Smith Cleaners 25 Key Dr. Boston  IA    60443       323-5555
 8 Mac's Mainframes   3500 Bacon Ct. Sparks   NV    89502       851-3991
 9
```

Although you would expect the records to be sorted in ascending order on the ADDRESS field, notice that the 2001 in row 6 appears before the 25 in row 7. This problem occurs because 1-2-3 sorts the numbers one character at a time when sorting labels.

Although it's unlikely that you would sort the company database by using the ADDRESS field as a key, some cases may require you to sort label fields that look like numbers. One solution is to make all labels that look like numbers the same length (as in the PHONE field) or add enough leading zeros (0) to ensure that all labels have the same format (that is, 0025 and 2001 are the same length). Figure 12.10 shows the result of sorting the database on ADDRESS after padding the address numbers with leading zeros so all are four characters long.

Chapter 12 ◆ Managing Data

```
A:B7: [W12] '2001 Ode Trail                                              READY
```

	A	B	C	D	E	F	G
1	COMPANY DATABASE		Database range name is COMPANY_DB				
2							
3	COMPANY	ADDRESS	CITY	STATE	ZIP	AREA	PHONE
4	A1 Computing	0001 Sun Lane	Waconia	MN	55660		459-0987
5	Ralph's Bar	0010 Lilac	Carmel	CA	95309		369-2468
6	Benson & Smith Cleaners	0025 Key Dr.	Boston	IA	60443		323-5555
7	Jay's Plumbing	2001 Ode Trail	San Fred	CA	95432		567-1234
8	Mac's Mainframes	3500 Bacon Ct.	Sparks	NV	89502		851-3991
9							

Fig. 12.10.
The corrected ascending sort.

Restoring the Presort Order

If you sort the original contents of the database on any field, such as the ADDRESS field shown in figure 12.10, you cannot restore the records to their original order. If you add a "record number" column to the database before any sort, however, you can reorder the records on any field and then restore the original order by re-sorting on the record number field. After you have sorted the database on a particular column, you can sort again on the record number field to restore the records to their original order. Later in this chapter you see how to use the /Data Fill command to automatically enter record numbers before sorting the database.

Searching for Records

You have learned how to use the /Data Sort option to reorganize information from the database by sorting records according to key fields. In this section of the chapter, you learn how to use /Data Query, the other data management command, to search for records and then edit, extract, or delete the records you find. The /Data Query commands can be used with a 1-2-3 database or an external table. In the latter case, you must first use the /Data External Use command (discussed later in this chapter) to establish a connection to the external table. Looking for records that meet certain conditions is the simplest form of searching a 1-2-3 database. To determine which companies are in California, for example, you can use a search operation to find records with CA as the value in the STATE field.

After you have located the records you want, you can extract them from the database and place them in another section of the worksheet, separate from the database. For example, you can extract all records with a California address, and print the extracted records. With 1-2-3's search operations, you also can look for only the first occurrence of a specified field value to develop a unique list of field entries. For example, you can search the STATE field to extract a list of the different states. Finally, if you do not want to do business in Iowa, you can delete all database records for which the state equals IA.

Using Minimum Search Requirements

To initiate any search operation, you need to select the appropriate operation from the /Data Query menu:

Input Criteria Output Find Extract Unique Del Modify Reset Quit

The 10 options of the **Query** menu perform the following search functions:

Option	Description
Input	Gives the location of the search area and must be specified in all **Query** operations.
Criteria	Gives the locations of the search conditions and must be specified in all **Query** operations.
Output	Specifies a range where a **Query** command copies records or parts of records to an area outside the database. Necessary only when you select a **Query** command that copies records or parts of records to an area outside the database (Extract, Unique, or Modify).
Find	Moves down through a database, and places the cell pointer on records that match given criteria. You can enter or change data in the records as you move the cell pointer through them.
Extract	Creates copies, in a specified area of the worksheet, of all or some of the fields in records that match the given criteria.
Unique	Similar to Extract, but recognizes that some of the field contents in the database may be duplicates of other cell entries in the same fields. Eliminates duplicates as entries are copied to the output range.
Del	Deletes from a database all the records that match the given criteria and shifts the remaining records to fill in the gaps.
Modify	Either inserts or replaces records in the input range with records from the output range. This command is used to add new records to a database, or to extract records from a database, modify them, and then reinsert them.
Reset	Removes all previous search-related ranges so that you can specify a different search location and conditions.
Quit	Returns 1-2-3 to READY mode.

To perform a **Query** operation, you must specify both an input range and a criteria range and select one of the four search options. Before issuing an Extract, Unique, or **Modify** command, you must also specify an output range.

Determining the Input Range

The input range for the /Data Query command is the range of records you want to search. The specified area does not have to include the entire database. In the company database shown in figure 12.10, specifying an input range of A3..G8 defines the search area as the entire database. Entering A3..G4 as the input range for the company database in figure 12.9 limits the search area to the records for Minnesota.

Chapter 12 ◆ Managing Data — 509

The input range can contain a single database or multiple-worksheet and/or external databases. Keep in mind that a worksheet database is limited to a single worksheet. An input range, however, can contain multiple databases from different worksheets.

Whether you search all or only a part of a database, you must include the field-name row in the input range. (Remember that you must not include the field names in a sort operation.) If field names occupy space on more than one row, specify only the bottom row to start the input range. In the company database, for example, because row 3 contains the field names, you would start the input range with row 3 (by entering A3..G8).

Select /Data Query Input, and specify the range by typing or pointing to a range name or by using an assigned range name. You do not have to specify the range again unless the search area changes. To search more than one database, you enter the ranges one after the other, separated by a semicolon.

Reminder:
The input range must include the row containing database field names. The Data-Range for record-sorting must exclude that row.

Entering the Criteria Range

When you want 1-2-3 to search for records that meet certain criteria, you must be able to talk to 1-2-3 in terms the program understands. Suppose that you want to identify all records in the database that contain CA in the STATE field. When the database is on-screen and **1-2-3** is in READY mode, type **STATE** in cell A12 and **CA** in cell A13 (see figure 12.11). Type **Criteria Range** in cell A11 only if you want the documentation it provides; cell A11 is not directly involved in the search command. (*Note:* You would normally place the criteria range to one side of the database range, not right below it. In this example it was placed below the database to allow the entire operation to appear on one screen.)

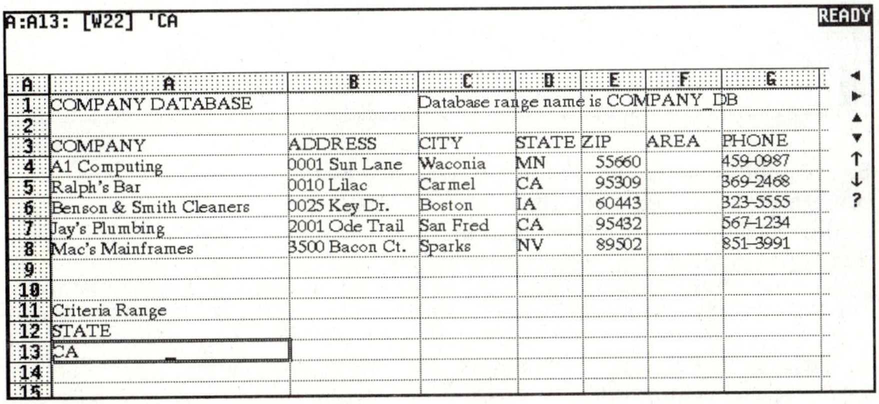

Fig. 12.11.
Adding a criteria range to the database.

Select /Data Query and specify **A3..G8** as the input range. The Query menu appears in the control panel as soon as you enter the input range. Select Criteria and then type, point to, or name the range **A12..A13** as the location of your search condition. The Query menu again returns to the screen.

Part III ◆ Customizing 1-2-3

Cue:
To ensure that the field names in the input range and the criteria range are exactly the same, copy the field names from the input range to the criteria range.

You can use numbers, labels, or formulas as criteria. A criteria range can be up to 32 columns wide and 2 or more rows long. The first row must contain the field names of the search criteria, such as STATE in row 12 of figure 12.11. The rows below the unique field names contain the actual criteria, such as CA in row 13. The field names of the input range and the criteria range must match exactly.

By entering one or more criteria in the worksheet and specifying the input and criteria ranges, you have completed the minimum steps necessary to execute a Find or Del command. Remember that you must enter field names in the first row of the criteria range, above the specific conditions.

Using the Find Command

When you select Find from the Query menu, the highlight rests on the first record (in the input range) that meets the conditions specified in the criteria range. In the current example, the highlight rests on the first field of the first record that includes CA in the STATE field (see fig. 12.12).

Fig. 12.12.

The first record highlighted in a Find operation.

	A	B	C	D	E	F	G
1	COMPANY DATABASE			Database range name is COMPANY_DB			
2							
3	COMPANY	ADDRESS	CITY	STATE	ZIP	AREA	PHONE
4	A1 Computing	0001 Sun Lane	Waconia	MN	55660		459-0987
5	Ralph's Bar	0010 Lilac	Carmel	CA	95309		369-2468
6	Benson & Smith Cleaners	0025 Key Dr.	Boston	IA	60443		323-5555
7	Jay's Plumbing	2001 Ode Trail	San Fred	CA	95432		567-1234
8	Mac's Mainframes	3500 Bacon Ct.	Sparks	NV	89502		851-3991
9							
10							
11	Criteria Range						
12	STATE						
13	CA						
14							
15							

Reminder:
Use the up- and down-arrow keys to highlight the previous and next records that meet the search criteria.

By using the down-arrow key, you can place the highlight on the next record that conforms to the criteria. You can continue pressing the down-arrow until the last record that meets the search conditions has been highlighted (see fig. 12.13). Notice that the mode indicator changes from READY to FIND during the search.

The down-arrow and up-arrow keys let you place the highlight on the next and previous records that meet the search criteria. The Home and End keys can be used to reach the first and last matching records. The right-arrow and left-arrow keys move the highlight to different fields in the current record. You can enter new values or use Edit (F2) to update the current values in any field; however, if you change the record so that it no longer satisfies the Find criteria and then move away from that record, you cannot return to the record during the Find operation.

To end the Find operation and return to the /Data Query menu, press Enter or Esc. To return directly to READY mode, press Ctrl-Break.

Chapter 12 ◆ Managing Data **511**

```
A:A7: [W22] 'Jay's Plumbing                                    FIND
```

A	A	B	C	D	E	F	G
1	COMPANY DATABASE		Database range name is COMPANY_DB				
2							
3	COMPANY	ADDRESS	CITY	STATE	ZIP	AREA	PHONE
4	A1 Computing	0001 Sun Lane	Waconia	MN	55660		459-0987
5	Ralph's Bar	0010 Lilac	Carmel	CA	95309		369-2468
6	Benson & Smith Cleaners	0025 Key Dr.	Boston	IA	60443		323-5555
7	Jay's Plumbing	2001 Ode Trail	San Fred	CA	95432		567-1234
8	Mac's Mainframes	3500 Bacon Ct.	Sparks	NV	89502		851-3991
9							
10							
11	Criteria Range						
12	STATE						
13	CA						
14							
15							

Fig. 12.13.
The last record highlighted in a Find operation.

Listing All Specified Records

The Find command has limited use, especially in a large database, because the command must scroll through the entire file if you want to view each record that meets the specified criteria. As an alternative, you can use the /Data Query Extract command to copy those records that meet the conditions to an output range. You can then view, print, or even use the /File Xtract command on the extracted records contained in the output range.

Cue:
Use /File Xtract to copy extracted records to a new file.

Defining the Output Range

Choose a blank area in the worksheet as the output range to receive records copied in an extract operation. Designate the range to the right of or below the database. In the first row of the output range, type or copy the field names of only those fields whose contents you want to extract. You do not have to include all of the field names. Also, the field names do not have to appear in the same order as in the database, although the field names that are used in both the criteria and output ranges must match exactly the corresponding field names in the input range. To avoid mismatch errors, use the /Copy command to copy the database field names in the criteria and output ranges.

Reminder:
Field names in the criteria and output ranges must match exactly the corresponding field names in the input range.

Note: Because Releases 3.1 and 3.1+ incorporate Wysiwyg report publishing features, there is a difference in the way 1-2-3 handles matching of field names between input and output ranges. In earlier releases, if you centered a database field name and left-justified the corresponding field name in the output range, an extract operation based on that field name would not work. Releases 3.1 and 3.1+, however, ignore the field name label prefixes, as you can see in the ZIP field of figure 12.14.

Select /Data Query Output; then type, point to, or name the range location of the output area. You can create an open-ended extract area by entering only the field-name row as the range, or you can set the exact size of the extract area.

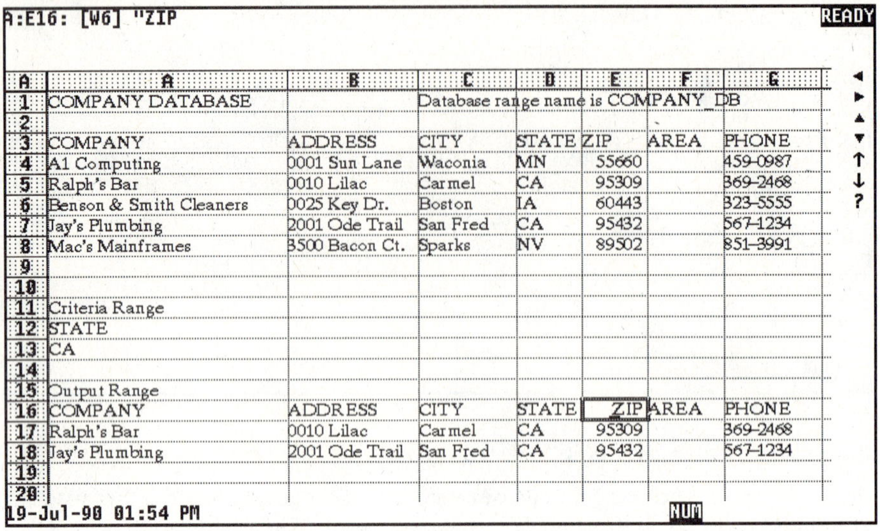

Fig. 12.14.
A full-record extract on an "exact match" label condition.

```
A:E16: [W6] "ZIP                                                    READY
     A              A              B            C        D      E      F        G
 1  COMPANY DATABASE                       Database range name is COMPANY_DB
 2
 3  COMPANY                  ADDRESS       CITY       STATE  ZIP    AREA  PHONE
 4  A1 Computing             0001 Sun Lane Waconia    MN     55660        459-0987
 5  Ralph's Bar              0010 Lilac    Carmel     CA     95309        369-2468
 6  Benson & Smith Cleaners  0025 Key Dr.  Boston     IA     60443        323-5555
 7  Jay's Plumbing           2001 Ode Trail San Fred  CA     95432        567-1234
 8  Mac's Mainframes         3500 Bacon Ct. Sparks    NV     89502        851-3991
 9
10
11  Criteria Range
12  STATE
13  CA
14
15  Output Range
16  COMPANY                  ADDRESS       CITY       STATE  ZIP    AREA  PHONE
17  Ralph's Bar              0010 Lilac    Carmel     CA     95309        369-2468
18  Jay's Plumbing           2001 Ode Trail San Fred  CA     95432        567-1234
19
20
19-Jul-90 01:54 PM                                                   NUM
```

To limit the size of the extract area, enter the upper left to lower right cell coordinates of the entire output range. The first row in the specified range must contain the field names; the remaining rows must accommodate the maximum number of records you expect to receive from the extract operation. Use this method when you want to retain additional data that is located below the extract area. For example, as you can see in figure 12.14, naming A16..G19 as the output range would limit incoming records to three (one row for field names and one row for each record). If you do not allow sufficient room in the fixed-length output area, the extract operation aborts and the message `Too many records` appears on-screen.

To create an open-ended extract area that does not limit the number of incoming records, specify as the output range only the row containing the output field names. For example, by naming A16..G16 as the output range in figure 12.14, you define the area to receive records from an extract operation without limiting the number of records.

Caution:
If you do not allow sufficient room in the output range for extracted records, the extract operation aborts.

An extract operation first removes all existing data from the output range. If you use only the field-name row to specify the output area, all data below that row is destroyed to make room for the unknown number of incoming extracted records. Make sure that you do not need any data contained below the output range before you issue the Extract command. Remember, with /Data Query Extract you also can specify an output range in another worksheet or in an external table; instead of destroying existing data in your current worksheet, use Release 3's three-dimensional worksheet features to extract to another worksheet level.

Caution:
If you use only the field-name row to specify the output area, all data below that row is destroyed to make room for the unknown number of incoming extracted records.

Executing the Extract Command

To execute an Extract command, you must type the search conditions in the worksheet, type the output field names in the worksheet, and set the input, criteria, and output ranges from the /Data Query menu.

Chapter 12 ◆ Managing Data **513**

To accelerate the set-up process, you need to establish standard input, criteria, and output areas. A criteria range can have up to 32 fields, which should enable you to establish a single criteria range that encompasses all the key fields on which you may search.

In the company database example, you have already established input, criteria, and output areas. Select /Data Query Extract and the two records from California companies are extracted.

You do not have to extract entire records or maintain the order of field names within the extracted records. For example, you can create an extract list containing only the COMPANY and AREA fields, as the next example on /Data Query Modify shows.

Modifying Records

You can use the /Data Query Modify command to extract records for modification and then return the modified records as new records or replacements of their original versions, or place them in an output range located in another worksheet or external table.

The first steps in using /Data Query Modify are exactly like those in using /Data Query Extract. You first specify input, criteria, and output ranges. Then select /Data Query Modify Extract to extract the matching records and copy them to the output range. The /Data Query Modify Extract command keeps a record of the original location of each extracted record so that you can later reinsert it correctly after any necessary editing. Do not, however, add or delete rows in the output range, or 1-2-3 cannot replace the records correctly.

You next select /Data Query Modify Replace or /Data Query Modify Insert. If you select Replace, the original records in the input range are replaced with the edited versions from the output range. If you select Insert, the records from the output range are appended at the end of the input range, and the original records remain in place. In both cases, the records in the output range are not deleted.

Figures 12.15 and 12.16 show an example of using /Data Query Modify. In this example, you add area code numbers for the companies located in California. You use an output range that contains only the COMPANY and AREA fields. In figure 12.15, you use /Data Query Modify Extract to extract those records for California companies and then add an area code to the AREA field. As figure 12.16 shows, the /Data Query Modify Replace command adds the area code to the AREA field of the replaced records in the input range.

Note that when you use /Data Query Modify Insert, the records being inserted (those in the output range) do not need to have been originally extracted from the database into which they are being inserted. You may, for example, use /Data Query Modify Insert as a simple data entry form for your database.

Reminder:
/Data Query Modify inserts or replaces records in the input range with records from the output range.

Caution:
1-2-3 does not replace records correctly if you add or delete rows in the output range when you use /Data Query Modify.

Fig. 12.15.
A worksheet data table after /Data Query Modify Extract has been executed.

```
A:B18: [W12] '805                                                    READY
     A                    B              C        D      E     F       G
 1  COMPANY DATABASE                    Database range name is COMPANY_DB
 2
 3  COMPANY              ADDRESS        CITY     STATE  ZIP   AREA    PHONE
 4  A1 Computing         0001 Sun Lane  Waconia  MN     55660         459-0987
 5  Ralph's Bar          0010 Lilac     Carmel   CA     95309         369-2468
 6  Benson & Smith Cleaners 0025 Key Dr. Boston  IA     60443         323-5555
 7  Jay's Plumbing       2001 Ode Trail San Fred CA     95432         567-1234
 8  Mac's Mainframes     3500 Bacon Ct. Sparks   NV     89502         851-3991
 9
10
11  Criteria Range
12  STATE
13  CA
14
15  Output Range
16  COMPANY              AREA
17  Ralph's Bar          916
18  Jay's Plumbing       805
19
20
```

Fig. 12.16.
The data table showing the replaced records.

```
A:B18: [W12] '805                                                    READY
     A                    B              C        D      E     F       G
 1  COMPANY DATABASE                    Database range name is COMPANY_DB
 2
 3  COMPANY              ADDRESS        CITY     STATE  ZIP   AREA    PHONE
 4  A1 Computing         0001 Sun Lane  Waconia  MN     55660         459-0987
 5  Ralph's Bar          0010 Lilac     Carmel   CA     95309 916     369-2468
 6  Benson & Smith Cleaners 0025 Key Dr. Boston  IA     60443         323-5555
 7  Jay's Plumbing       2001 Ode Trail San Fred CA     95432 805     567-1234
 8  Mac's Mainframes     3500 Bacon Ct. Sparks   NV     89502         851-3991
 9
10
11  Criteria Range
12  STATE
13  CA
14
15  Output Range
16  COMPANY              AREA
17  Ralph's Bar          916
18  Jay's Plumbing       805
19
20
```

Handling More Complicated Criteria Ranges

In addition to searching for an "exact match" to a single label field, 1-2-3 permits a wide variety of record searches: on exact matches to numeric fields; on partial matches of field contents; on fields that meet formula conditions; on fields that meet all of several conditions; and on fields that meet either one condition or another. Consider first some variations of queries on single fields.

Using Wild Cards in Criteria Ranges

You can use 1-2-3's wild card characters for matching labels in database operations. The characters ?, *, and ~ have special meaning when used in the criteria range. The ? character instructs 1-2-3 to accept any character in that specific position, and can be used only to locate fields of the same length. The * character, which tells 1-2-3 to accept any and all characters that follow, can be used on field contents of unequal length. By placing a tilde (~) symbol at the beginning of a label, you tell 1-2-3 to accept all values except those that follow. Table 12.2 shows how you can use wild cards in search operations.

Cue:
Use wild cards to match labels in database operations.

Table 12.2
Using Wild Cards in Search Operations

Enter	To Find
N?	Any two-character label starting with the letter N, such as NC, NJ, and NY
BO?L?	A five-character label such as BOWLE, but not a shorter label like BOWL
BO?L*	A four-or-more character label, such as BOWLE, BOWL, BOLLESON, and BOELING
SAN*	A three-or-more character label starting with SAN and followed by any number of characters, such as SANTA BARBARA and SAN FRANCISCO
SAN *	A four-or-more character label starting with SAN, followed by a space, and then followed by any number of characters, such as SAN FRANCISCO but not SANTA BARBARA
~N*	Strings that do not begin with the letter N

Use the ? and * wild-card characters when you are unsure of the spelling or when you need to match several records that are slightly different. Always check the results by using /Data Query Find or /Data Query Extract before you use wild cards in a Del command. If you are not careful, you may remove more records than you intend.

Using Formulas in Criteria Ranges

To set up formulas that query numeric or label fields in the database, you can use the following relational operators:

>   Greater than
>= Greater than or equal to
<   Less than
<= Less than or equal to
=   Equal to
<> Not equal to

Part III ◆ Customizing 1-2-3

Create a formula that references the first field entry in the numeric column you want to search. 1-2-3 tests the formula on each cell down the column until the program reaches the end of the specified input range.

Because the criteria formula specifies which field is being tested, you can place the formula below any of the criteria range's field names. This is unlike text criteria, which must appear directly below the associated field name. For example, you can use a formula to extract the records that have a ZIP code smaller than 90000. First, type the formula **+E4<=90000** in cell A13 (see fig. 12.17).

Fig. 12.17.
A relational formula condition to extract records.

	A	B	C	D	E	F	G
1	COMPANY DATABASE			Database range name is COMPANY_DB			
2							
3	COMPANY	ADDRESS	CITY	STATE	ZIP	AREA	PHONE
4	A1 Computing	0001 Sun Lane	Waconia	MN	55660		459-0987
5	Ralph's Bar	0010 Lilac	Carmel	CA	95309	916	369-2468
6	Benson & Smith Cleaners	0025 Key Dr.	Boston	IA	60443		323-5555
7	Jay's Plumbing	2001 Ode Trail	San Fred	CA	95432	805	567-1234
8	Mac's Mainframes	3500 Bacon Ct.	Sparks	NV	89502		851-3991
9							
10							
11	Criteria Range						
12	STATE						
13	1						
14							
15	Output Range						
16	COMPANY	AREA					
17	A1 Computing						
18	Benson & Smith Cleaners						
19	Mac's Mainframes						
20							

A:A13: [W22] +E4<=90000   READY
19-Jul-90 01:58 PM   NUM

Although the formula is displayed in the control panel, notice that a one (1) is displayed in cell A13. The formula checked whether the contents of cell E4 (in which ZIP equals 55660) were greater than or equal to 90000 and returned the one (1) to indicate a true condition.

After you have specified the input, criteria, and output ranges correctly, executing an extract operation produces three records for which ZIP is less than or equals 90000.

To reference cells outside the database, use formulas that include absolute cell addressing. (For addressing information, refer to Chapter 4.) For example, suppose that immediately after you issue the preceding command, you decide to use 80000 instead of 90000 as the upper limit for extracted zip codes. Although you can just edit the existing formula, in this case you want to make it easier to make fast changes. To make it easier, you first must return to READY mode. Enter the value **80000** in cell E13 and then type the formula **+E4<=$E$13** as the criterion in cell A13.

With the program still in READY mode, press Query (F7) to repeat the most recent query operation (Extract, in this example) and eliminate the need to select /Data Query Extract. Use the shortcut method only when you do not want to change the locations of the input, criteria, and output ranges. As you can see from figure 12.18, two records matched and were extracted.

```
A:A13: [W22] +E4<=$E$13                                                    READY

     A                    B              C        D    E      F     G
 1  COMPANY DATABASE                    Database range name is COMPANY_DB
 2
 3  COMPANY              ADDRESS        CITY     STATE ZIP    AREA  PHONE
 4  A1 Computing         0001 Sun Lane  Waconia  MN    55660        459-0987
 5  Ralph's Bar          0010 Lilac     Carmel   CA    95309 916    369-2468
 6  Benson & Smith Cleaners 0025 Key Dr. Boston  IA    60443        323-5555
 7  Jay's Plumbing       2001 Ode Trail San Fred CA    95432 805    567-1234
 8  Mac's Mainframes     3500 Bacon Ct. Sparks   NV    89502        851-3991
 9
10
11  Criteria Range
12  STATE
13                1                     ZIP CODE—>   80000
14
15  Output Range
16  COMPANY                             AREA
17  A1 Computing
18  Benson & Smith Cleaners
19
20
19-Jul-90 01:59 PM                                                NUM
```

Fig. 12.18.

A mixed formula condition to extract records.

Setting Up AND Conditions

Now that you have seen how to base a Find or Extract operation on only one criterion, you learn how to use multiple criteria for your queries. You can set up multiple criteria as AND conditions (in which *all* the criteria must be met) or as OR conditions (in which any *one* criterion must be met). For example, searching a music department's library for sheet music requiring drums AND trumpets is likely to produce fewer selections than searching for music appropriate for drums OR trumpets.

Cue:
Use AND or OR conditions to set up multiple criteria for your queries.

You indicate two or more criteria, *all* of which must be met, by specifying the conditions on the criteria row immediately below the field names. First, though, you must adjust your criteria range to add another field. Use /Range Erase **C13..E13** to clear the ZIP CODE entry. Next, add the field name to B12 by /Copy from C3 to B12. Finally, adjust the size of the criteria range by using the /Data Query Criteria command to indicate **A12..B13**. Now you can add the desired criteria to the criteria range.

For this example, suppose that you want only those records for companies not located in California and not in a city that starts with the letter *B*. In cell A13 place the formula **+D4<>"CA"** and in cell B13 place the criterion **~B***. Next, issue a /Data Query Extract command; 1-2-3 extracts two records that meet both conditions. The results should look like figure 12.19.

When you maintain a criteria range that includes many fields, you can quickly extract records based on an alternative condition. Enter the additional criteria only in the row immediately below the field name row.

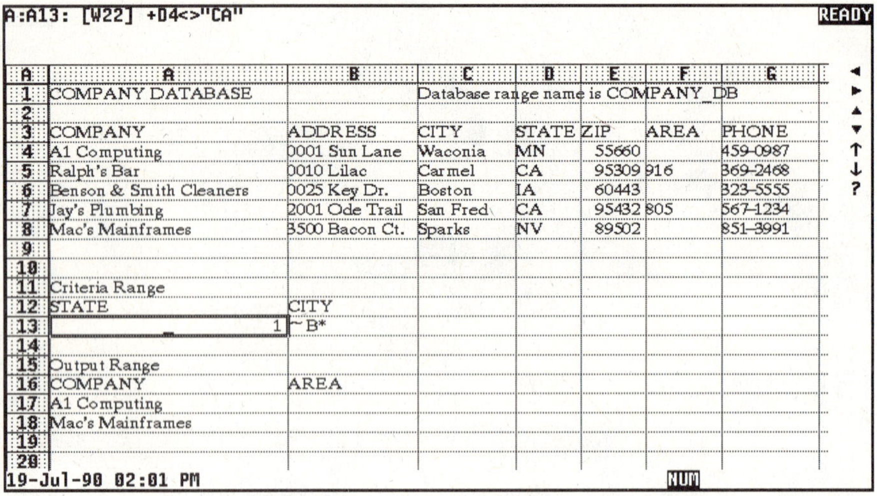

Fig. 12.19.
A two-field logical AND search.

```
A:A13: [W22] +D4<>"CA"                                          READY
         A              B          C      D     E      F       G
  1  COMPANY DATABASE            Database range name is COMPANY_DB
  2
  3  COMPANY         ADDRESS     CITY    STATE ZIP    AREA   PHONE
  4  A1 Computing    0001 Sun Lane Waconia MN   55660        459-0987
  5  Ralph's Bar     0010 Lilac  Carmel   CA   95309  916    369-2468
  6  Benson & Smith Cleaners 0025 Key Dr. Boston IA  60443   323-5555
  7  Jay's Plumbing  2001 Ode Trail San Fred CA 95432 805    567-1234
  8  Mac's Mainframes 3500 Bacon Ct. Sparks NV  89502        851-3991
  9
 10
 11  Criteria Range
 12  STATE                       CITY
 13                         1    ~B*
 14
 15  Output Range
 16  COMPANY                     AREA
 17  A1 Computing
 18  Mac's Mainframes
 19
 20
19-Jul-90 02:01 PM                                       NUM
```

Setting Up OR Conditions

Criteria placed on the same row have the effect of a logical AND; they tell 1-2-3 to find or extract on this condition AND this one, and so on. Criteria placed on *different* rows have the effect of a logical OR; that is, find or extract on this condition OR that one, and so on. You can set up a logical OR search on one or more fields.

Searching a single field for more than one condition is the simplest use of an OR condition. For example, you can extract those records where the STATE is MN or NV by placing MN in cell A13 and NV in cell A14 and expanding the criteria range to include the additional row.

You also can specify a logical OR condition on two or more different fields. For example, suppose that you want to search for records where either the state is not California or the city does not start with the letter *S*.

First, use /Range Erase to erase cell B13 and remove the AND condition. Next, place ~S* in cell B14 to add the OR condition. Then adjust the criteria range to include the specified OR condition by expanding the criteria range down a row. When you issue the Extract command, four records are copied to the output range. Although Ralph's Bar does not meet the condition of not being in California, it does meet the condition of being in a city that doesn't start with *S* and is therefore extracted to the output range along with the records for companies who are not in California. Only one condition OR the other had to be met before the copy was made. The results should look like figure 12.20.

To add additional OR criteria, drop to a new row, enter each new condition, and expand the criteria range. If you reduce the number of rows involved in an OR logical search, be sure to contract the criteria range. Remember, a blank row in the criteria range matches all records in the database.

Chapter 12 ◆ Managing Data

```
A:A13: [W22] +D4<>"CA"                                              READY

     A                    B              C        D     E     F       G
 1  COMPANY DATABASE              Database range name is COMPANY_DB
 2
 3  COMPANY              ADDRESS        CITY      STATE ZIP   AREA   PHONE
 4  A1 Computing         0001 Sun Lane  Waconia   MN    55660        459-0987
 5  Ralph's Bar          0010 Lilac     Carmel    CA    95309 916    369-2468
 6  Benson & Smith Cleaners 0025 Key Dr. Boston   IA    60443        323-5555
 7  Jay's Plumbing       2001 Ode Trail San Fred  CA    95432 805    567-1234
 8  Mac's Mainframes     3500 Bacon Ct. Sparks    NV    89502        851-3991
 9
10
11  Criteria Range
12  STATE                               CITY
13                   1
14                                      ~S*
15  Output Range
16  COMPANY              AREA
17  A1 Computing
18  Ralph's Bar          916
19  Benson & Smith Cleaners
20  Mac's Mainframes
19-Jul-90 02:02 PM                                                  NUM
```

Fig. 12.20.
A logical OR search on two fields.

Although no technical reason prevents you from mixing AND and OR logical searches, you may find it difficult to properly formulate such a mixed query. Follow the format of placing each AND condition in the row immediately below the criteria field-name row, and each OR condition in a separate row below. Be careful, however, to ensure that each row in the criteria range specifies all of the AND conditions that apply. For example, if you want to search for records in which STATE equals CA AND CITY starts with *S* OR STATE equals NV AND CITY starts with *S*, enter the AND/OR conditions in the following cells:

    A13:   +D4="CA"
    B13:   S*
    A14:   +D4="NV"
    B14:   S*

The criteria range remains unchanged. Repeating the *S** in cells B13 and B14 is critical because if 1-2-3 finds a blank cell within a criteria range, the program selects all records for the field name above that blank cell.

You should test the logic of your search conditions on a small sample database in which you can verify search results easily by scrolling through all records and noting which of them should be extracted. For example, if the database contains hundreds of records, you can test the preceding AND/OR search conditions on a small group or by using /**Data Query Find**.

Using String Searches

If you want to search on the partial contents of a field, you can use functions in a formula. For example, suppose that you can remember only the street name "Bacon" for a record you want to extract from the database. You can use the formula shown in

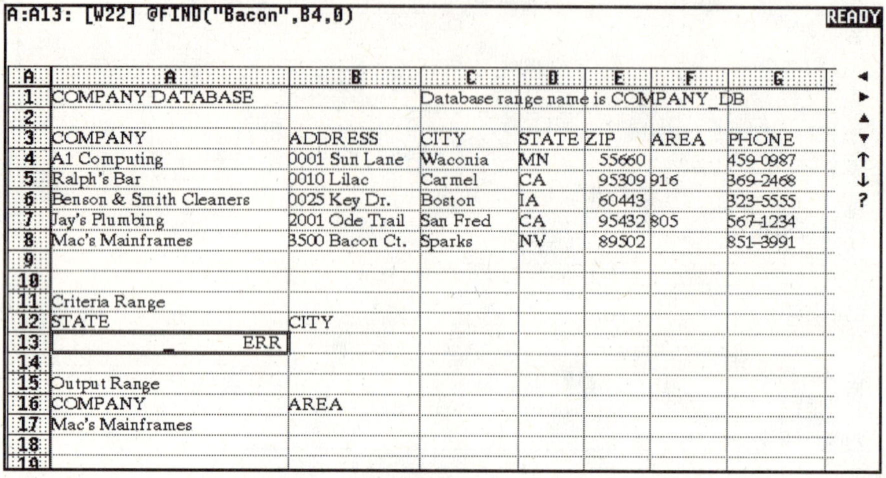

Fig. 12.21.

A function condition used for a string search.

```
A:A13: [W22] @FIND("Bacon",B4,0)                                  READY

      A                    B              C      D     E     F     G
 1  COMPANY DATABASE                   Database range name is COMPANY_DB
 2
 3  COMPANY              ADDRESS        CITY    STATE ZIP   AREA  PHONE
 4  A1 Computing         0001 Sun Lane  Waconia MN    55660       459-0987
 5  Ralph's Bar          0010 Lilac     Carmel  CA    95309 916   369-2468
 6  Benson & Smith Cleaners 0025 Key Dr. Boston IA    60443       323-5555
 7  Jay's Plumbing       2001 Ode Trail San Fred CA   95432 805   567-1234
 8  Mac's Mainframes     3500 Bacon Ct. Sparks  NV    89502       851-3991
 9
10
11  Criteria Range
12  STATE                              CITY
13                ERR
14
15  Output Range
16  COMPANY                            AREA
17  Mac's Mainframes
18
19
```

the control panel of figure 12.21 as the search criterion in cell A13 (making certain, of course, that you've adjusted the criteria range to eliminate the empty row 14).

Note that although ERR is displayed in cell A13, the formula still works properly when you issue the /Data Query Extract command. Remember that the @FIND function returns the starting position of the search string (Bacon) in the string being searched (the ADDRESS field). If @FIND does not find the search string, it returns ERR. Because "Bacon" does not occur in "0001 Sun Lane," the formula shows ERR. As 1-2-3 checks each record, however, it matches and returns a true value for the fifth record. In criteria formulas, 1-2-3 treats both ERR and zero as false and therefore nonmatching values. (See Chapter 6 for a detailed discussion of 1-2-3 @functions.)

Using Special Operators

To combine search conditions within a single field, use the special operators #AND# and #OR#. Use the special operator #NOT# to negate a search condition.

Use #AND# or #OR# to search on two or more conditions within the same field. For example, suppose that you want to extract all records with either Bacon or Lilac in their address. The formula shown in figure 12.22, @FIND("Bacon",B4,0)#OR#@FIND("Lilac",B4,0), matches the desired records.

You use the #AND#, #OR#, and #NOT# operators to enter (in one field) conditions that can be entered some other way (usually in at least two fields). For example, you can enter **+D4="CA"#AND#@FIND("Bar",A4,0)** in A13 or B13 to find any California companies with the word "Bar" in their name.

Use #NOT# at the beginning of a condition to negate that condition. For example, +D4="CA"#AND##NOT#@FIND("Bar",A4,0) would find all California companies without "Bar" in their name.

Chapter 12 ◆ Managing Data **521**

```
A:A13: [W22] @FIND("Bacon",B4,0)#OR#@FIND("Lilac",B4,0)                    READY
```

	A	B	C	D	E	F	G
1	COMPANY DATABASE		Database range name is COMPANY_DB			
2							
3	COMPANY	ADDRESS	CITY	STATE	ZIP	AREA	PHONE
4	A1 Computing	0001 Sun Lane	Waconia	MN	55660		459-0987
5	Ralph's Bar	0010 Lilac	Carmel	CA	95309	916	369-2468
6	Benson & Smith Cleaners	0025 Key Dr.	Boston	IA	60443		323-5555
7	Jay's Plumbing	2001 Ode Trail	San Fred	CA	95432	805	567-1234
8	Mac's Mainframes	3500 Bacon Ct.	Sparks	NV	89502		851-3991
9							
10							
11	Criteria Range						
12	STATE	CITY					
13	ERR						
14							
15	Output Range						
16	COMPANY	AREA					
17	Ralph's Bar	916					
18	Mac's Mainframes						
19							

Fig. 12.22.

The special operator #OR# used for extracting records.

Using the @FIND function to search for matching records can produce unexpected results, however, if you don't have a clear understanding of the information returned by the function. Suppose, for example, that you wanted to find all records with a "2" or the word "Lilac" in their address. As you can see in figure 12.23, something is wrong. Instead of the three expected records, **/Data Query Extract** (using the criteria formula @FIND("2",B4,0)#OR#@FIND("Lilac",B4,0) as shown in the control panel) only matched two records. The reason for this apparent error is simple; @FIND returns the position of the search string (2 or Lilac) within the target string (the ADDRESS field). Since Jay's Plumbing's address starts with a 2, @FIND reports the position as zero (0), which means the record is not extracted.

```
A:A13: [W22] @FIND("2",B4,0)#OR#@FIND("Lilac",B4,0)                        READY
```

	A	B	C	D	E	F	G
1	COMPANY DATABASE		Database range name is COMPANY_DB			
2							
3	COMPANY	ADDRESS	CITY	STATE	ZIP	AREA	PHONE
4	A1 Computing	0001 Sun Lane	Waconia	MN	55660		459-0987
5	Ralph's Bar	0010 Lilac	Carmel	CA	95309	916	369-2468
6	Benson & Smith Cleaners	0025 Key Dr.	Boston	IA	60443		323-5555
7	Jay's Plumbing	2001 Ode Trail	San Fred	CA	95432	805	567-1234
8	Mac's Mainframes	3500 Bacon Ct.	Sparks	NV	89502		851-3991
9							
10							
11	Criteria Range						
12	STATE	CITY					
13	ERR						
14							
15	Output Range						
16	COMPANY	AREA					
17	Ralph's Bar	916					
18	Benson & Smith Cleaners						
19							

Fig. 12.23.

A problem with the @FIND function.

Correcting this problem is simple because @FIND always returns ERR if the search string is not found. Adding any value to ERR still produces ERR. If you therefore modify the criteria formula as shown in figure 12.24, the /Data Query Extract returns the desired three records.

Fig. 12.24.
A solution to the problem.

```
A:A13: [W22] @FIND("2",B4,0)+1#OR#@FIND("Lilac",B4,0)+1                      READY

     A              A                B              C       D      E      F         G
 1  COMPANY DATABASE                         Database range name is COMPANY_DB
 2
 3  COMPANY                   ADDRESS        CITY        STATE ZIP    AREA   PHONE
 4  A1 Computing              0001 Sun Lane  Waconia     MN    55660         459-0987
 5  Ralph's Bar               0010 Lilac     Carmel      CA    95309 916     369-2468
 6  Benson & Smith Cleaners   0025 Key Dr.   Boston      IA    60443         323-5555
 7  Jay's Plumbing            2001 Ode Trail San Fred    CA    95432 805     567-1234
 8  Mac's Mainframes          3500 Bacon Ct. Sparks      NV    89502         851-3991
 9
10
11  Criteria Range
12  STATE                     CITY
13                ERR
14
15  Output Range
16  COMPANY                   AREA
17  Ralph's Bar               916
18  Benson & Smith Cleaners
19  Jay's Plumbing            805
20
19-Jul-90 02:07 PM                                                         NUM
```

Performing Other Types of Searches

In addition to the /Data Query Find commands, you can use the /Data Query menu's Unique and Del commands for searches. By issuing the /Data Query Unique command, you can produce (in the output range) a copy of only the first occurrence of a record that meets a specified criterion. /Data Query Del enables you to delete all records that meet specified criteria.

Extracting Unique Records

Ordinarily, the Unique command is used to copy into the output area only a small portion of each record that meets the criteria. For example, if you want a list of the states in the database, set up an output range that includes only the STATE field (cell D14 in fig. 12.25). To search all records, leave blank the row below the field-name row in the criteria range. Then set the output range at D14 and select /Data Query Unique to produce a list of the four states in the database.

As another example, if you have a large mailing list database, you can produce a list of the ZIP codes to assist with preparing mailings. To do so, you specify in the output area only the field name ZIP, leave blank the row under the field names in the criteria range, and execute the Unique command.

As with /Data Query Extract and /Data Query Modify Extract, you can specify as the output range an external table where 1-2-3 should place the results of a /Data Query Unique operation.

```
A:D14: [W6] 'STATE                                              READY

      A              B            C         D      E    F       G
 1  COMPANY DATABASE              Database range name is COMPANY_DB
 2
 3  COMPANY          ADDRESS      CITY      STATE  ZIP  AREA    PHONE
 4  A1 Computing     0001 Sun Lane Waconia  MN     55660         459-0987
 5  Ralph's Bar      0010 Lilac   Carmel    CA     95309 916    369-2468
 6  Benson & Smith Cleaners 0025 Key Dr. Boston  IA   60443      323-5555
 7  Jay's Plumbing   2001 Ode Trail San Fred CA  95432 805      567-1234
 8  Mac's Mainframes 3500 Bacon Ct. Sparks   NV   89502         851-3991
 9
10
11  Criteria Range
12  STATE                         CITY
13
14                                          STATE
15  Output Range                             CA
16  COMPANY          AREA                    IA
17  Ralph's Bar      916                     MN
18  Benson & Smith Cleaners                  NV
19  Jay's Plumbing   805
20
19-Jul-90 02:08 PM                                              NUM
```

Fig. 12.25.
The results of issuing a /Data Query Unique command.

Deleting Specified Records

As you learned in Chapter 4, you can use the /**W**orksheet **D**elete **R**ow command to remove rows from a worksheet. If you want a fast alternative to this "one-by-one" approach, use the /**D**ata **Q**uery **D**elete command to remove unwanted records from your database files. Before you select **D**el from the **Q**uery menu, simply specify the range of records to be searched (input range) and the conditions for the deletion (criteria).

For example, suppose that you want to remove all records with a STATE field beginning with the letter *N*. To do so, use the criterion **N*** in cell A13. Then issue the /**D**ata **Q**uery **D**el command to delete the rows and remove all records for states that begin with *N*. The remaining records pack together and the input range automatically adjusts.

Be extremely careful when you issue the /**D**ata **Q**uery **D**el command. To give you the opportunity to verify that you indeed want to select the **D**el command, 1-2-3 displays the following menu, on which the leftmost, least dangerous command is highlighted:

    Cancel   Delete

Choose **C**ancel to abort the **D**el command. Select **D**elete to verify that you want to execute the delete operation.

Although the /**D**ata **Q**uery **D**el command does not display the exact rows to be deleted, you can guard against deleting the wrong records by first saving the file or using the /**D**ata **Q**uery **F**ind (or /**D**ata **Q**uery **E**xtract) command to examine the records before deleting them.

Joining Multiple Databases

Cue:
Join multiple databases by using one or more key fields that the databases have in common.

A powerful feature of Release 3 is its capacity to create an output range that contains fields and/or calculated columns based on records contained in two or more databases. Performing a *join*, as it is called, is based on relating two or more databases that have one or more key fields in common.

You may wonder why you should keep two or more databases of related information instead of keeping all the information together in one large database. One reason is to increase efficiency. Suppose, for example, that you had several business contacts at each of the companies listed in the company database. You can just add a NAME field to the database and place each contact in a separate record. If you had three contacts at Jay's Plumbing, for example, just type in three complete records, one for each contact person. Of course, when Jay's Plumbing moves to a larger building, you have to change all three records. On the other hand, if you have one database with the company information and another with the contact persons and their company, you only have to update one record.

A key field is one whose content is unique for each record in the database. In our sample company database, for example, COMPANY is a key field because every company has a different name. STATE is not a key field because two companies may be in the same state.

To create room for the CONTACTS database and the examples that follow, use the /Worksheet Insert Sheet After command and add four worksheets. Then use /Worksheet Global Group Disable to ensure that work in the new worksheets does not interfere with the existing database. Figure 12.26 shows the CONTACTS database, which is in worksheet B.

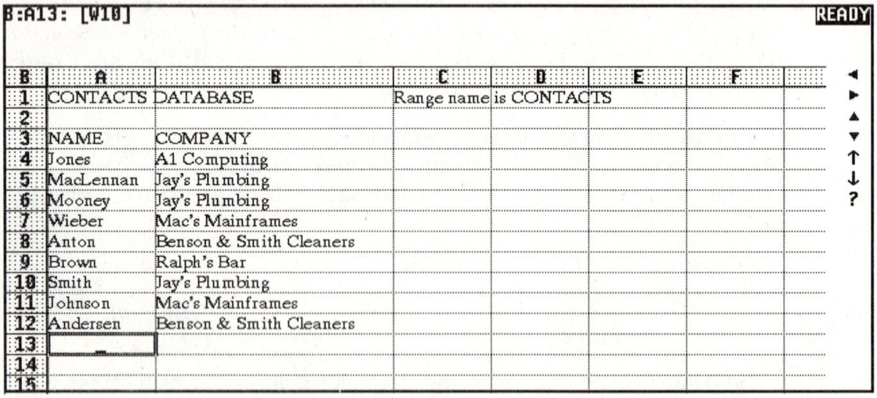

Fig. 12.26.
The Contacts database.

```
B:A13: [W10]                                                    READY

   B     A         B                C        D       E       F
   1  CONTACTS DATABASE         Range name is CONTACTS
   2
   3  NAME      COMPANY
   4  Jones     A1 Computing
   5  MacLennan Jay's Plumbing
   6  Mooney    Jay's Plumbing
   7  Wieber    Mac's Mainframes
   8  Anton     Benson & Smith Cleaners
   9  Brown     Ralph's Bar
  10  Smith     Jay's Plumbing
  11  Johnson   Mac's Mainframes
  12  Andersen  Benson & Smith Cleaners
  13
  14
  15
```

Press Ctrl-PgUp to move to worksheet C. The first step in joining multiple databases is to enter a *join formula* in the criteria range. The join formula specifies the relationship that must be satisfied between the key fields in the databases. In most applications, the required relationship is that the key fields are equal (=). Suppose, for example, that you have two databases, with the range names

COMPANIES and CONTACTS, which contain different information about your business contacts. Both databases have a company name, COMPANY, as a key field. To join these two databases, you use the following join formula:

+CONTACTS.COMPANY=COMPANIES.COMPANY

First use the /Range Name Create command to assign the range name COMPANIES to the range A:A3..A:G8, and the range name CONTACTS to the range B:A3..B:B12. Type the heading for the criteria range in C:A2. Notice that the heading (**CONTACTS.COMPANY**) is made up of one of the database's range names, a period, and the name of the key field. Then enter the formula (as shown in fig. 12.27) to create a criteria range. This joins from the two databases any records that have the same value in the COMPANY field. Use the /Data Query Criteria command to specify **C:A2..C:A3** as the criteria range.

	A	B	C	D	E	F	G	H
1	CRITERIA RANGE							
2	CONTACTS.COMPANY							
3	ERR							
4								
5	OUTPUT RANGE							
6	NAME	CONTACTS.COMPANY	ADDRESS	CITY	STATE	ZIP	AREA	PHONE
7	Jones	A1 Computing	0001 Sun Lane	Waconia	MN	55660		459-0987
8	Anton	Benson & Smith Cleaners	0025 Key Dr.	Boston	IA	60443		323-5555
9	Andersen	Benson & Smith Cleaners	0025 Key Dr.	Boston	IA	60443		323-5555
10	MacLennan	Jay's Plumbing	2001 Ode Trail	San Fred	CA	95432	805	567-1234
11	Mooney	Jay's Plumbing	2001 Ode Trail	San Fred	CA	95432	805	567-1234
12	Smith	Jay's Plumbing	2001 Ode Trail	San Fred	CA	95432	805	567-1234
13	Wieber	Mac's Mainframes	3500 Bacon Ct.	Sparks	NV	89502		851-3991
14	Johnson	Mac's Mainframes	3500 Bacon Ct.	Sparks	NV	89502		851-3991
15	Brown	Ralph's Bar	0010 Lilac	Carmel	CA	95309	916	369-2468
16								

C:A3: +CONTACTS.COMPANY=COMPANIES.COMPANY   READY

Fig. 12.27.
The criteria range and output of the joining of two databases.

Next, create an output range with column headings for the fields you want included. The output range must include one of the database's range names, a period, and the name of the key field (CONTACTS.COMPANY, for example). Select /Data Query Output and specify **C:A6..C:H6** for the output range.

After creating the output range, specify both databases as the input range. Select /Data Query Input, and in response to the prompt enter **CONTACTS;COMPANIES**.

Finally, select /Data Query Extract. The results are shown in figure 12.27. The output range contains complete address information for each of your business contacts. Although this type of list may be useful in many cases, sometimes you may just want to look up information on one contact person. As figure 12.28 shows, using @functions gives you another means of accessing multiple 1-2-3 databases.

Press Ctrl-PgUp to move to worksheet D and enter the labels shown down column A. Starting in cell B2, enter the formulas (shown in text format in column C). Finally, enter a name from the database in cell B1. As you can see, the result is more like calling Directory Assistance than searching through the phone book.

Fig. 12.28.
Using @VLOOKUP as an alternative type of join.

```
D:B1: [W13] 'Smith                                                    READY

     A         B              C         D         E         F      G    H
 1  NAME      Smith
 2  COMPANY   Jay's Plumbing  @VLOOKUP($B$1,$CONTACTS,1)
 3  ADDRESS   2001 Ode Trail  @VLOOKUP($B$2,$COMPANIES,1)
 4  CITY      San Fred        @VLOOKUP($B$2,$COMPANIES,2)
 5  STATE     CA              @VLOOKUP($B$2,$COMPANIES,3)
 6  ZIP                95432  @VLOOKUP($B$2,$COMPANIES,4)
 7  AREA      805             @VLOOKUP($B$2,$COMPANIES,5)
 8  PHONE     567-1234        @VLOOKUP($B$2,$COMPANIES,6)
 9
10
11
12
13
14
```

As a final example of relating databases, take a look at creating computed and aggregate columns in the output range. An output range can contain either computed or aggregate columns but not both.

Once again, press Ctrl-PgUp, and move to worksheet E. Notice that in the calculated-column output range of E:A4..B4 (see fig. 12.29), the second field is +CITY&", "&STATE. In the figure, the cell was formatted as **Text** to show the formula instead of ERR.

You may use nearly any valid formula to create a computed column. The exceptions are formulas containing the functions @AVG, @COUNT, @MIN, @MAX, @SUM, and any of the database @functions, such as @DSUM. All these functions, except the database @functions, create an aggregate column. Notice in figure 12.29 that the aggregate column uses the @COUNT function. With the same input and criteria ranges set, the output range is E:E4..E:F4. When you choose **Extract**, the unique STATE values are extracted to the output range with a count of the contacts in each state. The count is done with the column heading of the @COUNT(STATE) function. The computed and aggregate columns can be used with an output range for a single database (as the aggregate column shows), as well as in the output range of joined multiple databases (as the computed column shows).

Fig. 12.29.
Calculated and aggregate columns in output ranges.

```
E:F13:                                                                READY

     A          B              C       D      E          F           G    H
 1
 2
 3  CALCULATED COLUMN                        AGGREGATE COLUMN
 4  NAME       +CITY&", "&STATE              STATE      @COUNT(STATE)
 5  Jones      Waconia, MN                   CA              4
 6  Anton      Boston, IA                    IA              2
 7  Andersen   Boston, IA                    MN              1
 8  MacLennan  San Fred, CA                  NV              2
 9  Mooney     San Fred, CA
10  Smith      San Fred, CA
11  Wieber     Sparks, NV
12  Johnson    Sparks, NV
13  Brown      Carmel, CA
14
15
```

When creating join formulas, keep in mind the following guidelines:

Key field names used in a join formula cannot contain special characters, such as commas, spaces, or pound signs (#). If they do, 1-2-3 cannot calculate the formula properly.

Key field names do not have to be the same to join two databases. The names must only be key fields that contain the same type of data. Therefore, the company name field can be called COMPANY in one table and OFFICE in another and still be used as the basis for a join formula. If the field names are different, you need not include the database range names in the join formula:

+COMPANY=OFFICE

You can use more than one set of key fields in a join formula. You can use any of the logical operators (>, <, <>, >=, <=) in a join formula. 1-2-3 compares the join formula fields in every combination of records from the input ranges and creates a new record in the output range each time the join formula is TRUE.

Reminder:
You cannot use key fields that contain special characters in a join formula.

Creating Data Tables

In many situations, the variables used in your worksheet formulas are known quantities. For example, last year's sales summary deals with variables whose exact values are known. The results of calculations performed by using those values contain no uncertainties. Other situations, however, involve variables whose exact values are not known. Worksheet models for financial projections often fall into this category. For example, next year's cash flow projection depends on prevailing interest rates. Although you can make an educated guess at what interest rates may be, you cannot predict them exactly.

Data tables enable you to work with variables whose values are not known. With the /Data Table commands, you can create tables that show how the results of formula calculations vary as the variables used in the formulas change.

Here's a common example. You decide to purchase a new car that requires a $12,000 loan. Area banks offer you several combinations of loan periods and interest rates. You can use a data table to calculate your monthly payment with each combination of period and interest rate.

Another function of the /Data Table commands is to create *cross-tabulation tables*. A cross-tabulation table provides summary information categorized by unique information in two fields, such as the total amount of sales each sales representative made to each customer.

This section shows you how to use the /Data Table commands to perform "sensitivity" or "what-if" analysis, and to cross-tabulate information in data tables. First, however, you need to understand some terms and concepts.

General Terms and Concepts

A *data table* is an on-screen view of information in a column format, with the field names at the top. A data table contains the results of a /Data Table command plus some or all of the information that was used to generate the results. A data table range is a worksheet range that contains a data table.

A *variable* is a formula component whose value can change.

An *input cell* is a worksheet cell used by 1-2-3 for temporary storage during calculation of a data table. One input cell is required for each variable in the data table formula. The cell addresses of the formula variables are the same as the input cells.

An *input value* is a specific value that 1-2-3 uses for a variable during the data table calculations.

The *results area* is the portion of a data table where the calculation results are placed. One result is generated for each combination of input values. The results area of a data table must be unprotected.

The formulas used in data tables can contain values, strings, cell addresses, and @functions. You should not use logical formulas, because this type of formula always evaluates to either 0 or 1. Although using a logical formula in a data table does not cause an error, the results generally are meaningless.

The Four Types of Data Tables

When you select /Data Table, the following menu appears:

    1   2   3   Labeled   Reset

The first four menu selections correspond to the four types of data tables that 1-2-3 can generate. The four table types differ in the number of formulas and variables they can contain. In brief, the table types are these:

Data Table 1	One or more formulas with one variable
Data Table 2	One formula with two variables
Data Table 3	One formula with three variables
Data Table Labeled	One or more formulas with an unlimited number of variables

Creating a Type 1 Data Table

A data table created with the /Data Table 1 command shows the effects of changing one variable on the results of one or more formulas. Before using this command, you must set up the data table range and a single input cell.

The input cell can be a blank cell anywhere in the worksheet. The best practice is to identify the input cell by entering an appropriate label either above the input cell or to the left.

The data table range is a rectangular worksheet area. It can be placed in any empty worksheet location. The size of the data table range can be calculated as follows:

- The range will have one more column than the number of formulas being evaluated.
- The range will have one more row than the number of input values being evaluated.

The general structure of a type 1 data table range is as follows:

- The top-left cell in the data table range is empty.
- The formulas to be evaluated are entered across the first row. Each formula must refer to the input cell.
- The input values to be plugged into the formulas are entered down the first column.
- After the data table is calculated, each cell in the results range contains the result obtained by evaluating the formula at the top of that column with the input value at the left of that row.

Suppose, for example, that you plan to purchase a house with a 30-year mortgage in the $100,000 to $115,000 range, and a 10 percent or 11 percent interest rate. For each interest rate you want to determine the monthly payment that would result at each price.

For this example, you can use cell B2 as the input cell, and identify it with a label in cell A2. You need one formula for each interest rate. By using the @PMT function, enter the following in cell D2:

@PMT($B$2,0.1/12,360)

In cell E2, enter the following:

@PMT($B$2,0.11/12,360)

Because payments are monthly, each annual interest rate is divided by 12 to get the monthly interest rate. The 360 is the term of the loan in months.

Next, enter the four possible prices in cells C3 through C6. Select /Data Table 1, specify C2..E6 as the table range, and enter B2 as the input cell. The resulting table, which calculates the mortgage payments on four different amounts at two different interest rates, is shown in figure 12.30. Cells D2 and E2 have been formatted as Text so that you can see the formulas they contain.

	A	B	C	D	E
1			/Data Table 1		
2	INPUT:			@PMT($B$2,0.1/12,360)	@PMT($B$2,0.11/12,360)
3			100,000	$877.57	$952.32
4			105,000	$921.45	$999.94
5			110,000	$965.33	$1,047.56
6			115,000	$1,009.21	$1,095.17

Fig. 12.30.
/Data Table 1 used to calculate mortgage payments on four different house prices at two different interest rates.

Analyzing a 1-2-3 Database with /Data Table 1

/Data Table 1 also can be used with a database to create a cross-tabulation table. This type of analysis requires an input cell, which can be anywhere in the worksheet. For a cross-tabulation analysis, the cell immediately above the input cell must contain the name of the data table field on which the analysis is being based. (It may be easier to think of the input cell as being similar to a criteria range. The input cell is where 1-2-3 substitutes the unique values as it evaluates the formulas.)

The structure of a data table range for a cross-tabulation analysis is similar to that for a what-if analysis. The upper left cell is empty, and the top row contains the formula(s) that are to be evaluated. In most cases, these formulas may contain one or more database @functions.

The left column of the data table range again contains input values. Rather than being values that are plugged directly into the formulas, however, the input values for a cross-tabulation analysis are the values or labels that may be used as *criteria* for the analysis.

After the data table has been calculated, each cell in the results range contains the result of the formula at the top of the column applied to those database records that meet the criterion at the left of the row.

Imagine, for example, that you are the director of a week-long fishing tournament, and you are keeping a database of each contestant's catches. Each "catch" goes into one database record, which contains the contestant's name and the weight of the fish. At the end of the tournament, you want to calculate for each contestant the total weight and the maximum weight of a single catch. The database that handles this application is shown in figure 12.31.

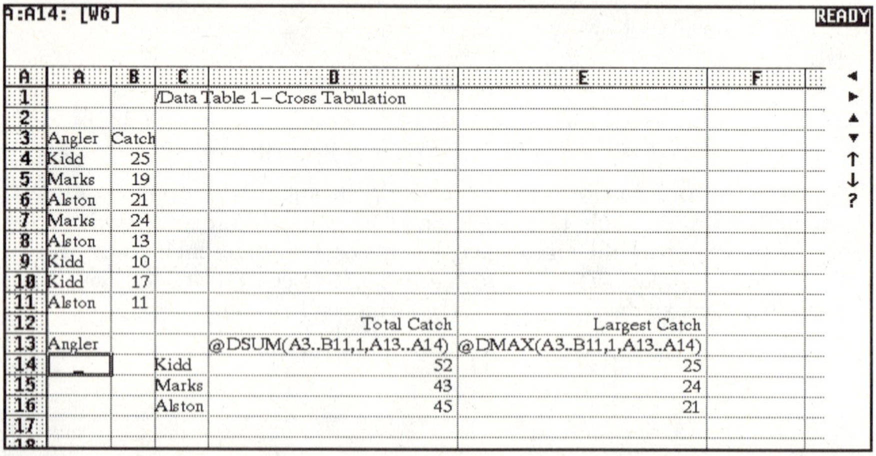

Fig. 12.31.
/Data Table 1 used to perform a cross-tabulation analysis on data in a data table.

To construct the data table, you can use A14 as the input cell. Because you want to select records based on the ANGLER field, enter the label ANGLER above the input cell, in cell A13.

The data table is in the range A3..B11. The three contestants' names are in the range C14..C16. The formulas are entered in cells D13 and E13.

In cell D13, for the total weight caught by each contestant, enter the following:

@DSUM(A3..B11,1,A13..A14)

In cell E13, for the maximum weight of a single catch for each contestant, enter the following:

@DMAX(A3..B11,1,A13..A14)

Note that each of these database @functions refers to the range containing the input cell (A14) and its identifying field name (A13) as the criteria range.

Select **/Data Table 1**, specify **C13..E16** as the table range, and enter **A14** as the input cell. The table of results appears, as shown in figure 12.31. Cells D13 and E13 have been formatted as **Text**.

Creating a Type 2 Data Table

The type 2 data table enables you to evaluate a single formula based on changes in two variables. The examples shown in figures 12.32 and 12.33 are type 2 data tables.

To use **/Data Table 2**, you need two blank input cells, one for each variable. They can be located anywhere in the worksheet, and need not be adjacent to each other. The input cells can be identified with an appropriate label in a cell next to or above each input cell.

The size of the data table range depends on the number of values of each variable you want to evaluate. The range is one column wider than the number of values of one variable, and one row longer than the number of values of the other variable.

A major difference between /Data Table 1 and /Data Table 2 is the location of the formula to be evaluated. In /Data Table 1, the formulas are placed along the top row of the table, and the upper left corner is blank. With /Data Table 2, the upper left cell of the data table range contains the formula to be evaluated. This formula must refer to the input cells.

The cells below the formula contain the various input values for one variable. These values are used for input cell 1. The cells to the right of the formula contain the various input values for the other variable. These values are used for input cell 2. Be sure that the formula refers correctly to the two input cells so that the proper input values get plugged into the correct part of the formula.

After the data table has been calculated, each cell in the results range contains the result of evaluating the formula with the input values in that cell's row and column.

Suppose, for example, that you want to create a data table that shows the monthly payments on a $12,000 loan at four interest rates: 9, 10, 11, and 12 percent; and three loan periods: 24, 36, and 48 months.

First, decide on a location for the two input cells. You can use cells B7 and B8. Put identifying labels in the adjacent cells A7 and A8.

Because you have three values of one variable and four values of the other, the data table range is four cells by five cells in size. You can use the range C3..F7. Enter the following @PMT formula in cell C3:

@**PMT(12000,B7/12,B8)**

Next, enter the values in the data table range. Enter the four interest rates in the range C4..C7, and the three loan terms in D3..F3.

Now, select /**Data Table 2**, specify **C3..F7** as the table range, enter **B7** as input cell 1, and enter **B8** as input cell 2. 1-2-3 calculates the data table, as shown in figure 12.32.

Fig. 12.32.
A table of loan payment amounts created with /Data Table 2.

	A	B	C	D	E	F
1			/Data Table 2			
2						
3			@PMT(12000,B7/12,B8)	24	36	48
4			9%	$548.22	$381.60	$298.62
5			10%	$553.74	$387.21	$304.35
6			11%	$559.29	$392.86	$310.15
7	INPUT 1:		12%	$564.88	$398.57	$316.01
8	INPUT 2:					
9						

If you create a data table larger than the screen, you can use /**Worksheet Titles** to freeze the input values on the screen as you scroll through the results cells.

Analyzing a 1-2-3 Database with /Data Table 2

/**Data Table 2** can be used to create a cross-tabulation analysis of records in a data table. A type 2 cross-tabulation analysis requires two blank input cells, which can be anywhere in the worksheet as long as they are in adjacent columns of the same row. The cell immediately above each input cell must contain the name of the data table field for which that input cell serves as a criterion.

The structure of a data table range for a type 2 cross-tabulation analysis is similar to that for a type 2 what-if analysis. The upper left cell contains the formula to be evaluated. When using a database @function, the function argument that specifies the criteria range should refer to the two input cells and the field names above them. The top row and left column contain the values or labels that are used as criteria when database records are selected for the formula calculations. The contents of the cells in the left column of the data table range are used as criteria in input cell 1, and the contents of the cells in the top row of the data table range are used as criteria in input cell 2. Be sure that the data table range input values correspond correctly with the input cells; otherwise, the analysis produces erroneous results.

Suppose that you want to create the type 2 cross-tabulation table shown in figure 12.33. To create a data table showing each sales representative's total sales of each item, you need a type 2 data table that is cross-tabulated based on the SALESREP and ITEM fields of the database table. Use cells F4 and G4 for the input cells, and put the field names above them in cells F3 and G3.

The data table range is A3..D9. Enter the following formula in cell A11:

@DSUM(A3..D9,3,F3..G4)

The criteria for input cell 1 (that is, the input cell under SALESREP) are the sales representatives' names. You have three names; enter them in cells A12..A14. For input cell 2, the criteria are the items. Enter them in B11..D11.

Note that the values or labels used as criteria in a type 2 cross-tabulation table must exactly match the entries in the database. When working with a large database, you can use **/Data Query Unique** to extract a nonduplicating list of all entries in a particular field, and then use this list as the left column or (after transposing) the top row of the data table range.

The next step is to select **/Data Table 2** and specify **A11..D14** as the table range, **F4** as input cell 1, and **G4** as input cell 2. The results are shown in figure 12.33.

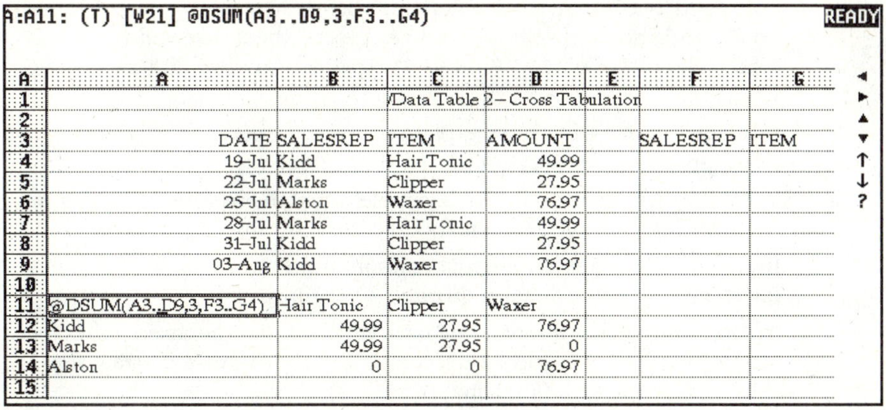

A:A11: (T) [W21] @DSUM(A3..D9,3,F3..G4) READY

A	A	B	C	D	E	F	G
1			/Data Table 2 – Cross Tabulation				
2							
3	DATE	SALESREP	ITEM	AMOUNT		SALESREP	ITEM
4	19-Jul	Kidd	Hair Tonic	49.99			
5	22-Jul	Marks	Clipper	27.95			
6	25-Jul	Alston	Waxer	76.97			
7	28-Jul	Marks	Hair Tonic	49.99			
8	31-Jul	Kidd	Clipper	27.95			
9	03-Aug	Kidd	Waxer	76.97			
10							
11	@DSUM(A3..D9,3,F3..G4)	Hair Tonic	Clipper	Waxer			
12	Kidd	49.99	27.95	76.97			
13	Marks	49.99	27.95	0			
14	Alston	0	0	76.97			
15							

Fig. 12.33.
/Data Table 2 used to create a cross-tabulation analysis of data contained in a data table.

Creating a Type 3 Data Table

A type 3 data table shows the effects of changing three variables in a single formula. The "third dimension" of a type 3 data table is represented by a three-dimensional worksheet range; the table spans two or more worksheets.

Reminder:
A type 3 data table shows the effects of changing three variables in a single formula.

The structure of a type 3 data table is an extension of the type 2 data table structure. The different values of variables 1 and 2 are represented by different rows and columns. The new variable, the third one, is located in the upper left corner of the data table range; the different values of variable 3 are represented by different worksheets.

A type 3 data table range spans a three-dimensional region. The size of the region is determined as follows:

Number of rows = (values of variable 1) + 1
Number of columns = (values of variable 2) + 1
Number of worksheets = (values of variable 3)

You also need three input cells. These cells can be located anywhere in any worksheet, but are often grouped together for convenience. You should identify the input cells with labels in adjacent cells.

The formula evaluated in a type 3 data table must correctly refer to all three input cells. Input cell 1 refers to the values in the first column of the data table range. Input cell 2 refers values in the first row of the data table range. Input cell 3 refers to the values in the upper left corner of the data table range in each worksheet.

Calculating loan payments is a perfect application for a type 3 data table because the relevant formula uses three variables: principal, interest rate, and term. You can create a data table that calculates monthly payments for three principal amounts, three interest rates, and three loan periods. To establish a type 3 data table range for this application, follow these steps:

1. You need two other worksheets for this data table. To insert these other worksheets, select /Worksheet Insert Sheet After and enter **2**. Next, select /Worksheet Window Perspective to view all three active worksheets.

2. By using the size guidelines explained in the preceding text, decide on an empty worksheet region for the data table.

   For this example, you need a data table range that is four rows by four columns by three worksheets in size. Use the range A:C2..C:F5.

3. In the top worksheet in the first column of the range, enter the values for variable 1 in the second through last cells.

   In this example, the interest rate is variable 1. Enter the three values for interest rate: **10, 11,** and **12** percent in cells A:C3..A:C5. Format these cells as **P**ercent with **0** decimal places.

4. In the same worksheet, enter the values for variable 2 in the second through last cells in the first row in the range.

   Term is variable 2 in the example. Enter the values for term: **24, 36,** and **48** months in cells A:D2..A:F2.

5. Copy the values for variables 1 and 2 to the other worksheets in the range.

   Select /Copy and enter **A:C2..A:F5** as the FROM range. Next, enter **B:C2..C:C2** as the TO range.

6. In the top left cell of the data table range, enter the values for variable 3. Enter a different value in the corresponding cell in each worksheet.

Cue:
Use the /Copy command to copy the variable information to other worksheets in the data table.

In this example, principal is variable 3. Enter the values for principal: **10000**, **15000**, and **20000** in cells A:C2..C:C2. Format these cells as Currency with **0** decimal places.

7. The range for the data table is now established. Next, you need to select the input cells. Use cells A:B2..A:B4 for input cells 1 to 3. Also, put identifying labels in cells A:A2..A:A4.

8. Enter the payment formula in any cell outside the data table range—for example, B6. Use the following 1-2-3 function for calculating loan payments:

    @PMT(A:B4,A:B2/12,A:B3)

    Because payment periods are expressed in months, you divide the annual interest rate by 12 to obtain the monthly interest rate. (Note that when you enter the @PMT function in B6, you see ERR. You may use /**R**ange **F**ormat **H**idden to hide the ERR from B6, or /**R**ange **F**ormat **T**ext to display the formula rather than ERR.)

9. Now, select /**D**ata **T**able **3** and specify **A:C2..C:F5** as the table range, **A:B6** as the formula cell, **A:B2** as input cell 1, **A:B3** as input cell 2, and **A:B4** as input cell 3. Format the results range A:D3..C:F5 as Currency. The results are shown in figure 12.34.

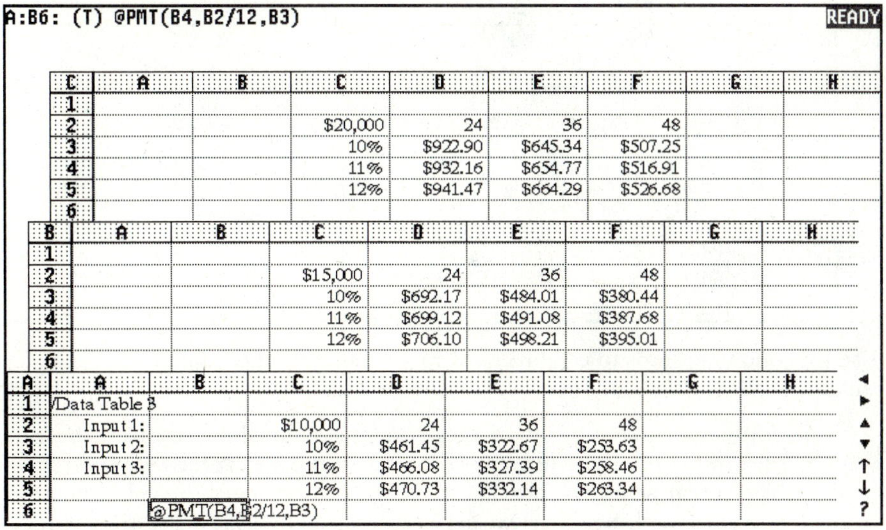

Fig. 12.34.
The three-dimensional table showing the loan payment amount for different interest rates, loan periods, and loan amounts.

Analyzing a Three-Dimensional Database

Using a type 3 data table for cross-tabulation analysis is analogous to using this table for what-if analysis. Instead of representing three variables plugged into a formula, the three dimensions of a type 3 cross-tabulation analysis hold labels or values used as criteria to select records from a data table. The cells in the results area each contain the result of a calculation based on the database records that meet the three intersecting criteria for that cell. For example, with information in a sales database, a manager can use a type 3 cross-tabulation analysis to determine the total dollar sales for each state, by each salesperson, for each month of the year.

To create a type 3 cross-tabulation table, you need three blank input cells in adjacent columns of the same row. The cells immediately above must contain the names of the database fields used as criteria.

You also need a formula located in any worksheet cell outside the data table range. If you use a database function, refer to the six-cell range that contains the input cells and field names as the criteria range.

The structure of a type 3 data table for cross-tabulation analysis is similar to the size and structure for type 3 what-if analysis.

Figure 12.35 shows a 1-2-3 database (A:A3..A:D13) of sales records. Each record shows the salesperson's name, the month and state of the sale, and the sale amount. The input cells are to the right of the database in cells F4..H4 with the fields used as criteria listed in F3..H3.

Fig. 12.35.
A database containing information to be analyzed with /Data Table 3.

	A	B	C	D	E	F	G	H
1	Database for /Data Table 3—Cross Tabulation							
2								
3	NAME	MONTH	STATE	AMOUNT		NAME	MONTH	STATE
4	Kidd	May	CA	$995				
5	Marks	May	NV	$4,590				
6	Alston	May	OR	$2,793				
7	Marks	June	NV	$2,345				
8	Kidd	June	NV	$5,217				
9	Kidd	June	CA	$9,142				
10	Alston	July	OR	$6,217				
11	Marks	July	NV	$3,741				
12	Alston	July	CA	$341				
13	Kidd	July	NV	$9,744				
14								

Use the following steps to establish a type 3 cross-tabulation data table range for this application:

1. You need three other worksheets for this data table. To insert these other worksheets, select /Worksheet Insert Sheet After and enter 3. Notice that when you add the three new worksheets, the cell pointer moves to worksheet B. Next, select /Worksheet Window Perspective to view the three new worksheets.

2. Place the state labels in cells B:B1..B:D1. Place the names of the sales reps down column A from B:A2..B:A4. /Copy B:A1..B:D4 to C:A1..D:A1.

   Note: You can use different values for the criteria in column A or row 1 for each of the three worksheets. The results, however, are difficult to compare because the three tables display different information. Remember that each cell in a /Data Table 3 cross-tabulation is reflecting the value of the formula based on the three intersecting criteria for that cell.

3. In the top left cell (B:A1) of the data table range, enter the values or labels to be used as criteria for the field (input cell 3). Enter a different criterion in the corresponding cell in each worksheet. In this example place **May** in B:A1, **June** in C:A1, and **July** in D:A1.

The data table range is now established. For this example, set the label prefix in cells B:B1..D:D1 to right-justification to better align the top row labels with the numeric values the table holds.

Enter the required formula in cell B:B6:

@DSUM(A:A3..A:D13,3,A:F3..A:H4)

Select /Data Table 3 and enter **B:A1..D:D4** as the table range. Enter **B:B6** as the formula cell, **A:F4** as input cell 1, **A:H4** as input cell 2, and **A:G4** as input cell 3. Your screen should look like the one shown in figure 12.36.

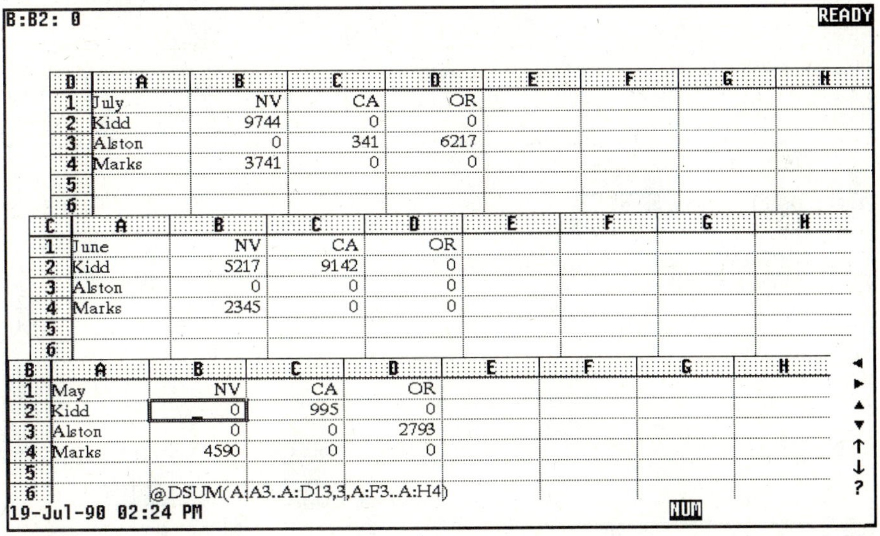

Fig. 12.36.
The completed three-dimensional cross-tabulation analysis.

Creating a Labeled Data Table

The most flexible type of data table is called a *labeled data table*, created with the /Data Table Labeled command.

A labeled data table provides significantly more flexibility than the other types of data tables. With /Data Table Labeled, you can do the following:

♦ Examine the effects of changing one or more variables on one or more formulas

Cue:
For more flexibility in creating data tables, use the /Data Table Labeled command.

Part III ♦ Customizing 1-2-3

- Include labels in the table to identify the table contents
- Use data in different worksheet areas as input for the data table
- Include blank rows and text in the table to improve its appearance
- Include formulas in the data table that perform calculations on the table results

Figures 12.37 and 12.38 show a table created with /Data Table Labeled.

Fig. 12.37.
One worksheet in a two-worksheet table created with /Data Table Labeled.

```
A:B7: (C2) 456.847422791730943                                    READY

         A              B              C              D         E
  1                        —Loan Payment—
  2            Loan amount
  3               $10,000                  Interest Rate
  4                           9.0%            10.0%         11.0%
  5
  6            Loan term
  7                  24       $456.85        $461.45       $466.08
  8                  36       $318.00        $322.67       $327.39
  9                  48       $248.85        $253.63       $258.46
 10                  60       $207.58        $212.47       $217.42
 11
 12
 13
 14           Loan Payment     Input 1:
 15    @PMT(C15,C14/12,C16)    Input 2:
 16                            Input 3:
 17
 18
```

Fig. 12.38.
Both worksheets in the two-worksheet table.

```
A:A2: [W22] "Loan amount                                          READY

         A              B              C              D         E
B 2           Loan amount
  3               $20,000                  Interest Rate
  4                           9.0%            10.0%         11.0%
  5
  6            Loan term
  7                  24       $913.69        $922.90       $932.16
  8                  36       $635.99        $645.34       $654.77
  9                  48       $497.70        $507.25       $516.91
 10                  60       $415.17        $424.94       $434.85
 11
A 2           Loan amount
  3               $10,000                  Interest Rate
  4                           9.0%            10.0%         11.0%
  5
  6            Loan term
  7                  24       $456.85        $461.45       $466.08
  8                  36       $318.00        $322.67       $327.39
  9                  48       $248.85        $253.63       $258.46
 10                  60       $207.58        $212.47       $217.42
19-Jul-90 02:26 PM                              CALC    NUM
```

When creating a labeled data table, keep in mind the following terms:

The *formula range* is the worksheet range that contains the formula(s). The formula(s) calculate(s) the data table results, plus contains labels that identify the formulas. In figure 12.37, A14..A15 is the formula range.

The *formula-label range* contains copies of the labels in the formula range. The formula-label range also may contain blank cells, other labels, and values. The placement of labels in the formula-label range is used to determine which formula is used with the various input values of the data table, and where the calculation results are placed. In figure 12.37, B1..D1 is the formula-label range.

A formula-label range also can contain *label-fill characters*—special formatting characters used to center a label. You generally use label-fill characters when the formula-label range covers two or more adjacent columns and your formula range contains a single formula.

A *row-variable range* is a region of the worksheet that contains rows of input values, organized by columns. A row-variable range may contain one or more columns, with each column containing a separate set of input variables. In figure 12.37, A7..A10 is the row-variable range.

A *column-variable range* is a region of the worksheet that contains columns of input values, organized by rows. A column-variable range may contain one or more rows, with each row containing a separate set of input values. In figure 12.37, B4..D4 is the column-variable range.

A *worksheet-variable range* is a three-dimensional region of the worksheet that contains one or more sets of input values. In figure 12.38, A:A3..B:A3 is the worksheet-variable range.

The *input cells* function just like the input cells used with other types of data tables. You need one input cell for each variable. In figure 12.37, C14..C16 are the input cells.

/Data Table Labeled does not require you to specify a data table range. The location of the results area is determined by the locations of the input ranges.

The specific variable ranges you need to create a labeled data table depend on the number of variables being evaluated by the table formulas and on the layout of the results. For example, a labeled data table that evaluates three variables can use all three types of variable ranges: column, row, and worksheet. You also can create a three-variable table by using any two of the three variable range types. A labeled data table that evaluates two variables can have any two variable ranges—a row-variable range and a column-variable range, for example, or a column-variable range and a worksheet-variable range.

Positioning the Results Area

The placement and structure of the variable ranges are important factors in determining the location and layout of the labeled data table. By changing the placement and structure of the variable ranges, you can control the location of the results area, and you can include blank rows, columns, and/or worksheets in the results area.

Where do you place the results of labeled data table calculations? In the worksheet cells at the intersection of the row(s) that contain(s) the nearest vertical range, and the column(s) that contain(s) the nearest horizontal range. A vertical range is one arranged in columns, such as a row-variable range. A horizontal range is one arranged in rows, such as a column-variable range. A formula-label range can be either vertical or horizontal.

To determine the placement of the results area, extend the rows that contain the row-variable range horizontally, both left and right, across the worksheet. Then extend the columns that contain the column-variable range, both up and down, along the worksheet. The cells where these "extended" rows and columns intersect are where 1-2-3 places the results area of the labeled data table.

In figure 12.37, the row- and column-variable ranges are adjacent to each other; therefore, there are no blank rows between the ranges and the results area.

Figure 12.39 shows the same table with the locations of the row- and column-variable ranges changed. The results are placed at the intersection of the rows and columns that contain these variable ranges. This placement inserts blank rows and columns between the variable ranges and the results area.

Fig. 12.39.
Blank rows included in the results area.

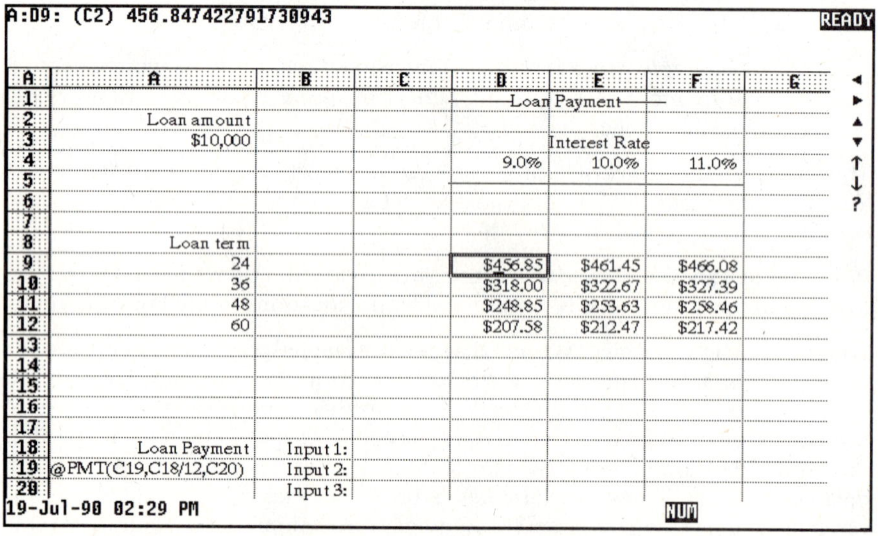

```
A:D9: (C2) 456.847422791730943                                          READY
          A              B          C         D          E          F         G
 1
 2              Loan amount                         Loan Payment
 3                  $10,000
 4                                                          Interest Rate
 5                                             9.0%       10.0%      11.0%
 6
 7
 8              Loan term
 9                       24                   $456.85    $461.45    $466.08
10                       36                   $318.00    $322.67    $327.39
11                       48                   $248.85    $253.63    $258.46
12                       60                   $207.58    $212.47    $217.42
13
14
15
16
17
18              Loan Payment   Input 1:
19       @PMT(C19,C18/12,C20)  Input 2:
20                             Input 3:
19-Jul-90 02:29 PM                                                   NUM
```

By placing the vertical and horizontal variable ranges adjacent to each other, you leave no space between the variable ranges and the results area. By placing the variable ranges in separate worksheet regions, you can leave blank rows and/or columns between the variable ranges and the results area.

The same principle applies when working in three dimensions (when using a worksheet-variable range). The results area is placed at the intersection of the rows, columns, and worksheets that contain the variable ranges. By controlling the worksheets in which the variable ranges are placed, you can include blank worksheets between some of the variable ranges and the results area. In a four-worksheet file, for example, you can place the row- and column-variable ranges in worksheet D and the worksheet-variable range in worksheets A and B. 1-2-3 places the results in worksheets A and B only, leaving worksheet C blank.

The blank rows, columns, or worksheets created with these formatting techniques can contain labels and formulas. You can enter these labels and formulas either before or after you create the labeled data table.

Formatting the Results Area

The preceding section discussed controlling the blank space *between* the results area and the variable ranges. You also can control the placement of blank rows, columns, and worksheets *within* the results area. You achieve such control by including blank cells in the input ranges you use to create the labeled data table.

For row- and column-variable ranges, the portion of the range closest to the results area is important. If the labeled data table includes a column-variable range, its bottom row is checked for blank cells. If the labeled data table includes a row-variable range, its rightmost column is checked for blank cells. If the formula-label range is the only vertical range or the only horizontal range in the labeled data table, this range is checked for blank cells. A blank cell or cells in any of these places results in the corresponding row(s) and/or column(s) of the results area being left blank (see fig. 12.40).

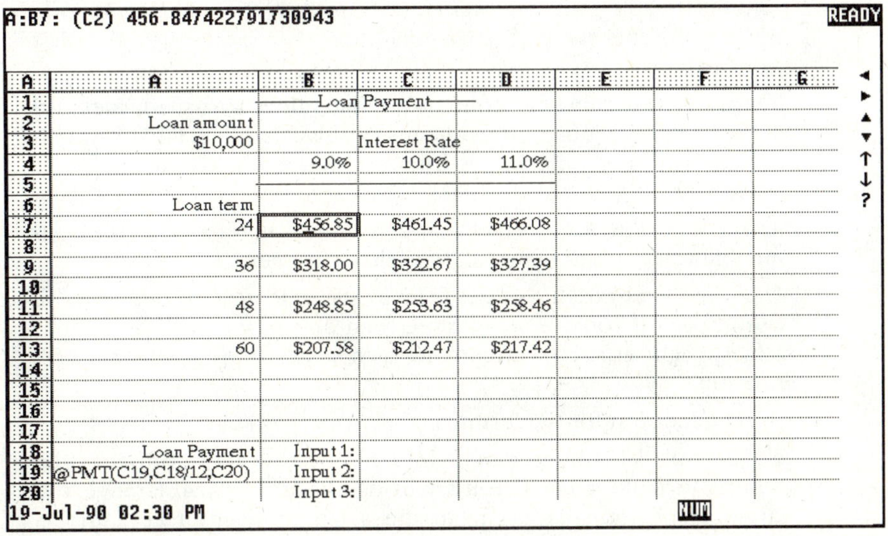

Fig. 12.40.
Blank cells included in the row-variable range.

Creating a Sample Labeled Data Table

This section shows you how to create a labeled data table. The following steps outline the procedure for specifying the variable ranges. After you understand what to enter for each range, you learn the steps you follow in 1-2-3 to enter these ranges.

1. Select a location for the labeled data table.

   The table's *minimum size* (rows × columns × worksheets) is determined by the number of values of each variable being evaluated. The actual size of the results area depends on its specific formatting (for example, inclusion of blank rows and/or columns).

2. Select a location for the input cell(s) and optionally identify the cells with labels in adjacent cells. You need one input cell for each variable being analyzed.

3. Select a worksheet area to hold the formula range.

   The size of this range is two rows by as many columns as you have formulas. Enter the formula(s) in the second row of this range and the formula label(s) in the top row. The formula range must be outside the region that contains the results and the input values.

4. If you are using a row-variable range, enter it either to the right or to the left of the results area. If you are using more than one set of row input values, enter them in adjacent columns in the range.

5. If you are using a column-variable range, enter it either above or below the results area. If you are using more than one set of column-variable range, enter them in adjacent rows in the range.

6. If you are creating a three-dimensional data table, each worksheet in which results are to be placed must contain values in the row- and/or column-variable ranges. Enter these values in the additional worksheet(s) in the same relative positions they occupy in the first worksheet.

   Because row-variable and column-variable values are usually identical in each worksheet of a three-dimensional labeled data table, you can use /Copy to copy the values from the first worksheet to the other worksheet(s).

7. If you are using a worksheet-variable range, enter one worksheet-variable value in the same cell of each worksheet.

   The worksheet-variable values form a "stack" that spans two or more worksheets. If you are using more than one set of worksheet input values, each set should occupy its own stack. These stacks must be adjacent.

8. Select a location for the formula-label range.

   The formula-label range can be located in a row above or below the column-variable range. If you are using a column-variable range, the formula-label range must span the same number of columns as the column-variable range. If you have only one formula label and more than one column, enter the formula and label-fill characters in the first cell of the formula-label range.

   The formula-label range also can be located in a column to the left or right of the row-variable range, or in a three-dimensional range between the worksheet-variable range and the results area. If the formula-label range does not span the same number of cells as the corresponding variable range, use the label-fill character.

At this point, you are ready to start working with the /Data Table commands to create the labeled data table. Select /Data Table Labeled and the following menu appears:

Formulas Down Across Sheets Input-Cells Label-Fill Go Quit

Table 12.3 at the end of this section explains the functions of these commands.

The following text describes how to create a payment table with /Data Table Labeled. First, start with a blank worksheet and select /Worksheet Global Group Enable to turn on GROUP mode. Next select /Worksheet Insert Sheet After 1 to insert a single worksheet (worksheet B) in the current file. Now, set /Worksheet Global Col-Width to **14** and /Worksheet Column Set-Width of column A to **22**. Also, set /Worksheet Global Label Right. Press Ctrl-PgDn to return to worksheet A.

Next, enter the following labels in the indicated cells of worksheet A:

```
     B1..D1:  '--------------- Loan Payment ---------------
        A2:  Loan amount
        A6:  Loan term
       A14:  Loan Payment
       B14:  Input 1:
       B15:  Input 2
       B16:  Input 3
        C3:  Interest Rate
     B5..D5:  \-
```

After you enter the labels, you can enter the variable values. In cells B4..D4, enter **9%**, **10%**, and **11%**; and then apply /Range Format Percent **1** to them. Next enter the term values **24**, **36**, **48**, and **60** in cells A7..A10. Enter **10000** in cell A3, and apply /Range Format Currency **0**.

Next, select /Copy and enter **A:A1..A:D10** as the FROM range and **B:A1** as the TO range. Press Ctrl-PgUp to move the cell pointer to worksheet B and change the value in cell B:A3 to **20000**.

Press Ctrl-PgDn to return the cell pointer to worksheet A. Select /Worksheet Global Group Disable to turn off GROUP mode.

In cell A15, enter the following formula:

   @PMT(C15,C14/12,C16)

Format that cell as **Text** so the formula is displayed on-screen.

To create the actual labeled data table, follow these steps:

1. Select /Data Table Labeled Formulas and enter **A:A14..A:A15** as the formula range and **A:B1..A:D1** as the formula-label range.

2. Select Down and enter **A:A7..A:A10** as the row-variable range. Press Enter to accept the highlighted range, and then enter **A:C16** as the corresponding input cell.

Part III ♦ Customizing 1-2-3

3. Select **Across** and enter **A:B4..A:D4** as the column-variable range. Press Enter to accept the highlighted range, and then enter **A:C14** as the corresponding input cell.

4. Next, select **Sheets** and enter **A:A3..B:A3** as the worksheet-variable range. Press Enter to accept the highlighted range, and then enter **A:C15** as the corresponding input cell.

Worksheet A now looks like figure 12.41.

5. You can select **Input-Cells** to verify and edit the addresses of variable ranges and input cells. 1-2-3 cycles through each set of variable ranges and input cells, displaying the addresses you initially entered. Press Enter to accept the original entries or specify new addresses.

6. If you are using label-fill characters but do not want to use the default hyphen (-), select **Label-Fill** and enter the character you want to use (for example, = or *).

7. Select **Go**.

1-2-3 evaluates the formulas by using the input values in the input ranges. The result of each calculation is placed in the location defined by the intersection of the corresponding row, column, and worksheet.

After formatting the results range A:B7..B:D10 as **Currency** with **2** decimal places, the data table is completed (see figures 12.41 and 12.42).

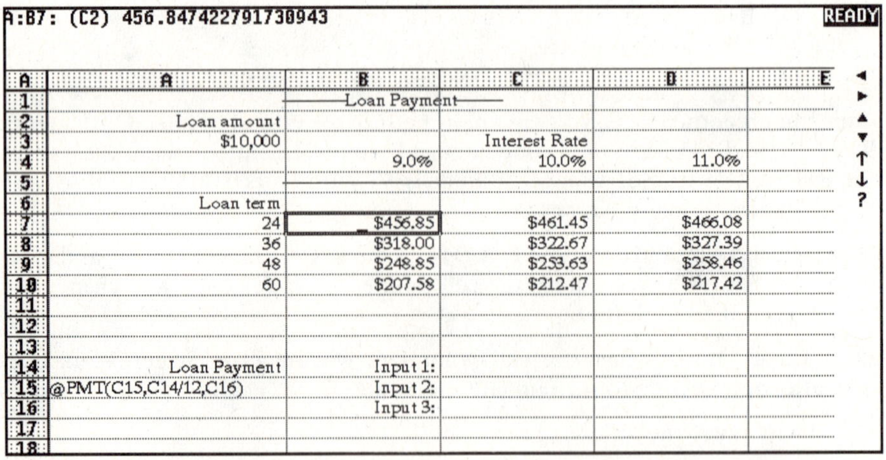

Fig. 12.41.
Worksheet A of the completed data table.

```
A:B7: (C2) 456.847422791730943                                READY

         A                    B              C              D          E
   ┌─────────────────Loan Payment──────────────────
 1
 2            Loan amount
 3              $10,000                  Interest Rate
 4                              9.0%         10.0%         11.0%
 5
 6            Loan term
 7              24             $456.85      $461.45       $466.08
 8              36             $318.00      $322.67       $327.39
 9              48             $248.85      $253.63       $258.46
10              60             $207.58      $212.47       $217.42
11
12
13
14            Loan Payment     Input 1:
15   @PMT(C15,C14/12,C16)      Input 2:
16                             Input 3:
17
18
```

You may have noticed that you can produce the same information in figures 12.41 and 12.42 with /Data Table **3**. By using a labeled data table, however, you have more flexibility than you do with a type 3 data table. You can produce a formatted, labeled table that is easier to understand.

After creating a labeled data table, if you return to the /Data Table Labeled menu and select **Down**, **Across**, or **Sheet**, 1-2-3 remembers the variable range you originally specified. If you accept the original variable range by pressing Enter, 1-2-3 "forgets" the input cell originally associated with that range. You must respecify the input cell. As an alternative, specify another input cell referenced by the formulas used in another data table. This method enables you to use the same sets of input values in different labeled data tables with only a few keystrokes.

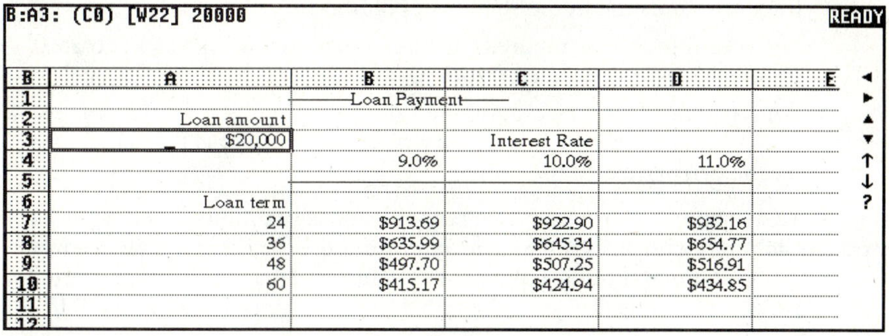

```
B:A3: (C0) [W22] 20000                                                  READY
```

	A	B	C	D
1		Loan Payment		
2	Loan amount			
3	$20,000		Interest Rate	
4		9.0%	10.0%	11.0%
5				
6	Loan term			
7	24	$913.69	$922.90	$932.16
8	36	$635.99	$645.34	$654.77
9	48	$497.70	$507.25	$516.91
10	60	$415.17	$424.94	$434.85

Fig. 12.42.
Worksheet B of the completed data table.

Table 12.3
/Data Table Labeled Commands

Option	Description
Formulas	Specifies the formula range and the formula-label range
Down	Specifies the row-variable range and input cells
Across	Specifies the column-variable range and input cells
Sheets	Specifies the worksheet-variable range and input cells
Input-Cells	Verifies and/or edits the input cells specified with **Down**, **Across**, or **Sheets**
Label-Fill	Specifies the label-fill character
Go	Calculates the results and generates the labeled data table
Quit	Returns 1-2-3 to READY mode

Using More Than Three Variables

A labeled data table can calculate formulas based on changing values of more than three variables. /**Data Table Labeled** can use only three types of variable ranges: column, row, and worksheet. How, then, can more than three types of variables be accommodated? You do so by including more than one variable in a particular variable range.

In the last section, you saw how each type of variable range can contain more than one part. A column-variable range can contain two or more rows. Each row is a separate variable with its own input cell. A row-variable range can contain two or more columns. Each column is a separate variable with its own input cell.

Reminder:
You can use more than three variables in a data table.

When setting up a variable range that contains more than one variable, you must organize the values in a certain way. For the three types of variable input ranges, note the following guidelines:

- For row-variable ranges, the values that change with the greatest frequency must be in the rightmost column.
- For column-variable ranges, the values that change with the greatest frequency must be in the bottom row.
- For worksheet-variable ranges, the values that change with the greatest frequency must be the bottom or rightmost group of cells, depending on the orientation of the range.

Figure 12.43 shows two row-variable ranges, each containing two variables. The row-variable range in B3..C11 is valid because the variable that changes fastest (10,20,30) is in the rightmost column. The values in F3..G11 do *not* constitute a valid row-variable range because the variable that changes the fastest is in the leftmost column.

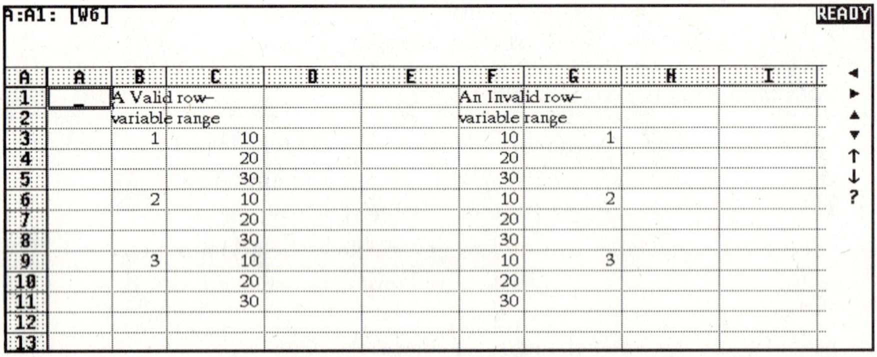

Fig. 12.43.
Valid and invalid row-variable ranges.

	A	B	C	D	E	F	G	H	I
1		A Valid row-				An Invalid row-			
2		variable range				variable range			
3		1	10			10	1		
4			20			20			
5			30			30			
6		2	10			10	2		
7			20			20			
8			30			30			
9		3	10			10	3		
10			20			20			
11			30			30			
12									
13									

Figure 12.44 shows a labeled data table that uses one variable range that contains two variables. This labeled data table provides the same information as the labeled data table in figures 12.40 and 12.41, but does so in a single worksheet. While this table contains only three variables, the principles are easily extended to four or more variables.

In this worksheet, the row-variable range is C7..D15. The input cell for the first row variable, Loan Amount, is B15. The input cell for the second row variable, Loan Term, is B16.

Analyzing a 1-2-3 Database with /Data Table Labeled

As with /Data Table 3, you can use /Data Table Labeled to perform a cross-tabulation analysis of data contained in a data table.

Chapter 12 ◆ Managing Data **547**

```
A:A19: (T) @PMT(B15,B14/12,B16)                                    READY

     A        B         C          D          E         F         G       H
 1                                                 Loan Payment
 2
 3                                                          Interest Rate
 4                                                  9.0%     10.0%     11.0%
 5                         Loan
 6                        amount     Loan term
 7                        $10,000        24      $456.85   $461.45   $466.08
 8                                       36      $318.00   $322.67   $327.39
 9                                       48      $248.85   $253.63   $258.46
10                                       60      $207.58   $212.47   $217.42
11
12                        $20,000        24      $913.69   $922.90   $932.16
13                                       36      $635.99   $645.34   $654.77
14          Input 1:                     48      $497.70   $507.25   $516.91
15          Input 2:                     60      $415.17   $424.94   $434.85
16          Input 3:
17
18   Loan Payment
19   @PMT(B15,B14/12,B16)
20
19-Jul-90 02:36 PM                                                   NUM
```

Fig. 12.44.
A variable range with two variables used to construct a three-variable labeled data table in a single worksheet.

The procedure used to create a cross-tabulation analysis with **/D**ata Table Labeled is similar to the procedures used in creating a what-if labeled data table. Follow the steps outlined in the section "Creating a Sample Labeled Data Table." In doing so, keep these points in mind:

◆ For a cross-tabulation analysis, the input cells must be in adjacent columns of the same row. Immediately above each input cell must be the name of the database field for which the input cell is going to serve as the criterion.

◆ For cross-tabulation analysis, the formulas are database functions. Each formula must refer to the input cells as the criteria range.

◆ When performing a cross-tabulation analysis, the variable ranges can contain multiple variables, as described in the previous steps for a **/D**ata Table Labeled what-if analysis.

◆ 1-2-3 evaluates the formulas based on the database records that meet the criteria in the input ranges. The result of each calculation is placed in the location defined by the intersection of the corresponding row, column, and worksheet.

◆ If, when creating either type of labeled table, you select **G**o and no error message appears, but the results area remains blank, compare the spelling of the labels in the formula range with those in the formula-label range. They must match exactly for **/D**ata Table Labeled to work. Also, if you are using label-fill characters, check to see that the fill character you are using is correct.

◆ Because of its complexity, **/D**ata Table Labeled offers many opportunities for error. You may obtain results that appear to be fine, but which are incorrect because of a misassigned input cell or some other error. Check the results carefully!

Cue:
If the results area of a labeled table is blank, check the spelling of the labels in the formula and formula-label ranges.

Caution:
Check the results of a labeled table carefully; if the table is not set up correctly, errors may result.

Filling Ranges

Cue:
Use /Data Fill to enter a series of numbers or dates that increment at the same value.

/Data Fill, the command for filling ranges, is useful when combined with the other database commands mentioned earlier in this chapter, particularly /Data Table and /Data Sort. /Data Fill fills a range of cells with a series of numbers (which can be in the form of numbers, formulas, or functions), dates, or times that increase or decrease by a specified increment or decrement.

When you issue the /Data Fill command, 1-2-3 first prompts you for the starting number of the series. The program then asks for the step (or incremental) value to be added to the previous value. Finally, 1-2-3 prompts you for the ending value.

Filling Ranges with Numbers

Consider, for example, using year numbers used as titles in a sales forecast worksheet. To enter a sequence of year numbers for a five-year forecast beginning in 1991, you need to start by specifying the range of cells to be filled (after you enter the /Data Fill command). For example, you can choose the range **B2..F2**. Then you would enter the start value of **1991**. The step value in this example is **1**. The ending value is **1995** for a five-year forecast. Figure 12.45 shows the result.

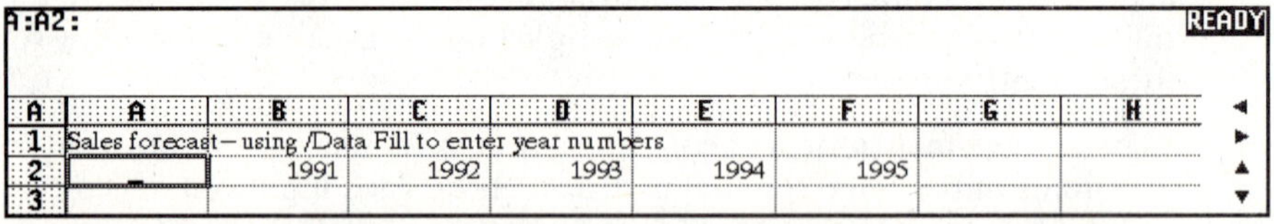

Fig. 12.45.
The year numbers entered in B2..F2 with /Data Fill.

```
A:A2:                                                           READY
    A           B        C        D        E        F       G       H
1  Sales forecast— using /Data Fill to enter year numbers
2              1991     1992     1993     1994     1995
3
```

One disadvantage of the /Data Fill command for year numbers is that you cannot center or left-justify the numbers after you have created them. As numbers, they always are right-justified. If you like the year numbers centered or left-justified, you should type them as labels instead of using this command.

The /Data Fill command also can work with the /Data Table command to build a list of interest rates. After you've specified the fill range, enter the starting value as a decimal fraction (**0.05** for 5 percent, for example), and another decimal fraction (**0.01** for 1 percent) for the step value. For the ending value, 1-2-3 defaults to 8192. The /Data Fill command, however, fills only the specified range and doesn't fill cells beyond the end of the range.

Cue:
Use /Data Fill with an added field in your database in case you need to restore the original order after sorting.

A third use for the /Data Fill command is in combination with /Data Sort. Suppose that you are going to sort a database, and you want to be able to restore the records to their original order if you make a mistake as you are sorting. All you need to do is add a field to the database and use /Data Fill to fill the field with consecutive numbers. Then you can sort your database. If you find that the results of the sort are unacceptable, you simply sort the database on the new field to return the database to its original order.

Using Formulas and Functions to Fill Ranges

Instead of using regular numbers for the start, step (incremental), and stop values, you also can use formulas and @functions. If you want to fill a range of cells with incrementing dates, after the range has been set, you can use the @DATE function to set the start value—for example, @DATE(91,6,1). You can use also a cell formula, such as +E4, for the incremental value. In this case, E4 may contain the increment 7 so that you can have increments of one week at a time. You can enter the stop value @DATE(91,10,1), for example; or, if the stop date is in a cell, you can give that cell address as the stop value. 1-2-3 provides many different combinations of commands.

Reminder:
You can use formulas and @functions as start and stop values with /Data Fill.

Filling Ranges with Dates or Times

/**D**ata **F**ill command also enables you to fill a worksheet range with a sequence of dates or times without using values, formulas, or @functions. You specify the starting and stopping values and the increment between values.

To fill a range with dates or times, you first should use the /**R**ange **F**ormat **O**ther **A**utomatic command (or one of the date or time formats if you prefer). Then select /**D**ata **F**ill and specify the worksheet range to be filled. Next, you enter the start value. To fill a range with dates, enter a start date in any of 1-2-3's date formats except Short International (D5). If you enter a date without the day or the year, 1-2-3 assumes the first day of the month and the current year. To fill a range with times, enter a start time in any of 1-2-3's time formats.

Next, you specify the increment. For dates, enter a value *n* followed by a letter to indicate the increment unit:

- **d** to increment by *n* days
- **w** to increment by *n* weeks
- **m** to increment by *n* months
- **q** to increment by *n* quarters
- **y** to increment by *n* years

For times, enter a value *n* followed by one of the following:

- **s** to increment by *n* seconds
- **min** to increment by *n* minutes
- **h** to increment by *n* hours

Then enter a stop value. For negative increments, the stop value must be smaller than the start value. Enter the stop value as a value or in a valid date or time format.

1-2-3 fills the range top-to-bottom, left-to-right. The first cell is filled with the start value, and each subsequent cell is filled with the value in the previous cell plus the increment. Filling stops when the stop value or the end of the fill range is reached, whichever happens first.

For example, to put a sequence of half-hourly times in column D, select /Data Fill and enter the range **D1..D10**. For the start value, type **1:00**; for the increment, enter **30min**; and for the stop value, enter **6:00**.

To put a sequence of biweekly dates in column F, select /Data Fill and enter the range **F1..F10**. Type **01-Jan** for the start value, **2w** for the increment, and **07-May** for the stop value.

The results of these commands are shown in figure 12.46. In this worksheet, columns D and F were formatted with /**Range Format Other Automatic** before the fill operation. When you fill a range formatted as **Automatic** with a date or time, 1-2-3 formats the range with the same format you use to specify the start and stop date or time.

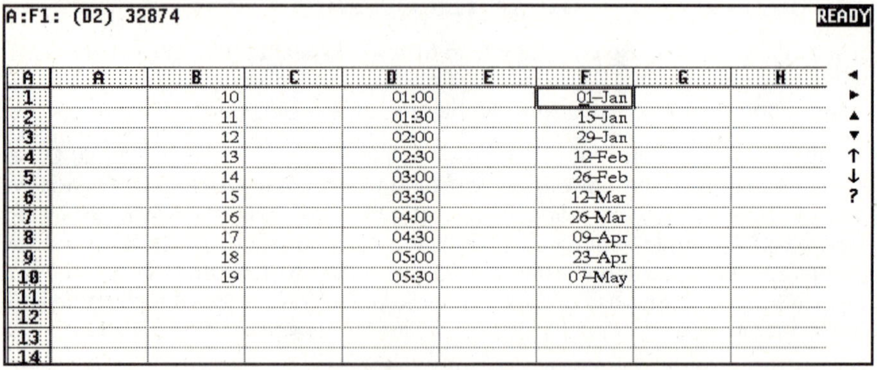

Fig. 12.46.

The results of using /Data Fill with dates and times.

```
A:F1: (D2) 32874                                              READY

      A         B         C         D         E         F         G         H
 1              10                  01:00               01-Jan
 2              11                  01:30               15-Jan
 3              12                  02:00               29-Jan
 4              13                  02:30               12-Feb
 5              14                  03:00               26-Feb
 6              15                  03:30               12-Mar
 7              16                  04:00               26-Mar
 8              17                  04:30               09-Apr
 9              18                  05:00               23-Apr
10              19                  05:30               07-May
11
12
13
14
```

Note that when you fill a range with times, 1-2-3 may put in the last cell of the fill range a time that is slightly different from the stop value you specified. A slight loss of accuracy sometimes occurs when 1-2-3 converts between the binary numbers it uses internally and the decimal numbers used for times. To avoid this problem, specify a stop value that is less than one increment larger than the desired stop value. For example, if the increment is 10 minutes and you want the last cell in the range to contain 10:30, specify a stop value between 10:30 and 10:40, such as 10:35.

Creating Frequency Distributions

The command for creating frequency distributions in 1-2-3 is the /**Data Distribution** command. A *frequency distribution* describes the relationship between a set of classes and the frequency of occurrence of members of each class. A list of consumers with their product preferences illustrates the use of the /**Data Distribution** command to produce a frequency distribution (see fig. 12.47).

To use the /**Data Distribution** command, you first specify a values range, which corresponds to the range of Taste Preference numbers in this example. After specifying **B3..B18** for the values range, you set up the range of intervals at **D3..D7**, in what 1-2-3 calls the *bin* range. If you have evenly spaced intervals, the /**Data Fill** command can be used to enter the values for the bin range. If the intervals are not evenly spaced, you cannot use the /Data Fill command to fill the range.

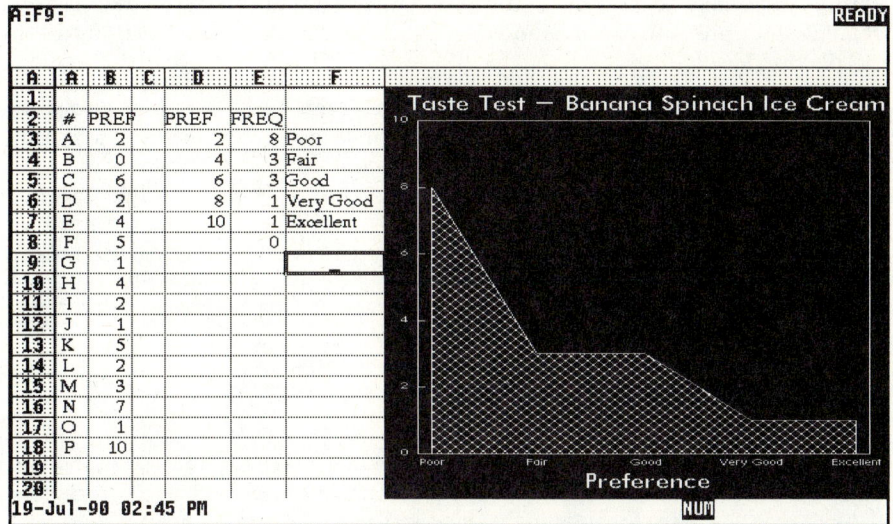

Fig. 12.47.
/Data Distribution used to analyze Taste Preference data.

When you specify these ranges and enter the /Data Distribution command, 1-2-3 creates the results column (E3..E8) to the right of the bin range (D3..D7). The results column, which shows the frequency distribution, is always in the column segment to the right of the bin range and extends one row farther down.

The values in the results column represent the frequency of distribution of the numbers in the values range for each interval. The first interval in the bin range is for values greater than zero and less than or equal to two; the second, for values greater than two and less than or equal to four, and so on. The last value in the results column, in cell E8 just below the corresponding column segment, shows the frequency of leftover numbers (that is, the frequency of numbers that do not fit into an interval classification).

The /Data Distribution command can help you create understandable results from a series of numbers. The results are easily graphed, as shown in figure 12.47. A manufacturer looking at this graph would probably start looking for another product or start trying to improve the taste of the current product. Banana Spinach Ice Cream probably won't be next summer's big seller!

Using the /Data Regression Command

The /Data Regression command gives you a multiple-regression analysis package within 1-2-3. Although most people don't have a need for this advanced feature, if you need to use it, 1-2-3 saves you the cost and inconvenience of buying a stand-alone statistical package for performing a regression analysis.

Part III ♦ Customizing 1-2-3

Cue:
Use /Data Regression to determine the relationship between sets of values.

Use **/Data Regression** when you want to determine the relationship between one set of values (the dependent variable) and one or more other sets of values (the independent variables). Regression analysis has a number of uses in a business setting, including relating sales to price, promotions, and other market factors; relating stock prices to earnings and interest rates; and relating production costs to production levels.

Think of linear regression as a way of determining the "best" line through a series of data points. Multiple regression does this for several variables simultaneously, determining the "best" line relating the dependent variable to the set of independent variables. Consider, for example, a data sample showing Annual Earnings versus Age. Figure 12.48 shows the data; figure 12.49 shows the data plotted as an XY graph (use A7..A20 for the X graph range and C7..C20 for the A graph range).

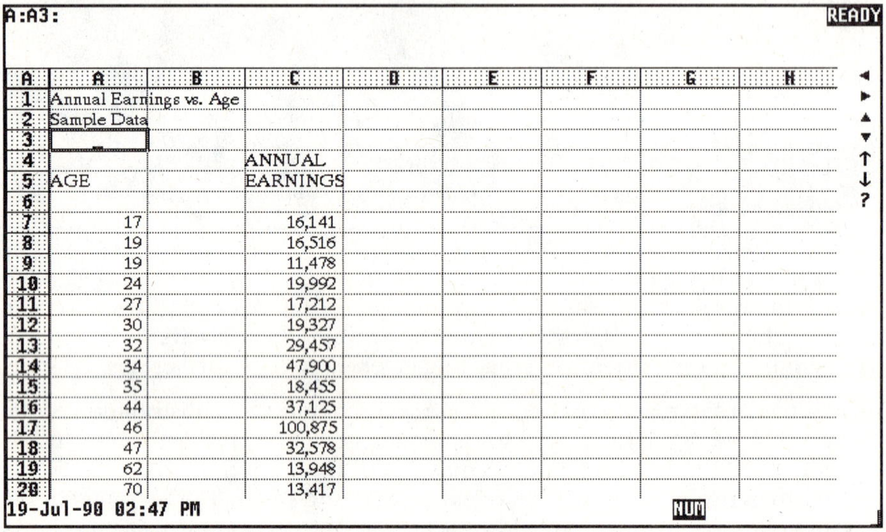

Fig. 12.48.
Annual Earnings versus Age data.

```
A:A3:                                                    READY
     A          B          C        D     E     F     G     H
 1  Annual Earnings vs. Age
 2  Sample Data
 3
 4                      ANNUAL
 5  AGE                 EARNINGS
 6
 7      17              16,141
 8      19              16,516
 9      19              11,478
10      24              19,992
11      27              17,212
12      30              19,327
13      32              29,457
14      34              47,900
15      35              18,455
16      44              37,125
17      46             100,875
18      47              32,578
19      62              13,948
20      70              13,417
19-Jul-90 02:47 PM                                        NUM
```

The **/Data Regression** command can simultaneously determine how to draw a line through these data points and how well the line fits the data. When you invoke the command, the following menu appears:

  X-Range   Y-Range   Output-Range   Intercept   Reset   Go   Quit

Use the **X-Range** option to select one or more independent variables for the regression. The **/Data Regression** command can use as many as 75 independent variables. The variables in the regression are columns of values, which means that any data in rows must be converted to columns with **/Range Transpose** before the **/Data Regression** command is issued. In this example, the **X-Range** is specified as **A7..A20**.

The **Y-Range** option specifies the dependent variable. The **Y-Range** must be a single column; in this example, **C7..C20** is the Y-Range.

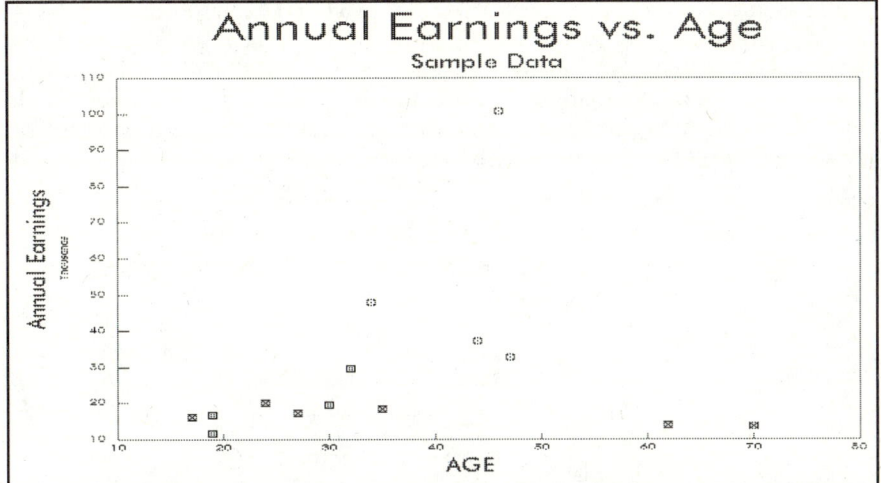

Fig. 12.49.
A graph of Annual Earnings versus Age data.

The **Output-Range** option specifies the upper left corner of the results range. This should be an unused section of the worksheet, because the output is written over any existing cell contents. In this example, **E5** was specified as the output range.

The **Intercept** option enables you to specify whether you want the regression to calculate a constant value. Calculating the constant is the default; in some applications, however, you may need to exclude a constant.

Figure 12.50 shows the results of using the **/Data Regression Go** command in the Annual Earnings versus Age example. The results (in cells E5..H13) include the value of the constant and the coefficient of the single independent variable that was specified with the **X-Range** option. The results also include a number of regression statistics that describe how well the regression line fits the data. In this case, the R-Squared value and the standard errors of the constant and the regression coefficient all indicate that the regression line does not explain much of the variation in the dependent variable.

The new data in column D is the computed regression line. These values consist of the constant plus the coefficient of the independent variable times its value in each row of the data. To calculate the regression line, place the formula **+$H$6+$G$12*A7** in cell D7. Then use the **/Range Format , (Comma) 0** command to format the result. Finally, use **/Copy** from **D7..D7** to **D8..D20** to copy the formula to the other cells in column D. This line can be plotted against the original data (as graph range B formatted to display lines only), as shown in figure 12.51.

When you look at the Annual Earnings versus Age plot, you notice that income appears to rise with age until about age 50; then income begins to decline. You can use the **/Data Regression** command to fit a line that describes such a relationship between Annual Earnings and Age. In figure 12.52, a column of data is added in column B containing the square of the age in column A. To include this new column in the regression, specify the range **A7..B20** for the **X-Range**, adjust the formulas in column D by changing D7 to +$H$6+$G$12*A7+$H$12*B7 (and then copying the formula to **D8..D20**) and recalculate the regression. Note that the regression statistics are much improved over the regression of Annual Earnings versus Age. This means that the new line fits the data more closely than the old one. (However, the regression statistics indicate that the regression only "explains" about one-third of the variation of the dependent variable.)

Fig. 12.50.
The results of /Data Regression on Annual Earnings versus Age data.

	A	B	C	D	E	F	G	H
1	Annual Earnings vs. Age							
2	Sample Data							
3								
4			ANNUAL	REGRESSION				
5	AGE		EARNINGS	LINE		Regression Output:		
6					Constant			18414.67
7	17		16,141	23,005	Std Err of Y Est			23930.2
8	19		16,516	23,545	R Squared			0.034195
9	19		11,478	23,545	No. of Observations			14
10	24		19,992	24,894	Degrees of Freedom			12
11	27		17,212	25,704				
12	30		19,327	26,514	X Coefficient(s)		269.9914	
13	32		29,457	27,054	Std Err of Coef.		414.2111	
14	34		47,900	27,594				
15	35		18,455	27,864				
16	44		37,125	30,294				
17	46		100,875	30,834				
18	47		32,578	31,104				
19	62		13,948	35,154				
20	70		13,417	37,314				

Fig. 12.51.
A plot of Annual Earnings versus Age data, with a regression line.

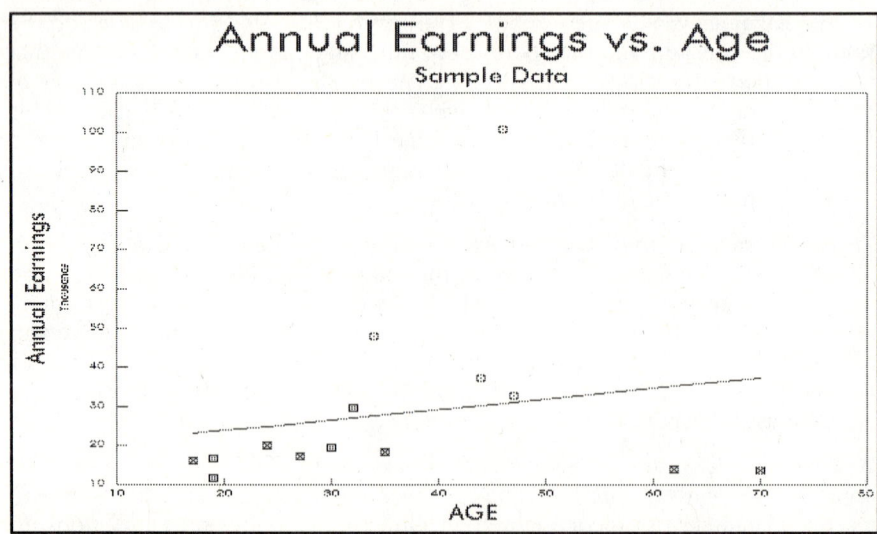

You must add the new regression coefficient (as mentioned above) to the equation that generates the regression line to generate the new plot in figure 12.53.

Note that the regression line is now a parabola that rises until age 45, and then declines. The regression line generated by a multiple regression may or may not be a straight line, depending on the independent variables that are used.

A:D7: (,0) +$H$6+$G$12*A7+$H$12*B7 READY

	A	B	C	D	E	F	G	H
1	Annual Earnings vs. Age							
2	Sample Data							
3								
4		AGE X	ANNUAL	REGRESSION				
5	AGE	AGE	EARNINGS	LINE		Regression Output:		
6					Constant			−56032.3
7	17	289	16,141	5,456	Std Err of Y Est			20621.17
8	19	361	11,478	10,789	R Squared			0.342593
9	19	361	16,516	10,789	No. of Observations			14
10	24	576	19,992	22,373	Degrees of Freedom			11
11	27	729	17,212	28,123				
12	30	900	19,327	32,973	X Coefficient(s)		4467.068	−50.0075
13	32	1024	29,457	35,706	Std Err of Coef.		1881.78	22.0141
14	34	1156	47,900	38,039				
15	35	1225	18,455	39,056				
16	44	1936	37,125	43,704				
17	46	2116	100,875	43,637				
18	47	2209	32,578	43,453				
19	62	3844	13,948	28,697				
20	70	4900	13,417	11,625				

19-Jul-90 02:55 PM NUM

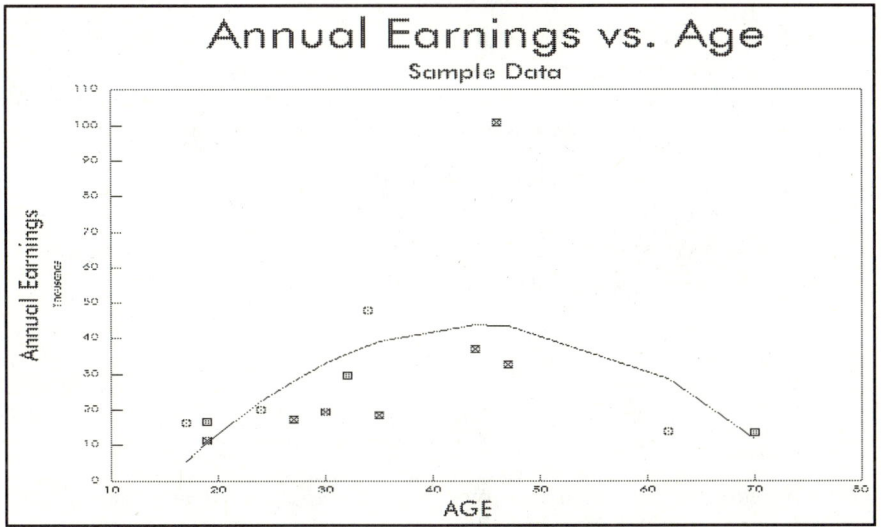

Fig. 12.52. *Annual Earnings versus Age data, and the square of Age.*

Fig. 12.53. *A plot of Annual Earnings versus Age data, with a revised regression line.*

Cue: *Use /Data Matrix for many types of economic analysis or for scientific or engineering calculations.*

Using the /Data Matrix Command

The /**D**ata **M**atrix command is a specialized mathematical command that enables you to solve systems of simultaneous linear equations and manipulate the resulting solutions. This command is powerful but has limited application in a

business setting. If you are using 1-2-3 for certain types of economic analysis or for scientific or engineering calculations, you may find this command valuable.

The **/Data Matrix** command has a menu with two options: **Invert** and **Multiply**. The **Invert** option enables you to invert a nonsingular square matrix of up to 90 rows and columns. Just select the **Invert** option and highlight the range you want to invert. Then select an output range to hold the inverted solution matrix. You can place the output range anywhere in the worksheet, including on top of the matrix you are inverting.

The time required to invert a matrix is proportional to the cube of the number of rows and columns. A 25-by-25 matrix takes about 10 seconds, and an 80-by-80 matrix takes almost 5 minutes on a 16-MHz 80386 computer with no numeric coprocessor. If you are going to use 1-2-3 to invert matrices, you may want to invest in a numeric coprocessor for your computer.

The **Multiply** option enables you to multiply two rectangular matrices together in accordance with the rules of matrix algebra. The number of columns in the first matrix must equal the number of rows in the second matrix. The result matrix has the same number of rows as the first matrix, and the same number of columns as the second.

When you select **/Data Matrix Multiply**, 1-2-3 prompts you for three ranges: the first matrix, the second matrix, and the output range. **Multiply** is fast compared to **Invert**, but still may take some time if you multiply large matrices.

Reminder:
In a three-dimensional input range, 1-2-3 performs matrix conversions and multiplications worksheet-by-worksheet.

Note how the **/Data Matrix** command affects three-dimensional worksheets. If you specify a three-dimensional input range, 1-2-3 performs inversions on a worksheet-by-worksheet basis. For example, if you specify **A:B2..D:D4** as the input range and **A:F2** as the output range, the following occurs:

A:B2..A:D4 is inverted and put in A:F2..A:H4

B:B2..B:D4 is inverted and put in B:F2..B:H4

C:B2..C:D4 is inverted and put in C:F2..C:H4

D:B2..D:D4 is inverted and put in D:F2..D:H4

1-2-3 also performs multiplications on a worksheet-by-worksheet basis if you specify three-dimensional ranges.

Loading Data from Other Programs

Lotus provides several means of importing data from other applications. The Translate utility (see Chapter 7) has options for converting data directly to 1-2-3 worksheets from DIF, dBASE II, dBASE III, and dBASE III Plus files, and from other file formats. You then can access the data by using the **/File Retrieve** or **/File Combine** commands from the current worksheet.

Use the **/File Import** command to read into a current worksheet the data stored on disk as a text file. Depending on the format, these files can be read directly to a range of cells or a column of cells. Specially formatted "numeric" data can be read directly to a range of worksheet cells. ASCII text can be stored as long labels in a single column with one line of the file per cell. You then must disassemble these labels into the appropriate data values or fields by using @functions or the /Data Parse command.

Finally, you can use certain advanced macro commands (see Chapter 14) to read and write an ASCII sequential file directly from within 1-2-3 advanced macro command programs.

Using the /Data Parse Command

The /Data Parse command is a flexible and easy method of extracting numeric, string, and date data from long labels and placing it in separate columns. For example, suppose that you printed to a disk file a report containing inventory data, and you want to load the ASCII file in 1-2-3. After you load the file by using the /File Import command, you must reformat the data with the /Data Parse command.

Cue:
Use /Data Parse to split long labels imported from text files into separate text, number, or date fields.

The /File Import command loads the inventory data into the range A1..A16 (see fig. 12.54). Visually, the data is formatted in a typical worksheet range, such as A1..G16, but the display is misleading. The current cell pointer location is A6; the entire contents of the row exist only in that cell as a long label.

To break the long label columns, move the cell pointer to the first cell to be parsed and select /Data Parse. The following menu appears:

   Format-Line Input-Column Output-Range Reset Go Quit

Use Format-Line to Create or Edit a newly inserted line in the data to be parsed. The Format-Line command specifies the pattern or patterns for splitting the long labels into numbers, labels, and dates.

```
A:A6: 'HAMMER                   10       EA       6.75    7/4/90                    READY

              B              C         D         E         F         G         H
 1    Inventory records
 2
 3
 4                                   ON HAND    UNIT OF    UNIT    P.O.
 5    DESCRIPTION                    QUANTITY   ISSUE      COST    DATE
 6    HAMMER                            10      EA         6.75    7/4/90
 7    SCREWDRIVER                       17      EA         8.75
 8    WRENCH                           100      EA        15.75    7/24/90
 9    HAMMER                            10      EA         6.75    7/4/90
10    SCREWDRIVER                       17      EA         8.75
11    WRENCH                           100      EA        15.75    7/24/90
12    SCREWDRIVER                       17      EA         8.75
13    WRENCH                           100      EA        15.75    7/24/90
14    HAMMER                            10      EA         6.75    7/4/90
15    SCREWDRIVER                       17      EA         8.75
16    WRENCH                           100      EA        15.75    7/24/90
17
```

Fig. 12.54.
The results of a /File Import command.

Use **Input-Column** to specify the range of cells to be parsed. The input range (contained in just one column) consists of the cell containing the format line, and all cells containing the long labels to be parsed.

Use **Output-Range** to specify the worksheet range where 1-2-3 puts the parsed data. You can specify a rectangular range or the single cell at the upper left of the range. The output data will have as many rows as there are long labels; the number of columns depends on the format line.

Reset clears the previously set Input-Column and Output-Range. **Go** performs the parse, based on the specified Input-Column, Format-Lines, and Output-Range.

To parse the data shown in figure 12.54, follow these steps:

1. Move the cell pointer to cell A4, which is the first cell in the range that has the data you want to break into columns. (You do not have to parse the title in cell A1.)
2. Parse the column headings in cells A4..A5, using one format line; and then parse the data in A6..A16, using another format line.

Different format lines are necessary because the data is a mixture of label, numeric, and date data, and because all the headings are labels. Select **Format-Line Create**. A suggested format line is inserted in the data at A4, in a step that moves the remaining worksheet contents down one line.

After creating a format line, you can edit it if necessary by selecting **Format-Line** again and choosing **Edit**. Use the format line to mark the column positions and the type of data in those positions. /Data Parse uses the format line to break down the data and move it to its respective columns in the output range.

Combinations of certain letters and special characters comprise format lines. The letters denote the beginning position and the type of data; special symbols define the length of a field and the spacing. Note the following letters and symbols:

Letter/Symbol	Purpose
D	Marks the beginning of a **Date** field
L	Marks the beginning of a **Label** field
S	Marks the beginning of a **Skip** position
T	Marks the beginning of a **Time** field
V	Marks the beginning of a **Value** field
>	Defines the continuation of a field; use one > for each position in the field (excluding the first position)
*	Defines blank spaces (in the data below the format line) that may be part of the block of data in the following cell

Add as many format lines as you need in the data. In the inventory example, you need to enter another format line at cell A6 (A7 after you added the first format line in A4) and specify the format criteria for the data records that follow. Suggested format lines are shown in figure 12.55. To restore the **Parse** menu, press Enter after you finish editing.

```
A:A7: |L>>>>>************************V>******L>******V>>>****D>>>>>            READY

      A          B          C          D          E          F          G          H
1   Inventory records
2
3
4   **************************L>*L>>>****L>>>*L>****L>>>****L>>>
5                             ON HAND    UNIT OF    UNIT    P.O.
6   DESCRIPTION               QUANTITY   ISSUE      COST    DATE
    L>>>>>************************V>******L>******V>>>****D>>>>>
8   HAMMER                        10       EA       6.75    7/4/90
9   SCREWDRIVER                   17       EA       8.75
10  WRENCH                       100       EA      15.75    7/24/90
11  HAMMER                        10       EA       6.75    7/4/90
12  SCREWDRIVER                   17       EA       8.75
13  WRENCH                       100       EA      15.75    7/24/90
14  SCREWDRIVER                   17       EA       8.75
15  WRENCH                       100       EA      15.75    7/24/90
16  HAMMER                        10       EA       6.75    7/4/90
17  SCREWDRIVER                   17       EA       8.75
18  WRENCH                       100       EA      15.75    7/24/90
19
```

Fig. 12.55. *A format line edited in a Parse operation.*

After setting up two format lines in the Physical Inventory example, select **Input-Range** from the **Parse** menu. Point to or type the range **A4..A18**, which includes format lines, column headings, and data. Continue by selecting **Output-Range** from the **Parse** menu and by specifying **A21** as the upper left corner of a blank range to accept the parsed data. Complete the operation by selecting the **Go** option (see fig. 12.56).

```
A:A21: 'ON                                                                    READY

      A          B          C          D          E          F          G          H
    ON         HAND       UNIT       OF         UNIT       P.O.
22  DESCRIPTIQUANTITY ISSUE      COST       DATE
23  HAMMER            10 EA            6.75      33058
24  SCREWDRIV         17 EA            8.75
25  WRENCH           100 EA           15.75      33078
26  HAMMER            10 EA            6.75      33058
27  SCREWDRIV         17 EA            8.75
28  WRENCH           100 EA           15.75      33078
29  SCREWDRIV         17 EA            8.75
30  WRENCH           100 EA           15.75      33078
31  HAMMER            10 EA            6.75      33058
32  SCREWDRIV         17 EA            8.75
33  WRENCH           100 EA           15.75      33078
34
35
```

Fig. 12.56. *The results of a Parse operation.*

The data displayed in individual cells may not be exactly what you want. You can make a few changes in the format and column width, and you also can add or delete information to make the newly parsed data more usable. These enhancements are not part of the **Parse** command, but they usually are necessary after importing and parsing data.

Part III ♦ Customizing 1-2-3

To produce the final inventory database shown in figure 12.57, follow these steps:

1. Delete rows A3..A20 to remove the unparsed data and to move the parsed data up under the title.
2. Expand column A to make it 25 characters wide, and contract column C to make it 8 characters wide.
3. Reformat the P.O. DATE range in column E to the **Date 4** format.
4. Insert at column E a column for the inventory value (the P.O. DATE now should be column F).
5. Widen the new column E to 10 characters.
6. Add the INVENTORY and VALUE headings in cells E3 and E4, respectively.
7. Enter in cell E5 the formula that computes the inventory value (**+B5*D5**).
8. Copy the formula in cell E5 to cells E6..E16.
9. Use the **/R**ange Format command to change the format of cells D5..E16 to the comma and **2** decimal places display.

Fig. 12.57.
The improved appearance of parsed data.

```
A:A1: [W25] 'Inventory records                                    READY
                           B       C         D      E        F
   Inventory records
 2
 3                      ON HAND  UNIT OF   UNIT  INVENTORY P.O.
 4 DESCRIPTION          QUANTITY ISSUE     COST    VALUE   DATE
 5 HAMMER                    10  EA        6.75    67.50  07/04/90
 6 SCREWDRIVER               17  EA        8.75   148.75
 7 WRENCH                   100  EA       15.75 1,575.00  07/24/90
 8 HAMMER                    10  EA        6.75    67.50  07/04/90
 9 SCREWDRIVER               17  EA        8.75   148.75
10 WRENCH                   100  EA       15.75 1,575.00  07/24/90
11 SCREWDRIVER               17  EA        8.75   148.75
12 WRENCH                   100  EA       15.75 1,575.00  07/24/90
13 HAMMER                    10  EA        6.75    67.50  07/04/90
14 SCREWDRIVER               17  EA        8.75   148.75
15 WRENCH                   100  EA       15.75 1,575.00  07/24/90
16
```

Caution:
Make sure that the column widths are wide enough to accept the complete value or label you want in the field.

Using Caution with /Data Parse

If you are parsing a value that continues past the end of the field, the data is parsed until a blank is encountered or until the value runs into the next field in the format line. This means that if you parse labels, you need to make sure that the field widths in the format line are wide enough so that you can avoid losing data because of blanks. If you parse values, the field widths are less critical.

Experiment on small amounts of data until you are comfortable using the **/D**ata **P**arse command. After you understand how this important command works, you may find many more applications for using it. Every time you develop a new application, you should consider whether existing data created with another software program can be imported and then changed to 1-2-3 format by using the **/D**ata **P**arse command.

Working with External Databases

1-2-3's /**Data External** commands access data in tables within an *external* database. An *external table* is a file that is created and maintained by a database program other than 1-2-3, such as dBASE III. Once a connection or link is established between 1-2-3 and an external table, you can perform the following tasks:

- Use /**Data Query** commands to find and manipulate data in the external table and then work with that data in the worksheet
- Use formulas and database functions to perform calculations based on data in the external table
- Create a new external table that contains data from the worksheet or from an existing external table

When you select /**Data External**, the following menu appears:

    Use List Create Delete Other Reset Quit

The functions of these commands are listed in table 12.4.

Cue:
Use /Data External to access data in tables created by external database programs.

Table 12.4
Data External Commands

Option	Description
Use	Establishes a connection to an external table (Use is the first step before using other /Data External commands)
List	Displays the names of the tables in an external database, or lists the names of the fields in an external table
Create	Establishes a new table in an external database and copies data from a worksheet data table or another external table to the new table
Delete	Deletes a table from an external database
Other	Includes three commands:
Refresh	Sets the interval for automatic updating of worksheet formulas that depend on an external table and for automatic reexecution of /Data Query and /Data Table commands
Command	Sends a command to a database management program
Translation	Permits translation of data created with foreign character sets
Reset	Breaks the connection to an external table
Quit	Returns to READY mode

Networks and database programs used on networks usually include controls to limit access to database files. These same controls apply when using 1-2-3 to access external database files. You may, for example, be prompted to enter your user ID and password. If so, type them, press Enter, and then continue with your 1-2-3 commands. You have your usual access to the network files. If you encounter problems, see your network administrator.

Understanding External Database Terminology

Data management in 1-2-3 is powerful and flexible because of Release 3's capability to use data from tables in external databases. Before you begin working with this feature, you should be familiar with several terms.

A *database driver* is a program that serves as an interface between 1-2-3 and an external database, allowing 1-2-3 to transfer data to and from the external tables in the database. A separate database driver is required for each external database format you use. The only database driver supplied with Releases 3 and 3.1 is for dBASE III, and the driver name is SAMPLE. 1-2-3 Release 3.1+ supplies an additional database driver for Bradox.

An *external database* is simply the path where the external tables reside.

> **Reminder:**
> To access an external table from 1-2-3, you must enter the full table name.

A *table name* identifies the external table with which you want to work. You must enter the full table name before you can access the table from 1-2-3. The full table name consists of three or four parts in the following order:

1. The name of the database driver
2. The name of the external database (path)
3. An owner name or user ID, if required by the database program
4. The name of a table in the database, or a 1-2-3 range name that has been assigned to the table

A *table-creation string* contains information used by a database driver to create a new external table. When you create a new external table from within 1-2-3, you may have to specify a table-creation string, depending on the specific database driver in use. The sample driver provided does not require a table-creation string. When in doubt, refer to the database driver documentation.

A *table definition* is a six-column worksheet range that contains information about a new external table. Information in a table definition always includes field names, data types, and field widths, and may include column labels, table creation-strings, and field descriptions.

Using an Existing External Table

> **Reminder:**
> To use an existing table, you must first establish a connection.

Using the data in an external table does not differ much from using a worksheet database. The major difference is that you need to establish a connection to the external table before you use it, and then break the connection when you are finished.

To use an existing external table, you must first set up the connection to the external table with the /Data External Use command. This command steps you through the components needed to define the full table name.

First, 1-2-3 displays a list of the available database drivers. After you select a driver (for example, SAMPLE), 1-2-3 lists the available external databases you can access with that driver. Then 1-2-3 displays a list of the table names, with each table name preceded by an owner name if appropriate. You can press Name (F3) to display a full-screen list for any of these components. Figure 12.58 shows a full-screen list of available external tables.

```
A:A4: 'LAST_NAME                                                      NAMES
Enter name of table to use: Sample C:\123R3\DATA

ADDRESS                                   COMPANY
EMPLOYEE
```

Fig. 12.58.
A list of available external tables.

You can enter a table name by typing it or by highlighting it in the list and pressing Enter. After you establish a connection to an external table, you are prompted to assign the table a 1-2-3 range name. As a default, the table name is supplied for the range name. To use the default, press Enter. Otherwise, type the range name you want and then press Enter. The range name is used to refer to the table as if it were a worksheet database.

Note that when you break the connection to an external table, the range name assigned to it is lost. Formulas and functions that reference the range name become undefined when the connection is broken. You must respecify the range name whenever you establish the connection. Be sure to use the same range name each time if your worksheet contains formulas or functions that reference the range.

By using the range name assigned to the table, you can treat the external table as if it were a worksheet database and perform the following tasks:

- Copy some or all records from the external table to your worksheet with /Data Query Extract
- Use /Data Query Extract to copy new records from your worksheet to the external table
- Use formulas and database @functions in your worksheet that reference data in the external table
- Modify records in the external table with /Data Query Modify (only if record modification is supported by the database driver in use; this command is not supported by the SAMPLE dBASE III driver)
- Use /Data External Other to perform special database functions not available in 1-2-3
- Terminate the connection to the external table with /Data External Reset

Listing External Tables

/Data External List offers the following options:

Option	Description
Tables	Lists the names of all the tables in an external database
Fields	Lists information about the structure of an external table to which you are connected (with /Data External Use)

Cue:
To find the location of a particular table, use /Data External List Tables.

A list of the tables in an external database file is useful when you do not remember the exact location of a particular table. To obtain such a list, select **/Data External List Tables.** You are prompted to supply the database driver name and database name, as for the **/Data External Use** command. After supplying the appropriate names, you are asked to provide an output range for the list.

Caution:
An external table list overwrites existing worksheet data.

This list consists of three columns and as many rows as there are tables in the database file. Because the list overwrites existing worksheet data, be sure that no important data is affected. Figure 12.59 shows a sample list. The first column of the list contains the table names, and the second column contains the table descriptions if they are used by the particular database, or NA (not applicable) if they are not. The third column contains the table owner IDs if used, or NA if they are not. The sample dBASE III driver does not use these table descriptions or table owner IDs.

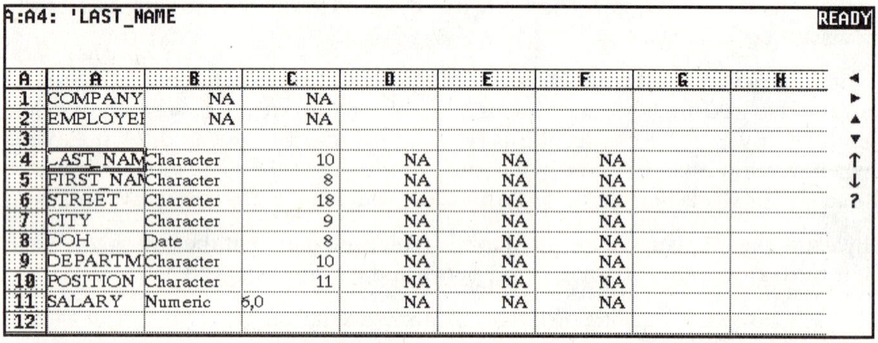

Fig. 12.59.
The rows containing information about the fields in the table.

```
A:A4: 'LAST_NAME                                              READY
     A            B          C        D       E       F     G    H
  1  COMPANY                 NA       NA
  2  EMPLOYEE                NA       NA
  3
  4  LAST_NAM    Character    10       NA      NA      NA
  5  FIRST_NA    Character     8       NA      NA      NA
  6  STREET      Character    18       NA      NA      NA
  7  CITY        Character     9       NA      NA      NA
  8  DOH         Date          8       NA      NA      NA
  9  DEPARTM     Character    10       NA      NA      NA
 10  POSITION    Character    11       NA      NA      NA
 11  SALARY      Numeric      6,0      NA      NA      NA
 12
```

Cue:
To review the contents of a particular table, use /Data External List Fields to list the structure.

You can use a list of a table's structure to remind yourself of the contents of a particular external table. You can use this list also as the basis for creating a new table definition, as explained in the next section. To create such a list, select **/Data External List Fields.** You are first prompted for the range name that identifies the external table, and then for the output range for the list.

The list consists of six columns and as many rows as there are fields in the table. Again, this list overwrites existing worksheet data, so be cautious. Each row in the list contains information about one field in the table (see fig. 12.59). The contents of the columns are the following:

Column 1	Field name
Column 2	Field data type
Column 3	Field width in characters
Column 4	Column label

Column 5   Field description

Column 6   Field-creation string

If the external table does not use column labels, field descriptions, or field-creation strings, these columns contain NA. The SAMPLE dBASE III driver does not use these three fields.

Creating a New External Table

You create a new external table with the /Data External Create command. When you select this command, the following menu appears:

Name   Definition   Go   Quit

Table 12.5 describes each of the menu options.

Table 12.5
/Data External Create Commands

Command	Description
Name	Specifies the external database that contains the new table and specifies the table name
Definition	Specifies the worksheet or external table that is used as a model for the structure of the new table. The two options are Create-Definition, which creates a table definition based on a range in the model, and Use-Definition, which uses a table definition that already exists in the model.
Go	Creates the external table
Quit	Returns to READY mode

The first step in creating an external table is to use the /Data External Create Name command to name the new external table. You are prompted to supply a name for the new table, followed by a range name to access the table, as for the /Data External Use command. Next, you are prompted for a table-creation string. Because the sample driver does not support the table-creation string, you simply press Enter at this prompt.

To create a new external table, 1-2-3 needs to know the number, order, data types, and names of the fields in the new table. This information is provided in a *table definition*. If the new external table has a structure identical to that of an existing table, 1-2-3 can create the table definition for you automatically. If the new table has a unique structure, you must create and edit a table definition.

Reminder:
To create a new external table, you must enter a table definition.

Duplicating an Existing Structure

You can duplicate the structure of either a worksheet database or an external table. To use a worksheet database, it must be in an active file and must contain a row of field names and at least one data record. When the /Data External Create Create-Definition command prompts you for an input range, you highlight the row of field names and the data record row (see fig. 12.60). Next, the command prompts you for an output range for the table definition (see fig. 12.61). Remember that 1-2-3 overwrites existing data in this range. Figure 12.62 shows the resulting table definition.

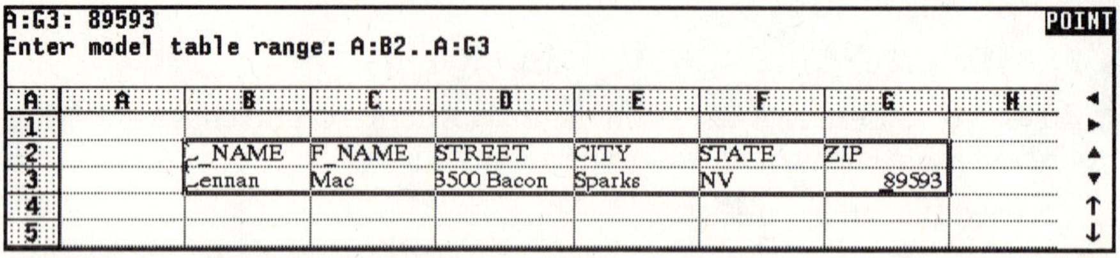

Fig. 12.60.
The prompt for an input range.

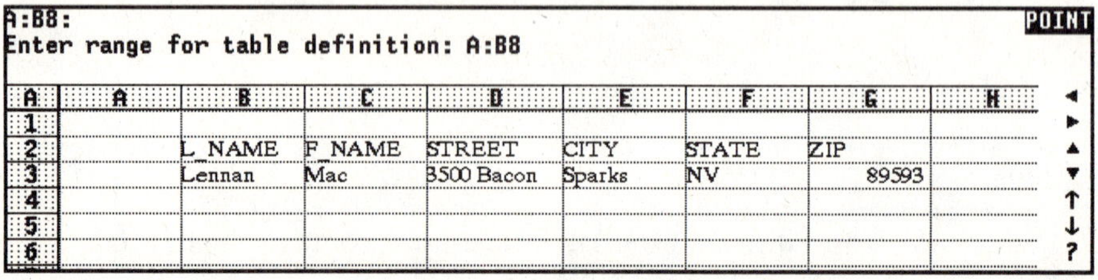

Fig. 12.61.
The prompt for an output range.

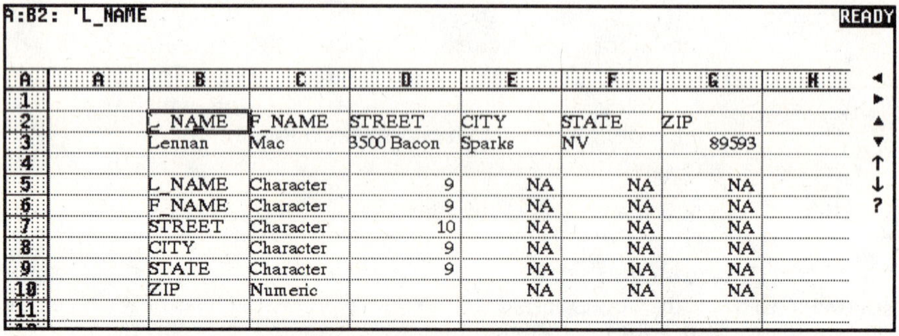

Fig. 12.62.
The resulting table definition.

To duplicate an external table, you first must establish a connection to that table and assign it a 1-2-3 range name. Then you use /Data External List Fields to create the table definition.

Creating a New Structure

To create a new external table with a new structure, you need to set up a table definition. If you look at figure 12.62, you can see that a table definition contains six columns and one row for each field in the table.

Column 1 contains the field names; this information is required.

Column 2 contains the data type of each field. Although 1-2-3 has only two data types (value and label), some external tables have additional data types. Refer to the database driver documentation for information on the data types supported.

Column 3 specifies the width, in characters, assigned to each field in the external table. Fields with a label data type always require a width; fields with a value data type may or may not require a width, depending on the database driver in use.

Column 4 may contain column labels, again depending on the database driver in use. A *column label* is an alternative label for a database field; such a label provides additional identification of the field. These labels are particularly useful for fields that have been assigned abbreviated field names. For example, the column label *part number* is more informative than the field name *pnum*.

Column 5 may contain field descriptions, depending on the database driver in use. A *field description* is another version of a column label.

Finally, column 6 may contain field-creation strings if they are required by the database driver in use. A *field-creation string* contains information needed by some database drivers to create a field in a new table. If your database driver requires field-creation strings, the details are explained in the database driver documentation.

If the database driver you are using does not require a certain piece of information, the corresponding location in the table description contains NA. The sample dBASE III driver provided does not use column labels, field descriptions, or field-creation strings. Thus, the corresponding locations in figure 12.62. contain NA.

You can use one of two approaches in creating a new table definition range. First, you can copy a table definition from an existing external table and then edit the definition to reflect the structure for the new external table. This method is usually the easier one. Second, you can type the table definition directly into a worksheet range. You use this method to create a new external table only if you know exactly what information is needed by the database driver in use.

Cue:
The easiest way to create a new table definition is to copy and then edit an existing one.

If you want to copy and modify an existing table definition, you can use the **/Data External List Fields** command to list information about that table. (Listing external tables is described in an earlier section.) The information provided by this command is actually a complete table definition.

The next step is to edit this information to reflect the structure you want the new external table to have. You edit the information as you would any other worksheet data. For example, you may need to make some of the following modifications: change field names, add or delete fields, change the order of the fields, change field widths and/or data types, add or modify column labels and field descriptions, or add field-creation strings if required.

Once the table has been named and the table definition is ready, you use the **/Data External Create Go** command to create the external table, and then use **/Data External Create Quit** to return to READY mode. You can now use the **Criteria, Extract, Input,** and **Output** commands on the **/Data Query** menu to copy data from worksheet databases or other external tables to this newly created table.

Deleting an External Table

You use the /**Data External Delete** command to delete external tables from the external database. As for the other /**Data External** commands, you must specify the database driver and database name, and then simply highlight the external table to be deleted (see fig. 12.63). The dBASE III SAMPLE driver provided does not support this command.

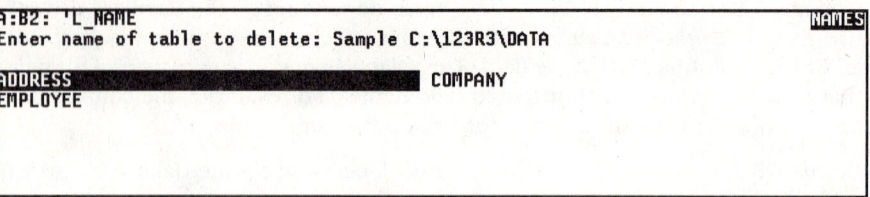

Fig. 12.63.
An external table highlighted for deletion.

Using Other /Data External Commands

In addition to the /**Data External** commands already discussed, you can use commands to update the table, send commands to the external database program, and use a different character set. When you select /**Data External Other**, the following menu appears:

    Refresh Command Translate

These options are discussed in the next sections.

/Data External Other Refresh

You use /**Data External Other Refresh** to specify the time interval at which Release 3 updates those worksheet portions that depend on data in an external table. When you are connected to a network and the external tables you are using may be modified by other users, you can use /**Data External Other Refresh** to ensure that the information in your worksheet is up-to-date.

The /**Data External Other Refresh** command offers the following options:

Option	Description
Automatic	Automatically updates the worksheet at a certain time interval
Manual	Does not automatically update the worksheet; updates must be done by the user
Interval	Specifies the time interval for **Automatic** refresh. The default is 1 second; you can enter any value from 0 through 3600 seconds (3600 seconds = 1 hour). The **Interval** setting has no effect if **Refresh** is set to **Manual**.

You can divide into two categories the worksheet components that depend on an external table: (1) formulas and database functions that depend on recalculation, and (2) /Data Query and /Data Table commands that do not depend on recalculation.

If you set /Data External Other Refresh to Automatic and also set worksheet recalculation to Automatic, all components of the worksheet are updated at the specified time interval.

If you set /Data External Other Refresh to Automatic but set worksheet recalculation to Manual (with /Worksheet Global Recalc), /Data Query and /Data Table commands are updated at the specified interval, but formulas and database functions are not. Formulas and database functions are updated only when a Calc (F9) command is executed.

If you set /Data External Other Refresh to Manual, you must update /Data Query and /Data Table commands manually. You must update formulas and database functions by issuing a Calc (F9) command.

1-2-3's background recalculation permits you to continue working during the recalculation process. If a recalculation cycle takes longer than the refresh interval, the next recalculation cycle begins immediately.

If you change the refresh interval with /Data External Other Refresh Interval, the new value is not saved with the worksheet. For the new value to be in effect for future work sessions, select /Worksheet Global Default Update.

/Data External Other Command

You use /Data External Other Command to send commands to a database management program, permitting you to perform database manipulations not possible with 1-2-3 alone. To use this command, 1-2-3 must be connected to an external table of a database management program having a database driver that supports this command. Again, the SAMPLE driver supplied does not support this command.

The capabilities of the commands you issue with /Data External Other Command (as well as the command syntax) depend on the database management program—the commands have no relationship to 1-2-3's database management commands. You must be familiar with the commands of the database program to which you want to send a command.

The /Data External Other Command prompts you first for the external table name, including driver and database, and then for the database command. The database command can be entered as either a string or the address of a cell that contains the command as a label. 1-2-3 sends the command and returns to READY mode.

Reminder:
To send commands to an external database program, use /Data External Other Command.

/Data External Other Translate

When transferring information to and from external tables, 1-2-3 normally copies each character exactly as it is found, with no modification. At times, however, you may be working with a database that was created with a character set different from the one for which your computer hardware is configured. With /Data External Other Translate, you can instruct 1-2-3 to use a different character set to translate between the external table and the worksheet.

To determine whether a particular external table requires translation, use the /Data Query commands to copy records from the external table to your worksheet. Examine the contents of the extracted records for strange-looking characters. If you find such characters, you may need to specify a translation character set. To translate an external table to which you are connected, you supply the full table name to the /Data External Other Translate command. The character sets available are displayed (see fig. 12.64). After you select the character set, the translation takes place, and 1-2-3 returns to READY mode.

Fig. 12.64.
The character sets available for translating the external table.

```
A:B2: 'L_NAME                                                        NAMES
Enter character set to use: United States (437)

United States (437)              Multilingual (850)
Portuguese (860)                 French-Canadian (863)
Nordic (865)
```

If only one character set is available, 1-2-3 automatically selects it. If more than one character set is available for the database in use, you may need to experiment to find the one that translates properly. The selected character set is used to translate all data transferred to and from all tables in the specified database, for the remainder of the current work session.

Disconnecting 1-2-3 and the External Table

Caution:
Once you break a connection, you lose the table range name; any formulas or queries that use this name may produce errors.

/Data External Reset severs the connection between 1-2-3 and an external table. If only one external table is in use, selecting /Data External Reset ends the connection to that table. If more than one table is in use, you must specify the database driver, database name, and table name of the specific table whose connection you want to break.

After you break the connection, the range name of the table becomes undefined. Any worksheet formulas or queries that use that range name may produce errors.

Summary

This chapter addressed all options on the /Data menu. **S**ort and **Q**uery, two options described extensively in the first half of the chapter, are true data management commands that require database organization by field name. **F**ill, **T**able, **D**istribution, **M**atrix, **R**egression, and **P**arse manipulate data and can be used in database or worksheet applications. **E**xternal enables you to access and modify data in files created by stand-alone database programs.

Data management is one of the advanced capabilities of 1-2-3. If you have mastered data management, you are a true "power user," and you probably are already using 1-2-3 macros. If not, be sure to continue your learning. Chapter 13 presents the creation and use of macros, and Chapter 14 introduces you to the powerful advanced macro commands.

Using Macros

13

Although 1-2-3's worksheet, database, and graphics features may provide much of the functionality you need, another feature of the program is often invaluable: the macro capability. Used in the most basic way, 1-2-3's macros provide a convenient method of automating the tasks you find yourself performing repeatedly, such as printing worksheets or changing global default settings. Macros and the advanced macro commands, however, enable you to do much more. You can construct sophisticated business applications that function, for example, in the same way as applications written in programming languages such as BASIC, C, or FORTRAN.

This chapter covers the following topics:

- The definition of a macro
- How to develop macros
- How to use the macro key names
- How to name and run macros
- How to plan the layout of a macro
- How to build a simple macro library
- How to use 1-2-3's Record feature to create and test macros
- How to document macros

The next chapter introduces you to the *advanced macro commands* (a set of advanced programming commands) and helps you learn the functions and applications of those commands.

Introducing Macros

Reminder:
Macros are short collections of keystrokes that 1-2-3 types for you.

The simplest macros are nothing more than keystrokes that 1-2-3 types for you. 1-2-3 stores these keystrokes in a cell as text which you can copy, edit, or move as you would any label. Consider the number of times you save and retrieve worksheet files, print reports, and perhaps set and reset worksheet formats. In each case, you perform the operation by typing a series of keystrokes—sometimes a rather lengthy series—on the computer keyboard. Using a macro, however, you can reduce any number of keystrokes to a simple two-keystroke abbreviation.

Consider a simple macro that enters text. Suppose, for example, that your company's name is *ABC Manufacturing, Incorporated*—an entry that takes 32 keystrokes to type in the worksheet (if you count pressing the Enter key). Suppose that you want to place this text in numerous locations in your worksheets. You can type the entry's 32 keystrokes or store them in a macro. If you store the keystrokes in a macro, the next time you want to type your company name, you can use just two keystrokes to invoke the macro, rather than 32 keystrokes to type the entire name. Later in this chapter, you learn how to create such a macro.

Developing Your Own Macros

The steps for creating any macro are basic and conform to the following outline. Later sections in this chapter give expanded detail on each of these steps.

Cue:
Planning your macro is an important step in the creation of the macro.

1. *Plan what you want the macro to do.* Write down the tasks you want the macro to perform and then arrange the steps in the order they should be completed.

2. *Identify the keystrokes the macro should repeat.* Keep in mind that macros are simply text (labels) that duplicate the keystrokes you want to replay.

3. *Find an area of the worksheet where you can enter macros.* When you choose the area, be aware that executed macros read text from cells starting with the top cell and working down through lower cells. Macros end when they come to a blank cell, a numeric cell, or a command that stops macro execution. Make certain that your macro stops executing where you want—leave at least one blank cell below it.

   Later in this chapter, you see that using 1-2-3 Release 3's 3-D capability enables you to store your macros in either a separate worksheet or a separate file. It's always a good idea to protect your macros by storing them in a different worksheet or file.

4. *Enter the keystrokes, keystroke equivalents, and commands into a cell or cells.* You must type an apostrophe (') before a slash (/) or backslash (\) to enter that keystroke in a cell as text rather than as a command request or as the repeating label-prefix. You also must type an apostrophe before a number, +, −, *, or (to enter that keystroke in a cell as text rather than as a number or formula.

Use range names rather than addresses in your macros. Addresses in a macro do not update when changes are made to the worksheet. As a consequence, moves, inserts, or deletions can cause a macro to use incorrect addresses. Creating your macros with range names instead of addresses corrects this problem, because range names in a macro (like range names in formulas) automatically update when the worksheet changes.

5. *Name the macro.* You can use one of three methods:
   - Assign an Alt-*letter* name, such as \a.
   - Choose a descriptive name, such as PRINT_BUDGET.
   - Use the name \0 (backslash zero) for a macro that runs automatically when the file is loaded.

6. *Document the macro.* You can document your macros in several ways. Using a descriptive name is a first step. You also can add comments in an adjacent column or use the /Range Name Note command.

Reminder:
Document the macro to help you remember what it does and why.

Even when your macros become more complex as your expertise increases, you always use these same basic steps to create a macro. Keep in mind that good planning and documentation are important for making macros run smoothly and efficiently.

Writing Some Sample Macros

The following sections explain how to write two simple macros. The first macro enters text into a cell. The second macro repeats commands specified in the macro. Later in this chapter, you learn to use the Record method of writing macros (see "Recording and Testing Macros").

Writing a Macro That Enters Text

In this section, you learn to create a macro that enters your company name in various locations in a worksheet.

Before you begin creating a macro, plan what you want the macro to do and then identify the keystrokes the macro is to type for you. In the case of a macro that enters a company name, you want the macro to type the letters, spaces, and punctuation that make up your company name. Then, as with any label, you want the macro to enter the typed characters into the cell by pressing the Enter key.

Cue:
Identify the keystrokes you want the macro to type for you.

You begin building your macro by storing the keystrokes as text in a worksheet cell. After manually typing the name, you enter a tilde (~) to represent the Enter key. If you forget to add the tilde at the end of your macro, 1-2-3 acts just as if you were entering the keystrokes at the keyboard and hadn't pressed Enter yet. Forgetting the tilde is the most common mistake macro writers make.

Cue:
Store the keystrokes for a macro as text in a worksheet cell.

Cell B3 in figure 13.1 shows the keystrokes, including the Enter (~) keystroke, that you want 1-2-3 to type for you as part of the macro:

```
ABC Manufacturing, Incorporated~
```

After you enter the text you want the macro to type for you, the next step is to name this sequence of keystrokes as a macro. To name this macro, follow these steps:

1. Move the cell pointer to cell B3 and select the /Range Name Create command.
2. At the `Enter name to create:` prompt, type the name **\n**. The backslash (\) represents the Alt key.
3. At the `Enter range:` prompt, specify the range to be named as the cell holding the keystrokes—in this case, cell A:B3. Because the cell pointer is already in this cell, you can just press Enter to accept B3.
4. Document the macro as shown in figure 13.1. Type the macro name one cell to the left of the first line of the macro—in this case, in cell A3. Documenting the macro in this way helps you remember the macro's name.

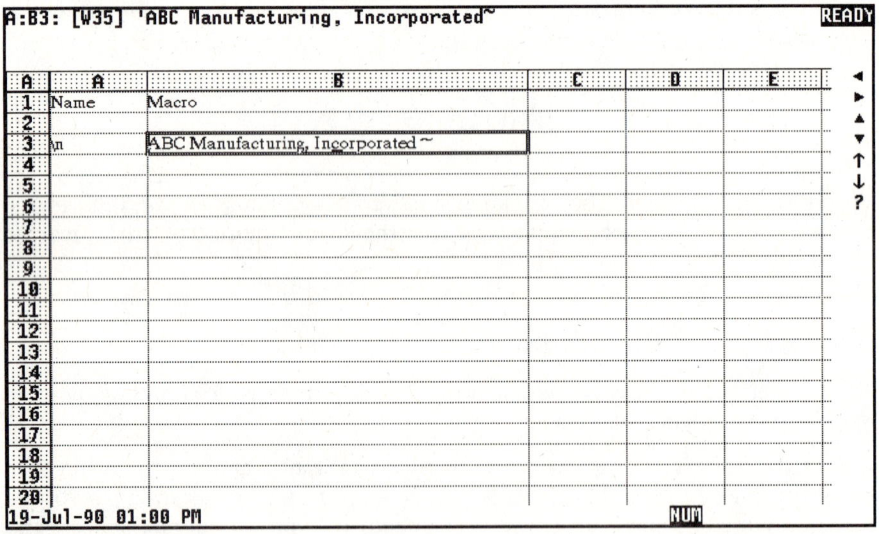

Fig. 13.1.
A simple macro for entering a company name.

Reminder:
Most users place the macro name in the cell to the left of the macro.

Note: Since the early days of 1-2-3, most texts have suggested placing the macro name in the cell to the *left* of the macro so that you can use the /Range Name Labels Right command to apply the name to the macro. Experienced programmers used to other programming languages often place the macro name in the cell immediately *above* the macro. The method you choose is up to you—1-2-3 doesn't require the macro names to be entered at all; they serve as documentation only.

To *execute*, or *run*, this simple macro, all you need to do is move the cell pointer to the cell where you want the company name to appear, press and hold the Alt key, and then press N. 1-2-3 enters the sequence of characters identified as the macro \n. Figure 13.2 shows the results of moving the cell pointer to B10 and then running the \n macro. To save this macro for future use, save the file in which the macro is located.

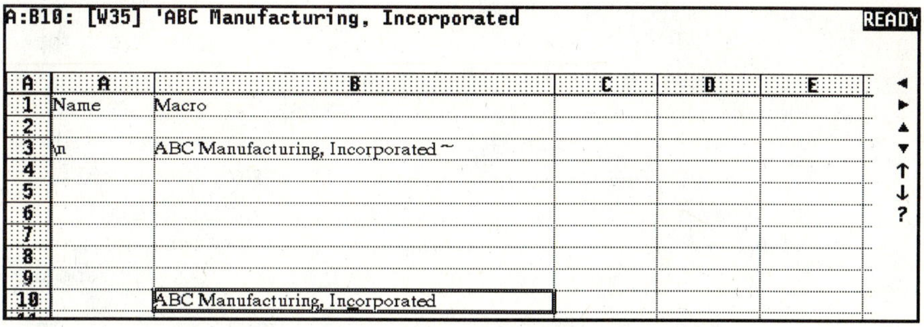

Fig. 13.2.
The results of running the \n macro.

Writing a Simple Command Macro

In addition to macros that repeat text, you can write macros that repeat commands. If you follow the same procedure each time, you find that macro writing can become second nature. This section describes a simple macro that enters commands. You use the same steps to create and name the macro that you used when you created and named the macro that entered the company name.

First, plan what you want the command macro to do. For instance, create a macro that changes the column width from the default 9-character width to 14. The keystrokes you normally use to enter this command are as follows:

1. Press the slash key (/) to access the 1-2-3 menu
2. Select **Worksheet**
3. Select **Column**
4. Select **Set-Width**
5. Enter the number for the desired column width (**14** in this example)
6. Press Enter

You can create a macro named \c to perform these same operations. When you type this macro into a cell, it should look like this (remember to type an apostrophe before the slash):

'/wcs14~

Notice that each character of the macro is what you normally press on the keyboard to enter this command. The tilde (~), for example, represents pressing the Enter key.

Reminder:
The tilde (~) represents pressing the Enter key.

Next, you need to name the macro. Because the macro changes the *column* width, name the macro \c. (The backslash represents the Alt key.) After the macro is given a name, you can press and hold the Alt key, and then press C to start the macro. Remember that the name you assign to the macro should remind you of the macro's function. In this case, the macro is named \c because it sets the *column* width.

In the following steps, you create the macro name, which you use to run the macro, and document the name by placing it in the worksheet:

1. Type the macro name one cell to the left of the first line of the macro. If the text of the macro is in cell AA1, for example, type the name of the macro in cell Z1. Not only does this step document the name of the macro, it aids you in naming the macro.

2. With the cursor in cell Z1, choose the /**R**ange **N**ame **L**abels **R**ight command and press Enter. This command uses the label in cell Z1 (the macro name) to name the macro one cell to the right (in cell AA1).

3. To document the macro further, type an explanation next to each line of the macro. Place the explanation one cell to the right of each line of the macro. Figure 13.3 shows the \c macro with appropriate documentation.

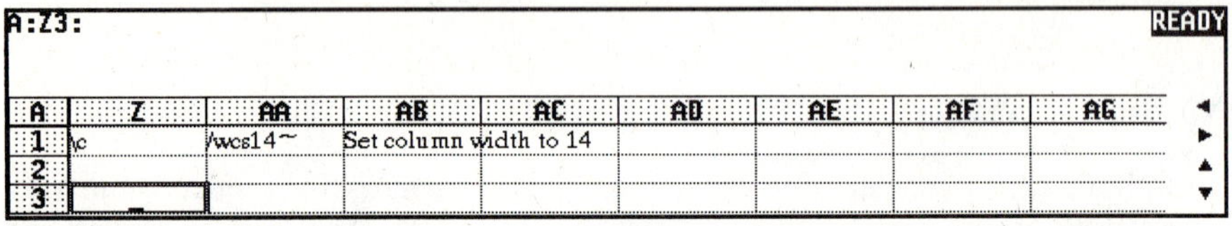

Fig. 13.3.
A simple command macro.

```
A:Z3:                                                           READY
   A       Z       AA        AB        AC        AD    AE    AF    AG
1         \c      /wcs14~   Set column width to 14
2
3
```

Using Macro Key Names

Reminder:
1-2-3 uses some special characters or words as equivalents for some keys and combinations of keys.

Because many keys on your keyboard aren't identifiable by obvious characters, 1-2-3 uses some special characters or words as equivalents for some keys and combinations of keys. Table 13.1 summarizes these *key names*—the special characters and words you use in macros to represent keystrokes that don't have obvious alphanumeric characters. Many of these key names are used in the examples throughout this chapter. (See Chapters 2 and 3 for explanations of the movement and function keys.)

Note: Some 1-2-3 keys, such as the tilde (~) and the braces ({ }), have special meanings in 1-2-3 macros. If you want to use these keys in a macro without invoking 1-2-3's special meanings, enclose them in braces ({ }). For example, to have a macro enter a tilde as a character (rather than interpreting the tilde as the Enter key), type {~} in the macro.

Table 13.1
Summary of Macro Key Names

1-2-3 Key	*Macro Key Name*
/ (slash) or < (less than)	/ or {MENU}
~ (tilde)	{~}
{ (open brace)	{{}
} (close brace)	{}}
↓	{DOWN} or {D}

1-2-3 Key	Macro Key Name
↑	{UP} or {U}
←	{LEFT} or {L}
→	{RIGHT} or {R}
Backspace	{BACKSPACE} or {BS}
(No keyboard equivalent; clears entry in EDIT mode)	{CE} or {CLEARENTRY}
Big Left (Ctrl-←) or BackTab (Shift-Tab)	{BIGLEFT}
Big Right (Ctrl-→) or Tab	{BIGRIGHT}
Ctrl-Break in MENU mode	{BREAK}
File (Ctrl-End)	{FILE}
Prev File (Ctrl-End Ctrl-PgDn)	{PREVFILE} or {PF} or {FILE}{PS}
First File (Ctrl-End Home)	{FIRSTFILE} or {FF} or {FILE}{HOME}
Last File (Ctrl-End End)	{LASTFILE} or {LF} or {FILE}{END}
Next File (Ctrl-End Ctrl-PgUp)	{NEXTFILE} or {NF} or {FILE}{NS}
First Cell (Ctrl-Home)	{FIRSTCELL} or {FC}
Prev Sheet (Ctrl-PgDn)	{PREVSHEET} or {PS}
Next Sheet (Ctrl-PgUp)	{NEXTSHEET} or {NS}
Del	{DELETE} or {DEL}
End	{END}
Last Cell (End Ctrl-Home)	{LASTCELL} or {LC}
Enter	~
Esc	{ESCAPE} or {ESC}
Help (F1)	{HELP}
Edit (F2)	{EDIT}
Name (F3)	{NAME}
Abs (F4)	{ABS}
GoTo (F5)	{GOTO}
Window (F6)	{WINDOW}
Query (F7)	{QUERY}
Table (F8)	{TABLE}
Calc (F9)	{CALC}
Graph (F10)	{GRAPH}
Zoom (Alt-F6)	{ZOOM}
App1 (Alt-F7)	{APP1}
App2 (Alt-F8)	{APP2}
App3 (Alt-F9)	{APP3}

continued

Table 13.1—(continued)

1-2-3 Key	Macro Key Name
Add-In (Alt-F10)	{ADDIN} or {APP4}
Home	{HOME}
Ins	{INS} or {INSERT}
PgDn or PageDown	{PGDN}
PgUp or PageUp	{PGUP}

You may have noticed that a few keys are not included in the table. These include Caps Lock, Compose (Alt-F1), Num Lock, Print Screen, Record (Alt-F2), Run (Alt-F3), Scroll Lock, and Shift. You cannot use these keystrokes in macros (although you see in later sections that the Run command does have a macro substitute).

Guidelines for Developing Macros

Earlier in this chapter, you learned how to write simple macros. You learned the importance of planning the macro and identifying the keystrokes the macro should perform. The following sections elaborate on the additional elements of successful macro creation and execution. These elements include formatting the macro, naming and running the macro, planning the layout of the macro, documenting the macro, and protecting the macro.

Formatting Macros

Certain formatting features are necessary to ensure the successful operation of 1-2-3 macros. Other conventions simplify the tasks of reading and analyzing your macros. These tasks are particularly important when you need to debug or edit a macro by changing or adding an operation.

The following list outlines certain rules you should follow so that your macros run properly:

1. When you type a macro into the worksheet, each cell of the macro must be entered as text. Certain keystrokes (such as numbers) cause 1-2-3 to change from READY mode to VALUE mode; other keystrokes (for example, the /) change 1-2-3 to MENU mode. Therefore, you must place an apostrophe (') before any of the following characters if you are typing that character as the first character in a macro cell:

    - A number from 0 to 9
    - /, +, -, @, #, $, ., <, (, or \

    The apostrophe (') switches 1-2-3 to LABEL mode from READY mode. Using an apostrophe before any of the preceding characters and numbers ensures that 1-2-3 does not misinterpret your text entry. If any character not in this list is the first keystroke in the cell, 1-2-3 automatically switches to LABEL mode, and 1-2-3 prefixes the entry with an apostrophe (') when you press Enter.

2. Macro key names should be entered as listed in table 13.1. Be sure to use braces to enclose the representations for function, movement, editing, and special keys.

   Two examples are {EDIT} and {DOWN}. When you use 1-2-3 key names in your macros, you must keep the entire key name in the same cell. Splitting the key name {EDIT} into two cells—{ED in one cell and IT} in the cell that follows—does not work. You should also be careful not to mix braces with parentheses. In other words, avoid a construction such as {DOWN).

   Reminder: *Don't split key names across cells in a macro.*

3. The syntax for advanced macro commands must be correct. See the tables in Chapter 14 for the correct syntax for all the macro commands used in 1-2-3. You must place each macro command within a single cell; you cannot write a macro command so that the opening brace is on one line and the closing brace is on another line.

4. You use the tilde (~) in a macro to represent the action of pressing the Enter key.

5. A macro can contain empty cells when such cells are filled by the macro. Suppose, for example, that you keep a list of file names in a separate worksheet. You can create a macro to retrieve any of the names in that list. The macro should contain one empty cell. When the macro runs, the file name on which you have placed the cell pointer is copied into the blank cell in the macro. When the /File Retrieve operation begins, 1-2-3 then retrieves the file whose name was copied into the blank cell.

6. Use repetition factors in macros whenever possible. For example, instead of typing {LEFT} three times, you can simply type {LEFT 3} or {L 3}. When you use repetition factors, be sure to place one space between the actual key name and the number of repetitions.

Naming and Running Macros

Depending on how you name a macro, you execute it in one of the following ways:

◆ Macros named with \ and a single letter can be executed with either Alt-*letter* or Run (Alt-F3).

◆ Macros named with a descriptive name of up to 15 characters can be executed with Run (Alt-F3).

◆ Macros named with \0 are executed when the file is loaded, and can also be executed with Run (Alt-F3).

Reminder: *You can name and run macros in three ways.*

Earlier in this chapter, you saw examples of the first method of running a macro; that is, by holding the Alt key and pressing a single letter key. Using the second method, you assign a descriptive name to the first cell of the range that holds the macro and execute it by pressing Run (Alt-F3), selecting the macro name from a list, and pressing Enter. The third method creates an automatic macro named \0; the macro is executed automatically when you load the file.

Notice that you can run any of the three types of macros with the Run (Alt-F3) key. Depending on how you name a macro, however, the macro also can be executed using alternative keystrokes or automatically.

> **Reminder:**
> *You can run any macro by pressing Run (Alt-F3) and selecting the macro name.*

Invoking a macro in Release 3 with the Run (Alt-F3) key is a much more user-friendly approach than the Alt-*letter* method available in early versions of 1-2-3. Selecting Run (Alt-F3) displays a prompt and a list of macro names from which you choose the macro you want to run.

Although you use the \0 name only when you want to invoke a macro automatically as soon as a file is retrieved, you can opt to use either the Alt-*letter* or descriptive name for any other macro. You have advantages with each type of name, however. Invoking a macro with an Alt-*letter* name can involve fewer keystrokes (if selected by pressing Alt and the letter) than invoking a macro that has a descriptive name. The disadvantage to using Alt-*letter* macro names, however, is that you may have difficulty remembering the specific functions of the macros, particularly when you have created many macros. Your chances of selecting the right macro are greater when you use descriptive names.

The following sections describe all three approaches to creating, naming, and running macros.

Using Alt-*Letter* Macros

As described earlier, one way to name a macro is using the backslash key (\) and a letter character. In earlier releases of 1-2-3, this was the only way you could name macros. A simple macro introduced earlier in this chapter, for example, was named \n. You can use either uppercase or lowercase letters to type the name of this macro; 1-2-3 doesn't differentiate between uppercase and lowercase for range names. You must, however, limit yourself to letters. Accordingly, \a, \B, and \C all are valid names for Alt-*letter* macros.

> **Reminder:**
> *1-2-3 uses the macro in the currently active file if more than one file is loaded into memory with the same macro name.*

To run a macro named with the backslash (\) and a letter character, press and hold the Alt key and then press the letter character that identifies the macro. For example, to run a macro named \c, you press Alt-C. If you have more than one file loaded into memory when you invoke a macro, and the same macro range name exists in more than one of the files, 1-2-3 uses the macro in the currently active file.

Using Macros with Descriptive Names

In 1-2-3 Release 3, you can give macros descriptive names. Instead of naming a macro to print your worksheet \p, for example, you can name it PRINT_BUDGET. You can have a descriptive name as long as 15 characters (the same length allowed for naming ranges). As a result, your macro names can be more descriptive and help with documentation.

Chapter 13 ◆ Using Macros

Avoid using macro names that also are used as 1-2-3 keystroke equivalents, such as CALC or RIGHT, or as one of the advanced macro commands listed in Chapter 14. Doing so leads to unpredictable and often incorrect results. Also avoid using cell addresses (such as IC1 or A4) as macro names. In addition, you should avoid the use of cell addresses within the macro; use range names (such as BUDGET) so the macro continues to function properly even if the range moves when you modify the worksheet.

Cue:
Give macros descriptive names, but avoid using the names of 1-2-3 keyboard equivalents.

Figure 13.4 shows four macros that demonstrate many of the rules and conventions for naming and running macros. Each of these macros is discussed in detail in "Building a Simple Macro Library," later in this chapter. Here they are used only to demonstrate the three ways to name and run a macro.

```
A:A11: [W14]                                                    READY

      A           B              C                    D
 1  Name        Macro          Description of macro
 2
 3    \s        /ppos{CE}015~qq  Sets printer setup string to 015
 4
 5  PRINT_BUDGET /pprBUDGET~gq   Prints the range named BUDGET
 6
 7    \0        /wgrm           Sets recalculation to manual
 8
 9  NEWSHEET    /wisa~          Adds a worksheet after the current one
10
11
```

Fig. 13.4.
Four macros that demonstrate naming rules.

Note: Before you run a macro, be sure that you've correctly positioned the cell pointer or that the macro positions the cell pointer correctly. That is, make sure that the cell pointer is in the cell where you want the macro to insert its text or start performing its commands.

To run any macro, press Run (Alt-F3). 1-2-3 lists all the range names in the current file. If you have other active files, 1-2-3 also lists these names. Figure 13.5 shows the full-screen listing of all range names that results after pressing Run (Alt-F3) and then pressing Name (F3).

Cue:
To run any macro, press Run (Alt-F3).

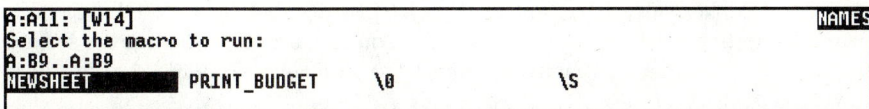

```
A:A11: [W14]                                                    NAMES
Select the macro to run:
A:B9..A:B9
NEWSHEET         PRINT_BUDGET      \0              \s
```

Fig. 13.5.
A list of range names in the current file.

You can select the macro you want to run from the list of macro names displayed in one of three ways. The first way is to highlight the name and press Enter. If you want to see the range names from one of the other active files, highlight the name of that file and press Enter; 1-2-3 then displays the range names from that file.

Reminder:
Active files are those in memory that you've either retrieved or opened.

The second method is to type the name of the macro or its starting address, and then press Enter. If you type the address without identifying the file, 1-2-3 assumes that you mean the *current file*. If you type an abbreviated address or one that doesn't include the worksheet letter, 1-2-3 assumes that you mean the *current worksheet*.

Reminder:
The current file and current worksheet are where the cell pointer is located.

For example, to execute a macro located in cell A1 in worksheet A in the file named BUDGET90.WK3, type the following:

    <<BUDGET90.WK3>>A:A1

Suppose that you want to execute a macro in cell A1 in worksheet A in file BUDGET90.WK3, and you are already working in that file. If worksheet B is current, press Run (Alt-F3) and enter the following:

    A:A1

The third approach to running a macro is to press the Esc key once after pressing Run (Alt-F3) to enter POINT mode. In POINT mode, you can move the cell pointer to the first cell of the macro (or the cell of the macro where you want to start executing the macro) and press Enter to execute the macro.

Using the third approach is best when you want to see the actual contents of a macro before executing it. This is especially useful when you are testing a new macro. The second method, typing the name or starting address of the macro, is useful when you want to invoke a macro located in a different file than the file you are currently working in. The first method, highlighting the macro name, is easiest, most intuitive, and less error-prone than the other two.

Using Macros That Execute Automatically

You may want some macros to run automatically when the worksheet is retrieved. For example, perhaps you always want to move the cell pointer to the end of a column. A handy trick, then, is to name a macro using the backslash key and the number 0. When you name a macro \0, 1-2-3 runs that macro whenever the file is loaded.

You also can use this feature in advanced macro command programs. For example, when you construct your own menus for a worksheet model, you may want the advanced macro command program to start automatically and place the first custom menu on the screen.

Reminder:
\0 macros work automatically as long as the /Worksheet Global Default Autoexec setting is Yes.

Caution: \0 macros work automatically as long as the /**W**orksheet **G**lobal **D**efault **A**utoexec setting is **Y**es, which is the default. You can, however, change the setting to **N**o, in which case \0 macros are not automatically executed when a file is retrieved or opened.

Figure 13.6 shows an automatic macro that moves the cursor to the bottom of column D. It tells 1-2-3 to perform the following keystrokes: press GoTo (F5), type D7, press Enter, press the End key, and then press the down-arrow key twice to move to the bottom of the column. These keystrokes are automatically performed when you create the macro, save the file, and then retrieve the file again.

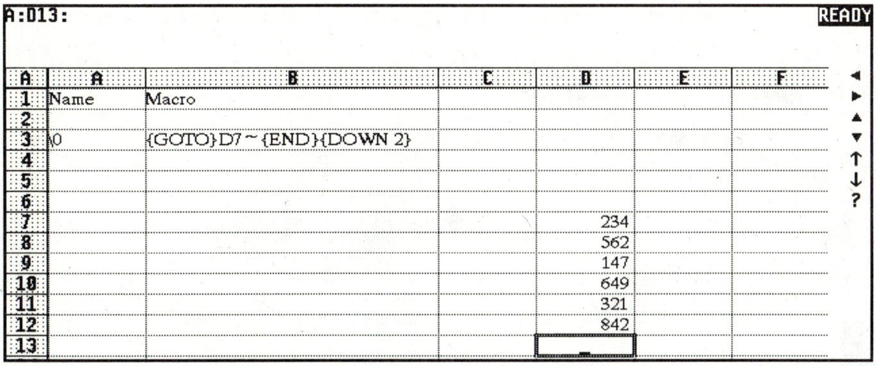

Fig. 13.6.

An automatic macro named \0.

Notice that the actual contents of cell B3 are as follows:

```
'{GOTO}D7~{END}{DOWN 2}
```

Because a macro is actually a text label, it is preceded by a label prefix—in this case, an apostrophe. You can use any of the label prefixes: ', ^, ", or \. The most common prefix, however, is the apostrophe.

To practice the method described in the preceding text, type the numbers in cells D7 through D12, as shown in figure 13.6. Next, type the keystrokes the macro performs: press F5, type **D7**, and press Enter; then press the End key once, notice the END indicator at the bottom of the screen, and press the down-arrow key twice. You have just accomplished what the macro is to perform.

Now move the cell pointer to cell B3, type the label prefix ' and the characters shown in cell B3 of figure 13.6. 1-2-3 collects the keystrokes as a label. By pressing Enter, you enter the label into cell B3.

Type '**\0** in cell A3. Then select /**R**ange **N**ame **L**abels **R**ight and press Enter with the cell pointer on cell A3. Save the worksheet and then retrieve it. You see that the macro works automatically. If you want to repeat the macro after it runs when the file is retrieved, press Run (Alt-F3) and select \0 from the list of macro range names.

Planning the Layout of a Macro

Although a macro containing fewer than 512 characters can be entered in one cell, you should get into the practice of breaking a long macro apart down a column of cells. Limit each cell to a single task or a few simple tasks and you can more easily debug, modify, and document a macro.

Figure 13.7, for example, shows two macros that execute the same sequence of keystrokes. The macros in figure 13.7 are enhancements of the macro in figure 13.1. Both enter the company name, move down two rows, enter the address, move down two rows again, and enter the city, state and ZIP. One macro is named \a and the other is named \b. In both cases, the range named is only one cell. \a is the range name given to the macro that starts in B3, and \b is the range name given to the macro that starts in B5.

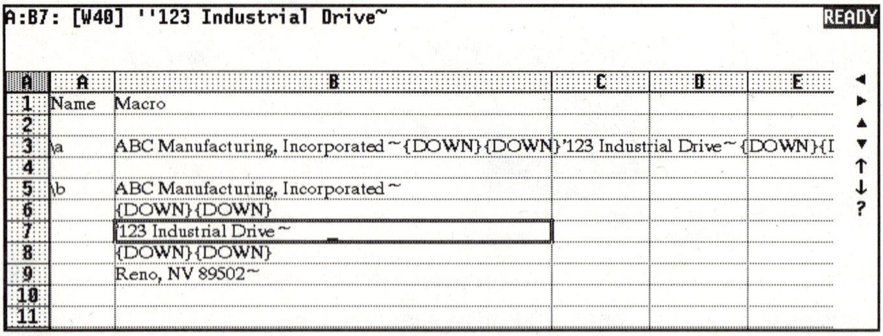

Fig. 13.7.

Two ways to store the keystrokes that make up a macro.

```
A:B7: [W40] ''123 Industrial Drive~                                    READY

       A          B                                          C         D         E
  1   Name       Macro
  2
  3   \a         ABC Manufacturing, Incorporated ~{DOWN}{DOWN}'123 Industrial Drive~{DOWN}{
  4
  5   \b         ABC Manufacturing, Incorporated ~
  6              {DOWN}{DOWN}
  7              '123 Industrial Drive ~
  8              {DOWN}{DOWN}
  9              Reno, NV 89502~
 10
 11
```

Reminder:

Keystrokes are executed starting at the cell in the upper left corner of the range.

The \b macro works correctly whether you name just cell B5 or the range of cells B5..B9. Keep in mind that for both simple keystroke macros and advanced macro command programs, the keystrokes are executed starting at the cell in the upper left corner of the range. After the keystrokes in B5 are executed, the macro moves down one cell and executes any keystrokes in that cell. Similarly, after completing those keystrokes, the macro again moves down one cell. The macro continues to move down and read until it encounters an empty cell, a cell that contains a numeric value, an error, or an advanced macro command that explicitly stops a macro. (These circumstances are discussed in Chapter 14.)

Although both macros perform the same functions, the \b macro is easier to read because it breaks the task down into simple steps:

1. Type the company name
2. Position the cell pointer
3. Type the address
4. Position the cell pointer again
5. Type the city, state, and ZIP

Macros are easier to read and understand later if you logically separate keystrokes and key names into separate cells. When you use key names such as {GOTO} and {NAME}, however, you must keep the entire key name in the same cell. Splitting the key name {NAME} into two cells—{NA in one cell and ME} in the cell that follows—doesn't work.

Cue:

Repeat certain key names by including a repetition factor.

Here's one other helpful hint: 1-2-3 allows you to repeat certain key names by including a *repetition factor*. A repetition factor tells 1-2-3 that you want a command repeated the specified number of times. Figure 13.8 shows another example of the same keystrokes performed by the \a and \b macros in figure 13.7. The \c macro uses a repetition factor to repeat the {DOWN} key name. Rather than typing {**DOWN**} two times, for example, you can simply type {**DOWN 2**} or {**D 2**} to repeat the {DOWN} key name. When you use a repetition factor, be sure to leave a space between the actual key name and the number.

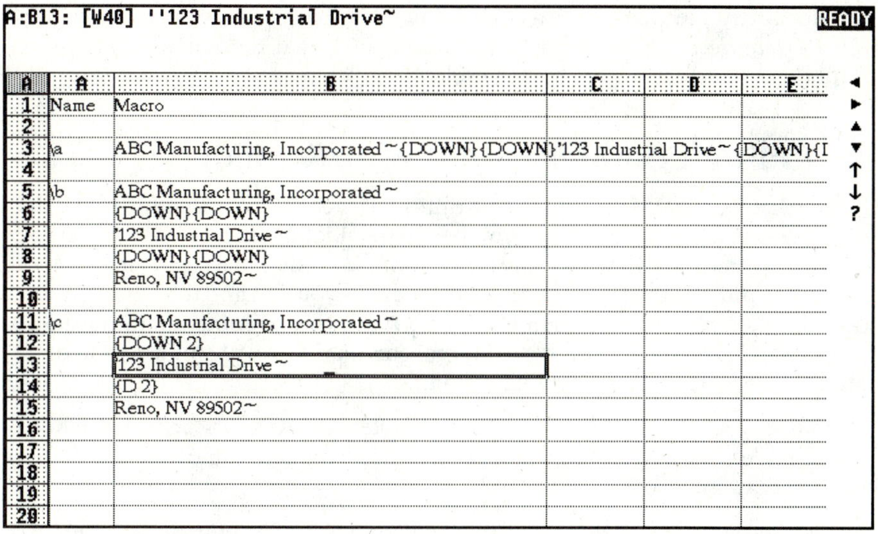

```
A:B13: [W40] ''123 Industrial Drive~                                    READY

         A    │            B                    │      C          │  D   │  E
     1  Name  Macro
     2
     3   \a   ABC Manufacturing, Incorporated ~{DOWN}{DOWN}'123 Industrial Drive~{DOWN}{D
     4
     5   \b   ABC Manufacturing, Incorporated ~
     6        {DOWN}{DOWN}
     7        '123 Industrial Drive ~
     8        {DOWN}{DOWN}
     9        Reno, NV 89502 ~
    10
    11   \c   ABC Manufacturing, Incorporated ~
    12        {DOWN 2}
    13        '123 Industrial Drive ~
    14        {D 2}
    15        Reno, NV 89502 ~
    16
    17
    18
    19
    20
```

Fig. 13.8.
A repetition factor used in the \c macro to repeat a key name.

Documenting Macros

As with other parts of a 1-2-3 worksheet, you should document your macros. You can document macros using many of the same techniques you use to document worksheets. Use the following techniques:

Reminder:
Use several techniques to document your macros.

- Use descriptive names as macro names.
- Use the /**R**ange **N**ame **N**ote feature.
- Include comments within your worksheet.
- Keep any external design notes.

Using Descriptive Names

Previous releases of 1-2-3 allowed only the backslash and a letter to name a macro. Although easy to execute, these names weren't very descriptive. Using descriptive macro names is better; use the Run (Alt-F3) key to execute macros with descriptive names.

Using the /Range Name Note Feature

Another 1-2-3 feature you can use to document your macros is /**R**ange **N**ame **N**ote, which allows you to attach a note to a range name. (Range name notes are described in detail along with other /**R**ange commands in Chapter 4.) You should find the /**R**ange **N**ame **N**ote capability particularly valuable in documenting macros originally created in previous releases of 1-2-3 and named with the backslash and a single letter. If you have a print macro named \p, for example, you

Cue:
Use /Range Name Note to document your macros.

can document the macro with a range name note that gives the description *Prints the 1991 budget*. This note gives you an idea of what the macro does without requiring you to review the macro itself.

Including Comments in the Worksheet

Reminder:
Comments provide information on what a macro is supposed to do and how it is supposed to do it.

Notice that figure 13.4 includes a description of each macro's function to the right of the actual macro. With these simple macros, identifying the tasks the macros perform is fairly easy. With longer and more complex macros—such as those discussed and demonstrated in the next chapter—you will find this sort of internal documentation immensely helpful. Later, when you or someone else wants to make changes in the macro, these internal comments provide information on the macro's purpose and its intended action.

Of course, you may not have to include complete documentation for each line of macro code. The following guidelines can help you determine a proper level of documentation:

- ◆ Simple macros using descriptive names may not require any additional documentation if their actions are quite clear.
- ◆ Notes that explain the overall operation of a macro instead of a note for each line are appropriate for macros that are less clear.
- ◆ Very complex macros and those that change during operation (such as by inserting a file name) should be fully documented.

Keeping External Design Notes

Cue:
Retain any paperwork you created as part of designing and constructing a macro.

Be sure to retain any paperwork you created as part of designing and constructing a macro. As with each form of macro documentation, this material eases considerably the burden of trying later to understand or modify a macro.

The most important piece of external documentation—which never should be neglected—is a hard copy printout of the macro. Examples of other external documentation that may be particularly valuable include notes on who requested a macro and why they requested it, who created a macro and who tested it, the underlying assumptions that determined the overall design, and any diagrams or outlines of macro operations or structure.

Protecting Macros

Warning:
Carefully locate your macros in the worksheet to protect them from accidental erasure.

If you create worksheet applications to be used by others, secure the macros to prevent their accidental erasure or alteration. Unlike most "programs," such as database management systems, 1-2-3 data and programs are in the same files. Even if you put all your macros into separate files, the files are still 1-2-3 worksheet files; they can be changed by anyone who knows 1-2-3 well enough.

Many users create macros in the same worksheet that contains the models with which the macros are to be used. You can, however, maintain a separate worksheet file containing nothing but macros (see the "Building a Simple Macro Library" section). Using a macro library is the best way to manage a large number of frequently used macros.

Most users store macros customized for particular applications in the same file that contains the application. In these instances, place the macros together—outside the area occupied by the main model. Storing the macros together makes it easier for you to find a macro for editing, and also helps you to avoid accidentally overwriting or erasing part of a macro as you create the model.

Generally, place the macros in a separate worksheet within the same file. For example, place the data in worksheet A and the macros in worksheet B. Be sure that your macros position the cell pointer in the correct worksheet. If you use this storage approach, you can avoid some common problems. Suppose, for example, that you want to use 1-2-3 commands to insert or delete columns or rows. When you use these commands—either manually or within macros—the macros may become corrupted if they are placed in the same worksheet. If you store your macros in a separate worksheet, you can use the /Worksheet Global Group Disable command to prevent inserted or deleted rows or columns from affecting the worksheet containing your macros.

Tip:
Use /Worksheet Global Group Disable to prevent inserted or deleted rows or columns from affecting the macros.

Inserting or deleting columns or rows also can cause problems with cell addresses used in macros because changes in cell references that occur as a result of the insertion or deletion are not reflected in the macros. Accordingly, use range names instead of cell addresses in macros.

Placing your macros in a separate worksheet also enables you to hide the macros if you want. To hide an entire worksheet, use the /Worksheet Hide Enable command and specify the letter of the worksheet that you want to hide.

Building a Simple Macro Library

A *macro library* is a file that contains macros you use frequently. By constructing a separate file that holds commonly used macros or by storing them in a separate worksheet within a file, you can run these macros anytime they are loaded. Such a library of macros can then be used with any of your worksheets.

Cue:
Construct a separate file that holds commonly used macros.

The macros shown in figure 13.4 can be the basis of a macro library. Each of these macros is described in the following sections along with some additional tips and techniques for writing and using macros.

A Macro To Define Printer Setup Strings

The first macro shown in figure 13.4 sets the printer setup string as 015. The actual sequence of keystrokes is stored in cell B3 as follows:

```
'/ppos{CE}015~qq
```

> **Reminder:**
> {CE} doesn't have a keyboard equivalent.

If you have ever defined a printer setup string, you may be familiar with most of the sequence that makes up this macro. Macro execution starts with an apostrophe (the label prefix), and then the / (slash), which activates the 1-2-3 menu. The letters *ppos* select the menu commands **P**rint **P**rinter **O**ptions **S**etup.

{CE}, which you also can write as {CLEARENTRY}, is a special macro key name that doesn't have a keyboard equivalent. {CE} clears the edit line of all data when 1-2-3 is in EDIT mode. In the case of this macro, {CE} clears any printer setup string that already has been entered. The number *015* is, in fact, a common printer setup string used to produce compressed print on many printers. The ~ (tilde) enters the setup string. Finally, the letters *qq* quit both the **P**rinter **O**ptions menu and the **/P**rint menu.

If you have difficulty visualizing the sequence of keystrokes, try typing them yourself starting with the slash key (/), which activates the 1-2-3 menu. Because {CE} doesn't have a keyboard equivalent, you won't be able to type that part of the macro sequence. Instead, use the Backspace or Esc key to remove any printer setup string you had previously defined.

The name of this macro is entered as \s in cell A3, the cell to the left of the cell storing the actual macro (B3). Select **/R**ange **N**ame **C**reate to name the macro. At the prompts, type the name **\s** and the cell address **B3**.

You can run this macro in any of three ways:

1. Press Alt-S.
2. Press Run (Alt-F3) and then choose the macro range name \s by highlighting that item on the list of range names that appears. Press Enter.
3. Press Run (Alt-F3), press the Esc key, and move the cell pointer to the cell that contains the appropriate macro: B3. Press Enter.

A Macro To Print a Report

The second macro shown in figure 13.4 prints the worksheet range BUDGET using the keystrokes stored in cell B5:

    '/pprBUDGET~gq

The macro starts with an apostrophe (the label prefix) and the / (slash), which activates the 1-2-3 menu. The letters *ppr* select the menu commands **P**rint **P**rinter **R**ange. *BUDGET* represents the name of the range you want to print. The ~ (tilde) sets the print range just as pressing the Enter key does. The letter *g* gives the **G**o print command. The letter *q* quits the menu.

> **Reminder:**
> Giving macros descriptive names makes remembering the names and purposes of macros easier.

The name of this macro, PRINT_BUDGET, is defined using the **/R**ange **N**ame **C**reate command and is documented in the cell A5, to the left of cell B5, which stores the actual macro. Because the macro is named with a descriptive range name, you run the macro using Run (Alt-F3).

A Macro To Set Worksheet Recalculation

The third macro shown in figure 13.4 sets the worksheet recalculation to manual. The keystrokes, which simply mirror the ones you use manually, are shown in cell B7:

    '/wgrm

Because the macro's name, documented in cell A7, is \0, the macro automatically executes whenever the file that contains this macro is retrieved or opened (as long as the /**W**orksheet **G**lobal **D**efault **A**utoexec setting is **Y**es). The macro starts with an apostrophe (the label prefix) and / (slash), which activates the 1-2-3 menu. The letters *wgrm* select the menu commands **W**orksheet **G**lobal **R**ecalc **M**anual.

In addition to running this macro automatically as part of retrieving or opening the file, you also can run this macro at other times. To run the macro, press Run (Alt-F3), and then choose the macro range name \0 by highlighting it on the list of range names that appears and pressing Enter. Another way to run the macro is to press Run (Alt-F3), and then the Esc key, move the cell pointer to the cell that contains the appropriate macro (in this case B7), and press Enter.

A Macro To Add a New Worksheet

The fourth macro in figure 13.4, named NEWSHEET, inserts a new worksheet after the current worksheet. The keystrokes for the macro, as shown in cell B9, are as follows:

    '/wisa~

The macro starts with an apostrophe (the label prefix) and / (slash), which activates the 1-2-3 menu. The letters *wisa* select the menu commands **W**orksheet **I**nsert **S**heet **A**fter. The ~ (tilde) represents the Enter key.

Because this macro is named with a descriptive range name, you can run it using the Run (Alt-F3) options discussed in the preceding sections.

Recording and Testing Macros

A powerful new feature provided in Release 3 of 1-2-3 is Record (Alt-F2). The Record feature records keystrokes, allows you to copy the keystrokes into a worksheet cell as a label, and automatically creates a macro.

Record works by displaying and letting you use information from a special storage area in your computer's memory called the *record buffer*. You can copy and play back keystrokes from the record buffer, clear the record buffer, and turn on STEP mode—so that you can run a macro one step at a time for testing purposes. The sections that follow describe in more detail the steps for using Record to create macros, play back your keystrokes, and step through macros.

Reminder:
Use the Record feature to capture keystrokes and create a macro.

Creating Macros with Record

Suppose that you want to create a macro that sets the global worksheet format to Currency with two decimal places. To make this setting manually, you select /Worksheet Global Format Currency, type 2, and then press Enter. You can write this macro easily; 1-2-3, however, gives you an even easier way to create the macro.

Reminder:
The Record feature records your keystrokes in the record buffer.

To record a macro, follow these steps:

1. Press Record (Alt-F2) and select **E**rase from the Record menu (see fig. 13.9). You don't have to erase, but doing so helps you find the characters you need more easily. Keep in mind that the record buffer holds roughly the last 512 characters you typed.

2. Type the keystrokes you want your macro to execute—for this example, type **/wgfc**, type **2**, and press Enter. The Record feature dutifully records your keystrokes in the record buffer.

Fig. 13.9.
The Record menu options.

Note: When you define a range within a macro you are recording, type the range address rather than pointing with the cursor-movement keys. You can much more easily identify a range in the record buffer from a typed address than from recorded cursor-movement keystrokes.

After you record the keystrokes of the macro, you must copy the keystrokes from the record buffer to the worksheet and assign a range name to the cells containing the keystrokes. To copy the keystrokes from the record buffer into the worksheet, press Record (Alt-F2) and select the **C**opy option from the Record menu. The keystrokes you typed since the beginning of the 1-2-3 session or since you last selected the **E**rase option appear in the control panel, as shown in figure 13.10.

Fig. 13.10.
Macro keystrokes in the record buffer, ready to be copied.

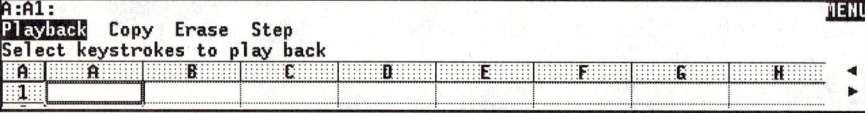

Identify the keystrokes you want to copy from the record buffer using a six-step process:

1. Move the cursor to the first character you want to copy to the worksheet.

2. Press Tab to anchor the cursor.

   Whenever you are in POINT mode, you can unanchor the cursor by pressing Esc. Otherwise, the cursor is anchored at the place it was located when you entered POINT mode.

Cue:
Press Esc to unanchor the highlight set with Tab.

Chapter 13 ◆ Using Macros 593

3. Use the arrow keys to highlight the remaining keystrokes you want to copy from the record buffer.

   Figure 13.11 shows highlighted the entire set of keystrokes necessary to set the global format to Currency with two decimal places.

4. After you highlight the characters you want to copy, press Enter. 1-2-3 asks where you want to copy the characters (see fig. 13.12).

5. Either move the cell pointer to the appropriate cell or range of cells, or type the cell or range address where you want to copy the characters. Whether you specify a single cell or a range of cells, 1-2-3 splits the recorded keystrokes to fit into the column width of the first cell.

6. Press Enter.

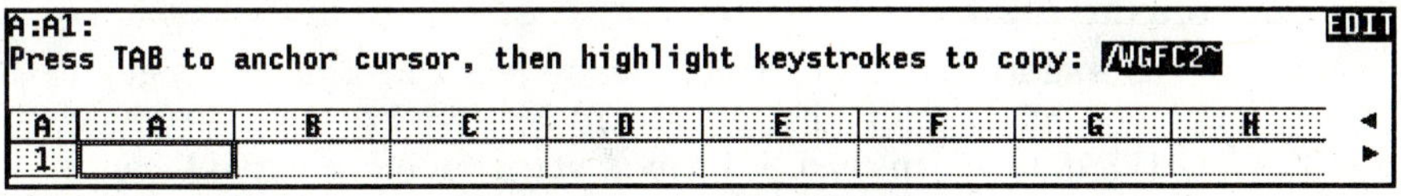

Fig. 13.11.
The highlighted characters.

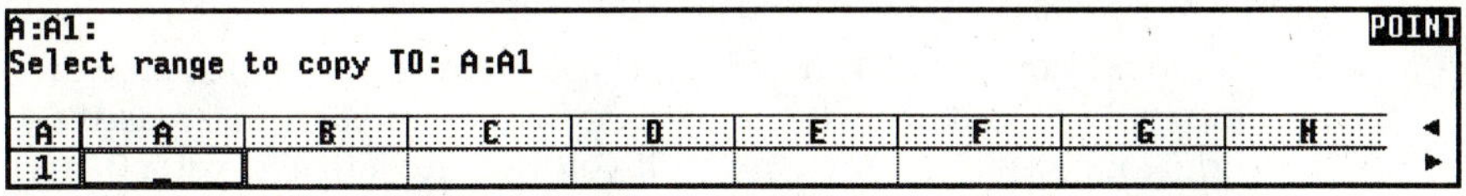

Fig. 13.12.
The prompt that asks where you want to copy the highlighted characters.

Note: You can edit the contents of the record buffer either before or after highlighting the contents, but not while you are highlighting the characters for the copy operation. Use the same editing keys you use to edit a formula.

The result of the copy operation appears as shown in figure 13.13 if you select cell B3 as the target range.

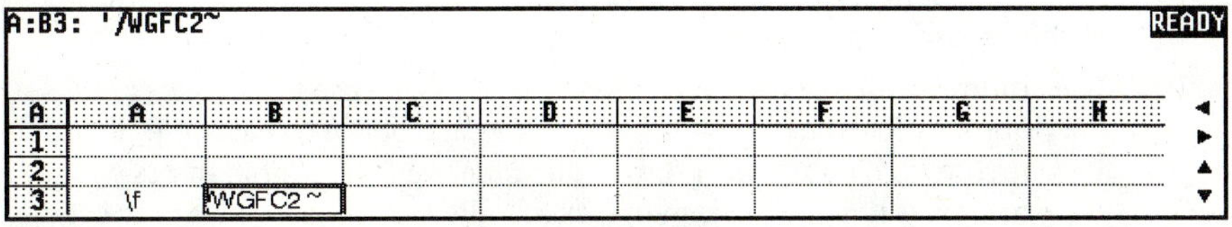

Fig. 13.13.
A recorded macro copied into the worksheet from the record buffer.

To use the macro, first name it. An unnamed macro can still be executed using the POINT mode of the Run (Alt-F3) command, but naming the macro allows you easier access. Type the label '\f in cell A3, as shown in figure 13.13. Place the cell pointer in cell A3 and select /Range Name Labels Right and press Enter. The label \f is assigned as the range name to the macro in cell B3. Now you can press Alt-F to start the macro.

You can use the steps given here with the Record feature to create more complex and lengthy macros as well. If you do use Record to build larger or more complex macros, however, keep the following information in mind:

Reminder:
The record buffer holds about 512 characters.

- The record buffer is limited in size to 512 bytes. Because a *byte* is roughly equal in size to one character, you have room for only the last 512 characters in the record buffer. When you type the 513th character, 1-2-3 "forgets" the first character—in effect, it removes from the record buffer the oldest characters to make room for the newest.

- Because some keys on your keyboard don't have character equivalents, several characters may be required to represent a keystroke. The F5 key, for example, is represented by six characters: {GOTO}.

- The Record feature doesn't record all your keystrokes. The keys which Record doesn't record include keys that have neither character symbols nor key names: Caps Lock, Compose (Alt-F1), Num Lock, Print Screen, Record (Alt-F2), Scroll Lock, and Shift. The Record feature also does not record Ctrl-Break and Ins.

- 1-2-3 uses shortcuts when possible. If you press the right-arrow key 10 times, you might guess that the record buffer records the key name {RIGHT} 10 times. Instead, 1-2-3 uses a repetition factor and the most abbreviated form of the key name—in this case, {R 10}—using 6 keystrokes instead of the 10 you actually typed.

- If you execute an Alt-*letter* macro while you are recording, the name of the macro is recorded in the record buffer rather than the macro's individual keystrokes. For example, if you execute a macro named \a, the record buffer shows the keystrokes as {\a}.

Caution:
1-2-3 may copy characters from the record buffer over data in your worksheet.

- You can specify one row or many rows for the range to which you want to copy the characters from the record buffer. 1-2-3 uses as many rows as needed to hold the characters you select to copy. If cells containing data are below the cells to which you have directed 1-2-3 to copy the record buffer contents, and 1-2-3 requires additional cells to store the characters being copied, 1-2-3 overwrites existing data with the contents of the record buffer.

- The column width of the range to which you copy the keystrokes affects the number of keystrokes 1-2-3 copies to each cell. For example, if you are copying 20 characters and the cell you specify is 10 characters wide, 1-2-3 attempts to split the keystrokes in half: 10 into the cell you specify and 10 into the cell below. 1-2-3 does not split key names between cells; doing so creates a macro error. Nonetheless, other keystrokes in the macro may be split into illogical segments. Regardless of the split, the macro will still work.

- If you specify a range of cells—not just a single cell—1-2-3 uses the width of the entire range to determine how many characters to put into the top left cell of the range and those below it. For example, if you specify D3..E3 as the range to hold 20 keystrokes and the column-width of each column is 20, 1-2-3 copies the full 20 characters into cell D3.

Using Playback To Repeat Keystrokes

One option of the Record feature is to "play back" the keystrokes in the record buffer. The steps to play back all or some portion of the keystrokes parallel the steps used to create the macro. You can play back a sequence of keystrokes as many times as you like. You should find this feature helpful when you want to repeat a sequence of keystrokes, but don't need to create an actual macro for them.

Cue:
Play back a sequence of keystrokes as many times as you like.

Before you play back keystrokes, position your cell pointer in the cell where the keystrokes should be repeated. Then, follow these steps to play back:

1. Press Record (Alt-F2) to access the Record menu.
2. Select the **P**layback option. The record buffer is displayed.
3. Select the keystrokes you want to repeat by positioning the cursor at the beginning or end of the sequence of keystrokes you want to repeat, pressing Tab to anchor the cursor, and then using the left-arrow or right-arrow key to highlight the entire range of keystrokes you want to repeat.
4. Press Enter.

Reminder:
Position the cell pointer in the specific location where you want the keystrokes repeated.

1-2-3 repeats the keystrokes and keystroke equivalents you highlighted. Keep in mind that you can edit the contents of the record buffer either before or after you anchor the cursor (but not while you're selecting the keystrokes).

Using Record To Test Macros

No matter how carefully you construct your macros, you may encounter errors the first time you execute them. By taking a series of precautions, however, you can minimize the efforts necessary to correct the errors.

Before you create a macro, always invest the time to design it carefully. Just as a carpenter never starts construction of a house without blueprints, neither should you start construction of a macro without a carefully conceived and well-documented design. Take time to map out the detailed steps a macro is to perform, to create good documentation, and to write descriptions of any range names used in the macro.

Even if you have a good design and documentation, however, you should plan to test and debug your macros. Testing lets you verify that your macro works precisely as you want it to. 1-2-3 provides a valuable aid in locating macro errors: the **S**tep option on the Record menu. The **S**tep option enables you to execute your macro one step at a time—giving you a chance to see, in slow motion, exactly what your macro does. Even though the **S**tep option is found on the Record menu, you can use **S**tep to test any macro—not just those you record.

Cue:
Even though the **S**tep option is located on the Record menu, you can use the option to test any macro.

Suppose that you want to use the **S**tep option to test the macro shown in figure 13.13, which you created using Record. Follow this procedure to use the **S**tep option to test that macro:

1. Press Record (Alt-F2).

2. Select **Step** to switch to STEP mode. The STEP indicator appears at the bottom of the screen, as shown in figure 13.14.

3. Execute the macro you want to step through one keystroke at a time. (Execute the macro by pressing Run (Alt-F3) or pressing Alt-*letter*, where *letter* is the single-character name of the macro.) The SST indicator, which represents Single STep, replaces the STEP indicator.

4. To have the macro begin operation, press any key—for example, the space bar. The first keystroke or keystroke equivalent is executed.

5. To execute each step in sequence, press the space bar after each subsequent step.

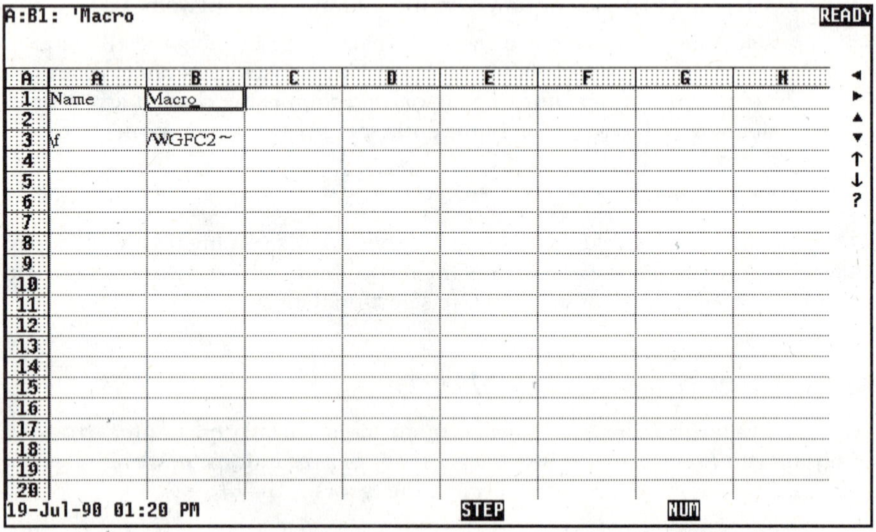

Fig. 13.14.

The STEP indicator, which appears when you select the Step option.

Figure 13.15 shows the first keystroke of the macro from figure 13.13 being executed. The first keystroke of that macro is the slash key (/); accordingly, the 1-2-3 menu is activated. Notice that the STEP indicator now appears as SST.

If you find an error, terminate the macro by pressing Ctrl-Break and then Esc or Enter. Edit the macro to correct the error. Then step through the macro again, repeating the process until no further errors remain.

Edit macros as you do any label. Move the cell pointer to the cell containing the label to edit (in this case, the macro line), press Edit (F2), and make your changes in the label. (The Edit (F2) key is described in detail in Chapter 3.)

When you want to execute the macro without single-stepping through one keystroke at a time, press Record (Alt-F2) and select **Step** to turn off the **Step** option. You also can turn off the option during execution of a macro by pressing Record (Alt-F2) when 1-2-3 is waiting for you to press another key to continue stepping.

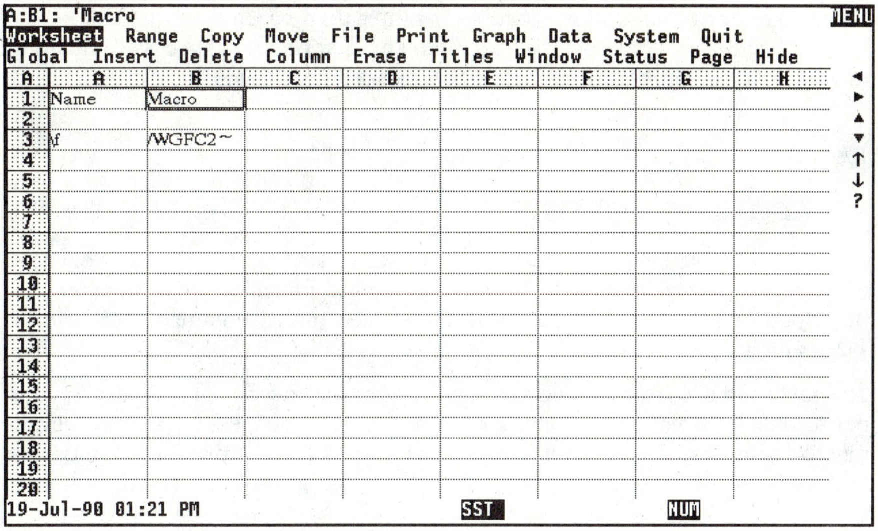

Chapter 13 ◆ Using Macros   **597**

Fig. 13.15.
The SST indicator, which appears when you begin to step through the macro.

Watching for Common Errors in Macros

As you test your macros, you should watch for some common errors, described in this section. You should find this material helpful as you begin testing and debugging your macros.

If 1-2-3 cannot execute a macro as written, the program displays an error message and the cell address where the error is located. Typically, this message should point you to the error. Occasionally, however, the real error—that is, the place 1-2-3 stops executing keystrokes the way you want them—may precede the error identified in the error message.

In the cell identified by the error message, check for the chronic macro errors everyone seems to make. If 1-2-3 stops on one of the 1-2-3 commands, you probably forgot to enter a tilde (~), representing the Enter key, to complete a command; or you forgot to press **Q** to quit a menu level. Sometimes, you need more than one **Q** because you actually have several menu levels to quit.

Even if 1-2-3 works all the way through a macro, the program may end with an error message or a beep. Remember that 1-2-3 continues to execute macro commands until it encounters an empty cell, a cell with a numeric value, or one of the advanced commands that stops macros and advanced macro command programs. If 1-2-3 encounters data in the cell directly below the last line of the macro, the program may interpret that cell as part of the macro. Always use the /**R**ange **E**rase command to empty the cell below the last line of your macro. If you discover that the cell is not empty, you may have identified one of the macro's problems.

If you get a message about an unrecognized macro key name or range name—which is followed by the cell address—check your key names and range names to make sure that they are spelled correctly. In addition, verify that you are using the

Reminder:
Check for common errors: missing tildes and missing **Q***uit commands.*

correct kind of punctuation—braces { } rather than parentheses ( ) or brackets [ ]; that arguments are correctly specified; and that no extra spaces are included in your macro—especially inside the braces { }.

Moving Up to the Advanced Macro Commands

If you find yourself writing larger and larger macros—macros that use dozens or hundreds of keystrokes—consider using 1-2-3's advanced macro commands, described in Chapter 14. You use the advanced macro commands in place of 1-2-3's menu commands.

Reminder:
Advanced macro commands are better suited than simple macro commands for writing large programs.

The advanced macro commands are much better suited for writing large programs because the commands are complete words and are much less cryptic than simple macro commands. For example, to erase a range in a macro program, you use the keystrokes /re; in an advanced macro command program, you use the command {BLANK}.

The advanced macro commands also enable you to perform operations that go beyond what's possible from the 1-2-3 menu—such as reading and writing records to external files and recalculating only a portion of a worksheet. If all this sounds like something you never want to get involved in, don't worry. You don't ever have to use the advanced macro commands. However, if you find yourself more and more restricted and frustrated by the limitations of your macro programs, consider moving up to 1-2-3's advanced macro commands.

Summary

This chapter has given you the information, and hopefully the confidence, to begin creating your own macros—tools that you can use to save time, reduce repetition, and automate your worksheet models. The chapter defined a macro and walked you through the steps to create some simple macros. The chapter also described the three ways you can name and run macros, explained how to build a simple macro library, showed you how to use 1-2-3 Release 3's Record feature to create and test macros, and reviewed techniques for documenting your macros. The chapter concluded with some ideas on when it's time for you to move up to 1-2-3's advanced macro commands, the subject covered in the next chapter.

Introducing the Advanced Macro Commands

14

In addition to the keyboard macro capabilities, 1-2-3 contains a powerful set of commands offering many of the aspects of a full-featured programming language. With the *advanced macro commands*, you can customize and automate 1-2-3 for your worksheet applications.

In Chapter 13, you learned how to automate keystrokes to save time by streamlining operations with macros. This chapter explains the advanced macro commands you can use to perform a variety of programming tasks.

This chapter is not designed to teach programming theory and concepts, but rather to introduce you to the capabilities of programming with the advanced macro commands. If you use 1-2-3 and want to learn some of the advanced techniques of macro programming, you should enjoy this chapter. The techniques presented can help you become a 1-2-3 macro expert.

Why Use the Advanced Macro Commands?

Programs created with the advanced macro commands give you added control and flexibility in the use of 1-2-3 worksheets. With the advanced macro commands, you control such tasks as accepting input from the keyboard during a program, performing conditional tests, repeating a sequence of commands, and creating user-defined command menus. You can use the advanced macro commands as a full-featured programming language to develop custom worksheets for specific business applications. For example, by developing advanced macro command programs that guide users to enter and change data on a worksheet, you can ensure that data is entered correctly. Even novice users who aren't familiar with 1-2-3's commands and operations can use program applications of this type.

After learning the concepts and the parts of the advanced macro commands discussed in this chapter, you will be ready to develop programs that perform the following tasks:

- Create menu-driven worksheet/database models
- Accept and control input from a user
- Manipulate data within and between files
- Execute tasks a predetermined number of times
- Control program flow
- Set up and print multiple reports
- Make intelligent decisions based on user input
- Execute multiple programs based on decisions made within programs

As you become more experienced with the advanced macro commands, you can take advantage of 1-2-3's full power to do the following:

- Disengage or redefine the function keys
- Develop a complete business system—from order entry to inventory control to accounting
- Operate 1-2-3 as a disk-based database system—limiting the size and speed of the file operation only to the size and speed of the hard disk

If you want to take 1-2-3 to its practical limits, the set of advanced macro commands is the proper vehicle, and your creativity can be the necessary fuel.

What Are the Advanced Macro Commands?

Reminder:
You can use advanced macro commands only within macro programs.

The 1-2-3 advanced macro commands are a set of 50 invisible commands. These commands are called *invisible* because, unlike the command instructions invoked through the 1-2-3 menus and function keys, the advanced macro commands cannot be invoked from the keyboard. These commands can be used only within macro and advanced macro command programs.

The \h program in figure 14.1 shows how you can use the advanced macro commands. With commands such as MENUBRANCH and BRANCH, you can create custom menus to assist and prompt the user.

The program in figure 14.1 begins by creating the range name HERE wherever the user has positioned the cell pointer before invoking the program. The second line continues by displaying a custom help screen. The third line uses the MENUBRANCH command to display a menu with three options: to select the next help screen, to select the previous help screen, or to return to the original cell-pointer position in the worksheet. The BRANCH command in the last line of the Next and Previous menu options causes the program to redisplay the menu after the user has selected either of these options.

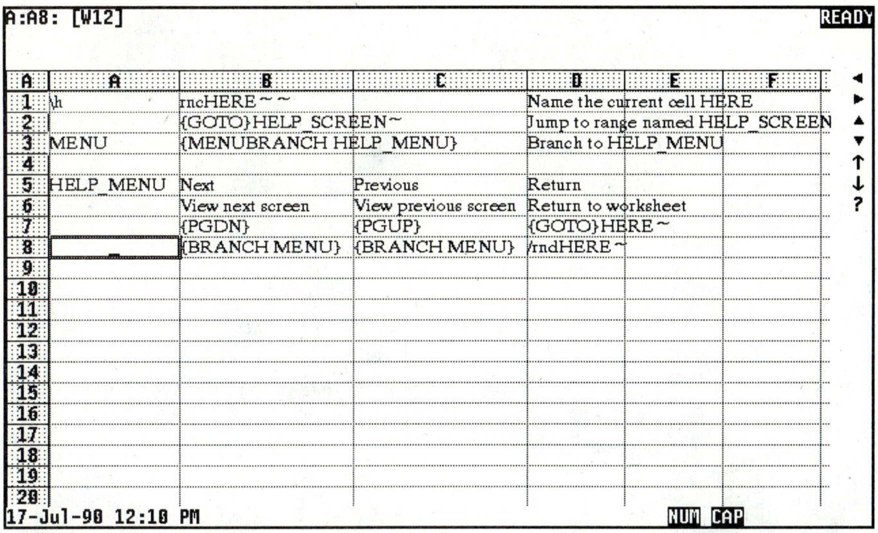

Chapter 14 ◆ Introducing the Advanced Macro Commands

```
A:A8: [W12]                                                              READY
     A        B                    C                   D         E        F
 1  \h        rncHERE~~                                Name the current cell HERE
 2            {GOTO}HELP_SCREEN~                       Jump to range named HELP_SCREEN
 3  MENU      {MENUBRANCH HELP_MENU}                   Branch to HELP_MENU
 4
 5  HELP_MENU Next                 Previous            Return
 6            View next screen     View previous screen Return to worksheet
 7            {PGDN}               {PGUP}              {GOTO}HERE~
 8            {BRANCH MENU}        {BRANCH MENU}       /rndHERE~
 9
10
...
20
17-Jul-90 12:10 PM                                                     NUM CAP
```

Fig. 14.1.
An advanced macro command program using the MENUBRANCH and BRANCH commands.

Notice that the program branches to *range names* and not to *cell addresses*. Using range names instead of cell addresses is an important convention. Not only does this practice make the program easier to read, but as you rearrange your worksheet, 1-2-3 updates the range name addresses so that your program continues to operate on the correct cells and ranges.

Tip:
Always use range names instead of cell addresses when branching within a macro program.

The examples in this chapter show you how to use the advanced macro commands for accepting input, for program control, for decision-making operations, for data manipulation, for program enhancement, and for file manipulation. You find tables that list and describe these commands throughout the chapter.

1-2-3's /x Commands

In addition to the 50 advanced macro commands, 1-2-3 includes a set of eight /x commands. These commands were included in 1-2-3 Release 1A to provide a "limited" programming capability that went beyond simple keystroke macros. All eight /x commands have advanced macro command counterparts. The /x commands and their advanced macro command counterparts include the following:

/x Command	Description	Advanced Macro Command Alternative
/xi	Sets up an if-then-else condition	IF
/xq	Quits execution	QUIT
/xg	Instructs a program to continue at a new location	BRANCH
/xc	Runs a subroutine	{*subroutine*}

/x Command	Description	Advanced Macro Command Alternative
/xr	Returns to the next line of the macro calling a subroutine	RETURN
/xm	Creates a menu	MENUBRANCH
/xn	Accepts input of numeric entries only	GETNUMBER
/xl	Accepts input of labels only	GETLABEL

Six of these commands work exactly like their advanced macro command counterparts: /xi, /xq, /xg, /xc, /xr, and /xm. For example, /xq performs exactly the same as the advanced macro command QUIT. When inserted into a program, both commands produce the same result.

The other two /x commands—/xn and /xl—work a little differently than their comparable advanced macro commands. These commands are used to prompt the user for text and numeric data and then place the data in the current cell. Before their advanced macro command counterparts (GETLABEL and GETNUMBER) can do the same tasks, some programming is required. /xn, unlike GETNUMBER, does not allow users to enter alphabetical characters (except for range names and cell addresses), nor does /xn let the user simply press Enter in response to the prompt.

The /x commands should not be used in new programs developed in Release 3 (except in very rare instances, where /xn and /xl perform differently from their advanced macro command counterparts). /x commands are beneficial, however, because they enable you to run and easily modify in Release 3 programs originally developed in Release 1A.

Understanding the Elements of Advanced Macro Command Programs

The examples in this chapter show you how to incorporate advanced macro commands into macros to produce complete, efficient programs that take 1-2-3's macro capability far beyond simply automating keystrokes. These programs contain advanced macro commands and all the elements that can be included in macros.

Programs can include the following:

- Keystrokes used for selecting 1-2-3 commands (for example, /rfc0)
- Range names and cell addresses
- Key names for moving the cell pointer, for function keys, for editing keys, and for special keys (see Chapter 13 for more information about key names)
- Advanced macro commands

Understanding Advanced Macro Command Syntax

Many of the examples in this chapter use advanced macro commands that have not yet been introduced in the text. In such cases, the text briefly describes the function of the command. Each command is, of course, fully described later in this chapter.

Like the key names used in keystroke macros (discussed in Chapter 13), all advanced macro commands are enclosed in braces. Just as you must represent the right-arrow key in a macro as {RIGHT} or {R}, you must enclose a command, such as QUIT, in braces: {QUIT}.

Note: When you write advanced macro command programs, press the Name (F3) key after you enter an open brace ({); 1-2-3 lists all the valid commands and key names, such as {QUIT} and {CALC}. Press Name (F3) again to see a full-page listing of the commands and key names. To enter the needed command or key name, select it by moving the cursor to highlight it and pressing Enter. Then, if you want to know the syntax, press Help (F1) to display that command.

Some commands are just a single command enclosed in braces. For example, to quit a macro during its execution, you use the command {QUIT}; no arguments are given. Many other commands, however, require additional arguments within the braces. The arguments that follow commands have a grammar, or syntax, similar to the syntax used in 1-2-3 @functions. The general syntax of commands that require arguments is as follows:

{COMMAND *argument1,argument2,...,argumentN*}

An *argument* can consist of numbers, strings, cell addresses, range names, formulas, or @functions. The command name and the first argument are separated by a space; for most commands, arguments are separated by commas (with no spaces). As you study the syntax for the specific commands described in this chapter, keep in mind the importance of following the conventions for spacing and punctuation. Consider this example:

{BRANCH *rangename*}

When you use the BRANCH command to transfer program control to a specific location in the program, for example, you must follow the command BRANCH with the cell address or range name indicating where the program should branch. In the command {BRANCH *rangename*}, *rangename* is the argument.

Creating, Using, and Debugging Advanced Macro Command Programs

Advanced macro command programs, like keystroke macros, must be efficient and error-free. You begin a macro command program by defining the actions you want

Reminder:
All advanced macro commands are enclosed in braces ({ }).

Reminder:
The command name and the first argument are separated by a space; subsequent arguments are separated by commas.

Tip:
If you don't know how to create keystroke macros, read Chapter 13 before continuing with this chapter.

Reminder:
A documented program is easier to debug and change than an undocumented one.

Tip:
Give a macro program both a descriptive name and an Alt-letter name.

the program to perform and the sequence of those actions. Then you develop the program, test it, debug it, and cross-check its results for all possible operations.

If you have created keystroke macros, you have a head start toward creating advanced macro command programs. These programs share many of the conventions used in the keyboard macros presented in Chapter 13. If you haven't yet experimented with 1-2-3 macros, take some time to review Chapter 13's simple keystroke macros before you try to develop advanced macro command programs. Review Chapter 13's discussions of creating, using, and debugging macros; many of the concepts are also related to advanced macro command programs.

Like keystroke macros, advanced macro command programs should be carefully planned and positioned on the worksheet. Locating your macros in a separate worksheet or file is the best practice. If you have macros that you use with many different worksheets, you may want to group them in a separate file. When the time comes to use those macros, issue the /File Open command to activate the macro file. If, however, you have a macro that is specific to one file, create a separate worksheet and store that macro on the separate worksheet in that file. Remember, though, that macros stored in a separate worksheet in a file can still be damaged or destroyed unless you use the /Worksheet Global Group Disable command.

You enter advanced macro command programs just as you enter keystroke macros—as text cells. You must use a label prefix to start any line that begins with a nontext character (such as / or <) so that 1-2-3 does not interpret the characters that follow as numbers or commands. After you decide where to locate your program and you begin entering program lines, keep several considerations in mind. Remember to document advanced macro command programs to the right of each program line. Because advanced macro command programs usually are more complex than keystroke macros, documenting each line is essential. A documented program, like the one shown in figure 14.1, is easier to debug and change than an undocumented one.

As described in Chapter 13, you can invoke macro and advanced macro command programs in one of three ways:

- Macros or advanced macro command programs you named using the backslash key and a letter character can be invoked by holding the Alt key while pressing the appropriate letter key.
- Macros or advanced macro command programs you named using complete range names can be invoked using the Run (Alt-F3) key. (As noted in Chapter 13, you can actually invoke *any* macro or advanced macro command program using the Run key.)
- Macros or advanced macro command programs you named using the backslash key and 0 are automatically executed when a file is loaded or opened as long as the /Worksheet Global Default Autoexec setting is Yes—which is the default.

You can give the same 1-2-3 range more than one name. You can, for example, give an often-used macro both a descriptive name and an Alt-*letter* name. By doing so, you gain the documentation benefit of the long, descriptive name and the ease of use of the Alt-*letter* name.

After you develop and run a program, you may need to debug it. Like keystroke macros, advanced macro command programs are subject to such problems as missing tildes (~) and misspelled key names and range names. Another problem is the use of cell addresses that have changed in a worksheet application. You can solve this problem by using range names in place of cell addresses wherever possible.

To debug advanced macro command programs, use 1-2-3's STEP mode in the same way you do for simple keystroke macros. Before you execute the program, press Record (Alt-F2) and select Step to invoke STEP mode. Then execute your advanced macro command program. Press any letter key or the space bar to continue with the next operation in the program. When you discover an error, press Ctrl-Break to stop execution. Press Esc to clear the error message, and then edit the program. Step through the program's execution again until all errors are found and corrected.

Reminder:
Debug macro programs using 1-2-3's STEP mode.

Understanding the Advanced Macro Command Categories

Using the power of 1-2-3's advanced macro commands, you can make 1-2-3 applications easier to use, enhance the features of 1-2-3's regular commands, and customize 1-2-3 for special worksheet applications. In the following sections, the advanced macro commands are grouped into six categories that reflect their functions: accepting input, controlling programs, making decisions, manipulating data, enhancing programs, and manipulating files.

Using Commands that Accept Input

The commands listed in table 14.1 provide for all possible types of user input into a 1-2-3 worksheet. You can use these commands to provide a more user-friendly interface than that of 1-2-3's standard commands and operations. For example, you can use these commands to create prompts and perform simple edit checks on the input before storing it in the worksheet.

Table 14.1
Commands for Accepting Input

Command	Description
{?}	Pauses the macro so that the user can enter any type of input
{GET}	Accepts a single character into the location specified
{GETLABEL}	Accepts a label into the location specified
{GETNUMBER}	Accepts a number into the location specified

continued

Table 14.1—(continued)

Command	Description
{LOOK}	Places the first character from the type-ahead buffer into the location specified
{FORM}	Interrupts macro execution so that data can be entered into an input range's unprotected cells

The ? Command

> **Reminder:**
> During the pause, no prompt is displayed in the control panel.

The ? command pauses the program so that the user can enter any type of information. During the pause, no prompt is displayed in the control panel; the user can move the cell pointer to direct the location of the input. The program continues executing after the user presses Enter. The format for the ? command is as follows:

{?}   Accepts any type of input

For example, the following one-line program combines macro commands and an advanced macro command to create a file-retrieve program:

/fr{NAME}{?}~

This program displays all files in the current drive and directory, and then pauses to accept input from the user. In this instance, the user can either type the name of a viewed file or simply move the cell pointer to a file name and press Enter.

Even if you press Enter after you type a {?} entry, you still must include a tilde (~) after the {?} if you want 1-2-3 to accept your input.

The GET Command

> **Reminder:**
> Use GET to place a single keystroke into a cell.

The GET command places a single keystroke into a target cell. The keystroke then can be analyzed or tested in a number of ways, and the results of these tests can be used to change the flow of the program. The format for the GET command is as follows:

{GET *location*}   Accepts single keystroke into range defined by *location*

The following example shows how you can use GET:

{GET CAPTURE}
{IF CAPTURE="q"}/fs~r
{GOTO}SALES~

The GET statement traps individual keystrokes in a cell named CAPTURE. The second line evaluates CAPTURE. If the keystroke in CAPTURE is the letter Q, the file is saved automatically. If CAPTURE contains any other keystroke, /fs~r is ignored. In either case, control then passes to the third line of the program, which places the cell pointer in the cell with the range name SALES.

Chapter 14 ♦ Introducing the Advanced Macro Commands

A more involved use of GET is to create a menu screen as shown in figure 14.2 and then use the GET command to accept the user's single key input.

```
A:A2: [W13]                                                        READY

      A              B              C         D         E              F              G              H
 1  \m            {PgDn}{GOTO}MENU ~
 2                {GET ANSWER}
 3                {IF ANSWER="A"}{PRINT_REPORT}
 4                {IF ANSWER="B"}{SAVE_FILE}
 5                {IF ANSWER="C"}{SHOW_GRAPH}
 6                {IF ANSWER="D"}{LEAVE_MACROS}
 7                {BRANCH \m}
 8
 9
10  ANSWER        d
11                                                           Please select your choice:
12  PRINT_REPORT  /ppgq                                       A. Print the report
13                                                           B. Save the file
14  SAVE_FILE     /fs~r                                       C. Show the graph
15                                                           D. Leave the macros
16  SHOW_GRAPH    {GRAPH}
17
18  LEAVE_MACROS  {QUIT}
19
20
MACRO.WK3                                                                        NUM
```

Fig. 14.2.
The GET command used to allow one-character input with a menu.

In this example, the GET command is used to pause the program while the user enters a single letter from the keyboard and to store that entry in a cell named ANSWER. Notice that since GET does not display a prompt, the program must first move the cursor so the menu screen is displayed. If you want a prompt to appear in the control panel rather than in the worksheet, you must use the GETLABEL or GETNUMBER command.

Note: The GET command returns the value as soon as the user presses a single key. If you are building a menu-driven worksheet program, GET offers you a great advantage: the user does not have to press Enter after making a selection. The three other major input commands, {?}, GETLABEL, and GETNUMBER, all require the user to press Enter to terminate input.

The GETLABEL Command

The GETLABEL command accepts any type of entry from the keyboard, but stores the input as a label. The prompt, which must be enclosed in quotation marks, is displayed in the control panel. With this command, the entry is placed in the location cell as a label when the user presses Enter. The format for the GETLABEL command is as follows:

{GETLABEL *prompt,location*}   Accepts label into *location*

The following example shows the use of the GETLABEL command:

{GETLABEL "Enter order date (MM/DD/YY):",ORDER_DATE}
{GOTO}ORDER_DATE~
{DOWN}~@DATEVALUE(ORDER_DATE)~/rfd1~

Reminder:
Use GETLABEL to display a prompt and accept any type of input from the user into a cell.

The GETLABEL statement displays a prompt and accepts a label into a cell named ORDER_DATE. The third line places a formula in the cell below ORDER_DATE; this formula converts the label date to a numerical date, and then formats the cell to appear as a date.

Figure 14.3 shows how to use GETLABEL with the IF, BRANCH, and BEEP commands (discussed later in this chapter) to improve the macro by adding error handling. If the user enters a label that cannot be converted to a date, the second GETLABEL command (in the DATE_ERR macro) displays an error message, the program pauses until the user presses Enter, and then branches back to prompt the user for a date in the correct format.

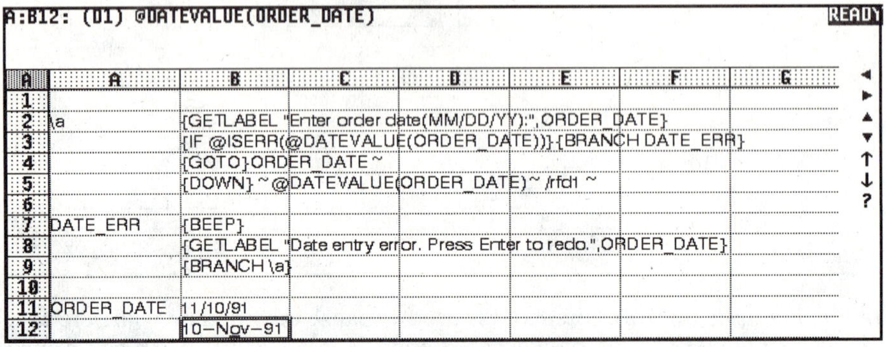

Fig. 14.3.
The GETLABEL command used with other commands to include string-input error checking.

```
A:B12: (D1) @DATEVALUE(ORDER_DATE)                                    READY

          A          B                   C              D              E              F              G
 1
 2   \a            {GETLABEL "Enter order date(MM/DD/YY):",ORDER_DATE}
 3                 {IF @ISERR(@DATEVALUE(ORDER_DATE))}{BRANCH DATE_ERR}
 4                 {GOTO}ORDER_DATE~
 5                 {DOWN}~@DATEVALUE(ORDER_DATE)~/rfd1~
 6
 7   DATE_ERR     {BEEP}
 8                 {GETLABEL "Date entry error. Press Enter to redo.",ORDER_DATE}
 9                 {BRANCH \a}
10
11   ORDER_DATE   11/10/91
12                10-Nov-91
```

GETLABEL versus /xl

GETLABEL and /xl are identical except for one /xl command feature. Suppose, for example, that you write the /xl command as follows:

   /xl*prompt*~~

The label entered in response to *prompt* is placed at the cell pointer's current location. You cannot write this kind of instruction with GETLABEL because 1-2-3 displays an error message if you don't specify a location for the argument. Using /xl is more convenient than using GETLABEL, for example, in a subroutine in which the location of the destination cell changes with each subroutine call. By using /xl in such a situation, you don't have to specify the location at which the label is to be placed.

Even with this difference between GETLABEL and /xl, however, you should use GETLABEL to specify exactly where the user input is to be placed by using a range name. That way, even if your worksheet is rearranged, the input ends up exactly where you expect.

The GETNUMBER Command

The GETNUMBER command accepts only numeric entries. The prompt, which must be a string enclosed in quotation marks, is displayed in the control panel,

Chapter 14 ♦ Introducing the Advanced Macro Commands

and the user's entry is placed in the results cell when Enter is pressed. If the user tries to enter a label, ERR is placed in the results cell. The format for the GETNUMBER command is as follows:

{GETNUMBER *prompt,location*}   Accepts the number into *location*

In the following example, the GETNUMBER statement displays a prompt and accepts a numeric entry into cell CLASS_CODE:

{GETNUMBER "Classification code:",CLASS_CODE}

Figure 14.4 shows how to use GETNUMBER in an inventory application by adding error trapping. As in the preceding example, GETNUMBER prompts the user for a classification number. If the user does not enter a number between 0 and 9999, the program displays the message `Class must be between 0 and 9999. Press Enter`. The program then branches back to prompt the user to enter another number.

Reminder:
Use GETNUMBER to display a prompt and accept numeric input from the user into a cell.

```
A:B8:                                                           READY

     A         B           C         D         E          F            G         H
 1        \a      {GETNUMBER "Classification code:",CLASS_CODE}
 2                {IF CLASS_CODE<0#OR#CLASS_CODE>9999}{BRANCH CODE_ERR}
 3
 4   CODE_ERR    {BEEP}
 5                {GETNUMBER "Class must be between 0 and 9999. Press Enter ",CLASS_CODE}
 6                {BRANCH \a}
 7
```

Fig. 14.4.
The GETNUMBER command with error trapping.

> **GETNUMBER versus /xn**
>
> The GETNUMBER and /xn commands work differently. With GETNUMBER, a blank entry or a text entry has a numeric value of ERR. With /xn, however, a blank entry or a text entry results in an error message, and the user is again prompted for a number. This difference can be useful in some applications. If, for example, you accidentally press **Q** (a letter) instead of **1**, the /xn command returns an error message. You also can use the /xn command in the following form:
>
> /xn*prompt*~
>
> This command reads a numeric value into the current cell instead of into a specified location. (See the discussion at the end of the GETLABEL section.)

The LOOK Command

The LOOK command is frequently used to interrupt processing when the user presses a key. The LOOK command checks 1-2-3's type-ahead buffer. If any keys are pressed after program execution begins, a copy of the first keystroke is placed in the target-cell location. Use the following syntax for LOOK:

{LOOK *location*}   Places the first character from the type-ahead buffer into *location*

Reminder:
LOOK copies the first keystroke in the type-ahead buffer to the specified location.

Reminder:
An IF statement can check the contents of location.

When you include the LOOK command in a program, the user can type a character at any time; the macro finds that single character when the LOOK command is executed. An IF statement can therefore check the contents of *location*. However, because the character is not removed from the type-ahead buffer, you must use the character or dispose of it before the program needs keyboard input or completes execution.

Note: The *type-ahead buffer* is a small storage area in memory where the computer holds a small number of keystrokes until they can be processed by a program such as 1-2-3.

LOOK is similar to GET, but there is an important difference: GET pauses the macro until the user presses a key. GET places the keystroke into a cell, thus removing it from the type-ahead buffer. LOOK, however, places a *copy* of the keystroke into the cell specified by *location* without pausing the macro, and without removing the keystroke from the buffer.

A test of the LOOK command is provided in figure 14.5. This program starts by placing the time that the macro starts in the cell named COUNTER (B15). Each time the program encounters the LOOK command, 1-2-3 checks the keyboard type-ahead buffer and copies—into the location ANSWER—the first character found. Then an IF statement checks the contents of ANSWER and branches to the CHECK_ANSWER macro if the user has typed a character. (The contents of ANSWER are compared with a *null string* by the IF command. You indicate a null string in a comparison test by placing two quotation marks side by side—""; the null string literally represents nothing.) The GET command at the beginning of the CHECK_ANSWER macro disposes of the keystroke that interrupted the loop; that is, the keystroke is removed from the buffer and placed in the cell ANSWER. The three IF statements in the CHECK_ANSWER macro form a simple test of the user's menu selections (two of the selections reset the time stored in COUNTER). Finally, if the user doesn't type a character, the IF statement in cell B4 is executed. It tests to see if the program has waited more than 30 seconds for user input and prompts the user if it has.

This example demonstrates a powerful use of the LOOK command. By storing the time the macro starts, you can give the user a limited amount of time to make a selection; then you can either prompt the user if too much time elapses or make a default selection. You could, for example, produce self-running demos which continue after a specified time even if the user doesn't make a selection.

Tip:
Use the LOOK command to process long commands.

The LOOK command is most helpful when you have a long program to process and you want to be able to stop processing at certain points in the program. You can enter a LOOK command followed by an IF statement, as in figure 14.5, at several places in the program. Then, if the user presses a key, the program stops the next time a LOOK command is executed. If no key is pressed, the program continues processing. In such cases, the LOOK command is preferable to the GET command, which *always* stops the program to wait for an entry.

Chapter 14 ◆ Introducing the Advanced Macro Commands

```
A:E16:                                                              READY

       A         B              C           D        E       F       G
 1              \0           {LET COUNTER,@NOW}
 2   LOOK_ANSWER {LOOK ANSWER}
 3              {IF ANSWER<>""}{CHECK_ANSWER}
 4              {IF @NOW<=COUNTER+@TIME(0,0,30)}{BRANCH LOOK_ANSWER}
 5              {BEEP}
 6              {GETLABEL "You're keeping me waiting.",ANSWER}{BRANCH \0}
 7
 8   CHECK_ANSWER {GET ANSWER}
 9              {IF ANSWER="Q"}{QUIT}
10              {IF ANSWER="1"}/fs~r{LET COUNTER,@NOW}
11              {IF ANSWER="2"}/wisa1~ {LET COUNTER,@NOW}
12              {RESTART}{BRANCH LOOK_ANSWER}
13
14   ANSWER     q
15   COUNTER    02:49:30 PM
16              Please choose one of the following:
17              Q            Leave the macros
18              1            Save the file
19              2            Add a new worksheet
20
18-Aug-90 03:05 PM                                             NUM CAP
```

Fig. 14.5.
The LOOK command used to examine the type-ahead buffer and place the first keystroke in the specified location.

The FORM Command

The FORM command interrupts macro execution temporarily so that the user can enter input into unprotected cells in a specified range. Although similar to the /Range Input command, FORM includes three added options: branching to another line of advanced macro command instructions if the user enters certain keys; specifying a set of keystrokes as valid; and specifying a set of keystrokes as invalid. The format for the FORM command is as follows:

{FORM *input,[call-table],*   Interrupts the macro temporarily
[include-keys],[exclude-keys]}   so that you can enter data into
                                  unprotected cells in the range
                                  specified as *input*

The *input* argument is a worksheet range with at least one cell previously unprotected using /Range Unprotect. Without the optional arguments, FORM functions just like /Range Input: you can use any keys to enter data into and move between the unprotected cells.

To complete execution of the FORM command, you press Enter or Esc while 1-2-3 is in READY mode. 1-2-3 then continues execution of the macro program; the cell pointer remains in the cell where it was when you completed FORM.

You can use FORM's three optional arguments—*call-table*, *include-keys*, and *exclude-keys*—either individually or in any combination.

Call-table represents a two-column range where the first column lists the names of keys on the keyboard, such as {CALC} or {GRAPH}, and the second column gives the commands to be executed when the key is pressed.

Reminder:
Use FORM to pause macro execution so that the user can enter input into unprotected cells in a specified range.

Include-keys specifies a range listing all acceptable keystrokes during execution of the FORM command. This list includes not only keystrokes entered into the unprotected field in the *input* range, but also any other keys needed to operate the macro or to deal with an error condition, such as {ESC}.

Exclude-keys specifies a range listing all unacceptable keystrokes during the execution of the FORM command. By specifying the unacceptable keys, you implicitly identify the acceptable keys; you probably use either the *include-keys* or the *exclude-keys* argument, but not both.

To omit an optional argument, use one of the following command structures:

{FORM *input*}	To omit all optional arguments
{FORM *input,call-table*}	To use only *call-table*
{FORM *input,,include-keys*}	To use only *include-keys*
{FORM *input,,,exclude-keys*}	To use only *exclude-keys*
{FORM *input,call-table,include-keys*}	To use *call-table* and *include-keys*
{FORM *input,,include-keys,exclude-keys*}	To use only *include-keys* and *exclude-keys* (although this format is often redundant or illogical)
{FORM *input,call-table,,exclude-keys*}	To use *call-table* and *exclude-keys*

Figure 14.6 shows an example of FORM used to accept data into the unprotected cells A1, B2, and A3 in the range INPUT (A1..B3). The *call-table* argument, KEYS (E3..F6), specifies additional keystrokes to be executed when certain keys are pressed—in this case, {HELP}, {EDIT}, {NAME}, and {ABS}—a series of beeps. The example doesn't use an *include-keys* argument, but does use an *exclude-keys* argument. The range EXCLUDE (E8..E11) shows the excluded keystrokes.

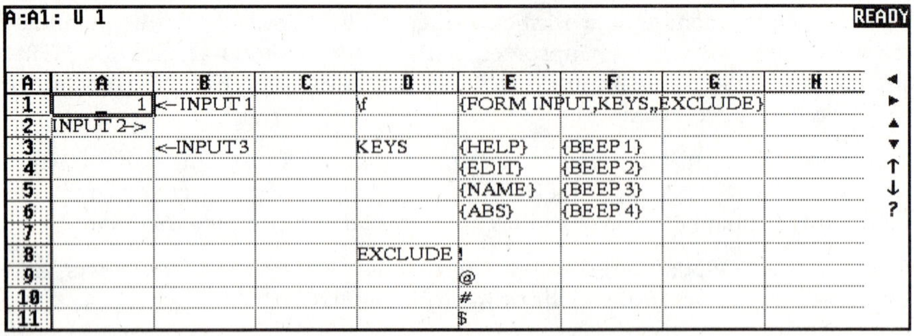
A:A1: U 1 READY

A	A	B	C	D	E	F	G	H
1	1	<-INPUT 1		\f	{FORM INPUT,KEYS,,EXCLUDE}			
2	INPUT 2->							
3		<-INPUT 3		KEYS	{HELP}	{BEEP 1}		
4					{EDIT}	{BEEP 2}		
5					{NAME}	{BEEP 3}		
6					{ABS}	{BEEP 4}		
7								
8				EXCLUDE	!			
9					@			
10					#			
11					$			

Fig. 14.6. *The FORM command used to collect input and specify valid keystrokes.*

Using Commands That Control Programs

The commands in table 14.2 allow varying degrees of control in 1-2-3 programs. These commands, used alone or in combination with decision-making commands, afford the programmer precise control of program flow.

Chapter 14 ◆ Introducing the Advanced Macro Commands

Table 14.2
Commands for Controlling Programs

Command	Action
{BRANCH}	Continues program execution at the location specified
{*subroutine*}	Performs a call to a subroutine before continuing to the next line of a macro
{MENUBRANCH}	Prompts the user with a dialog box menu found at the location specified
{MENUCALL}	Similar to MENUBRANCH, except that control returns to the statement after the MENUCALL
{RETURN}	Returns from a program subroutine
{QUIT}	Ends program execution
{ONERROR}	Traps errors, passing control to the branch macro specified
{BREAKON}	Enables the {BREAK} key
{BREAKOFF}	Disables the {BREAK} key
{WAIT}	Waits until the specified time
{DISPATCH}	Branches indirectly, through the location specified
{DEFINE}	Specifies cells for subroutine arguments
{RESTART}	Cancels a subroutine
{SYSTEM}	Executes a specified operating system command

The BRANCH Command

The BRANCH command causes program control to pass unconditionally to the cell address indicated in the BRANCH statement. The program begins reading commands and statements at the cell location indicated in the *location* argument. Program control does not return to the line from which it was passed unless directed to do so by another BRANCH statement. Use the following syntax for BRANCH:

{BRANCH *location*}   Continues program execution in the cell specified by *location*

BRANCH is an unconditional command unless it is preceded by an IF conditional statement, as in the following example:

```
{IF C22="alpha"}{BRANCH G24}
{GOTO}S101~
```

The IF statement must be in the same cell as the second command to act as a conditional testing statement. For more information, see the discussion of the IF command later in this chapter.

Consider a program where three separate company divisions are contained on different worksheets within the same file. When the user responds to the prompt

Tip:
BRANCH statements cause a permanent shift in the flow of statement execution; use them with IF statements.

Enter company division (A, B, or C):, the program should branch to a different place in the program and execute the instructions for moving to the correct worksheet. Figure 14.7 shows the program.

Fig. 14.7.
The BRANCH command used in a multiple-worksheet application.

	A	B	C
1	\m	{GETLABEL "Enter company division (A, B, or C):",ANSWER}	
2		{IF ANSWER="A"}{BRANCH A_DIVISION}	
3		{IF ANSWER="B"}{BRANCH B_DIVISION}	
4		{IF ANSWER="C"}{BRANCH C_DIVISION}	
5		{BRANCH \m}	
6			
7	ANSWER	B	
8			
9	A_DIVISION	{GOTO}A:A1 ~	
10	B_DIVISION	{GOTO}B:A1 ~	
11	C_DIVISION	{GOTO}C:A1 ~	

The BRANCH statements in the \m program cause the flow of program execution to shift to the different division routines. In this example, the BRANCH statements are coupled with IF statements to shift execution conditionally, depending on the user's response.

You may prefer that execution return to the \m program or to another program after completing the division routine. This can be accomplished in either of two ways: you can add {BRANCH \m} statements at the end of the subroutines to return to \m; or you can replace the BRANCH statements in \m with subroutine calls (discussed later in this chapter).

The MENUBRANCH Command

The MENUBRANCH command defines and displays in the control panel a menu from which up to eight individual programs can be initiated. Menu-item selection is identical to that of a 1-2-3 command menu. Following is the format of the MENUBRANCH command:

{MENUBRANCH *location*}   Executes menu structure at *location*

The menu invoked by the MENUBRANCH command consists of one to eight consecutive columns in the worksheet. Each column corresponds to one item in the menu. The upper left corner of the range named in a MENUBRANCH statement must refer to the first menu item; otherwise, you receive the error message Invalid use of Menu macro command.

Reminder:
Menu-option names should begin with unique letters, so that you can press the first letter of the option to select it.

Each menu item consists of three or more rows in the same column. The first row is the menu option name. The option-name items must fit on the top line of the control panel (typically 80 characters), or 1-2-3 displays the same error message. Option names should begin with different letters. If two or more options begin with the same letter and the user tries to use the first-letter technique to access an option, 1-2-3 selects the first option it finds with the specified letter.

Chapter 14 ◆ Introducing the Advanced Macro Commands

The second row in the menu range contains the descriptions of the menu items. These descriptions are displayed in the bottom row of the control panel when the cell pointer highlights the name of that menu option. Each description can contain up to 80 characters of text. The description row must be present, even if it is blank.

The third row begins the actual program command sequence. Because control branches to the individual programs, program control must be directed by statements at the end of each individual program.

No empty columns can exist between menu items; the column immediately to the right of the last menu item must be empty.

In figure 14.8, the MENUBRANCH command is used to produce a modification of the program shown in figure 14.7. The menu structure begins in cell B3; the individual programs each begin in row 5.

```
E:A5: [W12]                                                      READY

       A           B              C            D          E              F
 1     \m          {MENUBRANCH MAIN_MENU}
 2
 3     MAIN_MENU   A              B            C          Q
 4                 Use sheet A    Use sheet B  Use sheet C  Leave the macros
 5                 {GOTO}A:A1~    {GOTO}B:A1~  {GOTO}C:A1~  {QUIT}
 6
```

Fig. 14.8.
A program using the MENUBRANCH command.

When the MENUBRANCH statement is executed, 1-2-3 displays in the control panel the menu beginning at the cell named MAIN_MENU. (The /Range Name Labels Right command was used to assign the name MAIN_MENU to the cell in which the label A resides; A is the name of the first menu item.)

You can select from the menu either by moving the cell pointer with the arrow keys or by pressing the first letter of the menu item. The bottom line of the control panel contains a description of the menu item currently highlighted by the user. Moving the cursor to B, for example, changes the description to Use sheet B.

Suppose that you want to select the second menu item—B. Select it as you do any 1-2-3 menu item: press Enter after you position the cursor on your choice, or press the first letter of the menu item. After you select B, the next statement to be executed is {GOTO}B:A1~.

Note: If you have a multilevel menu structure, you can make the Esc key function as it does in the 1-2-3 command menus (backing up to the previous menu). If the user presses Esc instead of selecting a menu item, 1-2-3 stops displaying the menu items and executes the next program command after the MENUBRANCH command. To make the program return to the previous menu, place a BRANCH to the previous level's MENUBRANCH after the current MENUBRANCH command.

Reminder:
Select options from a menu created with MENUBRANCH in the same way you do from 1-2-3 menus.

The MENUCALL Command

The MENUCALL command is identical to the MENUBRANCH command except that 1-2-3 executes the menu program as a subroutine. After the individual menu

Part III ◆ Customizing 1-2-3

Reminder:
MENUCALL returns program control to the statement after the MENUCALL command; MENUBRANCH does not.

programs have been executed, program control returns to the cell immediately below the cell containing the MENUCALL statement. The format of the MENUCALL command is as follows:

{MENUCALL *location*}   Like MENUBRANCH except MENUCALL acts as a subroutine

Suppose that you replace the MENUBRANCH command in figure 14.8 with a MENUCALL command and add another BRANCH statement. The results are shown in figure 14.9.

Fig. 14.9.
Using MENUCALL in place of MENUBRANCH.

```
E:A1: [W12] ^\m                                                      READY

     A          B             C            D            E           F
1    \m         {MENUCALL MAIN_MENU}
2               {BRANCH BEEPER}
3
4    MAIN_MENU  A             B            C            Q
5               Use sheet A   Use sheet B  Use sheet C  Leave the macros
6               {GOTO}A:A1~   {GOTO}B:A1~  {GOTO}C:A1~  {QUIT}
7
8    BEEPER     {BEEP 4}{BEEP 4}
9               {BEEP 3}
```

When you use a MENUCALL, 1-2-3 returns to the statement immediately following the MENUCALL whenever it reads a blank cell or a {RETURN}. Selecting the B menu option, for example, causes 1-2-3 to execute {GOTO}B:A1~. When 1-2-3 encounters the blank cell in C7, however, the flow of execution shifts back to the statement following the MENUCALL: the {BRANCH BEEPER} statement.

Pressing Esc has the same effect with MENUCALL as it does with MENUBRANCH; execution shifts to the statement following the MENUCALL statement.

The advantage of MENUCALL is that you can call the same menu from several different places in a program and continue execution from the calling point after the MENUCALL is finished. This is an advantage of subroutines in general.

Subroutines {*subroutine*}

A *subroutine* is an independent program that can be run from within the main program. Calling a subroutine is as easy as enclosing the name of a routine in braces—for example, {SUB}. When 1-2-3 encounters a name in braces, the program passes control to the named routine. Then, when the routine is finished (when 1-2-3 encounters a blank cell or a RETURN command), program control passes back to the next command in the same cell or the cell below the cell that called the subroutine.

Using subroutines can decrease program-creation time. For example, rather than include the same program lines to display a help screen in each advanced macro command program you create, type the program lines once to create the help screen, and call those lines as a subroutine from each program.

Chapter 14 ◆ Introducing the Advanced Macro Commands **617**

> Isolating problems can be made easier by using subroutines. If you suspect that a subroutine is creating a problem, you can replace the call to the subroutine with a BEEP. If the program runs correctly, beeping when the subroutine should be called, you know that the problem is in the subroutine.
>
> Subroutines are easy to enhance. If you decide to add new commands, you can modify your subroutine. All programs that call that subroutine reflect the new commands.
>
> The greatest benefit of a subroutine, however, is that any program in the same file can use it. Simply create the subroutine once, and then call it at any time from any program. When the subroutine is finished, program execution returns to the originating program.

The RETURN Command

The RETURN command indicates the end of subroutine execution and returns program control to the cell immediately below the cell that called the subroutine (or to further commands in the same cell). Do not confuse RETURN with QUIT, which ends the program completely. RETURN can be used with the IF statement to return conditionally from a subroutine. The form of this command is as follows:

{RETURN}   Returns control from a subroutine

Figure 14.10 demonstrates the RETURN command. The first line of the \a macro places the cell pointer in INPUT_1 (B12) and then calls the subroutine INPUT_SUB. After INPUT_SUB is executed, the RETURN command passes control to the next command after the subroutine call (the {HOME} statement in cell B3), placing the cell pointer in the home position.

Reminder:
Use the RETURN command to end a subroutine and return to the cell that called the subroutine.

```
A:A2: [W11]                                            READY

     A          B          C      D      E      F      G
 1         \a     {GOTO}INPUT_1~
 2                {INPUT_SUB}
 3                {HOME}
 4
 5   INPUT_SUB    {?}~
 6                {DOWN}
 7                {?}~
 8                {RIGHT}
 9                {?}~
10                {RETURN}
11
12   INPUT_1
```

Fig. 14.10.
A macro that uses the RETURN command.

1-2-3 also ends a subroutine and returns to the calling routine when the program encounters, while executing the subroutine, a cell that either is blank or contains a numeric value.

The QUIT Command

Reminder:
The QUIT command causes the program to terminate unconditionally.

The QUIT command forces the program to terminate unconditionally. Even without a QUIT command, the program terminates if it encounters a cell that is empty or contains an entry other than a string (unless the program is a subroutine called by another program). A good practice, however, is always to include a QUIT statement at the point in your program where you want execution to stop. (Conversely, do not put a QUIT command at the end of a program you intend to call as a subroutine.) The form of the QUIT command is as follows:

{QUIT}   Halts program execution

In the following example, the QUIT command forces the program sequence to terminate unconditionally:

{HOME}/fs~r{QUIT}

This is not the case when QUIT is preceded by an IF conditional testing statement, as shown in the following example:

```
{GETNUMBER "Enter a number:",INPUT}
{IF INPUT<1}{QUIT}
```

The ONERROR Command

The processing of macro programs normally is interrupted if a system error (such as `Disk drive not ready`) occurs during execution. By sidestepping system errors that normally cause program termination, the ONERROR command allows programs to proceed. The general format of the command is as follows:

{ONERROR *branch,[message]*}   Traps errors; program control passes to *branch,* can display an error message

The ONERROR command passes program control to the cell indicated by *branch*. Any errors can be recorded in the *message* cell (the optional second argument).

Reminder:
ONERROR must be executed before it can trap errors; include the statement near the start of the program.

The ONERROR statement must be executed before it can trap an error. Therefore, you may want to include an ONERROR statement near the start of your programs. Note, however, that only one ONERROR statement is in effect at a time. You must take precautions to write your programs so that the correct ONERROR is active when its specific error is most probable.

In figure 14.11, the ONERROR statement acts as a safeguard against leaving drive A empty or not closing the drive door. If an error occurs, program control passes to the DISK_ERR macro, and an error message is displayed. Because ONERROR causes a program to branch, the DISK_ERR macro must contain the {BRANCH \a} command to continue the program after a disk is inserted in drive A and the drive door is closed.

In this example, the ONERROR statement causes the program to branch to a cell called DISK_ERR if an error occurs. A copy of the error message that 1-2-3 issues is entered in a cell called ERR_MESSAGE. The first statement in the DISK_ERR routine uses GETLABEL to give the user a customized error message. The program pauses for the user to press Enter. Finally, the program branches back to \a to try again.

Chapter 14 ♦ Introducing the Advanced Macro Commands

```
A:A4: [W14]                                                    READY

     A         B              C         D         E         F         G
1              \a      {ONERROR DISK_ERR,ERR_MESSAGE}
2                      /fs{CE}A:
3                      {?}~
4       _
5   ERR_MESSAGE  Break
6         ANSWER
7
8       DISK_ERR   {GETLABEL "Make sure the diskette is ready and press Enter",ANSWER}
9                  {BRANCH \a}
```

Fig. 14.11.
The ONERROR command used to prompt users to close the drive door.

In addition to the simple example shown in figure 14.11, notice that the ONERROR statement can be used in a sophisticated application that examines the error message and branches back to the appropriate subroutine to correct the error.

Ctrl-Break presents a special problem for the ONERROR statement. Because Ctrl-Break actually causes an error condition, the ONERROR statement is automatically invoked. Figure 14.11 shows how the Ctrl-Break is represented as Break in cell B5. Because this sample macro does not check the error message, Ctrl-Break displays the Make sure the diskette is ready and press Enter message, just as a true disk error would display the message. One possible technique for continuing the use of ONERROR is to disable Ctrl-Break after you debug your program. (See the following discussion of the BREAKOFF command.) By disabling Ctrl-Break, you can prevent the confusion that might arise with an untimely error message. Another technique is to immediately issue another, similar ONERROR command as the first statement in your error handling routine to trap any additional errors (such as a second Ctrl-Break) which immediately followed the first error.

The BREAKOFF Command

The easiest way to stop a program is to issue a Ctrl-Break command. However, 1-2-3 can eliminate the effect of a Ctrl-Break while a program is executing using the BREAKOFF command.

Before you use a BREAKOFF statement, be certain that the program is fully debugged. You may need to issue a Ctrl-Break command to halt the program and make a "repair" while debugging a macro program.

The format of the BREAKOFF command is as follows:

{BREAKOFF}   Disables Ctrl-Break sequence

Note: When a menu structure is displayed in the control panel, you can halt program execution by pressing Esc, regardless of the presence of a BREAKOFF command.

BREAKOFF is used primarily to prevent the user from interrupting a process and destroying the integrity of data in the worksheet. BREAKOFF can be an important safeguard against problems caused by users.

Reminder:
Make sure that the program is fully debugged before including the BREAKOFF command.

The BREAKON Command

To restore the effect of Ctrl-Break, use the BREAKON command. The format of this command is as follows:

{BREAKON}   Enables Ctrl-Break sequence

> **Reminder:**
> *Ctrl-Break is automatically turned back on when the macro program ends.*

Because any Ctrl-Break commands in the buffer are executed as soon as the BREAKON command is executed, be sure that BREAKON is located where the program can stop safely. Figure 14.12 shows how you can use BREAKOFF and BREAKON. Note, however, that BREAKON is actually unnecessary in this program, because Ctrl-Break is automatically turned back on when the macro program ends.

Fig. 14.12.
Use of the BREAKON and BREAKOFF commands.

```
A:B11: 720                                                        READY

        A              B         C         D          E         F         G
 1            \f         {LET PREVIOUS_NUMBER,1}
 2                       {GETNUMBER "Enter number: ",FACTORIAL}
 3                       {BREAKOFF}
 4                       {FOR COUNTER,1,FACTORIAL,1,FACT_RTN}
 5                       {BREAKON}
 6
 7      FACT_RTN         {LET PREVIOUS_NUMBER,+PREVIOUS_NUMBER*COUNTER}
 8
 9      COUNTER                 7
10      FACTORIAL               6
11      PREVIOUS_NUMBER       720
```

The WAIT Command

The WAIT command causes the program to pause until an appointed time. The general format of the WAIT command is as follows:

{WAIT *argument*}   Waits until time or elapsed time specified by *argument*

> **Tip:**
> *Use WAIT to make the program wait until a specific time or for a specified length of time.*

The WAIT statement in the following example pauses the BEEP sequence for 0.5 seconds (you can use this program to signal the user at the end of a long process).

```
{BEEP 2}
{BEEP 4}
{BEEP 4}
{BEEP 2}
{BEEP 3}{WAIT @NOW+@TIME(0,0.5)}
{BEEP 2}
{BEEP 1}
```

The serial time-number must contain a date plus a time. If you want the program to wait until 6:00 P.M. today to continue, you can use the following expression:

{WAIT @INT(@NOW)+@TIME(18,00,00)}

In this example, @INT(@NOW) returns the serial number for 12:00 A.M. on today's date. The +@TIME(18,00,00) adds 18 hours (or .75 days) to the serial number to make the WAIT statement pause macro execution until 6:00 P.M. today.

Chapter 14 ◆ Introducing the Advanced Macro Commands

To make the program pause for 50 seconds, use this expression:

```
{WAIT @NOW+@TIME(00,00,50)}
```

The DISPATCH Command

The DISPATCH command is similar to the BRANCH command. The DISPATCH command, however, branches indirectly to a location specified by the value contained in the *location* argument. The format of the command is as follows:

{DISPATCH *location*} Branches indirectly to the address stored in *location*

The *location* argument should contain a cell address or range name that is the destination of the DISPATCH. If the cell referred to by *location* does not contain a valid cell reference or range name, an error occurs and program execution either stops with an error message or transfers to the location in the current ONERROR command.

The *location* must contain a cell reference or range name that points to a single cell reference. If the location is either a multicell range or a range that contains a single cell, the DISPATCH acts like a BRANCH statement and transfers execution directly to the location.

In figure 14.13, the DISPATCH statement selects the subroutine to be executed based on the input in the cell ANSWER generated by the GETLABEL statement. The string formula in the DISPATCH command concatenates the word *SUB_* and the menu-selection label entered by the user. Because the name of every subroutine here begins with the word *SUB_*, the DISPATCH command passes program control to the subroutine specified by the user.

Reminder:
The DISPATCH argument must contain a cell reference or range name that points to a single cell reference.

```
A:A2:                                                              READY
      A         B              C            D          E         F         G         H
 1    \m        {GETLABEL "Enter number of menu selection: ",ANSWER}
 2              {DISPATCH +"SUB_"&ANSWER}
 3
 4    ANSWER
 5
 6    SUB_1     SUB_2          SUB_3        SUB_4      SUB_5     SUB_6     SUB_7
 7    ...       ...            ...          ...        ...       ...       ...
 8    ...       ...            ...          ...        ...       ...       ...
 9    ...       ...            ...          ...        ...       ...       ...
10    ...       ...            ...          ...        ...       ...       ...
```

Fig. 14.13.
An example of the DISPATCH command.

The DEFINE Command

An important subroutine feature of 1-2-3 is the capability of passing arguments, by using only the key name version of the subroutine call. A subroutine called with arguments must begin with a DEFINE statement that associates each argument with a specific cell location. The format of the subroutine call with arguments is as follows:

Reminder:
Use DEFINE if you want to call subroutines and pass arguments.

Part III ◆ Customizing 1-2-3

{DEFINE *loc1:[Type1]*,...}   Specifies cells for subroutine arguments where *loc1, loc2*, and so on are names or cell references for the cells in which to place the arguments passed from the main program

One or more arguments, separated by commas, can be used. *Type* can be either `STRING` or `VALUE`. *Type* is optional; if not present, the default is STRING. If an argument is of type STRING, the text of the corresponding argument in the subroutine call is placed in the indicated cell as a string value (label).

If an argument is of *type* VALUE, the corresponding argument in the subroutine call is treated as a formula, and its numeric or string value is placed in the argument cell. An error occurs if the corresponding argument in the subroutine call is not a valid number, string, or formula. You do not have to put a string in quotation marks or have a leading plus sign (+) in a formula that uses cell references.

Consider an application that repeatedly converts strings to numbers and displays the numbers in Currency format. Rather than enter the same code at several different places in the program, you decide to write a subroutine. Figure 14.14 shows how the subroutine might appear.

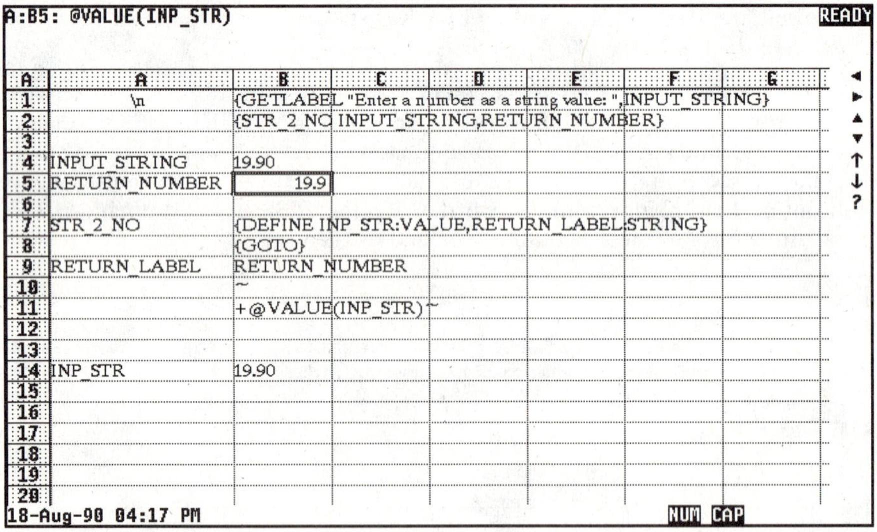

Fig. 14.14.
An example of a subroutine call with parameters.

```
A:B5: @VALUE(INP_STR)                                        READY

      A              B              C         D         E         F         G
 1          \n       {GETLABEL "Enter a number as a string value: ",INPUT_STRING}
 2                   {STR_2_NO INPUT STRING,RETURN NUMBER}
 3
 4   INPUT STRING    19.90
 5   RETURN NUMBER        19.9
 6
 7   STR_2_NO        {DEFINE INP_STR:VALUE,RETURN LABEL:STRING}
 8                   {GOTO}
 9   RETURN LABEL    RETURN NUMBER
10                   ~
11                   +@VALUE(INP_STR)~
12
13
14   INP_STR         19.90
15
16
17
18
19
20
18-Aug-90 04:17 PM                                          NUM CAP
```

The first statement in the main part of the \n program is a GETLABEL statement that reads a string value into the cell named INPUT_STRING. The second statement calls a subroutine named STR_2_NO and passes the arguments INPUT_STRING (the name of the cell containing the input string) and RETURN_NUMBER (the name of the cell where the formatted number is to be stored).

Reminder:
Any subroutine that receives arguments passed from its calling macro must begin with a DEFINE statement.

The STR_2_NO subroutine begins with a DEFINE statement, which defines where and how the arguments passed to the subroutine from the main part of the program are to be stored. Remember, any subroutine that receives arguments passed from its calling macro must begin with a DEFINE statement.

The DEFINE statement in STR_2_NO specifies two cells, INP_STR and RETURN_LABEL, which hold the two arguments passed from the caller. If the number of arguments in the subroutine call does not agree with the number of arguments in the DEFINE statement, an error occurs.

The DEFINE statement specifies that the first argument in the subroutine call is to be evaluated and its value placed in INP_STR. Because the first argument is the cell reference INPUT_STRING, the value in cell INPUT_STRING (in this case, the string 19.90) is placed in INP_STR.

The DEFINE statement specifies that the text of the second argument in the subroutine call is to be placed into the cell RETURN_LABEL as a string. Because the text of the second argument is RETURN_NUMBER, the string RETURN_NUMBER is placed in cell RETURN_LABEL.

The cell containing the second argument is located in the body of the subroutine. This technique is used to allow the subroutine to return a value to a location designated by the caller. In the example, the location RETURN_NUMBER is passed to the subroutine as a string value. The subroutine uses the passed value as the argument of a {GOTO} statement that places the cell pointer on the output cell. Notice that 19.90 is a left-aligned label in cells INPUT_STRING and INP_STR, and is displayed as a number in RETURN_NUMBER. After the subroutine places the cell pointer on the output cell, it continues by converting the string in INP_STR to a number and placing the resulting numeric value in the output cell.

This technique is one of two primary ways to return information to the calling routine. The other way to return information is to place it in a specified cell that is used every time the subroutine is called.

Passing arguments to and from subroutines is important if you want to get the most out of 1-2-3's subroutine capabilities. Subroutines with arguments simplify program coding and make the resulting macros easier to trace. Subroutine arguments are almost essential when you develop a subroutine to perform a common function you use again and again. Subroutines with arguments are also one of the trickiest parts of the 1-2-3 advanced macro commands.

Reminder: *Subroutine arguments are almost essential when you develop a subroutine to perform a common function you use frequently.*

The RESTART Command

Just as the main program can call subroutines, one subroutine can also call another. As 1-2-3 moves from one subroutine to the next, it saves the addresses of where it has been. This technique is called *stacking*, or *saving addresses on a stack*. By saving the addresses on a stack, 1-2-3 can trace its way back through the subroutine calls to the main program.

The RESTART command can eliminate the stack to prevent 1-2-3 from returning by the path it came, allowing a subroutine to be canceled at any time during execution. Although seldom used, RESTART can be quite helpful. The RESTART command normally is used with an IF statement under a conditional testing evaluation. The format for this command is as follows:

Tip: *Use RESTART to eliminate the stack and prevent 1-2-3 from returning by the same path.*

Part III ♦ Customizing 1-2-3

{RESTART}   Cancels a subroutine

Figure 14.15 shows how you can use RESTART to prevent a user from entering incorrect data in a database. In this example, the \b macro first prompts the user for his or her last name. Then a call is made to SUB_1, which starts with a call to SUB_2. SUB_2, in turn, calls SUB_3.

Fig. 14.15.
The RESTART command used in a database application.

```
A:B13: 'JONES                                                    READY

       A          B              C         D          E         F       G       H
 1    \b         {GETLABEL "What is your last name?",LAST_NAME}
 2               {SUB_1}
 3
 4    SUB_1     {SUB_2}
 5               {GETLABEL "What day is it?",DAY}
 6
 7    SUB_2     {SUB_3}
 8               {GETLABEL "How are you?",HOW}
 9
10    SUB_3     {IF LAST_NAME="SMITH"}{RESTART}{BRANCH \b}
11               {GETLABEL "What is your first name?",FIRST_NAME}
12
13    LAST_NAME  JONES
14    FIRST_NAME BOB
15    DAY        TUESDAY
16    HOW        FINE
```

The SUB_3 program first checks to see whether the user entered the LAST_NAME of *SMITH*. If the user entered *SMITH*, The program doesn't accept the entry and executes a RESTART and then a BRANCH back to the \b macro. If the user entered anything other than *SMITH*, SUB_3 prompts for the FIRST_NAME. When the user presses Enter, SUB_3 ends and control returns to the second line of SUB_2, which prompts for HOW. After the user's entry, SUB_2 ends and the second line of SUB_1 executes.

The SYSTEM Command

Reminder:
SYSTEM executes any operating system or batch command.

The SYSTEM command executes any operating system or batch command by using the following format:

{SYSTEM *command*}   Executes *command*

The following shows an example of the SYSTEM command executing the batch command PARK:

`{SYSTEM PARK}`

Caution:
If you try to load a memory-resident program, or use some batch commands, you may not be able to resume 1-2-3.

You can use up to 512 characters to specify the operating system or batch command. Keep in mind some rules when you use SYSTEM. First, if you attempt to load a memory-resident program, you may not be able to resume 1-2-3. Second, some batch commands may not let you resume 1-2-3. For these two reasons, be particularly careful to save your files before you begin testing a macro that uses SYSTEM. Also remember that if all you want to do is access the operating system during a 1-2-3 session, the /System menu command provides a convenient alternative way to do this (although the same warnings apply).

If you run into problems executing the operating system commands, test for successful completion of a command by following the SYSTEM command with @INFO("osreturncode"). See Chapter 6 for a description of this and other @functions.

Using Commands That Make Decisions

The advanced macro commands for decision-making, shown in table 14.3, give you the capabilities of true programming languages such as BASIC. With the three commands (IF, FOR, and FORBREAK) presented in the following sections, you can test for numeric and string values. The IF command provides the kind of conditional logic available in many high-level languages. FOR and FORBREAK offer a conditional looping capability, allowing you to control how many times a group of commands is activated.

Table 14.3
Commands for Making Decisions

Command	Description
{IF}	Conditionally executes statements after IF
{FOR}	Activates a loop a specified number of times
{FORBREAK}	Terminates a FOR loop

The IF Command

The IF command uses IF-THEN-ELSE logic to evaluate the existence of certain numeric and string values. The advanced macro command IF, commonly used to control program flow and enable the program to perform based on criteria provided by the user, is the functional equivalent of the IF command in BASIC. The format of the IF command is as follows:

{IF *condition*}{*true*}   Executes true or false statements based on
{*false*}   the result of a *condition*; if the logical
                           expression is true, the remaining commands
                           on the same line are executed

The commands to be executed if *condition* is true ordinarily include a BRANCH command to skip the {*false*} statements. If the expression is false, execution skips the commands (after the IF command) on the current line and continues on the next line.

IF statements can check for a variety of conditions, including the position of the cell pointer, a specific numeric value, or a specific string value. In figure 14.15, for

Reminder:
If the condition is true, the statements following the IF are performed; if the condition is false, execution continues with the next line.

example, the IF statement checks to see whether the user entered a LAST_NAME of *SMITH*. If so, program control passes to the \b macro, where the program starts over. If LAST_NAME is not *SMITH*, the second line of SUB_3 executes and the program continues by returning through the stack.

An IF statement is contained in a single cell. The part of the cell following the IF portion is called the *THEN clause*. The THEN clause executes only if the result of the logical test is true.

The second line contains the *ELSE clause*, which executes if the result of the logical statement in the IF statement is false or if the program statements in the THEN clause do not transfer control. In the example in figure 14.15, the THEN clause contains a BRANCH statement so that the ELSE does not execute when the IF statement is true.

The IF statement adds significant strength to 1-2-3's advanced macro commands. However, the one disadvantage of the IF statement is that if the code in the THEN clause does not branch or execute a QUIT command, the program continues its execution right through the ELSE clause.

The FOR and FORBREAK Commands

The FOR command is used to control the looping process in a program by calling a subroutine to be executed a certain number of times. FOR enables you to define the exact number of times the subroutine is to be executed. The format of the FOR command is as follows:

{FOR *counter,start,stop,step,routine*}   Activates a loop a specific number of times

Caution:
Although multiple loops are allowed in FOR structures, be careful of the logical flow of multiple looping structures.

The FOR statement contains five arguments. The first argument is a cell that acts as the counter for the loop. The second argument is the starting number for the counter, the third is the ending number, the fourth argument is the increment, and the fifth is the name of the subroutine that 1-2-3 executes on each pass through the loop. Arguments 2, 3, and 4 can be values, cell addresses, or formulas. Arguments 1 and 5, however, must be range names or cell addresses. Multiple loops are permitted; be careful of the logical flow of multiple looping structures.

Notice how FOR was used in the simple example in figure 14.12. The FOR statement controls how many times the program FACT_RTN executes. The FOR statement begins by using the range named COUNTER to keep track of how many times the program should loop. The second argument, 1, is the start number for the counter; the next argument, FACTORIAL, is the stop number. The program keeps track of the looping process by comparing the counter against the stop number, and stops executing if the counter value is larger than the stop number.

The FOR statement's next argument, 1, is the step number; this value is the one by which the counter is incremented after each loop. The last argument, FACT_RTN, is the name of the routine to be executed each time through the loop.

The FORBREAK command terminates processing of a FOR command based on something other than the number of iterations, such as a conditional test.

Chapter 14 ◆ Introducing the Advanced Macro Commands 627

FORBREAK interrupts the processing of the FOR command and continues execution with the command following the FOR statement. If, for example, FACT_RTN contained a second line with a test like the following, the loop ends as soon as the value in PREVIOUS_NUMBER exceeds 1000:

```
{IF PREVIOUS_NUMBER>1000}{FORBREAK}
```

Using Commands That Manipulate Data

The LET, PUT, CONTENTS, BLANK, APPENDBELOW, and APPENDRIGHT commands allow precise placement of data within worksheet files. These commands, listed in table 14.4, function similarly to menu commands such as /Copy, /Move, and /Range Erase but provide capabilities that go beyond these simple operations.

Table 14.4
Commands for Manipulating Data

Command	Description
{LET}	Places value of an expression in the location specified
{PUT}	Places value into cell within range
{CONTENTS}	Stores contents of the specified source in the specified destination
{BLANK}	Erases the cell or range
{APPENDBELOW}	Places contents of the specified source *below* the specified destination range and then expands the definition of the specified destination range to include the new data
{APPENDRIGHT}	Places contents of the specified source to the *right* of the specified destination range and then expands the definition of the specified destination range to include the new data

The LET Command

The LET command places a value or string in a target cell location without the cell pointer actually being at the location. LET is extremely useful, for example, for placing criteria in a database criteria range. The format of the LET command is as follows:

{LET *location,expression*}   Places value of *expression* in *location*

The LET command can use numeric values, string values, or formulas. Suppose, for example, that the cell named FIRST contains the string BOB and LAST holds the string JONES. The following statement stores BOB JONES in NAME:

Tip:
Use LET to assign a value to a location without first moving the cell pointer to the location.

{LET NAME,FIRST&" "&LAST}

Like the DEFINE command, the LET command enables you to specify :STRING and :VALUE suffixes after the argument. The :STRING suffix stores the text of the argument in *location*; the :VALUE suffix evaluates the argument as a string or numeric formula and places the result in *location*. When a suffix is not specified, LET stores the argument's numeric or string value if it is a valid formula; otherwise, the text of the argument is stored. For example, the following statement stores BOB JONES in NAME:

{LET NAME,FIRST&" "&LAST:VALUE}

The next statement, however, stores the string FIRST&" "&LAST in NAME:

{LET NAME,FIRST&" "&LAST:STRING}

Instead of using the LET command, you can move the cell pointer to the desired location with GOTO and enter the desired value into the cell. The LET command, however, has the major advantage that it does not disturb the current location of the cell pointer. Although you can use /Data Fill to enter numbers, you cannot use it to enter string values. Overall, the LET command is a convenient and useful means for setting the value of a cell from within a program. Figure 14.16 shows the three formats for the LET command and the results of each.

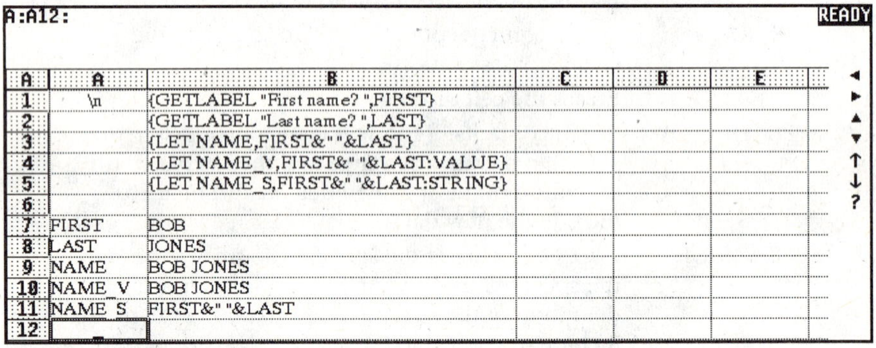

Fig. 14.16.

Examples of the LET command.

	A	B	C	D	E
1	\n	{GETLABEL "First name?",FIRST}			
2		{GETLABEL "Last name?",LAST}			
3		{LET NAME,FIRST&" "&LAST}			
4		{LET NAME_V,FIRST&" "&LAST:VALUE}			
5		{LET NAME_S,FIRST&" "&LAST:STRING}			
6					
7	FIRST	BOB			
8	LAST	JONES			
9	NAME	BOB JONES			
10	NAME_V	BOB JONES			
11	NAME_S	FIRST&" "&LAST			
12					

The PUT Command

The PUT command places a value in a target cell location determined by the intersection of a row and a column in a defined range. The format of the PUT command is as follows:

{PUT *range,col,row,value*}   Places *value* into the specified cell within *range*

The PUT statement contains four arguments. The first argument defines the range into which the value is placed. The second argument defines the column offset within the range; the third, the row offset within the range. The fourth indicates the value to be placed in the cell location. The first argument can be a range name or cell address. The second, third, and fourth arguments can be values, cell references, or formulas. Consider, for example, the following PUT statement:

`{PUT TABLE,S1,S2,ARG4}`

This statement places the contents of the cell named ARG4 in the range named TABLE (B5..D7) at the intersection defined by the values in cells S1 and S2. Figure 14.17 shows the results of different variations of this command. Keep in mind that the row and column offset numbers used with the PUT command follow the same conventions followed by @functions (the first column is number 0, the second is number 1, and so on). Also, the row and column values (contained in cells S1 and S2 in this example) must not place the value outside the range (the range is TABLE in this example); if this happens, the macro fails and 1-2-3 informs you that the PUT statement contains an invalid range.

Reminder:
The offset values you use with PUT are numbered starting with 0: the first column is column 0, the second row is row 1, and so on.

```
A:A2:                                                           READY
     A         B              C           D       E     F    G    H
 1        \p   {PUT TABLE,0,0,BOB}
 2             {PUT TABLE,1,1,JONES}
 3             {PUT TABLE,2,0,123}
 4
 5
 6   TABLE     BOB                       123
 7                            JONES
```

Fig. 14.17.
The PUT command used to enter numbers and labels.

The CONTENTS Command

The CONTENTS command stores the contents of the source cell in the destination cell, optionally assigning an individual cell width or cell format. If either width or format is not specified, the CONTENTS command uses the column width or format of the source location to format the string. The format of the CONTENTS command is as follows:

Tip:
Use CONTENTS to store a value in a cell, and optionally change the width or format of the cell.

    `{CONTENTS `*destination,source,width,format*`}`   Stores contents of *source* in *destination* as a string

Suppose that you want to copy the number 123.456 from cell SOURCE_1 to cell DEST_1, and change the number to a string while you copy. The statement for this operation is as follows:

`{CONTENTS DEST_1,SOURCE_1}`

The contents of cell DEST_1 are displayed as the string '123.456, with a left-aligned label-prefix character.

Suppose that you want to change the width of the string when you copy it. Rather than display the string as `123.456`, you want to display it as `123.5`. You can get the desired result by changing the statement to the following:

`{CONTENTS DEST_2,SOURCE_1,6}`

This second statement uses a width of 6 to display the string. The least significant digits of the number are rounded to create the string.

Now suppose that you want to change the display format of the string while you copy it and change its width. The following string changes the display format to **Currency 0**:

    {CONTENTS DEST_3,SOURCE_1,5,32}

The numbers you can use for the format number in this statement are listed in table 14.5. The result of the statement is the number $123.

Table 14.5
Numeric Format Codes for the CONTENTS Command

Code	Format of the Destination String
0–15	Fixed, **0** to **15** decimal places
16–31	Sci (scientific), **0** to **15** decimal places
32–47	Currency, **0** to **15** decimal places
48–63	Percent, **0** to **15** decimal places
64–79	, (Comma), **0** to **15** decimal places
112	+/– (bar graph)
113	General format
114	**D1** (DD-MMM-YY)
115	**D2** (DD-MMM)
116	**D3** (MMM-YY)
117	Text format
118	Hidden format
119	**D6** (HH:MM:SS AM/PM time format)
120	**D7** (HH:MM AM/PM time format)
121	**D4** (Long International Date)
122	**D5** (Short International Date)
123	**D8** (Long International Time)
124	**D9** (Short International Time)
127	The current window's default display format

In the following examples of the CONTENTS command, the number in cell SOURCE_2 (B2) is 123.456, the width of column B is 9, and the display format for cell SOURCE_2 (B2) is **Fixed 2**.

{CONTENTS DEST_4,SOURCE_2}	Displays the number 123.46 in cell DEST_4, using the **Fixed 2** format.
{CONTENTS DEST_5,SOURCE_2,4}	Displays the number in cell DEST_5, using a width of 4 and the **Fixed 2** format.
{CONTENTS DEST_6,SOURCE_2,5,0}	Displays the number 123 in cell DEST_6, using the **Fixed 0** format.

Figure 14.18 shows the results of each of these CONTENTS statements.

```
A:B2: (F2) 123.456                                          READY

    A         B        C              D              E    F
1  SOURCE_1  123.456  \c   {CONTENTS DEST_1,SOURCE_1}
2  SOURCE_2  123.46        {CONTENTS DEST_2,SOURCE_1,6}
3                          {CONTENTS DEST_3,SOURCE_1,5,32}
4  DEST_1    123.456       {CONTENTS DEST_4,SOURCE_2}
5  DEST_2    123.5         {CONTENTS DEST_5,SOURCE_2,4}
6  DEST_3    $123          {CONTENTS DEST_6,SOURCE_2,5,0}
7  DEST_4    123.46
8  DEST_5    ****
9  DEST_6    123
```

Fig. 14.18.
Examples of the CONTENTS command.

The CONTENTS command is somewhat specialized but useful in situations that require converting numeric values to formatted strings. Using the **Text** format, CONTENTS can convert long numeric formulas to strings which are useful for debugging purposes.

The BLANK Command

The BLANK command erases a range of cells in the worksheet. Although this command works similarly to the /Range Erase command, using BLANK has a few advantages over using /Range Erase in advanced macro command programs. Because BLANK works outside the menu structure, it is faster than /Range Erase. The format of the BLANK command is as follows:

{BLANK *location*}   Erases the range defined by *location*

The statement {BLANK RANGE_1}, for example, erases RANGE_1.

Reminder:
BLANK erases a range of cells.

The APPENDBELOW Command

The APPENDBELOW command copies the contents of one range to the rows immediately *below* another range. As part of the copy operation, APPENDBELOW also expands the range of the destination to include the new data. The format of the APPENDBELOW command is as follows:

{APPENDBELOW *source,destination*}   Copies contents of *source* to *destination* and expands the destination range to include the new data

Reminder:
APPENDBELOW copies the contents of one range to another, and expands the destination range to include the new data.

APPENDBELOW is a helpful companion to the FORM command, covered earlier in this chapter. The two commands provide an easy way to copy data from an input form to a storage table or database range. Figure 14.19 shows a simple example that collects first and last name information, stores that information in a range called TABLE_1, and uses APPENDBELOW to record the data in the database range called TABLE_2.

Fig. 14.19.
Using the APPENDBELOW command to copy data entered with the FORM command.

```
A:B7: U 'Q                                                    READY

       A         B              C          D       E       F       G
 1     \a        {FORM TABLE 1}
 2               {IF FIRST="Q"}{QUIT}
 3               {APPENDBELOW TABLE 2,TABLE 1}
 4               {BRANCH \a}
 5
 6               FIRST          LAST
 7    TABLE_1    Q              SMITH
 8
 9    TABLE_2
10               BOB            JONES
11               TOM            SMITH
```

Two situations can cause the APPENDBELOW command to fail. The first is if the number of rows in the specified source exceeds the number of rows left in the worksheet below the specified destination. When this happens, APPENDBELOW aborts. For example, if only 100 rows are left in the worksheet, you can't copy 200 rows of information.

A second condition that causes APPENDBELOW to fail is if executing the command would destroy data in the destination range by overwriting existing data. Actually, this condition is a handy safety feature, because APPENDBELOW does not destroy data in your worksheet.

APPENDBELOW copies calculated values, not the actual formulas. In this respect, APPENDBELOW is similar to /**R**ange Value.

The APPENDRIGHT Command

Reminder:
APPENDRIGHT works just like APPENDBELOW, except data is copied to the right of the destination range.

APPENDRIGHT's operation mirrors that of APPENDBELOW, with one exception: APPENDRIGHT copies the contents of *source* to the *right* of *destination*. (APPENDBELOW copies the contents of the source to just *below* the destination.) The APPENDRIGHT command uses the following format:

{APPENDRIGHT *source,destination*}   Expands the destination range to include newly copied data and converts formulas to values during the copy

APPENDRIGHT ends in an error when there isn't room to copy because of either existing data or insufficient worksheet space. Because 1-2-3 worksheets contain many more rows than columns, APPENDRIGHT runs out of space much sooner than APPENDBELOW. Figure 14.20 shows the result of changing the APPENDBELOW operation shown in figure 14.19 to APPENDRIGHT.

Using Commands That Enhance Programs

The commands listed in table 14.6 can "dress up" your program or recalculate a portion of your worksheet. With skillful placement, these commands can add the polish that a solid program structure needs to become a smooth, easy-to-use application. This catch-all group of maintenance-oriented commands includes commands to sound your computer's bell, control the screen display, and selectively recalculate portions of the worksheet. Two commands in this group—WINDOWSOFF and PANELOFF—can significantly increase the execution speed of large advanced macro command programs. The WINDOWSOFF and PANELOFF commands also suppress the menu display and range highlighting.

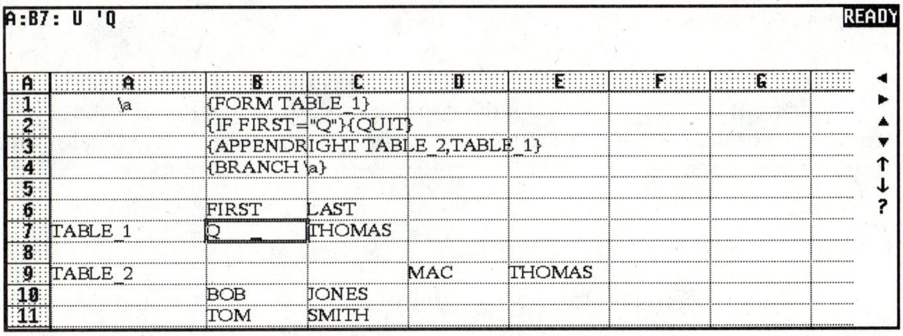

```
A:B7: U 'Q                                              READY

     A         B           C         D       E        F       G
 1         \a         {FORM TABLE 1}
 2                    {IF FIRST="Q"}{QUIT}
 3                    {APPENDRIGHT TABLE 2,TABLE 1}
 4                    {BRANCH \a}
 5
 6                    FIRST       LAST
 7  TABLE 1      Q               THOMAS
 8
 9  TABLE 2                             MAC     THOMAS
10               BOB         JONES
11               TOM         SMITH
```

Fig. 14.20.

Using the APPENDRIGHT command to copy data entered with the FORM command.

Table 14.6
Commands for Enhancing Programs

Command	Description
{BEEP}	Sounds one of the computer's four beeps
{PANELOFF}	Suppresses display in the control panel
{PANELON}	Reactivates the display in the control panel
{WINDOWSOFF}	Suppresses redisplay of the current window
{WINDOWSON}	Enables redisplay of the current window
{FRAMEOFF}	Suppresses display of the worksheet frame (worksheet letter, column letters, and row numbers)
{FRAMEON}	Displays the worksheet frame (worksheet letter, column letters, and row numbers)
{GRAPHON}	Displays the current graph and/or sets the named graph
{GRAPHOFF}	Removes the graph displayed by GRAPHON
{INDICATE}	Resets the control panel indicator to the string specified
{RECALC}	Recalculates a specified portion of the worksheet row by row
{RECALCCOL}	Recalculates a specified portion of the worksheet column by column

The BEEP Command

Tip:
Use BEEP to make the computer emit one of four beeps.

The BEEP command activates the computer's speaker system to produce one of four tones. Each argument (1 through 4) produces a different tone. The BEEP command is commonly used to alert the user to a specific condition in the program or to draw the user's attention. The format of the BEEP command is as follows:

{BEEP *number*} or {BEEP}   Sounds one of the computer's four beeps

Consider the following BEEP statement:

```
{IF A35>50}{BEEP 2}
```

This statement produces a sound if the condition presented in the IF statement is true. If the condition is not true, program control passes to the next cell below the IF statement.

The PANELOFF Command

The PANELOFF command freezes the control panel, suppressing the display of program commands in the control panel during program execution. Be aware, however, that the advanced macro commands such as MENUBRANCH, MENUCALL, GETLABEL, GETNUMBER, and INDICATE override the PANELOFF command. The format of the PANELOFF command is as follows:

{PANELOFF}   Suppresses display in the control panel

Consider the following example, where PANELOFF suppresses display in the control panel of the /Copy command in the second line:

```
{PANELOFF}
/cRANGE_1~RANGE_2~
```

The PANELON Command

The PANELON command unfreezes the control panel if it has been frozen with the PANELOFF command. The format of the PANELON command is as follows:

{PANELON}   Reactivates display in the control panel

In the following example, PANELOFF freezes the control panel display as RANGE_1 is copied to RANGE_2; the PANELON command reactivates the control panel:

```
{PANELOFF}
/cRANGE_1~RANGE_2~
{PANELON}
```

Reminder:
WINDOWSOFF freezes the main part of the screen, regardless of whether the macro program is executing.

The WINDOWSOFF Command

The WINDOWSOFF command freezes the main part of the screen but allows the control panel to display the program commands. The WINDOWSOFF command freezes the current screen display, regardless of whether the program is executing.

Chapter 14 ◆ Introducing the Advanced Macro Commands

WINDOWSOFF is particularly useful when you are creating applications used by beginning 1-2-3 users. WINDOWSOFF enables you to display only those screen changes that the user *must* see, preventing other changes (which might confuse beginners) from displaying. The format of the WINDOWSOFF command is as follows:

{WINDOWSOFF}   Suppresses screen display

Consider the following example:

```
{WINDOWSOFF}
/cRANGE_1~RANGE_2~{CALC}
```

In this example, WINDOWSOFF suppresses the automatic screen-rebuilding associated with the /Copy command or the Calc (F9) key. The WINDOWSOFF and PANELOFF commands can have a significant effect on program execution time; in some cases reducing execution time by as much as 50 percent. Performance improvements depend, of course, on the particular applications.

Tip:
WINDOWSOFF and PANELOFF reduce program execution time.

Figure 14.21 shows how to use WINDOWSOFF and PANELOFF to eliminate screen shifting and to reduce execution time for a graph "slide show" presentation. The program displays a sequence of graphs uninterrupted by intervening worksheet screens.

	A	B	C	D
1	\s	{PANELOFF}{WINDOWSOFF}	Suppress redrawing of panel and window	
2		/gnuFIG_1~	Display Figure 1	
3		q/gnuFIG_2~	Press space bar to display Figure 2	
4		q/gnuFIG_3~	Press space bar to display Figure 3	
5		q/gnuFIG_4~	Press space bar to display Figure 4	
6		{PANELON}{WINDOWSON}	Restore redrawing of panel and window	
7		q{HOME}	Return cursor to home position	

Fig. 14.21.
Using the WINDOWSOFF and PANELOFF commands for a graphics "slide show."

Be aware that if an error occurs while WINDOWSOFF is in effect, normal updating of the worksheet window does not occur. Develop and test programs without the WINDOWSOFF and WINDOWSON commands; add these commands to the debugged and tested program.

The WINDOWSON Command

The WINDOWSON command unfreezes the screen, allowing display of executing program operations. This command is commonly used to allow display of the 1-2-3 menu structures. The format of the WINDOWSON command is as follows:

{WINDOWSON}   Enables redisplay of the current window

In figure 14.21, the WINDOWSON command in B6 activates display of the worksheet screen after all the graphs have been shown.

Tip:
Use WINDOWSON to allow display of the 1-2-3 menu structures.

The FRAMEOFF Command

The FRAMEOFF command removes from the screen display the worksheet letter, column letters, and row numbers. The format of the command is as follows:

{FRAMEOFF}   Suppresses display of the worksheet frame

Reminder: *FRAMEOFF lasts until the end of program execution, if you don't specifically issue a FRAMEON command.*

After you execute a FRAMEOFF command within an advanced macro command program, the worksheet frame display is suppressed until the program encounters a FRAMEON command or completes execution.

FRAMEOFF does not work in Wysiwyg graphics mode. To accomplish the same effect as FRAMEOFF in Wysiwyg graphics mode, use the **:D**isplay **O**ptions **F**rame **N**one **Q**uit **Q**uit command sequence.

The FRAMEON Command

The FRAMEON command redisplays the worksheet frame—worksheet letter, column letters, and row numbers—originally suppressed by a FRAMEOFF command. The format for the FRAMEON command is as follows:

{FRAMEON}   Redisplays the worksheet frame

The following is an example showing a simple program using FRAMEOFF and FRAMEON. The program initially suppresses display of the worksheet frame until you press a key, redisplays the worksheet frame until you press a key, and then again suppresses the worksheet frame until you press a key.

```
{FRAMEOFF}{?}~
{DOWN 2}
{FRAMEON}{?}~
{RIGHT 3}
{FRAMEOFF}{?}~
```

If you construct this macro yourself, note that even though the last FRAMEOFF command doesn't have a matching FRAMEON command, the worksheet frame still redisplays when the macro program ends.

Tip: In Releases 3.1 and 3.1+, FRAMEOFF and FRAMEON do not function in Wysiwyg graphics mode. You must first switch to text mode (select **:D**isplay **M**ode **T**ext) if you want to use FRAMEOFF and FRAMEON.

The GRAPHON Command

The GRAPHON command can set the currently named graph, display the currently named graph, or first set and then display the currently named graph. The format for the GRAPHON command is as follows:

Chapter 14 ◆ Introducing the Advanced Macro Commands

{GRAPHON *[named-graph]*, [nodisplay]}   Displays the current graph or another named graph, or sets the current graph without displaying it

To display a full-screen view of the currently named graph, simply use the command alone, as in the following example:

    {GRAPHON}

To display a graph different from the one currently named, reset the currently named graph and then redisplay it. For example, if you have a graph setting named FIG_1, use the following structure:

    {GRAPHON FIG_1}

In either of the preceding cases, 1-2-3 continues to display a full-sized version of the graph until the macro program completes execution or until the macro program encounters a GRAPHOFF command, another GRAPHON command, or a command that displays a prompt or menu (such as GETLABEL or MENUCALL).

To change the named graph but not display it, use the nodisplay literal argument. For example, suppose that you have a graph setting named FIG_1 that you want as the current graph setting, but you don't want the graph displayed. Use the following structure:

    {GRAPHON FIG_1,nodisplay}

Figure 14.22 shows these alternative command formats. The first line of the \g program sets the current graph as FIG_1 and displays it for three seconds as indicated by the WAIT command in line 2. The third line sets the current graph setting as FIG_2, but does not display it. The fourth line displays FIG_2 for three seconds. The last line redisplays the worksheet by executing the GRAPHOFF command.

Reminder:
GRAPHON continues to display a full-screen graph until the program ends or encounters a GRAPHOFF or GRAPHON command.

	A	B	C
1	\g	{GRAPHON FIG_1}	Display graph FIG_1
2		{WAIT @NOW+@TIME(0,0,3)}	Wait 3 seconds
3		{GRAPHON FIG_2,nodisplay}	Make graph FIG_2 current but do not display
4		{GRAPHON}	Display graph FIG_2
5		{WAIT @NOW+@TIME(0,0,3)}	Wait 3 seconds
6		{GRAPHOFF}	Turn off graph display

Fig. 14.22.
The GRAPHON and GRAPHOFF commands used to display graphs and change the current graph.

The GRAPHOFF Command

The GRAPHOFF command removes the named graph from the display and redisplays the worksheet. The format for using the GRAPHOFF command is as follows:

    {GRAPHOFF}

For more information about the GRAPHOFF command, refer to the preceding section on GRAPHON.

The INDICATE Command

Tip:
Use INDICATE to create customized indicators.

The INDICATE command alters the mode indicator in the upper right corner of the 1-2-3 screen. This command is commonly used to provide custom indicators. The INDICATE command accepts a string argument as long as the screen width. The format of the INDICATE command is as follows:

{INDICATE *[string]*}   Resets the mode indicator to *string*

The following INDICATE command displays the message START in the upper right corner of the screen:

{INDICATE START}

Unless cleared, the START message displays until you exit 1-2-3. Restore the indicator to normal using the following command:

{INDICATE}

To blank out the indicator completely, use this command:

{INDICATE ""}

The INDICATE command can use a *string* argument; if you want to use the contents of a cell or range as the indicator, you must use a string formula. To display text stored in cell B1, for example, use the following formula:

+"{INDICATE """&B1&"""}"

Note: You use the three sets of quotation marks to ensure that the value of cell B1 is contained within a single set of quotation marks.

The RECALC and RECALCCOL Commands

Two macro commands, RECALC and RECALCCOL, recalculate a portion of the worksheet. Recalculating only a portion of the worksheet is useful in large worksheets where recalculation time is long and where you need to recalculate certain values in the worksheet before proceeding to the next processing step. The commands for partial recalculation have the following formats:

{RECALC *location,[condition],[iteration-number]*}
{RECALCCOL *location,[condition],[iteration-number]*}

In these commands, *location* is a range or range name that specifies the cells whose formulas are to be recalculated. The *condition* and *iteration-number* arguments are optional.

Reminder:
If you use the condition argument with RECALC or RECALCCOL, make sure the reference is to a cell within the recalculation range.

If the *condition* argument is included, the range is recalculated repeatedly until the condition has a logical value of TRUE (1). The *condition* must be either a logical expression or a reference to a cell within the recalculation range that contains a logical expression. If *condition* is a reference to a cell outside the recalculation range, the value of the condition—either TRUE (1) or FALSE (0)—does not change, and the condition does not control the partial recalculation.

If the *iteration-number* argument is included, the *condition* argument also must be specified (use the value 1 to make the condition always TRUE). The *iteration-number* specifies the number of times that the formulas in *location* are recalculated.

The RECALC and RECALCCOL commands differ in the order in which cells in the specified range are recalculated. RECALC performs the calculations of all the cells in the first row of the range, then all the cells in the second row, and so on. The RECALCCOL command performs the calculations of all the cells in the first column of the range, then all the cells in the second column, and so on. With either command, only cells within the specified range are recalculated.

Use RECALC if the formula to be recalculated is below and to the left of the cells on which it depends. Use RECALCCOL if the formula is above and to the right of the cells on which it depends.

The formulas in the recalculation range can refer to values in cells outside the range; however, those values are not updated by RECALC or RECALCCOL. When either the RECALC or RECALCCOL command is executed, the partial recalculation occurs immediately, although the results do not appear on-screen until the screen is redrawn. The recalculated numbers, however, are used in calculations and conditional tests.

If the macro program ends and you want to be sure that the recalculated numbers are on-screen, use the PgUp and PgDn keys to move the window away from and back to the recalculated range. The act of looking away and back again updates the screen and displays the current values in the recalculated range.

You may need to use {CALC}, RECALC, or RECALCCOL after commands such as LET, GETNUMBER, and ?, or after 1-2-3 commands such as /**R**ange **I**nput within a program. You do not have to recalculate after invoking 1-2-3 commands such as /**C**opy and /**M**ove; 1-2-3 automatically recalculates the affected ranges after such commands, even during program execution.

Caution: Recalculating a portion of the worksheet can cause some formulas (those outside a recalculated range that reference formulas within the range) to fail to reflect current data. Use {CALC} to correct this situation.

Caution:
You may have to use CALC if the formula is both above and to the left of cells on which it depends.

Tip:
Use PgUp and PgDn to redraw the screen and make sure that the recalculated formulas display on-screen.

Using Commands That Manipulate Files

Nine commands give 1-2-3 the capability of opening, reading, writing, and closing a sequential data file containing ASCII text data. These commands allow 1-2-3 applications to read and write files used by other business applications. The file manipulation commands provide an enhanced capability to manipulate foreign files beyond what is offered by the /**F**ile Import and /**P**rint File commands.

Part III ♦ Customizing 1-2-3

Table 14.7
Commands for Manipulating Files

Command	Description
{OPEN}	Opens a file for reading, writing, or both
{CLOSE}	Closes a file opened with OPEN
{READ}	Copies specified characters from the open file to the specified location
{READLN}	Copies the next line from a file to the specified location
{WRITE}	Copies a string to the open file
{WRITELN}	Copies a string plus a carriage-return line-feed sequence to the open file
{SETPOS}	Sets a new position for a file pointer
{GETPOS}	Records a file pointer position in the specified location
{FILESIZE}	Records the size of the open file in the specified location

Using the File Manipulation Commands

The file manipulation commands are programming commands. To read from and write to foreign files successfully, you must understand exactly how these commands work and how the sequential files you are manipulating are organized. If you write to a file containing another application, be sure to back up the file before trying to write to it from within 1-2-3.

Used with caution, this group of commands can open up the world of outside files to your 1-2-3 applications. If you need to process external data files, these commands make the task possible using 1-2-3.

The OPEN Command

The OPEN command opens a disk file, providing access so that you can write to or read from that file. In the command's second argument, you can specify whether you want to read only, write only, or both read from and write to the file.

Reminder:
You can open only one file at a time; 1-2-3 automatically closes a file before opening another.

1-2-3 allows only one file to be open at a time. If you want to work with more than one file in your application, you must open each file before using it; 1-2-3 automatically closes an open file before opening and using the next file.

The format of the OPEN command is as follows:

{OPEN *filename,access-mode*}   Opens file for reading, writing, or both

The *filename* argument can be a string, an expression with a string value, or a single-cell reference to a cell that contains a string or a string expression. The string must be a valid operating system file name or path name. A file in the current directory can be specified by its name and extension. A file in another directory

Chapter 14 ◆ Introducing the Advanced Macro Commands

may require a drive identification, a subdirectory path, or a complete operating system path in addition to the file name and extension.

The *access-mode* argument is a single-character string that specifies whether you want to read only, write only, or both read from and write to the file. The following chart lists the *access-mode* strings you can use:

Access-mode String	Description
"R"	Read access opens an existing file and allows access with the READ and READLN commands. You cannot write to a file opened with Read access.
"W"	Write access opens a new file with the specified name and enables access with the WRITE and WRITELN commands. Any existing file with the specified name is erased and replaced by the new file.
"A"	Append access opens an existing file and allows both read (READ and READLN) and write (WRITE and WRITELN) commands. Append access is like Modify access except that Append access places the byte pointer at the *end* of the file. (Modify places the byte pointer at the *beginning* of the file.)
"M"	Modify access opens an existing file with the specified name and allows both read (READ and READLN) and write (WRITE and WRITELN) commands. You cannot use the "M" (Modify) argument to create a new file.

The OPEN command succeeds if it can open the file with the access you requested. If the OPEN command succeeds, program execution continues with the cell below the OPEN statement. Any commands after OPEN in the current cell are ignored.

The OPEN command fails with an ERROR if the disk drive is not ready. Use the ONERROR command to handle the possibility of such an error.

If you specify an access mode of READ, APPEND, or MODIFY, but the file does not exist in the indicated directory, the OPEN command fails, and program execution continues with the commands after the OPEN command in the current cell. You can place one or more commands after the OPEN command in the same cell to deal with the failure (such as a BRANCH or a subroutine call to a macro that deals with the failure).

Tip:
To handle the possibility of ERROR, use the ONERROR command.

Following are some examples (with explanations) of the OPEN command:

{OPEN "PASTDUE",R}{BRANCH FIXIT}

Opens the existing file named PASTDUE in the current directory for reading. If the file cannot be opened, execution branches to the routine FIXIT.

Part III ♦ Customizing 1-2-3

    {OPEN "C:\DATA\CLIENTS.DAT",W}

Opens the new file named CLIENTS.DAT in drive C, subdirectory DATA, for writing.

    {OPEN FILE,A}{BRANCH RETRY}

Opens the file whose name is in the cell FILE for Append access. If the file cannot be opened, branches to the routine RETRY.

    {OPEN FILE,M}{BRANCH RETRY}

Opens the file whose name is in cell FILE for Modify access. If the file cannot be opened, branches to the routine RETRY.

Figure 14.23 shows an example that uses all the file commands except the READLN and WRITE commands (which are similar to the READ and WRITELN commands). The program named \r uses the OPEN command to open a file.

Fig. 14.23.

A program that uses the file manipulation commands.

	A	B	C	D	E	F	G	H
1	FILE_SIZE		\r	{OPEN "INPUT.TXT","R"}				
2	NUM_REC			{FILESIZE FILE_SIZE}				
3	REC_LEN	100		{LET NUM_REC,FILE_SIZE/REC_LEN}				
4	POINTER			{GETPOS POINTER}				
5	COUNTER			{FOR COUNTER,1,NUM_REC-1,1,READ_WRITE}				
6	INLINE			{CLOSE}				
7								
8	READ_WRITE	{READ REC_LEN,INLINE}						
9		{GETPOS POINTER}						
10		{OPEN "OUTPUT.TXT",R}{OPEN "OUTPUT.TXT",W}						
11		{OPEN "OUTPUT.TXT",A}						
12		{WRITELN INLINE}						
13		{CLOSE}						
14		{OPEN "INPUT.TXT","R"}						
15		{SETPOS POINTER}						

Figure 14.23 demonstrates the use of the file manipulation commands to read data from one file (INPUT.TXT) in 100-byte increments, and to write the same data to another file (OUTPUT.TXT) in lines ending with a carriage-return and line-feed. As you read through the following sections and follow the program in figure 14.23, take note of the following items:

1. The value stored in REC_LEN must be specified before executing the \r macro. This value determines the number of characters (bytes) to be read each time the READ_WRITE macro is executed.

2. The {OPEN "OUTPUT.TXT",R}{OPEN "OUTPUT.TXT",W} line in B10 is used to create OUTPUT.TXT if it does not already exist. If the OPEN with Read access fails, OPEN with Write access creates the file. The subsequent OPEN with Append access statement in cell B11 places the file pointer at the end of the file so that the WRITELN command extends the file.

3. GETPOS and SETPOS, like all file manipulation commands except OPEN, always refer to the currently open file. Cells B9 and B15, therefore, refer to the open file: INPUT.TXT.

The CLOSE Command

The CLOSE command closes a currently-open file. If no file is open, the CLOSE command has no effect. CLOSE does not take an argument. The CLOSE command is particularly important for files that you are writing or modifying; if you don't close a file, you can lose the last data written to the file. The format of the CLOSE command is as follows:

{CLOSE}   Closes a file opened with OPEN

Although under most circumstances 1-2-3 automatically closes a file you do not close, make it a practice to use CLOSE when you finish using any file opened with OPEN. (Better safe than sorry.) Use of the CLOSE command is shown in figure 14.23.

Tip:
Use CLOSE to close a file and make sure that data isn't damaged or lost.

The READ Command

The READ command reads a specified number of characters from the currently-open file, beginning at the present file pointer location. The characters read from the file are placed in the worksheet at the cell location indicated. The format of the READ command is as follows:

{READ *bytecount,location*}   Copies the specified number of characters from a file to *location*

The *bytecount* argument is the number of bytes to read, starting at the current position of the file pointer; *location* is the cell to read into. READ places the specified number of characters from the file into the location cell as a label. *Bytecount* can be any number between 1 and 240 (the maximum number of characters in a 1-2-3 label). If *bytecount* is greater than the number of characters remaining in the file, 1-2-3 reads the remaining characters into the specified location. After the READ command executes, the file pointer is positioned at the character following the last character read.

The following statement transfers information from the open file into the cell location named INLINE. The amount of information transferred is determined by the contents of the cell named REC_LEN, which can contain either a value or a formula.

    {READ REC_LEN,INLINE}

The READ command is useful when you want to read a specific number of characters into a specified location in the current worksheet. A data file that contains fixed-length records, for example, can be read conveniently by a READ command with the *bytecount* argument specified as the record length.

Reminder:
Use READ to copy up to 240 characters from the open file to a location in the current worksheet.

ASCII text files from a word processor or text editor may have each line terminated with a carriage-return and line-feed sequence, or they may have a carriage-return and line-feed sequence only at the end of a paragraph. Those with the carriage-return and line-feed at the end of each line can often be read using READLN (which reads a variable length line) instead of READ (which reads a fixed number of characters).

The READLN Command

The READLN command reads one line of information (up to the next carriage-return and line-feed) from the currently open file, beginning at the file pointer's current position. The characters read are placed in the cell location in the current worksheet. The READLN command format is as follows:

{READLN *location*}   Copies the next line from the file to *location*

Consider, for example, the following statement which copies a line from an open file into the cell named HERE:

{READLN HERE}

Tip:
Use READLN instead of READ to read lines that are delimited by a carriage-return and line-feed combination.

Use READLN to read a line of text from a file whose lines are delimited by a carriage-return and line-feed combination. Use READLN, for example, to read the next line of an ASCII text file. ASCII text files are created with 1-2-3's /Print File command. Also referred to as *print files*, ASCII text files are assigned the PRN file extension by 1-2-3.

> **Using READ and READLN**
>
> If you attempt to read past the end of the file, if no file is open, or if the file was opened with Write access, the READ or READLN command is ignored and program execution continues in the same cell. Otherwise, after the READ or READLN command is completed, program execution continues on the next line. Place a BRANCH or subroutine call after the READ or READLN to handle the problem of an unexecuted READ or READLN statement.

The WRITE Command

The WRITE command writes a string of text to the currently open file using the following format:

{WRITE *string*}   Copies *string* to the open file

Reminder:
WRITE does not append carriage returns or line feeds to the string.

The *string* argument can be a literal string, a range name or cell reference to a single cell that contains a string, or a string expression. Because WRITE does not place a carriage-return and line-feed sequence at the end of the string, you can use multiple WRITE statements to concatenate text on a single line. WRITE is well-suited to creating or updating a file that contains fixed-length database records.

Chapter 14 ♦ Introducing the Advanced Macro Commands

The WRITE command is used in much the same way as is the WRITELN command in figure 14.23.

If the file pointer is not at the end of the file, 1-2-3 overwrites existing characters in the file. If the file pointer is at the end of the file, 1-2-3 extends the file by the number of characters written. If the file pointer is past the end of the file (see the discussion of the SETPOS command later in this section), 1-2-3 extends the file by the amount indicated before writing the characters.

The WRITELN Command

The WRITELN command is identical to the WRITE command except that WRITELN places a carriage-return and line-feed sequence after the last character written from the string. The WRITELN command format is as follows:

{WRITELN *string*}   Copies *string* plus a carriage-return line-feed sequence to the open file

Reminder:
WRITELN places a carriage-return and line-feed sequence after the last character written.

WRITELN is useful when the file being written or updated uses the carriage-return and line-feed sequence to mark the end of its lines or records. In many applications, several WRITE statements are used to write a line to the file; then a WRITELN is used to mark the end of the line. The WRITELN command is shown in figure 14.23.

The SETPOS Command

The SETPOS command sets the position of the file pointer to a specified value. The format of the command is as follows:

{SETPOS *file-position*}   Sets a new position for a file pointer

The *file-position* argument is a number, or an expression resulting in a number, that specifies the character at which you want to position the pointer. The first character in the file is at position 0, the second at position 1, and so on. Suppose, for example, that you have a database file with 100 records that are each 20 bytes long. To access the first record, you can use the following commands:

Reminder:
The SETPOS command counts positions from the first character (position 0) to the last in the file.

```
{SETPOS 0}
{READ 20,buffer}
```

To read the 15th record, use the following commands:

```
{SETPOS (15-1)*20}
{READ 20,buffer}
```

Nothing prevents you from setting the file pointer past the end of the file. If the file pointer is set at or past the end and a READ or READLN command is executed, the command does nothing, and program execution continues with the next command on the same line as the READ or READLN. If the file pointer is set at or past the end and a WRITE or WRITELN command is executed, 1-2-3 first extends the file to the length specified by the file pointer, and then, starting at the file pointer, writes the characters.

Warning: If you inadvertently set the file pointer to a large number with SETPOS and write to the file, 1-2-3 attempts to expand the file and writes the text at the end of the file. If the file does not fit on the disk, the WRITE command does nothing, and program execution continues with the next command on the same line as the WRITE command. If the file does fit on the disk, 1-2-3 extends the file and writes the text at the end of the file.

If a file is not currently open, SETPOS does nothing, and execution continues with the next command on the same line as the SETPOS command. Otherwise, when the SETPOS command is completed, execution continues on the next line of the program. You can place a BRANCH command or a subroutine call after the SETPOS command to handle the problem of an unexecuted statement. SETPOS is shown in figure 14.23.

The GETPOS Command

Tip:
Use GETPOS to record the location of the file pointer if you want to return to that location again.

The GETPOS command allows you to record the file pointer's current position. The format of this command is as follows:

    {GETPOS *location*}   Records a file pointer position in the specified *location*

The current position of the file pointer is placed in the cell indicated by *location*, where *location* is either a cell reference or a range name.

The GETPOS command is useful if you record in the file the location of something you want to find again. You can use GETPOS to mark your current place in the file before you use SETPOS to move the file pointer to another position. You can use GETPOS to record the locations of important items in a quick-reference index. GETPOS is shown in figure 14.23.

The FILESIZE Command

The FILESIZE command returns the length of the file in bytes. The format of the command is as follows:

    {FILESIZE *location*}   Records the size of the open file in the specified *location*

The FILESIZE command determines the current length of the file and places this value in the cell referred to by *location*. *Location* can be a cell reference or range name. The FILESIZE command is shown in figure 14.23.

Summary

As you work with the 1-2-3 advanced macro commands, you discover that your powerful spreadsheet program has a rich programming language that can solve many of your application problems. Macro languages are slow, however, when compared to lower-level languages such as assembly language, C, Pascal, and BASIC. 1-2-3 does not always execute macro programming instructions with lightning speed. You almost always have a trade-off of capabilities; some applications may take a good deal of time to execute. But as you learn to integrate the powerful worksheet @functions, menu commands, macro key names, and advanced macro commands into worksheets, you can develop seamless applications that offer a nice balance between programming and development time, as well as program-execution time.

Macro programming offers many 1-2-3 users a sense of satisfaction and accomplishment when they see their ideas transformed into working applications. This chapter provided the groundwork for developing such applications. Experiment with the macro programs used as examples. As long as you exercise prudence when working with commands that manipulate disk files, you have little chance of damaging or destroying anything. Enjoy the adventure of exploring a new language and expressing new ideas!

As you become more experienced with the advanced macro commands, turn to other Que titles for help in becoming an expert advanced macro command programmer.

Part IV

1-2-3 Release 3.1+ Command Reference

1-2-3 Command Reference

Worksheet Commands /W

The /Worksheet commands control the display formats, screen organization, protection, and start-up settings for files. If you want to change these settings for only a portion of the worksheet, use the /Range commands. To change settings that affect the entire worksheet or file, however, use the /Worksheet commands shown in the following menu map.

Part IV ◆ 1-2-3 Release 3.1+ Command Reference

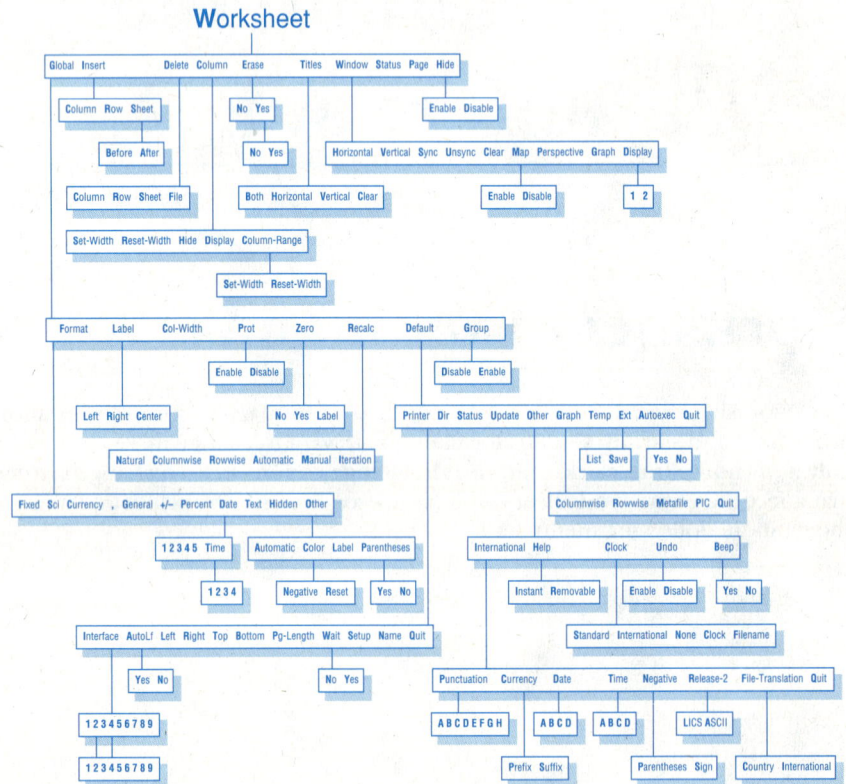

Worksheet Global Format /WGF

Purpose

Defines the display format for numeric values and formulas in the worksheet. The display format for the entire file is formatted if GROUP mode is on.

Formats previously entered with /Range Format are not affected.

Reminders

- Before you use /wgf, determine your most-used format for numeric data.
- If you want to format only a portion of the worksheet, use /Range Format instead of /wgf.

Procedures

1. Type /**wgf**.
2. Select one of the following formats:

Menu Item	Description
Fixed	Fixes the number of decimal places displayed. If the setting is 3 decimal places, for example, the number 1.2345 appears as `1.235`.
Sci	Displays in scientific notation large or small numbers. In a 2-decimal format, for example, the number 950000 appears as `9.50E+05`.
Currency	Displays the default currency symbol (for example, $ or £) and commas. Currency format is often used for the first row and the bottom line of financial statements. In a 2-decimal format, for example, 24500.254 appears as `$24,500.25`.
,	Marks thousands and multiples of thousands. In a 2-decimal format, for example, 24500.254 appears as `24,500.25`.
General	Suppresses zeros after the decimal point, uses scientific notation for large or small numbers, and serves as the default decimal display.
+/−	Creates horizontal bar graphs or time-duration graphs on computers that do not have graphics. A positive number displays as + symbols; a negative number as − symbols. The number of symbols equals the integer value of the cell contents. For example, 6.23 appears as `++++++`.
Percent	Displays a decimal number as a percentage followed by a percent sign (%). In a 2-decimal format, for example, .346 appears as `34.60%`.

Menu Item	Description

Date Displays the date in one of five customary formats. One selection under **Date** formats the time display. These are the **Date** selections:

	1 DD–MMM–YY	12–Jan–91
	2 DD–MMM	12–Jan
	3 MMM–YY	Jan–91
	4 MM/DD/YY	01/12/91
	5 MM/DD	01/12

Time:

	1 HH:MM:SS AM/PM	1:04:34 PM
	2 HH:MM AM/PM	1:04 PM
	3 HH:MM:SS	13:04:34
	4 HH:MM	13:04

Text Evaluates formulas as numbers but displays formulas as text. Numbers in cells appear in **General** format.

Hidden Hides cell contents from display and printing but evaluates contents. Use this command to hide confidential notes or variables.

Other Supplies additional formatting choices:

    Automatic Automatically recognizes and formats entries. Typed dates or times should match the date or time formats shown in the /wgfd menu. Improper formulas and labels beginning with numbers are entered as labels.

    Color Provides two options: **Negative**, which displays negative numbers brighter or in color; and **Reset**, which restores the default setting.

    Label Automatically enters a label prefix before the numeric values are entered in a cell. Existing values remain as numbers. New numeric entries appear as labels.

    Parentheses Provides two options: **Yes**, which puts parentheses around all values; and **No**, which removes parentheses.

3. After you select **Fixed**, **Sci**, **Currency**, **,** (Comma), or **Percent**, enter the number of decimal places. 1-2-3 normally truncates trailing zeros, but these appear for the number of decimal places you set.

4. Press Enter.

Important Cues

- Use **/R**ange Format to format only a portion of the worksheet.
- Use **T**ext format to display formulas as text while still using the numeric result from the formula.
- If you enter a number too large for the formatted cell, the cell fills with asterisks. To remove them, move the cell pointer to the cell, select **/W**orksheet **C**olumn **S**et-Width, and press the right arrow until the column is wide enough to display the entire number.
- To display non-USA formats with commands, use **/W**orksheet **G**lobal **D**efault **O**ther **I**nternational.

Cautions

- /wgf rounds displayed numbers to the specified decimal setting, but calculations are performed to 15-decimal precision. To keep apparently wrong values from being displayed, use @ROUND to round formula results so that calculated results match displayed values.
- Other users may enter percentage values incorrectly if you use the **P**ercent format. You should thus include a screen prompt to remind operators to place a percent sign (%) after percentages so that 1-2-3 automatically divides the entry by 100.

For more information, see **/R**ange **F**ormat, **/W**orksheet **G**lobal **D**efault, *and Chapter 5.*

Worksheet Global Label /WGL

Purpose

Specifies how you want text labels aligned throughout the worksheet. When GROUP mode is on, label alignment is changed for the entire file.

Labels narrower than the cell width can be aligned to the left, right, or center. Labels longer than the cell width are left-aligned. Previously entered labels do not change.

Reminders

- Before you begin building the worksheet, decide how to align the labels. Use /wgl to select left-alignment (the default setting), right-alignment, or center-alignment.
- If you use /wgl after you begin to build the worksheet, existing labels are not affected. Any alignment previously set with **/R**ange **L**abel is not altered by /wgl.
- To change the alignment of labels in a single cell or a range of cells, use **/R**ange **L**abel.

Procedures

1. Type **/wgl**.
2. Select one of the following:

Menu Item	Description
Left	Aligns label with cell's left edge.
Right	Aligns label with cell's right edge.
Center	Centers label in a cell.

3. Type the labels as you want them to appear on the worksheet.

Important Cues

- Align labels in a cell by entering one of the following prefixes before you type the label:

Label Prefix	Function
' (apostrophe)	Aligns label to the left (default).
" (quotation mark)	Aligns label to the right.
^ (caret)	Centers label in the cell.
\	Repeats character to fill the cell.

   Note: The backslash (\) label prefix cannot be selected with /wgl.

- The label prefix appears as the first character in the control panel when the cell pointer is positioned on a cell that contains a label. Use **/W**orksheet **S**tatus to show the global label prefix.

- You must enter a label prefix in front of labels that begin with a number or formula symbol. 1-2-3 automatically enters the label prefix if the worksheet is formatted with **/W**orksheet **G**lobal **F**ormat **O**ther **A**utomatic or **/R**ange **F**ormat **O**ther **A**utomatic. If the worksheet or range is not formatted, you must supply a prefix such as that in one of the following correct examples:

Correct	Incorrect
'2207Cheyenne Dr.	2207 Cheyenne Dr.
"34-567FB	34-567FB

- To turn a number into a label, position the cell pointer on the number you want to change and press Edit (F2). Then press Home to move the cursor to the beginning of the number; type the label prefix and press Enter. *Be careful*: if you format numbers as text, formulas evaluate the characters as zeros.

- Because every line of macro code must be entered as a string, a label prefix *must* precede text used as macro code. For example, if your macro line begins with the command sequence /ppooc, you must precede the entry with a label prefix such as '/ppooc; otherwise, the keystrokes in the macro select the command instead of typing macro code.

/Worksheet Commands 657

- Preserve a formula that has an unidentified error by adding a label prefix before the formula. (The **/Worksheet Global Format Other Automatic** and **/Range Format Other Automatic** commands also change incorrect formulas to labels.) Consider the following formula:

    +B5*@PMT(B16B12/12,B14*12)

    If you enter this formula, 1-2-3 signals an error and enters EDIT mode. (The problem is a missing comma after B16.) If you can't find the error, press Home to move to the beginning of the formula. Type an apostrophe and press Enter. The formula is accepted as a text label, and you can return to the formula later to look for the error and make the correction. Delete the apostrophe and press Enter after you make the correction.

- To turn a numeric label into a number, use EDIT mode and delete the label prefix.

Caution

Numbers or formulas preceded by a label prefix have the value of zero when evaluated by a numeric formula. In a database query, you must use text searches to search for numbers that have a label prefix.

*For more information, see **/Worksheet Global Format Other Automatic**, **/Range Format Other Automatic**, and Chapter 5.*

Worksheet Global Col-Width /WGC

Purpose

Sets the column width for the entire worksheet; sets the column width for the entire file if GROUP mode is on. Column widths set with **/Worksheet Column** are not affected.

Reminder

Before you use /wgc, decide on the column widths you need for the worksheet, and position the cell pointer so that an average column width is displayed.

Procedures

1. Type **/wgc**.
2. Enter a number for the column width used most frequently; or press the right- or left-arrow key to increase or decrease the column width.
3. Press Enter.

Important Cues

- Use **/Worksheet Column Set-Width** to set individual columns so that numbers and labels display correctly. When the column width is too narrow for the value entered, asterisks are displayed in the cell.

- Any global column width can be set to a new width with **/Worksheet Global Col-Width**. Column widths previously set with **/Worksheet Column Set-Width** keep their original setting.
- The default column width for all columns is 9 characters. Column width settings can range from 1 to 240 characters.
- You can see the current setting for the global column width by selecting **/Worksheet Status**.

Caution

If you use a split worksheet and change the column width in one or both windows, settings used in the bottom or right windows are lost when the windows are cleared. 1-2-3 keeps the column widths used in the top window of a horizontal split or the left window of a vertical split.

For more information, see **/Worksheet Column** *and Chapter 4.*

Worksheet Global Prot /WGP

Purpose

Protects the entire worksheet or file from being changed. If GROUP mode is on, the entire file is protected.

Cells previously marked with the **/Range Unprot** command are still unprotected when worksheet protection is on.

Reminder

Before you enable worksheet protection, save time by making sure that your worksheet is complete. After the worksheet is protected, you must disable protection or unprotect a range before you can modify the worksheet.

Procedures

1. Type **/wgp**.
2. Select one of the following options:

Menu Item	Description
Enable	Protects the worksheet. Only cells specified with /Range Unprot can be changed.
Disable	Unprotects the worksheet.

Important Cues

- Before or after you protect the entire worksheet, you can use **/Range Unprot** to specify cells that can be changed.
- Protected cells display P R on the status line. Unprotected cells display U on the status line.

- While **/W**orksheet **G**lobal **P**rot is enabled, the **/R**ange **I**nput commands restrict the cell pointer to cells unprotected by the **/R**ange **U**nprot command. This arrangement makes movement between data-entry cells easier.

Cautions

- Macros that change cell content can change only unprotected cells. When you program macros, include code necessary to enable or disable protection.
- **/W**orksheet **E**rase is one of the few commands that can be used while **/W**orksheet **G**lobal **P**rot is enabled.

For more information, see **/R**ange **U**nprot, **/R**ange **P**rot, and Chapter 4.

Worksheet Global Zero /WGZ

Purpose

Suppresses zeros in displays and printed reports so that only nonzero numbers appear; suppresses zeros in the entire file when GROUP mode is on. Also enables you to display a label instead of a zero.

When **/W**orksheet **G**lobal **Z**ero is in effect, zeros from formulas and typed entries are hidden.

Reminder

Protect hidden zeros in the worksheet by using the **/W**orksheet **G**lobal **P**rot and **/R**ange **U**nprot commands. Doing so prevents users new to 1-2-3 from typing over or erasing necessary hidden zero values or formulas.

Procedures

1. Type **/wgz**.
2. Choose one of the following options:

Menu Item	Description
No	Displays as zeros those cells containing a zero or a result of zero.
Yes	Displays as blank those cells containing a zero or a result of zero.
Label	Displays a custom label that replaces those cells containing a zero or zero result.

3. If you choose **Label**, enter the label you want displayed. Precede the label with an apostrophe (') for left-alignment or with a caret (^) for right-alignment. The default label alignment is right-alignment.

Important Cues

- Zeros that continue to display are actually values greater than zero; however, their format displays them rounded to a zero value.
- Suppressed zeros in formulas and typed entries are still evaluated as zeros by other formulas.

Caution

If zeros are suppressed, you can easily erase or write over portions of the worksheet that appear blank but contain suppressed zeros. To prevent accidental erasures and typeovers, use /**W**orksheet **G**lobal **P**rot **E**nable and /**R**ange **U**nprot.

For more information, see /**Worksheet Global Prot**, /**Range Prot and Unprot**, *and Chapter 4.*

Worksheet Global Recalc /WGR

Purpose

Defines how worksheets recalculate and how many times they calculate.

Reminders

- You may need to use this command more than once. The first time, use it to set whether calculation is automatic or manual. The second time, use the menu to define how you want calculations done or how many times calculations should be done.
- Recalculation can be set to **A**utomatic or **M**anual. Use **M**anual recalculation to increase data-entry speed on large worksheets or databases. By selecting either the **C**olumnwise or **R**owwise option, you can have 1-2-3 calculate formulas in a particular order. You also can use /wgr to calculate a formula many times to ensure correct results.
- If you change recalculation to **C**olumnwise or **R**owwise, enter formulas in a specific order so that they are calculated correctly. 1-2-3's default settings are **N**atural and **A**utomatic recalculation. In nearly all cases, you should leave recalculation in **N**atural mode.

Procedures

1. Type /**wgr**.
2. Select one of the following:

Menu Item	Description
Natural	Calculates formulas in the order the results are needed (the normal worksheet setting for the order of recalculation).

/Worksheet Commands

Menu Item	Description
Columnwise	Starts at the top of column A and recalculates downward; then moves to column B.
Rowwise	Starts at the beginning of row 1 and recalculates to the end; then continues through the following rows.
Automatic	Recalculates whenever cell contents change (the normal worksheet setting for when recalculation occurs).
Manual	Recalculates only when you press Calc (F9) or when {CALC} is encountered in a macro. The CALC indicator appears at the bottom of the screen when recalculation is advised.
Iteration	Recalculates the worksheet a specified number of times.

3. If you select Iteration, enter a number from 1 to 50. The default setting is 1. Iteration works with Columnwise and Rowwise recalculations or with Natural recalculation when the worksheet contains a circular reference.

4. If you selected Columnwise or Rowwise recalculation, you may need to repeat step 1 and select Iteration in step 2. In step 3, enter the number of recalculations necessary for correct results. Columnwise and Rowwise recalculations often require multiple calculations for all worksheet results to be correct.

Important Cues

◆ Display the current recalculation setting by selecting /Worksheet Status.

◆ Columnwise or Rowwise recalculation often requires multiple recalculations. Set the number of automatic recalculations by selecting /wgr and choosing Iteration.

Caution

When you use Manual recalculation, the screen display is not valid when the CALC indicator appears at the bottom of the screen. This indicator means that changes have been made to the worksheet, and that you should press Calc (F9) so that 1-2-3 recalculates the worksheet to reflect the changes.

*For more information, see /**Worksheet Status** and Chapter 4.*

Worksheet Global Default /WGD

Purpose

Specifies display formats and start-up settings for hardware.

With this command, you can control how 1-2-3 works with the printer; which disk and directory are accessed automatically; which international displays are used; and which type of clock is displayed. The settings can be saved so that each time you start 1-2-3, the specifications go into effect. For temporary changes, see the /File or /Print menu options.

Reminder

Before you set the interface for serial printers, find out the baud rate of your printer. The printer should be set to standard operating-system serial printer settings of 8 bits, no parity, and 1 stop bit (2 stop bits at 110 baud). These printer settings can be set with microswitches (DIP switches in your printer) and are normally preconfigured at the factory.

Procedures

1. Type **/wgd**.
2. Select the setting you want to change:

Menu Item	Description
Printer	Specifies printer settings and connections. Choose from the following options:
Interface	Selects parallel or serial port from 9 settings, **1** through **9**. The menu displays each of the 9 ports. The initial setting is **1** (Parallel 1).
AutoLf	Tells 1-2-3 whether your printer inserts its own line feed or whether 1-2-3 should insert a line feed. If the printer prints double spaces or overlapped text, choose the opposite setting.
Left	Sets left margin. The default is **4**, 0–1000.
Right	Sets right margin. The default is **76**, 0–1000.
Top	Sets top margin. The default is **2**, 0–240.
Bottom	Sets bottom margin. The default is **2**, 0–240.
Pg-Length	Sets page length. The default is **66**, 1–1000.
Wait	Pauses for page insert.
Setup	Creates initial printer-control code.
Name	Selects from multiple printers.
Quit	Returns to the **Printer** menu.
Dir	Specifies directory for read or write operations. Press Esc to clear. Type the new directory and press Enter.
Status	Displays settings for **/Worksheet Global Default**.
Update	Saves to disk the current global defaults for use during the next start-up.
Other	Provides the following five options:
International	Specifies display settings for **Punctuation**, **Currency**, **Date**, **Time**, **Negative** formats, **Release-2** character sets, and **File-Translation** of international characters.

/Worksheet Commands

Menu Item	Description
Help	Enables you to choose whether the Help file is immediately accessible from disk (**Instant**) or whether the Help file is on a removable disk (**Removable**).
Clock	Enables you to choose between **Standard** and **International** date and time formats or to have **None** displayed on the screen. **Clock** displays the date and time set by other commands, and **Filename** displays the file name instead of the date and time.
Undo	Offers two options: **Enable**, which enables the Undo feature; and **Disable**, which disables the Undo feature.
Beep	Offers two options: **Yes**, which turns the computer's sound on; and **No**, which turns it off.
Graph	Sets the directions used by 1-2-3 to divide cell ranges into automatic graph ranges. A range may be divided into data sets by column (**Columnwise**) or by row (**Rowwise**). **Graph** also specifies which type of format is used when you save a graph: **Metafile** (CGM) or **PIC** (picture).
Temp	Sets the directory where 1-2-3 saves temporary files used during operation.
Ext	Provides two options: **List**, which enables you to change the file extensions of files displayed by /**File** commands; and **Save**, which enables you to change the default file extensions under which files are saved.
Autoexec	Provides two options: **Yes**, which automatically executes autoexecute (\0) macros; and **No**, which stops autoexecute macros from executing.
Quit	Returns to the worksheet.

Important Cue

Changes made with /Worksheet Global Default are good only while 1-2-3 is running. To save the settings so that they load automatically at start-up, select /Worksheet Global Default Update.

For more information, see Chapter 5.

Worksheet Global Group /WGG

Purpose

While a file is in GROUP mode, transfers formatting changes made on one worksheet to the entire file.

Reminder

Use GROUP mode when you format files containing worksheets that are exact copies of each other (in terms of formatting).

Procedures

1. Type /**wgg**.
2. Select **Disable** to turn off GROUP, or select **Enable** to turn on GROUP.

Important Cues

- When GROUP mode is enabled, the GROUP status indicator appears at the bottom of the screen.
- When you are in GROUP mode, the following commands affect all worksheets:

  Of the /Range commands: **Format, Label, Prot,** and **Unprot**

  Of the /Worksheet commands: **Column, Delete Column, Delete Row, Insert Column, Insert Row, Page,** and **Titles**

  Of the /Worksheet Global commands: **Col-Width, Format, Label, Prot,** and **Zero**

For more information, see Chapter 4.

Worksheet Insert [Column, Row, Sheet] /WIC, /WIR, or /WIS

Purpose

Inserts one or more blank columns or rows in the worksheet or one or more blank worksheets in the file.

Use this command to add space for formulas, data, or text, or to add worksheets to a file to create three-dimensional worksheet files.

Reminders

Before you use /wi, do one of the following:

- Place the cell pointer in the column you want to move to the right when one or more columns are inserted.
- Place the cell pointer in the row you want to move down when one or more rows are inserted.
- Place the cell pointer in the worksheet you want to insert a worksheet before or after.

Procedures

1. Type /**wi**.
2. Select one of the following:

/Worksheet Commands **665**

Menu Item	Description
Column	Inserts column(s) at the cell pointer; moves the current column right.
Row	Inserts row(s) at the cell pointer; moves the current row down.
Sheet	Inserts worksheet(s) before or after the current worksheet.

3. If you choose **C**olumn, move the cell pointer right to highlight one cell for each column you want inserted.

   If you choose **R**ow, move the cell pointer down to highlight one cell for each row you want inserted.

   If you choose **S**heet, select **B**efore or **A**fter to indicate whether you want to insert the new worksheet(s) before or after the current worksheet. Indicate how many worksheets you want to insert. The total number of worksheets in memory cannot exceed 256.

Important Cues

- Addresses and ranges adjust automatically to the new addresses created when columns or rows are inserted.
- Check all worksheet areas for composition, lines, and layout that may have changed. Use /**M**ove to reposition labels, data, and formulas.

Cautions

- Cell addresses in macros do not adjust automatically. Adjust cell addresses in macros to reflect the inserted column(s) or row(s). Range names in macros remain correct.
- Make certain that inserted columns and rows do not pass through databases, print ranges, or a column of macro code. Macros stop execution if they reach a blank cell. Database and data-entry macros may stop or work incorrectly if they encounter unexpected blank columns or rows in the database or data-entry areas.

For more information, see /**Worksheet Delete**, /**File New**, and Chapter 4.

Worksheet Delete [Column, Row, Sheet, File]   /WDC, /WDR, /WDS, or /WDF

Purpose

Deletes one or more columns or rows from the worksheet; deletes one or more worksheets from a file; or deletes an active file from memory but not from the disk.

When you use /wd, the entire column, row, worksheet, or file and the information and formatting it contains are deleted from memory.

Reminders

- Before you delete a column or row, use the End and arrow keys to make sure that distant cells in that column or row do not contain needed data or formulas.
- Before you invoke /wd, place the cell pointer on the first column or row to be deleted. Place the cell pointer in the correct worksheet or in the file to be deleted.

Procedures

1. Type **/wd**.
2. Select one of the following:

Menu Item	Description
Column	Deletes column(s) at the cell pointer. Remaining columns to the right move left.
Row	Deletes row(s) at the cell pointer. Remaining rows below move up.
Sheet	Deletes worksheet(s) from memory.
File	Deletes the active file from memory but does not erase the file from disk.

3. Specify a range containing the columns, rows, or worksheets you want deleted. If you want to delete a file, specify the file.

Important Cues

- **/Worksheet Delete** deletes all the data and formulas in the column or row. To erase the contents of cells but leave the blank cells in their location, use **/Range Erase**.
- Formulas, named ranges, and ranges in command prompts are adjusted automatically to the new cell addresses after you delete a column or row.
- Use **/Move** when you need to reposition a portion of the worksheet and cannot delete a column or row.

Cautions

- Formulas that refer to deleted cells have the value ERR.
- Deleting all cells belonging to a named range leaves the named range in formulas, but as an undefined name. You must redefine the name by using **/Range Name**.
- Deleting a row that passes through an area containing macros can create errors in the macros. Deleting code in the middle of the macro causes problems, and deleting a blank cell between two macros merges their code.

For more information, see **/Worksheet Insert**, **/Range Erase**, *and Chapter 4.*

Worksheet Column [Set-Width, Reset-Width, Hide, Display, Column-Range]

/WCS, /WCR, /WCH, /WCD, or /WCC

Purpose

Changes the column-display characteristics of one or more columns.

Columns wider than 9 characters are needed to display large numbers, to display dates, and to prevent text from being covered by adjacent cell entries. Narrow column widths are useful for short entries, such as (Y/N), and for organizing the display layout.

Use **Hide** to hide columns you do not want to display or print. Redisplay these columns with the **Display** command.

Reminders

- Make certain that changing the width of a column does not destroy the appearance of another portion of the worksheet.
- Move the cell pointer to the widest entry in the column before you use /wcs.

Procedures

1. Type **/wc**.
2. Select one of the following menu items:

Menu Item	Description
Set-Width	Sets a new column width.
Reset-Width	Returns to the global width default.
Hide	Hides the column(s) from view or from printing.
Display	Displays the hidden column(s).
Column-Range	Sets the width of more than one column; provides the following two options:
	Set-Width Sets new column widths
	Reset-Width Returns to the global width default

3. If you chose **Set-Width**, enter the new column width by typing the number of characters or by pressing the left- or right-arrow key to shrink or expand the column.

    If you chose **Hide** or **Display**, indicate the columns you want changed. When you choose **Display**, hidden columns are displayed.

    If you chose **Column-Range**, choose **Set-Width** or **Reset-Width**; indicate the columns you want to change, and enter the column width as a number or press the left- or right-arrow key to shrink or expand the columns.

Important Cues

- Asterisks appear in a cell whose column is too narrow to display numeric or date information.
- Text entries wider than the cell may be partially covered by text or numeric entries in the cell to the right.
- Use /Worksheet Global Col-Width to set the column width for columns that were not set individually with /Worksheet Column.
- Column width settings from /Worksheet Column override settings from /Worksheet Global Col-Width.
- Use /wch to suppress the printing of unnecessary columns.
- You can use /wch to suppress columns in the current window without affecting the display in other windows. When the windows are cleared, the settings used in the top window of a horizontal split or the left window of a vertical split are kept; the settings used in the bottom or right windows are lost.
- When preparing reports, use /wch to hide the display of unnecessary data and reduce the number of printed columns.

Cautions

- Be sure that others who use your worksheet are aware of the hidden columns. Although the values and formulas of hidden columns work properly, the display may be confusing if data appears to be missing.
- When cells are hidden on an unprotected worksheet, ranges copied or moved to the hidden area overwrite existing data.

For more information, see Chapter 4.

Worksheet Erase /WE

Purpose

Erases all active worksheets from memory, leaving one blank worksheet on-screen.

Use this command to clear away old work after you have saved it and to start fresh with a blank worksheet.

Reminder

Be sure to save active worksheet(s) before you use /Worksheet Erase.

Procedures

1. Type **/we**.
2. Select one of the following:

/Worksheet Commands   **669**

Menu Item	Description
No	Cancels the command, leaving all worksheets in memory.
Yes	Erases all active worksheets if they have not changed since last saved. If worksheets have been changed, and the changes have not been saved, a No/Yes prompt appears, asking whether you still want to erase the worksheets. Press **Y** to erase; press **N** to keep the worksheets and return to READY mode.

Important Cue

Use **/Worksheet Delete** to delete individual worksheets from a file.

Caution

Files and worksheets erased from memory without first being saved are lost. Make sure that you save files and worksheets you want to use again.

For more information, see **/File Save** *and Chapter 4.*

Worksheet Titles   /WT

Purpose

Displays row or column headings that might otherwise scroll off the screen. When GROUP mode is on, **Titles** applies to all worksheets in the file.

Reminders

- ◆ You can "freeze" cell contents horizontally (in rows), vertically (in columns), or both ways.
- ◆ Rows are frozen across the top of the worksheet. Columns are frozen down the left edge.

Procedures

1. If you want column headings at the top of the screen, move the cell pointer so that the column headings you want frozen on-screen occupy the top row(s) of the worksheet.

    If you want row headings along the leftmost edge of the screen, move the cell pointer so that the column(s) containing the headings is (are) at the left edge of the screen.

    If you want both row and column headings, move the cell pointer so that the column headings are at the top of the screen and the row headings are in the leftmost column(s).

2. Move the cell pointer one row below the lowest row to be used as a title, and one column to the right of the column(s) to be used as title(s).

3. Type **/wt**.

4. Select one of the following:

Menu Item	Description
Both	Creates titles from the row(s) above the cell pointer and from the column(s) to the left of the cell pointer.
Horizontal	Creates titles from the row(s) above the cell pointer.
Vertical	Creates titles from the column(s) to the left of the cell pointer.
Clear	Removes all frozen title areas so that all worksheet areas scroll.

Important Cues

- To return the worksheet to normal, select the /Worksheet Titles Clear command.
- /Worksheet Titles does not work when the displaying of the titles and the cell pointer is impossible. This situation occurs when there is no room to display title rows or columns effectively, as when you use /Worksheet Window Perspective.
- If you split the worksheet into two windows with /Worksheet Window, each window can have its own titles.
- Press Home to move the cell pointer to the top left corner of the unfrozen area.
- Press GoTo (F5) to move the cell pointer inside the title area. This action creates duplicates of the frozen rows and columns. The double appearance can be confusing.
- The cell pointer can enter title areas when you are entering cell addresses in POINT mode.
- /Worksheet Titles can be useful for displaying protected screen areas when /Range Input is active. Position titles so that they display labels and instructions adjacent to the unprotected input range.
- /Worksheet Titles is especially useful for freezing column headings over a database or an accounting worksheet. You also can freeze rows of text that describe figures in adjacent cells.

For more information, see Chapter 4.

Worksheet Window /WW

Purpose

Displays your worksheet from many points of view. You can display portions of three worksheets, display two different views of the same worksheet, display part of a worksheet and a graph, or display a maplike overview of the worksheet.

Reminders

◆ If you want to see many views of the same worksheet, decide whether you want the worksheet split horizontally or vertically. If you want two horizontal windows, move the cell pointer to the top row of what is to be the lower window. To produce two vertical windows, move the cell pointer to the column that is to be the left edge of the right window. Position the worksheet so that the cell pointer is at midscreen.

◆ If you want to display a graph on-screen with the worksheet, use the cell pointer to define the column that divides the worksheet and graph. The left part of the screen shows the worksheet; the right part shows the graph.

Procedures

1. Type **/ww**.
2. Select one of the following:

Menu Item	Description
Horizontal	Splits the worksheet into two horizontal windows at the cell pointer.
Vertical	Splits the worksheet into two vertical windows at the cell pointer.
Sync	Synchronizes windows so that they move together. Windows are in sync when they are first opened.
Unsync	Unsynchronizes two windows so that they can move independently of each other. You can then simultaneously view different rows and columns in the same worksheet. A window moves only when it contains the cell pointer.
Clear	Removes the inactive window (the one that does not contain the cell pointer).
Map	Switches between the worksheet and a map view of the worksheet. The map view displays labels as "; in formulas or annotated numbers, the map view displays values as – and +. **Map** provides two options: **Enable**, which turns the map on; and **Disable**, which turns the map off.
Perspective	Displays three worksheets stacked so that portions of each are shown.
Graph	Displays the graph in the worksheet area to the right of the cell pointer. Changing data changes the graph.
Display	Switches between the two screen-display modes that you selected at installation. Choose **1** for the first mode you installed and **2** for the second mode.

3. Repeat steps 1 and 2 and select **Unsync** if you want the windows to move independently of each other. You can then simultaneously view different rows and columns in the worksheet.

Important Cues

- Each window can have different column widths. When /**Worksheet W**indow **C**lear is selected, the settings used in the top or left window determine the column width for the remaining worksheet.
- Press Ctrl-PgUp or Ctrl-PgDn to move the cell pointer between worksheets in **P**erspective view.
- Horizontal windows are useful when you work with databases. The criteria range and database column labels can appear in the upper window while the data or extracted data appears in the lower window.
- You can use /**W**orksheet **W**indow to display messages, instructions, warnings, help text, and so on, without having to leave the worksheet.

Caution

Always clear windows and reposition the screen before you invoke windows in a macro. Macros that split windows may become "confused" if the window configuration differs from what the macros "expect."

For more information, see Chapter 4.

Worksheet Status /WS

Purpose

Displays the current global settings and hardware options. You also can use /ws to check available memory.

Reminder

You can check the worksheet's status whenever a worksheet is displayed. The screen displays the status of the following information:

    Available Memory
    Math Coprocessor
    Recalculation (Method, Order, Iterations)
    Circular Reference (One cell in the circular error)
    Cell Display (Format, Label Prefix, Column Width, Zero Suppression)
    Global Protection

Procedures

1. Type /**ws**.
2. Press any key to return to the worksheet.

Important Cues

- You can reduce the size of a file by deleting unnecessary worksheets, formulas, labels, and values. Use /**R**ange **F**ormat **R**eset to reset the numeric format for unused areas; then save the revised worksheet to a file and retrieve a smaller version.

/Worksheet Commands **673**

♦ The Circular Reference status displays a single cell within a ring of formulas that reference each other. The Circular Reference status shows only one cell address from this ring.

For more information, see Chapter 4.

Worksheet Page /WP

Purpose

Manually inserts page breaks in printed worksheets. When GROUP mode is on, the page break is inserted in all worksheets in the file.

1-2-3 automatically inserts page breaks when the printing reaches the bottom margin. For some reports, however, you may want page breaks to occur at designated rows. The /**W**orksheet **P**age command indicates to the printer where manually selected page breaks should occur.

Reminders

♦ If you want to reuse the worksheet in a form without page breaks, save the worksheet before you insert the page breaks. The /**W**orksheet **P**age command inserts a row and inserts characters in that row, altering the worksheet so that it may be inconvenient for normal use.

♦ Before you use /wp, move the cell pointer to the leftmost column of the current print range and to the row where you want the page break to occur.

Procedures

1. Type /**wp**.
2. Press Enter. A row is inserted where the page is to break, and a double colon (::) appears in the left column.

Important Cues

♦ Use /**W**orksheet **D**elete **R**ow to delete the row containing a page break.
♦ /**W**orksheet **P**age overrides the /**P**rint **F**ile **O**ptions **O**ther **U**nformatted command, which normally suppresses page breaks. If you want to print to disk without using page breaks, make sure that you use /**R**ange **E**rase to remove the page-break markers.

Caution

Do not make entries in the row that contains the page-break marker (::). Entries in this row do not print.

For more information, see Chapter 8.

Worksheet Hide /WH

Purpose

Hides or displays one or more worksheets.

Reminder

Move the cell pointer into the topmost worksheet of the worksheets you want to hide or display.

Procedures

1. Type **/wh**.
2. Select **Enable** to hide worksheets, or select **Disable** to display worksheets.
3. Specify the range containing the worksheet(s) you want to hide or display. Hidden worksheets display with an asterisk (*) next to the worksheet letter.

Important Cues

- You cannot move the cell pointer into a hidden worksheet.
- Data and formulas in a hidden worksheet still work normally.
- Three-dimensional commands, such as @SUM commands, that pass through hidden worksheets evaluate the contents of the hidden worksheets.
- Data can be hidden in other ways. Use **/Worksheet Global Format Hidden** to hide the contents of a worksheet; use **/Range Format Hidden** to hide a range of cells in a visible worksheet; and use **/Worksheet Column Hide** to hide the contents of a column.

Caution

Be careful that you do not delete hidden worksheets when deleting across a range of worksheets.

For more information, see Chapter 4.

Range Commands /R

/**R**ange commands control the display formats, protection, and manipulation of portions of the worksheet. (If you want to affect the entire worksheet, as by inserting an entire column, look at the /**W**orksheet command menu.)

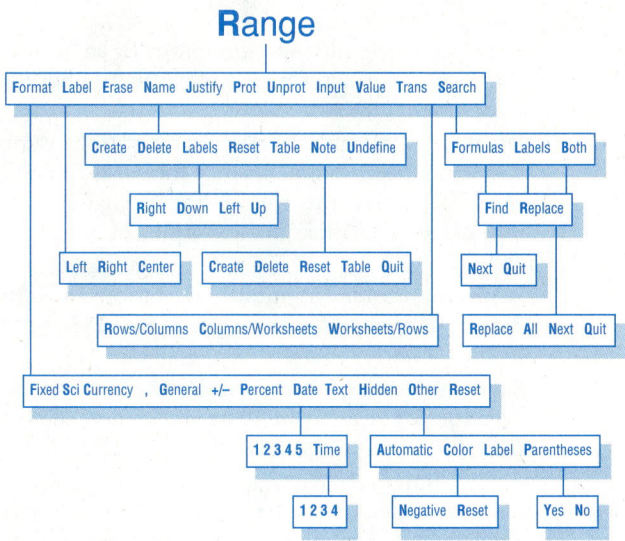

Range Format /RF

Purpose

Prepares cells so that they display with a specific format for both values (numbers) and formula results.

/**R**ange **F**ormat formats a cell or range of cells so that numbers appear in a specific format: with fixed decimal places; as currency; with commas only; in scientific notation; or as dates. The **H**idden and **T**ext formats affect text in cells. All these formats affect both screen display and printing.

Reminders

◆ Use /**W**orksheet **G**lobal **F**ormat to format the majority of the worksheet's cells that are to contain numeric data. Use /**R**ange **F**ormat to reset formats for areas that differ.

◆ Move the cell pointer to the upper left corner of the range you want to format.

Procedures

1. Type **/rf**.
2. Select a format from the following menu items:

Menu Item	Description
Fixed	Fixes the number of decimal places displayed. If the setting is 3 decimal places, for example, the number 1.2345 appears as `1.235`.
Sci	Displays in scientific notation large or small numbers. In a 2-decimal format, for example, the number 950000 appears as `9.50E+05`.
Currency	Displays the default currency symbol (for example, $ or £) and commas. Currency format is often used for the first row and the bottom line of financial statements. In a 2-decimal format, for example, 24500.254 appears as `$24,500.25`.
,	Marks thousands and multiples of thousands. In a 2-decimal format, for example, 24500.254 appears as `24,500.25`.
General	Suppresses zeros after the decimal point, uses scientific notation for large or small numbers, and serves as the default decimal display.
+/–	Creates horizontal bar graphs or time-duration graphs on computers that do not have graphics. A positive number displays as + symbols; a negative number, as – symbols. The number of symbols equals the integer value of the cell contents. For example, 6.23 appears as `++++++`.
Percent	Displays a decimal number as a percentage followed by a percent sign (%). In a 2-decimal format, for example, .346 appears as `34.60%`.
Date	Displays the date in one of five customary formats. One selection under **Date** formats the time display. These are the **Date** selections:

      1 DD–MMM–YY   12–Jan–91
      2 DD–MMM   12–Jan
      3 MMM–YY   Jan–91
      4 MM/DD/YY   01/12/91
      5 MM/DD   01/12

Time:

      1 HH:MM:SS AM/PM   1:04:34 PM
      2 HH:MM AM/PM   1:04 PM
      3 HH:MM:SS   13:04:34
      4 HH:MM   13:04

/Range Commands 677

Menu Item	Description
Text	Evaluates formulas as numbers but displays formulas as text. Numbers in cells appear in General format.
Hidden	Hides cell contents from display and printing but evaluates contents. Use this command to hide confidential notes or variables.
Other	Supplies additional formatting choices:
Automatic	Automatically formats numbers and dates when they are entered in a cell.
Color	Provides two options: Negative, which displays negative numbers brighter or in color; and Reset, which restores the default setting.
Label	Automatically enters a label prefix before the numeric values are entered in a cell. Existing values remain as numbers. New numeric entries appear as labels.
Parentheses	Provides two options: Yes, which puts parentheses around all values; and No, which removes parentheses.
Reset	Returns the format to current /Worksheet Global format.

3. If 1-2-3 prompts, enter the number of decimal places to be displayed. The full value of a cell—not the value displayed—is used for calculation. (See the first caution.)
4. If you select Date or Time, also select a format number to indicate how you want the date or time to appear.
5. Specify the range by entering the range address, highlighting the range, or using an assigned range name.
6. Verify that the specified range is correct.
7. Press Enter.

Important Cues

- ◆ To apply a format to the same cells in all the file's worksheets, put the file in GROUP mode by using /Worksheet Global Group Enable. Then use /Range Format.
- ◆ Use /Range Prot and /Worksheet Global Prot to protect cell contents hidden with /Range Format Hidden from being accidentally written over.
- ◆ /Range Format Hidden is the only format that affects labels. All other /Range Format commands work on values and numeric formulas.
- ◆ Redisplay hidden data with the Reset format or any other new format.
- ◆ Dates and times are generated from serial date and time numbers created with @DATE, @DATEVALUE, @TIME, @NOW, and @TIMEVALUE.

- If you use a format other than **General**, asterisks fill the cell when a value is too large to fit the cell's current column width. (In the **General** format, values that are too large are displayed in scientific notation.)
- Use /**W**orksheet **G**lobal **D**efault **O**ther **I**nternational to display non-USA formats. Select one of these international format options: **P**unctuation, **C**urrency, **D**ate, or **T**ime.
- Range formats take precedence over /Worksheet Global formats.

Cautions

- /**R**ange **F**ormat rounds only the appearance of the displayed number. The command does not round the number used for calculation. This difference can cause displayed or printed numbers to appear to be incorrect. In some worksheets, such as mortgage tables, results may be significantly different than expected. Enclose numbers, formulas, or cell references in the @ROUND function to ensure that the values in calculations are truly rounded.
- Use the **F**ixed decimal format to enter percentage data. Use the **P**ercent format to display or print results. The **P**ercent format displays a decimal number in percentage form; a decimal number such as .23 is displayed as 2 3 %. If the **P**ercent format is used for data entry, most users see numbers in percentage form (such as 23%) and attempt to enter similar percentages (.24 as 24, for example), producing grossly incorrect entries (such as 2400%). If the **P**ercent format is used, numeric entries should be followed by a percent sign, as in 24%. The trailing percent sign causes 1-2-3 to divide the value by 100.

*For more information, see /**Worksheet Global Format**, /**Worksheet Global Default**, /**Worksheet Global Group**, and Chapters 5 and 6.*

Range Label /RL

Purpose

Specifies how you want to align text labels in their cells.

Labels narrower than the cell width can be aligned to the left, right, or center. To change how numbers appear on-screen, use either /**R**ange **F**ormat or /**W**orksheet **G**lobal **F**ormat.

Reminders

- Move the cell pointer to the upper left corner of the range containing the cells you want to align.
- Use /Worksheet Global Label to align labels that have not been aligned with /Range Label.

Procedures

1. Type /**rl**.

/Range Commands

2. Select one of these menu items:

Menu Item	Description
Left	Aligns labels with cell's left edge.
Right	Aligns labels with cell's right edge.
Center	Centers labels in cell.

3. Specify the range by entering the range address, highlighting the range, or using an assigned range name.
4. Press Enter.

Important Cues

- If you want the align commands to apply to the same cells throughout a file, put the file in GROUP mode before aligning labels.
- The label prefix appears on the status line (the screen's first line), before the cell contents.
- To align labels in a cell manually, enter one of these label prefixes before typing the label:

Label Prefix	Function
' (apostrophe)	Aligns label to the left.
" (quotation mark)	Aligns label to the right.
^ (caret)	Centers label in the cell.
\ (backslash)	Repeats character to fill a cell (this prefix cannot be selected from the menu).

- Unmodified worksheets start with labels left-aligned. Use /Worksheet Global Label to set the label prefix used by text entries in areas not specified with /Range Label.
- /Range Label does not affect values (numeric cell entries). Values are always right-aligned.
- Labels beginning with numbers or formula symbols require label prefixes. Enter the label prefix before entering the numbers or symbols, or use /Range Format Other Label to create an area where numbers enter as labels. This process is necessary for such items as addresses, part numbers, Social Security numbers, and phone numbers, as in the following examples:

Correct	Incorrect
'2207 Cheyenne Dr.	2207 Cheyenne Dr.
"34-567FB	34-567FB

- Use a label prefix to preserve formulas that contain errors you have not yet identified. For example, if you have a problem with the formula +B5*@PMT(B16B12/12,B14*12), and you don't have time to look for the error (a comma is missing after B16), use an apostrophe label prefix to turn the formula into text. Later, when you have more time, use EDIT mode to remove the apostrophe to change the text back to a formula. Then correct the formula error.

- Document formulas by inserting a label prefix before each formula and copying the formula as a label to your worksheet documentation area. Later, remove the label prefix from the formula to restore it to its original, operable form.

Cautions

- **/R**ange **L**abel **C**enter does not center labels on the screen or page. You must center the text manually by moving the cell pointer with the text and following these steps:

  1. Enter the text if you have not done so already.
  2. Determine how many leading spaces are necessary to center the text on-screen.
  3. Press Edit (F2), and then press Home. The cursor moves to the label prefix at the beginning of the text.
  4. Move the cell pointer right one character and insert spaces in front of the first character to center the label.
  5. Press Enter.

- Numbers or formulas preceded by label prefixes have a value of zero when evaluated by a numeric formula. In a database query, you must use text searches to search for numbers that have label prefixes.

For more information, see **/Worksheet Global Label**, **/Range Format**, *and Chapter 5.*

Range Erase /RE

Purpose

Erases the contents of a single cell or range of cells while leaving the cell's format intact.

Reminders

- If you have any doubts about erasing a range of cells, use /File Save to save the worksheet to a file before erasing the range.
- Move the cell pointer to the upper left corner of the range to be erased.

Procedures

1. Type **/re**.
2. Specify the range to be erased by entering the range address, highlighting the range, or using an assigned range name.
3. Press Enter.

/Range Commands 681

Important Cues

- To erase protected cells, you must first remove worksheet protection by using /**W**orksheet **G**lobal **P**rotection **D**isable. You cannot remove protection if the file is sealed.
- Erasing data or formulas may produce an ERR display in formulas that depend on the erased data or formulas.
- Erasing a range does not change the format, label prefix, or protection status assigned to the cells. Use /**R**ange **F**ormat **R**eset, /**R**ange **P**rot, or /**R**ange **U**nprot to change these.

Caution

- Be careful not to erase formulas or values hidden with /**W**orksheet **G**lobal **F**ormat **H**idden or /**R**ange **F**ormat **H**idden.

For more information, see /**W**orksheet **D**elete, /**W**orksheet **E**rase, /**W**orksheet **G**lobal **D**efault **O**ther **U**ndo, *and Chapter 4.*

Range Name /RN

Purpose

Assigns an alphabetic or alphanumeric name to a cell or a range of cells. (See the caution about alphanumeric range names.)

Reminders

- You can use range names instead of cell references to make formulas and macros easier to understand. If you frequently print specific areas of a worksheet or go to specific areas, you can name these locations and use the easily remembered range name when asked for the print range or the GoTo location.
- There are two types of range names: defined and undefined. A *defined range name* refers to a cell or range address and can be used in formulas or command prompts. An *undefined range name* has not been assigned an associated address or range and can be used only in formulas. Formulas that use undefined range names result in ERR.

Procedures

To create a range name that describes a single cell or range of cells, follow these steps:

1. Move the cell pointer to the cell or upper left corner of the range of cells to be named.
2. Type /**rn**.

3. Select **Create**.
4. When prompted to enter the range name, press Name (F3) to see a full-screen display of names already in use. If the name you want to use is listed, delete it before you create another range by that name. Press Esc to exit from the list.
5. Type a range name of as many as 15 characters. Avoid using symbols other than the underline.
6. Press Enter.
7. To specify the range to be named, enter the range address or highlight the range.
8. Press Enter.

To delete one or more range names, follow these steps:

1. Type **/rn**.
2. Select **Delete** to delete a single range name. Select **Reset** to delete all range names.
3. If you select **Delete**, type or highlight the name you want to delete. Press Enter. Formulas containing the range names revert to using cell and range addresses.

To create range names from labels, follow these steps:

1. Move the cell pointer to the upper left corner of the column or row of labels.
2. Type **/rn**.
3. Select **Labels**.
4. Select one of these menu items:

Menu Item	Description
Right	Uses the labels to name the cell to the right of each label.
Down	Uses the labels to name the cell below each label.
Left	Uses the labels to name the cell to the left of each label.
Up	Uses the labels to name the cell above each label.

5. By entering the range address or highlighting the range, specify the range of labels to be used as names. Verify that the range encloses only labels.
6. Press Enter.

To display the addresses of existing range names, follow these steps:

1. Move the cell pointer to a clear area of the worksheet. The table you will create in these steps requires two columns and as many rows as there are range names, plus one blank row.
2. Type **/rn**.
3. Select **Table**.
4. Press Enter to create a table of range names and their associated addresses.

To attach or edit notes associated with a range name, follow these steps:

1. Type **/rn**.
2. Choose **N**ote **C**reate.
3. Type the range address or highlight the cells to which you want to attach a note.
4. Press Enter.
5. Type or edit a note of up to 512 characters.
6. Press Enter.
7. Choose **Q**uit to return to the previous menu.

To delete one or more notes associated with range names, follow these steps:

1. Type **/rn**.
2. Choose **N**ote **D**elete to delete one range name note, or **N**ote **R**eset to delete all range name notes.
3. If you choose **N**ote **D**elete, specify the range name whose note you want deleted.

To display a table of notes in the current file, follow these steps:

1. Move to a location where 1-2-3 can enter notes and addresses without destroying needed data. The table you will create in these steps is three columns wide and has as many rows as there are names, plus one.
2. Type **/rn**.
3. Choose **N**ote **T**able.
4. Press Enter.

To preserve an existing range name but separate it from its associated address, follow these steps:

1. Type **/rn**.
2. Choose **U**ndefined.
3. Select the name you want undefined.

Important Cues

- Use a range name when you enter a function. Instead of entering a function as **@SUM(P53..P65)**, for example, type it as **@SUM(EXPENSES)**. You do not have to create the name EXPENSES before entering the formulas; however, until the name is created, the @SUM formula returns ERR.
- Use range names when you respond to a prompt. For example, when the program requests a print range, provide a range name, as in the following:

    Enter print range: **JULREPORT**

- Undefined range names remain in formulas, although the formulas result in ERR. Use the **/R**ange **N**ame **C**reate or **L**abels command to redefine the name.

- ◆ To move the cell pointer rapidly to the upper left corner of any range, press GoTo (F5) and then enter the range name, or press Name (F3) to display a list of range names. After you enter the range name or select a name from the list, press Enter.
- ◆ To print a list of range names, use **/R**ange Name **T**able and press Shift-PrtSc after the list appears.
- ◆ **/M**ove moves range names with cells if the entire range is included in the block to be moved.
- ◆ Macro names are range names; therefore, macros must be named through the use of /rnc or /rnl.

Cautions

- ◆ A range name can be alphanumeric (as in SALES87), but avoid creating a range name that looks like a cell reference (for example, AD19). Such a range name does not function correctly in formulas.
- ◆ Be sure that you are in the correct file before deleting range names or range name notes.
- ◆ Always delete existing range names before re-creating them in a new location. If you don't delete an original range name, formulas that used the original name may be wrong.
- ◆ Do not delete columns or rows that form the corner of a named range. Doing so produces an ERR in formulas.
- ◆ Moving one or more corners of a range name can redefine the range name. To check the addresses that a range name applies to after a corner has been moved, issue **/R**ange **N**ame **C**reate and select the name in question. The name's range appears on-screen. Press Esc to return to the menu.
- ◆ When two named ranges have the same upper left corner, moving one of the corners moves the address location for both range names. To move a corner of overlapping named ranges, first delete one range name, move the range, and then re-create the deleted range name in its original location.
- ◆ **/R**ange **N**ame **T**able does not update itself automatically. If you move or copy ranges or change range names, you must re-create the range name table.

For more information, see Chapter 4.

Range Justify /RJ

Purpose

Fits text within a desired range by wrapping words to form complete paragraphs.

Use **/R**ange **J**ustify to join and "word wrap" automatically any lines of text in adjacent vertical cells to form a paragraph. **/R**ange **J**ustify redistributes words so that sentences are approximately the same length.

Reminders

- If you are uncertain about the results of /**R**ange **J**ustify, save your worksheet with /**F**ile **S**ave before using /**R**ange **J**ustify.
- Delete any blank cells or values between vertically adjacent cells you want to join. Blank cells or values stop text from justifying.
- Move the cell pointer to the top of the column of text you want justified. Make sure that the cell pointer is in the first cell containing the text. On the status line, you should see the first words of the text from the first row of the column.
- Remember that other cells are moved to reflect the justification unless you specify a range for /rj. In figure R.1, a range has been specified in which the text will be reformatted; this specification keeps the value in B10 from being displaced.

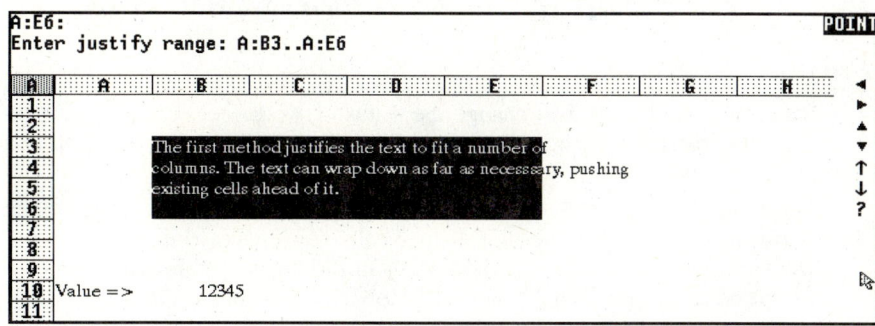

Fig. R.1.
The worksheet range marked for justification.

Procedures

1. Type /**rj**.
2. Highlight the range in which you want the text to be justified. If you choose not to specify a range for the justification, highlight only the first row of the text column.
3. Press Enter; the text is justified. If you specified a range, worksheet cells within the highlighted range are justified; cells outside the highlighted range are not moved.

Important Cues

- /**R**ange **J**ustify justifies all contiguous text in a column until justification is stopped by nonlabel cell contents (a blank cell, a formula, or a value).
- Use /**F**ile **I**mport to import text from word processing packages (ASCII text files only). Once in 1-2-3, the text can be justified with /**R**ange **J**ustify to fit the worksheet.

Cautions

- If the specified range is not large enough to hold the justified text, 1-2-3 displays an error message. To solve this problem, enlarge the range or move the text to a new location. If you enlarge the range, you may have to move other cell contents.
- Using /Range Justify on protected cells results in an error. Remove protection with /Worksheet Global Prot Disable.
- 1-2-3 is not a word processing software. Although /Range Justify wraps words, you are much better off learning the fundamental commands of a word processing software than using 1-2-3 for word processing.

For more information, see /Move, /File Import, and Chapter 5.

Range Prot and Range Unprot   /RP and /RU

Purpose

/Range Prot enables you to change the status of worksheet cells from unprotected to protected. /Range Unprot enables you to make changes to cells in a protected worksheet.

Use /Range Unprot and /Worksheet Global Prot to protect files from accidental changes. /Range Unprot identifies which cells' contents can be changed when /Worksheet Global Prot is enabled. Cells not identified with /Range Unprot cannot be changed when /Worksheet Global Prot is enabled.

Reminder

Move the cell pointer to the upper left corner of the range you want to identify as unprotected. /Worksheet Global Prot may be enabled or disabled. If the file has been sealed, the seal must be removed with /File Admin Seal Disable before worksheet global protection can be removed.

Procedures

To return an unprotected range to its original, protected identification, follow these steps:

1. Type /r.
2. Select Prot.
3. Specify the range by typing the range address, highlighting the range, or using an assigned range name.
4. Press Enter.

To identify a cell or a range of cells as unprotected, follow these steps:

1. Type /r.
2. Select Unprot.
3. Specify the range to be identified as unprotected by typing the range address, highlighting the range, or using a range name.
4. Press Enter.

Important Cues

- /Range Prot and /Range Unprot affect data entry only when /Worksheet Global Prot is enabled. The screen display of unprotected contents may be brighter or in a different color, depending on your graphics hardware. (See Chapter 4.)
- Use high-contrast characters in unprotected cells to attract attention to instructions or comments, even when worksheet protection is disabled.
- Use /Range Input to limit cell pointer movement to unprotected cells. Combine /Range Input with the advanced macro command FORM to create custom data-entry forms.
- Use /Worksheet Status to see whether worksheet protection is enabled or disabled.

Cautions

- When the file is in GROUP mode, identifying a range as unprotected on one worksheet identifies and removes the protection from the same range on all worksheets.
- Macros that make changes to cell contents do not work correctly if /Worksheet Global Prot is enabled and the macro attempts to change protected cells. Prevent this situation by limiting cell pointer movement to unprotected cells or by disabling worksheet protection when the macro starts. Macros should enable worksheet protection before they end.

For more information, see /Worksheet Global Prot, /Range Input /Worksheet Status, /File Admin Seal, and Chapter 4.

Range Input   /RI

Purpose

Restricts cell pointer movement to unprotected cells.

/Range Input is an excellent way to create fill-in-the-blank worksheets. Such worksheets prevent inexperienced users from making accidental changes to worksheet labels and formulas.

Reminders

- To use /Range Input effectively, organize your worksheet so that the data-entry cells are together. Include text and examples that show the operator the format and type of data to enter. Figure R.2 shows a worksheet arranged to maximize /Range Input.
- Before you use /Range Input, use /Range Unprot to identify unprotected data-entry cells. /Worksheet Global Prot does not have to be enabled.

Fig. R.2.
The Loan Calculator worksheet arranged to maximize /Range Input.

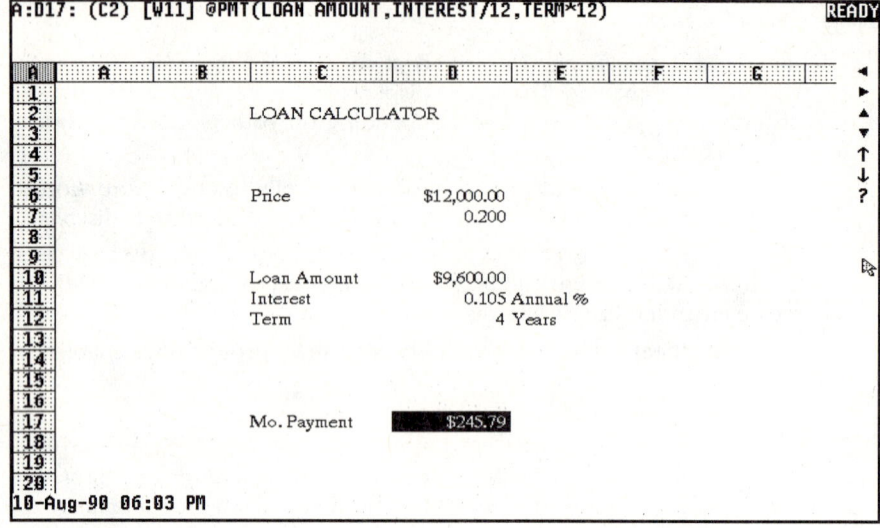

- Move the cell pointer to one corner of a range that includes the unprotected data-entry cells.

Procedures

1. Type **/ri**.
2. Specify the input range to be displayed. Include a range covering all cells in which you want to enter data. Type the range address, highlight the range, or use a range name.
3. Press Enter. The input range's upper left corner is moved to the screen's upper left corner. Cell pointer movements are restricted to unprotected cells in the designated input range.
4. Make data entries, using normal methods. Press Esc or Enter to exit from **/Range Input** and return to normal cell pointer movement.

Important Cues

- **/Range Input** restricts your key selections to Esc; Enter; Edit (F2); Help (F1); Home; End; and the left-, right-, up-, and down-arrow keys. Use standard alphanumeric keys for data entry.
- **/Range Input** is most valuable when used within macros. Within macros, the command can be used to restrict data entry to one worksheet range for one part of the macro and to another worksheet range for another part of the macro.

For more information, see **/Range Unprot** *and Chapter 4.*

Range Value /RV

Purpose

Copies formulas to the same or a new location and replaces the copied formulas with their resulting values.

Reminders

- Check to see that the destination area is large enough to hold the copied values, which will replace existing cell contents.
- Ensure that the source file is calculated. If CALC shows at the bottom of the screen, press Calc (F9) to recalculate the file. If the file is linked to other active files or to files on disk, use /File Admin Link-Refresh to update linked values.
- Move the cell pointer to the upper left corner of the range containing the formulas.

Procedures

1. Type /**rv**.
2. Specify the source range by typing the range address, highlighting the range, or using a range name.
3. Press Enter.
4. Specify the upper left corner cell of the destination range by typing a cell address or range name, or by moving the cell pointer to this location.
5. Press Enter. The values appear in the destination range and preserve the numeric formats used in the original formulas.

Important Cues

- /**R**ange Value also copies labels and string formulas and converts string (text) formulas to labels.
- Use /**C**opy to copy formulas without changing them into values.

Cautions

- /**R**ange Value overwrites data in the destination (TO) range. Be sure that the destination range is clear.
- If you make the destination range the same as the source range, formulas in the range are converted to their values. These values, however, overwrite the formulas they came from. The formulas are replaced permanently.

For more information, see /Copy and Chapter 4.

Range Trans /RT

Purpose

Copies formulas from one location and orientation to another location and orientation. Formulas are replaced by their values.

/Range Trans is useful when you want to change data from worksheet format (headings on left, data in rows) to database format (headings on top, data in columns), or vice versa. The command also can transpose data from rows and columns on one worksheet to individual rows or columns on multiple worksheets.

Reminders

- Transpose to a clear worksheet area. The transposed data overwrites any existing data.
- Move the cell pointer to the upper left corner of the range of cells you want to transpose.
- Ensure that the source file is calculated. If CALC shows at the bottom of the screen, press Calc (F9) to recalculate the file. If the file is linked to other active files or to files on disk, use **/File Admin Link-Refresh** to update linked values.

Procedures

1. Type **/rt**.
2. Specify the range to be transposed by typing the range address, highlighting the range, or using an assigned range name.
3. Press Enter.
4. When 1-2-3 displays the TO prompt, do one of two things:
    a. If you want to transpose rows to columns or columns to rows on a single worksheet, specify the upper left corner of the area where you want the transposed data to appear.
    b. If you want to transpose data across multiple worksheets, specify the upper left corner of the three-dimensional range for each of the multiple worksheets. Move the cell pointer to the upper left corner of the destination cells where the transposed data will be copied.
5. Press Enter. The data transposes immediately if you are working on a single worksheet.
6. If you are transposing across multiple worksheets, choose one of the following commands:

Menu Item	Description
Rows/Columns	Copies rows to columns or vice versa.
Columns/Worksheets	Copies each column to a succeeding worksheet in the TO range.
Worksheets/Rows	Copies each row to a succeeding worksheet in the TO range.

/Range Commands **691**

Figure R.3 shows data in A6..B10 transposed to D6..H7 on a single worksheet.

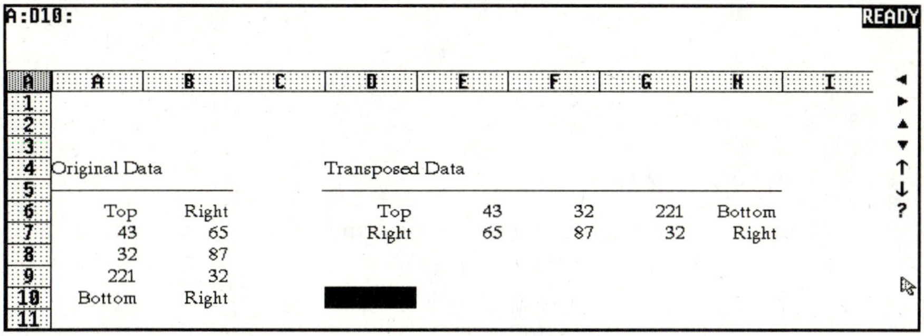

```
A:D10:                                              READY
     A      B      C      D      E      F      G      H      I
 1
 2
 3
 4  Original Data              Transposed Data
 5
 6       Top    Right               Top     43     32    221  Bottom
 7        43      65              Right     65     87     32   Right
 8        32      87
 9       221      32
10    Bottom    Right
11
```

Fig. R.3.
Data in A6..B10 transposed to D6..H7.

Important Cue

Transposing copies the cell format and protection status from the original cell.

Caution

Using the same upper left corner for the original and transposed data can result in incorrect data.

*For more information, see /**Range Value** and Chapter 4.*

Range Search   /RS

Purpose

Finds or replaces text within a label or formula. The search and replace can be limited to a specified range.

Use this command to search databases quickly or to find locations on a worksheet. The command also is useful for finding and replacing cell references, functions, and range names in formulas.

Reminders

♦ /**Range Search** makes it easy to correct or change formulas that use range names.

♦ /**Range Search** does not work with values.

Procedures

1. Type /**rs**.
2. Type the cell addresses or highlight or type a range name to specify the range you want searched.
3. Enter the text string you want to find or replace. You may use either uppercase or lowercase text; the /**Range Search** command is not case-sensitive.
4. Choose one of the following:

Menu Item	Description
Formulas	Searches through formulas.
Labels	Searches through labels.
Both	Searches through both formulas and labels.

5. Choose one of the following:

Menu Item	Description
Find	Finds the item, displays it, and pauses before continuing.
Replace	Finds the item; displays it; and requests a continue, replace, or quit action.

6. If you choose **Find**, 1-2-3 finds and displays the cell containing the text. You then are prompted to choose one of the following:

Menu Item	Description
Next	Finds the next occurrence.
Quit	Stops the search.

7. If you choose **Replace**, 1-2-3 finds and displays the cell containing the text. You then are prompted to choose one of the following:

Menu Item	Description
Replace	Replaces the found text with the replacement text, then finds the next occurrence.
All	Replaces all occurrences of found text.
Next	Finds the next occurrence without replacing the current text.
Quit	Stops the search.

Important Cues

- When no more matching text is found, an error message appears at the bottom of the screen. Press Enter or Esc to return to the worksheet.
- Use spaces and label prefixes to prevent finding unwanted text. For example, a search for *and* finds *and* and *sandwich*. A search for '*and* finds *and* as the first entry in a left-aligned text cell, but not *sandwich*. A search for <space>and<space> finds the phrase *this and that*, but not *sandwich*.
- Use /Range Search as a quick way to update text information in a database.

Cautions

- Beware of replacing with **All**. You can easily replace text or formulas you did not want to replace.
- /Range Search neither finds nor replaces values. It cannot be used to update numbers in the worksheet.

For more information, see Chapter 4.

Copy and Move Commands

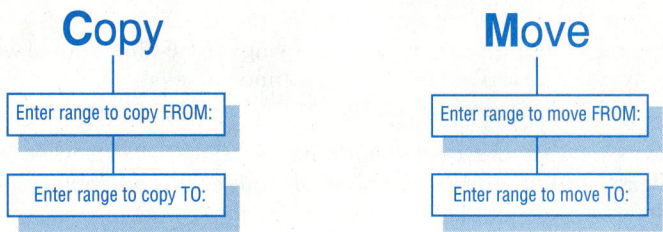

Copy /C

Purpose

Copies formulas, values, and labels to new locations. The copied data retains its format and its cell-protection status.

The cell addresses in copied formulas either change to reflect the new location or stay fixed, depending on whether you use relative or absolute cell references.

Reminders

- Make sure that the worksheets contain enough blank space to receive the cell or range of cells being copied. Three-dimensional worksheets must have enough room in the TO range to hold the entire three-dimensional duplicate. Copies replace the original contents of cells.
- If the receiving cell address is not close to the cell or range of cells being copied, make a note of the address before issuing /Copy, so that you can type the TO address. Pointing across a long distance to the TO address can be tedious.
- Before you issue the /Copy command, move the cell pointer to the upper left corner of the range you want copied. If you are copying one cell, put the cell pointer on that cell. If you are copying a three-dimensional range, put the cell pointer on the topmost worksheet.

Procedures

1. Type /**c**.
2. The FROM prompt requests the range of the cells to be copied. Enter the range to be copied by typing the range name or range address or by highlighting the range.

3. Press Enter.

4. At the TO prompt, specify on the topmost worksheet the upper left corner of the area where you want the duplicate to appear. If you want multiple adjacent duplicates, you can specify the top left corner where each duplicate should appear. If you are copying a three-dimensional worksheet, specify only the top left cell on the topmost worksheet.

5. Press Enter.

6. Make sure that the copied formulas produce correct answers. If the answers are not correct, the copy procedure has probably adjusted cell addresses that should have remained fixed.

Important Cues

- ◆ /Copy creates duplicates of labels and values. Formulas that use relative cell references are adjusted to the new location; formulas that use absolute cell references remain fixed.

- ◆ You can link files by copying formulas that use absolute range names. For example, copying @SUM($EXPENSES) from TRIP.WK3 to another file creates on the receiving worksheet the duplicate formula @SUM(<<C:\123\DIVISION\TRIP.WK3>>$EXPENSES)

- ◆ You can make single or multiple copies, depending on the range you enter at the TO prompt. Enter the ranges as follows:

Original Range FROM	Desired Copies	Duplicate Range TO
One cell	Fill an area	Row, column, or range on one or more worksheets
Rectangular range	One duplicate	Upper left cell of duplicate, outside original range, on one or more worksheets
Single column	Multiple columns	Adjacent cells across a row, formed from the top cell of each duplicate column, on one or more worksheets
Single row	Multiple rows	Adjacent cells down a column, formed from the left cell in each duplicate row, on one or more worksheets
Three-dimensional rectangular range	One duplicate	Upper left cell of topmost worksheet of duplicate's range

Cautions

- Overlapping FROM and TO ranges (original and duplicate) can cause formulas to yield incorrect results. To avoid producing incorrect results, move the cell pointer off the original cell before anchoring the TO range with a period.
- If the worksheet to be copied to does not have enough room to receive the copied range, the contents of the existing cells are covered by the copied data. If there are not enough worksheets to receive a three-dimensional copy, the copy is stopped, and a warning appears at the bottom of the screen. To fix this problem, use /Move to move existing data; use /Worksheet Insert to insert blank columns, rows, or worksheets.

For more information, see /Worksheet Insert [Column, Row, Sheet] /Range Value, /Range Name, and Chapter 4.

Move   /M

Purpose

Reorganizes your worksheet by moving blocks of labels, values, or formulas to different locations or worksheets.

Cell references and range names used in formulas stay the same, which means that formula results do not change. You cannot move data across files.

Reminders

- Make sure that you have enough blank space in the receiving worksheet(s) to receive the cell or range of cells being moved. The moved data replaces the original contents of the target range.
- Before you issue the /Move command, position the cell pointer on the top left corner of the range to be moved. If you want to move one cell, place the cell pointer on that cell.

Procedures

1. Type /**m**.
2. The FROM prompt requests the range of the cells to be moved. Highlight a range, or enter one by typing the range name or range address.
3. Press Enter.
4. At the TO prompt, enter the address of the single upper left corner of the range to which you want to move the cells. Do so by typing the cell address, typing a range name, or highlighting the cell with the cell pointer.
5. Press Enter.

Important Cues

- /Move does not change cell addresses. The range names and cell references in the formula remain the same.
- Use /Copy when you want to create at a new location a duplicate range of cells while keeping the original range intact.
- Range names move with the moved cells if the named area is completely enclosed.

Cautions

- The contents of moved cells replace the contents of existing cells. To make room for moved cells, use /Move to move existing data; use /Worksheet Insert to insert rows, columns, or worksheets to provide additional room for copies.
- You cannot move an original so that the duplicate is beyond the worksheet or file boundaries. Use /Worksheet Insert to insert additional rows, columns, or worksheets.
- Moving the anchor cell or the diagonally-opposite cell of a named range or formula's range moves the corner(s) of the named range or formula's range to the new location as well. If you have doubts about what is being moved, save the worksheet, delete the old range name, make the move, and then re-create the range name.
- Moving cell contents over the top of the corner in a formula's range creates an ERR in the referencing formula. The formula's range is replaced by ERR, and all dependent formulas show ERR.
- If a formula uses a named range, and cell contents are moved over a corner of the range, the name remains in the formula. The formula's results, however, display as ERR.
- Be careful when moving a named range that has the same upper left corner as another range. Moving one range changes the upper left corner of both named ranges.

For more information, see **/Worksheet Insert**, **/Copy**, **/Range Name**, *and Chapter 4.*

File Commands /F

File commands are used to save and retrieve worksheets, extract a small worksheet from a larger worksheet, combine two worksheets, import ASCII data, and select the drive and directory for storage.

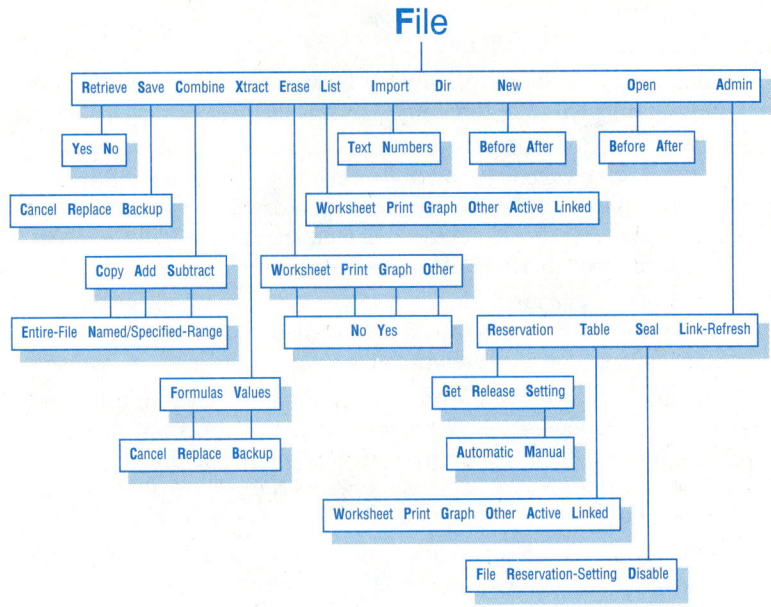

File Retrieve /FR

Purpose
Loads the requested file from disk.

Reminder
Before you retrieve a new file, use **/F**ile **S**ave to save the current worksheets in the active file. When a new file is retrieved, it replaces the file currently displayed.

Procedures
1. Type **/fr**.
2. Specify the name of the file you want to retrieve, either by typing the name or by using the right- or left-arrow key to highlight the file name.
3. Press Enter.

Important Cues

- You can display a listing of file names by pressing Name (F3) in response to the `Enter name of file to retrieve:` prompt. Use the arrow keys to move the highlight to the file name you want, and then press Enter. To return to the menu without making a selection, press Esc three times.

- Retrieve a single file from a different disk drive or directory by typing the drive designation, the path, and the file name, for example:

  `Enter name of file to retrieve:`
  C:\123\FORECAST\JUNEV3

  In this example, the file JUNEV3 is located on drive C in the FORECAST subdirectory of the 123 directory. To clear the previous path, you may have to press Esc twice after the prompt.

- Use the /File Open command to retrieve a file from disk without replacing the active files. If 1-2-3 has too little memory for you to open additional files, remove one or more active files from memory with /Worksheet Delete File. To remove all active files, use /Worksheet Erase.

- Protected worksheets require a password. When you enter a password, be sure to use the same uppercase and lowercase letter combination you originally used for the password.

- If you attempt to retrieve from a network a file that is in use by someone else, 1-2-3 displays a Yes/No menu. Press Y if you want the file without having the reservation. Doing so enables you to use the file, although you cannot save it under the same name. Press N if you do not want to retrieve the file. See /File Admin for more information on file reservations.

- When you start 1-2-3, the worksheet file loads automatically if you save it into the same directory as 123.EXE under the name AUTO123.

- To change the default drive or directory for the current work session, use the /File Dir command.

- Use /Worksheet Global Default Dir to change the directory that 1-2-3 uses on start-up. Use /Worksheet Global Default Update to save the settings to the disk.

- 1-2-3 Release 3 can retrieve Lotus 1-2-3 Release 1A and Symphony files, but they are saved as WK3 files. Use the Translate utility to convert the WK3 file back to 1-2-3 Release 1A or Symphony format.

Caution

The retrieved file replaces the active files on-screen. Use /File Save to store the current file or worksheet before retrieving a new one.

For more information, see /File Admin, /File Save, /Worksheet Global Default, /File Dir, and Chapter 7.

/File Commands **699**

File Save /FS

Purpose

Saves the active files and their settings.

/File Save stores files so that they can be retrieved later.

Reminders

- Remember to save frequently to guard against data loss.
- Name files so that they are easy to remember and group together. If you give related files similar names (such as TRENDV1, TRENDV2, and TRENDV3), you can use the wild cards * and ? to copy and erase files.

Procedures

1. Move the cell pointer so that it is in the active worksheet or file you want to save.
2. Type **/fs**.
3. If the file has not been saved before, 1-2-3 supplies a default name and extension, such as FILE0001.WK3. You can enter the file name for the worksheet by using the default name displayed; by highlighting an existing name; by typing a new name; or by entering a new drive designation, path name, and file name.

   If more than one file is active, 1-2-3 displays the message [ALL MODIFIED FILES]. Press Edit (F2) if you want to save a single file name. You can edit the file name.
4. Press Enter. If the message [ALL MODIFIED FILES] displays, all active modified files are saved under their original names.
5. If a file already exists under the name you have selected, choose one of the following:

Menu Item	Description
Cancel	Cancels the save operation.
Replace	Replaces an existing file with the current file.
Backup	Saves the active file and renames the existing file with the extension BAK.

Important Cues

- Create file names of up to eight characters by using the letters A through Z, the numbers 0 through 9, and the underline character (_) or hyphen (-). Spaces cannot be used.
- Password protection prevents unauthorized access to 1-2-3 worksheets. If you save worksheets with a password, the password must be entered before the file can be retrieved. To save a file with a password, follow these steps:

1. Move the cell pointer into the active file you want saved.
2. Type **/fs**.
3. Type the file name, press the space bar, and press **P**. (If the message [ALL MODIFIED FILES] appears, press Edit (F2) to see the file name.)
4. Press Enter.
5. Type a password of up to 15 characters (no spaces). An asterisk appears in place of each letter. Be sure to remember the uppercase and lowercase letter combination. When you retrieve the file, you must enter the password in exactly the same way.
6. Press Enter.
7. After the verification prompt appears, type the password again and press Enter.

- To change a protected file's password, use the Backspace key to erase the Password Protected message displayed when you use /File Save. Then repeat steps 3 through 7.
- From the list of existing files on disk, you can select a file name to save to. When prompted for a name, press Esc to remove the default file name. Press Name (F3), use the arrow keys to move to the file name you want to replace, and press Enter.
- Save single worksheets from 1-2-3 Release 3 (WK3) format to 1-2-3 Release 2 (WK1) format by typing the file extension **WK1** after the file name when you save. WK3 files that contain more than one worksheet or that are sealed cannot be saved to WK1 format. Remember to save a backup copy in WK3 format in case features or functions are lost during the conversion.
- Use /File List to display the size and the date of the existing files.
- If a file is too large to save in its entirety, use /File Xtract to save portions of it to disk as separate files.

Cautions

- Saving a file under an existing file name replaces the old file. This means that you can accidentally write over files you want to keep. A safer practice is to use the **Backup** option or to save each copy under a different name and delete old versions later, using /File Erase or the operating system's ERASE command.
- After executing /File Save, do not remove your data disk until the light on your disk drive goes off. Pay no attention to the READY indicator. Wait several seconds after the READY indicator disappears before you remove the disk. If you remove the disk prematurely, information can be lost.

*For more information, see **/File Dir**, **/File Erase**, **/File Xtract**, and Chapter 7.*

File Combine /FC

Purpose

Combines values or formulas from a file or worksheet on disk into the current file. Any part of a saved file can be combined with the current file.

Reminders

- ◆ Remember that /File Combine can be used three different ways: to copy the contents from the file on disk to the current file; to add values from the file on disk to the current file; and to subtract incoming values from the numeric values in the current file.
- ◆ Before starting the /File Combine operation, you must know the cell references or ranges you want from the disk and the name of the file on the disk.
- ◆ The /File Combine operation is easiest if the files on disk contain named ranges to be combined with the current file in memory.
- ◆ Use /File Import and /Data Parse to bring ASCII files into the current worksheet and organize them. To send your file to an ASCII text file, use /Print File to print the file to disk.
- ◆ The format of the cells coming in from disk takes priority over the formats in the current file. Global formats, range names, and column widths do not change.

Procedures

1. Move the cell pointer to the upper left corner of the range in which the data is to be combined.
2. Type /**fc**.
3. Select one of the following choices:

Menu Item	Description
Copy	Copies incoming cell contents over the cells in the current worksheet. Cells in the current worksheet that correspond to blank incoming cells do not change. Labels and formulas in the current worksheet are replaced.
Add	Adds values in the source file to cells containing blanks or values in the current worksheet. Labels and formulas in the current worksheet are not changed.
Subtract	Subtracts values in the source file from the corresponding blanks or values in the current worksheet. Labels and formulas in the current worksheet are not changed.

4. Select how much of the saved file you want to use:

Menu Item	Description
Entire-File	Combines the entire file with the current worksheet. Use when the disk file has been created with /File Xtract and contains only raw data.
Named/Specified-Range	Combines information from a named range or range address on the disk file into the current worksheet. Use when you want to retrieve only part of the information contained in a file on disk.

5. If you select **Entire-File**, choose a file name from the menu by pressing the right- or left-arrow key, by typing the file name, or by pressing Name (F3) to display a list of file names and using the arrow keys to select one. Press Enter. If you select **Named/Specified-Range**, you are asked to enter the range name (or the range address) and the file name.

Important Cues

- If you frequently combine a small portion from a file, first give that portion a range name. Use **/Range Name** to name the portion of the file and save the file back to disk. You then can use **/File Combine** and enter the range name of the part you want to combine.

- When creating worksheets, you can save time by using **/File Xtract** and **/File Combine** to merge parts of existing worksheets to form the new one.

- Use /fcc to copy sections of a macro file to your worksheet so that you don't have to type the macros on every new worksheet. Keep your favorite macros in one worksheet. You can use /fcc to copy the macro into the new worksheet, but you must use **/Range Name Create** or **/Range Name Labels** to rename the macro on the new worksheet.

- When you use **/File Combine Add**, cells in the incoming file that contain labels or string formulas are not added.

- Create a macro with **/File Combine** to consolidate worksheets.

Cautions

- /fcc combines values, labels, and formulas. All cell references, relative and absolute, are adjusted to reflect their new locations on the worksheet. Cell references are adjusted according to the upper left corner of the combined data range (the cell pointer location). Combined formulas adjust for the difference between the cell pointer and cell A1 on the current worksheet.

- Data copied into the current worksheet replaces existing data. Blank cells in the incoming worksheet take on the value of the cells in the current worksheet.

- Range names are not brought to the new worksheet when a file is combined. This arrangement prevents possible conflicts with range names

/File Commands 703

in the current worksheet. After combining files, you must re-create range names with **/Range Name Create** or **/Range Name Labels**.

For more information, see /Data Parse, /Range Name, /File Import, /File Xtract, /Print File, and Chapter 7.

File Xtract /FX

Purpose

Saves to disk a portion of the active file as a separate file. You can save the portion as it appears on the worksheet (with formulas) or save only the results of the formulas.

Reminders

- Extracted ranges that include formulas should include the cells the formulas refer to; otherwise, the formulas are not correct.
- If you want to create a 1-2-3 Release 2 file, extract only from a range on a single worksheet and from files that are not sealed.
- If the CALC indicator appears at the bottom of the screen, calculate the file before extracting values. Press Calc (F9) to calculate the file.

Procedures

1. Position the cursor at the upper left corner of the range you want to extract.
2. Type **/fx**.
3. Choose one of the following:

Menu Item	Description
Formulas	Saves as a new file both the formulas and cell contents from the current file.
Values	Saves as a new file the labels and results from formulas.

4. Specify a file name other than that of the current worksheet.
5. Specify the range of the file to be extracted as a separate file. Enter the range by typing the range address (such as B23..D46), by typing the range name, or by moving the cell pointer to the opposite corner of the range.
6. Press Enter.
7. If the name already exists, choose one of the following:

Menu Item	Description
Cancel	Cancels the extract operation.
Replace	Replaces the existing file with the extracted file.
Backup	Saves the extracted file and renames the existing file with the extension BAK.

Important Cues

- If you use /fxf to save a portion of a worksheet, the extracted file can function as a normal worksheet.
- To freeze a worksheet so that formulas and results don't change, extract a file with /fxv. The formulas are replaced with values.
- Use /fx to save memory when a worksheet becomes too large. Separate the worksheet into smaller worksheets that require less memory.
- Increase worksheet execution speed and save memory by breaking large worksheets into smaller ones with /fxf. Link the extracted worksheets so that they still pass data between them (see Chapter 3).
- You can protect an extracted file by using a password. For more information, read about /File Save, earlier in this section of the Command Reference.

Caution

Make sure that the extracted worksheet does not use values or formulas outside the extract range.

For more information, see /File Combine and Chapter 7.

File Erase /FE

Purpose

Erases 1-2-3 files from disk.

Use /fe to erase unnecessary files from disk so that you have more available disk space. You cannot erase files on disk that are in use with a reservation, as on a network drive. Use /Worksheet Erase or /Worksheet Delete to remove files from memory.

Reminders

- Use the operating system's ERASE or DEL command to remove a large number of files. From within 1-2-3, select the /System command, use ERASE or DEL at the system prompt, and return to 1-2-3 by typing **EXIT** and pressing Enter.
- You cannot restore an erased file. Before you erase a file, be sure that you do not need it.

Procedures

1. Type **/fe**.
2. Select the type of file you want to erase:

/File Commands 705

Menu Item	Description
Worksheet	Displays worksheet files with WK extensions as specified by /wgdel.
Print	Displays ASCII text files created with /Print or another program. The file extension must be PRN.
Graph	Displays files created with /Graph, which end with the extension PIC or CGM.
Other	Displays all files in the current drive and directory.

3. Type the path and the name of the file, or use the arrow keys to highlight the file you want to erase.
4. Press Enter.
5. By selecting Yes or No from the menu, verify that you do or do not want to erase the file.

Important Cues

◆ You can erase files from different drives or directories either by specifying the drive designation, path, and file name, or by changing these settings with /File Directory.

◆ Press Name (F3) at step 3 to see a full-screen listing of files.

For more information, see /**File Dir**, /**File List**, *and Chapter 7.*

File List /FL

Purpose

Displays all file names of a specific type that are stored on the current drive and directory.

/File List displays the size of the file (in bytes) and the date and time the file was created.

Reminder

Use /File List to select different directories and display the current files.

Procedures

1. Type /**fl**.
2. Select the type of file you want to display:

Menu Item	Description
Worksheet	Displays worksheet files with WK extensions as specified by /wgdel.
Print	Displays ASCII text files created with /Print or another program. The file extension must be PRN.

Menu Item	Description
Graph	Displays files created with /Graph, which end with the extension PIC or CGM.
Other	Displays all files in the current drive and directory.
Active	Displays all files in memory.
Linked	Displays all files linked to the current file.

3. Use the arrow keys to highlight individual file names and display their specific information. If the list of file names extends off the screen, use the arrow keys, PgDn, or PgUp to display the file names.
4. Display files from a different directory by moving the cell pointer to a directory name (such as \BUDGET) and pressing Enter. Move to a parent directory by pressing Backspace.
5. Press Enter to return to the worksheet.

Important Cues

- Use the /**File Admin Table** command to create a list of file information on the current worksheet. Be sure that you are in a blank part of the worksheet before you create a table; otherwise, data is erased.
- Use /fl to check your file listing before you use /**File Erase**. You don't want to erase files that are linked to files you still use.
- 1-2-3 displays the date and time each file was created so that you can find the most recent version of a file. (Date and time values are accurate only if you supply the correct entries when you start your computer. Date and time values can be reset at the system prompt through the DATE and TIME commands.)

For more information, see /**File Erase**, /**File Dir**, and Chapter 7.

File Import /FI

Purpose

Brings ASCII text files from other programs into 1-2-3 worksheets.

Many software programs use ASCII files to exchange data with other programs. Most databases, word processing packages, and spreadsheets have a method of printing ASCII files to disk.

Reminders

- Remember that you can use /**File Import** two different ways to transfer data into a 1-2-3 worksheet. The first method reads each row of ASCII characters as left-aligned labels in a column; the second method reads into separate cells text enclosed in quotation marks, or numbers surrounded by spaces or separated by commas.

/File Commands 707

- Be sure that you have enough room on the worksheet to receive the imported data; incoming characters replace the current cell contents. One row in an ASCII file is equal to one row on the worksheet. The number of columns depends on whether the incoming ASCII data is pure text (a single column) or delimited text (multiple columns).
- ASCII files must have the extension PRN. If you want to import a text file that does not have the PRN extension, use the operating system's RENAME command to change the extension.

Procedures

1. Move the cursor to the upper left corner of the range in which you want to import data.
2. Type /**fi**.
3. Choose how to import the ASCII file:

Menu Item	Description
Text	Makes each row of characters in the ASCII file a left-aligned label in the worksheet. Labels are in a single column from the cell pointer down.
Numbers	Enters each row of characters in the ASCII file into a row in the worksheet. Text enclosed in quotation marks is assigned to a cell as a label. Numbers surrounded by a space or separated by commas are assigned to a cell as values. Other characters are ignored.

4. Select or type the name of the ASCII print file. Do not type the PRN extension.
5. Press Enter.

Important Cues

- 1-2-3 cannot import ASCII files that have more than 8,192 rows. Lines longer than 512 characters wrap to the next worksheet row. If necessary, you can use a word processing software to read, modify, and divide the ASCII files into smaller files before saving them to disk as ASCII files.
- You can separate ASCII text files that are not delimited by quotation marks or commas. Use /**File Import Text** to bring the file into the worksheet. Use /**Data Parse** to separate the resulting long label into separate cells of data.

Cautions

- Incoming data replaces existing cell contents. If you are unsure of the size of the file you are importing, use the operating system's TYPE command to review the ASCII file.
- Word processing files contain special control codes that 1-2-3 cannot handle. Be sure to save your word processing document as an ASCII file before you try to import it into 1-2-3.

For more information, see /**Data Parse** *and Chapter 7.*

File Dir /FD

Purpose

Changes the current disk drive or directory for the current work session.

Reminder

Sketching how your directories and subdirectories are arranged on your hard disk makes /File Dir easier to use. Include the types of files stored in different directories.

Procedures

1. Type **/fd**.
2. If the displayed drive and directory are correct, press Enter. If you want to change the settings, type a new drive letter and directory name; then press Enter.

Important Cues

- Access another drive and directory temporarily by selecting /fr or /fs and pressing Esc twice to clear the current drive and directory from the command line. Then type the drive designation and directory name, including a final backslash (\). You then can either type a file name or press Enter to see a list of file names on that drive or directory; move the cursor and press Enter to select a name from the list.

- Access another directory on the same drive by selecting /fr or /fs and pressing the Backspace key as many times as necessary to clear the current directory from the command line. Then type the directory name, including a final backslash (\). You then can either type a file name or press Enter to see a list of file names on that drive or directory; move the cursor and press Enter to select a name from the list.

- Display current file names and directories by selecting /File List, choosing Other, and pressing Name (F3). Press Backspace to go to the parent directory.

- You can change 1-2-3's default start-up drive and directory by using /Worksheet Global Default Dir to enter a new drive or directory. Save this new setting to the System disk by using /wgdu.

Caution

When specifying drive letters and path names, be sure to enter the correct symbols. The most common mistakes include using a semicolon (;) instead of a colon (:) after the drive designation, using a slash (/) instead of a backslash (\) between subdirectory names, and inserting spaces in names.

For more information, see /Worksheet Global Default, /File List, /File Retrieve, /File Save, and Chapter 7.

/File Commands **709**

File New /FN

Purpose

Creates a new blank file on disk and positions a new worksheet on-screen either before or after the current file.

Reminders

- The new file contains one blank worksheet. The cell pointer appears at A1.
- Current files remain in memory.
- Use the /**F**ile **O**pen command to open existing files without deleting files currently in memory.

Procedures

1. Move the cell pointer to a file that will be adjacent to the new file's location.
2. Type /**fn**.
3. Choose the location for the new file:

Menu Item	Description
Before	Places the new file before the current file.
After	Places the new file after the current file.

4. Type a new file name to replace the default name given by 1-2-3.
5. Press Enter.

Important Cue

After entering data in the worksheet, you must use /**F**ile **S**ave to save the worksheet to disk if you want to use the worksheet later.

For more information, see /**F**ile **O**pen, /**F**ile **S**ave, and Chapter 7.

File Open /FO

Purpose

Opens a file from disk into memory without removing active files.

You choose whether the file opens before or after the current file. The cell pointer positions itself in the file at the same address that the cell pointer was at when the file was saved.

Reminder

Move to a file and its worksheet that are adjacent to where you want the opened file to appear.

Procedures

1. Type /**fo**.
2. Choose the location for the file to be opened:

Menu Item	Description
Before	Places the new file before the current file.
After	Places the new file after the current file.

3. Specify the name of the file by typing or highlighting the name with the left- or right-arrow key. Press Name (F3) to see all the names.

Important Cues

- Files saved with a password require a password entered exactly as originally recorded.
- Files under reservation display a No/Yes prompt. Press **Y** if you want to open the file (you must save it under a different name). Press **N** if you do not want to open the file.
- Close unneeded files if there is not enough memory to open the files you want.
- Use /**File New** to open a new blank file in memory.

Caution

The opened file controls recalculation and window settings for all active files. *For more information, see* /**File Retrieve**, /**File New**, *and Chapter 7.*

File Admin Reservation /FAR

Purpose

Controls the reservation status of a file. If more than one person has access to a file in a network, /**File Admin Reservation** controls how the file is shared.

Reminder

/**File Admin Reservation** enables you to get or release a file's reservation so that you can make changes to a file and save it under the original file name. You also can change the file setting so that the first person opening or retrieving the file automatically gets the file reservation.

Procedures

1. Type /**far**.
2. Choose one of the following commands:

/File Commands 711

Menu Item	Description
Get	Gets the file reservation for you after you have opened or retrieved the file and if no one has changed the file on disk since you opened it into memory. The read-only indicator (RO) disappears from screen.
Release	Releases the file reservation so that others can get the reservation. The read-only indicator (RO) appears on-screen.
Setting	Provides two options:
Automatic	Gives the file reservation to the first person to open or retrieve the file.
Manual	Requires the user to issue the /farg command to get the reservation.

3. If you changed the reservation setting, use **/File Save** to save the file and its new setting.

Important Cues

◆ Use **/File Admin Seal** to prevent unauthorized users from changing the setting.

◆ If you requested the reservation, but it was not available, a message appears to that effect.

◆ The **/File Save** command with the [ALL MODIFIED FILES] prompt saves active files only when you have the reservations for all files. Use the /farg command to get the reservations you need.

Caution

Do not release the reservation until you have saved your changes with **/File Save**. Releasing the reservation prevents you from making changes to the original file on disk.

For more information, see **/File Admin Seal** *and Chapter 7.*

File Admin Table   /FAT

Purpose

Enters a table of files on the worksheet. You select which type of files are in the table.

Reminder

To set up the table, first find on the worksheet an area that is blank or unneeded. Information in the table overwrites information in the same worksheet location.

Procedures

1. Move the cell pointer to an area where the table will not destroy needed information.
2. Type **/fat**.
3. Choose one of the following commands:

Menu Item	Description
Worksheet	Enters a table of worksheet files.
Print	Enters a table of PRN files.
Graph	Enters a table of CGM or PIC graph files.
Other	Enters a table of all files.
Active	Enters a table of active files.
Linked	Enters a table of files linked to the current file.

3. If you choose **Worksheet**, **Print**, **Graph**, or **Other**, press Enter to enter a table for the current directory. If you want a table from another directory, type a different directory path and press Enter.
4. Highlight the upper left corner of the range where you want the table.
5. Press Enter.

Important Cues

- Use **/File List** to see file information without creating a table on your worksheet.
- The table contains as many rows as there are files, plus one. Disk files or linked files use four columns. Active files use seven columns.
- The table columns for disk-based files are in the following order: file name, date, time, and file size. Use the **/Range Format** command to format the date and time columns so that their entries appear as dates or times.
- The table columns for active files are in the following order: file name, date, time, file size, number of worksheets in the file, modified file attribute, and file reservation attribute. A modified file attribute of 1 means that the file has been modified since you read it into memory; 0 means that the file is unmodified. A file reservation attribute of 1 means that you have the file reservation; 0 means that you do not.
- The **/fat** command is an excellent way to read file information into a worksheet so that macros can operate on selected files.
- A table of linked files shows the path name for each linked file, if the path was included in the linking formula.
- The graph or worksheet files are selected for listing by their file extensions. The file extensions selected are set by the **/Worksheet Global Default Graph** and **/Worksheet Global Default Ext List** settings.

Caution

Information in the table overwrites information in the worksheet. If you are unsure how many files will be in a table, limit the length of the table range in step 4 of the procedure.

For more information, see **/File Admin Reservation**, **/File List**, **/Worksheet Global Default**, and Chapter 7.

File Admin Seal /FAS

Purpose

Protects a file's format or its file reservation setting from being changed.

Reminders

- Sealing a file also seals the settings that result from these commands:

/File Admin Reservation Setting	/Range Name Note
/Graph Name	/Range Prot
/Print Options Name	/Range Unprot
/Range Format	/Worksheet Column
/Range Label	/Worksheet Global
/Range Name	/Worksheet Hide

- To set up a file for data entry yet protect formulas and macros, use **/Range Unprot** to mark ranges to receive data; then choose **/Worksheet Global Prot** to enable worksheet protection. Seal the file to prevent unauthorized changes to the protected ranges.

- The network administrator should use **/File Admin Seal Reservation-Setting** to prevent unauthorized changes to the file reservation settings.

Procedures

1. Type **/fas**.
2. Choose one of the following commands:

Menu Item	Description
File	Puts a seal on the current file and its reservation setting.
Reservation-Setting	Puts a seal only on the reservation setting for the current file.
Disable	Removes the seal from the current file and its reservation setting.

3. If you chose **File** or **Reservation-Setting**, type a password and press Enter.
4. If you are sealing the file or reservation setting, reenter the password and press Enter.

Important Cue

Ensure that the file is correctly formatted and well tested before putting a seal on it.

Cautions

- Use memorable passwords, but don't make them public. Keep backup copies of passwords with an alternate PC administrator or manager.
- In passwords, an uppercase letter and the corresponding lowercase letter are considered different characters. Remember exactly how you type the password, and always use that form.

For more information, see **/File Admin Reservation**, **/Range Unprot**, **/Range Prot**, **/Worksheet Global Prot**, *and Chapters 4 and 7.*

File Admin Link-Refresh /FAL

Purpose

Recalculates formulas in the active files that depend on data in other active files or files on disk. Link-Refresh ensures that your worksheet uses current data when all the files are not active or are shared among users.

Procedure

Type **/fal**.

Important Cue

Use the /File List Linked command to see whether other files are linked to the current file.

Caution

If the current file is linked to other files that may have changed, use Link-Refresh before printing or reviewing the final results. If you do not use Link-Refresh, your current file's results may be incorrect.

For more information, see **/File List Linked** *and Chapter 7.*

Print Commands /P

The /**Print** commands print worksheet contents as values or formulas. Use /**Print Printer** to send output to the printer and control the print queue; use /**Print File** to send output (as an ASCII file) to disk; use /**Print Encoded** to send a print-encoded file to disk.

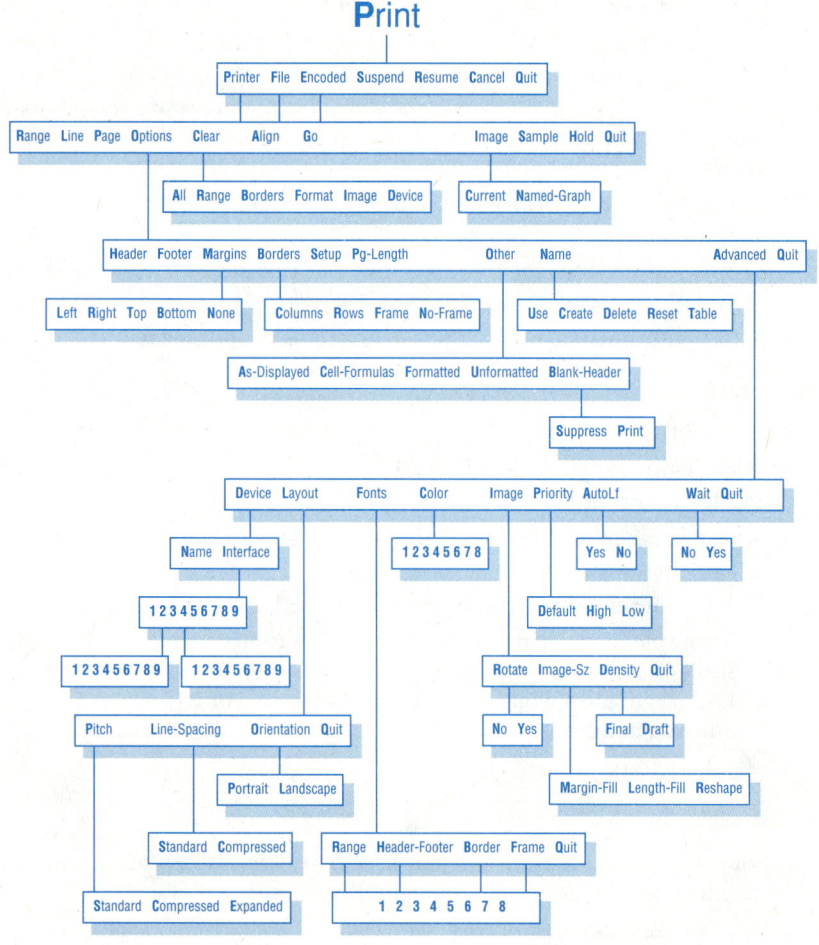

Print Printer /PP

Purpose

Prints worksheet contents (values or formulas) and graphs to the printer.

Reminders

- Before you print, check the lower right corner of the screen to see whether the CALC indicator is displayed. If it is, press Calc (F9) and wait until the WAIT indicator stops flashing before you proceed with the /Print commands.
- /Print Printer prints your worksheet range or graph directly to the printer.
- You do not have to wait for one print job to finish before starting another. 1-2-3 has a print queue that keeps jobs in sequence and remembers the order in which they print. You can continue to work as jobs wait to be printed.
- Remember that all /Print commands apply when output is printed directly to paper, but some do not apply when you use /Print File.
- Before you issue /Print Printer, move the cell pointer to the upper left corner of the range to be printed.
- Before printing, make sure that the printer is on, connected, and on-line.

Procedures

1. Type /**pp**.
2. Select **R**ange to print a worksheet range, or select **I**mage to choose the graph you want to print.
3. Type the range address, highlight the range, or enter a range name to specify the range to be printed.
4. Select from the other print options explained later in this section.

    For example, if the material to be printed is the beginning of a report or worksheet, adjust the top of the paper to the top of the print mechanism and select **A**lign to align the printer and the top of the paper. If you are printing an additional part onto an existing page, do not align the paper.

5. Select **G**o to print.

Important Cues

- For information on printing a graph, see the /Print [**P**, **E**] Image command later in this section of the Command Reference.
- You can use 1-2-3's /Print commands to set formats for your printouts. Use commands from /Print [**P**, **F**, **E**] Options to control formats for printing.
- Print an ASCII text file to disk by using /Print File. Most popular software programs, including word processing and database programs, can import ASCII text files.

Caution

Do not manually adjust paper in the printer once the **Align** command has been given. Use the **Line** or **Page** command to move paper after it is aligned. Moving paper manually misaligns the paper and 1-2-3's line counter, resulting in large blank spaces in your printout.

For more information, see /Print File, /Print [Printer, File, Encoded] Range, and Chapter 8.

Print File /PF

Purpose

Prints worksheet contents as an ASCII text file to disk. ASCII text files are a common means of transferring data to and from different software packages.

Reminders

◆ Before you print the file, check the lower right corner of the screen to see whether the CALC indicator is displayed. If it is, press Calc (F9) and wait until the WAIT indicator stops flashing before you proceed with the /**P**rint commands.

◆ Before you issue /**P**rint **F**ile, move the cell pointer to the upper left corner of the range to be printed.

Procedures

To create an ASCII file for use in word processing, follow these steps:

1. Type /**pf**.
2. Type a file name in response to the `Enter name of print file:` prompt. Limit the file name to eight characters (don't use spaces). 1-2-3 automatically gives the file name a PRN extension.
3. Select **R**ange.
4. Type the range address, highlight the range, or use a range name to specify the range to be printed to disk.
5. Select **O**ptions **M**argins. Set the top, left, and bottom margins to 0; set the right margin to 255.
6. Select **O**ther **U**nformatted to remove headers, footers, and page breaks. (These print options can cause extra work in reformatting when the file is imported by another program.)
7. Select **G**o from the second-level /**P**rint menu.

To create an ASCII file to be used with a database program, follow these steps:

1. Reset all numbers and dates to a format understood by the database program you are using.
2. Set column widths so that all data is displayed. Make a note of the column position in which each column begins and ends.
3. Type **/pf** and specify a file name.
4. Select **R**ange.
5. Specify the range to be printed; you may not want to include field names at the top of databases. Specify the range by typing the range address, highlighting the range, or using an assigned range name.
6. Select **O**ptions **M**argins. Set the top, left, and bottom margins to 0; set the right margin to 255.
7. Select **O**ther **U**nformatted to remove headers, footers, and page breaks.
8. Select **G**o from the second-level **/P**rint menu.

Important Cues

- 1-2-3 does not print a graph to a PRN file. To export a graph to a graphics program, save the graph with a picture file format (PIC) or metafile format (CGM).

- To add multiple ranges of data to an ASCII text file, stay in the **/P**rint menu; continue to choose new ranges and to select **G**o. The additional ranges append to the end of the ASCII text file you named with **/P**rint **F**ile. When you exit the **/P**rint menu, all final text ranges are printed to the ASCII file, and the file is closed so that you can no longer append data.

- To see an ASCII text file on-screen, return to the operating system. At the operating-system prompt, type the command **TYPE**, press the space bar, and type the path name and the name of the ASCII text file you want to review. For example, after the `C>` prompt you could enter **TYPE C:\123\BUDGET\VARIANCE.PRN** and press Ctrl-S to stop the data from scrolling off the screen. Press the space bar to continue scrolling.

- Before you print the file to disk, make sure that the columns are wide enough to display all the data. If a column is too narrow, values are changed to asterisks, and labels are truncated.

- Refer to your word processing documentation for instructions on importing ASCII files. Refer to your database documentation for instructions on importing column-delimited ASCII files.

Caution

Different database programs accept data in different formats; check to see in what form dates are imported and whether the receiving program accepts blank cells. Be sure to prepare your 1-2-3 file accordingly before printing to an ASCII file. As a general rule, remove numeric formats and align labels to the left before you print the data to disk. Because of an error in 1-2-3's method

/Print Commands 719

of calculating serial date numbers, dates in your worksheet may be one day different from dates used in your database package. If the right margin setting is too low, data may be moved to a following page when the file is printed to disk.

For more information, see */Print Printer*, */Print [Printer, File, Encoded] Range*, and Chapter 8.

Print Encoded /PE

Purpose

Prints worksheet contents (values or formulas) and graphs to an encoded file for later printing.

Reminders

- Before you print, check the lower right corner of the screen to see whether the CALC indicator is displayed. If it is, press Calc (F9) and wait until the WAIT indicator stops flashing before you proceed with the /Print commands.
- Remember that all /Print commands apply when output is printed directly to paper, but some do not apply when you use /Print Encoded.
- Before you issue /Print Encoded, move the cell pointer to the upper left corner of the range to be printed.
- /Print Encoded creates a file on disk that can later be sent to a printer through the operating system's COPY command.

Procedures

1. Type /**pe**.
2. Respond to the `Enter name of encoded file:` prompt. 1-2-3 automatically adds the file extension ENC.
3. Select **R**ange to print a worksheet range, or select Image to choose the graph you want to print.
4. Type the range address, highlight the range, or enter a range name to specify the range to be printed.
5. Select from the other print options explained in this section of the Command Reference.
6. Select **G**o to print.

Important Cues

- For information on printing a graph, see the /Print [**P**, **E**] Image command later in this section of the Command Reference.

- You can use 1-2-3's print commands to set formats for your printouts. Use commands from /Print [P, F, E] Options to control formats for printing.
- Print an ASCII text file to disk by using /Print File. Most popular software programs, including word processing and database programs, can import ASCII text files.
- You can print an encoded file by copying it to the printer at any time, whether or not 1-2-3 is in use. This capability is useful if you need to use a printer that isn't available where your PC is. When you create the ENC file, ensure that the designated printer is the same type that the file is to be copied to later. Once a file has been created, use the COPY command to copy the encoded file to the printer. For example, to copy the FRCST.ENC file in the C:\123 directory to the printer on the first parallel port, type **COPY C:\123\FRCST.ENC/B LPT1** and press Enter. Do not forget the /B part of the command. If you use a PostScript or Apple LaserWriter printer connected to a serial port, use COM1 or COM2 instead of LPT1 or LPT2.

For more information, see Chapter 8.

Print Suspend /PS

Purpose

Suspends (temporarily stops) the printer on the current print job.

1-2-3 may have in a queue more than one print job waiting to be printed. A print queue prints jobs in the "background" as you continue to work with the 1-2-3 worksheet or graph in the "foreground." This arrangement increases your efficiency with the computer.

Reminder

A printer may continue to print for a short time after the **S**uspend command is issued. The reason is that data has already been sent to and is stored in the printer.

Procedure

Type /**ps**.

Important Cues

- Suspending print jobs in the queue increases the performance of your operations and calculations in 1-2-3.
- To continue printing after selecting /**P**rint **S**uspend, select /**P**rint **R**esume.

/Print Commands   721

- Use the **/Print Cancel** command to cancel all print jobs.

*For more information, see **/Print Resume**, **/Print Cancel**, and Chapter 8.*

Print Resume   /PR

Purpose

Resumes printing after the queue has been suspended.

Reminder

Use **Resume** to restart the printer if it is waiting for the next sheet of paper.

Procedure

Type **/pr**.

Caution

Resume clears any printer error messages.

*For more information, see **/Print Printer Options Advanced**, **/Worksheet Global Default**, **/Print Suspend**, and Chapter 8.*

Print Cancel   /PC

Purpose

Cancels the current job in the printer and removes all other print jobs from the queue.

Important Cues

- Some printers contain memory called a *buffer* to store pages about to be printed. If you cancel a job, one or more pages that remain in the printer's buffer may still print. To clear them, turn the printer off, pause, and then turn it back on.
- Canceling print jobs in the queue increases the performance of your operations and calculations in 1-2-3.
- **/Print Cancel** realigns the printer and paper for the next job in the queue.

Procedure

Type **/pc**.

Caution

Printing may not stop when canceled if you are printing to a shared printer on a network. Refer to your network administrator for assistance.

*For more information, see **/Print Suspend** and Chapter 8.*

Print [Printer, File, Encoded] Range   /PPR or /PFR or /PER

Purpose

Defines the area of the worksheet to be printed.

Reminders

- Check the lower right corner of the screen to see whether the CALC indicator is displayed. If it is, press Calc (F9) and wait until the WAIT indicator stops flashing before you proceed with the /Print commands.
- Before you print, move the cell pointer to the upper left corner of the range to be printed.

Procedures

To define the worksheet area to be printed, follow these steps:

1. Type **/pp** to print directly to the printer; type **/pf** to print to disk; or type **/pe** to print an encoded file that can later be copied to a printer. Specify a file name if one is requested. 1-2-3 adds the appropriate file extension for **File** or **Encoded** files.
2. Select **Range**.
3. Type the range address, highlight the range, or enter an assigned range name to specify the range to be printed. You can enter a single range, multiple ranges, or a named graph. The following table shows sample entries:

Range Type	Example	Description
Single range	B12..R56 or MONTH_RPT	One range per print job.
Multiple range	B12..R56;MONTH_RPT	Multiple ranges within a single print job. You separate ranges with a semicolon (;).
Named graph	*BDGTGRF or B12..R56;*BDGTGRF	Graph or graph and worksheet in a single print job. Precede the named graph with an asterisk (*).

4. Verify that the range is correct and press Enter.

Important Cues

- /Print [P, F, E] Range "remembers" the last print range used, which means that you can reprint the specified worksheet portion without reentering the range. You also can edit existing print ranges.
- Hidden columns within a print range do not print.

/Print Commands 723

- To display the current print range, select **R**ange from the second-level /**P**rint menu. The status line displays the current range address, and the specified range is highlighted on the screen.
- To display each corner of the range, press the period key (.). Each time you press the period key, the next corner is displayed.
- Use /**P**rint [**P**, **F**, **E**] **O**ptions **B**orders to print headings at the top or side of every printed page. Use this technique, for example, when you want to print database field names at the top of every page.
- Use /**W**orksheet **P**age to insert mandatory page breaks in a range.
- After a range has been printed, 1-2-3 does not advance the paper to the top of the next page. Instead, 1-2-3 waits for you to print another range. To advance the paper, use the **P**age command in the second-level /**P**rint menu.
- If the print range is wider than the distance between the left and right margins, the remaining characters are printed on the following page (if printed to paper) or in the rows below the data (if printed to disk).

Caution

If you want long text labels to print, ensure that they are completely within the highlighted range. Highlighting only the cell containing text does not print text that extends beyond the cell.

*For more information, see /**W**orksheet **P**age, /**P**rint **P**rinter, /**P**rint **F**ile, and Chapter 8.*

Print [Printer, File, Encoded] Line /PPL or /PFL or /PEL

Purpose

Inserts blank lines. Use this command to put spaces between ranges on the same paper or between graphs and print ranges.

Reminder

/**P**rint [**P**, **F**, **E**] **L**ine puts a blank line on paper or in the ENC or PRN file.

Procedures

1. Type /**pp** or /**pf** or /**pe**
2. Select **L**ine to advance the paper one line or to insert a blank line in a file. Repeat the keystroke (or press Enter) as many times as necessary to advance the paper to the desired position.

Important Cue

Use this command to insert a blank line between printed ranges. You can get paper out of alignment with 1-2-3's internal line count if you change the position of paper in a printer manually (either by turning the platen knob or by pressing the printer's line feed button). Blank lines in the middle of printed output can signify that the printer and 1-2-3 are out of alignment. To realign the paper and reset 1-2-3, turn off the printer and roll the paper until the top of a page is aligned with the print head. Then turn on the printer again and use /Print Printer Align to reset 1-2-3.

For more information, see Chapter 8.

Print [Printer, File, Encoded] Page /PPP or /PFP or /PEP

Purpose

Ejects the page in the printer or marks the end of the current page in an ENC or PRN file. Paper alignment is maintained.

Reminder

- Use /Worksheet Page to create a page break in a worksheet. When you print the worksheet, a new page begins at the page break.

Procedures

1. Type /pp or /pf or /pe.
2. Select Page to advance to the next page and print the footer at the bottom of the page.

Important Cue

If the top of the paper is not in line with the print head when the paper is advanced, manually move the paper into position and reset 1-2-3 with /Print Printer Align.

Cautions

- The length of the printed page may not match the length of the paper. Check the paper-length settings with /Print [P, F, E] Options Pg-Length. This problem also occurs when the page-length setting does not match the number-of-lines-per-inch setting.
- The paper in the printer can get out of alignment if you manually advance the paper to the top of the next page. This misalignment causes printing over the paper perforation and blanks in the middle of the page. To realign the paper and reset 1-2-3, turn off the printer and roll the paper until the top of a page is aligned with the print head. Then turn on the printer again and use /Print Printer Align to reset 1-2-3.

For more information, see Chapter 8.

/Print Commands

Print [Printer, File, Encoded] /PPOH or
Options Header /PFOH or /PEOH

Purpose

Prints a header below the top margin on each page. Use the **H**eader option to print page numbers and dates in the heading. Two blank lines are inserted after the header.

Reminder

- A header uses the three lines below the top margin.

Procedures

1. Type **/ppo** or **/pfo** or **/peo**.
2. Select **H**eader.
3. Type a header as wide as the margin and paper width allow. The header can be up to 512 characters wide.
4. Press Enter.

Important Cues

- The date and page number can be printed automatically in a header. Enter an at sign (@) where you want the date to appear; enter a pound sign (**#**) where you want the page number. The **#** causes page numbering to begin with 1 and increase by 1 sequentially. Page numbering restarts at 1 whenever you issue an **A**lign command.

- Break the header into as many as three segments by entering a vertical bar (**|**) between segments. For example, to print at page 21 a three-segment header that uses the computer's internal date of October 30, 1991, enter the following:

    @|Hill and Dale XeriLandscaping|Page #

    The header appears as follows:

    ```
    30-Oct-91      Hill and Dale XeriLandscaping      Page 21
    ```

- To start page numbers at a specific number, use **##** (double-pound sign) followed by the starting number—for example, **##10** to start the page numbering at 10.

- Create a header from cell contents by typing a backslash (\) in the header, followed by the cell reference that contains header information. Typing **\B12**, for example, creates a header out of the information in cell B12. This capability cannot be used in combination with other header data, and the cell contents are left-aligned in the header.

- Use **/P**rint [**P**, **F**, **E**] **O**ptions **B**orders **R**ows to select worksheet rows that are printed above the data on each page. The **B**orders command is especially useful for printing database column headings above the data on each page.

Caution

Headers longer than margin settings print on the following page.

For more information, see /Print [Printer, File, Encoded] Options Margins, /Print [Printer, File, Encoded] Options Borders, /Print [Printer, Encoded] Options Setup, and Chapter 8.

Print [Printer, File, Encoded] Options Footer /PPOF or /PFOF or /PEOF

Purpose

Prints a footer above the bottom margin of each page.

Reminders

- Use /Print [**P**, **F**, **E**] Options Footer to print, for example, a title, department heading, or identifier. Footers can be used to print page numbers and dates automatically.
- Footers reduce the size of the printed area by three rows.

Procedures

1. Type **/ppo** or **/pfo** or **/peo**.
2. Select Footer.
3. Type a footer as wide as the margin and paper width allow. The footer can be up to 512 characters wide. Characters exceeding the margin width print on another page.
4. Press Enter.

Important Cues

- Use the same cues listed in the preceding section on Options Headers for creating footers that insert the date, page numbers, or data contained in cells.
- Footers occupy one line. Two blank lines are left between a footer and the body copy. The footer prints on the line above the bottom margin.

For more information, see /Print [Printer, File, Encoded] Options Header, /Print [Printer, File, Encoded] Options Margins, /Print [Printer, File, Encoded] Options Borders, /Print [Printer, Encoded] Options Setup, and Chapter 8.

/Print Commands **727**

Print [Printer, File, Encoded] Options Margins /PPOM or /PFOM or /PEOM

Purpose

Changes the left, right, top, and bottom margins from the default margin settings.

Reminder

If you are not sure how margins align on the paper, turn the printer off and on to reposition the print head to the zero position. Adjust the paper so that the left paper edge and the top of the paper align with the print head. Choose the **Align** command from the second-level **/P**rint menu. Now print a sample worksheet and check alignment.

Procedures

1. Type **/ppo** or **/pfo** or **/peo**.
2. Select **Margins**. Specify margins from these options:

Menu Item	Description
Left	Sets 0 to 1,000 characters.
Right	Sets greater than the left margin but not larger than 1,000.
Top	Sets 0 to 240 lines.
Bottom	Sets 0 to 240 lines.
None	Sets the left, top, and bottom margins to 0 and the right margin to 1,000.

Important Cues

- Most nonproportional fonts print at 10 characters per horizontal inch and 6 lines per vertical inch. Standard 8 1/2-by-11-inch paper is 85 characters wide and 66 lines long.

- You do not have to change margin settings if you use 1-2-3 commands to change between different character print modes. For example, if the print settings are for normal 10-pitch characters and you select /Print [**P**, **E**] **O**ptions **A**dvanced **L**ayout **P**itch **C**ompressed, the margins automatically compensate for the smaller characters.

- The size of a graph can be determined by the margins. Be sure that you set at least a right margin when printing graphs.

- When you want to print to disk, remember that you should set the left margin to 0 and the right margin to 255. These settings remove blank spaces on the left side of each row. Setting the right margin to 255 ensures that the maximum number of characters per row are printed to disk.

- Before printing to disk, select **None** for margins and **/Print File Options Other Unformatted** to remove page breaks, headers, and footers. Page breaks, headers, and footers confuse data transfer to a database. If you are importing the file to word processing, use the word processing package to insert margins, page breaks, headers, and footers.

Caution

If the line length is too short for the characters in a printed line, the additional characters are printed on the following page. To get a full-width print, use a condensed print setup string.

For more information, see **/Print File**, **/Print [Printer, Encoded] Options Setup**, *and Chapter 8.*

Print [Printer, File, Encoded] Options Borders — /PPOB or /PFOB or /PEOB

Purpose

Prints row or column headings from the worksheet on every page of the printout.

Use row borders to print database field names as headings at the top of each page. Use column borders to print worksheet labels at the left of each page.

When specifying your print range, do not include the rows or columns containing the borders. Doing so causes the row or column borders to print twice, once from the print range and again from Options Borders.

Reminders

- Before you issue **/ppob** or **/pfob**, move the cell pointer to the leftmost column of headings or to the top row of headings on the worksheet that you want repeated.
- The **B**orders command does not print borders around ranges or graphs.

Procedures

1. Type **/ppob** or **/pfob** or **/peob**.
2. Select from these menu items:

Menu Item	Description
Columns	Prints the selected column(s) at the left side of each page.
Rows	Prints the selected row(s) at the top of each page.
Frame	Prints the row and column frame around the top and left of the printed range.
No-Frame	Removes the frame.

/Print Commands 729

3. If necessary, press Esc to remove the current range. Move the cell pointer to the top row of the rows you want to use as a border or to the leftmost column you want to use. Press the period key (.) to anchor the first corner of the border. Then move the cell pointer, highlighting down for more rows or to the right for more columns.

4. Press Enter.

Important Cue

Including borders is useful when you want to print multiple pages. If you want to print sections of a wide worksheet, you can further condense the columns by using /Worksheet Column Hide to hide blank or unnecessary columns.

Cautions

♦ If you include in the print range the rows or columns specified as borders, the rows or columns are printed twice.

♦ When you use /Print [P, F, E] Options Borders Columns or Rows, the cell pointer's current location becomes a border automatically. To clear the border selection, use /Print [P, F, E] Clear Borders.

Print [Printer, Encoded] Options Setup   /PPOS or /PEOS

Purpose

Controls from within 1-2-3 the printing features offered by some printers.

The command gives you printing features controllable at the printer and not available through the /Print [P, E] Options Advanced commands. Such features may include underlining or strike-through.

Before using setup strings, check the /Print [P, E] Options Advanced commands to see whether an equivalent command is available.

Reminders

♦ Your printer manual contains lists of printer setup codes (also known as *printer control codes* or *escape codes*). These codes may be shown two ways: as a decimal ASCII number representing a keyboard character, or as the Escape key (Esc) followed by a character.

♦ 1-2-3 setup strings include decimal number codes (entered as three-digit numbers), preceded by a backslash (\). For example, the Epson printer control code for condensed print is 15. The 1-2-3 setup string is \015.

♦ Some codes start with the Esc character, followed by other characters. Because the Esc character cannot be typed in the setup string, the ASCII decimal number for Esc (27) is used instead. For example, the Epson printer code for emphasized print is Esc "E". In the 1-2-3 setup string, enter Esc "E" as \027E.

- Some printers retain previous control codes. Before sending a new code to the printer, clear the previous codes by turning your printer off and then on. You also can send the printer a reset code (\027@ for Epson-compatible printers). Put the reset code in front of the new code you send. For example, the 1-2-3 printer setup string that resets previous codes and switches to emphasized printing mode is \027@\027E.

Procedures

1. Type **/ppos** or **/peos**.
2. Enter the setup string. If a setup string has already been entered, press Esc to clear the string. Each string must begin with a backslash (\). Uppercase or lowercase letters must be typed as shown in your printer manual.
3. Press Enter.

Important Cues

- Setup strings can be up to 512 characters long.
- You cannot combine some character sets or print modes. Your printer manual may list combinations that work for your printer.
- Do not combine setup strings with the advanced macro commands. The result can be unpredictable.
- Use embedded setup strings in the print range to change printing features by row. Move the cell pointer to the leftmost cell in the print range row where you want the printing to change. Insert a row with **/W**orksheet **I**nsert **R**ow. Type two vertical bars (||), and then type the appropriate setup string. Notice that only one vertical bar displays. This setup string applies to all following rows. The row containing the double vertical bars does not print.
- When reading setup strings from the printer manual, don't confuse zero (0) with the letter O, or one (1) with the letter l.
- If you get the same several nonsense characters at the top of every printed page, you probably have those nonsense characters in your setup string.

Caution

Some printers retain the most recent printer control code. Clear the last code by turning off the printer for approximately five seconds or by preceding each setup string with the printer reset code. The reset code for Epson-compatible printers is \027@.

For more information, see /Print [Printer, File, Encoded] Sample, /Print [Printer, Encoded] Options Advanced Fonts, /Print [Printer, Encoded] Options Advanced Layout, and Chapter 8.

Print [Printer, File, Encoded] Options Pg-Length /PPOP or /PFOP or /PEOP

Purpose

Specifies the number of lines per page by using a standard 6 lines per inch of page height.

Reminders

- Setting the lines per inch with a setup string creates an incorrect number of lines per page from this command. This command assumes 6 lines per inch.
- Determine the printing area available for body copy by taking the page height at 6 lines per inch and subtracting the top and bottom margins. Also subtract 3 lines for each header and footer.

Procedures

1. Type **/ppop** or **/pfop** or **/peop**.
2. Enter the number of lines per page if that number is different from the number shown. The page length can be from 1 to 1,000 lines.
3. Press Enter.

Important Cue

Most printers print 6 lines per inch unless the ratio is changed with a setup string (printer control code). At 6 lines per inch, 11-inch paper has 66 lines, and 14-inch paper has 84 lines.

For more information, see **/Print [Printer, File, Encoded] Options Margins**, **/Print [Printer, Encoded] Options Setup**, *and Chapter 8.*

Print [Printer, File, Encoded] Options Other /PPOO or /PFOO or /PEOO

Purpose

Selects the form and formatting with which cells print. Worksheet contents can be printed as displayed on-screen or as formulas. You can print either option with or without formatting features.

Reminders

- **As-Displayed** (the default setting) is used with **Formatted** for printing reports and data.
- Use **Cell-Formulas** with **Formatted** to show formulas and cell contents. (**Cell-Formulas** often is used for documentation.)

- To print to disk the data to be used in word processing or a database, choose **As-Displayed** with **Unformatted**. If you are printing to disk (creating an ASCII file to export to word processing or a database), set the left, top, and bottom margins to 0 and the right margin to 255.

Procedures

1. Type **/ppoo** or **/pfoo** or **/peoo**.
2. Select the type of print from these options:

Menu Item	Description
As-Displayed	Prints the range as displayed on-screen. This is the default setting.
Cell-Formulas	Prints the formula, label, or value contents of each cell on one line of the printout. Contents match information that appears in the control panel: address, protection status, cell format, formula or value, and annotation.
Formatted	Prints with page breaks, headers, and footers. This default setting is normally used for printing to paper.
Unformatted	Prints without page breaks, headers, or footers. This setting is normally used for printing to disk.
Blank-Header	Removes the three blank lines at the top and bottom of each page if you don't use a header or footer. **Suppress** prevents the header and footer from printing. **Print** enables the header and footer to print.

3. Select **Quit** to exit from the **Options** submenu.

Important Cues

- Use **Cell-Formulas** to print documentation that shows the formulas and cell settings used to create the worksheet.
- In a **Cell-Formulas** listing many codes appear that indicate cell contents and formatting. P indicates a protected cell; U indicates an unprotected cell. Other codes, such as F2 for "fixed to 2 decimal places," may appear with control-panel codes for other format options.
- Document your worksheets by using the **Cell-Formulas** option to print a copy of all formulas. Use **/Range Name Table** to create a table of range names and addresses.
- Use **Unformatted** on files to be imported to databases. Databases expect ASCII-file data in a consistent order, and headers and footers can disrupt that order.

For more information, see **/Print [Printer, File, Encoded] Options Margins** *and Chapter 8.*

/Print Commands **733**

Print [Printer, File, Encoded] Options Name /PPON or /PFON or /PEON

Purpose

You can assign names to print settings you use frequently. These commands help you manage the library of print settings names you create.

Reminder

To ensure that the settings are what you want, do a test print before assigning names.

Procedures

To change print settings to the settings you have previously given a name, do the following:

1. Type **/ppo** or **/pfo** or **/peo**.
2. Select **Name Use**.
3. Select the name of the setting with which you want to print.

To name a print setting, do the following:

1. Type **/ppo** or **/pfo** or **/peo**.
2. Select **Name Create**.
3. Type for the settings a name of 15 characters or fewer. Do not use a double less-than sign (<<). Using an existing name replaces the previous settings for that name with the current settings.

To change settings assigned to an existing name, do the following:

1. Type **/ppo** or **/pfo** or **/peo**.
2. Select **Name Use**.
3. Select the name you want to modify.
4. Change settings by using **/Print** commands.
5. Type **/pponc** or **/pfonc** or **/peonc**, as though you were going to create a new name.
6. Select the same name.

To delete a print settings name, do the following:

1. Type **/ppo** or **/pfo** or **/peo**.
2. Select **Name Delete**.
3. Select the name you want to delete.

To delete all print settings names in the file, do the following:

1. Make sure that the cell pointer is in the file from which you want to delete names.
2. Type **/ppo** or **/pfo** or **/peo**.
3. Select **Name Reset**.

To create a table on the current worksheet containing a list of all the print settings names in the current file, do the following:

1. Move the cell pointer to a blank area in the worksheet that is one column wide and as many rows long as there are print settings names.
2. Type **/ppo** or **/pfo** or **/peo**.
3. Select **N**ame **T**able.
4. Press Enter.

Important Cue

If you switch between print settings frequently, write or record a keyboard macro that implements the change to the named settings most frequently used.

Caution

Ensure that you are in the correct file before assigning, deleting, or resetting print names.

For more information, see Chapter 8.

Print [Printer, Encoded] Options Advanced /PPOA or /PEOA

Purpose

Enables you to use the full printing capabilities of your printer to enhance printouts and graphs.

Menu items accessed through the **A**dvanced option include these:

Feature	Description
AutoLf	Switches between the printer supplying line feeds and 1-2-3 supplying line feeds.
Color	Prints color text, if your printer can print color.
Device	Changes between printers and printer interfaces that you chose during installation.
Fonts	Selects from as many as eight fonts for use with text.
Image Density	Specifies whether to print graphs in low density or high density.
Image Image-Sz	Selects the size and shape of a printed graph.
Image Rotate	Rotates a graph on the printed page.
Layout Line-Spacing	Selects standard or compressed spacing between lines.

/Print Commands

Feature	Description
Layout Orientation	Selects printing in portrait (vertical) or landscape (horizontal) mode.
Layout Pitch	Selects spacing between characters.
Priority	Selects the order of printing.
Wait	Waits for a page before resuming printing.

Reminders

♦ To see the capabilities of your printer, use the /Print [P, E] Sample command to print a sample page.

♦ Printers that cannot print graphs print an equivalent area of blank space.

Procedures

1. Type **/ppoa** or **/peoa**.
2. Select one of the following commands:

Menu Item		Description
Device		Selects the printer you want to print to. Device offers the following two options:
	Name	Enables you to select the printer you want.
	Interface	Enables you to select the interface for this printer. Nine different printer ports are available on the menu.
Layout		Selects printer characteristics that affect character and line spacing. These characteristics may vary with your printer. Layout offers the following four options:
	Pitch	Provides three options: **Standard**, which is approximately 10 cpi; **Compressed**, which is approximately 17 cpi; and **Expanded**, which is approximately 5 cpi.
	Line-Spacing	Provides two options: **Standard**, which is approximately 6 lines per inch; and **Compressed**, which is approximately 8 lines per inch.
	Orientation	Provides two options: **Portrait**, which designates vertical orientation on the page; and **Landscape**, which designates sideways or horizontal orientation on the page.
	Quit	Returns to the /Print [P, E] Options Advanced menu.

Menu Item	Description		
Fonts	Selects different typefaces and styles for a print range. Fonts offers the following five options:		
	Range	Enables you first to highlight the worksheet range you want to change, then select from fonts 1 through 8.	
	Header-Footer	Enables you to select from fonts 1 through 8 for both the header and footer.	
	Border	Enables you to select from fonts 1 through 8 for the border.	
	Frame	Enables you to select from fonts 1 through 8 for the frame.	
	Quit	Returns to the /Print [P, E] Options Advanced menu.	
Color	Enables you to select the color in which you want to print text. All text prints in the same color. Select a color from 1 to 8.		
Image	Selects the quality, size, and orientation of printed graphs. Image offers the following four options:		
	Rotate	Provides two options: **Yes**, which indicates that you want the graph rotated; and **No**, which indicates that you want to keep the graph oriented with the text.	
	Image-Sz	Sets the size and shape of the graph through three options: **Margin-Fill**, which creates the largest graph in the width entered; **Length-Fill**, which creates the largest graph in the length you enter; and **Reshape**, which creates a graph in the dimensions you enter. Length-Fill and Margin-Fill preserve proportions.	
	Density	Provides two options: **Final**, for high-quality graphs; and **Draft**, for less dark graphs.	
	Quit	Returns to the /Print [P, E] Options Advanced menu.	
Priority	Selects the priority for the current print job with respect to other jobs. Priority provides three options: **Default**, which prints the current job after high-priority and other default jobs but ahead of low-priority jobs; **High**, which prints the current job ahead of default and low-priority jobs; and **Low**, which prints the current job after all other jobs.		

/Print Commands **737**

Menu Item	Description
AutoLf	Selects when the chosen printer uses a line-feed setting different from the default printer's. Select **Yes** if your printer inserts a line feed; select **No** if you want 1-2-3 to insert the line feed. If your printer overlaps lines or prints double-spaced, choose the opposite setting.
Wait	Suspends printing after ejecting a page so that you can insert a new page. After inserting a page, use **/Print Resume** to continue. Choose **No** if you want continuous printing; choose **Yes** if you want to pause between pages.
Quit	Displays the **/Print [P, F, E] O**ptions menu.

Important Cues

◆ If you select COM1 or COM2 as the printer interface, you must use the operating system's MODE command to configure this printer port.

◆ 1-2-3 remembers the printer and interface used with the file if you save the file after printing.

◆ Change the margin settings and page length when you change the layout orientation.

◆ Use **/Print Printer Sample** to see which fonts correspond to fonts 1 through 8. You cannot see the fonts on-screen. The position of characters on-screen may not represent the position of characters when printed.

◆ On some printers, printing graphs in **Draft** quality may be faster.

Cautions

◆ Not all printers are capable of using advanced features. Use **/Print Printer Sample** to see a page printed with the full capabilities of your printer.

◆ Fonts of different sizes or proportional fonts may print narrower or wider than shown on-screen. Use different column widths to vary the printed position of different cells until columns print correctly. You also can change the width of the print range to vary the amount of text printed.

For more information, see **/Print Printer Sample** *and Chapter 8 for a description and illustration of available fonts.*

Print [Printer, File, Encoded] Clear /PPC or /PFC or /PEC

Purpose

Clears some or all print settings and options.

Reminders

- Cleared formats return to default settings.
- This option is the only way to clear borders after they have been set.

Procedures

1. Type **/ppc** or **/pfc** or **/pec**.
2. Choose one of the following:

Menu Item	Description
All	Clears all print options and resets all formats and setup strings to their defaults.
Range	Clears the print range.
Borders	Clears the borders and frame.
Format	Resets the margins, page length, layout, fonts, colors, setup strings, and graph settings to the default settings.
Image	Clears the name of the graph to be printed.
Device	Resets the printer name and interface to the default settings.

Important Cue

Use the /ppc, /pfc, and /pec commands in macros to cancel earlier print settings or to reestablish default settings you have specified. For example, use the /Worksheet Global Default Printer menu to create as default settings the settings you use most often for margins, the page length, and the setup string. Be sure to use /Worksheet Global Default Update to update the configuration file to make these settings the default settings for future sessions. Then when you place a /ppca command at the beginning of a macro (or use the command interactively), the default settings you specify are entered automatically.

Caution

In 1-2-3, print parameters remain in effect until you give different instructions. If you want to provide a new set of parameters, use /ppca to ensure that you are starting from the default parameters.

Print [Printer, File, Encoded] Go   /PPG or /PFG or /PEG

Purpose

Executes the /Print command, sending the print data in the range to the printer or file.

Reminders

- Before printing for the first time, align the top of the paper with the print head and choose the **Align** command from the second-level **/Print** menu.
- Use the **/Print [P, F, E] Range** command to specify the range to print.

Procedure

Type **/ppg** or **/pfg** or **/peg**.

Important Cue

Printing to a file is not complete until you exit all print menus.

Caution

Use the **/Print [P, F, E] Page** command to eject pages and keep the printer aligned. If you manually eject pages, realign the paper and print head and choose **/Print [P, F, E] Align**.

For more information, see /Print [Printer, File, Encoded] Align and Chapter 8.

Print [Printer, File, Encoded] Align /PPA or /PFA or /PEA

Purpose

Aligns 1-2-3's internal line counter with the physical page in the printer. Failure to use **Align** can cause blank gaps in the middle of printed documents.

Reminder

Use this command only after you have manually aligned the print head with the top of a sheet of printer paper. Use **Align** before printing for the first time or when printing to a printer that other operators have used.

Procedures

1. Position the printer paper so that the top of a page is aligned with the print head.
2. Type **/pp** or **/pf** or **/pe**.
3. Select **Align** to synchronize 1-2-3 with the printer.

Cautions

- Printed pages may have gaps (blank lines) if you do not use this command.
- **Align** resets the page counter to 1 so that the page number automatically starts over at 1 after each **Align** command.

For more information, see Chapter 8.

Print [Printer, Encoded] Image   /PPI or /PEI

Purpose

Selects the current or named graph you want to print.

Reminders

- If you want more than one graph associated with a file, use /Graph Name to name each of the graphs. You then can use these names when printing.
- Ensure that the cell pointer is in the file that contains the graph or graphs you want to print.

Procedures

1. Type /**pp** or /**pe**.
2. Select **Image**.
3. Select one of the following menu items:

Menu Item	Description
Current	Selects the current graph as the graph to be printed.
Named-Graph	Selects a named graph from the current file as the graph to be printed.

4. If you select **Named-Graph**, specify the name of the graph you want to print.
5. Select **Options Advanced Image** to format the image.
6. Select **Align** if you need to start the graph at the top of a page.
7. Select **Go** to print.

Important Cues

- Select **P**age from the second-level /**P**rint menu to eject a graph from the printer. Do not manually roll the paper from the printer.
- If you do not use the **Options Advanced Image Image-Sz** command to change the graph's printed size, the graph is the maximum size that fits within the left and right margins.
- Printers that cannot print a graph print a blank space of equivalent size.
- You can print a graph by entering the graph's name in the print range. When prompted for a print range, type an asterisk immediately followed by the graph's name, such as *BDGT.PIC.
- Use **L**ine to insert blank lines between graphs and worksheets on the printed page.
- A graph is not divided by a page break. The graph prints on the next page.

Caution

1-2-3 may not have enough memory available to print the graph when requested. To make more memory available, save files and then delete them from memory. Use /**P**rint **R**esume to resume printing of the graph. The graph

/Print Commands **741**

and worksheet do not have to be active to print, because the printing information was stored during the first print request.

Print Printer Sample /PPS

Purpose

Prints a sample page from the printer, using current settings and showing the capabilities of your printer.

Reminders

- ◆ A sample includes four sections:

    Print settings

    Sample worksheet

    Printer capabilities showing the following:

    - Fonts 1 through 8
    - Colors 1 through 8
    - Compressed and expanded pitch
    - Standard and compressed line spacing

    Sample graph and graph text, using current settings

- ◆ Before printing, ensure that your printer is on, that the paper is aligned, and that the printer is on-line.

Procedures

1. Set the print settings you plan to use with a worksheet or graph.
2. Type **/pp**.
3. Select **S**ample.
4. Select **A**lign, then **G**o.

Important Cues

- ◆ Because you cannot see on-screen how fonts, color, or pitch will appear when printed, save a copy of the sample printout for each printer you have and for each variation in printer settings. These samples can help you decide which **A**dvanced settings to use to improve printing appearance.
- ◆ If your printer does not support graphics, a blank space appears in the sample where the graphs should be.
- ◆ The data in the sample is preset. You cannot change the data or the graph.

Caution

The sample changes depending on the current print settings.

Print [Printer, File, Encoded] Hold   /PPH or /PFH or /PEH

Purpose

Enables you to change a print job "on the fly" while the job is still open.

Reminder

You can return to 1-2-3 and make changes such as the following:

- Correct a worksheet in the print queue or currently printing.
- Open additional worksheets.
- Use /**Print Resume** to continue printing after the printer has stopped because of an error or for additional paper.

Procedures

To leave a print job, do the following:

1. Type /**pp** or /**pf** or /**pe**.
2. Select **Hold**.

To take the print job off hold, do one of the following:

- Return to the main /Print menu and complete the job.
- Select /**Print Cancel**.
- Select a different printer or printer interface.
- Select a different type of printing (**Printer**, **File**, or **Encoded**).

Caution

If you attempt to end 1-2-3 with a print job still on hold, you are asked whether you want it completed. You can choose to complete the job or to end 1-2-3.

Print [Printer, File, Encoded] Quit   /PPQ or /PFQ or /PEQ

Purpose

Closes the print job so that it completes correctly; returns to READY mode.

Reminder

To properly finish a print job, exit the /**Print** menu by using **Quit**, or pressing **Esc** or **Ctrl-Break**.

Procedure

Type /**ppq** or /**pfq** or /**peq**.

For more information, see Chapter 8.

Graph Commands /G

/Graph commands control the graph's appearance and specify worksheet ranges to be used as graph data. Store multiple graphs with **/Graph Name** and display them at a later time. You can print either the current graph or a named graph. To send graphs to another program, use **/Graph Save** to create a PIC or CGM file.

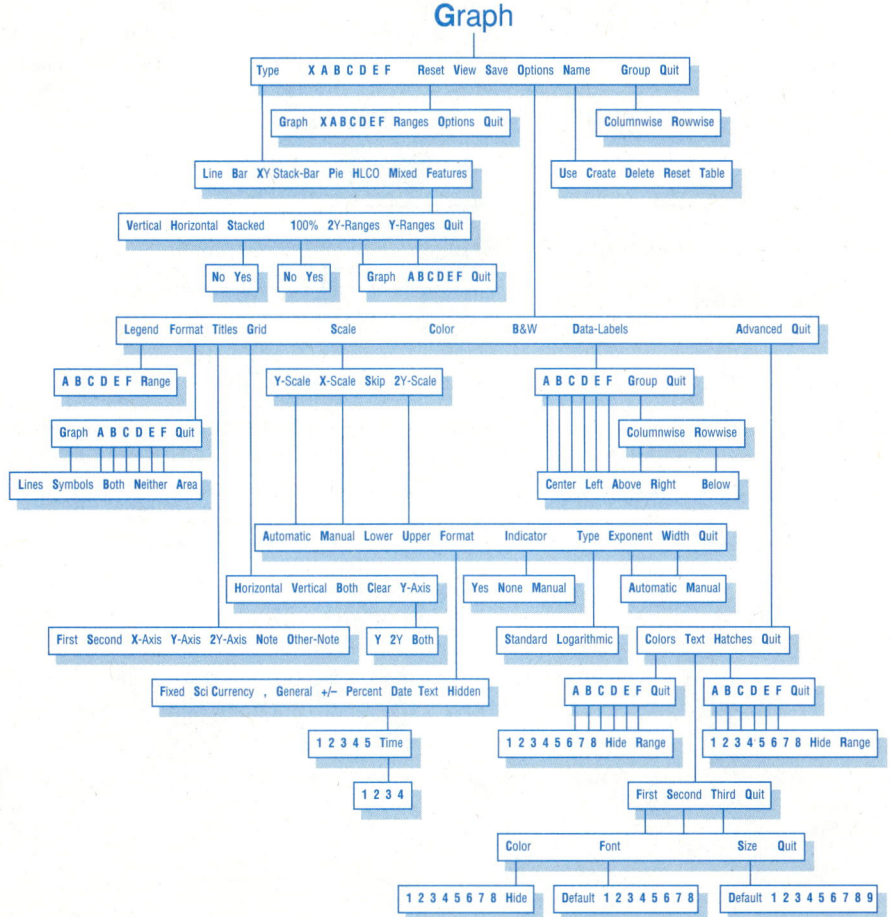

Graph Type /GT

Purpose

Selects from among the 1-2-3 graph types: **Line**; **Bar**; **XY**; **Stack-Bar**; **Pie**; **HLCO**, or high-low-close-open (stock market); and **Mixed** (bar and line). Each type of graph is best suited for displaying and analyzing a specific type of data.

Reminders

◆ Before you can create a graph, you must create a worksheet that has the same number of cells in each x-axis and y-axis range, similar to the one in figure G.1. Each y data item must be in the same range position as the corresponding x value. Figure G.2 shows the bar graph produced from the worksheet displayed in figure G.1. (The legends and titles were added separately.)

A:A1: [W14] READY

A	B	C	D	E	F	G	H	I
	Western Sales & Distribution Company Unlimited							
							Graph Axis	
Sales Region	Jan	Feb	Mar	Apr	May	Jun	<=X	
West	32	30	34	34	34	34	<=A	
Northwest	27	28	27	29	29	28	<=B	
Southwest	32	34	30	34	30	34	<=C	
Midwest	35	25	30	35	34	27	<=D	

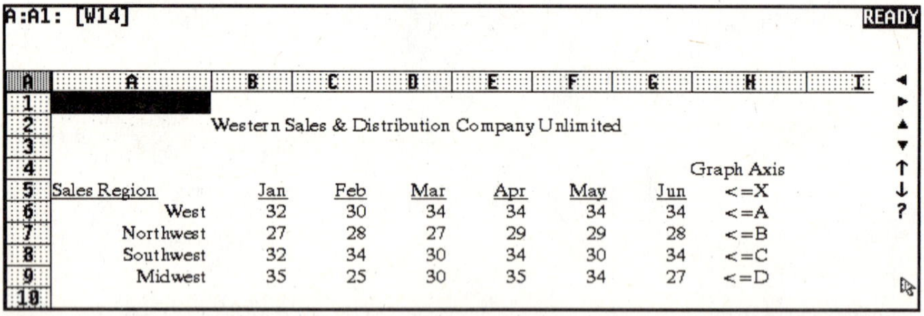

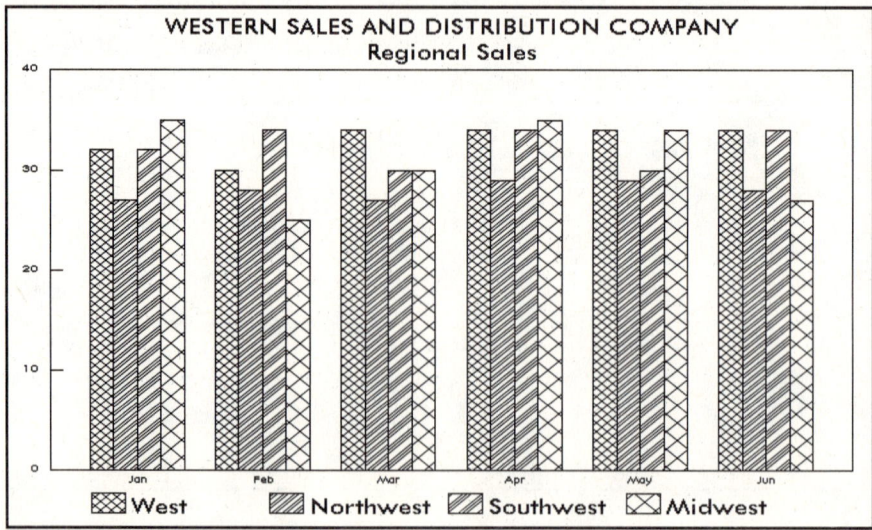

Fig. G.1.
A worksheet with the same number of cells in each x-axis and y-axis range.

Fig. G.2.
The bar graph produced from the worksheet in figure G.1.

◆ Except for pie graphs, graphs can have on the y-axis as many as six different series of data. The /Graph menu choices **A** through **F** are used to highlight the data series. The pie graph accepts data from only the A range.

Procedures

1. Type **/gt**.
2. Select the type of graph from the following options:

Menu Item	Description
Line	Usually depicts a continuous series of data. The change frequently occurs over time. Enter an x-axis label, such as Months, in the X range from the /Graph menu. Line graphs can be altered to appear as area graphs.
Bar	Usually displays discrete data series. The x-axis often represents time. Comparative weights between different y values are easier to judge in bar graphs than in line graphs. Enter x-axis labels in the X range from the /Graph menu.
XY	Graphs data sets of x and y data; good for plotting "clouds" of data. (Unlike line graphs with labels on the x-axis and data on the y-axis, XY graphs have data on both axes.) Each x value can have between one and six y values. Enter x-axis data in the X range of the /Graph menu.
Stack-Bar	Shows how proportions change within the whole. Enter x-axis labels in the X range from the /Graph menu. A bar can have as many as six portions.
Pie	Shows how the whole is divided into component portions. Use only the A range to contain the values of each portion. The X range is used to label the pie wedges. 1-2-3 automatically calculates each portion's percentage from the A values.
HLCO	Tracks items that vary over time. High-low-close-open graphs are most commonly used in the stock market to show the price at which a stock opens and closes and its high and low during the day.
Mixed	Contains elements of both bar and line graphs, and is therefore useful for relating trends in two distinct measurable quantities. If the scales for items vary significantly, you can add a second y-axis (**2Y-Axis**) that has a different scale. Mixed graphs can have up to three bars and three lines.
Features	Varies the original graph type with these options:
Vertical	Moves the x-axis to the bottom of the graph (default).

Menu Item	Description
Horizontal	Moves the x-axis to the left side. The y-axis runs across the top, and the 2Y-axis runs across the bottom.
Stacked	Works with line, bar, XY, and mixed graphs containing two or more data sets. **No** plots values separately (the default); **Yes** stacks values.
100%	Changes data values to a percentage of 100. **No** graphs the actual value; **Yes** graphs as percentages of the whole.
2Y-Ranges	Creates a second y-axis and specifies each data range. Choose **Graph** to assign all data ranges to the 2Y-axis. Choose **A** through **F** to specify individual data ranges on the 2Y-axis.
Y-Ranges	Enables you to move 2Y-Ranges back to the y-axis. **Y-Ranges** offers the same options as **2Y-Ranges**.
Quit	Displays the main /Graph menu.

3. After you make your selection, the /Graph menu reappears.
4. If you have already highlighted the X range and ranges A through F to indicate the data to graph, select View. If you are beginning the graph, see /Graph **X A B C D E F** in this section.

Important Cues

- With 1-2-3, you can build graphs interactively. After selecting /Graph Type and at least one x-axis and y-axis range, select View to see the graph as it is currently defined.
- When you save the worksheet to disk, you also save the most recently specified graph type and other graph settings.
- You can shade a pie graph's wedges with eight different shadings. You can even extract wedges from the pie. Use the B range to define the shade of a pie graph wedge and to extract the wedge. (To learn how to shade the pie graph, see /Graph **X A B C D E F** in this section.)

For more information, see **/Graph X A B C D E F** and Chapter 10.

Graph X A B C D E F　　　　/GX, /GA through /GF

Purpose

Specifies the worksheet ranges containing x-axis and y-axis data or labels.

Reminders

- The x-axis is the graph's horizontal (bottom) axis. The y-axis is the graph's vertical (left) axis. The labels or data assigned to the x-axis and the six possible sets of y-axis data (A through F) must have the same number of cells. To ensure that the x-axis and y-axis have an equal number of elements, place all the labels and data on adjacent rows. Figure G.3 shows the x-axis and y-axis labels and data in rows. Notice that some of the y values are blank but that each range has an equal number of elements.

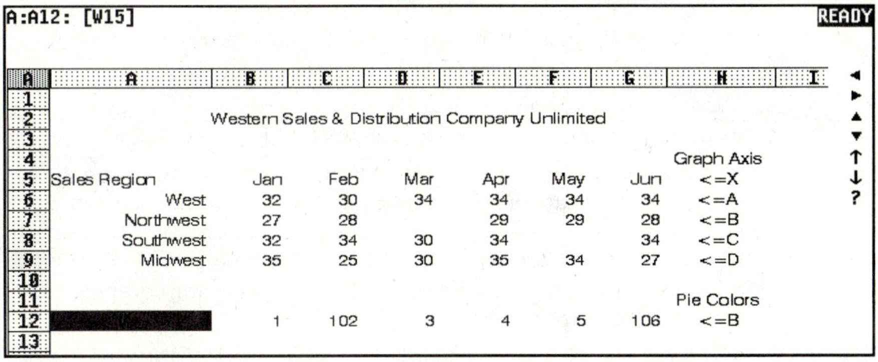

A:A12: [W15] READY

	A	B	C	D	E	F	G	H	I
1									
2		Western Sales & Distribution Company Unlimited							
3									
4								Graph Axis	
5	Sales Region	Jan	Feb	Mar	Apr	May	Jun	<=X	
6	West	32	30	34	34	34	34	<=A	
7	Northwest	27	28		29	29	28	<=B	
8	Southwest	32	34	30	34		34	<=C	
9	Midwest	35	25	30	35	34	27	<=D	
10									
11								Pie Colors	
12		1	102	3	4	5	106	<=B	
13									

Fig. G.3. *Worksheet with some blank y values but an equal number of elements.*

- Pie graph ranges are different from those of other graph types. Pie graphs use only the A range for data. (The B range contains code numbers to control shading and the extraction of wedges from the pie. The C range controls the removal of percentage labels on wedges.)

Procedures

1. Type /g.
2. From the following options, select the ranges for x-axis or y-axis data or labels to be entered:

Menu Item	*Description*
X	Enters x-axis label range. These are labels such as *Jan*, *Feb*, *Mar*, and so on. Creates labels for pie graph wedges and line, bar, and stacked-bar graphs (x-axis data range for XY graphs). The X range in figure G.3 is B5..G5.
A	Enters first y-axis data range, the only data range used by a pie graph. The A range in figure G.3 is B6..G6.
B	Enters second y-axis data range; enters pie graph shading values and extraction codes. (For more information, see this section's "Important Cues.") The B range in figure G.3 is B7..G7.
C	Enters third y-axis data range; enters pie graph control over percentage labels.
D to **F**	Enters fourth through sixth data ranges.

3. Indicate the data range by entering the range address, entering a range name, or highlighting the range.

4. Press Enter.

Important Cues

- If your graph data is in adjacent rows or columns like those in figure G.3, you may be able to save time by using /Graph Group.
- To ease the task of keeping track of graph data and labels, put the data and labels in labeled rows (see fig. G.3).
- You do not need to change the /Graph menu settings when you change or update the data in the ranges. /Graph remembers all the settings.
- Use /Graph Reset Graph to clear all graph settings. Use /Graph Reset [X through F] to clear individual ranges and their associated settings.
- 1-2-3 automatically updates graphs when you input new data in the worksheet (for new data or labels in the x-axis and y-axis ranges). Once you have set the graphs with the /Graph commands, you can view new graphs from the worksheet by pressing Graph (F10). If the computer beeps and no graph appears, you have not defined that graph, or your computer does not have graphics capability.
- Pie graphs do not use the x-axis and y-axis title options, grids, or scales.
- Pie graphs are limited because they often have too many elements in the A range, a situation that causes wedges to be small and labels to overlap. The A range is the only data range needed for pie graphs. Enter wedge labels in the X range, as you would for line graphs.
- Use the B range to enter the numbers from 1 to 14 that control the color or black-and-white patterns in each wedge. Add 100 to a shading code to extract one or more wedges from the pie. Enter a negative number in the B range to hide a wedge. To hide the percentage label for a wedge, enter a zero in the C range for that cell while leaving other cells in the C range blank.

Caution

If your graph has missing data or if the y values do not match the corresponding x positions, check to ensure that the x-axis and y-axis ranges have the same number of elements. The values in the y ranges (A through F) graph the corresponding x-range cells.

*For more information, see /**Graph** Type and Chapter 10.*

Graph Reset /GR

Purpose

Cancels all or some of a graph's settings so that you can either create a new graph or exclude from a new graph one or more data ranges from the old graph.

/Graph Commands

Reminder

The **Graph** option of this command (see "Procedures") enables you to reset all graph parameters quickly.

Procedures

1. Type **/gr**.
2. Choose one of the following:

Menu Item	Description
Graph	Resets all graph parameters but does not alter a graph named with /Graph Name Create. Use this option if you want to exclude all preceding graph parameters from the new graph.
X	Resets the X range and removes the labels (but not on XY graphs).
A through F	Resets a designated range and corresponding labels so that these are not displayed in the new graph.
Ranges	Resets all data ranges and all data labels.
Options	Resets all settings defined by /Graph Options.
Quit	Returns to the /Graph menu.

Important Cues

- Use /Graph **T**ype to change the type of graph.
- The **R**eset command enables you to remove unwanted features from a graph quickly so that you can update it.
- Create templates of graphs that can be used with different sets of data by defining a graph, then removing its data ranges with **R**eset. Respecify the data ranges to create a new graph with the same format.

Caution

If you delete too much from a graph, use /File Open to retrieve the original file containing the original graph settings.

For more information, see Chapter 10.

Graph View /GV

Purpose

Displays a graph on-screen.

Reminders

- What is displayed depends on the system hardware and the system configuration.

- On a nongraphics screen, no graph displays.
- If your system has a graphics card and either a monochrome display or a color monitor, you see a graph instead of the worksheet on the screen after you select View. You must select /Graph Options Color to see the graph in color.

Procedures

1. Select **View** from the /**Graph** menu when you are ready to see the graph you have created. The graph must be defined before you can view it.
2. Press any key to return to the /**Graph** menu.
3. Select **Quit** to return to the worksheet and READY mode.

Important Cues

- You can use /**Graph View** to redraw the graph, but an easier way is to press Graph (F10) while you are in READY mode. Graph (F10) is the equivalent of /**Graph View**, but the function key enables you to view a graph after making a change in the worksheet. You can use Graph (F10) without having to return to the /**Graph** menu. Graph (F10) does not function while the /**Graph** menu is visible. You can use Graph (F10) to toggle back and forth between the worksheet and the graph. You can therefore use Graph (F10) to do rapid "what if" analysis with graphics.
- If you want to see a portion of the worksheet at the same time that you see the graph, use /**Worksheet Window Graph** to split the screen between the worksheet and graph.
- If you want to create a series of graphs and view the series, you must use /**Graph Name** to name each graph.
- If the screen is blank after you select View, make certain that you have defined the graph adequately, that your system has graphics capability, and that 1-2-3 was installed for your particular graphics device(s). Press any key to return to the /**Graph** menu. Then select **Quit** to return to the worksheet.

For more information, see /***Worksheet Window Graph*** *and Chapter 10.*

Graph Save /GS

Purpose

Saves the graph so that it can be printed with a different program.

/**Graph Save** saves a graph file that cannot be viewed or retrieved from within 1-2-3. This file can be used by graphics programs to improve the quality of 1-2-3 graphs.

Use /**Graph Name Create** and /**File Save** to save the graph's settings with the worksheet so that you can view multiple graphs.

/Graph Commands 751

Reminders

- Select **V**iew or press Graph (F10) to review the graph. Ensure that the graph has the correct scaling, labels, and titles.
- Check the screen's lower right corner for a CALC indicator. If CALC appears and the worksheet is still visible, press Calc (F9) to update all worksheet values before you save the graph.
- If you need to return to this graph later, use /**G**raph **N**ame **C**reate to save the graph settings; then use /**F**ile **S**ave to save the worksheet to disk.
- The graph saved to a file is the current graph that displays on the screen.

Procedures

1. Type /**g**.
2. Select **S**ave.
3. Enter a new file name, or use the right- or left-arrow key to highlight a name already on the menu bar.
4. Press Enter.

Important Cues

- Saved graphs can have either PIC or CGM file extensions. Other software programs may use either a PIC or a CGM file format.
- Use the /**W**orksheet **G**lobal **D**efault **G**raph command to change the default file type and extension for graphs saved to disk. In step 3, you can type the file extension you want—either PIC or CGM—to override the default file format.

Caution

If you need to save graph settings and the worksheet's graph display, name the graph with /**G**raph **N**ame **C**reate and then use /**F**ile **S**ave to save the worksheet and graph together. /**G**raph **S**ave saves information used only to transfer the graph to another program. Files saved with /**G**raph **S**ave cannot be edited from the worksheet.

*For more information, see /**Graph Name**, /**File Save**, and Chapter 7.*

Graph Options Legend /GOL

Purpose

Legends indicate which line, bar, or point belongs to a specific y-axis data range.

Y-axis data is entered in ranges A, B, C, D, E, and F. Legend titles for each range also are assigned by A, B, C, D, E, and F. Figure G.2 shows a legend at the bottom of the bar graph, relating shading patterns to the division names West, Northwest, Southwest, and Midwest.

Reminder

As you create a graph, write on paper a list of the legend titles you want to associate with each data range (ranges A through F). If you have already created the graph, you can reenter the A through F data ranges to see the associated legend ranges. To reenter these legends, follow the steps outlined in the following section.

Procedures

1. Type **/go**.
2. Select **Legend**.
3. Select one of the following:

Menu Item	Description
A	Creates a legend for y-axis range A.
B	Creates a legend for y-axis range B.
C	Creates a legend for y-axis range C.
D	Creates a legend for y-axis range D.
E	Creates a legend for y-axis range E.
F	Creates a legend for y-axis range F.
Range	Assigns a legend to all y-axis ranges.

4. If you choose **A** through **F**, enter the text for the legend. If you choose **Range**, specify the range containing the legends.

Important Cues

- 1-2-3 displays the legend along the bottom of the graph.
- 1-2-3 may cut a legend short if there is not enough room or if the legend exceeds the graph's frame. If this happens, reenter a shorter legend.
- Create changeable legends by entering the text for a legend in cells. When **/Graph Options Legend** requests the legend title, you can enter a backslash (\) and the cell address or range name of a cell that holds the text.

Caution

If you relocate a graph by using **/Move**, **/Worksheet Insert**, or **/Worksheet Delete**, 1-2-3 does not adjust cell addresses used to create legends. Create your graphs by using range names to describe data and legend ranges to prevent this problem.

For more information, see **/Range Name**, **/Graph X A B C D E F**, *and Chapters 4 and 10.*

/Graph Commands   **753**

Graph Options Format   /GOF

Purpose

Selects the symbols and lines that identify and connect data points.

Some line and XY graphs present information better if the data is linked with data points or if the data is represented by a series of data points linked with a solid line. Use /**G**raph **O**ptions **F**ormat to select the type of data points used for each data range (symbols, lines, or both).

Reminders

- Time-related data is usually best represented by a continuous series of related data. Trends and slopes are more obvious when they are represented with lines rather than a cluster of data points.

- Data-point clusters representing multiple readings around different x-axis values are likely candidates for symbols instead of lines. (Symbols better reflect groupings.) The symbol for each y-axis range is unique so that you can keep data separated.

Procedures

1. Type /**gof**.
2. Select the data ranges to be formatted:

Menu Item	Description
Graph	Selects a format for the entire graph.
A to **F**	Selects a format for y-axis data points.

3. Select the data point type:

Menu Item	Description
Lines	Connects data points with a line.
Symbols	Encloses each data point in a symbol. Different ranges have different symbols. **Symbols** is most commonly used with XY graphs.
Both	Connects data points with a line and marks the data point.
Neither	Selects neither lines nor symbols. Use /**G**raph **O**ptions **D**ata-Labels to "float" labels or data within the graph.
Area	Fills the space between the line and the line or axis directly below.

Important Cues

- Figure G.4 shows the line graph created from the data in figure G.1. The A and D data ranges, West and Midwest, are each plotted with a line. The B and C data ranges, Northwest and Southwest, are each plotted with a particular symbol.

Fig. G.4.
A and C ranges plotted with lines, and B and D ranges plotted with symbols.

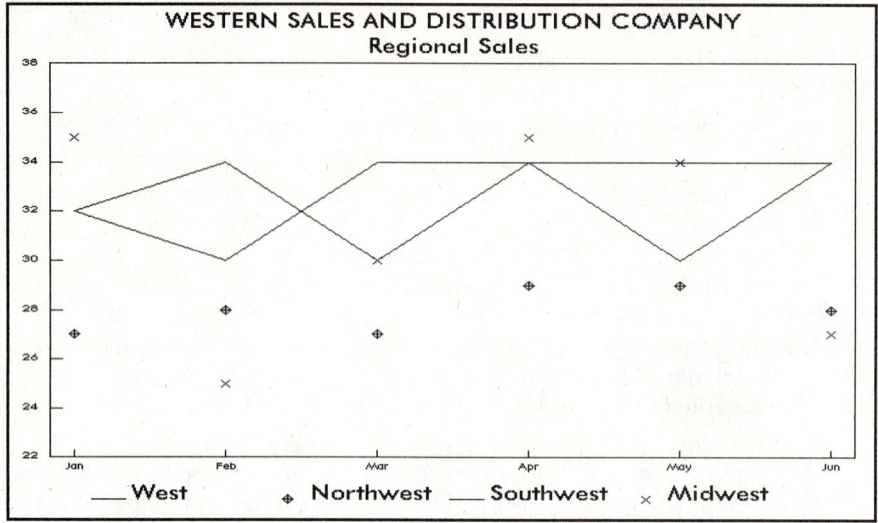

- Use the /**Graph Options Advanced Colors A** through **F** command to set the colors for a set of data.
- Use /**Graph Options Advanced Colors A** through **F Hide** to hide a set of data.
- If you are plotting a regression analysis trend line (/**Data Regression**), set the data points as symbols only and the regression's calculated y values as a line. This arrangement highlights the trend as a straight line through a swarm of data points.

Caution

If your XY line graphs are a confusing jumble of crossed lines, you must sort the data in x-axis order by arranging each x,y data pair in ascending or descending x-axis order within the worksheet range. Be sure to sort the y-axis data with the corresponding x-axis data.

*For more information, see /**Graph Options Advanced Text**, /**Graph Options Advanced Hatches**, and Chapter 10.*

Graph Options Titles   /GOT

Purpose

Adds headings to the graph and to each axis.

To increase the reader's understanding, use x-axis and y-axis titles.

Reminder

You must know the measurement units used in the x-axis and y-axis. 1-2-3 automatically scales graphs to fit accordingly and displays the scaling factor (for example, `Thousands`) along each axis.

/Graph Commands

Procedures

1. Type **/got**.
2. Select the title to be entered from the following options:

Menu Item	Description
First	Specifies the top heading of a graph.
Second	Specifies a second heading of a graph.
X-Axis	Specifies a title below the x-axis.
Y-Axis	Specifies a title to the left of the y-axis.
2Y-Axis	Specifies a title for the second y-axis.
Note	Specifies the first graph note at the lower left corner.
Other-Note	Specifies the second graph note at the lower left corner.

3. Type a title or enter the cell address of a cell containing a title. Use cell contents for a title by entering first a backslash (\) and then the cell address. If a title already exists, press Esc to cancel the title, or press Enter to accept it.
4. Press Enter.

Caution

You can lose titles and headings contained in cell addresses if you move the cells with **/Move**, **/Worksheet Insert**, or **/Worksheet Delete**. Using range names instead of cell addresses solves this problem.

*For more information, see **/Graph Options Data-Labels**, **/Graph Options Scale**, and Chapter 10.*

Graph Options Grid　　　　　　　　　　　　　　/GOG

Purpose

Overlays a grid on a graph to enhance readability. The grid lines can be horizontal, vertical, or both.

Reminders

- Before you add a grid, create a graph to view.
- Grid lines cannot be used with pie graphs.

Procedures

1. Type **/gog**.
2. Select the type of grid from the following options:

Menu Item	Description
Horizontal	Draws horizontal grid lines over the current graph from each major y-axis division.
Vertical	Draws vertical grid lines over the current graph from each major x-axis division.
Both	Draws both horizontal and vertical grid lines.
Clear	Removes all grid lines.
Y-Axis	Selects whether you want the grid lines to align with tick points on the y-axis, the 2y-axis, or **B**oth.

Important Cues

- Select grid lines that run in a direction that enhances the presentation of data.
- Use grid lines sparingly. Inappropriate grid lines can make some line and XY graphs confusing.
- Use **/G**raph **O**ptions **S**cale to change the graph's scale, thereby changing the number of grid lines shown on the graph. Note that although this technique changes the number of grid lines, it also magnifies or reduces the graph's proportion.
- Some data-point graphs are more accurate if you use data labels. Use **/G**raph **O**ptions **D**ata-**L**abels to create data labels that display precise numbers next to the point on the graph.

For more information, see **/G***raph* **O***ptions* **S***cale,* **/G***raph* **O***ptions* **D***ata-***L***abels, and Chapter 10.*

Graph Options Scale /GOS

Purpose

Varies the scale along either y-axis. The x-axis scale can be varied on XY graphs.

Options within this command include the following:

- Making changes manually to the upper-axis or lower-axis end points.
- Choosing formats for numeric display. (Options are identical to those in **/W**orksheet **G**lobal **F**ormat or **/R**ange **F**ormat.)
- Improving display of overlapping x-axis labels by skipping every specified occurrence, such as every second or third label.

Use **/G**raph **O**ptions **S**cale to change the axes' end points manually, thereby expanding or contracting the graph scale. Changing the end points expands or contracts the visible portion of the graph.

Use **/G**raph **O**ptions **S**cale to format numbers and dates that appear on the axes. These formats are the same as **/R**ange **F**ormat options.

/Graph Commands

Reminder

First create and view the graph. Notice which portions of the graph you want to view and which beginning and ending numbers you should use for the new X-scale or Y-scale. Also notice whether the x-axis labels overlap or seem crowded. You can thin the x-axis tick marks by using /Graph Options Scale Skip.

Procedures

1. Type **/gos**.
2. Select from the following options the axis or skip frequency to be changed:

Menu Item	Description
Y-Scale	Changes the y-axis scale or format.
X-Scale	Changes the x-axis scale or format.
Skip	Changes the frequency with which x-axis indicators display.
2Y-Scale	Changes the 2Y-axis scale or format.

3. If you select **Y**-Scale, **X**-Scale, or **2Y**-Scale, choose from the following:

Menu Item	Description
Automatic	Automatically scales the graph to fill the screen; the default (normal) selection.
Manual	Overrides automatic scaling with scaling you select.
Lower	Enters the lowest number for axis. Values are rounded.
Upper	Enters the highest number for axis. Values are rounded.

Format	Selects the formatting type and decimal display from the following 10 options (see /**R**ange Format for descriptions of these options):
	
	    Fixed +/−
	    Sci Percent
	    Currency Date
	    , Text
	    General Hidden

Indicator	Displays or suppresses the magnitude indicator (Thousands, Millions, and so on) that appears between the scale and axis titles. Select **Yes** to have 1-2-3 display its automatically calculated scaling factor; select **No** to suppress the display. Select Manual to be prompted for a display that you type.

Menu Item	Description
Type	Displays the scale, using either Standard (a linear scale) or Logarithmic (a logarithmic scale).
Exponent	Defines the order of magnitude (factor of 10) for numbers on the scale. Select Automatic to have 1-2-3 calculate a scaling factor; select Manual if you want to enter your own scaling factor.
Width	Defines how many characters display for each number on the scale. The width of 0 is used as a unit of measure. Select Automatic if you want 1-2-3 to set the maximum width; select Manual and enter a number from 1 to 50 to set your own width.
Quit	Leaves this menu and returns to the /Graph Options menu.

4. If you choose Skip, you must enter a number to indicate the intervals at which the x-axis scale tick marks are to appear. If you enter the number 25, for example, then the 1st, 26th, and 51st range entries appear. X-axis tick-mark spacing cannot be controlled from the menu.

Important Cues

- Selecting a scale inside the minimum and maximum data points creates a graph that magnifies an area within the data.
- If data points have grossly different magnitudes, you may not be able to see all the data; some ranges will be too large for the graph, and others will be too small. Scale down values on the y-axis by entering a larger exponent. An exponent of 3, for example, means that numbers on the y-axis are divided by 10 to the third power (1,000).

For more information, see /**Graph Options Grid** and Chapter 10.

Graph Options Color/B&W   /GOC or /GOB

Purpose

Defines the color 1-2-3 tries to use to display graphs on your monitor. If you have a monochrome display, use /Graph Options B&W; if you have a color display, use /Graph Options Color.

Reminder

If you have a monochrome monitor, use /Graph Options B&W. If you need to print to a color printer, however, you must change to /Graph Options Color. Color monitors set to /Graph Options Color automatically print black and white on printers that are capable of only black and white.

/Graph Commands **759**

Procedures

To set the color option, do the following:

Type **/goc**.

To set the B&W option, do the following:

Type **/gob**.

Important Cues

♦ To set color text, use the **/Graph Options Advanced Text** command.

♦ To set color shading, use the **/Graph Options Advanced Colors** command.

For more information, see ***/Graph Options Advanced*** *commands and Chapter 10.*

Graph Options Data-Labels /GOD

Purpose

Labels graph points from data contained in cells.

Graph labels can be numeric values that enhance the graph's accuracy, or text labels that describe specific graph points. The labels for graph points come from worksheet ranges.

Reminders

♦ First create the graph. Then view the graph and note future label locations that correspond to data they represent. Figure G.5 shows three ranges: the X range, the A range, and A-range labels.

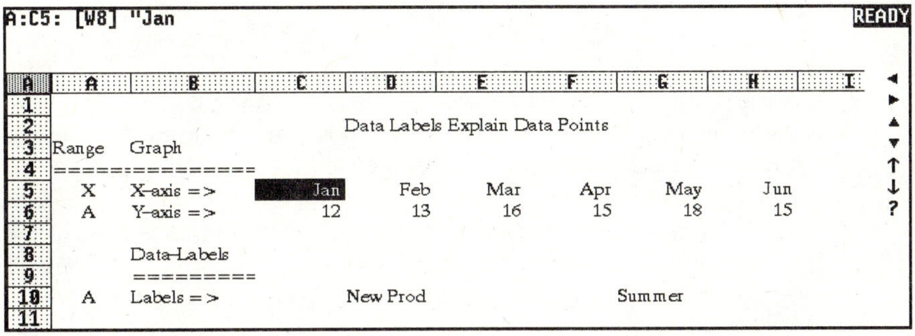

Fig. G.5.

X and A ranges used to plan the A-range labels.

♦ Enter labels in an order corresponding to the order of the data-entry points they describe.

♦ Figure G.6 shows the resulting graph with labels above data points. Note that you do not have to enter a label for every data point.

Fig. G.6.
The resulting graph with labels above the data points.

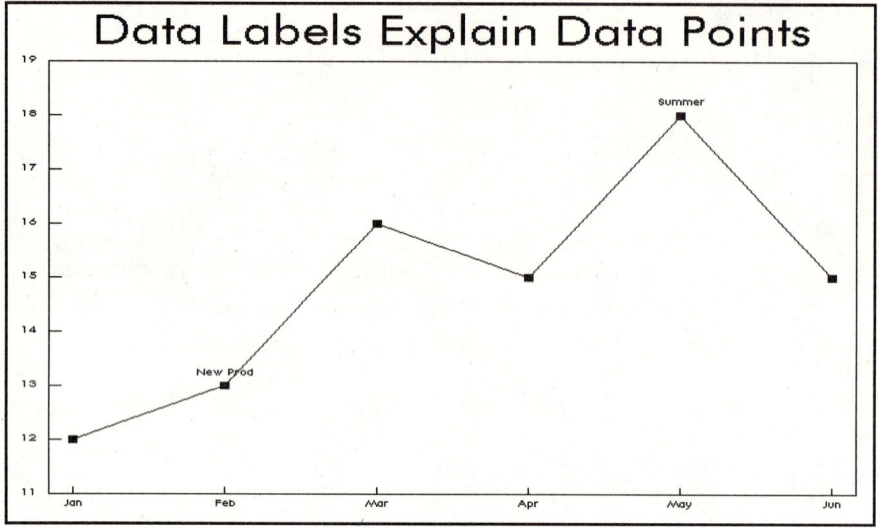

Procedures

1. Type **/god**.
2. From the following options, select the data range you want to label:

Menu Item	Description
A through F	Enters the range to be labeled.
Group	Enters at one time all the ranges to have labels. The **C**olumnwise and **R**owwise options appear. Select **C**olumnwise if data sets are in a column; select **R**owwise if data sets run across a row.
Quit	Exits the /god menu.

3. Specify the range containing the labels. This range should be the same size as the range you selected for A through F. If you are grouping data ranges, the range selected here must be the same size as all the data ranges combined.
4. From the following options, select the data label location relative to the corresponding data points. (Note that in fig. G.6, the **A**bove option was selected.)

Menu Item	Description
Center	Centers a label on a data point.
Left	Aligns a label left of a data point.
Above	Aligns a label above a data point.
Right	Aligns a label right of a data point.
Below	Aligns a label below a data point.

5. Choose **Quit** or return to step 2 to enter more data labels.

Important Cues

- Data labels can be formulas, values, or labels.
- Lines can have labels that are centered, left, right, above, or below. Bars can have labels that are above or below. If you choose a different option, the label appears above the bar. Pie graphs cannot have labels.
- Position "floating" labels that can be moved anywhere within the graph area by creating a set of labels assigned to invisible data points. To create floating labels, follow these steps:
  1. Set up two ranges that have the same number of cell locations and data points on the graph.
  2. In one range, enter floating labels in the left-to-right order in which you want them to appear in the graph.
  3. In the other range, enter the elevation of the y-axis labels. If the floating labels are to be positioned exactly where you want them, the cells in the elevation and label ranges must parallel actual data points on the x-axis and y-axis.
  4. Use **/Graph F** to enter the elevations for the F data range.
  5. Use **/Graph Options Data-Labels F** to specify the label range, and press Enter.
  6. Select **Center** to center the labels on the data points.
  7. To keep the F range data from plotting, use **/Graph Options Format F Neither** (invisible).

For more information, see **/Graph Options Titles**, **/Graph Options Scale**, and Chapter 10.

Graph Options Advanced Colors /GOAC

Purpose

Selects the colors used by data ranges A through F. **/Graph Options Advanced Colors** also can be used to hide data ranges.

Reminders

- **/Graph Options Advanced Colors** affects both the displayed and printed graph.
- Assign colors by choosing a number from 1 to 8. To see the color corresponding to each number, create a dummy bar graph and assign a different color to each bar. Test printer colors by using **/Print Printer Sample Go** to print the sample printout.
- You do not have to use the **Advanced Colors** settings to create color graphs. 1-2-3 defaults to the colors 2, 3, 4, 5, 6, and 7 for the respective data ranges A through F.

Procedures

1. Type **/goac**.
2. Select the data range you want to change—**A** through **F**.
3. From the following options, select the appearance of the data range:

Menu Item	Description
1 through 8	Colors 1 through 8 are set for the entire data range, A through F.
Hide	Hides this data range.
Range	Specifies colors for specific data items within the range A through F. Colors are entered as the numbers 1 through 14, in a range the same size as the range to which they are assigned.

4. If you select **Range**, specify the range containing the colors.

Important Cues

- Setting colors by choosing a number from 1 through 8 sets a color for the entire data range. For example, all the B data range has color 3. The **Range** method of setting colors enables you to set a specific color for each data item within a data range. For example, within the C data range, the first data item is color 4, the second data item is color 6, and so on.
- The size of the range containing **Range** colors should be the same size as the data range it is to color. Put the color numbers in the same relative cell location as the data item they are to color. Enter a negative number in a color range to hide a data item.
- Use formulas in the color range to assign colors based on data meeting certain criteria.
- The first color in a color range defines the color of the legend.
- Use **/Graph Options Advanced Text** to set text colors in a graph.

For more information, see **/Graph Options Advanced Text**, **/Graph Options Advanced Hatches**, and Chapter 10.

Graph Options Advanced Text   /GOAT

Purpose

Changes the font, size, and color for graph text.

Reminders

- **/Graph Options Advanced Text** affects both the displayed and printed graph.

/Graph Commands **763**

- Text on a graph is grouped into three types. The first group contains the first line of the graph title. The second group contains the second line of the graph title, as well as axes titles and legend titles. The third group contains other text on the graph.
- You must use **/Graph Options Color** to set the graph display to color if you want to print color text on a color printer.

Procedures

1. Type **/goa**.
2. Select **Text**.
3. Select the group of text you want to change: **First**, **Second**, or **Third**.
4. Select **Color**.
5. Select the color for the group of text you want to change. The choices are **1** through **8** or **Hide**.
6. Select **Font**.
7. Select the font you want for the group of text. The fonts are **1** through **8** or **Default**.
8. Select **Size**.
9. Select the size of font you want for the group of text. Sizes are **1** through **9** or **Default**.

Important Cues

- You can select **Color**, **Font**, and **Size** in any order.
- Text colors vary among printers. To see a sample of which printer colors are available, print the sample output by using **/Print Printer Sample Go**.

Cautions

- The display does not show how the printed graph will appear. Only three font sizes display on-screen. Printed font sizes vary among printers. Use **/Print Printer Sample** to print a sample output on your printer to see which font sizes are available.
- 1-2-3 may reduce font sizes automatically to keep text on-screen. If the text cannot be reduced enough, it is cut off.

For more information, see **/Graph Options Advanced Color**, **/Graph Options Advanced Hatches**, and Chapters 8 and 10.

Graph Options Advanced Hatches /GOAH

Purpose

Changes the hatching (shading) for each data range in a graph.

Reminder

/Graph Options Advanced Hatches affects both the displayed and printed graph.

Procedures

1. Type **/goah**.
2. Specify the range you want to hatch, **A** through **F**.
3. Select the hatch pattern from the following options:

Menu Item	Description
1 through 8	Uses the hatch pattern corresponding to this number.
Range	Specifies hatch patterns for specific data items within the range A through F. Hatches are entered as the numbers 1 through 14, in a range the same size as the range they are assigned to. Numbers **1** through **8** are hatches; numbers **9** through **14** are gray scales.

4. If you select **R**ange, specify the range containing the hatch values.

Important Cues

- The hatch patterns vary depending on the printer. To test the patterns your printer uses, print a test pattern with **/P**rint **P**rinter **S**ample **G**o.
- Use negative numbers in the hatch range to hide the corresponding data item.
- Use formulas within a hatch range to calculate a hatch pattern based on specific criteria. The first number in a hatch range determines the legend pattern for that data range.
- You can color and hatch at the same time by combining /goah with /Graph Options Advanced Colors.
- Adding 100 to a hatch range for pie graphs pulls out that wedge of the pie.

For more information, see **/Graph Options Advanced Tex**t, **/Graph Options Advanced Colors**, and Chapter 10.

Graph Name /GN

Purpose

Stores graph settings for later use with the same worksheet.

Because only one graph can be active at a time, use /Graph Name to name graphs and store their settings with the corresponding worksheets. To reproduce a stored graph, recall the graph and graph settings by name.

Reminders

- Before you can name a graph, you must create one that you can view.
- If you want to name a graph, make sure that it is the active graph.
- Before creating a table of graph names, make sure that you are in the file that contains the graphs you want to list.

Procedures

1. Type **/gn**.
2. From the following options, select the activity to name the file:

Menu Item	Description
Use	Retrieves previous graph settings with a saved graph name.
Create	Creates for the active graph a name of up to 15 characters. Make sure that no graph currently has the same name.
Delete	Removes the settings and name for the graph name chosen from the menu. Be sure that you have the correct name; you are not given the option to cancel.
Reset	Erases all graph names and their settings.
Table	Creates a table of graph names, types, and the first line of the graph title for names in the current file.

3. If you are switching to a new graph, creating a name, or deleting or resetting names, specify the name. If you are creating a table of graph names, specify the location for the table.

Important Cues

- Using /gn is the only way to store and recall graphs for later use with the same worksheet. /Graph Save saves graphs as PIC or CGM files for use with graphics-enhancement programs.
- The graph table overwrites existing cell contents.
- The graph table has three columns and as many rows as there are names.
- Graphs recalled by /Graph Name Use reflect changed data within the graph ranges.
- Create a slide-show effect by naming several graphs and recalling them in succession with a macro that controls /Graph Name Use.

Cautions

- You can recall graphs in later work sessions only if you have first saved the graph settings with /Graph Name Create and then saved the worksheet with /File Save. Even in the same work session, you cannot return to a previous graph unless you have saved the graph settings with /Graph Name Create.

- Respect the power of **/Graph Name Reset**. It deletes not only all graph names in the current worksheet, but also all graph parameters. The graph has no "Yes/No" confirmation step; once you press **R** for **Reset**, all graphs are gone.

*For more information, see /**Print [Printer**, **Encoded] Image**, /**File Save**, /**File Retrieve**, and Chapters 7 and 10.*

Graph Group   /GG

Purpose

Quickly selects the data ranges for a graph, X and A through F, when data is in adjacent rows and columns are in consecutive order. Designing worksheets with the /Graph Group command in mind can save you time later.

Reminder

In figure G.1, the /Graph Group range is B5..G9. /Graph Group automatically defines row 5 in this range as the X data range, row 6 as the A data range, row 7 as the B data range, and so on.

Procedures

1. Type /**gg**.
2. Specify the range containing **X** and **A** through **F** data values. The rows or columns must be adjacent and in the order X, A, B, C, and so on.
3. Select **Columnwise** if the data ranges are in columns; select **Rowwise** if the data ranges are in rows.

Important Cues

- /Graph Group assigns data ranges in the order X, A, B, and so on. Rows or columns that exceed the seven data ranges are ignored.
- Selecting a range for /Graph Group that contains blank rows or columns produces a graph containing blanks. For example, a rowwise group containing a blank row creates a bar graph with a missing set of bars.

*For more information, see /**Graph X A B C D E F** and Chapter 10.*

Data Commands   /D

/**D**ata commands work on data tables and enable you to perform three functions: database selection and maintenance, data analysis, and data manipulation. One of the most used /Data commands is **Query**. You use **Query** commands to rapidly find, update, extract, or delete information from within a large collection of data. You can use /Data commands to perform many different types of data manipulation, such as sorting, filling ranges with numbers, and parsing imported data.

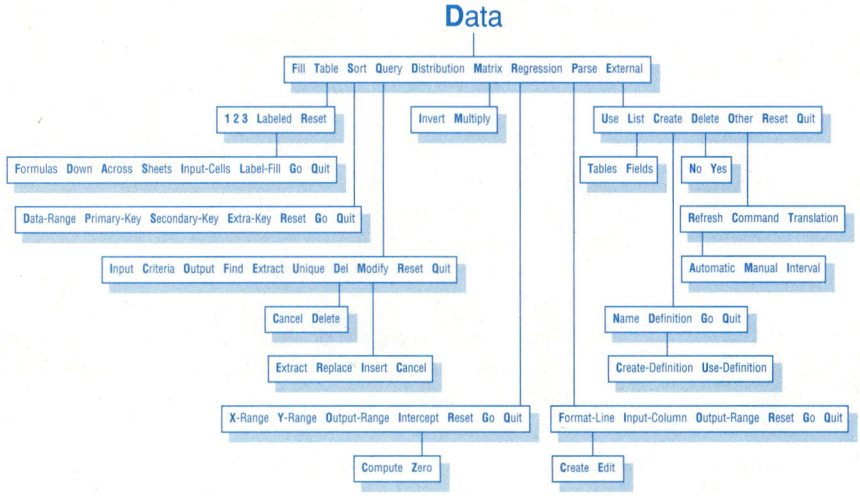

Data Fill   /DF

Purpose

Fills a specified range with a series of equally incremented numbers, dates, times, or percentages.

Use /Data Fill to create date or numeric rows or columns, headings for depreciation tables, sensitivity analyses, data tables, or databases.

Reminder

Before you issue /Data Fill, move the cell pointer to the upper left corner of the range you want to fill.

Procedures

1. Type /**df**.
2. Specify the range to be filled: type the address (such as **B23..D46**), type a range name, or highlight the range.
3. When a Start value is requested, enter the starting number, date, or time in the fill range, and then press Enter. You also can reference a cell or range that results in a value. Use a number or time format that 1-2-3 recognizes. (The default value is 0.)
4. When a Step value is requested, type the positive or negative number by which you want the value to be incremented. Date or time Step values can use special units described in this entry's "Important Cues." (The default value is 1.)
5. Enter a Stop value. You can use a date or time in any date or time format except Short International (D5). If the step is negative, make sure that the Stop value is less than the Start value. /Data Fill fills the cells in the range column-by-column from top to bottom and from left to right until the Stop value is encountered or the range is full. (The default value is 8191.)

Important Cues

- If you do not supply a Stop value, 1-2-3 uses the default, which may give you results you don't want. Supply a Stop value if you want 1-2-3 to stop at a particular value before the entire range is filled.
- Use /Data Fill to fill a range of numbers in descending order. Enter a positive or negative Start value and enter a negative Step value. The Stop value must be less than the Start value.
- Enter dates and times in valid date/time formats except Short International (D5). Entering a MMM-YY combination results in a date for the first of that month.

/Data Commands

- Enter date or time Step values by using one of the following formats:

Increment	Enter	Example
Days	# or #d	2 or 2d for two days
Weeks	#w	2w for two weeks
Months	#m	2m for two months
Quarters	#q	2q for two quarters
Years	#y	2y for two years

- Use /Data Fill to create an index numbering system for database entries. You can then sort the database on any column and return to the original order by sorting on the index column. To index a database so that you can return to the original sort order, follow these steps:

    1. Insert a column through the data.
    2. Use /Data Fill to fill the column with ascending numbers.
    3. Sort the data by any column. Include the column of index numbers in the sort range.
    4. To return to the original sort order, resort the data on the column containing the index numbers.

- Use data tables to change the input values in a formula so that you can see how the output changes. If the input values vary by constant amounts, use /df to create an input column or row for the data table.

Cautions

- Numbers generated by /Data Fill cover previous entries in the cell.
- If the Stop value is not large enough, a partial fill occurs. If the Stop value is smaller than the Start value with a positive Step value, /df does not work. Remember that if your increment is negative, however, the Stop value must be less than the Start value.

For more information, see ***/Data Table***, ***/Range Format Other Automatic***, *and Chapter 12.*

Data Table 1 /DT1

Purpose

Generates a table composed of one varying input value and the result from multiple formulas.

/Data Table 1 is useful for generating "what-if" models that show the results of changing a single variable.

Reminders

- ◆ /Data Table 1 is used to show how changes in one variable affect the output from one or more formulas.
- ◆ Formulas in /dt1 can include @functions.
- ◆ To change two variables in a single formula, use /Data Table 2.
- ◆ Before executing /dt1, enter data and formulas as though you are solving for a single solution (see cells B4..C8 in fig. D.1).

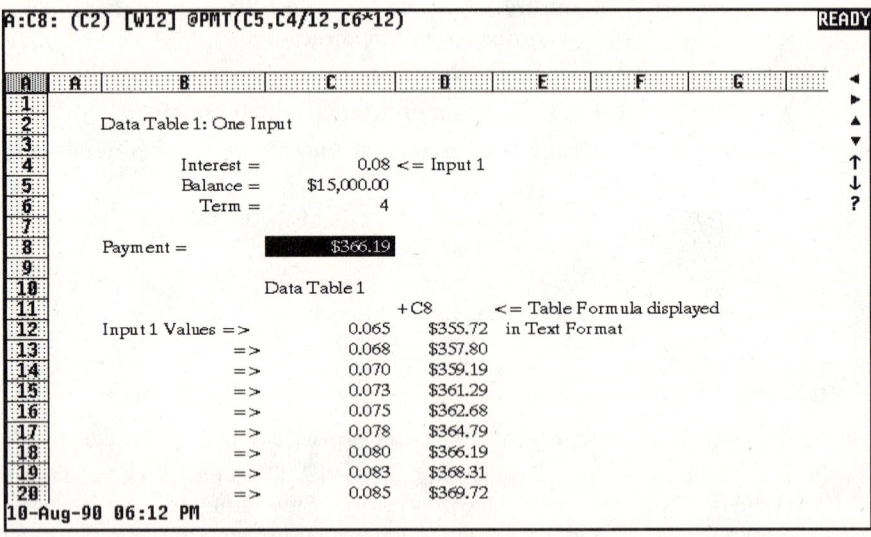

Fig. D.1.
/Data Table 1: solving with single inputs.

- ◆ In the leftmost column of the table, enter the numbers or text to be used as the replacement for the first variable (Input 1). In the second blank cell in the top row of the data table, type the address of the cell containing the formula. Enter additional formulas to the right on the same row. The upper left corner of the /Data Table 1 area (C11 in fig. D.1) remains blank.
- ◆ Display the cell addresses of the formulas at the top of the table by using /Range Format Text. You may need to widen the columns if you want to see entire formulas.

Procedures

1. Type /**dt1**.
2. Enter the table range so that it includes the Input 1 values or text in the leftmost column and the formulas in the top row. If a range has been previously specified, press Esc and define the new range: type the address, type a range name, or highlight the range.

3. Enter the address for Input 1 by moving the cell pointer to the cell in which the first input values are to be substituted. In figure D.1, the values from C12 to C20 are to be substituted into C4.

4. 1-2-3 then substitutes an Input 1 value into the designated cell and recalculates each formula at the top of the data table. After each substitution, the results are displayed in the data table. In figure D.1, the variable input for interest (.080) in cell C4 produces a monthly payment of $366.19. With /**Data Table 1**, you can see how "sensitive" the monthly payments are to variations in the interest rate.

Important Cues

- Make the formulas in the top row of the data table area easier to understand by using /**Range Name Create** to change address locations (such as C4) into descriptive text (such as *Interest*). /**Range Format Text** displays formulas as text, although the formulas still execute correctly.

- After you designate range and input values, you can enter new variables in the table and recalculate a new table by pressing Table (F8). You cannot recalculate a data table the same way you recalculate a worksheet—by setting /**Worksheet Global Recalc** to Automatic, by pressing Calc (F9), or by placing {CALC} in a macro.

- If input values vary by a constant amount, create them by using /**Data Fill**.

- /**Data Table 1**, combined with @D functions, is useful for cross-tabulating information from a data table. For example, suppose that you have a database of checks with amount and account code. Using an @DSUM function as the data table formula and an input range of account codes generates a table of the total for each account code.

Cautions

- The data table covers existing information in cells.
- Press the Table key (F8) to repeat the most recent /**Data Table** command so that you update the table after worksheet changes.

*For more information, see /**Data Fill** and Chapter 12.*

Data Table 2   /DT2

Purpose

Generates a table composed of two varying input values and their effect on a single formula.

/**Data Table 2** is useful for generating "what-if" models that show the results of changing two variables.

Reminders

- Formulas in /**Data Table 2** can include @functions.

- If you have to change a single input and see its result on many formulas, use /Data Table 1.
- Before executing /Data Table 2, enter data and formulas as though you were solving for a single solution (see cells B4..C8 in fig. D.2).

Fig. D.2.
/Data Table 2: solving with two inputs and a single formula.

```
A:C8: (C2) [W12] @PMT(C5,C4/12,C6*12)                              READY

         A           B              C           D         E         F         G
  1
  2         Data Table 2: Two Inputs
  3
  4               Interest =         0.08   <= Input 1
  5               Balance =    $15,000.00   <= Input 2
  6                  Term =             4
  7
  8            Payment =            $366.19
  9
 10                             Data Table 2  Input 2 Values =>
 11                                +C8            12000     13000     14000     15000
 12          Input 1 Values =>      0.065       $284.58   $308.29   $332.01   $355.72
 13                         =>      0.068       $286.24   $310.10   $333.95   $357.80
 14                         =>      0.070       $287.35   $311.30   $335.25   $359.19
 15                         =>      0.073       $289.03   $313.11   $337.20   $361.29
 16                         =>      0.075       $290.15   $314.33   $338.50   $362.68
 17                         =>      0.078       $291.83   $316.15   $340.47   $364.79
 18                         =>      0.080       $292.96   $317.37   $341.78   $366.19
 19                         =>      0.083       $294.65   $319.20   $343.76   $368.31
 20                         =>      0.085       $295.78   $320.43   $345.08   $369.72
10-Aug-90  06:12 PM
```

- In the leftmost column of the table, enter the numbers or text to be used by the first variable, Input 1 (**C12..C20** in fig. D.2). In the top row of the table, enter the numbers or text to be used by the second variable, Input 2 (**D11..G11**). In the blank cell in the upper left corner of the table (C11), type the address of the cell containing the formula (**+C8**).
- Make the cell address in the upper left corner of the table visible with /**R**ange Format **T**ext. You may need to widen the columns if you want to see all of the formula.

Procedures

1. Type /**dt2**.
2. Enter the table range so that it includes the Input 1 values in the leftmost column and the Input 2 values as the top row. If a range has been previously specified, press Esc and define the new range: type the address, type an assigned range name, or highlight the range.
3. Enter the address for Input 1 (C4) by moving the cell pointer to the cell in which the first input values are to be substituted. In figure D.2, the values from C12 to C20 are to be substituted in C4 as the interest amount. Press Enter.
4. Enter the address for Input 2 (C5) by moving the cell pointer to the cell in which the second input values are to be substituted. In the example, the values from D11 to G11 are to be substituted in C5 as the principal amount. Press Enter.

5. 1-2-3 then substitutes Input 1 and Input 2 and recalculates the formula in C8. After each combination of substitutions, the formula in C8 calculates a new answer and displays it in the table. In the example, the variable inputs for interest (0.08) and balance ($15,000) produce a monthly payment of $366.19. The monthly payment formula (C8) is referenced in cell C11.

Important Cues

- Make the formula in the top left corner of the table range easier to understand by using **/Range Name Create** to change address locations (C4) to descriptive text (*Interest*). Make the formula visible with **/Range Format Text**.
- After you designate range and input values, you can change input values in the input column and row, and recalculate a new table by pressing Table (F8).
- If input values are an evenly spaced series of numbers, create them with **/Data Fill**.
- **/Data Table 2**, combined with @D functions, is useful for cross-tabulating information from a database table.

For more information, see **/Data Fill**, **/Data Table 1**, and *Chapter 12*.

Data Table 3 /DT3

Purpose

Generates a three-dimensional table that shows how a single formula's results change when three input variables change.

/Data Table 3 is useful for generating "what-if" models that show the results of changing three variables.

Reminders

- Formulas in **/Data Table 3** can include @functions.
- If you have to change a single input and see its effect on many formulas, use **/Data Table 1**. If you have to change two variables and see the effect on a single formula, use **/Data Table 2**.
- Before executing **/Data Table 3**, enter data and formulas as though you were solving for a single solution. Make sure that you get the correct result for a single solution before attempting a table. Figure D.3 shows a table created with **/Data Table 3** that solves the @PMT formula in cell A:B2 for varying principal, interest, and term. The input variables are in cells A:B4, A:B5, and A:B6. The formula, instead of its results, appears in cell B2 because the cell was formatted as **/Range Format Text**.
- The table appears in the range A:C2..C:G6. In the leftmost column of the table, enter the numbers or text to be used by the first variable, Input 1 (**A:C3..C:C6** in fig. D.3). In the top row of the table, enter the numbers or text to be used by the second variable, Input 2 (**A:D2..C:G2**). At the top left corner of the table range, enter the third variable, Input 3 (**A:C2..C:C2**).

Use the /Copy command to copy the worksheet A table range (C2..G6) to additional worksheets behind it. Replace Input 3 at the top left of the table range on each worksheet with each value you want tested for Input 3.

Fig. D.3.
*/Data Table 3:
solving with
three inputs.*

```
A:B2: (T) @PMT(B5,B4/12,B6*12)                                           READY
         A      B       C        D         E         F         G       H
     1
     2                           5       $10,000   $12,500   $15,000   $17,500
     3                          0.09        208       259       311       363
     4                          0.10        212       266       319       372
     5                          0.11        217       272       326       380
     6                          0.12        222       278       334       389
         A      B       C        D         E         F         G       H
     1
     2                           4       $10,000   $12,500   $15,000   $17,500
     3                          0.09        249       311       373       435
     4                          0.10        254       317       380       444
     5                          0.11        258       323       388       452
     6                          0.12        263       329       395       461
         A      B       C        D         E         F         G       H
     1
     2  Evaluate @PMT(B5,B       3       $10,000   $12,500   $15,000   $17,500
     3                          0.09        318       397       477       556
     4  Input 1    0.09         0.10        323       403       484       565
     5  Input 2 $10,000         0.11        327       409       491       573
     6  Input 3    3            0.12        332       415       498       581
    10-Aug-90 06:13 PM                   GROUP
```

◆ Make the formula being evaluated, cell A:B2 in figure D.3, visible by using the /Range Format Text command. The formula is evaluated even though you can see the formula itself and not its result.

Procedures

1. Type **/dt3**.
2. Enter the table range so that it includes the Input 1 values in the leftmost column, the Input 2 values as the top row, and the Input 3 values at the top left corner. Press Ctrl-PgDn or Ctrl-PgUp to extend the range to additional worksheets.
3. Enter the address for the formula cell (cell **A:B2** in fig. D.3).
4. Enter the address for Input 1 (**A:B4**).
5. Enter the address for Input 2 (**A:B5**).
6. Enter the address for Input 3 (**A:B6**).
7. 1-2-3 then substitutes values from the table range into Input 1, Input 2, and Input 3 and recalculates the formula in A:B2. The result of that calculation is put in the table at the appropriate location. In the example, the variable inputs for Interest (.10) and Balance ($12,500) produce a monthly payment of $403 (cell A:C4).

/Data Commands   775

Important Cues

- Use /Data Table 3 with @D functions to create three-dimensional cross-tabulations on a data table.
- After you designate range and input values, you can change input values in the input column and row, and recalculate a new table by pressing Table (F8).
- If input values are an evenly spaced series of numbers, create them with /Data Fill.

Caution

Tables do not recalculate when the file recalculates. In some cases, you can enter a number that affects /Data Table results, but the CALC indicator does not display at the bottom of the screen. Recalculate data tables by pressing Table (F8).

For more information, see /**Data Table 1**, /**Data Table 2**, /**Data Table Labeled**, and Chapter 12.

Data Table Labeled   /DTL

Purpose

/Data Table Labeled is flexible but more complex than the /Data Table commands when creating tables that test one or more input changes on one or more formulas.

Reminders

- Practice creating /Data Table **1**, **2**, or **3** before using /Data Table Labeled. Although a labeled data table is more flexible and allows greater analysis, such a table is more complex to create. Figure D.4 shows a table created with /Data Table Labeled.
- The labeled data table in figure D.4 is in the range A:B3..B:I11. It is on two worksheets, uses three input variables, and produces a table showing the results of two formulas.
- Before building a table, solve a single-solution problem for each formula from which you want results. In figure D.4, cell A15 uses @PMT to calculate a monthly payment by using the input cells in B17..B19. Similarly, cell B15 calculates the total annual payments for the input cells in B17..B19. Both cells have been formatted with /Range Format Text so that you can read the formulas. (The formulas are repeated in cells E14 and E15.)
- Notice that A14 and B14 contain labels describing the formulas being calculated in the table. (This is the origin of the name of the command: /Data Table Labeled.)

Fig. D.4.
/Data Table Labeled: solving with multiple inputs and formulas.

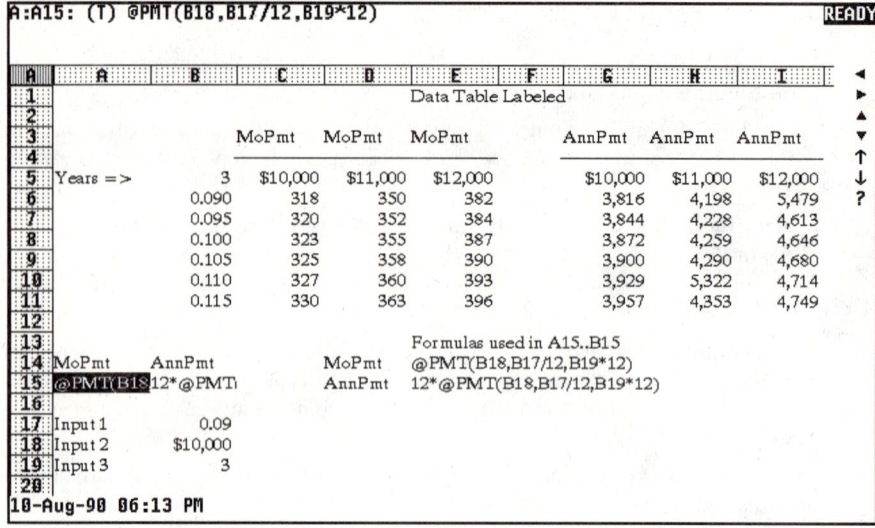

- The formula labels from A14 and B14 must be copied to the top row of the /Data Table Labeled range—row 3. For example, MoPmt is in cells C3..E3. This tells the /Data Table Labeled command in which columns the results from MoPmt calculations should be placed. Similarly, AnnPmt is copied into cells G3..I3 so that the /Data Table Labeled command knows where to put results from the AnnPmt formula.

- Row 4 and column F demonstrate that the table can contain text or blank areas that can make the table more readable.

- Variables for Input 1 are put in the range B6..B11. Variables for Input 2 are put in the range C5..E5 and again in G5..I5. Input 3 is in cell A:B5.

- You build three-dimensional tables by copying this framework to other worksheets. Use the /Copy command and Ctrl-PgUp to copy the table's framework into worksheets behind the current one. Enter different Input 3 values, such as years 4, 5, and so on, in these worksheets.

Procedures

1. Type **/dtl**.

2. Select **Formulas** and specify the range containing the formulas and the labels above the formulas. The formula range in figure D.4 is **A14..B15**. Next, enter the formula label range that defines the width of the table. In figure D.4, this range is **C3..I3**.

3. Select **Down** and specify the row variable range (**B6..B11** in fig. D.4). You are asked to confirm the range by pressing Enter again. Specify the cell for Input 1 (cell **B17** in fig. D.4).

4. Select **Across** and specify the column variable range (**C5..I5** in fig. D.4). You are asked to confirm this range by pressing Enter again. Specify the cell for Input 2 (cell **B18** in fig. D.4).

/Data Commands 777

5. Select **Sheets** and specify the worksheet variable range (**A:B5..B:B5** in fig. D.4). Use Ctrl-PgUp to specify the range to other worksheets. You are asked to confirm this range by pressing Enter again. Specify the cell for Input 3 (cell **B19** in fig. D.4).

6. Select **Input-Cells** if you want to review or change any of the variable ranges and their corresponding input cells.

7. Select **Go** to calculate and fill the table.

Important Cues

◆ You can leave blank or text-filled rows or columns in the /Data Table Labeled range to make the table easier to read.

◆ The formula labels at the top of the /Data Table Labeled range must match the labels above each formula. Use the /Copy command to create exact duplicates of the formula labels.

◆ The /Data Table Labeled command is flexible but complex. Refer to Chapter 12 for more examples and information on creating three-dimensional tables and tables that use more than three variables.

Caution

Plan your table arrangement and formulas before starting to build a labeled data table. Follow the steps in this entry's "Reminders" section to build the layout of your table before beginning the procedures to calculate the table.

For more information, see /Copy, /Data Fill, /Data Table 1, /Data Table 2, /Data Table 3, and Chapter 12.

Data Sort /DS

Purpose

Sorts the database in ascending or descending order, according to the entries in one or two columns.

Reminders

◆ Sorting can be done on one or more fields (columns). The first sort field is called the **Primary-Key**; the second is the **Secondary-Key**. Additional sorting using keys 3 through 253 is done with **Extra-Key**. All keys can be sorted in ascending or descending order.

◆ Save a copy of the worksheet with **/File Save** before sorting. Save to a different name to preserve your original file.

◆ If you want to return after sorting to records (rows) in the original order, insert a column and use **/Data Fill** to fill it with index numbers before selecting **/Data Sort**. Re-sort on the index numbers to return to the original order. Filling a range with sequential numbers is described in more detail in the **/Data Fill** entry.

Procedures

1. Type **/ds**.
2. Highlight the data range to be sorted. The range must include every field (column) in the database but does not have to include every record (row). Only records in the specified range are sorted, however. Do not include the field labels at the top of the database, or the labels are sorted with the data. Enter the range: type the address, type a range name, or highlight the range. Press Enter.
3. Move the cell pointer to the column of the database that is to be the **Primary-Key**; then press Enter.
4. Specify ascending or descending order by entering **A** or **D**.
5. Select **Secondary-Key** if you want duplicate copies of the **Primary-Key** sorted. Move the cell pointer to the column of the database that is to be the **Secondary-Key**, and then press Enter.
6. Specify ascending or descending order by selecting **A** or **D**.
7. Select **Extra-Key** if you want to sort on additional keys. Enter the number of the extra key, from 3 to 253. Enter a cell address from the column this key is to sort on.
8. Specify ascending or descending order by selecting **A** or **D**.
9. Repeat Steps 7 and 8 to sort on additional keys.
10. Select **Go**.

Important Cues

- Sorting occurs within each worksheet. If you select a three-dimensional sort range, data is sorted within each worksheet, but not across worksheets.
- Select **Quit** to return to READY mode at any time. Select **Reset** to clear previous settings.
- Sort settings are saved with the worksheet.
- During the Install process, you can change the order in which 1-2-3 sorts characters. The three sort precedences are ASCII, Numbers First, and Numbers Last. In ASCII and Numbers First formats, cell contents are sorted as follows:

    Blank spaces
    Special characters (!, #, $)
    Numeric characters
    Alpha characters
    Special composed characters

- In ASCII format, uppercase letters are sorted before lowercase; in Numbers First format, the case of characters is ignored. Numbers Last is similar to Numbers First except that numeric data is sorted after alpha characters.

Cautions

- If you sort a database without including the full width of records, the sorted portion is split from the nonsorted portion. Putting the records back together may be nearly impossible. If you saved the worksheet before sorting, you can retrieve the original file.
- Do not include blank rows or the data labels at the top of the database when you highlight the data range. Blank rows sort to the top or bottom of the database in ascending or descending order, and the data labels are sorted into the body of the database.
- Formulas in a sorted database may not be accurate because sorting switches rows to new locations. If the addresses do not use absolute and relative addressing correctly, the formulas in sorted records change. As a rule, use a relative address in a formula when the address refers to a cell in the same row. If the address refers to a cell outside the database, use an absolute address.

For more information, see **/Data Fill** and Chapter 12.

Data Query Input /DQI

Purpose

Specifies a range of data records to be searched. The records can be within a worksheet's database or within an external table. You can specify more than one database.

Reminders

- You must indicate an input range before you use the **Find**, **Extract**, **Unique**, or **Del** command from the **/Data Query** menu.
- The input range can be the entire database or part of it.
- The input range must include the field names.

Procedures

1. Type **/dqi**.
2. At the `Enter input range:` prompt, specify the range of data records you want searched. Either type the range address or move the cell pointer to highlight the range. Be sure to include in the range the field names at the top of the range and portions of the records that may be off the screen.
3. To specify more than one database, use an argument separator—a comma (,), period (.), or semicolon (;)—to separate the input ranges. Press Enter after specifying all the databases.

Caution

Redefine the input range if you add one or more rows to the bottom of the range, add one or more columns before or after the range, or delete the first or last row or column of the range. A defined input range is adjusted automatically if you insert or delete rows or columns within the range.

For more information, see /*Data Query Criteria*, /*Data Query Extract*, /*Data Query Find*, /*Data Query Output*, and Chapter 12.

Data Query Criteria /DQC

Purpose

Specifies the worksheet range containing the criteria that define which records are to be found.

Reminders

- You must indicate a criteria range before you use the Find, Extract, Unique, or Del options of the /Data Query command.
- You do not need to include in the criteria and output ranges all the field names in the database. If you do include all the field names, however, you won't have to alter the criteria range to apply a criterion to a new field.
- The first row of the criteria range must contain field names that exactly match the field names of the database. Use the /Copy command to copy field names from input ranges to ensure that criteria and input range field names exactly match.
- The row(s) below the first row of the criteria range contain(s) the search criteria.
- You can use more than one criterion for a search.
- More than one row can contain criteria, but no row in the criteria range should be blank.
- Criteria can be numbers, labels, or formulas. Numbers and labels must be positioned directly below the field name to which they correspond.
- Criteria labels can contain wild-card characters. An asterisk (*) stands for any group of characters; a question mark (?) represents a single character.
- A tilde (~) before a label excludes that label from a search.
- Criteria can contain logical operators (<, <=, >, >=, <>).
- You can use #AND#, #NOT#, or #OR# to create compound logical formulas as criteria.
- Criteria on the same row of the criteria range are treated as if they were linked by #AND# for every condition to be met. Criteria on separate rows are treated as if they were linked by #OR# for any condition to be met.

Procedures

1. Type /**dqc**.
2. At the Enter criteria range: prompt, specify or highlight the range that contains field names and criteria. The range should contain at least two

rows: the first row for field names from the top row of the database you want searched, and the second row for the criteria you specify. Allow two or more rows for criteria if you use them to specify #OR# conditions.

Important Cues

- Use wild cards in the criteria if you are unsure of spelling or want to find data that may have been misspelled. 1-2-3 searches only for exact matches for the characters in the criteria range.
- You can place the criteria range in the data-entry portion of the worksheet and use a split screen to view the criteria and output ranges simultaneously.

Cautions

- Including a blank row in the criteria range causes all records to be found, retrieved, or deleted with **Query** commands.
- If you alter the number of rows in a defined criteria range, you must redefine the range to reflect the change.

For more information, see **/Data Query Extract**, **/Data Query Find**, **/Data Query Input**, **/Data Query Output**, and Chapter 12.

Data Query Output /DQO

Purpose

Assigns a location to which found records can be copied by the /Data Query Extract or /Data Query Unique commands.

Reminders

- You must indicate an output range before you use the **Extract** and **Unique** options of the **/Data Query** command. The **Find** and **Del** options do not use an output range.
- Locate the output range so that there is nothing below its rows, and so that it does not overlap the input or criteria ranges.
- You can limit the output range by specifying the size of the (multiple-row) range. Or you can ensure that the output range is unlimited in size if you specify the range as the single row of field names. That way, the results of the search can be listed in the unlimited area below the field names.
- If the input range includes multiple databases with the same field names, precede field names in the output range with the database name, such as DBONE.AMOUNT and DBTWO.AMOUNT.
- The first row of the output range must contain field names that match the field names of the input and criteria ranges, but the field names in the output range can be in any order, and the label prefixes and the case of the letters can be different.

Procedures

1. Type **/dqo**.
2. At the `Enter output range:` prompt, specify or highlight the output field names. If you want a limited number of extracted records, include as many rows in the output range as you want extracted rows.

Caution

If you specify the row of field names as a single-row output range and use /Data Query Extract, matching records are listed below the output range. Any information in the cells in the row-and-column path from directly below the output range through the bottom of the worksheet, however, are erased. If you want to preserve any information in those cells, specify the output range as a multiple-row range. That way, cells below the last row of the output range are not affected by any results of a search.

For more information, see /Data Query Criteria, /Data Query Extract, /Data Query Input, /Data Query Unique, and Chapter 12.

Data Query Find /DQF

Purpose

Finds records in the database that meet conditions you have set in the criteria range.

Reminders

- ◆ /Data Query Find moves the cell pointer to the first cell of the first record that meets the condition(s). By pressing the up- or down-arrow key, you can display previous or succeeding records that meet the criteria. Using /Data Query Find can be the best way to access a record in a database quickly.
- ◆ /Data Query Find works only with a single input range or external database.
- ◆ You must define the input range, external database (if one is used), and criteria range before using /Data Query Find. Enter a criterion in the criteria range that specifies the type of records you want.

Procedures

1. Type **/dqf**.
2. The cell pointer highlights the first record that meets the criteria. You hear a beep if no record in the input range meets the criteria.
3. Press the up- or down-arrow key to move to the next record that meets the criteria. Pressing the Home key or the End key finds in the database the first or last record that meets the criteria.
4. You can edit contents within a record by moving the cell pointer right or left with the arrow keys. When the cell pointer highlights the cell you want to edit,

/Data Commands **783**

press the Edit (F2) key and edit the cell contents. Press Enter when you finish editing.

5. Return to the /Data Query menu by pressing Enter or Esc when you are not in EDIT mode.

Important Cues

- After you enter the /Data Query commands and ranges, you can repeat the operation simply by changing the criteria and pressing the Query (F7) key.
- /dqf remembers the last input and criteria range used from the /Data Query menu. You do not have to enter the input and criteria range if they are the same as those used by the previous database command. Check the current ranges by selecting **Input** or **Criteria**; then press Enter to accept the range, or Esc to clear the old range so that you can specify a new one.
- Use wild cards (* or ?) in the criteria if you are unsure of the spelling or if you want to find data that may have been misspelled. 1-2-3 finds only exact matches for the characters in the criteria range.
- Before you delete records with /Data Query **D**el, use /dqf to display the records to be deleted.

Cautions

- If /dqf does not find a record, use /**R**ange **E**rase to erase old criteria from the criteria range. A space character may have been used to "erase" a field in the criteria range. If so, /dqf looks for a space in the database, a process that can result in no found records.
- If /dqf finds all records, use the /Data Query **C**riteria command to check the size of the criteria range. Do not include blank rows in the criteria range; if you do, these commands find all records.

For more information, see /**Data Query Criteria**, /**Data Query Input**, and Chapter 12.

Data Query Extract   /DQE

Purpose

Copies to the output range of the worksheet those records that meet conditions set in the criteria range.

Reminders

- /Data Query Extract extracts copies of information from the input range that matches specific criteria found in the criteria range.
- You must define a 1-2-3 database complete with input, output, and criteria ranges. The criteria range must have field names entered exactly as they appear at the top of each database column.

- Choose an output range in a blank area of the worksheet. You can limit the output range to a specified number of rows, or you can give the output range an unlimited number of rows.

Procedure

Type **/dqe**.

Important Cues

- Records that match the criteria range are copied to the output range. If there is not enough room in the output range, 1-2-3 beeps, and an error message appears.
- After entering new criteria in the criteria range, press the Query (F7) key to repeat the most recent query.
- /dqe remembers the last input, criteria, and output ranges used from the /Data Query menu. You do not have to enter the ranges if they are the same as the previous ranges. Check the current ranges by selecting **Input**, **Criteria**, or **Output**; then press Enter to accept the ranges, or Esc to clear the old range so that you can specify a new one.
- Output ranges that are external ranges format and arrange extracted information according to the external database driver. Refer to your database driver documentation to learn more about this feature.
- Select the **Reset** command to clear all range settings.
- /Data Query Unique works the same way as /dqe, but /Data Query Unique extracts only unique records that meet the criteria.

Caution

If you select only the field names as the output range, you are given an unlimited amount of rows for the extracted report, but existing contents below the output field names are erased.

For more information, see /Data External Use, /Data Query Find, /Data Query Unique, and Chapter 12.

Data Query Unique /DQU

Purpose

Copies to the output range of the worksheet unique records that meet conditions set in the criteria range. Records are sorted after being copied.

Reminders

- /Data Query Unique extracts copies of information from the input range that match specific criteria found in the criteria range.
- You must define the input, output, and criteria ranges before using /Data Query Unique.

/Data Commands

Procedure

Type **/dqu**.

Important Cues

- Nonduplicate records that match the criteria range are copied to the output range. If there is not enough room in the output range, 1-2-3 beeps, and an error message appears.
- Only field names in the output range are used to test whether a record has a duplicate. A single copy of all duplicates appears in the output range.
- To include duplicate records in the extract range, use **/Data Query Extract**.
- After entering new criteria in the criteria range or copying new headings into the output range, press the Query (F7) key to repeat the most recent query.
- /dqu remembers the last input, criteria, and output ranges used from the /Data Query menu. You do not have to enter the ranges if they are the same as the previous ranges. Check the current ranges by selecting **Input**, **Criteria**, or **Output**; then press Enter to accept the ranges, or Esc to clear the old range so that you can specify a new one.
- Select **Reset** to clear all range settings.
- /dqu sorts the extracted records by the leftmost field.

Cautions

- As with other **/Data Query** commands, the field names in the criteria range must match the field names in the database.
- If you select only the field names as the output range, you are given an unlimited number of rows for the extracted report, but existing contents below the output field names are erased.

For more information, see **/Data External Use**, **/Data Query Criteria**, **/Data Query Extract**, **/Data Query Find**, **/Data Query Input**, **/Data Query Output**, and Chapter 12.

Data Query Del /DQD

Purpose

Removes from the input range any records that meet conditions in the criteria range.

Reminders

- Use **/Data Query Del** to "clean up" your database; remove records that are not current or that have been extracted to another worksheet.
- You must define a 1-2-3 database complete with input and criteria ranges.
- Create a backup file before using **/Data Query Del**. If data is incorrectly deleted, a copy of the worksheet is intact.

- Before deleting, use the /Data Query Find command to test that your criteria are accurate.
- To check which records will be deleted, select /Data Query Find after you enter the input and criteria ranges. Use the up- and down-arrow keys to display the records that meet the criteria.
- Another method of checking the records marked for deletion is to use /Data Query Extract to make a copy of the records. Check this copy against the records you want to delete.

Procedures

1. Type **/dqd**.
2. You are asked whether you want to delete the records. Select **Cancel** to stop the command and not delete records. Select **Delete** to remove the records from the input range.
3. Save the worksheet under a new file name by using /File Save. Do not save the worksheet under the same file name; doing so replaces the original database with the database from which records have been deleted.

Important Cues

- After entering new criteria, press the Query (F7) key to repeat the most recent query.
- Create a "rolling" database that stores only current records and removes old records to archive files. Use /Data Query Extract to extract old records from the file; save them to another worksheet by using /File Xtract. Then use /dqd to remove the old records from the database file.

Cautions

- As with other /Data Query commands, the field labels in the criteria range must match the field labels in the database. The labels can appear in a different order, but the spelling and cases must match. The easiest and safest method of creating criteria labels is to use /Copy.
- You can inadvertently delete more than you want with /dqd, particularly if a row in the criteria range is empty when you execute /dqd. Make sure that your criteria range is set up correctly before you use this command.

For more information, see **/Data Query Extract**, **/Data Query Find**, **/Range Erase**, **/Worksheet Delete**, and Chapter 12.

Data Query Modify /DQM

Purpose

Inserts or replaces records in the input range with records from the output range.

/Data Commands 787

Use this command to select a group of records, edit them, and then reinsert them into the database.

Reminder

Before using the **Extract** and **Replace** options, you must have correct input, output, and criteria ranges.

Procedures

1. Type **/dqm**.
2. Select one of the following options:

Menu Item	Description
Extract	Copies into the output range records that match the criteria.
Replace	Replaces records in the input range (1-2-3 database or external database) with the corresponding records from the **Modify Extract** output range.
Insert	Adds new records to the bottom of the original input range.
Cancel	Cancels the command without replacing records in the input range.

3. If you choose **Extract**, you can modify the records in the output range. Start again with step 1 and choose **Replace** or **Insert** to update the input range when you are finished. Choose **Cancel** if you do not want to modify the input range.

Cautions

- The **Replace** option can replace a formula in the input range with a value from the output range. Be careful not to accidentally change formulas to values in your database.
- Do not use the **/Data Query Extract** command if you want to modify records and replace them. **/Data Query Modify Replace** or **Insert** works only with data extracted by **/Data Query Modify Extract**.
- Do not insert or delete rows or sort records in the output range while using /dqm. Doing so reorganizes the records; 1-2-3 cannot recognize and restore the records to their correct locations.

For more information, see **/Data External Use**, **/Data Query Extract**, **/Data Query Input**, **/Data Query Output**, *and Chapter 12.*

Data Distribution /DD

Purpose

Creates a frequency distribution showing how often specific data occurs in a database.

For example, using data from a local consumer survey, you can have /Data Distribution determine how income is distributed. After you set up income brackets as a *bin*, /Data Distribution shows how many people's incomes fall within each bin. Figure D.5 shows an example of this type of distribution. The contents of column E (text values) were entered manually.

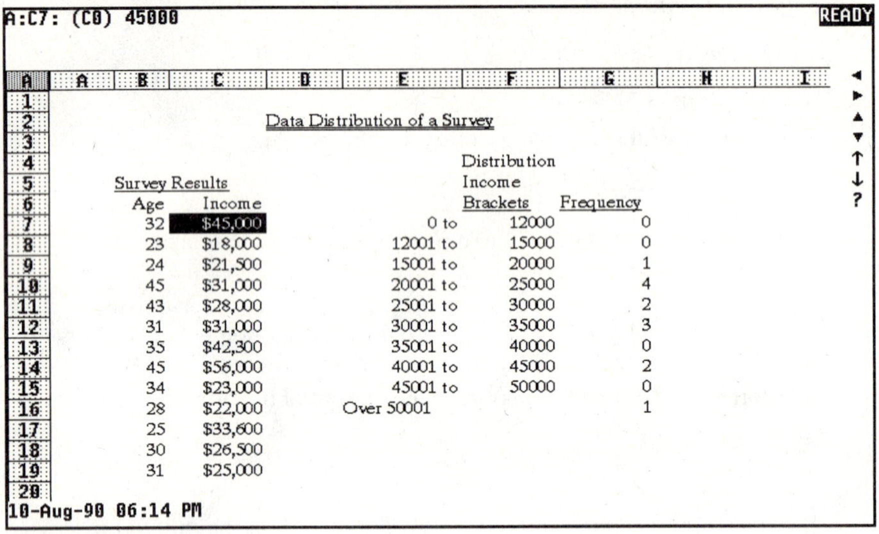

Fig. D.5.
An example of /Data Distribution.

```
A:C7: (C0) 45000                                                    READY

     A         B         C           D              E         F         G        H    I
 1
 2                          Data Distribution of a Survey
 3
 4                                              Distribution
 5       Survey Results                         Income
 6       Age       Income                       Brackets    Frequency
 7        32      $45,000          0 to          12000         0
 8        23      $18,000       12001 to         15000         0
 9        24      $21,500       15001 to         20000         1
10        45      $31,000       20001 to         25000         4
11        43      $28,000       25001 to         30000         2
12        31      $31,000       30001 to         35000         3
13        35      $42,300       35001 to         40000         0
14        45      $56,000       40001 to         45000         2
15        34      $23,000       45001 to         50000         0
16        28      $22,000       Over 50001                     1
17        25      $33,600
18        30      $26,500
19        31      $25,000
20
10-Aug-90 06:14 PM
```

Reminders

- /Data Distribution works only on numeric values.
- Data must be arranged in a value range: a column, row, or rectangular range.
- You must move the cell pointer to a worksheet portion that has two adjacent blank columns. In the left column, enter the highest value for each entry in the bin range. Enter bin values in ascending order.

Procedures

1. Type **/dd**.
2. Enter the value range, which contains the data being analyzed. The value range in figure D.5 is **C7..C19**.
3. Enter the bin range: type the range address, type a preset range name, or highlight the range. The bin range in figure D.5 is **F7..F15**.
4. The frequency distribution appears in the column to the right of the bin range. In figure D.5, the distribution appears in G7..G16. Notice that the frequency column extends one row beyond the bin range. The last frequency value is the number of values that are greater than the last bin value.

/Data Commands 789

Important Cues

- Use /**Data Fill** to create a bin range with evenly distributed values.
- You can find distribution patterns of subgroups in your database by first using /**Data Query Extract** to create a select database. Use /dd to find the distribution in the subgroup.
- You can make data distribution tables easier to read by including a text column at the left of the bin range.
- Use @DCOUNT with /**Data Table 1** to determine the data distribution for text in a database. Enter the text being counted down the left column of the data table. The input cell is the cell in the criteria range into which you would manually insert text. The @DCOUNT function should be placed in the top row of the data table area.
- Use @DCOUNT if you want to count items that match more than one criterion. (/dd uses the bin as the only criterion.) Insert criteria in the criteria range by using /**Data Table 1** or /**Data Table 2**.

Cautions

- Text labels and blanks are evaluated as zero in the value range.
- /dd overwrites any cell contents that previously existed in the frequency column.

For more information, see /**Data Fill**, /**Data Table 1**, /**Data Table 2**, /**Data Table 3**, /**Data Table Labeled**, *and Chapter 12.*

Data Matrix /DM

Purpose

Multiplies column-and-row matrices of cells. Inverts columns and rows in square matrices.

Reminder

/Data Matrix, a specialized mathematical command, enables you to solve simultaneous linear equations. You also can do array math or array manipulations.

Procedures

To invert a matrix, follow these steps:

1. Type /**dm**.
2. Choose Invert. You can invert a nonsingular square matrix of up to 80 rows and columns.
3. Enter the range address or range name of the range you want to invert.

4. Type or highlight an output range to hold the inverted solution matrix. You can indicate or point to just the upper left corner of the output range. You can locate the output range anywhere on the worksheet, including on top of the matrix you are inverting.

5. Press Enter.

To multiply matrices, follow these steps:

1. Type **/dm**.
2. Choose **Multiply**. You can multiply two rectangular matrices together in accordance with the rules of matrix algebra.
3. Enter the range address or range name of the first range to multiply. The number of columns of the first range must equal the number of rows of the second range. The maximum size of the matrix is 80 rows by 80 columns.
4. Enter the range address or range name of the second range to multiply.
5. Enter an output range to hold the multiplied solution matrix. You can type or point to just the upper left corner of the output range, and then press Enter. The resulting matrix has the same number of rows as the first matrix, and the same number of columns as the second.

Caution

The output matrix overwrites existing cell contents.

For more information, see Chapter 12.

Data Regression /DR

Purpose

Finds trends in data by using multiple linear regression techniques. Data regression calculates the "best straight line" relating dependent values to independent values.

Reminders

- **/Data Regression** measures the dependency of dependent values to independent values. The measure of this dependency is displayed as *R Squared*. The closer R Squared is to 1, the greater the dependency.
- A completed regression analysis produces the constant and X coefficients so that you can predict new values of Y from a given X. The following equation calculates Y values:

  Y = Constant + Coeff. of X1*X1 + Coeff. of X2*X2 + Coeff. of X3*X3 + .|.|.

- If there is a single X for each Y, the formula is the familiar formula for a straight line:

  Y = Constant + Coeff. of X1*X1

- The *Constant* term is the location where the best-fit line intersects the y-axis.

- The output area must be at least nine rows in length and two columns wider than the number of sets of X values (no less than four columns wide).

Procedures

1. Type /**dr**.
2. Select **X**-Range; then specify a range containing up to 75 independent variables. The values must be in adjacent columns.
3. Select **Y**-Range; then specify a range containing a single column of dependent variables. This single column must have the same number of rows as the X-Range.
4. Select **Intercept** and choose one of the following:

Menu Item	Description
Compute	Calculates the best-fit equation. The y-axis intercept finds its own value.
Zero	Calculates the best-fit equation but forces the equation to cross the y-axis at zero when all X values are zero.

5. Select **Output**-Range and enter the cell address of the upper left corner of the output range.
6. Select **Go**.

Important Cues

- You can enter a row of coefficient labels between the Degrees of Freedom row and the X Coefficient(s) rows that are not overwritten by the output range.
- To create a best-fit straight line from the results of /**Data Regression**, execute /dr, sort the original X and Y data in ascending order by using X data as the primary sort field (so that the graph plots correctly), and then enter the following formula in the top cell of the calculated Y column:

    Ycalc = Xvalue * Coeff. of X1 + Constant

  Copy this formula down a column to produce all the calculated Y values for each real X value. Use the /**Graph** commands to generate an XY graph where the X range for the graph is the real X value. The A graph range is the original Y data, and the B graph range is the calculated Y data.

Caution

/**Data Regression** produces the warning Cannot Invert Matrix if one set of X values is proportional to another set of X values. Values are proportional when one set of X values can be multiplied by a constant to produce the second set of X values.

*For more information, see the /**Graph** commands and Chapter 12.*

Data Parse /DP

Purpose

Separates the long labels resulting from /File Import into discrete text and numeric cell entries. The separated text and numbers are placed in individual cells in a row.

Reminders

- Import the data with /File Import Text. Each row of text from the file appears in a single cell. Rows of text appear down a single column.
- The long label resulting from /File Import Text may appear to be entries in more than one cell; however, the long label is located in the single cell at the far left of the worksheet.
- If the file you are importing includes numbers surrounded by spaces and text within quotation marks, use /File Import Numbers. This command automatically separates numbers and text in quotation marks into separate cells.
- Find in the worksheet a clear area to which the parsed data can be copied, and then note the cell addresses of the corners. Move the cell pointer to the first cell in the column you want to parse.
- /Data Parse separates the long label by using the rules displayed in the format line. You can edit the format line if you want the data to be separated in a different way.

Procedures

1. Move the cell pointer to the first cell in the row where you want to begin parsing.
2. Type **/dp**.
3. Select **Format-Line**.
4. Select **Create**. A format line is inserted at the cell pointer, and the row of data moves down. This format line shows 1-2-3's "best guess" at how the data in the cell should be separated.
5. You may want to edit the format line if a parsed area is not wide enough to include all the data in a field or if a field is not the correct type. If you want to change the format line, select Edit from the Format-Line menu. Edit the format line and press Enter.
6. If the imported data is in different formats, such as an uneven number of items or a mixture of field names and numbers, you must create additional format lines. Enter these lines at the row where the data format changed. Create additional format lines by selecting Quit and repeating the procedure.
7. Select **Input-Column**.
8. Specify the column containing the format line and the data it is to format. Do not highlight the columns to the right that appear to contain data but do not.

/Data Commands **793**

9. Select **Output-Range**.
10. Move the cell pointer to the upper left corner of the range to receive the parsed data, and press Enter.
11. Select **Go**.

Important Cues

♦ Figure D.6 shows two format lines generated automatically by 1-2-3. The first format line is for the field names; the second is for the data. The initial format lines separate inventory items that have a blank in the name. The asterisk (*) followed by an L shows where 1-2-3 "thinks" that a new field should begin.

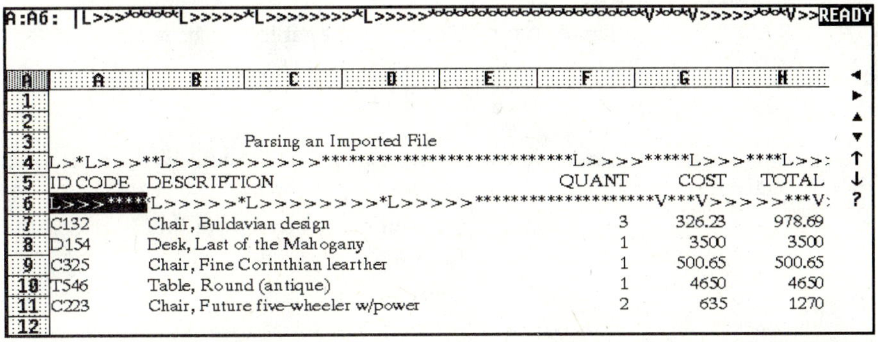

Fig. D.6.
Format lines for /Data Parse.

♦ Use symbols to indicate the first character of a label (L), value (V), date (D), or time (T). You also can choose to skip a character (S), specify additional characters of the same type (>), or add a blank space (*) if the data is longer than the > symbols indicate.

♦ Editing keys can be used on the format line to change the parsing rules. In addition, you can use the up- and down-arrow, PgDn, and PgUp keys to scroll the information on-screen. Use this method to see whether the format line has assigned enough space for each piece of data being parsed.

Caution

The output range should be blank. Parsed data covers any information previously in the output range.

*For more information, see /**File Import** and Chapter 12.*

Data External Use /DEU

Purpose

Links 1-2-3 database capabilities to a table in an external database created by another program.

Reminder

A link must be made to an external table and that table assigned a range name before the table's information can be used by 1-2-3.

Procedures

1. Type **/deu**.
2. Select the name of the database driver to use. Use SAMPLE if you want to use the dBASE III driver that comes with 1-2-3.
3. Enter or specify the path containing the external table you want to use.
4. Specify the table you want to use. Use EMPFILE to use the sample dBASE file that comes with 1-2-3.
5. Specify a range name to be assigned to the table you have selected. The range name can be up to 15 characters in length.

Important Cues

- The range name assigned in step 5 can be used with @D functions to analyze the contents of external tables.
- Issuing the **/Data External Reset** command breaks the link between the range name created in step 5 and the external table.

Caution

/Data External commands work only if you have an external database driver designed for your external database. 1-2-3 comes with a dBASE III driver.

For more information, see **/Data External List**, **/Data External Reset**, and Chapter 12.

Data External List /DEL

Purpose

Lists the tables and fields in an external database.

These lists can then be used with **/Data Query** commands to create criteria and output ranges used to extract information from a table in an external database.

Reminder

Before you use **/Data External List**, you must create a link to a table in an external database by using the **/Data External Use** command.

Procedures

1. Move the cell pointer to a blank area of the worksheet.
2. Type **/del**.
3. Select Fields to extract the field names used in the external table.

/Data Commands

4. Specify the name of the external table and location where you want the field names copied.
5. Select **Q**uit to return to the worksheet.
6. Use the **/R**ange **T**rans command to convert the column of field names into a row of field headings. Use these field headings as the top row for the **/D**ata **Q**uery **C**riteria range.
7. Copy the field names from the top of the criteria range to the top of where you want the output range. Use the **/D**ata **Q**uery **O**utput command to name the output range.
8. Enter a criterion in the criteria range.
9. Select **/D**ata **Q**uery **E**xtract to extract information from the external table into the output range in the worksheet.

Important Cue

If you are unfamiliar with entering criteria or extracting information, practice with a small worksheet database before using an external database.

Caution

A range name must be assigned to the table in the external database before you use this command. Use the **/D**ata **E**xternal **U**se command to create that range.

For more information, see **/D**ata **E**xternal **U**se, **/D**ata **Q**uery **C**riteria, **/D**ata **Q**uery **E**xtract, **/D**ata **Q**uery **O**utput, and Chapter 12.

Data External Create /DEC

Purpose

Creates the structure for a new table in an external database, using 1-2-3 to create the external table. The new table contains only field names.

Reminders

- Before you can define a new table in an external database, you must define its structure. The table structure is defined through the use of six columns with one row for each field name. The column and its contents appear in the following order:

Column	Contents
1	Field names as they will appear in the external table.
2	Data types as defined by the external database driver.
3	Field widths for fields containing labels. Numeric fields may or may not need a width.
4	Column label for the field. The column label is a synonym for the field name and makes the field name easier to read because some such names are abbreviations.

Column	Contents
5	Field descriptions that help users and programmers recognize the contents of the field.
6	Creation strings used by the external database driver to specify the field in the table.

- For more detailed information on table definitions, check the documentation for your database driver.
- Use the /Data External List Fields command to find the definition of tables in a similar external database.
- If a database structure similar to the one you want already exists, select /Data External Create Definition Create-Definition. Specify the table or 1-2-3 database that is to act as the model, and specify a location for the table definition. You can edit this definition and use it to create a new table definition.

Procedures

1. Type /**de**.
2. Select **Create Name** to connect to the external database and assign a name to the table. Specify the database driver you want to use. Then enter a range name of up to 15 characters and press Enter. You may enter a table creation string. If you do not have a table creation string, press Enter.
3. Select **Definition Use-Definition** and specify the range containing the six-column table definition. Include all rows for the fields you want in the table.
4. Select **Go**.

Important Cues

- Use /**Data Query Modify** to add information to the new table from an output range on the worksheet.
- Some databases require a user name, ID, or password. Type each as requested and press Enter. See the network or database administrator if you are unable to access data.

Caution

/Data External Create Name must be used to name the database you are creating before it can be used with any /Data Query or @D functions.

For more information, see /**Data External Use**, /**Data Query Modify**, /**Range Name**, and Chapter 12.

Data External [Delete, Reset]   /DED or /DER

Purpose

/Data External Delete deletes a table from an external database; /Data External Reset breaks the link to a table in an external database.

/Data Commands **797**

Reminder

/**Data External Delete** can be used even if a link has not been established to an external table by means of the /**Data External Use** command.

Procedures

To delete a table in an external database, follow these steps:

1. Type /**de**.
2. Select **Delete**.
3. Specify the name of the external database.
4. Specify the name of the table you want to delete in the external database.
5. Select **Yes** to delete the table or **No** to keep the table.

To break the link to a table in an external database, but preserve the table on disk, follow these steps:

1. Type /**de**.
2. Select **Reset**.
3. Specify the range name of the link you want to break.

Important Cue

If only a single table was in use when you reset the link, the database driver is removed from memory.

Caution

Either the database administrator or database driver can prevent you from deleting tables in an external database.

For more information, see /**Data External List**, /**Data External Use**, *and Chapter 12.*

Data External Other /DEO

Purpose

Sends commands directly to an external database to control the database, update worksheet /**Data Query** or **Table** functions, or translate data by using foreign-character sets.

Reminders

- ◆ A link to a table in an external database must be created with the /**Data External Use** command before you use /**Data External Other**.
- ◆ Commands used in /**Data External Other Command** are external database commands and are not related to 1-2-3 commands. Some database drivers may not allow the use of **Other Command**.

Procedures

To update the worksheet for changes that may have occurred in the database, follow these steps:

1. Type /**de**.
2. Select **O**ther **R**efresh.
3. Choose one of the following options:

Menu Item	Description
Automatic	Updates the worksheet's data from the external database and recalculates the worksheet with the time interval you specify with the Refresh Interval command.
Interval	Sets the frequency with which updates occur. Enter the number of seconds from 0 to 36000 (one hour). The default is 1 second.
Manual	Stops /**D**ata Query and /**D**ata Table commands and worksheet recalculations from automatically updating.

To send commands to an external database, follow these steps:

1. Type /**de**.
2. Select Other Command.
3. Specify the database driver.
4. Specify the name of the external database.
5. Enter a command or the cell address containing a command as a label. These commands are shown in your database driver documentation or in the database documentation.

To translate character sets used by an external database, follow these steps:

1. Type /**de**.
2. Select Other Translation.
3. Specify the name of the database driver.
4. Specify the name of the table you want translated.
5. Specify the name of a character set.

Important Cue

/Data External Other Refresh Interval resets with every work session.

For more information, see /**Data External** *commands and Chapter 12.*

System and Quit Commands /S and /Q

System /S

Purpose

Leaves the current worksheet, exits from 1-2-3 temporarily so that you can run operating-system commands, and enables you to return to 1-2-3 and the worksheet.

Reminders

- Be certain that the programs you run from within 1-2-3 can fit in your computer's available memory. Do not load or run memory-resident programs from the system level.
- If you want to run an external operating-system command, be sure that the command is available on your disk drive or is on the path for a hard disk system.

Procedures

1. Type /**S**.
2. Type the internal operating-system commands or program names that you want to run.
3. When you finish running a program, return to the operating system.
4. Return to 1-2-3 from the operating-system prompt by typing **EXIT**, and then pressing Enter.

Important Cue

For a complete discussion of the various operating-system commands, see *Using MS-DOS 5*; *Que's MS-DOS 5 User's Guide*, Special Edition; or *Using OS/2*, all published by Que Corporation.

For more information, see Chapter 2.

Quit /Q

Purpose

Leaves 1-2-3 for the current work session and returns to the operating system.

Reminder

Make sure that you have saved the current worksheet and graph before exiting from 1-2-3. If print jobs are pending and you want them completed, do not exit 1-2-3.

Procedures

1. Type **/q**.
2. Press **Y** to exit 1-2-3 and return to the operating system. Press **N** to return to 1-2-3 and the current worksheet.
3. If you made changes to the worksheet, press **Y** to exit without saving. Press **N** to return to the worksheet.
4. If you started 1-2-3 from the 1-2-3 Access Menu, you return to it. From the 1-2-3 Access Menu, choose **Exit** to leave 1-2-3. If you started 1-2-3 by typing **123**, you return to the operating system.

Important Cue

Use the DOS COPY or DISKCOPY command to create a backup of important files. To guard against data loss, be sure to make backup copies regularly and keep a weekly archival backup copy at a separate location. In most cases, your computer can be replaced, but your data and worksheets cannot.

Caution

Worksheets not saved with /**File Save** or /**File Xtract** are lost when you exit from 1-2-3. Changes to existing worksheets or graphs are not recorded unless the worksheet has been saved with /**File Save**.

For more information, see /**File Save**, /**File Xtract**, *and Chapter 2.*

:Worksheet Commands :W

:Worksheet commands set column widths, row heights, and page breaks.

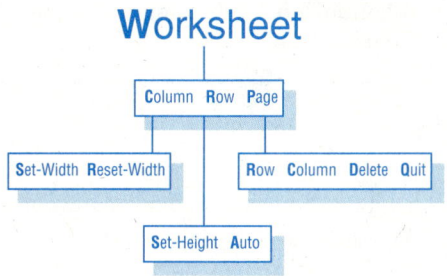

Worksheet Column :WC

Purpose

:Worksheet Column sets column widths.

Reminders

- Make certain that changing the width of a column does not destroy the appearance in another portion of the worksheet.
- Move the cell pointer to the widest entry in the column before you use :wc.

Procedures

1. Type :wc.
2. Select one of the following menu items:

Menu Item	Description
Set-Width	Sets the width for one or more columns in the worksheet.
Reset-Width	Resets the width of one or more columns to the global default column width.

3. If you selected Set-Width, specify the column(s) whose width you want to change. Then, enter the new column width by typing the number of characters or by pressing the left- or right-arrow keys to shrink or expand the column.

   If you selected Reset-Width, specify the column(s) whose widths you want to reset. 1-2-3 automatically sets the width of all specified columns to the global default column-width setting.

Important Cues

- Unlike most Wysiwyg commands, the column widths you set with :wc remain in the worksheet even when Wysiwyg is not loaded. In other words, the column-width settings are saved with the worksheet file and not with the Wysiwyg format settings.
- If you have GROUP mode enabled, using :wc sets the widths for specified columns in all worksheets in the file.

Worksheet Row :WR

Purpose

:Worksheet Row sets row heights in the worksheet.

Reminder

Make certain that changing the height of a row does not destroy the appearance of another portion of the worksheet.

Procedures

1. Type :wr.
2. Select one of the following menu items:

Menu Item	Description
Set-Height	Sets the height for one or more rows in the worksheet.
Auto	Sets the height of one or more rows to the height that best suits the largest font in the rows.

3. If you selected Set-Height, specify the row(s) whose height you want to change. Then, enter the new height by typing the number (in point sizes between 1 and 255) or by pressing the up- or down-arrow keys to shrink or expand the row.

    If you selected Auto, specify the row(s) whose height you want to reset. 1-2-3 automatically sets the height of all specified rows to the height that best fits the largest font used in those rows.

Important Cue

If you have GROUP mode enabled, using :wr sets the heights for specified rows in all worksheets in the file.

:Worksheet Commands **803**

Worksheet Page :WP

Purpose

Inserts or removes a page break in a worksheet.

Reminder

Before you use **:wp**, move the cell pointer to the row or column in the worksheet that you want to begin the new page. If you want to begin a new page with row 35, for example, move the cell pointer to any cell in row 35.

Procedures

1. Type **:wp**.
2. Choose one of the following menu items:

Menu Item	Description
Column	Insert a vertical page break (begin a new page at a specific column)
Row	Insert a horizontal page break (begin a new page at a specific row)
Delete	Remove a page break from the current column or row
Quit	Return to READY mode

Important Cues

- 1-2-3 only uses page breaks inserted with **:wp** when you print with the **:Print** command. To insert a page break to use with the **/Print** commands, type **/wp**.
- Use **:Display Options Page-Breaks No** to hide the page break lines that 1-2-3 displays.
- If GROUP mode is turned on, **:wp** inserts or deletes page breaks in the specified column or row in all worksheets in the file.
- A row page break is inserted at the top of the current row. A column page break is inserted to the left of the current column.

:Format Commands :F

:Format commands set the display of ranges in the worksheet. You use :Format commands to format both the screen display and printed output.

Format Font :FF

Purpose

Specifies the fonts you want to use for ranges in a worksheet and for default fonts.

Reminder

Each Wysiwyg font set contains eight fonts. You can use any or all of these fonts in the worksheet; however, depending on the printer and printer memory, you may not be able to print all eight fonts.

Procedures

1. Type **:ff**.
2. Choose one of the following:

Menu Item	Description
1 through 8	Sets characters in a range to a font in the current font set.
Default	Replaces the current font settings with the fonts from the default font set or updates the default font set with the current fonts.
Replace	Replaces one of the fonts in the current font set with a different font.
Library	Retrieves, erases, or saves a font library file on disk.
Quit	Returns to READY mode.

3. If you chose **1** through **8**, specify the range you want to display with the selected font.

   If you chose **Default**, select **Restore** to cancel the current font settings and replace them with the fonts from the default font set; select **Update** to copy the current font settings into the default font set file on disk.

   If you chose **Replace**, select one of the fonts in the current font set, **1** through **8**. Then select a new typeface from the following menu: **Swiss**, **Dutch**, **Courier**, **Xsymbol**, or **Other**. If you select **Other**, select one of the additional typefaces displayed. Finally, specify a font size by entering a number from 3 to 72, inclusive.

:Format Commands

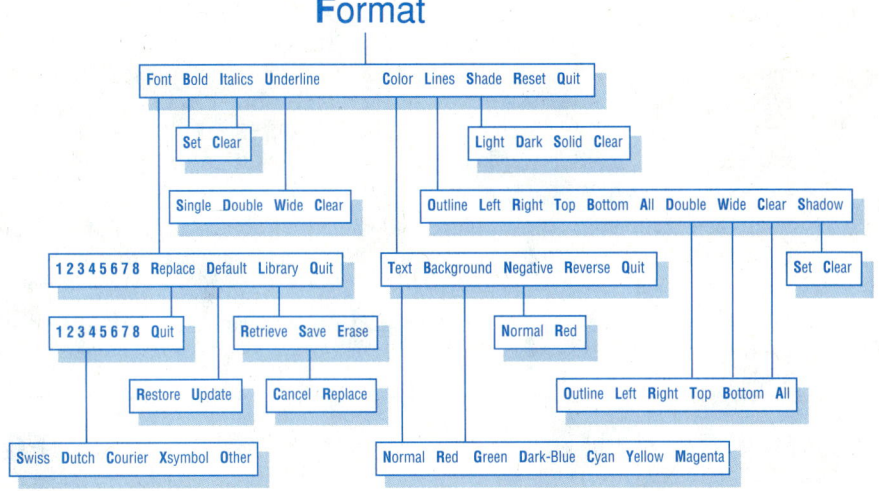

If you chose **Library**, select one of the following menu items:

Menu Item	Description
Retrieve	Retrieves the font settings from a font set file on disk and makes that the current font set.
Save	Saves the current font set in a font file on disk.
Erase	Deletes a font file from disk.

Then specify the name of the font file from which you want to retrieve settings, to which you want to save the current font set, or which you want to erase from disk. If you specified a font file to save that already exists, select **Cancel** to cancel the save or select **Replace** to save with the new font settings.

Important Cues

- When typing data, or in **:Text Edit** mode, you can also specify a font format for a range with a formatting sequence. To use a formatting sequence, move the cursor to the first character you want to format, press Ctrl-A, and type one of the following formatting codes: **1F** (font 1 in the current font set), **2F** (font 2 in the current font set), **3F**, **4F**, **5F**, **6F**, **7F**, or **8F**. Then move the cursor after the last character you want to format and press Ctrl-N.

- If you select **:Format Font Replace** and specify a font size that you have not previously installed, 1-2-3 selects the font size nearest to the size you specified.

- When you replace a font, all data previously formatted with the font number changes to the new font.

Format Bold :FB

Purpose

Adds or removes a bold format for characters in a range.

Reminders

- 1-2-3 displays Wysiwyg format settings only when Wysiwyg is in memory.
- Before you use the **:Format Bold** command, move the cell pointer to the first cell in the range you want to format.

Procedures

1. Type **:fb**.
2. Select **Set** to add the bold format to a range; select **Clear** to remove a bold format from a range.
3. Specify the range you want to format by typing the cell addresses, highlighting the range, or typing or highlighting the range name.

Important Cue

When typing data, or in **:Text Edit** mode, you can also specify a bold format for a range with a formatting sequence. To use a formatting sequence, move the cursor to the first character you want to boldface, press Ctrl-A, and type **b**. Then move the cursor after the last character you want to format and press Ctrl-N.

Format Italics :FI

Purpose

Adds or removes an italic format for characters in a range.

Reminders

- 1-2-3 displays Wysiwyg format settings only when Wysiwyg is in memory.
- Before you use the **:Format Italics** command, move the cell pointer to the first cell in the range you want to format.

Procedures

1. Type **:fi**.
2. Select **S**et to add the italic format to characters in a range; select **C**lear to remove the italics from characters in a range.
3. Specify the range you want to format by typing the cell addresses, highlighting the range, or typing or highlighting the range name.

Important Cue

When typing data, or in **:Text Edit** mode, you can also specify an italic format for characters in a range with a formatting sequence. To use a formatting sequence, move the cursor to the first character you want to italicize, press Ctrl-A, and type **i**. Then, move the cursor after the last character you want to format and press Ctrl-N.

Format Underline :FU

Purpose

Adds or removes an underline for characters in a range.

Reminders

- 1-2-3 displays Wysiwyg format settings only when Wysiwyg is in memory.
- Before you use the **:Format Underline** command, move the cell pointer to the first cell in the range you want to format.

Procedures

1. Type **:fu**.
2. Choose one of the following:

Menu Item	Description
Single	Adds a single underline to characters in a range.
Double	Adds a double underline to characters in a range.
Wide	Adds a wide underline to characters in a range.
Clear	Clears the underline from characters in a range.

3. Specify the range you want to format by typing the cell addresses, highlighting the range, or typing or highlighting the range name.

Important Cues

- When typing data, or in **:Text Edit** mode, you can also specify an underline format for characters in a range with a formatting sequence. To use a formatting sequence, move the cursor to the first character you want to underline, press Ctrl-A, and then type one of the following formatting codes: **1_** (single underline), **2_** (double underline), **3_** (wide underline). Then move the cursor after the last character you want to format and press Ctrl-N.
- **:Format Underline** does not underline blank cells or spaces in labels. Use **:Format Line** to underline entire cells, regardless of the cell contents.

Format Color   :FC

Purpose

Specifies colors for data in a range, both for screen display and for printed output.

Reminders

- 1-2-3 displays Wysiwyg format settings only when Wysiwyg is in memory.
- Before you use the **:Format Color** command, move the cell pointer to the first cell in the range you want to format.

Procedures

1. Type **:fc**.
2. Choose one of the following:

Menu Item	Description
Text	Sets data in a range to a specified color.
Background	Sets the background color for a range.
Negative	Sets the color for negative values in a range.

:Format Commands

Menu Item	Description
Reverse	Reverses the **Background** and **Text** colors in a range.
Quit	Returns to READY mode.

3. If you chose **Text** or **Background**, select one of the following colors: **N**ormal, **R**ed, **G**reen, **D**ark-Blue, **C**yan, **Y**ellow, or **M**agenta.

   If you chose **N**egative, select **N**ormal to use the same color as the **T**ext color or select **R**ed.

4. Specify the range you want to format by typing the cell addresses, highlighting the range, or typing or highlighting the range name.

Important Cues

- 1-2-3 uses the color you select for **Text** as the color for underlining in the range.
- You can display negative values in a color other than the **Text** color or red by selecting **:D**isplay **C**olors **N**eg and choosing an alternate color.

Caution

Some noncolor printers use very similar shading for different colors. If you are formatting your worksheet with many different colors, try printing a sample page first with /**P**rint **S**ample. Then select colors that work on both the display and on your printer.

Format Lines   :FL

Purpose

Specifies lines along the edges of cells and ranges on the worksheet.

Reminders

- 1-2-3 displays Wysiwyg format settings only when Wysiwyg is in memory.
- Before you use the **:F**ormat **L**ines command, move the cell pointer to the first cell in the range you want to format.

Procedures

1. Type **:fl**.
2. Choose one of the following:

Menu Item	Description
Outline	Creates a single-line outline around a range.
Left	Creates a vertical line along the left edge of a range.
Right	Creates a vertical line along the right edge of a range.

Menu Item	Description
Top	Creates a horizontal line along the top edge of a range.
Bottom	Creates a horizontal line along the bottom edge of a range.
All	Creates a single-line outline around every cell in a range.
Double	Creates a double-line outline around all or part of a range.
Wide	Creates a wide-line outline around all or part of a range.
Clear	Clears lines from cells in a range.
Shadow	Creates a drop shadow outline below and to the right of a range.

3. If you chose **Outline**, **Left**, **Right**, **Top**, **Bottom**, or **All**, specify the range you want to format.

   If you chose **Double**, **Wide**, or **Clear**, select one of the following menu items:

Menu Item	Description
Outline	Creates or removes an outline around a range.
Left	Creates or removes a vertical line along the left edge of each cell in a range.
Right	Creates or removes a vertical line along the right edge of each cell in a range.
Top	Creates or removes a horizontal line along the top edge of each cell in a range.
Bottom	Creates or removes a horizontal line along the bottom edge of each cell in a range.
All	Creates or removes an outline of the specified width around every cell in a range.

   If you chose **Shadow**, select **Set** to create a drop shadow outline or select **Clear** to remove a drop shadow outline.

4. Then specify the range you want to format.

   Figure F.1 shows several different line formats in a worksheet.

Important Cue

1-2-3 uses the color you select for **Text** as the color for the lines in the range.

Format Shade   :FS

Purpose

Adds or removes shading for a range.

:Format Commands

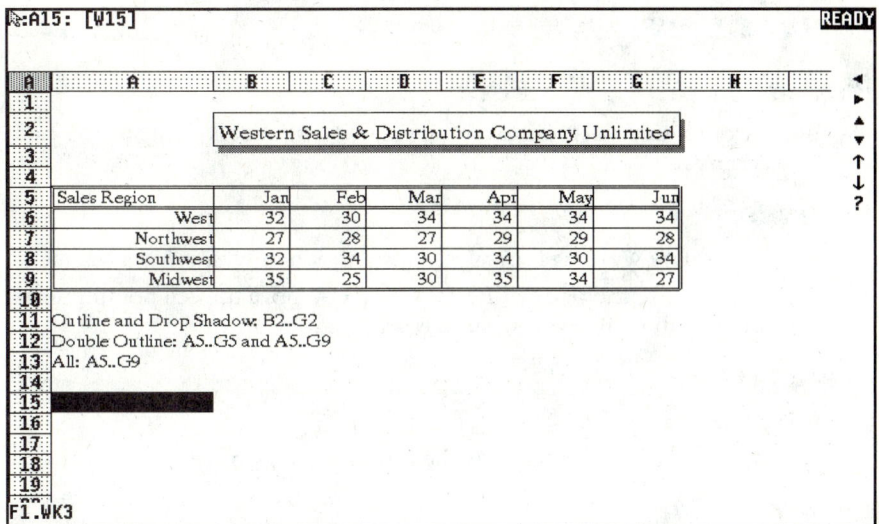

Fig. F.1.
Outlines and drop shadows created with :Format Line.

Reminders

- 1-2-3 displays Wysiwyg format settings only when Wysiwyg is in memory.
- Before you use the **:Format Shade** command, move the cell pointer to the first cell in the range you want to format.

Procedures

1. Type **:fs**.
2. Choose one of the following:

Menu Item	Description
Dark	Adds dark shading to a range.
Light	Adds light shading to a range.
Solid	Adds solid shading to a range.
Clear	Clears the shading from a range.

3. Specify the range you want to format by typing the cell addresses, highlighting the range, or typing or highlighting the range name.

Important Cue

Solid shading hides the data in a cell unless you select a different color for the data with **:Format Color Text**.

Caution

Solid shading always prints in black, even if you are using a color printer. For that reason, you should only use solid shading on areas of the worksheet that are blank or that contain data you do not want displayed in printed output.

Format Reset :FR

Purpose

Clears from a range all format settings created with the **:Format** and **:Named-Style** commands.

Reminders

- 1-2-3 displays Wysiwyg format settings only when Wysiwyg is in memory.
- Before you use the **:Format Reset** command, move the cell pointer to the first cell in the range you want to reset.

Procedures

1. Type **:fr**.
2. Specify the range that contains the format settings you want to clear.

Important Cue

:Format Reset does not reset formats that are set with /**R**ange Format, /**W**orksheet **G**lobal **F**ormat, or with special Wysiwyg formatting sequences.

Format Quit :FQ

Purpose

Returns the worksheet to READY mode.

Procedure

Type **:fq**.

:Display Commands :D

:Display commands specify the special Wysiwyg display characteristics you can set for a worksheet. Included in the :Display commands are format settings for the cell pointer and worksheet background colors, for the number of rows displayed, for zooming the display of selected cells, and for displaying the worksheet frame as a ruler.

Display Mode :DM

Purpose

Sets the display to either graphics or text mode and either color or monochrome.

Reminders

- Graphics mode is the default Wysiwyg display mode, in which the worksheet display echoes the way it would look when printed. All format settings you specify are displayed in graphics mode.
- Text mode is the default 1-2-3 display when Wysiwyg is not loaded in memory. Unlike the regular 1-2-3 display mode (when Wysiwyg is not in memory), you can continue to set formats; however, 1-2-3 does not display the formats in the worksheet until you reselect Graphics mode.

Procedure

1. Type :dm.
2. Choose one of the following:

Menu Item	Description
Graphics	Displays the worksheet in graphics mode (the default Wysiwyg display).
Text	Displays the worksheet in text mode (so that it resembles the default 1-2-3 display when Wysiwyg is not in memory).
B&W	Displays the worksheet in monochrome.
Color	Displays the worksheet in color.

Important Cue

1-2-3 uses the display mode you select for the current session of 1-2-3 only. If you want to set the display mode permanently, specify the mode and then select :Display Default Update.

Part IV ♦ 1-2-3 Release 3.1+ Command Reference

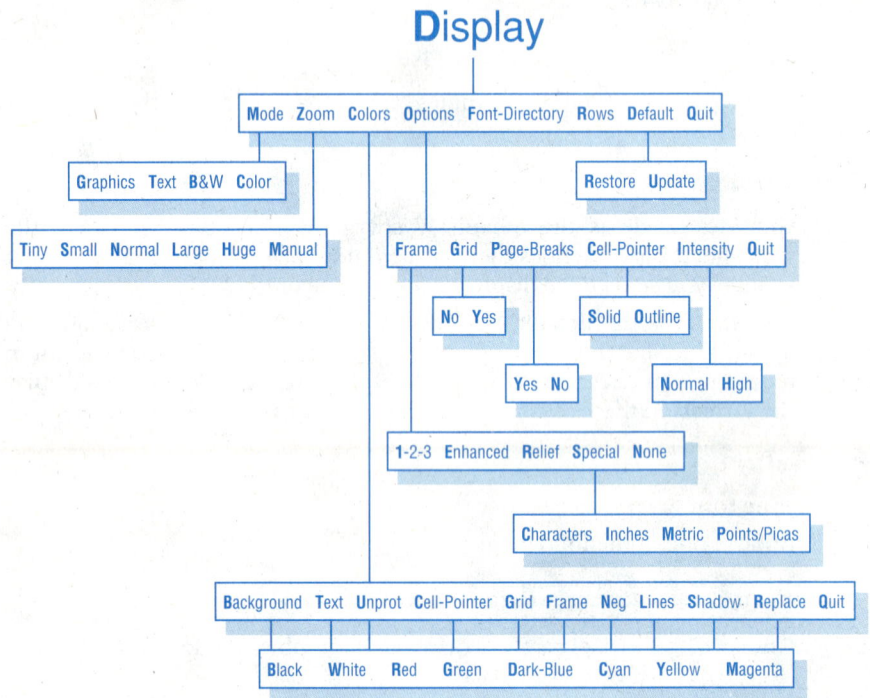

Display Zoom :DZ

Purpose

Enlarges or reduces the display of selected ranges in the worksheet. You can use **:Display Zoom** to get a better look at cell entries formatted with small fonts or to get an overview of a larger portion of the worksheet.

Reminder

Before you type **:dz**, move the cell pointer to the range you want to zoom.

Procedures

1. Type **:dz**.
2. Choose one of the following:

Menu Item	Description
Tiny	Displays cells at 63% of the standard display size.
Small	Displays cells at 87% of the standard display size.
Normal	Displays cells at their standard display size.
Large	Displays cells at 125% of the standard display size.
Huge	Displays cells at 150% of the standard display size.
Manual	Displays cells at a specified size, between 25% and 400% of the standard display size.

3. If you chose **Manual**, specify a new display size between 25 and 400, inclusive.

Important Cue

1-2-3 uses the display size you select for the current session of 1-2-3 only. If you want to set the display size permanently, specify the size and then select **:Display Default Update**.

Display Colors :DC

Purpose

Specifies the colors you want to use for the following worksheet characteristics: worksheet background, cell pointer, worksheet frame, grid lines, format lines, negative values, drop shadows, labels and nonnegative values, and unprotected cells.

Reminder

1-2-3 displays the colors you select only when Wysiwyg is in memory.

Procedures

1. Type **:dc**.
2. Choose one of the following:

Menu Item	Description
Background	Sets the worksheet background color.
Text	Sets the color for labels and nonnegative values in the worksheet.
Unprot	Sets the color for unprotected cells when global protection is enabled.
Cell-Pointer	Sets the cell pointer color.
Grid	Sets the color of grid lines created with **:Display Options Grid**.
Frame	Sets the color of the worksheet frame.
Neg	Sets the color of negative values in the worksheet.
Lines	Sets the color of format lines created with **:Format Lines**.
Shadow	Sets the color of drop shadows created with **:Format Lines Shadow**.
Replace	Specifies alternate colors you want 1-2-3 to use with the worksheet display.
Quit	Returns to the **:Display** menu.

3. Choose one of the following colors: **Black**, **White**, **Red**, **Green**, **Dark-Blue**, **Cyan**, **Yellow**, or **Magenta**.
4. If you chose **Replace**, specify a new color by typing a number between **0** and **63**, inclusive, or by pressing the left- or right-arrow keys to increase or decrease the current value.

Important Cue

1-2-3 uses the display colors you select for the current session of 1-2-3 only. If you want to set the display colors permanently, specify the colors and then select **:Display Default Update**.

Display Options :DO

Purpose

:Display Options specifies the display of the following worksheet characteristics: the cell pointer (solid or outline), the worksheet frame, grid lines, screen display intensity (brightness), and page-break lines.

:Display Commands

Reminder

1-2-3 uses the display settings you select with **:Display Options** only when Wysiwyg is in memory.

Procedures

1. Type **:do**.
2. Choose one of the following:

Menu Item	Description
Frame	Determines whether the worksheet frame is displayed or hidden.
Grid	Determines whether grid lines (set with **:dog**) are displayed or hidden.
Page-Breaks	Determines whether page-break lines (set with **:wp**) are displayed or hidden.
Cell-Pointer	Determines whether 1-2-3 displays the cell pointer as a solid rectangle or as an outline.
Intensity	Sets the brightness of the screen display.
Quit	Returns to the **:Display** menu.

3. If you chose **Frame**, choose one of the following:

Menu Item	Description
1-2-3	Displays the default 1-2-3 worksheet frame used when Wysiwyg is not in memory.
Enhanced	Displays the default Wysiwyg frame—column letters and row numbers are displayed in the center of separate rectangles.
Relief	Displays the enhanced worksheet frame, but changes the background color to gray and changes the display intensity to high.
Special	Displays the worksheet frame as rulers in one of the following measurements: inches, centimeters (metric), points and picas, or 10-point characters.
None	Hides the worksheet frame.

If you chose **Grid**, select **No** to hide the grid lines or select **Yes** to display grid lines.

If you chose **Page-Breaks**, select **No** to hide the page-break lines or select **Yes** to display the page-break lines.

If you chose **Cell-Pointer**, select **S**olid or **O**utline to specify the cell pointer type.

If you chose **Intensity**, select **N**ormal to display the worksheet at the standard 1-2-3 screen display brightness or select **H**igh to display the worksheet at high intensity.

4. If you chose Frame Special in steps 2 and 3, choose one of the following:

Menu Item	Description
Characters	Displays the worksheet frame as rulers measured in 10-point characters with six lines per inch.
Inches	Displays the worksheet frame as rulers measured in inches.
Metric	Displays the worksheet frame as rulers measured in centimeters.
Points/Picas	Displays the worksheet frame as rulers measured in points and picas.

Important Cue

1-2-3 uses the display options you select for the current session of 1-2-3 only. If you want to set the display options permanently, specify the options and then select **:Display Default Update**.

Display Font-Directory :DF

Purpose

Specifies the directory in which 1-2-3 searches for the Wysiwyg fonts used to display and print worksheets and graphs (the font directory).

Procedures

1. Type **:df**.
2. Specify the directory that contains the font files you want to use when Wysiwyg is in memory.

Important Cues

- If you specify a directory that does not contain Wysiwyg font files, 1-2-3 uses the default 1-2-3 fonts that are displayed when Wysiwyg is not in memory.
- 1-2-3 uses the display font directory you select for the current session of 1-2-3 only. If you want to set the font directory permanently, specify the directory and then select **:Display Default Update**.

Display Rows :DR

Purpose

Sets the number of rows that 1-2-3 displays in graphics mode (set with **:Display Mode Graphics**).

:Display Commands

Reminder

1-2-3 uses the display rows setting you select with **:Display R**ows only when Wysiwyg is in memory.

Procedures

1. Type **:dr**.
2. Specify the number of rows you want 1-2-3 to display in graphics mode. Enter a number between 16 and 60, inclusive.

Important Cue

1-2-3 uses the display rows setting you select for the current session of 1-2-3 only. If you want to set the display rows setting permanently, specify the setting and then select **:D**isplay Default Update.

Display Default :DD

Purpose

:Display Default restores the original Wysiwyg display settings or saves the new display settings you have specified with **:D**isplay commands in the Wysiwyg configuration file (WYSIWYG.CNF).

Reminder

1-2-3 uses the display settings you save with **:D**isplay Default each time you load Wysiwyg.

Procedures

1. Type **:dd**.
2. Select **R**estore to clear any new display settings you selected and use the display settings from the default configuration file.

   Select **U**pdate to save in the Wysiwyg configuration file new display settings you selected with the **:D**isplay commands.

Important Cue

Once you save new settings with **:D**isplay Default, the previous settings in the Wysiwyg configuration file are lost.

Display Quit :DQ

Purpose

Returns the worksheet to READY mode.

Reminder

1-2-3 uses the display settings you select for the current session of 1-2-3 only. If you want to set the display settings permanently, specify the settings and then select **:Display Default Update**.

Procedure

Type **:dq**.

:Special Commands :S

:Special commands copy and move Wysiwyg formats. You can use the :Special commands to transfer Wysiwyg format information and graphs from one worksheet file to another or from one range in a worksheet to another.

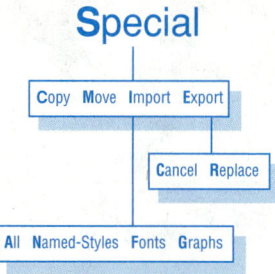

Special Copy :SC

Purpose

Copies Wysiwyg format information from a range to one or more other range(s).

Reminders

- Before you begin, decide which range you want to copy Wysiwyg format information from and which range(s) you want to copy the formats to. Remember that all Wysiwyg format information in the FROM range will be copied, including colors, shading, and lines.
- If the receiving address is not close to the FROM range, note the address before using :Special Copy, so that you can type the TO address. Pointing across a long distance to the TO address can be error-prone.

Procedures

1. Type :sc.
2. The FROM prompt requests the range of the cells that contain the format information to be copied. Enter the range by typing the range name or range address or by highlighting the range.
3. Press Enter.
4. At the TO prompt, specify on the topmost worksheet the upper left corner of the area where you want the duplicate Wysiwyg format information to appear. If you want to copy format information to multiple adjacent ranges, you can specify the top left corner where each duplicate should appear. If you are copying format information from a three-dimensional range, specify only the top left cell on the topmost worksheet.
5. Press Enter.

Important Cues

- If you copy Wysiwyg format information to a range that already contains Wysiwyg formats, 1-2-3 overwrites the old formats with the new settings.
- Use /Copy to copy data from one range to another.
- Use /Copy to copy formats set with /Range Format and /Worksheet Global Format.

Caution

Be sure you check the ranges to which you are copying Wysiwyg format information before you do the copy. Once you have copied new formats onto ranges, any previous Wysiwyg formats in those ranges are lost.

Special Move :SM

Purpose

Moves Wysiwyg format information from a range to one or more other range(s).

Reminders

- Before you begin, decide which range you want to move Wysiwyg format information from and which range(s) you want to move the formats to. Remember that all Wysiwyg format information in the FROM range will be moved, including colors, shading, and lines.
- If the receiving address is not close to the FROM range, note the address before using :Special Move, so that you can type the TO address. Pointing across a long distance to the TO address can be error-prone.

Procedures

1. Type **:sm**.
2. The FROM prompt requests the range of the cells that contain the format information to be moved. Enter the range by typing the range name or range address or by highlighting the range.
3. Press Enter.
4. At the TO prompt, specify on the topmost worksheet the upper left corner of the area where you want the Wysiwyg format information to appear. If you want to move format information to multiple adjacent ranges, you can specify the top left corner where each duplicate should appear. If you are moving format information from a three-dimensional range, specify only the top left cell on the topmost worksheet.
5. Press Enter.

:Special Commands 823

Important Cues

- If you move Wysiwyg format information to a range that already contains Wysiwyg formats, 1-2-3 overwrites the old formats with the new settings.
- Use /**M**ove to move data from one range to another.
- Use /**M**ove to move formats set with /**R**ange Format and /**W**orksheet Global Format.

Caution

Be sure you check the ranges to which you are copying Wysiwyg format information before you do the move. Once you have moved new formats onto ranges, any previous Wysiwyg formats in those ranges are lost.

Special Import   :SI

Purpose

Copies the formats, font set, graphs, and named styles from a Wysiwyg, Impress, or Allways format file into the current file.

Reminder

You can use **:S**pecial **I**mport to copy formatting information from any of the three 1-2-3 Release 3 formatting add-ins. Wysiwyg format files have the extension FM3; Impress format files (from 1-2-3 Release 3) have the extension FMT; Allways format files have the extension ALL.

Procedures

1. Type **:si**.
2. Choose one of the following:

Menu Item	Description
All	Copies all formats, the font set, graphs, and named styles from a format file on disk into the current file.
Fonts	Copies only the font set from a format file on disk into the current file.
Graphs	Copies only the graphs from a format file on disk into the current file. **Graphs** copies all information about Wysiwyg graphs settings, including their positions in the worksheet, but does not delete any graphs already in place in the current file.
Named-Styles	Copies only the named styles from a format file on disk into the current file.

3. Specify the name of the format file from which you want to copy formatting information.

Important Cues

- Remember that 1-2-3 copies the information in a format file into exactly the same cells as in the file for which the format file was originally created. For example, if you import information from a format file that contains information to boldface cells A6 through B20, those cells will be bold in the current file after the import.
- Once you have imported the formatting information into the current file, 1-2-3 also updates the Wysiwyg format file for that worksheet file.

Caution

:Special Import overwrites any Wysiwyg format information that already exists for the current file. Be sure you have saved your worksheet file before you do a :Special Import, just in case you need to return to the original format settings.

Special Export :SE

Purpose

Copies the formats, font set, graphs, and named styles from the current format file into another Wysiwyg, Impress, or Allways format file on disk.

Reminder

You can use :Special Export to copy formatting information to any of the three 1-2-3 Release 3 formatting add-ins. However, because some Wysiwyg formats are not available in Allways, some formatting information (such as drop shadows, named styles, and wide lines) will be lost if you copy into an ALL format file.

Procedures

1. Type **:se**.
2. Specify the name of the format file into which you want to copy information. If you are exporting formats into another Wysiwyg format file, you do not need to include the FM3 extension; if you want to export information into an Impress or Allways file, include the FMT or ALL extension, respectively.
2. If you are copying information into a format file that already exists, choose one of the following:

Menu Item	Description
Cancel	Cancels the command without exporting the formatting information.
Replace	Replaces the formatting information in the format file on disk with the new information from the current format file.

Important Cue

:Special Export does not copy graphs into the format file on disk; it only copies their positions in the worksheet and any special graphs formatting set with the :Graph Edit commands.

Caution

:Special Export overwrites any Wysiwyg format information that already exists for the format file on disk. Be sure you have saved a backup copy of the file before you do a :Special Export, just in case you need to return to the original format settings.

:Text Commands :T

:Text commands let you edit and enter text directly in the worksheet (as opposed to cell by cell in the control panel). The **:Text** commands are especially helpful when you are entering titles and longer passages of text in a worksheet.

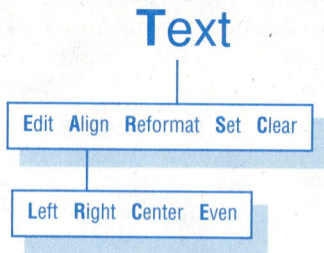

Text Edit :TE

Purpose

:Text Edit allows you to edit labels within a specified text range.

Reminder

Before you select **:te**, move the cell pointer to the first cell in the range in which you want to edit text.

Procedures

1. Type **:te**.
2. Specify the text range (the range in which you want to edit text). **:Text Edit** only edits text within the range you specify.
3. Enter or edit text in the range. You can use the following editing keys while in text editing mode:

Edit Key	Description
← or →	Moves the cursor one character to the left or right in the text range.
↑ or ↓	Moves the cursor one line up or down in the text range.
Backspace or Del	Deletes the character to the left or right of the cursor in the text range.
Ctrl-← or Ctrl-→	Moves the cursor left to the beginning of the previous word or right to the end of the next word.

:Text Commands

Edit Key	Description
Ctrl-Enter	Creates an end-of-paragraph symbol and begins a new line in the text range.
Enter	Begins a new line in the text range.
Esc	Returns 1-2-3 to READY mode.
Home or End	Moves the cursor to the first or last character in the line.
Home Home or End End	Moves the cursor to the first or last character in the text range.
Ins	Toggles between insert and overtype editing modes.
PgUp or PgDn	Moves the cursor up or down one screen.
F3	Displays format options (such as bold, outline, font choices) that you can set for the text in the text range.

4. Press Esc to stop editing text in the text range and return to READY mode.

To set formats for text in the text range:

1. Follow steps 1 and 2.
2. Move the cursor to the first character you want to format and press F3.
3. Choose one of the following:

Menu Item	Description
Bold	Boldfaces the text.
Color	Specifies a color for the text.
Font	Specifies a font for the text.
Italics	Italicizes the text.
–	Subscripts the text.
+	Superscripts the text.
Normal	Removes formatting from the text.
Outline	Formats text so that only the outline of each character is displayed.
Underline	Underlines the text.

4. Move the cursor past the last character you want to format, press F3 and select **Normal**.

Important Cue

You can edit text in an existing text range (specified with **:Text Set**) at any time by double-clicking the mouse on any text in the range.

Text Align   :TA

Purpose
Changes the label alignment for labels in the specified text range.

Reminder
Before you select **:ta**, move the cell pointer to the first cell in the range in which you want to change the label alignment.

Procedures

1. Type **:ta**.
2. Choose one of the following:

Menu Item	Description
Left	Left-aligns labels in the text range (aligns labels with the left edge of the text range).
Right	Right-aligns labels in the text range (aligns labels with the right edge of the text range).
Center	Centers labels in the text range (aligns labels so that they are centered in the text range).
Even	Aligns labels with both edges of the text range. Even does not align labels that end with a period (.), an exclamation point (!), a question mark (?), a colon (:), or an end-of-paragraph symbol (created with **:te**)

3. Specify the text range (the range in which you want to align labels). **:Text Align** only aligns labels within the range you specify.

Figure T.1 shows labels in two text ranges. The labels in range B2..B8 are centered; the labels in range D2..D8 are evenly aligned.

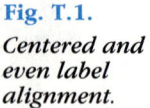

Fig. T.1.
Centered and even label alignment.

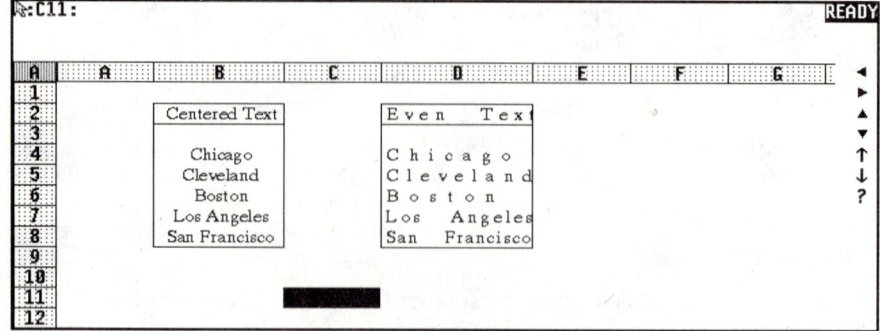

Important Cue

1-2-3 displays labels that are longer than the width of the text range as left-aligned, regardless of which alignment you select.

Text Reformat :TR

Purpose

Justifies a column of labels so that the labels fit in the specified text range.

Reminder

Before you select :tr, move the cell pointer to the first cell in the column of labels that you want to justify.

Procedures

1. Type :tr.
2. Specify the text range (the range in which you want the labels to be displayed). You must include all rows in the column that you want to reformat, as well as any other columns that you want to use to justify the labels. 1-2-3 reformats the labels in the first column of the text range, by using the label prefix of the first cell in the column, so that the labels are justified within the entire text range. For example, if the first cell is right-aligned, 1-2-3 displays the labels in the first column of the text range at the right edge of the text range.

Important Cue

You cannot use :tr if global protection is enabled. Type /wgpd to disable global protection before you select :Text Reformat.

Text Set :TS

Purpose

Specifies a text range that you can use with other :Text commands.

Reminder

Before you select :ts, move the cell pointer to the first cell you want to include in the text range.

Procedures

1. Type :ts.
2. Specify the range of cells you want to include in the text range.

Important Cues

- 1-2-3 displays the format description {Text} in the control panel whenever the cell pointer is located in a cell in a text range.
- You can edit text in an existing text range from READY mode by moving the cell pointer to any cell in the text range and double-clicking the mouse. Then use the text range editing keys to edit the text.

Text Clear :TC

Purpose

Clears the settings for a text range and removes any alignment in the range that was set with **:Text Align**.

Reminder

Before you select **:tc**, move the cell pointer to the first cell you want to include in the range you want to clear.

Procedures

1. Type **:tc**.
2. Specify the text range you want to clear. The range you specify does not need to be exactly the same as a previously defined text range.

Important Cue

:Text Clear does not remove formats specified with the **:Text Edit** or **:Text Reformat** commands.

:Named-Style Commands :N

:Named-Style commands define a set of Wysiwyg formats (such as cells you want displayed in boldface for titles, or an entire report or schedule format) that you can save and reuse.

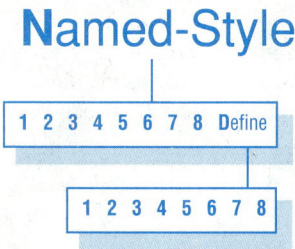

Named-Style 1 through   :ND1 through
Named-Style 8   :ND8

Purpose

Formats a range with a named set of Wysiwyg formats. Use these commands, in combination with **:Named-Style Define**, to set common Wysiwyg formats quickly.

Reminder

Before you format a range with a named style, you must define the named style with the **:Named-Style Define** command.

Procedures

1. Type **:n**.
2. Select the named style you want to use for a range (or ranges) from the menu (**1** through **8**). 1-2-3 displays the name and description of each named style next to its corresponding number. You can select any of the eight named styles, but only those named styles that have been previously defined with **:nd** will format a range.
3. Specify the range or ranges that you want to format with the named style.

Important Cue

1-2-3 automatically updates any cells you format with a named style whenever you change a named style with **:Named-Style Define**.

Named-Style Define :ND

Purpose

Defines and names a set of formats in a cell as a named style. You can define up to eight different named styles.

Reminder

Before you select **:Named-Style Define**, be sure you have formatted a cell with the Wysiwyg formats you want to use as the named style. Figure N.1 shows a cell formatted with Wysiwyg commands that can be used as a named style.

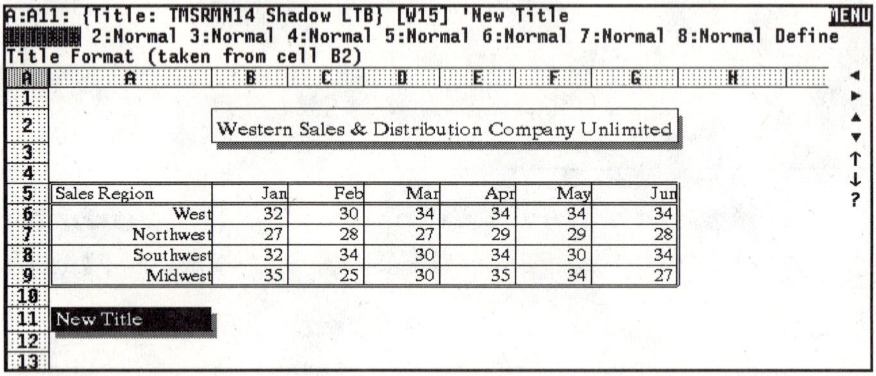

Fig. N.1.
Defining a cell's Wysiwyg formats as a named style.

Procedures

1. Type **:nd**.
2. Select the number for the named style you want to define (**1** through **8**).
3. Specify the cell that contains the Wysiwyg formats you want to define as a named style.
4. Enter a name (a maximum of six characters) for the named style.
5. Enter a description (a maximum of 37 characters) for the named style.

Important Cues

- When you define a named style, you should specify only the cell that contains the formats you want. You can specify a range of cells, but 1-2-3 uses the Wysiwyg formats from the first cell in the range only.
- Once you have defined a named style, 1-2-3 displays its name and description after its number each time you select **:nd**.

:Graph Commands :G

:Graph commands enable you to edit graphs and other graphics and place them in the worksheet for display and for printing.

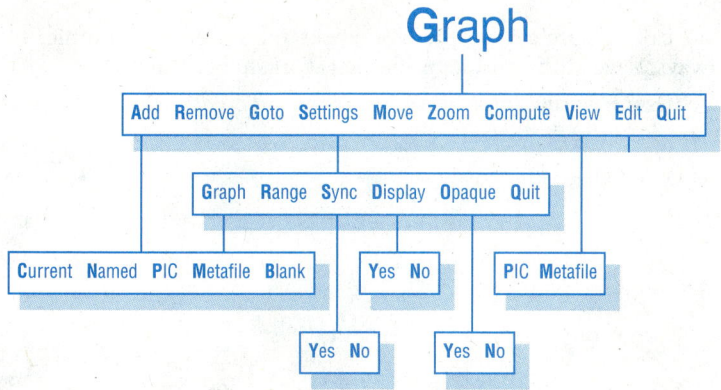

Graph Add :GA

Purpose

Inserts a graphic into the worksheet (both for display and for printing).

Reminder

Before you select **:Graph Add**, move the cell pointer to the first cell in the range in which you want to add the graphic.

Procedures

1. Type **:ga**.
2. Choose one of the following:

Menu Item	Description
Current	Inserts the current graph into the worksheet.
Named	Inserts a named graph into the worksheet.
PIC	Inserts a graphic in PIC format into the worksheet.
Metafile	Inserts a graphic in metafile (CGM) format into the worksheet.
Blank	Inserts a placeholder for a graphic into the worksheet.

3. If you chose **Named**, **PIC**, or **Metafile**, specify from the displayed list the graph or graphic you want to display in the worksheet. Then specify the range into which you want to place the graphic.

If you chose **Current** or **Blank**, specify the range into which you want to place the graphic.

Important Cues

- 1-2-3 automatically sizes the graphic you select so that it fits into the specified range.
- You can specify a multiple-worksheet range for the graphic, but 1-2-3 always places the graphic in the first worksheet of the range.
- Use **:Graph Add Blank** when you haven't yet created the graph you want to insert into the worksheet.

Graph Remove :GR

Purpose

Removes a graphic from the worksheet.

Reminder

:Graph Remove does not delete a graph you created with **/Graph**; it only removes the display of the graph from the worksheet. You can still view the graph by pressing Graph (F10) or by selecting **/Graph View**.

Procedures

1. Type **:gr**.
2. Specify the graphic you want to remove from the worksheet by specifying a cell in the range that includes the graphic or by pressing F3 and selecting the name of the graph.

Important Cues

- Removing a graphic does not affect any data in the range in which you displayed the graphic.
- You can remove more than one graphic at once by specifying a range that contains all the graphics you want to remove.

Caution

Any edits you have made to a graphic with **:Graph Edit** are lost when you remove it.

Graph Goto :GG

Purpose

Moves the cell pointer to the specified graphic.

Procedures

1. Type **:gg**.
2. Select the name of the graphic you want to move to by specifying a cell in the range that contains the graphic or by pressing F3 and selecting the name of the graphic.

Important Cue

If you have a small worksheet, use the mouse or arrow keys to move the cell pointer to the graphic.

Graph Settings :GS

Purpose

Sets the way a graphic is displayed in the worksheet.

Reminders

◆ Use **:Graph Settings** to replace one graphic with another, to hide the display of a graphic, to resize or move a graphic, to make a graphic opaque or transparent, and to synchronize updating a graph with changes in the worksheet's data.

◆ Before you select **:Graph Settings**, move the cell pointer to a cell in the range that contains the graphic you want to work with.

Procedures

1. Type **:gs**.
2. Choose one of the following:

Menu Item	Description
Graph	Replaces a graphic in the worksheet with a different graphic.
Range	Moves or changes the size of a graphic.
Sync	Synchronizes updating a graph with updates in the worksheet's data.
Display	Displays the data in the graphic or displays the graph as a shaded rectangle in the worksheet.
Opaque	Displays the data in the graphic (opaque) or displays the data in the range underneath the graphic (transparent).
Quit	Returns the worksheet to READY mode.

3. If you chose **Graph**, select the graphic you want to replace by specifying a cell in the range that contains the graphic or by pressing F3 and selecting the graphic's name. Then choose one of the following:

Menu Item	Description
Current	Replaces the graphic with the current graph.
Named	Replaces the graphic with a named graph.
PIC	Replaces the graphic with a graphic in PIC format.
Metafile	Replaces the graphic with a graphic in metafile (CGM) format.
Blank	Replaces the graphic with a placeholder for a graphic.

If you chose **Graph Named**, **P**IC, or **Metafile**, specify from the displayed list the graph or graphic you want to display in the worksheet.

If you chose **Range**, select the graphic you want to move or size by specifying a cell in the range that contains the graphic or by pressing F3 and selecting the graphic's name. Then use the arrow keys or the mouse to specify the new range for the graphic. Unlike **:Graph Move**, you must specify the entire range for the new graphic because 1-2-3 uses the new location information to resize the graphic as well as move it.

If you chose **Sync**, select **Yes** if you want 1-2-3 to update the graph each time data in the worksheet is recalculated; select **No** if you want 1-2-3 to update the graph only when you select **:Graph Compute**. Then select the graphic you want to sync by specifying a cell in the range that contains the graphic or by pressing F3 and selecting the graphic's name.

If you chose **Display**, select **Yes** to display the graphic in the worksheet or select **No** to display a shaded rectangle instead of the data in the graphic. Then select the graphic you want to display by specifying a cell in the range that contains the graphic or by pressing F3 and selecting the graphic's name.

If you chose **Opaque**, select **Yes** to display the data in the graphic or select **No** to hide the graphic and display the data in the range underneath. Then select the graphic you want to display by specifying a cell in the range that contains the graphic or by pressing F3 and selecting the graphic's name.

Important Cues

- When you replace a graphic with **:Graph Settings Graph**, you do not replace any enhancements made to the graphic with **:Graph Edit**. If you want to remove the graphic and its enhancements, select **:Graph Remove**.
- It is quicker to use **:Graph Move** instead of **:Graph Settings Range** if you are moving a graphic but do not want to change the size.
- Use **:Graph Settings Display No** when you want to make many changes to the data in a worksheet so that 1-2-3 will not need to redraw the graphics each time it recalculates the data. But don't forget to select **:Graph Settings Display Yes** to redisplay the graphics after you are done making changes.
- You can select multiple graphs to synchronize (or unsynchronize), display, or make opaque with **:Graph Settings Sync**, **:Graph Settings Display**, and **:Graph Settings Opaque** by specifying a range that contains all the graphs you want to work with.

:Graph Commands

Cautions

◆ If you unsynchronize graphs from their worksheet data, 1-2-3 will not update the graphs unless you select :Graph Compute. Be very sure you know about changes to the worksheet data if you choose to unsynchronize the graphs.

◆ Regardless of the setting you use for :Graph Settings Display, 1-2-3 always *prints* the graphic, and not a shaded rectangle.

Graph Move :GM

Purpose

Moves a graphic from one range to another in the worksheet.

Reminder

Before you select :Graph Move, move the cell pointer to a cell in the range that contains the graphic.

Procedures

1. Type :gm.
2. Select the graphic you want to move by specifying a cell in the range that contains the graphic or by pressing F3 and selecting the name from the displayed list.
3. Specify the first cell in the range to which you want to move the graphic.

Important Cue

1-2-3 does not resize the graphic when you move it to a new range. To change the size of the range in which a graphic is displayed, use :Graph Settings Range.

Caution

Before you move a graphic, make sure that the range to which you are moving it does not contain data that you do not want to hide.

Graph Zoom :GZ

Purpose

Temporarily displays a graphic in full-screen mode.

Reminder

To view a graphic saved in a PIC file or metafile format, select :Graph View.

Procedures

1. Type **:gz**.
2. Select the graphic you want to display by specifying a cell in the range that contains the graphic or by pressing F3 and selecting the name from the displayed list.
3. Press any key to remove the graphic from display and return to the worksheet.

Important Cue

Use **:Graph View** to display graphs created and saved in older versions of 1-2-3.

Graph Compute :GC

Purpose

Updates the data and display of graphics in all active worksheets.

Reminder

When you select **:Graph Compute**, 1-2-3 recalculates all worksheets in memory and updates the current and named graphs that are displayed in any active worksheet. If you have resaved any graphics in PIC or metafile format, 1-2-3 also updates the files with the newly saved graphics.

Procedure

Type **:gc**.

Important Cues

- If you delete a PIC or metafile graphic file from disk before you select **:Graph Compute**, 1-2-3 blanks the display of the range that contained that graphic. The data underneath the display, however, is not affected.
- If you do not want 1-2-3 to update graphics in the worksheet each time 1-2-3 recalculates active worksheet files, select **:Graph Settings Sync No**.

Graph View :GV

Purpose

Displays on the full screen a graphic saved in PIC or metafile format.

Reminder

To view a current graph, press Graph (F10) or select **/Graph View**.

Procedures

1. Type **:gv**.
2. Select **P**IC to display a list of graphs saved in PIC format; select **M**etafile to display a list of graphs saved in CGM format.
3. Select the graph you want to view from the list displayed.
4. Press any key to remove the graphic from display and return to the worksheet.

Important Cue

Use **:G**raph **V**iew to display graphs created and saved in older versions of 1-2-3.

Graph Edit :GE

Purpose

Edit a graph or graphic that you have positioned in the worksheet. Use **:G**raph **E**dit to create enhancements to the graph that are not available through the 1-2-3 /Graph commands. For example, you can add additional text, arrows, and freehand shapes.

Reminders

- To edit a graphic, you must first place it in the worksheet with **:G**raph **A**dd.
- There are two main types of changes you can make with the **:G**raph **E**dit commands—changes to the graphic appearance (such as background color) and changes to objects added to the graphic (such as arrows, additional text, and shapes).
- Remember that you use **:G**raph **E**dit to add or edit enhancements to a graphic only. If you want to change parts of the graph itself (such as ranges that you added to the graph with the /Graph commands) you must use the /Graph commands.
- Although you can use the cursor-movement keys to edit a graphic in the editing window, you'll find it much easier if you use the mouse. See Chapter 2 for information on mouse support in 1-2-3 Releases 3.1 and 3.1+.
- To use **:G**raph **E**dit (and the graphics editing commands it contains), you must first place a graphic in the Wysiwyg graphics editing window. The graphics editing window is a temporary separate display that 1-2-3 creates in which you edit a graphic. The following procedure explains how you add a graphic to the editing window.

Procedures

1. Type **:ge**.

2. Specify the graphic you want to copy into the graphics editing window by moving the cell pointer to a cell in the range that contains the graphic or by pressing F3 and choosing the graph name.

Important Cue

You can also copy a graphic into the graphics editing window from READY mode by moving the mouse pointer to the graphic and double-clicking.

Caution

To use **:Graph Edit** and the graphics editing window, you must be in Wysiwyg graphics mode. If you aren't sure whether you are in graphics mode, make sure Wysiwyg is in memory and then type **:dmg**.

Graph Edit Add :GEA

Purpose

Adds enhancements to a graphic.

Reminders

- Use **:Graph Edit Add** to include text, arrows, and shapes with a graphic displayed in the worksheet.
- Although you can use **:Graph Edit Add** with the cursor-movement keys, you'll find it much easier to create and place objects if you use the mouse.

Procedures

1. Type **:gea** and specify the graphic you want to edit.
2. Choose one of the following:

Menu Item	Description
Text	Adds text to a graphic.
Line	Adds lines (both single line and multiple, connected lines) to a graphic.
Polygon	Adds a polygon to a graphic.
Arrow	Adds an arrow to a graphic.
Rectangle	Adds a rectangle to a graphic.
Ellipse	Adds a circle or ellipse to a graphic.
Freehand	Adds a freehand form to a graphic.

3. If you chose **Text**, type the characters you want to add to the graphic and press Enter. Then use the mouse or the cursor-movement keys to specify the location of the text in the graphics editing window. When you've moved the cursor to the location where you want to place the text, press Enter or the left mouse button.

If you chose **Line**, use the mouse or the cursor-movement keys to specify the location of the first point on the line in the graphics editing window. When you've moved the cursor to the location, press Enter or the left mouse button. Then use the mouse or the arrow keys to draw the line. If you want to add an additional line connected to the first, press the space bar or click the mouse and draw the next line. Press Enter or double-click the mouse to finish drawing the line.

If you chose **Polygon**, use the mouse or the cursor-movement keys to specify the location of the first point in the polygon. When you've moved the cursor to the location, press Enter or the left mouse button. Then use the mouse or the arrow keys to draw the first line of the polygon and press the space bar or click the mouse. Continue drawing sides of the polygon, finishing each side by pressing the space bar or clicking the mouse. When you have finished drawing the polygon, press Enter or double-click the mouse. (You don't need to draw every side of a polygon. Once you have drawn enough sides of the polygon for 1-2-3 to guess the shape, you can have 1-2-3 finish the polygon for you by pressing Enter or double-clicking the mouse.)

If you chose **Arrow**, use the mouse or the cursor-movement keys to specify the location of the first point on the arrow in the graphics editing window. When you've moved the cursor to the location, press Enter or click the mouse. Then use the mouse or the arrow keys to draw the arrow. If you want to add an additional line connected to the first, press the space bar or click the mouse and draw the next line. Press Enter or double-click the mouse to finish drawing the arrow. 1-2-3 will place an arrowhead at the end of the line you drew.

If you chose **Rectangle** or **Ellipse**, use the mouse or the cursor-movement keys to specify the location of the first point of the rectangle or ellipse. When you've moved the cursor to the location, press Enter or click the mouse. Then use the cursor-movement keys or drag the mouse to stretch the rectangle or ellipse that 1-2-3 creates. When the rectangle or ellipse is the appropriate shape and size, press Enter or release the mouse button.

If you chose **Freehand**, use the mouse or the cursor-movement keys to specify the location of the first point of the shape. When you've moved the cursor to the location, press Enter or click the mouse. Then use the cursor-movement keys or drag the mouse to create the shape you want. Press Enter or release the mouse button to finish the shape.

Important Cues

- You can add a cell's contents to a graphic by selecting **:Graph Edit Add Text**, typing \ (backslash) and then specifying the cell address or range name.
- You can create a square from a rectangle or a circle from an ellipse by pressing Shift-Enter (or pressing Shift and double-clicking the mouse) to finish the object.

Graph Edit Select :GES

Purpose

Selects graphics and enhancements within the graphics editing window for editing.

Procedures

1. Type **:ges** and specify the graphic you want to edit.
2. Choose one of the following:

Menu Item	Description
One	Selects one object (either the graphic or an enhancement).
All	Selects all objects (both the graphic and its enhancements) in the editing window.
None	Cancels the selection of all objects (leaving no objects selected).
More/Less	Enables you to select more or fewer objects than are already selected.
Cycle	Lets you cycle through all objects and graphics so that you can select or not select each of them.
Graph	Selects the graphic without its enhancements.
Quit	Returns you to the :Graph Edit menu.

3. If you chose **One**, move the cursor to the object and press Enter.

   If you chose **More/Less**, move the cursor to the object you want to select (or cancel as a selection) and press the space bar. Continue selecting objects (or canceling objects) by moving to the object and pressing the space bar. When you have finished, press Enter.

   If you chose **Cycle**, use the cursor-movement keys to cycle through the objects in the editing window. Press the space bar to select an object. When you have finished selecting objects, press Enter.

Important Cue

You can select a single object in the editing window by moving the cursor to the object and clicking the mouse. You can select several objects in the editing window by holding the mouse down and dragging the mouse over all the objects you want to select.

:Graph Commands 843

Graph Edit Edit :GEE

Purpose

Edit enhancements to a graphic that you created with other :Graph Edit commands.

Reminders

◆ Use :Graph Edit Edit to change or remove arrowheads; edit, align, or change the font of text enhancements; and edit shapes you added to a graphic.

◆ You use :Graph Edit Edit to edit enhancements you make to graphics with other :Graph Edit commands. Use /Graph if you want to edit parts of a graph that you created with the /Graph commands.

Procedures

1. Type :gee and specify the graphic you want to edit.
2. Choose one of the following:

Menu Item	Description
Text	Edits text in a text enhancement.
Centering	Aligns text enhancements.
Font	Changes the font of text enhancements in a graphic.
Line-Style	Changes the line style of one or more shapes added to a graphic.
Width	Changes the width of lines or of shape outlines.
Arrowheads	Adds arrowheads to lines and edits existing arrowheads.
Smoothing	Smooths (rounds) the edges of shapes added to a graphic.

3. If you chose Text, move the cursor to the text you want to edit and press Enter or double-click the mouse. 1-2-3 displays the text in the control panel. Use the 1-2-3 editing keys to edit the text. When you are finished editing the line, press Enter or double-click the mouse.

   If you chose Centering, select one of the following alignments: Left, Center, or Right. Then select the text enhancements that you want to align.

   If you chose Font, select one of the eight fonts 1-2-3 displays. Then select the text enhancements that you want to change.

   If you chose Line-Style, select one of the following line styles: 1:Solid, 2:Dashed, 3:Dotted, 4:Long-Dashed, 5:Chain-Dotted, 6:Chain-Dashed, or 7:Hidden. Then select the objects that you want to change. You can change both lines and arrows and the outlines of shape enhancements, such as rectangles and circles.

   If you chose Width, select one of the following width settings: 1:Very-Narrow, 2:Narrow, 3:Medium, 4:Wide, or 5:Very-Wide. Then select the objects that you want to change. You can change both line and arrow widths and the widths of the outlines of shape enhancements, such as rectangles and circles.

If you chose **Arrowheads**, select one of the following options: **S**witch (move the arrowhead to the other end of a line), **O**ne (add an arrowhead at the end of a line), **T**wo (add arrowheads at both ends of a line), or **N**one (remove the arrowheads from a line). Then select the lines or arrows that you want to change.

If you chose **S**moothing, select one of the following smoothing styles:

Menu Item	Description
None	Removes smoothing (changes a circle into a square, for example).
Tight	Smooths the edges of an outline, but doesn't change the shape (rounds the edges of a square, but doesn't change it into a circle, for example).
Medium	Completely rounds the edges of an outline, changing lines into curves (changes a square into a circle, for example).

Then select the shapes that you want to smooth.

Important Cues

- You can select a single object in the editing window by moving the cursor to the object and clicking the mouse. You can select several objects in the editing window by holding the left mouse button down and dragging the mouse over all the objects you want to select. However, you cannot select several objects with **:Graph Edit Edit Text**.
- If you have previously selected an object in the graphics editing window with **:Graph Edit Select**, you do not need to reselect the object in step 3.
- Instead of using **:Graph Edit Edit Text** to edit a text enhancement in the graphics editing window, you can also move the cursor to the text and press F2.

Graph Edit Color :GEC

Purpose

Changes the color of graphics and enhancements within the graphics editing window.

Reminder

Even though 1-2-3 uses the colors you choose with **:Graph Edit Color** for both the display and printed output, not all printers can print in color. Check your printer specifications before you use **:Graph Edit Color** if your goal is to print graphics in color.

:Graph Commands

Procedures

1. Type **:gec** and specify the graphic you want to edit.
2. Choose one of the following:

Menu Item	Description
Lines	Changes the color of a line, an arrow, or an outline.
Inside	Changes the inside color of an object.
Text	Changes the color of text enhancements.
Map	Changes the color palette for the specified graphic.
Background	Changes the background color of the range that contains the graphic.
Quit	Returns to the **:Graph Edit** menu.

3. If you chose **Lines**, select the graphic or enhancements that you want to change and then choose one of the following colors: **B**lack, **W**hite, **R**ed, **G**reen, **D**ark-Blue, **C**yan, **Y**ellow, **M**agenta, or **H**idden.

   If you chose **Inside**, select the graphic or enhancements that you want to change. Then, choose an inside color from the color palette that 1-2-3 displays.

   If you chose **Text**, select the text enhancements that you want to change and then choose one of the following colors: **B**lack, **W**hite, **R**ed, **G**reen, **D**ark-Blue, **C**yan, **Y**ellow, **M**agenta, or **H**idden.

   If you chose **Map**, select one of the sixteen colors you want to change on the color palette (**1–9, A–G**) or select **Q**uit to return to the **:Graph Edit** menu. If you choose a color to change, 1-2-3 displays the color palette for the selected graphic and outlines the current color for the number or letter that you specified. Select a new color from the palette, or press Esc to return to the **:Graph Edit Color Map** menu without changing the current selection.

   If you chose **B**ackground, choose a background color from the palette that 1-2-3 displays.

Important Cue

If you have previously selected an object in the graphics editing window with **:Graph Edit Select**, you do not need to reselect the object in step 3.

Graph Edit Transform :GET

Purpose

Changes the size and shape of graphics and enhancements within the graphics editing window.

Reminder

Some printers can only rotate text in 90-degree increments. Check your printer specifications before you use **:Graph Edit Transform** to rotate text in graphics to make sure that printed copies match the display.

Procedures

1. Type **:get** and specify the graphic you want to edit.
2. Choose one of the following:

Menu Item	Description
Size	Resizes graphics or enhancements.
Rotate	Rotates graphics or enhancements.
Quarter-Turn	Rotates graphics or enhancements in 90-degree increments.
X-Flip	Flips graphics or enhancements vertically.
Y-Flip	Flips graphics or enhancements horizontally.
Horizontal	Slants graphics or enhancements horizontally.
Vertical	Slants graphics or enhancements vertically.
Clear	Cancels all **:Graph Edit Transform** changes on the selected objects.

3. Select the object (or objects) you want to transform.

   If you chose **Size**, **Rotate**, **Horizontal**, or **Vertical**, use the cursor-movement keys or the mouse to adjust the graphics or enhancements. Press Enter to finish the transformation.

Important Cue

If you have previously selected an object in the graphics editing window with **:Graph Edit Select**, you do not need to reselect the object in step 3.

Graph Edit Rearrange :GER

Purpose

Rearranges graphics and enhancements within the graphics editing window.

Reminder

Use **:Graph Edit Rearrange** to copy and delete graphics and enhancements in the editing window, to move graphics and enhancements to the front or back of other objects, and to save graphics and enhancements from changes.

Procedures

1. Type **:ger** and specify the graphic you want to edit.

2. Choose one of the following:

Menu Item	Description
Delete	Removes objects from the editing window.
Restore	Retrieves the last object deleted from the editing window.
Move	Moves objects within the editing window.
Copy	Copies objects within the editing window.
Lock	Protects an object from changes within the editing window.
Unlock	Enables changes to an object within the editing window.
Front	Moves an object in front of others in the editing window.
Back	Moves an object in back of others in the editing window.

3. Select the object (or objects) you want to rearrange in the editing window.

   If you chose **Move** in step 2, use the mouse or the arrow keys to move the object. Press Enter to finish the move.

Important Cues

- If you have previously selected an object in the graphics editing window with **:Graph Edit Select**, you do not need to reselect the object in step 3.
- You can delete a previously selected object in the graphics editing window by pressing Del.
- You can copy a previously selected object in the graphics editing window by pressing Ins.

Caution

:Graph Edit Rearrange Restore can only restore the most recently deleted object in the graphics editing window. If you have used **:Graph Edit Rearrange Delete** or the Del key more than once in an editing session, only the last object you deleted can be restored.

Graph Edit View :GEV

Purpose

Sets the size of areas in the graphics editing window.

Reminder

:Graph Edit View does not change the size or placement of graphics in the worksheet—only the size of areas in the graphics editing window.

Procedures

1. Type **:gev** and specify the graphic you want to edit.
2. Choose one of the following:

Menu Item	Description
Full	Displays the graphics in the editing window at their normal size.
In	Makes an area of the editing window full screen.
Pan	Allows you to use + (plus), – (minus), and the other cursor-movement keys so that you can enlarge, reduce, or move graphics in the editing window.
+	Enlarges the size of the contents of the editing window (use up to a maximum of five times).
–	Reduces the size of the contents of the editing window (use up to a maximum of five times).
Up	Moves the contents of the editing window up one half-screen in the editing window.
Down	Moves the contents of the editing window down one half-screen in the editing window.
Left	Moves the contents of the editing window left one half-screen in the editing window.
Right	Moves the contents of the editing window right one half-screen in the editing window.

3. If you chose **In**, use the arrow keys or the mouse to specify the first corner of the area you want to enlarge. Anchor the corner by pressing the space bar or by holding down the left button on the mouse. Then drag the mouse or use the arrow keys to specify the diagonally-opposite corner of the area. Press Enter or release the mouse button to complete the command.

   If you chose **Pan**, use the +, –, and cursor-movement keys to move and size the graphics in the editing window.

Important Cues

- You can use the + (plus) and – (minus) keys to enlarge and reduce the contents of the graphics editing window instead of using **:Graph Edit View +** and **:Graph Edit View –**.
- You can use the up- and down-arrow keys to move the contents of the graphics editing window instead of using **:Graph Edit View Up** and **:Graph Edit View Down**.

:Graph Commands

Graph Edit Options :GEO

Purpose

Sets options for the graphics editing window, such as grid lines, the size of the cursor, and the text size in the graphic.

Reminder

Use **:Graph Edit Options Grid** when you want to see which parts of a graphic are located in the cells in the range that contains the graphic. The grid lines 1-2-3 displays in the graphics editing window are temporary and are not displayed when you return to the worksheet.

Procedures

1. Type **:geo** and specify the graphic you want to edit.
2. Choose one of the following:

Menu Item	Description
Grid	Adds or clears grid lines in the graphics editing window.
Cursor	Specifies the size of the cursor in the graphics editing window.
Font-Magnification	Specifies the text size for graphics in the graphics editing window.

3. If you chose **Grid**, select **No** to hide the grid lines or select **Yes** to display grid lines that correspond to the cells in the range that contains the graphic.

   If you chose **Cursor**, select **Small** to display the default editing cursor (a small cross); select **Big** to display the cursor as a large cross that fills the graphics editing window.

   If you chose **Font-Magnification**, specify the number (between 1 and 1000, inclusive) that corresponds to the percentage by which you want to enlarge (or reduce) the size of text you add to the graphic with other **:Graph Edit** commands. Specify **0** if you want to display the text as it is displayed in the graphic in the worksheet.

Important Cues

- When you are in the graphics editing window, you can also set and remove grid lines by pressing F4.
- When you return to the worksheet, 1-2-3 automatically scales the text in a graphic so that it corresponds to the size of the graphic as it fits in the specified range.

Graph Edit Quit :GEQ

Purpose
Leaves the graphics editing window and returns 1-2-3 to READY mode.

Reminder
You can also use Ctrl-Break to leave the graphics editing window and return to READY mode.

Procedure
Type **:geq**.

Important Cue
Any changes you made to a graphic with **:Graph Edit** are saved in the graph in memory when you leave the graphics editing window. However, you must use **/File Save** to save the editing changes for the worksheet.

Graph Quit :GQ

Purpose
Returns the worksheet to READY mode.

Procedure
Type **:gq**.

:Print Commands :P

:Print commands enable you to include Wysiwyg format settings in printed copies of your worksheets. You can print to either a printer or an encoded file.

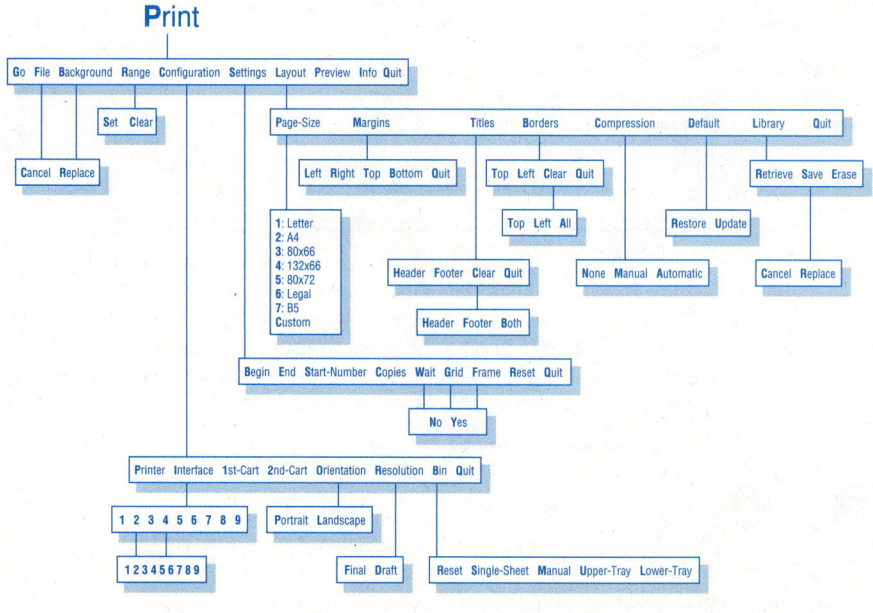

Print Go :PG

Purpose

Prints the specified range to the current printer.

Reminders

- Before you print in 1-2-3, you must first specify the ranges and special print settings you want to use. See **:Print Range** for information on specifying the print range; see **:Print Layout** and **:Print Settings** for information on print settings.
- Before you select **:Print Go**, make sure that the printer you want to use is currently selected and is on-line. Otherwise, 1-2-3 will not be able to complete the print job. Select **:Print Configuration Printer** to select the current printer.

Procedure

Type **:pg**

Important Cues

- Use **/Print Cancel** to stop printing all 1-2-3 print jobs. To temporarily halt a print job (so that you can change the paper or fix a paper jam, for example), select **/Print Suspend**. When you are ready to continue printing, select **/Print Resume**.
- Use **:Print Go** when you want to print ranges that include Wysiwyg format settings. If you just want to print a quick, unformatted range, you can also use **/Print [Printer, File, Encoded] Go**. (You must set a range through the /Print menu, however.) Remember that **/Print Go** will not print any Wysiwyg formats.

Print File :PF

Purpose

Prints the specified range to an encoded file on disk.

Reminder

- Before you print in 1-2-3, you must first specify the ranges and special print settings you want to use. See **:Print Range** for information on specifying the print range; see **:Print Layout** and **:Print Settings** for information on print settings.

:Print Commands

◆ Before you select **:Print File**, make sure that the printer you want to eventually use to print the file to is currently selected. Otherwise, the print settings 1-2-3 uses in the file may not be compatible with the printer. Select **:Print Configuration Printer** to select the current printer.

Procedures

1. Type **:pf**.
2. Specify the name for the file to which you want to print.
3. If you specify a file that already exists, select **Cancel** to return to READY mode without printing or select **Replace** to overwrite the existing file with a file that contains the new output.

Important Cues

◆ 1-2-3 automatically adds the extension ENC to the file you print. If you want a different extension, include it when you specify the file name in step 2.

◆ Use **:Print File** when you want to print ranges that include Wysiwyg format settings. If you just want to print a quick, unformatted range, you can also use **/Print File** or **/Print Encoded**. Remember, though, that **/Print File** and **/Print Encoded** will not print any Wysiwyg formats.

◆ The file 1-2-3 creates with **:Print File** is not an ASCII text file. Instead, it contains print codes specific to the printer so that 1-2-3 can include formatting information in the file. If you want to print an ASCII text file, select **/Print File**.

Caution

Don't name print files with names that might be confused with other files you use because you are taking the chance of overwriting a file you may need. For example, don't name a print file with a name that begins with the characters 123 because it may coincide with a file that 1-2-3 uses.

Print Range   :PR

Purpose

Specifies the ranges you want to print or clears all ranges from the print settings. 1-2-3 includes the format settings in the ranges you select when you print them.

Reminder

You must select **:P**rint **R**ange and specify ranges to print before you can select either **:P**rint **G**o or **:P**rint **F**ile. This is true even if you have selected ranges with the **/P**rint **R**ange command.

Procedures

1. Type **:pr**.
2. Select **S**et to specify ranges in the worksheet that you want to print; select **C**lear to cancel the ranges currently specified.
3. If you chose **S**et, specify the range or ranges you want to print. To specify a single range, enter the range address or range name or use the arrow keys to highlight the range or range name. To specify multiple ranges, type or highlight the first address, type a comma or semicolon, and then type or highlight the next range. Continue to enter ranges, separating each range with a comma or semicolon.

Important Cues

- If you include a hidden column in the print range, 1-2-3 will ignore that column when it prints.
- 1-2-3 displays the print range with dashed lines when you are in graphics mode.

Print Configuration :PC

Purpose

Sets options for the printer you want to use.

Reminders

- Before you use **:P**rint **C**onfiguration, make sure you have correctly installed the printers you have available through the 1-2-3 Install program.
- Use **:P**rint **C**onfiguration to set the following printer options: the paper bin you want to use, the font cartridges you are using, the interface/port the printer is connected to, the printer you want to use, and the page orientation (landscape or portrait).
- Many configuration settings apply to selected printers only. If your printer does not use those settings, you can ignore those settings. For example, if you are using an Apple LaserWriter, you do not need to select **B**in, **1**st-**C**art, or **2**nd-**C**art because the printer does not make use of these features.

Procedures

1. Type **:pc**.
2. Choose one of the following:

Menu Item	Description
Printer	Specifies the printer you want to use (from the list of printers you selected during 1-2-3 Install).
Interface	Specifies the interface/port with which the printer is connected.
1st-Cart	Specifies the first font cartridge you are using in the printer.
2nd-Cart	Specifies the second font cartridge you are using in the printer.
Orientation	Specifies whether you want to print in portrait or landscape mode.
Resolution	Specifies the quality of the output, either draft or final.
Bin	Specifies the paper bin you want to use.
Quit	Returns to the :Print menu.

3. If you chose **Printer**, select from the displayed list of printers the number that corresponds to the printer you want to use. 1-2-3 displays only the names of the printers you selected during Install.

   If you chose **Interface**, select the correct interface or port from the menu. If you specify a serial port, select the appropriate baud rate for the printer.

   If you chose **1st-Cart** or **2nd-Cart**, select from the list of available cartridges the one that you want to use.

   If you chose **Orientation**, select **Portrait** if you want to print across the width of the paper; select **Landscape** if you want to print across the length of the paper.

   If you chose **Resolution**, select **Draft** to print more quickly but with less clarity; select **Final** to print less quickly but with better clarity.

   If you chose **Bin**, choose one of the following:

Menu Item	Description
Reset	Clears the bin setting.
Single-Sheet	Specifies single-sheet feed.
Manual	Specifies manual paper-feed.
Upper-Tray	Specifies the top bin on the printer.
Lower-Tray	Specifies the bottom bin on the printer.

Important Cues

◆ If you selected a printer and interface with **/Print Printer Options Advanced Device**, 1-2-3 will use that printer and interface as the default.

◆ If you are using a printer that does not use font cartridges, specifying **1st-Cart** or **2nd-Cart** has no effect.

- If you are using a printer that does not have multiple bins, specifying **B**in has no effect.

Cautions

- When you specify a printer and interface, 1-2-3 saves that information with the worksheet file. So, if you retrieve the file again to print, 1-2-3 defaults to the last printer and interface you specified with **:P**rint **C**onfiguration. If you copy the worksheet file to another computer, you should first use **/P**rint **P**rinter **C**lear **D**evice to clear the printer and interface information so that other potential users of the file do not become confused when they attempt to print.
- Do not select a font cartridge that you are not using in the printer because 1-2-3 may generate unexpected characters in the output.
- If you are using a printer that does not print in landscape mode, do not select **:P**rint **C**onfiguration **O**rientation **L**andscape. If you do, 1-2-3 displays an error message when you attempt to print.
- Do not select **:P**rint **C**onfiguration **B**in **S**ingle-Sheet if your printer does not have a single-sheet feed option because 1-2-3 sends a form feed after each page, and this may confuse the printer and the paper alignment.

Print Settings :PS

Purpose

Specifies the settings for the printed output. You use **:P**rint **S**ettings to specify the following: the page number of the first and last pages you want to print, the number of copies you want to print, the page number for the first page of the print job, whether the printer should pause after each page, and whether you want to print the worksheet frame and the worksheet grid.

Reminder

The print settings you specify with **:P**rint **S**ettings are not applicable to print jobs you create with **/P**rint.

Procedures

1. Type **:ps**.
2. Choose one of the following:

Menu Item	Description
Begin	Specifies the first page to print in the print job (from 1 to 9999, inclusive).
Copies	Specifies the number of copies to print (from 1 to 99, inclusive).

:Print Commands **857**

Menu Item	Description
End	Specifies the last page to print in the print job (from 1 to 9999, inclusive).
Frame	Specifies whether to print the worksheet frame.
Grid	Specifies whether to print the worksheet grid.
Reset	Resets all print settings to the default settings.
Start-Number	Specifies the page number for the first page you print (from 1 to 9999, inclusive).
Wait	Pauses the printer after printing each page.
Quit	Returns to the :Print menu.

3. If you chose **Begin**, **Copies**, **End**, or **Start-Number**, specify the number.

   If you chose **Frame** or **Grid**, select **No** if you do not want to print the worksheet frame or worksheet grid, respectively. Select **Yes** if you want to print the worksheet frame or worksheet grid.

   If you chose **Wait**, select **No** if you do not want 1-2-3 to pause after it prints each page. Select **Yes** if you want 1-2-3 to pause after it prints each page. (If you select **Yes**, 1-2-3 prompts you after each page; you must select /**P**rint **R**esume to continue printing the next page.)

Important Cues

- After you set the print settings, use :**P**rint **P**review to view the output on the screen before you print to a printer. It is far less time-consuming to make preliminary changes based on the previewed pages than to wait for printed output after each tweak to the settings.

- Make sure you keep page numbering consistent when you select **Begin**, **End**, and **Start-Number** pages to print. 1-2-3 uses the **Start-Number** as the first number for the print job. So, if you select a **Start-Number** of 20 and a **Begin** number of 19, for example, 1-2-3 will not print any pages.

- Use :**P**rint **L**ayout **T**itles to tell 1-2-3 to include a page number on pages of the printed output. :**P**rint **S**ettings **B**egin, **E**nd, and **S**tart-Number all tell 1-2-3 about which pages to print, but do not print page numbers themselves.

Caution

With the exception of the frame and grid settings, none of the settings you specify with :**P**rint **S**ettings are saved with the file. You need to respecify the settings each time you begin a new 1-2-3 session, each time you reload Wysiwyg into memory, and each time you select /**W**orksheet **E**rase or /**F**ile **R**etrieve.

Print Layout Page-Size :PLP

Purpose

Sets the size of the paper you are using to print.

Reminder

The default page size 1-2-3 assumes when you print is 8 1/2 inches by 11 inches.

Procedures

1. Type **:plp**.
2. Choose one of the following:

Menu Item	Description
1:Letter	Standard 8 1/2-by-11-inch pages.
2:A4	210 mm × 297 mm pages.
3:80x66	8 1/2-by-11-inch fanfold pages.
4:132x66	14-by-11-inch fanfold pages.
5:80x72	8 1/2-by-12-inch fanfold pages.
6:Legal	Standard 8 1/2-by-14-inch pages.
7:B5	176 mm × 250 mm pages.
Custom	Specifies a custom length and width.

3. If you chose **Custom**, specify a page length and width. You can specify the size to be in inches, millimeters, or centimeters by typing **in**, **mm**, or **cm** after the length or width value.

Important Cue

Because 1-2-3 automatically formats print ranges so that they fit properly on each page, it is important that you specify the correct page size.

Print Layout Margins :PLM

Purpose

Sets new margin settings for printed output.

Reminder

The default page margins are .5 inches for the top, left, and right sides, and .55 inches for the bottom.

Procedures

1. Type **:plm**.
2. Select **Top**, **Left**, **Right**, **Bottom**, or **Quit**.

3. If you chose **Top**, **Left**, **Right**, or **Bottom**, specify the number that corresponds to the new margin setting.

Important Cue

You can specify a margin size in a measurement different from the default by including a code with the new setting. If you want to specify a margin in inches, type **in** after the number; if you want to specify a margin in centimeters, type **cm** after the number; if you want to specify a margin in millimeters, type **mm** after the number. For example, to specify a right margin of 3 centimeters, select **:plmr** and type **3cm**.

Caution

You cannot set left and right margins that together are larger than the size of the page. The same is true of the top and bottom margins. For example, if you are using a page that is 8 1/2 inches wide, you cannot set a left margin of 4 inches and a right margin of 5 inches because the total margin size would be 9 inches, 1/2 inch larger than the paper is wide.

Print Layout Titles :PLT

Purpose

Sets the headers and footers you want to include on each page.

Reminder

Headers and footers are the lines you want to print at the top and bottom of each page. For example, if you wanted to include the date at the top of each page and the page number at the bottom of each page, you would specify a header that included the date and a footer that included the page number.

Procedures

1. Type **:plt**.
2. Choose one of the following:

Menu Item	Description
Header	Specifies the text you want to print at the top of each page.
Footer	Specifies the text you want to print at the bottom of each page.
Clear	Removes the header and footer text.
Quit	Returns you to the **:Print Layout** menu.

3. If you chose **Header** or **Footer**, specify the text you want to print. You can enter any text you want (up to a maximum of 512 characters), or one of the following special characters:

@ Prints the current date (formatted in the global international default date format).

\# Prints the page number.

| Specifies the location in the header or footer for text. 1-2-3 left-aligns header and footer text unless you specify otherwise. To center text, type | and then the text you want to center; to right-align text, type another | and then the text you want to right-align. For example, the header @|Sales|# would print a header that has the date left-aligned, the centered title Sales, and the page number right-aligned.

\ Specifies that you want to use the contents of a cell as the header or footer. To use a cell's contents in a header or footer, type \ followed by the cell address. For example, the footer \D2 would print the contents of cell D2 at the bottom of each page.

If you chose Clear, select **H**eader to clear the header text, select **F**ooter to clear the footer text, or select **B**oth to clear both the header and footer text.

Important Cues

- 1-2-3 prints the header on the line immediately below the top margin and prints two blank lines between the header and the first line of text; it prints the footer on the line immediately above the bottom margin and prints two blank lines between the last line of text on the page and the footer.

- You can format text in the header and footer by using the formatting sequences. See Chapter 2 for information on the Wysiwyg formatting sequences.

Caution

Although a header or footer can be up to 512 characters long, 1-2-3 only prints as much of the header or footer as it can fit on a single line across the page. If there is not enough room to print the entire line, 1-2-3 truncates the text.

Print Layout Borders :PLB

Purpose

Specifies the column and row borders you want to print at the left and top of each page and print range.

Reminder

Before you select **:Print Layout Borders**, move the cell pointer to the first cell in the range that you want to use as a border.

Procedures

1. Type **:plb**.

2. Choose one of the following:

Menu Item	Description
Left	Specifies the columns you want to print at the left side of each page and to the left of every print range.
Top	Specifies the rows you want to print at the top of each page and at the top of every print range.
Clear	Clears one or more borders.
Quit	Returns to the :Print Layout menu.

3. If you chose Left or Top, specify the range that contains the columns or rows you want to use as borders. You only need to include a single cell from each column you want to use as a left border and from each row you want to use a top border.

If you chose Clear, select Top to clear only the top border rows, select Left to clear only the left border columns, or select All to clear both the top and left borders.

Important Cue

Don't include the columns and rows you specified as borders when you specify a print range unless you want those columns and rows repeated in the output.

Print Layout Compression :PLC

Purpose

Shrinks or enlarges the font used for the print range.

Reminder

Use :Print Layout Compression when you want to try to print a large range on a single page.

Procedures

1. Type :plc.
2. Choose one of the following:

Menu Item	Description
None	Turns off compression.
Automatic	Tells 1-2-3 to attempt to shrink the print range so that it fits on a single page. 1-2-3 can shrink the print range up to a maximum of seven times smaller than normal.
Manual	Lets you specify the percentage you want to shrink or enlarge the font used to print the range (between 15 and 1000 percent).

3. If you chose Manual, specify the amount you want to change the font. For example, if you want to double the size of the print range, select 200 (for 200 percent of the original size).

Important Cue

Do not include any page breaks in the print range if you are using :Print Layout Compression to shrink the range to a single page. 1-2-3 starts a new page at each page break, even if you have compressed the print range.

Caution

Depending on the printer you use and the font sizes you installed, some compression settings may not look the way you intended because the printer cannot print the fonts that would equal the percentage you specified.

Print Layout Default :PLD

Purpose

Updates the default layout settings 1-2-3 uses to print output through Wysiwyg; replaces the current layout settings with the default settings.

Reminder

Before you select :Print Layout Default Update to save the new default layout library, be sure you have specified all the layout settings you want to include. Use the other :Print Layout commands to specify the settings.

Procedures

1. Type :pld.
2. Select Restore if you want to replace the current layout settings with the default settings; select Update if you want to save the current layout settings as the default settings (so that they are the initial layout settings you see each time you begin a new 1-2-3 session).

Important Cue

1-2-3 saves the default page-layout settings in the file layout CNF. When you select :Print Layout Default Update, 1-2-3 overwrites this file with a new file that contains the new settings.

Caution

Once you update the default page layout file, the original settings are gone. If, for some reason, you want to recreate the original default layout settings file, clear all layout settings, set the page size to 8 1/2-by-11 inches, set the left, right, and top margins to .5 inches, set the bottom margin to .55 inches, and set compression to None.

:Print Commands

Print Layout Library :PLL

Purpose

Retrieves, creates, and edits page-layout library files. A page-layout library file contains the layout settings you specify for any given print job. For example, if you print a report each week for which you specify layout settings, you can create a page-layout library file for that report. Then, each time you print the report, you can retrieve the library file instead of re-creating the settings.

Reminder

Before you select **:Print Layout Library** to save a layout library file, be sure you have specified all the layout settings you want to include in the library. Use the other **:Print Layout** commands to specify the settings.

Procedures

1. Type **:pll**.
2. Choose one of the following:

Menu Item	Description
Retrieve	Replaces the current layout settings with the settings from a layout library file on disk.
Save	Saves the current layout settings in a layout library file on disk.
Erase	Erases a layout library file from disk.

3. If you chose **Retrieve**, specify the name of the layout library file from which you want to retrieve layout settings.

   If you chose **Save**, specify the name you want to use for the layout library file. If a file with the specified name already exists, select **Cancel** to return to READY mode without saving the file or select **Replace** to save the file with the new layout settings.

   If you chose **Erase**, specify the name of the layout library file you want to delete from disk.

Important Cues

- When you save a layout library file, 1-2-3 automatically adds the extension AL3 to the file. If you want to use a different extension, include that extension in the file name. Remember, though, that 1-2-3 does not automatically display library files with extensions other than AL3 when you select **:Print Layout Library Retrieve** or **Erase**.

- Use names that you can easily identify with a set of layouts when you name a library file. For example, a name such as SALESRPT.AL3 makes more sense than the name LIBRARY1.AL3 for a set of layouts you want to use for a monthly sales report.

Caution

Once you erase a library file, it is gone for good. Be sure you no longer need a library file that you erase.

Print Layout Quit :PLQ

Purpose

Returns you to the **:Print** menu.

Reminder

Selecting **:Print Layout Quit** does not clear any of the layout settings you have specified.

Procedure

Type **:plq**.

Print Preview :PP

Purpose

Temporarily displays the specified print ranges as they appear when printed with **:Print Go** or **:Print File**.

Reminder

Before you print in 1-2-3, you must first specify the ranges and special print settings you want to use. See **:Print Range** for information on specifying the print range; see **:Print Layout** and **:Print Settings** for information on print settings.

Procedures

1. Type **:pp**.
2. 1-2-3 temporarily clears the screen and displays the first page of output on the screen. Type any key except Esc to display the next page, or press Esc to redisplay the worksheet and return to READY mode.

Important Cue

Depending on the size of the ranges you are previewing and the number of format settings in those ranges, 1-2-3 may take some time to prepare the preview.

Print Info :PI

Purpose

Displays or clears the Wysiwyg print settings screen that contains the current print settings.

Reminder

You cannot specify print settings directly from :Print Info; it is only for information.

Procedures

1. Type :pi.
2. 1-2-3 displays the print settings screen, or, if it is already displayed, removes the screen and redisplays the worksheet.

Important Cue

You can also view and remove the print settings screen by pressing F6 at any time while you are in the :Print menu.

Print Quit :PQ

Purpose

Returns the worksheet to READY mode.

Procedure

Type :pq.

Quit Command :Q

Purpose

Leaves the Wysiwyg menu and returns 1-2-3 to READY mode.

Reminder

Unlike the /Quit command, :Quit does not exit from 1-2-3.

Procedure

Type :q.

Important Cue

To use the Wysiwyg menu again, type : (colon) or reinvoke the Wysiwyg add-in.

Part V

Appendixes

Installing 1-2-3 Release 3.1+

Using the Auditor Add-In

Using the Solver and Backsolver Add-Ins

Using the Viewer Add-In

Compose Sequences for the Lotus Multibyte Character Set

Installing 1-2-3 Release 3.1+

The Install program for installing 1-2-3 Release 3.1+ makes installation very simple; after you start the program, follow the on-screen instructions. You must install Release 3.1+ on a hard disk; the Install program is designed for this type of installation. You cannot run Release 3.1+ from a floppy disk.

The Install program begins by creating several subdirectories on your hard disk and then copying the program files to the appropriate subdirectory. Install asks you to specify the type of video display and printer you use, so verify the brand and model of your printer before installing Release 3.1+ (the program can detect the type of video display). Finally, Install generates the font files you need to use the Wysiwyg add-in.

Installation takes about 20 minutes; another 10 to 20 minutes is necessary to generate the basic font set for Wysiwyg. When you are ready to begin, turn on your computer and follow the instructions in this appendix.

Checking DOS Configuration

Before you install 1-2-3 Release 3.1+ to run under DOS, you must complete a preliminary step: make sure that DOS is configured adequately to run 1-2-3. Check your CONFIG.SYS file for the FILES statement. CONFIG.SYS is found on your start-up hard disk in the root directory. Type **TYPE C:\CONFIG.SYS** and press Enter to see the contents of CONFIG.SYS (assuming that drive C is your start-up hard disk). The screen displays something like the following:

```
FILES=25
BUFFERS=20
DEVICE=C:\DOS\ANSI.SYS
```

The FILES statement tells DOS how many files can be open at once. The minimum number of files you need for 1-2-3 is 20 (FILES=20). If you don't have a FILES statement or if the number of files is less than 20, change the CONFIG.SYS file. You can edit CONFIG.SYS with any text editor (such as EDLIN) or with a word processing software that can save files as ASCII unformatted text.

After modifying the CONFIG.SYS file, restart your computer by pressing Ctrl-Alt-Del. (A change in CONFIG.SYS doesn't modify DOS until you reload DOS.) Be sure that your version of DOS is 3.0 or higher and that you have at least 1M of memory available for 1-2-3.

To use 1-2-3 Release 3.1+ with Windows 3.0, your system must have at least 4.25M of free Windows memory. To determine how much memory you have available, choose "Help" at the "Windows Program Manager" and then choose "About Program Manager." For more information about using 1-2-3 Release 3.1+ with Windows 3.0, refer to your Lotus documentation.

Starting the Install Program

To install 1-2-3, place the Install disk in drive A. Switch to drive A by typing **A:** and pressing Enter. At the DOS A> prompt, type **INSTALL** and press Enter. The first screen you see is 1-2-3's welcome screen. Read the information on-screen and then press Enter to continue the installation and register your disks.

Registering Your Original Disks

To make your disks usable, you must register them by entering and saving your name and company name on the Install disk. When you see the screen shown in figure A.1, type your name, press Enter, and type your company name. When everything is correct, press Ins to continue.

The Install program asks whether you want to record what you typed on the disk. Press **Y** and press Enter. The information you typed is recorded, and your copy of 1-2-3 is now registered. Your name, company name, and serial number appear every time you start 1-2-3.

Choosing Files To Copy

In the next step of the installation procedure, you can choose to copy the Translate files. Translate is a program that converts outside data files (such as those created by Symphony and dBASE) and data file formats (such as DCA and DIF) to 1-2-3 format and vice versa.

Translate is useful if you plan to transfer data between 1-2-3 and other programs. To copy the Translate files during the installation, press **Y** and then Enter.

Next, specify whether you want to install Wysiwyg fonts. As with the Translate procedure, press **Y** and then Enter when this screen appears.

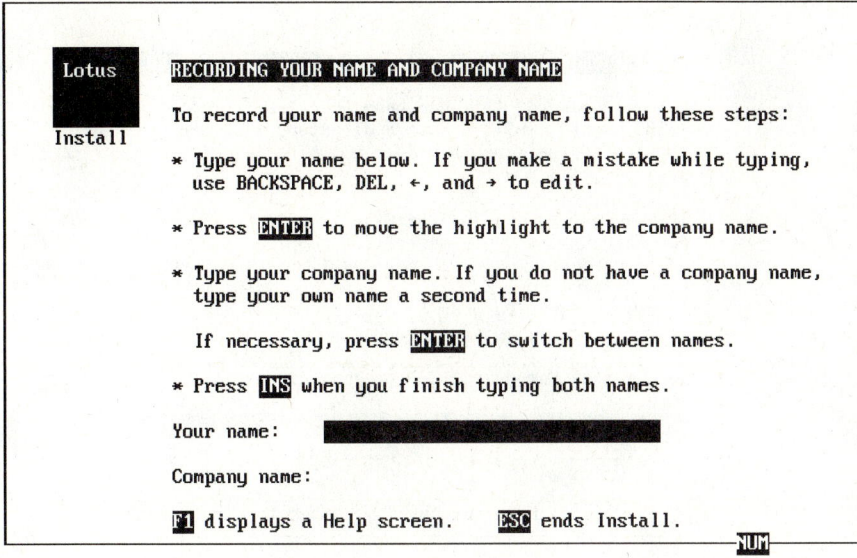

Fig. A.1.
Directions for registering Install disks.

Creating a Directory for the 1-2-3 Files

The next screen enables you to choose the hard disk on which to install 1-2-3. Most often, you install programs on drive C. To install 1-2-3 on drive C, press Enter. To install 1-2-3 on a different drive, type the letter of the drive (for example, **D**) and press Enter.

After you choose the drive, Install prompts you for the name of the directory where you want to copy the 1-2-3 files. The default directory name is \123R3 (see fig. A.2). You can type another name if you prefer. Press Enter to continue.

Copying Files

After you name the drive and directory, Install begins copying files to the hard disk, beginning with disk 1. After copying the files from disk 1, Install prompts you to insert the next disk. (Follow the screen prompts to insert the correct disk.) 1-2-3 copies the necessary files from the disks and prompts you to insert other disks as necessary.

Configuring 1-2-3 for Your Computer

After the program copies the system files, the second part of the installation begins. The first screen provides information about making selections in this part of the installation. Press Enter to continue to the Main menu (see fig. A.3).

Fig. A.2.
Specifying the directory in which to install 1-2-3.

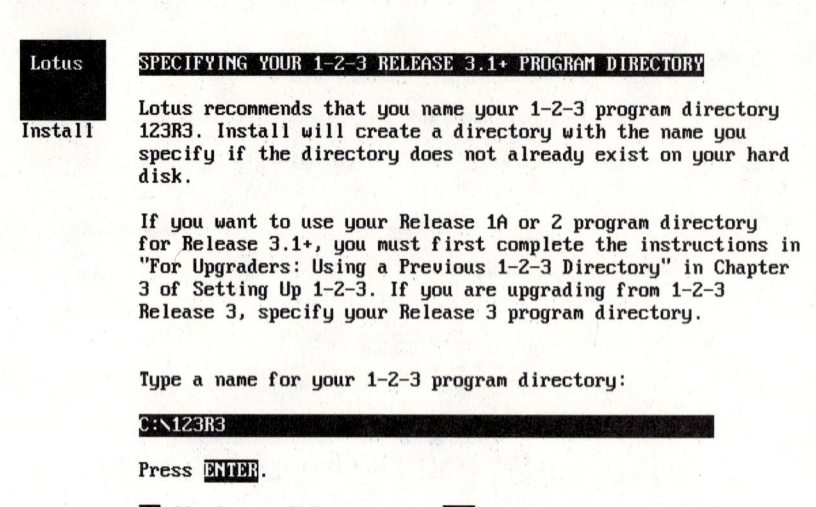

On the Main menu, the `First-Time Installation` option is highlighted. To make a different selection, press the up-arrow or down-arrow key to highlight the desired selection and then press Enter. Because you are installing 1-2-3 for the first time, highlight `First-Time Installation` and press Enter.

Fig. A.3.
The Main menu of the Install program.

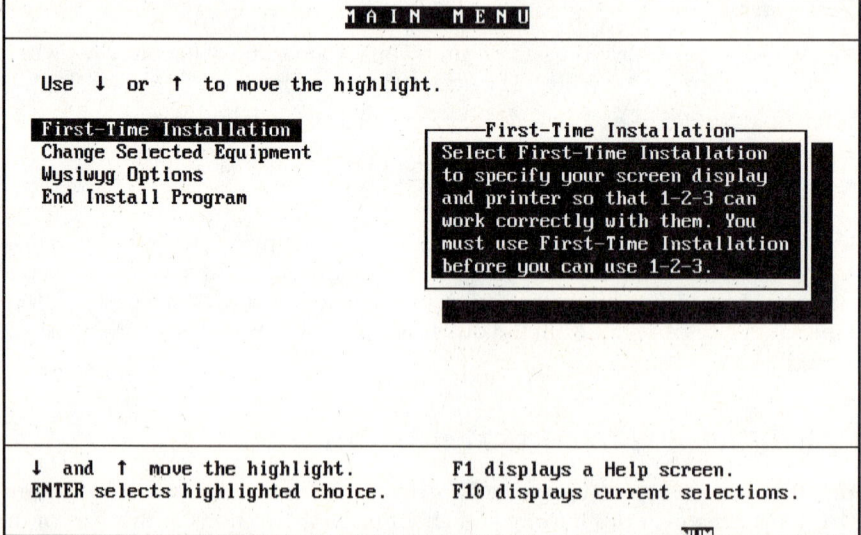

Install lists the type of video display detected in your computer system. Make a note of this information and press Enter. When the Screen Selection menu appears, highlight the correct display for your system and press Enter (see fig. A.4).

Often a video display can show information on-screen in multiple ways. After you specify the type of display you use, the program lists the available modes for that display. If your video display offers more than one mode, choose the one that best suits your needs. (After installing 1-2-3, you can change this selection.)

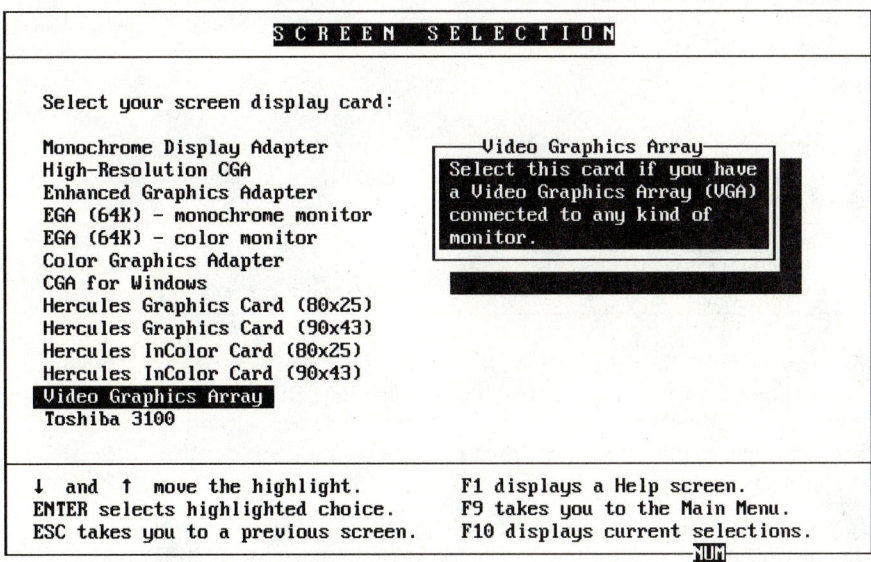

Fig. A.4.
The Screen Selection menu.

If your video display doesn't offer different modes for showing information on-screen, the Install program records the display you chose and moves on to installing a printer.

You may have more than one video display card in your computer, or you may want to install more than one video mode. 1-2-3 enables you to install a primary display and a secondary display. As you use 1-2-3, you can issue the /Worksheet Window Display command and instruct 1-2-3 to activate the primary or secondary display driver.

Install asks whether you want to use a printer with 1-2-3. If you don't have a printer or don't want to install a printer now, select **N**o and press Enter to continue. Otherwise, press Enter to select **Y**es.

Selecting **Y**es displays the Printer Selection menu (see fig. A.5). Highlight the brand of printer you use and press Enter. In figure A.5, HP (Hewlett-Packard) is specified as the brand of printer to install.

After you specify the brand of printer, specify the model by highlighting the correct model and pressing Enter. Depending on the specified equipment (such as whether your printer uses a font cartridge), 1-2-3 may prompt you with additional screens. Highlight the appropriate selection and press Enter to continue.

Fig. A.5.
The Printer Selection menu.

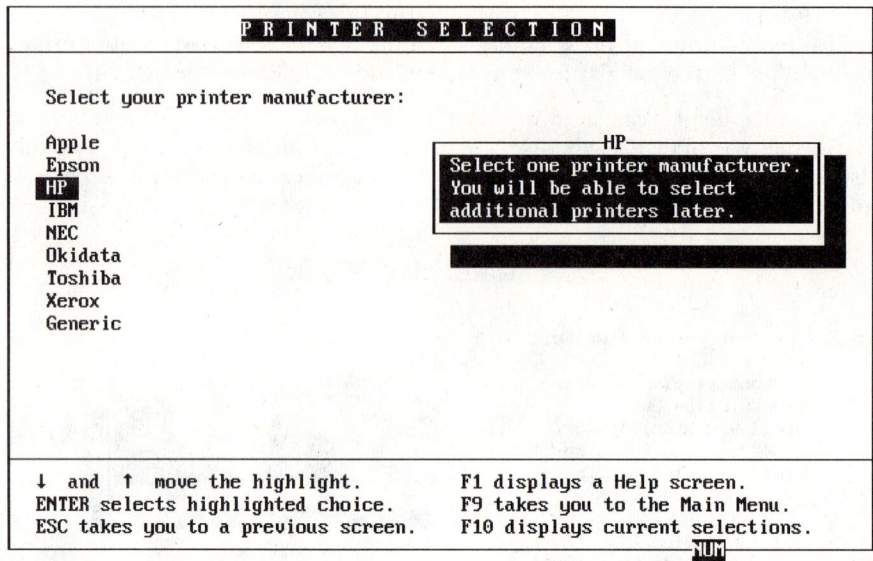

After you specify the printer, Install asks whether you want to specify another printer. Answering Yes returns Install to the Printer Selection menu; to install the additional printer, follow the same procedure. If you have only one printer or if you don't want to install another printer now, press Enter to select No (the default answer).

After you make your video and printer selections, the program prompts you to name your driver configuration file (DCF). The DCF contains all the information from your responses to questions about your display type and printer. If you select No at the prompt, Install names the file 123.DCF. If you prefer, answer Yes and give the file a different name.

If you give the DCF a name other than 123.DCF, you must supply the DCF's name when you start 1-2-3. If you create a DCF called 60LINE.DCF, for example, you must type **123 60LINE** and press Enter to start 1-2-3. If you use the default name, you don't have to specify the DCF name when you start 1-2-3.

For first-time installation, choose No and press Enter to accept the default name. The benefits of having multiple DCF files on your disk (with different names) are explained in the "Changing 1-2-3's Configuration" section of this appendix.

The Install program copies files to the hard disk to complete the installation. The specific files copied depends on your selection of video display and printer.

Install prompts you to insert disks based on your 1-2-3 configuration. When all files are copied to the hard disk with no errors, a screen appears stating that the installation was successful. Press Enter to continue to the font generation screen.

Note: The screens for generating fonts don't appear if you opted not to install the Wysiwyg fonts.

Press Enter at the font generation screen to continue the installation process. The Generating Fonts menu appears. From this menu, you can choose between Basic, Medium, and Extended font sets. Each successive font set provides a broader range of fonts and font sizes to use with Wysiwyg, but also takes a longer time to install. Choose one of the font sets and press Enter. Then select Yes to begin generating fonts now, or No to generate fonts at another time.

The installation process generates the fonts needed to work with your printer and with your type of display. The font names and point sizes are shown on-screen as each is generated. When the fonts are generated, the Install program prompts you to press any key to return to the DOS prompt.

Installing the Release 3.1+ Add-Ins

1-2-3 Release 3.1+ includes four new add-ins—Auditor, Backsolver, Solver, and Viewer—that you install after the 1-2-3 program. In the following sections, you learn how to install these add-ins, whether you install the entire 1-2-3 Release 3.1+ program or upgrade from 1-2-3 Release 3.1.

Understanding the System Requirements

Before you can install the Release 3.1+ add-ins, you must have installed Release 3.1 or 3.1+ (as covered earlier in this appendix). You don't have to install all four add-ins, but you must install an add-in before you can use it with 1-2-3. You must have sufficient space available on your hard disk for each add-in you install, and each add-in requires available system memory in addition to that required by 1-2-3. The following table shows the approximate disk and memory space required to install each of the Release 3.1+ add-ins (requirements for the specific equipment you use may vary):

Add-In	Disk Space Required	Approximate Memory Required
Auditor	41K	45K
Backsolver	26K	45K
Solver	666K	650K
Viewer	213K	66K

Checking Available Memory

To determine if sufficient system memory is available before attempting to use the Release 3.1+ add-ins, use the /Worksheet Status command in 1-2-3. If necessary, you can remove the Wysiwyg add-in to free approximately 181K of system memory by pressing Alt-F10 (Add-in), selecting **R**emove, and selecting WYSIWYG. Select **Q**uit and press Enter to return to READY mode.

Installing the Add-Ins

To begin the installation, place the Enhancement Add-Ins Disk (or Enhancement Add-Ins Disk 1, if you are installing with 3 1/2-inch disks) in drive A or B, type **A:** (or **B:**), and press Enter to make the drive current. Then start the add-ins installation program by typing **AINSTALL** and pressing Enter.

Press Enter to continue to the next screen. As mentioned previously, considerable disk space is required to install all four add-ins. If your hard disk has sufficient space, install all the add-ins—you later can free the space occupied by an add-in (if necessary) by deleting it. Remember that you must install an add-in before you can use the add-in.

Figure A.6 shows the second AINSTALL screen. Each add-in is listed with the approximate amount of disk space required. Add-ins marked Y will be installed; those marked with N will not be installed. Use the up-arrow and down-arrow keys to move the highlight, and press **N** for each add-in you don't want to install. After making your selections, press Enter to continue.

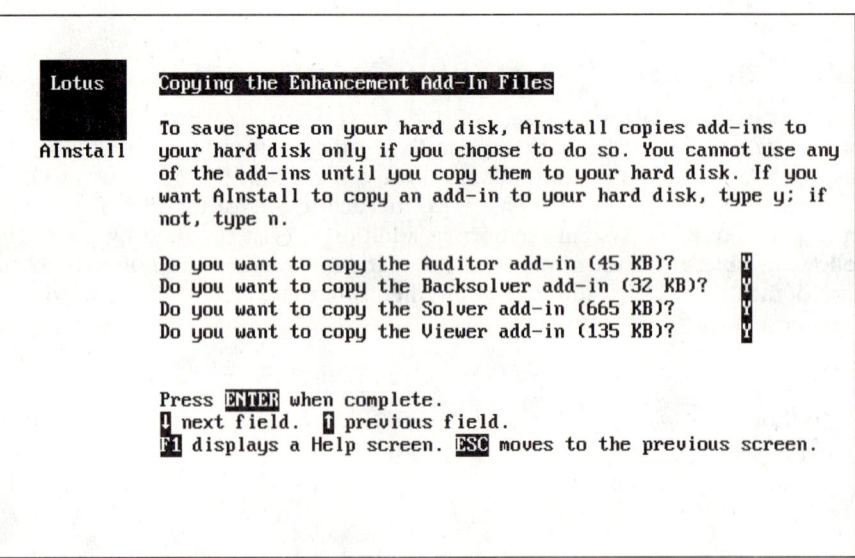

Fig. A.6.
Selecting add-ins for installation.

You must specify the letter assigned to your hard disk. Normally the default C is correct; if you installed 1-2-3 Release 3.1 or 3.1+ on another drive, however, type the appropriate drive letter and press Enter.

After you specify the drive containing the 1-2-3 program files, the installation program searches for the appropriate directory. The Release 3.1+ add-ins usually are stored in a subdirectory called ADDINS, located in the 1-2-3 program files directory. If the 1-2-3 Release 3.1+ program directory is not found, the installation program offers to create a subdirectory called ADDINS in the root directory of the specified disk.

Appendix A ◆ Installing 1-2-3 Release 3.1+   **877**

You can edit the directory name suggested for the add-ins. To change the directory shown, type your changes in the box and press Enter.

The Install program now installs each of the selected Release 3.1+ add-ins in the designated directory, prompting you to change disks if you are installing with 3 1/2-inch disks. When the installation is complete, a screen appears, indicating that your installation was successful. The Release 3.1+ add-ins are ready to use. The following appendixes provide information on using each of these add-ins.

If the installation was unsuccessful due to insufficient disk space, clear some space by removing from the disk any files you no longer need. When you have enough space for the add-ins, run the AINSTALL program again.

Changing 1-2-3's Equipment Configuration

In some cases, you may want to change 1-2-3's configuration. If you purchase a new printer or a new video display, for example, you must reconfigure 1-2-3 for that printer or video display. Also, if you want to create additional DCFs, you must start the Install program again.

After installing 1-2-3 on your hard disk, you can start and run the Install program easily. Begin by making the directory containing 1-2-3 the current directory; for example, if the directory is C:\123R3, type **CD\123R3** at the operating system prompt and press Enter.

Type **INSTALL** and press Enter. Press Enter at the welcome screen to continue to the Main menu. From the Main menu, choose Change Selected Equipment. The Change Selected Equipment menu appears. The menu selections have the following actions:

Selection	Action
Return to Main Menu	Returns to the Main menu
Modify Current DCF	Enables you to change the configuration of the current DCF (normally 123.DCF)
Choose Another DCF to Modify	Enables you to choose a different DCF to place in memory for changing
Save Changes	Saves any modifications in the current DCF to disk
End Install Program	Exits the Install program

Changing the Selected Display or Printer

If you purchase a new printer or video display, modify the current DCF by selecting Modify Current DCF. The Modify Current DCF menu appears. You can change the selected display, printer, or country with this menu. Press F10 to display a screen showing the current configuration.

The selections for display and printer are similar to those available when you installed 1-2-3. To change the video display mode, for example, select `Change Selected Display`. In figure A.7, notice that the `Video Graphics Array` selection on the Display screen shows 1 to indicate that this item is currently selected. With `Video Graphics Array` highlighted, press Enter. The `80x25 color` mode selection also has 1 in front of it (see fig. A.8).

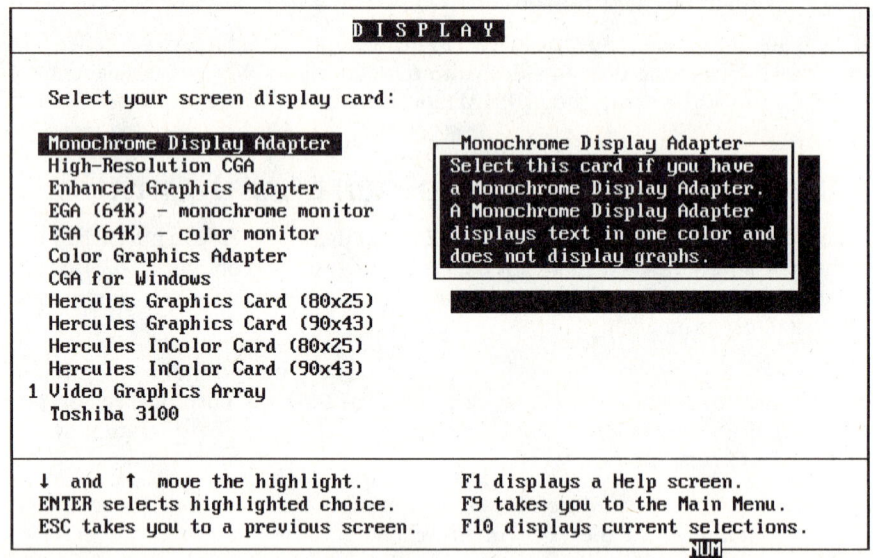

Fig. A.7.
The screen showing the currently selected display.

To select a new mode—for example, 80x34 color (80 characters per line, 34 lines, in color)—deselect `80x25 color`. Highlight `80x25 color` (or your display's mode) and press the space bar. Notice that the 1 disappears. Use the down-arrow key to highlight `80x34 color` and press the space bar. The 1 appears in front of `80x34 color`. (If you don't deselect `80x25 color`, the 1 continues to appear next to that option, and `80x34 color` shows 2. If you include two display modes, you can use **/W**orksheet **W**indow **D**isplay to select the primary or secondary color.) Press Enter to return to the Modify Current DCF menu.

From the Modify Current DCF menu, select `Return to Menu`; this option returns Install to the Change Selected Equipment menu. Select `Save Changes`. Install prompts you to name the DCF. Because the current file (123.DCF) contains the video mode selection for 80 characters per line and 25 lines, and you selected a display mode with 80 characters per line and 34 lines, you may want to change the name of the DCF. Assigning a new name enables you to start 1-2-3 in either video mode. Using the Backspace key, delete 123. Type **34LINE** (as shown in figure A.9) and press Enter. The file 34LINE.DCF is created in the \123R3 directory.

As you save the DCF, be prepared to insert any disks that the Install program needs. Depending on the changes you made in the configuration, the Install program may need to read files from the disks. When a screen appears stating that the installation was completed successfully, press Enter.

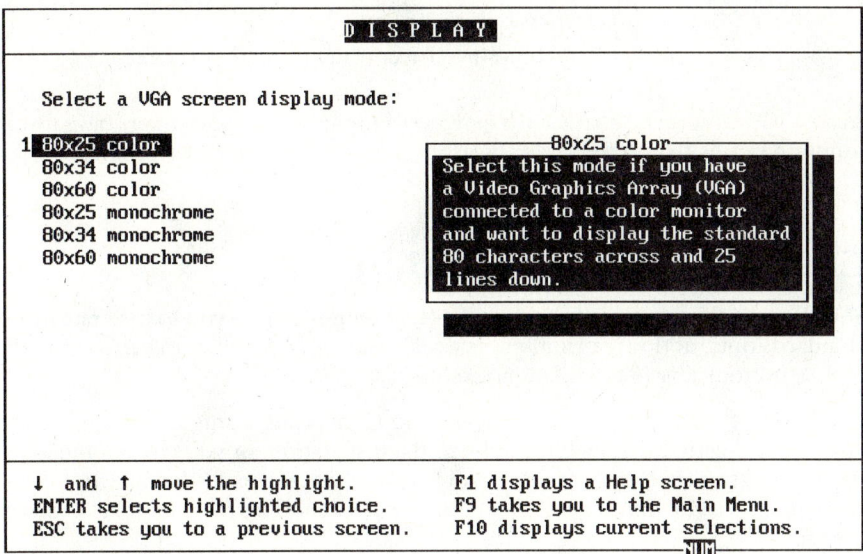

Fig. A.8.
The screen showing the currently selected display mode.

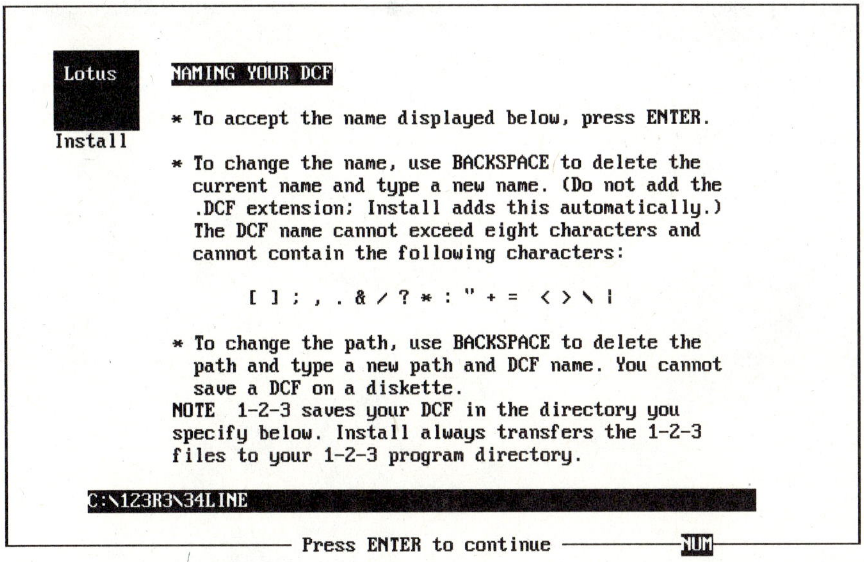

Fig. A.9.
Saving the new configuration file 34LINE.DCF.

Changing the Selected Country

The Change Selected Country option on the Modify Current DCF menu changes the sorting order 1-2-3 uses. The following options are available when you select Change Selected Country:

Selection	Description
Numbers First	Numbers sorted before letters
Numbers Last	Letters sorted before numbers
ASCII	Characters sorted according to the ASCII table

In an ASCII table, each character is assigned a numeric value. Numbers have lower numeric values than letters. Uppercase letters have a lower numeric value than lowercase letters.

Changing Wysiwyg Options

Selecting `Wysiwyg Options` from Install's Main menu enables you to generate more standard fonts, add fonts from an external source, and switch the left and right mouse buttons (for left-handed mouse users).

If you select the `Generate Fonts` option, the Generating Fonts menu appears. If you didn't create the fonts during the initial installation, or you created the `Basic` font set and want to create the `Medium` or `Extended` font set, make that selection now. Select the `Extended` font set and press Enter. 1-2-3 generates the Extended Wysiwyg font set.

If you select the `Switch Mouse Buttons` option, specify which mouse button you want to use to select items. The left mouse button is the default. Choose `Right` or `Left` and press Enter.

If you choose `Add Fonts`, Install asks which disk drive contains the fonts you want to add. (These soft fonts are available from your software dealer.) Specify the drive; Install copies the fonts to your 1-2-3 directory.

Using the Auditor Add-In

B

1-2-3 Release 3.1+ includes several add-in programs that enhance or expand upon the existing features of 1-2-3. Throughout this book, you have seen and used one of these programs: Wysiwyg. This appendix describes another add-in program called Auditor. You can use Auditor to diagnose the formulas in a worksheet and to help verify the accuracy of your figures. Auditor is particularly useful when you fine-tune or debug formulas. With Auditor, you can ensure that the formulas refer to the proper cells and that certain cells are used in the proper worksheet calculations. Auditor also is useful for finding and correcting circular references and for determining the recalculation order 1-2-3 uses within a range.

This appendix shows you how to use Auditor to perform the following tasks:

- Highlight all formulas in the worksheet
- Find all cells supplying data to a formula
- Find all formulas relying on a particular cell
- Trace the path of circular references
- Check the order of recalculation

Attaching and Detaching Auditor

You must install Auditor before you can use this add-in. If you have not already installed Auditor, see Appendix A of this book for installation instructions.

After installing Auditor, you must attach the add-in in the same way as any other add-in program. With 1-2-3 loaded, press Alt–F10 (Add-in) and select **Load**. 1-2-3 displays a list of add-in program files with the extension PLC. Select `AUDITOR.PLC` and press Enter.

1-2-3 asks which key to assign to Auditor. The key you assign invokes (runs) the add-in. The key numbers 1 through 3 refer to APP1, APP2, and APP3—which correspond to the function keys labeled F7, F8, and F9, respectively. After you select one of the numbers, you invoke the add-in by holding down the Alt key and pressing the specified function key. If you select 1, for example, you invoke Auditor by holding down Alt and pressing F7. You also can assign **No-Key** to the add-in. If you don't assign a key to Auditor, you must invoke the add-in using Alt-F10 (Add-in) **Invoke**. For this example, assign a key to Auditor and press Enter. 1-2-3 assigns the key, and the Add-In menu reappears. Select **Quit** to return to the worksheet.

To remove Auditor from memory, use Alt-F10 (Add-in) **Remove**. 1-2-3 displays a list of currently attached add-ins. Highlight AUDITOR and press Enter. You also can select Alt-F10 (Add-in) **Clear** to remove all add-ins from memory. At this point, however, leave Auditor in memory so you can try the features described in this appendix.

Invoking and Using Auditor

To invoke Auditor, hold down the Alt key and press the function key you assigned to Auditor. 1-2-3 displays the Auditor menu and Auditor Settings box shown in figure B.1. Auditor is in the computer's memory, integrated with 1-2-3. You can use Auditor with the current worksheet; or exit Auditor, load another worksheet, and invoke Auditor again with the Alt-function key combination.

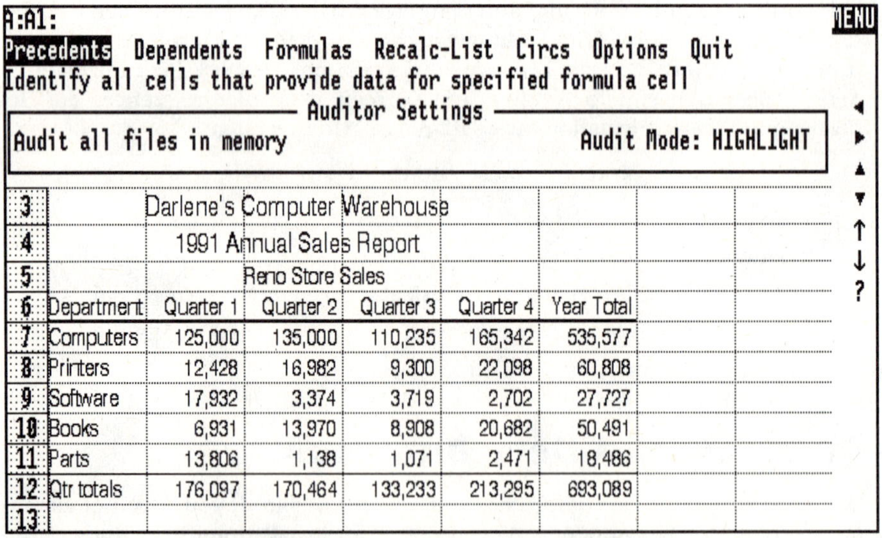

A:A1: MENU
Precedents Dependents Formulas Recalc-List Circs Options Quit
Identify all cells that provide data for specified formula cell
Auditor Settings
Audit all files in memory Audit Mode: HIGHLIGHT

3		Darlene's Computer Warehouse				
4		1991 Annual Sales Report				
5			Reno Store Sales			
6	Department	Quarter 1	Quarter 2	Quarter 3	Quarter 4	Year Total
7	Computers	125,000	135,000	110,235	165,342	535,577
8	Printers	12,428	16,982	9,300	22,098	60,808
9	Software	17,932	3,374	3,719	2,702	27,727
10	Books	6,931	13,970	8,908	20,682	50,491
11	Parts	13,806	1,138	1,071	2,471	18,486
12	Qtr totals	176,097	170,464	133,233	213,295	693,089
13						

Fig. B.1.
The Auditor add-in menu.

To leave Auditor and return to 1-2-3 READY mode, select **Quit** from the Auditor menu. From READY mode, you can select /**File Retrieve** to load a worksheet. You redisplay Auditor by invoking the add-in with the Alt-function key combination or with Alt-F10 (Add-in) **Invoke**.

Understanding the Auditor Menu

The Auditor menu contains seven options. Table B.1 describes each option.

Table B.1
Auditor Menu Selections

Selection	Action
Precedents	Finds all cells supplying data to a formula
Dependents	Finds all formulas dependent on a specified cell
Formulas	Identifies all cells containing formulas
Recalc-List	Shows the path 1-2-3 follows when recalculating the worksheet
Circs	Lists all cells involved in a circular reference
Options	Modifies or resets the audit range and audit mode
Quit	Leaves Auditor and returns to 1-2-3

Setting the Audit Range

By default, Auditor assumes that you want to diagnose the entire area of all worksheet files in memory; that is, every cell from A:A1 to IV:IV8192 of every open file. Auditor calls this range the *audit range*. Auditor displays the current audit range on the left side of the Auditor Settings box, as shown in figure B.1. At the right side of the Auditor Settings box, Auditor displays the Audit Mode setting (detailed later in the "Changing the Audit Mode" section).

Suppose that you want to fine-tune a small section of a large worksheet. You checked the rest of the worksheet and found it correct, and you want Auditor to diagnose only the last few changes made. You generally can change the audit range to include only the modified cells, even if the cells refer to other formulas or cells outside the audit range.

To change the audit range, select **O**ptions **A**udit-Range from the Auditor menu. Auditor highlights the current audit range in the worksheet and changes to POINT mode. Press Esc to unanchor the range, and highlight a new range. To specify the range in the sample worksheet shown in figure B.1, for example, highlight the range A:B7..A:F12. After highlighting the correct range of cells, press Enter. Auditor displays the new range in the Auditor Settings box.

If the audit range is off by one or two cells, you can edit the current range in the control panel when you select **O**ptions **A**udit-Range. Press F2 (Edit); Auditor displays a cursor at the end of the audit range. Edit the address as necessary and press Enter to accept the new range.

Changing the Audit Mode

By default, Auditor highlights all worksheet cells matching the selected report option. Highlighting matched cells works well for small worksheets. When you have a large worksheet, however, you cannot see all the highlighted cells on one screen; you must scroll through the worksheet to see all matching cells. To correct this limitation, Auditor uses two other audit modes to display the results of an option. With these two modes, you can create a list of matching cells in a separate range of the worksheet, or you can move a highlight through the worksheet and display one matching cell at a time. The second method is called *tracing* through the worksheet. To change the audit mode, select **Highlight**, **List**, or **Trace** from the **Options** menu.

If you select **Options Trace**, Auditor highlights the first cell matching the current Auditor command selection, and displays a menu with the options **Forward**, **Backward**, and **Quit**. Select **Forward** to trace through the worksheet and find the next matching cell, or **Backward** to move to the preceding matching cell. When no more matching cells exist in the selected direction, Auditor beeps instead of moving the cell pointer. After looking at the matching cells, select **Quit** to return to the main Auditor menu.

Use the same procedure to change the audit mode to **List**. The only difference between **List** and **Trace** is that **List** prompts for a range to hold the list of matching cell addresses and contents. Be sure to specify an empty range; Auditor doesn't write over existing data, instead displaying an error message and forcing you to respecify the range. If you specify a single row target range, Auditor expands the range as far as necessary, to the bottom of the worksheet.

Note: Auditor doesn't remove highlights automatically if you select a different Auditor command option. To remove highlights, select **Options Reset Highlight** before selecting a new Auditor command.

Finding Cells Used by One Formula (Precedents)

When you make corrections in a worksheet, you don't want to inadvertently change other (correct) parts of the worksheet. If you change the value of one cell, for example, the value of a formula in another area of the worksheet also may change, if the formula depends on that cell's value. The formula also may depend—directly or indirectly—on another cell.

In certain applications, you may want to know every cell used by a formula. Suppose that you want to revise a formula to make the formula more efficient. Before editing, you may want to see every cell affected by a change in that formula. Or perhaps, when debugging a formula, you cannot find the reason for an erroneous result. You need to know which cells the formula uses so you can determine why the result is incorrect.

To find all the cells supplying information to a particular formula, select the **Precedents** option. Auditor prompts you for the formula to use. Point to or type the address of the cell containing the formula and press Enter. Auditor finds all cells that the formula uses and displays the results in the selected audit mode.

Figure B.2 shows the cells used by the formula in cell A:F11. The audit mode selected was Options List.

```
A:F11: {B} @SUM(B11..E11)                                            MENU
Precedents  Dependents  Formulas  Recalc-List  Circs  Options  Quit
Identify all cells that provide data for specified formula cell
                        ─── Auditor Settings ───
Audit all files in memory                       Audit Mode: LIST

  3              Darlene's Computer Warehouse
  4                  1991 Annual Sales Report
  5                      Reno Store Sales
  6    Department  Quarter 1  Quarter 2  Quarter 3  Quarter 4  Year Total
  7    Computers    125,000    135,000    110,235    165,342    535,577
  8    Printers      12,428     16,982      9,300     22,098     60,808
  9    Software      17,932      3,374      3,719      2,702     27,727
 10    Books          6,931     13,970      8,908     20,682     50,491
 11    Parts         13,806      1,138      1,071      2,471     18,486
 12    Qtr totals   176,097    170,464    133,233    213,295    693,089
 13
 14    Precedents of cell A:F11
 15    A:B11: 13806
 16    A:C11: 1138
 17    A:D11: 1071
 18    A:E11: 2471
 19
 20                                                              NUM
```

Fig. B.2.
Displaying the precedent cells of a formula.

Finding Formulas That Refer to One Cell (Dependents)

To find all formulas that may be affected by a change you make in one cell, use the **Dependents** option. **Dependents** finds all formulas in the audit range dependent on a specific cell. When you select **Dependents**, Auditor prompts you for the dependent source cell. Highlight or type the address of the cell whose value you want to change and press Enter. Using the selected audit mode (**Highlight, List,** or **Trace**), Auditor reports formulas (if any) dependent on the information in the cell.

Suppose that you want to find all formulas dependent on cell A:B11 in the sample worksheet. Select **Dependents** and specify cell A:B11. Auditor shows you all the formulas directly or indirectly dependent on the value in A:B11 for calculations. Figure B.3 shows the cells found for cell A:B11. In figure B.3, the selected audit mode is Options List.

Finding Formulas

The **Formulas** option of the Auditor menu locates all cells containing formulas in the worksheet. If the audit mode is set to **Options Highlight,** Auditor highlights the cells containing formulas. On a color monitor, Auditor displays the cells in a different color. On a monochrome monitor, the cells show as high intensity.

Fig. B.3.
Displaying formula cells dependent on a specified cell.

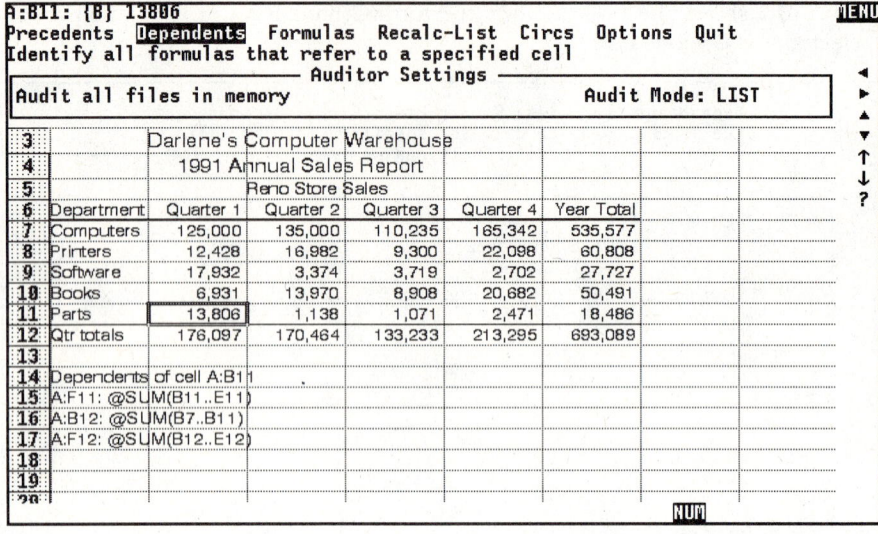

Using the **Highlight** audit mode, you can see all cells containing formulas. As you examine these cells, you may notice an error in one of the formulas. If you edit the cell to correct the mistake, the highlight remains. If the correction involves a change in the worksheet such as moving cells, inserting or deleting rows or columns, or redefining range names, however, Auditor removes all highlights. You must select **Formulas** again to redisplay the formula cells.

If you select the **Options List** audit mode, Auditor places in the worksheet a list of all formulas contained in the audit range.

Examining Recalculation Order

For some worksheets, the order 1-2-3 uses to recalculate the worksheet is important. You may want to make sure that 1-2-3 recalculates net sales before recalculating net income, for example. As discussed earlier in this book, you can use /**Worksheet Global Recalc** to set the recalculation order to one of the following methods: **Natural**, **Columnwise**, or **Rowwise**.

During recalculation, 1-2-3 may skip around the worksheet. With **Natural** recalculation, for example, 1-2-3 begins by determining the dependencies among the worksheet's formulas. If no formulas depend on other formulas, 1-2-3 begins recalculating formula cells starting at the top left corner of the first worksheet. If you have a formula referring to another formula cell, however, 1-2-3 performs the calculation in the referenced formula first.

To determine the recalculation order that 1-2-3 uses, select the **Recalc-List** option. Before using this option, change the audit mode to **Trace** or **List**. Then select **Recalc-List** from the Auditor main menu. If you select **Trace** for the audit mode, Auditor

Appendix B ◆ Using the Auditor Add-In   **887**

highlights the first cell that 1-2-3 calculates in the audit range. Select **Forward** to move to the next cell to be recalculated. Select **Backward** to move back through the cells. Select **Quit** to exit the **Trace** display and return to Auditor.

If you select **List** for the audit mode, Auditor copies the list of formula cells from the worksheet, in the order the cells are recalculated. Figure B.4 shows the **Recalc-List** command in use.

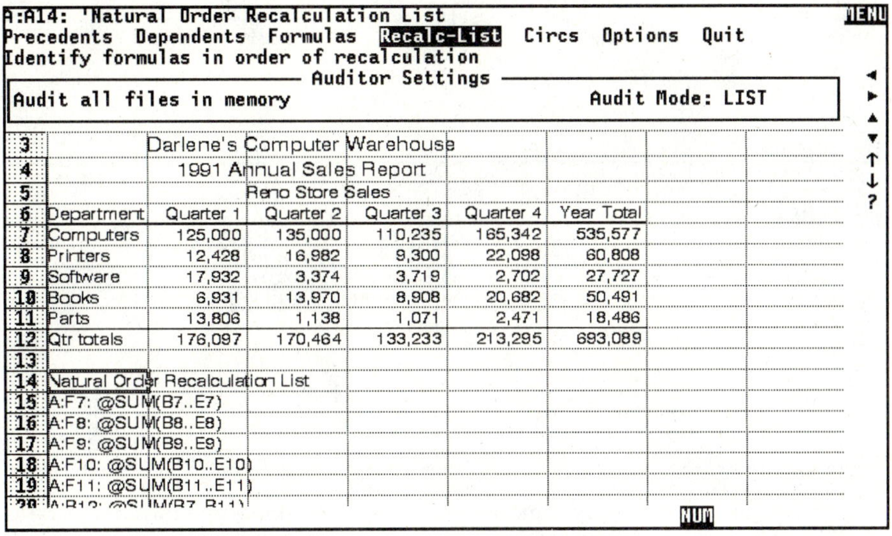

Fig. B.4.
Determining the formula recalculation order with the Recalc-List option.

Note: Unlike other Auditor options, **Recalc-List** is not limited to the audit range. Because of this difference, the **Recalc-List** option can require a considerable amount of space in your worksheet. Consider using three-dimensional worksheets, specifying a report range in a new, blank worksheet.

Examining Circular References

In 1-2-3 worksheets, circular references are among the most complicated and difficult errors to correct. In rare cases, you intentionally create circular references to perform calculations, but the CIRC indicator usually is an unwelcome surprise.

Circular references in formulas are hard to find because these errors often result from an indirect reference that seems reasonable. Suppose that you want to make the number of sales staff hired contingent on your company's net income. You reason that if net income is too far in the red (negative numbers), you may need to increase the number of sales staff to bring in more revenue. Because the number of sales staff depends on net profit, net profit depends on sales, and sales depends on the number of sales staff, you have a circular reference.

Part V ◆ Appendixes

More often, however, circular references result from an error made when entering or editing a formula. In figure B.5, for example, the formula in cell A:F13 reads as follows:

    @SUM($A:E$12..$A:F13)

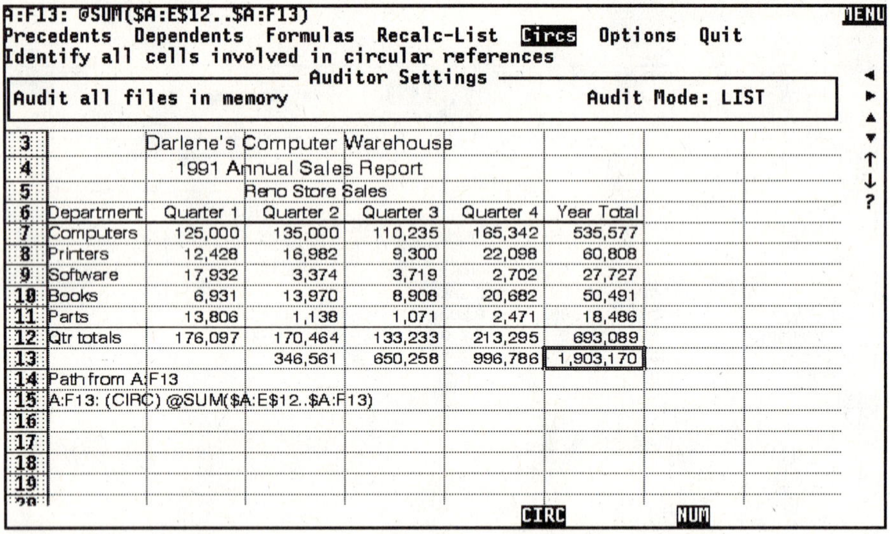

Fig. B.5.
Displaying circular references with the Circs option.

```
A:F13: @SUM($A:E$12..$A:F13)                                          MENU
Precedents  Dependents  Formulas  Recalc-List  Circs  Options  Quit
Identify all cells involved in circular references
─────────────────────── Auditor Settings ───────────────────────
Audit all files in memory                        Audit Mode: LIST

  3           Darlene's Computer Warehouse
  4              1991 Annual Sales Report
  5                    Reno Store Sales
  6   Department  Quarter 1  Quarter 2  Quarter 3  Quarter 4  Year Total
  7   Computers    125,000    135,000    110,235    165,342    535,577
  8   Printers      12,428     16,982      9,300     22,098     60,808
  9   Software      17,932      3,374      3,719      2,702     27,727
 10   Books          6,931     13,970      8,908     20,682     50,491
 11   Parts         13,806      1,138      1,071      2,471     18,486
 12   Qtr totals   176,097    170,464    133,233    213,295    693,089
 13                            346,561    650,258    996,786  1,903,170
 14   Path from A:F13
 15   A:F13: (CIRC) @SUM($A:E$12..$A:F13)
 16
 17
 18
 19
 20
                                                    CIRC        NUM
```

The **Circs** option of the Auditor menu helps you determine why a formula (such as the one just described) causes a circular reference. Select **Circs** from the Auditor main menu. Auditor displays a list of the cells involved with circular references. (The worksheet may have more than one circular reference.) Highlight the cell to use and press Enter. Auditor lists all cells referring to this cell.

Even without Auditor, 1-2-3 shows one circular reference when you select **/Worksheet Status**. The Auditor Circs report is considerably more comprehensive, however.

Resetting Auditor Options

After using Auditor to correct one worksheet, you may want to check your other worksheets. Before retrieving another worksheet, reset the audit range and audit mode as necessary. If you highlighted a range of cells by using **Highlight** and **Precedents**, **Dependents**, or **Formulas**, you may need to turn off the highlighted cells.

To reset the audit range and audit mode, select **Options Reset Options**. Auditor resets the audit range to `Audit all files in memory` and the audit mode to `HIGHLIGHT`. (These changes appear in the Auditor Settings box.) Select **Quit** to return to the Auditor main menu.

To remove the highlight set by the **Highlight** audit mode, select **Options Reset Highlight** from the Auditor main menu. Auditor removes the highlights (or color) from cells in the worksheet. Select **Q**uit twice to return to the worksheet and READY mode.

Using the Solver and Backsolver Add-Ins

C

1-2-3 Release 3.1+ includes two very powerful new add-ins, Solver and Backsolver, to analyze and find answers to complex problems. These utilities enable you to create *what-if scenarios* using a number of different values for one or more variables in a problem. What-if scenarios are a common way of collecting a number of different solutions to a problem, based on different assumptions.

Suppose that you want to determine the best product mix based on your production capacity. You can use Solver to perform a what-if analysis that maximizes bottom-line profits by determining the optimal production ratio for each product.

Backsolver works slightly differently than Solver—you supply the target and Backsolver shows you the correct path to follow to reach the goal. Backsolver can help you reach a specific target, but Solver may present several answers.

This appendix describes some of the ways in which you can use Solver and Backsolver to solve what-if problems.

Attaching and Detaching Solver and Backsolver

To use Solver and Backsolver, you first must install these add-ins. If you have not installed the Solver and Backsolver add-ins, see Appendix A for installation instructions.

After installing Solver or Backsolver, you must attach the add-in to use it, as with any other add-in program. To attach an add-in in 1-2-3, press Alt–F10 (Add-in) and select Load. 1-2-3 displays a list of add-in program files with the extension PLC. Select SOLVER.PLC or BSOLVER.PLC and press Enter.

1-2-3 asks which function key to assign to Solver or Backsolver. You use this key to invoke (run) the add-in. The key numbers **1**, **2**, and **3** correspond to the function keys F7, F8, and F9, respectively. After selecting a number, you invoke Solver or Backsolver by holding down the Alt key and pressing the selected function key. If you chose **1** for Solver and **2** for Backsolver, for example, you invoke Solver by holding down Alt and pressing F7, and Backsolver by holding down Alt and pressing F8.

You can assign **N**o-Key to the add-in. If you don't assign a key to Solver or Backsolver, you must invoke these add-ins with Alt–F10 (Add-in) **I**nvoke. Select a key to assign to Solver or Backsolver and press Enter. 1-2-3 assigns the selected key(s) and returns to the Add-In menu. Select **Q**uit to return to the worksheet.

To remove Solver or Backsolver from memory, select Alt–F10 (Add-in) **R**emove. 1-2-3 displays a list of currently attached add-in programs. Highlight `SOLVER` or `BSOLVER` and press Enter. You also can select Alt–F10 (Add-in) **C**lear to remove all add-ins from memory. At this point, leave Solver and Backsolver in memory so you can try the features described in this appendix.

The Solver add-in is the largest of the four new add-ins in 1-2-3 Release 3.1+. Solver requires approximately 666K of disk space and a considerable amount of available memory (RAM) to load—over 638K in addition to that required for 1-2-3 Release 3.1+. Depending on the memory available in your system, you may need to free additional memory before you can load Solver. If you receive an `Out of memory` message when you attempt to load Solver, issue the **/W**orksheet **G**lobal **D**efault **O**ther **U**ndo **D**isable command. If this procedure doesn't free enough memory to load Solver, select Alt–F10 (Add-in) **C**lear to remove all add-ins from memory. If you still cannot load Solver, you may need to add memory or make a larger percentage of your system memory available to 1-2-3. Because 1-2-3 Release 3.1+ uses extended memory, you may find reducing the extended memory used by system utilities like disk caching programs provides enough additional memory for Solver.

Invoking Solver

To invoke Solver, hold down the Alt key and press the function key you assigned to Solver. 1-2-3 displays the Solver menu shown in figure C.1.

The Solver utility analyzes data in a problem to determine a set of possible answers. Depending on the defined problem, Solver may find no answer, several answers, the best available answer based on the supplied data, or the optimal answer. This utility is fairly easy to use but—because the types of problems Solver analyzes tend to be very complex—you may need to experiment before arriving at the final result. Fortunately, Solver is extremely powerful and includes many reports explaining the answers Solver finds.

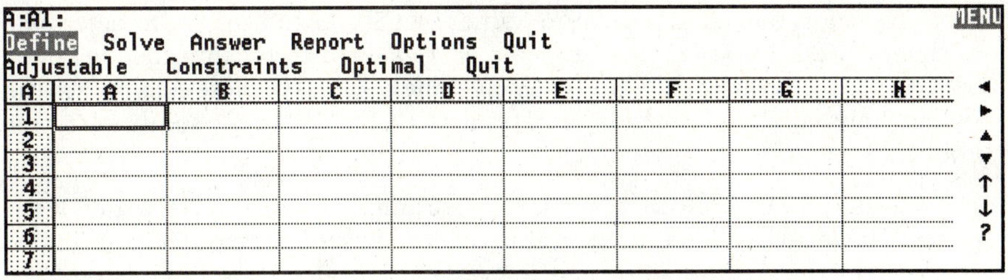

Appendix C ◆ Using the Solver and Backsolver Add-Ins

Fig. C.1.
The Solver menu.

This appendix shows you how to accomplish the following tasks with Solver and Backsolver:

- Define what-if scenarios to use with Solver
- Solve complex problems with Solver
- Analyze the Solver results
- Use Backsolver to reach a desired result

Using Solver

The Solver add-in analyzes data in your worksheets to determine a series of possible answers to a specific problem. You can use Solver, for example, to find the maximum price house you can afford to buy; to determine the combination of sales items yielding the greatest profit; to search for an investment strategy yielding the highest return subject to your tolerance for risk; or to maximize the profit potential of your business by determining the best way to use your manufacturing capacity.

You can solve problems like these by inserting different amounts for each of the variables. Using this "manual" method is time-consuming and frustrating, however, because you must guess at possible answers, saving each set of answers for comparison later. The Solver add-in tracks each possible answer and displays the answer on demand. Solver also determines the best answer from the set of all possible answers and, with its report capacity, shows how the conclusion was derived.

The following sections describe the Solver add-in and the reports generated by Solver.

Understanding Solver Terminology

Before you begin using Solver, you must understand a few terms. Solver finds answers to problems by using data you specify in a worksheet. Each problem you give Solver must contain one or more values that Solver can change to determine possible answers. These values are called *adjustable values*, and the cells containing the values are *adjustable cells*. Solver changes the contents of these cells (which can contain only numbers, not text or formulas) to find different solutions to the problem.

Each Solver problem must contain one or more limits (or *constraints*) to define the scope of the problem. If you use Solver to determine a mortgage rate, for example, you may limit the possible answers to interest rates between 8 and 15 percent. You enter the constraints in *constraint cells*, as logical formulas evaluating to TRUE (1) or FALSE (0). Solver accepts only those answers in which all constraints are TRUE.

You can include an optimal cell in your worksheet. An *optimal cell* contains a value you want to maximize (or minimize) to obtain the best answer. If you don't select an optimal cell, Solver determines possible answers to the problem but doesn't sort answers according to their value for the optimal cell.

Optimizing Production for Maximum Profit

Determining the best mix of products to optimize a company's profits can be a difficult problem. Many factors can be involved, including production capacity, relative costs of production, warehousing costs, and so on. The following sections demonstrate how Solver analyzes a problem and provides an optimal solution.

Creating a Sample Worksheet for Solver

Figure C.2 shows a sample worksheet that details how a small premium ice cream business calculates its production levels and profits. The company makes two flavors, chocolate and vanilla, and wants to determine how much of each flavor to produce each month. Chocolate costs more to produce than vanilla but both sell for the same price. Storage costs at the roadside store are $2 per gallon plus $50 per month per flavor. The factory has a 250 gallon-per-month production capacity.

Before Solver can begin solving your problem, you must define both the adjustable cells and the constraint cells. When you select **Define** on the Solver main menu, the **Define** menu appears, as shown in figure C.3.

In this problem, the adjustable cells are the projected sales shown in A:B2..A:C2. As you adjust the values in these cells, the overall profit calculated in A:C10 is affected. Figure C.4 shows the adjustable cells being defined.

The constraint cells place limits on values in the worksheet. Because the factory can produce only 250 gallons of ice cream per month, one constraint must be to limit the sum of cells A:B2 and A:C2 to 250. Other reasonable constraints include setting minimum production levels for each flavor, making sure that you produce enough of each flavor to pay for fixed costs (such as the $50-per-flavor storage charge), and production of full gallons. Figure C.5 shows several constraint formulas placed in

Appendix C ◆ Using the Solver and Backsolver Add-Ins

cells A:A11..A:A17. You write constraints as a series of logical formulas. The **Define Constraints** command provides Solver with the limits the add-in must use to solve the problem.

```
A:C10: (C2) [W10] @SUM(B8..C8)                                        READY

       A              B          C         D      E      F      G
  1        Flavor  Chocolate   Vanilla
  2        Sales      125        125
  3   Cost/Gallon    $5.50      $4.50
  4     Prod Cost   $687.50    $562.50   +C2*C3
  5       Storage   $300.00    $300.00   50+C2*2
  6   Price/Gallon   $10.00     $10.00
  7     Total Sale $1,250.00  $1,250.00  +C2*C6
  8        Profit   $262.50    $387.50   +C7-C4-C5
  9
 10                            $650.00   @SUM(B8..C8)
 11
```

Fig. C.2.
Sample ice cream production worksheet.

```
A:C10: (C2) [W10] @SUM(B8..C8)                                         MENU
Adjustable  Constraints  Optimal  Quit
Specify the adjustable cells for the problem
       A              B          C         D      E      F      G
  1        Flavor  Chocolate   Vanilla
  2        Sales      125        125
  3   Cost/Gallon    $5.50      $4.50
  4     Prod Cost   $687.50    $562.50   +C2*C3
  5       Storage   $300.00    $300.00   50+C2*2
  6   Price/Gallon   $10.00     $10.00
  7     Total Sale $1,250.00  $1,250.00  +C2*C6
  8        Profit   $262.50    $387.50   +C7-C4-C5
  9
 10                            $650.00   @SUM(B8..C8)
 11
```

Fig. C.3.
The Solver Define menu.

In this example, the following constraints were used: chocolate sales (B2) of at least 10 gallons; vanilla sales (C2) of at least 5 gallons; total sales of 250 gallons; no losses on either product; and both products sold by full gallon only.

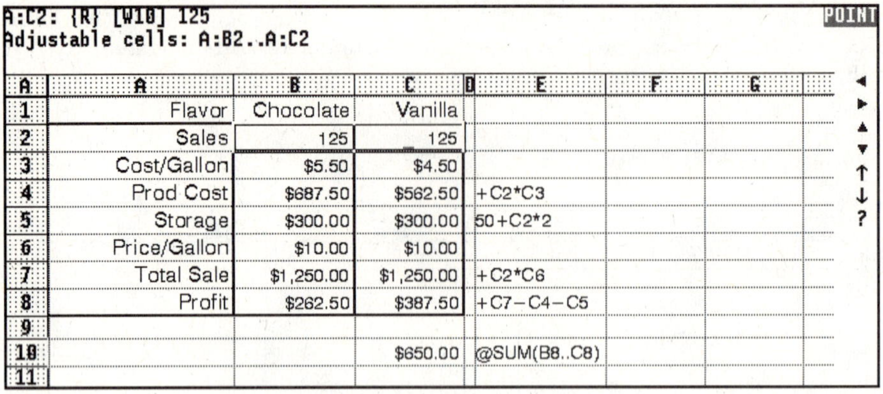

Fig. C.4.
Defining the adjustable cells.

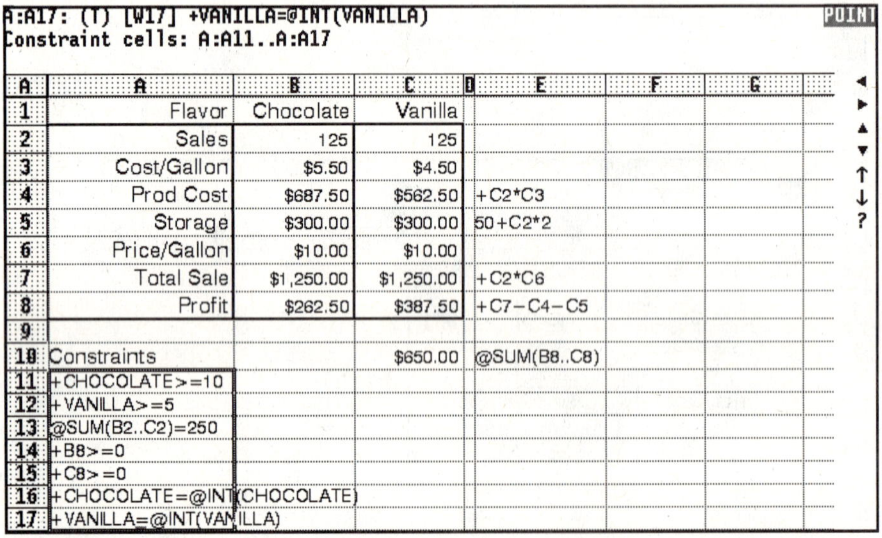

```
A:C2: {R} [W10] 125                                                POINT
Adjustable cells: A:B2..A:C2
```

	A	B	C	D	E	F	G
1	Flavor	Chocolate	Vanilla				
2	Sales	125	125				
3	Cost/Gallon	$5.50	$4.50				
4	Prod Cost	$687.50	$562.50		+C2*C3		
5	Storage	$300.00	$300.00		50+C2*2		
6	Price/Gallon	$10.00	$10.00				
7	Total Sale	$1,250.00	$1,250.00		+C2*C6		
8	Profit	$262.50	$387.50		+C7−C4−C5		
9							
10			$650.00		@SUM(B8..C8)		
11							

Fig. C.5.
Defining constraints.

```
A:A17: (T) [W17] +VANILLA=@INT(VANILLA)                            POINT
Constraint cells: A:A11..A:A17
```

	A	B	C	D	E	F	G
1	Flavor	Chocolate	Vanilla				
2	Sales	125	125				
3	Cost/Gallon	$5.50	$4.50				
4	Prod Cost	$687.50	$562.50		+C2*C3		
5	Storage	$300.00	$300.00		50+C2*2		
6	Price/Gallon	$10.00	$10.00				
7	Total Sale	$1,250.00	$1,250.00		+C2*C6		
8	Profit	$262.50	$387.50		+C7−C4−C5		
9							
10	Constraints		$650.00		@SUM(B8..C8)		
11	+CHOCOLATE>=10						
12	+VANILLA>=5						
13	@SUM(B2..C2)=250						
14	+B8>=0						
15	+C8>=0						
16	+CHOCOLATE=@INT(CHOCOLATE)						
17	+VANILLA=@INT(VANILLA)						

Generally, you define the optimal cell with a formula that Solver optimizes by maximizing or minimizing the value. If you don't define an optimal cell, Solver provides several answers meeting the defined constraints, and you decide which answer you prefer. In this example, the goal is making the maximum profit on production. Select **Define Optimal**; Solver asks whether you want to maximize or minimize the value of the optimal cell (see fig. C.6).

Because you want maximum profits, select **X-Maximize**. Because cell A:C10 contains the formula that Solver will optimize, specify cell A:C10 at the `Optimal cell:` prompt (see fig. C.7).

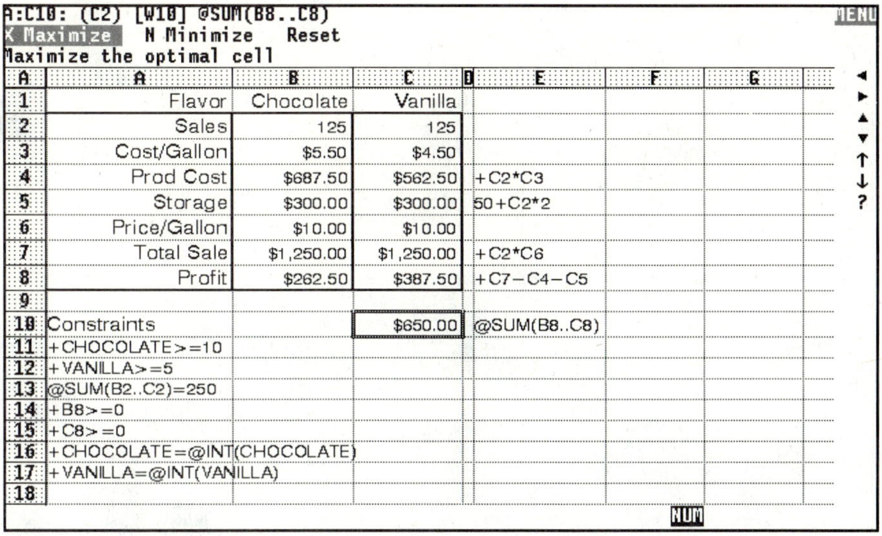

```
A:C10: (C2) [W10] @SUM(B8..C8)                                    MENU
X Maximize  N Minimize  Reset
Maximize the optimal cell
   A           A            B         C        D        E         F        G
  1         Flavor      Chocolate  Vanilla
  2          Sales         125        125
  3       Cost/Gallon    $5.50      $4.50
  4        Prod Cost    $687.50    $562.50  +C2*C3
  5         Storage    $300.00    $300.00  50+C2*2
  6       Price/Gallon   $10.00     $10.00
  7       Total Sale  $1,250.00  $1,250.00  +C2*C6
  8          Profit     $262.50    $387.50  +C7-C4-C5
  9
 10 Constraints                    $650.00  @SUM(B8..C8)
 11 +CHOCOLATE>=10
 12 +VANILLA>=5
 13 @SUM(B2..C2)=250
 14 +B8>=0
 15 +C8>=0
 16 +CHOCOLATE=@INT(CHOCOLATE)
 17 +VANILLA=@INT(VANILLA)
 18
                                                                   NUM
```

Fig. C.6.
The Solver Define Optimal menu.

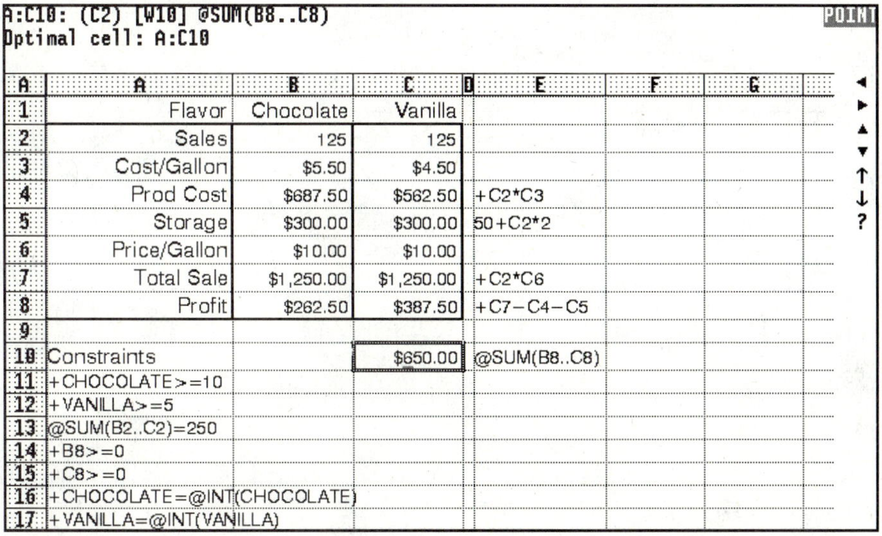

```
A:C10: (C2) [W10] @SUM(B8..C8)                                    POINT
Optimal cell: A:C10
   A           A            B         C        D        E         F        G
  1         Flavor      Chocolate  Vanilla
  2          Sales         125        125
  3       Cost/Gallon    $5.50      $4.50
  4        Prod Cost    $687.50    $562.50  +C2*C3
  5         Storage    $300.00    $300.00  50+C2*2
  6       Price/Gallon   $10.00     $10.00
  7       Total Sale  $1,250.00  $1,250.00  +C2*C6
  8          Profit     $262.50    $387.50  +C7-C4-C5
  9
 10 Constraints                    $650.00  @SUM(B8..C8)
 11 +CHOCOLATE>=10
 12 +VANILLA>=5
 13 @SUM(B2..C2)=250
 14 +B8>=0
 15 +C8>=0
 16 +CHOCOLATE=@INT(CHOCOLATE)
 17 +VANILLA=@INT(VANILLA)
```

Fig. C.7.
Defining the optimal cell.

After defining the problem, select **Q**uit to return to the Solver menu; then select **S**olve **P**roblem (as shown in fig. C.8) to begin searching for the best answer. Solver displays a message at the bottom of the screen, informing you of progress made as the add-in attempts to find the optimal solution.

Solver finds answers by substituting values in the adjustable cells, testing to see if all defined constraints are met, and repeating the process until Solver finds the best answer. If the constraints you set are valid, at least one outcome is possible. An optimal answer appears, as shown in figure C.9.

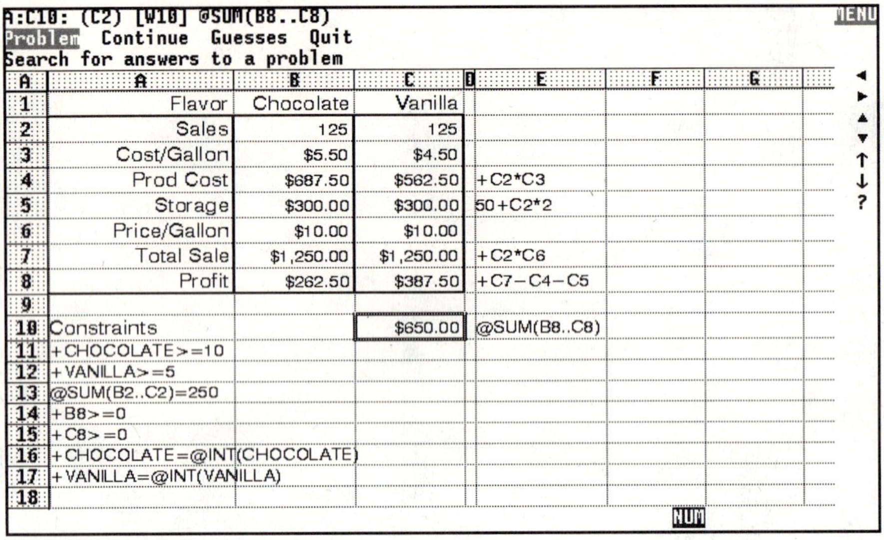

Fig. C.8.
The Solver Solve menu.

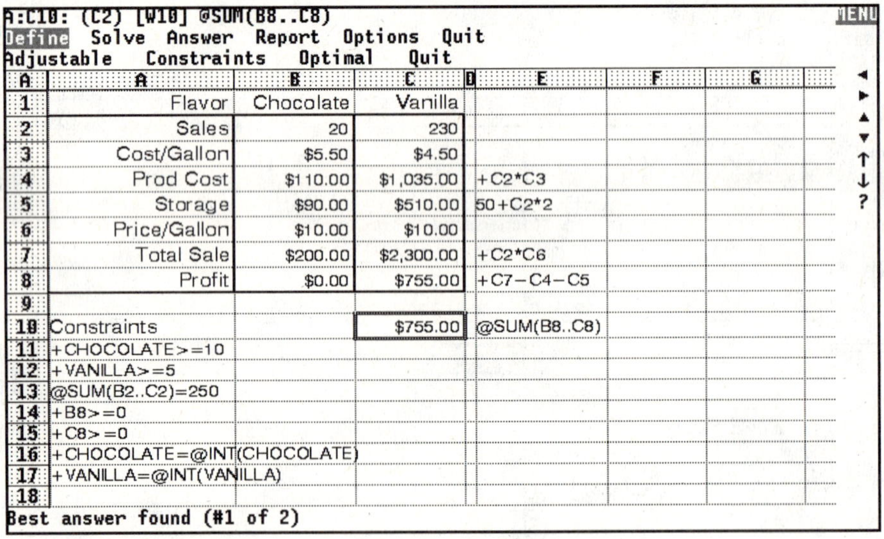

```
A:C10: (C2) [W10] @SUM(B8..C8)                                    MENU
Problem  Continue  Guesses  Quit
Search for answers to a problem
      A              B           C         D      E         F      G
 1    Flavor      Chocolate   Vanilla
 2    Sales          125         125
 3    Cost/Gallon   $5.50       $4.50
 4    Prod Cost    $687.50    $562.50         +C2*C3
 5    Storage      $300.00    $300.00         50+C2*2
 6    Price/Gallon  $10.00     $10.00
 7    Total Sale  $1,250.00  $1,250.00        +C2*C6
 8    Profit       $262.50    $387.50         +C7-C4-C5
 9
10   Constraints              $650.00         @SUM(B8..C8)
11   +CHOCOLATE>=10
12   +VANILLA>=5
13   @SUM(B2..C2)=250
14   +B8>=0
15   +C8>=0
16   +CHOCOLATE=@INT(CHOCOLATE)
17   +VANILLA=@INT(VANILLA)
18
                                                                   NUM
```

Fig. C.9.
Solver's best answer to the ice cream production problem.

```
A:C10: (C2) [W10] @SUM(B8..C8)                                    MENU
Define  Solve  Answer  Report  Options  Quit
Adjustable  Constraints  Optimal  Quit
      A              B           C         D      E         F      G
 1    Flavor      Chocolate   Vanilla
 2    Sales           20         230
 3    Cost/Gallon   $5.50       $4.50
 4    Prod Cost    $110.00   $1,035.00        +C2*C3
 5    Storage       $90.00    $510.00         50+C2*2
 6    Price/Gallon  $10.00     $10.00
 7    Total Sale   $200.00   $2,300.00        +C2*C6
 8    Profit         $0.00    $755.00         +C7-C4-C5
 9
10   Constraints              $755.00         @SUM(B8..C8)
11   +CHOCOLATE>=10
12   +VANILLA>=5
13   @SUM(B2..C2)=250
14   +B8>=0
15   +C8>=0
16   +CHOCOLATE=@INT(CHOCOLATE)
17   +VANILLA=@INT(VANILLA)
18
Best answer found (#1 of 2)
```

Evaluating Solver's Answers

For the simple problem presented here, Solver reports that its best answer is one of two possible answers. In most cases, Solver finds multiple answers while seeking the best solution. By default, Solver finds up to ten answers, but you can use **Options Number-Answers** to instruct Solver to find a larger or smaller number of answers.

To display Solver's additional answers in the worksheet, select **Answer Next** to cycle through the answers. As figure C.9 shows, the optimal answer increases profit to

$755. Figure C.10 shows Solver's next best answer as $105 less, for a total of $650. With more complex problems, you may see several more solutions as you cycle through Solver's answers.

```
A:C10: (C2) [W10] @SUM(B8..C8)                                    MENU
Next  First  Previous  Last  Optimal  Reset  Quit
Show the next answer the Solver found to the problem
     A              B          C          D          E        F    G
 1           Flavor      Chocolate   Vanilla
 2           Sales          125        125
 3           Cost/Gallon    $5.50      $4.50
 4           Prod Cost     $687.50    $562.50   +C2*C3
 5           Storage       $300.00    $300.00   50+C2*2
 6           Price/Gallon   $10.00     $10.00
 7           Total Sale   $1,250.00  $1,250.00  +C2*C6
 8           Profit        $262.50    $387.50   +C7-C4-C5
 9
10  Constraints                        $650.00  @SUM(B8..C8)
11  +CHOCOLATE>=10
12  +VANILLA>=5
13  @SUM(B2..C2)=250
14  +B8>=0
15  +C8>=0
16  +CHOCOLATE=@INT(CHOCOLATE)
17  +VANILLA=@INT(VANILLA)
18
Sample answer #2 of 2
```

Fig. C.10.
Solver's sample answer #2.

Instead of cycling through the different answers, you can view the optimal or best answer by selecting **Optimal** from the Solver Answer menu. Select **Reset** to view the original values in the worksheet at any time as you cycle through the answers.

Solver often cannot provide an optimal answer. Suppose that the constraints for the ice cream production problem don't include the 250 gallon per month production limit. The values of the adjustable cells have no defined limit, and Solver is unable to provide a solution because the problem is unconstrained.

Other situations also can prevent Solver from finding an optimal solution. If constraint formulas conflict, Solver cannot find an answer that allows all constraints to be met. Depending on the difficulty involved, Solver attempts to inform you of the changes necessary to find an optimal answer.

Remember that Solver's answers are only as good as the information you provide. Your customers are unlikely to buy 230 gallons of vanilla and only 20 gallons of chocolate. Use care in determining the problem definition.

In some cases, the default number of solutions doesn't produce an optimal answer, but Solver hasn't exhausted all possibilities. To instruct Solver to seek additional answers, select **Solve Continue**. Solver attempts to find an additional set of answers (up to the **Number-Answers** setting).

Supplying Guesses

Sometimes Solver cannot solve a problem as initially stated because the problem is too complex, or because Solver lacks pertinent information to establish starting values for the adjustable cells. In such cases, the following message appears:

```
Guesses required
```

Before Solver can proceed, you must supply a new starting value for one or more of the adjustable cells. Select **Solve Guesses Guess** to specify a new value for the currently highlighted adjustable cell. To specify a new value for a different adjustable cell, select **Solve Guesses Next** and cycle through the adjustable cells until the correct cell is highlighted. Select **Solve Guesses Guess** to specify a new value for the adjustable cell.

After you specify new starting values for the adjustable cells, select **Solve Guesses Solve** to tell Solver to attempt another solution. Solver discards the previous attempted solutions if the new values lead to a successful solution.

Understanding Best and Optimal Answers

Solver differentiates between best and optimal answers. An optimal answer is determined mathematically to be the highest or lowest, depending on whether the **X**-Maximize or **N**-Minimize command is selected. A best answer is reported when Solver cannot verify precisely the mathematical optimum. The best answer is the highest or lowest found, but the best answer may not be the overall highest or lowest possible answer.

Displaying Attempted Answers

If Solver cannot find an answer meeting all constraint criteria, the add-in displays attempted answers. An attempted answer is really a partial answer, because at least one of the constraint cells doesn't evaluate to TRUE. Inconsistent constraints are described more fully in the section of this appendix called "The Inconsistent Constraints Report."

Selecting an Answer

By selecting **Quit** on the Solver menu, you can exit Solver. Before selecting **Quit**, decide which of the answers you want to keep in the worksheet. Be sure to save the worksheet after leaving Solver if you want to retain the solution. You can keep alternate solutions in separate worksheets of the same file or in separate files if you prefer.

1-2-3 doesn't remove the alternate answers immediately when you leave Solver. Alternate answers are removed when 1-2-3 recalculates the worksheet, but you can restart Solver and recover all previous solutions if the worksheet hasn't been recalculated. Changing the worksheet eliminates previous solutions.

Using the Solver Reports

You can access the following different types of reports on the answers found by Solver:

- Answer
- How solved
- What-If
- Differences
- Inconsistent constraints
- Unused constraints
- Cells used

Most of these reports can be viewed in two report formats. *Table format* shows the report in a table in a separate worksheet. *Cell format* shows information about one cell at a time in a display window. Figure C.11 shows the Solver Report menu.

The Answer Report

Selecting the **Report Answer** command causes Solver to create a new worksheet file named ANSWER*xx*.WK3, containing an overview of all answers. The *xx* in the file name is replaced with a number supplied by Solver; for example, the first **Answer** report is named ANSWER01.WK3. The report number is incremented by 1 for each subsequent **Answer** report. Solver stores the file in the default drive and directory. Figure C.12 shows the Answer report for the ice cream production example.

The **Answer** report is divided into areas covering the optimal cell, the adjustable cells, and the supporting formula cells.

Because Solver places the **Answer** report in a separate file (replacing the current worksheet on-screen), you may think that the **Answer** report wrote over your worksheet, but you can toggle between the worksheet files using the Ctrl–PgUp and Ctrl–PgDn key combinations.

Column B of figure C.12 shows the cell addresses for all cells in the problem. Solver automatically assigns to column C the range names for cells (displayed in uppercase), or, when a cell has no range name, the closest column and row labels (displayed in lowercase). This naming convention can lead to duplicate names for different cells if the closest row and column labels are the same for each cell.

Columns D and E of the Answer report show the lowest and highest value for all cells across the set of answers found. Answers appear starting in column F.

The optimal cell row in the Answer report (row 7 in fig. C.12) shows that the expected profit on ice cream production varies from a high of $755 for the optimal answer to a low of $650 for the second answer. The optimal answer generates the highest return by reducing chocolate production to the minimal level necessary to prevent a loss on chocolate while maximizing the more profitable vanilla. You can gather information on how adjustable cells are set for the current application by reviewing rows 15 through 23.

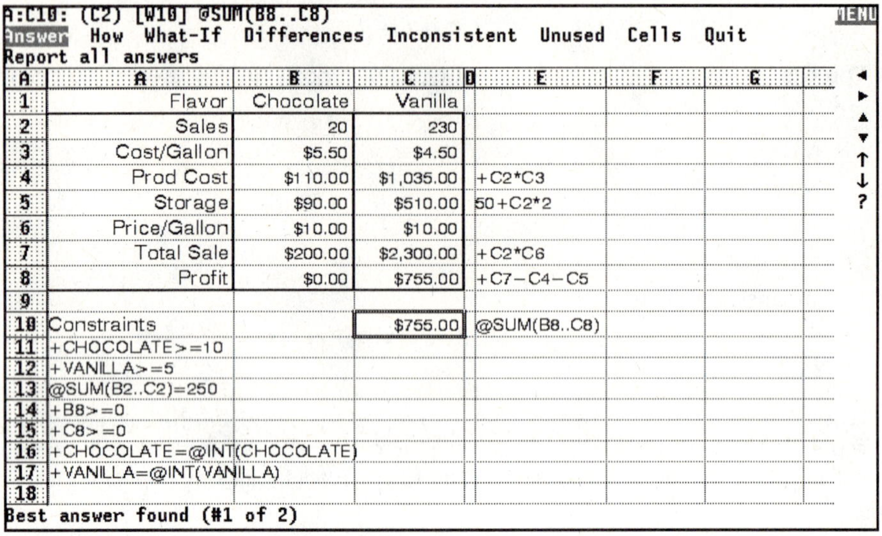

Fig. C.11.
The Solver Report menu.

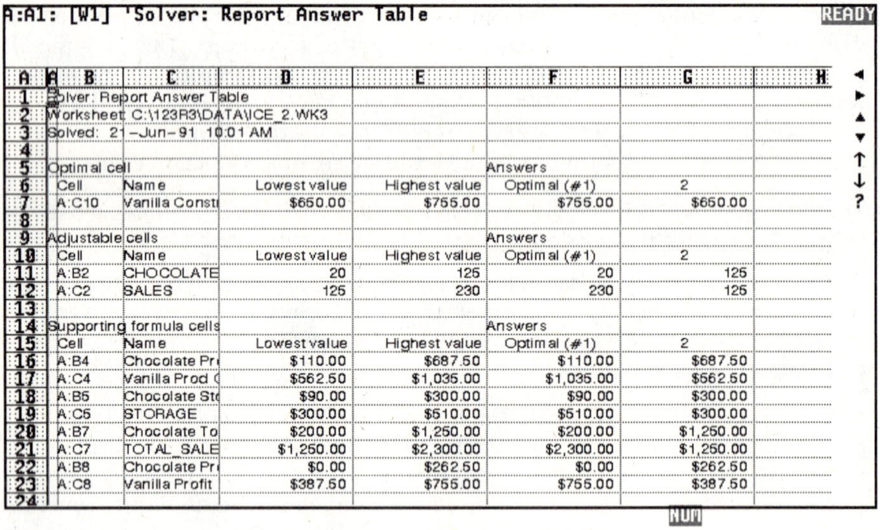

```
A:C10: (C2) [W10] @SUM(B8..C8)                                    MENU
Answer  How What-If  Differences  Inconsistent  Unused  Cells  Quit
Report all answers
```

	A	B	C	D	E	F	G
1	Flavor	Chocolate	Vanilla				
2	Sales	20	230				
3	Cost/Gallon	$5.50	$4.50				
4	Prod Cost	$110.00	$1,035.00	+C2*C3			
5	Storage	$90.00	$510.00	50+C2*2			
6	Price/Gallon	$10.00	$10.00				
7	Total Sale	$200.00	$2,300.00	+C2*C6			
8	Profit	$0.00	$755.00	+C7–C4–C5			
9							
10	Constraints		$755.00	@SUM(B8..C8)			
11	+CHOCOLATE>=10						
12	+VANILLA>=5						
13	@SUM(B2..C2)=250						
14	+B8>=0						
15	+C8>=0						
16	+CHOCOLATE=@INT(CHOCOLATE)						
17	+VANILLA=@INT(VANILLA)						
18							

Best answer found (#1 of 2)

Fig. C.12.
The Answer report.

```
A:A1: [W1] 'Solver: Report Answer Table                          READY
```

	A	B	C	D	E	F	G	H
1	Solver: Report Answer Table							
2	Worksheet C:\123R3\DATA\ICE_2.WK3							
3	Solved: 21-Jun-91 10:01 AM							
4								
5	Optimal cell				Answers			
6	Cell	Name	Lowest value	Highest value	Optimal (#1)	2		
7	A:C10	Vanilla Const	$650.00	$755.00	$755.00	$650.00		
8								
9	Adjustable cells				Answers			
10	Cell	Name	Lowest value	Highest value	Optimal (#1)	2		
11	A:B2	CHOCOLATE	20	125	20	125		
12	A:C2	SALES	125	230	230	125		
13								
14	Supporting formula cells				Answers			
15	Cell	Name	Lowest value	Highest value	Optimal (#1)	2		
16	A:B4	Chocolate Pr	$110.00	$687.50	$110.00	$687.50		
17	A:C4	Vanilla Prod	$562.50	$1,035.00	$1,035.00	$562.50		
18	A:B5	Chocolate St	$90.00	$300.00	$90.00	$300.00		
19	A:C5	STORAGE	$300.00	$510.00	$510.00	$300.00		
20	A:B7	Chocolate To	$200.00	$1,250.00	$200.00	$1,250.00		
21	A:C7	TOTAL_SALE	$1,250.00	$2,300.00	$2,300.00	$1,250.00		
22	A:B8	Chocolate Pr	$0.00	$262.50	$0.00	$262.50		
23	A:C8	Vanilla Profit	$387.50	$755.00	$755.00	$387.50		
24								

The How Solved Report

The **How** solved report exists only in **Table** format. Figures C.13 and C.14 show the How solved report for this example.

This report is for the first answer, which maximizes profit on ice cream production. Solver reports this result to the user by displaying the following message in row 9:

Appendix C ◆ Using the Solver and Backsolver Add-Ins

```
This answer is the best answer Solver could find maximizing
the value of cell A:C10 (Vanilla Constraints)
```

In row 10, Solver notes Better answers may be possible.

```
A:A1: [W1] 'Solver: Report How Solved                                    READY

   A  AB   C            D                    E                   F              G
 1    Solver: Report How Solved
 2    Worksheet: C:\123R3\DATA\ICE_2.WK3
 3    Solved: 25-Jun-91 08:41 AM
 4
 5    Optimal answer (#1)
 6
 7    Answer #1 is one of 2 which satisfies all of the constraints.
 8
 9    This answer is the best answer Solver could find maximizing the value of cell A:C10 (Vanilla Cons
10    Better answers may be possible.
11
12    For this answer, the optimal cell attained the following value:
13
14    Optimal Cell
15       Cell       Name                    Value
16       A:C10      Vanilla Const          $755.00
17
18    For this answer, Solver changed the values in the following adjustable cells:
19
20    Adjustable cells
                                                                            NUM
```

Fig. C.13.
Page 1 of the How solved report.

```
A:A21: [W1]                                                              READY

   A  AB   C            D                    E                   F              G
21       Cell       Name                    Value
22       A:B2       CHOCOLATE                20
23       A:C2       SALES                    230
24
25    These values make the following constraints binding:
26
27    Binding constraints
28       Cell       Name        Formula
29       A:A13      Constraints  @SUM(B2..C2)=250
30       A:A14      Constraints  +B8>=0
31       A:A16      Constraints  +CHOCOLATE=@INT(CHOCOLATE)
32       A:A17      Constraints  +VANILLA=@INT(VANILLA)
33
34    The following constraints are not binding for this answer:
35
36    Unused constraints
37       Cell       Name        Formula          Becomes binding if written as
38       A:A11      Constraints  +CHOCOLATE>=10   +CHOCOLATE>=10+10
39       A:A12      Constraints  +VANILLA>=5      +VANILLA>=5+225
40       A:A15      Constraints  +C8>=0           +C8>=0+755
                                                                            NUM
```

Fig. C.14.
Page 2 of the How solved report.

Solver displays the highest value attained by the optimal cell and the corresponding values for the adjustable cells. The following block of rows reports on the *binding constraints*, which actively bind a solution. Seven constraints were applied in this problem, but only four of these constraints actively restricted the search for the optimal answer.

The **H**ow solved report concludes by listing unused constraints, showing how these constraints can be transformed to make them binding for the current solution.

The What-If Report

The What-If report notes the range of values an adjustable cell can assume (with all constraints in the current answer still evaluating to TRUE) in the current answer and for any other answer. The what-if range for the current answer assumes no other adjustable cells change. The range for limits is occasionally approximate so that at least one constraint doesn't evaluate to TRUE; you can fix this problem by modifying the limit slightly in the direction that makes the constraint TRUE.

You can display the What-If report in both **Cell** and **Table** formats. This report applies to the answer displayed in the worksheet before invoking the Solver **R**eport command. Figure C.15 shows the report in **T**able format and figure C.16 in **C**ell format.

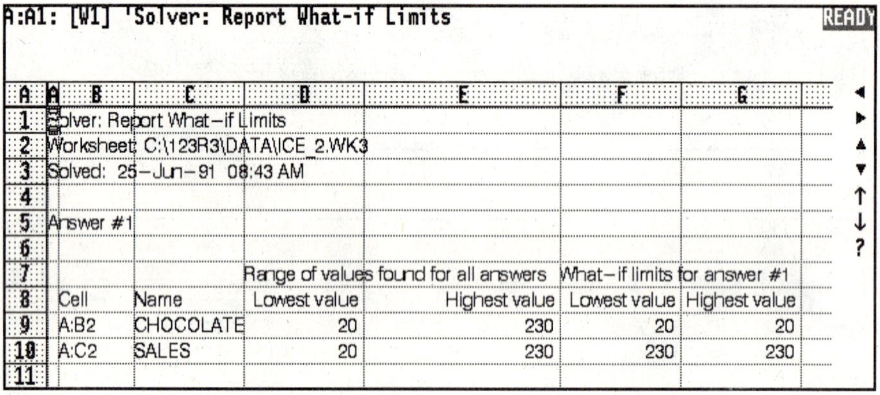

Fig. C.15.
The What-If report in Table format.

	A	B	C	D	E	F	G
1	Solver: Report What-if Limits						
2	Worksheet C:\123R3\DATA\ICE_2.WK3						
3	Solved: 25-Jun-91 08:43 AM						
4							
5	Answer #1						
6							
7				Range of values found for all answers		What-if limits for answer #1	
8		Cell	Name	Lowest value	Highest value	Lowest value	Highest value
9		A:B2	CHOCOLATE	20	230	20	20
10		A:C2	SALES	20	230	230	230
11							

When you select the **R**eport **W**hat-If **T**able command from the Solver menu, Solver creates a new worksheet file containing a table showing the highest and lowest values for all adjustable cells. As figure C.15 shows, the What-If Table shows all adjustable cells in one report. If you are interested in seeing a single adjustable cell—perhaps because the problem contains a large number of adjustable cells— the **R**eport **W**hat-If **C**ell report shown in figure C.16 may be a better choice for you. After viewing the **W**hat-If **C**ell report box, select **N**ext to view the next adjustable cell or **Q**uit to return to the menu. What-If Cell doesn't create a new worksheet file.

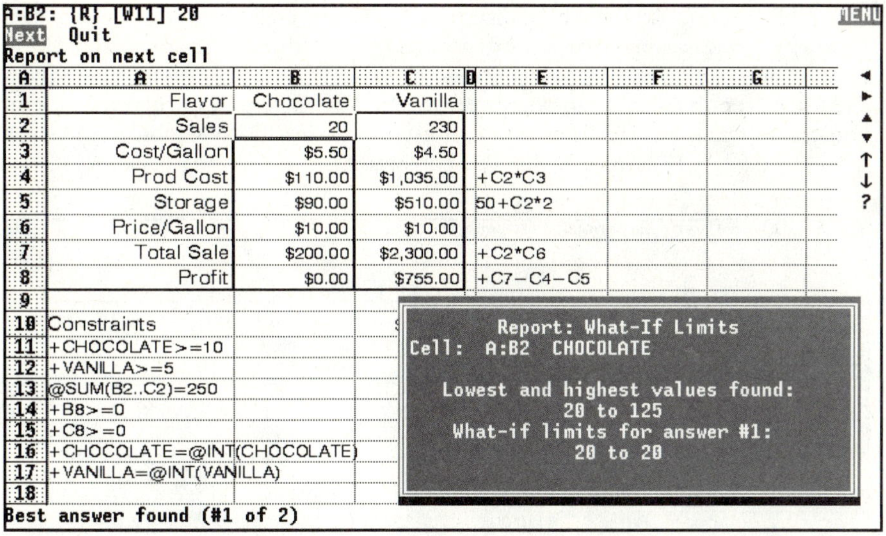

Fig. C.16.
The What-If report in Cell format.

The Differences Report

The **Differences** report shows how answers compare with each other. The report compares only two solutions at a time, but you can contrast different pairs of answers by repeatedly invoking the report, specifying a new pair each time.

To see the **Differences** report, select **Report Differences** from the Solver menu. Select **Cell** or **Table**, depending on whether you want to view the differences between the values in one cell or in a complete report format. Solver asks you to specify which two answers you want to compare, and requests the minimum size of differences to report. The default (0) displays all differences. After reviewing an initial **Difference** report, you may want to screen the differences by setting the minimum difference to a value greater than 0.

If you select **Table** format, Solver generates the DIFFS*xxx*.WK3 worksheet file, replacing *xxx* with 001 for the first **Differences** report. The report number is increased by 1 each time a **Differences** report is generated with the same default drive and directory. Figure C.17 shows the **Differences** report in **T**able format.

If you requested **Cell** format for the **Differences** report, the Solver Cell report box appears, displayed in the same manner as the **What-If** report box shown in figure C.16. By repeatedly selecting the **Next** command, you can view the cells that contribute to the result shown in the worksheet.

The Inconsistent Constraints Report

Constraints sometimes are mutually exclusive; if one constraint is TRUE, the other constraint cannot be TRUE. Solver calls mutually exclusive constraints *inconsistent constraints*. Suppose that the constraints in the ice cream example specify that production levels cannot exceed 250 gallons per month, but total profit must be at least $1,500 per month. If you make this change in the worksheet and start Solver, the add-in reports that no answers were found, but one attempt with inconsistent constraints was tried. The 0 for the "We must make at least $1,500" constraint in cell A:A18 (see fig. C.18) suggests that this constraint is causing the problem.

Fig. C.17. *The Differences report.*

A:A1: [W1] 'Solver: Report Differences READY

A	A	B	C	D	E	F	G
1	Solver: Report Differences						
2	Worksheet: C:\123R3\DATA\ICE_2.WK3						
3	Solved: 26–Jul–91 02:17 PM						
4							
5	Comparing answers 1 and 2						
6	For differences >= 0						
7							
8		Cell	Name	Answer 1	Answer 2	Difference	Difference %
9		A:B2	CHOCOLATE	20	125	–105	–84.00%
10		A:C2	SALES	230	125	105	84.00%
11		A:B4	Chocolate Pro	$110.00	$687.50	($577.50)	–84.00%
12		A:C4	Vanilla Prod C	$1,035.00	$562.50	$472.50	84.00%
13		A:B5	Chocolate Sto	$90.00	$300.00	($210.00)	–70.00%
14		A:C5	STORAGE	$510.00	$300.00	$210.00	70.00%
15		A:B7	Chocolate To	$200.00	$1,250.00	($1,050.00)	–84.00%
16		A:C7	TOTAL_SALE	$2,300.00	$1,250.00	$1,050.00	84.00%
17		A:B8	Chocolate Pro	$0.00	$262.50	($262.50)	–100.00%
18		A:C8	Vanilla Profit	$755.00	$387.50	$367.50	94.84%
19		A:C10	Vanilla Constr	$755.00	$650.00	$105.00	16.15%
20							

NUM

Fig. C.18. *A problem that cannot be solved because of inconsistent constraints.*

A:A18: [W17] +C10>=1500 MENU
Define Solve Answer Report Options Quit
Adjustable Constraints Optimal Quit

A	A	B	C	D	E	F	G
1	Flavor	Chocolate	Vanilla				
2	Sales	20	230				
3	Cost/Gallon	$5.50	$4.50				
4	Prod Cost	$110.00	$1,035.00	+C2*C3			
5	Storage	$90.00	$510.00	50+C2*2			
6	Price/Gallon	$10.00	$10.00				
7	Total Sale	$200.00	$2,300.00	+C2*C6			
8	Profit	$0.00	$755.00	+C7–C4–C5			
9							
10	Constraints		$755.00	@SUM(B8..C8)			
11	+CHOCOLATE>=10						
12	+VANILLA>=5						
13	@SUM(B2..C2)=250						
14	+B8>=0						
15	+C8>=0						
16	+CHOCOLATE=@INT(CHOCOLATE)						
17	+VANILLA=@INT(VANILLA)						
18	0						

No answers found: Attempt #1 of 1

Appendix C ♦ Using the Solver and Backsolver Add-Ins

The Inconsistent constraint report option from the Solver Report menu provides a definitive way of determining which constraints are inconsistent. Figure C.19 shows the result of selecting this report in a worksheet without inconsistent constraints (see the prompt at the bottom of the screen). Figure C.20 shows the result of issuing the Solver Report Inconsistent Table command after modifying the constraints to make them inconsistent.

```
A:B2: {R} [W11] 20                                              ERROR
Cell   Table
Report unsatisfied constraints in a report window
   A              A          B          C       D          E          F          G
   1           Flavor    Chocolate   Vanilla
   2            Sales       20         230
   3       Cost/Gallon    $5.50       $4.50
   4         Prod Cost   $110.00    $1,035.00  +C2*C3
   5          Storage    $90.00     $510.00   50+C2*2
   6      Price/Gallon   $10.00      $10.00
   7        Total Sale  $200.00    $2,300.00  +C2*C6
   8           Profit     $0.00     $755.00   +C7-C4-C5
   9
  10  Constraints                  $755.00   @SUM(B8..C8)
  11  +CHOCOLATE>=10
  12  +VANILLA>=5
  13  @SUM(B2..C2)=250
  14  +B8>=0
  15  +C8>=0
  16  +CHOCOLATE=@INT(CHOCOLATE)
  17  +VANILLA=@INT(VANILLA)
  18
This answer has no inconsistent constraints.
```

Fig. C.19.
A worksheet with no inconsistent constraints.

```
A:A1: [W1] 'Solver: Report Inconsistent Constraints             MENU
Answer  How  What-If  Differences  Inconsistent  Unused  Cells  Quit
Report unsatisfied constraints for the current answer
   A      B         C              D                      E
   1  Solver: Report Inconsistent Constraints
   2  Worksheet C:\123R3\DATA\ICE_3.WK3
   3  Solved: 25-Jun-91 11:47 AM
   4
   5  Attempt #1
   6
   7  Cell    Name       This constraint was not satisfied  Becomes satisfied if written as
   8  A:A18   Constraints  +C10>=1500                       +C10>=1500+-745
   9
  10
  ...
  20
No answers found: Attempt #1 of 1
```

Fig. C.20.
The result of adding inconsistent constraints.

As figure C.20 shows, Solver indicates which constraints were not satisfied, and notes which changes are necessary before those constraints can be satisfied. Because Solver cannot determine which constraints you can modify in a "real world" situation, you may have to examine other possibilities to determine which constraints to change.

The Unused Constraints Report

In some situations, knowing which constraints don't bind or limit a solution may be helpful. Constraints may bind some answers but not others. If you select **Report Unused Table**, Solver generates an UNUSED*xx*.WK3 worksheet file listing the unused constraints for the current answer (see fig. C.21). You can select **Report Unused Cell** to report unused constraints one cell at a time.

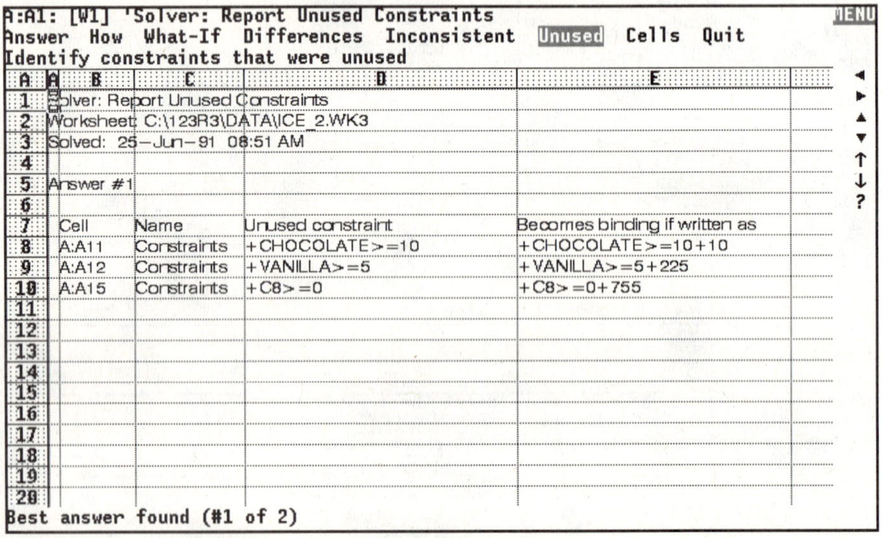

Fig. C.21.
The Unused constraints report.

Cell	Name	Unused constraint	Becomes binding if written as
A:A11	Constraints	+CHOCOLATE>=10	+CHOCOLATE>=10+10
A:A12	Constraints	+VANILLA>=5	+VANILLA>=5+225
A:A15	Constraints	+C8>=0	+C8>=0+755

The Unused constraint report in figure C.21 shows that three constraints had no effect on the solution found by Solver. Row 8 indicates that the constraint requiring the manufacture of at least ten gallons of chocolate ice cream is not binding, because at least 20 gallons of chocolate are necessary to pay production and storage costs. The Unused constraint report shows how to transform the constraint to make it binding (add ten to the amount).

Similarly, the requirement of making at least five gallons of vanilla isn't binding. Because the profit is greater on vanilla, the best answer indicates that the business should sell as much vanilla as possible after meeting a minimum volume requirement on chocolate. Because the optimal answer specifies 230 gallons of vanilla, the requirement to sell at least five gallons isn't binding. Row 9 of the figure specifies that the minimum amount of vanilla is binding if you increase it to 230.

The Cells Used Report

The **Cells** used report provides a summary of the cells used in a Solver problem, including all adjustable, constraint, and optimal cells. Figure C.22 shows the report in **Table** format. The **Cells** used report also can be displayed in **Cell** format.

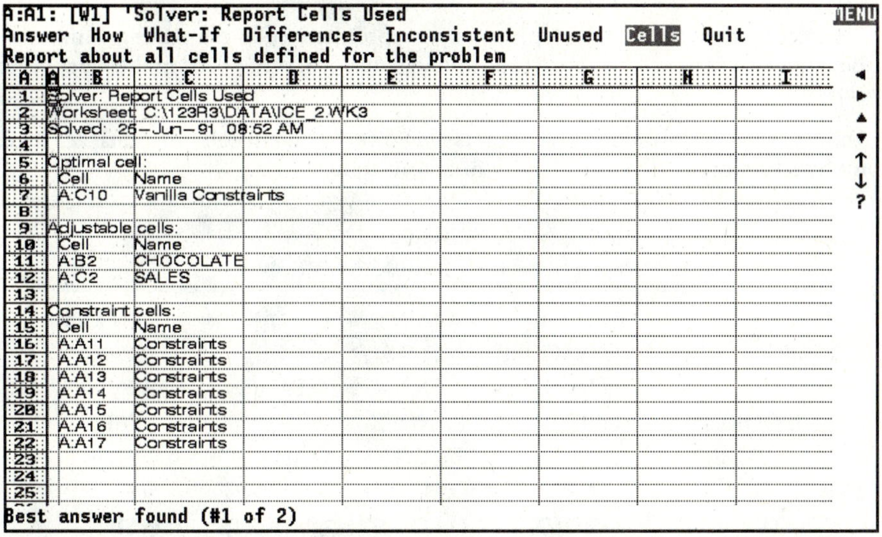

Fig. C.22.
The Cells used report.

For each cell used in solving the problem, the **Cells** used report indicates the following: the type of cell—adjustable, constraint, or optimal; the cell's address; the cell's range name or (if the cell has no range name) the closest row and column labels (used to label the cell).

If you select **Cell** format instead of **Table** format, two menu commands appear. The **Next** command advances the cell shown in the display box to the next cell. The natural progression starts with the first adjustable cell and moves through all remaining adjustable cells before advancing to the first constraint cell. After noting the constraint cells, Solver highlights the optimal cell before starting the cycle again with the first adjustable cell. Select **Quit** to return to the Solver **Report** menu.

Using Functions with Solver

You can use 1-2-3 functions in the cell formulas that Solver uses to determine solutions, if you obey the following basic rules:

- ◆ Functions in problem cells must use only numbers as arguments.

    Problem cells cannot contain functions requiring strings, date or time values, or values from a database. You can use @AVG in a Solver problem cell because @AVG uses only numbers to determine a numeric average, but you cannot use @TRIM or @DAVG because those functions require a string argument and a value from a database, respectively.

- Functions in problem cells must return numbers.

    In problem cells, you cannot use any functions returning a string (such as @STRING), a date or time value (such as @DATE), or a value from a database (such as @DQUERY). You can use functions returning Boolean values (such as @ERR and @ISNA) because 1-2-3 Release 3.1+ considers Boolean values to be regular numbers.

Remember that these rules apply only to problem cells containing functions. Because Solver uses only those cells to find solutions, other cells in the worksheet can contain any functions or formulas.

Table C.1 lists the functions you can use in Solver problem cells. See Chapter 6 for information on using each of these functions in formulas.

Table C.1
Functions Compatible with Solver

@ABS	@ACOS	@ASIN	@ATAN	@ATAN2
@AVG	@CHOOSE	@COLS	@COS	@COUNT
@CTERM	@DDB	@EXP	@FALSE	@FV
@HLOOKUP	@IF	@INDEX	@INT	@IRR
@ISNUMBER	@LN	@LOG	@MAX	@MIN
@MOD	@NPV	@PI	@PMT	@PV
@RATE	@ROUND	@ROWS	@SHEETS	@SIN
@SLN	@SQRT	@STD	@STDS	@SUM
@SUMPRODUCT	@SYD	@TAN	@TERM	@TRUE
@VAR	@VARS	@VDB	@VLOOKUP	

Using Solver with Macros

The Solver add-in adds a new function called @SOLVER to 1-2-3. This function is used with macros to determine the state of Solver. Following is the syntax for @SOLVER:

@SOLVER("*query_string*")

@SOLVER has eight possible arguments you can use as the *query_string*, as shown in table C.2.

Table C.2
@SOLVER Arguments

Argument	Value Returned	Description
"*consistent*"	1	All constraints met
	2	At least one constraint not met
	ERR	No answer in file
"*done*"	1	Solver finished
	2	Solver in progress
	3	Problem not yet solved
"*moreanswers*"	1	No more answers exist
	2	Solve Continue may produce additional answers
	ERR	Problem not yet solved
"*needguess*"	1	No guesses needed
	2	Guesses needed
	ERR	No answer in file
"*numanswers*"	x	x number of answers found
	ERR	Problem not yet solved
"*optimal*"	1	Optimal answer found
	2	Best answer found
	3	No binding constraints
	4	No optimal cell defined or no answer found
	ERR	Problem not yet solved
"*progress*"	x	x fraction of problem solved
	ERR	Problem not yet solved
"*result*"	1	One or more answers found
	2	Answers not found but Solver can display attempts
	ERR	Problem not yet solved

Chapter 14 provides more information on using functions with 1-2-3 macros.

Using Backsolver

The Backsolver add-in finds values for variables based on a given goal value by manipulating one cell in the worksheet. Backsolver offers a quick and efficient way of making preliminary estimates for the variables in any what-if problem.

Figure C.23 shows a sample problem for which Backsolver can help you find answers to what-if questions. In this example, the worksheet shows that you can repay a loan of $50,000 at 10% interest in 12 months with a monthly payment of $4,395.79. But suppose that you can pay $5,000 per month—how much more money can you borrow, assuming the same term and interest rate?

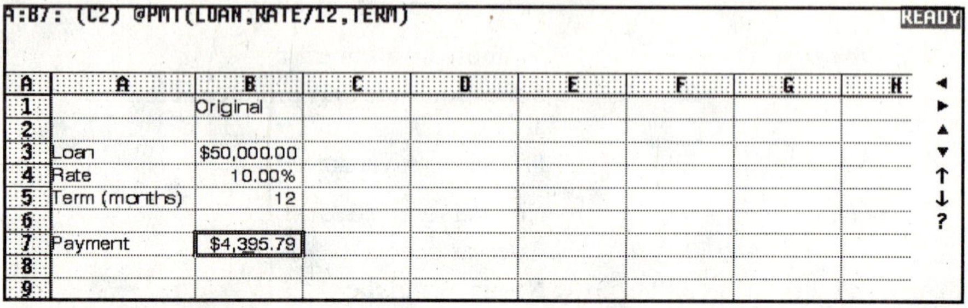

Fig. C.23.
Calculating a loan payment.

To use Backsolver to solve the problem, you first must attach the Backsolver add-in, as described in the "Attaching and Detaching Solver and Backsolver" section of this appendix. With Backsolver attached, press the function key combination you assigned to invoke Backsolver. Figure C.24 shows the resulting Backsolver menu.

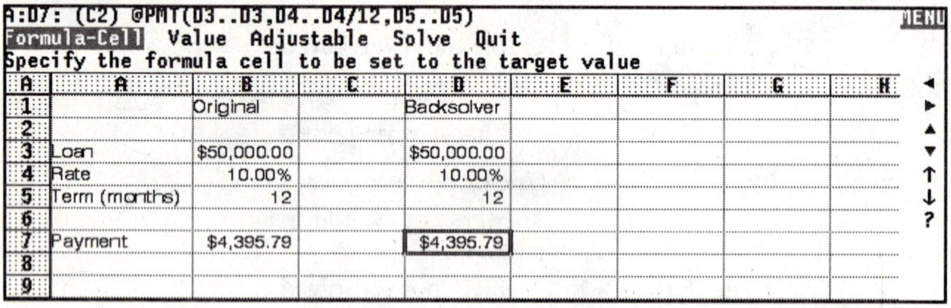

Fig. C.24.
The Backsolver menu.

Because Backsolver makes permanent changes in your worksheet, save the worksheet before using the add-in. As an alternative, you can create a duplicate copy of the problem cells (as shown in fig. C.24) and use Backsolver in the duplicate area. With Undo active, you can reverse changes made by Backsolver if you use Undo immediately after using Backsolver.

Before Backsolver can solve a problem, you must specify all of the following: which cell contains the formula you want to return a specific value; the desired value; and which cell contains the variable that you want to change to achieve the desired result. Select Formula-Cell from the Backsolver menu. Backsolver prompts you to specify the range address of the formula, as shown in figure C.25.

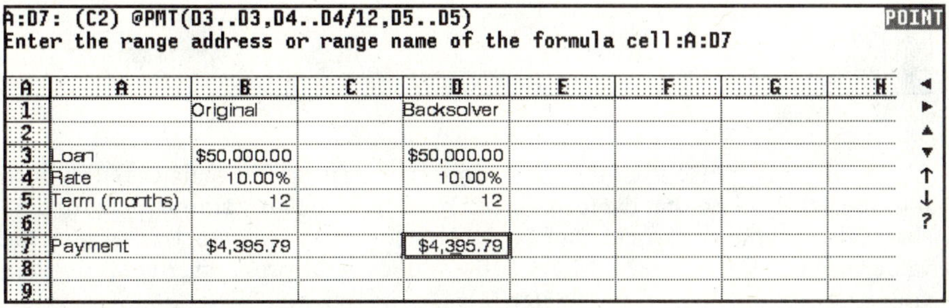

```
A:D7: (C2) @PMT(D3..D3,D4..D4/12,D5..D5)                                POINT
Enter the range address or range name of the formula cell:A:D7
     A           B              C         D           E      F      G     H
1                Original                 Backsolver
2
3    Loan        $50,000.00               $50,000.00
4    Rate        10.00%                   10.00%
5    Term (months)   12                   12
6
7    Payment     $4,395.79                $4,395.79
8
9
```

Fig. C.25.
Entering the Formula-Cell address.

Select Value and specify the desired value you want the formula to attain. In figure C.26, the value shown is $5,000—the maximum monthly payment.

```
A:D7: (C2) @PMT(D3..D3,D4..D4/12,D5..D5)                                EDIT
Enter the desired result value:5000_
     A           B              C         D           E      F      G     H
1                Original                 Backsolver
2
3    Loan        $50,000.00               $50,000.00
4    Rate        10.00%                   10.00%
5    Term (months)   12                   12
6
7    Payment     $4,395.79                $4,395.79
8
9
```

Fig. C.26.
Entering the desired value for the formula cell.

Backsolver changes one value to achieve the specified goal. In this example, the value to be adjusted is the loan amount in cell A:D3. Select **Adjustable** from the Backsolver menu and specify cell A:D3 as the adjustable cell, as shown in figure C.27. If you duplicate the problem cells, the original worksheet figures remain intact, and you can compare Backsolver's solution with the original answer.

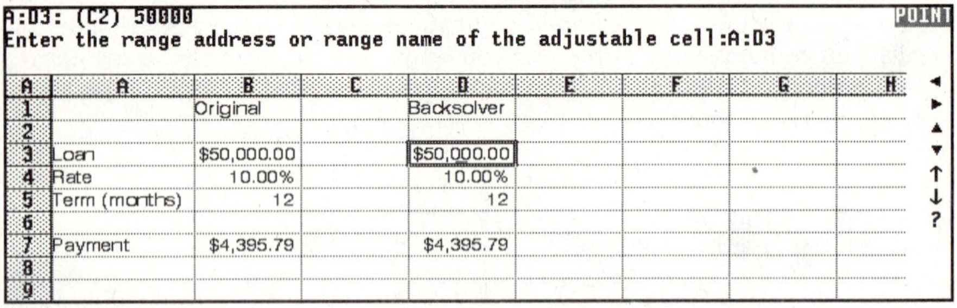

Fig. C.27.
Specifying the adjustable cell.

```
A:D3: (C2) 50000                                                    POINT
Enter the range address or range name of the adjustable cell:A:D3
```

	A	B	C	D	E	F	G	H
1		Original		Backsolver				
2								
3	Loan	$50,000.00		$50,000.00				
4	Rate	10.00%		10.00%				
5	Term (months)	12		12				
6								
7	Payment	$4,395.79		$4,395.79				
8								
9								

When you select **Solve** from the Backsolver menu, the add-in changes the value in the adjustable cell so that the formula cell returns the desired amount. Figure C.28 shows the sample worksheet after Backsolver solves the problem by changing the value in cell A:D3 to $56,872.54. If all other values in the problem remain constant, you can borrow a maximum of $56,872.54.

If Backsolver cannot find a solution that adjusts the value of the formula to the desired amount, an error message appears describing the problem. If Backsolver cannot find a value that adjusts the value of the formula to the desired figure, you may want to run Solver on the data in your problem to determine reasonable estimates.

If the resulting answer is better than the original answer, Backsolver places the best possible answer in the adjustable cell.

When you use Backsolver, remember that the value of the adjustable cell is permanently changed. If you plan to use Backsolver to try a number of different values, save the worksheet file before you begin; then you can return to the original worksheet containing the starting values. If you forget to save the worksheet before using Backsolver, return to the last value in the adjustable cell with the Undo command. (Note that Undo only returns the preceding set of values.) If you use Backsolver a number of times, Undo cannot return the initial values, but returns the values that existed before you selected **Solve** from the Backsolver menu. Consider placing each Backsolver attempt in a separate worksheet.

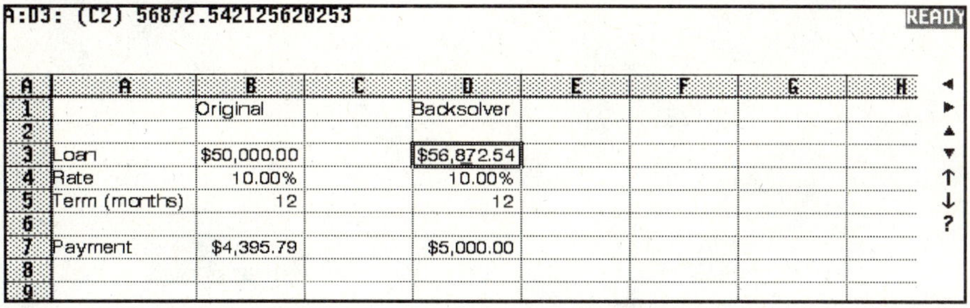

Appendix C ◆ Using the Solver and Backsolver Add-Ins

```
A:D3: (C2) 56872.542125620253                                READY

       A          B          C          D        E     F    G    H
  1               Original              Backsolver
  2
  3   Loan       $50,000.00             $56,872.54
  4   Rate          10.00%                  10.00%
  5   Term (months)    12                      12
  6
  7   Payment     $4,395.79              $5,000.00
  8
  9
```

Fig. C.28.
The worksheet after selecting Solve from the Backsolver menu.

Using the Viewer Add-In

D

This appendix describes the 1-2-3 Release 3.1+ add-in program called Viewer. Viewer enables you to examine a file before opening or retrieving it, makes file linking much easier, and enables you to browse worksheet and text files.

This appendix shows you how to use Viewer to perform the following tasks:

- ◆ View and retrieve worksheet files
- ◆ View and open additional worksheet files
- ◆ Create worksheet linking formulas
- ◆ Browse worksheet and text files

Attaching and Detaching Viewer

To use Viewer, you must first install the add-in. If you haven't installed Viewer, see Appendix A for installation instructions.

After installing Viewer, you must attach the add-in to make it available for use, just as with any other add-in program. To attach an add-in, press Alt–F10 (Add-in) and select Load. 1-2-3 displays a list of add-in program files with the extension PLC. Select VIEWER.PLC and press Enter.

1-2-3 asks which key to assign to Viewer. You use this key to invoke (run) the add-in. The key numbers **1**, **2**, and **3** correspond to the function keys labeled F7, F8, and F9, respectively. After you choose one of the numbers, you invoke Viewer by holding down the Alt key and pressing the function key you selected. If you selected **1**, for example, you invoke Viewer by holding down Alt and pressing F7. You also can assign No-Key to the add-in. If you don't assign a key to Viewer, you must invoke Viewer using Alt–F10 (Add-in) **Invoke**. For this example, select a key to assign to

917

Viewer and press Enter. 1-2-3 assigns the key you selected and returns to the Add-In menu. Select **Q**uit to return to the worksheet.

To remove Viewer from memory, use Alt–F10 (Add-in) **R**emove. 1-2-3 displays a list of currently attached add-in programs. Highlight `VIEWER` and press Enter. You also can select Alt–F10 (Add-in) **C**lear to remove all add-ins from memory. At this point, however, leave Viewer in memory so you can try the features described in this appendix.

Invoking and Using Viewer

To invoke Viewer, hold down the Alt key and press the function key you assigned to Viewer. 1-2-3 displays the Viewer menu shown in figure D.1. Viewer is in the computer's memory and integrated with 1-2-3. You can use any Viewer function, leave Viewer, and invoke Viewer again with the Alt-function key combination.

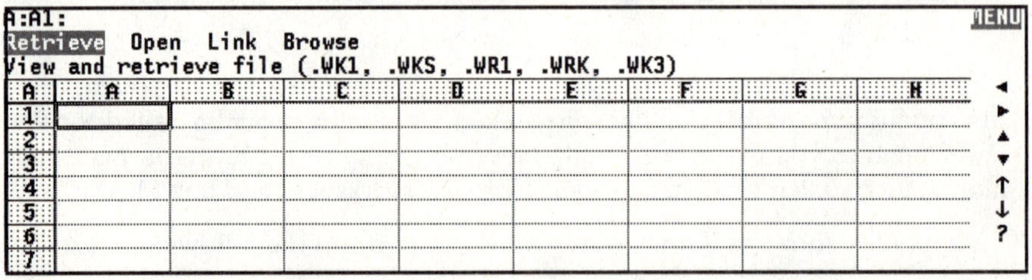

Fig. D.1.
The Viewer add-in menu.

To leave Viewer and return to 1-2-3 READY mode, press Esc. You can redisplay Viewer by invoking the add-in with the Alt-function key combination or with Alt–F10 (Add-in) **I**nvoke.

Understanding the Viewer Menu and Screen

The Viewer menu contains four options. Table D.1 describes the Viewer options.

Table D.1
Viewer Menu Selections

Selection	Description
Retrieve	Reads a worksheet file into memory after displaying its contents
Open	Opens a worksheet file in memory after displaying its contents; you specify whether the file goes **B**efore or **A**fter the current worksheet

Appendix D ♦ Using the Viewer Add-In

Selection	Description
Link	Enters one or more linking formulas in the current worksheet; you point at cells or ranges in the files to be linked
Browse	Displays the contents of worksheet and text files; doesn't retrieve, open, or link to files being browsed

After you select a Viewer command, 1-2-3 removes the worksheet from the screen and displays the Viewer screen (see fig. D.2). Table D.2 describes the elements of the Viewer screen.

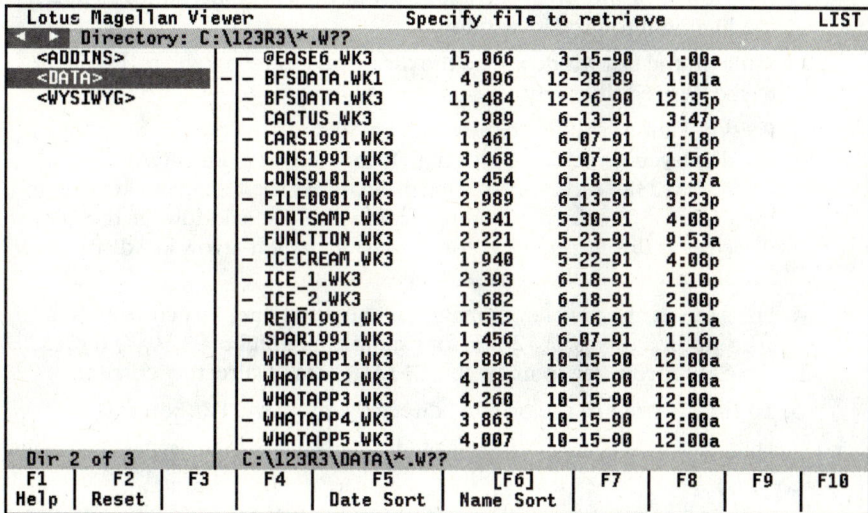

Fig. D.2.
The Viewer screen.

**Table D.2
Viewer Screen Elements**

Screen Element	Description
Status line	A line displaying prompts and an indicator showing whether the highlight is in the List or View window (top of the screen)
Directory path	The file directory shown on the second line of the display (below the status line)
List window	The left window, containing a list of file names in the current Viewer directory
View window	The right window, displaying the contents of the file highlighted in the List window
Information line	The line below the View window, showing the number of worksheets in the file
Key bar	The area at the bottom of the screen that displays the list of available function keys

Navigating Viewer

Viewer displays different directories, files, or portions of files when you move the highlight on the Viewer screen. You use the same movement keys with all Viewer commands; you cannot use a mouse with Viewer. Use the up-arrow and down-arrow keys to move the highlight up or down one or more lines—regardless of whether the highlight is in the List or View window.

When you start Viewer, the current 1-2-3 directory is displayed. To change the directory, follow these steps:

1. Make sure that the highlight is in the List window. If the highlight is in the View window, press the left-arrow key one or more times to move the highlight to the List window.
2. While in the List window, use the direction keys to move the highlight to the desired directory.
3. Press the left-arrow key to move the highlight to the parent directory of the displayed directory. To change from the C:\123R3\DATA directory to the C:\123R3 directory, for example, press the-left arrow key when the <DATA> directory is highlighted in the List window. If the root directory is the current directory, pressing the left-arrow key displays a list of currently-available disk drives.
4. Press the right-arrow key to make a highlighted directory current. If the current directory is C:\123R3, for example, highlight <DATA> and press the right-arrow key to make the C:\123R3\DATA directory current.
5. To reset Viewer to the original directory, press the F2 (Reset) key.

Retrieving a File

As your collection of worksheet files grows, remembering which file serves which purpose may become increasingly difficult. Is MYREC91.WK3 or MYFILE91.WK3 the business expense worksheet for 1991? Without the Viewer add-in, you can keep written records documenting each worksheet's purpose, or try retrieving each worksheet in turn until you find the correct one. Both methods are too time-consuming.

Viewer's **Retrieve** command displays the contents of worksheet files as you scroll through the list of files in the current Viewer directory. After highlighting the correct file, press Enter to retrieve the file. The major advantage to retrieving with Viewer instead of /**F**ile **R**etrieve is that you can display the file contents before retrieving, to ensure that you have the right file.

Viewer displays each worksheet as it appears in READY mode without Wysiwyg attached. Graphs, special fonts, and cell formatting are not displayed. Figure D.3 shows how Viewer displays a typical worksheet file.

Appendix D ◆ Using the Viewer Add-In   **921**

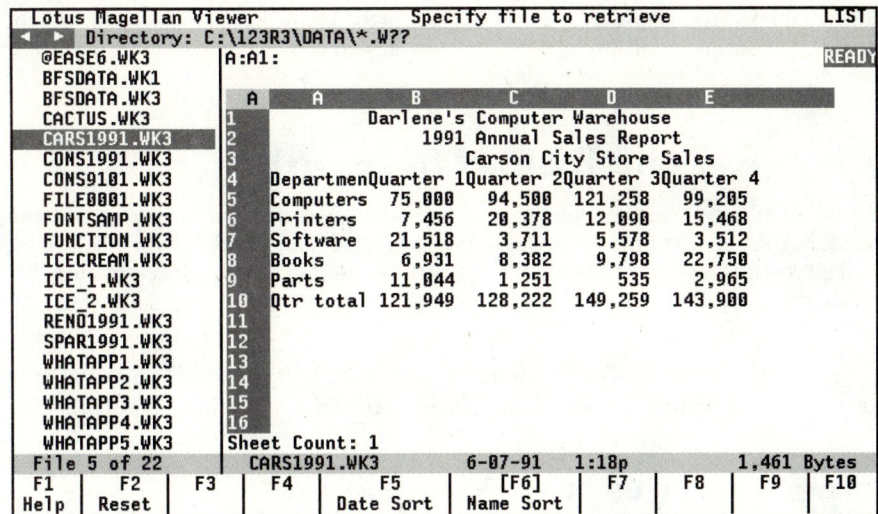

Fig. D.3.
Displaying a worksheet file with Viewer prior to retrieving the file.

If you select the Viewer **R**etrieve command but have not saved the current worksheet, Viewer prompts you with the following message:

```
WORKSHEET CHANGES NOT SAVED! Retrieve file anyway?
```

Select **N**o to return to READY mode and save the worksheet with **/**File **S**ave. If you select **Y**es, Viewer replaces the current worksheet without saving.

Viewing a File Before Retrieving

When a file is displayed in the View window, you can see areas of the file that aren't currently displayed by pressing the right-arrow key to switch to the View window. With the highlight in the View window, scroll through the file using the same direction keys you use to navigate a worksheet in 1-2-3.

To retrieve a worksheet file, press Enter while the file name is highlighted in the List window and the worksheet contents are displayed in the View window.

Note: If you are scrolling through the worksheet in the View window, you need not return to the List window before pressing Enter to retrieve the file.

Returning to the List Window

Suppose that the file you're viewing is not the correct file. To view and select another file, move the highlight back to the List window by pressing the left-arrow key when the highlight is in column A of the displayed worksheet. Depending on the worksheet's structure, several keystrokes may be required to move the highlight to the A column. You can save keystrokes by using the Home key to move the highlight to the A column. Then press the left-arrow key to move the highlight to the List window.

Changing the Display Sort Order

By default, Viewer displays file names in alphabetical order, but the add-in also can list files using a date sort. Suppose that you have several hundred worksheet files, but all you know about the file you need is that someone in your office updated that file within the past week. To change the display so that Viewer shows the newest files at the top of the list, press F5 (Date Sort).

To return to alphabetical order, press F6 (Name Sort). Viewer continues to use the last sort order setting you selected until you remove the add-in from memory.

Opening Files with Viewer

With 1-2-3 Release 3, you can load multiple worksheet files into memory at the same time. When you open an additional worksheet file, any worksheet files already in memory remain open and available for use.

The Viewer **O**pen command functions much like the Viewer **R**etrieve command discussed in the preceding section. Instead of warning you if the current worksheet has been modified, however, **O**pen prompts with two choices, **B**efore and **A**fter. The **B**efore option reads a file into memory in front of the current file. After reads a file into memory behind the current file. After you select **B**efore or **A**fter, the Viewer Open screen appears.

When you open a new file, 1-2-3 moves the cell pointer to the new file. To see both open files, select /Worksheet Window Perspective. 1-2-3 displays a three-dimensional perspective view of the open worksheets, as shown in figure D.4.

Each worksheet in figure D.4 displays the letter A in the upper left corner of the frame. This visual cue reminds you that 1-2-3 is displaying two files—not two worksheets in a single file.

Linking Files with Viewer

Using links between 1-2-3 worksheet files, you can consolidate data from several files automatically. Before file linking was available, consolidating data was difficult at best. You could use the /File Combine command and automate the process with macros, but this method is sometimes dangerous; for example, errors can result if changes in your worksheet insert or delete rows or columns.

The process of linking formulas between files offers many advantages over /File Combine. The file links are updated automatically when you retrieve the master file;

you need not perform a manual or macro-driven /File Combine operation to ensure that you are using the latest data. Because file linking uses formulas, if you rearrange your master worksheet, the links remain updated. One disadvantage of file linking formulas, however, is the complexity of the formulas. You must specify the file name of the linked file as well as the desired cell address or range name. The Viewer add-in makes creating linking formulas much easier because with Viewer you can point to the cell or address in another file.

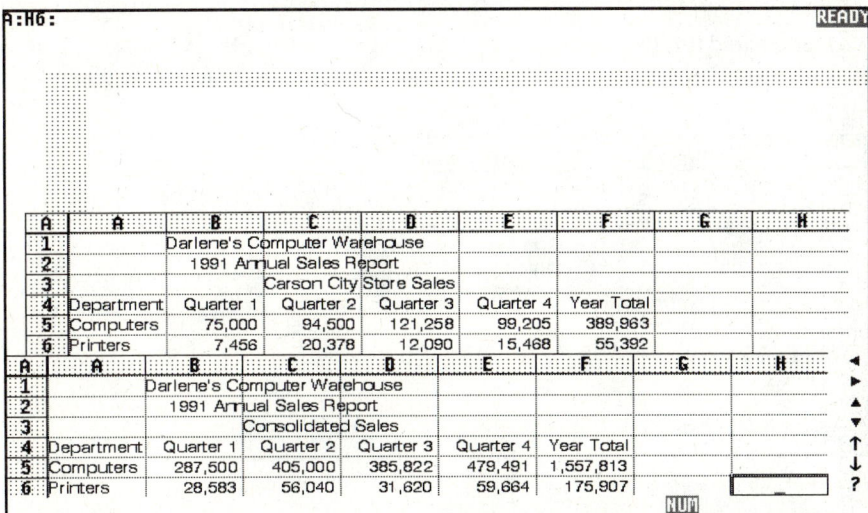

Fig. D.4.
Two open worksheets displayed in Perspective view.

Suppose that you run a chain of small discount computer stores located in Reno, Sparks, and Carson City, Nevada. Separate worksheet files contain the sales results from the three stores. The sales manager decides to run a contest with prizes for the store with the best performance in each department. The sales manager wants a single report comparing each store's results, not three separate worksheets. A consolidation worksheet can show the combined results for all stores. Figure D.5 shows the consolidation worksheet.

To consolidate the data, you use the Viewer Link command. Place the cell pointer in cell A:B5, the first cell to contain a linking formula. Invoke Viewer and select Link. Because you consolidate data for the Reno store first, move the highlight in the List window to RENO1991.WK3. With the file name highlighted, press the right-arrow key to move the highlight to the View window. Move the highlight to the beginning of the range you want to link (cell A:B7). Press the period key to anchor the range, and move the highlight down until A:B7..A:B11 is highlighted. (Fig. D.6 shows the highlighted range.) Press Enter to complete the selection and enter the linking formulas in the consolidation worksheet.

Continue the linking process by moving the cell pointer in the master worksheet to the next cell where you want to start a series of linking formulas (A:C5) and use Viewer to create links to SPAR1991.WK3. Finally, move the cell pointer to A:D5 and create the links to CARS1991.WK3. Figure D.7 shows the completed consolidation worksheet.

Notice the following formula in cell A:B5 of the consolidation worksheet:

```
+<<C:\123R3\DATA\RENO1991.WK3>>A:B7..A:B7
```

Viewer created this formula and similar ones in the range A:B5..A:D9—a total of 15 linking formulas. You can see the advantage of using Viewer to create file links.

Fig. D.5.

A consolidation worksheet before adding formula links.

A:B5: {SWISS14} READY

A	A	B	C	D	E	F	G
1		Darlene's Computer Warehouse					
2		1991 1st Quarter Sales Report					
3			Consolidated Sales				
4	Department	Reno	Sparks	Carson City	Dept Totals		
5	Computers				0		
6	Printers				0		
7	Software				0		
8	Books				0		
9	Parts				0		
10	Qtr totals	0	0	0	0		
11							

Browsing Files with Viewer

Viewer's **Browse** command enables you to look at 1-2-3 and Symphony worksheet and text files. **Browse** is for viewing only; you cannot retrieve, open, or link to the file displayed in the View window.

The **Browse** command is very useful for examining text files before issuing a /**F**ile **I**mport **T**ext or /**F**ile **I**mport **N**umbers command. With **Browse**, you can verify that you are importing the correct file.

Browse displays 1-2-3 and Symphony worksheet files as they would appear if you retrieved the file, and treats all other files as text files. As a result, if you **Browse** program files, you see unintelligible characters with the text of any messages contained in the file.

Appendix D ◆ Using the Viewer Add-In

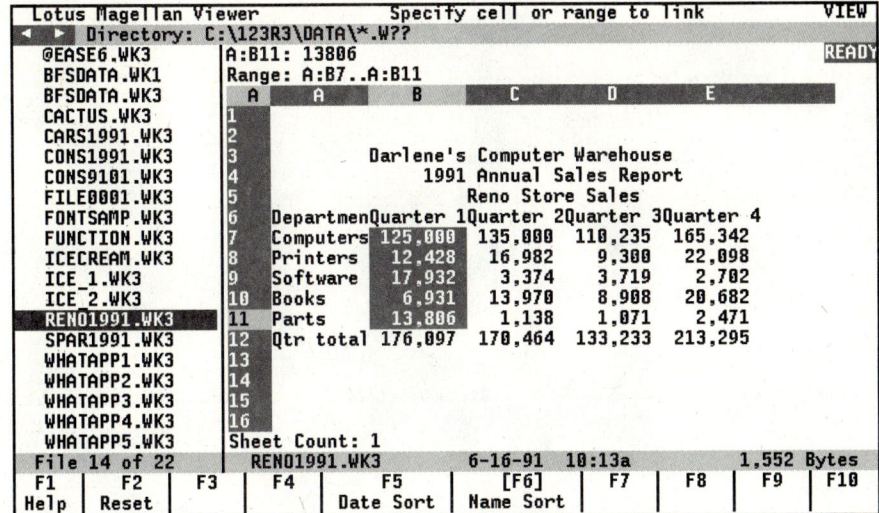

Fig. D.6.
Setting up a link with Viewer.

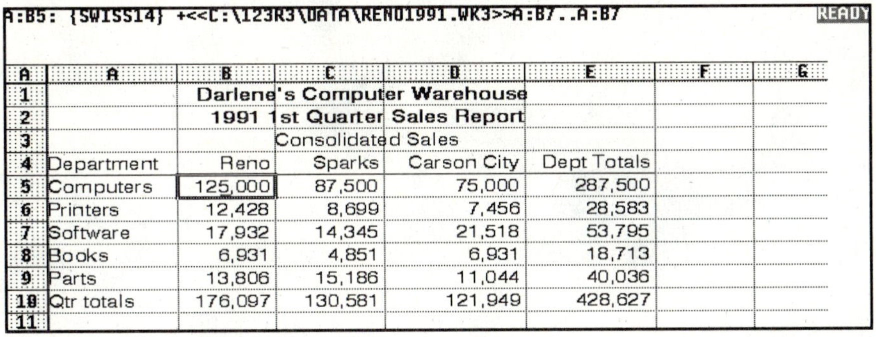

Fig. D.7.
The completed consolidation worksheet.

Compose Sequences for the Lotus Multibyte Character Set

E

The Lotus Multibyte Character Set (LMBCS) includes characters you may not find on your keyboard. These special characters include monetary symbols, mathematical symbols and operator signs, and diacritical marks.

To enter a character that is not on your keyboard, press Compose (Alt-F1) and then a series of keystrokes that Lotus calls a *compose sequence*. To create some characters, you can use one of several compose sequences. For example, to enter the British pound sign (£), you press Compose (Alt-F1) and then type **L=** or **l=**. Depending on your hardware, some LMBCS characters may not display on your monitor or print from your printer. If a character does not display on your screen, print a sample range to see whether the character is available from your printer.

The table that follows lists the special characters with their LMBCS codes, a description of each character, and the compose sequence(s) used to create each character.

If you use some characters frequently, you can easily create macros to perform the compose sequences for you. You then can store the macros in a macro library and access them as you need them. (See Chapters 13 and 14 to learn how to create macros and macro libraries.)

LMBCS characters also can be generated by using the @CHAR function. For example, @CHAR(156) enters the British pound symbol (£) into the worksheet. See Chapter 6 for a complete discussion of the @CHAR function.

927

Group 0

This section defines the Group 0 LMBCS characters.

Note: Codes 1 through 31 are not LMBCS codes. Using the @CHAR function with the numbers 1 through 31 produces the characters for LMBCS codes 256 through 287, listed in the Group 1 table.

LMBCS code	Compose sequence	Description	Character
32		Space	Space
33		Exclamation point	!
34		Double quotes	"
35	+ +	Pound sign	#
36		Dollar sign	$
37		Percent	%
38		Ampersand	&
39		Close single quote	'
40		Open parenthesis	(
41		Close parenthesis	)
42		Asterisk	*
43		Plus sign	+
44		Comma	,
45		Minus sign	-
46		Period	.
47		Slash	/
48		Zero	0
49		One	1
50		Two	2
51		Three	3
52		Four	4
53		Five	5
54		Six	6
55		Seven	7
56		Eight	8
57		Nine	9
58		Colon	:
59		Semicolon	;
60		Less than	<
61		Equal sign	=
62		Greater than	>
63		Question mark	?
64	aa or AA	At sign	@
65		A, uppercase	A
66		B, uppercase	B
67		C, uppercase	C
68		D, uppercase	D
69		E, uppercase	E
70		F, uppercase	F
71		G, uppercase	G
72		H, uppercase	H
73		I, uppercase	I
74		J, uppercase	J
75		K, uppercase	K
76		L, uppercase	L
77		M, uppercase	M
78		N, uppercase	N

Appendix E ◆ Compose Sequences for the Lotus Multibyte Character Set

LMBCS code	Compose sequence	Description	Character
79		O, uppercase	O
80		P, uppercase	P
81		Q, uppercase	Q
82		R, uppercase	R
83		S, uppercase	S
84		T, uppercase	T
85		U, uppercase	U
86		V, uppercase	V
87		W, uppercase	W
88		X, uppercase	X
89		Y, uppercase	Y
90		Z, uppercase	Z
91	((	Open bracket	[
92	//	Backslash	\
93	))	Close bracket	]
94	v v	Caret	^
95		Underscore	_
96		Open single quote	`
97		a, lowercase	a
98		b, lowercase	b
99		c, lowercase	c
100		d, lowercase	d
101		e, lowercase	e
102		f, lowercase	f
103		g, lowercase	g
104		h, lowercase	h
105		i, lowercase	i
106		j, lowercase	j
107		k, lowercase	k
108		l, lowercase	l
109		m, lowercase	m
110		n, lowercase	n
111		o, lowercase	o
112		p, lowercase	p
113		q, lowercase	q
114		r, lowercase	r
115		s, lowercase	s
116		t, lowercase	t
117		u, lowercase	u
118		v, lowercase	v
119		w, lowercase	w
120		x, lowercase	x
121		y, lowercase	y
122		z, lowercase	z
123	(-	Open brace	{
124	^ /	Bar	|
125	)-	Close brace	}
126	- -	Tilde	~
127		Delete	⌂
128	C,	C cedilla, uppercase	Ç
129	u"	u umlaut, lowercase	ü
130	e'	e acute, lowercase	é
131	a^	a circumflex, lowercase	â
132	a"	a umlaut, lowercase	ä
133	a'	a grave, lowercase	à

Part V ◆ Appendixes

LMBCS code	Compose sequence	Description	Character
134	a*	a ring, lowercase	å
135	c,	c cedilla, lowercase	ç
136	e^	e circumflex, lowercase	ê
137	e"	e umlaut, lowercase	ë
138	e'	e grave, lowercase	è
139	i"	i umlaut, lowercase	ï
140	î	i circumflex, lowercase	î
141	i'	i grave, lowercase	ì
142	A"	A umlaut, uppercase	Ä
143	A*	A ring, uppercase	Å
144	E'	E acute, uppercase	É
145	ae	ae diphthong, lowercase	æ
146	AE	AE diphthong, uppercase	Æ
147	o^	o circumflex, lowercase	ô
148	o"	o umlaut, lowercase	ö
149	o'	o grave, lowercase	ò
150	u^	u circumflex, lowercase	û
151	u'	u grave, lowercase	ù
152	y"	y umlaut, lowercase	ÿ
153	O"	O umlaut, uppercase	Ö
154	U"	U umlaut, uppercase	Ü
155	o/	o slash, lowercase	ø
156	L = l = L- or l-	British pound sterling symbol	£
157	O/	O slash, uppercase	Ø
158	xx or XX	Multiplication sign	×
159	f f	Guilder	ƒ
160	a'	a acute, lowercase	á
161	i'	i acute, lowercase	í
162	o'	o acute, lowercase	ó
163	u'	u acute, lowercase	ú
164	n~	n tilde, lowercase	ñ
165	N~	N tilde, uppercase	Ñ
166	a _ or A _	Feminine ordinal indicator	ª
167	o _ or O _	Masculine ordinal indicator	º
168	??	Question mark, inverted	¿
169	RO ro R0 or r0	Registered trademark symbol	®
170	-]	End of line symbol/Logical NOT	¬
171	1 2	One half	½
172	1 4	One quarter	¼
173	!!	Exclamation point, inverted	¡
174	‹ ‹	Left angle quotes	«
175	› ›	Right angle quotes	»
176		Solid fill character, light	░
177		Solid fill character, medium	▒
178		Solid fill character, heavy	▓
179		Center vertical box bar	│
180		Right box side	┤
181	A '	A acute, uppercase	Á
182	A ^	A circumflex, uppercase	Â
183	A `	A grave, uppercase	À
184	CO co C0 or c0	Copyright symbol	©
185		Right box side, double	╣
186		Center vertical box bar, double	║
187		Upper right box corner, double	╗
188		Lower right box corner, double	╝
189	cl c/ Cl or c/	Cent sign	¢

Appendix E ◆ Compose Sequences for the Lotus Multibyte Character Set

LMBCS code	Compose sequence	Description	Character
190	Y= y= Y- or y-	Yen sign	¥
191		Upper right box corner	┐
192		Lower left box corner	└
193		Lower box side	┴
194		Upper box side	┬
195		Left box side	├
196		Center horizontal box bar	─
197		Center box intersection	┼
198	a˜	a tilde, lowercase	ã
199	A˜	A tilde, uppercase	Ã
200		Lower left box corner, double	╚
201		Upper left box corner, double	╔
202		Lower box side, double	╩
203		Upper box side, double	╦
204		Left box side, double	╠
205		Center horizontal box bar, double	═
206		Center box intersection, double	╬
207	XO xo X0 or x0	International currency sign	¤
208	d-	Icelandic eth, lowercase	ð
209	D-	Icelandic eth, uppercase	Ð
210	Ê	E circumflex, uppercase	Ê
211	E"	E umlaut, uppercase	Ë
212	E'	E grave, uppercase	È
213	i‹space›	i without dot (lowercase)	ı
214	I'	I acute, uppercase	Í
215	Î	I circumflex, uppercase	Î
216	I"	I umlaut, uppercase	Ï
217		Lower right box corner	┘
218		Upper left box corner	┌
219		Solid fill character	█
220		Solid fill character, lower half	▄
221	/‹space›	Vertical line, broken	¦
222	I'	I grave, uppercase	Ì
223		Solid fill character, upper half	▀
224	O'	O acute, uppercase	Ó
225	ss	German sharp (lowercase)	ß
226	Ô	O circumflex, uppercase	Ô
227	O'	O grave, uppercase	Ò
228	o˜	o tilde, lowercase	õ
229	O˜	O tilde, uppercase	Õ
230	/u	Greek mu, lowercase	µ
231	p-	Icelandic thorn, lowercase	þ
232	P-	Icelandic thorn, uppercase	Þ
233	U'	U acute, uppercase	Ú
234	Û	U circumflex, uppercase	Û
235	U'	U grave, uppercase	Ù
236	y'	y acute, lowercase	ý
237	Y'	Y acute, uppercase	Ý
238	¯	Overline character	¯
239		Acute accent	´
240	-=	Hyphenation symbol	-
241	+-	Plus or minus sign	±
242	-- or ==	Double underscore	═
243	3 4	Three quarters sign	¾
244		Paragraph symbol	¶
245		Section symbol	§

932 Part V ◆ Appendixes

LMBCS code	Compose sequence	Description	Character
246	:-	Division sign	÷
247	,,	Cedilla accent	¸
248	o	Degree symbol	°
249		Umlaut accent	¨
250	^.	Center dot	·
251	1	One superscript	¹
252	3	Three superscript	³
253	2	Two superscript	²
254		Square bullet	■
255		Null	

Group 1

This section defines the Group 1 LMBCS Characters.

LMBCS code	Key code	Compose sequence	Description	Character
256	(000)		Null	
257	(001)		Smiling face	☺
258	(002)		Smiling face, reversed	☻
259	(003)		Heart suit symbol	♥
260	(004)		Diamond suit symbol	♦
261	(005)		Club suit symbol	♣
262	(006)		Spade suit symbol	♠
263	(007)		Bullet	•
264	(008)		Bullet, reversed	◘
265	(009)		Open circle	○
266	(010)		Open circle, reversed	◉
267	(011)		Male symbol	♂
268	(012)		Female symbol	♀
269	(013)		Musical note	♪
270	(014)		Double musical note	♫
271	(015)		Sun symbol	☼
272	(016)		Forward arrow indicator	►
273	(017)		Back arrow indicator	◄
274	(018)		Up-down arrow	↕
275	(019)		Double exclamation points	‼
276	(020)	!p or !P	Paragraph symbol	¶
277	(021)	SO so S0 or s0	Section symbol	§
278	(022)		Solid horizontal rectangle	
279	(023)		Up-down arrow, perpendicular	↨
280	(024)		Up arrow	↑
281	(025)		Down arrow	↓
282	(026)		Right arrow	→
283	(027)	mg	Left arrow	←
284	(028)		Right angle symbol	∟
285	(029)		Left-right symbol	↔
286	(030)	ba	Solid triangle	▲
287	(031)	ea	Solid triangle inverted	▼
288	(032)	" ‹space›	Umlaut accent, uppercase	
289	(033)	~ ‹space›	Tilde accent, uppercase	
290	(034)	° ‹space›	Ring accent, uppercase	°
291	(035)	^ ‹space›	Circumflex accent, uppercase	
292	(036)	` ‹space›	Grave accent, uppercase	
293	(037)	' ‹space›	Acute accent, uppercase	

Appendix E ◆ Compose Sequences for the Lotus Multibyte Character Set

LMBCS code	Key code	Compose sequence	Description	Character
294	(038)	″∧	High double quotes, opening	"
295	(039)		High single quote, straight	'
296	(040)		Ellipsis	…
297	(041)		En mark	–
298	(042)		Em mark	—
299	(043)		Null	
300	(044)		Null	
301	(045)		Null	
302	(046)		Left angle parenthesis	‹
303	(047)		Right angle parenthesis	›
304	(048)	‹space›″	Umlaut accent, lowercase	¨
305	(049)	‹space›~	Tilde accent, lowercase	~
306	(050)		Ring accent, lowercase	°
307	(051)	‹space›^	Circumflex accent, lowercase	^
308	(052)	‹space›`	Grave accent, lowercase	`
309	(053)	‹space›'	Acute accent, lowercase	´
310	(054)	″v	Low double quotes, closing	„
311	(055)		Low single quote, closing	‚
312	(056)		High double quotes, closing	"
313	(057)	_ ‹space›	Underscore, heavy	—
314	(058)		Null	
315	(059)		Null	
316	(060)		Null	
317	(061)		Null	
318	(062)		Null	
319	(063)		Null	
320	(064)	OE	OE ligature, uppercase	Œ
321	(065)	oe	oe ligature, lowercase	œ
322	(066)	Y″	Y umlaut, uppercase	Ÿ
323	(067)		Null	
324	(068)		Null	
325	(069)		Null	
326	(070)		Left box side, double joins single	╞
327	(071)		Left box side, single joins double	╟
328	(072)		Solid fill character, left half	▌
329	(073)		Solid fill character, right half	▐
330	(074)		Null	
331	(075)		Null	
332	(076)		Null	
333	(077)		Null	
334	(078)		Null	
335	(079)		Null	
336	(080)		Lower box side, double joins single	╧
337	(081)		Upper box side, single joins double	╤
338	(082)		Upper box side, double joins single	╥
339	(083)		Lower single left double box corner	╙
340	(084)		Lower double left single box corner	╘
341	(085)		Upper double left single box corner	╒
342	(086)		Upper single left double box corner	╓
343	(087)		Center box intersection, vertical double	╫
344	(088)		Center box intersection, horizontal double	╪
345	(089)		Right box side, double joins single	╡
346	(090)		Right box side, single joins double	╢
347	(091)		Upper single right double box corner	╖
348	(092)		Upper double right single box corner	╕

Part V ◆ Appendixes

LMBCS code	Key code	Compose sequence	Description	Character
349	(093)		Lower single right double box corner	╜
350	(094)		Lower double right single box corner	╛
351	(095)		Lower box side, single joins double	┴
352	(096)	ij	ij ligature, lowercase	ij
353	(097)	IJ	IJ ligature, uppercase	IJ
354	(098)	fi	fi ligature, lowercase	fi
355	(099)	fl	fl ligature, lowercase	fl
356	(100)	'n	n comma, lowercase	'n
357	(101)	l.	l bullet, lowercase	l·
358	(102)	L.	L bullet, uppercase	L·
359	(103)		Null	
360	(104)		Null	
361	(105)		Null	
362	(106)		Null	
363	(107)		Null	
364	(108)		Null	
365	(109)		Null	
366	(110)		Null	
367	(111)		Null	
368	(112)		Single dagger symbol	†
369	(113)		Double dagger symbol	‡
370	(114)		Null	
371	(115)		Null	
372	(116)		Null	
373	(117)		Null	
374	(118)	TM Tm or tm	Trademark symbol	™
375	(119)	lr	Liter symbol	ℓ
376	(120)		Null	
377	(121)		Null	
378	(122)		Null	
379	(123)		Null	
380	(124)	KR Kr or kr	Krone sign	Kr
381	(125)	-[	Start of line symbol	⌐
382	(126)	LI Li or li	Lira sign	₤
383	(127)	PT Pt or pt	Peseta sign	Pt

Note: LMBCS codes 384 through 511 duplicate LMBCS codes 128 through 255, for use with code groups of other countries. Refer to LMBCS codes 128 through 255 in the Group 0 table for a list of these characters.

Index

Symbols

– (negative operator), 78
– (subtraction operator), 15, 78
& (concatenation operator), 79
* (multiplication
 operator), 15, 78
+ (addition operator), 15, 78
+ (positive operator), 78
+/– format, 174
/ (division operator), 15, 78
< (less than), 80
<= (less than or equal to), 80
<> (not equal to), 80
= (equal), 80
> (greater than), 80
>= (greater than or equal
 to), 80
? advanced macro command, 606
@@ function, 268
@functions, *see* functions
^ (exponentiation operator), 78
1-2-3
 Access Menu, 37
 exiting, 36-39
 starting, 34-39
 tutorial, 56-57
 using mouse, 47
 with Wysiwyg, 367
1-2-3 Release 3
 using earlier 1-2-3 files in, 308
 using earlier Symphony files
 in, 308
 windows, 57-58
1-2-3 Release 3.1+
 hardware requirements, 29-32
 installing, 869
 system requirements, 14-15,
 875

A

@ABS function, 206-206
absolute addresses, 146-147
absolute value, calculating
 206-207
@ACOS function, 265
add-ins
 Auditor, 881-889
 Backsolver, 891-892, 911-914
 installing, 875-877

menus, 35
Solver, 891-901
    Answer Report, 901
    attaching, 891-892
    Cells Used Report, 909
    Differences Report, 905
    How Solved Report, 902-904
    Inconsistent Constraints Report, 905
    invoking, 892
    terminology, 893
    Unused Constraints Report, 908
    using functions in, 909
    using with macros, 910
    What-If Report, 904
Viewer, 917-920
    attaching and detaching, 917-918
    browsing files, 924
    invoking and using, 918
    linking files, 922-923
    opening files, 922
    retrieving files, 920-922
addresses
    absolute, 82, 146-147
    cell, 271-272, 601
    indirect, 268
    mixed, 82, 147, 151-152
    range names, 682
    relative, 82, 145-146
advanced macro commands
    see macro commands
alphanumeric keys, 41-43
anchoring ranges, 101-103
#AND# operator, 520
angles, 491
Answer Report, Solver add-in, 901
APPENDBELOW advanced macro command, 631-632
APPENDRIGHT advanced macro command, 632
arccosine, finding, 265

arcsine, finding, 265
arctangent, finding, 265
arguments
    guess, 220
    input, 611
    precision, 209
    search, 253
arrow keys, 68
arrows in graphs, 475-476, 482
ASCII
    files, 305, 706-707
    printing files to disk, 717-718
@ASIN function, 265
@ATAN function, 265
@ATAN2 function, 265
attributes
    cell, 269-271
    text, 406
Auditor add-in
    attaching and detaching, 881-882
    Audit Mode, 884
    Audit Range, 883
    circulation references, 887
    formulas, 884-885
    invoking and using, 882
    menu, 883
    options, 888-889
    recalculation order, 886
Automatic format, 181-183
@AVG function, 205, 234-235

B

background printing, 360
Backsolver, 891-892, 911, 914
Backup option, 287
bar graphs, 449
batch files
    loading mouse driver, 38
    start-up, 34-35
BEEP advanced macro command, 634
BLANK advanced macro command, 631

blank-header, 344
borders, 728-729
    column, 346, 860-861
    printing, 390-391
    row, 346, 860-861
boxes, 377-378
BRANCH advanced macro
    command, 613
BREAKOFF advanced macro
    command, 619
BREAKON advanced macro
    command, 620
buffers, 610

C

calculating
    absolute value, 206-207
    arithmetic mean, 234-235
    compound growth rate, 222
    days, 212
    depreciation
        double declining-balance,
            230
        straight-line, 229
        sum-of-the-years'-digits, 231
        variable declining-
            balance, 232
    deviation, 243
    future value, 226-227
    internal rate of return,
        220-222
    investment term, 227-228
    loan payment amounts,
        222-223
    net present value, 224-225
    present value, 225-226
    square roots, 210
    standard deviation, 237-238
    variance, 240, 243
calculation, *see also* recalculation
@CELL function, 269-271
cell pointer, 14, 49, 80-81, 399
    keyboard control, 66-67
    mouse control, 67-68
    restricting, 687-688
cell references, 80-82
@CELLPOINTER function,
    269-271
cells, 13-14, 62
    adding, 299-300
    addresses, 82, 100, 271-272,
        601
    attributes, 269-271
    blank, 180
    calculating, 137
    contents
        erasing, 680-681
        listing, 344
    copying, 144-148
    counting, 235
    formats, 82-83
    hiding, 133-135
    in Wysiwyg, 370-371
    input, 528, 539
    moving, 140
    notes, 83
    protecting, 131-132
    ranges, 99-100
    referencing, 268
    strings, 259
    testing contents, 250-251
    text, 199-201
Cells Used Report, Solver
    add-in, 909
@CHAR function, 262
characters
    formatting, 402-403
    special, 262-263, 927
    subscripted, 403
    superscripted, 403
@CHOOSE function, 272
circular references, 138-140, 887
@CLEAN function, 261
CLOSE advanced macro
    command, 643

@CODE function, 263
Color Graphics Adapter (CGA), 31
colors, 184, 358, 396-397, 438-439, 808-809, 815-816
  adding, 483-484
  changing, 129, 192-193, 762-763
  labels, 192
  numbers, 192
  selecting, 761-762
  viewing graphs in, 444
@COLS function, 272-273
column-variable range, 539
columns
  adjusting number, 129
  borders, 860-861
  converting to rows, 154
  deleting, 115-116, 665-666
  hiding, 133-135
  inserting, 120
  labels, 567
  width, 111-113, 380-381, 657, 801-802
comma format, 171-172
commands
  /Copy, 21, 144, 693-695
  /Data Distribution, 550
  /Data External, 27, 309, 561, 568-569
  /Data External Create, 565-566
  /Data External Delete, 568
  /Data External List, 563-566
  /Data External Other, 569
  /Data External Use, 563
  /Data Fill, 548
  /Data Matrix, 555-556
  /Data Parse, 306, 557-560
  /Data Query, 180, 241, 497
  /Data Query Extract, 287
  /Data Query Find, 522
  /Data Regression, 551
  /Data Sort, 502
  /Data Table, 26, 180
  /Data Table 1, 531
  /Data Table 2, 531
  /Data Table Labeled, 537
  /File Admin, 302
  /File Admin Link-Refresh, 91, 312
  /File Admin Reservation, 310-311
  /File Admin Seal, 136, 181, 302, 312
  /File Admin Table, 304, 312
  /File Combine, 295
  /File Combine Add, 299-301
  /File Combine Copy, 297, 383
  /File Dir, 282, 289
  /File Erase, 281-282, 303
  /File Import, 261, 305
  /File Import Numbers, 306
  /File Import Text, 305
  /File List, 281, 304
  /File New, 87, 282, 289
  /File Open, 87, 282, 287
  /File Retrieve, 282, 287
  /File Save, 98, 282, 285
  /File Xtract, 282, 291
  /File Xtract Formulas, 294
  /File Xtract Values, 294
  /Graph Options Advanced Colors, 439
  /Graph Options Advanced Hatches, 440
  /Graph Options Color, 444
  /Graph View, 443
  /Move, 21, 140-141, 695-696
  /Print, 319, 361
  /Print File, 305
  /Print Printer, 106, 317, 346
  /Print Resume, 361
  /Print Suspend, 361
  /Range, 21
  /Range Erase, 95, 100-115, 518

Index 939

/Range Format, 82, 166-168
/Range Format Date, 175, 213
/Range Format Date Time, 178, 217
/Range Format Fixed, 171
/Range Format Hidden, 133, 181, 340
/Range Format Other Automatic, 214
/Range Format Other Color Negative, 184
/Range Format Percent, 173
/Range Format Reset, 133
/Range Format Text, 242
/Range Input, 132-133
/Range Justify, 186, 199
/Range Label, 185
/Range Name Create, 108-109
/Range Name Labels, 108-109
/Range Name Note, 575, 587
/Range Name Table, 109
/Range Prot, 181
/Range Search, 155-158
/Range Transpose, 154
/Range Unprot, 131
/Range Value, 152-153, 216, 256
/Worksheet, 20
/Worksheet Column Display, 340
/Worksheet Column Hide, 134, 340
/Worksheet Delete File, 87, 117-119, 303
/Worksheet Delete Row, 116
/Worksheet Delete Sheet, 87, 117
/Worksheet Erase, 119
/Worksheet Global Col-Width, 112
/Worksheet Global Default, 85, 162, 172
/Worksheet Global Format, 82, 168, 175
/Worksheet Global Group, 87
/Worksheet Global Prot, 132
/Worksheets Global Recalc, 138
/Worksheet Global Zero, 188
/Worksheet Insert Column, 120
/Worksheet Insert Row, 120
/Worksheet Insert Sheet, 87, 120
/Worksheet Status, 162
/Worksheet Titles, 127, 532
/Worksheet Window Clear, 123-124
/Worksheet Window Display, 129
/Worksheet Window Graph, 125, 443
/Worksheet Window Horizontal, 122-123
/Worksheet Window Perspective, 87, 534
/Worksheet Window Vertical, 122
/x commands, 601-602
:Display, 22
:Display Colors, 129, 397
:Display Mode, 128
:Display Options, 129
:Display Zoom, 129
:Format, 22, 82
:Format Color Text, 194
:Format Font, 372
:Format Font Replace, 373
:Format Lines, 194, 377
:Format Shade, 194, 378
:Graph Add, 469
:Graph Edit Add Text, 480
:Graph Edit Color Background, 440

:Graph Edit Color Map, 483
:Graph Edit Options, 441-443
:Graph Edit Rearrange, 480
:Graph Goto, 471
:Graph Move, 471
:Graph Remove, 472
:Graph Settings Display, 472
:Graph Settings Graph, 470
:Graph Settings Range, 472
:Graph Settings Sync, 472
:Named-Style, 23
:Print Configuration, 289, 385-386
:Print Layout 289, 389-390
:Print Preview, 388
:Print Range, 386
:Special, 23
:Special Copy, 194, 381
:Special Import, 383
:Special Move, 194, 382
:Text, 22, 84
:Text Align, 185, 199, 403
:Text Edit, 84, 186, 198
:Text Reformat, 84, 186, 199
:Text Set, 201
:Worksheet, 20
selecting from menus, 94-98
complex operators
   #AND#, 248
   #NOT#, 248
   #OR#, 248
compound growth, calculating, 222
compressing print, 392
concatenation, 79
conditional tests, 246-247
configuration
   changing, 877-878
   of 1-2-3, 871-875
   of DOS, 869-870
   printer, 385

CONTENTS advanced macro command, 629-630
control panel, 49-50, 634
@COORD function, 271-272
/Copy command, 21, 144, 693-695
@COS function, 265
cosine, calculating, 265
@COUNT function, 235
criteria range, 509-510, 514
   formulas, 515-516
   wild cards, 515
@CTERM function, 228-229
Currency format, 172-173
cursor movement, 44, 66, 88, 401
   arrow keys, 43, 68
   End key, 70-72
   GoTo (F5), 72
   in text, 198
   keys, 41

D

@D360 function, 212
/Data Distribution command, 550, 787-789
/Data External command, 27, 309, 561, 568-569
/Data External Create command, 565-566, 795-796
/Data External Delete command, 568, 796-797
/Data External List command, 563-566, 794-795
/Data External Other command, 569, 797-798
/Data External Use command, 563, 793-794
/Data External Use commands, 793-794
/Data Fill command, 548, 768-769

Index 941

/Data Matrix command,
    555-556, 789-790
/Data Parse command, 306,
    557-560, 792-793
/Data Query command, 180, 241,
    497
/Data Query Criteria command,
    780-781
/Data Query Del command,
    785-786
/Data Query Extract command,
    287, 783-784
/Data Query Find command,
    522, 782-783
/Data Query Input command,
    779
/Data Query Modify command,
    786-787
/Data Query Output command,
    781-782
/Data Query Unique command,
    784-785
/Data Regression command,
    551, 790-791
/Data Sort command, 502,
    777-779
/Data Table command, 26, 180
/Data Table 1 command,
    531, 769-771
/Data Table 2 command,
    531, 771-773
/Data Table 3 command, 773-775
/Data Table Labeled command,
    537, 775-777
data
    analysis, 61-62
    entering, 73
    extracting, 291-293
    management, 275-276, 495
    parsing, 306, 792-793
    regression, 790-791
    retrieving, 275-276

data tables, 527-529
    labeled, 537-547
    type 1, 530-531
    type 2, 531-533
    type 3, 533-535
database(s)
    creating, 498
    entering data, 500
    designing, 497-498
    drivers, 562
    external, 309, 561-562
        listing tables, 794-795
    fields, 496
    functions, 241
    joining, 524-527
    management, 25-26
    modifying, 501-502
    records, 496
    sorting, 502-507, 777-779
    table, 497
    three-dimensional, 535-537
    worksheets and, 498
@DATE function, 212-213
date and time formats, 175-177
date and time functions, 18
dates
    converting to serial numbers,
        212-213
    current, 215-216
    filling ranges with, 549-550
@DATEVALUE function, 214
@DAY function, 215
@DDB function, 230
defaults, global, 161-162
DEFINE advanced macro
    command,
    621-623
delimited files, 306
dependent variables, 456
depreciation
    double declining-balance, 230
    straight-line, 229
    sum-of-the-years'-digits 231

variable declining-balance, 232
deviation, calculating, 243
@DGET function, 244
Differences Report, Solver add-in, 905
dingbats, 373
directories, 818, 871
   changing, 284, 708
   default, 282, 285
   paths, 284
   subdirectories, 284
disks
   registering, 870
   saving graphs on, 445
   shared, 309
DISPATCH advanced macro command, 621
:Display Colors command, 129, 397, 815-816
:Display Default command, 819
:Display Font-Directory command, 818
:Display Mode command, 128, 813
:Display Options command, 129, 816-818
:Display Rows command, 818
:Display Zoom command, 129, 815
display, 395
   colors, 129, 396-397, 815-816
   format, 121-122
   modes, 128, 396
   primary, 122
   secondary, 122
   zoom, 396, 815
displaying
   file names, 705-706
   global settings, 672
   graphs, 749-750
DOS, 869-870
@DQUERY function, 244-245

drawing
   boxes, 377-378
   lines, 377-378
drop shadows, 378
@DSTDS function, 243
duplicating
   databases, 565
   external tables, 565
   worksheets, 565
@DVARS function, 243

E

editing
   in Wysiwyg, 84
   with keyboard, 83-84
editing keys, 401
ellipses, 476-477
Enhanced Graphics Adapter (EGA), 31
entering
   formulas, 77-78
   numbers, 76
@ERR function, 273-274
error trapping, 248-249, 273-274
@EXACT function, 257
exiting 1-2-3, 36-37
@EXP function, 264
exponents, 174
exporting files, 363
extensions, 283-284
external tables, 561-570
   deleting, 568
   disconnecting, 570
   listing, 563-565
   table definition, 565
   transferring information, 570
extra-key sort, 505

F

@FALSE function, 249
field descriptions, 567
field-creation strings, 567

Index

fields, 496
  key fields, 497
  names, 497-499
/File Admin command, 302
/File Admin Link-Refresh command, 91, 312, 714
/File Admin Reservation command, 310-311, 710-711
/File Admin Seal command, 136, 181, 302, 312, 713-714
/File Admin Table command, 304, 312, 711-713
file and clock indicator, 53
/File Combine command, 295, 701-702
/File Combine Add command, 299-301
/File Combine Copy command, 297, 383
/File Dir command, 282, 289, 708
/File Erase command, 281-282, 303, 704-705
/File Import command, 261, 305, 706-707
/File Import Numbers command, 306
/File Import Text command, 305
/File List command, 281, 304, 705-706
/File New command, 87, 282, 289, 709
/File Open command, 87, 282, 287, 709-710
/File Retrieve command, 282, 287, 697-698
/File Save command, 98, 282, 285, 699-700
/File Xtract command, 282, 291, 703-704
/File Xtract Formulas command, 294
/File Xtract Values command, 294
file linking, 90-92
file management, 23, 281-282
file sharing, 310
files
  active, 282-283
  ASCII, 717-718
  batch, 34-35
  closing, 643
  combining, 282, 295-296, 701-702
  consolidating, 291-293, 297-298
  converting, 40-41
  copying, 871
  deleting, 117-119, 665-666
  delimited, 306
  directories, 282
  disk, 282, 640
  erasing, 282, 303-304, 704-705
  exporting, 363
  extensions, 283-284
  importing, 305-306
  linking, 64
  listing, 705-706
  lists, 304-305
  loading, 697-698
  multiple, 290
  multiple-worksheet, 62-63, 86-92
  naming, 283-284
  network, 302-303
  new, 282
  nonsharable, 309
  opening, 289-290
  printing, 395
    to disk, 852-853
  protecting, 24, 136, 301, 658
    formats, 713-714
    in a network, 302
    reservation, 303
  RAM, 282
  reservation in network, 303
  retrieving, 287-289

retrieving with wild cards, 287-288
saving, 98-99, 285-287, 699-700
   over existing files, 286
   with passwords, 136
sealed, 136, 282, 302, 312
shared, 282
tables, 304-305
transferring, 305-307
FILESIZE advanced macro command, 646
financial functions, 17
@FIND function, 253
Fixed format, 171
flipping objects, 491
font
   libraries, 374-375
   magnification, 485
font formats, 190-191
fonts, 190-191, 354-355, 804-806
   changing, 480, 762-763
   directories, 818
   fixed-space, 373
   in Wysiwyg, 371
   point size, 371
   proportional, 373
   replacing, 373
   serif, 373
   soft, 371
footers, 341-344, 726, 859-860
FOR advanced macro command, 626
FORBREAK advanced macro command, 626
FORM advanced macro command, 611-612
:Format Bold command, 806-807
:Format Color command, 194, 808-809
:Format command, 22, 82, 194
:Format Font command, 372, 804-806
:Format Font Replace command, 373
:Format Italics command, 807
:Format Lines command, 377, 809
:Format Reset command, 812
:Format Shade command, 194, 378, 810-811
:Format Underline command, 807-808
formats
   +/−, 174
   Automatic, 181-183
   bold, 806-807
   cell, 82-83
   color, 184, 808-809
   Comma, 171-172
   contents vs. cell, 165-166
   copying, 194-196, 381-382
   Currency, 164, 172-173
   Date, 175-177
   Date and Time, 175
   display, 165
   exporting, 384
   file, 713-714
   Fixed, 164, 171
   font, 190-191
   formulas, 653
   General, 170-171
   Hidden, 164, 180
   importing, 195-196, 383-384
   international, 184
   italics, 807
   Label, 181
   line, 193, 809
   moving, 194-196, 381-382
   parentheses, 183-184
   Percent, 173
   ranges, 168
   scientific, 173-174
   shade, 194
   text, 180

Index

Time, 177-179
values, 653
formatting, 161, 663-665
   attributes, 375-376
   cells, 164
   characters, 402-403
   columns, 111-114, 185
   display, 121-122
   justified text, 186-188
   macros, 580-581
   rows, 114
   with Wysiwyg, 369-371
   worksheets, 129
formatting sequences, 378-379
formulas, 62, 203-204
   converting to values, 152-153
   copying, 145-147, 689-691
   creating, 15-16
   entering, 77-78
      with multiple-worksheet
         files, 90-91
   errors in, 81-82
   extracting, 294
   filling ranges with, 549
   logical, 77
   numeric, 77-78
   string, 77-79
FRAMEOFF advanced macro
  command, 636
frequency distributions, 550-551
full-screen mode, 58
functions, 16-18, 203-204
     @CHAR, 262
     @CODE, 263
   database, 241
     @DGET, 244
     @DQUERY, 244-245
     @DSTDS, 243
     @DVARS, 243
     @FALSE, 249
     @ISERR, 248-249
     @ISNA, 248-249
     @ISNUMBER, 250-251
     @ISRANGE, 249-250
     @ISSTRING, 250-251
     @TRUE, 249
   date and time, 18, 210
     @D360, 212
     @DATE, 212-213
     @DATEVALUE, 214
     @DAY, 215
     @HOUR, 218
     @MINUTE, 218
     @MONTH, 215
     @NOW, 215-216
     @SECOND, 218
     @TIME, 216-217
     @TIMEVALUE, 218
     @TODAY, 215-216
     @YEAR, 215
   entering, 204-205
   filling ranges with, 549
   financial, 17, 218
     @CTERM, 228-229
     @DDB, 230
     @FV, 226-227
     @IRR, 220-222
     @NPV, 224-225
     @PMT, 222-223
     @PV, 225-226
     @RATE, 222
     @SLN, 229
     @SYD, 231
     @TERM, 227-228
     @VDB, 232
   logarithmic
     @EXP, 264
     @LN, 264
     @LOG, 263
   logical, 17
     @IF, 246-247
   mathematical, 17
     @ABS, 206-207
     @INT, 207-208
     @MOD, 208
     @RAND, 210

@ROUND, 209
@SQRT, 210
special, 17
   @@, 268
   @CELL, 269-271
   @CELLPOINTER, 269-271
   @CHOOSE, 272
   @COLS, 272-273
   @COORD, 271-272
   @ERR, 273-274
   @HLOOKUP, 274
   @INDEX, 275-276
   @INFO, 277-278
   @NA, 273-274
   @ROWS, 272-273
   @SHEETS, 272-273
   @VLOOKUP, 274
statistical, 17, 234
   @AVG, 234-235
   @COUNT, 235
   @MAX, 236
   @MIN, 236
   @STD, 237-238
   @SUM, 238-239
   @SUMPRODUCT, 239
   @VARS, 240
string, 17
   @CLEAN, 261
   @EXACT, 257
   @FIND, 253
   @LEFT, 255-256
   @LENGTH, 257
   @LOWER, 257-259
   @MID, 254-255
   @N, 259
   @PROPER, 257-259
   @REPEAT, 259
   @REPLACE, 256
   @RIGHT, 255-256
   @S, 259
   @STRING, 260
   @TRIM, 259
   @UPPER, 257-259

   @VALUE, 260-261
trigonometric
   @ACOS, 265
   @ASIN, 265
   @ATAN, 265
   @ATAN2, 265
   @COS, 265
   @PI, 264
   @SIN, 265
   @TAN, 265
functions keys, 41, 44-45
future value, calculating, 226-227
@FV function, 226-227

G

General format, 170-171
GET advanced macro command, 606-607
GETLABEL advanced macro command, 607-608
GETNUMBER advanced macro command, 608-609
GETPOS advanced macro command, 646
graph settings, 445-446
/Graph Group command, 766
/Graph Name command, 764-765
:Graph Move command, 471, 837
:Graph Settings Sync command, 472
graph options, 437-441
/Graph command, 746-748
/Graph Options Advanced command, 440, 762-763
/Graph Options Advanced Colors command, 439, 761-762
/Graph Options Advanced Hatches command, 763-764
/Graph Options Color command, 444, 758-759

Index

/Graph Options Data-Labels
command, 759-761
/Graph Options Format
command, 753-754
/Graph Options Grid command,
755-756
/Graph Options Legend
command, 751-752
/Graph Options Scale command,
756-758
/Graph Options Titles
command, 754-755
/Graph Reset command, 748-749
/Graph Save command, 750-751
/Graph Type command, 744-746
/Graph View command, 443,
749-750
:Graph Add command, 469, 833
:Graph Compute command, 838
:Graph Edit command, 839-840
:Graph Edit Add command,
480, 840-841
:Graph Edit Color command,
440, 483, 844-845
:Graph Edit Edit command,
843-844
:Graph Edit Options command,
441-443, 849
:Graph Edit Rearrange
command, 480, 846-847
:Graph Edit Select command,
842
:Graph Edit Transform
command, 845-846
:Graph Edit View command,
847-848
:Graph Goto command, 471,
834
:Graph Remove command, 472,
834
:Graph Settings command,
835-836
:Graph Settings Display
command, 472
:Graph Settings Graph
command, 470
:Graph Settings Range
command, 472
:Graph View command, 838
:Graph Zoom command, 837
graphics editor, 473-474
GRAPHOFF advanced macro
command, 637
GRAPHON advanced macro
command, 636-637
graphs, 24-25
arrows, 475-476
bar, 449
colors, 438-439, 444
density, 463
displaying in worksheet, 125
editing, 473-474, 839-840
grids, 755-756
hatch patterns, 440
HLCO, 459
in reports, 466, 469-471
in worksheets, 835-836
inserting into worksheets, 833
line, 448, 475-476
mixed, 452
moving, 471, 837
objects, 474
pie, 453-455
polygons, 476
printing, 27-28, 463-464
removing, 472, 834
repositioning, 471
resetting, 446, 748-749
resizing, 472
saving, 445, 750-751
settings, 472-473
saving, 445-465
size, 462-463, 845-846

stacked-bar, 450-452
text, 440-441, 474-475
types, 744-746
viewing, 443
XY, 456-457
GROUP mode, 114, 117

H

hardware requirements, 1-2-3, 29-31
hatch patterns, 440
hatching, *see* shading
headers, 341-344, 859-860
  blank, 344
  printing, 725-726
Help, 54-56
Hercules Graphics Adapter, 31
Hidden format, 180
hiding parts of
  worksheet, 133-135
HLCO graphs, 459
@HLOOKUP function, 274
@HOUR function, 218
How Solved Report, Solver
  add-in, 902-904

I

icon panel, 67
@IF function, 246-247
IF advanced macro
  command, 625-626
importing
  data from other programs, 556-557
  formats, 195-196
Inconsistent Constraints Report,
  Solver add-in, 905
independent variables, 456
@INDEX function, 275-276
INDICATE advanced macro
  command, 638
@INFO function, 277-278

input
  cells, 528, 539
  range, 508-509
  value, 528
Install program, 39-40
installing
  add-ins, 875-877
  disks, 870
  Install program, 870
  printers, 460-461, 873
  Release 3.1+, 869-870
  registering disks, 870
  settings, 37
@INT function, 207-208
integers, 207-208
internal rate of return calculating, 220-222
international formats, 184
investment term, calculating, 227-228
@IRR function, 220-222
@ISERR function, 248-249
@ISNA function, 248-249
@ISNUMBER function, 250-251
@ISRANGE function, 249-250
@ISSTRING function, 250-251

J–L

justified text, 186-188
keyboard, 41, 66-67
Label format, 181
label-fill characters, 539
labels, 61-62, 607-608
  aligning, 403-404, 678-680
  color, 192
  editing, 826-827
  extracting, 244
  justifying, 186
  prefixes, 73-75, 185
  text, 655
LABEL mode, 67
layout

default options, 323-324
defining, 389-390
designing reports, 341
line spacing, 351
margins, 347-350
orientation, 351-352
page breaks, 330-333
page length, 347-350
pitch, 351
settings, 392
@LEFT function, 255-256
legends in graphs, 751-752
@LENGTH function, 257
LET advanced macro
  command, 627-628
libraries
  font, 374-375
  macro, 589
line graphs, 448, 475-476
line spacing, 351
linear equations, 555-556
lines, 377-378, 809
  drawing, 193
  style, 480
  width, 481
linking files, 64, 90-92
listing files, 304-305
LMBCS (Lotus Multibyte
  Character Set), 927
  Group 0, 928
  Group 1, 932
  with @CHAR, 262
  with @CODE, 263
@LN function, 264
loading
  data from other programs,
    556-557
  mouse driver, 36
  Wysiwyg, 35-36, 366
loan payment amount,
  calculating, 222-223
@LOG function, 263

logarithms
  computing, 263
  natural, 264
logical formulas, 77
logical functions, 17, 246
logical operators, 247
LOOK advanced macro
  command, 609-610
Lotus Multibyte Character Set
  (LMBCS), see LMBCS
@LOWER function, 257-259

M

macro commands
  ?, 606
  APPENDBELOW, 631-632
  APPENDRIGHT, 632
  BEEP, 634
  BLANK, 631
  BRANCH, 613
  BREAKOFF, 619
  BREAKON, 620
  CLOSE, 643
  CONTENTS, 629-630
  DEFINE, 621-623
  DISPATCH, 621
  FILESIZE, 646
  FOR, 626
  FORBREAK, 626
  FORM, 611-612
  FRAMEOFF, 636
  GET, 606-607
  GETLABEL, 607-608
  GETNUMBER, 608-609
  GETPOS, 646
  GRAPHOFF, 637
  GRAPHON, 636-637
  IF, 625-626
  INDICATE, 638
  LET, 627-628
  LOOK, 609-610
  MENUBRANCH, 614-615

MENUCALL, 615-616
ONERROR, 618
OPEN, 640-642
PANELOFF, 634
PANELON, 634
PUT, 628-629
QUIT, 618
READ, 643-644
READLN, 644
RECALC, 638-639
RECALCCOL, 638-639
RESTART, 623-624
RETURN, 617
SETPOS, 645-646
SYSTEM, 624-625
WAIT, 620
WINDOWSOFF, 634-635
WINDOWSON, 635
WRITE, 644
WRITELN, 645
macros, 28-29
  /x commands, 601-602
  advanced, 598-605
  Alt-*letter*, 582
  automatic, 584-585
  comments, 588
  creating, 592-594
  developing, 574-575
  documenting, 587
  errors, 597
  formatting, 580-581
  key names, 578-580
  layout, 585-586
  libraries, 589
  naming, 581-584
  notes, 588
  playback, 595
  protecting, 588-589
  recording, 591
  running, 576, 581-582
  testing, 591, 595-596
  using in Solver, 910
  writing, 575-578
mantissa, 174
margins, 347-350, 727-728, 858
mathematical functions, 17
@MAX function, 236
memory, 875
MENUBRANCH advanced macro
  command, 614-615
MENUCALL advanced macro
  command, 615-616
menus
  add-in, 35
  commands, 48
  selecting commands from,
    94-98
  selecting objects, 479
  Wysiwyg, 18-22, 367-368
@MID function, 254-255
@MIN function, 236
@MINUTE function, 218
mixed addressing, 147-152
@MOD function, 208
mode indicator, 51
modes
  display, 128
  full-screen, 58
  GROUP, 114, 117
  LABEL, 67
  POINT, 67, 100
  READY, 67
  VALUE, 67
Monochrome Display Adapter
  (MDA), 31
@MONTH function, 215
mouse
  clicking, 47
  controlling cell pointer, 67-68
  dragging, 101-103
  icons, 47
  in 1-2-3, 47
  loading driver, 36
  pointer, 47

Index

selecting menu commands, 48
selecting objects, 479
/Move command, 21, 140-141, 695-696
Multicolor Graphics Array (MCGA), 31
multiple regression, 26
multiple-worksheets
   displaying, 65-66
   files, 62-63, 86, 92
   formulas, 90-92
   moving in, 87-90
multiuser environment, *see* networks

N

@N function, 259
@NA function, 273-274
:Named-Style command, 23, 831-832
net present value, calculating, 224-225
networks, 302-303
   file sharing, 310
   reading files, 309
nonsharable files, 309
#NOT# operator, 520
@NOW function, 215-216
@NPV function, 224-225
null strings, 610
numbers
   color, 192
   combined, 298
   entering, 76
   filling ranges with, 548
   negative, 184
   random, 210
   rounding, 209
numeric formulas, 77-78
numeric keys, 41, 44

O

objects, 474
   copying, 487-488
   deleting, 487
   editing, 479
   flipping, 491
   freehand, 478
   locking, 489
   moving, 487-488
   rearranging, 487
   restoring, 487
   rotating, 490
   selecting, 478-479
   selecting with mouse, 479
   sizing, 490
   transforming, 489
one-key sort, 503-504
ONERROR advanced macro command, 618
OPEN advanced macro command, 640-642
operating system, 277-278
   accessing, 158
operators
   #AND#, 520
   #NOT#, 520
   #OR#, 520
   arithmetic
      – (negative operator), 78
      – (subtraction operator), 15, 78
      * (multiplication operator), 15, 78
      + (addition operator), 15, 78
      + (positive operator), 78
      / (division operator), 15, 78
      ^ (exponentiation operator), 78

complex
- #AND#, 248
- #NOT#, 248
- #OR#, 248

in numeric formulas, 78
in string formulas, 79
logical
- #AND#, 80
- #NOT#, 80
- #OR#, 80
- < (less than), 80, 247
- <= (less than or equal to), 80, 247
- <> (not equal to), 80, 247
- = (equal), 80, 247
- > (greater than), 80, 247
- >= (greater than or equal to), 80, 247

string
- & (concatenation), 79

#OR# operator, 520
orientation, printing, 351-352
output
- formatted, 344
- unformatted, 344

output range, 511-512

P

page breaks, 673, 803
- horizontal, 332-333
- inserting, 388-389
- screens, 399
- vertical, 330-332

page length, 347-350
PANELOFF advanced macro command, 634
PANELON advanced macro command, 634
passwords, 136, 301-302
paths, 284
patterns, 483-484
payment amounts, calculating, 222-223

Percent format, 173
Perspective view, 65
@PI function, 264
pie graphs, 453-455
pitch, printer, 351
playback of macros, 595
@PMT function, 222-223
POINT mode, 67, 100
point size, 371
polygons, 476
present value, calculating, 225-226
/Print command, 319, 361, 721
:Print Configuration command, 289, 385-386, 854-856
/Print Encoded command, 719-720
/Print File command, 305, 717-718
:Print File command, 852-853
:Print Go command, 852
:Print Info command, 865
:Print Layout command, 289, 389-390, 858-864
:Print Preview command, 388, 864
/Print Printer command, 106, 346, 317, 716-717
/Print Printer Align command, 739
/Print Printer Clear command, 737-738
/Print Printer Go command, 738-739
/Print Printer Hold command, 742
/Print Printer Image command, 740
/Print Printer Line command, 723
/Print Printer Options Advanced command, 734-737
/Print Printer Options Borders command, 728-729

Index

/Print Printer Options Footer command, 726
/Print Printer Options Header command, 725-726
/Print Printer Options Margins command, 727-728
/Print Printer Options Name command, 733-734
/Print Printer Options Other command, 731-732
/Print Printer Options Pg-Length command, 731
/Print Printer Options Setup command, 729-730
/Print Printer Page command, 724
/Print Printer Range command, 346, 722-723, 106
/Print Printer Sample command, 741
:Print Range command, 386, 853
/Print Resume command, 361, 721
:Print Settings command, 856-857
/Print Suspend command, 361, 720
printers, 31-32
   changing, 877-878
   configuring, 385
   controlling, 358
   installing, 873
   laser, 387
   pausing, 361
   specifying, 358
   status, 321
   stopping, 361-362
printing
   background, 360
   borders, 346, 390-391
   cancelling, 721
   compressing, 392
   controlling paper movement, 359
   default
      hardware, 322-323
      settings, 321, 324
   files, 395
      encoded, 320
   footers, 726
   graphs, 27-28, 460
      customized, 464
      default settings, 463-465
      with text, 362
   headers, 725-726
   holding, 360
   layout, 323-324
   options
      clearing, 363
      default, 323-324
   page breaks, 388-389
   page set up, 389
   pausing, 361
   previewing, 388
   priorities, 360
   ranges, 333, 386-387
      excluding, 339-341
      hiding segments, 336
   reports, 27-28, 317-319, 325-329
   resume, 721
   sample page, 741
   settings, 394
      naming, 362
      saving, 362, 392
   stopping, 361-362
   suspending, 720
   titles, 390-391
   with Wysiwyg, 384
   worksheets, 716-717
programs
   controlling, 612
   pausing, 606
@PROPER function, 257-259
PUT advanced macro command, 628-629
@PV function, 225-226

Q–R

QUIT advanced macro command, 618
@RAND function, 210
random numbers, generating, 210
/Range command, 21
/Range Erase command, 95, 100, 115, 518, 680-681
/Range Format command, 82, 166-168, 178, 217, 675-678
/Range Format Date command, 175, 213
/Range Format Fixed command, 171
/Range Format Hidden command, 133, 181, 340
/Range Format Other Automatic command, 214
/Range Format Other Color Negative command, 184
/Range Format Percent command, 173
/Range Format Reset command, 133
/Range Format Text command, 242
/Range Input command, 132-133, 687-688
/Range Justify command, 186, 199, 684-685
/Range Label command, 185, 678-680
/Range Name command, 681-684
/Range Name Create command, 108-109
/Range Name Labels command, 108-109
/Range Name Note command, 575, 587
/Range Name Table command, 109
/Range Prot command, 181, 686-687
/Range Search command, 155-158, 691-692
/Range Trans command, 690-691
/Range Transpose command, 154
/Range Unprot command, 131, 686-687
/Range Value command, 152-153, 216, 256, 689
ranges, 20, 99
  adding notes, 109
  addresses, 100
  anchored, 101-103
  color, 192-193
  column-variable, 539
  columns, 340
  copying, 149-151
    between files, 296
  criteria, 241, 509-510, 514
    formulas, 515-516
    wild cards in, 515
  dimensions, 272-273
  erasing, 115
  excluding while printing, 340-341
  filling
    dates, 549-550
    formulas, 549
    functions, 549
    times, 549-550
    with numbers, 548
  formats, 168
  global formats, 163
  hiding segments, 336
  highlighting, 101-103
  in multiple worksheets, 110-111
  input, 241, 508-509
  labels, 826-827
  moving contents, 141-144
  names, 72, 106-108, 152, 601
    addresses, 682

Index

checking, 249-250
deleting, 682
listing, 109
output, 511-512
preselecting, 105
printing, 333, 336
remembered, 106
row-variable, 539
rows, 339
saving, 291
searching, 779
specifying, 100
specifying to print, 386-387
three-dimensional, 111, 151
two-dimensional, 150
worksheet-variable, 539
@RATE function, 222
rate of return, calculating, 220-222
READ advanced macro command, 643-644
READLN advanced macro command, 644
READY mode, 67
RECALC advanced macro command, 638-639
RECALCCOL advanced macro command, 638-639
recalculation, 886
automatic, 137
background, 137
forced, 137
optimal, 137
order, 137-140
record buffer, 591
records, 496
deleting, 523
extracting, 522
modifying, 513
searching, 507-508
sorting, 502-507
specified, 511

rectangles, in graphs, 476-477
relative addressing, 82, 145-146
@REPEAT function, 259
@REPLACE function, 256
reports
designing, 341
graphs in, 466, 469-471
printing, 27-28, 325-329
RESTART advanced macro command, 623-624
RETURN advanced macro command, 617
@RIGHT function, 255-256
rotating objects, 490
@ROUND function, 209
row-variable range, 539
@ROWS function, 272-273
rows, 818
adjusting number, 129
borders, 860-861
converting to columns, 154
deleting, 115-116
height, 114, 380-381, 802
inserting, 120

S

@S function, 259
scatter plots, 456
scientific format, 173-174
screen, *see also* windows
control panel, 49
display, 49
freezing, 634-635
options
cell pointer, 399
default, 399
frame, 397-398
grid, 398
intensity, 399
page breaks, 399
rows, 399

splitting, 122-124
status line, 49
worksheet area, 49
worksheet frame, 49
Wysiwyg, 369
scrolling, 68-70
searching, 155-158, 507-508, 522, 691-692
   with strings, 519
   with wild cards, 515
@SECOND function, 218
serif fonts, 373
setup strings, 355-357
SETPOS advanced macro command, 645-646
shade format, 194
shading, 194, 378, 763-764, 810-811
@SHEETS function, 272-273
simultaneous equations, 26
@SIN function, 265
sine, 265
@SLN function, 229
soft fonts, 371
Solver add-in, 893, 897, 900
   Answer Report, 901
   attaching, 891-892
   Cells Used Report, 909
   Differences Report, 905
   functions used in, 909
   How Solved Report, 902-904
   Inconsistent Constraints Report, 905
   invoking, 892
   terminology, 893
   Unused Constraints Report, 908
   What-If Report, 904
   with macros, 910
:Special command, 23
:Special Copy command, 194, 381, 821-822
:Special Export command, 824-825
:Special Import command, 383, 823-824
:Special Move command, 194, 822-823, 382
special keys, 41, 44-46
@SQRT function, 210
square roots, calculating, 210
stacked-bar graphs, 450-452
stacking, 623
standard deviation, calculating, 237-238
starting
   1-2-3, 34-35, 58
   Wysiwyg, 35
statistical functions, 17
status indicators, 52-53
status line, 49
@STD function, 237-238
@STRING function, 260
string formulas, 77-79
string functions, 18
strings, 251
   case, 257-259
   comparing, 257
   converting, 260-261
   extracting from another, 254-256
   length, 257
   linking, 253
   null, 610
   repeating, 259
   replacing within another, 256
   retrieving from tables, 274
   searching with, 519
   table-creation, 562
   testing for, 259
   within another string, 253
subdirectories, 284
   retrieving files from, 288-289
subroutines, 616-617
subscripted characters, 403
@SUM function, 238-239
@SUMPRODUCT function, 239
superscripted characters, 403

Index

suppressing zeros, 188-189, 659-660
@SYD function, 231
/System command, 799
SYSTEM advanced macro command, 624-625
system requirements, 1-2-3, 14-15, 875

T

table definition, 562-565
table names, 562
table-creation strings, 562
tables
   creating, 769-777
   entries, 274
   external, 244-245
   of files, 304-305
@TAN function, 265
tangent, 265
@TERM function, 227-228
testing
   cells, 250-251
   for strings, 259
   for values, 259
:Text command, 22, 84
:Text Align command, 185, 199, 403, 828-829
:Text Clear command, 830
:Text Edit command, 84, 186, 198, 826-827
:Text Reformat command, 84, 186, 199, 829
:Text Set command, 201, 829
text
   aligning, 199-201
   attributes
      clearing, 406
      setting, 406
   centering, 480
   correcting, 400-401
   editing, 197-198, 480

   in graphs, 440-441, 474-475
   labels, 655, 678-680
   typing, 400-401
Text format, 180
@TIME function, 216-217
time
   converting to numbers, 210
   current, 215-216
   expressing as decimal, 216-217
Time format, 177-179
@TIMEVALUE function, 218
titles
   freezing, 126-128
   printing, 390-391
@TODAY function, 215-216
Translate Utility, 40-41, 307
@TRIM function, 259
@TRUE function, 249
tutorial, 56-57
two-key sort, 504
type-ahead buffer, 610
typeface, *see* fonts

U

Undo, 84-86
Unused Constraints Report, Solver add-in, 908
@UPPER function, 257-259

V

@VALUE function, 260-261
VALUE mode, 67
values
   converted from formulas, 152-153
   converting to strings, 260
   extracting, 244, 295
   input, 528
   multiplying lists of, 239
   strings, 260-261
   testing for, 259

totaling, 238-239
variables, 528
   dependent, 456
   independent, 456
variance, 240
   calculating, 243
@VARS function, 240
@VDB function, 232
video displays, 31
Video Graphics Array (VGA), 31
Viewer add-in, 917
   attaching and detaching, 917-918
   files
      browsing, 924
      linking, 922-923
      opening, 922
      retrieving, 920-922
   invoking and using, 918
   menu, 918
   navigating, 920
@VLOOKUP function, 274

W

WAIT indicator, 309
WAIT advanced macro command, 620
"what-if" analysis, 16
   see also Backsolver, Solver
What If Report, Solver add-in, 904
wild cards, 287-288, 515
windows, 57-58, 121-123
   moving between, 124
   viewing graphs with, 443
   zooming, 124
WINDOWSOFF advanced macro command, 634-635
WINDOWSON advanced macro command, 635
/Worksheet command, 20
/Worksheet Column command, 667-668
/Worksheet Column Display command, 340
/Worksheet Column Hide command, 134, 340
/Worksheet Delete command, 665-666
/Worksheet Delete File command, 87, 117-119, 303
/Worksheet Delete Row command, 116
/Worksheet Delete Sheet command, 87, 117
/Worksheet Erase command, 119, 668-669
/Worksheet Erase Yes command, 119
/Worksheet Global Col-Width command, 112, 657-658
/Worksheet Global Default command, 85, 162, 172, 661-663
/Worksheet Global Format command, 82, 168, 175, 653-655
/Worksheet Global Format Date command, 175
/Worksheet Global Group command, 87, 663-665
/Worksheet Global Label command, 655-657
/Worksheet Global Prot command, 132, 658-659
/Worksheet Global Recalc command, 138, 660-661
/Worksheet Global Zero command, 188, 659-660
/Worksheet Hide command, 674
/Worksheet Insert Column command, 120
/Worksheet Insert Row command, 120
/Worksheet Insert Sheet command, 87, 120

Index

/Worksheet Page command, 673
/Worksheet Status command, 162, 672
/Worksheet Titles command, 127, 532, 669-670
/Worksheet Window commands, 670-672
/Worksheet Window Clear command, 123-124
/Worksheet Window Graph command, 125, 443
/Worksheet Window Horizontal command, 122-123
/Worksheet Window Perspective command, 87, 534
/Worksheet Window Vertical command, 122
:Worksheet command, 20
:Worksheet Column command, 801-802
:Worksheet Page command, 803
:Worksheet Row command, 802
worksheets
   appearance, 129-130
   area, 49
   cells, 13-14, 62
   consolidated, 111
   databases and, 498
   deleting, 115-119, 665-666
   entering data in, 73
   erasing, 119
   formats, 163
   formatting, 129
   formulas, 62
   frame, 49
   graphics, 24-25
   graphs, 125, 835-836
      inserting, 833
      removing, 834
   hiding, 674
   inserting, 120
   macro comments, 588
   moving in, 66
   printing, 716-717
   protecting, 24, 130-131, 303, 658
   ranges in, 110-111
   recalculating, 638, 660-661
   scrolling, 68-70
   text, 197-198
   variable range, 539
   viewing graphs from, 443
workspace, 64-65
WRITE advanced macro command, 644
WRITELN advanced macro command, 645
Wysiwyg, 18
   cells, 370-371
   changing options, 880
   display options, 128
   editing in, 84
   fonts, 371
   formatting, 189-190, 369-371
   loading, 35-36, 366
   menu, 19, 22, 98, 367-368
   printing with, 384
   starting, 35
   screen, 369
   text commands, 400
   viewing graphs in, 443
   with 1-2-3, 367

X–Z

/x commands, 601-602
XY graphs, 456-457
@YEAR function, 215
zooming, 124, 396, 815, 837

Computer Books From Que Mean PC Performance!

Spreadsheets

1-2-3 Database Techniques	$29.95
1-2-3 Graphics Techniques	$24.95
1-2-3 Macro Library, 3rd Edition	$39.95
1-2-3 Release 2.2 Business Applications	$39.95
1-2-3 Release 2.2 PC Tutor	$39.95
1-2-3 Release 2.2 QueCards	$19.95
1-2-3 Release 2.2 Quick Reference	$ 8.95
1-2-3 Release 2.2 QuickStart, 2nd Edition	$19.95
1-2-3 Release 2.2 Workbook and Disk	$29.95
1-2-3 Release 3 Business Applications	$39.95
1-2-3 Release 3 Workbook and Disk	$29.95
1-2-3 Release 3.1 Quick Reference	$ 8.95
1-2-3 Release 3.1 QuickStart, 2nd Edition	$19.95
1-2-3 Tips, Tricks, and Traps, 3rd Edition	$24.95
Excel Business Applications: IBM Version	$39.95
Excel Quick Reference	$ 8.95
Excel QuickStart	$19.95
Excel Tips, Tricks, and Traps	$22.95
Using 1-2-3/G	$29.95
Using 1-2-3, Special Edition	$27.95
Using 1-2-3 Release 2.2, Special Edition	$27.95
Using 1-2-3 Release 3.1, 2nd Edition	$29.95
Using Excel: IBM Version	$29.95
Using Lotus Spreadsheet for DeskMate	$22.95
Using Quattro Pro	$24.95
Using SuperCalc5, 2nd Edition	$29.95

Databases

dBASE III Plus Handbook, 2nd Edition	$24.95
dBASE III Plus Tips, Tricks, and Traps	$24.95
dBASE III Plus Workbook and Disk	$29.95
dBASE IV Applications Library, 2nd Edition	$39.95
dBASE IV Programming Techniques	$24.95
dBASE IV Quick Reference	$ 8.95
dBASE IV QuickStart	$19.95
dBASE IV Tips, Tricks, and Traps, 2nd Edition	$24.95
dBASE IV Workbook and Disk	$29.95
Using Clipper	$24.95
Using DataEase	$24.95
Using dBASE IV	$27.95
Using Paradox 3	$24.95
Using R:BASE	$29.95
Using Reflex, 2nd Edition	$24.95
Using SQL	$29.95

Business Applications

Allways Quick Reference	$ 8.95
Introduction to Business Software	$14.95
Introduction to Personal Computers	$19.95
Lotus Add-in Toolkit Guide	$29.95
Norton Utilities Quick Reference	$ 8.95
PC Tools Quick Reference, 2nd Edition	$ 8.95
Q&A Quick Reference	$ 8.95
Que's Computer User's Dictionary	$ 9.95
Que's Wizard Book	$ 9.95
Quicken Quick Reference	$ 8.95
SmartWare Tips, Tricks, and Traps 2nd Edition	$24.95
Using Computers in Business	$22.95
Using DacEasy, 2nd Edition	$24.95
Using Enable/OA	$29.95
Using Harvard Project Manager	$24.95
Using Managing Your Money, 2nd Edition	$19.95
Using Microsoft Works: IBM Version	$22.95
Using Norton Utilities	$24.95
Using PC Tools Deluxe	$24.95
Using Peachtree	$27.95
Using PFS: First Choice	$22.95
Using PROCOMM PLUS	$19.95
Using Q&A, 2nd Edition	$23.95
Using Quicken: IBM Version, 2nd Edition	$19.95
Using Smart	$22.95
Using SmartWare II	$29.95
Using Symphony, Special Edition	$29.95
Using Time Line	$24.95
Using TimeSlips	$24.95

CAD

AutoCAD Quick Reference	$ 8.95
AutoCAD Sourcebook 1991	$27.95
Using AutoCAD, 3rd Edition	$29.95
Using Generic CADD	$24.95

Word Processing

Microsoft Word 5 Quick Reference	$ 8.95
Using DisplayWrite 4, 2nd Edition	$24.95
Using LetterPerfect	$22.95
Using Microsoft Word 5.5: IBM Version, 2nd Edition	$24.95
Using MultiMate	$24.95
Using Professional Write	$22.95
Using Word for Windows	$24.95
Using WordPerfect 5	$27.95
Using WordPerfect 5.1, Special Edition	$27.95
Using WordStar, 3rd Edition	$27.95
WordPerfect PC Tutor	$39.95
WordPerfect Power Pack	$39.95
WordPerfect Quick Reference	$ 8.95
WordPerfect QuickStart	$19.95
WordPerfect 5 Workbook and Disk	$29.95
WordPerfect 5.1 Quick Reference	$ 8.95
WordPerfect 5.1 QuickStart	$19.95
WordPerfect 5.1 Tips, Tricks, and Traps	$24.95
WordPerfect 5.1 Workbook and Disk	$29.95

Hardware/Systems

DOS Tips, Tricks, and Traps	$24.95
DOS Workbook and Disk, 2nd Edition	$29.95
Fastback Quick Reference	$ 8.95
Hard Disk Quick Reference	$ 8.95
MS-DOS PC Tutor	$39.95
MS-DOS Power Pack	$39.95
MS-DOS Quick Reference	$ 8.95
MS-DOS QuickStart, 2nd Edition	$19.95
MS-DOS User's Guide, Special Edition	$29.95
Networking Personal Computers, 3rd Edition	$24.95
The Printer Bible	$29.95
Que's PC Buyer's Guide	$12.95
Understanding UNIX: A Conceptual Guide, 2nd Edition	$21.95
Upgrading and Repairing PCs	$29.95
Using DOS	$22.95
Using Microsoft Windows 3, 2nd Edition	$24.95
Using Novell NetWare	$29.95
Using OS/2	$29.95
Using PC DOS, 3rd Edition	$24.95
Using Prodigy	$19.95
Using UNIX	$29.95
Using Your Hard Disk	$29.95
Windows 3 Quick Reference	$ 8.95

Desktop Publishing/Graphics

CorelDRAW Quick Reference	$ 8.95
Harvard Graphics Quick Reference	$ 8.95
Using Animator	$24.95
Using DrawPerfect	$24.95
Using Harvard Graphics, 2nd Edition	$24.95
Using Freelance Plus	$24.95
Using PageMaker: IBM Version, 2nd Edition	$24.95
Using PFS: First Publisher, 2nd Edition	$24.95
Using Ventura Publisher, 2nd Edition	$24.95

Macintosh/Apple II

AppleWorks QuickStart	$19.95
The Big Mac Book, 2nd Edition	$29.95
Excel QuickStart	$19.95
The Little Mac Book	$ 9.95
Que's Macintosh Multimedia Handbook	$24.95
Using AppleWorks, 3rd Edition	$24.95
Using Excel: Macintosh Version	$24.95
Using FileMaker	$24.95
Using MacDraw	$24.95
Using MacroMind Director	$29.95
Using MacWrite	$24.95
Using Microsoft Word 4: Macintosh Version	$24.95
Using Microsoft Works: Macintosh Version, 2nd Edition	$24.95
Using PageMaker: Macinsoth Version, 2nd Edition	$24.95

Programming/Technical

Assembly Language Quick Reference	$ 8.95
C Programmer's Toolkit	$39.95
C Quick Reference	$ 8.95
DOS and BIOS Functions Quick Reference	$ 8.95
DOS Programmer's Reference, 2nd Edition	$29.95
Network Programming in C	$49.95
Oracle Programmer's Guide	$29.95
QuickBASIC Advanced Techniques	$24.95
Quick C Programmer's Guide	$29.95
Turbo Pascal Advanced Techniques	$24.95
Turbo Pascal Quick Reference	$ 8.95
UNIX Programmer's Quick Reference	$ 8.95
UNIX Programmer's Reference	$29.95
UNIX Shell Commands Quick Reference	$ 8.95
Using Assembly Language, 2nd Edition	$29.95
Using BASIC	$24.95
Using C	$29.95
Using QuickBASIC 4	$24.95
Using Turbo Pascal	$29.95

For More Information, Call Toll Free!
1-800-428-5331

All prices and titles subject to change without notice. Non-U.S. prices may be higher. Printed in the U.S.A.

Que—The Top Name In Spreadsheet Information!

Using 1-2-3 Release 3.1, 2nd Edition
Que Development Group

This comprehensive resource for Release 3.1 features a tear-out **Menu Map** and an extensive reference section. Easy-to-read text and tutorials introduce worksheet basics with detailed coverage of advanced features, including multiple worksheet and file applications.

Releases 3 & 3.1

Order #1216   **$29.95 USA**
0-88022-621-8, 900 pp., 7 3/8 x 9 1/4

1-2-3 Release 3.1 QuickStart, 2nd Edition
Que Development Group

This illustrated guide provides a step-by-step introduction to Release 3.1 worksheets. Beginners will learn how to enter and change data, develop multiple worksheet and file applications, and create presentation quality graphs and reports.

Releases 3 & 3.1

Order #1208   **$19.95 USA**
0-88022-613-7, 400 pp., 7 3/8 x 9 1/4

1-2-3 Release 3.1 QuickReference
Que Development Group

Releases 3 & 3.1

Order #1267   **$8.95 USA**
0-88022-656-0, 160 pp., 4 3/4 x 8

To Order, Call:
(800) 428-5331 OR (317) 573-2510

Teach Yourself
With QuickStarts From Que!

The ideal tutorials for beginners, Que's QuickStart books use graphic illustrations and step-by-step instructions to get you up and running fast. Packed with examples, QuickStarts are the perfect beginner's guides to your favorite software applications.

1-2-3 Release 2.2 QuickStart, 2nd Edition
Releases 2.01 & 2.2

| Order #1207 | $19.95 USA |

0-88022-612-9, 400 pp., 7 3/8 x 9 1/4

1-2-3 Release 3.1 QuickStart, 2nd Edition
Releases 3 & 3.1

| Order #1208 | $19.95 USA |

0-88022-613-7, 400 pp., 7 3/8 x 9 1/4

dBASE IV QuickStart
dBASE IV

| Order #873 | $19.95 USA |

0-88022-389-8, 384 pp., 7 3/8 x 9 1/4

dBASE IV QuickStart, 2nd Edition
Through Version 1.1

| Order #1209 | $19.95 USA |

0-88022-614-5, 400 pp., 7 3/8 x 9 1/4

Excel QuickStart
IBM Version 1 & Macintosh Version 2.2

| Order #957 | $19.95 USA |

0-88022-423-1, 334 pp., 7 3/8 x 9 1/4

MS-DOS QuickStart, 2nd Edition
Version 3.X & 4.X

| Order #1206 | $19.95 USA |

0-88022-611-0, 400 pp., 7 3/8 x 9 1/4

Q&A QuickStart
Versions 3 & 4

| Order #1264 | $19.95 USA |

0-88022-653-6, 400 pp., 7 3/8 x 9 1/4

Quattro Pro QuickStart
Through Version 2.0

| Order #1305 | $19.95 USA |

0-88022-693-5, 450 pp., 7 3/8 x 9 1/4

WordPerfect QuickStart
WordPerfect 5

| Order #871 | $19.95 USA |

0-88022-387-1, 457 pp., 7 3/8 x 9 1/4

WordPerfect 5.1 QuickStart
WordPerfect 5.1

| Order #1104 | $19.95 USA |

0-88022-558-0, 427 pp., 7 3/8 x 9 1/4

Windows 3 QuickStart
Ron Person & Karen Rose

This graphics-based text teaches Windows beginners how to use the feature-packed Windows environment. Emphasizes such software applications as Excel, Word, and PageMaker and shows how to master Windows' mouse, menus, and screen elements.

Version 3

| Order #1205 | $19.95 USA |

0-88022-610-2, 400 pp., 7 3/8 x 9 1/4

MS-DOS 5 QuickStart
Que Development Group

This is the easy-to-use graphic approach to learning MS-DOS 5. The combination of step-by-step instruction, examples, and graphics make this book ideal for all DOS beginners.

DOS 5

| Order #1293 | $19.95 USA |

0-88022-681-1, 400 pp., 7 3/8 x 9 1/4

To Order, Call:
(800) 428-5331 OR (317) 573-2510

Find It Fast With Que's Quick References!

Que's Quick References are the compact, easy-to-use guides to essential application information. Written for all users, Quick References include vital command information under easy-to-find alphabetical listings. Quick References are a must for anyone who needs command information fast!

1-2-3 for DOS Release 2.3 Quick Reference
Release 2.3
Order #1352 $9.95 USA
0-88022-725-7, 160 pp., 4 3/4 x 8

1-2-3 Release 3.1 Quick Reference
Releases 3 & 3.1
Order #1267 $8.95 USA
0-88022-656-0, 160 pp., 4 3/4 x 8

Allways Quick Reference
Version 1.0
Order #1193 $8.95 USA
0-88022-605-6, 160 pp., 4 3/4 x 8

Assembly Language Quick Reference
IBM Version
Order #934 $8.95 USA
0-88022-428-2, 160 pp., 4 3/4 x 8

AutoCAD Quick Reference, 2nd Edition
Releases 10 & 11
Order #1217 $8.95 USA
0-88022-622-6, 160 pp., 4 3/4 x 8

Batch File and Macros Quick Reference
Through DOS 5.0
Order #1311 $9.95 USA
0-88022-699-4, 160 pp., 4 3/4 x 8

C Quick Reference
IBM Version
Order #868 $8.95 USA
0-88022-372-3, 160 pp., 4 3/4 x 8

CorelDRAW Quick Reference
Through Version 1.2
Order #1186 $8.95 USA
0-88022-597-1, 160 pp., 4 3/4 x 8

dBASE IV Quick Reference
Version 1.0
Order #867 $8.95 USA
0-88022-371-5, 160 pp., 4 3/4 x 8

DOS and BIOS Functions Quick Reference
Version 4
Order #932 $8.95 USA
0-88022-426-6, 160 pp., 4 3/4 x 8

Excel Quick Reference
Version 2.1
Order #1023 $8.95 USA
0-88022-473-8, 160 pp., 4 3/4 x 8

Fastback Quick Reference
Version 2.1
Order #1260 $8.95 USA
0-88022-650-1, 160 pp., 4 3/4 x 8

Hard Disk Quick Reference
Through DOS 4.01
Order #974 $8.95 USA
0-88022-443-6, 160 pp., 4 3/4 x 8

Harvard Graphics Quick Reference
Version 2.3
Order #1084 $8.95 USA
0-88022-538-6, 160 pp., 4 3/4 x 8

Laplink Quick Reference
Laplink III
Order #1314 $9.95 USA
0-88022-702-8, 160 pp., 4 3/4 x 8

Microsoft Word 5 Quick Reference
Version 5.5
Order #976 $8.95 USA
0-80822-444-4, 160 pp., 4 3/4 x 8

Microsoft Works Quick Reference
Through IBM Version 2.0
Order #1306 $9.95 USA
0-88022-694-3, 160 pp., 4 3/4 x 8

MS-DOS 5 Quick Reference
Version 5.0
Order #1256 $9.95 USA
0-88022-646-3, 160 pp., 4 3/4 x 8

MS-DOS Quick Reference
Through Version 3.3
Order #865 $8.95 USA
0-88022-369-3, 160 pp., 4 3/4 x 8

Norton Utilities Quick Reference
Norton Utilities 5 & Norton Commander 3
Order #1053 $8.95 USA
0-88022-508-4, 160 pp., 4 3/4 x 8

PC Tools Quick Reference, 2nd Edition
Through Version 6.0
Order #1185 $8.95 USA
0-88022-596-3, 160 pp., 4 3/4 x 8

Q&A Quick Reference
Versions 2, 3, & 4
Order #1165 $8.95 USA
0-88022-581-5, 160 pp., 4 3/4 x 8

Quattro Pro Quick Reference
Through Version 2.0
Order #1304 $8.95 USA
0-88022-692-7, 160 pp., 4 3/4 x 8

Quicken Quick Reference
IBM Through Version 4
Order #1187 $8.95 USA
0-88022-598-X, 160 pp., 4 3/4 x 8

Turbo Pascal Quick Reference
Version 5
Order #935 $8.95 USA
0-88022-429-0, 160 pp., 4 3/4 x 8

UNIX Programmer's Quick Reference
AT&T System V, Release 3
Order #1081 $8.95 USA
0-88022-535-1, 160 pp., 4 3/4 x 8

UNIX Shell Commands Quick Reference
AT&T System V, Releases 3 & 4
Order #1147 $8.95 USA
0-88022-572-6, 160 pp., 4 3/4 x 8

Windows 3 Quick Reference
Version 3
Order #1230 $8.95 USA
0-88022-631-5, 160 pp., 4 3/4 x 8

WordPerfect 5.1 Quick Reference
WordPerfect 5.1
Order #1158 $8.95 USA
0-88022-576-9, 160 pp., 4 3/4 x 8

WordPerfect Quick Reference
WordPerfect 5
Order #866 $8.95 USA
0-88022-370-7, 160 pp., 4 3/4 x 8

To Order, Call:
(800) 428-5331 OR (317) 573-2510

Complete Coverage From A To Z!

The Ultimate Glossary Of Computer Terms— Over 200,000 In Print!

Que's Computer User's Dictionary

Que Development Group

This compact, practical reference contains hundreds of definitions, explanations, examples, and illustrations on topics from programming to desktop publishing. You can master the "language" of computers and learn how to make your personal computers more efficient and more powerful. Filled with tips and cautions, *Que's Computer User's Dictionary* is the perfect resource for anyone who uses a computer.

IBM, Macintosh, Apple, & Programming

Order #1086 $10.95 USA

0-88022-540-8, 500 pp., 4 3/4 x 8

"Dictionary indeed. This whammer is a mini-encyclopedia...an absolute joy to use...a must for your computer library...."

Southwest Computer & Business Equipment Review

**To Order, Call:
(800) 428-5331 OR (317) 573-2510**